PEARSON

mybusinesslab™

Improve Your Grade

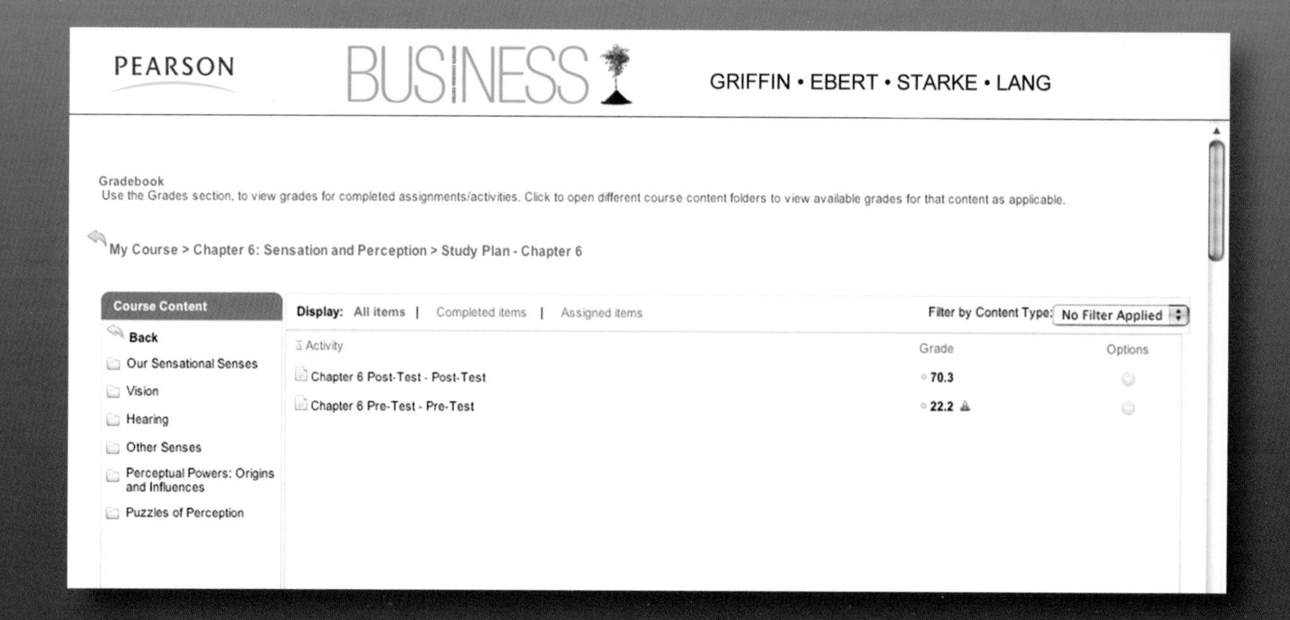

MyBusinessLab helps you focus your efforts where they are needed. Know your strengths and weaknesses before your first in-class exam.

Go to **www.mybusinesslab.com** and follow the simple registration instructions on the Student Access Code Card provided with this text. Your unique access code is hidden there.

Save Time. Improve Results. **www.pearsoned.ca/mybusinesslab**

Pearson eText

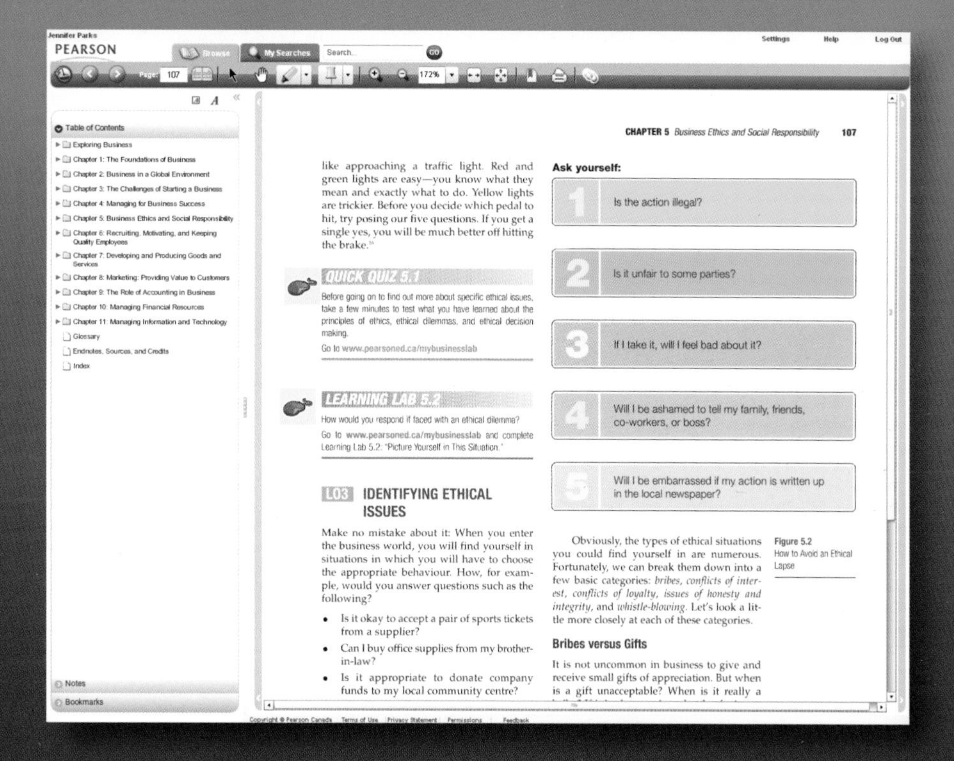

Pearson eText gives students access to the text whenever and wherever they have access to the internet. eText pages look exactly like the printed text, offering powerful new functionality for students and instructors.

Users can create notes, highlight text in different colours, create bookmarks, zoom, click hyperlinked words and phrases to view definitions, and choose single-page or two-page view.

Pearson eText allows for quick navigation using a table of contents and provides full-text search. The eText may also offer links to associated media files, enabling users to access videos, animations, or other activities as they read the text.

Personalized Learning

In MyBusinessLab you are treated as an individual with specific learning needs.

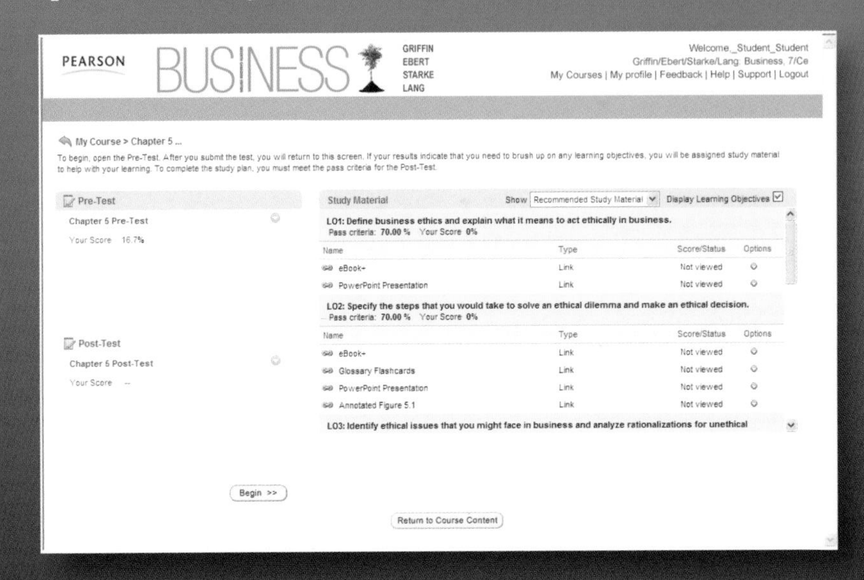

The study and assessment resources that come with your textbook allow you to review content and develop what you need to know, on your own time, and at your own pace.

MyBusinessLab provides

- Auto-graded quizzes, assignments, and mini-cases
- A personalized study plan that tells you where to study based on your quiz results
- BizSkills mini-simulations that help you analyse and make decisions in common business situations; these assess you and include reinforcement quizzes, outlines, and glossaries
- Glossary Flashcards to help you study key terms
- Acadia/Pearson video portal featuring interviews with more than 70 executives from a variety of companies, including some featured in your textbook
- Crafting a Business Plan, including templates to guide you through the steps of creating your own business plan

SEVENTH CANADIAN EDITION

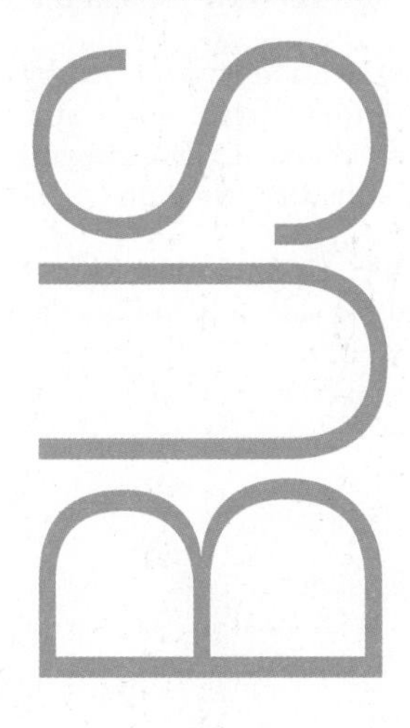

RICKY W. GRIFFIN
Texas A & M University

RONALD J. EBERT
University of Missouri-Columbia

FREDERICK A. STARKE
University of Manitoba

MELANIE D. LANG
University of Guelph

With portions of Chapter 4 written by
Monica Diochon, St. Francis Xavier University
and the Entrepreneurship and New Ventures boxes written by
Sherry Finney, Cape Breton University

Pearson Canada
Toronto

To Ann, Eric, and Grant — F. A. S.
For Paul, Hannah, and Beth — M. D. L

Library and Archives Canada Cataloguing in Publication
Business / Ricky W. Griffin ... [et al.]. — 7th Canadian ed.

Includes bibliographical references and index
ISBN 978-0-13-715120-2

1. Industrial management. 2. Business enterprises. 3. Industrial management—Canada.
4. Business enterprises—Canada. I. Griffin, Ricky W.

HD31.G75 2010 658 C2009-906650-5

ISBN 978-0-13-715120-2

Vice-President, Editorial Director: Gary Bennett
Acquisitions Editor: Karen Elliott
Executive Marketing Manager: Cas Shields
Developmental Editors: Pamela Voves/Catherine Belshaw
Production Editor: Cheryl Jackson
Copy Editor: Patricia Jones
Proofreaders: Strong Finish/Marnie Lamb
Production Coordinator: Andrea Falkenberg
Compositor: Hermia Chung
Photo and Permissions Researcher: Heather Jackson
Art Director: Julia Hall
Cover and Interior Designer: Anthony Leung
Cover Image: Veer.com

2 3 4 5 13 12 11

Printed and bound in United States of America.

Business Accountability Counterfeit Products: Who's Accountable? 87
Responsibility Toward Employees 88
Responsibility Toward Investors 90
Implementing Social Responsibility Programs 91
Approaches to Social Responsibility 91
Corporate Charitable Donations 93
Managing Social Responsibility Programs 93
Social Responsibility and the Small Business 95
Entrepreneurship and New Ventures How Green Is That Orange? 95

Summary of Learning Objectives 96
KEY TERMS 97
QUESTIONS FOR ANALYSIS 97
APPLICATION EXERCISES 97
Building Your Business Skills 98
Exercising Your Ethics: Team Exercise 99
Concluding Case 3-1 The Debate over Global Warming 100
Concluding Case 3-2 Pollution on the High Seas 102

4 Understanding Entrepreneurship, Small Business, and New Venture Creation 104

Opening Case Family Businesses 105

Small Business, New Venture Creation, and Entrepreneurship 106
Small Business 106
The New Venture/Firm 108
Entrepreneurship 108
The Role of Small and New Businesses in the Canadian Economy 109
Small Businesses 109
The Greening of Business Small Businesses Go Green 110
New Ventures 111
The Entrepreneurial Process 112
The Entrepreneur 113
Identifying Opportunities 113
Accessing Resources 117
Business Accountability Looking for Angels 119
Assessing the "Fit" Between Elements in the Entrepreneurial Process 120
After the Start-Up 121
Starting Up a Small Business 121
Forms of Business Ownership 123
The Sole Proprietorship 123
The Partnership 125
The Corporation 126
The Co-operative 128
Success and Failure in Small Business 130
Reasons for Success 130
Reasons for Failure 131

Summary of Learning Objectives 132
KEY TERMS 134
QUESTIONS FOR ANALYSIS 134
APPLICATION EXERCISES 134
Building Your Business Skills 135
Exercising Your Ethics: Team Exercise 135
Concluding Case 4-1 Mompreneurs 136
Concluding Case 4-2 Getting In on the Ground Floor 138

5 Understanding International Business 140

Opening Case Bombardier's Global Strategy 141

The Contemporary Global Economy 142
The Major World Marketplaces 143
Forms of Competitive Advantage 145
Import–Export Balances 147
Exchange Rates 149
International Business Management 151
"Going International" 151
Entrepreneurship and New Ventures Epic Entrepreneurs: Have Camera, Will Travel 152
Levels of Involvement in International Business 153
International Organizational Structures 154
Barriers to International Trade 156
Social and Cultural Differences 156
Business Accountability High Risk in the Mining Business 157
Economic Differences 158
Legal and Political Differences 159
Overcoming Barriers to Trade 162

Summary of Learning Objectives 166
KEY TERMS 167
QUESTIONS FOR ANALYSIS 167
APPLICATION EXERCISES 167
Building Your Business Skills 168
Exercising Your Ethics: Team Exercise 169
Concluding Case 5-1 Bribery on the International Scene 170
Concluding Case 5-2 International Challenges in the Clothing Industry 171
CBC Video Case 1-1: Whistle-blowers at the RCMP 172
CBC Video Case 1-2: Mompreneurs 173
Crafting a Business Plan Part 1: The Contemporary Business Environment 174

Part Two
The Business of Managing 176

6 Managing the Business Enterprise 178

Opening Case Corporate Culture 179

Who Are Managers? 180
The Management Process 180
Planning 181
Organizing 182
Leading 182
Controlling 182
Business Accountability What Do Managers Actually Do? 184
Types of Managers 184
Levels of Management 184
Areas of Management 186

Basic Management Skills 187
Technical Skills 187
Human Relations Skills 188
Conceptual Skills 188
Time Management Skills 188
Decision-Making Skills 189
Strategic Management: Setting Goals and Formulating Strategy 192
Setting Goals 193
Formulating Strategy 194
The Greening of Business Setting Green Goals 195
Levels of Strategies 196
Entrepreneurship and New Ventures From a Missouri Garage to Hollywood 198
Contingency Planning and Crisis Management 199
Contingency Planning 199
Crisis Management 200
Management and the Corporate Culture 200
Forces Shaping Corporate Culture 201
Communicating the Culture and Managing Change 202

Summary of Learning Objectives 203
KEY TERMS 204
QUESTIONS FOR ANALYSIS 205
APPLICATION EXERCISES 205
Building Your Business Skills 205
Exercising Your Ethics: Team Exercise 206
Concluding Case 6-1 The Business of Bagging Customers 207
Concluding Case 6-2 If at First You Don't Succeed... 208

7 Organizing the Business Enterprise 210

Opening Case Reorganizing the Irving Empire 211
What Is Organizational Structure? 212
Determinants of Organizational Structure 212
The Chain of Command 213
The Building Blocks of Organizational Structure 214
Specialization 214
Departmentalization 215
Business Accountability Product vs. Geographical Departmentalization: What's the Right Choice? 217
Establishing the Decision-Making Hierarchy 218
Assigning Tasks 219
Performing Tasks 219
Distributing Authority 219
Basic Organizational Structures 224
The Functional Structure 224
The Divisional Structure 224
Project Organization 225
International Organization 227
Organizational Design for the Twenty-first Century 228
The Greening of Business Green Structures 229
The Informal Organization 231
Informal Groups 231
Summary of Learning Objectives 233
KEY TERMS 234
QUESTIONS FOR ANALYSIS 234
APPLICATION EXERCISES 234
Building Your Business Skills 235
Exercising Your Ethics: Team Exercise 235
Concluding Case 7-1 Structure Evolves at Frantic Films 236
Concluding Case 7-2 Cooking Up a New Structure 238

8 Managing Human Resources 240

Opening Case Are More Cracks Appearing in the Glass Ceiling? 241
The Foundations of Human Resource Management 242
The Strategic Importance of HRM 242
Human Resource Planning 242
Staffing the Organization 245
Recruiting Human Resources 245
Selecting Human Resources 246
The Greening of Business Green Recruiting 247
Developing Human Resources 249
New Employee Orientation 250
Training and Development 250
Evaluating Employee Performance 252
The Performance Appraisal Process 252
Methods for Appraising Performance 253
Providing Compensation and Benefits 254
Determining Basic Compensation 255
Performance-Based Compensation 256
Benefits 258
Business Accountability The Importance of Perks 260
The Legal Context of HRM 261
Equal Employment Opportunity 261
Comparable Worth 262
Sexual Harassment 263
Employee Safety and Health 264
Retirement 264
New Challenges in the Changing Workplace 265
Managing Workforce Diversity 265
Managing Knowledge Workers 266
Managing Contingent Workers 267

Summary of Learning Objectives 269
KEY TERMS 270
QUESTIONS FOR ANALYSIS 270
APPLICATION EXERCISES 271
Building Your Business Skills 271
Exercising Your Ethics: Team Exercise 272
Concluding Case 8-1 Who Should Get Overtime Pay? 273
Concluding Case 8-2 Galt Contracting 274

9 Understanding Labour–Management Relations 276

Opening Case Reports from the Battlefield 277
Why Do Workers Unionize? 278
The Development of Canadian Labour Unions 279
Unionism Today 280

Trends in Union Membership 280
Trends in Union–Management Relations 282
Trends in Bargaining Perspectives 282
The Future of Unions 282
The Legal Environment for Unions in Canada 283
Federal Legislation: The Canada Labour Code 283
Provincial Labour Legislation 285
Union Organizing Strategy 286
Certifying a Union: An Example 286
Types of Unions 286
Union Security 287
Collective Bargaining 288
Reaching Agreement on the Contract's Terms 288
Contract Issues 289
Business Accountability Butting Heads Around the World 291
When Bargaining Fails 292
Mediation and Arbitration 295
Administering a Labour Agreement 295

Summary of Learning Objectives 296
KEY TERMS 297
QUESTIONS FOR ANALYSIS 297
APPLICATION EXERCISES 298
Building Your Business Skills 298
Exercising Your Ethics: Team Exercise 299
Concluding Case 9-1 It's the Latest Crisis in the Automobile Business 299
Concluding Case 9-2 Labour Relations in Hollywood 301

10 Motivating and Leading Employees 302

Opening Case What Do Employees Want? 303
Forms of Employee Behaviour 304
Individual Differences Among Employees 305
Personality 305
Attitudes 307
Matching People and Jobs 307
Psychological Contracts 307
The Person-Job Fit 308
Motivation in the Workplace 308
Classical Theory and Scientific Management 308
Early Behavioural Theory 309
Contemporary Motivation Theory 311
Strategies for Enhancing Motivation 313
Reinforcement/Behaviour Modification Theory 313
Entrepreneurship and New Ventures Employee Engagement: The Ultimate Win-WIn 314
Goal Setting Theory 315
Participative Management and Empowerment 316
Business Accountability Encouraging Employees to Share Ideas 317
Team Management 318
Job Enrichment and Job Redesign 318
Modified Work Schedules 319
The Greening of Business The Four-Day Workweek and Telecommuting: Are They Really Green? 322
Leadership and Motivation 322
Approaches to Leadership 323
Recent Trends in Leadership 325

Summary of Learning Objectives 329
KEY TERMS 331
QUESTIONS FOR ANALYSIS 331
APPLICATION EXERCISES 331
Building Your Business Skills 332
Exercising Your Ethics: Team Exercise 332
Concluding Case 10-1 What About Telecommuting? 333
Concluding Case 10-2 Leadership and Management 334
CBC Video Case 2-1: Flair Bartending 336
CBC Video Case 2-2: Clash of the Co-workers 336
Crafting a Business Plan Part 2(a): The Business of Managing 338
Crafting a Business Plan Part 2(b): The Business of Managing 339

Part Three
Managing Operations and Information 340

11 Producing Goods and Services 342

Opening Case Mattel: Getting a Toy Recall Right 343
What Does "Production" Mean Today? 344
The Growth of Global Operations 345
Entrepreneurship and New Ventures Move Over, George Jetson 346
Creating Value Through Production 346
Operations Processes 347
Business Strategy as the Driver of Operations 349
Differences Between Service and Manufacturing Operations 351
Operations Planning 353
Capacity Planning 354
Location Planning 355
Layout Planning 356
Business Accountability The People's Car 359
Quality Planning 360
Methods Planning 360
Operations Scheduling 363
Scheduling Goods Operations 363
Scheduling Service Operations 363
Operations Control 365
Materials Management 366
Tools for Operations Process Control 367
The Greening of Business For the Greener Good 368
Quality Control 369

Summary of Learning Objectives 370
KEY TERMS 371
QUESTIONS FOR ANALYSIS 372
APPLICATION EXERCISES 372
Building Your Business Skills 372
Exercising Your Ethics: Team Exercise 373
Concluding Case 11-1 How to Keep a Project Afloat 374
Concluding Case 11-2 Bailout or Bust? 375

12 Increasing Productivity and Quality 378

Opening Case Quality Problems in Service Businesses 379

The Productivity–Quality Connection 380
- Responding to the Productivity Challenge 380

Total Quality Management 384

Business Accountability Rating the Quality of Diamonds 385
- Managing for Quality 386

Entrepreneurship and New Ventures A Cut Above 387

Tools for Total Quality Management 389
- Value-Added Analysis 389
- Statistical Process Control 390
- Quality/Cost Studies 391
- Quality Improvement Teams 392
- Benchmarking 392
- Getting Closer to the Customer 392
- ISO 9000:2000 and ISO 14000 393
- Process Re-engineering 394
- Adding Value Through Supply Chains 394

The Greening of Business Green Changes in Steel Making 397

Productivity and Quality as Competitive Tools 398
- Invest in Innovation and Technology 398
- Adopt a Long-Run Perspective 399
- Emphasize Quality of Work Life 399
- Improve the Service Sector 400

Summary of Learning Objectives 400
- KEY TERMS 402
- QUESTIONS FOR ANALYSIS 402
- APPLICATION EXERCISES 402
- Building Your Business Skills 403
- Exercising Your Ethics: Team Exercise 403
- Concluding Case 12-1 Poor Productivity: Canada's Biggest Problem? 404
- Concluding Case 12-2 Supply Chain Management at Loblaw 406

13 Understanding Information Systems and Communication Technology 408

Opening Case The Instapreneur 409

Information Management 410
- Information Systems 411
- Key Users of Information Systems 411
- Types of Information Systems 412

Information Technology 414
- Information Technology and Organizational Processes 415
- IT Building Blocks 419

Business Accountability Social Matters 423

IT Risks and Threats 424
- Hackers 424
- Software Piracy 425
- Identity Theft 425
- Intellectual Property Theft 426
- Computer Viruses, Worms, and Trojan Horses 426
- Spyware 426
- Spam 427

IT Protection Measures 427
- Firewalls 427
- Preventing Identity Theft 428
- Preventing Viruses: Anti-virus Software 428
- Encryption Software 428
- Avoiding Spam and Spyware 428

Summary of Learning Objectives 429
- KEY TERMS 431
- QUESTIONS FOR ANALYSIS 431
- APPLICATION EXERCISES 431
- Building Your Business Skills 432
- Exercising Your Ethics: Team Exercise 433
- Concluding Case 13-1 Sharing the Wealth 434
- Concluding Case 13-2 Internet Wars 435

14 Understanding Accounting Issues 438

Opening Case Accounting for Pensions 439

What Is Accounting? 440

Who Are Accountants and What Do They Do? 441
- Financial and Managerial Accounting 441
- Professional Accountants 442
- Accounting Services 443

Business Accountability Who's Accountable for Offshore Oversight? 444
- Private Accountants 445

Entrepreneurship and New Ventures New Opportunities in Forensic Accounting 446

The Accounting Equation 447

Financial Statements 447
- Balance Sheets 448
- Income Statements 450
- Statement of Cash Flows 452
- The Budget: An Internal Financial Statement 453
- Reporting Standards and Practices 453

Analyzing Financial Statements 455
- Solvency Ratios 456
- Profitability Ratios 457
- Activity Ratios 458

International Accounting 459
- Foreign Currency Exchange 459
- International Transactions 459
- International Accounting Standards 460

The Greening of Business The Green Revolution Hits Accounting 460

Summary of Learning Objectives 461
- KEY TERMS 462
- QUESTIONS FOR ANALYSIS 462
- APPLICATION EXERCISES 463
- Building Your Business Skills 463
- Exercising Your Ethics: Team Exercise 464
- Concluding Case 14-1 Do We Need to Audit the Auditors? 465
- Concluding Case 14-2 Continuing Concerns in the Accounting Profession 466
- CBC Video Case 3-1: Tree Planters 468
- CBC Video Case 3-2: African Accountants 469
- Crafting a Business Plan Part 3: Managing Operations and Information 470

Part Four Managing Marketing 472

15 Understanding Marketing Processes and Consumer Behaviour 474

Opening Case Why So Serious? 475
What Is Marketing? 476
Providing Value and Satisfaction 476
Goods, Services, and Ideas 477
Business Accountability When Smoke Gets in Your Eyes 478
The Marketing Environment 480
The Greening of Business Guelph Thinks Green 482
Strategy: The Marketing Mix 483
Target Marketing and Market Segmentation 485
Identifying Market Segments 487
Market Segmentation: A Caution 489
Market Research 490
The Research Process 491
Research Methods 492
Data Warehousing and Data Mining 493
Understanding Consumer Behaviour 494
Influences on Consumer Behaviour 494
The Consumer Buying Process 495
Organizational Marketing and Buying Behaviour 497
Organizational Markets 497
Organizational Buying Behaviour 497
The International Marketing Mix 498
International Products 498
International Pricing 499
International Promotion 499
International Distribution 499
Small Business and the Marketing Mix 500
Small Business Products 500
Small Business Pricing 501
Small Business Promotion 501
Small Business Distribution 501

Summary of Learning Objectives 501
KEY TERMS 503
QUESTIONS FOR ANALYSIS 503
APPLICATION EXERCISES 504
Building Your Business Skills 504
Exercising Your Ethics: Team Exercise 505
Concluding Case 15-1 Dell-ivering on Consumer Electronics 506
Concluding Case 15-2 An Old Company with New Potential 508

16 Developing and Promoting Goods and Services 510

Opening Case Psst! Did You Hear the Latest? 511
What Is a Product? 512
Product Features and Benefits 512
Classifying Goods and Services 513
The Product Mix 514
Developing New Products 514
The Time Frame of New Product Development 514
The Seven-Step Development Process 515
The Product Life Cycle 516
Stages in the Product Life Cycle (PLC) 517
Identifying Products 518
Branding Products 518
Packaging Products 522
Labelling Products 522
Promoting Products and Services 522
Information and Exchange Values 523
Promotional Objectives 523
The Greening of Business Promoting a Green Business Image 524
Promotional Strategies 525
The Promotional Mix 525
Advertising Promotions 527
Advertising Strategies 527
Advertising Media 527
Entrepreneurship and New Ventures Fuelling the World of Branded Entertainment 532
Types of Advertising 533
Preparing an Advertising Campaign 533
Personal Selling 534
Sales Force Management 535
Sales Promotions 536
Types of Sales Promotions 537
Publicity and Public Relations 538
International Promotion Strategies 538
Emergence of the Global Perspective 538
The Movement Toward Global Advertising 539
Promotional Practices in Small Business 540
Small Business Advertising 540
The Role of Personal Selling in Small Business 540
Small Business Promotions 541

Summary of Learning Objectives 541
KEY TERMS 543
QUESTIONS FOR ANALYSIS 543
APPLICATION EXERCISES 543
Building Your Business Skills 544
Exercising Your Ethics: Team Exercise 545
Concluding Case 16-1 Measuring the Effectiveness of Advertising 546
Concluding Case 16-2 The Changing Face of Advertising 547

17 Pricing and Distributing Goods and Services 550

Opening Case Buyers and Sellers Jockey for Position 551
Pricing Objectives and Tools 552
Pricing to Meet Business Objectives 552
Price-Setting Tools 553
Entrepreneurship and New Ventures Men and Cars: Unrequited Love 555
Pricing Strategies and Tactics 556
Pricing Strategies 556
Pricing Tactics 558
International Pricing 559
The Distribution Mix 559
Intermediaries and Distribution Channels 559

Distribution Strategies 563
Channel Conflict and Channel Leadership 564

Wholesaling 564
Merchant Wholesalers 565
Agents and Brokers 565

Retailing 565
Types of Retail Outlets 565

The Greening of Business Green Retailing 567
Non-store Retailing 567

Physical Distribution 570
Warehousing Operations 570
Transportation Operations 571
Companies Specializing in Transportation 574
Distribution as a Marketing Strategy 574

Summary of Learning Objectives 575
KEY TERMS 577
QUESTIONS FOR ANALYSIS 577
APPLICATION EXERCISES 578
Building Your Business Skills 578
Exercising Your Ethics: Team Exercise 578
Concluding Case 17-1 This Distribution Net's for You 579
Concluding Case 17-2 Changing Distribution Channels in the Music Business 581
CBC Video Case 4-1: The "Feel-Better" Bracelet 583
CBC Video Case 4-2: Shall We Dance? 584
Crafting a Business Plan Part 4: Principles of Marketing 585

Part Five
Managing Financial Issues 586

18 Understanding Money and Banking 588

Opening Case Money, Money, Money 589

What Is Money? 590
The Characteristics of Money 590
The Functions of Money 591
The Spendable Money Supply: M-1 592
M-1 Plus the Convertible Money Supply: M-2 593
Credit Cards: Plastic Money? 593

The Canadian Financial System 595
Financial Institutions 595
Changes Affecting Financial Institutions 595
The Bank of Canada 597
Operation of the Bank of Canada 597

Financial Pillar #1—Chartered Banks 598
Services Offered by Banks 598

The Greening of Business Ebanking: Easy and Eco-friendly 600
Bank Deposits 601
Bank Loans 602
Banks as Creators of Money 602

Business Accountability Canadian vs. U.S. Banks: Quite a Difference 604

Financial Pillar #2—Alternate Banks 605
Trust Companies 605
Credit Unions/Caisses Populaires 605

Financial Pillar #3—Specialized Lending and Savings Intermediaries 606
Life Insurance Companies 606
Factoring Companies 606
Financial Corporations 606
Venture Capital Firms 606
Pension Funds 607

Financial Pillar #4—Investment Dealers 607

Other Sources of Funds 607

International Banking and Finance 608
Exchange Rates and International Trade 608
The International Payments Process 609
The International Bank Structure 610

Summary of Learning Objectives 611
KEY TERMS 613
QUESTIONS FOR ANALYSIS 613
APPLICATION EXERCISES 613
Building Your Business Skills 613
Exercising Your Ethics: Team Exercise 614
Concluding Case 18-1 Coping with Currency Fluctuations 615
Concluding Case 18-2 The Struggle to Finance Fish Farming 616

19 Understanding Securities and Investments 618

Opening Case And the Markets Came Tumbling Down—Again 619

Securities Markets 620
Primary and Secondary Markets for Securities 620

Stocks 621
Common Stock 621
Preferred Stock 622
Stock Exchanges 623

Business Accountability Accountability Goes Professional 625

Bonds 627
Corporate Bonds 628
The Retirement of Bonds 628
Government Bonds 629
Secondary Markets for Bonds 630

Other Investments 630
Mutual Funds 630
Hedge Funds 631
Commodities 632
Stock Options 632
Making Choices for Diversification, Asset Allocation, and Risk Reduction 633

Buying and Selling Securities 634
Using Financial Information Services 634
Buying and Selling Stocks 637
Financing Securities Purchases 637

The Greening of Business Green Trading 639

Securities Regulation 640
Canadian Securities Regulations 640
U.S. Securities Regulation 640

Summary of Learning Objectives 641
KEY TERMS 643
QUESTIONS FOR ANALYSIS 643

APPLICATION EXERCISES 643
Building Your Business Skills 644
Exercising Your Ethics: Team Exercise 645
Concluding Case 19-1 Scandal in the Mutual Fund Industry 646
Concluding Case 19-2 Stock Market Shenanigans 648

20 Financial Decisions and Risk Management 650

Opening Case A Financial Meltdown 651

The Role of the Financial Manager 652
Objectives of the Financial Manager 652
Responsibilities of the Financial Manager 653

Why Do Businesses Need Funds? 654
Short-Term (Operating) Expenditures 654
Long-Term (Capital) Expenditures 655

Sources of Short-Term Funds 656
Trade Credit 656
Secured Short-Term Loans 656
Unsecured Short-Term Loans 657
Factoring Accounts Receivable 658

Sources of Long-Term Funds 659
Debt Financing 659
Equity Financing 660
Hybrid Financing: Preferred Stock 661
Choosing Between Debt and Equity Financing 661

Entrepreneurship and New Ventures An Online Community for People 50 and Older 663
The Risk-Return Relationship 664

Financial Management for Small Businesses 664
Establishing Bank Credit and Trade Credit 665
Venture Capital 665
Planning for Cash Flow Requirements 665

Business Accountability A Quicken Course in Accountability 666

Risk Management 667
Coping with Risk 667
Insurance as Risk Management 669

Summary of Learning Objectives 673
KEY TERMS 675
QUESTIONS FOR ANALYSIS 675
APPLICATION EXERCISES 675
Building Your Business Skills 676
Exercising Your Ethics: Team Exercise 676
Concluding Case 20-1 The Commercial Paper Crisis 677
Concluding Case 20-2 Pursuing Effective Risk Management 678
CBC Video Case 5-1: Debt Nation 681
CBC Video Case 5-2: Card Tricks 682
Crafting a Business Plan Part 5: Financial Issues 683

Appendix A Business Law A-1

Appendix B Managing Your Personal Finances B-1

Appendix C Comprehensive Cases C-1

Google's Way—Don't Be Evil C-1
A Midsummer Day's Nightmare C-12
The Last Resort Retirement Community C-16
MediaSpark C-20
Security Breach at TJX C-25

Endnotes, Sources, and Credits N-1
Name and Organization Index I-1
Subject Index I-10

PREFACE

In this, the seventh Canadian edition of *Business*, we continue to emphasize our long-standing principle of "Doing the Basics Best." Cutting-edge firsts, up-to-date issues that shape today's business world, and creative pedagogy help students build a solid foundation of business knowledge. This new edition continues with the strengths that made the first six editions so successful—comprehensiveness, accuracy, currency, and readability.

What's New to the Seventh Canadian Edition

The impact of one of the most significant events of the past 60 years—the **financial crisis** that began in **2008—is examined in depth in several chapters of the text**. For example, the opening case in Chapter 20 explains the causes of the financial meltdown and its impact on banks, the stock market, sub-prime mortgages, and the economy and business in general. Chapter 20 also includes an end-of-chapter case describing the commercial paper crisis that hit Canada just prior to the more general financial crisis. The opening case of Chapter 19 describes the ups and downs of the world's stock markets during the last decade and explains how the financial crisis of 2008 led to dramatic declines in shareholder wealth. The impact of the financial crisis on business firms is also analyzed in many other places in the text.

The seventh Canadian edition of *Business* incorporates many of the changes suggested by professors and students who used the sixth edition, as well as changes suggested by reviewers. The following changes have been made:

- The book opens with a **dynamic new Prologue** that describes the four basic perspectives from which students can approach business—as an employee, as an owner or manager, as a customer, and as an investor. In the Prologue, we introduce eight actual "stories of business" that help students see the excitement, challenge, and satisfaction that are essential parts of business activity in Canada.
- Each chapter opens with a section called **"How Will This Help Me?"** This section shows students why the content in the chapter really matters to them and to their careers in business.
- The text contains three series of boxed inserts that are positioned at strategic points in the chapters. The first of these—**brand-new to this edition—is entitled "The Greening of Business."** It analyzes the steps that businesses are taking to be more environmentally friendly, and identifies both the opportunities and challenges that businesses are encountering as they try to be more socially responsible. The second series—entitled **"Entrepreneurship and New Ventures"**—provides all new, real-life examples of Canadian entrepreneurs who saw an opportunity to provide a new product or service in the marketplace, and the activities they carried out to be successful. The third series—entitled **"Business Accountability"**—focusses student attention on business behaviour that is of significant public concern. Each insert describes an accountability issue that is currently confronting a real Canadian or international company, and the steps that are being taken to make business managers more accountable for their actions.

- A completely rewritten business plan project, tailor-made to match and reinforce book content, appears at the end of each major section of the text. This new business plan project is software-independent and provides students with an easy-to-understand template that they work from as they create their business plans. Based on reviewer feedback, we've divided the business plan project into logical sections, placing each part of the project at the end of each main section of the text. With five parts in all, students can gradually apply the concepts they've learned in the chapters to their business plans throughout the course. You will find the templates for the Business Plan project online in MyBusinessLab.
- **90% of the opening cases, boxed inserts, end-of-chapter cases, and video cases are either new or updated.**
- Significant **new material has been added** in Chapter 6 **on the topic of managerial decision making**. Sound decision-making processes are particularly important during difficult economic times.
- **A completely new section on the topic of leadership has been added** to Chapter 10. This section describes the latest trends in thinking about the crucial topic of leadership.
- **New material on business strategy and its impact on operations management has been added** in Chapter 11.
- **Information technology (IT)** has dramatically changed the business landscape, and we include a totally rewritten chapter on IT (Chapter 13) that reflects those changes. We discuss the impact IT has had on the business world, the many IT resources businesses have at their disposal, the threats IT poses for businesses, and the ways in which businesses protect themselves from these threats.
- Many **new examples of business practice have been included** in each of the chapters. Some of these examples are brief and some are more detailed, but they all help students to better understand important business concepts.
- A **new team ethics exercise** is found at the end of each chapter. These exercises ask students to take on the role of employee, owner, customer, or investor and examine a chapter-related business ethics dilemma through the perspective of that role. By working together as a team, students learn how to cooperate with each other, see an ethical dilemma from various points of view, and decide what outcome is ultimately best in each situation.
- **Nine of the ten video cases are new.** There are two cases at the end of each part; see the table of contents for a listing.
- Five supplementary cases are included in Appendix C, and three of these cases are new to this edition. These cases are more detailed than the end-of-chapter cases, and they provide students with more extensive information to consider as they analyze the case material and make recommendations about how to resolve the problems presented in the case.

Major Themes

Five major themes continue to be evident in this new edition: change, international business, ethics and social responsibility, the importance of small business, and the quality imperative. Students need to understand these themes since their careers in business will be significantly affected by them.

The Theme of Change

The dramatic changes that have been occurring in business practice during the past decade continue apace, and these changes have been complicated by the financial crisis that began in 2008. The development of new business processes, new products, and new services all make the study of change in business exciting and necessary. New ways of doing things are replacing traditional business practices, usually with surprising speed and often with better competitive results. As authors, we have tried to communicate the theme of change by describing how real-world business firms cope with planned and unplanned events that test the mettle of managers.

The Growth of International Business

The globalization of the economy is one of the dominant challenges of the twenty-first century. To keep students aware of this challenge, we've included many examples and cases that describe the experiences of Canadian companies in the global marketplace. We also describe how global companies have impacted the domestic Canadian market. In addition to these examples—which are found throughout the text—we devote an entire chapter to international business (Chapter 5, International Business).

The Role of Ethics and Social Responsibility

During the last decade, the topics of business ethics and social responsibility have generated a sharply increased level of discussion and debate as a result of the highly-publicized trials of top managers at companies like Enron, WorldCom, and Livent, as well as concern about questionable financial practices that led to the financial meltdown of 2008. We devote an entire chapter to the discussion of ethical and social responsibility issues (Chapter 3, Conducting Business Ethically and Responsibly) because these issues are so important to modern business. Ethical issues are also raised in many other chapters of the text, and a team ethics exercise is found at the end of every chapter.

The Significance of Small Business

College and university graduates will develop careers in both large and small businesses. We have therefore provided coverage of both large and small companies throughout the text. For those students who are interested in a career in small business, we discuss the implications of various ideas for small business. As well, a major section in Chapter 4 (Understanding Entrepreneurship, Small Business, and New Venture Creation) is devoted to small business and new business startups. The boxed series entitled "Entrepreneurship and New Ventures" gives additional information about small business activity in Canada.

The Importance of Information and Communication Technology

In our information-based society, the people and organizations that learn how to obtain and use information will be the ones that succeed. The explosive growth and change in these systems is recognized as we provide a substantially revised chapter on the management of information (Chapter 13, Managing Information Systems and Communication Technology).

The Quality Imperative

Quality and productivity became the key to competitive success for many companies in the global marketplace during the 1990s. These topics continue to dominate the thinking of managers in the twenty-first century, and we devote a full chapter to their coverage (Chapter 12, Increasing Productivity and Quality).

Major Features of the Text

The text contains the following features to stimulate student interest in and understanding of the material that is presented about business.

Part Opener

At the beginning of each of the five major parts of the book is a brief outline introducing the material that will be discussed in that part. These outlines give students a glimpse of the "big picture" as they start reading about a new area of the business world.

Chapter Materials

Each chapter contains several features that are designed to increase student interest in and understanding of the material being presented. These features are as follows:

Chapter Learning Objectives. A list of numbered learning objectives is presented at the beginning of each chapter. These objectives—which guide students in determining what is important in each chapter—are also referenced in the margins opposite the relevant content in the chapter.

Chapter Opening Case. Each chapter begins with a description of a situation that is faced by a real Canadian or international company. The subject matter of the opening case is relevant to the material presented in the chapter and therefore helps students bridge the gap between theory and practice.

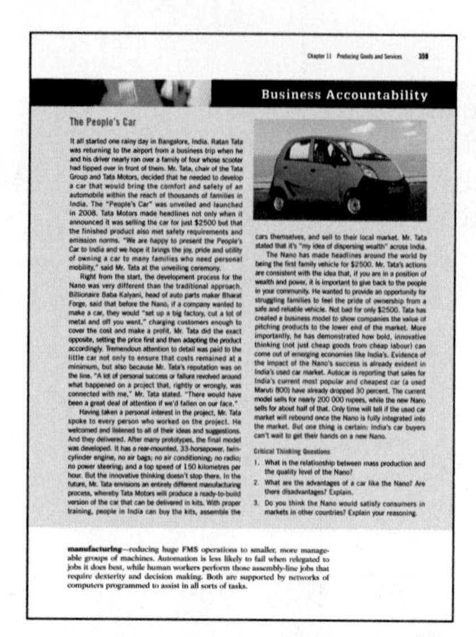

Boxed Inserts. There are three series of boxed inserts: "Business Accountability," "Entrepreneurship and New Ventures," and "The Greening of Business." As noted above, the Business Accountability boxes raise student consciousness about business responsibility to its constituents. The Entrepreneurship and New Ventures boxes tell interesting stories of how Canadian entrepreneurs identified a need for a new product or service and how they set up a company to effectively satisfy that need. The Greening of Business boxes describe how business firms are responding to concerns about the environment.

Examples. In addition to the boxed inserts, each chapter contains numerous examples of how businesses operate so that students can gain a better understanding of the dynamics of business practice in Canada and elsewhere. These examples—which range in length from one sentence to several paragraphs—help students understand concepts which are discussed in the text.

Figures and Tables. The latest available data have been used to update tables and figures throughout the text.

End-of-Chapter Materials

Several important pedagogical features are found at the end of each chapter. These are designed to help students better understand the contents of the chapter.

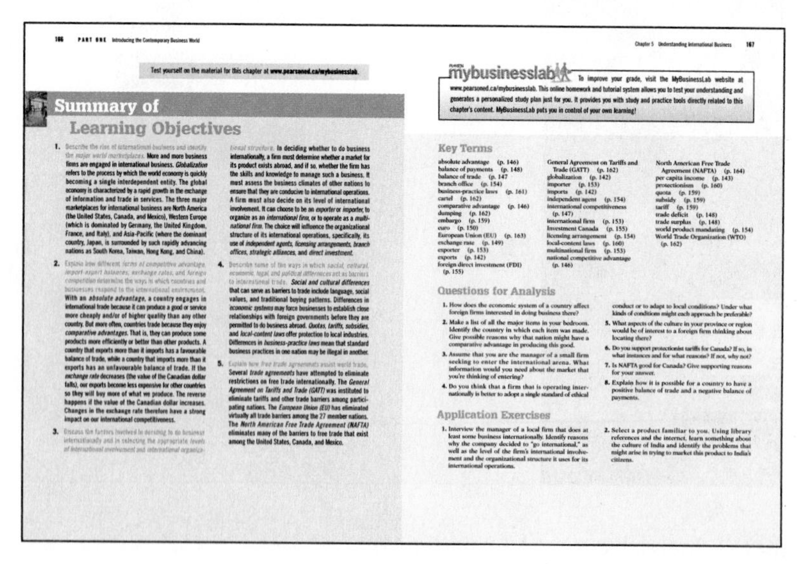

Summary of Learning Objectives. The material in each chapter is concisely summarized, using the learning objectives as the organizing scheme. This helps students understand the main points that were presented in the chapter.

Key Terms. In each chapter, the key terms that students should know are highlighted in the text, defined in the margin, and listed alphabetically at the end of the chapter (with page references).

Questions and Exercises. There are two types of questions here: analysis questions (which require students to think beyond simple factual recall and apply the concepts they have read about) and application exercises (which require students to visit local businesses or to interview managers and gather additional information that will help them understand how business firms operate).

Building Your Business Skills Exercise. This feature involves in-depth exercises that allow students to examine some specific aspect of business in detail. The exercise may ask students to work individually or in a group to gather data about an interesting business issue and to then develop a written report or a class presentation based on the information that was gathered. Each exercise begins with a list of goals, a description of the situation, a step-by-step methodology for proceeding, and follow-up questions to help students focus their responses to the challenge.

Exercising Your Ethics: Team Exercise. In these new exercises, students are presented with a description of a situation that leads to an ethical dilemma and are then asked several questions that focus on how to approach and resolve the ethical challenge. Students take on the role of employee, owner, customer, or investor and examine the ethical dilemma through the perspective of that role.

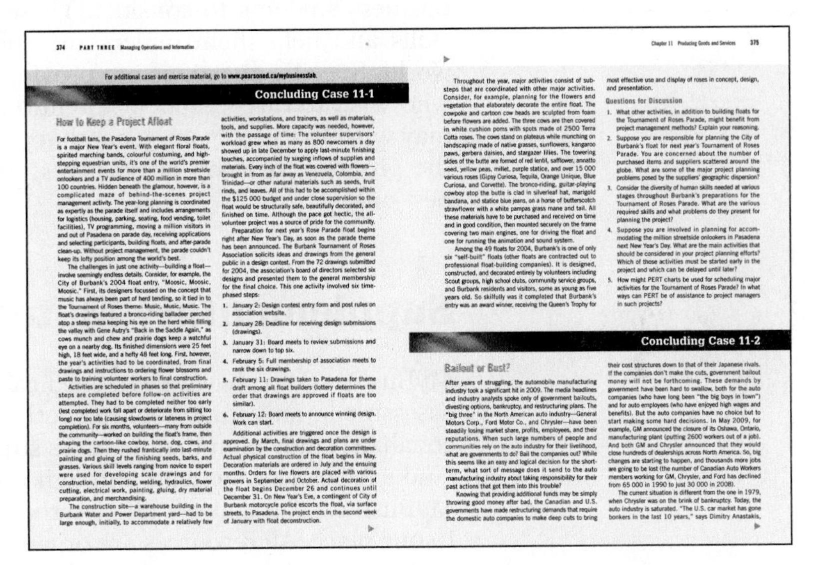
Concluding Case 11-1

How to Keep a Project Afloat

Concluding Case 11-2

Bailout or Bust?

Concluding Cases. Each chapter concludes with two case studies that focus on real Canadian or international companies. These cases are designed to help students apply the chapter material to a real company that is currently in the news. At the end of each case, several questions guide students in their analysis.

End-of-Part Material

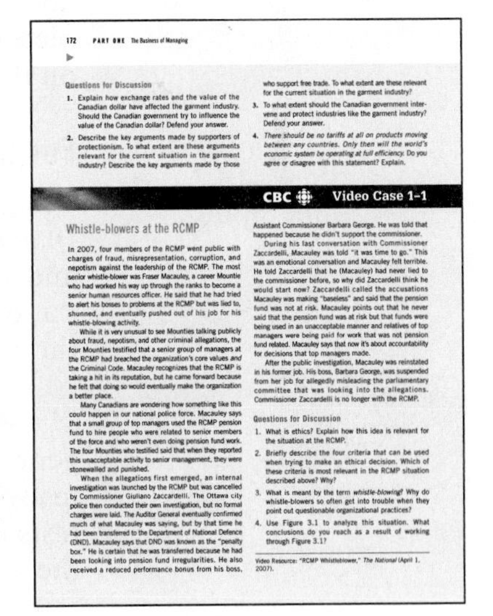
Questions for Discussion

CBC Video Case 1-1

Whistle-blowers at the RCMP

Video Cases. Two new video cases are presented at the end of each of the five major parts of the text. The instructor can show the video in class and then either conduct a class discussion, using the questions at the end of the written case summary as a guide, or ask students to complete a written assignment which requires answering the questions at the end of the case. This approach to teaching adds a major new dynamic to classes because students will be able to relate text material to actual Canadian business situations. These video cases are also available on MyBusinessLab for *Business*, Seventh Canadian Edition.

Crafting a Business Plan. As noted above, this new, software-independent feature helps students gain key insights into what is involved in starting a new business.

Appendices

Three appendices accompany the text.

Appendix A—Business Law. The material on Business Law includes key topics such as contracts, the concept of agency, warranties, and bankruptcy.

Appendix B—Managing Your Personal Finances (provided on the accompanying MyBusinessLab). This feature has been overwhelmingly requested by students and instructors, and presents a down-to-earth hands-on approach that will help students manage their personal finances. The practical information found in this feature includes a worksheet for determining net worth, insightful examples demonstrating the time value of money, a method for determining how much to invest now in order to build a future nest egg of a certain size, suggestions on how to manage credit card debt, guidelines for purchasing a house, and a personalized worksheet for setting financial goals. The information contained in this feature will be immensely useful to students.

Appendix C—Supplementary Case Studies. Five supplementary cases are presented for student consideration. These cases are longer than the end-of-chapter cases, and they raise several issues that are important for beginning business students to consider. These cases further build students' analytical skills and help them understand the complexities of the modern business world. Specific questions are provided at the end of each case for instructors who wish to direct student attention to certain problems. Other instructors may wish to use a more general approach that simply asks students to define the problem, develop alternatives, analyze the alternatives, and choose the best one.

Supplementary Materials

MyBusinessLab (www.pearsoned.ca/mybusinesslab) is an online grading, assessment, and study tool for both faculty and students. It generates a personalized study plan that focusses students on what they, individually, need to study. It engages students through an interactive and focussed environment. MyBusinessLab delivers all classroom resources for instructors and students in one place. All resources are organized by learning objective so that lectures and studying can be customized more conveniently than ever before. A complete description of the student and instructor resources available is provided on the MyBusinessLab insert included with this text.

For Instructors

Instructor's Resource Centre. Instructor resources are password protected and available for download via www.pearsoncanada.ca. For your convenience, these resources are also available on the Instructor's Resource CD-ROM and through the instructor's area of MyBusinessLab.

MyTest. MyTest from Pearson Canada is a powerful online assessment-generation program that helps instructors easily create and print quizzes, tests, and exams, as well as homework or practice handouts. Questions and tests can all be authored online, allowing instructors ultimate flexibility and the ability to efficiently manage assessments at any time, from anywhere.

Pearson TestGen. Pearson TestGen is a special computerized test item file that enables instructors to view and edit the existing questions, add questions, generate tests, and print the tests in a variety of formats. Powerful search and sort functions make it easy to locate questions and arrange them in any order desired. TestGen also enables instructors to administer tests on a local area network, have the tests graded electronically, and have the results prepared in electronic or printed reports. The Pearson TestGen is compatible with PC or Macintosh systems. This edition's test item file was written by text author Frederick A. Starke.

Instructor's Resource Manual. The Instructor's Resource Manual contains chapter outlines, teaching tips, in-class exercises, and suggestions on how to use the text effectively. The manual also provides answers to the end-of-chapter questions and cases (including Building Your Business Skills, Exercising Your Ethics, and the Video Cases). This edition's Instructor's Manual is written by text author Frederick A. Starke.

PowerPoint® Presentations. PowerPoint Presentations offer about 40 PowerPoint slides per chapter, outlining the key points in the text. The slides include lecture notes that provide page references to the text, summaries, and suggestions for student activities or related questions from the text. This edition's PowerPoint slides were written by Valerie Miceli (Seneca College).

CBC Video Library. The Video Library for *Business*, Seventh Canadian Edition, includes 10 new video segments that focus on Canadian companies and discuss business issues from a Canadian point of view. The cases can also be viewed online at www.pearsoned.ca/highered/videocentral and answers to the discussion questions are provided in the Instructor's Resource Manual. (Please contact your Pearson Canada Inc. sales representative for details.)

Pearson Custom Publishing (www.prenhall.com/custombusiness). Pearson Custom Publishing can provide you and your students with texts, cases, and articles to enhance your course. Choose material from Darden, Ivey, Harvard Business School Publishing, NACRA, and Thunderbird to create your own custom casebook. Contact your Pearson Canada Inc. sales representative.

Online Learning Solutions. Pearson Canada Inc. supports instructors interested in using online course management systems by providing text-related content in Blackboard/WebCT and Course Compass. To find out more about creating an online course using Pearson content in one of these platforms, contact your Pearson Canada Inc. sales representative.

Your Pearson Canada Inc. Sales Representative. Your Pearson sales rep is always available to ensure that you have everything you need to teach a winning course. Armed with experience, training, and product knowledge, your Pearson rep will support your assessment and adoption of any of the products, services, and technologies outlined here to ensure that our offerings are tailored to suit your individual needs and the needs of your students. Whether it's getting instructions on TestGen software or specific content files for your new online course, your Pearson sales representative is there to help. Ask your Pearson sales representative for details.

Technology Specialists. Pearson's Technology Specialists work with faculty and campus course designers to ensure that Pearson technology products, assessment tools, and online course materials are tailored to meet your specific needs. This highly qualified team is dedicated to helping schools take full advantage of a wide range of educational resources by assisting in the integration of a variety of instructional materials and media formats. Your local Pearson Education sales representative can provide you with more details on this service program.

CourseSmart. CourseSmart is a new way for instructors and students to access textbooks online anytime from anywhere. With thousands of titles across hundreds of courses, CourseSmart helps instructors choose the best textbook for their class and give their students a new option for buying the assigned textbook as a lower cost eTextbook. For more information, visit www.coursesmart.com.

For Students

MyBusinessLab (www.pearsoned.ca/mybusinesslab) is an online grading, assessment, and study tool for both faculty and students. It generates a personalized study plan that focusses students on what they, individually, need to study. It engages students through an interactive and focussed environment. All resources are organized by learning objective so that studying can be customized more conveniently than ever before. A complete description of the student and instructor resources available is provided on the MyBusinessLab insert included with this text.

Crafting a Business Plan. A completely rewritten business plan project, tailor-made to match and reinforce book content, appears at the end of each major section of the book. This new business plan project is *software-independent* and provides students with an easy-to-understand template that they work from as they create their business plans.

ACKNOWLEDGMENTS

We owe special thanks to Patricia Jones for her excellent copyediting; Heather Sangster for her careful proofreading; Cheryl Jackson, Senior Production Editor, for her efficient management of this project; and Heather Jackson for her fine photo research. Thanks are also due to Karen Elliott, Acquisitions Editor; Pamela Voves, Developmental Editor; Cas Shields, Executive Marketing Manager, Business and Economics; and all the members of the Pearson Canada Inc. sales team.

In addition, we would like to acknowledge the contributions of Sherry Finney of Cape Breton University who prepared the Entrepreneurship and New Venture boxed features.

We appreciate the insights and suggestions of the following individuals who provided feedback on the sixth edition or reviewed the manuscript for the new edition: Donald S. Ausman (JR Shaw School of Business, NAIT), Chuck Bridges (Saint Mary's University), Choon Hian Chan (Kwantlen Polytechnic University), Randall Fisher, PhD (Mount Saint Vincent University), Allan Fraser (Cape Breton University), David Laurentiu (Centennial College of Applied Arts and Technology), Valerie Miceli, MBA (Seneca College), and Frank Saccucci (Grant MacEwan College). Their comments were carefully considered and implemented wherever possible.

Frederick A. Starke
Melanie D. Lang

About the Authors

Ronald J. Ebert is Emeritus Professor at the University of Missouri-Columbia where he lectures in the Management Department and serves as adviser to students and student organizations. Dr. Ebert draws upon more than 30 years of teaching experience at such schools as Sinclair College, University of Washington, University of Missouri, Lucian Blaga University of Sibiu (Romania), and Consortium International University (Italy). His consulting alliances include such firms as Mobay Corporation, Kraft Foods, Oscar Mayer, Atlas Powder, and John Deere. He has designed and conducted management development programs for such diverse clients as the American Public Power Association, the United States Savings and Loan League, and the Central Missouri Manufacturing Training Consortium.

His experience as a practitioner has fostered an advocacy for integrating concepts with best business practices in business education. The five business books he has written have been translated into Spanish, Chinese, Malaysian, and Romanian. Dr. Ebert has served as the editor of the *Journal of Operations Management*. He is a past-president and fellow of the Decision Sciences Institute. He has served as consultant and external evaluator for *Quantitative Reasoning for Business Studies*, an introduction-to-business project sponsored by the National Science Foundation.

Ricky W. Griffin is Distinguished Professor of Management and holds the Blocker Chair in Business in the Mays School of Business at Texas A&M University. Dr. Griffin currently serves as executive associate dean. He previously served as head of the Department of Management and as director of the Center for Human Resource Management at Texas A&M. His research interests include workplace aggression and violence, executive skills and decision making, and workplace culture. Dr. Griffin's research has been published in such journals as *Academy of Management Review, Academy of Management Journal, Administrative Science Quarterly,* and *Journal of Management.* He has also served as editor of *Journal of Management*. Dr. Griffin has consulted with such organizations as Texas Instruments, Tenneco, Amoco, Compaq Computer, and Continental Airlines.

Dr. Griffin has served the Academy of Management as chair of the organizational behaviour division. He also has served as president of the southwest division of the Academy of Management and on the board of directors of the Southern Management Association. He is a fellow of both the Academy of Management and the Southern Management Association. He is also the author of several successful textbooks, each of which is a market leader. In addition, the books are widely used in dozens of countries and have been translated into numerous foreign languages, including Spanish, Polish, Malaysian, and Russian.

Frederick A. Starke is Emeritus Professor of Organizational Behaviour in the Asper School of Business at the University of Manitoba. He began his career at the University of Manitoba in 1968 and has taught courses in organizational behaviour, organization theory, decision making, and marketing. He has served in several administrative positions, including head of the Department of Business Administration from 1982–87 and from 1989–94, and as associate dean from 1996–2005.

Dr. Starke earned his B.A. and M.B.A. from Southern Illinois University and his Ph.D. in Organizational Behaviour from Ohio State University. He has published research articles in such scholarly journals as the *Administrative Science Quarterly, the Journal of Applied Psychology, the Academy of Management Journal, the Journal of Management Studies,* and the *Review of Religious Research*. He has also written articles for professional journals, such as the *Journal of Systems Management*, *Information Executive*, and the *Canadian Journal of Nursing Administration*.

Dr. Starke writes textbooks that are used by university and community college students in business programs across Canada. These titles include *Organizational Behaviour*, *Business Essentials*, *Management*, and *Business*. Dr. Starke also presents seminars on the topics of decision making and goal setting to practising managers in both the public and private sectors.

Melanie D. Lang is Assistant Professor at the University of Guelph. She served as Academic Advisor to the BComm. Marketing Management major from 2005 to 2008 and is currently Director of the Centre for Business and Social Entrepreneurship (CBaSE). As Director, Ms. Lang oversees the experiential learning opportunities of students working with local businesses and community-based organizations. The Centre promotes student engagement and social responsibility while encouraging entrepreneurship in its broadest sense: the translation of ideas into action for the betterment of society.

Ms. Lang began her career at the University of Guelph in 2004 and has taught courses in marketing, consumer behaviour, and business. One of the areas of discipline that Ms. Lang teaches includes an interdisciplinary product/business development course involving students from various academic backgrounds who work in teams to develop real products and accompanying business plans. Her research interests include the acceptance of new and emerging agrifood products into culturally dynamic consumer markets as well as evaluating innovative teaching and learning models.

Ms. Lang earned her BComm and MSc. from the University of Guelph in Marketing and Consumer Studies. She has research papers and case studies in the International Food and Agribusiness Management Association's professional journal. She has contributed to textbooks that are used by business students in commerce programs across Canada.

From the Authors

Ron Ebert, Ricky Griffin, Fred Starke, and Melanie Lang

Businesses today face constant change—change in their competitive landscape, change in their workforce, change in government regulations, change in the economy, change in technology, change in... well, you get the idea. As we began planning this revision, we too recognized the need for change—changing demands from instructors, changing needs and preferences of students, and changing views on what material to cover in this course and how to cover it. These have all affected how we planned and revised the book.

The business world provided us with dozens of new examples, new challenges (particularly the financial crisis of 2008-09), new success stories, and new perspectives on what businesses must do to remain competitive. A new dedication to relevance guided our work from beginning to end. For example, we know that some business students will go to work for big companies. Others will work for small firms. Some will start their own business, and others may join a family business. We have therefore tried to make the book as relevant and useful as possible to all students, regardless of their personal and career goals and objectives.

We have incorporated many new features in this seventh Canadian edition of *Business* (see the Preface for a description of these new features). We also carefully reviewed the existing book line by line. New material was added, and older examples were updated or replaced with newer ones. We worked extra hard to make our writing as clear and as crisp as possible. We think that these changes will help make the material even more alive and personal for you.

We believe that we have taken this book to a new, higher level of excellence. Its content is stronger, its learning framework is better, its design is more reader-friendly, and its support materials are the best on the market. We hope that you enjoy reading and learning from this book as much as we enjoyed creating it. And who knows? Perhaps one day we can tell your story of business success to other students.

Prologue

If you're like many students, you may be starting this term with some questions about why you're here. You may be taking this course at a community college or at a university, and you may be taking it in a traditional classroom setting or online. Whatever the case, you may be wondering just what you're supposed to get from this course and how it will benefit you. In short, you may be wondering, "How will this help me?"

First, regardless of what it may be called at your school, this is a survey course designed to introduce you to the exciting and challenging world of business, both in Canada and elsewhere. The course is designed to fit the needs of a wide variety of students. You may be taking this course as the first step toward earning a degree in business, or you may be thinking about business and want to know more about it, or you may know you want to study business but are unsure of the area you want to pursue. You may plan to major in another field but want some basic business background and are taking this course as an elective. Or you may be here because, frankly, this course is required or is a prerequisite for another course. Whatever your situation, this course will be helpful to you.

If you don't have a lot of work experience, you may be uncertain as to what the business world is all about. If you have a lot of work experience, you might be a bit skeptical as to what you can actually learn about business from an introductory course. One of our biggest challenges as authors is to write a book that meets the needs of such a diverse student population, especially when we acknowledge the legitimacy of your right to ask "How will this help me?" We also want to do our best to ensure that you find the course challenging, interesting, and useful. To help lay the foundation for meeting these challenges, let's look at the various "hats" that you may wear, both now and in the future.

Wearing the Hats

There's an old metaphor that refers to people wearing different "hats." In general, this is based on the idea that any given person usually has different roles to play in different settings. For example, your roles may include student, child, spouse, employee, friend, and/or parent. You could think of each of these roles as needing a different hat—when you play the role of a student, for example, you wear one hat, but when you leave campus and go to your part-time job, you put on a different hat. From the perspective of studying and interfacing with the world of *business*, there are at least four distinct "hats" that you might wear:

- *The Employee Hat.* One hat is "worn" as an employee working for a business. Most people wear this hat throughout their working career. To wear the hat successfully, you will need to understand your "place" in the organization—your job duties and responsibilities, how to get along with others, how to work with your boss, what your organization is all about, and so on. You'll begin to see how best to wear this hat as you learn more about organizing business enterprises in Chapter 7 and how organizations manage their human resources in Chapter 8, as well as in several other places in this book.
- *The Employer or Boss Hat.* Another business hat that many people wear is as an employer or boss. Whether you start your own business or get promoted within someone else's business, people will be working for you.

You'll still need to know your job duties and responsibilities, but you'll also need to understand how to manage other people—how to motivate and reward them, how to lead them, how to deal with conflict among them, and the legal parameters that may affect how you treat them. Chapters 3, 6, 9, and 10 provide a lot of information about how you can best wear this hat, although information about the role of employer is found throughout the book.

- *The Consumer Hat.* Even if you don't work for a business, you will still wear the hat of a consumer. Whenever you fill your car with PetroCanada gasoline, bid for something on eBay, buy clothes at Urban Outfitters, or download a song from iTunes, you're consuming products or services created by businesses. To wear this hat effectively, you need to understand how to assess the value of what you're buying, your rights as a consumer, and so on. We discuss how you can best wear this hat in Chapters 2, 15, 16, and 17.
- *The Investor Hat.* The final business hat many people wear is that of an investor. You may buy your own business or work for a company that allows you to buy its stock. You may also invest in other companies through the purchase of stocks or shares of a mutual fund. In order for you to invest wisely, you must understand some basics, such as financial markets, business earnings, and the costs of investment. Chapters 4, 18, 19, 20, and Appendix B will help you learn how to best wear this hat.

Most people wear more than one of these hats at the same time. Regardless of how many hats you wear or when you may be putting them on, you will interface with many different businesses in different ways. Knowing how to best wear all of these hats is what this book is all about.

The Stories of Business

How do businesses get started? How do they work? Why do some businesses grow, and others struggle or even fail? How do businesses affect us regardless of the hats we may be wearing? These are the questions we'll discuss throughout this book. But first, let's "meet" a few people and see how these questions have affected them.

Let's Google It

Sergey Brin and Larry Page decided they were tired of internet search engines that yielded an overwhelming mass of random returns, so they decided to create their own search engine. Their creation—Google—has become the world's most popular web search engine, conducting hundreds of millions of searches everyday. The word "google" has become virtually synonymous with the word "search" among many computer users.

But Brin and Page are not resting on their laurels as they push and expand Google into more corners of our daily lives. Google now offers an improved search engine (Google Chrome), Google Talk (instant messaging), Google Maps, Gmail, and Google Desktop. It has even started a venture capital firm to provide funding for new business start-ups. Google generates more than one-quarter of its revenues from markets outside the United States, and it has been translated into 97 languages. When Google began selling its stock to the public in 2004, it generated over $1.6 billion that it is using for even faster expansion. In Chapters 13, 16, and 17 we'll discuss how Google used information technology on its path to success and how companies like it create their own line-up of products (their so-called "product mix"), as well as how a company's public stock offerings affect its balance sheet.

Google founders Sergey Brin and Larry Page.

Roll up the Rim

The Tim Hortons coffee and donut chain is one of the most famous and well-recognized businesses in Canada. It was founded by NHL player Tim Horton in 1964 in Hamilton, Ontario. In 1967, entrepreneur Ron Joyce became Horton's partner. When Horton was killed in an automobile accident in 1974, Joyce bought out the Horton family and became the sole owner of the business. Joyce then embarked on a dramatic expansion of the business. By 1991, there were 500 Tim Hortons stores across Canada, and by 2008 the number had increased to 3000. In 2006, the company went public. The company has surpassed even McDonald's as Canada's largest food service provider. There are also 500 Tim Hortons outlets in the northeastern United States, but these stores have not fared as well as the Canadian stores.

In Canada, the company is legendary for its community support activities and for the Tim Hortons Children's Foundation, which sponsors underprivileged children so they can attend summer camps in Canada and the United States. The company also has very high visibility with the Canadian military, and many of its outlets are located near military bases. It has even opened an outlet in Afghanistan to serve Canadian Forces troops that are stationed there. Why has Tim Hortons been such a dramatic success in Canada? Why has it not been as successful in the United States? We'll look at answers to these and other related questions in Chapters 1, 5, and 16.

Hip Hop Hoops

When most people think of athletic footwear, global brands such as Nike and Adidas come to mind. But a small upstart company called And1 is fast making a name for itself as well. Founded by Jay Coen Gilbert, Seth Berger, and Tom Austin, And1 takes a "streetball" approach to basketball. At the core of its business is a growing line of tapes highlighting the skills—and swagger—of playground legends showing incredible moves and turning basketball purists on their heads.

But if the tapes are the catalyst, And1's shoes and shirts are the drivers. Indeed, And1 now trails only Nike in terms of NBA player endorsements. The counterculture firm has 165 employees, generates $180 million in annual revenues, and sells its products in over 125 countries. Among its more recent activities was a smash summer tour showcasing the talents—and footwear—of more than 15 top streetball players. And to help keep itself fresh, And1 hires mostly younger staffers and pays close attention to their advice. And1 is successful because it knows, hires, and promotes to its target market. You'll learn more about these factors in Chapters 3, 8, 16, and 17.

Dell Computer founder Michael Dell.

A Boy and His Computer

When Michael Dell was 13, he ran a successful mail-order stamp trading business out of his bedroom, grossing over $2000 a month. When he entered university in 1983, personal computers were just coming onto the market, and Michael saw them as the wave of the future. He realized he could buy computer parts from manufacturers, assemble the computers himself, and then sell them directly to consumers for 40 percent below retail. Soon he was grossing $80 000 from his dorm room, so he decided to drop out of school and launch a mail-order computer business.

He named his business Dell Computer, and over the next two decades Dell became the world's biggest PC maker. It also expanded into other product lines such as printers, MP3 players, and LCD televisions. Michael handed over day-to-day control of the company to Kevin Rollins in 2004, but when Dell's sales slumped in 2006 and Hewlett-Packard became the number one computer company, Michael took over again as CEO. Why and how did a business like Dell prosper, and then run into difficulties? How can you make your own business successful? Chapters 1, 3, 4, 11, and 15 will help you better understand the key reasons for business success and failure.

A Good Cup of Java

Starbucks has become an important part of the urban landscape in most major cities in Canada. In less than 30 years, the firm has grown to become the largest coffee retailer in the world. The three people who founded Starbucks did not have ambitious retail plans for the firm; they were primarily interested in wholesaling high-quality coffee beans to independent coffeehouses. In 1987, Howard Schultz (a former employee) bought the company from its three original owners and began an aggressive expansion campaign. By combining tight quality control with an uncanny sense of consumer tastes and preferences, Schultz built Starbucks into one of the strongest brand names in the world.

Starbucks founder Howard Schultz.

It's difficult to provide an accurate count of the number of Starbucks outlets because the firm had been opening a new store somewhere in the world almost every day. But when the recession of 2008 hit, consumer demand for its luxury coffee products declined, and Starbucks began closing stores and laying off staff.

The firm has also become a surprisingly important force in the music industry. Managers determined that many premium coffee drinkers also share a passion for music, so the company started selling a small number of handpicked CDs in its store. As a result, music company executives now line up to try and get their latest offerings on the Starbucks play list. What are the secrets behind Starbucks' success? Can Starbucks regain its former runaway success? How do Starbucks marketers apply their skills to understand Starbucks' customers' preferences? You'll find the answers to these and other related questions in Chapters 4, 6, 8, and 15.

Going Where Others Fear to Go

Inuktun Services Ltd. is a Nanaimo, B.C.-based company that designs and produces small, waterproof, remotely operated vehicles (ROVs) that are equipped with lights and video cameras. These ROVs are used to inspect industrial equipment that is located in places where humans can't easily work—in very small spaces, in dangerous places, and underwater. The ROVs are used by companies in industries like electrical generation, oil and gas, and nuclear, and by the military.

Inuktun was founded in 1989 by Al Robinson and Terry Knight, who chose the name "Inuktun" because in the Inuit language it means "service to mankind." Robinson and Knight originally thought that their ROVs would be of primary interest to boat owners who could guide the robots down into the water to inspect the bottom of their boat and view its condition on a TV monitor. As it turned out, boat owners weren't too interested, but lots of companies were. Now, Inuktun's ROVs travel up and down stairs, around corners, and over obstacles. They can work in water as deep as 300 metres and in pipes that are as little as 15 centimetres in diameter. Inuktun has been successful, even though its customer base turned out to be somewhat different than the company founders originally planned. In Chapters 15 and 16, we'll look at the issues of customer needs and the new product development process, and how these factors influence business success.

Planting the Seeds: A Blast From the Past

During the heady days of the dot-com boom, new web-based businesses were popping up left and right. Garden.com was founded in 1996 by three friends, Cliff and Lisa Sharples and Jamie O'Neill. In early 2000, their company employed over 200 people, and Garden.com was acclaimed by *Fortune, Forbes,* and *Inc.* as one of the best internet-based retailers in the world. The company also had more cash than it needed and was in the enviable position of being able to turn down investment proposals from venture capitalists.

But by the end of that very same year, the business environment had changed dramatically. Venture capital dried up, operating costs escalated, and investors sought lower risk. These forces combined to drive many of the dot-com companies out of business. Cliff, Lisa, and Jamie were sufficiently realistic to see that their business wasn't going to succeed, and they shut down their operations in a relatively orderly manner. They also managed to pay off all of their obligations and still have a tidy nest egg left over to explore future opportunities. In Chapters 4, 6, and 14 we'll discuss why some businesses succeed and others fail, and we'll look at some of the forces that influence business success and failure.

Changing the Urban Landscape

Urban Outfitters sells clothes, accessories, gifts, housewares, and shoes to young metropolitan customers seeking affordable but fashionable lifestyle brands. Urban Outfitters may not have the retailing presence of, say, Old Navy, but the hip retailer nevertheless is a real success story. The company has stores in fashion centres in or near large cities in Canada, the United States, the United Kingdom, Sweden, Denmark, and Ireland.

Urban Outfitters also owns Anthropologie, a similarly focussed store that targets consumers in the 30- to 45-year-old range. Another venture—called Free People—offers merchandise similar to Urban Outfitters and Anthropologie, but at slightly lower prices. Free People also offers a wider range of houseware merchandise geared to apartment dwellers. How is one company able to open different kinds of retail stores and operate at different "price points," and do so in several different countries? You'll learn more about these important aspects of business in Chapters 1, 4, 5, and 14.

So, How *Will* This Help Me?

The world is populated with a breathtaking array of businesses and business opportunities. We hope that these brief business stories have piqued your interest about what lies ahead in this book. Big and small businesses, established and new businesses, broad-based and niche businesses, successful and unsuccessful businesses, global and domestic businesses—regardless of where your future plans take you, we hope that you will look back on this course as one of your positive first steps.

Keep in mind that what you get out of this course depends on at least three factors. One factor is this book and the information about business that you will acquire as a result of reading it. Another factor is your instructor, who is a dedicated professional who wants to help you grow and develop intellectually and academically. The third factor is YOU. Learning is an active process that requires you to be a major participant. Simply memorizing the key terms and concepts in this book may help you achieve an acceptable course grade, but true learning requires that you read, study, discuss, question, review, experience, evaluate—and wear the four hats—as you go along. Tests and homework are necessary, but we hope that you will finish this course with new knowledge and increased enthusiasm for the world of business. Your instructor will do his or her part to facilitate your learning. The rest, then, is up to you. We wish you success.

Part One

Introducing the Contemporary Business World

In the Opening Cases in Chapters 1 to 5, you will read about five interesting situations: (1) fluctuations in the prices of commodities, (2) inflation and deflation, (3) the unethical behaviour of some business managers, (4) family business stories, and (5) Bombardier's global strategy. All of these situations and many more that are described in this text have a common thread—they all demonstrate the key elements of business as well as the excitement and complexity of business activity. Each case tells a part of the story of our contemporary business world.

Part One, Introducing the Contemporary Business World, provides a general overview of business today, including its economic roots, the environment in which it operates, the ethical problems and opportunities facing business firms, the importance of entrepreneurship, the various forms of ownership available to business firms, and the globalization of business.

- We begin in **Chapter 1, Understanding the Canadian Business System,** by examining the role of business in the economy of Canada and other market economies. We also present a brief history of business in Canada.
- Then, in **Chapter 2, Understanding the Environments of Business,** we examine the external environments that influence business activity. These include the economic, technological, socio-cultural, political-legal, and general business environments.
- Next, in **Chapter 3, Conducting Business Ethically and Responsibly,** we look at individual ethics and corporate social responsibility and how these affect the firm's customers, employees, and investors.
- In **Chapter 4, Understanding Entrepreneurship, Small Business, and New Venture Creation,** we examine the important concepts of entrepreneurship and small business, and the various forms of business ownership that have evolved to facilitate business activity.
- Finally, in **Chapter 5, Understanding International Business,** we look at why countries engage in international trade, how companies organize to operate internationally, the development of free trade agreements, and factors that help or hinder international trade.

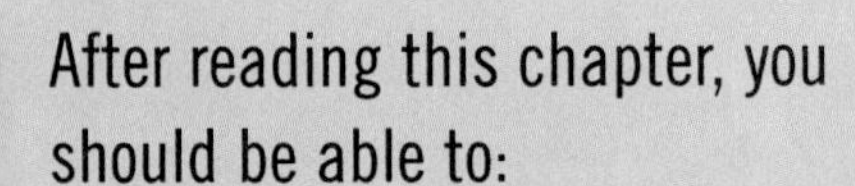

Chapter 1

Understanding the Canadian Business System

After reading this chapter, you should be able to:

1. Define the nature of Canadian *business* and identify its main goals.
2. Describe different types of global *economic systems* according to the means by which they control the *factors of production* through *input* and *output markets*.
3. Show how *demand* and *supply* affect resource distribution in Canada.
4. Identify the elements of *private enterprise* and explain the various *degrees of competition* in the Canadian economic system.
5. Trace the *history of business* in Canada.

The Ups and Downs of Commodities

Canada is blessed with a rich supply of natural resources such as oil, gas, gold, nickel, copper, and diamonds. Canadian business firms profit from extracting and selling these commodities, and they also create jobs for millions of Canadians. But businesses that hitch their success to commodities have to cope with big swings in their fortunes because the prices of commodities can fluctuate wildly. When that happens, company profits can be threatened and employees can be put out of work.

The experience of companies trying to develop the Alberta oil sands illustrates this potential. Development began in 1967, but ups and downs in oil prices in the 1970s and 1980s led many business people to conclude that the oil sands were really not economically viable, because oil extraction costs were so high and the price of oil fluctuated so much. Nevertheless, over the last 40 years, companies like Suncor Energy Inc., Canadian Natural Resources Ltd., Petro-Canada, and Syncrude Canada Ltd. have spent more than $30 billion to develop the oil sands, and billions more are likely to be spent over the next decade. The megaprojects at these companies generated a huge demand for both people and raw materials. One project at Suncor alone required 21 million construction hours, 3 million engineering hours, and 150 000 cubic metres of concrete. At its peak, the Syncrude upgrader project employed 6000 workers.

All this investment looked pretty good as oil prices rose to record levels during the last few years. The concerns about the high costs of extraction were muted, and the rate of oil sands development increased dramatically. There were predictions that Canada would soon rival Saudi Arabia as a major player in world oil markets. But several developments occurred that were not under the control of the oil companies. First, the financial crisis that occurred in 2008 was closely followed by a worldwide recession. Millions of people lost their jobs, business activity declined, and consumers reduced their spending. This reduction in consumer and business activity caused "demand extinction" for oil. As demand declined, so did the price of oil, from $140 a barrel in mid-2008 to less than $40 a barrel by the end of 2008. This created a big problem for oil sands companies because they needed a price of about $70 a barrel in order to make any profit.

Second, environmentalists became increasingly vocal about the environmental damage that was being done by the large amount of greenhouse gases that were being emitted by oil sands developments. The province of Alberta began imposing tighter restrictions on development, and it increased the royalty rates that oil companies had to pay on each barrel of oil they extracted.

Third, there was a sharp drop in the demand from China for commodities. Everyone had assumed that China would provide so much demand that commodity prices would remain high, but between July and October 2008, the commodity price index declined from 475 to 280, Chinese car sales dropped 20 percent, and real estate values dropped 40 percent. These declines depressed prices for commodities like oil, steel, coal, copper, and iron ore.

The steep decline in the price of oil during 2008 forced oil companies to put many of their oil sands development projects on hold, but it's not just oil producers who have to cope with price fluctuations in commodities. Consider what is happening with palm oil. The price of palm oil is rising because of increased food demand in China and India and because it is a key ingredient in the production of biodiesel fuel. Several big companies in Southeast Asia had big plans to build biodiesel refineries to capitalize on European demand for biodiesel, but the increase in the price of palm oil means that it is difficult to make a profit, because raw material inputs to the production process are too expensive. So, while a decline in the price of oil hurts Canadian producers, an increase in the price of palm oil hurts Asian producers. Sometimes you just can't win.

Another commodity that has fluctuated in price is palladium, a greyish metal that is used in automobile catalytic converters. It is produced mostly by Russian and South African companies. In the 1990s, car makers switched from platinum to palladium because palladium does a better job of cleaning auto emissions and because, at that time, palladium was much cheaper than platinum. But the increased demand for palladium caused its price to rise from less than $200 an ounce to over $1000 an ounce. Fearing further price rises, Ford Motor

Company stockpiled supplies at then-current prices. At the same time, however, engineers at automobile companies were figuring out ways to reduce the amount of palladium they needed, and the price started dropping again. Ford eventually had to write off $1 billion in costs that it incurred trying to cope with palladium's fluctuating price. During 2008, the price of palladium dropped to below $200 an ounce because the worldwide recession reduced demand for automobiles. North American Palladium Ltd. suspended operations at its Thunder Bay mine in 2008 because the price of palladium had dropped to $180 an ounce; the company cannot make a profit unless the price is at least $300 an ounce. ◆

How will this help me?

The opening case reflects both the opportunities and challenges you'll find in today's business world. All businesses are subject to the influences of economic forces. But these same economic forces also provide astute managers and entrepreneurs with opportunities for profits and growth. By understanding these economic forces and how they interact, you'll be better able to (1) appreciate how managers must contend with the challenges and opportunities resulting from economic forces (from the standpoint of an employee and a manager or business owner), and (2) understand why prices fluctuate (from the perspective of a consumer).

In this chapter, we begin your introduction to Canadian business by looking at its role in our economy and society. Because a variety of economic systems are found around the world, we will first consider how the dominant ones operate. Once you have some understanding of different systems, you can better appreciate the workings of the Canadian system. As you will see, the effect of economic forces on Canadian businesses and the effect of Canadian businesses on our economy produce dynamic and sometimes volatile results. We conclude the chapter by briefly tracing the history of Canadian business.

The Concept of Business and Profit

business An organization that seeks to earn profits by providing goods and services.

profit What remains (if anything) after a business's expenses have been subtracted from its revenues.

1 Define the nature of Canadian *business* and identify its main goals.

The opening case illustrates three key concepts: business, profit, and risk taking. But what do you think of when you hear the word *business*? Large corporations like Shoppers Drug Mart and Wal-Mart? Smaller companies like your local supermarket or favourite restaurant? Successful companies like CN and Manulife Financial? Less successful companies like Nortel Networks or GM Canada? Actually, each of these firms is a **business**—an organization that produces or sells goods or services in an effort to make a profit. **Profit** is what remains after a business's expenses have been subtracted from its revenues. Profits reward the owners of businesses for taking the risks involved in investing their time and money. In 2008, the most profitable Canadian companies were Encana Corp. ($6.3 billion), the Canadian Wheat Board ($5.7 billion), and Canadian Natural Resources Ltd. ($4.9 billion).[1]

In Canada's economic system, businesses exist to earn profits for owners who are free to set them up. But consumers also have freedom of choice, so businesses must take into account what consumers want or need. No matter how efficient a business is, it won't survive if there is no demand for its goods or services. Neither a snow blower shop in Victoria nor a beach-umbrella store in Rankin Inlet is likely to do very well. But a person who can spot a promising opportunity and then develop a good plan for capitalizing on it can succeed. The opportunity always involves goods or services that consumers want or need—especially if no one else is supplying them or if existing businesses are doing so inefficiently or incompletely.

Businesses produce most of the goods and services we consume and they employ the majority of working people. They create most new innovations and

"Your Honor, my client pleads guilty to an overzealous but well-intentioned pursuit of the profit motive."

provide opportunities for other businesses, which serve as their suppliers. A healthy business climate contributes directly to our quality of life and standard of living. New forms of technology, service businesses, and international opportunities promise to keep production, consumption, and employment growing indefinitely (but not always smoothly). Business profits enhance the personal incomes of millions of owners and stockholders, and business taxes help to support governments at all levels. Many businesses also support charities and provide community leadership.

Economic Systems Around the World

2 Describe different types of global *economic systems* according to the means by which they control the *factors of production* through *input* and *output markets.*

A Canadian business is different in many ways from a business in China. And both are different from businesses in Japan, France, or Peru. A major determinant of how organizations operate is the kind of economic system that characterizes the country in which they do business. An **economic system** allocates a nation's resources among its citizens. Economic systems differ in terms of who owns and controls these resources.

economic system The way in which a nation allocates its resources among its citizens.

Factors of Production

The key difference between economic systems is the way in which they manage the **factors of production**—the basic resources that a country's businesses use to produce goods and services (see Figure 1.1). Traditionally, economists have focussed on four factors of production: *labour*, *capital*, *entrepreneurs*, and *natural resources*. Information resources are now often included as well.[2]

factors of production The resources used to produce goods and services: labour, capital, entrepreneurs, and natural resources.

Labour

The people who work for a company represent the first factor of production, **labour**. Sometimes called **human resources**, labour is the mental and physical capabilities of people. Carrying out the business of such a huge company as Imperial Oil, for example, requires a labour force with a wide variety of skills

labour (or human resources) The mental and physical training and talents of people.

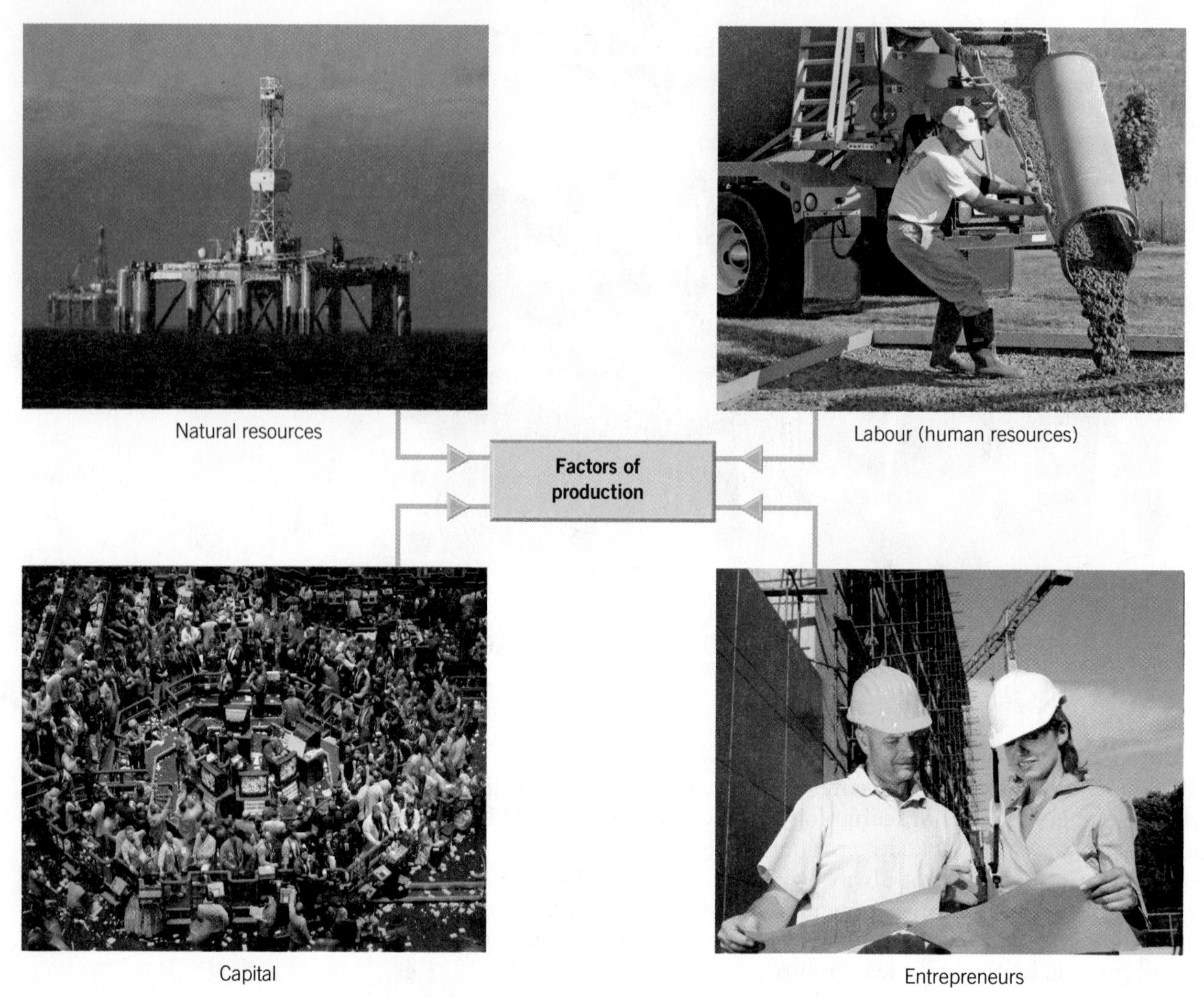

Figure 1.1 Factors of production are the basic resources a business uses to create goods and services. The four factors are natural resources, labour, capital, and entrepreneurs.

ranging from managerial to geological to transportation. Employees who are well trained and knowledgeable can provide a real competitive advantage for a company.

Capital

capital The funds needed to operate an enterprise.

Obtaining and using labour and other resources requires **capital**—the financial resources needed to operate an enterprise. Capital is needed to start a new business and then to keep it running and growing. Imperial Oil needs millions of dollars in cash, and millions more in equipment and other assets, to run its operations. A major source of capital for small businesses is personal investment by owners. Investments can come from individual entrepreneurs, from partners who start businesses together, or from investors who buy stock. Revenue from the sale of products is a key and ongoing source of capital once a business has opened its doors.[3]

Entrepreneurs

entrepreneur An individual who organizes and manages labour, capital, and natural resources to produce goods and services to earn a profit but who also runs the risk of failure.

Entrepreneurs are people who accept the opportunities and risks involved in creating and operating businesses. James Balsillie (Research in Motion), Sergie Brin and Larry Page (Google), Michael Dell (Dell Computer), and Mark Zuckerberg (Facebook) are well-known entrepreneurs.

Natural Resources

Natural resources include all physical resources such as land, water, mineral deposits, and trees. Imperial Oil makes use of a wide variety of natural resources. It obviously has vast quantities of crude oil to process each year. But Imperial Oil also needs the land where the oil is located, as well as land for its refineries and pipelines.

natural resources Items used in the production of goods and services in their natural state, including land, water, mineral deposits, and trees.

Information Resources

Information resources include the specialized knowledge and expertise of people who work in businesses, as well as information that is found in market forecasts and various other forms of economic data. Much of what businesses do results in either the creation of new information or the repackaging of existing information for new users and different audiences. The boxed insert entitled "A Shrine to Wine" gives you an opportunity to think about the factors of production in a specific business.

information resources Information such as market forecasts, economic data, and specialized knowledge of employees that is useful to a business and that helps it achieve its goals.

Entrepreneurship and New Ventures

A Shrine to Wine

"Wine... the intellectual part of the meal," said Alexandre Dumas, famous French author of such literary works as *The Three Musketeers* and *The Count of Monte Cristo*. For wine connoisseurs, also known as oenophiles, this couldn't be truer. These people have a love for and devotion to wine and take just as much care in the procurement and storage of their "vino" as they do in the tasting. Had Genuwine Cellars of Winnipeg, Manitoba, been around in 1873, owners Robb Denomme and Lance Kingma probably would have sold one of their custom-designed cellars to the famous Parisian writer. Apparently Dumas was known for his lavish spending, and with some of the cellars boasting six-figure price tags, custom cellars are certainly suited to those with a taste for the finer things in life.

Genuwine Cellars began in 1995, somewhat by accident, when someone asked Kingma if he thought he could build a wine cellar. He took on the challenge, and the first order led to another. Kingma eventually partnered with Denomme, who was just 17 at the time, and, as the saying goes, the rest is history. Today, the business is a multimillion-dollar operation selling to clients around the world, with the majority of sales going to the United States. But Genuwine's international success probably wouldn't have happened, or at least not as easily, without the help of the Department of Foreign Affairs and International Trade (DFAIT). According to Robb Denomme, "Working with the TCS [Trade Commissioner Service] you get results, you get where you want to go. Trade Commissioners are there to help and always get back to you with the answers you need." The TCS is a division of Foreign Affairs and their goal is to help companies succeed globally. Not only did TCS help Genuwine Cellars get connected with a business consultant, they also helped with financing. Other governmental agencies, including the Prairie Centre for Business Intelligence and the National Research Council, have also provided business support.

In addition to market development strategies, Genuwine Cellars is also credited with some other good moves. "Genuwine is doing all the right things a growing company should do—lean manufacturing, continual investments in technology, importing contract manufactured goods from Asia, setting up a design office in Latin America to take advantage of a lower cost structure and access to skilled professionals, the list goes on," says Joanne MacKean, Senior Manager, Business Development Canada. Further, Genuwine Cellars is one of the largest wine cellar manufacturers in North America and the only company with a manufacturing facility in Canada. Very little competition, niche market, upscale consumer—so just what's "in store" for this business?

According to Denomme, the recession is having some effect, but the company is still experiencing growth. Year 2008 sales are expected to be more than the year prior but are certainly not expanding like they have been historically. Denomme's enthusiasm and drive are not quashed, however. He says, "You've got to keep a positive attitude." Sounds like this entrepreneur looks upon his wineglass as being half full and not half empty!

Critical Thinking Questions

1. Discuss the factors of production as they apply to Genuwine Cellars.
2. What do you think about the company's decision to move some of its operations to Latin America because of a lower cost structure?

Types of Economic Systems

Different types of economic systems manage the factors of production in different ways. In some systems, ownership is private; in others, the government owns the factors of production. Economic systems also differ in the way that decisions are made about production and allocation. A **command economy**, for example, relies on a centralized government to control most factors of production and to make most production and allocation decisions. In **market economies**, individuals—producers and consumers—control production and allocation decisions through supply and demand.

command economy An economic system in which government controls all or most factors of production and makes all or most production decisions.

market economy An economic system in which individuals control all or most factors of production and make all or most production decisions.

Command Economies

The two most basic forms of command economies are communism and socialism. As originally proposed by the nineteenth-century German economist Karl Marx, **communism** is a system in which the government owns and operates all sources of production. Marx envisioned a society in which individuals would ultimately contribute according to their abilities and receive economic benefits according to their needs. He also expected government ownership of production factors to be only temporary. Once society had matured, government would "wither away" and the workers would gain direct ownership. But Marx's predictions were faulty, and most countries abandoned communism in favour of a more market-based economy.

communism A type of command economy in which the government owns and operates all industries.

A GlobeScan poll of over 20 000 people in 20 different countries asked people whether they agreed with the following statement: "The free market economy is the best system." Where do you think the highest support for capitalism was found? Not in Canada, the United States, Germany, or Japan, but in *China*, where 74 percent of people polled agreed with the statement.[4] This is a surprising finding, given the Chinese government's strong support of the communist economic ideology. It seems hard to believe now, but before 1979 people who sold watches on street corners in China were sentenced to years of hard labour. After China's constitution was amended to legitimate private enterprise, the private sector has become incredibly productive. It is estimated that China produces 60 percent of all the toys in the world.[5] China's reputation for being a low-cost producer of goods is legendary. China is also a vast and rapidly growing market for many of the products that Canadian firms produce—chemicals, ores, cereals, and wood products.

In a less extensive command economic system called **socialism**, the government owns and operates only selected major industries. Smaller businesses such as clothing stores and restaurants may be privately owned. Although workers in socialist countries are usually allowed to choose their occupations or professions, a large proportion generally works for the government. Many government-operated enterprises are inefficient, since management positions are frequently filled based on political considerations rather than on ability. Extensive public welfare systems have also resulted in very high taxes. Because of these factors, socialism is generally declining in popularity.[6]

socialism A kind of command economy in which the government owns and operates the main industries, while individuals own and operate less crucial industries.

Market Economies

A **market** is a mechanism for exchange between the buyers and sellers of a particular good or service. For example, the internet is a technologically sophisticated market that brings buyers and sellers together through ecommerce. People usually think of ecommerce as being business-to-consumer (B2C) transactions such as buying books over the internet for personal use. But business-to-business (B2B) transactions are also very important. B2B involves businesses joining together to create ecommerce companies that

market A mechanism for exchange between the buyers and sellers of a particular good or service.

make them more efficient when they purchase the goods and services they need. B2B transactions actually far exceed B2C transactions in dollar value.

A market economy is one where B2C and B2B exchanges take place without much government involvement. To understand how a market economy works, consider what happens when a customer goes to a fruit stand to buy apples. Assume that one vendor is selling apples for $1 per kilogram and another is charging $1.50. Both vendors are free to charge what they want, and customers are free to buy what they choose. If both vendors' apples are of the same quality, the customer will likely buy the cheaper ones. But if the $1.50 apples are fresher, the customer may buy them instead. Both buyers and sellers enjoy freedom of choice.

Input and Output Markets. Figure 1.2 shows how the factors of production work in a pure market economy. Businesses and households interact in two different market relationships.[7] In the **input market**, firms buy resources from households, which are thus resource suppliers. In the **output market**, firms supply goods and services in response to demand on the part of households. (We will provide a more detailed discussion of supply and demand later in this chapter.)

input market Firms buy resources that they need in the production of goods and services.

output market Firms supply goods and services in response to demand on the part of consumers.

As you can see, the activities of these two markets create a circular flow. GM Canada, for example, relies on various kinds of inputs. It buys labour directly from households, which may also supply capital from accumulated savings in the form of stock purchases. Consumer buying patterns provide information that helps GM decide which models to produce and which to discontinue. In turn, GM uses these inputs in various ways and becomes a supplier to households when it designs and produces various kinds of automobiles, trucks, and sports utility vehicles and offers them for sale to consumers.

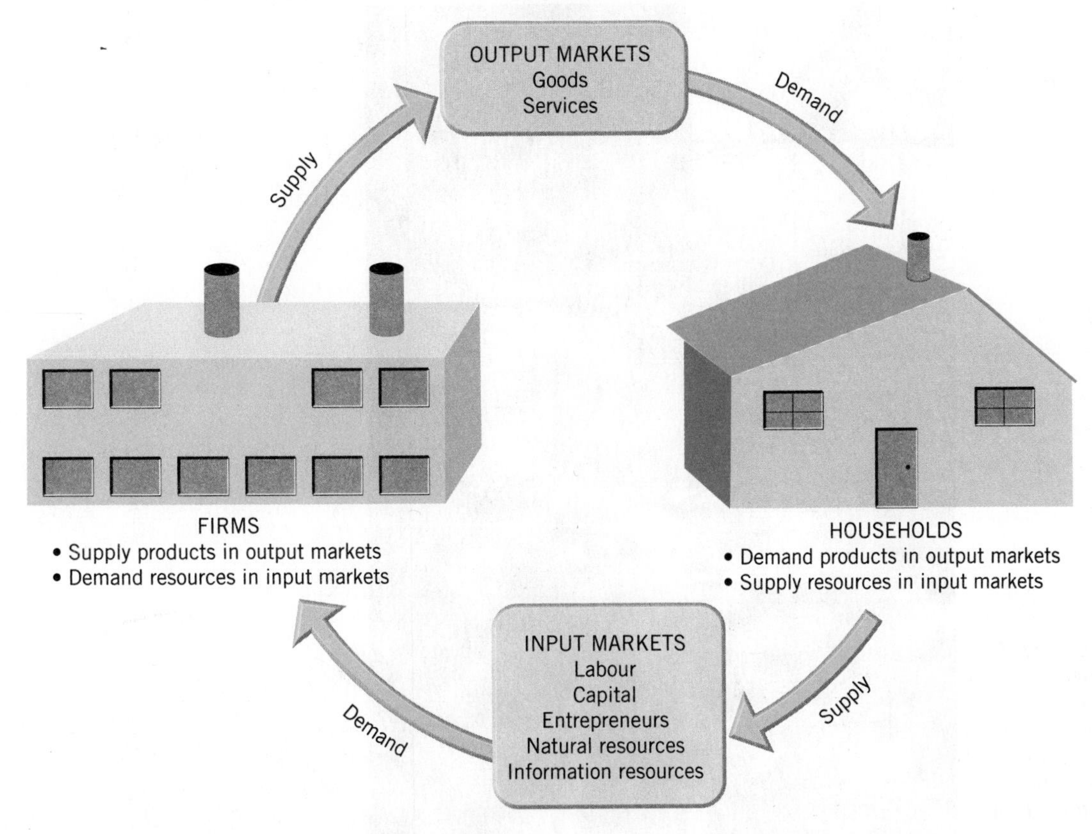

Figure 1.2 Circular flow in a market economy.

Capitalism. Individuals, meanwhile, are free to work for GM or an alternative employer and to invest in GM stock or alternative forms of saving or consumption. Similarly, GM can create whatever vehicles it chooses and price them at whatever value it chooses. But consumers are then free to buy their next car from GM, Ford, or Toyota. This process contrasts markedly with that of a command economy, in which individuals may be told where they can and cannot work, companies are told what they can and cannot manufacture, and consumers may have little or no choice as to what they purchase or how much they pay for items. The political basis of market processes is called **capitalism**, which sanctions the private ownership of the factors of production and encourages entrepreneurship by offering profits as an incentive. The economic basis of market processes is the operation of supply and demand.

capitalism An economic system in which markets decide what, when, and for whom to produce.

Mixed Market Economies

mixed market economy An economic system with elements of both a command economy and a market economy; in practice, typical of most nations' economies.

privatization The transfer of activities from the government to the private sector.

Command and market economies are two extremes or opposites. In reality, most countries rely on some form of **mixed market economy**—a system featuring characteristics of both command and market economies. Beginning in the 1990s, a trend developed toward **privatization**—converting government enterprises into privately owned companies. In Canada, for example, the air traffic control system was privatized, and the federal government sold several other corporations, including Canadian National Railway and Air Canada. The Netherlands privatized its TNT Post Group N.V., and India privatized 18 different industries, including iron, steel, machinery, and telecommunications.[8] However, when a worldwide recession began in 2008, the trend slowed. Government bailouts in the United States meant that the government was once again a part-

Despite becoming a territory of the communist People's Republic of China in 1997, Hong Kong remains one of the world's freest economies. In Hong Kong's Lan Kwai Fong district, for example, traditional Chinese businesses operate next door to well-known international chains.

owner of some business firms. A few countries are even pursuing a policy of **nationalization**—converting private firms into government-owned firms. Venezuela, for example, nationalized its telecommunications industry.

nationalization The conversion of private firms into government-owned firms.

Deregulation—the reduction in the number of laws affecting business activity and in the powers of government enforcement agencies—is another trend that developed during the 1990s but has now reversed due to the world-wide recession. Deregulation originally freed companies to do what they wanted without much government intervention, thereby simplifying the task of management. Deregulation occurred in many industries, including airlines, pipelines, banking, trucking, and communication. In 2008 and 2009, there were calls for a dramatic tightening up of the laws regulating business activity, particularly in the financial sector.

deregulation A reduction in the number of laws affecting business activity and in the powers of government enforcement agencies.

Interactions Between Business and Government

In Canada's mixed economic system, there are many important interactions between business and government. We look first at how government influences business and then at how business influences government.

How Government Influences Business

Government plays several different roles in the Canadian economy, and each of these roles influences business activity in some way.

Government as Customer

Government buys thousands of different products and services from business firms, including office supplies, office buildings, computers, battleships, helicopters, highways, water treatment plants, and management and engineering consulting services. The government is also the largest purchaser of advertising in Canada. Many businesses depend on government purchasing, if not for their survival, at least for a certain level of prosperity. Total government expenditures in 2008 were $243.4 billion.[9]

Government as Competitor

Government also competes with business through Crown corporations, which are accountable to a minister of parliament for their conduct. Crown corporations exist at both the provincial and federal level and account for a significant amount of economic activity in Canada (see Table 1.1).

Government as Regulator

Federal and provincial governments in Canada regulate many aspects of business activity through administrative boards, tribunals, and commissions. Examples include the **Canadian Radio-Television and Telecommunications Commission (CRTC),** which issues and renews broadcast licences; the **Canadian Transport Commission (CTC),** which makes decisions about route and rate applications for commercial air and railway companies; and the **Canadian Wheat Board,** which regulates the price of wheat. Sometimes business people claim that government is unfair in the way it performs its role as regulator (see Concluding Case 1-2).

Canadian Radio-Television and Telecommunications Commission (CRTC) A federal regulatory agency that issues and renews broadcast licences.

Canadian Transport Commission (CTC) A federal regulatory agency that makes decisions about route and rate applications for commercial air and railway companies.

Canadian Wheat Board A federal regulatory agency that regulates the price of wheat.

There are several important reasons for regulating business activity. These include promoting competition, protecting consumers, achieving social goals, and protecting the environment.

Table 1.1 The Top 10 Crown Corporations in Canada, 2008

Company	Annual Revenues (in billions of $)
1. Hydro-Quebec	$ 12.7
2. Canada Mortgage and Housing Corp.	9.5
3. Canadian Wheat Board	8.4
4. Canada Post Corp.	7.4
5. Ontario Lottery and Gaming Corp.	6.2
6. Ontario Power Generation Inc.	6.0
7. B.C. Hydro and Power Authority	4.8
8. Crown Investments Corp. of Saskatchewan	4.4
9. Workplace Safety & Insurance Board	4.3
10. Alberta Gaming and Liquor Commission	4.3

Promoting Competition. One of the reasons that government regulates business is to ensure that healthy competition exists among business firms, because competition is crucial to a market economy. Without restrictions, a large company with vast resources could drive smaller firms out of the market. Competition policy tries to eliminate restrictive trade practices and thereby stimulate maximum production, distribution, and employment.

The guidelines for Canada's competition policy are contained in The Competition Act, which prohibits a variety of practices (see Table 1.2). One of the important provisions of the act prohibits agreements that are designed to reduce competition among companies. Formerly, the government had to prove that such agreements actually reduced competition, but recent changes to the legislation mean that the mere existence of a conspiracy is assumed to be proof that competition has been reduced.[10]

Businesses often complain that the Competition Bureau—which investigates suspected anti-competitive behaviour—is too slow in approving or denying merger plans. For example, when Labatt Brewing wanted to take over Lakeport Brewing, it was told that the Competition Bureau would need up to six months to determine whether the takeover would lessen competition. Labatt therefore appealed to the Competition Tribunal—which hears applications relating to the Competition Act—to speed up the process. The Tribunal agreed with Labatt, and the merger went ahead sooner than it otherwise would have.[11] There was, however, some interesting fallout later. The federal Industry Minister began an investigation after a Federal Court judge accused the Competition Bureau of providing misleading information in order to get a court order for Labatt's records during its review of the proposed merger.[12]

Hazardous Products Act Requires poisonous, flammable, explosive, or corrosive products to be appropriately labelled.

Tobacco Act Prohibits cigarette advertising on billboards and in stores.

Weights and Measures Act Sets standards of accuracy for weighing and measuring devices.

Textile Labelling Act Regulates the labelling, sale, importation, and advertising of consumer textile articles.

Food and Drug Act Prohibits the sale of food that contains any poisonous or harmful substances.

Protecting Consumers. The federal government has passed various laws that are designed to protect consumers. Consumer and Corporate Affairs Canada administers these laws. Important legislation includes the **Hazardous Products Act**, which requires poisonous, flammable, explosive, or corrosive products to be appropriately labelled; the **Tobacco Act**, which prohibits cigarette advertising on billboards and in stores; the **Weights and Measures Act**, which sets standards of accuracy for weighing and measuring devices; the **Textile Labelling Act**, which regulates the labelling, sale, importation, and advertising of consumer textile articles; and the **Food and Drug Act**, which prohibits the sale of food that contains any poisonous or harmful substances. Consumers are also protected by municipal bylaws such as the "no-smoking" bylaws that are so common in Canadian cities.

Table 1.2	The Competition Act
Section 45	Prohibits conspiracies and combinations formed for the purpose of unduly lessening competition in the production, transportation, or storage of goods. Persons convicted may be imprisoned for up to five years or fined up to $1 million or both.
Section 50	Prohibits illegal trade practices. A company may not, for example, cut prices in one region of Canada while selling at a higher price everywhere else if this substantially lessens competition. A company may not sell at "unreasonably low prices" if this substantially lessens competition. (This section does not prohibit credit unions from returning surpluses to their members.)
Section 51	Prohibits giving allowances and rebates to buyers to cover their advertising expenses, unless these allowances are made available proportionally to other purchasers who are in competition with the buyer given the rebate.
Section 52	Prohibits marketing (promotion) activities that are false or misleading. Includes telemarketing activities.
Section 53	Prohibits the deceptive notice that a person has won a prize if the recipient is asked to pay money as a condition of winning the prize.
Section 54	Prohibits charging the higher price when two prices are shown on a product.
Section 55.1	Prohibits pyramid selling (a participant in the plan receives compensation for recruiting other individuals into the plan).
Section 61	Prohibits resale price maintenance. No person who produces or supplies a product can attempt to influence upward, or discourage reduction of, the price of the good in question. It is also illegal for the producer to refuse to supply a product to a reseller simply because the producer believes the reseller will cut the price.
Section 74	Prohibits bait-and-switch selling. No person can advertise a product at a bargain price if there is no supply of the product available to the consumer. (This tactic baits prospects into the store, where salespeople switch them to higher-priced goods.) This section also controls the use of contests to sell goods, and prohibits the sale of goods at a price higher than the advertised one.

Hazardous products must have warning labels to protect consumers who use them.

Achieving Social Goals. Social goals promote the well-being of our society. They include universal access to health care, safe workplaces, employment insurance, and decent pensions. All of these goals require the interaction of business firms and government. The decisions of foreign governments—as they pursue their own social goals—can also affect Canadian businesses. For example, when the U.S. government introduced legislation making it difficult for online gambling companies to operate in the United States, the stock prices of many companies in that industry, including Canadian firms CryptoLogic Inc. and Chartwell Technology, dropped sharply.[13]

Canada Water Act Controls water quality in fresh and marine waters.

Fisheries Act Controls the discharge of any harmful substance into water.

Environmental Contaminants Act Establishes regulations for airborne substances that are a danger to human health or the environment.

Protecting the Environment. Key government legislation designed to protect the environment includes the **Canada Water Act**, which controls water quality in fresh and marine waters; the **Fisheries Act**, which controls the discharge of any harmful substance into water; and the **Environmental Contaminants Act**, which establishes regulations for airborne substances that are a danger to human health or the environment.

Government as Taxation Agent

revenue taxes Taxes whose main purpose is to fund government services and programs.

progressive revenue taxes Taxes levied at a higher rate on higher-income taxpayers and at a lower rate on lower-income taxpayers.

regressive revenue taxes Taxes that cause poorer people to pay a higher percentage of income than richer people pay.

restrictive taxes Taxes levied to control certain activities that legislators believe should be controlled.

Taxes are imposed and collected by federal, provincial, and local governments. **Revenue taxes** (e.g., income taxes) are levied by federal and provincial governments primarily to provide revenue to fund various services and programs. **Progressive revenue taxes** are levied at a higher rate on higher-income taxpayers and at a lower rate on lower-income taxpayers. **Regressive revenue taxes** (e.g., sales tax) are levied at the same rate regardless of a person's income. They cause poorer people to pay a higher percentage of their income for these taxes than rich people pay. **Restrictive taxes** (e.g., taxes on alcohol and tobacco) are levied partially for the revenue they provide, but also because legislators believe that the products should be controlled.

Government as Provider of Incentives

Federal, provincial, and municipal governments offer incentive programs that help stimulate economic development. In Quebec, for example, Hyundai Motors received $6.4 million to build a production facility and an additional $682 000 to train workers. Both Toyota and Hyundai have received millions of dollars in incentives from government in the form of training incentives, interest-free loans, and the suspension of customs duties.[14]

Governments also offer incentives through the many services they provide to business firms through government organizations. Examples include the *Export Development Corporation*, which assists Canadian exporters by offering export insurance against non-payment by foreign buyers and long-term loans to foreign buyers of Canadian products; *Natural Resources Canada*, which provides geological maps of Canada's potential mineral-producing areas; and *Statistics Canada*, which provides data and analysis on almost every aspect of Canadian society.

Industry Canada offers many different programs designed to help small businesses. The Canada Business program, for example, provides information on government programs, services, and regulations in order to improve the start-up and survival rates of small and medium-sized businesses. It also encourages businesses to focus on sound business planning and the effective use of market research. The Department of Foreign Affairs and International Trade (DFAIT) helps Canadian companies doing business internationally by promoting Canada as a good place in which to invest and carry on business activities. It also assists in negotiating and administering trade agreements.

There are many other government incentive programs, including municipal tax rebates for companies that locate in certain areas, design assistance programs, and remission of tariffs on certain advanced technology production equipment. Government incentive programs may or may not have the desired effect of stimulating the economy. They may also cause difficulties with our trading partners, as we shall see in Chapter 5. Some critics also argue that business firms are too willing to accept government assistance—in the form of incentives or bailouts—and that managers should put more emphasis on innovation and creativity so business firms can better cope with economic difficulties when they arise, as they did during the 2008–09 recession.

Government as a Provider of Essential Services

Federal, provincial, and municipal governments facilitate business activity through the wide variety of services they supply. The federal government provides highways, the postal service, the minting of money, the armed forces, and statistical data on which to base business decisions. It also tries to maintain stability through fiscal and monetary policy. Provincial and municipal governments provide streets, sewage and sanitation systems, police and fire departments, utilities, hospitals, and education. All of these activities create the kind of stability that encourages business activity.

How Business Influences Government

While government activity influences what businesses do, businesses also try to influence the government through lobbyists, trade associations, and advertising (see Figure 1.3). A **lobbyist** is a person hired by a company or industry to represent its interests to government officials. The Association of Consulting Engineers of Canada, for example, regularly lobbies the federal and provincial governments to make use of the skills possessed by private sector consulting engineers on projects like city water systems. Some business lobbyists have training in the particular industry, public relations experience, or a legal background. A few have served as legislators or government regulators.

lobbyist A person hired by a company or an industry to represent its interests to government officials.

The federal Lobbying Act requires lobbyists to register with the Commissioner of Lobbying so that it is clear which individuals are being paid for their lobbying activity. It also sets rules for accountability and transparency and requires lobbyists to report detailed information about their communications with so-called Designated Public Office Holders (DPOH).[15]

For many lobbying efforts, there are opposing points of view. The Canadian Cancer Society and the Tobacco Institute present very different points of view on cigarette smoking and cigarette advertising. Owners of small businesses that cannot afford lobbyists often join **trade associations**, which may act as an industry lobby to influence legislation. Trade associations also conduct

trade association An organization dedicated to promoting the interests and assisting the members of a particular industry.

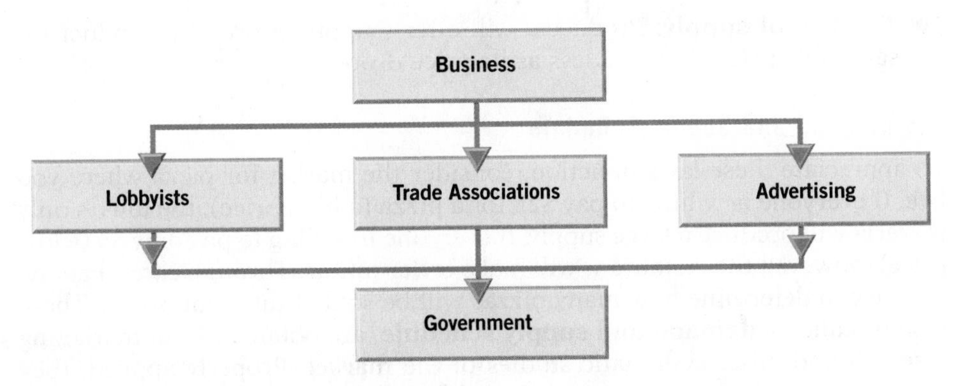

Figure 1.3 Business influences the government in a variety of ways.

training programs relevant to the particular industry, and they arrange trade shows at which members display their products or services to potential customers. Most publish newsletters featuring articles on new products, new companies, changes in ownership, and changes in laws affecting the industry.

Corporations can influence legislation indirectly by influencing voters. A company can, for example, launch an advertising campaign designed to get Canadians to write their MPs, MPPs, or MLAs demanding passage—or rejection—of a particular bill that is before parliament or the provincial legislature.

The Canadian Market Economy

3 Show how *demand* and *supply* affect resource distribution in Canada.

Understanding the complex nature of the Canadian economic system is essential to understanding Canadian businesses. In the next few pages, we will examine the workings of our market economy in more detail. Specifically, we will look at demand and supply in a market economy, private enterprise, and degrees of competition.

Demand and Supply in a Market Economy

As we have seen, a market is not a specific place, like a supermarket, but an exchange process between buyers and sellers. A market economy consists of many different markets. We have already described input and output markets, but we need to remember that the inputs used by business and the products created by business have their own markets. In each of these markets, businesses decide what inputs to buy, what to make and in what quantities, and what prices to charge. Likewise, customers decide what to buy and how much they want to pay. Literally billions of such exchanges take place every day between businesses and individuals, between businesses, and among individuals, businesses, and governments. Moreover, exchanges conducted in one area often affect exchanges elsewhere.

The Laws of Demand and Supply

demand The willingness and ability of buyers to purchase a product or service.

supply The willingness and ability of producers to offer a good or service for sale.

law of demand The principle that buyers will purchase (demand) more of a product as its price drops.

law of supply The principle that producers will offer (supply) more of a product as its price rises.

In a market economy, decisions about what to buy and what to sell are determined primarily by the forces of demand and supply.[16] **Demand** is the willingness and ability of buyers to purchase a product (a good) or a service. **Supply** is the willingness and ability of producers to offer a good or service for sale. Generally speaking, demand and supply follow basic "laws":

- **The law of demand**: Buyers will purchase (demand) more of a product as its price drops and less of a product as its price increases.
- **The law of supply**: Producers will offer (supply) more of a product for sale as its price rises and less as its price drops.

The Demand and Supply Schedule

demand and supply schedule Assessment of the relationships among different levels of demand and supply at different price levels.

To appreciate these laws in action, consider the market for pizza where you live. If everyone is willing to pay $25 for a pizza (a high price), the town's only pizzeria will produce a large supply. If everyone is willing to pay only $5 (a low price), however, the restaurant will make fewer pizzas. Through careful analysis, we can determine how many pizzas will be sold at different prices. These results, called a **demand and supply schedule**, are obtained from marketing research and other systematic studies of the market. Properly applied, they help managers better understand the relationships among different levels of demand and supply at different price levels.

Demand and Supply Curves

The demand and supply schedule, for example, can be used to construct demand and supply curves for pizza in your town. A **demand curve** shows how many products—in this case, pizzas—will be demanded (bought) at different prices. A **supply curve** shows how many pizzas will be supplied (cooked) at different prices.

Figure 1.4 shows hypothetical demand and supply curves for pizzas. As you can see, demand increases as price decreases, and supply increases as price increases. When the demand and supply curves are plotted on the same graph,

demand curve A graph showing how many units of a product will be demanded (bought) at different prices.

supply curve A graph showing how many units of a product will be supplied (offered for sale) at different prices.

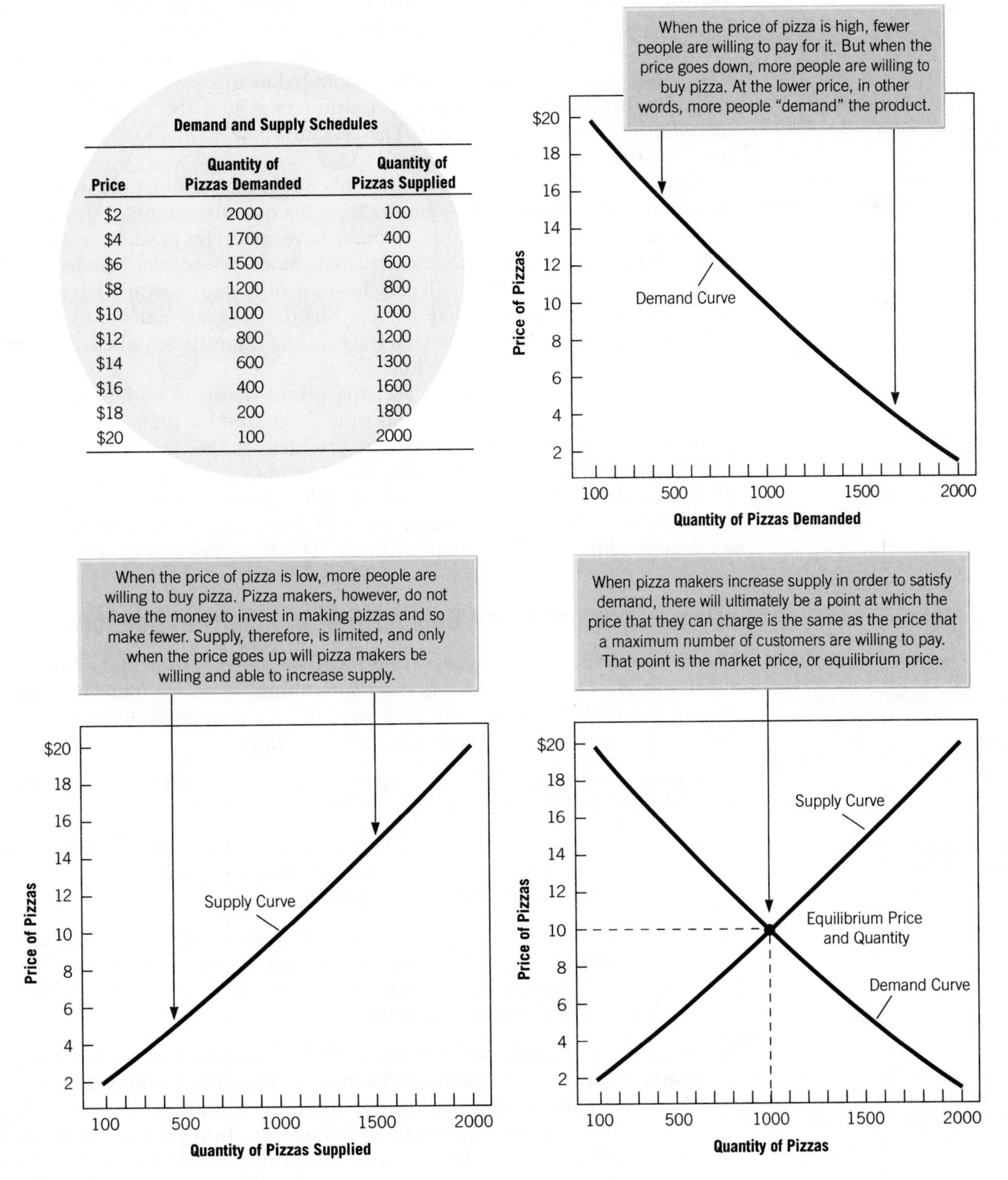

Demand and Supply Schedules

Price	Quantity of Pizzas Demanded	Quantity of Pizzas Supplied
$2	2000	100
$4	1700	400
$6	1500	600
$8	1200	800
$10	1000	1000
$12	800	1200
$14	600	1300
$16	400	1600
$18	200	1800
$20	100	2000

Figure 1.4 Demand and supply.

market price (or equilibrium price) Profit-maximizing price at which the quantity of goods demanded and the quantity of goods supplied are equal.

the point at which they intersect is the **market price or equilibrium price**—the price at which the quantity of goods demanded and the quantity of goods supplied are equal. Note in Figure 1.4 that the equilibrium price for pizzas is $10. At this point, the quantity of pizzas demanded and the quantity of pizzas supplied are the same: 1000 pizzas per week.

Surpluses and Shortages

What would happen if the owner tried to increase profits by making more pizzas to sell? Or what if the owner wanted to reduce overhead, cut back on store hours, and reduce the number of pizzas offered for sale? In either case, the result would be an inefficient use of resources—and perhaps lower profits. For example, if the restaurant supplies 1200 pizzas and tries to sell them for $10 each, 200 pizzas will not be purchased. The demand schedule clearly shows that only 1000 pizzas will be demanded at this price. The pizza maker will therefore have a **surplus**—a situation in which the quantity supplied exceeds the quantity demanded. The restaurant will thus lose the money it spent making those extra 200 pizzas.

surplus A situation in which quantity supplied exceeds quantity demanded.

shortage A situation in which quantity demanded exceeds quantity supplied.

Conversely, if the pizzeria supplies only 800 pizzas, a **shortage** will result—the quantity demanded will be greater than the quantity supplied. The pizzeria will "lose" the extra money that it could have made by producing 200 more pizzas. Even though consumers may pay more for pizzas because of the shortage, the restaurant will still earn lower profits than it would have if it had made 1000 pizzas. To optimize profits, businesses must constantly seek the right combination of the price charged and the quantity supplied. This combination is found at the equilibrium point.

As we saw in the opening case, the prices of many commodities have fluctuated dramatically as the supply of and demand for them fluctuates. The price of that quintessential Canadian product—maple syrup—increased in 2009 because of unfavourable spring weather in Quebec. A 540 ml bottle cost $5–$6 in 2008 but had risen to $8–$11 in 2009. Quebec produces 71 percent of the entire world's supply of maple syrup.[17] The consequences of high prices are described in the boxed insert entitled "The High Price of High Prices."[18]

Private Enterprise and Competition in a Market Economy

4 Identify the elements of *private enterprise* and explain the various *degrees of competition* in the Canadian economic system.

Market economies rely on a **private enterprise** system—one that allows individuals to pursue their own interests with minimal government restriction. Private enterprise requires the presence of four elements: private property rights, freedom of choice, profits, and competition.

private enterprise An economic system characterized by private property rights, freedom of choice, profits, and competition.

- *Private property rights.* Ownership of the resources used to create wealth is in the hands of individuals.[19]
- *Freedom of choice.* You can sell your labour to any employer you choose. You can also choose which products to buy, and producers can usually choose whom to hire and what to produce.
- *Profits.* The lure of profits (and freedom) leads some people to abandon the security of working for someone else and to assume the risks of entrepreneurship. Anticipated profits also influence individuals' choices of which goods or services to produce.
- *Competition.* If profits motivate individuals to start businesses, competition motivates them to operate those businesses efficiently. **Competition** occurs when two or more businesses vie for the same resources or customers. To gain an advantage over competitors, a business must produce its goods or services efficiently and be able to sell at a reasonable profit. To achieve these goals, it must convince customers that its products are either better

competition The vying among businesses in a particular market or industry to best satisfy consumer demands and earn profits.

Business Accountability

The High Price of High Prices

Economic theory tells us that when demand for a commodity increases, its price goes up and people try to find substitutes that are cheaper. For example, when the price of oil is high, companies use corn to make ethanol to add to gasoline and palm oil to make diesel fuel (called biodiesel). That sounds okay, but by definition, as more producers start using corn or palm oil, the demand for those commodities goes up and so does their price. During 2006, for example, the price of palm oil rose from less than US$400 per metric tonne to more than US$500 per metric tonne.

When the prices of commodities rise rapidly, there are usually some unanticipated outcomes. One of these is increased criminal activity. As the price of stainless steel and aluminum rose during the last few years, thieves began stealing items such as beer kegs, railway baggage carts, railroad tracks, light poles, highway guard rails, and plastic milk crates. These items were then sold to scrapyards for cash. As oil prices soared early in 2008, thieves started tapping into pipelines and stealing oil out of storage tanks. Devon Energy Corporation had 600 barrels of oil stolen in just one night. Oil companies were forced to spend extra money on security, since most oil fields are in remote areas where there are no observers to detect thieves. The sharp decline in the price of oil in 2009 should mean that theft will be less of a problem.

High commodity prices can result in rather bizarre thefts. When a statue was stolen from city property in Brea, California, it was initially reported to the FBI as art theft. But local police conclude that the 250-pound statue was stolen because it had a lot of copper in it, which was very valuable. The rise in the price of copper has also motivated thieves to steal all sorts of other items that contain copper, particularly water pipes for new homes and for irrigation systems.

The impact of stealing is limited to lost revenue (it's only money), but sky-high prices for food can actually threaten people's lives. Global food prices increased 83 percent between 2005 and 2008, and that put a lot of stress on the world's poorest countries. In some countries, families are spending one-half of their income just on food. One culprit is the push to convert corn into biofuel; ironically, the urge to avoid high oil prices has led to higher food prices. In many countries, including Haiti, Cameroon, Senegal, and Ethiopia, citizens have rioted over higher prices for important staple items like beans and rice. In Pakistan and Thailand, army troops were deployed to prevent the theft of food from warehouses. The World Bank said that 33 countries were at risk for serious social upheaval because of high food prices. To cope with the problem, some countries are slashing import duties and imposing export duties. This is just the reverse of what countries normally do.

Vancouver-based Western Rice Mills Ltd. discovered this development first-hand. It imports rice, which it then sells to grocery stores and restaurants across Canada. But in 2008, the rice it normally imported from Thailand suddenly became unavailable, and the company had to scramble to get supplies from elsewhere. The price of rice was reflected in these shortages: Rice futures rose from $11 per 100 pounds in mid-2007 to more than $24 per 100 pounds by mid-2008.

Critical Thinking Questions

1. The material presented above describes some of the negative outcomes that can occur with high prices. Can high prices ever lead to positive outcomes? Explain.
2. Consider the following statement: *The high price of commodities like copper is not a concern because we do not need copper to survive, but the high price of food is a concern because it threatens people's lives. The central governments of the world should therefore coordinate their efforts and put in place rules to ensure that food prices are kept low.* Do you agree or disagree with the statement? Explain your reasoning.
3. Consider the following statement: *Fluctuation in the prices of commodities is usually not caused by actual shortages of supply. Rather, it is caused by manipulation of the market by speculators.* Do you agree or disagree with the statement? Explain your reasoning.

or less expensive than those of its competitors. Competition, therefore, forces all businesses to make products better or cheaper. A company that produces inferior, expensive products is likely to fail. There are several degrees of competition.

Degrees of Competition

Even in a free enterprise system, not all industries are equally competitive. Economists have identified four degrees of competition in a private enterprise

Table 1.3 Degrees of Competition

Characteristic	Perfect Competition	Monopolistic Competition	Oligopoly	Monopoly
Example	Local farmer	Stationery store	Steel industry	Public utility
Number of competitors	Many	Many, but fewer than in perfect competition	Few	None
Ease of entry into industry	Relatively easy	Fairly easy	Difficult	Regulated by government
Similarity of goods or services offered by competing firms	Identical	Similar	Can be similar or different	No directly competing goods or services
Level of control over price by individual firms	None	Some	Some	Considerable

system: *perfect competition*, *monopolistic competition*, *oligopoly*, and *monopoly* (see Table 1.3).

perfect competition A market or industry characterized by a very large number of small firms producing an identical product so that none of the firms has any ability to influence price.

Perfect Competition. For **perfect competition** to exist, two conditions must prevail: (1) all firms in an industry must be small, and (2) the number of firms in the industry must be large. Under these conditions, no single firm is powerful enough to influence prices, so they are determined by the market forces of supply and demand. These two conditions reflect four principles:

1. The products of each firm are so similar that buyers view them as identical to those of other firms.
2. Both buyers and sellers know the prices that others are paying and receiving in the marketplace.
3. Because each firm is small, it is easy for firms to enter or leave the market.
4. Going prices are set exclusively by supply and demand and accepted by both sellers and buyers.

Canadian agriculture is a good example of perfect competition. The wheat produced on one farm is the same as that on another. Both producers and buyers are aware of prevailing market prices. It is relatively easy to start producing wheat and relatively easy to stop when it's no longer profitable.

monopolistic competition A market or industry characterized by a large number of firms supplying products that are similar but distinctive enough from one another to give firms some ability to influence price.

Monopolistic Competition. Fewer sellers are involved in **monopolistic competition** than in perfect competition, but because there are still many buyers, sellers try to make their products at least *seem* different than those of competitors. Differentiating strategies include brand names (Tide and Cheer), design or styling (Polo and Tommy Hilfiger jeans), and advertising (Coca-Cola and Pepsi). For example, in an effort to attract health-conscious consumers, the Kraft Foods division of Philip Morris promotes such differentiated products as low-fat Cool Whip, low-calorie Jell-O, and sugar-free Kool-Aid.

Monopolistically competitive businesses may be large or small, but they can still enter or leave the market easily. For example, many small clothing stores compete successfully with large apparel retailers such as Liz Claiborne and Limited Brands. bebe Stores is a good case in point. The small clothing chain controls its own manufacturing facilities and can respond just as quickly as firms like Gap Inc. to changes in fashion tastes.[20] Many single-store clothing businesses in college towns compete by developing their own T-shirt and cap designs with copyrighted slogans and logos.

Consumers often buy products under conditions of monopolistic competition. For example, there are few differences between various brands of toothpaste, cold tablets, detergents, canned goods, and soft drinks.

Product differentiation also gives sellers some control over prices. For instance, even though Sears shirts may have similar styling and other features, Ralph Lauren Polo shirts can be priced with little regard for the lower Sears prices. But there are limits. Although Polo might be able to sell shirts for, say, $20 more than a comparable Sears shirt, it could not sell as many shirts if they were priced at $200 more.

Oligopoly. When an industry has only a handful of sellers, an **oligopoly** exists. As a general rule, these sellers are quite large, and it is difficult for new competitors to enter the industry because large capital investment is needed. Oligopolistic industries like the automobile, airline, and steel industries tend to stay that way.[21] For example, only two companies make large commercial aircraft: Boeing (a U.S. company) and Airbus (a European consortium). Furthermore, as the trend toward globalization continues, most experts believe that, as one forecaster puts it, "global oligopolies are as inevitable as the sunrise."[22]

oligopoly A market or industry characterized by a small number of very large firms that have the power to influence the price of their product and/or resources.

The actions of any one firm in an oligopolistic market can significantly affect the sales of all other firms. When one company reduces prices or offers some type of incentive to increase its sales, the others usually do the same to protect their sales. Likewise, when one company raises its prices, the others generally follow suit. As a result, the prices of comparable products are usually quite similar. Since substantial price competition would reduce every seller's profits, most oligopolistic firms use product differentiation to attract customers. The four major cereal makers (Kellogg, General Mills, General Foods, and Quaker Oats) control almost all of the cereal market, and each charges roughly the same price for its cereal. But each also advertises that its cereals are better tasting or more nutritious than the others. Competition within an oligopolistic market is often fierce.[23]

Monopoly. When an industry or market has only one producer, a **monopoly** exists. Being the only supplier gives a firm complete control over the price of its product. Its only constraint is how much consumer demand will fall as its price rises. The long-distance telephone business was formerly a monopoly in Canada, and cable TV, which had a local monopoly for years, lost it when telephone companies and satellite broadcasters like Bell ExpressVu were allowed into the cable business.

monopoly A market or industry with only one producer, who can set the price of its product and/or resources.

natural monopoly A market or industry in which having only one producer is most efficient because it can meet all consumer demand for the product.

In Canada, laws such as the Competition Act forbid many monopolies, and the prices charged by so-called "natural monopolies" are closely watched by provincial utilities boards. **Natural monopolies** are found in industries in which one company can most efficiently supply all the product or service that is needed. For example, the argument is typically made that a single provincial electric company can supply all the power (product) needed in an area. Duplicate facilities—such as two nuclear power plants, two sets of power lines, and so forth—would be wasteful.

But the assumption that certain activities qualify as natural monopolies is increasingly being challenged. For example, the Royal Mail Group's 350-year monopoly of the British postal service ended in 2006 and rival companies are now allowed to compete with Royal Mail.[24] India Post had a monopoly on mail delivery for several hundred years, but now private couriers like FedEx and United Parcel Service provide more than half the delivery business in India after they were allowed to compete.[25]

A Brief History of Business in Canada

5 Trace the history of business in Canada.

A look at the history of business in Canada shows a steady development from sole proprietorships to the complex corporate structures of today. In this section, we will trace the broad outlines of the development of business in Canada. Table 1.4 highlights some of the specific events in Canadian business history.

The Early Years

Business activity and profit from commercial fishing were the motivation for the first European involvement in Canada. In the late 1400s, ships financed by English entrepreneurs came to the coast of Newfoundland to fish for profit. By the late 1500s, the Newfoundland coast was being visited by hundreds of fishing vessels each year.

Beginning in the 1500s, French and British adventurers began trading with the Aboriginal peoples. Items such as cooking utensils and knives were exchanged for beaver and other furs. One trading syndicate made over 1000 percent profit on beaver skins sold to a Paris furrier. Trading was aggressive and, over time, the price of furs rose as more and more Europeans bid for them. Originally the fur trade was restricted to eastern Canada, but by the late 1600s, *coureurs de bois* were travelling far to the west in search of new sources of furs.

European settlers who arrived in Canada in the sixteenth and seventeenth centuries initially had to farm or starve. Gradually, however, they began to produce more than they needed for their own survival. The governments of the countries from which the settlers came (notably England and France) were strong supporters of the mercantilist philosophy. Under *mercantilism*, colonists were expected to export raw materials like beaver pelts and lumber at low prices to the mother country. These raw materials were then used to produce finished goods such as fur coats, which were sold at high prices to settlers in Canada. Attempts to develop industry in Canada were thwarted by England and France, who enjoyed large profits from mercantilism. As a result, Canadian manufacturing was slow to develop.

Industrial Revolution A major change in goods production that began in England in the mid-eighteenth century and was characterized by a shift to the factory system, mass production, and specialization of labour.

The Factory System and the Industrial Revolution

British manufacturing took a great leap forward around 1750 with the coming of the **Industrial Revolution**. A new level of production was made possible by

Table 1.4 Some Important Dates in Canadian Business History

Year	Event	Year	Event
1490	English fishermen active off the coast of Newfoundland	1926	U.S. replaces Great Britain as Canada's largest trading partner
1534	Account of first trading with Aboriginal peoples written by Jacques Cartier	1927	Armand Bombardier sells first "auto-neige" (forerunner of the snowmobile)
1670	Hudson's Bay Company founded	1929	Great stock market crash
1779	North West Company forms	1929–33	Great Depression
1785	Molson brewery opens	1930	Canadian Airways Limited formed
1805	First Canadian paper mill built at St. Andrew's, Quebec	1932	Canadian Radio Broadcasting Corporation formed (it became the CBC in 1936)
1809	First steamboat (the *Accommodation*) put into service on the St. Lawrence River by John Molson	1935	Bank of Canada begins operations
		1947–51	Early computer built at the University of Toronto
1817	Bank of Montreal chartered	1947	Leduc Number 1 oil well drilled in Alberta
1821	Hudson's Bay Company and North West Company merge	1949	A.V. Roe (Avro) makes Canada's first commercial jetliner
1830–50	Era of canal building	1965	Auto Pact signed with the U.S.
1850–60	First era of railroad building	1969	Canada becomes world's largest potash producer
1855	John Redpath opens first Canadian sugar refinery in Montreal	1989	Free trade agreement with U.S. comes into effect
1857–58	First oil well in Canada drilled near Sarnia, Ontario	1993	North American Free Trade Agreement comes into effect
1861	Toronto Stock Exchange opens	2000	Tech bubble bursts; stock prices drop sharply
1869	Eaton's opens for business in Toronto	2003	Canadian internet pharmacies begin selling prescription drugs to U.S. citizens
1880–90	First western land boom		
1885	Last spike driven to complete the Canadian Pacific Railroad	2006	Softwood lumber dispute with U.S. settled
		2007	Canadian dollar reaches par with U.S. dollar
1897–99	Klondike gold rush	2008	Oil prices reach record high of $147 per barrel
1917–22	Creation of Canadian National Railways	2008–09	Worldwide recession occurs; stock markets drop sharply

advances in technology and by the development of the **factory system**. Instead of hundreds of workers turning out items one at a time in their cottages, the factory system brought together in one place all of the materials and workers required to produce items in large quantities, along with newly created machines capable of **mass production**.

factory system A process in which all the machinery, materials, and workers required to produce a good in large quantities are brought together in one place.

mass production The manufacture of products of uniform quality in large quantities.

specialization The breaking down of complex operations into simple tasks that are easily learned and performed.

Mass production offered savings in several areas. It avoided unnecessary duplication of equipment. It allowed firms to purchase raw materials at better prices by buying large lots. And most important, it encouraged **specialization** of labour. No longer did production require highly skilled craftspeople who could do all the different tasks required to make an item. A series of semi-skilled workers, each trained to perform only one task and supported by specialized machines and tools, greatly increased output.

In spite of British laws against the export of technology and against manufacturing in North America, Canadian manufacturing existed almost from the beginning of European settlement. Modest manufacturing operations were evident in sawmills, breweries, gristmills, tanneries, woollen mills, shoemakers' shops, and tailors' shops. These operations were so successful that, by 1800, exports of manufactured goods were more important than exports of fur.

With the advent of steam power in the early 1800s, manufacturing activity began to increase rapidly. By 1850, more than 30 factories—employing more than 2000 people—lined the Lachine Canal in Montreal alone. Exports of timber to England in 1850 were 70 times greater than what they had been in 1800. The demand for reliable transportation was the impetus for canal building in the mid-1800s and then the railroad-building boom in the mid- and late 1800s.

The Entrepreneurial Era

One of the most significant features of the last half of the nineteenth century was the emergence of entrepreneurs willing to take risks in the hope of earning huge profits. Adam Smith, in his book *The Wealth of Nations*, argued that the government should not interfere in the economy but should let businesses function without regulation or restriction. The Canadian government often adopted this laissez-faire attitude. As a result, some individuals became immensely wealthy through their aggressive business dealings. Some railway, bank, and insurance executives made over $25 000 per year in the late 1800s, and their purchasing power was immense. Entrepreneurs such as Joseph Flavelle, Henry Pellatt, and John MacDonald lived in ostentatious mansions.

The size and economic power of some firms meant that other businesses had difficulty competing against them. At the same time, some business executives decided that it was more profitable to collude than to compete. They decided among themselves to fix prices and divide up markets. Hurt by these actions, Canadian consumers called for more regulation of business. In 1889, the first anti-combines legislation was passed in Canada, and legislation regulating business has increased ever since.

The Production Era

The concepts of specialization and mass production that originated in the Industrial Revolution were more fully refined as Canada entered the twentieth century. The Scientific Management Movement focussed management's attention on production. Increased efficiency via the "one best way" to accomplish tasks became the major management goal.

production era The period during the early twentieth century when businesses focussed almost exclusively on improving productivity and manufacturing methods.

In the United States, Henry Ford's introduction of the moving assembly line in 1913 ushered in the **production era**. During the production era, less attention was paid to selling and marketing than to technical efficiency when producing goods. By using fixed workstations, increasing task specialization, and moving the work to the worker, the assembly line increased productivity and lowered prices, making all kinds of products affordable for the average person. It also increased the available labour pool because many people could be trained to carry out assembly line tasks. Formerly, the labour pool was limited because relatively few people had the high skill levels of craftspeople.

During the production era, large businesses began selling stock—making shareholders the owners—and relying on professional managers. The growth of corporations and improved production output that resulted from assembly lines came at the expense of worker freedom. The dominance of big firms made it harder for individuals to go into business for themselves. Company towns run by the railroads, mining corporations, and forest products firms gave individuals little freedom of choice over whom to work for and what to buy. To restore some balance within the overall system, both government and labour had to develop and grow. Thus, this period saw the rise of labour unions and collective bargaining (more detail is provided in Chapter 9). The Great Depression of the 1930s and the Second World War caused the federal government to intervene in the economic system on a previously unimaginable scale.

Business, government, and labour are the three *countervailing powers* in our society. All are big. All are strong. Yet, none totally dominates the others.

The Sales and Marketing Eras

By the 1930s, business' focus on production had resulted in spectacular increases in the amount of goods and services for sale. As a result, buyers had more choices and producers faced greater competition in selling their wares.

Thus began the so-called **sales era**. According to the ideas of that time, a business's profits and success depended on hiring the right salespeople, advertising heavily, and making sure products were readily available. Business firms were essentially production- and sales-oriented, and they produced what they thought customers wanted or simply what the company was good at producing. This approach is still used by firms that find themselves with surplus goods that they want to sell (e.g., used-car dealerships).

sales era The period during the 1930s and 1940s when businesses focussed on sales forces, advertising, and keeping products readily available.

Following the Second World War, pent-up demand for consumer goods kept the economy rolling. While brief recessions did occur periodically, the 1950s and 1960s were prosperous times. Production increased, technology advanced, and the standard of living rose. During the **marketing era**, business adopted a new philosophy of how to do business—use market research to determine what customers want, and then make it for them. Firms like Procter & Gamble and Molson were very effective during the marketing era and continue to be profitable today. Each offers an array of products within a particular field (toothpaste or beer, for example) and gives customers a chance to pick what best suits their needs.

marketing era The period during the 1950s and 1960s when businesses began to identify and meet consumer wants in order to make a profit.

The Finance Era

In the 1980s, emphasis shifted to finance. In the **finance era** there was a sharp increase in mergers and in the buying and selling of business enterprises. Some people now call it the "decade of greed." As we will see in Chapter 2, during the finance era there were many hostile takeovers and a great deal of financial manipulation of corporate assets by so-called corporate raiders. Critics charged that these raiders were simply enriching themselves and weren't creating anything of tangible value by their activity. They also charged that raiders were distracting business managers from their main goals of running the business. The raiders responded that they were making organizations more efficient by streamlining, merging, and reorganizing them.

finance era The period during the 1980s when there were many mergers and much buying and selling of business enterprises.

The Global Era

The last few years have seen the continuation of technological advances in production, computer technology, information systems, and communication capabilities. A truly global economy has also emerged. Canadians drive cars made in Japan, wear sweaters made in Italy, drink beer brewed in Mexico, and

global era The emergence of a truly global economy, facilitated by advances in production, computer technology, and communication systems.

China opened its economy to foreign investors in the 1980s and joined the World Trade Organization in 2001. Now the Chinese buy as many cars as the Germans and more photographic film than the Japanese. They also buy more cellphones than anyone anywhere, and the opening of the Chinese market has created a windfall for makers of wireless handsets, including Motorola (U.S.), Siemens (Germany), Samsung (South Korea), and Nokia (Finland).

Most of these software developers are among the 65 000 engineers that the Indian State of Andhra Pradesh graduates every year—up from 7500 just 10 years ago. Microsoft operates an R&D centre in the capital city of Hyderabad, where Oracle, Computer Associates, and IBM also have facilities. The city is prospering as a hub not only for software programming, but also for telephone call centres and pharmaceuticals.

listen to stereos made in Taiwan. But we're not alone in this. People around the world buy products and services from foreign companies.

Many Canadian businesses have been hurt by foreign imports, but numerous others have profited by exploring new foreign markets. Domestic competition has forced many businesses to work harder than ever to cut costs, increase efficiency, and improve product and service quality. We will explore a variety of important trends, opportunities, and challenges of the global era throughout this book.

The Internet Era

The turn of the century has been accompanied by what many experts are calling the **internet era** of business. The growth of the internet affects business in at least three different ways:

internet era The rapid growth of the internet has opened up new growth possibilities for both small and large businesses.

1. The internet gives a dramatic boost to trade in all sectors of the economy, especially services. If the internet makes it easier for all trade to grow, this is particularly true for trade in services on an international scale.
2. The internet levels the playing field, at least to some extent, between larger and smaller enterprises, regardless of what products or services they sell. In the past, a substantial investment was typically needed to enter some industries and to enter foreign markets. Now, however, a small business based in central Alberta, southern Italy, eastern Malaysia, or northern Brazil can set up a website and compete quite effectively with much larger businesses located around the world.
3. The internet holds considerable potential as an effective and efficient networking mechanism among businesses. Business-to-business (B2B) networks can link firms with all of their suppliers, business customers, and strategic partners in ways that make it faster and easier for them to do business together.

Test yourself on the material for this chapter at **www.pearsoned.ca/mybusinesslab**.

Summary of Learning Objectives

1. **Define the nature of Canadian *business* and identify its main goals.** *Businesses* are organizations that produce or sell goods or services to make a profit. *Profits* are the difference between the revenues and expenses of a business. The prospect of earning profits encourages individuals and organizations to open and expand businesses. The benefits of business activities also extend to wages paid to workers and to taxes that support government functions.
2. **Describe different types of global *economic systems* according to the means by which they control the *factors of production* through *input* and *output markets*.** An *economic system* is a nation's system for allocating its resources among its citizens. Economic systems differ in terms of who owns or controls the basic *factors of production*: labour, capital, entrepreneurs, natural resources, and information resources. In command economies, the government controls all or most of these factors. In *market economies*, which are based on the principles of capitalism, individuals and businesses control the factors of production and exchange them through input and output markets. Most countries today have mixed market economies that are dominated by one of these systems but include elements of the other. The process of *privatization* is an important means by which many of the world's planned economies moved toward mixed market systems.

3. **Show how *demand* and *supply* affect resource distribution in Canada.** The Canadian economy is strongly influenced by markets, demand, and supply. *Demand* is the willingness and ability of buyers to purchase a good or service. *Supply* is the willingness and ability of producers to offer goods or services for sale. Demand and supply work together to set a *market* or *equilibrium price*—the price at which the quantity of goods demanded and the quantity of goods supplied are equal.

4. **Identify the elements of *private enterprise* and explain the various *degrees of competition* in the Canadian economic system.** The Canadian economy is founded on the principles of *private enterprise: private property rights, freedom of choice, profits,* and *competition.* Degrees of competition vary because not all industries are equally competitive. Under conditions of *perfect competition,* numerous small firms compete in a market governed entirely by demand and supply. In *monopolistic competition,* there are a smaller number of sellers, and each one tries to make their product seem different than the products of competitors. An *oligopoly* involves only a handful of sellers who fiercely compete with each other. A *monopoly* involves only one seller.

5. **Trace the *history of business* in Canada.** Modern business structures reflect a pattern of development over centuries. Throughout much of the colonial period, sole proprietors supplied raw materials to English manufacturers. The rise of the factory system during the Industrial Revolution brought with it mass production and specialization of labour. During the entrepreneurial era in the nineteenth century, large corporations—and monopolies—emerged. During the production era of the early twentieth century, companies grew by emphasizing output and production. During the sales and marketing eras of the 1950s and 1960s, business began focussing on sales staff, advertising, and the need to produce what consumers wanted. In the 1980s there was increased buying and selling of businesses, and in the 1990s a significant global economy emerged. Many Canadian companies have profited from exporting their goods to foreign markets. The most recent development is the use of the internet to boost business. To some extent, the internet should level the playing field between large and small companies.

PEARSON mybusinesslab™

To improve your grade, visit the MyBusinessLab website at www.pearsoned.ca/mybusinesslab. This online homework and tutorial system allows you to test your understanding and generates a personalized study plan just for you. It provides you with study and practice tools directly related to this chapter's content. MyBusinessLab puts you in control of your own learning!

Key Terms

business (p. 6)
Canada Water Act (p. 16)
Canadian Radio-Television and Telecommunications Commission (CRTC) (p. 13)
Canadian Transport Commission (CTC) (p. 13)
Canadian Wheat Board (p. 13)
capital (p. 8)
capitalism (p. 12)
command economy (p. 10)
communism (p. 10)
competition (p. 20)
demand (p. 18)
demand and supply schedule (p. 18)
demand curve (p. 19)
deregulation (p. 13)
economic system (p. 7)
entrepreneur (p. 8)
Environmental Contaminants Act (p. 16)
factors of production (p. 7)
factory system (p. 25)
finance era (p. 27)
Fisheries Act (p. 16)
Food and Drug Act (p. 14)
global era (p. 27)
Hazardous Products Act (p. 14
Industrial Revolution (p. 24)
information resources (p. 9)
input market (p. 11)
internet era (p. 28)
labour (or human resources) (p. 7)
law of demand (p. 18)
law of supply (p. 18)
lobbyist (p. 17)
market (p. 10)
market economy (p. 10)
market price (or equilibrium price) (p. 20)
marketing era (p. 27)
mass production (p. 25)
mixed market economy (p. 12)
monopolistic competition (p. 22)
monopoly (p. 23)
nationalization (p. 13)
natural monopoly (p. 24)
natural resources (p. 9)
oligopoly (p. 23)
output market (p. 11)
perfect competition (p. 22)
private enterprise (p. 20)
privatization (p. 12)

production era (p. 26)
profit (p. 6)
progressive revenue taxes (p. 16)
regressive revenue taxes (p. 16)
restrictive taxes (p. 16)
revenue taxes (p. 16)
sales era (p. 27)
shortage (p. 20)
socialism (p. 10)
specialization (p. 25)
supply (p. 18)
supply curve (p. 19)
surplus (p. 20)
Textile Labelling Act (p. 14)
Tobacco Act (p. 14)
trade association (p. 17)
Weights and Measures Act (p. 14)

Questions for Analysis

1. Is one factor of production more important than the others? If so, which one? Why?
2. On various occasions, government provides financial incentives to business firms. For example, the Canadian government provided expert assistance to Bombardier Inc. with its Technology Transfer Program. Is this consistent with a basically free market system? Explain how this might distort the system.
3. In recent years, many countries have moved from planned economies to market economies. Why do you think this has occurred? What recent events might cause a resurgence of planned economies? Explain.
4. For a product that is not discussed in Chapter 1, find an example where a surplus led to decreased prices. Then find an example where a shortage led to increased prices. What eventually happened in each case? Why? Is what happened consistent with what economics predicts?
5. Familiarize yourself with a product or service that is sold under conditions of perfect competition. Explain why it is an example of perfect competition and identify the factors that make it so. Then do the same for a product in each of the other three competitive situations described in the chapter.
6. Analyze how the factors of production work together for a product or service of your choice.
7. Government plays a variety of roles in the Canadian mixed economy. Consider each of the roles discussed in the text and state the criteria you would use to decide whether government involvement in each role is excessive, insufficient, or about right.

Application Exercises

1. Choose a locally owned business. Interview the owner to find out how the business uses the factors of production and have the owner describe the means of acquiring them.
2. Visit a local shopping mall or shopping area. List each store that you see and determine what degree of competition it faces in its *immediate environment*. For example, if there is only one store in the mall that sells shoes, that store represents a monopoly. Note those businesses with direct competitors (e.g., two jewellery stores) and show how they compete with one another.
3. Go to the library or log onto the internet and research 10 different industries. Classify each according to their degree of competition.

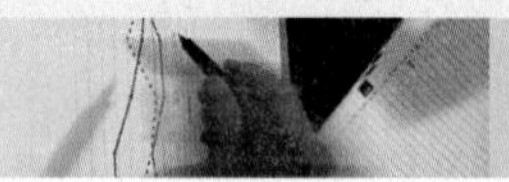

Building Your Business Skills

Analyzing the Price of Doing eBusiness

The Purpose of the Assignment

To encourage students to understand how the competitive environment affects a product's price.

The Situation

Assume that you own a local business that provides internet access to individuals and businesses. (This kind of business is called an ISP or internet service provider). Yours is one of four such businesses in the local market. Each of the four companies charges the same price: $20 per month for unlimited dial-up service. Your business also provides users with email service; two of your competitors also offer email service. One of these same two competitors, plus the third, also provides the individual user with a free, basic personal webpage. One competitor just dropped its price to $14 per month, and the other two have announced their intentions to follow suit. Your break-even price is $10 per customer; that is, you must charge $10 for your service package to cover your costs (but not earn any profit). You are concerned about getting into a price war that may destroy your business.

Method

Divide into groups of four or five people. Each group is to develop a general strategy for handling competitors' price changes. In your discussion, take the following factors into account:

- how the demand for your product is affected by price changes
- the number of competitors selling the same or a similar product
- the methods—other than price—you can use to attract new customers and/or retain current customers

Analysis

Develop specific pricing strategies based on each of the following situations:

- Within a month after dropping the price to $14, one of your competitors raises its price back to $18.
- Two of your competitors drop their prices further—to $12 per month. As a result, your business falls off by 25 percent.
- One of your competitors that has provided customers with a free webpage has indicated that it will start charging an extra $4 per month for this optional service.
- Two of your competitors have announced that they will charge individual users $12 per month but will charge businesses a higher price (not yet announced).
- All four providers (including you) are charging $11 per month. One goes out of business, and you know that another is in poor financial health.

Questions for Discussion

1. Discuss the role that various inducements other than price might play in affecting demand and supply in the market for internet service.
2. Is it always in a company's best interest to feature the lowest prices?
3. Eventually, what form of competition is likely to characterize the market for internet service?

Exercising Your Ethics: Team Exercise

Making the Right Decision

The Situation

Hotel S is a large hotel in a Maritime city. The hotel is a franchise operation run by an international hotel chain. The primary source of revenue for the hotel is convention business. A major tropical storm is working its way up the east coast and is about to hit the city. When that happens, heavy flooding is likely.

The Dilemma

Because Hotel S is a licensed operation, it must maintain numerous quality standards in order to keep its licence. This licence is important because the international management company handles advertising, reservations, and so on. If it were to lose its licence, the hotel would almost certainly have to reduce its staff.

For the past few years, members of the Hotel S team have been lobbying the investors who own the hotel to undertake a major renovation. They fear that without such a renovation, the hotel will lose its licence when it comes up for renewal in a few months. The owners, however, have balked at investing more of their funds in the hotel itself but have indicated that hotel management can use revenues earned above a specified level for upgrades.

The approaching storm has cut off most major transportation avenues, and land lines and cellphone service are also down. The Hotel S staff are unable to reach the general manager, who has been travelling on business. Because the city is full of conventioneers, hotel rooms are in high demand. Unfortunately, because of the disrepair at the hotel, it has only about 50 percent occupancy. Hotel S staff have been discussing what to do and have identified three options:

1. The hotel can reduce room rates in order to help local citizens as well as out-of-town visitors. The hotel can also provide meals at reduced rates. A few other hotels are also doing this.
2. The hotel can maintain its present pricing policies. Most of the city's hotels are adopting this course of action.
3. The hotel can raise its rates by approximately 15 percent without attracting too much attention. It can also start charging for certain things it has been providing for free, such as parking and morning coffee. The staff members see this option as one way to generate extra profits for the renovation and thus protect jobs.

Team Activity

Assemble a group of four students and assign each group member to one of the following roles:

- a member of the hotel staff
- the Hotel S manager
- a customer at the hotel
- a Hotel S investor

Action Steps

1. Before discussing the situation with your group, and from the perspective of your assigned role, which of the three options do you think is the best choice? Write down the reasons for your position.
2. Before discussing the situation with your group, and from the perspective of your assigned role, what are the underlying ethical issues, if any, in this situation? Write down the issues.
3. Gather your group together and reveal, in turn, each member's comments on the best choice of the three options. Next, reveal the ethical issues listed by each member.
4. Appoint someone to record the main points of agreement and disagreement within the group. How do you explain the results? What accounts for any disagreement?
5. From an ethical standpoint, what does your group conclude is the most appropriate action that should be taken by the hotel in this situation?
6. Develop a group response to the following question: Can your team identify other solutions that might help satisfy both extreme views?

For additional cases and exercise material, go to **www.pearsoned.ca/mybusinesslab**.

Concluding Case 1-1

Are We Running Out of Oil?

Oil is a product that is much in the news these days, and several important questions have been raised about this important commodity: Are we running out of oil? If so, when will it happen? Is oil production going to peak and then rapidly decline? Answers to these questions are hotly debated. Much of the debate is focussed on an idea called "peak oil theory," which says that oil production will soon peak and will then decline rapidly, causing a major oil crisis in the world. Opponents of the peak oil theory reject the argument and point to several earlier predictions of peak oil theorists that have turned out to be wrong. Illustrative claims of each group are summarized below.

The Arguments of Peak Oil Supporters

Those who support the idea of peak oil make the following arguments:

- Output from oil fields around the world is declining (in some fields the decline is about 18 percent a year). Declines are particularly evident in the Middle East, Europe, and the United States. That means that 3–4 million barrels a day of new oil will have to be found for global oil production just to remain steady.
- Many big oil-producing countries are very secretive about their year-to-year production rates, so it is difficult to know just how fast their output is really declining. Their oil fields may be in worse shape than they will admit.
- Several top-level executives in the oil industry say that there is a limit to how much oil can be produced each year (about 100 million barrels per day), and that ceiling may be reached as early as 2012. The International Energy Agency (IEA) also predicts that oil production of more than 100 million barrels of oil per day will be difficult to achieve.
- Oil production will peak because of factors such as restricted access to oil fields, shortages of oil field workers, rapidly increasing costs, political crises, and complex oil field geology.
- The IEA has questioned the 174 billion barrel reserves figure commonly cited for the Alberta oil sands, saying that uncertain project economics make it unlikely that that much oil could be extracted. It says that a number closer to 15 billion barrels is more accurate.
- New oil discoveries have declined sharply. For example, new discoveries in the Middle East during 1963–72 totalled 187 billion barrels, but new discoveries during 1993–2002 totalled only 16 billion barrels.
- In 1956, M.K. Hubbert predicted that U.S. oil production would peak in the early 1970s, and he was right. The same thing will happen with world oil production.

The Arguments of Peak Oil Opponents

Those who reject the peak oil theory make the following arguments:

- World oil production has been steadily increasing and in 2006 was the highest in history, averaging over 85 million barrels per day (over 31 billion barrels per year). Oil output will eventually plateau, but it will not peak and then fall rapidly.
- A widely used measure of oil reserves is "ultimate recoverable reserves" (URR). TrendLines, a Canadian research company, notes that the world's URR is growing at an increasing rate. For example, during the period 1957–2006, URR grew at an annual rate of 2.4 percent, but during 2000–07, it grew at an annual rate of 6 percent.

- The U.S. Geological Services (USGS) predicts that URR will grow by about 2.4 percent annually for the next few years. The URR was 1.6 trillion barrels in 1995 and was predicted to rise to 3.3 trillion barrels in 2025, but it had already reached 3.2 trillion barrels in 2006, years ahead of schedule.
- In 1979, the "life index" of oil was estimated to be about 35 years (at 1979 consumption rates). That meant that we would experience an oil crisis early in the twenty-first century. But by 2003, the life index had actually risen to 40 years, and by 2007 it had risen to 45 years. These increases have occurred even though oil consumption rates now far exceed those of 1979.
- There have been several major new discoveries in the last couple of years (for example, off the coast of Brazil and in the Gulf of Mexico). The new Gulf of Mexico oil field may contain up to 15 billion barrels of oil. If it does, that single new field would increase U.S. oil reserves by 50 percent. The new oil field off the coast of Brazil may contain 33 billion barrels of oil.
- M.K. Hubbert's prediction for United States oil production was correct, but his prediction for world production was far off the mark. He predicted that global oil production would peak at 12 billion barrels per year by early in the twenty-first century, but actual production in 2006 was 31 billion barrels.

Critics of peak oil also use several general arguments from economics to support their claims that the peak oil idea is not correct. First, they note that the higher the price of oil, the greater the amount of oil that can be extracted in an economically viable way. Second, higher oil prices will also discourage consumption, and that will make the existing supply of oil last longer. Third, higher oil prices will motivate the development of alternate sources of fuel, and that will also make the existing oil supply last longer. Fourth, new technologies for extracting oil are constantly being developed and old technologies are being refined. This means that more oil can be extracted than was originally thought. For example, Canadian and Japanese researchers have succeeded in extracting natural gas from structures called gas hydrates. The energy locked in gas hydrates may exceed the total world supply of energy available from coal, oil, and natural gas combined. If this new technology becomes commercially viable, it will have a dramatic effect on the total supply of fossil fuels.

Irrespective of what the supporters and opponents of peak oil say, there is another factor that bears on this argument: the business cycle. Most of the arguments presented above were generated before the worldwide recession began in 2008. The recession has substantially reduced demand for oil and caused its price to drop from $147 a barrel to less than $40. In an attempt to prop up the price, the OPEC countries cut output by four million barrels per day. This reduced output will extend the supply of oil even further into the future. Some experts are now predicting that weak economic growth around the world will mean that the demand for oil will be low for many years to come. So, these developments support the opponents of peak oil. But peak oil supporters point out that that low demand for oil will cause less exploration for oil, and that means we will be facing an oil shortage in the future.

It is difficult to know what is going to happen, isn't it?

Questions for Discussion

1. Which group—peak oil supporters or their opponents—do you think makes more persuasive arguments about the future of oil production and the demand for oil? Explain your reasoning.
2. After considering the arguments in support of peak oil theory and the arguments against it, draw a graph that shows your predictions of world oil production from now until the year 2100 (measure annual world oil production in billions of barrels on the vertical axis and time on the horizontal axis). Defend your predictions.
3. Consider the following statement: *There are so many uncertainties that must be taken into account when trying to predict world oil production that it is impossible to have any confidence in anyone's predictions.* Do you agree or disagree with the statement? Explain your reasoning.

Concluding Case 1-2

Business vs. Government in the Liquor Industry

Controversy is a fact of life in the liquor industry. In addition to the long-standing moral and health issues associated with the use of alcohol, two relatively new controversies have arisen regarding (1) the monopoly role of provincial liquor boards, and (2) the issue of privatization of the retail trade in alcohol.

The Monopoly Role of Provincial Liquor Boards

In December 2008, an arbitration panel ruled in favour of a group of private wine stores who claimed that the

Manitoba Liquor Control Commission (MLCC) had engaged in behaviour that was designed to damage the business of the private wine stores. The arbitration panel denied a claim by the wine stores that the MLCC pay them $2.5 million in punitive damages. The wine stores have appealed that part of the decision.

The relationship between the private wine stores and the MLCC has been rocky ever since private wine stores first opened in Manitoba in the 1990s. Wine store owners filed their first lawsuit against the MLCC in 2000, claiming that the MLCC had engaged in various unfair business practices in an attempt to steal customers from the private wine stores. In 2006, it was disclosed that the MLCC had paid $8 million to the wine stores in an out-of-court settlement. In 2004, several other disputes were also settled.

The private wine store owners have long argued that the MLCC has a conflict of interest because it is a distributor, a regulator, and a competitor to the private wine stores. The 2008 arbitration panel found these multiple roles questionable and concluded that it is time to reconsider the how the MLCC operates. The panel is not alone in its views. A Probe Research poll showed that 90 percent of Winnipeggers didn't want the province to phase out private wine stores. More than half of those polled said that private wine stores forced the MLCC stores to improve their service by providing competition.

The issue of the role of government in the liquor industry has also been an issue in Ontario. In the late 1990s, for example, Magnotta Winery Corporation was denied shelf space for its products by the Liquor Control Board of Ontario (LCBO). Magnotta therefore started selling its wine at its own on-site store at its vineyard. The company wanted to charge $3.95 for a 750-mL bottle, which was lower than the LCBO's price of $5.15. But the LCBO ruled that Magnotta couldn't sell its products for less than the cheapest wine carried in an LCBO store. The province of Ontario eventually stripped the government-owned liquor stores of their regulatory status to make competition fairer.

Privatization of the Retail Trade in Alcohol

Another major controversy in the liquor industry concerns the idea of privatization. For many years, all provincial governments held a monopoly on the sale of liquor. But with the worldwide move to privatization that began in the 1990s, various provinces began looking at the possibility of privatizing liquor sales. In 2005, a government-appointed panel in Ontario called for the privatization of the LCBO. But the Ontario finance minister rejected the idea, apparently because the Crown corporation is popular with consumers and because liquor suppliers like dealing with just one big buyer instead of many smaller ones. The LCBO's unionized employees were also very vocal in their opposition to privatization.

Critics of the LCBO say that it should be privatized because it is inefficient and it doesn't make any profit. Supporters, on the other hand, argue that it is profitable. Who's right? In its financial statements, the LCBO counts the provincial liquor tax it collects as part of its profit. Critics point out that if this tax is subtracted from the LCBO's net income, there is no profit at all. The critics say this tax revenue should be subtracted, since private sector firms are not allowed to claim government taxes they collect as profit.

The Ontario dispute is just one example of the long-running debate about privatization. In 1993, the province of Alberta announced that it was getting out of the liquor business and that it would allow private sector operators to begin selling liquor. It was doing so because it said it would save $65 million annually in salaries and operating costs. Within a year, 500 privately owned liquor stores had opened up. In 2003, a policy research group at the University of Alberta analyzed the province of Alberta's 10-year experience with privatized liquor stores and concluded that the benefits of privatization were modest at best.

Also in 2003, the British Columbia branch of the Consumers Association of Canada (CAC) compared liquor prices in British Columbia (where the government had a monopoly on liquor sales) with prices in Alberta. It found that B.C. prices were competitive with, or lower, than prices in Alberta. The study also concluded that if British Columbia privatized its liquor sales, consumers would pay 10–20 percent more. The B.C. government had, in fact, been looking at the possibility of closing 224 government liquor stores and replacing them with privately owned stores. But the provincial government put the plan on hold so they could do more analysis of the situation. Not surprisingly, the Government and Service Employees Union expressed concerns about what privatization would do to its members' jobs.

Another interesting comparison involves Quebec and Ontario, both of which have provincial monopolies in the sale of liquor. Prices of most liquor products are higher in Quebec than they are in Ontario. Even when a Société des alcools du Québec (SAQ) store in Quebec has a sale, prices may be higher than non-sales prices in Ontario. For example, during one period in 2006, a bottle of Australian Wyndham Estate Cabernet Merlot that was on sale at SAQ cost $17, while the regular price in Ontario was just $14.60. Critics of the Quebec government's liquor monopoly argue that SAQ's new "Customer First" slogan is a joke. The government's position was not helped when newspapers reported that several European wine distributors claimed that SAQ had urged them to raise their prices rather than pass on savings to Quebec consumers as a result of the rising value of the Canadian dollar relative to the euro. Australian winemakers have also expressed surprise that Canadians tolerate provincial

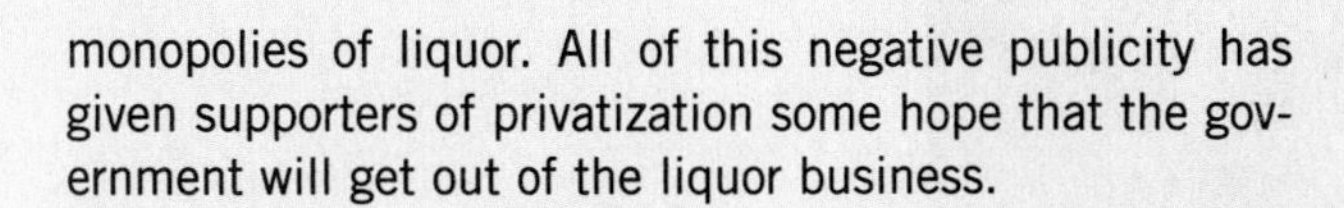

monopolies of liquor. All of this negative publicity has given supporters of privatization some hope that the government will get out of the liquor business.

Questions for Discussion

1. What are the different roles that government plays in Canada's mixed economic system? How do these roles play out in practice in, say, retail trade and manufacturing? Should the government's role in the liquor business be different from its role in retail trade or manufacturing? Explain your reasoning.
2. Should the sale of liquor be a government monopoly, or should other provinces do what Alberta did? Defend your answer.
3. Critics argue that government-run monopolies like liquor stores should make a profit. Is this a reasonable claim? Explain.

apter 2

Understanding the Environments of Business

After reading this chapter, you should be able to:

1. Explain the concepts of *organizational boundaries* and *multiple organizational environments*.
2. Explain the importance of the *economic environment* to business and identify the factors used to evaluate the performance of an economic system.
3. Describe the *technological environment* and its role in business.
4. Describe the *political-legal environment* and its role in business.
5. Describe the *socio-cultural environment* and its role in business.
6. Identify emerging challenges and opportunities in the *business environment*.
7. Understand recent trends in the *redrawing of corporate boundaries*.

Inflation or Deflation?

In 2008 and 2009, there was great fear and confusion in financial markets, and it wasn't just because of the credit crisis, the housing crisis, and the worldwide recession. There was also uncertainty about whether *inflation* or *deflation* was going to add to the problems that already existed. On the one hand, it seemed logical to predict that inflation was going to get worse because central governments around the world had cut interest rates and were injecting billions of dollars into their financial systems in an attempt to resolve the credit crisis and get their economies moving again. On the other hand, the recession had gotten so bad that the demand for goods and services was declining, commodity prices (including oil) were falling fast, banks were not loaning money (because they feared that borrowers wouldn't be able to repay their loans), consumers were reluctant to spend money, and everyone was hoarding cash. All of those factors suggested that deflation was going to occur.

To see how this complicated situation developed, we have to back up a year. In the first half of 2008, prices increased for many different products and services, including food, metals, energy, air transportation, gasoline, cablevision services, and mortgages. The Bank of Canada became concerned that inflation was becoming a real threat. The weakening of the Canadian dollar against the U.S. dollar also increased the threat since imported goods would be more expensive for Canadians. The Bank of Canada's conclusions seemed pretty much in line with what was happening elsewhere in the world. In India, for example, inflation was running at a 12 percent annual rate, and poor people were being forced to spend an ever-increasing percentage of their income on food. In an attempt to slow price increases, the Indian government cut import duties on edible oils and butter, and banned exports of certain farm commodities, including rice and wheat, in order to make more food available.

The International Monetary Fund (IMF) expressed concern that the strong demand for food and other resources in rapidly growing countries like India and China was going to cause increased inflation elsewhere in the world. The IMF's deputy managing director noted that there were about 50 countries in the world with inflation rates *above* 10 percent, mostly developing nations.

The interconnectedness of the global economy was also a problem. The U.S. Federal Reserve cut interest rates in an attempt to get the U.S. economy moving, but that caused the value of the U.S. dollar to decline relative to other currencies (at least for a while). That, in turn, meant that U.S. consumers would have to pay more for imported products. The rate cut also created problems for Middle Eastern and Asian countries that had pegged their dollar to the U.S. dollar in an attempt to stabilize their economies. When the United States reduced interest rates, those countries really had to follow suit; if they didn't, people would move more money into their country (because they could earn a higher rate of return than they could in the United States). That, in turn, would create upward pressure on the currency of those Middle Eastern and Asian countries. It would also cause increased inflation, because when interest rates decline, it is easier for people to borrow money.

All of these factors suggested that inflation was going to be a problem. But economic circumstances can change very quickly. Just a few months after the Bank of Canada expressed concerns about inflation, it decided to *cut* interest rates, even though doing so typically increases the chance of inflation. The Bank of Canada did this because commodity prices had suddenly declined and a worldwide recession had started. In spite of the rate cut, prices soon started dropping for housing, meat, automobiles, computers, fresh fruit, furniture, appliances, tools, hardware, and a wide range of commodities including oil. In China, overproduction of everything from laptop computers to building materials raised fears that many products would soon be dumped on world markets at cut-rate prices. That increased the chance of deflation (negative inflation). Support for deflation fears could be found in the fact that the rate of inflation in the U.S. economy between March 2008 and March 2009 was –0.1 percent. That was the first year of negative inflation since 1955.

These fears about deflation were not without foundation. Japan experienced deflation for 15 years after its housing bubble burst in the early 1990s. Then, just when it looked like Japan would escape from that problem, the U.S. Federal Reserve cut interest rates to almost 0 percent in an attempt to get the U.S. economy moving. Japan's central bank followed suit; it didn't want the yen to rise in value because that would depress Japan's exports.

It is difficult to predict whether inflation or deflation is more likely partly because both situations are influenced by self-fulfilling prophecies. For example, if people think inflation is going to be a problem, they are motivated to buy things now in order to avoid paying the higher prices that they assume are soon to come. But buying things now creates more demand, and that causes prices to rise. Conversely, if people think deflation is going to occur, they are motivated to put off purchases to the time when the price will be lower. But putting off purchases lowers demand, and that causes prices to fall.

Given all this complexity, we should not be surprised if economists have trouble accurately predicting whether inflation or deflation will be the next problem we face. Inflation definitely lurks in the background. If the crisis in confidence can be overcome, people will start spending again, and with all that money that governments dished out still in the system, demand could soar and inflation could become a big problem. On the other hand, if the recession is long and deep, deflation is a distinct possibility because there will be very little demand for goods and services, and that will cause prices to fall. ◆

How will this help me?

By understanding the material in this chapter, you'll be better able to assess (1) the impact that events outside a business can have on its owners and managers, (2) how environmental change affects you as a consumer, and (3) the challenges and opportunities that environmental change provides you as an employee or an investor.

In this chapter, we first introduce the ideas of organizational boundaries and organizational environments. We then describe five key external environments that all businesses must deal with—economic, technological, political-legal, socio-cultural, and business. We conclude with a discussion of how changes in the external environment have motivated businesses to redraw their corporate boundaries through activities like mergers, employee stock ownership plans, and strategic alliances.

Organizational Boundaries and Environments

1 Explain the concepts of *organizational boundaries* and *multiple organizational environments.*

external environment Everything outside an organization's boundaries that might affect it.

All businesses, regardless of their size, location, or mission, operate within a larger external environment. This **external environment**—which consists of everything outside an organization's boundaries that might affect it—plays a major role in determining the success or failure of any organization. Managers must therefore have an accurate understanding of the environment facing their company and then strive to operate and compete within it. While no single firm can control the environment, managers should not simply react to changes; they should also be proactive and at least try to influence their environment.

To better explain the environment of business, we begin by discussing *organizational boundaries* and *multiple organizational environments*.

Organizational Boundaries

organizational boundary That which separates the organization from its environment.

An **organizational boundary** separates the organization from its environment. Boundaries were once relatively easy to identify, but they are becoming increasingly complicated and hard to pin down. Consider the simple case of a small neighbourhood grocery that includes a retail customer area, a storage room, and an owner/manager's office. In many ways, the store's boundary coincides with its physical structure. When you walk through the door, you're crossing the boundary into the business, and when you go back onto the sidewalk, you cross the boundary back into the environment.

But even this simple example isn't as straightforward as it seems. During the course of the business day, distributors of soft drinks, beer, snack foods, ice, and bread products may enter the store, inventory the products that they distribute, and automatically refill coolers and shelves just as if they were employees. Although these distributors are normally considered part of the environment rather than the organization, during the time that they're inside the store, they are essentially part of the business. Customers may assume they are employees and ask them questions as they restock shelves. The bread distributor may even offer someone a fresh loaf instead of the one that he or she has taken from the shelf.

Now consider the case of a large domestic business (such as GM Canada) that is owned by an even larger international corporation (U.S.–based General Motors). The domestic business has a complex network of relationships with other businesses. GM Canada, for example, deals with companies that supply tires, glass, steel, and engines. But GM Canada also functions within the boundaries of its international parent, which has its own network of business relationships, some overlapping and some distinct from GM Canada's network.

We can also examine similar complexities from the customer's perspective. McDonald's, for example, has a contract with Coca-Cola, stipulating that it will sell only Coke soft-drink products. McDonald's also has partnerships with Wal-Mart and Disney that allow it to open stores inside those firms' facilities. So when you buy a Coca-Cola soft drink from a McDonald's restaurant located inside a Wal-Mart store or Disney theme park, you are essentially affecting, and being affected by, multiple businesses.

Multiple Organizational Environments

Although we tend to speak of the external environment as if it were a single entity, organizations actually have multiple environments. Some of them are relatively general. Prevailing economic conditions, for instance, will affect the performance of almost every business. But other dimensions are much more precise. Our neighbourhood grocery will be influenced not only by an increase in unemployment in the area but also by the pricing and other marketing policies of its nearest competitor.

Figure 2.1 shows the major dimensions and elements of the external environment as it affects most businesses. As you can see, these include economic conditions, technology, political-legal considerations, social issues, the global environment, issues of ethical and social responsibility, the business environment itself, and numerous other emerging challenges and opportunities. Because this book provides detailed coverage of global and ethical issues in Chapters 3 and 5, respectively, we will introduce them here only as they relate directly to the other areas in this chapter.

The Economic Environment

Explain the importance of the *economic environment* to business and identify the factors used to evaluate the performance of an economic system. **2**

The **economic environment** refers to the conditions of the economic system in which an organization operates.[1] For example, McDonald's Canadian operations are (as of this writing) functioning in an economic environment characterized by negative growth, rising unemployment, and low inflation. Rising unemployment means that people are less likely to eat out at expensive restaurants (but perhaps more likely to eat at lower-priced restaurants like McDonald's). It also means that McDonald's will likely have little trouble hiring employees at reasonable wage rates because many people are searching for work. Low inflation means that McDonald's pays relatively constant prices for

economic environment Conditions of the economic system in which an organization operates.

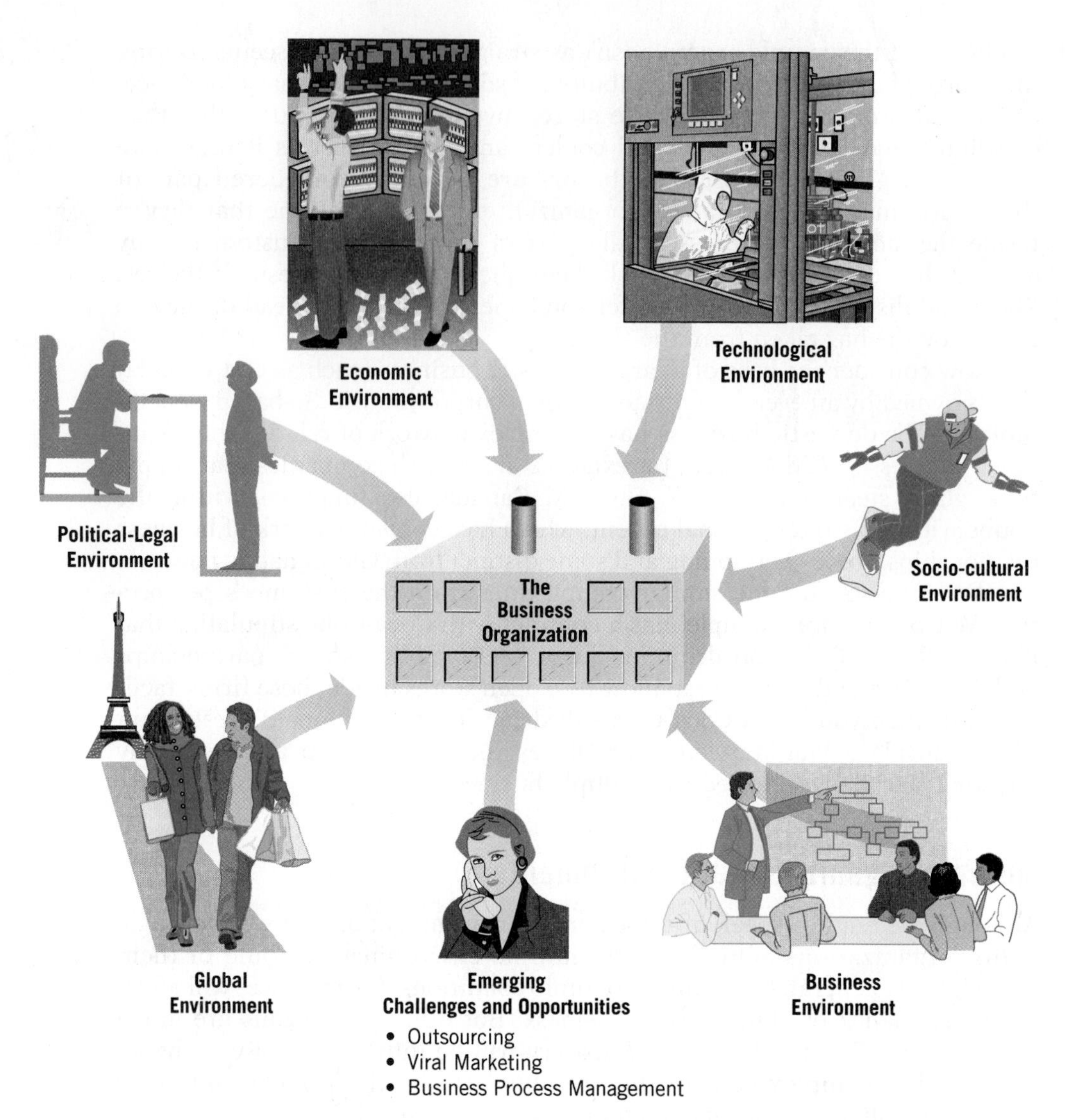

Figure 2.1 Dimensions of the external environment.

its supplies, but it also means that McDonald's can't really increase the prices it charges consumers, because of competitive pressures from Burger King and Wendy's.

There are three key goals in the Canadian economic system: *economic growth*, *stability*, and *full employment*. We look first at the tools we use to measure economic growth, including *aggregate output*, *standard of living*, *gross domestic product*, and *productivity*. We then discuss the main threats to stability: *inflation* and *unemployment*. We conclude this section by discussing government attempts to manage the Canadian economy so that national economic goals are met.

Economic Growth

At one time, about half the population of Canada was involved in producing food. Today, less than 2.5 percent of the population works in agriculture. Agricultural efficiency has improved because we devised better ways of producing agricultural commodities. We can therefore say that agricultural production has grown because we have been able to increase total output in the agricultural sector.

The Business Cycle

We can apply the same concepts to a nation's economic system, but the computations are much more complex because we are dealing with many more sectors of the economy. We can tell whether or not an economic system is growing by examining the **business cycle**—the pattern of ups and downs in an economy. The business cycle has four recognizable phases: peak, recession, trough, and recovery (see Figure 2.2). A **recession** is usually defined as two consecutive quarters when the economy shrinks, but it is probably more helpful to say that a recession starts just after the peak of the business cycle is reached and ends when the trough is reached.[2] A **depression** occurs when the trough of the business cycle extends two or more years. During that period, economic activity declines, unemployment is very high, and consumer buying declines. Periods of expansion and contraction can vary from several months to several years. During the latter half of the 1990s, the Canadian economy was continuously expanding, leading some people to believe that the business cycle was a thing of the past. That belief was shattered twice in the last 10 years: in 2000, when the high-tech bubble burst, and in 2008, when a major financial crisis and worldwide recession occurred. Economists fear that the most recent recession will be long and deep, and some are even predicting that a depression similar to the Great Depression of the 1930s will occur.

business cycle Pattern of short-term ups and downs (expansions and contractions) in an economy.

recession Period during which aggregate output, as measured by real GDP, declines.

depression Particularly severe and long-lasting recession.

Aggregate Output and the Standard of Living

The main measure of growth in the business cycle is **aggregate output**—the total quantity of goods and services produced by an economic system during a given period.[3] To put it simply, an increase in aggregate output is growth (or economic growth).[4] When output grows more quickly than the population, two things usually follow: Output per capita—the quantity of goods and services per person—goes up, and the system provides relatively more of the goods and services that people want.[5] When these two things occur, people benefit from a higher **standard of living**, which refers to the total quantity and quality of goods and services that they can purchase with the currency used in their economic system.

aggregate output Total quantity of goods and services produced by an economic system during a given period.

standard of living Total quantity and quality of goods and services that a country's citizens can purchase with the currency used in their economic system.

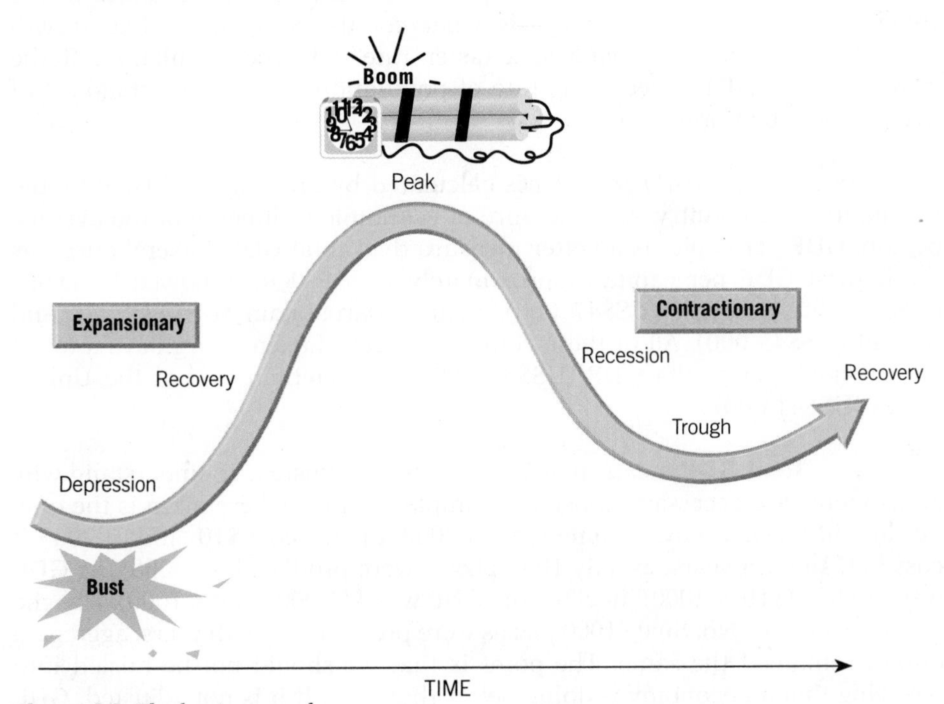

Figure 2.2 The business cycle.

Gross Domestic Product and Gross National Product

gross domestic product (GDP) Total value of all goods and services produced within a given period by a national economy through domestic factors of production.

The term **gross domestic product (GDP)** refers to the total value of all goods and services produced within a given period by a national economy through *domestic* factors of production. Canada's GDP in 2008 was $1.6 trillion.[6] Global GDP is approximately $55 trillion, with five countries—the United States, China, Japan, Germany, and India—accounting for nearly half of the total.[7] If GDP is going up, the nation is experiencing economic growth.

gross national product (GNP) Total value of all goods and services produced by a national economy within a given period regardless of where the factors of production are located.

Economists also use the term **gross national product (GNP)**, which refers to the total value of all goods and services produced by a national economy within a given period *regardless of where the factors of production are located*. Thus, the profits earned by a Canadian company abroad are included in GNP but not in GDP. Conversely, profits earned by foreign firms in Canada are included in GDP. Consider the example of a Canadian-owned manufacturing plant in Brazil. The profits earned by the factory are included in Canadian GNP—but not in GDP—because its output is not produced domestically (that is, in Canada). Conversely, those profits are included in Brazil's GDP—but not GNP—because they are produced domestically (that is, in Brazil). As you can imagine, calculations like these quickly become very complex because of different factors of production. The labour, for example, will be mostly Brazilian but the capital mostly Canadian. Thus, wages paid to Brazilian workers are part of Brazil's GNP even though profits are not.

GDP and GNP are useful measures of economic growth because they allow us to track an economy's performance over time. But simply tracking growth may lead to a distorted view of the economic environment. An organization called Redefining Progress has proposed a more realistic measure to assess economic activity—the Genuine Progress Indicator (GPI). The GPI treats activities that harm the environment or our quality of life as costs and gives them negative values. The GPI measure shows that while GDP has been increasing for many years, GPI has been falling since the 1970s.[8]

Real Growth Rates. GDP and GNP usually differ slightly, but GDP is the preferred method of calculating national income and output. The *real growth rate of GDP*—the growth rate of GDP adjusted for inflation and changes in the value of the country's currency—is what counts. Remember that growth depends on output increasing at a faster rate than the population. If the growth rate of GDP exceeds the rate of population growth, our standard of living should be improving.

GDP per Capita. *GDP per capita* is calculated by dividing total GDP by the population of a country. As a measure of economic well-being of the average person, GDP per capita is a better measure than total GDP. Luxembourg has the highest GDP per capita (approximately US$69 000), followed by Qatar (US$68 000), Norway (US$47 000), Brunei Darussalam (US$47 000), and Kuwait (US$45 000). All of these countries except Luxembourg have a lot of oil. Canada's per capita GDP (US$35 000) is lower than that of the United States (US$41 600).[9]

real GDP GDP calculated to account for changes in currency values and prices.

Real GDP. **Real GDP** means that GDP has been adjusted. To understand why adjustments are necessary, consider a simple example where pizza is the only product in an economy. Assume that in 2008 a pizza cost $10, and in 2009 it cost $11. In both years, exactly 1000 pizzas were produced. In 2008, the GDP was $10 000 ($10 × 1000); in 2009, the GDP was $11 000 ($11 × 1000). Has the economy grown? No. Since 1000 pizzas were produced in both years, aggregate output remained the same. The point is that we should not be misled into believing that an economy is doing better than it is. If it is not adjusted, GDP for 2009 is **nominal GDP.** Nominal GDP is measured in current dollars or with all components valued at current prices.[10]

nominal GDP GDP measured in current dollars or with all components valued at current prices.

Purchasing Power Parity. In our example, current prices would be 2009 prices. On the other hand, we calculate real GDP when we account for *changes in currency values and price changes*. When we make this adjustment, we account for both GDP and **purchasing power parity**—the principle that exchange rates are set so that the prices of similar products in different countries are about the same. Purchasing power parity gives us a much better idea of what people can actually buy with the financial resources allocated to them by their economic system. In other words, it gives us a better sense of standards of living around the world.

purchasing power parity Principle that exchange rates are set so that the prices of similar products in different countries are about the same.

Productivity

Productivity is a measure of economic growth that compares the output of an economic system with the resources that are needed to produce the output. Suppose that it takes one Canadian worker and one Canadian dollar to make 10 soccer balls in an eight-hour workday. Let's also say that it takes 1.2 Saudi workers and the equivalent of $1.20 (in riyals, the currency of Saudi Arabia) to make 10 soccer balls in the same eight-hour workday. The Canadian soccer-ball industry is said to be more *productive* than the Saudi soccer-ball industry. The two factors of production in this extremely simple case are labour and capital.

productivity Any activity that adds value to some input, transforming it into an output for a customer (whether external or internal).

If more products are being produced with fewer factors of production, the prices of these products go down. As a consumer, you would need less of your currency to purchase the same quantity of these products, so your standard of living—at least with regard to these products—has improved. If your entire economic system increases its productivity, then your overall standard of living improves. In fact, *standard of living improves only through increases in productivity*.[11] Real growth in GDP reflects growth in productivity. We examine productivity in detail in Chapter 12.

There are several factors that can help or hinder the growth of an economic system, but we'll focus on just two of them: the *balance of trade* and the *national debt*.

Balance of Trade. The **balance of trade** is the economic value of all the products that a country *exports* minus the economic value of those it *imports*. A positive balance of trade results when a country exports (sells to other countries)

balance of trade The total of a country's exports (sales to other countries) minus its imports (purchases from other countries).

High productivity levels can be attained using automated equipment such as that shown in this soft-drink bottling operation. Productivity is high because relatively few workers, supported by specialized machines, are able to produce large quantities of the product.

more than it imports (buys from other countries). A *positive* balance of trade facilitates economic growth. A *negative* balance of trade results when a country imports more than it exports. A negative balance of trade inhibits economic growth because the money that flows out of a country can't be used to invest in productive enterprises, either at home or overseas. More information on the balance of trade is presented in Chapter 5.

national debt The total amount of money that a country owes its creditors.

National Debt. A country's **national debt** is the amount of money that the government owes its creditors. Like a business, the government has both revenues (primarily in the form of taxes) and expenses (military spending, social programs, and so forth). For many years, the government of Canada incurred annual **budget deficits**; that is, the government spent more money each year than it took in. These accumulated annual deficits created a huge national debt ($590 billion in 2008). A typical recession causes an 86 percent increase in the national debt.[12]

budget deficit The result of the government spending more in one year than it takes in during that year.

From Confederation (1867) to 1981, the *total* accumulated debt was only $85.7 billion, but in the period 1981–94, *annual deficits* were in the $20- to $40-billion range. During the period 1997–2008, Canada was the only highly industrialized country in the world that had annual budget surpluses. Canada's budget surplus in 2008 was $3.9 billion, but a 2009 report by the parliamentary budget officer predicted that because of the worldwide recession that began in 2008, Canada will run annual deficits of between $46 and $105 billion for the next five years.[13] Big increases in annual deficits are also predicted for the United States because of the multibillion-dollar bailouts that were given to companies in the financial sector. In spite of this, the United States is still able to borrow large amounts of money from countries like China because the United States is seen as a strong economy and a safe haven in troubled economic times.[14]

A country's national debt affects economic growth, and here's why: While taxes are the most obvious way the government raises money, it also sells *bonds*—securities through which it promises to pay buyers certain amounts of money by specified future dates. The government sells bonds to individuals, households, banks, insurance companies, industrial corporations, non-profit organizations, and government agencies, both at home and overseas.[15] These bonds are attractive investments because they are extremely safe; the Canadian government is not going to *default* on them (that is, fail to make payments when due). Even so, these bonds must offer a decent return for the buyers, so the Canadian government pays interest at a competitive rate. But when it sells bonds, the Canadian government competes with every other potential borrower—individuals, households, businesses, and other organizations—for the available supply of loanable money. The more money the government borrows, the less money is available for the private borrowing and investment that increases productivity.

Economic Stability

stability Condition in an economic system in which the amount of money available and the quantity of goods and services produced are growing at about the same rate.

An important goal of an economic system is **stability**, a condition where the amount of money available and the quantity of goods and services produced are growing at about the same rate. Several factors threaten stability—namely, *inflation*, *deflation*, and *unemployment*.

Inflation

inflation Occurrence of widespread price increases throughout an economic system.

Inflation means that widespread price increases occur throughout an economic system. Inflation occurs when the amount of money injected into an economy outstrips the increase in actual output. When this happens, people will have more money to spend, but there will still be the same quantity of products available for them to buy. As they compete with one another to buy available products, prices go up. Before long, high prices will erase the increase in the amount of money injected into the economy. Purchasing power, therefore, declines.

Inflation varies widely across countries. One of the most dramatic recent examples of inflation occurred in Zimbabwe in 2008, when inflation reached an astonishing annual rate of more than 40 million percent (most countries have rates between 2 and 15 percent). One Zimbabwean dollar from 2005 would have been worth one trillion Zimbabwean dollars in 2008. Many workers simply stopped going to their jobs because their pay was not enough to cover their bus fare.[16] The problem was finally solved in 2009 when the government began allowing people to pay their bills using other currencies like the U.S. dollar or the South African rand.[17]

Inflation hurts consumers because price is a primary concern when consumers are deciding whether to purchase a product. You will probably decide to make a purchase if the value of the product justifies the price that you'll have to pay. Table 2.1 reduces a hypothetical purchase decision to three bare essentials:

1. Your household income over a three-year period
2. The price of a hamburger over a three-year period
3. The rates of increase for both over a three-year period

In which year did the cost of a hamburger go up? At first glance, you might say in both YR2 and YR3 (to $4 in YR2 and to $7.50 in YR3). In YR2, your income kept pace; although a hamburger cost twice as much, you had twice as much money to spend. In effect, the price to you was actually the same. In YR3, however, your income increased by 250 percent while the price of a hamburger increased by 275 percent. In YR3, therefore, you got hit by inflation (how hard, of course, depends on your fondness for hamburgers). Inflation, therefore, can be harmful to you as a consumer because *inflation decreases the purchasing power of your money.*

Measuring Inflation: The CPI. Remember that inflation means widespread price increases throughout an economic system. It stands to reason, therefore, that we can measure inflation by measuring price increases. To do this, we can turn to such price indexes as the **consumer price index (CPI)**, which measures changes in the cost of a "basket" of 600 different goods and services that a typical family might buy. What is included in the basket has changed over the years as new products and services have become available and old ones fell out of favour. The first CPI in 1913 included items like coal, spirit vinegar, and fruit, but now the CPI includes DVD home theatre systems, MP3 portable players, and plasma televisions.[18] These changes in the CPI also reflect changes in consumer purchasing patterns. For example, in 1961, about 53 percent of consumer spending went to necessities like food, housing, and

consumer price index (CPI) Measure of the prices of typical products purchased by consumers living in urban areas.

Table 2.1 When Did the Cost of a Hamburger Go Up?

YR1 Income	YR2 Income	YR2 % Increase Over YR1 Base	YR3 Income	YR3 % Increase Over YR1 Base
$5000	$10 000	100	$17 500	250
YR1 Hamburger Price	**YR2 Hamburger Price**	**YR2 % Increase Over YR1 Base**	**YR3 Hamburger Price**	**YR3 % Increase Over YR1 Base**
$2	$4	100	$7.50	275

clothing. By 2000, only 40 percent of consumer spending went to necessities.[19] Figure 2.3 shows how inflation has varied over the last 20 years in Canada.

Deflation

deflation A period of generally falling prices.

When **deflation** (generally falling prices) occurs, the Bank of Canada reduces interest rates in an attempt to increase consumer demand. Prices may fall because industrial productivity is increasing and cost savings can be passed on to consumers (this is good) or because consumers have high levels of debt and are therefore unwilling to buy very much (this is bad). As we saw in the opening case, it can be difficult to predict whether inflation or deflation is the bigger threat for Canada at the moment.

Unemployment

unemployment Level of joblessness among people actively seeking work in an economic system.

In 2008, there were 7.7 million men and 6.8 million women (over age 25) working in Canada's labour force.[20] But there were many additional people who wanted a job but could not get one. **Unemployment** is the level of joblessness among people actively seeking work. There are various types of unemployment: *frictional unemployment* (people are out of work temporarily while looking for a new job); *seasonal unemployment* (people are out of work because of the seasonal nature of their jobs); *cyclical unemployment* (people are out of work because of a downturn in the business cycle); and *structural unemployment* (people are unemployed because they lack the skills needed to perform available jobs). Unemployment rates have varied greatly over the years, as Figure 2.4 shows, with the rates in recent years being higher for men than for women.

When unemployment is low, there is a shortage of labour available for businesses. As these businesses compete with one another for the available supply of labour, they raise the wages that they are willing to pay. Then, because higher labour costs eat into profit margins, businesses raise the prices of their products. Thus, although consumers have more money, this increase is soon erased by higher prices. Purchasing power declines.

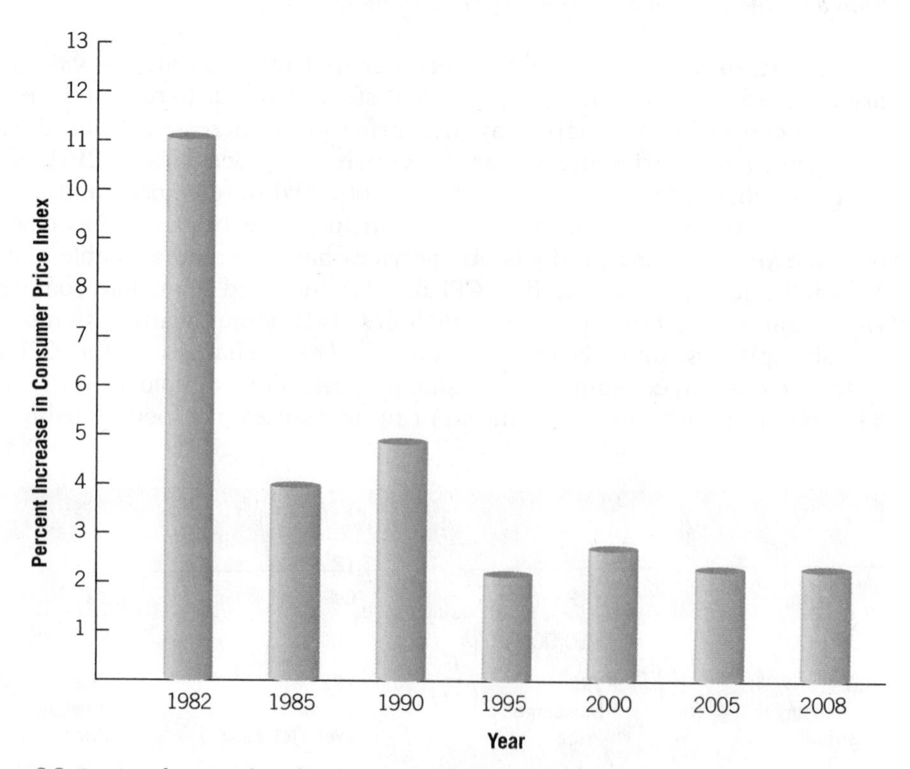

Figure 2.3 During the past decade, the rate of price increases in Canada has been low and quite stable.

During the depression of the 1930s, unemployment was very high, with nearly one-quarter of the population unable to find work. Lines of unemployed workers outside soup kitchens were an unfortunate reality during those difficult economic times.

If wage rates get too high, businesses will respond by hiring fewer workers and unemployment will go up. But if that happens, demand may decline because unemployed workers don't purchase as much. Because of reduced sales, companies may further cut back on hiring and unemployment will go even higher. If the government tries to correct this situation by injecting more money into the economic system—by cutting taxes or spending more money—

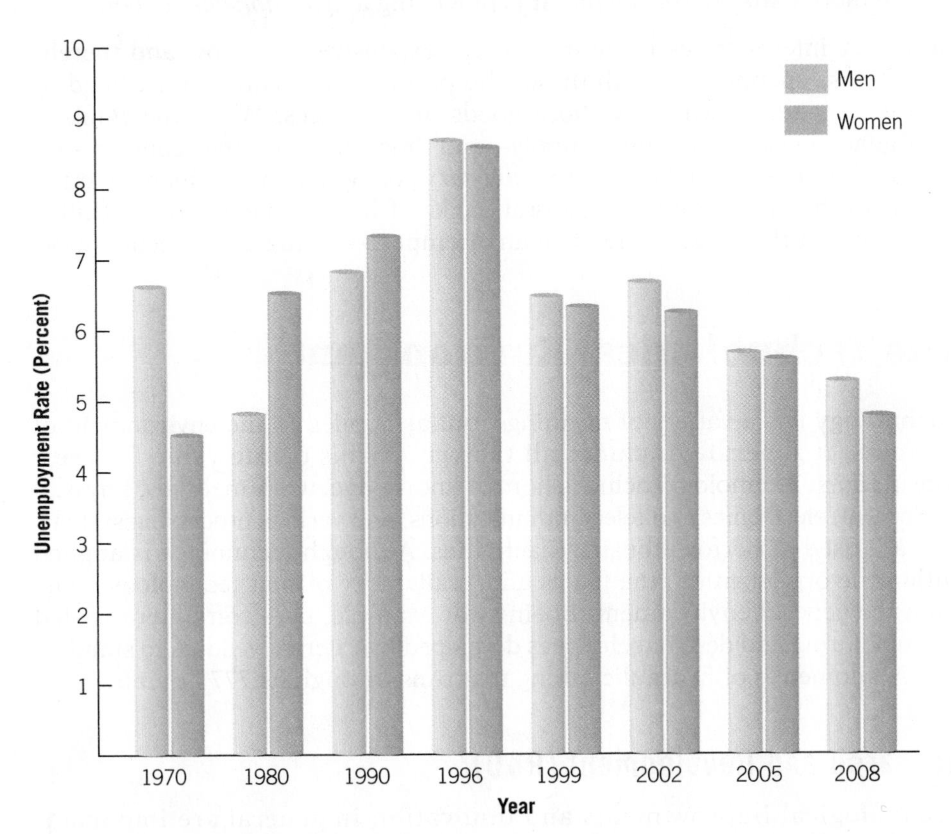

Figure 2.4 Historical unemployment rate.
During the period 1970–96, there was a steady upward trend in unemployment rates, but the rate began to decline in the late 1990s.

prices in general may go up because of increased consumer demand, but then inflation sets in and purchasing power declines.[21] Many economists are predicting that the United States will experience high inflation rates beginning in about 2011 because of the trillion-dollar stimulus package that was implemented in 2009.

Managing the Canadian Economy

The government manages the Canadian economic system through both fiscal and monetary policies. Taken together, fiscal policy and monetary policy make up **stabilization policy**, the goal of which is to smooth out fluctuations in output and unemployment and to stabilize prices.

stabilization policy Government policy, embracing both fiscal and monetary policies, the goal of which is to smooth out fluctuations in output and unemployment and to stabilize prices.

fiscal policies Policies by means of which the government collects and spends revenues.

monetary policies Policies by means of which the government controls the size of the nation's money supply.

The Canadian government manages the collection and spending of its revenues through **fiscal policies**. Tax increases can function as fiscal policies, not only to increase revenues but also to manage the economy. For example, when the growth rate of the economy is decreasing, tax cuts will normally stimulate renewed economic growth. **Monetary policies** focus on controlling the size of the nation's money supply. Working primarily through the Bank of Canada (the nation's central bank), the government can influence the ability and willingness of banks throughout Canada to lend money. It can also influence the supply of money by prompting interest rates to go up or down. The power of the Bank of Canada to make changes in the supply of money is the centrepiece of the Canadian government's monetary policy. The principle is fairly simple:

- Higher interest rates make money more expensive to borrow and thereby reduce spending by both those who produce goods and services and by those who buy those goods and services. When the Bank of Canada restricts the money supply, we say that it is practising a *tight monetary policy.*
- Lower interest rates make money less expensive to borrow and thereby increase spending by both those who produce goods and services and by the consumers who buy those goods and services. When the Bank of Canada loosens the money supply—and thus stimulates the economy—we say that it is practising an *easy monetary policy*. When the financial crisis hit in the fall of 2008, the central banks of both Canada and the United States cut their interest rates in an attempt to stimulate their economies.

The Technological Environment

3 Describe the *technological environment* and its role in business.

technology All the ways firms create value for their constituents.

Technology has a variety of meanings, but as applied to the environment of business, it generally includes all the ways firms create value for their constituents. Technology includes human knowledge, work methods, physical equipment, electronics and telecommunications, and various processing systems that are used to perform business activities. Although technology is applied within the organization, the forms and availability of that technology come from the general environment. Boeing, for example, uses computer-assisted manufacturing and design techniques developed by external vendors to simulate the six kilometres of hydraulic tubing that runs through its 777 aircraft.

Research and Development (R&D)

research and development (R&D) Those activities that are necessary to provide new products, services, and processes.

Technological improvements and innovation in general are important contributors to the economic development of a country. The innovation process includes **research and development (R&D)**, which provides new ideas for products, services, and processes. (See Chapter 16 for a discussion of the importance of R&D in the marketing of products.) There are two types of R&D. **Basic (or pure) R&D** involves improving knowledge in an area without focussing on whether any discoveries will be immediately marketable. For example, chemists are continually experimenting with how chemical compounds behave, but this activity might or might not result in a marketable product. **Applied R&D**, on the other hand, means focussing specifically on how a technological innovation can be put to use in the making of a product or service that can be sold in the marketplace. For example, H.J. Heinz developed a tomato that is sweeter than the variety that it had previously been using in making its ketchup. This reduced the need for corn syrup, which had been rapidly increasing in price.[22]

basic (or pure) R&D Improving knowledge in an area without primarily focussing on whether any discoveries that might occur are immediately marketable.

applied R&D Focussing specifically on how a technological innovation can be put to use in the making of a product or service that can be sold in the marketplace.

Another example: Several Canadian companies share an office in Shanghai called the Textile Canada Business Centre. Instead of trying to sell traditional apparel fabric, they want to sell "technical textiles" for the medical, construction, and sports industries. These include heat- and flame-resistant fabric for firefighters and sheets to protect crops from sun or hail. One niche product—SilverClear—is an antibacterial liquid that is applied to bed linen. It is produced by TransTex Technologies in Saint-Hyacinthe, Quebec, and sold to Chinese companies who apply it to the sheets they make. In 1989, only 10 percent of Canadian textiles were exported, but now half are.[23]

The boxed insert entitled "The Hydrogen Fuel Cell" describes how complex and time-consuming research and development work can be.

R&D spending in Canada in 2008 totalled about $16.3 billion.[24] The Canadian private sector accounts for about 54 percent of R&D, the government 9 percent, and universities 35 percent.[25] In the private sector, just 100 businesses account for over half of all R&D money that is spent.[26] The largest expenditures on R&D in Canada are concentrated in industries like computer system design, information, communications equipment, and scientific research.[27]

As a proportion of GDP, Canada's level of R&D lags behind that of other countries (see Figure 2.5). This lag exists partly because many Canadian businesses are subsidiaries of large U.S. companies that carry out their R&D in the United States. When we take into account that the GDP of countries like Japan, the United States, and Germany is much larger than the GDP of Canada, it means that R&D spending in Canada (in terms of absolute dollars) is a tiny fraction of what is spent in other countries.

Product and Service Technologies

Technology is used to create physical goods and services for customers. Although many people associate technology with manufacturing, it is also a significant force in the service sector. Just as an automobile is built following a predetermined pathway along an assembly line, a hamburger at McDonald's is cooked, assembled, wrapped, and bagged as it moves along a predefined path. The rapid advancement of the internet into all areas of business is also a reflection of the technological environment. Indeed, new technologies continue to revolutionize nearly every aspect of business, ranging from the ways that customers and companies interact to where, when, and how employees perform their work.

Companies must constantly be on the lookout for technological breakthroughs that might make their current products or services obsolete and thereby threaten their survival. Many of these breakthroughs do not come from direct competitors or even from the industry the company is part of. Microsoft, for example, originally didn't pay much attention to internet technology because it was busy competing with companies like WordPerfect in the word processing and operating software market. When Netscape entered the

The Greening of Business

The Hydrogen Fuel Cell

In the 1990s, Vancouver-based Ballard Power Systems generated great excitement when it announced that it was going to develop a fuel cell that would solve the world's energy problems and save the environment at the same time. The hydrogen fuel cell combines hydrogen (one of earth's most common elements) with oxygen to produce electricity. The only exhaust is warm water. The electricity generated by the fuel cell can be used to power anything that runs on electricity, including cars. The fuel cell greatly interested car makers because they had been trying for years to develop a new engine to replace the internal combustion engine that has powered automobiles for over a century.

Initially, enthusiasm for the hydrogen fuel cell was high. DaimlerChrysler and Ford Motor Company invested hundreds of millions of dollars to pursue the development of fuel cells, Ballard sold prototypes to several automobile companies for testing, the Chicago Transit Authority put three fuel cell–powered buses into service, and the British Columbia government purchased three buses. But 15 years have passed, and the hydrogen fuel cell is nowhere near ready for the mass market. The revolution, which was always said to be just around the corner, has stayed tantalizingly in the future. Skeptics (and investors) wonder if the fuel cell will ever be available to the mass market.

What happened? Why has the fuel cell—which looks like a fantastic product—taken so long to develop? Consider the daunting list of development problems facing the fuel cell:

- Hydrogen must first be extracted from substances that contain it (e.g., natural gas), but stripping the hydrogen from natural gas creates carbon dioxide, which is precisely what the standard internal combustion car engines emit.
- Safety is an issue. (When the word "hydrogen" is mentioned, many people immediately think of the spectacular explosion and fire that destroyed the hydrogen-powered Hindenburg dirigible in 1937.)
- If insufficient numbers of hydrogen-dispensing gas stations are built, consumer demand will never be high enough to encourage mass production of cars that are powered by fuel cells.
- The hydrogen fuel cell is likely to be very expensive because the most environmentally sound way to make hydrogen—extracting it from water using electricity made from solar or wind power—is costly and requires large areas of land covered in solar panels that produce the required electricity.
- Hybrid cars like the Toyota Prius and the Honda Civic have been very successful and are providing strong competition for the hydrogen fuel cell.

A lot of time and money have been invested in the development of hydrogen fuel cells for environmental (less air pollution) and political (less reliance on foreign oil) reasons. The fuel cell may be commercially viable in 20 or 30 years, but there are still many developmental problems to be overcome. Progress continues to be slow. In 2005, Honda began production of the FCX, a zero-emission hydrogen fuel cell car, and in 2008 it began producing the FCX Clarity, an improved version. It expects to lease 200 of the vehicles by 2011. The goal for mass market sales is 2018. The company says that the biggest impediments to sales are the high price of the car and the lack of availability of hydrogen fuelling stations.

Maybe the hydrogen fuel cell will eventually become popular. Keep in mind what critics said when internal combustion–powered automobiles were introduced early in the twentieth century. "They'll never become popular because there would have to be gas stations all over the place." Well, now we have gas stations all over the place, so maybe in the future we will see hydrogen fuelling stations all over the place.

Critical Thinking Questions

1. Summarize in your own words the key factors that have limited the development of the hydrogen fuel cell.
2. Look at the section on new product development in Chapter 16. At what stage of the new product development process is the hydrogen fuel cell?
3. Consider the following statement: *The hydrogen fuel cell will never be widely used as a power source for automobiles. If the fuel cell had any value, it would have been fully developed by now and there would already be many cars on the road that are powered by the fuel cell.* Do you agree or disagree with the statement? Explain your reasoning.

market with a browser program that threatened to make operating systems unnecessary, Microsoft had to spend a lot of time and money developing its own Internet Explorer browser.[28]

R&D intensity R&D spending as a percentage of a company's sales revenue.

Companies must decide how much emphasis they are going to place on R&D as a competitive tool. **R&D intensity** refers to R&D spending as a

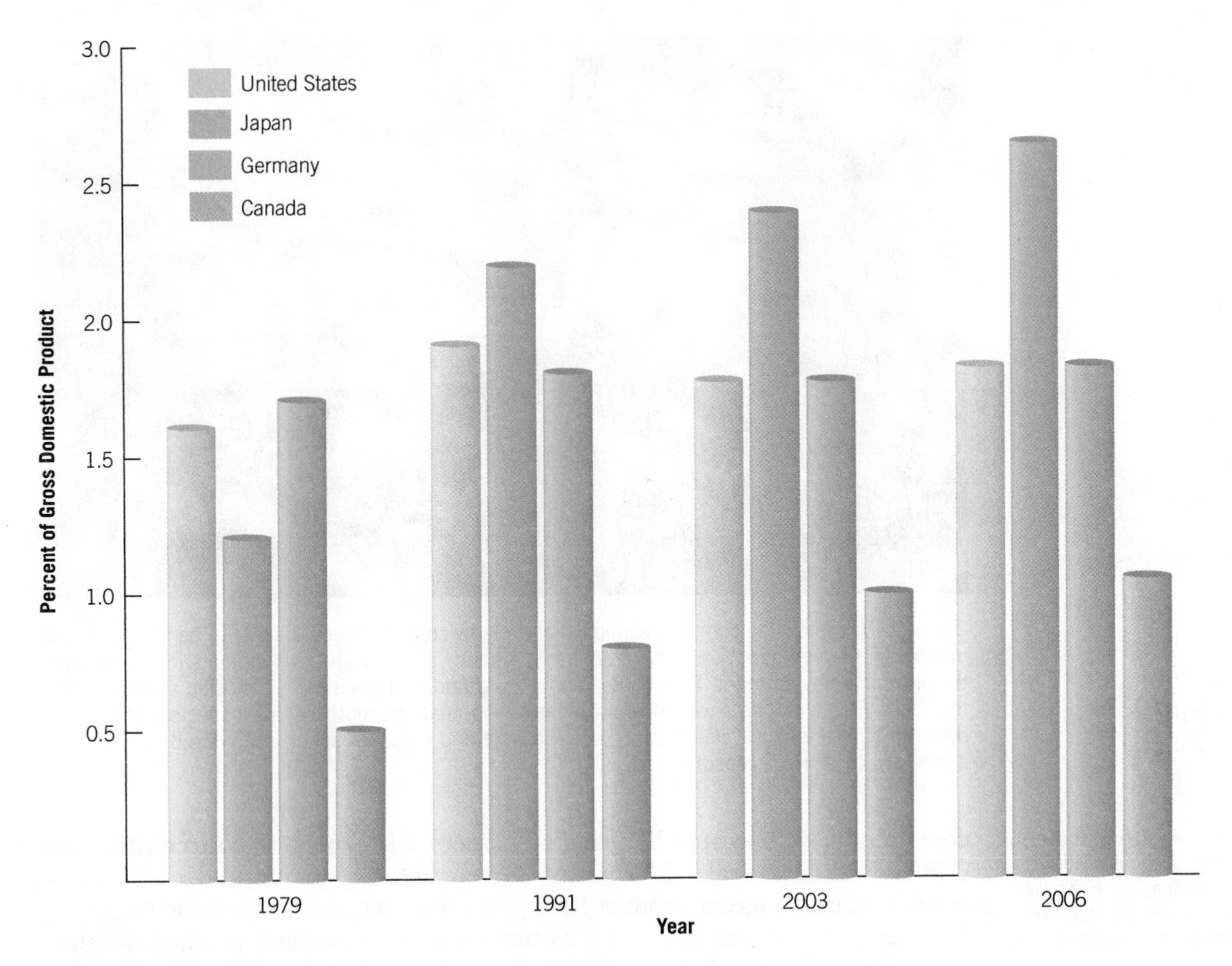

Figure 2.5 R&D expenditures as a proportion of GDP.

percentage of the company's sales revenue. Companies with a high R&D intensity are better able to gain market share in global markets.[29] If a company has a strategy to be the technological leader in its industry, it will likely have a high R&D intensity. Alternatively, if its strategy is to be a technology follower, it will likely have a much lower R&D intensity. Companies that have efficient **technology transfer**—the process of getting a new technology out of the lab and into the marketplace—generate more profits.

technology transfer Process of getting a new technology out of the lab and into the marketplace.

Technology is an important basis of competition for some firms. For example, a company might focus its efforts on being the lowest-cost producer or always having the most technologically advanced products on the market. One challenge is meeting constant demands to decrease *cycle time*—the time that it takes a firm to accomplish some recurring activity or function from beginning to end. Businesses are more competitive if they can decrease cycle times. Twenty years ago, it took an automaker about five years from the decision to launch a new product until it was available in dealer showrooms. Now, most companies can complete the cycle in less than two years. The speedier process allows them to respond more quickly to changing economic conditions, consumer preferences, and new competitive products while recouping their product-development costs more quickly.

Process Technologies

Process technologies are used to improve a firm's performance of its internal operations (such as accounting, managing information flows, creating activity reports, and so forth). They also help create better relationships with external

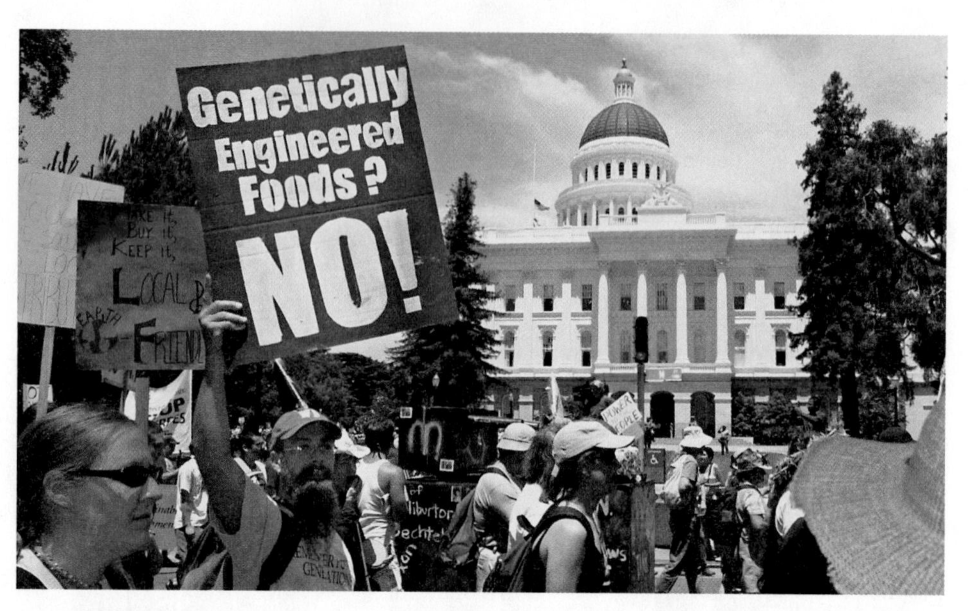

On the surface, low-fat corn and salmon that grow twice as fast would seem to be a good way of improving the food supply. But not everybody is happy about such developments in the modern technological environment. Environmentalists are afraid that genetically modified crops (which they call "Frankenfoods") will sneak into natural populations, outbreed wild species, and threaten biodiversity. Or else they'll cross-pollinate and engineer species that are downright dangerous for human consumption.

enterprise resource planning (ERP) Large-scale information system for organizing and managing a firm's processes across product lines, departments, and geographic locations.

constituents such as suppliers and customers. **Enterprise resource planning (ERP)** is a large-scale information system for organizing and managing a firm's processes across product lines, departments, and geographic locations. Company-wide processes—such as materials management, production planning, order management, and financial reporting—can all be managed by ERP. Figure 2.6 shows some of the areas in which ERP can be applied, including some of the common processes performed in each area.[30]

In developing its ERP system, a firm starts by identifying the processes that need critical attention, such as supplier relationships, materials flows, or customer order fulfillment. The resulting system would thus integrate the sales process with production planning and then both of these operations into the financial accounting system. Let's say that a customer in Rome orders a product to be manufactured in Ireland. The ERP-integrated seller can schedule the order shipment via air cargo to Rome, where it can be picked up by a truck at the airport and delivered to the customer's warehouse by a specified date. All of these activities are synchronized in one massive database.

The ERP also stores updated real-time information on activities, reports recent and upcoming transactions, and posts electronic notices that certain action is required if certain schedules are to be met. It coordinates internal operations with activities by outside suppliers and notifies customers of current order status and upcoming deliveries and billings. It can integrate financial flows among the firm, its suppliers, customers, and banks and generate up-to-the-minute financial reports at a moment's notice (reduced from the traditional one-month time span).

One Canadian company that uses ERP is Crestline Coach Ltd., a relatively small company in Saskatoon that builds customized emergency vehicles and replacement parts. When problems developed with Crestline's old software—for example, customers had to wait days for parts—management decided to buy an ERP system called Business One from SAP Canada Inc. This was a scaled-down, less expensive version of the ERP systems that are usually sold

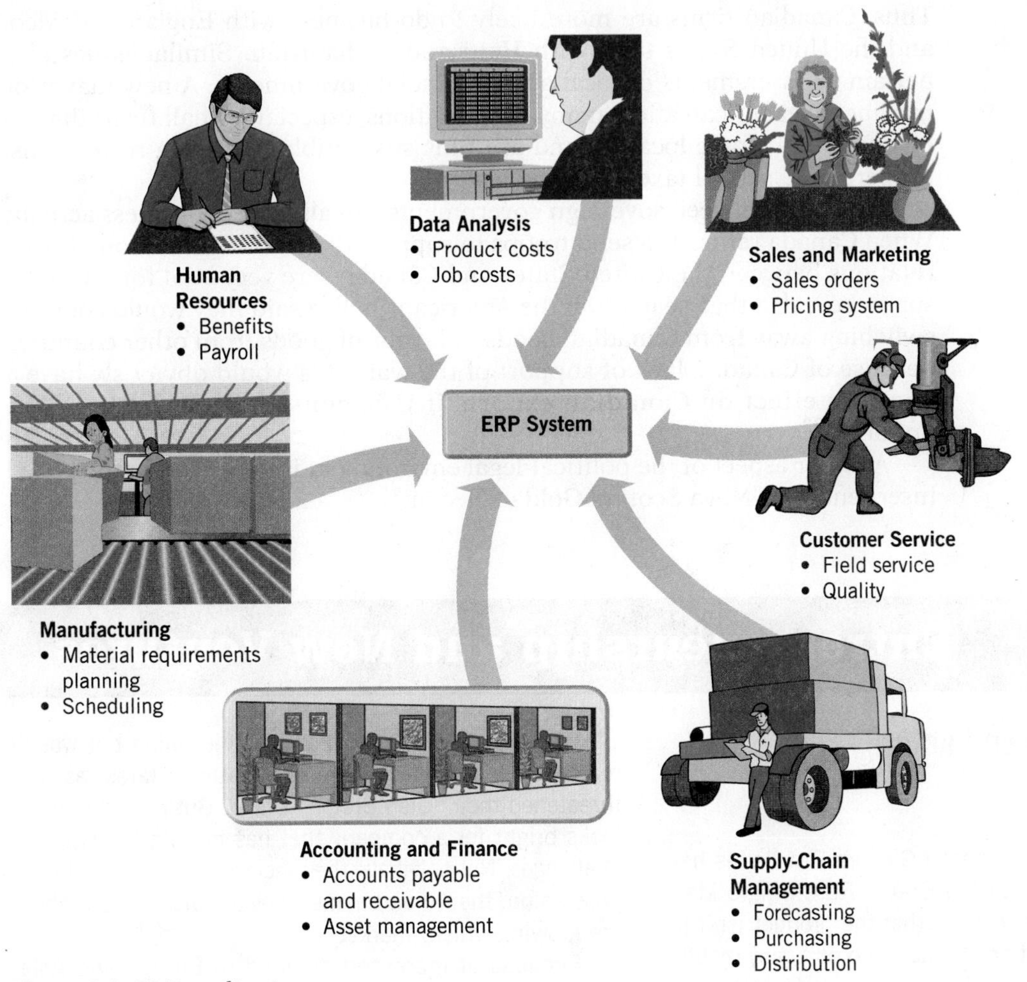

Figure 2.6 ERP applications.

to large companies. With the new ERP system, when Crestline receives an order for a replacement part, it can usually ship it the same day.[31]

The Political-Legal Environment

Describe the *political-legal environment* and its role in business. **4**

political-legal environment Conditions reflecting the relationship between business and government, usually in the form of government regulation.

The **political-legal environment** reflects the relationship between business and government, usually in the form of government regulation of business. The legal system defines in part what an organization can and can't do. Although Canada is a free market economy, it still has major regulation of business activity, as we saw in Chapter 1.

Pro- or anti-business sentiment can further influence business activity. During periods of pro-business sentiment, firms find it easier to compete and have fewer concerns about antitrust issues. During a period of anti-business sentiment, firms may find their competitive activities more restricted. For example, there may be fewer opportunities for mergers and acquisitions because of antitrust concerns. When the Royal Bank wanted to merge with the Bank of Montreal, the Canadian government blocked the merger on the grounds that it would reduce competition and harm consumers.

Political stability is also an important consideration, especially for international firms. No business wants to set up shop in another country unless trade relationships with that country are relatively well defined and stable.

Thus, Canadian firms are more likely to do business with England, Mexico, and the United States than with Haiti and Afghanistan. Similar issues also pertain to assessments of local and provincial governments. A new mayor or provincial leader can affect many organizations, especially small firms that do business in a single location and are thus susceptible to zoning restrictions, property and school taxes, and the like.

Relations between sovereign governments can also affect business activity. When Canada refused to send troops to support the U.S.–led invasion of Iraq, relations between the United States and Canada were very cool for a time. A survey revealed that nearly half the Americans polled said they would consider switching away from Canadian goods in favour of goods from other countries because of Canada's lack of support of the war. This would obviously have a negative effect on Canadian exports if U.S. consumers acted on these opinions.[32]

Another aspect of the political-legal environment is described in the boxed insert entitled "Nova Scotia's Golden Nectar."

Entrepreneurship and New Ventures

Nova Scotia's Golden Nectar: Glen Breton Rare

Cape Breton, Nova Scotia–based Glenora Distilleries has been battling to keep its Glen Breton Rare Single Malt Whisky on store shelves. It's not that the product isn't in demand—quite the contrary, in fact. The company distills a single-malt whisky, the only one produced in Canada, and they have been in a court battle since 2000 over the use of "Glen" in their brand name. The Scotch Whisky Association, a group representing over 50 whisky distillers in Scotland, claims the company's use of "Glen" in its brand is confusing consumers and leading them to believe that the product is distilled in Scotland

Lauchie MacLean, Glenora's president, strongly disagrees. He argues the name is referring to Glenville, Cape Breton, which is Glenora Distillery's home community. Fortunately, a Canadian Federal Court of Appeal's ruling in January 2009 allowed the company to continue to use the name. The Scotch Whisky Association can take the case to the Supreme Court of Canada if they wish, but MacLean hopes the battle is over, since he "doesn't want Glen Breton to go the way of being a collector's memorabilia."

The latest clash hasn't been the only form of legal restriction imposed on Glenora Distillery and other whisky producers around the globe. Distillers based in Scotland have set out to protect the use of the label "scotch." One such move was an agreement signed by Canada and the European Union in 2003 that prevented Canadian whisky distillers from using "scotch" in their label. This term is reserved for Scotland-based distillers only. "In the sense that only true champagne comes from France's Champagne region, so real scotch whisky is distilled only in Scotland." Glenora has always complied with this ruling but wasn't ready to lie down when the association's latest assault threatened their "Glen Breton" brand. But now, the future looks bright for a company that has had its fair share of challenges. Not only have they secured their most valuable possession, their brand name, they are also excited about the growing whisky market.

Because of increased demand in Europe and Asia, some single-malt whisky distillers have found their products in short supply. As a result, many distillers are pulling out of some markets and entering others. It's simple economics according to MacLean: "They [distillers] have an asset, and they're looking at selling that asset for the most money that they can get out of it." Glenora is a relatively small producer, but the company hopes to increase production at a later date to better match demand. Currently, Glenora is not "heavily into the Asian market," but expect that to change over the next few years.

Glenora's successes have partly been due to their entrepreneurial flexibility. The company experienced serious cash flow problems not long after its launch in 1991 because distilling doesn't happen overnight—it can take 10 to 12 years before a distillery will see revenues. However, some innovative approaches, which involved selling whisky futures and adding rum bottling and complementary tourism operations to the business, brought the company through the tough times. The business environment hasn't always been kind to Glenora, but in true entrepreneurial fashion, they have persevered. Sláinte!

Critical Thinking Question

1. Which of the external environments have had the most effect on Glenora Distilleries?

The Socio-Cultural Environment

Describe the *socio-cultural environment* and its role in business. 5

The **socio-cultural environment** includes the customs, values, attitudes, and demographic characteristics of the society in which an organization functions. Socio-cultural processes determine the goods and services as well as the standards of business conduct that a society is likely to value and accept.

socio-cultural environment Conditions including the customs, values, attitudes, and demographic characteristics of the society in which an organization functions.

Customer Preferences and Tastes

Customer preferences and tastes vary both across and within national boundaries. In some countries, consumers are willing and able to pay premium prices for designer clothes with labels such as Armani or Calvin Klein. But the same clothes have virtually no market in other countries. Product usage also varies between nations. In China, bicycles are primarily seen as a mode of transportation, but in Canada, they are marketed primarily for recreational purposes.

Similarly, consumer preferences can also vary widely within the same country. Customs and product preferences in Quebec, for example, differ from those in other parts of Canada. In the United States, pre-packaged chili is more popular in the southwest states than in the northeast. McDonald's is just one company that is affected by socio-cultural factors. In response to concerns about nutrition and health, McDonald's has added salads to its menus and experimented with other low-fat foods. It was the first fast-food chain to provide customers with information about the ingredients in its products, and it attracted media attention when it announced that it would reduce the fat content in its popular french fries.

Consumer preferences and tastes also change over time. Preferences for colour, style, and so forth change from season to season. In some years, brightly coloured clothes sell best, while in other years people want more subdued colours. Some of these changes are driven by consumers, and some are driven by companies trying to convince consumers to adopt new styles. Soft drinks usually sell better during the hot summer months than in the cold winter months. Whisky, vodka, gin, and cigarettes are consumed less today than they were just a few years ago.

Socio-cultural factors influence the way workers in a society feel about their jobs and organizations. In some cultures, work carries meaningful social significance, with certain employers and job titles being highly desired by workers. But in other cultures, work is simply a means to an end, and people are concerned only with pay and job security. McDonald's has occasionally struggled with its operations in the Middle East because many people there are not interested in working in food-service operations. These and many other related issues regarding businesses and their customers are explored more fully in Chapters 15 through 17.

Ethical Compliance and Responsible Business Behaviour

Ethics and social responsibility are critical elements of the socio-cultural environment. We cover these areas in detail in Chapter 3, but a preview of them is justified here. The central issue revolves around the fact that rapid changes in business relationships, organizational structures, and financial flows pose difficulties in keeping accurate track of a company's financial position. The public—current and potential investors—often gets blurred pictures of a firm's competitive health. The stakeholders of business firms—employees, stockholders, consumers, unions, creditors, and government—are entitled to a fair accounting so they can make enlightened personal and business decisions.

Keeping up with today's increasingly fast-paced business activities is putting a strain on the accounting profession's traditional methods for auditing, financial reporting, and time-honoured standards for professional ethics.

The now-famous Enron scandal in the United States, for example, involved fast-moving financial transactions among layers of subsidiary firms, which were designed to conceal Enron's shaky financial condition. In a blatant display of social irresponsibility and unethical behaviour, Enron's public reports concealed many of its partnerships (and obligations) with other companies, thus hiding its true operating condition. This activity netted prison terms for several Enron executives. Arthur Andersen LLP, the accounting firm that audited Enron's finances, did not catch its client's distorted reports. Skeptics wonder if Andersen's desire for future high-revenue consulting services with Enron motivated the auditors to turn a blind eye to questionable practices that eventually showed up during audits of Enron's finances. Andersen's unethical and illegal practices—including obstruction of justice for shredding and doctoring documents related to Enron audits—destroyed the public's trust and Arthur Andersen as a company.

These activities were not limited to U.S. companies. In a report released on July 28, 2003, court-appointed examiner Neal Batson charged that the Canadian Imperial Bank of Commerce, one of Enron's lenders, knew that Enron was concealing billions of dollars in debts. The report further charged that CIBC helped Enron executives manipulate their financial statements. In 2004, CIBC agreed to pay $480 million to settle allegations that it facilitated accounting fraud at Enron. The CEO of CIBC admitted that the company had "stumbled" in the area of trust and reputation.[33]

Appropriate standards of business conduct vary across cultures. In Canada, accepting bribes in return for political favours is unethical and illegal. In some other countries, however, payments to local politicians are expected in return for favourable responses to such common business transactions as zoning and operating permits. The shape of the market, the ethics of political influence, and the attitudes of its workforce are only a few of the many ways in which culture can affect an organization. We examine these issues in more detail in Chapter 6.

The Business Environment

6 Identify emerging challenges and opportunities in the *business environment.*

Business today is faster paced, more complex, and more demanding than ever before. A 2007 C-Suite survey found that the three most important issues facing Canadian businesses are (1) the value of the Canadian dollar, (2) a skilled labour shortage, and (3) the environment. These three issues are all important elements of the business environment.[34]

The business environment is complex. As businesses aggressively try to differentiate themselves, there has been a trend toward higher-quality products, planned obsolescence, and product life cycles measured in weeks or months rather than years. This, in turn, has created customer expectations for instant gratification. Consumers and business customers want high-quality goods and services—often customized—with lower prices and immediate delivery. Sales offices, service providers, and production facilities are shifting geographically as new markets and resources emerge in other countries. Employees want flexible working hours and opportunities to work at home. Stockholder expectations also add pressure for productivity increases, growth in market share, and larger profits. At the same time, however, a more vocal public demands more honesty, fair competition, and respect for the environment.

The Industry Environment

Each business firm operates in a specific industry, and each industry has different characteristics. The intensity of the competition in an industry has a big influence on how a company operates. To be effective, managers must understand the company's competitive situation and then develop a competitive strategy to exploit opportunities in the industry.

One of the best known examples of an effective competitive strategy is Wal-Mart's satellite-based distribution system. And WestJet has a unique management system that helps it minimize aircraft turnaround time and thus keep its costs lower than its competitors. Managers try hard to find a competitive strategy for their firm, because doing so will slow down or stop new competitors from entering the industry.

One of the most popular tools to analyze competitive situations in an industry is Michael Porter's five forces model.[35] The model (see Figure 2.7) helps managers analyze five important sources of competitive pressure and then decide what their competitive strategy should be. We briefly discuss each of the elements of the model in the following paragraphs.

Rivalry Among Existing Competitors

The amount of rivalry among companies varies across industries. Rivalry can be seen in activities like intense price competition, elaborate advertising campaigns, and an increased emphasis on customer service. For many years, the rivalry among Chartered Accountants, Certified General Accountants, and Certified Management Accountants in Canada was low key, but it has recently become much more intense. These organizations are responding by trying to attain more market power, cutting costs, making pricing deals with clients, and trying to find ways to differentiate themselves from their competitors.

Threat of Potential Entrants

When new competitors enter an industry, they may cause big changes. For example, when Microsoft introduced Encarta, it caused the sale of hard-copy encyclopedias by companies like Encyclopaedia Britannica to drop sharply. If it is easy for new competitors to enter a market, competition will likely be intense and the industry will not be very attractive. Some industries (for example,

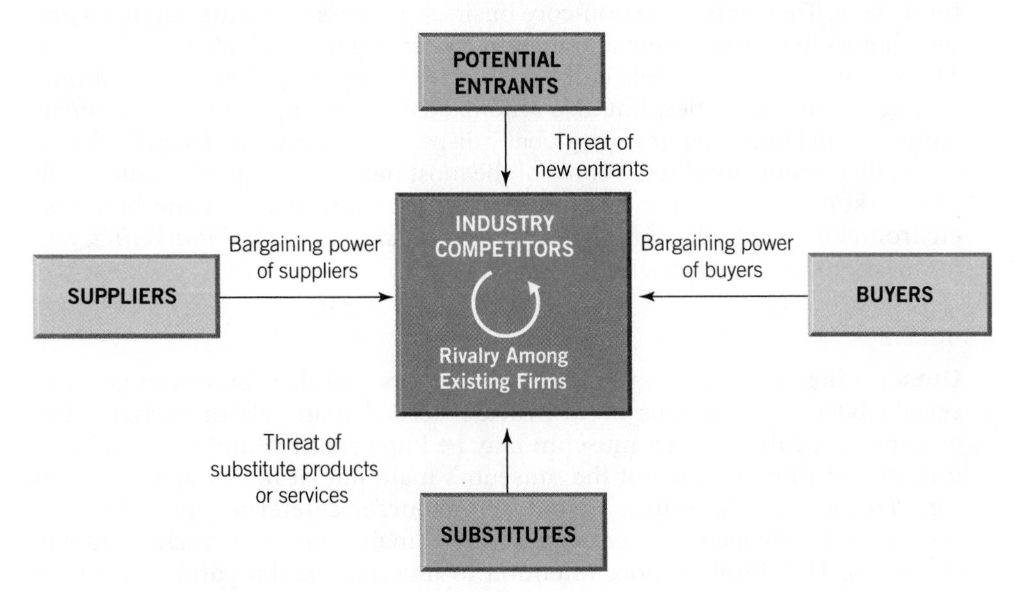

Figure 2.7 Michael Porter's five forces model.

automobile manufacturing) are very capital intensive and are therefore difficult to enter, but others (for example, home cleaning or lawn care services) are relatively easy to enter.

Suppliers

The amount of bargaining power that suppliers have in relation to buyers helps determine how competitive an industry is. When there are only a few suppliers in an industry, they tend to have great bargaining power. The power of suppliers is influenced by the number of substitute products that are available (i.e., products that perform the same or similar functions). When there are few substitute products, suppliers obviously have more power.

Buyers

When there are only a few buyers and many suppliers, the buyers have a great deal of bargaining power. Wal-Mart, for example, is often cited as a buyer that puts tremendous pressure on its suppliers to reduce their prices. Wal-Mart can do this because it buys so much from these suppliers.

Substitutes

If there are many substitute products available, the industry is more competitive. For example, various synthetic fibres can be used as substitutes for cotton.

Managers use Porter's ideas to help them decide the level of competitive intensity in an industry. A good example is the emergence of the internet in the sale of airline tickets. By making it easier for consumers to compare prices, the internet has increased the competitive intensity of the airline industry (and many other industries, for that matter). In the airline industry, the internet increased the bargaining power of ticket buyers.

Emerging Challenges and Opportunities in the Business Environment

core competency Skills and resources with which an organization competes best and creates the most value for owners.

The most successful firms are dealing with challenges and opportunities in today's business environment by focussing on their **core competencies**—the skills and resources with which they compete best and create the most value for owners. They outsource non-core business processes, paying suppliers and distributors to perform them and thereby increasing their reliance on suppliers. These new business models call for unprecedented coordination—not only among internal activities, but also among customers, suppliers, and strategic partners—and they often involve globally dispersed processes and supply chains.

In this section, we discuss some of the most publicized steps that companies have taken to respond to challenges and opportunities in the business environment. These developments include *outsourcing*, *viral marketing*, and *business process management*.

Outsourcing

outsourcing Strategy of paying suppliers and distributors to perform certain business processes or to provide needed materials or services.

Outsourcing is the strategy of paying suppliers and distributors to perform certain business processes or to provide needed materials or services. For example, the cafeteria in a museum may be important to employees and customers, but running it is not the museum's main line of business and expertise. That's why museums usually outsource cafeteria operations to food-service management companies whose main line of business is to run cafeterias. The result is more attention to museum exhibits and better food service for customers. Firms today outsource numerous activities, including payroll, employee training, and research and development. The boxed insert

Much concern has been expressed by government officials and labour unions that the outsourcing of jobs will hurt the Canadian economy. Here, women work in one of the many call centres in New Delhi, India, that do work for Canadian and U.S. companies.

entitled "Is Outsourcing a Good Idea?" describes some of the dilemmas associated with outsourcing.

Business Accountability

Is Outsourcing a Good Idea?

During the last decade or so, outsourcing has become increasingly popular because (1) it helps firms to focus attention on their core activities and avoid getting sidetracked by secondary activities, and (2) it reduces costs. The Bank of Montreal (BMO), for example, outsourced its human resource processing services to Exult Inc., which now manages payroll and benefits administration, employee records, HR call centre services, and other functions that used to be performed in-house at BMO. The new arrangement means a 20 percent reduction in HR costs for BMO, and it also frees up BMO managers to concentrate on more value-added work.

Outsourcing decisions like the one at BMO involve moving jobs from one company to another within Canada, but a lot of outsourcing involves moving jobs from Canada to a foreign country (often called *offshoring*). Because of this, much concern has been expressed about Canadian job losses. But outsourcing may actually be beneficial to Canada. If you wonder how that could be possible, the reasoning goes something like this: Canadian companies outsource certain kinds of work in order to take advantage of low-cost foreign suppliers. This allows Canadian companies to reduce their costs and increase their productivity which, in turn, helps them to be more competitive in global markets. Greater competitiveness of Canadian firms in international markets means more success, more jobs, and a higher standard of living for Canadians.

Even if we accept this line of reasoning, that doesn't mean that outsourcing is without problems. A 2006 study by the Toronto-based Centre for Outsourcing Research and Education found that less than 50 percent of companies that have tried outsourcing are satisfied with it. A study by Dun & Bradstreet found that one-quarter of all outsourcing relationships fail within two years, and one-half fail within five years. One of the problems is that members of the "stay-back team"—the individuals who are responsible for managing the new outsourcing relationship—are under pressure not only to cut costs, but also to increase the quality of the services that have been outsourced. In addition, managers complain that suppliers don't understand what they are supposed to do, they charge too much, and they provide poor service. Moreover, when disruptions occur in the supply chain, the costs to both parties can be high. Replacing failed outsourced operations can be very expensive, especially if the firm wants to go back to performing the outsourced activity itself. Another risk is the loss of control over both operations and information.

▶

The problem that Boeing has had getting its new 787 Dreamliner jet to market illustrates the problems that can arise because of outsourcing. Boeing was supposed to deliver the first 787 to All Nippon Airways in May 2008, but now the date has been pushed back until 2010. These delays will cost Boeing millions of dollars in penalties for failure to deliver the new aircraft on time to the 50 different airlines that have placed orders for nearly 900 of the new jets. To reduce development costs for the 787, Boeing decided to outsource and have different parts suppliers build different sections of the plane. These parts suppliers are located all over the world. For example, the nose section is made by a subsidiary of Toronto-based Onex Corp., the rear fuselage section is made at a factory in South Carolina, the middle fuselage section is made in Italy, and the wings are made in Japan. The idea was that these various sections (subassemblies) would then be put together at Boeing's Seattle, Washington, production facility.

To make this system work, a great deal of discretion was given to the various makers of these subassemblies. But several major problems have arisen: (1) the first 787 subassembly that was sent to Seattle by a supplier was missing literally thousands of parts; (2) parts suppliers have had trouble handling tasks that Boeing employees knew how to do because of their many years of experience in building airplanes; (3) suppliers further outsourced key tasks like engineering to other companies; and (4) subassemblies were not completed on time.

What can managers do to reduce the risks of outsourcing? They can monitor the procedures that suppliers use when making the product or providing the service, visit suppliers to inspect the premises, talk to the people who are actually making the product or delivering the service, and ensure that needed information flows from the suppliers back to the company. Overall, companies who outsource must clearly stipulate how the outsourcing process is going to work and how much authority and responsibility suppliers have. For example, the company doing the outsourcing must determine whether the supplier has the right to do further outsourcing. They must also stipulate performance expectations for the supplier and specify how the product is to be made. When Terrapin Communications Inc. outsourced production of its main product—a high-tech bracelet called Safety Turtle, which has an alarm that goes off if it is immersed in water—to Baja Technology Inc. in Zhuhai, China, it stipulated that Baja had to follow detailed instructions when making the bracelet. For example, Baja cannot substitute parts, and they must adhere closely to the bill of materials.

In spite of the potential problems with outsourcing, the practice is likely here to stay because of the increasingly global nature of business. Indian companies like Wipro and Infosys are now offering more sophisticated services than previously. For example, Wipro now offers to manage all of a company's information technology (IT) needs rather than just troubleshooting for the company's IT department, and Infosys has entered the management consulting field. These companies are also opening offices in other countries. Tata Consultancy Service has offices in Canada as well as in several South American countries, while Wipro has offices in Canada, the United States, and the Middle East. All of this change means that a Canadian company with an Anglo-German parent firm might outsource its IT functions to a firm in India, and that firm would send the actual work to the Czech Republic. That's globalization in action.

Critical Thinking Questions

1. What is outsourcing? Why do Canadian companies outsource work?
2. Do you think that Canadian companies are treating Canadian workers unfairly when they outsource jobs to foreign countries? Defend your answer.
3. *Canadian companies really don't have any alternative but to outsource. If they don't, they will not be cost-competitive and will lose out in the global market. If that happens, all Canadians will be hurt.* Do you agree or disagree with this statement? Explain.

Viral Marketing

viral marketing Strategy of using the internet and word-of-mouth marketing to spread product information.

Viral marketing, which uses word of mouth that spreads information like a virus from customer to customer, relies on the vast reaches of the internet to replace face-to-face communications. Messages about new cars, sports events, and numerous other goods and services travel on the internet among potential customers who pass the information on to others. Using various formats—games, contests, chat rooms, and bulletin boards—marketers encourage potential customers to try out products and tell other people about them.[36]

The Organic Trade Association (OTA), which promotes organic foods, created a successful viral marketing program when it partnered with Free Range Graphics and produced a five-minute online spoof of the latest *Star Wars* movie. The film—which is called *Store Wars: The Organic Rebellion*—has characters such as Cuke Skywalker and Darth Tater and has been passed around the internet by consumers who favour organic foods.[37]

Viral marketing leads to faster consumer awareness and a wider reach than traditional media messages, and at a lower cost. The OTA's short film, for example, was seen by 10 million people in its first four months. Viral marketing works because people increasingly rely on the internet for information that they used to get from other media and because the customer becomes a participant in the process of spreading the word by forwarding information to other internet users.

Business Process Management

Every company performs numerous processes that provide goods or services for both external customers or for other departments within the firm. Human resource departments perform interviewing and hiring processes, payroll departments perform the employee payment process, the purchasing department performs the process of ordering materials, accounting performs the financial reporting process, and marketing performs the process of taking orders from customers. A **process**, in short, is any activity that adds value to some input, transforming it into an output for a customer (whether external or internal).[38]

In today's business environment, many firms are moving away from the department-oriented structures and toward process-oriented team structures that cut across old departmental boundaries. This approach is called **business process management**. Often, companies begin by asking, "What must we do well to stay in business and win new orders?" Next, they identify the major processes that must be performed well to satisfy these general goals. Then they organize resources and skills around those essential processes. By organizing according to processes rather than departments, they gain a number of benefits. Decision making is faster and more customer-oriented, materials and operations are coordinated, and products get to customers more rapidly.[39]

process Any activity that adds value to some input, transforming it into an output for a customer (whether external or internal).

business process management Approach by which firms move away from department-oriented organization and toward process-oriented team structures that cut across old departmental boundaries.

Redrawing Corporate Boundaries

Understand recent trends in the *redrawing of corporate boundaries.* 7

Successful companies are responding to challenges in the environment by redrawing traditional organizational boundaries and by joining together with other companies to develop new goods and services. Some of these relationships are permanent, but others are temporary alliances formed on short notice so that, working together, partners can produce and deliver products with shorter lead times than either firm could manage alone.

Several trends in redrawing corporate boundaries have become evident in recent years. They include *acquisitions and mergers, divestitures and spinoffs, employee-owned corporations, strategic alliances,* and *subsidiary/parent corporations.*

Acquisitions and Mergers

In an **acquisition**, one firm simply buys another firm. For example, in 2008, Mars Inc. bought Wm. Wrigley Jr. Co. for $23 billion.[40] The transaction is similar to buying a car that then becomes your property. In contrast, a **merger** is a consolidation of two firms, and the arrangement is more collaborative. In recent years, Canadian National Railways merged with the Illinois Central Railroad, Jean Coutu Group Inc. merged with Eckerd Drugs, Toronto-Dominion Bank merged with Canada Trust, and Molson Inc. merged with Adolph Coors Co.

When the companies are in the same industry, as when Agricore and United Grain Growers merged to form Agricore United, it is called a **horizontal merger**. When one of the companies in the merger is a supplier or customer to the other, it is called a **vertical merger**. When the companies are in unrelated businesses, it is called a **conglomerate merger**.

acquisition One firm buys another firm.

merger The consolidation of two firms.

horizontal merger A merger of companies in the same industry.

vertical merger A merger of companies where one is a supplier or customer of the other.

conglomerate merger A merger of companies in unrelated businesses.

friendly takeover A merger where the acquired company welcomes the acquisition.

hostile takeover A merger where one company buys enough of the other company's stock to take control even though the other company is opposed to the takeover.

poison pill A defence adopted by management to make a firm less attractive to a hostile suitor in a takeover attempt.

A merger or acquisition can take place in one of several different ways. In a **friendly takeover**, the acquired company welcomes the acquisition, perhaps because it needs cash or sees other benefits in joining the acquiring firm. But in a **hostile takeover**, the acquiring company buys enough of the other company's stock to take control even though the other company is opposed to the takeover. In 2007, mergers and acquisitions together were valued at a record $370 billion; that compared to the former record of $187 billion, which was set in 2006.[41]

A **poison pill** is a defence that management adopts to make a firm less attractive to an actual or potential hostile suitor in a takeover attempt. The objective is to make the "pill" so distasteful that a potential acquirer will not want to swallow it. BCE Inc., for example, adopted a poison pill that allowed its shareholders to buy BCE stock at a 50 percent discount if another company announced its intention to acquire 20 percent or more of BCE's shares.[42]

Divestitures and Spinoffs

divestiture Occurs when a company decides to sell part of its existing business operations to another corporation.

A **divestiture** occurs when a company decides to sell part of its existing business operations to another corporation. For example, Unilever—the maker of Close-Up toothpaste, Dove soap, Vaseline lotion, and Q-tips—at one time owned several specialty chemical businesses that made ingredients for its consumer products. The company decided that it had to focus more on consumer products, so it sold the chemical businesses to ICI, a European chemical company.

spinoff Occurs when a company sets up one or more corporate units as new, independent businesses.

In other cases, a company might set up one or more corporate units as new, independent businesses because a business unit might be more valuable as a separate company. This is known as a **spinoff**. For example, PepsiCo spun off Pizza Hut, KFC, and Taco Bell into a new, separate corporation called Tricon Global Restaurants (now called Yum! Brands Inc.). Canadian Pacific spun off Canadian Pacific Railways, CP Ships, PanCanadian Petroleum, and Fording Coal.

Employee-Owned Corporations

employee stock ownership plans (ESOPs) Plans that allow employees to buy significant stakes of larger corporations.

Corporations are sometimes owned by the employees who work for them, and there is a growing trend today for employees to buy significant stakes of larger corporations. The current pattern is for this ownership to take the form of **employee stock ownership plans (ESOPs)**.

A corporation might decide to set up an ESOP to stimulate employee motivation or to fight a hostile takeover attempt. Here's how it works: The company first secures a loan, which it then uses to buy shares of its stock on the open market. Some of the future profits made by the corporation are used to pay off the loan. The stock, meanwhile, is controlled by a bank or other trustee. Employees gradually gain ownership of the stock, usually on the basis of seniority. But even though they might not have physical possession of the stock for a while, they control its voting rights immediately.

A survey of 471 Canadian and U.S. companies conducted by Western Compensation & Benefits Consultants of Vancouver found that three-quarters of the companies that have adopted ESOPs have experienced improvement in both sales and profits. Charlie Spiring, the CEO of Wellington West Holdings Inc., says that one of the fundamental principles of his business is employee ownership. People really have to be entrepreneurs to work well in the company.[43]

Strategic Alliances

strategic alliance (or joint venture) Involves two or more enterprises co-operating in the research, development, manufacture, or marketing of a product.

A **strategic alliance**, or **joint venture**, involves two or more enterprises co-operating in the research, development, manufacture, or marketing of a product.

Companies form strategic alliances for two main reasons: (1) to help spread the risk of a project, and (2) to get something of value (like technological expertise) from their strategic partner. GM and Suzuki formed a strategic alliance at the Ingersoll, Ontario, plant where Trackers and Grand Vitaras are made. Northern Empire, Stornoway, and Hunter Exploration Group formed a three-way joint venture to explore for diamonds on Melville Island in the Arctic Ocean.[44]

Subsidiary and Parent Corporations

Sometimes corporations own other corporations. A **subsidiary corporation** is one that is owned by another corporation. The corporation that owns the subsidiary is called the **parent corporation**. For example, Unilever is the parent corporation of Lever Brothers, Lipton, and Chesebrough Ponds.

subsidiary corporation A company that is owned by another corporation.

parent corporation A corporation that owns subsidiary corporations.

Test yourself on the material for this chapter at **www.pearsoned.ca/mybusinesslab**.

Summary of Learning Objectives

1. **Explain the concepts of *organizational boundaries* and *multiple organizational environments*.** All businesses operate within a larger external environment. An *organizational boundary* is that which separates the organization from its environment. Boundaries were once relatively easy to identify, but they are becoming harder to pin down. Organizations have *multiple environments*. Some environments are relatively general, such as prevailing economic conditions. Others are much more precise, such as the pricing policies of competitors. A full picture of a company's organizational environments would include the following elements: economic conditions, technology, political-legal considerations, social issues, the global environment, issues of ethics and social responsibility, the business environment itself, and numerous other emerging challenges and opportunities.

2. **Explain the importance of the *economic environment* to business and identify the factors used to evaluate the performance of an economic system.** The *economic environment* is the economic system in which business firms operate. The health of this environment affects business firms. The three key goals of the Canadian system are economic growth, economic stability, and full employment. *Economic growth* is influenced by the pattern of short-term ups and downs in an economy known as the *business cycle*. The main measure of growth in this cycle is aggregate output. An increase in aggregate output is growth. *Gross domestic product (GDP)* is the total value of all goods and services produced within a given period by a national economy through domestic factors of production. If GDP is going up, so is aggregate output; if aggregate output is going up, we have economic growth.

   Economic stability means that the amount of money available in an economic system and the quantity of goods and services produced in it are growing at about the same rate. There are three threats to stability: inflation, deflation, and unemployment.

   Unemployment is the level of joblessness among people actively seeking work. If people in different sectors lose their jobs at the same time, overall income and spending drop and businesses cut spending further—including spending on labour—and unemployment goes up further. Meanwhile, producers also start producing less because they can't sell as much. Aggregate output then decreases and we have a recession. A prolonged and deep recession is a depression.

   The government manages the economy through *fiscal policies and monetary policies*. Through the Bank of Canada, the Canadian government can influence the ability and willingness of banks to lend money. It can also influence the supply of money by prompting interest rates to go up or down.

3. **Describe the *technological environment* and its role in business.** *Technology* refers to all the ways by which firms create value for their constituents, including human knowledge, work methods, physical equipment, electronics

and telecommunications, and various processing systems. There are two general categories of business-related technologies: product and service technologies and business process technologies. *Product and service technologies* create products—both physical goods and services—for customers. *Business process technologies* are used to improve a firm's performance of internal operations (such as accounting) and to help to create better relationships with external constituents, such as suppliers and customers. Enterprise resource planning (ERP) is a large-scale information system for organizing and managing a firm's processes across product lines, departments, and geographic locations.

4. **Describe the *political-legal environment* and its role in business.** The *political-legal environment* reflects the relationship between business and government, usually in the form of government regulation. The legal system defines in part what an organization can and can't do. Various government agencies regulate important areas such as advertising practices, safety and health considerations, and acceptable standards of business conduct. Pro- or anti-business sentiment in government can further influence business activity. During periods of pro-business sentiment, firms find it easier to compete and have fewer concerns about antitrust issues. During periods of anti-business sentiment, firms may find their competitive activities more restricted.

5. **Describe the *socio-cultural environment* and its role in business.** The *socio-cultural environment* includes the customs, values, and demographic characteristics of the society in which an organization functions. Socio-cultural processes determine the goods and services as well as the standards of business conduct that a society values and accepts. Appropriate standards of conduct also vary across cultures. The shape of the market, the ethics of political influence, and the attitudes of its workforce are only a few of the many ways in which culture can affect an organization.

6. **Identify emerging challenges and opportunities in the *business environment*.** Successful companies are responding to challenges in new ways. The innovative ways in which companies respond to emerging challenges and opportunities include outsourcing, viral marketing, and business process management. *Outsourcing* is the strategy of paying suppliers and distributors to perform certain business processes or to provide needed materials or services. *Viral marketing* relies on the internet to replace face-to-face communications. Many firms are moving away from the department-oriented organization and toward process-oriented team structures that cut across old departmental boundaries—an approach called *business process management*.

7. **Understand recent trends in the *redrawing of corporate boundaries*.** An *acquisition* occurs when one firm buys another outright. A *merger* occurs when two firms combine to create a new company. A *divestiture* occurs when a corporation sells a part of its existing business operations or sets it up as a new and independent corporation. When a firm sells part of itself to raise capital, the strategy is known as a *spinoff*. The *employee stock ownership plan (ESOP)* allows employees to own a significant share of the corporation through trusts established on their behalf. In a *strategic alliance*, two or more organizations collaborate on a project for mutual gain.

PEARSON mybusinesslab™ To improve your grade, visit the MyBusinessLab website at **www.pearsoned.ca/mybusinesslab**. This online homework and tutorial system allows you to test your understanding and generates a personalized study plan just for you. It provides you with study and practice tools directly related to this chapter's content. MyBusinessLab puts you in control of your own learning!

Key Terms

acquisition (p. 61)
aggregate output (p. 41)
applied R&D (p. 49)
balance of trade (p. 43)
basic (pure) R&D (p. 49)
budget deficit (p. 44)
business cycle (p. 41)
business process management (p. 61)
conglomerate merger (p. 61)
consumer price index (CPI) (p. 45)
core competency (p. 58)
deflation (p. 46)
depression (p. 41)
divestiture (p. 62)
economic environment (p. 39)
employee stock ownership plan (ESOP) (p. 62)
enterprise resource planning (ERP) (p. 52)
external environment (p. 38)

fiscal policies (p. 48)
friendly takeover (p. 62)
gross domestic product (GDP) (p. 42)
gross national product (GNP) (p. 42)
horizontal merger (p. 61)
hostile takeover (p. 62)
inflation (p. 44)
merger (p. 61)
monetary policies (p. 48)
national debt (p. 44)
nominal GDP (p. 42)
organizational boundary (p. 38)
outsourcing (p. 58)
parent corporation (p. 63)
poison pill (p. 62)
political-legal environment (p. 53)
process (p. 61)
productivity (p. 43)
purchasing power parity (p. 43)
R&D intensity (p. 50)
real GDP (p. 42)
recession (p. 41)
research and development (R&D) (p. 48)
socio-cultural environment (p. 55)
spinoff (p. 62)
stability (p. 44)
stabilization policy (p. 48)
standard of living (p. 41)
strategic alliance (p. 62)
subsidiary corporation (p. 63)
technology (p. 48)
technology transfer (p. 51)
unemployment (p. 46)
vertical merger (p. 61)
viral marketing (p. 60)

Questions for Analysis

1. It has been argued that inflation is both good and bad. How can this be? Explain. Are government efforts to control inflation well advised? Explain.
2. What are the benefits and risks of outsourcing? What, if anything, should be done about the problem of Canadian companies outsourcing jobs to foreign countries? Defend your answer.
3. Why is it important for managers to understand the environment in which their businesses operate?
4. Explain how current economic indicators such as inflation and unemployment affect you personally. Explain how they might affect you as a manager.
5. Using a product or service of your choice, explain how the various environments of business affect the sales possibilities of the product or service.
6. What is the current climate regarding the regulation of business? How might it affect you if you were a manager today?
7. At first glance, it might seem as though the goals of economic growth and stability are inconsistent with one another. How can you reconcile this apparent inconsistency?

Application Exercises

1. Select two businesses with which you are familiar. Identify the major elements of their external environments that are most likely to affect them in important and meaningful ways.
2. Using the internet, identify the major suppliers of software for enterprise resource planning. Try to locate information about their primary customers.
3. Interview two business owners or managers. Ask them to describe for you the following things: (1) what, if any, business functions they outsource; (2) whether or not they are focussing more attention on business process management now than in the past; and (3) how the events of September 11, 2001, have affected their work.

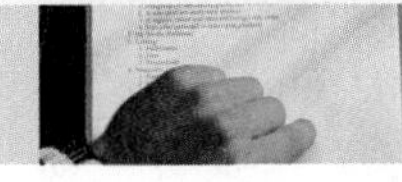
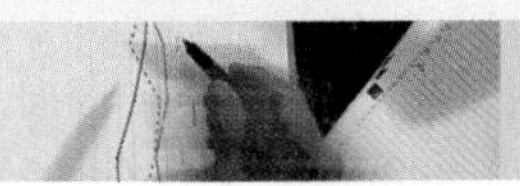

Building Your Business Skills

The Letdown from Environmental Upheaval

Purpose of the Assignment

To encourage students to understand how local events can affect other businesses in a number of ways.

The Situation

The collapse of Enron affected literally hundreds of other businesses. While attention was directed primarily at the demise of Arthur Andersen, many other businesses suffered as well. For example, Enron's headquarters were located in a large office building on the edge of Houston's downtown business district. Because of both Enron's rapid growth and the prosperity of its employees, numerous other service providers had set up shop nearby—a shoeshine stand, a coffee shop, a bank branch, a dry cleaner, and two restaurants. When Enron collapsed, the demand for services provided by these small businesses dropped sharply.

Larger businesses were also caught up in the ripple effect. Enron, for example, had bought the rights to name the new home of baseball's Houston Astros Enron Field. The Astros were forced to remove all Enron signage and

seek a new sponsor. Continental Airlines dominates the air traffic market out of Houston, and Enron was one of Continental's largest corporate clients. Combined with the events of September 11, 2001, and major staff reductions at Compaq Computer, another big Continental client, the end of business travel by Enron managers cost the airline considerable revenue.

Assignment

Divide up into groups of four or five students. Each group should begin by doing the following:

Step 1

Identify five kinds of small businesses likely to have been affected by Enron's collapse. You can include some of those identified above, but identify at least two others.

Step 2

Identify five kinds of large businesses likely to have been affected by Enron's collapse. Again, you can use some of those identified above, but identify at least two others.

Step 3

Now Respond to the Following Items:

1. For each company that you identify, both small and large, describe the specific effects of the Enron collapse on its business.
2. Describe the most logical organizational response of each company to these effects.
3. What kinds of plans, if any, should each organization develop in the event of similar future events?
4. Identify businesses that might have benefitted economically from the collapse of Enron.

Alternative Assignment

Select a different high-profile environmental upheaval, such as the latest U.S. duties that have been placed on Canadian softwood lumber being shipped to the United States, and substitute it for Enron. Then proceed with Steps 1–3 above.

Questions for Discussion

1. What does this exercise demonstrate about the pitfalls of relying too heavily on one business?
2. Could any of these businesses have been better prepared for the Enron collapse?
3. Managers must be on the alert for environmental changes that may negatively affect their business. Is it possible for a manager to spend too much time trying to anticipate future events? Why or why not?

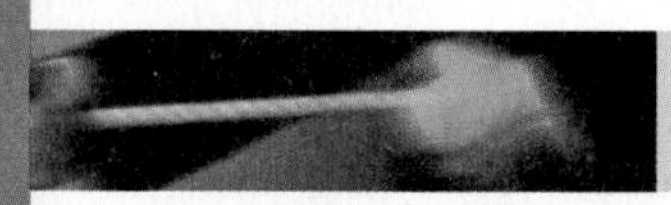

Exercising Your Ethics: Team Exercise

Finding the Balance

The Situation

Managers often find it necessary to find the right balance among the interests of different stakeholders. For instance, paying employees the lowest possible wages can enhance profits, but paying a living wage might better serve the interests of workers. As more businesses outsource production to other countries, these trade-offs become even more complicated.

The Dilemma

The Canadian Delta Company currently uses three different suppliers in Southeast Asia for most of its outsourced production. Due to increased demand for its products, it needs to double the amount of business it currently subcontracts to one of these suppliers. (For purposes of this exercise, assume that the company must award the new supplier contract to a single firm and that it must be one of these three. You can also assume that the quality provided is about the same for all three companies.)

Subcontractor A provides a plain but clean work environment for its workers. Even though the local weather conditions are hot and humid much of the year, the plant is not air conditioned. Canadian Delta safety experts have verified that the conditions are not dangerous but are definitely uncomfortable at times. The firm pays its workers the same prevailing wage rate that is paid by its local competitors. While it has never had a legal issue with its workforce, Subcontractor A does push its employees to meet production quotas and it has a very tough policy regarding discipline for tardiness. For instance, an employee who is late gets put on probation; a second infraction within three months results in termination. This subcontractor provides production to Canadian Delta at a level such that it can attach a 25 percent markup.

Subcontractor B also provides a plain work environment. It pays its workers about 5 percent above local wage levels and hence is an attractive employer. Because of its higher pay, this firm is actually quite ruthless with some of its policies, however. For instance, any employee who reports to work more than 15 minutes late without a medical excuse is automatically terminated. This supplier's costs are such that Delta Company can achieve a 20 percent markup.

Subcontractor C runs a much nicer factory than either A or B, and the plant is air conditioned. It also pays its workers about 10 percent above local wage levels. The company also operates an on-site school for the children of its employees and provides additional training for its workers so they can improve their skills. Due to its higher costs, Canadian Delta's markup on this firm's products is only around 15 percent.

Team Activity

Assemble a group of four students and assign each group member to one of the following roles:

- Canadian Delta executive
- Canadian Delta employee
- Canadian Delta customer
- Canadian Delta investor

Action Steps

1. Before discussing the situation with your group, and from the perspective of your assigned role, which firm do you think should get the additional business? Which firm is your second choice? Write down the reasons for your position.
2. Before discussing the situation with your group, and from the perspective of your assigned role, what are the underlying ethical issues in this situation? Write down the issues.
3. Gather your group together and reveal, in turn, each member's comments on their choices. Next, reveal the ethical issues listed by each member.
4. Appoint someone to record the main points of agreement and disagreement within the group. How do you explain the results? What accounts for any disagreement?
5. From an ethical standpoint, what does your group conclude is the most appropriate choice for the company in this situation? Why?

For additional cases and exercise material, go to **www.pearsoned.ca/mybusinesslab**.

Concluding Case 2-1

The Impact of the External Environment on Business Firms

There are various "environments of business" that managers must pay attention to: economic, technological, socio-cultural, political-legal, and global. In the political-legal environment, for example, terrorism is a risk that must be dealt with. Lloyd's of London is a famous insurance company that is one of the world's largest underwriters of terrorism insurance. In a speech in Toronto in 2007, a Lloyd's spokesman warned about terrorism and political risk and said that it is not simply a threat to governments, but also to businesses. In a typical year, there are 150–200 incidents of terrorism against businesses worldwide. Canadian businesses are operating in some dangerous places and their assets are difficult to protect.

In the socio-cultural environment, there is increasing activity by various pressure groups who have concluded that business firms cannot be counted on to behave in a socially responsible fashion. For example, in 2007, Greenpeace—a well-known environmental pressure group—launched a media campaign against AbitibiBowater Inc., a large Canadian forest products company. As part of the campaign, it put up a banner at the company's head office that read "Looters of our forest." In the Netherlands in 2007, Greenpeace blocked the unloading of a ship containing newsprint made by AbitibiBowater.

The "environment" is not limited simply to factors like those mentioned above. Another very important environment for many business firms is the *physical* environment. The most highly publicized physical environment issue at the moment is global warming. It presents both challenges and opportunities for business firms.

Challenges. Consider the challenge that global warming presents for forestry companies. If climate predictions are accurate, British Columbia's forestry companies will be significantly affected by global warming because different species of trees thrive at different latitudes. The predicted temperature change will mean that trees that do well in Prince George today will grow best north of the Yukon border in 80 years. Whitebark pine, for example, will almost disappear from its current range, and lodgepole pine, white spruce, sitka spruce, and western hemlock will all decrease in importance over the next 80 years. By contrast, ponderosa pine will triple, and Douglas fir and western red cedar will both increase substantially. These are dramatic changes that forestry companies will have to take into account, particularly since they have such a long planning horizon.

Global warming also means that new tree diseases will have to be dealt with. Whitebark pine, for example, can't fend off insects and fungi that exist in a warmer climate. Tree companies are now conducting tests to determine if the tree can be planted much further north to reduce the threat from insects. The most significant tree disease at the moment is the mountain pine beetle, which has killed millions of acres of trees in British Columbia. The warming climate has allowed the beetle population to explode, and the infestation threatens to destroy jobs, communities, and companies that are dependent on forestry. By 2013, as much as 80 percent of the lodgepole pine will be dead as a result of the beetles' boring activity. What's worse, the infestation is spreading into neighbouring Alberta.

To complicate matters further, a dispute has erupted about how to deal with the beetle infestation. Lumber companies want to cut vast swaths of dead pine because it still has some market value. Environmentalists oppose such massive cutting, and some even argue that nothing at all should be done and that nature should be allowed to take its natural course. They accept that the pine beetle may eventually destroy 30 percent of Alberta's pine trees, but they say that's better than having logging companies cut 100 percent of them. Homeowners in areas that are infested have their own agenda. They know that if dead pine trees are not cut, an increased fire risk will develop that will threaten their homes. All of these conflicting views have created a significant challenge for Canadian forestry companies.

Opportunities. Global warming may also provide opportunities for Canadian businesses. Consider the wine industry. The highest quality grapes historically have been grown in France, Spain, Australia, and California, where the climate was just right for them. But with global warming, excessive heat is beginning to be a problem in these areas. Global warming means that grapes can now be grown further and further north. In Tappen, British Columbia, for example, Gary Kennedy is experimenting with growing Pinot Noir grapes at latitudes where they formerly could not have survived. Grapes of this variety can survive winter temperatures down to about minus 20 degrees Celsius. Fifty years ago, it was not uncommon for temperatures to drop that low in the Okanagan Valley, but during the last decade temperatures almost never dropped that low. This has opened up a whole new geographical area for growing high-quality grapes, and the number of B.C. wineries has increased from 17 in 1990 to 136 in 2007. Wines made in this region are starting to win gold medals at European wine competitions.

Questions for Discussion

1. Describe in general terms how each element of the external environment (economic, technological, socio-cultural, political-legal, global, and business) affects business firms.
2. Choose a specific industry (for example, automobile, fashion, construction, fast food, etc.) and describe how each element of the external environment is likely to affect firms in that industry.
3. Can managers in business firms control the elements in the external environment, or do they simply have to react to changes that are beyond their control? Give examples that support your conclusion.
4. Explain how the factors in Porter's five forces model (rivalry among competitors, threat of potential entrants, suppliers, substitutes, and buyers) differ from the other environmental elements (economic, technological, socio-cultural, political-legal, and global).

Concluding Case 2-2

Corporate Reputations Are on the Line

During the last few years, there has been a great deal of negative publicity about business firms because of illegal and unethical behaviour by business executives and the economic woes that started in 2008. But some corporations continue to perform well, and to do good things for their stakeholders.

Each year, the Reputation Institute publishes *Global Pulse,* which ranks the world's 1000 largest companies according to their reputation with their stakeholders. Each company's score is determined by how well it scores on key performance indicators like products/services, innovation, workplace, citizenship, governance, and leadership. In the 2008 survey, the top companies were Toyota (Japan), Google (United States), IKEA (Sweden), Ferrero (Italy), and Johnson & Johnson (United States). The highest-ranked Canadian company was Jean Coutu Group, which ranked eighteenth.

A list of the most respected corporations in Canada is published by KPMG/Ipsos-Reid. Several hundred leading Canadian CEOs were asked to assess Canadian corporations on eight performance categories such as long-term investment value, innovation and product/service development, financial performance, corporate social responsibility, corporate governance, human resource management, and customer service. In one recent survey, the top-ranked companies were the Royal Bank of Canada, Research in Motion, EnCana Corp., and WestJet Airlines.

Surveys about corporate reputations are also conducted in the United States. The Reputation Quotient study is a joint effort of Harris Interactive Inc., a Rochester, New York–based research firm, and the Reputation Institute of New York. Its 2008 survey asked more than 20 000 people to name two companies with the best reputation and two companies with the worst reputation. Respondents evaluated the companies on factors such as emotional appeal, financial performance, social responsibility, vision and leadership, and workplace environment. In total, 60 companies were ranked. In the survey, 88 percent of respondents rated the reputation of American business as either "not good" or "terrible."

The company with the best reputation was Johnson & Johnson, a manufacturer of baby products and pharmaceuticals. The next four companies (in order) were Google, Sony Corporation, Coca-Cola, and Kraft Foods. Apparently, consumers have warm feelings about Johnson & Johnson because of its baby products.

The worst company was AIG, the recipient of a multi-billion dollar bailout by the U.S. government. General Motors, Chrysler, and Citigroup were also rated poorly. All of these companies received negative publicity in 2009 because of their financial problems.

It's not just individual companies that can run into difficulty. During the last few years, the reputations of entire industries have declined. For example, the reputations of the financial and automobile industries have diminished sharply since the recession began in 2008. Consumer impressions of the pharmaceutical and oil industries are also negative because of a widely held belief that these industries are overcharging consumers for the products they sell. The tobacco industry has also had problems because consumers think that information about the negative effects of smoking and nicotine was withheld from the public.

When we consider negative information about business firms, we must remember that only a very small proportion of them are actually engaging in illegal or unethical behaviour. A review of the global, Canadian, and U.S. reputation lists—and the criteria that are used to generate them—provides some reassuring testimony on the vitality and values of many businesses. It also shows the manner in which they conduct their operations and gives us some insights into how companies must perform to gain the kind of stellar reputation necessary to get on the list.

These criteria all have one underlying theme: They reflect in one way or another the extent to which an organization and its managers effectively meet or exceed the needs and expectations of their external constituents. For example, hiring and developing the brightest and most motivated people from the labour market results in high levels of employee talent. Likewise, respecting the needs of shareholders and other investors affects several criteria, including financial soundness, use of corporate assets, and long-term investment value. Says one expert, "We admire companies that cater to their constituents."

Questions for Discussion

1. What is your opinion of the value of rankings like these? How might the different ways that the Canadian and U.S. surveys are conducted influence the results?
2. Do you think the criteria that are used are appropriate? Can you suggest others?
3. Is the ranking something that investors should rely on in buying stock?
4. If you were a top manager and wanted your firm to move up in the rankings, how would you proceed?

apter 3

Conducting Business Ethically and Responsibly

After reading this chapter, you should be able to:

1. Explain how individuals develop their personal *codes of ethics* and why ethics are important in the workplace.
2. Distinguish *corporate social responsibility* from *ethics*, identify *organizational stakeholders*, and characterize social consciousness today.
3. Show how the concept of social responsibility applies both to environmental issues and to a firm's relationships with customers, employees, and investors.
4. Identify four general *approaches to social responsibility* and describe the four steps a firm must take to implement a *social responsibility program.*
5. Explain how issues of social responsibility and ethics affect small businesses.

What Really Happened at Livent?

Livent Inc. was founded by Garth Drabinsky and Myron Gottlieb. It was a live theatre company with outlets in Toronto, Vancouver, Chicago, and New York. In 1998, questions were raised about Livent's finances by new owners who had bought in to the company. Shortly thereafter, Drabinsky and Gottlieb were fired. They were eventually charged with producing false financial statements to make the company look more profitable than it actually was. The fraud allegedly cost investors and creditors $500 million. Drabinsky and Gottlieb denied any wrongdoing and claimed that the financial manipulations were carried out by subordinates without their knowledge. After a long delay, their trial finally started in 2008.

During the trial, prosecutors called several witnesses who admitted that they had participated in the financial manipulations, but they said that they had done so at the direction of Drabinsky and Gottlieb. Some of their charges were as follows:

- A computer technician said he was asked by the accounting controller to modify accounting software so that changes could be made without auditors detecting them. He said that the vice-president, Gordon Eckstein, told him to carry out the controller's instructions.
- Gordon Eckstein said that he was told by Drabinsky and Gottlieb to carry out the fraud (Eckstein had previously pled guilty).
- John Beer, a private investigator who was hired by KPMG's forensic unit to look into allegations of accounting manipulations, said he found a document in Drabinsky's briefcase that described $21 million of expenses that were omitted from one year's financial statements and "rolled" to the next year.
- Gary Gill, another investigator for KPMG, also testified that he saw an internal company document that contained information about financial manipulations.
- Chris Craib, Livent's accounting controller, testified that he had prepared the document and had given it to Drabinsky and Gottlieb, and that he had attended a meeting where accounting manipulations were openly discussed.
- Another accounting employee said he was amazed to learn of a plan to reclassify $10 million of expenses as fixed assets.
- Chief financial officer Maria Messina (who had formerly worked at KPMG) said she didn't tell her former colleagues about the fraud because she wanted to try to cope with it in-house (she finally exposed the fraud after new investors had taken over managing the company).
- Former controller Grant Malcolm testified that he spent all of his time recording fraudulent manipulations to the company's books. He said he routinely deleted expenses for shows, or moved them to future periods, or transferred them to different shows. He said he prepared a memo for Drabinsky that summarized all the improperly transferred production costs. He also said that two advertising agencies helped with the fraud by moving their billings from an earlier year to a later year. That allowed profit to be higher in the earlier year.

Drabinsky and Gottlieb's defence attorneys repeatedly attacked the credibility of the witnesses and argued that accounting staff had circumvented the accounting controls that Drabinsky had put in place. The defence presented no witnesses, and Drabinsky and Gottlieb did not testify.

In 2009, Drabinsky and Gottlieb were found guilty of fraud and forgery. Drabinsky was sentenced to seven years in jail and Gottlieb to six years. In a related case, the Institute of Chartered Accountants of Ontario found three senior Deloitte & Touche LLP auditors guilty of making errors during an audit of Livent's financial statements. The three were fined $100 000 each.

Drabinsky and Gottlieb are not the only executives who have been charged with wrongdoing in the recent past. In 2005, Bernie Ebbers, the CEO of WorldCom, was found guilty of nine charges of securities fraud and filing false documents. He was sentenced to 25 years in prison. In 2006, Ken Lay, the CEO of Enron, was convicted of conspiracy and securities fraud, but he died before he was sentenced. In 2007, Conrad Black, CEO of Hollinger International, was convicted of fraud and obstruction of justice and was sentenced to six and a half years in prison. In December 2008, Bernie Madoff pleaded guilty to swindling investors in a $50 billion fraud. He is likely to spend the rest of his life in prison. ◆

How will this help me?

There is a growing dilemma in the business world today involving the economic imperatives (real or imagined) facing managers and the pressure to function as good citizens. By understanding the material in this chapter, you'll be better able to assess the ethical and social responsibility issues that you will face as an employee and as a boss or business owner. It will also help you understand the ethical and social responsibility actions of businesses you deal with as a consumer and as an investor.

In this chapter, we'll look at ethics and social responsibility—what they mean and how they apply to a firm's relationships with customers, employees, and investors. Along the way, we look at some general approaches to social responsibility, the steps businesses must take to implement social responsibility programs, and how issues of social responsibility and ethics affect small businesses. But first, we begin this chapter by discussing ethics in the workplace—individual, business, and managerial.

Ethics in the Workplace

1 Explain how individuals develop their personal *codes of ethics* and why ethics are important in the workplace.

Ethics are beliefs about what is right and wrong or good and bad. An individual's personal values and morals and the social context in which they occur determine whether a particular behaviour is perceived as ethical or unethical. **Ethical behaviour** is behaviour that conforms to individual beliefs and social norms about what is right and good. **Unethical behaviour** is behaviour that individual beliefs and social norms define as wrong and bad. **Business ethics** refers to ethical or unethical behaviour by a manager or employee of an organization.

ethics Individual standards or moral values regarding what is right and wrong or good and bad.

ethical behaviour Behaviour that conforms to individual beliefs and social norms about what is right and good.

unethical behaviour Behaviour that individual beliefs and social norms define as wrong and bad.

business ethics Ethical or unethical behaviour by a manager or employee of an organization.

Individual Ethics

Because ethics are based on both individual beliefs and social concepts, they vary from person to person, from situation to situation, and from culture to culture. Social standards are broad enough to support differences in beliefs. Without violating these general standards, therefore, people may develop personal codes of ethics reflecting a wide range of attitudes and beliefs.

Thus ethical and unethical behaviour is determined partly by the individual and partly by culture. Virtually everyone would agree that if you see someone drop a $20 bill in a store, it would be ethical to return it to the owner. But there will be less agreement if you find $20 and don't know who dropped it. Should you turn it in to the lost-and-found department? Or, since the rightful owner isn't likely to claim it, can you just keep it? The real problem is that each person has a different standard of ethics.

The difference between unethical and illegal behaviour can complicate matters. When CIBC World Markets sued six former employees after they left the company and started a new rival firm, Genuity Capital Markets, CIBC was making a claim of illegal behaviour. But the defendants argued that they had done nothing illegal, or unethical for that matter, because the employees they took with them had already decided to leave CIBC.[1] In another case, damages were awarded to RBC Dominion Securities after one of its branch managers and his subordinates abruptly left as a group to work for a competitor.[2]

Because every situation has some degree of ambiguity, societies may adopt formal laws that reflect prevailing ethical standards or social norms. For example, because most people regard theft as unethical, we have laws against such behaviour and ways of punishing those who steal. We try to make unambiguous laws, but real-world situations can often be interpreted in different ways, and it isn't always easy to apply statutory standards to real-life behaviour. The epidemic of financial scandals in recent years shows how willing people can be to take advantage of potentially ambiguous situations.

In some cultures, ethically ambiguous practices are hallmarks of business activity. Brazilians, for example, apply the philosophy of *jeitinho*—meaning "to find a way"—by using personal connections, bending the rules, or making a "contribution."[3] Suppose you needed to get an official document. You might start out determined to take all the proper bureaucratic steps to get it. However, when you find yourself in a complex maze of rules and regulations and think you'll never get your document, you're likely to resort to *jeitinho* to get the job done.

Individual Values and Codes

How should we deal with business behaviour that we regard as unethical—especially when it's legally ambiguous? We must start with the individuals in a business—its managers, employees, agents, and other legal representatives. Each of these people's personal code of ethics is determined by a combination of factors. We start to form ethical standards as children in response to our perceptions of the behaviour of parents and other adults. Soon we enter school, where peers influence us, and as we grow into adulthood, experience shapes our lives and contributes to our ethical beliefs and our behaviour. We also develop values and morals that contribute to ethical standards. If you put financial gain at the top of your priority list, you may develop a code of ethics that supports the pursuit of material comfort. If you set family and friends as a priority, you'll no doubt adopt different standards.

Because ethics are both personally and culturally defined, differences of opinion can arise as to what is ethical or unethical. For example, many people who would never think of taking a candy bar from a grocery store routinely take home pens and pads of paper from their offices. Other people who view themselves as law-abiding citizens have no qualms about using radar detectors to avoid speeding tickets. In each of the situations, people will choose different sides of the issue and argue that their actions are ethical.

Managerial Ethics

Managerial ethics are the standards of behaviour that guide managers in their work.[4] Although ethics can affect managerial work in any number of ways, it's helpful to classify behaviour in terms of three broad categories.

managerial ethics Standards of behaviour that guide individual managers in their work.

Behaviour Toward Employees

This category covers such matters as hiring and firing, wages and working conditions, privacy, and respect. Ethical and legal guidelines suggest that hiring and firing decisions should be based solely on the ability to perform a job. A manager who discriminates against any ethnic minority in hiring exhibits both unethical and illegal behaviour. But what about the manager who hires a friend or relative when someone else might be more qualified? Such decisions may not be illegal, but in Canada they may be objectionable on ethical grounds (but not necessarily in some other countries).

Wages and working conditions, though regulated by law, are also areas for controversy. Consider a manager who pays a worker less than what is deserved because the manager knows that the employee can't afford to quit. While some people will see the behaviour as unethical, others will see it as simply smart business. It is much easier to judge the behaviour of Enron managers, who encouraged employees to invest retirement funds in Enron stock and then, when financial problems began to surface, refused to permit employees to sell the stock (even though top officials of the company were allowed to sell their stock).

Behaviour Toward the Organization

conflict of interest Occurs when an activity benefits an individual at the expense of the employer.

Ethical issues also arise from employee behaviour toward employers, especially in such areas as conflict of interest, confidentiality, and honesty. A **conflict of interest** occurs when an activity benefits an individual at the expense of the employer. Most companies have policies that forbid buyers from accepting gifts from suppliers. Businesses in highly competitive industries—software or fashion apparel, for example—have safeguards against designers selling company secrets to competitors. Relatively common problems in the general area of honesty include such behaviour as stealing supplies, padding expense accounts, and using a business phone to make personal long-distance calls. Most employees are honest, but most organizations are nevertheless vigilant.

Behaviour Toward Other Economic Agents

Ethics also come into play in the relationship between the firm and its so-called primary agents of interest—mainly customers, competitors, stockholders, suppliers, dealers, and unions. In dealing with such agents, there is room for ethical ambiguity in just about every activity—advertising, financial disclosure, ordering and purchasing, bargaining and negotiation, and other business relationships.

For example, businesses in the pharmaceuticals industry are under criticism because of the rising prices of drugs. They argue that high prices cover the costs of research and development programs to develop new drugs. The solution to such problems seems obvious: Find the right balance between reasonable pricing and *price gouging* (responding to increased demand with steep price increases). But like so many questions involving ethics, there are significant differences of opinion about the proper balance.[5]

Another area of concern is competitive espionage. In 2004, Air Canada sued WestJet for $220 million, claiming that a WestJet executive had accessed Air Canada's confidential reservations database, which contained important competitive information that would be beneficial to WestJet.[6] WestJet eventually admitted its actions were unethical and paid Air Canada $5 million to cover expenses Air Canada incurred while investigating the unauthorized accessing of its website. WestJet also agreed to contribute $10 million to children's charities.

Most people would probably see the WestJet incident as a fairly clear case of unethical behaviour. But what if a manager is given confidential information by an unhappy former employee of a competitor who wants to get revenge on his former employer? Is it acceptable in that case for the manager to use the information? Some people would say it's still unethical, but others might feel that since the manager didn't go looking for the information, it's acceptable to use it.[7]

Difficulties also arise because business practices vary globally. In many countries, bribes are a normal part of doing business, but in Canada and the United States, bribes are seen as clearly unethical and illegal. In 2006, the Gemological Institute of America (GIA) fired several employees after they had accepted bribes from diamond dealers. In return for the bribes, the GIA

The intense competition between Air Canada and WestJet motivated a WestJet executive to access Air Canada's confidential reservations database in the hope of gaining a competitive edge for WestJet.

employees rated the dealers' diamonds higher than they should have been, and this allowed the dealers to sell them for a much higher price.[8]

Assessing Ethical Behaviour

Given the difficulties of distinguishing ethical and unethical behaviour, how can we go about deciding whether a particular action or decision is ethical?[9] A three-step model can be used for applying ethical judgments to situations that may arise during the course of business activities:

1. Gather the relevant factual information.
2. Determine the most appropriate moral values.
3. Make an ethical judgment based on the rightness or wrongness of the proposed activity or policy.

Let's see how this process might work for a common dilemma faced by managers involving their expense accounts. Companies routinely provide managers with accounts to cover work-related expenses when they are travelling on company business and/or entertaining clients for business purposes. Common examples of such expenses include hotel bills, meals, rental cars, and so forth. Employees are expected to claim only those expenses that are accurate and work related. If a manager takes a client to dinner while travelling on business and spends $100, submitting a receipt for that dinner and expecting to be reimbursed for $100 is clearly appropriate. Suppose, however, that the manager also has a $100 dinner the next night in that same city with a good friend for purely social purposes. Submitting that receipt for full reimbursement would be seen by most managers as unethical (although a few might rationalize that it is acceptable because they are underpaid and this is a way to increase their pay).

Other principles that come into play in a case like this include various ethical norms. Consider four such norms and the issues that they raise:

Utility: Does the act optimize what is best for those who are affected by it?

Rights: Does it respect the rights of the individuals involved?

Justice: Is it consistent with what we regard as fair?

Caring: Is it consistent with people's responsibilities to each other?

Figure 3.1 incorporates the consideration of these ethical norms.

Now, let's return to the case of the inflated expense account. The utility norm would acknowledge that the manager benefits from padding an expense account, but others (co-workers and owners) do not. Likewise, most experts would agree that this behaviour does not respect the rights of others. Moreover, it is clearly unfair and compromises the manager's responsibilities to others. This particular act, then, appears to be clearly unethical.

Figure 3.1 also provides mechanisms for considering unique circumstances—those that apply only in certain limited situations. Suppose, for example, that the manager loses the receipt for the legitimate dinner but retains the receipt for the social dinner. Some people will argue that it is acceptable to submit the illegitimate receipt because the manager is only doing so to be reimbursed for what he or she is entitled to. Others, however, will argue that submitting the other receipt is wrong under any circumstances. Changes in the situation can obviously make issues more or less clear-cut.

When judging the ethics of a given behaviour, one of the simplest tests to use is the so-called "newspaper test." This means asking yourself this question:

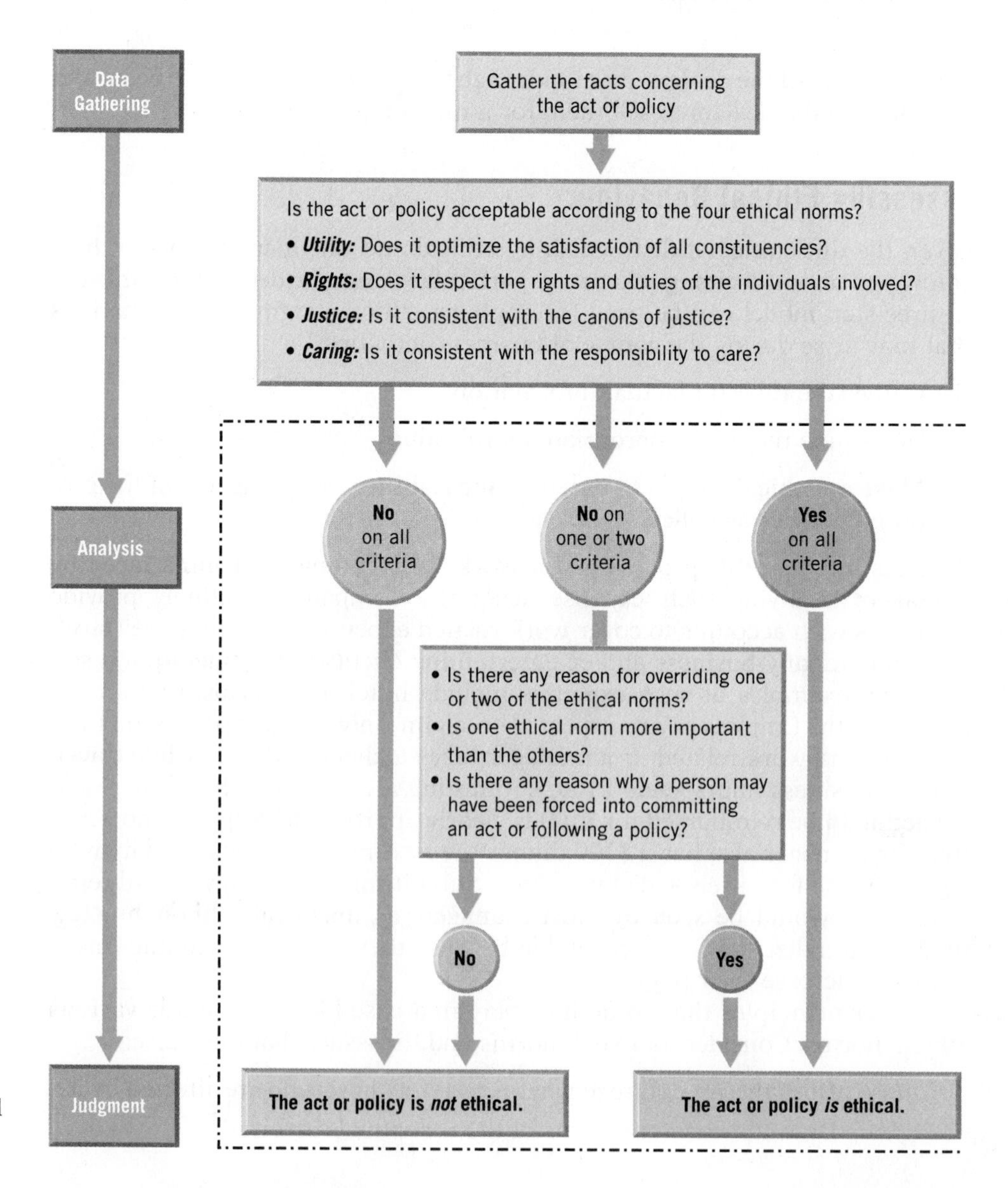

Figure 3.1 Expanded model of ethical judgment making.

If you were to make a decision on an ethical issue and then read about it on the front page of tomorrow's paper, how would you feel? If you would feel embarrassed, you are very likely violating ethical standards and should make a different decision.

Company Practices and Business Ethics

As unethical and even illegal behaviour by both managers and employees plagues more and more companies, many firms have taken steps to encourage ethical behaviour in the workplace. Many, for example, establish codes of conduct and develop clear ethical positions on how the firm and its employees will conduct its business.

Technological developments are creating all sorts of new ethical problems—cloning, satellite reconnaissance, email snooping, and bioengineered foods, to name just a few. For every innovation that promises convenience or safety, there seems to be a related ethical issue. The internet and email, for example, are certainly convenient and efficient, but they present business people with a variety of ethics-related problems. In one sense, electronic communications are merely the modern version of traditional forms of communication, such as regular mail or the telephone. However, they make it possible to run classic swindles, such as Ponzi or pyramid schemes, with greater efficiency than ever before. Federal law-enforcement personnel routinely surf the web looking for illegal or unethical practices, often finding hundreds of questionable sites in a typical sting. Employers are also using email to test employee loyalty, as in the case of the manager who sent false emails to his workers, pretending to be a recruiter from a competing firm. Any employees who responded were skipped for promotion.

If a company truly wishes to promote ethical behaviour on the part of its employees, the single most effective step a company can take is to demonstrate top management commitment to high ethical standards. A now-classic illustration of the power of ethical commitment involved Johnson & Johnson (J&J). In 1982, it was discovered that capsules of the company's Tylenol pain reliever had been laced with cyanide. Managers at J&J quickly recalled all Tylenol bottles still on retailers' shelves and then went public with candid information throughout the crisis. J&J's ethical choices proved to be a crucial factor in its campaign to rescue its product. Both the firm and the brand bounced back much more quickly than anyone had thought possible. When food products made by Maple Leaf Foods were found to be contaminated with listeria, the company took quick action to manage the crisis (see Chapter 6 for more details).[10]

Two of the most common approaches to formalizing commitment are adopting written codes and instituting ethics programs.

Adopting Written Codes

Many companies have adopted written **codes of ethics** that formally acknowledge their intent to do business in an ethical manner. Most codes of ethics are designed to perform one or more of the following functions:

code of ethics Formal, written acknowledgment of a company's intent to do business in an ethical manner.

- They may increase public confidence in a firm or its industry.
- They may help stem the tide of government regulation—that is, aid in self-regulation.
- They may improve internal operations by providing consistent standards of both ethical and legal conduct.
- They can help managers respond to problems that arise as a result of unethical or illegal behaviour.

Our Purpose To support people in achieving the benefit of wilderness-oriented recreation.	Our **purpose** is what we resolve to do.
Our Vision Mountain Equipment Co-op is an innovative, thriving co-operative that inspires excellence in products and services, passion for wilderness experiences, leadership for a just world, and actionfor a healthy planet.	Our **vision** is our picture of the future and outlines where we want to go.
Our Mission Mountain Equipment Co-op provides quality products and services for self-propelled wilderness-oriented recreation, such as hiking and mountaineering, at the lowest reasonable price in an informative, respectful manner. We are a member-owned co-operative striving for social and environmental leadership.	Our **mission** tells us what business we are in, who we serve, and how. It represents the fundamental reason for MEC's existence.
Our Values We conduct ourselves ethically and with integrity. We show respect for others in our words and actions. We act in the spirit of community and co-operation. We respect and protect our natural environment. We strive for personal growth, continual learning, and adventure.	Our **values** influence our conduct both collectively as an organization, and individually as employees, directors and members of our community. We strive to have our actions reflect these values, demonstrate personal accountability, and be publicly defensible.

Figure 3.2 Mountain Equipment Co-op's statements of purpose, vision, mission, and values make up their code of ethics.

Figure 3.2 shows the code of ethics adopted by Mountain Equipment Co-op.

Figure 3.3 illustrates the central role that corporate ethics and values should play in corporate policy. Although strategies and practices can change frequently and objectives can change occasionally, an organization's core principles and values should remain steadfast.

Two-thirds of Canada's largest corporations have codes of ethics (90 percent of large U.S. firms do). More and more regulatory and professional associations in Canada are recommending that corporations adopt codes of ethics. The Canada Deposit Insurance Corp., for example, requires that all deposit-taking institutions have a code of conduct that is periodically reviewed and ratified by the board of directors. The Canadian Competition Bureau, the Canadian Institute of Chartered Accountants, and the Ontario Human Rights Commission are all pushing for the adoption of codes of ethics by corporations.[11] Many Canadian and U.S. firms are also adding a position called ethics director or ethics officer.

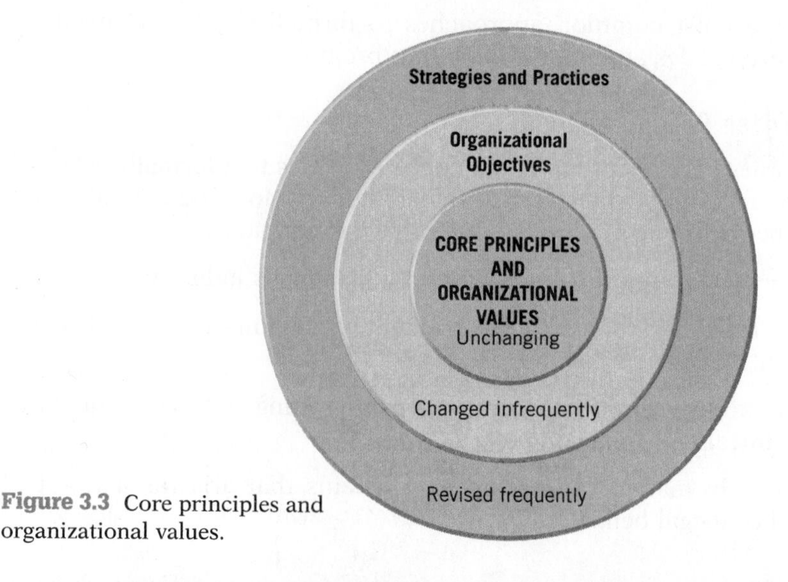

Figure 3.3 Core principles and organizational values.

Instituting Ethics Programs

Can business ethics be "taught," either in the workplace or in schools? While business schools have become important players in the debate about ethics education, most analysts agree that companies must take the chief responsibility for educating employees. In fact, more and more firms are doing so. Imperial Oil, for example, conducts workshops that emphasize ethical concerns for employees. The purpose of these workshops is to help employees put Imperial's ethics statement into practice.

But some firms struggle with ethical dilemmas, particularly in international business situations. A few years ago, a scathing report on Nike's manufacturing partners in Asia called their practices just short of slave labour. Nike responded to the report by acknowledging its mistakes and made a commitment to improve working conditions. Nike plants in Asia, for example, no longer force employees to work on Sundays. Wages have been increased, and supervisors are forbidden to use the extreme punishments that were formerly doled out.[12]

Social Responsibility

Distinguish *corporate social responsibility* from *ethics*, identify *organizational stakeholders*, and characterize social consciousness today. **2**

Corporate social responsibility (CSR) refers to the way in which a business tries to balance its commitments to **organizational stakeholders**—those groups, individuals, and organizations that are directly affected by the practices of an organization and that therefore have a stake in its performance.[13] Galen Weston, the executive chair of Loblaw Companies Ltd., says that companies that want to be successful need to embrace CSR as part of their core strategy. It can no longer simply be an "add-on." In fact, corporate boards of directors are increasingly considering CSR issues in addition to financial and operational issues.[14]

corporate social responsibility (CSR) Refers to the way in which a business tries to balance its commitments to organizational stakeholders.

organizational stakeholders that are directly affected by the practices of an organization and that therefore have a stake in its performance.

Everyone seems to accept the idea that attention must be paid to organizational stakeholders. But which ones should be given the most attention? One view, often called *managerial capitalism*, is that a company's only responsibility is to make as much money as possible for its shareholders, as long as it doesn't break any laws. In recent years, this view has been strongly challenged by an opposing view that says that companies must be responsible to a variety of stakeholders, including *customers, employees, investors, suppliers*, and the *local communities* in which they do business.

Most companies that strive to be responsible to their stakeholders concentrate on the five groups shown in Figure 3.4. They may also select other

Starbucks is helping local farmers gain access to credit, working to develop and maintain sustainability of the coffee crop, and building farmer support centres in Costa Rica, Ethiopia, and Rwanda to provide local farmers with agricultural and technical education and support.

stakeholders that are particularly important to the organization and try to address their needs and expectations as well.

Contemporary Social Consciousness

Canadian society and Canadian business have changed dramatically in the last two centuries, and so have views about social responsibility. The late nineteenth century was characterized by the entrepreneurial spirit and the laissez-faire philosophy. During this era of labour strife and predatory business practices, individual citizens and the government both became concerned about unbridled business activity. This concern was translated into laws regulating basic business practices.

During the Great Depression of the 1930s, many people blamed the failure of businesses and banks and the widespread loss of jobs on a general climate of business greed and lack of restraint. Out of the economic turmoil emerged new laws that described an increased expectation that business should protect and enhance the general welfare of society.

During the social unrest of the 1960s and 1970s, business was often characterized as a negative social force. Eventually, increased activism prompted increased government regulation in a variety of areas. Health warnings, for example, were placed on cigarettes, and stricter environmental protection laws were enacted.

Social consciousness and views toward social responsibility continue to evolve in the twenty-first century. The financial excesses that caused the recession that started in 2008 are likely to result in new laws governing business conduct. As well, an increased awareness of the global economy and heightened

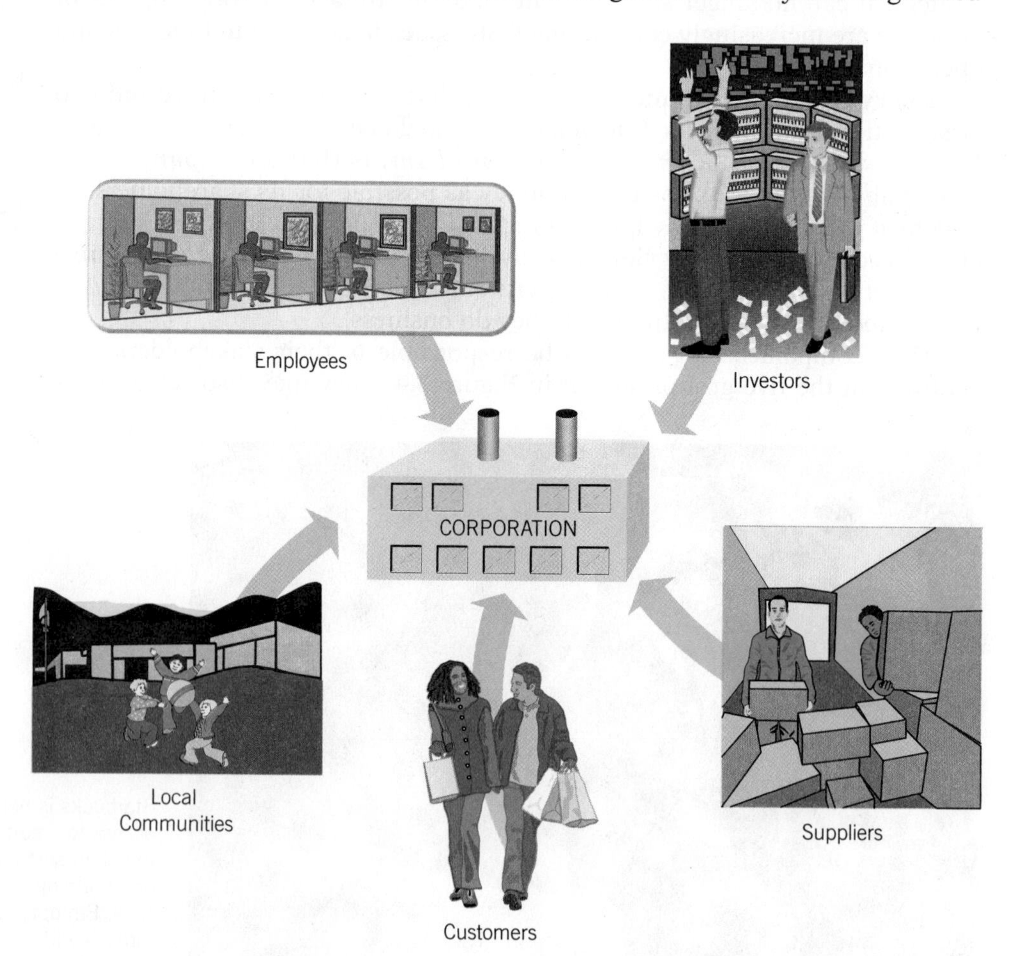

Figure 3.4 Major corporate stakeholders.

campaigning on the part of environmentalists and other activists means that businesses are becoming more sensitive to their social responsibilities.

The production of environmentally safe products has become a potential boom area, as many companies introduce products designed to be "environmentally friendly." Electrolux, a Swedish appliance maker, has developed a line of water-efficient washing machines, a solar-powered lawnmower, and the first refrigerators that are free of ozone-depleting refrigerants. The boxed insert entitled "This Is One Green (and Socially Responsible) Company!" describes the efforts that have been made by retailer Mountain Equipment Co-op to protect the environment and the workers who make the products it sells.

The Greening of Business

This Is One Green (and Socially Responsible) Company!

In 2008, Mountain Equipment Co-op (MEC) opened its twelfth Canadian store in Burlington, Ontario. The retailer was started in 1971 by four students from the University of British Columbia who were committed to protecting the environment. MEC is a co-operative (see Chapter 4), and shares in the company cost $5. The company does not try to maximize shareholder wealth; rather it seeks a balance between financial and social/environmental goals.

MEC directs 1 percent of its sales to charity and to running energy-efficient stores. Jantzi Research Inc. rates MEC as the top company in Canada's retail sector for sustainability practices. MEC also received top marks in North America from the Certified Chartered Accountants for its first sustainability report.

Practising social and environmental responsibility means more than simply giving money to environmental causes and organizations. It also means being conscious of other aspects of social responsibility. For example, products that are sold in MEC stores must be manufactured in safe and healthy workplaces where human and civil rights are respected. The co-op has even stricter standards for MEC-brand products (58 percent of which are manufactured in Canada), which comprise approximately 60 percent of sales. MEC conducts its own Supply Team Evaluation Process, but it also has other organizations do independent audits of its suppliers. These audits ensure that suppliers who produce MEC-brand products:

- Implement and maintain systems to minimize negative impacts of manufacturing and packaging on the environment.
- Implement programs to ensure that waste is disposed of in an environmentally responsible manner.
- Do not use child labour or forced labour.
- Treat their workers with dignity.
- Do not subject their workers to harassment, discrimination, or abuse.
- Allow their workers to join unions and to bargain collectively.
- Pay their workers fairly and directly.
- Provide safe and healthy work environments for workers, which comply with local health and safety laws and regulations.

In its retail outlets, MEC practises what it preaches. The design of its buildings and the material and construction methods used are consistent with care for the environment. MEC's stores are designed to enhance (or at least not detract from) the natural environment, and they are built with resources from the local area. Energy efficiency, pollution control, and recycling potential are all important considerations in MEC buildings. Innovations found in MEC's green buildings include the use of geothermal energy heat pumps in Montreal, a demonstration straw-bale wall in Ottawa, and composting toilets in Winnipeg. When it was built, MEC's Winnipeg store was only the second retail building in Canada that met the national C2000 Green Building Standard (the first one was MEC's Ottawa store). (For information on other green buildings in Canada, see the The Greening of Business box in Chapter 7.)

Critical Thinking Questions

1. Which of the two major views about business—"managerial capitalism" or the "variety of stakeholders" idea—would most likely be held by MEC's shareholders? Why?
2. What are the arguments for and against "managerial capitalism" and the "variety of stakeholders" idea?
3. Consider the following statement: *Businesses should not give money to charity because (1) business executives do not have any training that would help them decide which charities to give money to, (2) businesses are biased in their decisions about which charities to give money to, and (3) business managers don't have any right to give away shareholders' money.* Do you agree or disagree with the statement? Explain your reasoning.

Areas of Social Responsibility

3 Show how the concept of social responsibility applies both to environmental issues and to a firm's relationships with customers, employees, and investors.

In defining their sense of social responsibility, most firms must confront four areas of concern: *responsibilities toward the environment, customers, employees,* and *investors*.

Responsibility Toward the Environment

pollution The injection of harmful substances into the environment.

One critical area of social responsibility involves how the business relates to its physical environment. Controlling **pollution**—the injection of harmful substances into the environment—is a significant challenge for contemporary business. Air, water, and land pollution are the subjects of most anti-pollution efforts by business and governments.[15]

Air Pollution

air pollution When several factors converge to lower air quality.

Air pollution results when several factors converge to lower air quality. Chemicals like the carbon monoxide emitted by automobiles contribute to air pollution. So does smoke and other chemicals emitted by manufacturing plants. Air pollution is particularly bad in China, where 100 coal-fired power plants are being built each year. Each plant uses 1.3 million tonnes of coal and gives off 3.4 million tonnes of carbon dioxide. Only 5 percent of the coal-fired power plants in China are equipped with pollution control equipment.[16] Many industrial companies were forcibly shut down by the Chinese government in advance of the 2008 Olympics in an attempt to improve air quality.

The Kyoto Summit in 1997 was an attempt by various governments to reach an agreement on ways to reduce the threat of pollution. Australia is the world's largest greenhouse gas emitter per capita, contributing 7.3 percent of the world's total. The United States (at 6.5 percent) and Canada (at 6.4 percent) are close behind. Canada is the only one of the three leading emitters that signed the Protocol, but in 2006 the Conservative government said Canada would not be able to meet the targets for reducing pollution and that it would continue with the Protocol only if the targets were renegotiated.[17]

The United Nations is spearheading a move to get rich countries to reduce the impact of their own pollution by paying for cleanups in the developing world. Companies can buy carbon credits, which essentially give them the right to pollute the atmosphere with carbon dioxide. The money collected is then used to help fund clean-air projects in China and other developing countries; these projects would not be affordable otherwise.[18]

Figure 3.5 shows atmospheric carbon dioxide (CO_2) levels for the period 1750 to 2000, and it offers three possible scenarios for future levels under different sets of conditions. The three projections—lowest, middle, highest—were developed by the Intergovernmental Panel on Climate Change, which calculated likely changes in the atmosphere during this century if no efforts were made to reduce so-called greenhouse emissions (waste gases that trap heat in the atmosphere). The criteria for estimating changes are population, economic growth, energy supplies, and technologies; the less pressure exerted by these conditions, the less the increase in CO_2 levels. Energy supplies are measured in exajoules—roughly the annual energy consumption of a large metropolitan area like New York or London.

Under the lowest (or best-case) scenario, by 2100 the population would grow to only 6.4 billion people, economic growth would be no more than 1.2 to 2.0 percent a year, and energy supplies would require only 8000 exajoules of conventional oil. However, under the highest (or worst-case) scenario, the population would increase to 11.3 billion people, annual economic growth would be between 3.0 and 3.5 percent, and energy supplies would require as much as 18 400 exajoules of conventional oil.

There is currently a great deal of discussion and debate about climate change and **global warming**—an increase in the earth's average temperature. Almost everyone agrees that global warming is happening, but there is debate about what is causing it (see Concluding Case 3-1 for more information on this issue). In difficult economic times, like those that developed in 2008–09, the general public is less willing to make personal sacrifices in order to battle climate change. A poll of 12 000 people in 11 different countries showed that less than half of the respondents were willing to make lifestyle changes to reduce carbon emissions, and only 20 percent said they would be willing to spend extra money to fight climate change.[19]

global warming An increase in the earth's average temperature.

Water Pollution

For years, businesses and municipalities dumped their waste into rivers, streams, and lakes with little regard for the effects. Thanks to new legislation and increased awareness on the part of businesses, water quality is improving in many areas. Millar Western Pulp Ltd. built Canada's first zero-discharge pulp mill at Meadow Lake, Saskatchewan. There is no discharge pipe to the river, no dioxin-forming chlorine, and almost no residue. Dow Chemical built a plant at Fort Saskatchewan that will not dump any pollutants into the nearby river.[20]

Land Pollution

Toxic wastes are dangerous chemical and/or radioactive by-products of various manufacturing processes. For example, thousands of hectares of agricultural

toxic wastes Dangerous chemical and/or radioactive by-products of various manufacturing processes.

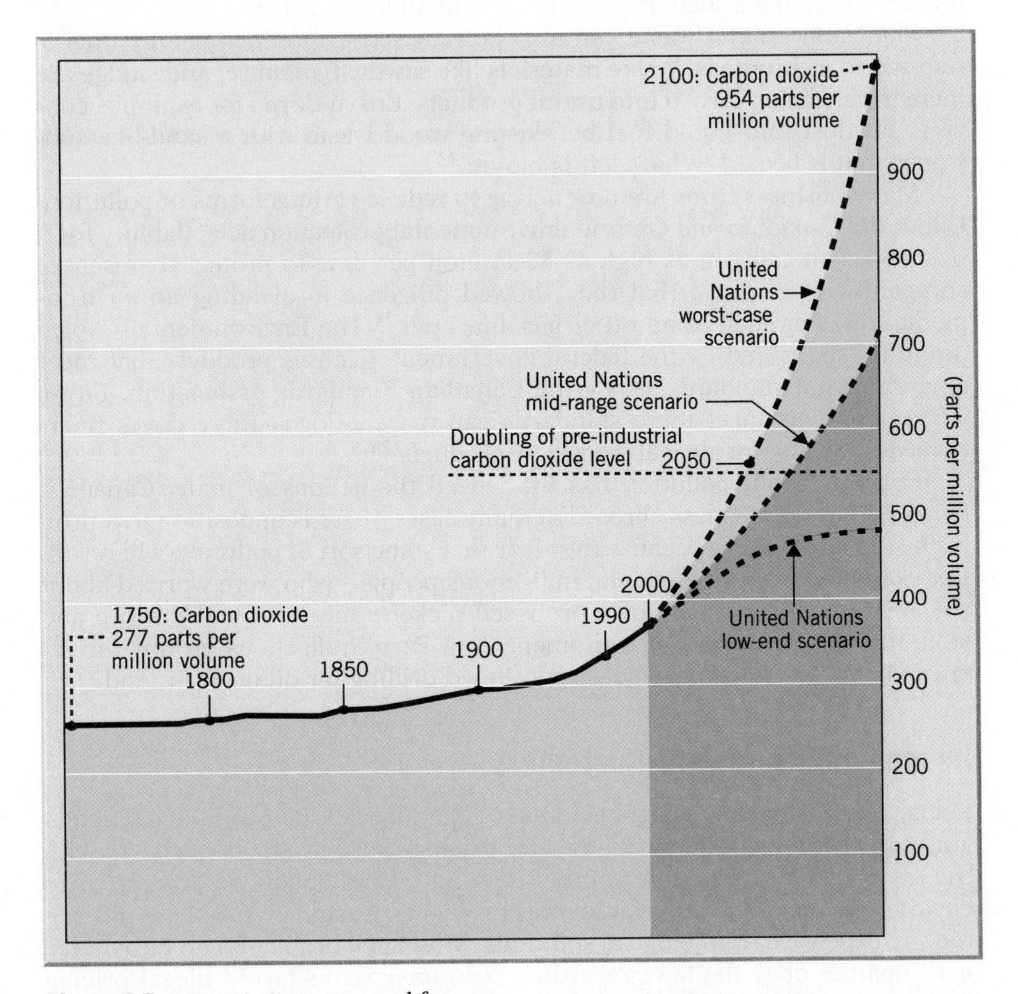

Figure 3.5 CO_2 emissions, past and future.

land were contaminated when five million cubic litres of toxic waste escaped from a holding pond at a zinc mine in Spain that was operated by the Canadian firm Boliden Ltd.[21] Restoring the quality of land is time consuming and costly. Because toxic waste cannot usually be processed into harmless material or destroyed, it must be stored somewhere. The problem is—where? Few people want a toxic waste storage facility in their town.

Recycling. Changes in forestry practices, limits on certain types of mining, and new forms of solid waste disposal are all attempts to address the issue of land pollution. The conversion of certain waste materials into useful products—**recycling**—has developed as a response to the increased consciousness about land pollution. Some products, such as aluminum beverage cans and glass, can be very efficiently recycled. Others, such as plastics, are more troublesome. Many local communities actively support various recycling programs, including curbside pickup of aluminum, plastics, glass, and pulp paper.

recycling The conversion of certain waste materials into useful products.

An interesting problem that highlights some of the complexities in recycling involves wooden pallets—those splintery wooden platforms used to store and transport consumer goods. Pallets are popular because they provide an efficient method for stacking and moving large quantities of smaller items. Pallets of merchandise can be easily and efficiently moved from factories to trucks to retail stores. Pallets are very recyclable, but since the cost of new ones is so low, many companies just toss used ones aside and get new ones. Many landfills refuse to take pallets, and others assess surcharges for recycling them. Ironically, some environmentalists argue that abandoned pallets actually serve a useful purpose because, in urban areas, they often become refuges for animals such as raccoons and abandoned pets.[22]

Plant and animal waste can also be recycled to produce energy; this is referred to as **biomass**. Waste materials like sawdust, manure, and sludge are increasingly being turned into useful products. Ensyn Corp., for example, converts sawdust into liquid fuel by blasting wood waste with a sand-like substance that is heated. What's left is bio-oil.[23]

biomass Plant and animal waste that can be recycled to produce energy.

Many business firms are now acting to reduce various forms of pollution. Under the Canadian and Ontario environmental protection acts, liability for a business firm can run as high as $2 million per day. To protect themselves, companies must prove that they showed diligence in avoiding an environmental disaster such as an oil or gasoline spill.[24] The Environmental Choice program, sponsored by the federal government, licenses products that meet environmental standards set by the Canadian Standards Association. Firms whose products meet these standards can put the logo—three doves intertwined to form a maple leaf—on their products.[25]

Concern about pollution has influenced the actions of many Canadian firms as they do business abroad. In many cases, there is opposition to a project by the local people because they fear that some sort of pollution will result. For example, in New Caledonia, indigenous people—who were worried about the environmental impact of a proposed nickel mine—stormed the site and stole millions of dollars of equipment.[26] In Peru, indigenous groups threatened violence if Talisman Energy continued drilling for oil on their land.[27]

Responsibility Toward Customers

Social responsibility toward customers generally falls into one of two categories: providing quality products and pricing those products fairly. As with the environment, firms differ in their level of concern about responsibility to customers. Yet unlike environmental problems, customer problems do not require expensive technological solutions. Most such problems can be avoided if companies obey the laws regarding consumer rights, avoid illegal pricing practices, and behave ethically when advertising their products.

Rights of Consumers

Much of the current interest in business responsibility toward customers can be traced to the rise of consumerism. **Consumerism** is a form of social activism dedicated to protecting the rights of consumers in their dealings with businesses. Consumers have the following rights:

consumerism A social movement that seeks to protect and expand the rights of consumers in their dealings with businesses.

1. *The right to safe products*. The right to safe products is not always honoured. In 2008, 20 people died after eating meat made by Maple Leaf Foods that was contaminated with listeria. Company sales dropped by nearly 50 percent once this became public.[28] The government of China has become concerned that negative publicity about faulty toys and contaminated pet food and toothpaste has damaged the "Made in China" label. In a surprising development, Mattel Inc. apologized to China for claiming that a recall of 18 million playsets with dangerous magnets was necessitated by poor quality control at one of its Chinese suppliers. Mattel eventually admitted that its own product design was flawed.[29]
2. *The right to be informed about all relevant aspects of a product*. Food products must list their ingredients. Clothing must be labelled with information about its proper care. And banks must tell you exactly how much interest you are paying on a loan. Cereal companies have come under fire for some of the claims they have made about the oat bran content of their cereals, as well as its likely effects.
3. *The right to be heard*. Many companies today have complaints offices. Retailers like Kmart offer a money-back guarantee if consumers aren't satisfied. Procter & Gamble puts a toll-free number on many of its products; customers can call this number if they have questions or complaints. When companies refuse to respond to consumer complaints, consumer protection agencies such as the Better Business Bureau and consumer interest groups such as the Airline Passengers Association may intervene.
4. *The right to choose what they buy*. Central to this right is free and open competition among companies. In times past, "gentlemen's agreements" were often used to avoid competition or to divide up a market so that firms did not have to truly compete against each other. Such practices are illegal today, and any attempts by business to block competition can result in fines or other penalties.
5. *The right to be educated about purchases*. All prescription drugs now come with detailed information regarding dosage, possible side effects, and potential interactions with other medications.
6. *The right to courteous service*. This right is hard to legislate, but as consumers become increasingly knowledgeable, they are more willing to complain about bad service. Consumer hotlines can also be used to voice service-related issues.

Unfair Pricing

Interfering with competition can also mean illegal pricing practices. **Collusion** among companies—including getting together to "fix" prices—is against the law. Arctic Glacier Inc. of Winnipeg was one of several companies served with subpoenas by the U.S. government as it investigated collusion in the U.S. market for packaged ice. One of Arctic's employees, who claimed he was fired for refusing to take part in a conspiracy to divide up markets, went to the U.S. government and helped them in their investigation. The investigation is underway at the time of this writing.[30] The Canadian Competition Bureau also launched an investigation after hearing allegations from a confidential informant that Mars, Hershey, Nestle, and Cadbury had teamed up in a candy price-fixing

collusion An illegal agreement among companies in an industry to "fix" prices for their products.

scheme.[31] A law firm in Toronto is organizing a class-action lawsuit against the major chocolate companies, alleging a conspiracy to fix prices.[32] Also in 2008, Ultramar, Les Petroles Therrien Inc., and Petro-T pleaded guilty to price-fixing in the retail gasoline market. Ultramar was fined $1.85 million, and the other two companies were both fined $179 000.[33]

Under some circumstances, firms can also come under attack for price gouging. For example, when DaimlerChrysler first launched its PT Cruiser, demand for the vehicles was so strong that some dealers sold them only to customers willing to pay thousands of dollars over sticker prices. Some Ford dealers adopted a similar practice when the new Thunderbird was launched. As we saw in Chapter 1, this illustrates what can happen when there is a shortage of a product.

Ethics in Advertising

In recent years, increased attention has been given to ethics in advertising and product information. Because of controversies surrounding the potential misinterpretation of words and phrases such as *light*, *reduced calories*, *diet*, and *low fat*, food producers are now required to use a standardized format for listing ingredients on product packages. There are several key ethical issues in advertising, including truth-in-advertising claims, the advertising of counterfeit brands, the use of stealth advertising, and advertising that is morally objectionable.

Truth in Advertising. Concerns about truth in advertising are becoming more noticeable on the international scene. In July 2005, for example, Chinese government officials investigated Procter & Gamble's claim that its Pantene shampoo made hair "10 times stronger." A few months earlier, P&G paid a $24 000 fine after one consumer complained that SK-II Skin Cream was not the "miracle water" it claimed to be and that it did not make her skin "look 12 years younger in 28 days."[34]

Advertising of Counterfeit Brands. Another issue concerns the advertising and sale of counterfeit brand names. Canadians tourists who visit New York often go to booths on Canal Street, which is famous for the "bargains" that can be had on supposedly name brand items like Cartier, Panerai, Vacheron, Montblanc, and Louis Vuitton. Many of the items being sold are counterfeit, although it can be very hard to tell the difference between these "knock-offs"

Of all roadway accidents, 25 percent are distraction-related, and the biggest distractions for motorists are handheld gadgets such as cellphones, pagers, and the like. In fulfilling their responsibility to consumers, some companies are conducting tests, which yield important data about roadway accidents. Ford Motor Company, for example, has a Virtual Test Track Experiment simulator that determines how often drivers get distracted. Under normal circumstances, an adult driver will miss about 3 percent of the simulated "events" (like an ice patch or a deer on the road) that Ford contrives for a virtual road trip. If they're on the cellphone, they'll miss about 14 percent. Teenagers miss a scary 54 percent of the events.

and the genuine article. For example, knock-offs of Suzuki motorcycles hit the market just a few weeks after the genuine product became available. These knock-offs were sold to customers as the real thing, but they had not been subjected to rigorous quality control like real Suzuki motorcycles are. Naturally, legitimate manufacturers of these high-end products are trying to stamp out this counterfeit trade in their products.[35] The boxed insert entitled "Counterfeit Products: Who's Accountable?" provides more information about this issue.

Business Accountability

Counterfeit Products: Who's Accountable?

Counterfeit goods are a problem in many different product lines, including perfume, luggage, handbags, pharmaceuticals, designer clothing, shoes, cigarettes, watches, sports memorabilia, and fine wines, to name just a few. An FBI investigation in the United States revealed, for example, that up to 75 percent of sports memorabilia was fake. Wine makers are concerned about the counterfeiting of their products because some of the top names in wine (e.g., Château Mouton Rothschild and Penfolds Grange) cost as much as $3000 a bottle, and this is an incentive for counterfeiters to make a lot of easy money. The counterfeiters buy cheaper wine and then put it in bottles with fake labels. Wineries are fighting counterfeiting by embedding microchips in the label that can be read with an optical scanner, and by laser-etching the wine's name and vintage year into the bottle's glass.

The International Chamber of Commerce estimates that the counterfeit goods trade may be worth as much as $500 billion annually. According to Interpol—the international police organization in Lyon, France—organized crime groups like the Chinese triads and terrorist groups like Hezbollah have gotten into the business of counterfeiting products because of the high rate of return they can make (about as high as the illegal drug trade). Consider an example: One Vietnamese group in New York imported watch components that cost them about 27 cents and then sold them to wholesalers for $12 to $20. The wholesalers then sold them to street vendors for $20 to $30, and the street vendors sold them as Cartier watches for as much as $250. That was still well below the price of a real Cartier watch (about $1800).

While many counterfeit products are sent from China to other countries, shopping for knock-offs in China itself is also very popular with visiting tourists because prices are incredibly low (for example, $10 for a Gucci bag, $15 for a Samsonite suitcase, $7 for a Polo shirt, and $3 for a Rolex watch). While regular tourists are the most frequent purchasers of knock-offs, celebrities are also attracted to counterfeit products. In 2008, for example, Céline Dion was spotted shopping at a knock-off store in Shanghai. But China is not the only country where counterfeit products are made: North Korea turns out two billion packs of cigarettes each year, many of which are fake Marlboros.

The trade in counterfeit goods is harmful to the companies that have spent a lot of time and money developing brand name goods for sale. Every counterfeit product that is sold reduces the sales revenues of the legitimate producers. It also harms governments by denying them tax revenues (most counterfeiters do not pay taxes). Consumers are hurt, too. While it may seem that consumers benefit because they spend very little money for goods that look like the real thing, in fact consumers often pay far too much for counterfeit goods because those goods have very low quality. As well, some counterfeit goods are downright dangerous to use. While a fake handbag simply costs money, fake pharmaceuticals, electrical products, and motorcycles can kill the people who use them.

There is increasing pressure on the Canadian government to do something about counterfeit goods. The Canadian Anti-Counterfeiting Network (CACN) was formed in 2005 to lobby the government for changes in laws. But changes are slow in coming, and other countries (most notably the United States) feel that Canada is not doing enough to discourage the sale of counterfeit goods. Unlike the United States, France, and Italy, Canada doesn't have many famous brand exports, so there aren't very many businesses putting pressure on the government to crack down on counterfeiters. The United States has placed Canada on its official list of countries that don't do enough to control counterfeit products (the list also includes Turkey, Belarus, Vietnam, and Uzbekistan). Canada is moving slowly toward bringing its laws into conformity with the World Intellectual Property Organization (WIPO).

A new approach to reducing counterfeiting is to prosecute anyone who facilitates the sale of counterfeit products, including landlords (who own the buildings where counterfeit goods are being sold), shipping companies, credit-card companies, and others in the supply chain. The argument is that these people are benefitting from the sale of knock-offs, so they should be held accountable. There is also a move in some countries to hold the consumers who buy counterfeit goods accountable. In France and Italy, for example, it is now a crime to buy counterfeit goods.

Individual companies are becoming more aggressive in pursuing counterfeiters. Louis Vuitton, for example, sued

▶

eBay for selling knock-offs of Vuitton products, and in June 2008, a French court levied a fine of $60.8 million against eBay, saying that it should be doing much more to curtail the sale of counterfeit goods. Tiffany & Co., the high-end jeweller, also filed a lawsuit against eBay, charging that it had ignored the sale of fake Tiffany jewellery on eBay's website. But in July 2008, a U.S. federal judge ruled that Tiffany, not eBay, had the responsibility for protecting the Tiffany brand name. A court in Belgium also ruled in favour of eBay after it had been sued by L'Oréal, the cosmetics company.

Critical Thinking Questions

1. How might cultural and individual differences lead to conflicting views about the ethics of selling counterfeit goods?
2. The production and sale of knock-offs obviously benefits some people—for example, the seller of counterfeit goods and perhaps consumers who get products cheap. But it also hurts others—for example, the legitimate manufacturers of products, and consumers who are injured by knock-offs that are faulty. Do you think the benefits of knock-offs exceed the costs, or vice versa? Defend your answer.
3. Consider the following statement: *eBay should not be responsible for monitoring the authenticity of products that are sold through its online business. The responsibility for that lies with the companies who are worried that someone is selling a counterfeit version of their product.* Do you agree or disagree with this statement? Defend your answer.

stealth advertising (undercover or guerrilla advertising) Involves companies paying individuals to extol the virtues of their products to other individuals.

Stealth Advertising. A variation of viral advertising, **stealth advertising** (also called **undercover or guerrilla advertising**) involves companies paying individuals to extol the virtues of their products to other individuals. For example, Student Workforce hires individuals who are 18–30 years old to market products to other people in the same age bracket. One of the people hired is Leanne Plummer, a student at Toronto's Humber College. She says that stealth advertising is more about sharing information than it is about sales.[36]

The ethics of stealth advertising are questionable if the paid individuals do not reveal that they are being paid by a company. In that case, the recipient of the advertising is not aware that it *is* advertising. For example, one advertising agency hired models to pose as "tourists." These models asked real tourists to take their picture with a new Sony Ericsson camera cellphone. The models then talked up the advantages of the new product to the unsuspecting real tourists. Commercial Alert, a U.S.–based consumer protection group, wants a government investigation of these undercover marketing tactics.[37]

Morally Objectionable Advertising. A final ethical issue concerns advertising that is morally objectionable. Benetton, for example, aired a series of commercials featuring inmates on death row. The ads, dubbed "We, on Death Row," prompted such an emotional outcry that Sears dropped the Benetton USA clothing line.[38] Other ads receiving criticism include Victoria's Secret models in skimpy underwear, and campaigns by tobacco and alcohol companies that allegedly target young people.

Responsibility Toward Employees

Organizations also need to employ fair and equitable practices with their employees. In Chapter 8, we describe the human resource management activities essential to a smoothly functioning business. These same activities—recruiting, hiring, training, promoting, and compensating—are also the basis for social responsibility toward employees. A company that provides its employees with equal opportunities for rewards and advancement without regard to race, sex, or other irrelevant factors is meeting its social responsibilities. Firms that ignore their responsibility to employees leave themselves open to lawsuits. They also miss the chance to hire better and more highly motivated employees.

Legal and Social Commitments

Some progressive companies go well beyond legal requirements, hiring and training the so-called hard-core unemployed (people with little education or training and a history of unemployment) and those who have disabilities. The Bank of Montreal, for example, sponsors a community college skills upgrading course for individuals with hearing impairments. The Royal Bank provides managers with discrimination awareness training. Rogers Cablesystems Ltd. provides individuals who have mobility restrictions with telephone and customer-service job opportunities.[39] Bell Canada employs more than 1000 people with disabilities (2 percent of its permanent workforce). But, in Canada, over 50 percent of those with physical disabilities are still unemployed.[40]

In addition to their responsibility to employees as resources of the company, firms have a social responsibility to their employees as people. Firms that accept this responsibility ensure that the workplace is safe, both physically and emotionally. They would no more tolerate an abusive manager or one who sexually harasses employees than they would a gas leak.

Business firms also have a responsibility to respect the privacy of their employees. While nearly everyone agrees that companies have the right to exercise some level of control over their employees, there is great controversy about exactly how much is acceptable in areas such as drug testing and computer monitoring. When Canadian National Railways instituted drug testing for train, brake, and yard employees, 12 percent failed. Trucking companies have found that nearly one-third of truckers who have been involved in accidents were on drugs.[41]

whistle-blower An employee who discovers and tries to put an end to a company's unethical, illegal, or socially irresponsible actions by publicizing them.

Employees are often unaware that they are being monitored by computer software programs like "Spy" and "Peek." This type of monitoring increases employee stress levels because they don't know exactly when the boss is watching them. A lawsuit was brought against Nortel Networks by employees who charged that the firm installed telephone bugs and hidden microphones in one of its plants.[42]

Whistle-Blowers. Respecting employees as people also means respecting their behaviour as ethically responsible individuals. Suppose, for instance, an employee discovers that a business has been engaging in practices that are illegal, unethical, or socially irresponsible. Ideally, this employee should be able to report the problem to management, but management often does not want to hear about such issues. The employee might then decide to inform a regulatory agency or perhaps the media. At this point, he or she becomes a **whistle-blower**—an employee who discovers and tries to put an end to a company's unethical, illegal, or socially irresponsible actions by publicizing them.[43]

Melvin Crothers, who worked in the marketing department at WestJet, paid a price for his whistle-blowing. In 2003, he discovered that a fellow WestJet employee was accessing a restricted Air Canada website in order to obtain data about Air Canada's "load factor" (the proportion of seats filled) on certain flights. He felt that this was unethical, so he tried to talk to WestJet president Clive Beddoe and tell him what was going on. Beddoe was out of town, so Crothers called a former WestJet president who was heading up an Air Canada

The safety of workers is an important consideration for all organizations. The required use of hardhats is just one example of precautions that companies can take to protect workers while they are on the job.

discount airline. The conversation led to Air Canada discovering what WestJet was up to, and before long, Air Canada filed a lawsuit against WestJet. Crothers resigned from WestJet four days later.[44] Video Case I-1 describes a whistle-blowing situation at the RCMP.

Whistle-blowers are often demoted—and even fired—when they take their accusations public. Even if they retain their jobs, they may still be treated as outsiders and suffer resentment or hostility from co-workers. Many co-workers see whistle-blowers as people who simply can't be trusted. One recent study suggests that about half of all whistle-blowers eventually get fired, and about half of those who get fired subsequently lose their homes and/or families.[45] New federal legislation to protect whistle-blowers was introduced in Canada in 2003.

Responsibility Toward Investors

It may sound odd to say that a firm can be irresponsible toward investors, since they are the owners of the company. But if managers abuse their firm's financial resources, the ultimate losers are the owners, since they do not receive the earnings, dividends, or capital appreciation due them.

Improper Financial Management

Occasionally, organizations are guilty of financial mismanagement. In the most highly publicized recent case, managers at American International Group became involved in very high-risk insurance that caused the company to be on the hook for billions of dollars. The U.S. government ended up giving hundreds of billions of dollars to the company to keep it afloat. Financial mismanagement can also take many other forms, including executives paying themselves outlandish salaries and bonuses and spending huge amounts of company money for their own personal comfort. In these cases, creditors don't have much leverage and shareholders have few viable options. Trying to force a management changeover is not only difficult, it can also drive down the price of the company's stock, and this is a penalty shareholders are usually unwilling to assign themselves.

Cheque Kiting

cheque kiting Involves writing a cheque from one account, depositing it in a second account, and then immediately spending money from the second account while the money from the first account is still in transit.

Cheque kiting involves writing a cheque from one account, depositing it in a second account, and then immediately spending money from the second account while the money from the first account is still in transit. A cheque from the second account can also be used to replenish the money in the first account, and the process starts all over again. This practice obviously benefits the person doing the cheque kiting, but is irresponsible because it involves using other peoples' money without paying for it.

Insider Trading

insider trading The use of confidential information to gain from the purchase or sale of stock.

Insider trading occurs when someone uses confidential information to gain from the purchase or sale of stock. The most famous case is that of Martha Stewart, but there are many others as well. Barry Landen of Agnico-Eagle Mines was found guilty of insider trading when he sold shares he owned before it became publicly known that the company was going to report poor results. He was sentenced to 45 days in jail and fined $200 000.[46] Andrew Rankin, an investment banking star with RBC Dominion Securities, was originally convicted in 2005 for "tipping" a friend about several big corporate deals that were pending. The friend used this insider information to make over $4 million by buying and selling the stocks of these companies. In 2008, the Ontario Securities Commission agreed to a deal where criminal charges were withdrawn; Rankin was fined $250 000, and he was barred for life from working in the securities industry.[47]

Misrepresentation of Finances

Certain behaviours regarding financial representation are also illegal. In maintaining and reporting its financial status, every corporation must conform to generally accepted accounting principles (see Chapter 14). Sometimes, however, unethical managers project profits far in excess of what they actually expect to earn. As we saw in the opening case, managers at Livent hid losses and/or expenses to boost on-paper profits.

A few years earlier, the same sorts of things happened at Enron, where CFO Andrew Fastow had set up a complex network of partnerships that were often used to hide losses. This allowed Enron to report all the earnings from a partnership as its own while transferring all or most of the costs and losses to the partnership.[48]

"From a purely business viewpoint, taking what doesn't belong to you is usually the cheapest way to go."

Implementing Social Responsibility Programs

Thus far, we have discussed corporate social responsibility (CSR) as if a consensus exists on how firms should behave in most situations. In fact, dramatic differences of opinion exist as to the appropriateness of CSR as a business goal. Some people oppose any business activity that cuts into profits to investors, while others argue that responsibility must take precedence over profits.

Supporters of CSR believe that corporations are citizens just like individuals and therefore need to help improve our lives. Others point to the vast resources controlled by businesses and note that since businesses often create many of the problems social programs are designed to alleviate, they should use their resources to solve the problems. Still others argue that CSR is wise because there is a payoff for the firm.

Opponents of CSR fear that if businesses become too active in social concerns, they will gain too much control over how those concerns are addressed. They point to the influence many businesses have been able to exert on the government agencies that are supposed to regulate them. Other critics of business-sponsored social programs argue that companies lack the expertise needed. For example, they believe that technical experts, not business managers, should decide how best to clean up a polluted river.

The late Max Clarkson, formerly a top-level business executive and director of the Centre for Corporate Social Performance and Ethics at the University of Toronto, said that business firms that had a strong consciousness about ethics and CSR outperform firms that do not. After designing and applying a CSR rating system for companies, he found that companies that had the highest marks on questions of ethics and CSR also had the highest financial performance.[49]

Approaches to Social Responsibility

Identify four general approaches to social responsibility and describe the four steps a firm must take to implement a social responsibility program. **4**

Given these differences of opinion, it is little wonder that corporations have adopted a variety of approaches to social responsibility. As Figure 3.6 illustrates, the four stances an organization can take concerning its obligations to society fall along a continuum ranging from the lowest to the highest degree of CSR practices.

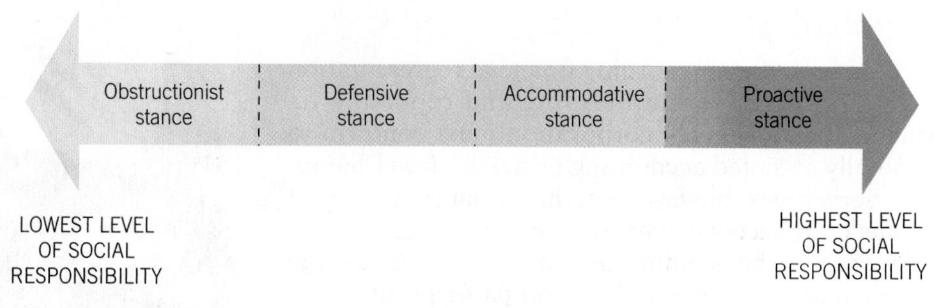

Figure 3.6 Spectrum of approaches to social responsibility.

Obstructionist Stance

obstructionist stance A business does as little as possible to solve social or environmental problems and denies or covers up their wrongdoings.

Businesses that have an **obstructionist stance** to social responsibility do as little as possible to solve social or environmental problems. When these businesses cross the ethical or legal line that separates acceptable from unacceptable practices, their typical response is to deny or cover up their actions. Firms that adopt this position have little regard for ethical conduct and will generally go to great lengths to hide wrongdoing.

Defensive Stance

defensive stance An organization does only what is legally required and nothing more.

One step removed from the obstructionist stance is the **defensive stance**, where the organization does everything that is required of it legally, but nothing more. For example, a company would install pollution-control equipment dictated by law but would not install higher-quality equipment even though it might further limit pollution. Managers who take a defensive stance insist that their sole job is to generate profits. Tobacco companies generally take this position in their marketing efforts. In Canada and the United States, they are legally required to include warnings to smokers on their products and to limit advertising to prescribed media. Domestically, they follow these rules to the letter of the law, but they use more aggressive marketing methods in countries that have no such rules.

Accommodative Stance

accommodative stance A company meets all of its legal and ethical requirements, and in some cases even goes beyond what is required.

A firm that adopts an **accommodative stance** meets its legal and ethical requirements but also goes further in certain cases. Such firms voluntarily agree to participate in social programs but only after they are convinced that these programs are worthy of their support. Many organizations respond to requests for donations to community hockey teams, Girl Guides, youth soccer programs, and so forth. The point, however, is that someone has to knock on the firm's door and ask; accommodative organizations are not generally proactively seeking avenues for contributing.

Proactive Stance

proactive stance An organization actively seeks opportunities to be socially responsible.

The highest degree of social responsibility a firm can exhibit is the **proactive stance**. Firms that adopt this approach take to heart the arguments in favour of CSR. They view themselves as citizens in a society and proactively seek opportunities to contribute. The most common—and direct—way to implement this stance is by setting up a foundation to provide direct financial support for various social programs.

Keep in mind that organizations do not always fit neatly into one category or another. The Ronald McDonald House program has been widely applauded, for example, but McDonald's has also come under fire for allegedly misleading consumers about the nutritional value of its food products. The Exercising Your Ethics exercise at the end of the chapter gives you an opportunity to think about the pros and cons of the various stances toward CSR.

Corporate Charitable Donations

Donating money to different causes is one way that business firms try to show that they are socially responsible. In 2008, for example, Great-West Life, London Life, and Canada Life donated $100 000 to the Salvation Army's Christmas campaign.[50] A 2008 survey of 93 large Canadian companies found that 97 percent made a charitable contribution of some sort and that the median value of their contributions was $340 000.[51] Another survey of 2200 companies that was conducted by Imagine Canada found that 91 percent gave to charities or non-profit organizations. Cash donations were provided by 76 percent of the companies, products by 51 percent, and services by 43 percent. More than 80 percent of the companies said that they made contributions because it was a good thing to do, irrespective of any financial benefits they might achieve from giving.[52]

Imagine Canada's "Caring Company" program recommends that corporations give 1 percent of pre-tax profits to charity, but only half of the corporations met that goal in 2008. A survey conducted by the Centre for Philanthropy found that the most of the money given to charities comes from individuals, not corporations. Canadians think that corporations give about 20 percent of the total and that it should be 30 percent.[53]An Environics survey of people in 23 different countries found that two-thirds of them thought that businesses are not doing enough if they simply abide by the law and provide employment.[54]

Businesses have also demonstrated a willingness to give money and products when disasters strike. When seven people died in Walkerton, Ontario, as a result of drinking contaminated water, companies such as Petro-Canada, Shoppers Drug Mart, Sobeys, and Zellers contributed products such as bleach and bottled water. And when tens of thousands of people died in the Asian tsunamis of 2004, companies from around the world rushed aid to the stricken areas. Global Fortune 500 firms donated $580 million in drugs, cellphones, machinery, medical equipment, and water to the relief effort.[55]

Some companies go beyond simply giving money or products. For example, Unilever Canada gives employees four afternoons a year for community activities.[56] Mars Canada sets aside one day each year for employees to volunteer. At Telus Corp.'s annual "day of service" in 2008, employees helped out at a soup kitchen.[57] Many companies take a community-based approach; they try to determine how they can achieve value for the community (and the company) with their donations of time and money.

Managing Social Responsibility Programs

Making a company truly socially responsible takes an organized and managed program (see Figure 3.7).

1. Top management must state strong support for CSR and be considered a factor in strategic planning. Without the support of top management, no program can succeed.
2. A committee of top managers must develop a plan detailing the level of management support. Some companies set aside percentages of profits for social programs. Mountain Equipment Co-op, for example, earmarks 1 percent of its sales revenue for charity. Managers must also set specific priorities. For instance, should the firm train the hard-core unemployed or support the arts?
3. One executive must be put in charge of the firm's agenda. Whether the role is created as a separate job or added to an existing one, the selected individual must monitor the program and ensure that its implementation is consistent with the firm's policy statement and strategic plan.

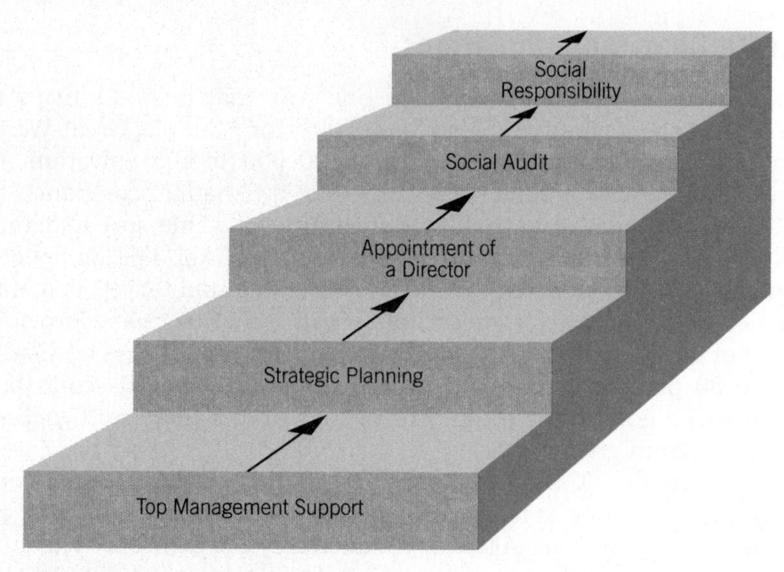

Figure 3.7 Establishing a social responsibility program involves four basic steps.

social audit A systematic analysis of how a firm is using funds earmarked for social-responsibility goals and how effective these expenditures have been.

4. The organization must conduct **social audits**, which are systematic analyses of its success in using funds earmarked for its CSR goals.[58] Suppose a company has a strategic plan calling for spending $100 000 to train 200 hard-core unemployed people and to place 180 of them in jobs. If the firm actually spends $98 000, trains 210 people, and fills 175 jobs, a social audit will confirm the program's success. But if the program costs $150 000, trains only 90 people, and places only 10 of them, the audit will reveal the program's failure. Such failure should prompt a rethinking of the program's implementation and its priorities.

triple bottom line reporting Measuring the social, environmental, and economic performance of a company.

In addition to social audits, Canadian businesses are increasingly publishing sustainability reports. These reports go beyond simple financial reporting and explain how the company is performing on issues such as the environment, employee relations, workplace diversity, and business ethics. The majority of Canadian companies now report at least some sustainability performance information, and about 60 percent of the 100 largest companies in Canada prepare sustainability reports.[59] Social audits and sustainability reports together constitute **triple bottom line reporting**—measuring the social, environmental, and economic performance of a company.[60]

Ronald McDonald House helps the families of children who are in hospital. It is supported by McDonald's and is an example of socially responsible behaviour by a business corporation.

Social Responsibility and the Small Business

Explain how issues of social responsibility and ethics affect small businesses. 5

Ethics and CSR issues must be faced by managers in all organizations, regardless of size. One key to business success is to decide in advance how to respond to these issues. As the owner of a garden supply store, how would you respond to a building inspector's suggestion that a cash payment would expedite your application for a building permit? As the manager of a nightclub, would you call the police, refuse service, or sell liquor to a customer whose ID card looks forged? As the owner of a small laboratory, would you call the board of health to make sure that it has licensed the company you want to contract to dispose of the lab's medical waste? Who will really be harmed if a small firm pads its income statement to help get a much-needed bank loan?

Can a small business afford to set CSR objectives? Should it sponsor hockey teams, make donations to the United Way, and buy light bulbs from the Lions Club? Would you join the Chamber of Commerce and support the Better Business Bureau because it is the responsible thing to do or just because it is good business? The boxed insert entitled "How Green Is That Orange?" describes the social responsibility initiatives of one small business.

Entrepreneurship and New Ventures

How Green Is That Orange?

Ahhh . . . the delicious taste of a fresh wild blueberry juice smoothie! What could be better to quench your thirst? The super juices offered by Arthur's Fresh, an Ontario-based beverage producer, offer much more than just thirst quenching. And it's a good thing because consumers are looking for more than that these days . . . much more. Today's consumers insist on products that are both good for them and good for the environment. Arthur's Fresh is meeting the demands on both fronts. Their fruit smoothies are known for their nutritional benefits. Adding sugar is taboo, and one 325 mL serving is 25 to 50 percent of your required daily intake of fruits and vegetables. The product is sweet; pardon the pun! But what's even sweeter about this product is the way it's produced.

In 2008, Travis Bell, president and founder of Arthur's Fresh, along with his brother Scott (the company CEO), decided to get serious about reducing the environmental footprint of their manufacturing business. Their strategy involved reducing bottle weight (which also reduced transportation costs and emissions), reducing packaging (plastic and cardboard), making responsible raw material sourcing decisions (like "buying local"), changing to bulk hauling transportation providers, and utilizing renewable energy for power generation. They expect to recover their $330 000 investment by 2011, mostly from cost savings associated with transportation and packaging.

The Packaging Association of Canada thought the changes made by the brothers were commendable and recognized them in 2009 with an award for sustainable packaging leadership. Apparently, their customers liked the changes too, since Arthur's Fresh has experienced a 1250 percent increase in sales since 2004. Company sales were $10 million in 2007, and in 2008, *Profit* magazine ranked Arthur's Fresh among Canada's fastest-growing companies.

The company is also involved in social responsibility initiatives that extend beyond concern for the environment. Through its "Seeds of Change" program, Arthur's Fresh gives at least 10 percent of its annual pre-tax profits back to the community for "kid-oriented programs." In 2008, the company was a corporate sponsor for See-Them-Run, a campaign involving two Canadians—Erin van Wiltenburg and Reuben Jentink—who ran 4200 kilometres across the African continent to raise money for youth education programs in Africa. Arthur's Fresh is also a regular donor of juice to food banks throughout the Toronto area. Along with making healthy products and ethical procurement decisions, the company also strongly believes in enriching the lives of children.

For Travis Bell, a fifth-generation fruit farmer from Goderich, Ontario, the decision to develop his part-time business to full-time operations has taken him to greener pastures in more ways than one. So, the next time you pull your chair up to the breakfast table to enjoy a glass of cold O.J., ask yourself, "Exactly how green is that orange?"

Critical Thinking Questions

1. How has Arthur's Fresh addressed the various areas of social responsibility?
2. What further actions might the company take?

Test yourself on the material for this chapter at **www.pearsoned.ca/mybusinesslab**.

Summary of Learning Objectives

1. **Explain how individuals develop their personal *codes of ethics* and why ethics are important in the workplace.** Individual codes of ethics are derived from social standards of right and wrong. Ethical behaviour is behaviour that conforms to generally accepted social norms concerning beneficial and harmful actions. Unethical behaviour can result in loss of business, fines, and even imprisonment. Because ethics affect the behaviour of individuals on behalf of the companies that employ them, many firms are adopting formal statements of ethics.
2. **Distinguish *corporate social responsibility* from ethics, identify *organizational stakeholders*, and characterize social consciousness today.** *Corporate social responsibility* refers to the way a firm attempts to balance its commitments to organizational stakeholders. One way to understand social responsibility is to view it in terms of stakeholders—those groups, individuals, and organizations that are directly affected by the practices of an organization and that therefore have a stake in its performance. Until the second half of the nineteenth century, businesses often paid little attention to stakeholders. Since then, however, both public pressure and government regulation, especially as a result of the Great Depression of the 1930s and the social activism of the 1960s and 1970s, have forced businesses to consider public welfare, at least to some degree. A trend toward increased social consciousness, including a heightened sense of environmental activism, has recently emerged.
3. **Show how the concept of corporate social responsibility (CSR) applies to environmental issues and to a firm's relationships with customers, employees, and investors.** With respect to the environment, CSR requires firms to minimize pollution of air, water, and land. With respect to customers, CSR requires firms to provide products of acceptable quality, to price products fairly, and to respect consumers' rights. With respect to employees, CSR requires firms to respect workers both as resources and as people who are more productive when their needs are met. With respect to investors, CSR requires firms to manage their resources and to represent their financial status honestly.
4. **Identify four general *approaches to social responsibility* and describe the four steps a firm must take to implement a *social responsibility program*.** An *obstructionist stance* on social responsibility is taken by a firm that does as little as possible to address social or environmental problems. The *defensive stance* emphasizes compliance with minimum legal requirements. Companies adopting the *accommodative stance* go beyond minimum activities, if they are asked. The *proactive stance* commits a company to actively contribute to social projects. Implementing a social responsibility program entails four steps: (1) drafting a policy statement with the support of top management, (2) developing a detailed plan, (3) appointing a director to implement the plan, and (4) conducting social audits to monitor results.
5. **Explain how issues of social responsibility and ethics affect small businesses.** Managers and employees of small businesses face many of the same ethical questions as their counterparts at larger firms. Small businesses also face the same issues of social responsibility and the same need to decide on an approach to social responsibility. The differences are primarily differences of scale.

Key Terms

accommodative stance (p. 92)
air pollution (p. 82)
biomass (p. 84)
business ethics (p. 72)
cheque kiting (p. 90)
code of ethics (p. 77)
collusion (p. 85)
conflict of interest (p. 74)
consumerism (p. 85)
corporate social responsibility (CSR) (p. 79)
defensive stance (p. 92)
ethical behaviour (p. 72)
ethics (p. 72)
global warming (p. 83)
insider trading (p. 90)
managerial ethics (p. 97)
obstructionist stance (p. 92)
organizational stakeholders (p. 79)
pollution (p. 82)
proactive stance (p. 92)
recycling (p. 84)
social audit (p. 94)
stealth (undercover) advertising (p. 88)
toxic wastes (p. 83)
triple bottom line reporting (p. 94)
unethical behaviour (p. 72)
whistle-blower (p. 89)

Questions for Analysis

1. Write a one-paragraph description of an ethical dilemma that you or someone you know faced recently. What was the outcome in the situation? Was it consistent with what you thought should have occurred? Why or why not? Analyze the situation using the ideas presented in the chapter. Make particular reference to the ethical norms of utility, rights, justice, and caring in terms of how they influenced the situation. What would each of these suggest about the correct decision? Does this analysis lead you to a different conclusion about the best outcome? Explain.
2. Develop an example of the way in which your personal code of ethics might clash with the operations of a specific company. How might you try to resolve these differences?
3. What kind of wrongdoing would be most likely to prompt you to be a whistle-blower? What kind of wrongdoing would be least likely? Why?
4. In your opinion, which area of social responsibility is most important? Why? Are there areas other than those noted in the chapter that you consider important?
5. Identify some specific ethical or social responsibility issues that might be faced by small business managers and employees in each of the following areas: environment, customers, employees, and investors.
6. Choose a product or service and explain the social responsibility concerns that are likely to be evident in terms of the environment, customers, employees, and investors.
7. Analyze the forces that are at work from both the company's perspective and the whistle-blower's perspective. Given these forces, what characteristics should a law to protect whistle-blowers have in order to be effective?
8. Pick a product or service that demonstrates the defensive approach to social responsibility. What has been the impact of that stance on the company that is using it? Why did the company adopt a defensive stance?

Application Exercises

1. Develop a list of the major stakeholders of your college or university. As a class, discuss the ways in which you think the school prioritizes these stakeholders. Do you agree or disagree with this prioritization?
2. Using newspapers, magazines, and other business references, identify and describe three companies that take a defensive stance to social responsibility, three that take an accommodative stance, and three that take a proactive stance.

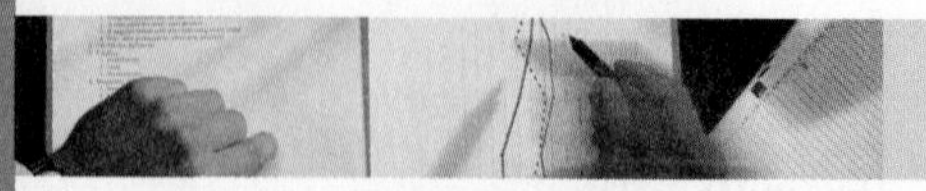

Building Your Business Skills

To Lie or Not to Lie: That Is the Question

The Purpose of This Assignment

To encourage students to apply general concepts of business ethics to specific situations.

Background

Workplace lying, it seems, has become business as usual. According to one survey, one-quarter of working adults said that they had been asked to do something illegal or unethical on the job. Four in 10 did what they were told. Another survey of more than 2000 administrative assistants showed that many employees face ethical dilemmas in their day-to-day work.

Assignment

Step 1

Working with four other students, discuss ways in which you would respond to the following ethical dilemmas. When there is a difference of opinion among group members, try to determine the specific factors that influence different responses.

- Would you lie about your supervisor's whereabouts to someone on the phone?
- Would you lie about who was responsible for a business decision that cost your company thousands of dollars to protect your own or your supervisor's job?
- Would you inflate sales and revenue data on official company accounting statements to increase stock value?
- Would you say that you witnessed a signature when you did not if you were acting in the role of a notary?
- Would you keep silent if you knew that the official minutes of a corporate meeting had been changed?
- Would you destroy or remove information that could hurt your company if it fell into the wrong hands?

Step 2

Research the commitment to business ethics at Johnson & Johnson (www.jnj.com/our_company/our_credo/index.htm) and Texas Instruments (www.ti.com/corp/docs/company/citizen/ethics/index.shtml) by visiting their respective websites. As a group, discuss ways in which these statements are likely to affect the specific behaviours mentioned in Step 1.

Step 3

Working with group members, draft a corporate code of ethics that would discourage the specific behaviours mentioned in Step 1. Limit your code to a single typewritten page, but make it sufficiently broad to cover different ethical dilemmas.

Questions for Discussion

1. What personal, social, and cultural factors do you think contribute to lying in the workplace?
2. Do you agree or disagree with the following statement? *The term* business ethics *is an oxymoron.* Support your answer with examples from your own work experience or that of a family member.
3. If you were your company's director of human resources, how would you make your code of ethics a "living document"?
4. If you were faced with any of the ethical dilemmas described in Step 1, how would you handle them? How far would you go to maintain your personal ethical standards?

Exercising Your Ethics: Team Exercise

Assessing the Ethics of Trade-Offs

The Situation

Managers must often make choices among options that are presented by environmental circumstances. This exercise will help you better appreciate the nature and complexity of the kinds of trade-offs that often result.

The Dilemma

You are the CEO of a medium-sized, unionized manufacturing corporation that is located in a town of about 15 000 people. The nearest major city is about 200 kilometres away. With about 500 workers, your company is one of the five largest employers in town. A regional recession has caused two of the other largest employers to close down (one went out of business and the other relocated to another area). A new foreign competitor has set up shop in the area, but local unemployment has still risen sharply. All in all, the regional economic climate and the new competitor are hurting your business. Your company's sales have dropped 20 percent this year, and you forecast another drop next year before things begin to turn around.

You face two unpleasant choices:

Choice 1: You can tell your employees that you need them to take cuts in pay and benefits. You know that because of the local unemployment rate, you can easily replace anyone who refuses. Unfortunately, you may need your employees to take another cut next year if your forecasts hold true. At the same time, you have reason to believe that when the economy rebounds (in about two years, according to your forecasts), you can begin reversing pay cuts. Here are the advantages of this choice: You can probably (1) preserve all 500 jobs, (2) maintain your own income, (3) restore pay cuts in the future, and (4) keep the business open indefinitely. And the disadvantages: Pay cuts will (1) pose economic hardships for your employees, and (2) create hard feelings and undercut morale.

Choice 2: You can maintain the status quo as far as your employees are concerned, but in that case, you'll be facing two problems: (1) you'll have to cut your own salary (while you can certainly afford to live on less income, doing so would be a blow to your personal finances); and (2) if economic conditions get worse and/or last longer than forecast, you may have to close down altogether. The firm has a cash surplus, but because you'll have to dip into that fund to maintain stable wages, it will soon run out. The advantages of this option: You can (1) avoid economic hardship for your workers, and (2) maintain good employee relations. The downside: You will reduce your own standard of living and may eventually cost everyone his or her job.

Team Activity

Assemble a group of four students and assign each group member to one of the following roles:

- CEO of the company
- the vice-president of production
- a stockholder
- an employee who is a member of the union

Action Steps

1. Before discussing the situation with your group, and from the perspective of your assigned role, which of the two options do you think is the best choice? Write down the reasons for your position.
2. Before discussing the situation with your group, and from the perspective of your assigned role, what are the underlying ethical issues in this situation? Write down the issues.
3. Gather the group together and reveal, in turn, each member's comments on the best choice of the two options. Next, reveal the ethical issues listed by each member.
4. Appoint someone to record the main points of agreement and disagreement within the group. How do you explain the results? What accounts for any disagreement?
5. From an ethical standpoint, what does your group conclude is the most appropriate action that should be taken by the company? (You may find the concepts of *utility, rights, justice,* and *caring* helpful in making your decision.)

For additional cases and exercise material, go to **www.pearsoned.ca/mybusinesslab.**

Concluding Case 3-1

The Debate over Global Warming

In the 1990s, many scientists came to the conclusion that air pollution and greenhouse gases were causing the temperature of the earth to rise (global warming) and that serious problems were going to be evident in the future unless something was done to reduce carbon dioxide emissions. Recently, a debate has arisen in the scientific community with respect to global warming. The two most extreme positions are held by "Malthusian pessimists" (those who think we are heading toward an inevitable crisis) and the "technological optimists" (those who think that advances in technology will be able to overcome any crisis that might occur). These extreme views make for great party conversation, but what is needed is a careful analysis of the empirical data about climate change. This analysis needs to address two questions: (1) is the global average surface temperature of the earth really increasing, and (2) if it is, what is causing that to happen?

Is Global Warming Occurring?

A strong majority of scientists have concluded that global warming is real, and they point to data generated by the United Nations Intergovernmental Panel on Climate Change (IPCC), which shows that the average global temperature has risen about 0.6 degrees Celsius during the last century. Some scientists who agree that warming is occurring don't think the magnitude is as large as the IPCC claims; their main argument is that the IPCC data are contaminated and therefore exaggerate the amount of warming that has actually occurred. For example, taking temperatures in urban areas—so-called "heat islands"—leads to overestimates of temperature levels.

To the untrained person, it might seem that measuring temperature is a pretty straightforward thing to do, but it is more complex than it appears at first glance. One problem is that the number and location of weather stations is constantly changing, so the comparability of weather data over time is not as good as scientists would like. Another problem is that the methods used to measure temperature change over time. For example, many years ago, the temperature of sea water was measured by lifting a bucket of sea water into a ship and then measuring the temperature of the water. Now, water is pumped into the engine room of a ship and then measured. But doing that might cause the reading to increase because of the warmer temperature in the engine room. Deciding *where* to measure temperature is another problem. Urban heating must be taken into account, but it is not clear what proportion of urban and rural sites should be included in temperature calculations.

Is Global Warming Caused by Human Activity?

Let us assume for the moment that global warming is a fact. The next obvious question is "What is causing global warming?" Many scientists argue that the rapid increase in carbon dioxide emissions that has occurred during the last 200 years is the cause of global warming. These emissions—which are the result of human industrial activity—trap heat in the atmosphere (the "greenhouse effect") and cause the temperature of the earth to rise. The views of scientists who hold this belief have been widely publicized, and many people accept them as fact. The IPCC has also concluded that greenhouse gases are the cause of global warming.

Other scientists have expressed skepticism about human-caused global warming. Consider some illustrative (and controversial) comments from the skeptics:

- Reid Bryson, emeritus professor of meteorology and one of the most-cited meteorologists in the world, says the idea that global warming is caused by the release of carbon dioxide into the atmosphere is absurd. He says that warming is occurring simply because we are still coming out of the "little ice age" of the early 1800s.
- Tad Murty, a professor in the Departments of Civil Engineering and Earth Sciences at the University of Ottawa, says that global warming is the biggest hoax ever perpetrated on humanity. He notes that there have always been cycles of warming and cooling.
- Tim Patterson, a professor of geology at Carleton University, points out that, 450 million years ago, carbon dioxide levels were ten times higher than they are now and yet the planet was in the depths of an ice age. He also points out that 10 000 years ago, when the earth was coming out of a particularly cold period, temperatures rose as much as 6 degrees Celsius in one decade. That is one hundred times more rapid than the current rise.

Scientists who reject the idea that human activity is the cause of global warming make other, more general arguments. First, they point out that there have been variations in the earth's temperature in the past and that these variations couldn't possibly have been caused by human activity because there weren't any humans. Second, since the thermometer wasn't invented until 1602, we don't have a very long time period of accurate temperature records to examine as we look for warming trends. Records going back thousands of years are needed before we can say with any confidence that a warming (or cooling) trend is actually occurring. Third, research shows that changes in the earth's climate correlate better with fluctuations in the brightness of the sun than they do with fluctuations in carbon dioxide levels. Analysis of core samples from the sediment in British Columbia fjords shows a consistent 11-year cycle in marine productivity which correlates closely with the known 11-year cycle of sunspots. Scientists predict that by the year 2020 the sun will be entering a phase of weaker output, and they conclude that a period of unusually cool temperatures is likely. Several other research studies of tree rings and freshwater river levels also strongly suggest that the sun drives climate change.

What Does All This Mean?

If the scientists who say that global warming is caused by human activity are right, we had better get moving on initiatives to reduce carbon dioxide emissions. But if the scientists who say that global warming is not caused by human activity are right, there isn't much that we can do about climate change. Regardless of whether global warming is human caused or is a natural occurrence, there are some likely outcomes that will occur because of it. There will be both winners and losers if the average global temperature goes up significantly. In Greenland, for example, rising temperatures mean that more pasture area can be grazed by sheep and cows, and a greater variety of vegetables can be grown than was formerly the case; this will improve Greenland's economic performance. But rising temperatures will also undermine the seal hunting by Greenland's Inuit because of thinning ice and may also cause a decline in polar bear populations.

Questions for Discussion

1. Given the information presented above, as well as other information you have read, do you think the evidence supports the argument that global warming is occurring?
2. Given the information presented above, as well as other information you have read, do you think the evidence supports the argument that global warming is caused by human activity?
3. List some additional winners and losers that are likely as a result of global warming.
4. *While there are some uncertainties about global warming, the problem is significant enough that we need to take immediate action to reduce carbon dioxide emissions. If we don't, in 40 or 50 years it will be too late.* Do you agree or disagree with this statement? Defend your answer.

Concluding Case 3-2

Pollution on the High Seas

A study by the International Council on Clean Transportation provides some interesting statistics on the global shipping industry.

- Ships transport more than 90 percent of the world's products by volume.
- Ships release more sulfur dioxide than all of the world's cars, trucks, and buses combined.
- Only six countries in the world release more greenhouse gases than ships collectively do.
- Ships produce about one-quarter of the entire world's output of nitrogen-oxide emissions (the ones that cause smog).
- In 1990, land-based sulfur dioxide emissions in Europe were about 10 times higher than sea-based emissions; by 2030, sea-based emissions will exceed land-based emissions.

Pollution from cargo ships is unusually high because they use bunker fuel, which is a tar-like sludge that is left over from the process of refining petroleum. Bunker fuel releases more pollutants than high-grade fuel, but ship owners use it because it is cheap. And refineries are happy to sell it to shippers because it gives them an outlet for a product that would otherwise not have a market.

While increasing concerns are evident about the global shipping industry, regulating ships on the high seas has always been something of a problem. This difficulty is obvious in the work of the International Maritime Organization, which is a United Nations agency that regulates shipping. The 167 nations that comprise its membership have had extreme difficulty agreeing on what to do about the problem of pollution. For example, it took the group 17 years to agree that the sulfur content in marine fuel should not exceed 4.5 percent. But the sulfur content in bunker fuel had already been reduced to half that level by the time the regulation was passed. One frustrated member of the committee said it spent most of one meeting discussing procedural details and the punctuation in its report.

A more effective approach is for ports to set emission rules, since cargo ships obviously have to unload their cargo *somewhere*. Some ports—particularly those in the Baltic Sea region and in the state of California—have already passed laws that prohibit ships from docking unless they use cleaner-burning fuels. California, for example, does not allow ships that use low-grade fuel to sail within 24 miles of its shores. Ports in Germany, Sweden, and Canada have also set targets to reduce air pollution from ships. But this patchwork of regulations has caused ship owners big problems, because it means that ships need to switch from low- to high-grade fuel as they sail to different locations. Because this process is complicated and dangerous, the International Association of Independent Tanker Owners and the Hong Kong Ship Owners Association both think the UN should simply require ships to stop using bunker fuel.

The problem of pollution is not restricted to ships that carry merchandise; there is also a problem with ships that carry people. More than eight million passengers take an ocean voyage each year, cruising many areas of the world's oceans in search of pristine beaches and clear tropical waters. The tourists and the giant ships that carry them are usually welcomed for the revenues that they bring, but these ships also bring pollution.

A modern cruise ship generates a lot of waste—on a typical day, a ship will produce seven tonnes of solid garbage, 30 000 gallons of sewage, 7000 gallons of bilge water containing oil, and 225 000 gallons of "grey" water from sinks and laundries. Multiply these numbers by more than 167 ships worldwide, cruising 50 weeks per year, and the scope of the environmental damage is staggering.

Environmental groups see the top pollution-related problem as the death of marine life, including extinction. Foreign animals bring parasites and diseases, and in some cases, replace native species entirely. Bacteria that are harmless to human beings can kill corals that provide food and habitat for many species. Oil and toxic chemicals are deadly to wildlife, even in minute quantities. Turtles swallow plastic bags, thinking they are jellyfish, and starve, while seals and birds drown after becoming entangled in the plastic rings that hold beverage cans.

Here again, lack of regulation is the biggest obstacle to solving the problem. Laws and enforcement policies vary considerably from country to country, and even when laws are strict, enforcement may be limited. Cruise lines should be very concerned about clean seas for their own economic well-being, but this is often not the case. Intentional illegal dumping may actually be growing in scope. Over the last decade, for instance, as enforcement has tightened, 10 cruise lines have collectively paid $48.5 million in fines related to illegal dumping. In the largest settlement to date, Royal Caribbean paid $27 million for making illegal alterations to facilities, falsifying records, lying to the U.S. Coast Guard, and deliberately destroying evidence.

Critics are speaking out against the cruise lines' profiteering from an environment that they are destroying, but they note that the companies won't stop as long as the profits continue. Technology exists to make the waste safe, but industry experts estimate that dumping can save a firm millions of dollars annually. From that perspective, the cruise lines are making understandable decisions.

Questions for Discussion

1. What are the major legal issues in this case? What are the major ethical issues?
2. Aside from personal greed, what factors might lead a cruise line to illegally dump waste into the ocean? What factors might cause cargo ships to use low-grade fuel?
3. Are the approaches to social responsibility by the cargo and cruise lines similar or different? Explain.
4. Distinguish between ethical issues and social responsibility issues as they apply to this problem.

Chapter 4*

Understanding Entrepreneurship, Small Business, and New Venture Creation

*With contributions from Dr. Monica Diochon, St. Francis Xavier University.

After reading this chapter, you should be able to:

1. Explain the meaning of and interrelationship among the terms *small business*, *new venture creation*, and *entrepreneurship*.
2. Describe the role of small and new businesses in the Canadian economy.
3. Explain the *entrepreneurial process* and describe its three key elements.
4. Describe three alternative strategies for becoming a business owner—*starting a business, buying an existing business*, and *buying a franchise*.
5. Describe four forms of *legal organization* for a business and discuss the advantages and disadvantages of each.
6. Identify four key reasons for success in small businesses and four key reasons for failure.

Family Businesses

Family businesses are a prominent feature in many countries of the world. Most family businesses are small, but some are very large. In addition to the usual challenges facing business firms, family businesses often are threatened by disagreements between family members about how the business should be run. Here are some classic examples.

The Irving Family

The Irving family of New Brunswick is one of the great success stories of Canadian business. The company owns scores of businesses in oil refining, forestry, shipbuilding, food processing, publishing, transportation, and home improvement. The business was started in the nineteenth century by J.D. Irving and was expanded by his son K.C. The empire is now run by K.C.'s three sons, Arthur, J.K., and Jack, who are all in their seventies. In 2007, it became clear that J.K.'s son Jim and Arthur's son Kenneth were competing for a chance to shape the company's fortunes, and they were at odds over the strategic direction the company should take. That disagreement drove a wedge between J.K. and his brothers.

This is a new situation for the Irving family, which has always presented a remarkably united front. The three brothers have a great deal of respect for each other, so when these succession tensions developed, they decided they would try to amicably divide up the businesses. The energy business will go to Arthur's family, and the forestry business to J.K.'s family. Their approach contrasts sharply with what happened to the McCain family, another New Brunswick business dynasty.

The McCain Family

For many years, brothers Wallace and Harrison McCain were the key players at McCain Foods Ltd., the world's largest french fry producer. But in the mid-1990s, the two brothers had a falling out over the question of who would succeed Harrison as the CEO. Wallace wanted his son Michael to get the job, but Harrison wanted someone from outside the family to take over. After a nasty battle, Wallace was removed from the firm. He then took over Maple Leaf Foods and his son Michael eventually became CEO of that company.

The Redstone Family

Shari Redstone is the daughter of Sumner Redstone, the CEO of Viacom Inc., the company that owns MTV, Nickelodeon, Comedy Central, and Paramount Pictures. In 2006, it looked like Shari was being groomed to take over her father's position, but by 2007 their relationship had soured and her father decided that he didn't want her to succeed him when he died. So he negotiated with her to end her involvement in the company. She was not happy.

The dispute came just six months after Mr. Redstone had settled a lawsuit filed by his son Brent that alleged that his father had tried to freeze him out of the business. Sumner eventually bought out his son's interest for $240 million. Mr. Redstone also faced another lawsuit, from a nephew who claimed that he was deprived of his inheritance.

The Mitchell Family

Mitchell's Gourmet Foods Inc. was a Saskatchewan-based family business. A family feud developed when Fred Mitchell claimed that his mother and his brother Charles were trying to wrest control of the business from him. Both sides in the dispute then sued each other. An accommodation of sorts was reached when the disputing parties agreed to divide up the assets of the company. Fred (and his wife, LuAn) kept Mitchell's, and Charles (and his wife, Camille) kept a beef plant the company owned.

Cuddy International

Cuddy International Corp. was founded by Mac Cuddy, who was known as "the turkey king of Canada." Cuddy was a brilliant entrepreneur who created a great company, but then couldn't manage it, partly because he couldn't get along with his five sons and one daughter. All of Mac's sons worked in the family business at one time or another, but Mac was doubtful about their ability to manage the company. Three of his sons—Peter, Bruce, and Brian—made several attempts to take control of the business, but they failed. Eventually, Mac fired Peter and Brian and demoted Bruce (who then quit the business and became a competitor of his father). Squabbles of various sorts were evident, such as the time Peter sued the company, claiming that he had not been given financial information that he was entitled to. He was then sued by the company for making allegedly defamatory remarks at a press conference.

The Antinori Family

Some family businesses manage to avoid feuds. The Antinori family business in Florence, Italy, has been making wine since 1385, and for 26 generations the family has somehow managed to pass on management of the company to the next generation without getting in a big fight. How do they do it? By going against conventional wisdom—which says that you should clearly separate the family's interest from the interest of the business—and instead blurring the two interests as much as possible. For example, the current CEO and his wife live on the top two floors of their fifteenth-century mansion, and the business operates on the bottom two floors. Perhaps more importantly, the company plans far into the future for a company the grandchildren can run.

Maybe there is something about the wine business that makes family feuds less likely. For example, Catherine and Anne Monna and their father, Bernard, run Cassis Monna & Filles near Quebec City. The sisters are the fifth generation of the family to be involved in the wine business.◆

How will this help me?

By understanding the material discussed in this chapter, you'll be better prepared to (1) identify the challenges and opportunities provided in new venture start-ups, (2) assess the risks and benefits of working in a new business, and (3) evaluate the investment potential inherent in a new business.

In this chapter, we begin by looking at the important role that small and new businesses play in the Canadian economy. We then examine entrepreneurship and the process that entrepreneurs use to start a new business from scratch. We also describe two other ways that entrepreneurs can get into business: buying an existing business or buying a franchise. When operating a business, an entrepreneur must also decide which legal form of organization to adopt—sole proprietorship, partnership, corporation, or co-operative—and we discuss the advantages and disadvantages of each form. We conclude the chapter with a discussion of the reasons for success and failure of small businesses.

Small Business, New Venture Creation, and Entrepreneurship

1 Explain the meaning of and interrelationship among the terms *small business, new venture creation*, and *entrepreneurship.*

Every day, approximately 380 businesses are started in Canada.[1] New firms create the most jobs, are noted for their entrepreneurship, and are typically small.[2] But does this mean that most small businesses are entrepreneurial? Not necessarily.

The terms *small business, new venture*, and *entrepreneurship* are related terms, but each idea is distinct.

Small Business

Defining a "small" business can be tricky. Various measures might be used, including the number of people the business employs, the company's sales revenue, the size of the investment required, or the type of ownership structure the business has. Some of the difficulties in defining a small business are evident when we consider the way the Canadian government collects and reports information on small businesses.

Industry Canada relies on two distinct sources of information, both provided by Statistics Canada: the Business Register (which tracks businesses) and the Labour Force Survey (which tracks individuals). To be included in the Business Register, a business must have at least one paid employee and annual sales revenues of $30 000 or more, or be incorporated. A goods-producing business in the register is considered small if it has fewer than 100 employees, while a service-producing business is considered small if it has fewer than 50 employees.

The Labour Force Survey uses information from *individuals* to make estimates of employment and unemployment levels. Individuals are classified as self-employed if they are working owners of a business that is either incorporated or unincorporated, if they work for themselves but do not have a business (some musicians, for example, would fall into this category), or if they work without pay in a family business.

In its publication *Key Small Business Statistics* (July 2008), Industry Canada reports that there are 2.3 million "business establishments" in Canada and about 2.5 million people who are "self-employed." There is no way of identifying how much overlap there is in these two categories, but we do know that an unincorporated business operated by a self-employed person (with no employees) would *not* be counted among the 2.3 million *businesses* in the Business Register. This is an important point because the majority of businesses in Canada have no employees (just the owner), nor are they incorporated. A study conducted by members of the Entrepreneurship Research Consortium (ERC) tracked a sample of Canadian *nascent entrepreneurs*—people who were trying to start a business—over four years. Only 15 percent of those who reported establishing an operating business had incorporated their firm.[3] These facts need to be kept in mind when considering statistics or research that excludes these firms. When either of these indicators is used to find businesses to study, the number of new firms will be underestimated.

Given all this, we define a **small business** as an owner-managed business with fewer than 100 employees. We do so because it enables us to make better use of existing statistics and because you now are aware of how definitions can influence our understanding of small businesses.

small business An owner-managed business with fewer than 100 employees.

Each year, the Queen's Centre for Business Venturing develops a ranking of the top 50 small- and medium-sized employers to work for. The Top 10 firms in the 2008 study are shown in Table 4.1. Each of these companies exhibited superiority in employee recognition, managing performance, career opportunities, and organizational reputation.[4]

Table 4.1 Top 10 Small- and Medium-Sized Employers in Canada, 2008

Company	Location
1. Protegra Inc.	Winnipeg, Manitoba
2. Miele Canada Limited	Vaughan, Ontario
3. Gibraltar Solutions Inc.	Mississauga, Ontario
4. ISL Engineering and Land Services	Edmonton, Alberta
5. Hood Group	Sherwood Park, Alberta
6. Solutions 2 GO Inc.	Mississauga, Ontario
7. DRN Commerce Inc.	London, Ontario
8. PDL Contact Centres Ltd.	Calgary, Alberta
9. Benefits by Design Inc.	Port Coquitlam, B.C.
10. Heathtech Consultants	Toronto, Ontario

The New Venture/Firm

Various criteria can also be used to determine when a new firm comes into existence. Three of the most common are when it was formed, whether it was incorporated, and if it sold goods and/or services.[5] A business is considered to be new if it has become operational within the previous 12 months, if it adopts any of the main organizational forms (proprietorship, partnership, corporation, or co-operative), and if it sells goods or services. Thus, we define a **new venture (or new firm)** as a recently formed commercial organization that provides goods and/or services for sale.

new venture (or new firm) A recently formed commercial organization that provides goods and/or services for sale.

Entrepreneurship

Entrepreneurship is the process of identifying an opportunity in the marketplace and accessing the resources needed to capitalize on that opportunity.[6] **Entrepreneurs** are people who recognize and seize opportunities. For example, Mark Zuckerberg created the website Facebook, and just a few years later it had close to 40 million active users. By 2008, Zuckerberg was widely thought to be the richest person in the world under the age of 25, with a net worth of over $1.5 billion. It takes more than a good idea to be successful. Zuckerberg worked long hours, and he is constantly tailoring the website to suit its expanding audience.[7]

entrepreneurship The process of identifying an opportunity in the marketplace and accessing the resources needed to capitalize on that opportunity.

entrepreneur A business person who accepts both the risks and the opportunities involved in creating and operating a new business venture.

Another example: Ken Woods and John Gagliardi are two entrepreneurs who recognized an opportunity in the marketplace for higher-quality beer and formed the Ontario-based Black Oak Brewing Company. They've already developed several award-winning beers, such as Black Oak Nut Brown Ale, Pale Ale, and Premium Lager. A website for Toronto beer lovers called The Bar Towel rates these beers very positively.[8]

Each year, the Heritage Foundation publishes an index of economic freedom, which assesses the extent to which entrepreneurs have freedom to pursue new business opportunities. In 2009, the top three countries were Hong Kong, Singapore, and Australia, with freedom scores of 90.0, 87.1, and 82.6, respectively. Canada ranked seventh with a score of 79.6 and North Korea ranked last with a score of 2.0.[9]

Creativity is an important personal attribute that has come to be associated with entrepreneurs, and small businesses provide a great environment to use creativity.[10] But do not assume that only small business owners exhibit entrepreneurial characteristics. Many successful managers in large organizations in both the public and private sectors also exhibit similar characteris-

There are many areas in which small businesses excel. This entrepreneur, for example, has a lucrative business as a dog walker.

tics.[11] Entrepreneurship is evident in a wide range of contexts: in small or new firms, in old firms, in large firms, in firms that grow slowly, in firms that grow rapidly, in non-profit organizations, and in the public sector.[12]

Historically, most innovations have come from individuals in small businesses. As businesses increase in size, however, innovation and creativity tend to become casualties in the battle for higher sales and profits. In some large companies, new ideas are even discouraged, and champions of innovation have been stalled in mid-career. But people who exhibit entrepreneurial characteristics can often create and maintain the innovation and flexibility of a small-business environment within the confines of a large, bureaucratic structure. This is known as **intrapreneuring**, and it is supported by many large firms, including Compaq Computer, Rubbermaid, 3M, and Xerox.

intrapreneuring Entrepreneurial characteristics that can create and maintain the innovation and flexibility of a small-business environment within the confines of a large, bureaucratic structure.

Compaq, which is now part of Hewlett-Packard, is an excellent example of how intrapreneuring works. The firm has one major division called the New Business Group. When a manager or engineer has an idea for a new product or product application, he or she takes it to the New Business Group and "sells" it. The managers in the group are then encouraged to help the innovator develop the idea for field testing. If the product takes off and does well, it is then spun off into its own business group or division. If it doesn't do as well as hoped, it may be maintained as part of the New Business Group or phased out.

Procter & Gamble is also known for encouraging intrapreneurship. It has earned this reputation by having divisions that focus on creating new products for specific markets.[13] The Swiffer product line is one example. Once the basic Swiffer mop was launched successfully, a whole range of products was added, such as the Swiffer WetJet and Swiffer Dusters. A key difference between intrapreneurs and entrepreneurs is that intrapreneurs typically don't have to concern themselves with getting the resources needed to bring the new product to market, since their employer provides the resources.

The Role of Small and New Businesses in the Canadian Economy

Describe the role of small and new businesses in the Canadian economy. 2

Small and new businesses play a key role in the Canadian economy, but recognition of this role is relatively recent. Prior to the 1980s, large businesses were the focus of attention in terms of economic impact within industrialized nations.

Small Businesses

There are 2.3 million business establishments in Canada. Of these, 1.1 million are classified as "employer businesses" (i.e., they have a payroll of at least one person), while the other 1.2 million are classified as "indeterminate" because they have no employees registered with the Canada Revenue Agency.[14]

It may surprise you to learn that 97.8 percent of all employer businesses in Canada are small (they have fewer than 100 employees), and more than half of these have fewer than 5 employees. Medium-sized businesses (100–499 employees) comprise just 1.9 percent of employer businesses, and large businesses (those with 500 or more employees) represent just 0.3 percent of all employer businesses.[15] This pattern is consistent across all provinces in Canada. While one large business has many more employees than one small business, as a group, small businesses provide more jobs than large businesses. Small businesses also lead the way when it comes to innovation and new technology.

Ontario and Quebec together account for the largest proportion of business establishments in Canada (about 56 percent), followed by the western provinces (36 percent) and the Atlantic provinces (7 percent). The Northwest

A common type of small business in Canada is the convenience store. As the name suggests, it emphasizes convenience. It attracts customers from its immediate area through its long hours of operation and the product lines it carries.

Territories, the Yukon, and Nunavut represent just 0.3 percent of Canada's businesses.[16]

The distribution of employment by size of firm varies considerably across industries. Small businesses account for over two-thirds of employment in four industries: non-institutional health care (90 percent), the construction industry (77 percent), other services (73 percent), and accommodation and food (69 percent).[17] In another five industries, at least half of the workforce is employed by small businesses.

The boxed insert entitled "Small Businesses Go Green" provides information on the developing interest in the environment among small business owners.

The Greening of Business

Small Businesses Go Green

Most entrepreneurs and small business owners have plenty of operational problems and crises that demand their attention, so they might not spend much time thinking about how their company could become more eco-friendly. Even if they did find the time, they might think that they couldn't afford to go green. But there are a lot of resources available to help small business owners who are interested in showing more concern for the environment.

John Walker is the CEO of Transition Plus Sustainability Solutions (TPSS), an environmental consulting firm. He says that small business owners are always interested in ways to reduce energy costs, and doing so will make small businesses greener. Making simple changes like choosing energy-efficient lighting and turning off photocopiers and computers overnight is a good place to start. The energy departments in most provinces have websites that provide information on how companies can save money by using water and energy more efficiently.

For more aggressive or longer-term projects, small business owners can access the federal government's ecoACTION program website, which contains information about programs that help organizations reduce energy costs. The ecoENERGY Retrofit program provides financial incentives of up to 25 percent of project costs to help small- and medium-sized companies implement energy saving projects.

Saving energy is just one possible area for improvement. There are also many other ideas that will appeal to small business owners because implementing the ideas will be inexpensive. Consider the following:

- Use recycled paper.
- Use eco-friendly cleaning supplies.
- Buy pens made of compostable material, not plastic.

- Help staff to organize car pools.
- Encourage staff to bicycle to work by giving them a place to lock their bikes.
- Encourage staff to use public transit.

Various other approaches and resources are also available to small businesses. For example, a Toronto-area initiative called greenTbiz—a project of the Toronto Association of Business Improvement Areas—works free with small businesses to implement environmental programs. The project focusses on recommendations that make financial sense for the small business. Most of the companies that have used the service have fewer than 20 employees.

Another example is Green Enterprise Toronto (GET), which is a group of 385 eco-minded businesses that pay $195 each year to belong to a network where they can trade business, advice, and referrals. All of the businesses in the group are committed to activities like sustainable purchasing, manufacturing, and recycling of products. GET runs regular workshops on topics of importance to small businesses—for example, finance and marketing—but it also offers information on environmental and social responsibility initiatives. Chris Lowry, the director, says that many small business owners have gotten interested in going green after being asked "uncomfortable" questions by their children and staff members about why they aren't doing more for the environment. John Walker, CEO of TPSS, also notes that small business owners are starting to respond to social pressure from customers.

One small business that wants to become more environmentally friendly is the Gladstone Hotel on trendy Queen Street West in Toronto. It occupies a building that is well over 100 years old, so a lot of work is necessary to make the building more energy efficient. The company hired Green Shift consultants to do an environmental audit of the property and to draw up a long-term strategy, which will take several years to implement. A variety of relatively inexpensive actions are being taken, including

- using non-toxic cleaning supplies
- composting waste from the hotel restaurant
- using compostable take-out food containers
- revamping the heating and lighting system

Upgrading an existing business is just one approach; another is to start a business whose whole purpose is to be green. Shannon Boase, for example, founded Earthcycle, a company that makes packaging from palm fibre, a renewable resource that is typically thrown away. She got the idea after working in Malaysia for a company that was developing a new technology that could turn palm husks into biodegradable packaging material for fruits and vegetables. The production activities of Earthcycle are fully integrated, all the way from the plantation to the marketing of the packaging.

Julie Jonas is an environmentalist who thought there would be a market for organic products. So she started an ecommerce business called Zia and Tia Luxury Organics that sells a diverse line of organic products. Customers place orders and Jonas has them shipped directly from the manufacturer to the customer. This reduces the amount of greenhouse gases that are produced because less transportation is required.

Critical Thinking Questions

1. Find a small business in your local area that is committed to being eco-friendly. How did the owner decide to commit to having an eco-friendly business?
2. Interview the owners of several small businesses in your local area. Ask them what they have done to become more environmentally friendly. If they have not done anything, ask them what has prevented them from taking the initiative to be more environmentally friendly.
3. Consider the following statement: *It is unrealistic to expect small business owners to spend much time thinking about or implementing green practices. The failure rate of small businesses is high, so small business owners have to focus all their energies on trying to ensure the survival of their businesses. They simply don't have the time (or money) to "go green."* Do you agree or disagree with the statement? Explain your reasoning.

New Ventures[18]

New ventures are important as a source of job creation and for the introduction of new products and services.[19] In 2007, small business created 100 000 jobs in Canada; this represented 40 percent of all jobs that were created.[20] Between 2002 and 2006, approximately 130 000 new small businesses were started each year in Canada.[21] During that same period, an equal number of small businesses ceased operations each year.[22]

According to Statistics Canada, there were about 877 000 women entrepreneurs in Canada in 2006, and 47 percent of small- and medium-sized enterprises have some degree of female ownership.[23] Between 1996 and 2006, the number of self-employed women increased by 18 percent (compared to 14 percent for men). Women are playing a more prominent role than ever before in starting new ventures. Kyla Eaglesham, the owner of Madeleines, Cherry Pie and Ice Cream, is typical. After doing a lot of research on the ice cream and dessert industry, she left her job as a flight attendant and opened a dessert café in Toronto's trendy Annex neighbourhood. The store attracts customers who want "a little bit of cottage country in the heart of Toronto."[24]

More and more women are starting and successfully operating their own small businesses, and women now account for half of all new businesses that are formed. But women lead only 12 percent of the small- and medium-sized businesses that export goods and services.[25] Women who run businesses from their homes are sometimes called "mompreneurs."[26] One such person is Crystal Dallner, who started a marketing business called Outright Communication soon after her first child was born. The Mompreneur Networking Group organizes seminars and publishes *Mompreneur*, a free magazine that helps women who want to start a business.[27] More information on mompreneurs is provided in Concluding Case 4-1 and Video Case I-1.

Female entrepreneurs are honoured each year at the Canadian Woman Entrepreneur Awards. In 2008, winners included Christina Jennings (Shaftesbury Films, Toronto), Baljit Gill (Kitwanga Lumber Company, Surrey, B.C.), and Nina Gupta (Greenlite Lighting Corp., Pointe Claire, Quebec).[28]

Young entrepreneurs—both men and women—are also involved in creating new ventures in Canada. Consider the following examples:

- Geraldine McManus, who started Ab-Original Wear, buys artwork from Aboriginal artists and then reproduces it on T-shirts, crew-neck shirts, and sweatshirts. The clothing products feature Aboriginal artwork on the front and an inspirational message from a chief or elder on the back. The store also sells crafts made by local Aboriginal artists and miniature log cabins that McManus makes herself from recycled wood.[29]
- The Ben Barry Agency is an Ottawa-based modelling business that promotes models who are considered unorthodox—models of various sizes and ages, different racial backgrounds, and who have physical disabilities. The models have appeared in government advertising campaigns and on fashion runways in shopping malls. Barry works with company management to define their clientele and then chooses models who will best reflect the store's typical shoppers.[30]
- Tell Us About Us (TUAU) is a Winnipeg-based company specializing in market research and customer satisfaction programs. Owners Tyler Gompf and Scott Griffith recently signed a seven-figure deal to provide mystery shopper service to Dunkin' Donuts, Baskin-Robbins, and Togo's in the United States and Canada. The mystery shoppers will note any problems at a retail site and TUAU will then measure how quickly the problems are fixed.[31]
- Sean McCormick is the owner of Blue Moose Clothing Company, the largest manufacturer of mukluks in Canada. McCormick employs 25 people, many of them Aboriginal. He credits Aboriginal Business Canada, which provides money to native entrepreneurs to help them start small businesses.[32]

The Entrepreneurial Process

3 Explain the *entrepreneurial process* and describe its three key elements.

The entrepreneurial process is like a journey. To get to the destination (the start-up of a new venture), the entrepreneur must identify a business opportunity and access the resources needed to capitalize on it. Along the way, social, economic, political, and technological factors in the broader environment will have an influence, but we will focus our attention on understanding the three key process elements—the entrepreneur, the opportunity, and the resources—and how they interact.

As these key elements interact, they may be mismatched or well matched. If elements are mismatched (a "misfit"), the journey may be abandoned before the destination is reached. For example, if an entrepreneur identifies an opportunity for a new health service but does not have the relevant background and skills to deliver the service, the business may never get off the ground. Conversely, if the process elements are well matched (a "fit"), the new business venture will likely become operational. After start-up, the venture's next phase of development will result in one of the following outcomes: growth, stability (staying the same), decline, or demise (ceasing to exist). These ideas are illustrated in Figure 4.1.

The Entrepreneur

Since the entrepreneur is at the heart of the entrepreneurial process, researchers have paid considerable attention to identifying the personal characteristics of entrepreneurs. The profiles provided in Table 4.2 illustrate how wide ranging these characteristics are.[33] Some are behavioural (for example, high energy level), others are personality traits (for example, independence), and still others are skills (for example, problem solving).

While the idea that people are "born" entrepreneurs is still quite popular, nothing could be further from the truth.[34] In fact, entrepreneurial characteristics have been found to be widely distributed in the population.[35] We also know that personal characteristics often have less impact on a person's actions than the situation a person is in.[36] What is really important is not who the person *is* but what the person *does*.[37] The two main things that entrepreneurs need to do are to identify an opportunity and to access resources.

Identifying Opportunities

Identifying opportunities involves generating ideas for new (or improved) products, processes, or services, then screening those ideas so that the one that presents the best opportunity can be developed, and then developing the opportunity.

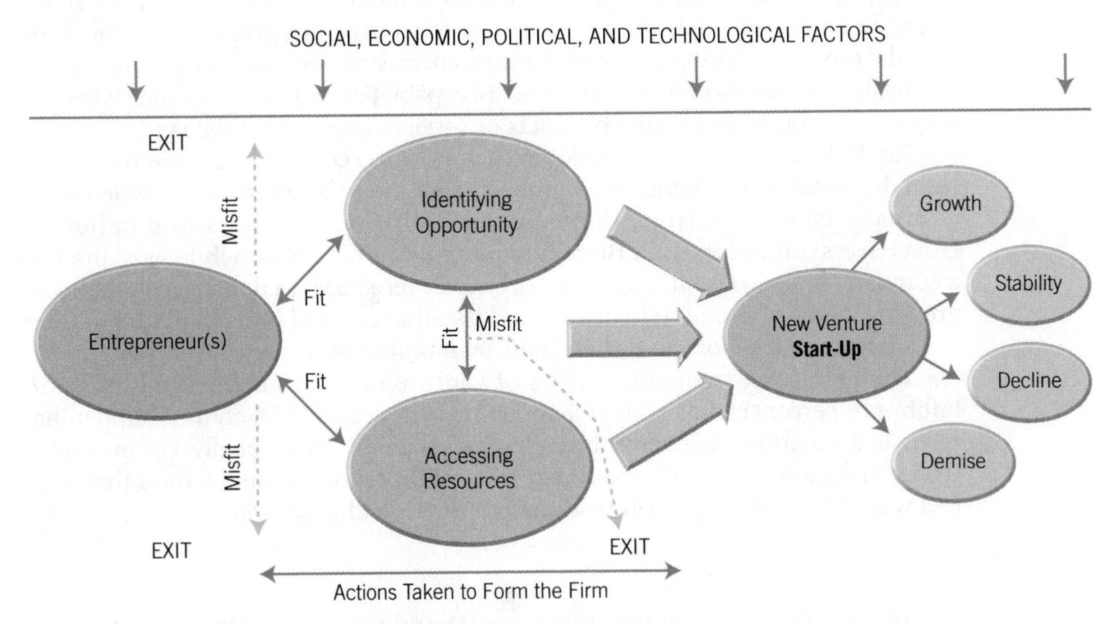

Figure 4.1 The entrepreneurial process in a new venture context.

Table 4.2 Entrepreneurial Characteristics

Kuratko and Hodgetts (2007)	Hornday (1982)	Timmons and Spinelli (2007)
Commitment, Determination, and Perseverance	Self-Confidence	Commitment and Determination
Drive to Achieve	Perseverance, Determination	Leadership
Opportunity Orientation	Drive to Achieve	Opportunity Obsession
Initiative and Responsibility	Energy, Diligence	Tolerance of Risk, Ambiguity, and Uncertainty
Persistent Problem Solving	Resourcefulness	Creativity, Self-Reliance, and Adaptability
Seeking Feedback	Calculated Risk Taking	Motivation to Excel
Internal Locus of Control	Need to Achieve	Courage
Tolerance for Ambiguity	Creativity	Creativity and Innovativeness
Calculated Risk Taking	Initiative	Energy, Health, and Emotional Stability
Integrity and Reliability	Flexibility	Values
Tolerance for Failure	Positive Response to Challenges	Capacity to Inspire
High Energy Level	Independence	Intelligence
Creativity and Innovativeness	Perceptiveness	
Vision	Dynamism, Leadership	
Self-Confidence and Optimism	Positive Attitude	
Independence	Ability to Get Along with People	
Team Building	Responsiveness to Suggestions and Criticism	
	Profit Orientation	
	Perceptiveness	

Idea Generation

Typically, generating ideas involves abandoning traditional assumptions about how things work and how they ought to be and involves seeing what others do not. If the prospective new (or improved) product, process, or service can be profitably produced and is attractive relative to other potential venture ideas, it might present an opportunity.

Where do ideas come from? Most new ventures do not emerge from a deliberate search for viable business ideas but from events relating to work or everyday life.[38] Approximately half of all new business ideas come from insights gained or skills learned at a previous job. As employees, prospective entrepreneurs are familiar with the product or service and with the customers, suppliers, and competitors. They can relate those needs to their own personal capabilities and can determine whether they are capable of producing products or services that can fill the void.

Jay Hagan and Scott Gaidano learned how to recover data from damaged hard drives while working for a company that manufactured them. When that company went bankrupt, they started their own business and called it DriveSavers. Likewise, Gina Bianchini met Marc Andreessen while working for a company that also went bankrupt. They discovered a shared interest in the fast-growing world of social networking and together created Ning, a platform that gives users the freedom to design their own online networks.[39]

The next most frequent sources of venture ideas are a personal interest/hobby (16 percent) and a chance happening (11 percent).[40] A chance happening refers to a situation where a venture idea comes about unexpectedly. For example, while on vacation in another country you might try a new snack food that you feel would be in demand if introduced to the Canadian market.

Screening

Entrepreneurs often generate many ideas, and screening them is a key part of the entrepreneurial process. The faster you can weed out the "dead-end" venture ideas, the more time and effort you can devote to the ones that remain. The more of the following characteristics that an idea has, the greater the opportunity it presents.

The Idea Creates or Adds Value for the Customer. A product or service that creates or adds value for the customer is one that solves a significant problem or meets a significant need in new or different ways. Consider Sally Fox's idea for eliminating the dyeing process in textile operations.[41] By cross-breeding long-fibre white cotton and short-fibre coloured cotton, she developed Foxfibre, an environmentally friendly new cotton fibre that is naturally grown in several colours and is long enough to be spun commercially.

The Idea Provides a Competitive Advantage That Can Be Sustained. A competitive advantage exists when potential customers see the product or service as being better than that of competitors. Sustaining a competitive advantage involves maintaining it in the face of competitors' actions or changes in the industry. All other things being equal, the longer markets are in a state of flux, the greater the likelihood of being able to sustain a competitive advantage. Lacking a competitive advantage or developing a competitive advantage that is not sustainable constitute two fatal flaws of many new ventures.[42]

To continue with Sally Fox's story, not too long after she sold her first crop she was running a $10 million business and had well-known companies like Levi's, L.L. Bean, Land's End, and Esprit as customers. But Fox's journey turned out to be bumpy. She had to relocate twice in response to pressure from powerful cotton growers who were afraid that her coloured varieties would contaminate their own crops. Also, once spinning mills began moving to Southeast Asia and South America, Fox's cotton lost the financial advantage it had over traditional cotton. Because the overseas mills were unwilling or unable to process the relatively small quantities of cotton her farmers produced, she lost her big customers. Fox now concentrates on smaller mills and smaller customers, and she is rebuilding her business and her network of growers.

The Idea Is Marketable and Financially Viable. While it is important to determine whether there are enough customers who are willing to buy the product or service, it is also important to determine whether sales will lead to profits.[43] Estimating market demand requires an initial understanding of who the customers are, what their needs are, and how the product or service will satisfy their needs better than competitors' products will. It also requires a thorough understanding of the key competitors who can provide similar products, services, or benefits to the target customer. For example, 10 years ago few people thought that manufacturers of cellphones would be competitors of camera manufacturers in providing real-time photos through digital imaging. Customers define the competition in terms of who can satisfy their needs best.

After learning about the competition and customers, the entrepreneur must prepare a sales forecast. A **sales forecast** is an estimate of how much of a product or service will be purchased by the prospective customers for a specific period of time—typically one year. Total sales revenue is estimated by multiplying the units expected to be sold by the selling price. The sales forecast forms the foundation for determining the financial viability of the venture and the resources needed to start it.

sales forecast An estimate of how much of a product or service will be purchased by the prospective customers for a specific period of time.

Determining financial viability involves preparing financial forecasts, which are two- to three-year projections of a venture's future financial position and performance. They typically consist of an estimate of *start-up costs*, a *cash budget*, an *income statement*, and a *balance sheet* (see Chapter 14 for more detail about these financial documents). A cash budget forecasts the cash receipts and cash disbursements of the business; the income statement shows the profit or loss; and the balance sheet shows the assets (what the business owns), the liabilities (what it owes), and the owners' equity (owners' investment, including any profits that the business retains). These projections serve as the basis for decisions regarding whether to proceed with the venture, and if so, the amount and type of financing to be used in financing the new business.

exit costs The costs in terms of time, money, and reputation that are incurred when a business shuts down.

The Idea Has Low Exit Costs. The final consideration is the venture's **exit costs**. Exit costs are low if a venture can be shut down without a significant loss of time, money, or reputation.[44] If a venture is not expected to make a profit for a number of years, its exit costs are high, since the project cannot be reasonably abandoned in the short term. On the other hand, if the venture is expected to make a profit quickly, its exit costs will be lower, making the idea more attractive.

Developing the Opportunity

As the "dead-end" venture ideas are weeded out, a clear notion of the business concept and an entry strategy for pursuing it need to be developed. As the process proceeds, the business concept often changes from what was originally envisioned. Some new ventures develop entirely new markets, products, and sources of competitive advantage once the needs of the marketplace and the economies of the business are better understood. So, while a vision of what is to be achieved is important, it is equally important to be responsive to new information and to be on the lookout for opportunities that were not originally anticipated. For example, if customers are not placing orders, as was the case with Sally Fox, it is important to find out why and to make the appropriate adjustments.

New ventures use one or more of three main entry strategies: They introduce a totally new product or service; they introduce a product or service that will compete directly with existing competitive offerings but add a new twist (such as offering the option of customizing the standard product); or they franchise.[45] A **franchise** is an arrangement in which a buyer (franchisee) purchases the right to sell the product or service of the seller (franchiser). We discuss franchising in more detail later in this chapter.

franchise An arrangement in which a buyer (franchisee) purchases the right to sell the product or service of the seller (franchiser).

When capital requirements are high, such as when a manufacturing operation is being proposed, there is a need for considerable research and planning. Similarly, if product development or operations are fairly complex, research and analysis will be needed to ensure that the costs associated with effectively coordinating tasks will be minimized. In these circumstances, or when the aim is to attract potential investors, a comprehensive written business plan will be required. A **business plan** is a document that describes the entrepreneur's proposed business venture, explains why it is an opportunity, and outlines its marketing plan, its operational and financial details, and its managers' skills and abilities.[46] The contents of a business plan are shown in Table 4.3.

business plan A document that describes the entrepreneur's proposed business venture, explains why it is an opportunity, and outlines its marketing plan, its operational and financial details, and its managers' skills and abilities.

If market conditions are changing rapidly, the benefits gained from extensive research and planning diminish quickly. By the time the entrepreneur is ready to start, new competitors may have entered the market, prices may have changed, a location may no longer be available, and so on. Similarly, if the product is highly innovative, market research is of less value because the development of entirely new products involves *creating* needs and wants rather than simply responding to existing needs. Consequently, measuring the capacity of the product or service to fill existing customer needs or wants is less critical.

Contrary to what many people might think, planning does not have to be completed before action is taken. For example, if an electrical contracting business is being proposed in an area where there is a shortage of tradespeople,

Table 4.3 A Business Plan

A well-written business plan is formally structured, easy to read, and avoids confusion. By organizing the information into sections, it makes dealing with the information more manageable. The amount of detail and the order of presentation may vary from one venture to another and according to whom the plan is being prepared for (an investor will require more detail than if the plan is being prepared for internal use by the entrepreneur). An outline for a standard business plan is provided below. While formats vary, with some better suited to the type of venture being proposed than others, most contain the following elements.

I.	**Cover Page**: Name of venture and owners, date prepared, contact person, his/her address, telephone and fax numbers, email address, and the name of the organization the plan is being presented to. The easier it is for the reader to contact the entrepreneur, the more likely the contact will occur.
II.	**Executive Summary**: A one- to three-page overview of the total business plan. Written after the other sections are completed, it highlights their significant points, and aims to create enough excitement to motivate the reader to continue.
III.	**Table of Contents:** This element lists major sections with page numbers for both the body and the appendices of the plan.
IV.	**Company Description**: Explains the type of company and tells whether it is a manufacturing, retail, service, or other type of business. It also describes the proposed form of organization: sole proprietorship, partnership, corporation, or co-operative. A typical organization of this section is as follows: name and location; company objectives; nature and primary product or service of the business; and current status (start-up, buyout, or expansion) and history if applicable.
V.	**Product or Service Description:** Describes the product or service and indicates what is unique about it. This section explains the value that is added for customers—why people will buy the product or service; features of the product or service providing a competitive advantage; legal protection (patents, copyrights, trademarks, if relevant); and dangers of technical or style obsolescence.
VI.	**Marketing:** This section has two key parts, the market analysis and the marketing plan. The market analysis convinces the reader that the entrepreneur understands the market for the product or service and can deal effectively with the competition to achieve sales projections. The marketing plan explains the strategy for achieving sales projections.
VII.	**Operating Plan**: Explains the type of manufacturing or operating system to be used. Describes the facilities, labour, raw materials, and processing requirements.
VIII.	**Management:** Identifies the key players—the management team, active investors, and directors—and cites the experience and competence they possess. This section includes a description of the management team, outside investors and directors and their qualifications, outside resource people, and plans for recruiting and training employees.
IX.	**Financial Plan**: Specifies financial needs and contemplated sources of financing. Presents projected financial statements, including a cash budget, a balance sheet, and an income statement.
1X.	**Supporting Details/Appendix**: Provides supplementary materials to the plan such as résumés and other important supporting data.

it would be important to seek out qualified employees prior to conducting other analyses that are needed to complete the business plan. Such early action also helps to build relationships that can be drawn on later. Obviously, some ventures do not lend themselves to early action, particularly those that are capital intensive. Since most entrepreneurs have limited resources, it is important to concentrate on the issues that can be dealt with *and* that will help determine whether to proceed and how to proceed.[47]

Accessing Resources

Typically, entrepreneurs acquire the various resources needed to make the venture a reality by **bootstrapping**, which means "doing more with less." Usually the term refers to financing techniques whereby entrepreneurs make do with as few resources as possible and use other peoples' resources wherever they can. However, bootstrapping can also refer to the acquisition of other types of resources, such as people, space, equipment, or materials that are loaned or provided free by customers or suppliers.

bootstrapping Financing techniques whereby entrepreneurs make do with as few resources as possible and use other peoples' resources wherever they can. Can also refer to the acquisition of other types of resources, such as people, space, equipment, or materials that are loaned or provided free by customers or suppliers.

Financial Resources

There are two main types of financing—*debt* and *equity* (see Chapter 20 for a detailed discussion of debt and equity). Briefly, *debt financing* refers to money that is borrowed. The borrower is obliged to repay the full amount of the loan in addition to interest charges on the debt. The most common sources of debt financing are banks (who provide personal loans), trust companies, co-operatives, finance companies, equipment companies, credit unions, government agencies, and suppliers (who provide goods such as inventory to the entrepreneur with an agreement to bill the entrepreneur later).

Equity financing refers to money that the entrepreneur (or others) invests in a business in return for an ownership interest. Equity investors, as owners, are keenly interested in how any profit will be distributed. The most common sources of equity financing are personal savings (new venture founders draw heavily on their own finances to start their businesses), love money (investments from friends, relatives, and business associates), venture capitalists (who loan money to promising new ventures in return for a share of ownership in the business), and private investors (also known as *angels*), who are financially well-off entrepreneurs who wish to recycle their wealth by investing in new businesses. The boxed insert entitled "Looking for Angels" gives more details about angel investing.

Choosing between debt and equity financing involves trade-offs with regard to potential profitability, financial risk, and control. On the one hand, borrowing money increases the potential for higher rates of return to the entrepreneur when the business is performing well. On the other hand, equity makes it possible to reduce risk by giving up some control. Since a business is at its riskiest point during the start-up phase, equity is usually more appropriate and accessible than debt. However, most new venture founders prefer debt because they are reluctant to give up any control to outsiders. To obtain debt financing the entrepreneur must have an adequate equity investment in the business—typically 20 percent of the business's value—and collateral (or security). **Collateral** refers to items (assets) owned by the business (such as a building and equipment) or by the individual (such as a house or car) that the borrower uses to secure a loan or other credit. These items can be seized by the lender if the loan isn't repaid according to the specified terms. To lenders, equity investment demonstrates the commitment of the entrepreneur, because individuals tend to be more committed to a venture if they have a substantial portion of what they own invested in it.

collateral Items (assets) owned by the business (such as a building and equipment) or by the individual (such as a house or car) that the borrower uses to secure a loan or other credit.

Entrepreneurs who want to obtain financing for a start-up business must have collateral like a house or car in order to get a loan. Would you be willing to give your house or car as collateral, knowing that if you couldn't repay the loan the bank would take your house or car?

Business Accountability

Looking for Angels

When small business owners come up with a great idea for a new product, they often find themselves in a Catch-22: They need money to get their product known in the market, but they can't get money because their product is not known in the market. How can they escape from this vicious circle? One answer is angel investors. Consider these stories.

Saxx & Co. makes high-performance men's underwear. The company was started by Trent Kitsch, who developed the idea as part of a project requirement in his MBA program. He put $18 000 of his own money into the company—and he did manage to sell 2000 pairs of Saxx underwear and generate $50 000 in revenue in the process—but he needed a major cash injection to compete with the bigger companies in the industry. Eventually, he received $50 000 from a private investor in return for a 5 percent ownership stake in the business. Kitsch wants to get an additional $500 000, and he is willing to give such an investor 15 percent of the business; he also wants a mentor who has experience in the business.

Kevin Quinn started PowerForward Inc., a company that makes a machine that automatically attaches labels, scratch-and-win cards, or coupons to printed material as it runs through high-speed printing presses. Quinn needed $300 000 to produce the machines so that he could demonstrate that they actually did what he claimed. After several false starts, he approached the ISCM Investment Network in Markham, Ontario. The network does not lend money, but it provides free coaching from mentors who help entrepreneurs like Quinn to better prepare to seek capital. It then introduces the entrepreneurs to angel investors. Quinn was introduced to an angel who invested $250 000. The angel will get a royalty on all machines that Quinn sells.

Chris Beaver, Mark Kerbel, and Roman Kulyk started REGEN Energy Inc., which makes devices to help companies reduce electricity use. The partners needed cash to expand their business, so they approached several venture capital firms. Those firms weren't interested, so they approached angel investors. They found an organization called Maple Leaf Angels, which was in the energy-efficient lighting business. Maple Leaf agreed to sign on as an investor, and one of the individuals at Maple Leaf introduced the partners to the buildings where he was already doing business.

It is important that the angel investor and the small business owner have a clear understanding about issues like who has control over what, the kinds of decisions the angel has to approve, and the amount of regular progress reporting the small business owner will give to the angel.

There are various information sources for small business owners who want to find angels to invest in their business. Angelinvestor.ca, for example, is a Canadian not-for-profit organization that has a directory of angel investors. Another website that contains information about angels is www.angelinvestmentnetwork.ca. Canada has about 25 angel groups. The National Angels Organization is a not-for-profit group that promotes better investment practices and advocates for private investors.

Critical Thinking Questions

1. How are angel investors different from venture capitalists?
2. Are entrepreneurs more accountable to venture capitalists or to angels? Explain your reasoning.
3. Consider the following statement: *Entrepreneurs who have a great new product idea should not try to get money from either venture capitalists or angels. Rather, they should pursue debt or equity capital because they can get larger sums of money that way. They can then use the money to more effectively develop their new product idea.* Do you agree or disagree with the statement? Explain your reasoning.

Besides these conventional sources of financing, the possibilities for creative bootstrap financing are almost endless. For example, an entrepreneur might require an advance payment from customers, in full or in part. Equipment can be leased rather than purchased (which reduces the risk of equipment becoming obsolete). Office furniture can be rented, premises can be shared, and the manufacture of products can be subcontracted, thereby avoiding the expense of procuring material, equipment, and facilities. All of these activities free up cash, which can then be used for other purposes.

Other Resources

Businesses may be owned by one person, but entrepreneurship is not a solo process. There are various stakeholders who provide resources to the venture, including partners, employees, customers, suppliers, professionals, consultants, government agencies, lenders, shareholders, and venture capitalists. Sometimes ownership is shared with one or more of these stakeholders in order to acquire the use of their resources. When ownership is shared, decisions must be made about who to share it with, how much each stakeholder will own, at what cost, and under what conditions. The form of legal organization chosen affects whether ownership can be shared and whether resources can be accessed. We discuss this important point later in the chapter.

Some small businesses are started by friends who decide to team up. For example, Eryn Green and Tamar Wagman teamed up to start Sweetpea, a Toronto-based organic baby food company. Sari Nisker and Casey Soer started Spynga, a Toronto fitness club that focusses on yoga, spinning classes, and holistic health. Candice Versace and Dolly Woo started an upscale clothing shop in Winnipeg. There have been some interpersonal conflicts in all three businesses, but the partners have learned to work together. Stewart Thornhill, who teaches entrepreneurship at the Richard Ivey School of Business, says that friends who operate a business together sometimes have trouble deciding when to quit. He says they should ask themselves this question: "If the person I'm working with wasn't my friend, would I want to be in business with them?"[48]

Deciding whether to share ownership by forming a team involves considering whether having a team is desirable or necessary and whether the aim is to build a company with high growth potential. Whether a team is *necessary* depends upon certain conditions:

- *The size and scope of the venture*: How many people does the venture require? Is it a one-person operation or does it need contributions from others? Can people be hired to fill the key roles as they are required?
- *Personal competencies*: What are the talents, know-how, skills, track record, contacts, and resources that the entrepreneur brings to the venture? How do these match up with what the venture needs to succeed? If gaps are identified, the entrepreneur needs to decide what competencies are needed to complement his or hers and when they are needed.

The nature of the team depends upon the match-up between the lead entrepreneur and the opportunity and how fast and aggressively he or she plans to proceed. Most teams tend to be formed in one of two ways: (a) one person has an idea (or wants to start a business), and then several associates join the team over the first few years of the venture's operation; or (b) an entire team is formed at the outset based on such factors as a shared idea, a friendship, or an experience.

The ideal team consists of people with complementary skills covering the key success areas for the business (for example, marketing, finance, production). Small founding teams tend to work better than big ones. It is quite common for the initial team to consist of just two people—a craftsperson and a salesperson.

If the entrepreneur does not intend to establish a high-growth venture, going solo may be a realistic option. Some new venture founders bring on additional team members only as the business can afford them. Most successful solo businesses are simple types of ventures, such as small retail stores or services.[49] The odds for survival, growth, profitability, and attracting capital are increased by a team approach.[50]

Assessing the "Fit" Between Elements in the Entrepreneurial Process

Assessing the "fit" between the key elements in the entrepreneurial process is an ongoing task, since the shape of the opportunity, and consequently the resources and people needed to capitalize on it, typically changes as the opportunity is developed. It is the entrepreneur who stands to gain the most by attending to these "fits" and any changes they may require, although other stakeholders, such as investors, will be considering them as well.

The Entrepreneur–Opportunity Fit

The entrepreneur needs to decide whether the opportunity, as identified, is something he or she *can do* and *wants to do*. A realistic self-assessment is important. Prospective ventures that are of limited personal interest and that require skills and abilities that do not fit well with those of the entrepreneur should be quickly eliminated. For example, it does little good to identify an opportunity for an ecotourism business in a wilderness area if the entrepreneur is a sedentary urban dweller.

Once the entrepreneur has chosen the opportunity he or she wants to pursue, the success of the venture depends heavily upon the individual or individuals involved. No matter how good the product or service concept is, as the opportunity changes shape, it may demand skills a single entrepreneur lacks. This may prompt a decision to acquire the needed skills either by forming a team or by getting further training.

The Opportunity–Resources Fit

Assessing the opportunity-resources fit involves determining whether the resources needed to capitalize on the opportunity can be acquired. As the opportunity changes shape, so too will the resource requirements. When challenges or risks arise, the aim is to determine whether they can be resolved and, if so, to deal with them as quickly as possible. For example, if the venture requires a greater financial investment than originally anticipated, this does not necessarily mean that the venture should be abandoned. Other options, such as taking on partners or leasing rather than building a facility, may be viable. Of course, some ventures may not be viable regardless of the alternatives considered.

The Entrepreneur–Resources Fit

Once the resource requirements of the venture have been determined, the entrepreneur needs to assess whether he or she has the capacity to meet those requirements. For example, an entrepreneur with a stellar reputation for software development will have an easier time attracting employees for a venture specializing in software development than someone with no track record. If that same entrepreneur is well connected with people in the industry, he or she will be more likely to gain commitments from customers and, in turn, investors.

After the Start-Up

Entrepreneurs must make the right decisions as they work toward the start-up of their new venture, but they must also pay attention to how the business will be run beyond the start-up phase. In this section, we examine three important topics that are relevant to these issues. First, we describe the three main ways that entrepreneurs start up a small business. Next, we look at the four main organizing options that are available to entrepreneurs. We conclude the chapter with a look at the reasons for success and failure in small business.

Starting Up a Small Business

4 Describe three alternative strategies for becoming a business owner—*starting a business, buying an existing business*, and *buying a franchise*.

In the previous section, we looked in detail at how entrepreneurs start a business from scratch. But there are two additional ways that entrepreneurs can go into business: buy an already-existing business or buy a franchise.

Buying an Already Existing Business

About one-third of all new businesses that were started in the past decade were bought from someone else. Many experts recommend buying an existing business because the odds of success are better. An existing business has already proven its ability to attract customers. It has also established relationships with lenders, suppliers, and other stakeholders. Moreover, an existing track record gives potential buyers a much clearer picture of what to expect than any estimate of a new business's prospects.

But an entrepreneur who buys someone else's business may not be able to avoid certain problems. For example, the business may have a poor reputation, its location may be poor, it may be difficult to determine an appropriate purchase price, and there may be uncertainty about the exact financial shape the business is in.

Taking Over a Family Business. A special case of buying an existing business involves family businesses. Taking over a family business poses both challenges and opportunities. On the positive side, a family business can provide otherwise unobtainable financial and management resources because of the personal sacrifices of family members. Family businesses often have a strong reputation or goodwill that can result in important community and business relationships. As well, employee loyalty is often high, and an interested, unified family management and shareholders group may emerge. Toronto-based hosiery manufacturer Phantom Industries Inc. is an example of a family-owned business that has been successful through three generations of family members.[51]

On the other hand, major problems can arise in family businesses (see the Opening Case for examples). There may be disagreements over which family members assume control. If the parent sells his or her interest in the business, the price to be paid may be an issue. The expectation of other family members may also be problematic. Some family members may feel that they have a right to a job, promotion, and impressive title simply because they are part of the family.[52] Two other problem areas are choosing an appropriate successor and handling disagreements among family members about the future of the business.

Buying a Franchise

If you drive or walk around any Canadian town, you will notice retail outlets with names like McDonald's, Pizza Pizza, Swiss Chalet, Yogen Früz, 7-Eleven, RE/MAX, Comfort Inn, Blockbuster Video, Sylvan Learning Centre, and Super Lube. What do all these businesses have in common? They are all franchises, operating under licences issued by parent companies to local entrepreneurs who own and manage them.

Franchising became very visible in the 1950s with fast-food franchisers like McDonald's, but it actually started in the early 1800s. In the late 1800s, General Motors began franchising retail dealerships, and similar systems were created by Rexall (pharmacies) in 1902 and by Howard Johnson (restaurants and motels) in 1926. Franchising continues to increase in importance in the twenty-first century. Depending on how it is defined, franchising now accounts for 43 percent of retail sales in Canada. There are thousands of franchise establishments in Canada, and they generate approximately $30 billion in annual sales revenue.[53]

franchising agreement Outlines the duties and responsibilities of the franchiser and the franchisee.

A franchise is an arrangement that gives franchisees (buyers) the right to sell the product of the franchiser (the seller). A **franchising agreement** outlines the duties and responsibilities of each party. For example, it stipulates the amount and type of payment that franchisees must make to the franchiser. Franchisees usually make an initial payment for the right to operate a local outlet of the franchise; they also make royalty payments to the franchiser ranging from 2 to 30 percent of the franchisee's annual revenues or profits. The franchisee

Franchising is very popular in Canada. It offers individuals who want to run their own business an opportunity to establish themselves quickly in a local market.

also pays an advertising fee so that the franchiser can advertise in the franchisee's local area. Franchise fees vary widely: $30 000 for a Fantastic Sam's hair salon, to $1 million for a Burger King franchise, to hundreds of millions for a professional sports franchise.

The Advantages of Franchising. Both franchisers and franchisees benefit from the franchising way of doing business (see Table 4.4).

Is Franchising for You? Do you think you would be happy being a franchisee? The answer depends on a number of factors, including your willingness to work hard, your ability to find a good franchise to buy, and the financial resources you possess. If you are thinking seriously of going into franchising, you should consider several areas of costs that you will incur:

- the franchise sales price
- expenses that will be incurred before the business opens
- training expenses
- operational expenses for the first six months
- personal financial needs for the first six months
- emergency needs

Forms of Business Ownership

Describe four forms of *legal organization* for a business and discuss the advantages and disadvantages of each. **5**

Whether they intend to run a small farm, a large factory, an online retail business, a hair salon, or any one of many other types of business, entrepreneurs must decide which form of legal ownership best suits their needs. Four options are available: the sole proprietorship, the partnership, the corporation, and the co-operative.

The Sole Proprietorship

sole proprietorship A business owned and operated by one person.

The **sole proprietorship** is a business owned and operated by one person. Legally, if you set up a business as a sole proprietorship, your business is

Table 4.4 The Benefits of Franchising

For the Franchiser	For the Franchisee
■ The franchiser can attain rapid growth for the chain by signing up many franchisees in many diffeent locations. ■ Franchisees share in the cost of advertising. ■ The franchiser benefits from the investment money provided by franchisees. ■ Advertising money is spent more efficiently (the franchiser teams up with local franchisees to advertise only in the local area). ■ The franchiser benefits because franchisees are motivated to work hard for themselves; the more revenue the franchisee generates, the more money the franchiser makes. ■ The franchiser is freed from all details of a local operation, which are handled by the franchisee.	■ Franchisees own a small business that has access to big business management skills. ■ The franchisee does not have to build up a business from scratch. ■ Franchisee failure rates are lower than are rates for those who start their own business. ■ A well-advertised brand name comes with the franchise and the franchisee's outlet is recognizable because it looks like all other outlets in the chain. ■ The franchiser may send the franchisee to a training program run by the franchiser (e.g., the Canadian Institute of Hamburgerology run by McDonald's). ■ The franchiser may visit the franchisee and provide expert advice on how to run the business. ■ Economies in buying allow franchisees to get lower prices for the raw materials they must purchase. ■ Financial assistance is provided by the franchiser in the form of loans; the franchiser may also help the franchisee obtain loans from local sources. ■ Franchisees are their own bosses and get to keep most of the profit they make.

considered to be an extension of yourself (and not a separate legal entity). Though usually small, a sole proprietorship may be as large as a steel mill or as small as a lemonade stand. While the majority of businesses in Canada are sole proprietorships, this form of ownership accounts for only a small proportion of total business revenues.

Advantages of a Sole Proprietorship

Freedom may be the most important benefit of a sole proprietorship. Sole proprietors answer to no one but themselves since they don't share ownership. A sole proprietorship is also easy to form. If you operate the business under your own name, with no additions, you don't even need to register your business name to start operating as a sole proprietor; you can go into business simply by putting a sign on the door. The simplicity of legal set-up procedures makes this form appealing to self-starters and independent spirits, as do low start-up costs.

Another attractive feature is tax benefits. Most businesses suffer losses in their early stages. Since the business and the proprietor are legally one and the same, these losses can be deducted from income the proprietor earns from personal sources other than the business.

Disadvantages of a Sole Proprietorship

unlimited liability A sole proprietor is personally liable (responsible) for all debts incurred by the business.

A major drawback is **unlimited liability**. A sole proprietor is personally liable (responsible) for all debts incurred by the business. If the business fails to generate enough cash, bills must be paid out of the owner's pocket. Another disadvantage is the lack of continuity; a sole proprietorship legally dissolves when the owner dies. Finally, a sole proprietorship depends on the resources of one person, and that person's managerial and financial limitations may constrain the business. Sole proprietors often find it hard to borrow money to start up or expand. Many bankers fear that they won't be able to recover loans if the owner becomes disabled.

The Partnership

The **partnership**, a form of organization often used by professionals like accountants and lawyers, is established when two or more individuals (partners) agree to combine their financial, managerial, and technical abilities for the purpose of operating a business for profit. Partnerships are often an extension of a business that began as a sole proprietorship. The original owner may want to expand, or the business may have grown too big for a single person to handle.

There are two basic types of partners in a partnership. **General partners** are actively involved in managing the firm and have unlimited liability. **Limited partners** don't participate actively in the business, and their liability is limited to the amount they invested in the partnership. A **general partnership** is the most common type of partnership and is similar in nature to the sole proprietorship in that all the (general) partners are jointly liable for the obligations of the business. The other type of partnership—a **limited partnership**—consists of at least one general partner (who has unlimited liability) and one or more limited partners (who have limited liability). The limited partners cannot participate in the day-to-day management of the business or they risk the loss of their limited liability status.

partnership A form of organization established when two or more individuals (partners) agree to combine their financial, managerial, and technical abilities for the purpose of operating a business for profit.

general partners Partners who are actively involved in managing the firm and have unlimited liability.

limited partners Partners who generally do not participate actively in the business, and whose liability is limited to the amount they invested in the partnership.

general partnership A type of partnership where all partners are jointly liable for the obligations of the business.

limited partnership A type of partnership with at least one general partner (who has unlimited liability) and one or more limited partners. The limited partners cannot participate in the day-to-day management of the business or they risk the loss of their limited liability status.

Advantages of a Partnership

The most striking advantage of a general partnership is the ability to grow by adding talent and money. Partnerships also have a somewhat easier time borrowing funds than do sole proprietorships because banks and other lending institutions prefer to make loans to enterprises that are not dependent on a single individual. Partnerships can also invite new partners to join if they agree to invest money in the firm.

Like a sole proprietorship, a partnership is simple to organize, with few legal requirements. Even so, all partnerships must begin with an agreement of some kind. It may be written, oral, or even unspoken. Wise partners, however, insist on a written agreement to avoid trouble later. This agreement should answer several questions:

- How will disagreements be resolved?
- Who invested what sums of money in the partnership?
- Who will receive what share of the partnership's profits?
- Who does what and who reports to whom?
- How will the partnership be dissolved?
- How will leftover assets be distributed among the partners?

The partnership agreement is strictly a private document. Partners are not required by law to file an agreement with some government agency, and partnerships are not regarded as legal entities. In the eyes of the law, a partnership is nothing more than two or more persons working together. The partnership's lack of legal standing means that the partners are taxed as individuals.

Disadvantages of a Partnership

As with sole proprietorships, unlimited liability is the greatest drawback of a general partnership. By law, each general partner may be held personally liable for all debts incurred in the name of the partnership. And if any partner incurs a debt, even if the other partners know nothing about it, they are all liable if the offending partner cannot pay up. Another problem with partnerships is lack of continuity. When one partner dies or pulls out, the partnership dissolves, even if the other partners agree to stay to continue the business.

A related drawback is the difficulty of transferring ownership. No partner may sell out without the other partners' consent. Thus, the life of a partnership may depend on the ability of retiring partners to find someone compatible with the other partners to buy them out. Finally, a partnership provides little or no guidance in resolving conflict between the partners. For example, suppose one partner wants to expand the business rapidly and the other wants it to grow slowly. If under the partnership agreement the two are equal, it may be difficult for them to decide what to do.

The Corporation

When you think of corporations you probably think of giant businesses such as Air Canada, Imperial Oil, or CN. The very word *corporation* suggests bigness and power. Yet, the tiny corner newsstand has as much right to incorporate as does a giant oil refiner. And the newsstand and oil refiner have the same basic characteristics that all corporations share: legal status as a separate entity, property rights and obligations, and an indefinite lifespan. The Top 10 corporations in Canada are listed in Table 4.5.

corporation A business that is a separate legal entity that is liable for its own debts and whose owners' liability is limited to their investment.

A **corporation** has been defined as "an artificial being, invisible, intangible, and existing only in contemplation of the law."[54] As such, corporations may sue and be sued; buy, hold, and sell property; make and sell products to consumers; and commit crimes and be tried and punished for them. Simply defined, a corporation is a business that is a separate legal entity that is liable for its own debts and whose owners' liability is limited to their investment.

stockholders Investors who buy shares of ownership in the form of stock.

Stockholders—investors who buy shares of ownership in the form of stock—are the real owners of the corporation (the different kinds of stockholders are described in Chapter 19). Profits may be distributed to stockholders in the form of dividends, although corporations are not required to pay dividends. Instead, they often reinvest any profits in the business.

board of directors The governing body of a corporation whose basic responsibility is to ensure that the corporation is run in a way that is in the best interests of the shareholders.

The **board of directors** is the governing body of a corporation. Its basic responsibility is to ensure that the corporation is run in a way that is in the best interests of the stockholders. The board chooses the president and other officers of the business and delegates the power to run the day-to-day activities of the business to those officers. The board sets policy on paying dividends, on financing major spending, and on executive salaries and benefits. Large corporations tend to have large boards with as many as 20 or 30 directors. Smaller corporations, on the other hand, tend to have no more than 5 directors.

Each year, the *Globe and Mail* analyzes the governance practices of Canadian companies in four areas: board composition, compensation, shareholder rights,

Table 4.5 Top 10 Corporations in Canada, 2008 (ranked by sales revenues)

Company	Sales Revenues (in billions of dollars)
1. Royal Bank of Canada	$37.5
2. Power Corp. of Canada	37.0
3. Manulife Financial Corp.	33.0
4. George Weston Ltd.	32.0
5. EnCana Corp.	32.0
6. Imperial Oil Ltd.	31.2
7. Suncor Energy Inc.	29.0
8. Petro-Canada	27.5
9. Onex Corp.	26.8
10. The Bank of Nova Scotia	26.6

and disclosure. The top-ranked companies in 2008 were Gildan Activewear Inc., Potash Corporation of Saskatchewan, and Manulife Financial Corp. The lowest-ranked companies were TriStar Oil & Gas Ltd., ACE Aviation Holdings Inc., and Galleon Energy Inc.[55]

Inside directors are employees of the company and have primary responsibility for the corporation. That is, they are also top managers, such as the president and executive vice-president. **Outside directors** are not employees of the corporation in the normal course of its business. Attorneys, accountants, university officials, and executives from other firms are commonly used as outside directors.

inside directors Members of a corporation's board of directors who are employees of the company and have primary responsibility for the corporation.

outside directors Members of a corporation's board of directors who are not also employees of the corporation on a day-to-day basis.

Corporate officers are the top managers hired by the board to run the corporation on a day-to-day basis. The **chief executive officer (CEO)** is responsible for the firm's overall performance. Other corporate officers typically include the president, who is responsible for internal management, and various vice-presidents, who oversee functional areas such as marketing or operations.

chief executive officer (CEO) The person responsible for the firm's overall performance.

Types of Corporations

There are two types of private sector corporations (corporations can also be found in the municipal, provincial, federal, and nonprofit sectors). The **public corporation** is a business whose shares of stock are widely held and available for sale to the general public. The shares of public corporations like George Weston, Air Canada, and Canadian Pacific are traded on securities exchanges and are widely available to the general public for purchase (see Chapter 19). By contrast, the shares of stock of a **private corporation** are held by only a few shareholders, are not widely available for purchase, and may have restrictions on their sale. For example, Kroeker Farms, a large agri-business in Manitoba, is owned by nine members of one family. Other private corporations are Para Paints of Canada and Bata Shoes. Most corporations are privately held.

public corporation A business whose shares of stock are widely held and available for sale to the general public.

private corporation A business whose shares of stock are held by only a few shareholders, are not widely available for purchase, and may have restrictions on their sale.

Most new corporations start out as private corporations, because few investors will buy an unknown stock. As the corporation grows and develops a record of success, it may issue shares to the public ("go public") as a way of raising additional money. This is called its **initial public offering (IPO)**. MasterCard went public in 2006 and Visa did the same in 2008. IPOs are not very attractive to investors during stock market declines, but they become more popular when stock markets recover. Globally, there were 1449 IPOs in 2007, and they raised $285 billion.[56]

initial public offering (IPO) The sale of shares of stock in a company for the first time to the general investing public.

A public corporation can also "go private," which is the reverse of going public. In 2008, Clearwater Seafoods Income Fund announced that it would be taken private by a consortium led by Clearwater Fine Foods.[57]

During the period from 2000 to 2005, many corporations converted to an **income trust** structure, which allowed them to avoid paying corporate income tax if they distributed all or most of their earnings to investors. For example, Bell Canada Enterprises could have avoided an $800-million tax bill in one year by becoming an income trust. The federal government estimated that it was going to lose billions of dollars of tax revenue because so many corporations were becoming income trusts. In a surprise move in 2006, the Canadian government announced that it would begin taxing income trusts more like corporations by 2011. This announcement caused a significant decline in the market value of income trusts, and it also means that very few corporations will now convert to an income trust structure.[58]

income trust Involves corporations distributing all or most of their earnings to investors and thereby reducing the corporation's income tax liability.

Formation of the Corporation

The two most widely used methods to form a corporation are federal incorporation under the Canada Business Corporations Act and provincial incorporation under any of the provincial corporations acts. The former is used if the company is going to operate in more than one province; the latter is used if the founders intend to carry on business in only one province. Except for banks and certain insurance and loan companies, any company can be federally incorporated under the Canada Business Corporations Act. To do so, it must draw up articles of incorporation. These articles include such information as the name of the corporation, the type and number of shares to be issued, the number of directors the corporation will have, and the location of the company's operations. The specific procedures and information required for provincial incorporation vary from province to province.

All corporations must attach the word *Limited* (Ltd./Ltée), *Incorporated* (Inc.), or *Corporation* (Corp.) to the company name to indicate clearly to customers and suppliers that the owners have limited liability for corporate debts. The same sorts of rules apply in other countries. British firms, for example, use PLC for "public limited company" and German companies use AG for "Aktiengesellschaft" (corporation).

Advantages of Incorporation

limited liability The liability of investors is limited to their personal investment in the corporation.

The biggest advantage of the corporate structure is **limited liability**, which means that the liability of investors is limited to their personal investment in the corporation. In the event of failure, the courts may seize a corporation's assets and sell them to pay debts, but the courts cannot touch the investors' personal possessions. If, for example, you invest $1000 in a corporation that goes bankrupt, you may lose your $1000 but no more. In other words, your liability is limited to $1000.

Another advantage of a corporation is continuity. Because it has a legal life independent of its founders and owners, a corporation can, in theory, continue forever. Shares of stock may be sold or passed on to heirs, and most corporations also benefit from the continuity provided by professional management. Finally, corporations have advantages in raising money. By selling shares of stock, they expand the number of investors and the amount of available funds. The term **stock** refers to a share of ownership in a corporation. Continuity and legal status tend to make lenders more willing to grant loans to corporations.

stock A share of ownership in a corporation.

Disadvantages of Incorporation

One of the disadvantages for a new firm in forming a corporation is the cost (approximately $2500). Corporations also need legal help in meeting government regulations because they are far more heavily regulated than are proprietorships or partnerships. Some people say that **double taxation** is another problem with the corporate form of ownership. By this they mean that a corporation must pay corporate income taxes on its profits, and then shareholders must also pay personal income taxes on the dividends they receive from the corporation. The **dividend** a corporation pays is the amount of money, normally a portion of the profits, which is distributed to the shareholders. Since dividends paid by the corporation are not tax deductible for the corporation, this amounts to double taxation. Others point out that shareholders get a "dividend tax credit," which largely offsets the effect of double taxation.

double taxation A corporation must pay corporate income taxes on its profits, and then shareholders must also pay personal income taxes on the dividends they receive from the corporation.

dividend The amount of money, normally a portion of the profits, which is distributed to the shareholders by the corporation.

The Co-operative

co-operative An incorporated form of business that is organized, owned, and democratically controlled by the people who use its products and services, and whose earnings are distributed on the basis of their use of the co-operative rather than their level of investment.

A **co-operative** is an incorporated form of business that is organized, owned, and democratically controlled by the people who use its products and services, and whose earnings are distributed on the basis of their use of the co-operative rather than their level of investment. As such, it is formed to benefit its owners in the form of reduced prices and/or the distribution of surpluses at year-end. The process works like this: Suppose some farmers believe they can get cheaper fertilizer prices if they form their own company and purchase in large volumes. They might then form a co-operative, which can be either federally or provincially chartered. Prices are generally lower to buyers and, at the end of the fiscal year, any surpluses are distributed to members on the basis of how much they purchased. If Farmer Jones bought 5 percent of all co-op sales, he would receive 5 percent of the surplus.

The co-operative's start-up capital usually comes from shares purchased by the co-operative's members. Sometimes all it takes to qualify for membership in a co-operative is the purchase of one share with a fixed (and often nominal) value. Federal co-operatives, however, can raise capital by issuing investment shares to members or non-members. Co-operatives, like investor-owned corporations, have directors and appointed officers. In a co-operative, each member is entitled to one vote, regardless of how many shares he or she owns.

Types of Co-operatives

There are hundreds of different co-operatives, but they generally function in one of six main areas of business:

- *Consumer co-operatives*. These organizations sell goods to both members and the general public (e.g., co-op gasoline stations, agricultural implement dealers).
- *Financial co-operatives*. These organizations operate much like banks, accepting deposits from members, giving loans, and providing chequing services (e.g., credit unions).
- *Insurance co-operatives.* These organizations provide many types of insurance coverage, such as life, fire, and liability (for example, the Co-operative Hail Insurance Company of Manitoba).
- *Marketing co-operatives.* These organizations sell the produce of their farm members and purchase inputs for the production process (e.g., seed and fertilizer). Some, like Federated Co-operatives, also purchase and market finished products.
- *Service co-operatives.* These organizations provide members with services, such as recreation.
- *Housing co-operatives.* These organizations provide housing for members who purchase a share in the co-operative, which holds the title to the housing complex.

In terms of numbers, co-operatives are the least important form of ownership. However, they are of significance to society and to their members since they may provide services that are not readily available or that cost more than the members would otherwise be willing to pay. Table 4.6 compares the various forms of business ownership using different characteristics.

Advantages of a Co-operative

Co-operatives have many of the same advantages of investor-owned corporations, such as limited liability of owners and continuity. A key benefit of a co-operative relates to its structure. As noted above, each member has only one vote in the affairs of the co-operative, regardless of how many shares he or she holds. This system prevents voting and financial control of the business by a few wealthy individuals. This is particularly attractive to the less-wealthy members of the co-operative.

Vancouver-based Mountain Equipment Co-op is one of the best-known co-operatives in Canada.

Unlike corporations, which are not allowed a tax deduction on dividend payments made to shareholders, co-operatives are allowed

Table 4.6 A Comparison of Four Forms of Business Ownership

Characteristic	Sole Proprietorship	Partnership	Corporation	Co-operative
Protection against liability for bad debts	low	low	high	high
Ease of formation	high	high	medium	medium
Permanence	low	low	high	high
Ease of ownership transfer	low	low	high	high
Ease of raising money	low	medium	high	high
Freedom from regulation	high	high	low	medium
Tax advantages	high	high	low	high

to deduct patronage refunds to members out of before-tax income. Thus, income may only be taxed at the individual member level rather than at both the co-operative and member level.[59]

Disadvantages of a Co-operative

One of the main disadvantages of co-operatives relates to attracting equity investment. Since the benefits from being a member of a co-operative arise through the level of use of the co-operative rather than the level of equity invested, members do not have an incentive to invest in equity capital of the co-operative. Another drawback is that democratic voting arrangements and dividends based purely on patronage turn off some entrepreneurs from forming or joining a co-operative.

Success and Failure in Small Business

6 Identify four key reasons for success in small businesses and four key reasons for failure.

Of every 100 small businesses that begin operation, 96 will still be operating after one year, 85 after three years, and 67 after five years.[60] A study conducted by CIBC World Markets found that small businesses with above-average revenue growth were run by owners who had more education, used professional advisers, adopted the corporate form of ownership, did outsourcing work for other companies, had a high level of internet connectivity, and used the internet to sell outside of Canada.[61]

Reasons for Success

In addition to the specific findings of the CIBC study, four general factors typically explain the success of small business owners:

1. *Hard work, drive, and dedication.* Small business owners must be committed to succeeding and be willing to put in the time and effort to make it happen. Long hours and few vacations generally characterize the first few years of new business ownership.
2. *Market demand for the product or service.* Careful analysis of market conditions can help small business owners assess the probable reception of their products. If the area around a college has only one pizza parlour, a new pizzeria is more likely to succeed than if there are already 10 in operation.
3. *Managerial competence.* Successful small business people have a solid understanding of how to manage a business. They may acquire competence through training (taking courses), experience, or by using the expertise of

others. Few, however, succeed alone or straight out of university or college. Most spend time in successful companies or partner with others to bring expertise to a new business.

4. *Luck.* Luck also plays a role in the success of some firms. For example, after one entrepreneur started an environmental clean-up firm, he struggled to keep his business afloat. Then the government committed a large sum of money for toxic waste clean-up. He was able to get several large contracts, and his business is now thriving.

Reasons for Failure

Small businesses collapse for a number of reasons (see Table 4.7). Entrepreneurs may have no control over some of these factors (for example, weather, fraud, accidents), but they can influence most items on the list. Four general factors are particularly important:

1. *Managerial incompetence or inexperience.* Some entrepreneurs put their faith in common sense, overestimate their own managerial skills, or believe that hard work alone ensures success. If entrepreneurs don't know how to make basic business decisions or don't understand basic management principles, they aren't likely to succeed in the long run.
2. *Neglect.* Some entrepreneurs try to launch ventures in their spare time, and others devote only limited time to their new business. But starting a small business demands an overwhelming time commitment. If you aren't willing to put in the time and effort that a business requires, you aren't likely to survive.
3. *Weak control systems.* Effective control systems keep a business on track and alert owners to potential trouble. If your control systems don't signal impending problems, you may be in serious trouble before you spot more obvious difficulties.

Table 4.7 Causes of Small Business Failure

Poor management skills ■ poor delegation and organizational ability ■ lack of depth in management team ■ entrepreneurial incompetence, such as a poor understanding of finances and business markets ■ lack of experience	**Personal reasons** ■ loss of interest in business ■ accident, illness ■ death ■ family problems
Inadequate marketing capabilities ■ difficulty in marketing product ■ market too small, non-existent, or declining ■ too much competition ■ problems with distribution systems	**Disasters** ■ fire ■ weather ■ strikes ■ fraud by entrepreneur or others
Inadequate financial capabilities ■ weak skills in accounting and finance ■ lack of budgetary control ■ inadequate costing systems ■ incorrect valuation of assets ■ unable to obtain financial backing	**Other** ■ mishandling of large project ■ excessive standard of living ■ lack of time to devote to business ■ difficulties with associates or partners ■ government policies change
Inadequate production capabilities ■ poorly designed production systems ■ old and inefficient production facilities and equipment ■ inadequate control over quality ■ problems with inventory control	

4. *Insufficient capital.* Some entrepreneurs are overly optimistic about how soon they'll start earning profits. In most cases, it takes months or even years. Amazon.com didn't earn a profit for 10 years but obviously still required capital to pay employees and to cover other expenses. Experts say you need enough capital to operate at least six months without earning a profit; some recommend enough to last a year.[62]

Test yourself on the material for this chapter at **www.pearsoned.ca/mybusinesslab**.

Summary of Learning Objectives

1. **Explain the meaning of and interrelationship among the terms *small business, new venture creation,* and *entrepreneurship.*** A *small business* has fewer than 100 employees. A *new venture* is one that has become operational within the previous 12 months, has adopted any of four main organizational forms—sole proprietorship, partnership, corporation, or co-operative—and sells goods or services. *Entrepreneurship* is the process of identifying an opportunity in the marketplace and accessing the resources needed to capitalize on it. In relation to small and/or new businesses, entrepreneurship is the process by which a small business or a new business is created.

2. **Describe the role of small and new businesses in the Canadian economy.** New firms create the most jobs, are noted for their entrepreneurship, and are typically small. The small business sector's capacity for entrepreneurship and innovation accounts for much of the job creation this sector contributes to the economy, with start-ups accounting for most of the growth. As the number of businesses has increased, so too has the number of firms led by women. About 98 percent of employer businesses in Canada are small (they have fewer than 100 employees), and the majority of those have fewer than 5 employees. The distribution of employment by size of firm varies considerably across industries. Small businesses account for over two-thirds of employment in four industries: non-institutional health care, construction, other services, and accommodation and food. In another five industries, at least half of the workforce is employed by small businesses.

3. **Explain the *entrepreneurial process* and describe its three key elements.** The *entrepreneurial process* occurs within a social, political, and economic context and consists of three key elements: the entrepreneur, the opportunity, and resources. The *entrepreneur* is the driving force in identifying an opportunity and accessing the resources to capitalize on it. Opportunities don't simply materialize; entrepreneurs create them. *Opportunity* identification involves generating ideas, screening them to determine their potential, and developing the ones that remain. Entrepreneurs typically access the various *resources* needed by *bootstrapping*—doing more with less. These resources are both financial and non-financial. Two types of financing—debt and equity—can be accessed from a range of sources.

4. **Describe three alternative strategies for becoming a business owner—*starting a business, buying an existing business,* and *buying a franchise.*** It is necessary to work through the entrepreneurial process when *starting a business* from scratch. Whether start-up efforts will result in a new business often depends upon how well matched the entrepreneur's skills and abilities are with the opportunity and the resources required, as well as how well matched the opportunity and resources are. Of the ventures that are brought to fruition, some will grow, while others will decline, die, or remain stable.

   Generally, when *buying an existing business*, the odds of success are better. An existing business has already proven its ability to attract customers. It has also established relationships with lenders, suppliers, and other stakeholders. Moreover, an existing track record gives potential buyers a much clearer picture of what to expect than any estimate of a new business's prospects. On the other hand, there may be uncertainty about the exact financial shape the business is in, the business may have a poor reputation, the location may be poor, or it may be difficult to determine an appropriate purchase price. A special case of buying an existing business involves family businesses, which pose both opportunities and challenges.

In *buying a franchise*, the buyer (franchisee) purchases the right to sell the product or service of the seller (franchiser) according to the terms of the franchising agreement. In return the franchiser provides assistance with the business's start-up as well as with ongoing operations once the business opens its doors.

5. Describe four forms of *legal organization* for a business and discuss the advantages and disadvantages of each. A *sole proprietorship* is a business owned and operated by one person. Answering only to themselves, sole proprietors enjoy considerable freedom in running the business. The ease of setting up a sole proprietorship makes it appealing to self-starters, as do the low start-up costs and the tax benefits. A major drawback is unlimited liability. A sole proprietor is personally liable for all debts incurred by the business. Another disadvantage is lack of continuity. A sole proprietorship dissolves when the owner dies. Finally, a sole proprietorship depends on the resources of a single individual.

A *general partnership* is similar to a sole proprietorship in that all partners have unlimited liability for the obligations of the business. The biggest advantage is its ability to grow by adding new talent and money. Because banks prefer to make loans to enterprises that are not dependent on single individuals, it's easier for partnerships to borrow money. They can also invite new partners to join by investing. Although a partnership is easy to form and has few legal requirements, all partnerships should have a partnership agreement. Partners are taxed as individuals, and unlimited liability is a drawback. Each partner may be liable for all partnership debts. Partnerships may lack continuity, and transferring ownership may be hard. No partner may sell out without the consent of the others.

All *corporations* share certain characteristics. They are separate legal entities, they have property rights and obligations, and they have indefinite lifespans. They may sue and be sued; buy, hold, and sell property; make and sell products; and be tried and punished for crimes committed. The biggest advantage of incorporation is limited liability; that is, investor liability is limited to one's personal investments in the corporation. If the business fails, the courts may sell a corporation's assets but cannot touch the personal possessions of investors. Another advantage is continuity—a corporation can continue forever. Shares can be sold or passed on to heirs, and most corporations benefit from the continuity of professional management. Finally, corporations have advantages in raising money. By selling stock, they expand the number of investors and the amount of available funds. Legal protections tend to make lenders more willing to grant loans. Start-up costs and complexity are among the disadvantages of incorporating. Corporations are heavily regulated and must meet complex legal requirements in the provinces in which they're chartered. A potential drawback to incorporation is *double taxation*. A corporation pays income taxes on company profits, and its stockholders pay taxes on income returned by their investments. Thus, corporate profits are taxed twice—at the corporate and at ownership levels (but the dividend tax credit given to owners may offset the effects of double taxation). Of the two types of private sector corporations—public and privately held—the vast majority are privately held. In forming a corporation, a business will incorporate federally if it is going to operate in more than one province and provincially if it is going to operate in only one province.

A *co-operative* is an organization that is formed to benefit its owners in the form of reduced prices and/or the distribution of surpluses at year-end. It is an incorporated business that is organized, owned, and democratically controlled by the people who use its products and services. The distribution of its earnings (or surpluses) is based upon the use of the co-operative rather than the level of investment. In addition to the two main advantages co-operatives share with corporations—limited liability and continuity—they also have two benefits that corporations don't have. Since all members have one vote, this democratic control means that a few people cannot dominate the decision making. Additionally, co-operatives aren't subject to double taxation, since surpluses are distributed to members from pre-tax profits. Co-operatives are not without disadvantages. The main drawback is that co-operatives often have difficulty raising equity, since members gain financial benefit according to their use of the co-operative, not according to the amount they have invested. While there are hundreds of different co-operatives, they usually function in one of six areas of business: consumer co-operatives, financial co-operatives, insurance co-operatives, marketing co-operatives, service co-operatives, or housing co-operatives.

6. Identify four key reasons for success in small businesses and four key reasons for failure. Four basic factors explain most small business success: (1) hard work, drive, and dedication; (2) market demand for the product or service; (3) managerial competence; and (4) luck. Four factors contribute to small business failure: (1) managerial incompetence or inexperience; (2) neglect; (3) weak control systems; and (4) insufficient capital.

Key Terms

board of directors (p. 126)
bootstrapping (p. 117)
business plan (p. 116)
chief executive officer (CEO) (p. 127)
collateral (p. 118)
co-operative (p. 128)
corporation (p. 126)
dividend (p. 128)
double taxation (p. 128)
entrepreneur (p. 108)
entrepreneurship (p. 108)
exit costs (p. 116)
franchise (p. 116)
franchising agreement (p. 122)
general partners (p. 125)
general partnership (p. 125)
income trust (p. 127)
initial public offering (IPO) (p. 127)
inside directors (p. 127)
intrapreneuring (p.109)
limited liability (p. 128)
limited partners (p. 125)
limited partnership (p. 125)
new venture/firm (p. 108)
outside directors (p. 127)
partnership (p. 125)
private corporation (p. 127)
public corporation (p. 127)
sales forecast (p. 115)
small business (p. 107)
sole proprietorship (p. 123)
stock (p. 128)
stockholders (p. 126)
unlimited liability (p. 124)

Questions for Analysis

1. What are some of the problems that are encountered when we try to define the term *small business*?
2. Why are new ventures the main source of job creation and new product/service ideas?
3. Do you think that you would be a successful entrepreneur? Why or why not?
4. Consider a new product or service that has recently become available for purchase by consumers. To what extent did this product or service possess the "screening" characteristics that are described in the chapter (adding value, providing competitive advantage, etc.)?
5. Using the product or service you described in Question 4, analyze the extent to which there is a good "fit" between the various elements in the entrepreneurial process.
6. Why might a corporation choose to remain private? Why might it choose to "go public"?

Application Exercises

1. Identify two or three of the fastest-growing businesses in Canada. What role has entrepreneurship played in the growth of these firms?
2. Find a newspaper or magazine article that describes someone who is an entrepreneur. Use the information provided to explain what makes this person an entrepreneur.
3. Spend some time watching what people do and how they do it, and then (1) identify two ways to make what they do easier, and (2) describe two problems you observed and identify strategies for resolving those problems.
4. Interview the owner/manager of a sole proprietorship or general partnership. What characteristics of that business form led the owner to choose it? Does the owner ever contemplate changing the form of ownership of the business? Why or why not?

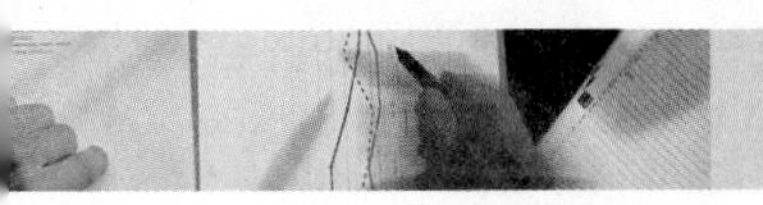

Building Your Business Skills

Working the Internet

The Purpose of the Assignment

To encourage students to define opportunities and problems for small companies doing business on the internet.

The Situation

Suppose you and two partners own a gift basket store, specializing in special occasion baskets for individual and corporate clients. Your business is doing well in your community, but you believe there may be opportunity for growth through a virtual storefront on the internet.

Assignment

Step 1

Join with two other students and assume the role of business partners. Start by researching internet businesses. Look at books and articles at the library and check the following websites for help:

- Canada Business—Services for Entrepreneurs: www.cbsc.org
- U.S. Small Business Administration: www.sba.gov
- IBM Small Business Center: www.businesscenter.ibm.com
- Apple Small Business Home Page: www.apple.com/business/

These sites may lead you to other sites, so keep an open mind.

Step 2

Based on your research, determine the importance of the following small business issues:

- an analysis of changing company finances as a result of expansion to the internet
- an analysis of your new competitive marketplace (the world) and how it affects your current marketing approach, which focusses on your local community
- identification of sources of management advice as the expansion proceeds
- the role of technology consultants in launching and maintaining the website
- customer service policies in your virtual environment

Questions for Discussion

1. Do you think your business would be successful on the internet? Why or why not?
2. Based on your analysis, how will internet expansion affect your current business practices? What specific changes are you likely to make?
3. Do you think that operating a virtual storefront will be harder or easier than doing business in your local community? Explain your answer.

Exercising Your Ethics: Team Exercise

Public or Private? That Is the Question

The Situation

The Thomas Corporation is a very well-financed private corporation with a solid and growing product line, little debt, and a stable workforce. However, in the past few months, there has been a growing rift among the board of directors that has created considerable differences of opinion as to the future directions of the firm.

The Dilemma

Some board members believe the firm should "go public" with a stock offering. Since each board member owns a large block of corporate stock, each would make a considerable amount of money if the company went public.

Other board members want to maintain the status quo as a private corporation. The biggest advantage of this approach is that the firm maintains its current ability to remain autonomous in its operations.

The third faction of the board also wants to remain private but clearly has a different agenda. Those board members have identified a small public corporation that is currently one of the company's key suppliers. Their idea is to buy the supplying company, shift its assets to the parent firm, sell all of its remaining operations, terminate employees, and then outsource the production of the parts it currently buys from the firm. Their logic is that the firm would gain significant assets and lower its costs.

Team Activity

Assemble a group of four students and assign each group member to one of the following roles:

- an employee at the Thomas Corporation
- a customer of the Thomas Corporation

- an investor in the Thomas Corporation
- a board member who has not yet decided which option is best

Action Steps

1. Before discussing the situation with your group, and from the perspective of your assigned role, which option do you think is best? Write down the reasons for your position.
2. Before discussing the situation with your group, and from the perspective of your assigned role, what are the underlying ethical issues, if any, in this situation? Write down the issues.
3. Gather your group together and reveal, in turn, each member's comments on the situation. Next, reveal the ethical issues listed by each member.
4. Appoint someone to record the main points of agreement and disagreement within the group. How do you explain the results? What accounts for any disagreement?
5. From an ethical standpoint, what does your group conclude is the most appropriate action that should be taken by the Thomas Corporation in this situation?
6. Develop a group response to the following question: What do you think most people would do in this situation?

For additional cases and exercise material, go to **www.pearsoned.ca/mybusinesslab**.

Concluding Case 4-1

Mompreneurs

A Vanier Institute survey revealed that 90 percent of Canadians think that, for two-parent families, the ideal situation is to have one parent stay at home as the primary caregiver. But families often need more income than can be earned by just one parent, so the parent who stays home is often under some pressure to also generate income. How can this be done? One answer is found in the increasing number of Canadian women who have decided to be stay-at-home entrepreneurs (called mompreneurs). They aren't trying to be supermoms who can do everything; rather, they want to use their skills to run a business and at the same time achieve a better work-life balance. Here are some of their interesting success stories.

ABZ for Me

When Tammy Levitt of Thornton, Ontario, learned her son had autism, she stopped working as a graphic artist so she could spend more time with him. Levitt then started an at-home business called ABZ for Me, a children's home decor business. Levitt says running such a business gives her the flexibility to set her own hours. It also allows her to take her son to 20 hours of therapy each week.

Spoon Fed Soup

Carmie Nearing of Calgary had a career as a chef, but when her children came along, the hours she needed to work didn't fit with raising children. She quit and got a 9-to-5 job. But that didn't satisfy her, so she decided to start her own company—called Spoon Fed Soup—to provide gourmet soups to customers. Nearing found that as her business grew, she had to hire employees and spend more and more time dealing with customers. She now realizes that she has a passion for entrepreneurship that goes beyond the simple desire to stay at home with her children.

The Enamoured Heart

When her daughter was born, Lori Bettig of Winnipeg gave up her job in publishing to become a full-time mom. But when a friend showed her a line of personalized "motherhood bracelets," Bettig saw an opportunity to start a home-based business. She set up a website and the business took off. In 2008, Bettig's business—The Enamoured Heart—was nominated for Savvy.com's Mom Entrepreneur of the Year Award. Bettig's daughter has now taken an interest in designing jewellery, and Bettig hopes to someday pass the business on to her daughter.

Zia and Tia Pure Luxury Organics

Julie Jonas of Beaconsfield, Quebec, started an ecommerce company called Zia and Tia Pure Luxury Organics, which sells 450 different organic products, ranging from baby clothes and bedding to adult grooming products, hemp pet beds, and hand-painted furniture. Jonas got the idea for the business after a friend gave her an article about a company that sold organic cotton baby clothes. Jonas likes being a mompreneur because she can be a stay-at-home mother while also building a socially responsible business. She contributes 10 percent of the company's profits to the Half the Sky Foundation, which provides care for orphanages in China.

Outside/In Cosmetics Inc.

Consuelo Clarke of Chilliwack, B.C., started this company, which makes mineral makeup and organic skin care products. However, in just a few months she noticed that work demands were making her family relations deteriorate. She came close to quitting the business, but then decided to let go of some of the business functions, like bookkeeping and sales. That made life simpler for her and freed up time for her to focus on the part of the business that she enjoys.

Robeez

One of the most highly publicized mompreneurs in recent years is Sandra Wilson. After she was downsized out of her airline job, she handcrafted a pair of brightly coloured, soft-soled leather shoes for her 18-month-old son Robert. She thought that other mothers might find them a good product for their children, so she started her own business and called the footwear Robeez after her son. She hand-stitched 20 pairs of her footwear, then went to the Vancouver Gift Show trade exhibition. The orders flooded in and she signed up 15 retailers ready to sell her product.

Wilson's basement became Robeez Footwear's early headquarters, and she quickly learned all there was to know about leather, cutting, sewing, design, sales, and distribution. Wilson hired her first sales representative in March 1995, and by May 1997 Robeez was online. The company moved out of Wilson's basement in May 1999 and into its first commercial space. Since then, the company has relocated and expanded into larger premises to accommodate its rapidly expanding operations. Today, Robeez is recognized as the world's leading manufacturer of soft-soled leather footwear for newborns to four-year-olds. The company has 450 employees and sells more than 90 designs of shoes and booties in over 6500 stores in countries throughout North America, Europe, Australia, and parts of Asia. In 2006, Robeez joined The Stride Rite Corporation's family of well-known footwear brands, including Keds, Sperry Top-Sider, Tommy Hilfiger Footwear, Stride Rite, and Saucony.

Some observers of the mompreneur trend have noted that things are not always as positive as they seem. Barbara Orser, a management professor at the University of Ottawa's School of Management, says that most mompreneurs work long hours, run low-growth businesses, don't make much money, and don't get benefits. She cites a Statistics Canada report showing that only 17 percent of self-employed women earn more than $30 000 per year. In spite of this, increasing numbers of women are becoming mompreneurs (the number of self-employed women increased 18 percent between 1996 and 2006).

It isn't just women who are trying to achieve a better work-life balance. There are also dadpreneurs doing the same thing. For example, Craig Ellis of Calgary (Shift Selling Inc.) and Greg Thorpe (MonkeyRed Designs) are just two examples of men who have started home businesses in order to help raise their children. There do, however, seem to be fewer dadpreneurs than mompreneurs.

Questions for Discussion

1. What is the difference between small business and entrepreneurship? Are mompreneurs entrepreneurs? Explain.
2. Interview a mompreneur and ask the following questions: (a) Why did you start your business? (b) What are the advantages of being a mompreneur? and (c) What are the disadvantages?
3. Why do you think the number of self-employed women is increasing?
4. Why do you think so little attention is been paid to dadpreneurs?

Concluding Case 4-2

Getting In on the Ground Floor

Larry Gibson, 51, oversees a business empire that employs 80 people full time (plus 110 under contract) and is projected to have sales of $30 million this year. But things didn't start out that way. Gibson got into the flooring business after finding university too slow for his liking. After working as a flooring installer in Halifax, he went west in the late 1970s and worked in Calgary and in the Arctic, honing his commercial estimating skills before returning to Nova Scotia in 1983.

After five years of managing Eaton's flooring business in Halifax, he got word that his division was closing in May 1988. At the time Eaton's still had contracts and warranties outstanding. "So they came to me and said, 'Will you take these contracts on and go out on your own?'" Using personal savings, he and his wife, Patricia, bought a dilapidated Halifax building from which to launch a floor-covering business and took over the chain's local flooring accounts, setting up shop under the Install-a-Flor name.

The weekend before opening the doors in July 1988, Patricia started to cry, wondering if they were doing the right thing. Reassurance was not long in coming. Gibson's phone rang at 8:30 opening day, and on the line—unaware that Gibson's phone was resting on a sawhorse, since his office wasn't furnished yet—was Atlantic property developer Armour Construction. Gibson's earlier bid to install flooring in a 185-unit complex had been accepted. The deal was worth $440 000 over 15 months.

He says that first sale taught him that "if you believe you can do something, then put your mind and heart to it. There's always an element of surprise and the unforeseen, and it can be good or it can be bad. In my case, it was good and lucky." Indeed, Larry Gibson is known for his commitment to hard work, providing the best possible service, and delivering a quality product at a competitive price. He credits the nuns at the convent school in Herring Cove for instilling discipline in him and says the unexpected death of his father when he was 10 helped give him drive.

Mr. Gibson said the first few years of heads-down, all-out work took its toll on his health. "I was gritting my teeth at night and my stomach had a big knot in it, basically, because we started with nothing and always worried about turning that dollar and getting financial institutions and suppliers to believe in me," he recalled. "It was always tight."

Mr. Gibson credits his wife, who handles the business's finances and administration, with helping him through the early days. "I'd go home, we'd sit at the table—most people have salt shakers; we had a calculator. We would do quantity measures on plans and I would bid, bid, bid." That effort resulted in a 633 percent growth over the company's first five years. "When we first started, it was difficult to convince suppliers to sell us their products," recalls Patricia, "because selling to a newcomer is sometimes a bit of a risk. But Larry and I have a policy of 'Never take no for an answer. There's always another way.' We stuck with it and gained people's confidence."

Today, the business includes seven Floors Plus retail stores in Nova Scotia and New Brunswick, as well as specialty and contract divisions that operate internationally and have specialties such as clean room technology—on-site thermal welding and moulding of plastics—that is used in medical operating theatres and food-processing facilities. "Right now we're doing a school in Bermuda," said Mr. Gibson, adding that the business has opened offices in China and Ontario.

Contracting represents 40 percent of the company's business, with retail accounting for another 40 percent and the growing wholesale business, named Dantra (after his two children, Daniel and Tracy, who both work in the family firm), representing 20 percent.

"We have a lack of supply here of specialty products," Mr. Gibson said in explaining the company's diversification. "Nobody's going to come in here and say, 'Listen, I want you to do clean rooms.' You've got to search this stuff out and find a market for it. It's not just about money, it's about service, being a leader and having knowledge about the market."

Market knowledge is market power, and Mr. Gibson has gained that by going all over the world in search of new business opportunities. "We know from travelling the styles that are coming," he said, noting that he is largely in the business of selling fashion. "The (Atlantic) area is a couple of years behind Toronto, New York, and even European or Asian markets. So we know we've got time to react if we react quickly."

Questions for Discussion

1. According to Statistics Canada's Business Register, would Install-a-Flor be considered a small business? Why or why not?

2. Assess the fit between Larry Gibson and the opportunity when Install-a-Flor was started. What personal characteristics contributed most to his success?
3. To what extent did Larry Gibson use bootstrapping in getting his business started? Explain.
4. Assess Larry Gibson's capacity for identifying opportunities according to the characteristics outlined in the opportunity screening section of the chapter.
5. What benefits or drawbacks are evident in this family business?
6. Would you recommend that Install-a-Flor go public?
7. Clearly, Install-a-Flor is no longer a new business. But is it entrepreneurial?

Chapter 5

Understanding International Business

After reading this chapter, you should be able to:

1. Describe the rise of international business and identify the *major world marketplaces*.
2. Explain how different forms of *competitive advantage*, *import-export balances*, *exchange rates*, and *foreign competition* determine the ways in which countries and businesses respond to the international environment.
3. Discuss the factors involved in deciding to do business internationally and in selecting the appropriate *levels of international involvement* and *international organizational structure*.
4. Describe some of the ways in which *social*, *cultural*, *economic*, *legal*, and *political differences* act as barriers to international trade.
5. Explain how *free trade agreements* assist world trade.

Bombardier's Global Strategy

Photo courtesy of Bombardier Inc. and used under license.

Montreal-based Bombardier Inc. is a diversified Canadian company that specializes in transportation, recreational products, and aerospace products, as well as financial and real estate services. Bombardier was founded in 1942 to manufacture a now-classic Canadian product—tracked vehicles for transportation across snow-covered terrain. Many of the Bombardier snowmobiles that were manufactured decades ago can still be seen in various areas of Canada. One such half-track sits on the windswept shores of Yathkyed Lake in Nunavut, hundreds of kilometres from any town. It is a mute reminder of the important role Bombardier played in opening up Canada's remote North.

Bombardier's headquarters are in Montreal, but its employees also work in the United States, Mexico, Europe, and the Middle East. More than 90 percent of company revenues come from outside Canada. Bombardier's strategy is to achieve accelerated growth in foreign markets, so it is continually refining its strategy to find new business opportunities in global markets.

Bombardier has historically been very successful in the commercial airplane market with its regional jets, which seat 50–90 passengers. But competition is fierce. In the mid-1990s, Bombardier held two-thirds of the market; then Brazilian rival Embraer entered the market and became a strong competitor. In 2007, Embraer finally overtook Bombardier to become the market leader in regional jets. Along the way, Bombardier had complained to the World Trade Organization that the Brazilian government was unfairly subsidizing Embraer by giving it large sums of money. But the Canadian government was also giving loans to Bombardier's customers to help them purchase Bombardier's planes.

Irrespective of how the competitive wars in the regional jet market turn out, an inescapable fact is that the regional jet market is declining because airline companies want jets with longer ranges, lower operating costs, and wider cabins. Bombardier planners reasoned that if they did not develop a new jet, they would gradually be forced out of the commercial airplane business. In 2008, at the famous Farnborough International Airshow near London, England, the company announced that it would go ahead with its new transcontinental C Series commercial jet, a plane that will seat 110–130 passengers and is designed for transcontinental flights. The plane will be more fuel efficient than current models and much quieter due to technological improvements in the new engines that will be used on the plane. Bombardier also announced that Deutsche Lufthansa AG had signed a letter of intent for 30 of the planes, as well as an option for 30 more. Other leading potential customers include Qatar Airways and the International Lease Finance Corp., which is the world's largest aircraft leasing company.

The introduction of the C Series means Bombardier will be going head-to-head with global giants Airbus and Boeing. That strategy is risky, but if it succeeds, it will mean huge sales revenues and profits for Bombardier. It will also mean that Canada is one of only three countries in the world that produce intercontinental commercial jet aircraft. Market research suggests that the market for commercial jets like the C Series will be 5000–6000 units over the next 20 years, and Bombardier hopes to get 50 percent of that market. The price of each plane is about $46 million, so if the company achieves its market share goal, it will receive approximately $147 *billion* in revenues over the next 20 years.

That sounds impressive, but there are three areas of risk associated with Bombardier's strategy. First, there may (or may not) be competing products from other airplane manufacturers. Here, Bombardier may get lucky. There is little evidence that Airbus or Boeing is planning to develop a plane that will compete directly with the C Series. That's because there are large order backlogs (4–5 years) for both the Airbus A320 and the Boeing 737, and the companies are fully engaged trying to fill those orders. However, Embraer may be developing a jet to compete with the C Series.

Second, there is some risk associated with Bombardier's alleged "cozy" relationship with the Canadian government. In the past, the federal government has loaned money to Bombardier's customers so they can purchase the planes and trains the company manufactures. But will the government decide to stop handing out money? When he was opposition leader, Stephen Harper said he wanted to end this type of support to private sector companies, but as prime minister he has now reversed his position. Industry Minister Jim Prentice says that Canada wants to maintain its position as a global supplier in the airplane business. The Liberal industry critic, Scott Brison, says the Canadian government doesn't have an industrial strategy and is just making ad hoc decisions based on which way the political winds are blowing. But given the uncertain economic times, it appears that government loans are likely to continue.

Third, there is a risk that Boeing, Airbus, and Embraer will argue at the World Trade Organization that Canada is illegally subsidizing Bombardier. There is a long and contentious history between Bombardier and Embraer about government subsidies, and each company has claimed at various times in the past that the other is being illegally subsidized by its government. The outcome of any legal action by other airplane manufacturers against Bombardier is very uncertain.

Bombardier's strategy also includes shifting some of the risk of the C Series to suppliers and to government. About $3.3 billion will be spent on developing the plane, but help with financing will come from three sources: (1) Pratt & Whitney (the maker of the plane's engines, who will contribute over $1 billion); (2) the Canadian government and the province of Quebec (who will contribute $513 million); and (3) the United Kingdom (the wings will be built there and the U.K. government will contribute $311 million). The various governments will be paid a royalty on each plane that is sold. The project will create 3500 high-paying jobs in Quebec and about 800 jobs in the United Kingdom. ◆

How will this help me?

Whether you see yourself living abroad, working for a big company, or starting your own business, the global economy will affect you in some way. Exchange rates for different currencies and global markets for buying and selling are all of major importance to everyone, regardless of their role or perspective. The material in this chapter will help you to understand (1) how global forces affect you as a customer, (2) how globalization affects you as an employee, and (3) how global opportunities and challenges can affect you as a business owner and as an investor.

We begin this chapter with an exploration of the major world marketplaces. Next, we examine several factors that help determine how countries and businesses respond to international opportunities and challenges. We identify the decisions managers must make if they intend to compete in international markets, and we discuss the social, cultural, economic, legal, and political factors that affect international business. We conclude with a description of international trade agreements and how they facilitate international trade.

The Contemporary Global Economy

globalization The integration of markets globally.

imports Products that are made or grown abroad and sold in Canada.

exports Products that are made or grown in Canada and sold abroad.

The total volume of world trade today is immense—around $8 trillion each year. As more and more firms engage in international business, the world economy is fast becoming a single, interdependent system—a process called **globalization**. But we often take for granted the diversity of goods and services available today as a result of international trade. Your television set, your shoes, and even the roast lamb on your dinner table may all be **imports**—that is, products made or grown abroad but sold in Canada. At the same time, the success of many Canadian firms depends on **exports**—products made or grown domestically and shipped for sale abroad. An Ontario company called 1867 Confederation Log Homes has found a way to export entire houses. It makes the homes at its factory, then dismantles them, numbers all the components, and ships them to foreign countries. When they arrive, they are easily reassembled by the buyer using only basic construction skills. Confederation exports 40 percent of its output.[1]

Trade between nations can be traced back at least as far as 2000 BCE, when North African tribes took dates and clothing to Assyria and Babylonia in the Middle East and traded them for olive oil and spices. So, international business is nothing new. In fact, MIT professor Paul Krugman argues that what we now regard as an extremely active "global economy" is not as big a change as you might imagine. He points out that imports now represent only a slightly higher proportion of GDP than they did 100 years ago, and that capital mobility (the movement of money from country to country) is about the same as it was in 1914. In that era, for example, England's trade surplus—4 percent of GDP—was the same as the surplus enjoyed by Japan during the 1980s.

Even so, international trade is becoming increasingly central to the fortunes of most nations of the world, as well as to their largest businesses. Whereas in the past many nations followed strict policies to protect domestic businesses, today more and more countries are aggressively encouraging international trade. They are opening their borders more freely to foreign businesses, offering incentives for their own domestic businesses to expand internationally, and making it easier for foreign firms to partner with local firms through various alliances.

Several forces have combined to spark and sustain globalization. For one thing, governments and businesses have simply become more aware of the benefits of globalization to their countries and stockholders. For another, new technologies have made international travel, communication, and commerce easier, faster, and cheaper than ever before. Overseas phone calls and seaborne shipping costs per tonne have both declined sharply over the last several decades. Likewise, transatlantic travel that once required several days aboard a ship now takes only a few hours by air. Finally, there are competitive pressures: Sometimes, a firm simply must enter foreign markets just to keep up with its competitors.

Globalization is not without its critics, who charge that it allows businesses to exploit workers in less developed countries and bypass domestic environmental and tax regulations. They also charge that globalization leads to the loss of cultural heritages and often benefits the rich more than the poor. As a result, many international gatherings of global economic leaders—including the G8 meetings in Germany in 2007—have been marked by protests and demonstrations. The recession that began in 2008 has also been a negative influence; the World Trade Organization (WTO) predicted that the volume of world trade would drop by 9 percent in 2009 as a result of the recession that began in 2008, and Export Development Canada predicted that Canada's exports would drop 22 percent.[2] Many nations will be influenced by reductions in trade because of their interconnectedness.

The Major World Marketplaces

Describe the rise of international business and identify the *major world marketplaces*. 1

The World Bank, an agency of the United Nations, uses **per capita income**—the average income per person in a country—as a measure to divide countries into one of four groups.[3]

per capita income The average income per person in a country.

- *High-income countries* are those with per capita income greater than US$11 115. These include Canada, the United States, most countries in Europe, Australia, New Zealand, Japan, South Korea, Kuwait, the United Arab Emirates, Israel, Singapore, and Taiwan. Hong Kong, while technically no longer an independent nation, also falls into this category.
- *Upper-middle-income countries* are those with per capita income between US$3595 and US$11 115. This group includes, among others, the Czech Republic, Greece, Hungary, Poland, most countries composing the former Soviet Bloc, Turkey, Mexico, Argentina, and South Africa.
- *Low middle-income countries* are those with per capita income between US$905 and US$3595. Among the countries in this group are China, Colombia, Guatemala, India, Samoa, and Thailand.
- *Low-income countries* (often called developing countries) are those with annual per-capita income of less than US$905. Due to low literacy rates, weak infrastructures, unstable governments, and related problems, these

countries are less attractive to international business. For example, the East African nation of Somalia is plagued by drought, civil war, and starvation, and plays virtually no role in the world economy.

Geographic Clusters

The world economy revolves around three major marketplaces: North America, Europe, and Asia-Pacific. In general, these clusters include relatively more of the upper-middle and high-income nations, but relatively few low- and low-middle-income countries. For instance, because Africa consists primarily of low- and low-middle-income countries, it is not generally seen as a major marketplace. The three geographic regions that do warrant this designation are home to most of the world's largest economies, biggest corporations, most influential financial markets, and highest-income consumers.

North America. The United States dominates the North American business region. It is the single largest marketplace and enjoys the most stable economy in the world. Canada also plays a major role in the international economy. Moreover, the United States and Canada are each other's largest trading partner. Many U.S. firms, such as General Motors and Procter & Gamble, have maintained successful Canadian operations for years, and many Canadian firms, such as Bombardier and Alcan Aluminum, are also major international competitors.

Mexico has also become a major manufacturing centre, especially along its border with the southern U.S., where cheap labour and low transportation costs have encouraged many firms, from the United States and other countries, to build manufacturing plants. The auto industry has been especially active. For example, Chrysler, General Motors, Volkswagen, Nissan, and Ford have large assembly plants in this region. However, the emergence of China as a low-cost manufacturing centre may lead companies to shift their production from Mexico to China.[4]

Europe. Europe has often been regarded as two regions—Western Europe and Eastern Europe. Western Europe, dominated by Germany, the United Kingdom, France, and Italy, has long been a mature but fragmented marketplace. But the transformation of the European Union (EU) in 1992 into a unified marketplace has further increased the region's importance. Major international firms such as Unilever, Renault, Royal Dutch/Shell, Michelin, Siemens, and Nestlé are all headquartered in Western Europe.

Ecommerce and technology have also become increasingly important in this region.[5] There has been a surge in internet start-ups in southeast England, the Netherlands, and the Scandinavian countries, and Ireland is now one of the world's largest exporters of software. Strasbourg, France, is a major centre for biotech start-ups; Barcelona, Spain, has many flourishing software and internet companies; and the Frankfurt region of Germany is dotted with both software and biotech start-ups.[6]

Eastern Europe, once primarily communist, has also gained in importance, both as a marketplace and as a producer. For example, such multinational corporations as Daewoo, Nestlé, General Motors, and ABB Asea Brown Boveri have set up operations in Poland. Similarly, Ford, General Motors, Suzuki, and Volkswagen have all built new factories in Hungary. On the other hand, government instability has hampered economic development in Russia, Bulgaria, Albania, Romania, and other countries in this region, and the recession that began in 2008 worsened their financial troubles.

Asia-Pacific. Asia-Pacific consists of Japan, China, Thailand, Malaysia, Singapore, Indonesia, South Korea, Taiwan, the Philippines, and Australia

The growth in international commerce has led to the emergence of several major marketplaces. Much of the international commerce in these marketplaces, in turn, is managed from major cities. Traditional centres of international commerce include New York, London, Paris, and Tokyo, but in recent years, cities like Shanghai, Beijing, Hong Kong, Dubai, Vancouver, Bangalore, and Kuala Lumpur have taken on increased importance. For example, international business now defines the glittering skyline of Shanghai.

(which technically is not in Asia, but is included here because of its proximity to that region). Some experts still distinguish Hong Kong, though now part of China, as a part of the region, and others include Vietnam. Fuelled by strong entries in the automobile, electronics, and banking industries, the economies of these countries grew rapidly in the 1970s and 1980s. A currency crisis in the late 1990s slowed growth in virtually every country of the region for a few years.

Asia-Pacific is an important force in the world economy and a major source of competition for North American firms. Led by firms such as Toyota, Toshiba, and Nippon Steel, Japan dominates the region. South Korea (home to such firms as Samsung and Hyundai), Taiwan (owner of Chinese Petroleum and the manufacturing home of many foreign firms), and Hong Kong (a major financial centre) are also successful players in the international economy. China, the world's most densely populated country, has emerged as an important market and now boasts the world's third largest economy behind only the European Union and the United States.[7] India, though not part of Asia-Pacific, is also rapidly emerging as one of the globe's most important economies.[8]

As in North America and Western Europe, technology promises to play an increasingly important role in this region. In Asia, however, the emergence of technology firms has been hampered by a poorly developed electronic infrastructure, slower adoption of computers and information technology, and a higher percentage of lower-income consumers.[9]

Forms of Competitive Advantage

2

Explain how different forms of *competitive advantage, import-export balances, exchange rates,* and *foreign competition* determine the ways in which countries and businesses respond to the international environment.

There are high levels of importing, exporting, and other forms of international business activity because no country can produce all the goods and services that its people need. Countries tend to export products that they can produce better or less expensively than other countries and then use the proceeds to import products that they cannot produce as effectively.

But this general idea does not explain why various nations export and import specific products and services. Such decisions hinge partly on the kind of advantages a particular country may enjoy regarding its ability to create and/or sell various products and resources.[10] Traditionally, economists assessed *absolute* and *comparative advantage* to explain international trade. But because this approach focusses narrowly on such factors as natural resources and labour costs, a perspective has emerged that emphasizes the more complex idea of *national competitive advantage*.

Absolute Advantage

absolute advantage A nation's ability to produce something more cheaply or better than any other country.

An **absolute advantage** exists when a country can produce something more cheaply and/or of higher quality than any other country. Saudi oil, Brazilian coffee beans, and Canadian timber approximate absolute advantage, but examples of true absolute advantage are rare. In reality, absolute advantages are always relative. For example, most experts say that the vineyards of France produce the finest wines in the world. But the burgeoning wine business in California, British Columbia, and Ontario attests to the fact that producers there can also produce very good values in wine—wines that are perhaps almost as good as French wines and that are available in more varieties and at lower prices.

Comparative Advantage

comparative advantage A nation's ability to produce some products more cheaply or better than it can others.

A country has a **comparative advantage** in goods that it can produce more efficiently or better than other goods. For example, if businesses in a given country can make computers more efficiently than they can make automobiles, that nation's firms have a comparative advantage in computer manufacturing. Canada has a comparative advantage in farming (because of capital-intensive and efficient land use), while South Korea has a comparative advantage in electronics manufacturing (because of efficient operations and cheap labour). As a result, Canadian firms export grain to South Korea and import electronic equipment from South Korea.

Almost all countries have a comparative advantage in *some* products, but no country has a comparative advantage in *all* products. Developed countries tend to have a comparative advantage in making high-tech products, while developing countries tend to have a comparative advantage in making products that require a lot of low-cost labour.

National Competitive Advantage

national competitive advantage A country will be inclined to engage in international trade when factor conditions, demand conditions, related and supporting industries, and strategies/structures/rivalries are favourable.

In recent years, a theory of **national competitive advantage** has become a more widely accepted model of why nations engage in international trade.[11] Basically, national competitive advantage derives from four conditions:

1. *Factor conditions* are the factors of production that we identified in Chapter 1.
2. *Demand conditions* reflect a large domestic consumer base that promotes strong demand for innovative products.
3. *Related and supporting industries* include strong local or regional suppliers and/or industrial customers.
4. *Strategies, structures, and rivalries* refer to firms and industries that stress cost reduction, product quality, higher productivity, and innovative new products.

Figure 5.1 shows why these four attributes are referred to as a national diamond. The interaction of the four elements determines the environment in which a nation's firms compete. When all of these conditions exist, a nation will naturally be inclined to engage in international business. Japan, for instance, has strong domestic demand for automobiles. Its automobile producers have well-oiled supplier networks, and domestic firms have competed intensely with each other for decades. This set of circumstances explains why Japanese automobile companies such as Toyota, Honda, Nissan, and Mazda are generally successful in foreign markets.

International competitiveness refers to the ability of a country to generate more wealth than its competitors in world markets. Each year, the World Economic Forum publishes a global competitiveness ranking based on both economic data and a poll of business leaders in many countries. In 2008, the top three countries on the list were the United States, Switzerland, and Denmark (Canada ranked tenth).[12]

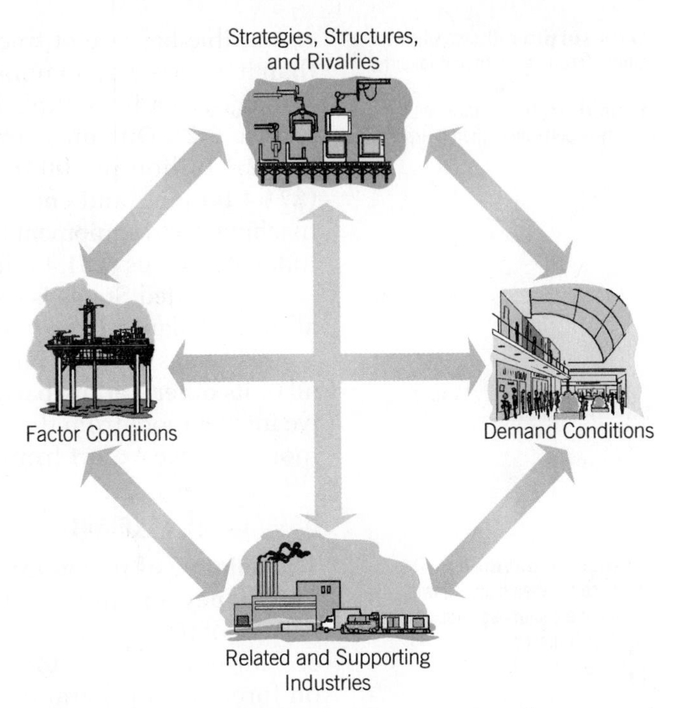

Figure 5.1 Attributes of national competitive advantage.

international competitiveness The ability of a country to generate more wealth than its competitors in world markets.

Import–Export Balances

Although international trade offers many potential advantages, trading with other nations can pose problems if a country's imports and exports are not balanced. In deciding whether an overall balance exists, economists use two measures: *balance of trade* and *balance of payments*.

Balance of Trade

balance of trade The difference in value between a nation's total exports and its total imports.

A nation's **balance of trade** is the difference in value between its total exports and its total imports. A country that exports more than it imports has a

If local boosters have their way, the success of *The Lord of the Rings*—whose fictional Middle Earth is really New Zealand's South Island—will turn the dramatic scenery of New Zealand into an advantage in competing for global business. The national film promotion board appeals to foreign producers by stressing the country's variety of unspoiled landscapes (and largely non-union workforce), and *Rings*-related tourism has already become a thriving business. On the web, Tourism New Zealand invites you to "Experience the Home of Middle Earth," and Air New Zealand bills itself as the "Airline to Middle Earth."

trade surplus Occurs when a country exports more than it imports.

trade deficit Occurs when a country imports more than it exports.

favourable balance of trade, or **trade surplus**. A country that imports more than it exports has an unfavourable balance of trade, or **trade deficit**. Canada has enjoyed a favourable balance of merchandise trade for many years (see Figure 5.2). Our most important exports are machinery and equipment ($102.1 billion in 2008), motor vehicles ($79.1 billion), industrial goods ($74.4 billion), and energy ($54.1 billion). Our most important imports are machinery and equipment ($172.1 billion in 2008), motor vehicles ($89.3 billion), industrial goods ($81.4 billion), and consumer goods ($75.3 billion).[13]

The United States is Canada's largest trading partner by far, and our overall trade balance is favourable only because we export so much more to the United States than we import from them. Canada's trade balance with almost all of its other trading partners is unfavourable (see Table 5.1). As you can see, we import more from the European Union than we export to it, and we import more than we export from the category "other countries" as well.

Balance of Payments

balance of payments The difference between money flowing into and out of a country as a result of trade and other transactions.

The **balance of payments** refers to the flow of money into or out of a country. The money a nation pays for imports and receives for exports—that is, its balance of trade—comprises much of its balance of payments, but other financial exchanges are also factors. For example, money spent by tourists, money spent on foreign aid programs, and money spent and received in the buying and selling of currency on international money markets all affect the balance of payments.

An unfavourable balance means that more money is flowing out than in. For Canada to have a favourable balance of payments for a given year, the total of (1) our exports, (2) foreign tourist spending in this country, (3) foreign investments here, and (4) earnings from overseas investments must be greater than the total of (1) our imports, (2) Canadian tourist spending overseas, (3) our foreign aid grants, (4) our military spending abroad, (5) the investments made by Canadian firms abroad, and (6) the earnings of foreigners from their investments in Canada. These relationships are summarized in Figure 5.3.

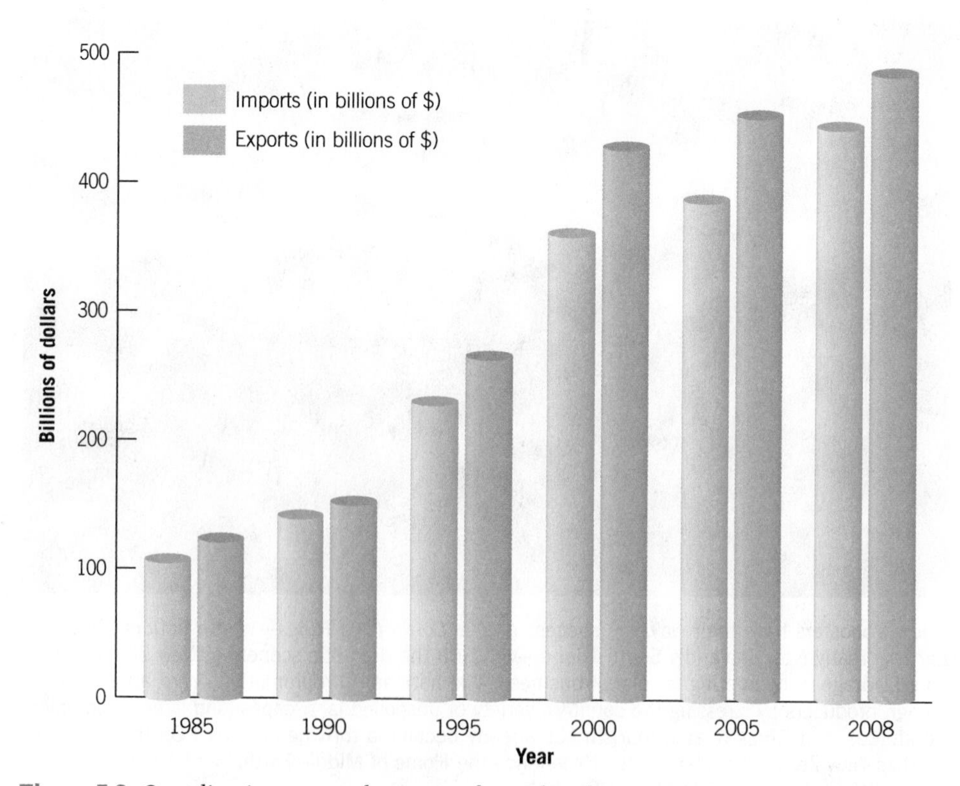

Figure 5.2 Canadian imports and exports of merchandise.

Table 5.1 Canadian Exports to and Imports from Selected Countries, 2008

Country	Exports to (in billions of $)	Imports from (in billions of $)
United States	$369.7	$280.6
European Union	39.5	46.6
Japan	11.8	11.6
All others	68.3	103.8

Canada has had an unfavourable balance of payments for many years. In 2008, for example, $102 billion more money flowed out of Canada than flowed in.[14]

Exchange Rates

The balance of imports and exports between two countries is affected by the rate of exchange between their currencies. An **exchange rate** is the rate at which the currency of one nation can be exchanged for that of another.[15] For

exchange rate The rate at which the currency of one nation can be exchanged for that of another.

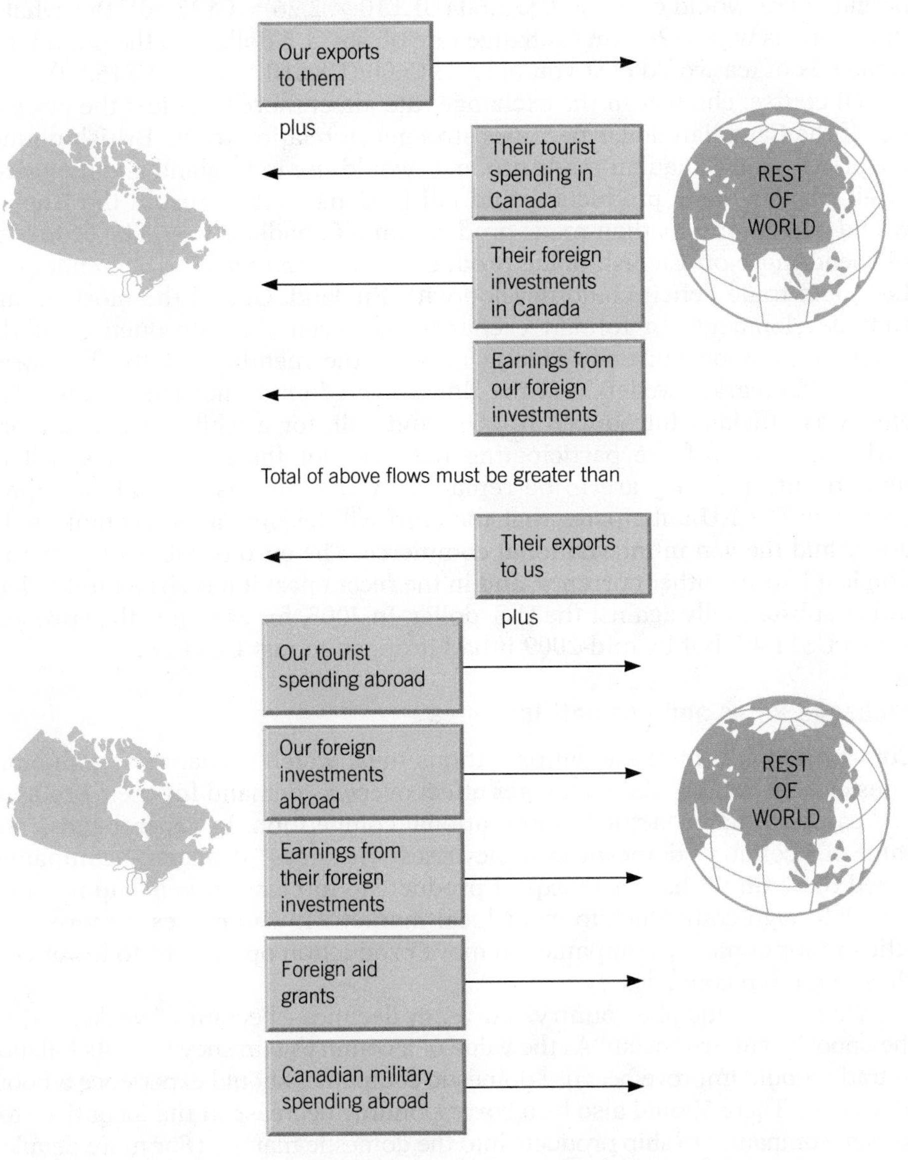

Figure 5.3 Requirements for Canada to have a favourable balance of payments. (The arrows indicate the direction of the flow.)

example, in recent years, UK£1 has been worth about US$2.00. This means that it costs one British pound to "buy" two U.S. dollars, or US$1.00 to buy 0.50 of a British pound. This exchange rate means that 0.50 of a British pound and one U.S. dollar should have exactly the same purchasing power. If English citizens start spending a lot of pounds to buy U.S. dollars (or goods), *demand* for the U.S. dollar goes up, and the value of the dollar relative to the pound increases. A currency is said to be "strong" when demand for it is high and when there is high demand for the goods manufactured by using that currency.

At the end of the Second World War, the major nations of the world agreed to establish *fixed exchange rates* so that the value of any country's currency relative to that of another country remained constant. Today, however, *floating exchange rates* are the norm, and the value of one country's currency relative to that of another country varies with market conditions. The Canadian dollar, for example, fluctuates in value compared to the U.S. dollar. Exchange rates typically fluctuate by very small amounts on a daily basis, with more significant variations occurring over greater spans of time.

Fluctuations in exchange rates can have an important impact on the balance of trade. Suppose, for example, that you wanted to buy some English tea for UK£10 per box. At an exchange rate of 2.26 Canadian dollars to the British pound, a box would cost you C$22.60 (UK£10 × 2.26 = C$22.60). But what if the pound is weaker? At an exchange rate of, say, 1.5 dollars to the pound, the same box of tea would cost you only C$15.00 (UK£10 × 1.5 = C$15.00).

Of course, changes in the exchange rate affect more than just the price of tea. If the Canadian dollar becomes stronger in relation to the British pound, the prices of all Canadian-made products would rise in England and the prices of all English-made products would fall in Canada. As a result, the English would buy fewer Canadian-made products, and Canadians would be prompted to spend more on English-made products. If the trend was strong enough, a Canadian trade deficit could develop with England. One of the most significant developments in foreign exchange has been the introduction of the **euro**—a common currency among most of the members of the European Union (Denmark, Sweden, and the United Kingdom do not participate). The euro was officially introduced in 2002 and will, for a while, circulate along with currencies of the participating nations. But those currencies will be phased out, and they are to be replaced by the euro as the only accepted currency. The EU anticipates that the euro will become as important as the dollar and the yen in international commerce. The euro is subject to fluctuation just like any other currency, and in the recent past it has risen (and fallen) rather substantially against the U.S. dollar. In 2008, for example, the euro was worth US$1.47, but by mid-2009 it had dropped to just US$1.30.

euro A common currency shared among most of the members of the European Union (excluding Denmark, Sweden, and the United Kingdom).

Exchange Rates and Competition

Companies with international operations must watch exchange rate fluctuations closely because these changes affect overseas demand for their products and can be a major factor in international competition. In general, when the value of a country's domestic currency rises—becomes "stronger"—companies based there find it harder to export products to foreign markets and it is easier for foreign companies to enter local markets. It also makes it more cost-efficient for domestic companies to move production operations to lower-cost sites in foreign countries.

When the value of a country's currency declines—becomes "weaker"—just the opposite patterns occur. As the value of a country's currency falls, its balance of trade should improve because domestic companies should experience a boost in exports. There should also be a corresponding decrease in the incentives for foreign companies to ship products into the domestic market. (For more detailed information on the effect of exchange rates, see Chapter 18.)

International Business Management

Discuss the factors involved in deciding to do business internationally and in selecting the appropriate *levels of international involvement* and *international organizational structure.* 3

Wherever a firm is located, its success depends largely on how well it is managed. International business is so challenging because the basic functions of management—planning, organizing, directing, and controlling—are much more difficult to carry out when a business operates in several markets scattered around the globe. (We discuss the functions of management in detail in Chapter 6.)

Managing means making decisions, and in this section we examine the three most basic decisions a company's management must make when faced with the prospect of globalization. The first decision is whether or not to "go international." Once that decision has been made, managers must decide on the company's level of international involvement and on the organizational structure that will best meet its global needs.

"Going International"

"Going international" isn't for everyone. For example, if you buy and sell fresh fish, you'll probably find it more profitable to confine your activities to a limited geographic area in order to minimize storage and transportation costs. As Figure 5.4 shows, several factors enter in to the decision to go international.

Gauging International Demand

In considering international expansion, a company must determine if there is demand for its products abroad. Products that are successful in one country may be useless in another. Snowmobiles are popular for transportation and recreation in Canada, and they have actually revolutionized reindeer herding in Lapland, but there's no demand for them in Central America. Even when there is demand, advertising may still need to be adjusted. For instance, in Canada bicycles and small motorcycles are mainly used for recreation, but in many parts of Asia they are seen as transportation. Market research and/or the prior market entry of competitors may indicate whether there's an international demand for a firm's products.

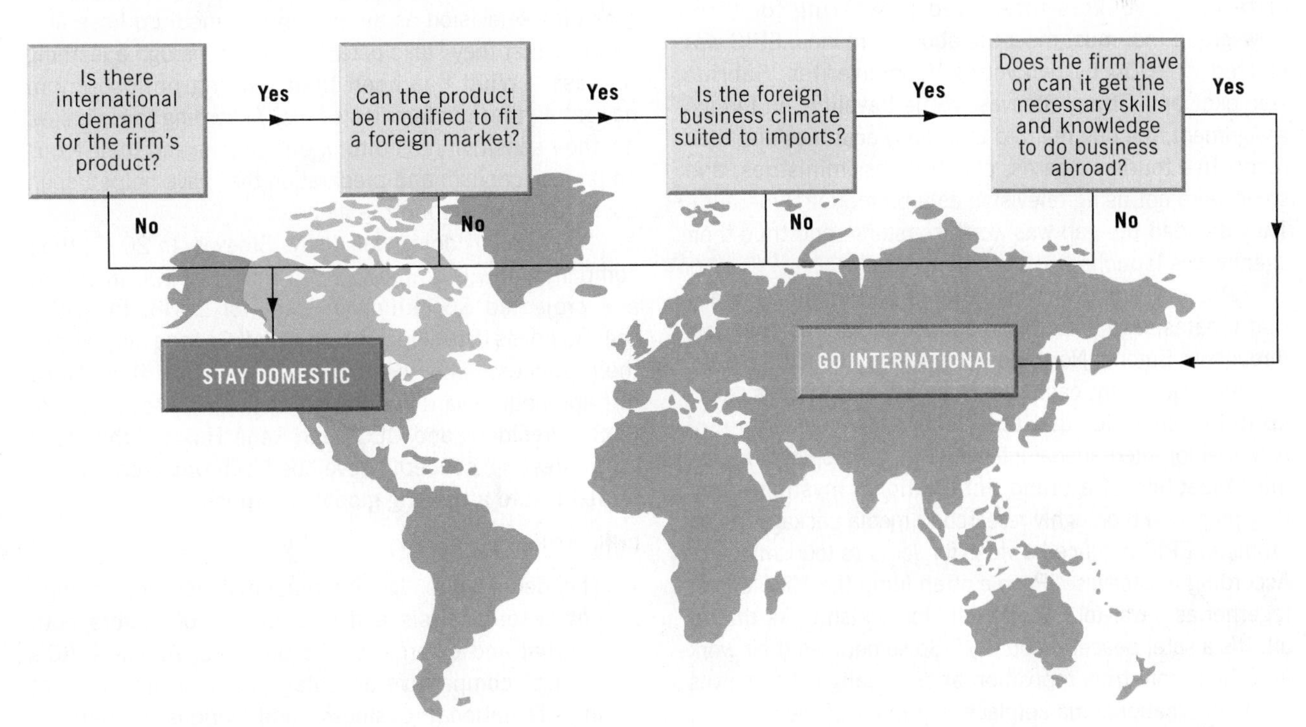

Figure 5.4 The decision to go international.

Adapting to Customer Needs

If there is international demand for its product, a firm must consider whether and how to adapt that product to meet the special demands and expectations of foreign customers. Movies, for example, have to be dubbed into foreign languages. Likewise, McDonald's restaurants sell wine in France, beer in Germany, and meatless sandwiches in India to accommodate local tastes and preferences. Ford products must have their steering wheels mounted on the right if they are to be sold in England and Japan. When Toyota launches upscale cars at home, it retains the Toyota nameplate; but those same cars are sold under the Lexus nameplate in Canada because the firm has concluded that Canadian consumers there will not pay a premium price for a Toyota.

In addition to these issues of demand and the need to adapt products, consideration must also be given to the business climate that exists in the foreign market (these issues are discussed in detail later in this chapter). The company must also assess the specific business skills that will be needed to be successful in the foreign country. Businesses can deal with this issue by adopting various levels of involvement in international business. The boxed insert entitled "Epic Entrepreneurs" describes one company's experience in going international.

Entrepreneurship and New Ventures

Epic Entrepreneurs: Have Camera, Will Travel

Help wanted: Dynamic and innovative company seeks staff who are adventurous, love to travel, and are willing to spend most of the year in some of the world's most exotic locations, many of them very warm! Sounds like a dream job, right? Well, while there's sure to be other mandatory criteria, jobseekers interested in working for EPIC Newsgroup Inc. must meet the above demands. EPIC was started in 2004 by two young Vancouverites, Sabrina Heinekey and Tiffany Steeves. While travelling on foreign assignment, the duo realized that many countries and their respective tourism boards, corporations, ministries, and so on were not using television as a promotional medium. They decided the gap was worth pursuing, and thus their agency was launched.

EPIC is a production and media placement company that creates segments for broadcast on various channels throughout Europe, North America, Africa, the Middle East, and Asia. Generally, each year Heinekey and Steeves select up to five countries that they believe have some form of potential for international interest (e.g., developing a brand, misconception of a brand, international mystique) and they prepare a thoroughly researched media package. As an example, EPIC produced a video for Jordan's tourism board. According to Steeves, "People often lump the Middle East together as a war-torn area. Well, Jordan isn't like that at all. It's a safe, peaceful country." So sometimes their work is to help countries reposition and/or realign themselves in the international marketplace. For many of their clients, there had been a perception that television production as a form of media exposure was difficult and out of reach; EPIC provides a solution. However, in doing so, Heinekey and Steeves haven't always found the exotic, international locations easy to navigate themselves.

The pair learned early on that young women don't often play a role in the business environment of some countries. Heinekey and Steeves state, "In some countries, for example, we've had to disprove local attitudes towards working with two women..." The cultural differences regarding television as an appropriate medium have also required that they "take potential clients through a learning process." What has been their guiding philosophy in navigating these unfamiliar waters? According to Heinekey, it's their sensitivity to cultural differences and their focus on professionalism and preparation that have helped open doors for them around the globe.

"We're really doing well," says Steeves. In 2007, their company had 20 employees (up from just two in 2004) and projected $5 million in sales for 2008. In 2007, the Business Development Bank of Canada applauded their success and bestowed upon them the Young Entrepreneur Award for British Columbia. According to BDBC President and CEO Jean-René Halde, "they took an interesting concept, developed a novel product and turned it into a thriving global enterprise."

Critical Thinking Question

1. The decision to "go international" requires a high degree of analysis and examination of factors both internal and external to the business. Assess EPIC's form of competitive advantage, level of involvement in international business, and various barriers to international trade.

Levels of Involvement in International Business

Several different levels of involvement in international business are possible. A firm may act as an *exporter* or *importer*, organize as an *international firm*, or operate as a *multinational firm*. Most of the world's largest industrial firms are multinationals.

Exporters and Importers

Exporting and importing represent the lowest level of involvement in international operations, but they are excellent ways to learn the fine points of global business. An **exporter** is a firm that makes products in one country and then distributes and sells them in other countries. An **importer** buys products in foreign markets and then imports them for resale in its home country. Exporters and importers tend to conduct most of their business in their home nations, but some companies export a large proportion of what they produce. Both Coke and IBM entered international markets as exporters to Europe before they actually set up production facilities there.

exporter A firm that makes products in one country and then distributes and sells them in others.

importer A firm that buys products in foreign markets and then imports them for resale in its home country.

Canada ranks first among the G8 countries in the proportion of its production that is exported (almost 40 percent).[16] Large and small Canadian firms export products and services. For example, McCain Foods is a formidable presence in Europe, where it holds a 75 percent share of the market for "oven fries" in Germany; Sabian Cymbals sells 90 percent of its products in 80 different countries; Electrovert Ltd. does 95 percent of its business outside Canada; and Lingo Media Inc. is the largest supplier of English-language textbooks in China's primary school system.[17]

Exporting is also important to many other countries. Perhaps the most obvious examples are countries like Venezuela, Saudi Arabia, and Nigeria, which rely heavily on revenues generated from oil exports. But there are other not-so-obvious exports that are important, like the exporting of movies from Hollywood. Although U.S. movie revenues have been declining during the past few years, Hollywood has been very successful at exporting its product around the world. In 2007, for example, nearly half the total revenue from movie theatres came from outside the United States. International sales accounted for 81 percent of *The Golden Compass*'s total earnings and 68 percent of the total earnings of *Pirates of the Caribbean: At World's End*.[18]

International Firms

As firms gain experience and success as exporters and importers, they may move to the next level of involvement. An **international firm** conducts a substantial portion of its business abroad, and it may have some manufacturing facilities in foreign countries. Hershey, for example, sells its products in about 50 foreign countries, and it buys ingredients for its chocolates from several foreign suppliers. But it manufactures all of its products in the United States and still generates most of its revenue in the United States.[19] So an international firm may be large and influential in the global economy, but remain basically a domestic firm with international operations. Its central concern is its own domestic market. Despite its obvious presence (and impact) in Canada, Wal-Mart still earns 90 percent of its revenues from U.S. sales.

international firm A company that conducts a significant portion of its business abroad and maintains manufacturing facilities overseas.

Multinational Firms

Most **multinational firms** ordinarily do not think of themselves as having domestic and international divisions. Instead, planning and decision making are geared to international markets.[20] The locations of headquarters are almost irrelevant. Royal Dutch/Shell, Nestlé, IBM, and Ford are well-known multinationals.

multinational firm Controls assets, factories, mines, sales offices, and affiliates in two or more foreign countries.

The economic importance of multinational firms should not be underestimated. Consider, for example, the economic impact of the 500 largest multinational corporations. In 2007, these 500 firms generated $10.6 trillion in revenues and $645 billion in owner profits. They employed tens of millions of people; bought supplies, parts, equipment, and materials from thousands of other firms; and paid billions of dollars in taxes. Their activities and products have affected the lives of hundreds of millions of consumers, competitors, and investors (sometimes in a not very positive way).[21]

International Organizational Structures

Different levels of involvement in international business require different kinds of organizational structure. For example, a structure that would help coordinate an exporter's activities would be inadequate for the activities of a multinational firm. In this section, we briefly consider the spectrum of international organizational strategies, including *independent agents, licensing arrangements, branch offices, strategic alliances,* and *direct investment.*

Independent Agents

independent agent A foreign individual, or organization, who agrees to represent an exporter's interests in foreign markets.

An **independent agent** is a foreign individual or organization that agrees to represent an exporter's interests in foreign markets. Independent agents often act as sales representatives as well—they sell the exporter's products, collect payment, and ensure that customers are satisfied. Independent agents often represent several firms at once and usually do not specialize in a particular product or market. Levi Strauss uses agents to market clothing products in many small countries in Africa, Asia, and South America.

Licensing Arrangements

licensing arrangement An arrangement by an owner of a process or product to allow another business to produce, distribute, or market it for a fee or royalty.

Companies seeking more substantial involvement in international business may opt for **licensing arrangements**, where the exporting firm gives individuals or companies in a foreign country the exclusive right to manufacture or market their products in that market. In return, the exporting firm typically receives a fee plus ongoing payments called royalties.[22] Royalties are usually calculated as a percentage of the licence holder's sales. For example, Can-Eng Manufacturing, Canada's largest supplier of industrial furnaces, exports its furnaces under licensing arrangements with businesses in Japan, Brazil, Germany, Korea, Taiwan, and Mexico.

Franchising is a special form of licensing that is very popular.[23] McDonald's and Pizza Hut franchise around the world. Similarly, Accor SA, a French hotel chain, franchises its Ibis, Sofitel, and Novotel hotels. Allied Domecq PLC, a British firm, owns and franchises Baskin-Robbins and Dunkin' Donuts stores in dozens of countries.

Branch Offices

branch office A location that an exporting firm establishes in a foreign country in order to sell its products more effectively.

world product mandating When a business operates branches, plants, or subsidiaries in several countries, it may assign to one plant or subsidiary the responsibility for researching, developing, manufacturing, and marketing one product or line of products.

Instead of developing relationships with foreign companies or independent agents, a firm may simply send some of its own managers to overseas **branch offices**, where it has more direct control than it does over agents or licence holders. Branch offices also give a company a more visible public presence in foreign countries. Potential customers tend to feel more secure when a business has branch offices in their country. When a business operates branches, plants, or subsidiaries in several countries, it may assign to one plant or subsidiary the responsibility for researching, developing, manufacturing, and marketing one product or line of products. This is known as **world product mandating**.

Strategic Alliances

Recall from Chapter 2 that a *strategic alliance* is formed when a company finds a partner in a foreign country where it would like to conduct business. Each party agrees to invest resources and capital in a new business or else to co-operate in some way for mutual benefit. This new business—the alliance—is then owned by the partners, who divide its profits. For example, Canadian publisher Lingo Media Inc. is involved in a strategic alliance with the state-owned People's Education Press, the market leader in providing textbooks to Chinese schools.[24] Manulife Financial Corp. also entered the Chinese market through a strategic alliance with Sinochem, a state-owned trading company. Manulife trains raw recruits by emphasizing training and team building so that its sales agents can provide good service to customers. The venture now has 8 percent of the Chinese market and Manulife is the second-ranking foreign insurance firm in China.[25]

In many countries, including Mexico, India, and China, laws make alliances virtually the only way to do international business within their borders. Mexico, for example, requires all foreign firms investing there to have local partners. Similarly, Disney's new theme park near Hong Kong is a joint venture with local partners. Vancouver-based Westport Innovations, which makes natural gas engines, is now selling its products to China through a strategic alliance with Cummins Inc., a U.S.-based company that is selling buses powered by clean air technology to the city of Beijing.[26]

In addition to easing the way into new markets, strategic alliances give firms greater control over their foreign activities than independent agents and licensing arrangements. Perhaps most important, alliances allow firms to benefit from the knowledge and expertise of their foreign partners. Microsoft, for example, relies heavily on strategic alliances as it expands into new international markets. This approach has helped the firm to learn the intricacies of doing business in China and India, two very large emerging markets that are difficult to crack.

While there are many positive aspects to strategic alliances, serious conflicts can develop. For example, in 2003 oil giant BP formed a strategic alliance with a Russian company called TNK. When a bitter power struggle erupted in 2008, investors feared that the government of Russia might kick BP out of the alliance without compensation. An agreement was eventually reached that allowed BP to remain a 50/50 partner, but CEO Robert Dudley was removed and BP's control of operations was reduced.[27]

Foreign Direct Investment

Foreign direct investment (FDI) means buying or establishing tangible assets in another country.[28] There has been a long-running debate in Canada about how FDI in Canada affects Canadians. The *Foreign Investment Review Agency (FIRA)*, which was established in 1973, was designed to ensure that FDI benefitted Canadians. In 1985, FIRA's title was changed to **Investment Canada**, and its mandate was changed to focus on attracting foreign investment to Canada. Foreign ownership of Canadian industry has recently been on the rise and may actually be higher than it appears, since many firms that look Canadian are actually multinational companies. For example, before it was bought by Paris-based Vivendi, Seagram had been run from New York City, and Nortel Networks ran all of its business divisions from Dallas, Texas.

foreign direct investment (FDI) Buying or establishing tangible assets in another country.

Investment Canada Replaced FIRA in 1985; designed primarily to attract and facilitate foreign investment in Canada.

Recently, foreign buyouts of major firms like Inco, Four Seasons Hotels, and Alcan have caused some Canadian business leaders to express renewed fears about FDI in Canada. For example, a study by Secor Consulting concluded that Canada is the easiest country in the world for foreigners to come into and take over a business. It also found that only three countries in the world were net

Table 5.2 Top 10 Foreign-Controlled Companies in Canada, 2008 (based on sales revenue)

Company	Annual Revenues (in billions of $)
1. Imperial Oil Ltd.	$31.2
2. Husky Energy Inc.	24.7
3. Wal-Mart Canada Corp.	16.6
4. Novelis Inc.	11.6
5. Honda Canada Inc.	11.5
6. Direct Energy Marketing Ltd.	11.3
7. Ultramar Ltd.	11.1
8. Costco Wholesale Canada	10.1
9. Gerdau Ameristeel Corp.	9.0
10. Ford Motor Co. of Canada Ltd.	8.3

sellers of their companies: Canada, the United States, and Great Britain.[29] The most general concern is that foreign buyouts of Canadian firms will damage the Canadian economy because the head offices will be moved to foreign countries and major decisions will be made there, not in Canada.

Another concern is that foreign takeovers will mean large job losses in Canada. But a Statistics Canada study showed that between 1999 and 2005, foreign companies were responsible for creating *all* of the new head offices that were created in Canada and about two-thirds of the jobs in those new head offices.[30] Another survey of 150 senior Canadian executives showed that the issue of foreign ownership ranked low on their list of perceived economic challenges.[31] Many experts also argue that limitations on foreign investment in Canada essentially shield companies from competition and make them less efficient.[32] Table 5.2 lists the top 10 foreign-owned companies in Canada.

Barriers to International Trade

4 Describe some of the ways in which *social, cultural, economic, legal,* and *political differences* act as barriers to international trade.

Success in foreign markets depends largely on the way businesses respond to the social, economic, legal, and political barriers that exist in international trade. The boxed insert entitled "High Risk in the Mining Business" describes some of the problems that one industry has had.

Social and Cultural Differences

Any firm involved in international business needs to understand something about the society and culture of the countries in which it plans to operate. Unless a firm understands these cultural differences—either by itself or by acquiring a partner that does—it will probably not be successful in its international business activities.

Some differences are relatively obvious. Language barriers can cause inappropriate naming of products (see Chapter 16 for examples). The physical stature of people in different countries can make a difference. For example, the Japanese and French are slimmer and shorter on average than Canadians, and this is an important consideration for firms that intend to sell clothes in these markets.

Differences in the average age of the local population can also have ramifications for product development and marketing. Countries with growing

Business Accountability

High Risk in the Mining Business

Any company that does business abroad has to accept the fact that unexpected events may occur that complicate the conduct of their business or threaten its very survival. These unexpected events can be clearly seen in the mining business.

Sometimes changes in government policy cause significant problems. In 2008, the Democratic Republic of the Congo (DRC) made a surprise announcement: All mining contracts would have to be renegotiated because the royalty rate that foreign mining firms were paying was far too low. In essence, the government of the DRC wanted more profit from foreign companies who were mining in the DRC. After the announcement, shares of foreign mining firms dropped significantly because investors were concerned that the mining projects could be delayed or cancelled entirely.

The DRC is not the only government taking actions like these with foreign mining companies:

- In Zambia, the government proposed to increase the tax rate on foreign mining companies from 25 to 30 percent, increase the royalty rate on copper from 0.6 percent to 3 percent, and introduce a large windfall profits tax.
- Argentina slapped a 10 percent tariff on metals that are exported.
- In Mongolia, the government introduced a 68 percent windfall profits tax on gold and copper.
- In Zimbabwe, Metallon Corp. had to close all five of its mines because the government didn't pay it for the gold Metallon sold them.

Sometimes problems arise when a foreign mining company runs into difficulties with local customs. When Calgary-based Niko Resources tried to develop two natural gas fields in Bangladesh, it discovered that it was common for companies to give "gifts" to members of the media so that they would report favourably on company activities. After Niko refused to give any "gifts" (and after two unfortunate accidents in Niko's gas fields), the media began portraying Niko as an irresponsible company. Then, feuding politicians seized the opportunity to use Niko as a scapegoat during a political campaign. Niko's reputation in Bangladesh suffered greatly, even before the government demanded $12 million for environmental damage. What's worse, in 2009 the RCMP started an investigation into allegations that Niko made improper payments to public officials.

In some cases, local people oppose a foreign mining company's project even before it starts because they are concerned the project will damage the environment:

- Calgary-based TVI Pacific Inc.'s planned open-pit mine and cyanide processing plant in the Philippines led to violent clashes between the company and the Subanon people.
- Critics of Inco Ltd.'s Goro mine in New Caledonia claimed that it would damage the second-largest barrier reef system in the world; indigenous people stormed the site and stole millions of dollars of equipment.
- A group of villagers in Thailand objected to a potash mine that was proposed by Asia Pacific Potash Corp., arguing that the project would increase salt levels in the soil and damage the ability to grow rice.
- After the Ecuadorian government gave the Argentine Oil Company a concession to explore for oil, a protest began that included lodging a legal complaint against the government, demonstrations, letter writing, sabotage, theft of oil company equipment, and detention of oil company workers.

Critical Thinking Questions

1. Why do you think foreign governments introduce significant changes to the rules that govern mining companies?
2. What can mining companies do to reduce the risk of carrying on operations in foreign countries?
3. Do you think that there is something about the mining industry that causes it to have more problems than other industries? Explain.

populations tend to have a high percentage of young people. Thus, electronics and fashionable clothing would likely do well. Countries with stable or declining populations tend to have more old people. Generic pharmaceuticals might be more successful in such markets.

In addition to such obvious differences, a wide range of subtle value differences can have an important impact on international business. For example, many Europeans shop daily. To Canadians used to weekly trips to the supermarket, the European pattern may seem like a waste of time. But for Europeans, shopping is not just "buying food." It is also about meeting friends, exchanging political views, gossiping, and socializing.

Tunisian-born French entrepreneur Tawfik Mathlouthi doesn't like U.S. policy in the Middle East, but he does like the American way of doing business. He created Mecca-Cola for Muslims who like Coke but want to protest U.S. foreign policy by boycotting American products. With a core market of Muslims in France, Mecca-Cola is now sold elsewhere in Europe, and Coke (which has taken no legal action regarding the look-alike label) admits that Mecca-Cola and similar products have hurt its international business, mostly in such countries as Egypt and Morocco.

Even more subtle behavioural differences that can influence business activity exist. For example, crossing your legs in a business meeting in Saudi Arabia is inappropriate, because showing the sole of your foot is viewed as an insult to the other people in the room. In Portugal, it is considered rude to discuss business during dinner, and in Taiwan, tapping your fingers on the table is a sign of appreciation for a meal.

In Japan, the word *yes* is often used to mean "I understand." So, if a Canadian businesswoman asks a Japanese business supplier to lower prices, and he says "Yes," he may simply mean "I understand that you want me to lower prices." But that doesn't mean he will actually lower prices. These kinds of subtleties (and thousands of others) demonstrate that knowledge of local culture and local dos and don'ts is important in international business activity.

Jonathan Fischer, the president of Georgetown, Ontario–based Mold-Masters Ltd., discovered how different cultures can be when he went to Shanghai to visit some of his firm's customers. At one meeting he attended, he was dismayed to hear Chinese buyers yelling at his salespeople. When he asked his Chinese managers what was wrong, they explained that the buyers were simply demanding lower prices and faster delivery times and that the shouting was typical of negotiations in China. Fischer learned that the Chinese negotiating style is tough, focusses on price, appears theatrical, and emphasizes hierarchy, but it also requires giving the other side the opportunity to "save face" somewhere in the negotiations.[33]

If companies do their homework, they can benefit from being sensitive to foreign cultures. McCain Foods Ltd., which entered the South African market in 2000, was initially unsuccessful at selling frozen food products to black South Africans. The company discovered that blacks didn't eat frozen food because they were unfamiliar with it and because most lived in areas that did not have the electricity needed to run freezers (and they couldn't afford freezers anyway). But there is a growing middle class in South Africa, so McCain began trying to reach this group by providing single-serving packages of frozen vegetables that could be consumed in one meal. This eliminated the need for a freezer. McCain also discovered that funerals are significant events in the South African culture and that the cost of hosting the traditional funeral lunch is very high for the family of the deceased. So, the company offered to help grieving families by matching the family's purchases of frozen foods on a one-for-one basis. The families were grateful for the support and were happy to have the McCain name prominently displayed at their funerals. When these individuals go shopping in the future, they will immediately recognize the McCain brand.[34]

Economic Differences

Although cultural differences are often subtle, economic differences can be fairly pronounced. In dealing with economies like those of France and Sweden, for example, firms must be aware of when—and to what extent—the government is involved in a given industry. The French government, for example, is heavily involved in all aspects of airplane design and manufacturing.

Similarly, a foreign firm doing business in a command economy must understand the unfamiliar relationship of government to business, including a host of idiosyncratic practices. General Motors, which entered a $100-million joint venture to build pickup trucks in China, found itself faced with an economic system that favoured state-owned companies over foreign investors. So, while its Chinese suppliers passed on inflation-based price increases for steel and energy, GM could not in turn pass increases on to Chinese consumers. With subsidized state-owned automakers charging considerably less per truck, GM had no choice but to hold its own prices—and lose money on each sale.

Despite such problems, however, not all companies have had negative experiences. When Motorola opened a factory in China to manufacture paging devices, it planned to export most of the pagers because it forecast limited internal demand. But Motorola was forced to reassess the Chinese market after repeatedly selling out its weekly output of 10 000 units. This experience helped convince Motorola to build a $120-million plant in the northern port city of Tianjin to manufacture pagers, simple integrated circuits, and cellphones. As part of the largest manufacturing venture in China, Motorola involved Chinese technicians in the production process. Chinese designers and engineers also played key roles in creating an operation that integrates manufacturing, sales, research, and development.

Legal and Political Differences

Legal and political differences are often closely linked to the structure of the economic systems in different countries. These issues include *tariffs* and *quotas, local-content laws,* and *business-practice laws.*

Quotas, Tariffs, and Subsidies

Even free market economies often use some form of quota and/or tariff that affects the prices and quantities of foreign-made products in those nations. A **quota** restricts the total number of certain products that can be imported into a country. It indirectly raises the prices of those imports by reducing their supply. For example, the United States imposes a quota on the number of Japanese automobiles that can be imported into the country. The ultimate form of quota is an **embargo**: a government order forbidding exportation and/or importation of a particular product—or even all products—of a particular country. For example, Cuban products cannot be legally sold in the United States because there is a long-standing embargo on all Cuban products. Many other countries also impose quotas and embargoes.

quota A restriction by one nation on the total number of products of a certain type that can be imported from another nation.

embargo A government order forbidding exportation and/or importation of a particular product—or even all products—of a particular country.

A **tariff** is a tax charged on imported products. Tariffs raise the price of imports to consumers, who must pay not only for the products but also for the tariff. A *revenue tariff* is imposed strictly to raise money for the government. But most tariffs in effect today are *protectionist tariffs,* which are meant to discourage the importation of a particular product. In 2004, for example, the Canadian government placed a 34.6 percent tariff on barbecues made in China after complaints were received that Chinese companies were unfairly subsidizing the production of barbecues.[35]

tariff A tax charged on imported products.

In 2002, the U.S. Commerce Department imposed a 29 percent tariff on softwood lumber exported from Canada to the United States (84 percent of Canadian lumber is exported to the United States). Ottawa immediately appealed the decision under the provisions of both the North American Free Trade Agreement (NAFTA) and the World Trade Organization (WTO). During 2002 and 2003, both the WTO and NAFTA ruled against the United States on various points in the appeal and said that duties on Canadian lumber must be cut drastically. In spite of these rulings, the United States continued to impose the duties. After the duties were imposed, the Canadian lumber industry paid over $5 billion in duties to the United States.[36] An agreement that resolved the dispute was eventually reached in 2006.[37]

A **subsidy** is a government payment to help a domestic business compete with foreign firms. When the government of a country pays subsidies to one of its domestic industries, it can have a negative effect on producers in other countries. The European Union, for example, pays subsidies to encourage sugar cultivation in unlikely places like Sweden and Finland. This has created a surplus of sugar on the world market, reducing prices and contributing to poverty-level income for sugar producers in some developing countries in the

subsidy A government payment to help domestic business compete with foreign firms.

The long-standing softwood lumber dispute between the United States and Canada has hurt Canadian companies in the forestry industry. The dispute was settled in 2006, but much unhappiness is evident, and critics have charged that the Conservative government caved in to American pressure.

tropics.[38] In 2005, the WTO ruled that the U.S. government's subsidies to its cotton growers broke trade rules, depressed world cotton prices, and hurt Brazilian cotton producers.[39] These subsidies also hurt small cotton farmers in Africa.[40] Canada's supply management system, which restricts imports and guarantees markets for producers of chickens, turkeys, eggs, and milk, could also come under fire since the WTO views the system as an unfair subsidy to producers.[41]

protectionism Protecting domestic business at the expense of free market competition.

Protectionism—the practice of protecting domestic business at the expense of free market competition—has both advocates and critics. Supporters argue that tariffs and quotas protect domestic firms and jobs. In particular, they protect new industries until they are truly able to compete internationally. Some claim that, since other nations have such measures, so must we. Still others justify protectionism in the name of national security. They argue that a nation must be able to produce goods needed for its survival in the event of war and that advanced technology should not be sold to potential enemies.

But opponents of protectionism are equally vocal. They note that protectionism reduces competition and drives up prices to consumers. They cite it as a cause of friction between nations. They maintain that, while jobs in some industries would be lost if protectionism ceased, jobs in other industries would expand if all countries abolished tariffs and quotas.

Protectionism sometimes takes on almost comic proportions. Neither the United States nor European countries grow bananas, but American and European firms both buy and sell bananas in foreign markets. Problems arose when the EU put a quota on bananas imported from Latin America—a market dominated by two U.S. firms, Chiquita and Dole—to help firms based in current and former European colonies in the Caribbean. To retaliate, the United States imposed a 100 percent tariff on certain luxury products imported from Europe, including Louis Vuitton handbags, Scottish cashmere sweaters, and Parma ham.[42]

Local-Content Laws

local-content laws Laws requiring that products sold in a particular country be at least partly made in that country.

A country can affect how a foreign firm does business there by enacting **local-content laws**, which require that products sold in a particular country be at least partly made in that country. These laws typically mean that firms seeking to do business in a country must either invest directly in that country or have a joint-venture partner from that country. In this way, some of the profits from doing business in a foreign country are shared with the people who live there.

Many countries have local-content laws. In a fairly extreme case, Venezuela forbids the import of any product if a like product is made in Venezuela. In 2005, Venezuela's president said he would cancel all mining licences and stop issuing new ones to foreign companies. This move was designed to protect the many small, local miners operating in Venezuela. Oil and gas licences held by foreign companies had already been cancelled. These actions have made foreign companies much more reluctant to invest in Venezuela.[43]

Local-content laws may even exist within a country; when they do, they act just like trade barriers. In Canada, for example, a low bid on a bridge in British Columbia was rejected because the company that made the bid was from Alberta. The job was given to a B.C. company. A New Brunswick window manufacturer lost a contract in Nova Scotia despite having made the lowest bid; the job went to a Nova Scotia company.

The Agreement on Internal Trade (AIT) requires all 10 Canadian provinces to remove barriers to agricultural trade. But when Quebec—which has a strong dairy lobby—prohibited margarine coloured to look like butter, it was in violation of the agreement.[44] Unilever Canada Ltd. challenged the legality of the ban on coloured margarine in 2002, but it was not until 2008 that the province of Quebec repealed the law.[45] In another case, Prince Edward Island ignored a dispute panel ruling that P.E.I.'s milk import restrictions violated the AIT.[46] A third case involves the question of who is allowed to audit the financial statements of public companies. At present, only Chartered Accountants (CAs) are allowed to do this in Quebec. This rule is being challenged by the Certified General Accountants (CGAs), who have auditing rights in most other provinces.[47] If provincial governments do not honour their obligations, the AIT will become meaningless.

Business-Practice Laws

Many businesses entering new markets encounter problems in complying with stringent regulations and bureaucratic obstacles. Such **business-practice laws** are passed by host countries to regulate business practices within their jurisdictions. Wal-Mart left Germany and South Korea because it did not effectively adapt to local tastes and was unable to achieve economies of scale.[48] In Germany, for example, Wal-Mart had to stop refunding price differences on items sold for less by other stores because the practice is illegal in Germany.

business-practice laws Law or regulation passed by host countries to regulate business practices within their jurisdictions.

Sometimes, what is legal (and even accepted) business practice in one country is illegal in another. For example, in 2007, the U.S. government crackdown on internet gambling led to the arrest of Canadian entrepreneur John Lefebvre, who was charged with laundering billions of dollars in gambling proceeds through Neteller PLC, an internet payment company he helped create. U.S. authorities have vowed to prosecute online gambling companies even when their executives are outside the United States. Calvin Ayre, the Canadian entrepreneur who runs the gambling site Bodog.com, does not enter the United States, because he fears he will be arrested.[49]

Paying bribes to government officials to get business is another problem area. The Canadian Corruption of Foreign Public Officials Act prohibits bribery of foreign officials, but as more Canadian companies do business abroad, they find themselves competing against companies that are willing to pay bribes in order to get business. As a result, Canadian companies are losing business to these companies.[50] In an attempt to create fairer competition among multinational companies, ministers from 29 member countries of the Organisation for Economic Co-operation and Development (OECD) agreed in

1997 to criminalize bribery of foreign public officials.[51] More information on bribery is found in Concluding Case 5-1.

Transparency International (TI), an organization devoted to stamping out global corruption, says that companies from Belgium and Canada are least likely to pay bribes to win business in foreign countries; Russian firms are most likely to pay bribes.[52] TI publishes a "Corruption Perceptions Index," which ranks countries based on the amount of corruption that is perceived to exist, based on ratings by business people, academics, and risk analysts. The 2008 index showed that the least corrupt countries are Denmark, New Zealand, and Sweden (all tied for first place), while the most corrupt countries are Iraq, Myanmar, and Somalia. Canada ranked ninth and the United States eighteenth.[53] The U.S. government is investigating scores of different companies in anti-corruption cases.[54]

cartel Any association of producers whose purpose is to control supply of and prices for a given product.

Cartels and Dumping. A **cartel** is an association of producers whose purpose is to control the supply and price of a commodity. The most famous cartel is the Organization of Petroleum Exporting Countries (OPEC), which has given oil-producing countries considerable power in the last 25 years. At various times, other cartels have been evident in diamonds, shipping, and coffee. While nothing much can be done when governments form a cartel like OPEC, private sector businesses can be prosecuted for doing so. In 2008 alone, the European Union imposed fines on importers of Dole and Del Monte bananas (who were fined $95.5 million), on makers of car glass (fined $2 billion), and on makers of paraffin wax used in paper plates and cups (fined $1 billion).[55]

dumping Selling a product for less abroad than in the producing nation; illegal in Canada.

Many countries forbid **dumping**—selling a product abroad for less than the comparable price charged at home. Anti-dumping legislation typically views dumping as occurring if products are being sold at prices less than "fair value," or if the result unfairly harms domestic industry. In 1992, Canada imposed anti-dumping duties on bicycles made in China, but in 2004 the duties were dropped because Chinese companies provided evidence that they could indeed make bicycles as cheaply as they said they could.[56] India has accused China of dumping products on the Indian market that it can't sell elsewhere.[57]

Overcoming Barriers to Trade

5 Explain how *free trade agreements* assist world trade.

Despite the barriers to trade described so far, international trade is flourishing. This is because both organizations and free trade treaties exist to promote international trade. The most significant of these are the General Agreement on Tariffs and Trade (GATT), the World Trade Organization (WTO), the European Union (EU), and the North American Free Trade Agreement (NAFTA).

General Agreement on Tariffs and Trade

General Agreement on Tariffs and Trade (GATT) International trade agreement to encourage the multilateral reduction or elimination of trade barriers.

The **General Agreement on Tariffs and Trade (GATT)**, which has often been humorously referred to as the General Agreement to Talk and Talk, was signed after the Second World War. Its purpose was to reduce or eliminate trade barriers, such as tariffs and quotas. It did so by encouraging nations to protect domestic industries within agreed-upon limits and to engage in multilateral negotiations. While 92 countries signed GATT, not all complied with its rules. The United States was one of the worst offenders. A revision of GATT went into effect in 1994, but many issues remained unresolved—for example, the opening of foreign markets to most financial services.

World Trade Organization (WTO) Organization through which member nations negotiate trading agreements and resolve disputes about trade policies and practices.

The World Trade Organization

On January 1, 1995, the **World Trade Organization (WTO)** came into existence as the successor to GATT. The 140 member countries are required to open

Fisher Ratish Karthikeyan can sometimes double the revenue from a day's take by phoning around to compare prices at markets within reach of his boat. India is a thriving export market for cellphones. About half of India's 600 000 rural communities aren't even wired for fixed-line phone service. The number of cellphone users in India should jump from 3 million to 30 million in the next few years.

markets to international trade, and the WTO is empowered to pursue three goals:

1. Promote trade by encouraging members to adopt fair trade practices
2. Reduce trade barriers by promoting multilateral negotiations
3. Establish fair procedures for resolving disputes among members

The WTO is overseeing reductions in import duties on thousands of products that are traded between countries. Canada, the United States, and the European Union are founding members of the WTO.[58] Unlike GATT, the WTO's decisions are binding, and many people feared that it would make sweeping decisions and boss countries around. But the WTO has not been very successful in toppling global barriers to trade, because political leaders from various countries are fearful of the consequences of freer trade.[59]

The WTO has had significant trouble dealing with the issue of agricultural subsidies. Many attempts have been made during the last few years to resolve this problem (the so-called Doha Round of trade talks). The general idea was that developing countries would lower their tariffs on industrial goods and European and American governments would lower subsidies on agricultural products. In 2008, however, these efforts collapsed, with negotiators from China and India blaming the United States, and negotiators from the United States blaming China and India.[60]

WTO talks on trade liberalization have often been disrupted by protestors who resent the power of the WTO and who are concerned about what world trade is doing to both the environment and the developing countries.[61] Protestors include labour unions (who regard Third World imports as unfair), environmentalists (who are concerned about business activity harming the environment), social activists (who are concerned about poor working conditions in developing countries), and farmers (who are concerned about the effect of free trade on grain prices).

The European Union (EU)

Originally called the Common Market, the **European Union (EU)** initially included only the principal Western European nations like Italy, Germany, France, and the United Kingdom. But by 2009, 27 countries belonged to the EU, including eight former communist countries and two Mediterranean islands. Several other countries are in the process of applying for membership, including Turkey, Macedonia, and Croatia (see Figure 5.5). The EU has eliminated most

European Union (EU) Agreement among major Western European nations to eliminate or make uniform most trade barriers affecting group members.

quotas and set uniform tariff levels on products imported and exported within their group. The EU is the largest free marketplace in the world and produces nearly one-quarter of global wealth.[62]

The North American Free Trade Agreement

North American Free Trade Agreement (NAFTA) Agreement to gradually eliminate tariffs and other trade barriers among the United States, Canada, and Mexico.

The **North American Free Trade Agreement (NAFTA)** came into effect in 1994. It removes tariffs and other trade barriers among Canada, the United States, and Mexico. An earlier agreement, the Canada–U.S. Free Trade Agreement (FTA), took effect in 1989. Its goal was to achieve freer trade between Canada and the United States. Surveys conducted prior to the introduction of the FTA showed that the majority of Canadians were opposed to free trade. They feared that (1) jobs would be lost to other countries, (2) Canada would be flooded with products manufactured in lower-wage countries such as Mexico, (3) Canada would lose the right to control its own environmental standards, (4) the United States might take our natural resources, and (5) Canadian cultural sovereignty would be lost.

Supporters of free trade, by contrast, argued that (1) access to U.S. markets would be guaranteed by free trade, and this would protect Canadian employment; (2) Canadian exports would increase because of free trade; (3) the environment was not covered in free trade agreements; (4) there was nothing in the free trade agreement that threatened Canada's control over its energy resources; and (5) the free trade agreement was about trade and tariffs, not cultural sovereignty.

What has actually happened since NAFTA took effect? In 2004, a group of economists at the Canadian Economics Association concluded that free trade has not been as good for Canada as predicted by its supporters, nor as bad for Canada as predicted by its detractors.[63] Several specific effects are noticeable:

- NAFTA has created a much more active North American market.
- Direct foreign investment has increased in Canada.

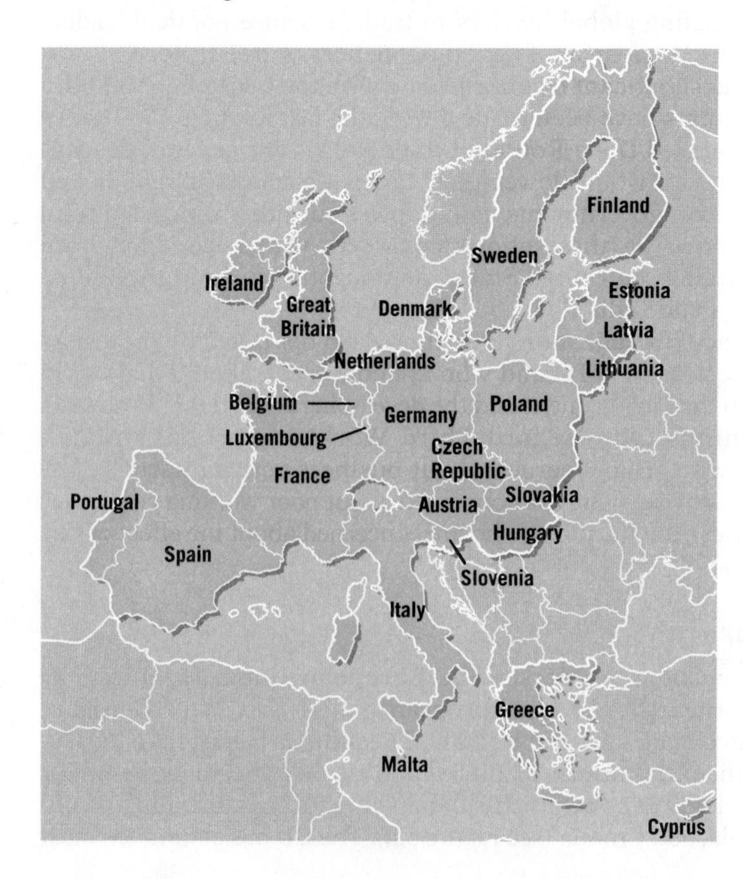

Figure 5.5 The nations of the European Union (EU).

- U.S. imports from (and exports to) Mexico have increased.
- Canada has become an exporting powerhouse.
- Trade between the United States and Canada has risen sharply, and Canada enjoys a large trade surplus with the United States.

In the last few years, there is evidence that the benefits of NAFTA are slowly being eroded by ever-increasing delays at border crossings, caused mostly by heavy U.S. border security as a result of the terrorist attacks in 2001. Studies by the Conference Board of Canada and the Canadian and U.S. chambers of commerce show that companies are not able to take advantage of the efficiencies of integrated supply chains because there are so many cross-border delays. Those delays are forcing companies to spend extra time and money just trying to ensure that their deliveries will get through to customers on time.[64]

Other Free Trade Agreements in the Americas

NAFTA is the most publicized trade agreement in the Americas, but there has been a flurry of activity among other countries as well. On January 1, 1995, a free trade agreement known as Mercosur went into effect between Argentina, Brazil, Uruguay, and Paraguay. By 2005, tariffs were eliminated on 80 percent of the goods traded between those four countries. Brazil has proposed enlarging Mercosur into a South American Free Trade Area (SAFTA), which might eventually negotiate with NAFTA to form an Americas Free Trade Area (AFTA).

There are several other free trade areas in existence in the Americas as well: the Andean Pact (Bolivia, Ecuador, Colombia, Peru, and Venezuela), the Central American Common Market (Costa Rica, El Salvador, Guatemala, Honduras, and Nicaragua), the G-3 group (Colombia, Mexico, and Venezuela), and the Caribbean Common Market (many of the island nations of the Caribbean).[65] The population of the various free trade areas of the Americas totals nearly 900 million. The economies of many of these nations are growing rapidly, and they will become increasingly important to Canada during the next decade.

Free Trade Agreements Elsewhere

Free trade agreements are not restricted to the Americas. A high level of activity is evident around the world as groups of nations band together to form regional trade associations for their own benefit. Here are some examples:

- the Association of Southeast Asian Nations (ASEAN) (see Figure 5.6)
- the Asia-Pacific Economic Cooperation (many nations of the Pacific Rim, as well as the United States, Canada, and Mexico)
- the Economic Community of Central African States (many nations in equatorial Africa)
- the Gulf Cooperation Council (Bahrain, Kuwait, Oman, Qatar, Saudi Arabia, and the United Arab Emirates)

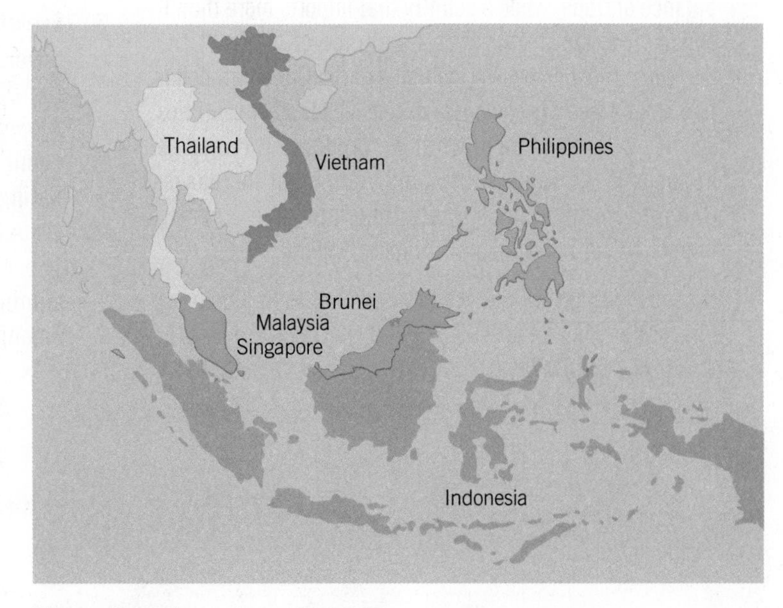

Figure 5.6 The nations of ASEAN.

Test yourself on the material for this chapter at **www.pearsoned.ca/mybusinesslab.**

Summary of Learning Objectives

1. **Describe the rise of international business and identify the *major world marketplaces*.** More and more business firms are engaged in international business. *Globalization* refers to the process by which the world economy is quickly becoming a single interdependent entity. The global economy is characterized by a rapid growth in the exchange of information and trade in services. The three major marketplaces for international business are North America (the United States, Canada, and Mexico), Western Europe (which is dominated by Germany, the United Kingdom, France, and Italy), and Asia-Pacific (where the dominant country, Japan, is surrounded by such rapidly advancing nations as South Korea, Taiwan, Hong Kong, and China).

2. **Explain how different *forms of competitive advantage, import-export balances, exchange rates,* and *foreign competition* determine the ways in which countries and businesses respond to the international environment.** With an *absolute advantage*, a country engages in international trade because it can produce a good or service more cheaply and/or of higher quality than any other country. But more often, countries trade because they enjoy *comparative advantages*. That is, they can produce some products more efficiently or better than other products. A country that exports more than it imports has a favourable balance of trade, while a country that imports more than it exports has an unfavourable balance of trade. If the *exchange rate* decreases (the value of the Canadian dollar falls), our exports become less expensive for other countries so they will buy more of what we produce. The reverse happens if the value of the Canadian dollar increases. Changes in the exchange rate therefore have a strong impact on our international competitiveness.

3. **Discuss the factors involved in deciding to do business internationally and in selecting the appropriate *levels of international involvement* and *international organizational structure*.** In deciding whether to do business internationally, a firm must determine whether a market for its product exists abroad, and if so, whether the firm has the skills and knowledge to manage such a business. It must assess the business climates of other nations to ensure that they are conducive to international operations. A firm must also decide on its level of international involvement. It can choose to be an *exporter* or *importer,* to organize as an *international firm*, or to operate as a *multinational firm.* The choice will influence the organizational structure of its international operations, specifically, its use of *independent agents*, *licensing arrangements*, *branch offices*, *strategic alliances*, and *direct investment.*

4. **Describe some of the ways in which *social, cultural, economic, legal,* and *political differences* act as barriers to international trade.** *Social and cultural differences* that can serve as barriers to trade include language, social values, and traditional buying patterns. Differences in *economic systems* may force businesses to establish close relationships with foreign governments before they are permitted to do business abroad. *Quotas, tariffs, subsidies,* and *local-content laws* offer protection to local industries. Differences in *business-practice laws* mean that standard business practices in one nation may be illegal in another.

5. **Explain how *free trade agreements* assist world trade.** Several *trade agreements* have attempted to eliminate restrictions on free trade internationally. The *General Agreement on Tariffs and Trade (GATT)* was instituted to eliminate tariffs and other trade barriers among participating nations. The *European Union (EU)* has eliminated virtually all trade barriers among the 27 member nations. The *North American Free Trade Agreement (NAFTA)* eliminates many of the barriers to free trade that exist among the United States, Canada, and Mexico.

Key Terms

absolute advantage (p. 146)
balance of payments (p. 148)
balance of trade (p. 147)
branch office (p. 154)
business-practice laws (p. 161)
cartel (p. 162)
comparative advantage (p. 146)
dumping (p. 162)
embargo (p. 159)
euro (p. 150)
European Union (EU) (p. 163)
exchange rate (p. 149)
exporter (p. 153)
exports (p. 142)
foreign direct investment (FDI) (p. 155)
General Agreement on Tariffs and Trade (GATT) (p. 162)
globalization (p. 142)
importer (p. 153)
imports (p. 142)
independent agent (p. 154)
international competitiveness (p. 147)
international firm (p. 153)
Investment Canada (p. 155)
licensing arrangement (p. 154)
local-content laws (p. 160)
multinational firm (p. 153)
national competitive advantage (p. 146)
North American Free Trade Agreement (NAFTA) (p. 164)
per capita income (p. 143)
protectionism (p. 160)
quota (p. 159)
subsidy (p. 159)
tariff (p. 159)
trade deficit (p. 148)
trade surplus (p. 148)
world product mandating (p. 154)
World Trade Organization (WTO) (p. 162)

Questions for Analysis

1. How does the economic system of a country affect foreign firms interested in doing business there?
2. Make a list of all the major items in your bedroom. Identify the country in which each item was made. Give possible reasons why that nation might have a comparative advantage in producing this good.
3. Assume that you are the manager of a small firm seeking to enter the international arena. What information would you need about the market that you're thinking of entering?
4. Do you think that a firm that is operating internationally is better to adopt a single standard of ethical conduct or to adapt to local conditions? Under what kinds of conditions might each approach be preferable?
5. What aspects of the culture in your province or region would be of interest to a foreign firm thinking about locating there?
6. Do you support protectionist tariffs for Canada? If so, in what instances and for what reasons? If not, why not?
7. Is NAFTA good for Canada? Give supporting reasons for your answer.
8. Explain how it is possible for a country to have a positive balance of trade and a negative balance of payments.

Application Exercises

1. Interview the manager of a local firm that does at least some business internationally. Identify reasons why the company decided to "go international," as well as the level of the firm's international involvement and the organizational structure it uses for its international operations.
2. Select a product familiar to you. Using library references and the internet, learn something about the culture of India and identify the problems that might arise in trying to market this product to India's citizens.

Building Your Business Skills

Putting Yourself in Your Place

The Purpose of the Assignment

To encourage students to apply global business strategies to a small business situation.

Background

Some people might say that Yolanda Lang is a bit too confident. Others might say that she needs confidence—and more—to succeed in the business she's chosen. But one thing is certain: Lang is determined to grow INDE, her handbag design company, into a global enterprise. At only 28 years of age, she has time on her side—if she makes the right business moves now.

These days, Lang spends most of her time in Milan, Italy. Backed by $50 000 of her parents' personal savings, she is trying to compete with Gucci, Fendi, and other high-end handbag makers. Her target market is women willing to spend $200 on a purse. Ironically, Lang was forced to set up shop in Italy because of the snobbishness of these customers, who buy high-end bags only if they're European made. "Strangely enough," she muses, "I need to be in Europe to sell in North America."

To succeed, she must first find ways to keep production costs down—a tough task for a woman in a male-dominated business culture. Her fluent Italian is an advantage, but she's often forced to turn down inappropriate dinner invitations. She also has to figure out how to get her 22-bag collection into stores worldwide. Retailers are showing her bags in Italy and Japan, but she's had little luck in the United States. "I intend to be a global company," says Lang. The question is how to succeed first as a small business.

Assignment

Step 1

Join together with three or four other students to discuss the steps that Lang has taken so far to break into the U.S. retail market. These steps include the following:

- buying a mailing list of 5000 shoppers from high-end department store Neiman Marcus and selling directly to these customers
- linking with a manufacturer's representative to sell her line in major U.S. cities while she herself concentrates on Europe

Step 2

Based on what you learned in this chapter, suggest other strategies that might help Lang grow her business. Working with group members, consider whether the following options would help or hurt Lang's business. Explain why a strategy is likely to work or likely to fail.

- Lang could relocate to the United States and sell abroad through an independent agent.
- Lang could relocate to the United States and set up a branch office in Italy.
- Lang could find a partner in Italy and form a strategic alliance that would allow her to build her business on both continents.

Step 3

Working alone, create a written marketing plan for INDE. What steps would you recommend that Lang take to reach her goal of becoming a global company? Compare your written response with those of other group members.

Questions for Discussion

1. What are the most promising steps that Lang can take to grow her business? What are the least promising?
2. Lang thinks that her trouble breaking into the U.S. retail market stems from the fact that her company is unknown. How would this circumstance affect the strategies suggested in Steps 1 and 2?
3. When Lang deals with Italian manufacturers, she is a young, attractive woman in a man's world. Often, she must convince men that her purpose is business and nothing else. How should Lang handle personal invitations that get in the way of business? How can she say no while still maintaining business relationships? Why is it often difficult for women to do business in male-dominated cultures?
4. The American consulate has given Lang little business help because her products are made in Italy. Do you think the consulate's treatment of an American business person is fair or unfair? Explain your answer.
5. Do you think Lang's relocation to Italy will pay off? Why or why not?
6. With Lang's goals of creating a global company, can INDE continue to be a one-person operation?

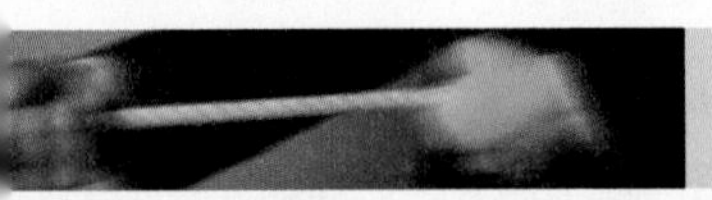

Exercising Your Ethics: Team Exercise

Weighing the Trade-offs

The Situation

There is a small bank that is headquartered in western Canada. The firm is privately owned and all the managers own stock in the bank. The company's senior managers (and majority owners) have decided to sell the bank to a major international banking company within the next two to three years. First, though, the bank corporation needs to trim its expenses in order to make it more attractive to a potential buyer.

The Dilemma

Because the bank corporation has been a locally owned and operated enterprise, it has maintained a full slate of operations within the local market. For instance, its corporate offices, many banking outlets, and all of its support activities are housed locally. The latter category includes a large call centre—a staff of 30 people who handle most customer calls involving questions about their accounts.

There has been a growing trend in banking, though, to outsource call centres to foreign countries, most notably India. Such markets have an abundance of potential English-speaking employees, excellent technology, and low wages. One senior manager has argued that the bank corporation should outsource its call centre immediately. This would enable the firm to lower its costs, thus making it even more attractive to a potential buyer. When confronted with the prospect of cutting 30 jobs, the manager acknowledges that will be tough, but he is certain that any buyer will eventually do the same anyway.

Another vocal senior manager, though, is opposed to this idea. This person argues that because the bank corporation was started locally and has strong ties to the local community, it should maintain its current operations until the bank is sold. Then, this manager argues, if a new owner decides to cut jobs, "it will be on their conscience, not ours."

Team Activity

Assemble a group of four students and assign each group member to one of the following roles:

- senior manager (majority owner) of the bank
- call centre employee
- bank customer
- bank corporation investor

Action Steps

1. Before discussing the situation with your group, and from the perspective of your assigned role, do you think that the call centre should be outsourced immediately? Write down the reasons for your position.
2. Before discussing the situation with your group, and from the perspective of your assigned role, what are the underlying ethical issues, if any, in this situation? Write down the issues.
3. Gather your group together and reveal, in turn, each member's comments on whether the call centre should be outsourced immediately. Next, reveal the ethical issues listed by each member.
4. Appoint someone to record the main points of agreement and disagreement within the group. How do you explain the results? What accounts for any disagreement?
5. From an ethical standpoint, what does your group conclude is the most appropriate action for the bank to take in this situation?
6. Develop a group response to the following question: Can your team identify other solutions that might help satisfy both senior managers' views?

For additional cases and exercise material, go to www.pearsoned.ca/mybusinesslab.

Concluding Case 5-1

Bribery on the International Scene

Historically, European countries have had relatively lax bribery laws. At one point, companies were even allowed to pay "commissions" to foreign officials and deduct such payments from their taxes. But that practice was outlawed in Germany in 1999 and in France in 2000. European countries are starting to take a much tougher stance on practices that have often been employed in the past by companies as they attempted to win contracts.

Recently there have been two high-profile cases where European companies have been charged with bribing potential customers in order to obtain business. One case involves Siemens AG, Europe's largest engineering company. It does business in nearly 200 countries around the world and manufactures a wide range of products, including light bulbs, medical scanners, steam turbines, and high-speed trains. The other company is Alstom SA, a French engineering firm that makes power turbines, high-speed trains, and subway cars.

Siemens AG

In 2006, German police raided the company's headquarters looking for evidence that Siemens managers had bribed potential customers in order to win projects in various foreign countries. After an internal investigation in the fall of 2007, the company said it found US$1.3 billion in suspicious transactions during the period 2000–2006. The investigation triggered the resignation of the company's CEO and its supervisory board chairman. The U.S. Justice Department had also been investigating Siemens under its Foreign Corrupt Practices Act. In 2007, a German court fined Siemens US$284 million after the company admitted that it bribed government officials in Nigeria, Russia, and Libya in order to win telecommunications equipment contracts in those countries.

In July 2008, Reinhard Siekaczek, a sales executive at the company, was found guilty of breach of trust. He had funnelled US$77 million into a slush fund that was used to pay bribes to help win infrastructure contracts. He was fined US$170 000 and given a two-year suspended sentence. He also testified that his superiors were aware of what was going on. In fact, he said they told him to organize a new way of raising money to pay bribes. So he created fake contracts that he used to extract US$83 million from Siemens' regular accounts. He received a lenient sentence because he co-operated. In October 2008, a Munich court ruled that Siemens had paid US$17.5 million in bribes to government officials in Nigeria, Libya, and Russia. These bribes were facilitated by Siekaczek. In December 2008, Siemens agreed to pay US$1.6 billion in fines levied by the German and U.S. governments. As a result of the scandal, there has been a massive personnel shakeup at Siemens. All but one management board member has been replaced.

Alstom SA

Alstom is alleged to have given hundreds of millions of dollars of bribes to go-betweens to win contracts in South America and Asia. Suspicious contracts include a subway expansion and hydroelectric plant in Brazil and electric power stations in Singapore and Venezuela. In Brazil, for example, it is alleged that a mysterious intermediary arranged payments to Brazilian politicians so that they would award lucrative public works contracts to Alstom. The intermediary was paid US$5 million, but so far there is no evidence that any Brazilian politicians actually received any money. If it loses its case, Alstom could be banned from bidding on contracts in fast-growing economies like Brazil. The company denies any wrongdoing and says it is a victim, not a perpetrator.

Documents seized by prosecutors allegedly show that the scheme was run by senior Alstom officials in Paris and that cash was channelled through shell companies and Swiss bank accounts to make it look like Alstom was not involved. Investigators claim that the alleged bribery started in 1997, when a Paris-based Alstom executive wrote a memo proposing that an intermediary be paid a big commission to help win political support in Brazil for Alstom's bids. In another memo, the executive noted that the intermediary was close to the governor of Sao Paulo and could "get things done" if he (the intermediary) was paid 7.5 percent of the value of any contract that was signed. Shortly after that, a team of executives was formed to work with the intermediary. Records of the "commission" payments were sent to a Swiss banker for safekeeping. The banker kept the records at the home of a secretary. The documents were discovered during the course of an unrelated probe after the banker was arrested and charged with laundering money for a South American drug ring. The identity of the intermediary is still unknown.

Questions for Discussion

1. Each year Transparency International publishes a Corruption Perceptions Index that ranks various countries based on the amount of corruption that is perceived to exist in each one. Which countries are least corrupt? Most corrupt? Do you notice any patterns? Explain.

2. Bribery of public officials seems to be an accepted practice in some countries and absolutely forbidden in others. Why is this the case? How can companies that operate in different international settings cope with these differences?
3. Refer back to Chapter 3, where four ethical norms are noted (utility, rights, justice, and caring). Briefly summarize the essence of each of these ethical norms. Which of the four approaches do you think was operative at Siemens? At Alstom? Explain your answer.
4. Again referring back to Chapter 3, use Figure 3.1 to analyze the Siemens and Alstom cases. What do you conclude? Explain your reasoning.

Concluding Case 5-2

International Challenges in the Clothing Industry

On January 1, 2005, import quotas in Canada were lifted for members of the World Trade Organization. Prior to that time, the amount of textiles and apparel that could be imported into Canada from countries like China and India was limited to protect domestic Canadian industries. The Canadian government unveiled a $600-million aid package to help Canadian companies cope with the expected increase in cheap imports, but many in the industry didn't think this would help much. A mere seven months after the import quotas were lifted, the Canadian apparel industry had lost about 20 percent of its workforce. Many of these jobs were shifted to low-wage countries as companies tried to reduce their costs to compete with Chinese imports.

The town of Huntingdon, Quebec (population 2600), discovered first-hand what the new trade rules meant even before they were implemented. In December 2004, townspeople learned that Huntingdon Mills was bankrupt and that 215 jobs would be lost, and that Cleyn & Tinker would soon shut down, costing 600 workers their jobs. The closing of the two textile mills meant a 25 percent decline in the town's tax revenue and increased the unemployment rate (already at 20 percent). Workers don't put all the blame on China. They feel that the Canadian government is accountable because it gave undue import preferences to Caribbean and other poor countries and that it didn't do enough to keep the Canadian dollar from rising and making Canada's textile exports more expensive.

Two successful apparel companies in Quebec—Peerless Clothing Inc. and Gildan Activewear—are also trying to determine what the dropping of import quotas will mean for them. Peerless operates the largest men's tailored clothing factory in North America, producing 30 000 suits and 40 000 pairs of trousers each week. Annual sales exceed $300 million, and Peerless has captured 20 percent of the U.S. men's suit market. A U.S. retailer who orders a suit on a Monday knows it will show up the next *day* at Peerless's shipping centre in St. Albans, Vermont, ready to be sent anywhere in the United States. Part of Peerless's success is attributed to owner Alvin Segal's invention of the "engineered suit," where a high-quality suit is made using assembly line efficiencies. The company has also benefitted from the Canada–U.S. free trade agreement; Segal landed contracts with major U.S. retailers and with labels like Ralph Lauren and Calvin Klein.

Gildan Activewear has become a global T-shirt powerhouse by focussing on being the highest-quality, lowest-cost provider of "blank" 100 percent cotton T-shirts, which are sold to wholesalers and then imprinted with logos and designs. Using this strategy, Gildan has achieved annual sales of $600 million and has captured 29 percent of the U.S. imprinted T-shirt market. Its goal is 40 percent of the U.S. market. Unlike Peerless, Gildan aggressively uses offshore manufacturing facilities, mostly in the Caribbean where labour costs are low.

Both Peerless and Gildan have to keep an eye on future imports from China. The vice-chair of Peerless says that since Peerless imports most of its textiles from abroad, the elimination of the 16 percent tariff on yarn that Peerless imports will enable it to enjoy a significant reduction in costs, allowing it to be price competitive. Gildan's executive vice-president said his company will be able to meet the threat from China because of Gildan's economies of scale, its state-of-the-art factories, and its already low labour costs.

The government aid package is designed to help both the capital-intensive textile industry and the labour-intensive apparel industry, but the interests of these two industries often do not coincide. The apparel industry pays relatively low wages, buys the lowest-cost fabric it can find, and is able to shift production to wherever it makes the most economic sense. By contrast, the textile industry pays higher wages and invests in new technology to remain competitive in its Canadian base. The irony is that the new regulations will allow Canadian apparel makers to import yarn duty-free. That means that they can use textiles that are not made in Canada, thus hurting Canadian textile mills.

Questions for Discussion

1. Explain how exchange rates and the value of the Canadian dollar have affected the garment industry. Should the Canadian government try to influence the value of the Canadian dollar? Defend your answer.
2. Describe the key arguments made by supporters of protectionism. To what extent are these arguments relevant for the current situation in the garment industry? Describe the key arguments made by those who support free trade. To what extent are these relevant for the current situation in the garment industry?
3. To what extent should the Canadian government intervene and protect industries like the garment industry? Defend your answer.
4. *There should be no tariffs at all on products moving between any countries. Only then will the world's economic system be operating at full efficiency.* Do you agree or disagree with this statement? Explain.

CBC Video Case 1-1

Whistle-blowers at the RCMP

In 2007, four members of the RCMP went public with charges of fraud, misrepresentation, corruption, and nepotism against the leadership of the RCMP. The most senior whistle-blower was Fraser Macauley, a career Mountie who had worked his way up through the ranks to become a senior human resources officer. He said that he had tried to alert his bosses to problems at the RCMP but was lied to, shunned, and eventually pushed out of his job for his whistle-blowing activity.

While it is very unusual to see Mounties talking publicly about fraud, nepotism, and other criminal allegations, the four Mounties testified that a senior group of managers at the RCMP had breached the organization's core values *and* the Criminal Code. Macauley recognizes that the RCMP is taking a hit in its reputation, but he came forward because he felt that doing so would eventually make the organization a better place.

Many Canadians are wondering how something like this could happen in our national police force. Macauley says that a small group of top managers used the RCMP pension fund to hire people who were related to senior members of the force and who weren't even doing pension fund work. The four Mounties who testified said that when they reported this unacceptable activity to senior management, they were stonewalled and punished.

When the allegations first emerged, an internal investigation was launched by the RCMP but was cancelled by Commissioner Giuliano Zaccardelli. The Ottawa city police then conducted their own investigation, but no formal charges were laid. The Auditor General eventually confirmed much of what Macauley was saying, but by that time he had been transferred to the Department of National Defence (DND). Macauley says that DND was known as the "penalty box." He is certain that he was transferred because he had been looking into pension fund irregularities. He also received a reduced performance bonus from his boss, Assistant Commissioner Barbara George. He was told that happened because he didn't support the commissioner.

During his last conversation with Commissioner Zaccardelli, Macauley was told "it was time to go." This was an emotional conversation and Macauley felt terrible. He told Zaccardelli that he (Macauley) had never lied to the commissioner before, so why did Zaccardelli think he would start now? Zaccardelli called the accusations Macauley was making "baseless" and said that the pension fund was not at risk. Macauley points out that he never said that the pension fund was at risk but that funds were being used in an unacceptable manner and relatives of top managers were being paid for work that was not pension fund related. Macauley says that now it's about accountability for decisions that top managers made.

After the public investigation, Macauley was reinstated in his former job. His boss, Barbara George, was suspended from her job for allegedly misleading the parliamentary committee that was looking into the allegations. Commissioner Zaccardelli is no longer with the RCMP.

Questions for Discussion

1. What is ethics? Explain how this idea is relevant for the situation at the RCMP.
2. Briefly describe the four criteria that can be used when trying to make an ethical decision. Which of these criteria is most relevant in the RCMP situation described above? Why?
3. What is meant by the term *whistle-blowing*? Why do whistle-blowers so often get into trouble when they point out questionable organizational practices?
4. Use Figure 3.1 to analyze this situation. What conclusions do you reach as a result of working through Figure 3.1?

Video Resource: "RCMP Whistleblower," *The National* (April 1, 2007).

CBC Video Case 1–2

Mompreneurs

The term *mompreneur* is often used to describe women who are trying to take care of kids and run a business at the same time. But just being a mom and being in business doesn't make a woman a mompreneur. Rather, a mompreneur is a woman who starts a business because she is inspired by being a mother. Consider two stories.

Darlene Martin

Darlene Martin has been teaching skating for 17 years, and while the money is great, the hours are awful, and Darlene has not been able to spend as much time with her daughter as she would like. So she has started a home-based business making and selling expensive jewellery called Bijouxbead (prices range from $100 to $1000 per piece). As a mompreneur, she wants to be able to set her own hours, and she is hoping that Bijouxbead will also make big money.

So far, Darlene has spent $75 000 on her business, and her products are carried in three high-end stores. She also sells her products at invitation-only parties. She wants her business to break even this year, and to do that she must sell $45 000 worth of product in the next five weeks. She's planning a big jewellery show, and she has invited more than 200 people. She checks out craft shows to see how other jewellers display their products, then stops in at the boutiques that are selling her products. The boutiques take a cut of up to 50 percent of sales revenue, but at the craft show she will keep all the profit.

On sale day, family and friends help Darlene with the set-up. She has just six hours to sell $45 000 worth of beads. The first visitors are skaters and their parents. Most other visitors are family and friends (her dentist comes as well). At the end of the day, Darlene has sold just $8500 worth of products. She is far short of her goal, and she realizes that she has to do things differently in order to be successful. She wants to get more publicity for her products in magazines like *Lou Lou* and *Flair*, and she hopes to get her jewellery worn by celebrities.

Sandra Wilson

When Sandra Wilson lost her job at Canadian Airlines in the 1990s, she decided to start a home-based business that would give her flexibility and some extra income. Since she had experienced difficulty in getting non-slip soft shoes for her son Robert, she decided to make a soft shoe out of leather. She named her company Robeez. In 1994, she went to the Vancouver Gift Show trade exhibition with 20 pairs of her new footwear. They were an instant hit. Sales in the first year of her business were $20 000 and doubled every year thereafter. By 2002, sales reached $2 million. A lot of celebrity moms now use her products. She says her business was built largely on word of mouth.

Robeez is the world's leading manufacturer of soft-soled leather footwear. It employs 450 people and sells a diverse product line in 6500 stores located in North America, Europe, Australia, and parts of Asia. In 2006, Sandra sold her company to Stride Rite Corporation for $30 million. She can now enjoy the fruits of her labour. She is still with Stride Rite as a consultant, and she also meets with various mompreneurs once a month to help them.

Questions for Discussion

1. What are the advantages and disadvantages of being a mompreneur?
2. Why do you think that so much publicity is currently being given to mompreneurs? Why is so little publicity given to dadpreneurs?
3. Consider the following statement: *Mompreneurs say they want to spend more time with their children, but many hours of hard work are required each day in order to make a new business successful. This means that mompreneurs will not actually be able to spend any more time with their children.* Do you agree or disagree with the statement? Explain your reasoning.

Video Resource: "Mompreneurs," *Marketplace* (February 16, 2008).

Crafting a Business Plan

Part 1: The Contemporary Business Environment

Goal of the Exercise

In Chapter 4 we discussed how the starting point for virtually every new business is a *business plan.* Business plans describe the business strategy for any new business and demonstrate how that strategy will be implemented. One benefit of a business plan is that, in preparing it, would-be entrepreneurs must develop their idea on paper and firm up their thinking about how to launch their business before investing time and money in it. In this exercise, you'll get started on creating your own business plan.

Exercise Background: Part 1 of the Business Plan

The starting point for any business plan is coming up with a "great idea." This might be a business that you've already considered setting up. If you don't have ideas for a business already, look around. What are some businesses that you come into contact with on a regular basis? Restaurants, childcare services, and specialty stores are a few examples you might consider. You may also wish to create a business that is connected with a talent or interest you have, such as crafts, cooking, or car repair. It's important that you create a company "from scratch" rather than use a company that already exists. You'll learn more if you use your own ideas.

Once you have your business idea, your next step is to create an "identity" for your business. This includes determining a name for your business and an idea of what your business will do. It also includes identifying the type of ownership your business will take, topics we discussed in Chapter 4. The first part of the plan also briefly looks at who your ideal customers are and at how your business will stand out from the crowd. It also looks at how the business will interact with the community and demonstrate social responsibility, topics we discussed in Chapter 3. Finally, almost all business plans today include a perspective on the impact of global business, which we discussed in Chapter 5.

Your Assignment

Step 1

To complete this assignment, you first need to download the *Business Plan Student Template* file from MyBusinessLab at www.pearsoned.ca/mybusinesslab. This is a Microsoft Word file you can use to complete your business plan. For this assignment, you will fill in Part 1 of the plan.

Step 2

Once you have the *Business Plan Student Template* file, you can begin to answer the following questions in Part 1: The Contemporary Business Environment.

1. What is the name of your business?

Hint: When you think of the name of your business, make sure that it captures the spirit of the business you're creating.

2. What will your business do?

Hint: Imagine that you are explaining your idea to a family member or a friend. Keep your description to 30 words or less.

3. What form of business ownership (sole proprietorship, partnership, or corporation) will your business take? Why did you choose this form?

Hint: For more information on types of business ownership, refer to the discussion in Chapter 4.

4. Briefly describe your ideal customers. What are they like in terms of age, income level, and so on?

Hint: You don't have to give too much detail in this part of the plan; you'll provide more details about customers and marketing in later parts of the plan.

5. Why will customers choose to buy from your business instead of your competition?

Hint: In this section, describe what will be unique about your business. For example, is the product special or will you offer the product at a lower price?

6. All businesses have to deal with ethical issues. One way to address these issues is to create a code of ethics. List three core principles your business will follow.

Hint: To help you consider the ethical issues that your business might face, refer to the discussion in Chapter 3.

7. A business shows social responsibility by respecting all of its stakeholders. What steps will you take to create a socially responsible business?

Hint: Refer to the discussion of social responsibility in Chapter 3. What steps can you take to be a "good citizen" in the community? Consider also how you may need to be socially responsible toward your customers and, if applicable, investors, employees, and suppliers.

8. Will you sell your product in another country? If so, what countries and why? What challenges will you face?

Hint: To help you consider issues of global business, refer to Chapter 5. Consider how you will expand internationally (i.e., independent agent, licensing, etc.). Do you expect global competition for your product? What advantages will foreign competitors have?

Note: Once you have answered the questions, save your Word document. You'll be answering additional questions in later chapters.

Part Two

The Business of Managing

Corporate culture, organizational structure, women in top management positions, labour–management relations, and employee motivation and satisfaction are five issues you will read about in the opening cases of Chapters 6 through 10. These and many other issues must be effectively managed if companies hope to grow and prosper. Managers in all business firms—indeed, in any kind of organization—must carry out the basic management functions of planning, organizing, leading, and controlling. These important functions are the basis for this section of the text.

Part Two, The Business of Managing, provides an overview of business management today. It includes a look at the importance of managers in business firms, how businesses are structured to achieve their goals, the management of the firm's human resources, labour–management relations, and the importance of motivating and leading employees.

- We begin in **Chapter 6**, **Managing the Business Enterprise**, by describing the basic functions of management—planning, organizing, leading, and controlling. We also look at the different types and levels of managers, the skills that managers must possess, the importance of goal setting and strategic management, and the idea of corporate culture.
- In **Chapter 7**, **Organizing the Business Enterprise**, we look at the basic organizational structures that companies have adopted and the different kinds of authority that managers have. The impact of the informal organization is also analyzed.
- In **Chapter 8**, **Managing Human Resources**, we explore the activities that are necessary to effectively manage employees, including assessing employee needs, training, promoting, and compensating employees.
- In **Chapter 9**, **Understanding Labour–Management Relations**, we look at the development of the union movement in Canada, why and how workers organize, and how government legislation has affected workers' rights to organize into unions.
- Finally, in **Chapter 10**, **Motivating and Leading Employees**, we examine the important issues of motivation and leadership. We look at the reasons why managers should establish good relationships with their employees, strategies for enhancing employee job satisfaction, and the various approaches to leadership that have been evident over time.

apter 6

Managing the Business Enterprise

After reading this chapter, you should be able to:

1. Describe the four basic functions that constitute the *management process*.
2. Identify *types of managers* by level and area.
3. Describe the five basic *management skills*.
4. Explain the importance of *setting goals* and *formulating strategies*.
5. Discuss *contingency planning* and *crisis management*.
6. Explain the idea of *corporate culture* and why it is important.

Corporate Culture

The term *corporate culture* refers to the shared experiences, values, norms, and ethical stance that characterize an organization. It is important for managers to understand the concept of corporate culture because culture influences the behaviour of employees. Managers can use that knowledge to be more effective in leading and motivating employees. Consider these examples of corporate culture:

- At WestJet, employees have a big stake in the company's success because of profit-sharing, and they contribute ideas about how best to run the airline. For example, a group has formed that calls itself the WestJesters. They do things like developing the cornball jokes that WestJet flight attendants tell during flights.
- Paul Godfrey, the CEO of the Toronto Blue Jays Baseball Club, says the culture of the club is to make employees feel like they are part of a family. To facilitate the culture, Godfrey invites small groups of employees to have "snacks with the president" so they can talk about how the organization is operating. Godfrey encourages questions from employees on virtually any topic.
- Rick George, the CEO of Suncor, says the company's culture is open and non-bureaucratic, and that it has a clear strategy that employees can relate to. The company hires many new people, so it must take steps to ensure that the new employees understand the "soul" of Suncor because they have different experiences and different expectations.
- At Wellington West Holdings Inc., the culture is simple, personal, and fun.

Companies that focus largely on one type of product (for example, Starbucks Coffee Company) may have a fairly homogeneous culture throughout the organization. But large companies with many different divisions and many different types of customers (for example, the Royal Bank of Canada) are likely to have several different subcultures because the various divisions pursue different goals and because different types of people are found in the different divisions. Even in smaller firms, there may be noticeable differences in the culture of the marketing and finance departments.

Culture Surveys

Each year, Waterstone Human Capital conducts in-depth interviews with senior managers at many different Canadian companies and asks them which corporate cultures they admire most. The top three companies named in the 2008 survey were Boston Pizza, Four Seasons Hotels and Resorts, and Intuit Canada. The majority of managers who are interviewed typically say that the culture of their company is not what they want it to be, that their corporate culture is "weak," and that they don't monitor their organization's culture through surveys.

Starbucks is one company that systematically assesses its corporate culture. Once every 18 months employees fill out a Partner View Survey, which contains questions that are designed to help the company determine whether it is making progress toward one of its key values—providing a work environment where people treat one another with respect and dignity. The survey is voluntary, but about 90 percent of employees fill it out (on company time). One reason the participation rate is so high is that the company actually pays attention to what employees say in the survey. For example, when one survey showed that employees were not clear about career progression possibilities in the company, Starbucks held career fairs in several Canadian cities, where company managers spoke with employees about management opportunities at Starbucks.

Cultural Change

Companies sometimes decide that they need to change their culture. A realization of the need for change usually comes after top management sees that changes in the company's external environment are going to require some sort of response from the company. But just because someone recognizes the need does not mean that it will actually be implemented because changing an organization's culture can be very difficult.

In 2007, several RCMP officers alleged that senior management was covering up mismanagement of the RCMP's pension and insurance plans. As a result of these charges, lawyer David Brown was appointed by the government to look into the matter. His report concluded that Commissioner Giuliano Zaccardelli had exercised absolute power, that no one questioned his management style, and that there was a "tone" at the top of the organization that resulted in little respect for employees and put pressure on the employees not to challenge authority. The report also said that whistle-blowers within the RCMP were punished when they pointed out that there were problems. The report concluded that the culture and management structure at the RCMP were "horribly broken." These developments are discouraging because a few years earlier the RCMP had completed a "visioning" process that resulted in a new mission statement, a new set of core values, and a commitment to the communities where it worked. At that time, it was reported that the culture of the RCMP were quite different than it was in the days when military tradition dominated the organization, but subsequent events suggested that the culture had not actually changed.

A similar story can be told about the Canadian Imperial Bank of Commerce. It supposedly had a conservative culture, but as the commercial paper crisis unfolded in 2007 (see Chapter 20), it became clear that CIBC was going to incur billions of dollars of losses because of its exposure to subprime mortgages in the United States. This happened in spite of CIBC's supposed shift to a low-risk culture. ◆

How will this help me?

After reading this chapter, you will have a clearer understanding of how to effectively carry out various management responsibilities. From the perspective of a consumer or investor, you'll be better able to assess and appreciate the quality of management in various companies.

In this chapter, we begin by introducing the idea of the management process and the functions that are necessary in this process. We then identify the different types of managers that are likely to be found in an organization (by level and by area). Next, we describe the basic management skills, paying particular attention to decision-making skills. We then explore the importance of strategic management and effective goal setting in organizational success. We conclude the chapter by examining the concept of corporate culture.

Who Are Managers?

All organizations depend on effective management. Regardless of the type of business they work in, managers perform the same basic functions, are responsible for many of the same tasks, and have many of the same responsibilities. All managers plan, organize, direct, and control day-to-day operations.

Although our focus is on managers in business settings, remember that the principles of management apply to all kinds of organizations. Managers work in charities, churches, social organizations, educational institutions, and government agencies. The prime minister of Canada, the president of the University of Toronto, the executive director of the United Way, the dean of your business school, and the chief administrator of your local hospital are all managers. Remember, too, that managers bring to small organizations many of the same kinds of skills—the ability to make decisions and to respond to a variety of challenges—that they bring to large ones. Regardless of the nature and size of an organization, managers are among its most important resources.

1 Describe the four basic functions that constitute the *management process.*

management The process of planning, organizing, leading, and controlling an enterprise's financial, physical, human, and information resources to achieve the organization's goals of supplying various products and services.

The Management Process

Management is the process of planning, organizing, leading, and controlling an enterprise's financial, physical, human, and information resources to achieve the organization's goals of supplying various products and services. Thus, the CEO of Walt Disney Productions is a manager because he regularly carries out these four functions as films are being made. Actors such as Julia Roberts or Tom Cruise, while they may be the stars of the movies, are not managers because they don't carry out the functions of management.

There are two important overall points to keep in mind when thinking about the management process. First, the planning, organizing, leading, and controlling aspects of a manager's job are interrelated. These activities generally follow one another in a logical sequence, but sometimes they are performed simultaneously or in a different sequence altogether. In fact, a manager is likely to be engaged in all these activities during the course of a business day. Second, it is important to make the distinction between management effectiveness and management efficiency. **Efficiency** means achieving the greatest level of output with a given amount of input. **Effectiveness**, on the other hand, means achieving the organizational goals that have been set. Put another way, efficiency means doing things right, while effectiveness means doing the right things. A manager who focuses on being effective will likely also be efficient, but a manager who focuses on being efficient may or may not be effective.

efficiency Achieving the greatest level of output with a given amount of input.

effectiveness Achieving the organizational goals that have been set.

Planning

Planning is the process of determining the firm's goals and developing a strategy for achieving them. It has five basic steps. In *step 1*, goals are established for the organization. WestJet, for example, may set a goal to fill 90 percent of the seats on every flight. In *step 2*, managers identify whether a gap exists between the company's desire and actual position. Examination of the load factor data may show that the load factor is only 86 percent. In *step 3*, managers develop plans to achieve the desired goal. For example, the fare from Calgary to Winnipeg may be reduced by 10 percent in an attempt to increase the load factor to 90 percent. Note that goals indicate *what* results are desired, while plans indicate *how* these goals are to be achieved. In *step 4*, the plans that have been decided upon are implemented. This involves actually charging the new reduced fare. This is the point in the planning process where thinking is converted into action. In *step 5*, the effectiveness of the plan is assessed. Actual results are compared with planned performance, that is, the load factor data are analyzed to determine whether the 90 percent goal has been achieved. Plans may then have to be modified and a different goal may have to be set.

planning The process of determining the firm's goals and developing a strategy for achieving them.

This is how the planning process worked when Yahoo was created. The company's top managers set a strategic goal of becoming a top firm in the then-emerging market for internet search engines. They started by assessing the ways in which people actually use the web and concluded that people wanted an easy-to-understand web interface. Yahoo also wanted to be able to satisfy a wide array of needs, preferences, and priorities by having people go to as few sites as possible to find what they were looking for. One key component of Yahoo's strategy was to foster partnerships and relationships with other companies so that potential web surfers could draw upon several sources through a single portal. Yahoo managers then began fashioning alliances with such diverse partners as Reuters, Standard & Poor's, the Associated Press (for news coverage), RE/MAX (for real estate information), and a wide array of information providers specializing in sports, weather, entertainment, shopping, and travel.

It may be difficult to predict which plans will be successful. One tool that helps managers assess future possibilities is called **prediction markets**. It involves creating a market where people can buy "shares" in various answers to important questions that need to be answered. At Cisco Systems, for example, 20 employees in a chip-design unit bought shares based on how many defects they thought they would find in a new product (each stock represented a range of possible numbers of defects). The winner of the game received an iPod. The actual number of defects found in the new chip was in the range that was predicted by the group. Other companies that use prediction markets include Microsoft, Best Buy, and Hewlett-Packard.[1]

prediction markets Creating a market where people can buy "shares" in various answers to important questions that need to be answered.

A Hierarchy of Plans

strategic plans Set by top management; reflect decisions about resource allocations, company priorities, and the steps needed to meet strategic goals.

tactical plans Shorter-range plans concerned with implementing specific aspects of the company's strategic plans. They typically involve upper and middle management.

operational plans Plans developed by middle and lower-level managers that set short-term targets for daily, weekly, or monthly performance.

Plans can be made on three general levels, with each level reflecting plans for which managers at that level are responsible. These levels constitute a hierarchy because implementing plans is practical only when there is a logical flow from one level to the next. **Strategic plans**, which are set by top management, reflect decisions about resource allocations, company priorities, and the steps needed to meet strategic goals (we look at strategic planning later in this chapter). General Electric's plan to be number one or number two in all the markets in which it competes is an example of a strategic plan. **Tactical plans** are shorter-range plans concerned with implementing specific aspects of the company's strategic plans. They typically involve upper and middle management. Coca-Cola's plan to increase sales in Europe by building European bottling facilities is an example of a tactical plan. **Operational plans**, which are developed by middle and lower-level managers, set short-term targets for daily, weekly, or monthly performance. McDonald's, for example, establishes operational plans when it stipulates precisely how Big Macs are to be cooked, warmed, and served.

Organizing

organizing Mobilizing the resources that are required to complete a particular task.

Organizing involves mobilizing the resources that are required to complete a particular task (we examine this topic in detail in Chapter 7). The importance of organizing can be seen by considering what happened at Hewlett-Packard, which lost some of its competitive edge a few years ago. One of the major reasons for its slide could be traced back to what had once been a major strength. Specifically, HP had long prided itself on being a corporate confederation of individual businesses. Sometimes these businesses even ended up competing against each other. This approach had been beneficial for much of the firm's history. It was easier for each business to make its own decisions quickly and efficiently, and the competition kept each unit on its toes. By 1998, however, problems had become apparent, and no one could quite figure out what was going on.

Enter Ann Livermore, then head of the firm's software and services business. Livermore realized that the structure that had served so well in the past was now holding the firm back. To regain its competitive edge, HP needed an integrated, organization-wide internet strategy. Unfortunately, the company's highly decentralized organization made that impossible. Livermore led the charge to create one organization to drive a single internet plan. A reorganized HP has bounced back and it has regained its competitive strength.[2]

Leading

leading (or directing) Involves the interactions between managers and their subordinates as they both work to meet the firm's objectives.

Leading (or directing) involves the interactions between managers and their subordinates as they both work to meet the firm's objectives. By definition, managers have the power to give orders and demand results. Leading, however, goes beyond merely giving orders. Leaders attempt to guide and motivate employees to work in the best interests of the organization. Managers at WestJet, for example, have been very successful in motivating employees to go above and beyond normal work practices to ensure the company's (and their own) financial success. We discuss leadership in more detail in Chapter 10; topics include the various approaches to leadership (trait, behavioural, and situational), leadership styles (autocratic, democratic, and free-rein), and recent trends in leadership (e.g., charismatic leadership, ethical leadership, and strategic leadership).

Controlling

controlling The process of monitoring a firm's performance to make sure that it is meeting its goals.

Controlling is the process of monitoring a firm's performance to make sure that it is meeting its goals. Managers at WestJet and Air Canada, for example,

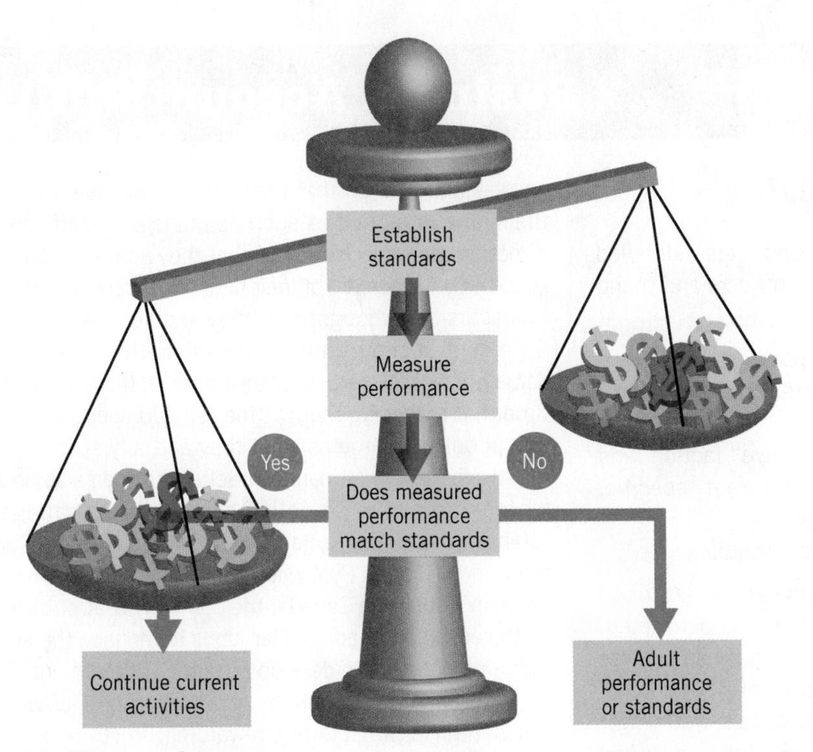

Figure 6.1 The control process.

focus relentlessly on indicators of performance like on-time arrivals, baggage-handling errors, the number of empty seats on an airplane, and results of surveys of employees and customers. If, say, on-time arrivals start to slip, managers focus on the problem and get it fixed. No single element of the firm's performance can slip too far before it's noticed and fixed.

Figure 6.1 illustrates the control process that begins when management establishes standards, often for financial performance. If, for example, a company wants to increase sales by 20 percent over the next 10 years, then an appropriate standard might be an increase of about 2 percent a year. Managers then measure actual performance against standards. If the two amounts agree, the organization continues along its present course. If they vary significantly, however, one or the other needs adjustment.

Control can also show where performance is better than expected and thus can serve as a basis for providing rewards or reducing costs. Volkswagen Canada cancelled a scheduled advertising campaign for its new Eos automobile because the cars were rapidly being sold due to positive word of mouth about the car among consumers.[3]

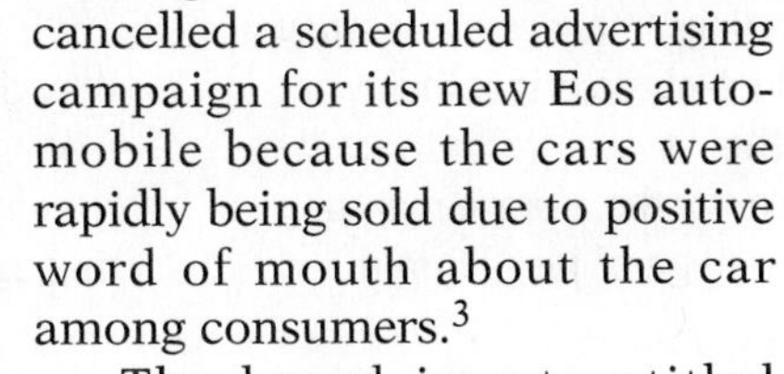

The boxed insert entitled "What Do Managers Actually Do?" explains in practical terms what it means to be a manager.

Japanese organizations don't usually like radical restructuring, but when Senichi Hoshino took over the hapless Hanshin Tigers, he axed 24 of the team's 70 players and replaced them with free agents. He required everyone on the roster to compete for a position, tracked performance daily, and made individual coaches directly responsible for seeing that players executed certain skills. Soon after that, the Tigers won the pennant—a particularly important achievement because superstition says that when the Tigers win, Japan will soon enjoy a period of prolonged prosperity.

Business Accountability

What Do Managers Actually Do?

Henry Mintzberg of McGill University conducted a detailed study of the work of five chief executive officers and found the following:

1. Managers work at an unrelenting pace.
2. Managerial activities are characterized by brevity, variety, and fragmentation.
3. Managers have a preference for "live" action and emphasize work activities that are current, specific, and well defined.
4. Managers are attracted to the verbal media.

Mintzberg believes that a manager's job can be described as 10 roles (in three categories) that must be performed. The manager's formal authority and status give rise to three interpersonal roles: (1) figurehead (duties of a ceremonial nature, such as attending a subordinate's wedding); (2) leader (being responsible for the work of the unit); and (3) liaison (making contact outside the vertical chain of command). These interpersonal roles give rise to three informational roles: (1) monitor (scanning the environment for relevant information); (2) disseminator (passing information to subordinates); and (3) spokesperson (sending information to people outside the unit).

The interpersonal and informational roles allow the manager to carry out four decision-making roles: (1) entrepreneur (improving the performance of the unit); (2) disturbance handler (responding to high-pressure disturbances, such as a strike at a supplier); (3) resource allocator (deciding who will get what in the unit); and (4) negotiator (working out agreements on a wide variety of issues, such as the amount of authority an individual will be given).

Consistent with Mintzberg's findings, managers in a study conducted by Toronto's Pace Productivity said that their work lives were very hectic and that their focus shifted rapidly from activity to activity. For example, for the average manager, 43 different activities lasted an average of just 16 minutes each. Managers felt that they should have spent about half their time on activities such as managing staff, providing direction, and coaching, but that they actually were able to spend only 18 percent of their time on "people management." Managers also thought that they should have spent about 6 percent of their time on administrative tasks, but they actually spent 25 percent of their time on those activities. The time that managers thought they should spend on planning was about the same as what they actually spent.

Insight into what managers actually do can also be gained by looking at the so-called functions of management (planning, organizing, leading, and controlling). Consider the work of Marina Pyo, who is publisher, School Division, at Pearson Education Canada, the company that publishes the textbook you are reading. Her job is to manage the activities that are necessary to develop resources in math and science for the Canadian elementary school market. Her work is at times intense, fragmented, rewarding, frustrating, and fast paced. In short, she is a typical manager.

Pyo carries out the planning function when she drafts a plan for a new book. She is organizing when she develops a new organization chart to facilitate goal achievement. She is leading when she meets with a subordinate to discuss that person's career plans. And she is controlling when she checks sales prospects for a book before ordering a reprint.

Some of Pyo's activities do not easily fit into this "functions of management" model. For example, it is not clear which function she is performing when she negotiates the size of a reprint run with the manager of the sales division. But this activity is captured in Mintzberg's role approach to management (Pyo is carrying out the negotiator role).

Critical Thinking Questions

1. What exactly is it that managers are accountable for?
2. Why do you think managers spend less time on "people management" than they think they should and more time on administrative tasks? How does this affect managerial accountability?

Types of Managers

2 Identify *types of managers* by level and area.

Although all managers plan, organize, lead, and control, not all managers have the same degree of responsibility for each activity. Moreover, managers differ in the specific application of these activities. We can divide managers by their *level* of responsibility or by their *area* of responsibility.

Levels of Management

The three basic levels of management are top, middle, and first-line management. As shown in Figure 6.2, in most firms there are more middle managers than

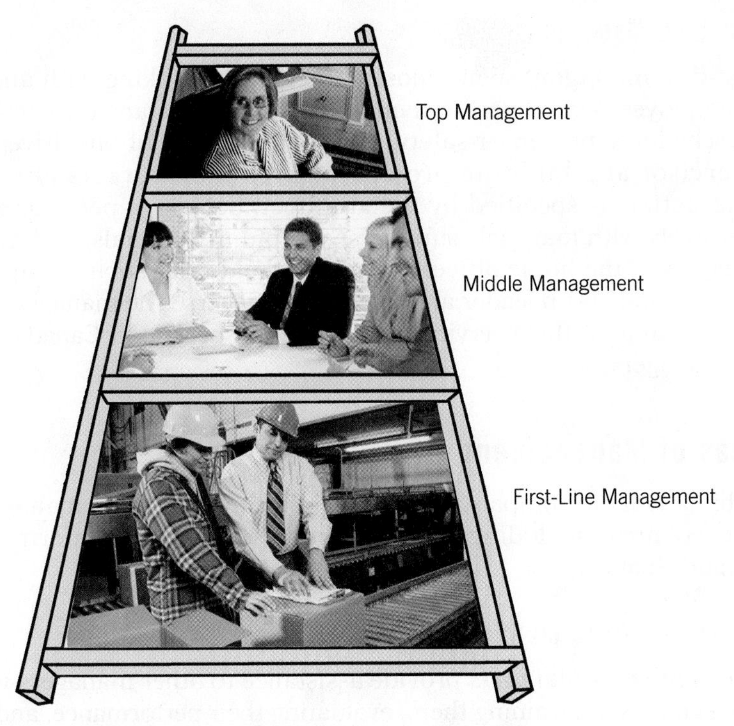

Figure 6.2 Most organizations have three basic levels of management.

top managers and more first-line managers than middle managers. Moreover, as the categories imply, the power of managers and the complexity of their duties increase as we move up the pyramid.

Top Managers

The small number of executives who guide the fortunes of companies are **top managers**. Common titles for top managers include president, vice-president, chief operating officer (COO), chief executive officer (CEO), and chief financial officer (CFO). Top managers are responsible to the board of directors and shareholders of the firm for its overall performance and effectiveness. They set general policies, formulate strategies, oversee significant decisions, and represent the company in its dealings with other businesses and government.[4] In 2006, *Canadian Business* magazine named Denis Turcotte, CEO of Algoma Steel, as the top Canadian CEO for his work in making Algoma the most efficient steel producer in the world.[5]

top managers Those managers responsible for a firm's overall performance and effectiveness and for developing long-range plans for the company.

In some companies, top managers temporarily do the jobs of front-line workers in order to get insights into what employees are actually doing each day and to think of ways to help employees do their jobs better. For example, 150 managers of Loews Hotels in Canada and the United States spend one day every year in an entry-level job at the company. At Amazon.com, top managers deal with customers' phone or email questions one day every two years.[6]

Middle Managers

Middle managers occupy positions between top and first-line managers. Titles such as plant manager, operations manager, and division manager are typical of middle-management jobs. Middle managers are responsible for implementing the strategies, policies, and decisions of the top managers. For example, if top management decides to bring out a new product in 12 months or to cut costs by 5 percent in the next year, middle management will have to decide whether to increase the pace of new product development or to reduce the plant's workforce. With companies increasingly seeking ways to cut costs, the job of middle manager has lately become precarious in many large companies.

middle managers Those managers responsible for implementing the decisions made by top managers.

First-Line Managers

first-line managers Those managers responsible for supervising the work of employees

First-line managers spend most of their time working with and supervising the employees who report to them. For example, a transit supervisor monitors bus schedules, passenger safety, and the behaviour of bus drivers. A first-line supervisor at a building project ensures that workers are carrying out construction as specified by the architect, but the supervisor also interacts extensively with materials suppliers, community officials, and middle and top managers at the home office. Those who hold titles such as supervisor, office manager, and group leader are first-line managers. The manager of a Canadian Tire store and the flight-services manager for a specific Air Canada flight are first-line managers.

Areas of Management

Within any large company, the top, middle, and first-line managers work in a variety of areas, including human resources, operations, information, marketing, and finance.

Human Resource Managers

Human resource managers provide assistance to other managers when they are hiring employees, training them, evaluating their performance, and determining their compensation level. In unionized companies, human resource managers are also involved in negotiations with the union. Imperial Oil has separate departments to deal with recruiting and hiring, wage and salary levels, and labour relations. Smaller firms may have a single department, while very small organizations may have only a single person responsible for all human resource activities. Chapters 8 to 10 address issues involved in human resource management.

Operations Managers

Operations managers are responsible for the production systems that create goods and services. These include production control, inventory control, and quality control, among others. Manufacturing companies like Steelcase, Bristol Aerospace, and Sony need operations managers at many levels. Such firms typically have a vice-president for operations (top manager), plant managers (middle managers), and foremen or supervisors (first-line managers). In recent years, operations management practices have been receiving increasing attention in service organizations, hospitals, universities, and the government. Operations management is the subject of Chapters 11 and 12.

Information Managers

Information managers are responsible for designing and implementing systems that gather, process, and disseminate information. Dramatic increases in both the amount of information available to managers and the ability to manage it have led to the emergence of this important function. Many firms, including Federal Express, have a chief information officer (CIO). Middle managers engaged in information management help design information systems for divisions or plants. Computer systems managers within smaller businesses or operations are first-line managers. Information management is discussed in Chapter 13.

Marketing Managers

Marketing managers are responsible for getting products and services to buyers. Consumer product firms like Procter & Gamble and Coca-Cola often have large numbers of marketing managers at various levels. A large firm will have a vice-president of marketing (top manager), regional marketing managers (middle managers), and several district sales managers (first-line managers). Firms that produce industrial products such as machinery and janitorial supplies tend to put less emphasis on marketing and to have fewer marketing managers. We look at marketing in detail in Chapters 15 to 17.

Financial Managers

Management of a firm's finances, including its investments and accounting functions, is extremely important to its survival. Nearly every company has *financial managers* to plan and oversee its financial resources. Levels of financial management may include a vice-president for finance (top manager), division controllers (middle managers), and accounting supervisors (first-line managers). Financial management is covered in Chapters 14 and 18 to 20.

Basic Management Skills

Describe the five basic *management skills.* 3

The degree of success that managers enjoy is determined by the skills and abilities they possess. Effective managers must have five key skills: *technical, human relations, conceptual, time management*, and *decision-making skills*.

Technical Skills

Skills associated with performing specialized tasks within a company are called **technical skills**. An administrative assistant's ability to type, an animator's ability to draw a cartoon, and an accountant's ability to audit a company's records are all technical skills. People develop their technical skills through education and experience. The administrative assistant, for example, probably took a keyboarding course and has had many hours of practice both on and off the job. The animator may have received training in an art school and probably learned a great deal from experienced animators on the job. The accountant earned a university degree and a professional certification.

technical skills Skills associated with performing specialized tasks within a company.

As Figure 6.3 shows, technical skills are especially important for first-line managers. Most first-line managers spend considerable time helping employees solve work-related problems, monitoring their performance, and training them

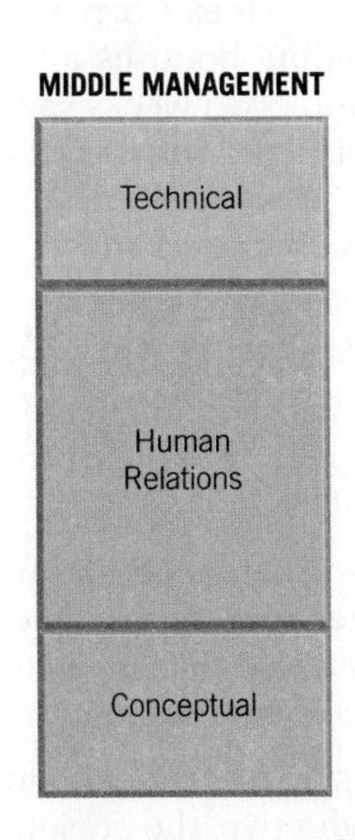

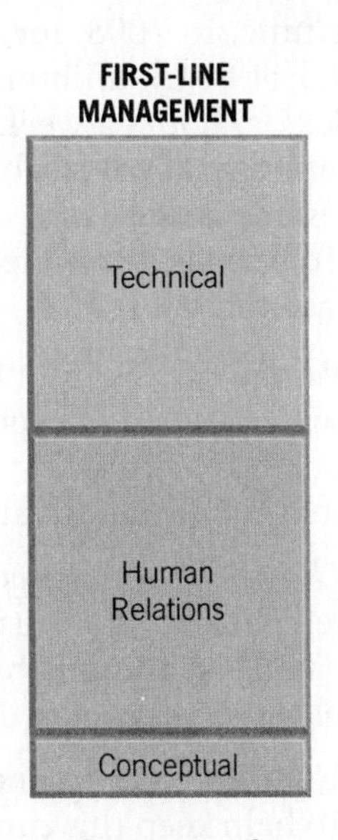

Figure 6.3 Different levels in an organization require different combinations of managerial skills.

in more efficient work procedures. Such managers need a basic understanding of the jobs they supervise. As a manager moves up the corporate ladder, however, technical skills become less and less important. Top managers, for example, often have only a cursory familiarity with the mechanics of basic tasks performed by their subordinates. Michael Eisner, the former CEO of Disney, freely admits that he can't draw Mickey Mouse or build a ride for Disney World.

Human Relations Skills

human relations skills Skills that enable managers to understand and get along with other people.

Human relations skills enable managers to understand and get along with other people. A manager with poor human relations skills will have trouble getting along with subordinates, which will, in turn, cause valuable employees to quit or transfer, and contribute to poor morale. When Development Dimensions International (DDI) asked 944 human resource professionals to state the reasons why newly promoted managers fail, 53 percent said it was because of poor people skills.[7]

Human relations skills are important at all levels, but they are probably most important for middle managers, who must often act as bridges between top managers, first-line managers, and managers from other areas of the organization. Effective managers possess communication skills that help them to understand others (and to get others to understand) and that can go a long way in maintaining good relations in an organization.

Conceptual Skills

conceptual skills A person's ability to think in the abstract, to diagnose and analyze different situations, and to see beyond the present situation.

Conceptual skills refer to a person's ability to think in the abstract, to diagnose and analyze different situations, and to see beyond the present situation. Conceptual skills help managers recognize new market opportunities (and threats). They can also help managers analyze the probable outcomes of their decisions. Top managers depend most on conceptual skills and first-line managers least, although some level of conceptual skill is needed in almost any job-related activity.

Time Management Skills

time management skills The productive use that managers make of their time.

Time management skills refer to the productive use that managers make of their time. In 2008, for example, Onex Corp. CEO Gerald Schwartz was paid a total of $61.7 million (including bonuses and options).[8] Assuming that he worked 50 hours a week and took two weeks vacation, Schwartz earned about $24,680 per hour, or about $411 per minute. Any time that Schwartz wastes represents a large cost to Onex and its stockholders.

To manage time effectively, managers must address the four leading causes of wasted time:

- *Paperwork.* Some managers spend too much time deciding what to do with letters and reports. Most documents of this sort are routine and can be handled quickly. Managers must learn to recognize those documents that require more attention.
- *The telephone.* Experts estimate that managers are interrupted by the telephone every five minutes. To manage time more effectively, they suggest having an administrative assistant screen all calls and setting aside a certain block of time each day to return the important ones.
- *Meetings.* Many managers spend as much as four hours per day in meetings. To help keep this time productive, the person handling the meeting should specify a clear agenda, start on time, keep everyone focussed on the agenda, and end on time.

- *Email.* More and more managers are also relying heavily on email and other forms of electronic communication. Like memos and telephone calls, many email messages are not particularly important, and some are trivial. As a result, time is wasted when managers have to sort through a variety of electronic folders, in-baskets, and archives. As the average number of electronic messages grows, the potential time wasted also increases.

Decision-Making Skills

Decision making means choosing one alternative from among several options. **Decision-making skills** are critical for managers because decision making affects all the functions of management and all managers at all levels in all organizations. Managers can improve their decision-making effectiveness by following a rational decision-making process.

decision making Choosing one alternative from among several options.

decision-making skills Skills in defining problems and selecting the best courses of action.

The Rational Decision-Making Process

Figure 6.4 shows the steps in the rational decision-making process. The key elements of each step are described below.

Recognizing and Defining the Decision Situation. The first step in rational decision making is recognizing that a decision is necessary. There must be some stimulus or spark to initiate this process. For example, when equipment malfunctions, managers must decide whether to repair it or to replace it. The stimulus for a decision may be either a problem or an opportunity. A manager

Step	Detail	Example
1. Recognizing and defining the decision situation	Some stimulus indicates that a decision must be made. The stimulus may be positive or negative.	The plant manager sees that employee turnover has increased by 5 percent.
2. Identifying alternatives	Both obvious and creative alternatives are desired. In general, the more important the decision, the more alternaticves should be generated.	The plant manager can increase wages, increase benefits, or change hiring standards.
3. Evaluating alternatives	Each alternatives is evaluated to determine its feasibility, its satisfactoriness, and its consequences.	Increasing benefits may not be feasible. Increasing wages and changing hiring standards may satify all conditions.
4. Selecting the best alternative	Consider all situational factors and choose the alternative that best fits the manager's situation.	Changing hiring standards will take an extended period of time to cut turnover, so increase wages.
5. Implementing the chosen alternative	The chosen alternative is implemented into the organizational system.	The plant manager may need permission from corporate headquarters. The human resource department establishes a new wage structure.
6. Following up and evaluating the results	At some time in the future, the manager should ascertain the extent to which the alternative chosen in step 4 and implemented in step 5 has worked.	The plant manager notes that six months later, turnover dropped to its previous level.

Figure 6.4 Steps in the rational decision-making process.

problem decision A decision that is necessary when actual results do not conform to those expected.

opportunity decision Taking new initiatives or doing a current activity more effectively even if no problem exists.

facing cost overruns on a project is faced with a **problem decision**, while a manager who is trying to decide how to invest surplus funds is faced with an **opportunity decision**. Managers also need to understand precisely what the problem or opportunity is. This understanding comes from careful analysis and thoughtful consideration of the situation.

Consider the situation in the international air travel industry. Because of the growth of international travel related to business, education, and tourism, global carriers such as Singapore Airlines, KLM, Japan Air Lines, British Airways, and American Airlines need to increase their capacity for international travel. Because most major international airports are already operating at or near capacity, adding new flights to existing schedules is not feasible. Rather, the most logical alternative is to increase capacity on existing flights. Thus, Boeing and Airbus recognized an important opportunity and defined their decision situation as how best to respond to the need for increased global travel capacity.[9]

Identifying Alternatives. Once the need for a decision is recognized, the second step is to identify possible alternative courses of action. In general, the more important the decision, the more attention is directed to developing alternatives. If the decision involves a multimillion-dollar relocation, a great deal of time and expertise should be devoted to identifying alternatives, but if the decision involves choosing a name for the company softball team, much fewer resources should be devoted to the task (although it may be difficult to keep the players from arguing about what the name should be!).

Factors such as legal restrictions, moral and ethical norms, and available technology can limit alternatives. After assessing the question of how to increase international airline capacity, Boeing and Airbus identified three different alternatives. They could independently develop new large planes, they could collaborate in a joint venture to create a single new large plane, or they could modify their largest existing planes to increase their capacity.

Evaluating Alternatives. Once alternatives have been identified, they must be carefully evaluated. During its analysis of alternatives, Airbus concluded that it would be at a disadvantage if it tried to simply enlarge its existing planes because the competitive Boeing 747 is already the largest aircraft being made and could readily be expanded. Boeing, meanwhile, was seriously concerned about the risk inherent in building a new and even larger plane, even if it shared the risk with Airbus as a joint venture.

Selecting the Best Alternative. Choosing the best available alternative is the real crux of decision making. Many situations do not lend themselves to objective mathematical analysis, but managers and leaders can often develop subjective estimates for choosing an alternative. Decision makers should also remember that finding multiple acceptable alternatives may be possible, so selecting just one alternative and rejecting all the others might not be a good decision. Airbus proposed a joint venture with Boeing, but Boeing decided that its best course of action was to modify its existing 747 to increase its capacity. Airbus then decided to proceed on its own to develop and manufacture a new jumbo jet called the A380. Meanwhile, Boeing decided that in addition to modifying its 747, it would also develop a new plane (the 787).

Implementing the Chosen Alternative. After an alternative has been selected, managers must implement it. In some situations implementation is fairly easy, but in others it is very difficult. In the case of an acquisition, for example, managers must decide how to integrate all the activities of the new business into the firm's existing organizational framework. When Hewlett-Packard first announced its acquisition of Compaq, managers acknowledged that it would take at least a year to integrate the two firms into a single one.

After a long decision-making process, Airbus decided to design its own jumbo jet. The Airbus A380's design allows seating for up to 850 people, and major airports around the world have been building new runways and terminal areas to accommodate the behemoth. Boeing, meanwhile, went through a similar decision-making process but concluded that the risks were too great to gamble on such an enormous project. Instead, the firm decided to modify its existing 747 design and develop a new fuel-efficient aircraft, the 787.

One of the key things that managers must deal with during implementation is employee resistance to change. The reasons for such resistance include insecurity, inconvenience, and fear of the unknown. Managers must also recognize that even when all alternatives have been evaluated as precisely as possible and the consequences of each alternative have been weighed, unanticipated consequences are still likely.

Following Up and Evaluating the Results. The final step in the decision-making process requires managers to evaluate the effectiveness of their decision—that is, they should make sure that the chosen alternative has served its original purpose. If an implemented alternative appears not to be working, managers can respond in several ways. One possibility is to adopt an alternative that had previously been discarded. Or they might recognize that the situation was not correctly defined to begin with and start the process all over again. In the Boeing/Airbus case, both companies are getting feedback that they made a good decision because they have large order backlogs. But both companies are experiencing delays in meeting their new product development schedules.

Behavioural Aspects of Decision Making

Many managers make decisions with too little consideration for logic and rationality. Peter Tingling, a professor at the Segal School of Business at Simon Fraser University, says that managers too often decide what they want to have happen and then later conduct analyses to support their decision. In his words, instead of using "evidence-based decision making," managers often use "decision-based evidence making."[10] Even when managers try to be logical, they sometimes fail. When Starbucks opened its first coffee shops in New York, it relied on scientific marketing research, taste tests, and rational deliberation in making a decision to emphasize drip over espresso coffee. However, that decision proved wrong when it became clear that New Yorkers strongly preferred the same espresso-style coffees that were Starbucks' mainstays on the west coast. Hence, the firm had to reconfigure its stores hastily to meet customer preferences.

Non-logical and emotional factors often influence managerial decision making. These factors include *organizational politics*, *intuition*, *escalation of commitment*, and *risk propensity*.

organizational politics The actions that people take as they try to get what they want.

Organizational Politics. The term **organizational politics** refers to the actions that people take as they try to get what they want. These actions may or may not be beneficial to the organization, but they do influence decision making, particularly if the person taking the action is powerful and can get his or her way.

intuition An "inner sense" or "hunch" usually based on years of experience and practice in making decisions in similar situations.

Intuition. Managers sometimes decide to do something because it "feels right" or because they have a "hunch." **Intuition** is usually based on years of experience and practice in making decisions in similar situations. Such an inner sense may actually help managers make an occasional decision without going through a rational sequence of steps. For example, the New York Yankees once contacted three major sneaker manufacturers—Nike, Reebok, and Adidas—and informed them that they were looking to make a sponsorship deal. While Nike and Reebok were carefully and rationally assessing the possibilities, managers at Adidas quickly responded to the idea and ended up hammering out a contract while the competitors were still analyzing details.[11] These occasional successes can be very dramatic, but they should not cause managers to rely too heavily on intuition.

escalation of commitment When a manager makes a decision and then remains committed to its implementation in spite of clear evidence that it was a bad decision.

Escalation of Commitment. When a manager makes a decision and then remains committed to its implementation in spite of clear evidence that it was a bad decision, **escalation of commitment** has occurred. A good example of this is Expo 86, the world's fair that was held in Vancouver. When the project was first conceived, the deficit was projected at about $56 million. Over the next few years, the projected deficit kept rising until it was over $300 million. In spite of that, the project went forward. Managers can avoid over-commitment by setting specific goals ahead of time that deal with how much time and money they are willing to spend on a given project. These goals make it harder for managers to interpret unfavourable news in a positive light.[12]

risk propensity How much a manager is willing to gamble when making decisions.

Risk Propensity. **Risk propensity** refers to how much a manager is willing to gamble when making decisions. Managers who are very cautious when making decisions are more likely to avoid mistakes, and they are unlikely to make decisions that lead to big losses (or big gains). Other managers are extremely aggressive in making decisions and are willing to take big risks.[13] They rely heavily on intuition, reach decisions quickly, and often risk big money on their decisions. These managers are more likely than their conservative counterparts to achieve big successes with their decisions, but they are also more likely to incur greater losses.[14] The organization's culture is a prime ingredient in fostering different levels of risk propensity.

Strategic Management: Setting Goals and Formulating Strategy

strategic management The process of aligning the organization with its external environment.

strategic goals The overall objectives that a business wants to achieve.

Strategic management is the process of aligning the organization with its external environment. The starting point in effective strategic management is setting **strategic goals**—the overall objectives that a business wants to achieve. Remember, however, that deciding what it intends to do is only the first step for an organization. Managers must also make decisions about what actions will and will not achieve company goals. Decisions cannot be made on a problem-by-problem basis or merely to meet needs as they arise. In most companies, a broad program underlies those decisions. That program is called a **strategy**—the broad set of organizational plans for implementing the decisions made for achieving organizational goals.

strategy The broad set of organizational plans for implementing the decisions made for achieving organizational goals.

Setting Goals

Explain the importance of *setting goals* and *formulating strategies.* 4

Goals are performance targets, the means by which organizations and their managers measure success or failure at every level. In this section, we identify the main purposes for which organizations establish goals, classify the basic levels of business goals, and describe the process that is commonly used to set goals.

The Purposes of Goal Setting

goals Performance targets, the means by which organizations and their managers measure success or failure at every level.

There are four main purposes in organizational goal setting:

1. *Goal setting provides direction, guidance, and motivation for all managers.* If managers know precisely where the company is headed, there is less potential for error in the different units of the company.
2. *Goal setting helps firms allocate resources.* Areas that are expected to grow will get first priority. The company allocates more resources to new projects with large sales potential than it allocates to mature products with established but stagnant sales potential.
3. *Goal setting helps to define corporate culture.* General Electric's goal, for instance, is to push each of its divisions to #1 or #2 in its industry. The result is a competitive, often stressful, environment and a culture that rewards success and has little tolerance for failure.
4. *Goal setting helps managers assess performance.* If a company sets a goal to increase sales by 10 percent in a given year, managers in units that attain or exceed the goal can be rewarded. Units failing to reach the goal will also be compensated accordingly.

Kinds of Goals

Goals differ from company to company, depending on the firm's purpose and mission. Every enterprise, of course, has a *purpose*—a reason for being. Businesses seek profit, universities work to discover and transmit new knowledge, and government agencies exist to provide service to the public. Most enterprises also have a **mission statement**—a statement of how an organization will achieve its purpose. Bell Canada's mission, for example, is to be a world leader in helping communicate and manage information. Chrysler's mission statement emphasizes "delighted customers." Atco Ltd.'s mission is to provide products and services to the energy and resource industries and to invest principally in energy-related assets in North America. The mission of Investors Group is to satisfy clients who need general and comprehensive financial planning.

mission statement An organization's statement of how it will achieve its purpose in the environment in which it conducts its business.

Two business firms may have the same purpose—for example, to sell watches at a profit—but very different missions. Timex sells low-cost, reliable watches in outlets ranging from department stores to corner drugstores. Rolex, on the other hand, sells high-quality, high-priced fashion watches through selected jewellery stores. Regardless of a company's purpose and mission, every firm needs to set long-term, intermediate, and short-term goals:

- **Long-term goals** relate to extended periods of time—typically five years or more into the future. MasterCard, for example, might set a long-term goal of doubling the number of participating merchants during the next 10 years. Similarly, Sony might adopt a long-term goal to increase its share of the digital SLR market by 10 percent during the next five years.

long-term goals Goals set for extended periods of time, typically five years or more into the future.

intermediate goals Goals set for a period of one to five years.

- **Intermediate goals** are set for a period of one to five years into the future. For example, the marketing department's goal might be to increase sales by 3 percent in two years. The production department might want to decrease expenses by 6 percent in four years. Human resources might want to cut turnover by 10 percent in two years. Finance might aim for a 10 percent increase in return on investment in three years.

short-term goals Goals set for the very near future, typically less than one year.

- **Short-term goals** are set for one year or less. For example, Four Seasons Hotels may set a goal to increase the revenue generated by each hotel room by 10 percent over the next six months. Or WestJet may set a goal to increase the proportion of occupied seats on the average flight by 8 percent over the next three months.

SMART goals Goals that are specific, measurable, achievable, relevant, and time-framed.

Whatever the time frame of the goals that are set, research shows that managers who set **SMART goals** (*S*pecific, *M*easurable, *A*chievable, *R*elevant, and *T*ime-framed) have higher performance than managers who don't. The boxed insert entitled "Setting Green Goals" describes the importance of setting goals that take the environment into account.

Formulating Strategy

strategy formulation Creation of a broad program for defining and meeting an organization's goals.

After a firm has set its goals, it must develop a strategy for achieving them. In contrast to planning, strategy is wider in scope and is a broad program that describes how a business intends to meet its goals, how it will respond to new challenges, and how it will meet new needs. **Strategy formulation** involves three basic steps: (1) setting strategic goals, (2) analyzing the organization and its environment, and (3) matching the organization and its environment (see Figure 6.5).

Setting Strategic Goals

Strategic goals are long-term goals derived directly from the firm's mission statement. General Electric Co., for example, is pursuing four strategic goals to ensure continued success for the company: an emphasis on quality control, an emphasis on selling services and not just products, a concentration on niche acquisitions, and global expansion.

Analyzing the Organization and Its Environment

SWOT analysis Identification and analysis of organizational strengths and weaknesses and environmental opportunities and threats as part of strategy formulation.

After strategic goals have been set, managers assess both their organization and its environment using a **SWOT analysis**. This involves identifying organizational **S**trengths and **W**eaknesses, and identifying environmental **O**pportunities and **T**hreats. Strengths and weaknesses are factors *internal* to

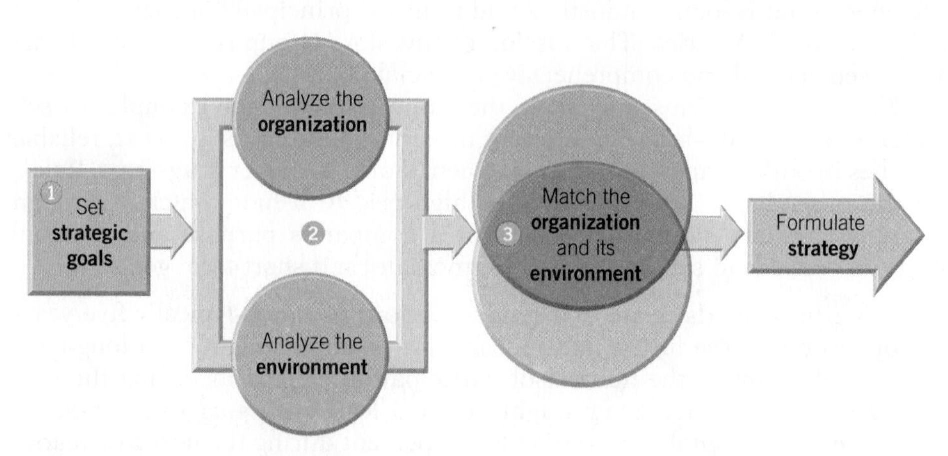

Figure 6.5 Strategy formulation.

The Greening of Business

Setting Green Goals

The logic of goal setting is being extended to making businesses greener. Consider the following:

- Wal-Mart set a goal to reduce the amount of packaging used by 5 percent throughout its huge supply chain; it wants to achieve that goal by 2013.
- The province of Ontario has set a goal to reduce plastic bag usage by 50 percent by 2012.
- Loblaws set a goal of reducing by one billion the number of plastic bags given to customers by 2009.
- Scotiabank has set a goal to be in the top 10 percent of the companies listed on the Dow-Jones World Sustainability Index.

For some organizations, their entire mission is being green. For example, the mission of B.C.–based Greener Footprints (a non-profit organization) is to reduce the use of plastic bags in Canada. For other organizations, the setting of green goals is closely tied to the success of their business. For example, the CEO of Honda, Takeo Fukui, recognized that Toyota's popular Prius hybrid automobile outsold Honda's hybrid car by a wide margin during the last decade, so he set a goal to make Honda the greenest company in the automobile industry. Honda has set a goal to sell 500 000 hybrid automobiles each year (Toyota's goal is one million). In 2008, Honda introduced its Clarity FCX, which is the most advanced green vehicle ever made. It is powered by a hydrogen fuel cell that generates no pollution at all. Honda also launched a new gas-electric hybrid in 2009 and plans to launch several other hybrids by 2015.

Rona Inc., the home renovation chain, has set a goal of doing business only with suppliers who address environmental sustainability and who do not contribute to deforestation. The goal for 2009 was to have all the plywood panels Rona sells made only from lumber that comes from forests that have been certified as sustainable. By 2010, the same goal will apply to spruce, pine, and fir. By 2012, Rona's goal is to have 25 percent of its total wood sales come from forests that are certified by the Forest Stewardship Council.

Sometimes companies get involved in green activities that are quite different than their main business. For example, Google is involved in a strategic initiative called RE<C, whose goal is to develop electricity from renewable energy resources (solar, wind, and geothermal) that will actually be cheaper than electricity that is produced by burning coal. Larry Page, the co-founder of Google, says the company gained expertise as it developed efficient data centres, and it wants to apply that expertise to the development of generating renewable electricity. The first goal is to produce one gigawatt of renewable energy that is cheaper than that produced by coal. He thinks that can be done within a few years. Once that goal is achieved, the next goal will be to produce renewable electricity on a much larger scale.

Green goals may be developed by managers, or they may be imposed on companies by external groups. In 2007, for example, the federal government notified Canada's biggest industrial polluters that they had six months to provide emissions data that the government would use in setting new emission reduction targets. Discussions also continue at the international level about what the goal for emissions should be, but to date there has been no agreement. A spokesperson for 77 developing nations says that unless there is a goal, there can be no progress.

Critical Thinking Questions

1. What are the advantages associated with setting green goals? Are there disadvantages? Explain.
2. What difficulties might Rona encounter as it tries to reach the goal of having 25 percent of its total wood sales come from forests that are certified by the Forest Stewardship Council?
3. What are the advantages of the government setting emission reduction targets? What are the disadvantages?

the firm and are assessed using **organizational analysis**. Strengths might include surplus cash, a dedicated workforce, an ample supply of managerial talent, technical expertise, or weak competitors. For example, Pepsi's strength in beverage distribution through its network of soft drink distributors was successfully extended to distribution of its Aquafina brand of bottled water. Weaknesses might include a cash shortage, aging factories, and a poor public image. Garden.com's total reliance on the emerging internet-based retailing model became its downfall when the dot-com bubble burst.

organizational analysis The process of analyzing a firm's strengths and weaknesses.

Opportunities and threats are factors *external* to the firm and are assessed using **environmental analysis**. Opportunities include things like market demand for new products, favourable government legislation, or shortages of

environmental analysis The process of scanning the environment for threats and opportunities.

raw materials that the company is good at producing. For example, when Pepsi managers recognized a market opportunity for bottled water, they moved quickly to launch their Aquafina brand and to position it for rapid growth. Threats include new products and processes developed by competitors, changes in government regulations, and shifting consumer tastes. For example, Eastman Kodak Co. realized that that it needed to convert from its long-standing silver-halide film business to digital photography, and manufacturers of CDs and CD players now recognize the threat that online music services like iTunes pose.[15]

Matching the Organization and Its Environment

The final step in strategy formulation is matching environmental threats and opportunities with corporate strengths and weaknesses. This matching process is the heart of strategy formulation. More than any other facet of strategy, matching companies with their environments lays the foundation for successfully planning and conducting business. Over the long term, this process may also determine whether a firm typically takes risks or behaves more conservatively. Just because two companies are in the same industry does not mean that they will use the same strategies. The Toronto-Dominion Bank, for example, has been aggressively expanding into the U.S. retail banking industry by acquiring U.S. banks, but the Royal Bank of Canada has been much less aggressive in this area.[16]

corporate-level strategy Identifies the various businesses that a company will be in and how these businesses will relate to each other.

business-level (competitive) strategy Identifies the ways a business will compete in its chosen line of products or services.

functional strategies Identify the basic courses of action that each department in the firm will pursue so that it contributes to the attainment of the business's overall goals.

concentration strategy Focussing the company on one product or product line.

market penetration Boosting sales of present products by more aggressive selling in the firm's current markets.

product development Developing improved products for current markets.

geographic expansion Expanding operations in new geographic areas or countries.

Levels of Strategies

There are three levels of strategy in a business firm (see Figure 6.6). A **corporate-level strategy** identifies the various businesses that a company will be in and how these businesses will relate to each other. A **business-level (competitive) strategy** identifies the ways a business will compete in its chosen line of products or services. **Functional strategies** identify the basic courses of action that each department in the firm will pursue so that it contributes to the attainment of the business's overall goals.

Corporate-Level Strategies

There are several different corporate-level strategies that a company might pursue, including concentration, growth, integration, diversification, and investment reduction.

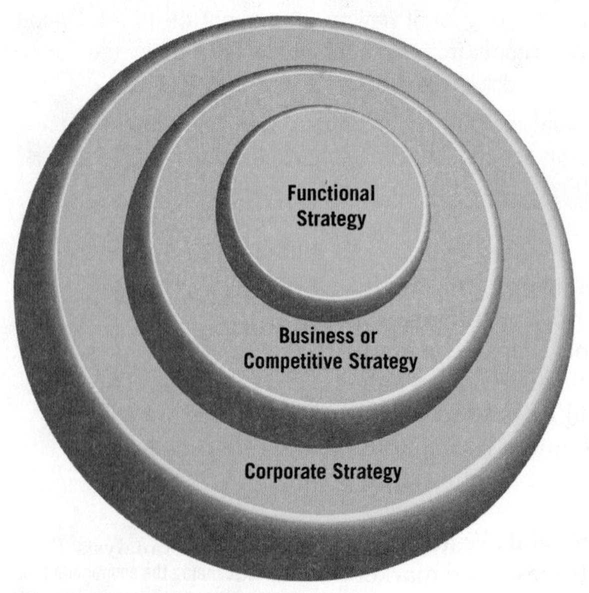

Figure 6.6 Hierarchy of strategy.

Concentration. A **concentration strategy** involves focussing the company on one product or product line. Organizations that have successfully pursued a concentration strategy include McDonald's and Canadian National Railway. The main advantage of a concentration strategy is that the company can focus its strengths on the one business it knows well. The main disadvantage is the risk inherent in putting all of one's eggs in one basket. These risks can be overcome to some extent by adhering to the following principle: "If you put all your eggs in one basket, watch the basket!"

Growth. Several growth strategies are available, all of which focus on *internal* activities that will result in growth. These strategies include **market penetration** (boosting sales of present products by more aggressive selling in the firm's current markets), **product development** (developing improved products for current markets), and **geographic expansion** (expanding

In the wake of an industry-wide slump a few years ago, Cisco Systems, a giant maker of communications equipment, radically revised its strategic plans. Where engineers once pursued their own pet projects, engineering is now centralized under a group of top managers. Where individual units once chose their own suppliers, a committee now oversees all partnerships. Where the product line once consisted solely of networking apparatus, the company has branched out into a variety of new high-tech markets.

operations in new geographic areas or countries). WestJet, for example, has used a geographic expansion strategy, since it started by offering service in Western Canada but has now added flights to various other cities.

Integration. Integration strategies focus on *external* activities that will result in growth. **Horizontal integration** means acquiring control of competitors in the same or similar markets with the same or similar products. For example, Hudson's Bay Company purchased Kmart and Zellers. **Vertical integration** means owning or controlling the inputs to the firm's processes and/or the channels through which the products or services are distributed. Thus, major oil companies like Shell not only drill and produce their own oil, but refine the oil into different products and then sell those products through company-controlled outlets across Canada. Another example of vertical integration is Irving Forest Products' purchase of Royale Tissue from Procter & Gamble.

horizontal integration Acquiring control of competitors in the same or similar markets with the same or similar products.

vertical integration Owning or controlling the inputs to the firm's processes and/or the channels through which the products or services are distributed.

Diversification. **Diversification** means expanding into related or unrelated products or market segments. Diversification helps the firm avoid the problem of having all of its eggs in one basket by spreading risk among several products or markets. *Related diversification* means adding new, but related, products or services to an existing business. For example, CN diversified into trucking, an activity that is clearly related to railway operations. Maple Leaf Gardens Ltd., which already owned the Toronto Maple Leafs, also acquired the Toronto Raptors basketball team. *Conglomerate diversification* means diversifying into products or markets that are not related to the firm's present businesses. For example, Brookfield Asset Management (formerly known as Brascan Ltd.) used to own companies in the mining, real estate, electric power generation, and financial services businesses but has now moved away from a diversification strategy.

diversification Expanding into related or unrelated products or market segments.

Investment Reduction. **Investment reduction** means reducing the company's investment in one or more of its lines of business. One investment-reduction strategy is *retrenchment*, which means the reduction of activity or operations. For example, Federal Industries formerly was a conglomerate with interests in trucking, railways, metals, and other product lines, but it retrenched and now focusses on a more limited set of customers and products. *Divestment* is another investment-reduction strategy; it involves selling or liquidating one or more of a firm's businesses. For example, BCE sold its *Yellow Pages* and *White Pages* for $4 billion.

investment reduction Reducing the company's investment in one or more of its lines of business.

Business-Level (Competitive) Strategies

cost leadership Becoming the low-cost leader in an industry.

differentiation strategy A firm seeks to be unique in its industry along some dimension that is valued by buyers.

focus strategy Selecting a market segment and serving the customers in that market niche better than competitors.

Whatever corporate-level strategy a firm decides on, it must also have a competitive strategy. A *competitive strategy* is a plan to establish a profitable and sustainable competitive position.[17] Michael Porter identifies three competitive strategies. **Cost leadership** means becoming *the* low-cost leader in an industry. Wal-Mart is the best-known industry cost leader. Montreal-based Gildan Activewear is dedicated to achieving the lowest possible costs in producing its T-shirts. The company has captured 29 percent of the U.S. imprinted T-shirt market with this strategy.[18] A firm using a **differentiation strategy** tries to be unique in its industry along some dimension that is valued by buyers. For example, Caterpillar Tractor emphasizes durability, Volvo stresses safety, Apple Computer stresses user-friendly products, and Mercedes-Benz emphasizes quality. A **focus strategy** means selecting a market segment and serving the customers in that market niche better than competitors. Before it was acquired by Nexfor, Fraser Inc. focussed on producing high-quality, durable, lightweight paper that is used in bibles. While it still has a good reputation in the production of bible paper, Nexfor Fraser Papers is now more diversified and produces papers for a variety of uses, including dog food bags and doughnut boxes.

Functional Strategies

Each business's choice of a competitive strategy (cost leadership, differentiation, or focus) is translated into supporting functional strategies for each of its departments to pursue. A functional strategy is the basic course of action that each department follows so that the business accomplishes its overall goals. To implement its cost-leadership strategy, for example, Wal-Mart's distribution department pursued a functional strategy of satellite-based warehousing that ultimately drove down distribution costs.

The strategy of one small company is described in the boxed insert entitled "From a Missouri Garage to Hollywood."

Entrepreneurship and New Ventures

From a Missouri Garage to Hollywood

The feature films *The Red Canvas* and *Way of the Guardian* were not developed by your typical Hollywood production team. For starters, one of the films' co-creators lives and works in Missouri. Adam Boster and his partner, Ken Chamitoff, started Photo-Kicks—a marketing company specializing in action photography—in their garages in 2002. From their beginnings photographing students at local martial arts schools, Boster and Chamitoff built Photo-Kicks into a multimillion-dollar business employing photographers, graphic designers, and marketers throughout the United States and Canada. In 2007, Photo-Kicks came in at number 592 on *Inc.* magazine's list of the 5000 fastest-growing private companies in America.

Just a quick glance at the many photographs on display on the Photo-Kicks website (www.photo-kicks.com) provides an eye-opening introduction to action photography. Athletes young and old punch, kick, and leap their way across the frames. But it's the countless other services that Photo-Kicks provides to its customers that have allowed it to grow so rapidly. Photo-Kicks bills itself as "a fully equipped graphic design and marketing organization," creating such products as customized logos, brochures, websites, posters, and trading cards.

Then, of course, there are the movies. *Way of the Guardian* began as a card game and animated series also developed by Boster and Chamitoff. *The Red Canvas* is more personal. It tells the story of a struggling immigrant who finds success and redemption in the sport of mixed martial arts. Chamitoff acknowledges that the film could not have happened without the years he and Boster spent travelling the country photographing martial arts students. "I learned the stories of every person I encountered," said Chamitoff. "Those stories shaped not only *The Red Canvas*, but Photo-Kicks as well."

Critical Thinking Question

1. What are the key differences between the various types of corporate and business-level strategies? Which strategies do you believe Photo-Kicks is pursuing?

Contingency Planning and Crisis Management

Discuss *contingency planning* and *crisis management.* 5

Business environments are often difficult to predict because unexpected events may occur. Managers know that such things can happen, so they often develop alternative plans in case things go awry. Two common methods of dealing with the unknown and unforeseen are *contingency planning* and *crisis management*.

Contingency Planning

contingency planning Identifying aspects of a business or its environment that might entail changes in strategy.

Contingency planning attempts to (1) identify in advance important aspects of a business or its market that might change, and (2) identify the ways in which a company will respond to changes. Suppose, for example, that a company develops a plan to create a new business. It expects sales to increase at an annual rate of 10 percent for the next five years and develops a marketing strategy for maintaining that level. But suppose that an unexpected financial crisis and recession occurs (as happened in 2008) and sales do not reach planned levels. Does the company abandon the business, invest more in advertising, or wait to see what happens in the second year? Any of these alternatives is possible. However, things will go more smoothly if managers have decided in advance what to do in the event of problems like a financial crisis. Contingency planning helps managers do that.

In the summer of 2008, a strike at the PotashCorp. of Saskatchewan created a shortage of potassium acetate, which is the key ingredient in runway de-icer that airports use to prevent airplanes from sliding off runways in sub-freezing weather. The strike ended in November 2008, but by then airports were having trouble obtaining potassium acetate. The U.S. Federal Aviation Administration informed all airports that they should develop contingency plans to get their potassium acetate from alternate sources. Cryotech Technologies, the biggest supplier of potassium acetate to airports, responded by getting supplies of a corn-based de-icer instead. [19]

Commercial airlines have contingency plans to deal with problems like major snowstorms. These contingency plans involve making sure that planes are not stranded at airports that are experiencing snow delays.

Crisis Management

crisis management An organization's plan for dealing with emergencies that require an immediate response.

Crisis management involves an organization's plan for dealing with emergencies that require an immediate response. The listeria problem at Maple Leaf Foods in 2008 is an example of a crisis that needed to be effectively managed. CEO Michael McCain acted quickly to handle the crisis and did not hide behind lawyers or let financial implications get in the way of his decisions. The company recalled 686 000 kilograms of tainted meat (which cost the company $19 million). McCain publicly apologized at news conferences and in television commercials and assured consumers that the company would solve the problem.[20] By January 1, 2009, a survey revealed that 78 percent of respondents had recently purchased a Maple Leaf product. That was up from only 20 percent in September 2008.[21]

Italian food giant Parmalat Finanziaria SpA also faced a crisis when it couldn't account for $11.7 billion in funds. Its Canadian division, headed by CEO Marc Caira, responded by auditing the Canadian operation's accounting practices to make sure his division wasn't part of the problem. After he had determined it wasn't, he then took a variety of actions to reassure customers, employees, and investors that everything was fine in the Canadian division. He did this by continuously communicating with the company's key constituents. Caira's actions worked. The year after the Parmalat scandal broke in Italy, the Canadian division recorded its highest sales and profits ever.[22]

Disruption management (DM) stresses internal self-reliance in planning for and preparing responses to disruptions in an organization's external environment. Consider a shutdown caused by a snowstorm at Toronto's Pearson International Airport. An airline's least costly solution would be to simply cancel all incoming flights immediately. This approach cuts the airline's operating costs, but it is a terrible option for passengers who can't get where they're going. A DM approach would consider alternatives such as rescheduling flights into neighbouring airports and providing ground transportation into Toronto. A DM model would quickly simulate the costs and benefits of these and other options to help managers make an effective decision.

Management and the Corporate Culture

6 Explain the idea of *corporate culture* and why it is important.

corporate culture The shared experiences, stories, beliefs, norms, and ethical stance that characterize an organization.

Every organization—big or small, more successful or less successful—has an unmistakable "feel" to it. Just as every individual has a unique personality, every company has a unique identity, called its **corporate culture**—the shared experiences, stories, beliefs, norms, and ethical stance that characterize an organization. This culture helps define the work and business climate that exists in an organization.

The opening case provides several examples of corporate cultures. Here are some more:

- Magna International, a large Canadian producer of auto parts, is a firm with a strong culture. Its founder, Frank Stronach, is well known for his views about employees, working conditions, daycare centres, unions, the free enterprise system, and profit distribution.[23]
- Four Seasons Hotels and Resorts has a different, but equally strong, culture. Managers are judged by deeds, not words, and act as role models; employees take their cues from the managers.[24]
- At Toyota's Cambridge, Ontario, plant the corporate culture stresses values, principles, and trust. The culture is one of continuous improvement.[25]
- At WestJet Airlines, the corporate culture emphasizes profit maximization. Most of the employees own shares in the company, and all of them get to

keep some of the profits. This is a powerful incentive for them to work productively.[26]

In 2008, executives at 340 Canadian companies participated in the Waterstone Human Capital corporate culture survey and expressed the following views:[27]

- Eighty-two percent said that culture has a strong or very strong impact on corporate performance.
- Three-year average revenue growth for the top 10 firms on the list was 63 percent higher than that of the 60 largest public companies in Canada that are listed on the S&P/TSX.
- Fifty-three percent felt that a strong culture reduced turnover, and 57 percent felt that a strong culture gave employees a sense of belonging. This finding is important, since an online survey conducted by Ipsos Reid found that many workers feel that they don't fit in well at work.[28]

A strong corporate culture guides everyone to work toward the same goals and helps newcomers learn accepted behaviours. Cameron Herold is a Vancouver entrepreneur who has had a string of successes in franchising, including College Pro Painters, Boyd Autobody, and 1-800-GOT-JUNK. He says that a cult-like culture is crucial for attracting great employees. He says what's needed is a culture that is "more than a business and slightly less than a religion."[29]

In a strong culture where financial success is the key issue, newcomers quickly learn that they are expected to work long, hard hours and that the "winner" is the one who brings in the most revenue. But if quality of life is more fundamental to the culture, newcomers learn that it's more acceptable to spend less time at work and that balancing work and non-work is encouraged. The survey mentioned above found that only 36 percent of executives felt that the culture of their company was strong.

Forces Shaping Corporate Culture

A number of forces shape corporate cultures. First, the values held by top management help set the tone of the organization and influence its business goals and strategies. Frank Stronach (Magna International), Timothy Eaton (Eaton's), Max Ward (Wardair), Larry Clark (Spar Aerospace), and Jean de Grandpré (BCE) are just a few of the leaders who have had a profound impact on the culture of their respective organizations. Even a large, long-time firm like Ford still bears the traces of founder Henry Ford.

The firm's history also helps shape its culture. The championship banners that line the arena where the Montreal Canadiens play signify that they are winners. Maintaining a corporate culture draws on many dimensions of business life. Shared experiences resulting from norms sustain culture. Thus, working long hours on a special project becomes a shared experience for many employees. They remember it, talk about it among themselves, and wear it as a badge of their contribution to the company.

Stories and legends are also important. Walt Disney has been dead for many years now, but his spirit lives on in the businesses he left behind. Quotations from Disney are affixed to portraits of him throughout the company's studios. And Disney's emphasis on family is still visible in corporate benefits such as paying for spouses to accompany employees on extended business trips. In fact, employees are often called "the Disney family."

Finally, strong behavioural norms help define and sustain corporate cultures. For example, a strong part of the culture at Hewlett-Packard Canada is that everyone wears a name tag and that everyone is called by his or her first name. And at Sony Corporation every employee wears a corporate smock.

These banners hanging in Centre Bell, the home of the Montreal Canadiens, are a dramatic illustration of the history of the team and its winning culture.

Communicating the Culture and Managing Change

Managers must carefully consider the kind of culture they want for their organization, then work to nourish that culture by communicating with everyone who works there. Wal-Mart, for example, assigns veteran managers to lead employees in new territories. As we saw in the opening case, Starbucks surveys employees every 18 months regarding several aspects of its culture. Royal Bank of Canada and Four Seasons Hotels and Resorts also survey their employees to determine how well they are progressing toward their corporate culture goals.[30]

Communicating the Culture

To use its culture to the firm's advantage, managers must accomplish several tasks, all of which hinge on effective communication. First, managers themselves must have a clear understanding of the culture. Second, they must transmit the culture to others in the organization. Communication is thus one aim in training and orienting newcomers. A clear and meaningful statement of the organization's mission is also a valuable communication tool. Finally, managers can maintain the culture by rewarding and promoting those who understand it and work toward maintaining it.

Managing Change

Organizations must sometimes change their cultures. Ontario Hydro, for example, had an "engineering" culture for many years. That meant that everything was planned and analyzed down to the last detail before any action was taken. But Ontario Hydro's culture has changed to a more consumer-oriented, risk-taking culture as it tries to cope with large debt and changes in its markets. When cultural change is required, the process usually goes through three stages:

1. At the highest level, analysis of the company's environment highlights extensive change as the most effective response to its problems. Conflict and resistance typically characterize this period.

2. Top management begins to formulate a new vision and culture for the company. Whatever that vision is, it must include a renewed focus on the activities of competitors and the needs of customers.
3. The firm sets up new systems for appraising and compensating employees, systems that enforce its new values. The purpose is to give the new culture solid shape from within the firm.

Robert Nardelli, the CEO of troubled Chrysler, is trying to change the "old Detroit mind-set" culture of the company, which was characterized by managers focussing on priorities that were important to the company—like running at full capacity—rather than what was important to the customer. As part of the process, Nardelli himself led a management development seminar on what the culture of a customer-driven company should look like.[31] Given the major problems that Chrysler was facing in 2009, it is imperative that the company develop a customer-driven culture if it hopes to survive.

Sometimes the three-stage change process is not completed. Consider what happened at Nortel Networks, which hired a new president and a new chief technology officer in an attempt to resolve some of the company's problems. Both of these individuals had worked at Cisco Systems Inc., and it was thought that they would be a great addition to a troubled company like Nortel. But Cisco has a hard-driving sales culture, while Nortel's culture is much less intense. Within three months, both new managers resigned from Nortel. Nortel's CEO said that their departure was due to different management styles and a different vision for the future of the company. In short, there was a culture clash that caused the new hires to leave the company, and the culture they envisioned will not be implemented at Nortel.[32] In 2009, Nortel declared bankruptcy.

Test yourself on the material for this chapter at **www.pearsoned.ca/mybusinesslab**.

Summary of Learning Objectives

1. **Describe the four basic functions that constitute the *management process*.** *Management* is the process of planning, organizing, leading, and controlling an organization's financial, physical, human, and information resources to achieve the organization's goals. *Planning* means determining what the company needs to do and how best to get it done. *Organizing* means determining how best to arrange a business's resources and the necessary jobs into an overall structure. *Leading* means guiding and motivating employees to meet the firm's objectives. *Controlling* means monitoring the firm's performance to ensure that it is meeting its goals.
2. **Identify *types of managers* by level and area.** Managers can be differentiated in two ways: by level and by area. By *level, top managers* set policies, formulate strategies, and approve decisions; *middle managers* implement policies, strategies, and decisions; and *first-line managers* work with and supervise employees. By *area*, managers work in areas like marketing, finance, operations, human resources, and information. Managers at all levels may be found in every area of a company.
3. **Describe the five basic *management skills*.** Most managers agree that five basic management skills are necessary for success. *Technical skills* are associated with performing specialized tasks ranging from typing to auditing. *Human relations skills* are associated with understanding and getting along with other people. *Conceptual skills* refer to the ability to think in the abstract, to diagnose and analyze different situations, and to see beyond present circumstances. *Time management skills* refer to managers' ability to make productive use of the time available to them. *Decision-making skills* allow managers to define problems and to select the best course of action.

4. **Explain the importance of *setting goals* and *formulating strategies*.** *Goals*—the performance targets of an organization—can be long term, intermediate, and short term. They provide direction for managers, they help managers decide how to allocate limited resources, they define the *corporate culture*, and they help managers assess performance. *Strategies*—the methods that a company uses to meet its stated goals—involve three major activities: setting *strategic goals*, analyzing the organization and its environment, and matching the organization and its environment. These strategies are translated into *strategic, tactical*, and *operational plans*.

5. **Discuss *contingency planning* and *crisis management*.** To deal with crises or major environmental changes, companies develop contingency plans and plans for crisis management. *Contingency planning* means identifying in advance certain key aspects of a business or its market that might change and thereby affect the operation of the business. This type of planning also identifies the ways the business will respond if the changes actually occur. *Crisis management* means developing methods and actions for dealing with an emergency that requires an immediate response. To prepare for such emergencies, organizations develop crisis plans.

6. **Explain the idea of *corporate culture* and why it is important.** *Corporate culture* is the shared experiences, stories, beliefs, norms, and ethical stance that characterize an organization. A strong, well-defined culture can help a business reach its goals and can influence management styles. Culture is determined by several factors, including top management; the organization's history, stories and legends; and behavioural norms. If carefully communicated and flexible enough to accommodate change, corporate culture can be managed for the betterment of the organization.

Key Terms

business-level (competitive) strategy (p. 196)
concentration strategy (p. 196)
conceptual skills (p. 188)
contingency planning (p. 199)
controlling (p. 182)
corporate culture (p. 200)
corporate-level strategy (p. 196)
cost leadership (p. 198)
crisis management (p. 200)
decision making (p. 189)
decision-making skills (p. 189)
differentiation strategy (p. 198)
diversification (p. 197)
effectiveness (p. 181)
efficiency (p. 181)
escalation of commitment (p. 192)
environmental analysis (p. 195)
first-line managers (p. 186)
focus strategy (p. 198)
functional strategies (p. 196)
geographic expansion (p. 196)
goals (p. 193)
horizontal integration (p. 197)
human relations skills (p. 188)
intermediate goals (p. 194)
intuition (p. 192)
investment reduction (p. 197)
leading (or directing) (p. 182)
long-term goals (p. 193)
management (p. 180)
market penetration (p. 196)
middle managers (p. 185)
mission statement (p. 193)
operational plans (p. 182)
opportunity decision (p. 190)
organizational analysis (p. 195)
organizational politics (p. 192)
organizing (p. 182)
planning (p. 181)
prediction markets (p. 181)
problem decision (p. 190)
product development (p. 196)
risk propensity (p. 192)
short-term goals (p. 194)
SMART goals (p. 194)
strategic goals (p. 192)
strategic management (p. 192)
strategic plans (p. 182)
strategy (p. 193)
strategy formulation (p. 194)
SWOT analysis (p. 194)
tactical plans (p. 182)
technical skills (p. 187)
time management skills (p. 188)
top managers (p. 185)
vertical integration (p. 197)

Questions for Analysis

1. How are the four functions of management related to the five basic management skills? Use examples to clarify your answer.
2. What is the relationship between Mintzberg's roles of management and the more traditional functions of management? Use examples to clarify your answer.
3. Select any group of which you are a member (your company, your family, or a club or organization, for example). Explain how planning, organizing, directing, and controlling are practised in that group.
4. Identify managers by level and area at your school, college, or university.
5. In what kind of company would the technical skills of top managers be more important than human relations or conceptual skills? Are there organizations in which conceptual skills are not important?
6. How can managers determine if they are being efficient and effective?
7. Perform a SWOT analysis for the school you are currently attending.
8. Consider the various corporate-level strategies discussed in the text (concentration, growth, integration, diversification, investment reduction). What is the relationship between these various strategies? Are they mutually exclusive? Are they complementary? Explain.

Application Exercises

1. Interview a manager at any level of a local company. Identify that manager's job according to level and area. Show how planning, organizing, directing, and controlling are part of this person's job. Inquire about the manager's education and work experience. Which management skills are most important for this manager's job?
2. Interview managers at several different companies and determine their views on government bailouts of companies that are in financial trouble. Include in your list of interview questions the following one: "Do you think managers should accept bailout money from government during difficult economic times like those that companies experienced in 2008 and 2009?"

Building Your Business Skills

Speaking with Power

The Purpose of This Assignment

To encourage students to appreciate effective speaking as a critical human relations skill.

Background

A manager's ability to understand and get along with supervisors, peers, and subordinates is a critical human relations skill. At the heart of this skill, says Harvard University professor of education Sarah McGinty, is the ability to speak with power and control. McGinty defines "powerful speech" in terms of the following characteristics:

- the ability to speak at length and in complete sentences
- the ability to set a conversational agenda
- the ability to deter interruption
- the ability to argue openly and to express strong opinions about ideas, not people
- the ability to make statements that offer solutions rather than pose questions
- the ability to express humour

Taken together, says McGinty, "all this creates a sense of confidence in listeners."

Assignment

Step 1

Working alone, compare your own personal speaking style with McGinty's description of powerful speech by taping yourself as you speak during a meeting with classmates or during a phone conversation. (Tape both sides of the conversation only if the person to whom you are speaking gives permission.) Listen for the following problems:

- unfinished sentences
- an absence of solutions
- too many disclaimers ("I'm not sure I have enough information to say this, but...")
- the habit of seeking support from others instead of making definitive statements of personal conviction (saying, "As Emily has stated in her report, I also recommend consolidating the medical and fitness functions," instead of "I recommend consolidating the medical and fitness functions")
- language fillers (saying, "you know," "like," and "um" when you are unsure of your facts or uneasy about expressing your opinion)

Step 2

Join with three or four other classmates to evaluate each other's speaking styles.

- Have a 10-minute group discussion on the importance of human relations skills in business.
- Listen to other group members, and take notes on the "power" content of what you hear.
- Offer constructive criticism by focussing on what speakers say rather than on personal characteristics (Say, "Bob, you sympathized with Paul's position, but I still don't know what you think," instead of "Bob, you sounded like a weakling").

Questions for Discussion

1. How do you think the power content of speech affects a manager's ability to communicate? Evaluate some of the ways in which effects may differ among supervisors, peers, and subordinates.
2. How do you evaluate yourself and group members in terms of powerful and powerless speech? List the strengths and weaknesses of the group.
3. Do you agree or disagree with McGinty that business success depends on gaining insight into your own language habits? Explain your answer.
4. In our age of computers and email, why do you think personal presentation continues to be important in management?
5. McGinty believes that power language differs from company to company and that it is linked to the corporate culture. Do you agree, or do you believe that people express themselves in similar ways no matter where they are?

Exercising Your Ethics: Team Exercise

Clean Up Now, or Clean Up Later?

The Situation

The top management team of a medium-sized manufacturing company is on a strategic planning "retreat," and the members are formulating ideas and plans for spurring new growth in the company. As one part of this activity, the team, working with the assistance of a consultant, has conducted a SWOT analysis. During this activity, an interesting and complex situation has been identified. Next year, the federal government will be issuing new—and much more stringent—pollution standards for the company's industry. The management team sees this as a potential "threat" in that the company will have to buy new equipment and change some of its manufacturing methods in order to comply with the new standards.

The Dilemma

One member of the team, James Smith, has posed an interesting option—not complying. His logic can be summarized as follows:

1. The firm has already developed its capital budgets for the next two years. Any additional capital expenditures will cause major problems with the company's cash flow and budget allocations.
2. The company has a large uncommitted capital budget entry available in three years; those funds could be used to upgrade pollution control systems at that time.
3. Because the company has a spotless environmental record so far, Smith argues that if the company does not buy the equipment for three years, the most likely outcomes will be (a) a warning in year 1, (b) a small fine in year 2, and (c) a substantial fine in year 3. However, the total amounts of the fines in years 2 and 3 will be much lower than the cost of redoing the company budgets and complying with the new law next year.

Team Activity

Assemble a group of four students and assign each group member to one of the following roles:

- management team member
- lower-level employee at the company
- company customer
- company investor

Action Steps

1. Before discussing the situation with your group, and from the perspective of your assigned role, do you think that James Smith's suggestion regarding ignoring pollution standards is a good one? Write down the reasons for your position.
2. Before discussing the situation with your group, and from the perspective of your assigned role, what are the underlying ethical issues in this situation? Write down the issues.
3. Gather your group together and reveal, in turn, each member's comments on James Smith's suggestion. Next, reveal the ethical issues listed by each member.
4. Appoint someone to record the main points of agreement and disagreement within the group. How do you explain the results? What accounts for any disagreement?

5. From an ethical standpoint, what does your group conclude is the most appropriate action that should be taken by the company in this situation?
6. Develop a group response to the following questions: (a) What are the respective roles of profits, obligations to customers, and obligations to the community for a firm in this situation? and (b) Is it possible to simultaneously make an ethical decision and maximize company revenue?

For additional cases and exercise material, go to **www.pearsoned.ca/mybusinesslab.**

Concluding Case 6-1

The Business of Bagging Customers

Coach Inc. started out in 1941 making virtually indestructible, high-quality handbags. In the 1970s it was bought by Sara Lee Corp., a big company that was pursuing a strategy of diversification. Because Coach was just one of literally dozens of businesses owned by Sara Lee, it suffered from the lack of focussed management attention. Coach's CEO, Lew Frankfort, knew that his company's success depended on finding the right industry niche. In 2000, he convinced Sara Lee to spin off Coach as an independent company.

By 2007, Coach had sales of $2.6 billion, and the company's net income growth had averaged 51 percent per year for the previous five years. In spite of the recession that started in 2008, the company planned to open many new stores in North America and in China. And it had big plans to compete with the best-known brand names in the industry. For example, just a few years ago in China, Louis Vuitton had the largest market share (33 percent), followed by Gucci and Prada (more than 10 percent each). Coach had only 2 percent. By 2007, Coach's share market share had increased to 12 percent, Louis Vuitton's share had dropped to 27 percent, and Gucci and Prada had less than 10 percent each.

These successes have come in the high-fashion business, where fickle customers and rapid changes make planning difficult. Most fashion designers—Ralph Lauren, Donna Karan, Prada, Gucci, Fendi—have adopted a design-driven business model, in which the designer dictates style to the customers. Coach, however, has taken a different approach. The company asks the customers what they want and then provides it. Coach's customer focus has created a competitive advantage for the firm, which annually sells $865 of merchandise for every square foot of store space, compared to an industry average of $200–$300.

Frankfort introduced many new analytical tools for tracking market trends, evaluating effectiveness, and managing risk. The firm's leaders look at sales data for each store and each product type on a daily basis (several times a day during busy seasons). But extensive and intensive customer research remains the cornerstone of his planning. Indeed, the company spends $2 million per year on surveys. The surveys are supplemented with one-on-one interviews with customers from locations around the world, to quiz them on everything from appearance and quality to the correct length for a shoulder strap.

"The tremendous amount of testing they do differentiates them from a lot of other fashion companies," says industry analyst Robert Ohmes. Analyst Bob Drbul says, "Their execution and business planning is in the league of a Wal-Mart or a Target" (two much larger firms known for their effective business planning). New Coach products are first shown to selected buyers in 12 worldwide markets to gauge initial customer reaction. An initial demand forecast is then made, and six months before introduction, they are tested in another 12 markets. At launch time, sales are monitored closely and adjustments made quickly.

For example, an unexpected spike in sales was investigated, and managers found that buying by Hispanic customers was on the increase. Within a week, the firm had moved up the opening date of a South Miami store and began advertising in Spanish for the first time. Frankfort understands that, to be effective, plans must be translated into appropriate actions. "Not only do you need to know your business and your customers... you also need to be nimble to adapt," he says.

A host of other changes have also aided Coach in its rapid rise. Lew Frankfort hired a former Tommy Hilfiger designer, Reed Krakoff, to update the firm's classic but clunky styles. "Something was missing," says Krakoff. "I had to take these ideas and make them fun—young in spirit." Instead of introducing new products twice a year, a common practice in the fashion industry, Coach releases new styles monthly. Customers now have a reason to visit the stores more often. Outsourcing the production function allowed the company to increase gross profit margins by 24 percent over five years. The firm has diversified into many other related lines of business, including shoes, jewellery, and furniture. There is even a Coach car, a co-branded Lexus, with a Coach leather interior.

Women's Wear Daily, the bible of the fashion industry, named Coach as the "most splurgeworthy luxury brand." Customers agree. Investors, too, like Coach. The firm's share price rose an astonishing 900 percent during its first four years as an independent firm. Krakoff gives the credit for the firm's achievements to Frankfort's planning skills, saying, "The key to Lew's success... is his ability to orchestrate a decision-making process that is both inclusive and incisive."

Questions for Discussion

1. Describe examples of each of the management functions illustrated in this case.
2. Which management skills seem to be most exemplified in Lew Frankfort?
3. Explain the role of goals and strategy in the success of Coach.
4. What corporate culture issues might exist when a former division of a big company is spun off?

Concluding Case 6-2

If at First You Don't Succeed . . .

Warner Music Group Corp. is one of four companies that control about 80 percent of the global recording business. The others are Vivendi Universal Music Group, Sony BMG Music Entertainment, and EMI Group PLC. Warner is trying to profit from increased sales of downloaded music from the web and from cellphone networks. In 2006, downloaded music accounted for just 10 percent of the market, but the International Federation of the Phonographic Industry (IFPI) predicts that figure will rise to 25 percent by 2010.

In the spring of 2007, EMI Group became the first of the Big Four labels to remove so-called Digital Rights Management (DRM) software that restricts how consumers can play and copy music files. The CEO of Warner thought that was a bad idea, but when Universal Music Group followed EMI's lead, Warner finally agreed in December 2007 to remove the software and sell its music on Amazon.com Inc.'s digital music store. Up to that time, Warner had refused to offer songs by its artists in the MP3 format because they can be copied and burned onto CDs and played on Apple's iPod. In July 2008, cellphone maker Nokia announced that it had signed three of the Big Four labels for its "Comes with Music" phone service. It is rumoured that Nokia paid the record companies millions of dollars for the right to offer songs free for downloading.

Industry observers are very interested in whether Warner's strategy will work, partly because Warner's CEO—Edgar Bronfman Jr.—is the person who made a series of disastrous decisions when he was CEO of Seagram, the iconic Canadian company. Seagram was started by his grandfather Sam Bronfman in the 1920s. In 1957, Sam's son Edgar Sr. became CEO of Seagram, and for the next 40 years the company focussed on the production of wine and distilled spirits with well-known brand names like Chivas Regal, Absolut Vodka, and Crown Royal. In the process, Seagram became a household name in Canada and the Bronfman family became very wealthy.

In 1994, Edgar Jr. took over leadership of the company from his father and before long was making some dramatic strategic moves that steered the company away from its traditional products and toward the high-risk entertainment business. For example, the company bought MCA Inc. (now Universal) and Polygram NV. These high-risk moves caused some people to recall founder Sam Bronfman's observation that third-generation family members often dissipate the family fortune. Edgar Jr. was well aware of this criticism, and he was determined not to fulfill his grandfather's prophecy.

Under Edgar Jr.'s leadership, things went reasonably well for a time. Then he met Jean-Marie Messier, the CEO of Vivendi SA, who was trying to convert a French water and utility company into a media conglomerate. In 2000, Edgar sold Seagram to Vivendi for $33 billion of Vivendi stock. But when Vivendi got into financial trouble shortly thereafter, its stock price dropped sharply and the Seagram family fortune declined—from about US$7 billion to less than US$1 billion. Critics charged that Edgar Jr. had exchanged the Bronfman family fortune for a relatively worthless piece of the New Economy dream. Some people started thinking Sam Bronfman was right after all.

After the Vivendi debacle, Edgar moved on to other things in an attempt to repair his reputation as a manager. Determined to get back on the winning path, he first tried to buy Vivendi's film and TV assets, but he was unsuccessful. Later, he and several partners were able to purchase Warner Music Group, which includes record labels such as Warner Bros., Atlantic, Electra, and the Christian music producer Word Records. As CEO of Warner, Edgar Jr. adopted a corporate strategy premised on the belief that consumers would increasingly bypass traditional music stores and instead buy online digital music.

It is not yet clear what the latest developments in digital music mean for Edgar Bronfman Jr. and for Warner Music Group. If Warner's strategy works, Edgar Jr. will be seen as a manager who had the vision and insight to position Warner so that it could capitalize on a major trend. Also, if Vivendi somehow overcomes its financial problems, Edgar Jr. will benefit from its increased stock price because he still holds a lot of its shares. If neither of these possibilities works out, critics will say that old Sam Bronfman was right.

Questions for Discussion

1. What are the various corporate-level strategies that a company might use? Which of these corporate-level strategies did Seagram use under Edgar Bronfman Sr.? Under Edgar Bronfman Jr.? Which strategy is Warner Music Group using now?
2. What is involved in each of the four functions of management? Which of these four functions caused Edgar Bronfman Jr. the most difficulty when he was CEO of Seagram?
3. How do you tell if a person is a good manager? Is Edgar Bronfman Jr. a good manager?
4. What skills do managers need to be effective? In what skill did critics say Edgar Bronfman Jr. was weak? Explain.

apter 7

Organizing the Business Enterprise

After reading this chapter, you should be able to:

1. Discuss the elements that influence a firm's *organizational structure*.
2. Explain how *specialization* and *departmentalization* are the building blocks of organizational structure.
3. Distinguish between *responsibility* and *authority* and explain the differences in decision making in *centralized* and *decentralized* organizations.
4. Explain the differences between *functional, divisional, project,* and *international organizational structures* and describe the most popular new forms of organizational design.
5. Explain the idea of the *informal organization*.

Reorganizing the Irving Empire

The Irving family of New Brunswick is a legendary success story in Canadian business. The company owns nearly 300 businesses in areas as diverse as oil refining, forestry, shipbuilding, food processing, publishing, transportation, and home improvement, and it has dominated corporate life in New Brunswick for decades. The company represents Canada's third largest fortune and is valued at about $6 billion. The company was founded by J.D. Irving in 1882 when he opened a sawmill in Bouctouche, New Brunswick. The business expanded dramatically under his son K.C. Irving, who then passed it on to his sons J.K., Arthur, and Jack. These three brothers—who are now in their seventies—have five sons working in the business. Two of the most active sons are Ken (Arthur's son), who heads the oil and gas operation, and Jim (J.K.'s son), who oversees the forestry operations. Over time, tensions developed between Ken and Jim regarding the strategic direction of the company because they each wanted more control over the business. These tensions made relations between J.K. and his brothers more difficult and threatened the company's tradition of passing on control of the company to the next generation.

Originally, K.C. Irving set up a structure that saw J.K. (and later his son Jim) running the forestry empire, trucking, food processing, and newspapers. Arthur (and later his son Ken) was in charge of oil refineries and service stations. Jack's responsibilities were in construction, steel, and real estate. The grand plan began to fall apart when Jim began to feel restricted by the structure because it tied his strategy to Ken's. As well, the third brother—Jack—began to feel like an also-ran in the company. As a result, a coalition—composed of Arthur and Jack and their families—developed and began to oppose Jim and his family.

These tensions were surprising because the Irving family had always presented a united front. But once the conflict became public, the key players in the business decided to avoid the problems that many other family businesses have faced when family members disagree. To their credit, the brothers wanted to avoid a bitter family feud like the one that engulfed the McCain brothers in the 1990s. So they started talking about how to achieve an amicable parting. They basically decided to restructure the company and let the two main parts go their separate ways. Jim and his relatives took control of the forestry end of the business, and Ken and his relatives took over the oil and gas business.

The restructuring is a bit complicated because the various businesses in the family empire are controlled by trusts that were set up by K.C. Irving many years ago. In order to divide up the company, the dozens of family members who have an interest will have to agree on what the restructuring will look like. Irving descendants will likely be offered cash or business interests in return for the original trusts being phased out.

The complexity involved in dividing up the trusts is only one problem. The other is the shifting fortunes of the two main businesses (energy and forestry). In 2007, the energy business was in good shape (because of high oil prices) while forestry was suffering (the high Canadian dollar had a negative effect on exports of lumber). This was just the reverse of the situation that existed in the 1990s, when forestry was booming and the energy business was suffering (partly because of cost overruns on a new refinery that was being built in Saint John). At that time, the energy business needed a bailout, and the forestry side of the business provided it. By 2009, however, oil prices had dropped dramatically and so had the Canadian dollar, so the fortunes of the two main parts of the Irving empire were converging once again. ◆

How will this help me?

Companies frequently introduce changes that are designed to improve their organization structures. When this happens, people have to understand their "place" in the organization. By understanding the material in this chapter, you will also be prepared to understand your "place" in the organization that employs you. Similarly, as a boss or owner, you'll be better equipped to create the optimal structure for your own organization.

This chapter examines factors that influence a firm's formal organizational structure. We discuss the building blocks of organizational structure—specialization, departmentalization, and decision-making hierarchy. We also describe a variety of organizational structures and the most popular new forms of organizational design. The chapter concludes with an explanation of the important elements of the informal organization.

What Is Organizational Structure?

1 Discuss the elements that influence a firm's *organizational structure.*

In many ways, a business is like an automobile. All automobiles have an engine, four wheels, fenders and other structural components, an interior compartment for passengers, and various operating systems including those for fuel, brakes, and climate control. Each component has a distinct purpose but must also work in harmony with the others. Automobiles made by competing firms all have the same basic components, although the way they look and fit together may vary.

Similarly, all businesses have common structural and operating components, each of which has a specific purpose. Each component must fulfill its own purpose while simultaneously fitting in with the others. And, just like automobiles made by different companies, how these components look and fit together varies from company to company. Thus, **organizational structure** is the specification of the jobs to be done within a business and how those jobs relate to one another.

organizational structure The specification of the jobs to be done within a business and how those jobs relate to one another.

Every institution—be it a for-profit company like Frantic Films, a not-for-profit organization like the University of Saskatchewan, or a government agency like the Canadian Wheat Board—must develop a structure that is appropriate for its own unique situation. What works for Air Canada will not work for Canada Revenue. Likewise, the structure of the Red Cross will not work for the University of Toronto.

Determinants of Organizational Structure

How is an organization's structure determined? Does it happen by chance or is there some logic that managers use to create structure? Does it develop by some combination of circumstance and strategy? Ideally, managers should carefully assess a variety of important factors as they plan for and then create a structure that will allow their organization to function efficiently. But with the busyness that is evident in most organizations, structure may also develop without much planning.

Many elements work together to determine an organization's structure. Chief among these are the organization's purpose, mission, and strategy. A dynamic and rapidly growing enterprise, for example, achieved that position because of its purpose and successful strategies for achieving it. Such a firm will need a structure that contributes to flexibility and growth. A stable organization with only modest growth will function best with a different structure.

Size, technology, and changes in environmental circumstances also affect structure. A large manufacturer operating in a strongly competitive environment requires a different structure than a local barbershop or video store. Moreover, even after a structure has been created, it is rarely free from tinkering—or even outright re-creation. Indeed, most organizations change their structures almost continually.

Since it was first incorporated in 1903, for example, Ford Motor Co. has undergone literally dozens of major structural changes, hundreds of moderate changes, and thousands of minor changes. In just the last 15 years, Ford has initiated several major structural changes. In 1994, the firm announced a major restructuring plan called Ford 2000, which was intended to integrate all of Ford's vast international operations into a single, unified structure by 2000. By 1998, however, midway through implementation of the plan, top Ford executives announced major modifications, indicating that (1) additional changes would be made, (2) some previously planned changes would not be made, and (3) some recently realigned operations would be changed again. In 1999, managers announced another sweeping set of changes intended to eliminate corporate bureaucracy, speed up decision making, and improve communication and working relationships among people at different levels of the organization.[1] In 2001, still more changes were announced that were intended to boost the firm's flagging bottom line and stem a decline in product quality.[2] The problems that developed in the automobile industry in 2007 and 2008 have resulted in further significant structural changes.

The Chain of Command

Most businesses prepare **organization charts** that illustrate the company's structure and show employees where they fit into the firm's operations. Figure 7.1 shows the organization chart for a hypothetical company. Each box represents a job within the company. The solid lines that connect the boxes define the

organization chart Illustrates the company's structure and show employees where they fit into the firm's operations.

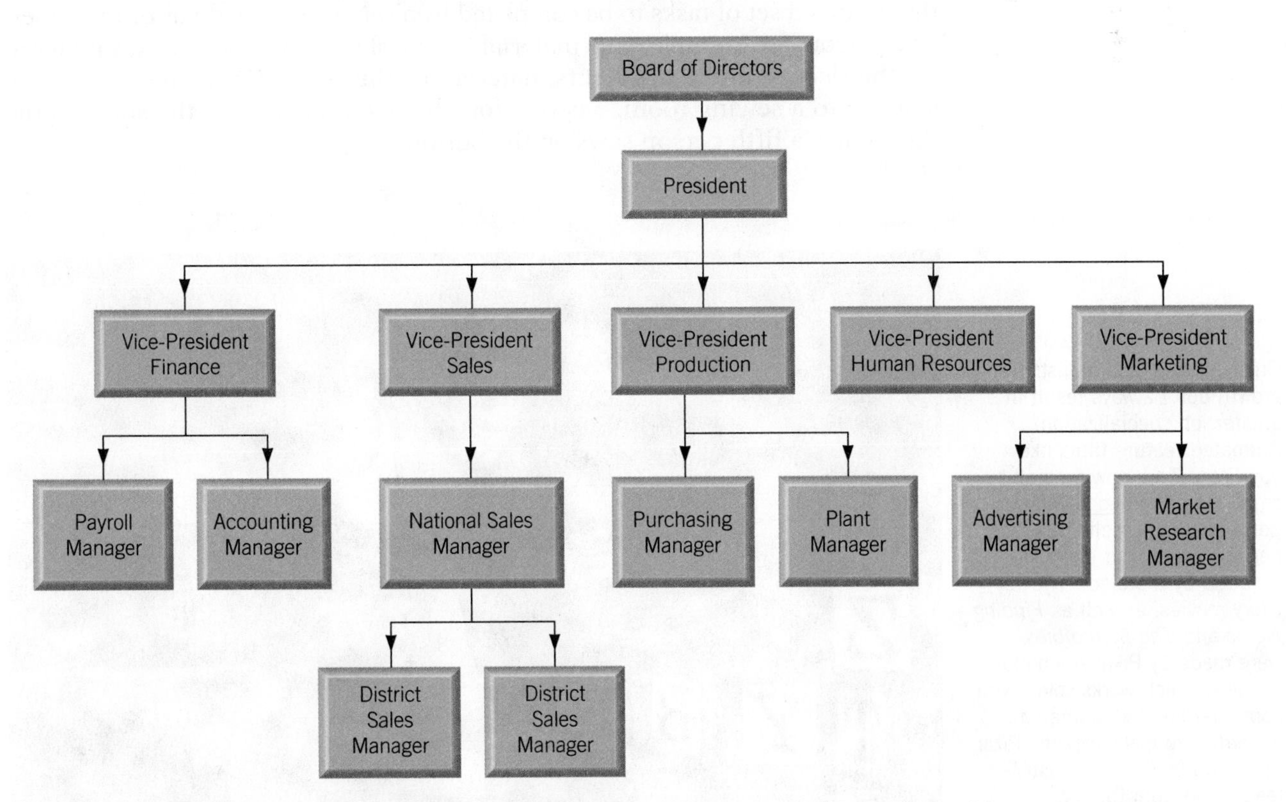

Figure 7.1 An organization chart shows key positions in the organization and interrelationships among them.

chain of command The reporting relationships within the company.

chain of command, or the reporting relationships within the company. For example, the plant manager reports directly to the vice-president of production, who, in turn, reports to the president. When the chain of command is not clear, many different kinds of problems can result.

An actual organization chart would, of course, be far more complex and include individuals at many more levels. Large firms cannot easily draw an organization chart with everyone on it.

The Building Blocks of Organizational Structure

2 Explain how *specialization* and *departmentalization* are the building blocks of organizational structure.

The first step in developing the structure of any business, large or small, is twofold:

- Specialization: determining who will do what
- Departmentalization: determining how people performing certain tasks can best be grouped together

These two tasks are the basic building blocks of all business organization.

Specialization

job specialization The process of identifying the specific jobs that need to be done and designating the people who will perform them.

Job specialization is the process of identifying the specific jobs that need to be done and designating the people who will perform them. In a sense, all organizations have only one major "job"—for example, making a profit by manufacturing and selling something. But this overall job needs to be broken down into smaller components. In turn, each component is assigned to an individual. Consider the manufacture of men's shirts. Because several steps are required to produce a shirt, each job is broken down into its component parts—that is, into a set of tasks to be completed by a series of individuals or machines. One person, for example, cuts material for the shirt body, another cuts material for the sleeves, and a third cuts material for the collar. Components are then shipped to a sewing room, where a fourth person assembles the shirt. In the final stage, a fifth person sews on the buttons.[3]

Organizational and industry-wide growth don't always result in greater job specialization. Animated feature films like *Toy Story 2* are now created by small teams of people who use point-and-click techniques to perform just about every job required by a project. The *Toy Story* movies, as well as *Finding Nemo* and *The Incredibles*, were made by Pixar Animation Studios, which works solely with computer-created animation. According to many experts, Pixar may soon take over industry leadership from Disney.

Specialization and Growth

In a very small organization, the owner may perform every job. As the firm grows, however, so does the need to specialize jobs so that others can perform them. To see how specialization can evolve in an organization, consider the case of Mrs. Fields Cookies. When Debbi Fields opened her first store, she did everything herself: bought the equipment, negotiated the lease, baked the cookies, operated the store, and kept the records. As the business grew, however, Fields found that her job was becoming too much for one person. She first hired a bookkeeper to handle her financial records. She then hired an in-store manager and a cookie baker. She herself concentrated on advertising and promotions. Her second store required another set of employees—another manager, another baker, and some salespeople. While Fields focussed her attention on other expansion opportunities, she turned promotions over to a professional advertising director. Thus the job that she once did all by herself was increasingly broken down into components and assigned to different individuals.

Job specialization is a natural part of organizational growth. It is neither a new idea nor limited to factory work. In the ancient art of winemaking, for example, a high degree of specialization has existed for centuries. The activities necessary to make wine—picking and crushing grapes, fermenting the juice, aging and clarifying the wine, and selling it through specialized intermediaries—are performed by individuals who can draw on the knowledge and experience of their predecessors.

Job specialization has certain advantages—individual jobs can be performed more efficiently, the jobs are easier to learn, and it is easier to replace people who leave the organization. On the other hand, if job specialization is carried too far and jobs become too narrowly defined, people get bored, derive less satisfaction from their jobs, and often lose sight of how their contributions fit into the overall organization.

Departmentalization

After jobs are specialized, they must be grouped into logical units. This process is called **departmentalization**. Departmentalized companies benefit from the division of activities. Control and coordination are narrowed and made easier, and top managers can see more easily how various units are performing. Departmentalization allows the firm to treat a department as a **profit centre**—a separate unit responsible for its own costs and profits. Thus, by assessing profits from sales in a particular area—for example, men's clothing—Sears can decide whether to expand or curtail promotions in that area.

departmentalization The process of grouping jobs into logical units.

profit centre A separate company unit responsible for its own costs and profits.

Managers do not group jobs randomly. They group them logically, according to some common thread or purpose. In general, departmentalization may occur along functional, customer, product, geographic, or process lines (or any combination of these).

Functional Departmentalization

Many service and manufacturing companies develop departments according to a group's functions or activities—a form of organization known as **functional departmentalization**. Such firms typically have production, marketing and sales, human resource, and accounting and finance departments. Departments may be further subdivided. For example, the marketing department might be divided geographically or into separate staffs for market research and advertising.

functional departmentalization Departmentalization according to functions or activities.

Customer Departmentalization

Some retail stores actually derive their generic name—department stores—from the manner in which they are structured. Stores like HMV are divided

Many department stores are departmentalized by product. Concentrating different products in different areas of the store makes shopping easier for customers.

into departments—a classical music department, an R&B department, a pop department, and so on. Each department targets a specific customer category (people who want to buy different genres of music). **Customer departmentalization** makes shopping easier by providing identifiable store segments. Thus, a customer shopping for Shania Twain's latest CD can bypass World Music and head straight for Country. Stores can also group products in locations designated for deliveries, special sales, and other service-oriented purposes. In general, when it is departmentalized the store is more efficient and customers get better service—in part because salespeople tend to specialize and gain expertise in their departments.[4]

customer departmentalization Departmentalization according to the types of customers likely to buy a given product.

Product Departmentalization

Both manufacturers and service providers often opt for **product departmentalization**—dividing an organization according to the specific product or service being created. 3M Corp., which makes both consumer and industrial products, operates different divisions for Post-it brand tape flags, Scotch-Brite scrub sponges, and the Sarns 9000 perfusion system for open-heart surgery.

product departmentalization Dividing an organization according to the specific product or service being created.

Geographic Departmentalization

Some firms may be divided according to the area of the country—or even the world—they serve. This is known as **geographic departmentalization**. In 2009, Nike introduced a new structure that was organized around six geographic regions: North America, Western Europe, Eastern/Central Europe, Greater China, Japan, and emerging markets.[5] Levi Strauss has one division for the United States, one for Europe, and one for the Asia-Pacific region.

geographic departmentalization Departmentalization according to the area of the country or world supplied.

The boxed insert entitled "Product vs. Geographical Departmentalization" describes some dilemmas that companies face when they try to choose between product and geographic departmentalization.

Process Departmentalization

process departmentalization Departmentalization according to the production process used to create a good or service.

Other manufacturers favour **process departmentalization**, in which the organization is divided according to the production processes that are used to

Product vs. Geographical Departmentalization: What's the Right Choice?

Geographic departmentalization ensures quick, responsive reaction to the needs of the company's customers in certain geographic areas. On the other hand, it may also lead to duplicate production and other facilities and compartmentalization of knowledge in those same geographic areas. So it's not easy to decide whether to organize geographically or around products.

Organizing geographically grew in popularity as globalization occurred and firms expanded across national borders. Years ago, when relatively limited communications made it difficult to take the pulse of consumer needs or monitor operations abroad, it made sense to let local managers in foreign countries run their regional or country businesses as more or less autonomous companies. However, two trends are making this structure less popular today. First, information technology is reducing the impediments to cross-border communication. Second, global competition is so intense that firms can't afford to miss an opportunity to quickly transfer product improvements from one region to another.

Many firms are therefore switching from geographic to product departmentalization. For example, food company H.J. Heinz abandoned geographical departmentalization and is now organized by products. Managers in the United States work with those in Europe, Asia, and other regions to apply the best ideas from one region to all the others.

The Canadian Imperial Bank of Commerce (CIBC) also reorganized to break down the walls between the conservative and traditional retail/commercial banking side and the more volatile investment banking side. The company is now organized around product lines.

Exide Corp., the world's largest producer of automotive and industrial batteries, has also shifted from geographical to product departmentalization. Previously, Exide's structure consisted of about 10 "country organizations." The head of each country organization had considerable latitude to make decisions that were best for that country. It also meant that each country manager focussed on products that were marketable in that country. Under the new product system, global business units have been formed to oversee the company's various product lines, such as car and industrial batteries. But the change has not been without problems. For example, when Exide made an acquisition, some top executives got upset when their unit was made subordinate to the newly acquired unit. It wasn't long before Exide was tinkering with its organization chart again.

PepsiCo was formerly organized around geographic areas. The company had two major divisions: North America and International. When Indra Nooyi became CEO, she reorganized the company into three divisions: Americas Foods, Americas Beverages, and International. The new structure—which is something of a compromise between product and geographic departmentalization—better reflects PepsiCo's focus on snack foods (which accounted for 45 percent of total revenue in 2007).

Either approach—products or geography—can cause problems if taken to an extreme. If a company organizes by products, it can standardize manufacturing, introduce new products around the world faster, and eliminate overlapping activities. But if too much emphasis is placed on product and not enough on geography, a company is likely to find that local decision making is slowed, pricing flexibility is reduced, and products are not tailored to meet the needs of a specific country's customers. Ford Motor Co. experienced exactly these problems when it decided to move toward product departmentalization. The reorganization saved the company $5 billion in its first few years of operation, but Ford's market share declined during the same period. This is what we would expect to happen when too much emphasis is placed on product departmentalization. Ford responded to this drop in market share by giving executives in various regions more authority to decide what types of vehicles were best for their local market. In other words, it moved back a bit toward the geographical model.

Procter & Gamble also encountered problems after it replaced country organizations with global business units in an attempt to globalize P&G brands like Tide, Pampers, and Crest. The reorganization caused great upheaval within the company as thousands of employees shifted into new jobs. As many as half of all company executives took on new roles. The CEO who ordered the change left the company just 17 months into his job.

Questions for Discussion

1. In your own words, explain the dilemma that managers face when they are trying to decide between product and geographic departmentalization.
2. How does the notion of managerial accountability enter into the product vs. geographic departmentalization decision?

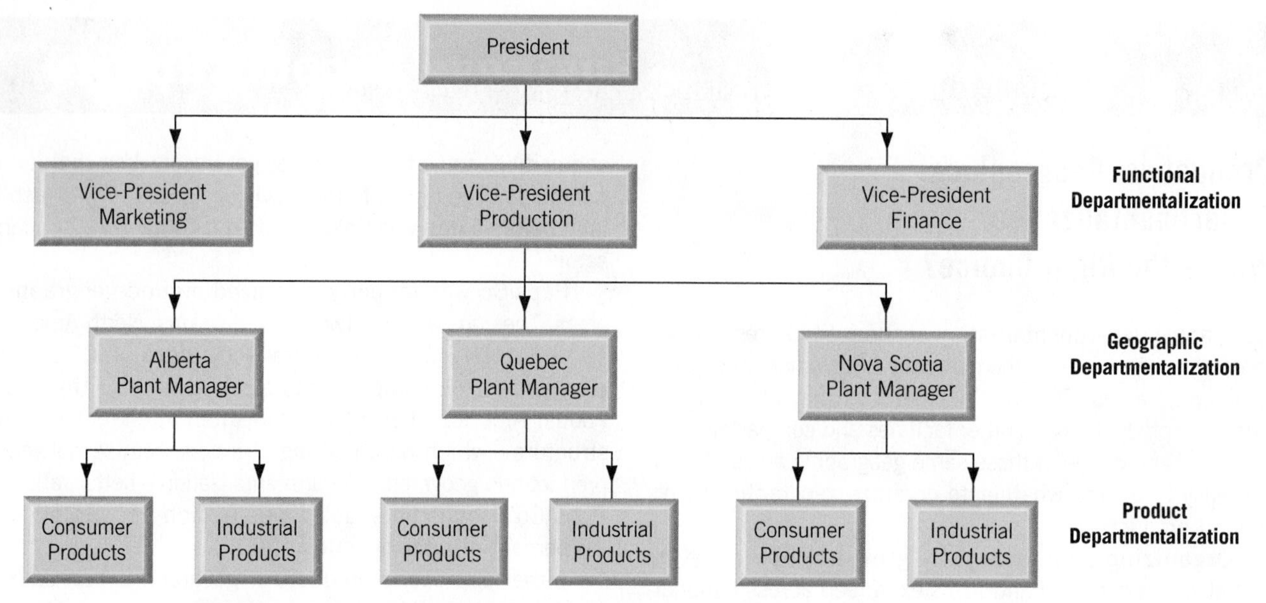

Figure 7.2 Most organizations use multiple bases of departmentalization. This organization, for example, is using functional, geographic, and product departmentalization.

make the product. This principle, for example, is logical for a pickle maker like Vlasic, which has separate departments to transform cucumbers into fresh-packed pickles, pickles cured in brine, and relishes. Cucumbers destined to become fresh-packed pickles must be packed into jars immediately, covered with a solution of water and vinegar, and prepared for sale. Those slated for brined pickles must be aged in brine solution before packing. Relish cucumbers must be minced and combined with a host of other ingredients. Each process requires different equipment and worker skills.

Because different bases of departmentalization have different advantages, larger companies tend to adopt different types of departmentalization for various levels. For example, the company illustrated in Figure 7.2 uses functional departmentalization at the top level. At the middle level, production is divided along geographic lines. At a lower level, departmentalization is based on product groups.

Establishing the Decision-Making Hierarchy

After jobs have been appropriately specialized and grouped into manageable departments, the next step is to answer the question "Who makes which decisions?" This requires the establishment of a decision-making hierarchy, that is, managers must explicitly define reporting relationships among positions so that everyone will know who has responsibility for various decisions and operations. The development of this hierarchy generally involves a three-step process:

1. Assigning tasks: determining who can make decisions and specifying how they should be made
2. Performing tasks: implementing decisions that have been made
3. Distributing authority: determining whether the organization is to be centralized or decentralized

Assigning Tasks

Distinguish between *responsibility* and *authority* and explain the differences in decision making in *centralized* and *decentralized* organizations. 3

The question of who is supposed to do what and who is entitled to do what in an organization is complex. In any company with more than one person, individuals must work out agreements about responsibilities and authority. **Responsibility** is the duty to perform an assigned task. **Authority** is the power to make the decisions necessary to complete the task.

responsibility The duty to perform an assigned task.

authority The power to make the decisions necessary to complete the task.

For example, imagine a mid-level buyer for a department store who encounters an unexpected opportunity to make a large purchase at an extremely good price. Let's assume that an immediate decision is absolutely necessary—but that this decision is one that this buyer has no authority to make without confirmation from above. The company's policies on delegation and authority are inconsistent, since the buyer is responsible for purchasing the clothes that will be sold in the upcoming season but lacks the authority to make the needed purchases.

Performing Tasks

Trouble occurs when appropriate levels of responsibility and authority are not clearly spelled out in the working relationships between managers and subordinates. Here, the issues become delegation and accountability. **Delegation** begins when a manager assigns a task to a subordinate. **Accountability** falls to the subordinate, who must then complete the task. If the subordinate does not perform the assigned task properly and promptly, he or she may be reprimanded or punished, possibly even dismissed.

delegation Assignment of a task, a responsibility, or authority by a manager to a subordinate.

accountability Liability of subordinates for accomplishing tasks assigned by managers.

Fear of Delegating

Unfortunately, many managers have trouble delegating tasks to others. Managers who have trouble delegating typically exhibit several characteristics: they assume that employees can never do anything as well as they can; they fear that their subordinates will "show the manager up" in front of others by doing a superb job; they want to control everything; they fail to do long-range planning because they are bogged down in day-to-day operations; and they are in the dark about industry trends and competitive products because they are too involved in day-to-day operations.

There are remedies for these problems. First, managers should recognize that they cannot do everything themselves. Second, if subordinates cannot do a job, they should be trained so that they can assume more responsibility. Third, managers should recognize that if a subordinate performs well, it reflects favourably on that employee's manager. Effective managers surround themselves with a team of strong subordinates and then delegate sufficient authority to those subordinates so they can get the job done. There are four things to keep in mind when delegating:

- Decide on the nature of the work to be done.
- Match the job with the skills of subordinates.
- Make sure the person chosen understands the objectives he or she is supposed to achieve.
- Make sure subordinates have the time and training necessary to do the task.

Distributing Authority

Delegation involves a specific relationship between managers and subordinates. Most businesses must also make decisions about general patterns of authority throughout the company. This pattern may be largely centralized or decentralized.

Centralized Organizations

centralized organization Top managers retain most decision-making rights for themselves.

In a **centralized organization**, top management retains the right to make most decisions, and top management must approve most lower-level decisions before they can be implemented.[6] McDonald's practises centralization as a way to maintain standardization. All restaurants must follow precise steps in buying products and making and packaging burgers and other menu items. Most advertising is handled at the corporate level, and a regional manager must approve any local advertising. Restaurants even have to follow prescribed schedules for maintenance and upgrades like floor polishing and parking lot cleaning.[7]

Decentralized Organizations

decentralized organization Lower- and middle-level managers are allowed to make significant decisions.

In a **decentralized organization**, much of the decision-making authority is delegated to levels of management at various points below the top level. The purpose of decentralization is to make a company more responsive to its environment by breaking the company into more manageable units and giving those units more autonomy. Reducing top-heavy bureaucracies is also a common goal of decentralization.

At FedEx, the commitment to decentralization promotes innovation. Managers are encouraged and rewarded for questioning, challenging, and developing new ideas, which are always given serious consideration. Developments have included teaming up with Motorola and Microsoft to create a proprietary pocket-size PC, sending package information to cellphones, and creating software products for small business logistics.[8]

Jack Welch, the former CEO of General Electric and a long-time proponent of decentralized management, says, "If you don't let managers make their own decisions, you're never going to be anything more than a one-person business."

McDonald's emphasis on centralization ensures standardization in its product offerings. Customers will have a consistent dining experience whenever and wherever they eat at a McDonald's restaurant.

The idea of autonomy for managers sounds pretty reasonable, but decentralization can also cause difficulties for companies. Consider what happened at General Motors. For many years, GM had a decentralized structure that allowed each car division to produce cars that would attract whatever market segment the division was pursuing. This decentralized structure worked so well that GM became the largest automobile manufacturer in the world. But the autonomy given to managers resulted in widely differing car designs that were very expensive to produce. As GM's costs soared, and as competition from foreign car makers became ferocious, GM's sales and overall profitability plummeted. To cope, GM recentralized and head office took away much of the autonomy that managers in various international divisions had.

Now, GM requires its worldwide units to work much more closely together to design cars that can be sold (with modest variations) worldwide. The new, more centralized structure means that engineers in various regions have less authority than they used to have when they are designing cars. A "Global Council" in Detroit now makes key decisions about how much will be spent on new car development. And the council can say "no" to proposed new car designs. For example, when GM engineers at its Daewoo joint venture with South Korea wanted to develop a sport utility vehicle especially suited for the South Korean market, the request was denied.[9] Even with all of these changes, GM's future is in doubt.

Tall and Flat Organizations

Related to the concept of centralized or decentralized authority is the concept of tall or flat organizational structures. With relatively fewer layers of management, decentralized firms tend to have a **flat organizational structure** such as the one shown in Figure 7.3. In contrast, companies with centralized authority systems typically require multiple layers of management and thus have a **tall organizational structure**. The Canadian Forces is an example of such an organization. Because information, whether upward or downward bound, must pass through so many organizational layers, tall structures are prone to delays in information flow.

flat organizational structure An organization with relatively few layers of management.

tall organizational structure An organization with many layers of management.

As organizations grow in size, they typically become at least somewhat taller. For instance, a small firm with only an owner-manager and a few employees is likely to have two layers—the owner-manager and the employees who report to that person. But as the firm grows, more layers will be needed.

Span of Control

As you can see in Figure 7.3, the distribution of authority in an organization also affects the number of people who work for any individual manager. In a flat organizational structure, the number of people managed by one supervisor—the manager's **span of control**—is usually wide. In tall organizations, span of control tends to be relatively narrow. Span of control, however, depends on many factors. Employees' abilities and the supervisor's managerial skills help determine whether span of control is wide or narrow, as do the similarity and simplicity of those tasks performed under the manager's supervision and the extent to which they are interrelated.[10]

span of control The number of people managed by one manager.

If lower-level managers are given more decision-making authority, their supervisor's workload will be lightened because some of the decisions the supervisor previously made are now made by subordinates. The supervisor may then be able to oversee and coordinate the work of more subordinates, resulting in an increased span of control. Similarly, when several employees perform either the same simple task or a group of interrelated tasks, a wider span of control is possible (for example, one supervisor may control an entire assembly line). Because each task is interdependent, if one work station stops, they all

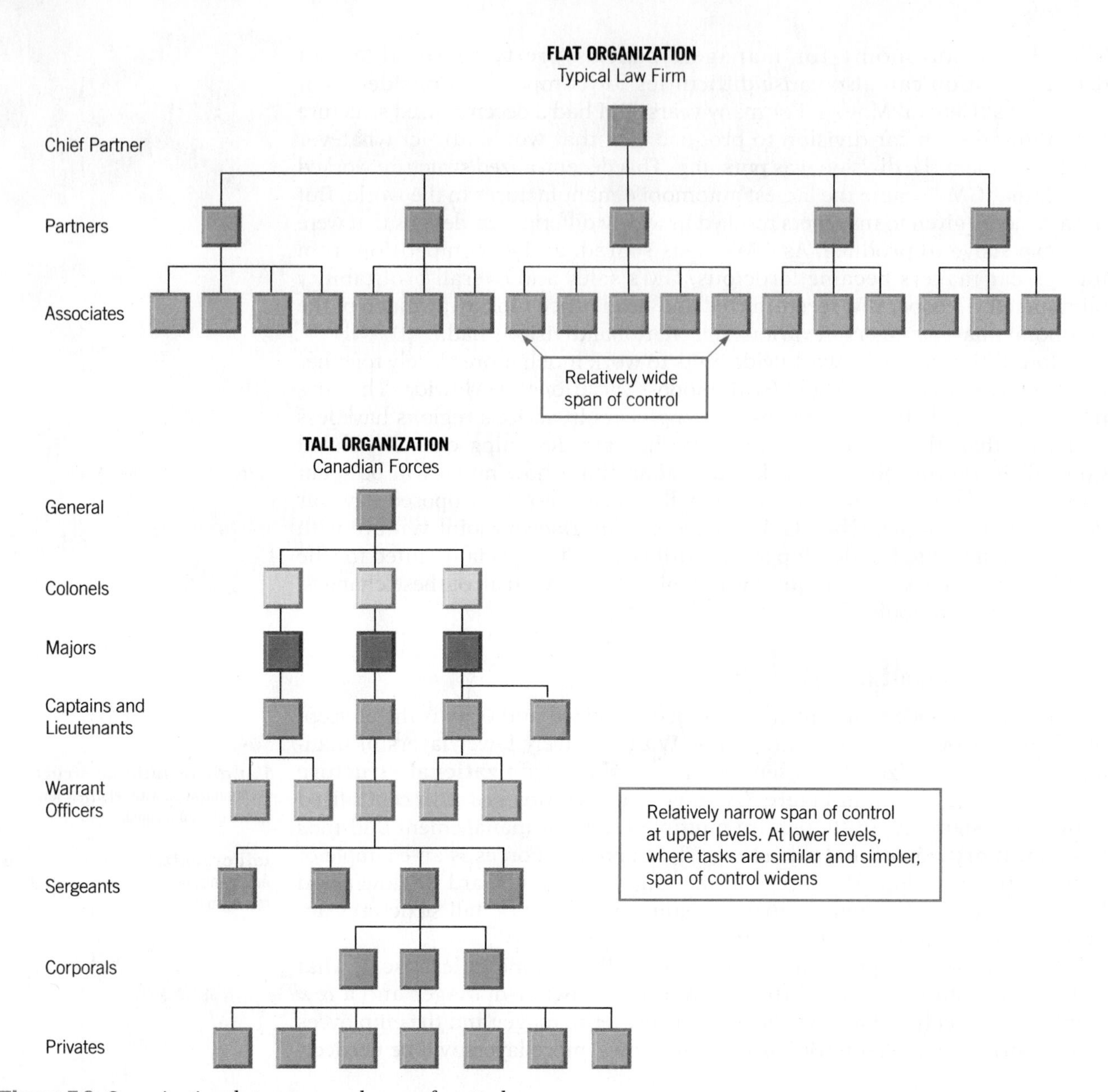

Figure 7.3 Organizational structure and span of control.

stop. Having one supervisor ensures that all stations receive equal attention and are well coordinated. **Downsizing**—the planned reduction in the scope of an organization's activity—also affects the span of control. It usually means cutting substantial numbers of managers and workers and reducing the number and variety of products the company produces. Downsizing may eliminate entire layers of management (creating a flatter corporate structure), and the remaining managers end up with larger spans of control.

downsizing The planned reduction in the scope of an organization's activity.

When jobs are more diversified or prone to change, a narrow span of control is preferable. At Case Corp., farm tractors are made to order in five to six weeks. Farmers can select from among a wide array of options, including engines, tires, power trains, and CD players. A wide assortment of machines and processes is used to construct each tractor. Although workers are highly skilled operators of their assigned machines, each machine is different. In this kind of set-up, the complexities of each machine and the advanced skills needed by each operator mean that one supervisor can oversee only a relatively small number of employees.[11]

Three Forms of Authority

In an organization, it must be clear who will have authority over whom. As individuals are delegated responsibility and authority in a company, a complex web of interactions develops. These interactions may result in one of three forms of authority: line, staff, or committee and team. In reality, like departmentalization, all three forms may be found in a given company, especially a large one.

Line Authority. **Line authority** is authority that flows up and down the chain of command (refer back to Figure 7.1). Most companies rely heavily on **line departments**—departments directly linked to the production and sales of specific products. For example, Clark Equipment Corp. has a division that produces forklifts and small earth movers (see Figure 7.4). In this division, line departments include purchasing, materials handling, fabrication, painting, and assembly (all of which are directly linked to production) along with sales and distribution (both of which are directly linked to sales).

line authority Authority that flows up and down the chain of command.

line departments Departments directly linked to the production and sales of specific products.

Each line department is essential to an organization's success. Line employees are the "doers" and producers in a company. If any line department fails to complete its task, the company cannot sell and deliver finished goods. Thus, the authority delegated to line departments is important. A bad decision by the manager in one department can hold up production for an entire plant. For example, say that the painting department manager at Clark Equipment changes a paint application on a batch of forklifts, which then show signs of peeling paint. The batch will have to be repainted (and perhaps partially reassembled) before the machines can be shipped.

Staff Authority. Most companies also rely on **staff authority**, which is based on technical expertise and involves advising line managers about decisions. Common staff positions include specialists in areas such as law, engineering, accounting, marketing research, and human resource management. Staff members help line departments in making decisions but do not generally have the authority to make final decisions.

staff authority Based on technical expertise and involves advising line managers about decisions.

Suppose that the fabrication department at Clark Equipment has an employee with a drinking problem. The manager of the department could consult a human resource staff expert for advice on handling the situation. The staff expert might suggest that the worker stay on the job but enter a counselling program. But if the line manager decides that the job is too dangerous to be handled by a person whose judgment is impaired by alcohol, the line manager's decision will most likely prevail.

Typically, the separation between line authority and staff responsibility is clearly delineated. As Figure 7.4 shows, this separation is usually shown in organization charts by solid lines (line authority) and dotted lines (staff responsibility). It may help to understand this separation by remembering that while staff members generally provide expert advice and services to management, line managers are the ones who are directly involved in producing and selling the firm's products.

Committee and Team Authority. Recently, more and more organizations have started to use **committee and team authority**—authority granted to committees or work teams that play central roles in the firm's daily operations. A committee, for example, may consist of top managers from several major areas. If the work of the committee is especially important, and if the committee will be working together for an extended time, the organization may even grant it special authority as a decision-making body that goes beyond the individual authority possessed by each of its members.

committee and team authority Authority granted to committees or work teams that play central roles in the firm's daily operations.

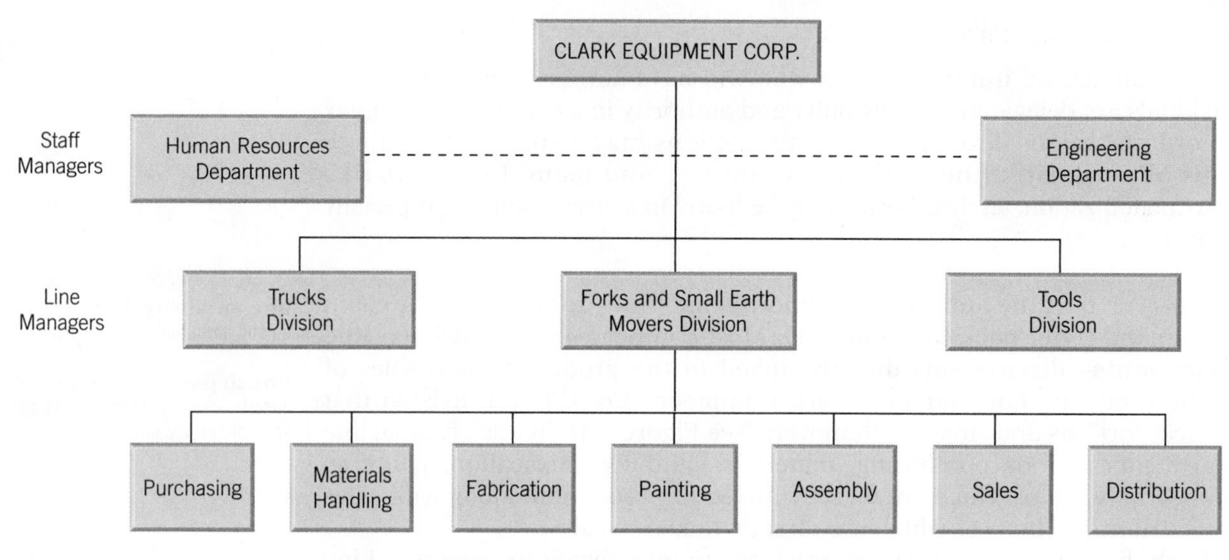

Figure 7.4 Line and staff organization: Clark Equipment Corp.

At the operating level, many firms today are also using work teams—groups of operating employees empowered to plan and organize their own work and to perform that work with a minimum of supervision. As with permanent committees, the organization will usually find it beneficial to grant special authority to work teams so that they will function more effectively.[12]

Basic Organizational Structures

Explain the differences between *functional, divisional, project,* and *international organizational structures* and describe the most popular new forms of organizational design.

A glance at the organization charts of many organizations reveals what appears to be an almost infinite variety of structures. However, closer examination shows that it is possible to identify four basic forms: functional, divisional, project, and international.

functional structure The various units in the organization are formed based on the functions that must be carried out to reach organizational goals.

divisional structure Divides the organization into several divisions, each of which operates as a semi-autonomous unit and profit centre.

The Functional Structure

In the **functional structure**, the various units in the organization are formed based on the functions that must be carried out to reach organizational goals. The functional structure makes use of departmentalization by function. Refer back to Figure 7.1 for an example of a functional structure. The advantages and disadvantages of the functional structure are summarized in Table 7.1.

Business firms are increasingly using work teams and allowing groups of employees to plan and organize their own work with a minimum of supervision. This contributes to employee empowerment.

The Divisional Structure

The **divisional structure** divides the organization into several divisions, each of which operates as a semi-autonomous unit and profit centre (see Figure 7.5). Divisions in organizations can be based on products, customers, or geography. In 2008, Teck Resources Ltd. (formerly Teck Cominco Ltd.)

Table 7.1 Advantages and Disadvantages of a Functional Structure

Advantages	Disadvantages
1. It focusses attention on the key activities that must be performed.	1. Conflicts may arise among the functional areas.
2. Expertise develops within each function.	2. No single function is responsible for overall organizational performance.
3. Employees have clearly defined career paths.	3. Employees in each functional area have a narrow view of the organization.
4. The structure is simple and easy to understand.	4. Decision making is slowed because functional areas must get approval from top management for a variety of decisions.
5. It eliminates duplication of activities.	5. Coordinating highly specialized functions may be difficult.

reorganized its business into separate product divisions for gold, copper, zinc, metallurgical coal, and energy. The company felt that the new structure would increase its competitiveness and allow it to act on opportunities in the five different commodity segments.[13]

H.J. Heinz, one of the world's largest food-processing companies, is divisionalized along seven product lines: food service, infant foods, condiments, Star-Kist tuna, pet foods, frozen foods, and miscellaneous products. Because of its divisional structure, Heinz can evaluate the performance of each division independently. Because divisions are relatively autonomous, a firm can take actions (like selling unprofitable divisions) with minimal disruption to its remaining business operations. The advantages and disadvantages of the divisional structure are summarized in Table 7.2.

Project Organization

Most organizations are characterized by unchanging vertical authority relationships because such a set-up facilitates the production of a product in a routine and repetitive way. Procter & Gamble, for example, produces millions of tubes of Crest toothpaste each year using standardized production methods. The company has done this for years and intends to do so indefinitely.

But some organizations find themselves faced with projects that have a definite starting and ending point. These organizations often use a project structure to deal with the uncertainty encountered in new situations. **Project organization** involves forming a team of specialists from different functional areas of the organization to work on a specific project.[14] A project structure

project organization Involves forming a team of specialists from different functional areas of the organization to work on a specific project.

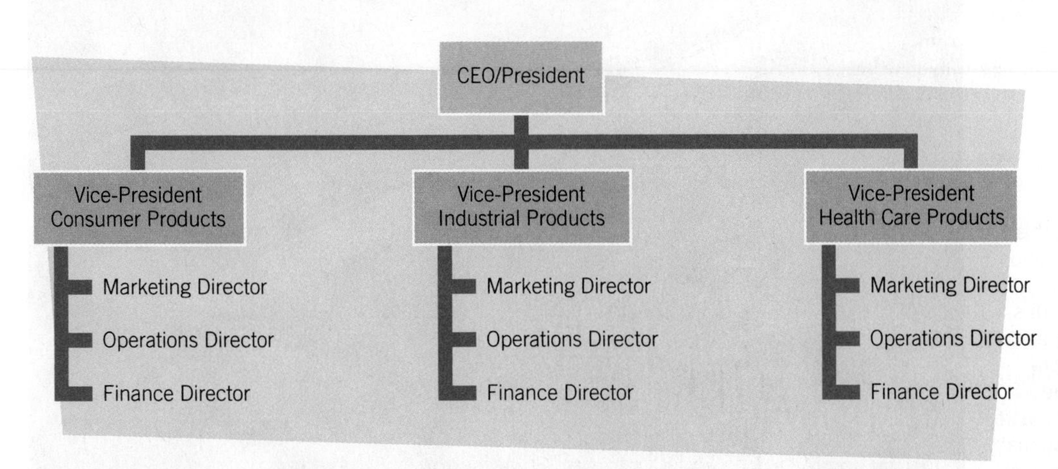

Figure 7.5 Divisional structure.

Table 7.2 Advantages and Disadvantages of a Divisional Structure	
Advantages	**Disadvantages**
1. It accommodates change and expansion.	1. Activities may be duplicated across divisions.
2. It increases accountability.	2. A lack of communication among divisions may occur.
3. It develops expertise in the various divisions.	3. Adding diverse divisions may blur the focus of the organization.
4. It encourages training for top management.	4. Company politics may affect the allocation of resources.

may be temporary or permanent; if it is temporary, the project team disbands once the project is completed and team members return to their regular functional area or are assigned to a new project.

Project organization is used extensively by Canadian firms, for example, in the construction of hydroelectric generating stations like those developed by Hydro-Quebec on La Grande River and by Manitoba Hydro on the Nelson River. Once the generating station is complete, it becomes part of the traditional structure of the utility. Project organization is also used at shipyards. Each ship that is built is treated as a project and supervised by a project manager. The project manager for a given ship is responsible for ensuring that the ship is completed on time and within budget.[15] Project organization has proven useful for coordinating the many elements needed to extract oil from the tar sands. Project management is also used in other kinds of tasks, including construction, military weapons, aerospace, and health-care delivery.[16]

matrix organization A variation of project structure in which the project manager and the regular line managers share authority.

A **matrix organization** is a variation of project structure in which the project manager and the regular line managers share authority. Ford, for example, used a matrix organization to redesign the Ford Thunderbird. A design team composed of people from engineering, marketing, operations, and finance was created to design the new car. During the time the team was working on the Thunderbird project, the engineering, marketing, operations, and finance experts reported primarily to the project manager, but the line managers of the departments they came from also had some say about what work they did. After the team's work was done, team members moved back to their permanent functional jobs.

The project organization structure is very useful for construction projects like this hydroelectric generating station on the La Grande River in Quebec. Installations like this have a specific beginning and ending point. Once the construction is completed, the generating station becomes part of the traditional organizational structure of the provincial utility.

In other companies, the matrix organization is a semi-permanent fixture. Martha Stewart Living Omnimedia Inc. has created a permanent matrix organization for its burgeoning lifestyle business. The company is organized broadly into media and merchandising groups, each of which has specific product and product groups. Layered on top of this structure are teams of lifestyle experts organized into groups such as cooking, crafts, weddings, and so forth. Although each group targets specific customer needs, they all work across all product groups. A wedding expert, for example, might contribute to an article on wedding planning for a Martha Stewart magazine, contribute a story idea for a Martha Stewart cable television program, and supply content for a Martha Stewart website. This same individual might also help select fabrics suitable for wedding gowns that are to be retailed.[17]

The matrix structure does not always work well. In 2009, Carol Bartz—the new CEO at Yahoo—announced a restructuring that was designed to make managers more accountable and to speed up decision making. The new structure essentially did away with the matrix structure and workers no longer report to multiple bosses.[18]

International Organization

As we saw in Chapter 5, many businesses today manufacture, purchase, and sell in the global market. As a result, several different **international organizational structures** have emerged. Moreover, as competition on a global scale becomes more complex, companies often find that they must experiment with the ways in which they respond.

international organizational structures Organizational structures that are designed to help a company succeed in international markets. International departments, international divisions, or an integrated global organization are all variations of the international organizational structure.

For example, when Wal-Mart opened its first store outside the United States in 1992, it set up a special projects team to handle the logistics. As more stores were opened abroad in the mid-1990s, the firm created a small international department to handle overseas expansion. By 1999, however, international sales and expansion had become such a major part of Wal-Mart's operations that the firm created a separate international division headed up by a senior vice-president. And by 2002, international operations had become so important to Wal-Mart that the international division was further divided into geographic areas where the firm does business, such as Mexico and Europe. Wal-Mart typifies the form of organization outlined in Figure 7.6.

Other firms have also developed a wide range of approaches to international organization structure. The French food giant Danone Group, for instance,

All the signs at this 85 000-square-foot store in Numazu identify it as a Seiyu outlet run by Japan's fifth largest supermarket chain. However, Wal-Mart owns 38 percent of Seiyu, and this giant store is part of Wal-Mart's effort to enter the world's second largest retail market.

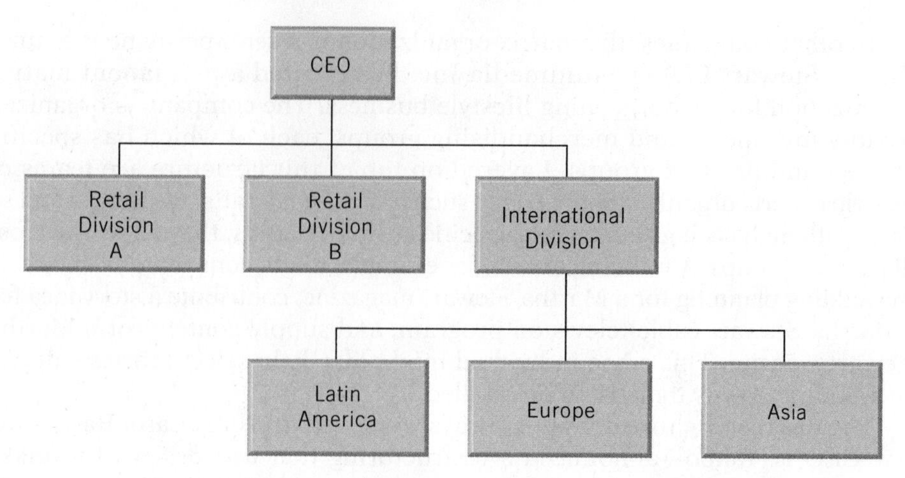

Figure 7.6 International division structure.

has three major product groups: dairy products (Danone yogourt), bottled water (Evian), and cookies (Pim's). Danone's structure does not differentiate internationally, but rather integrates global operations within each product group.[19] In contrast, U.S. entertainment companies are finding it advantageous to create a more local identity when they enter foreign markets. For instance, Columbia TriStar, known for such U.S. television programs as *Seinfeld* and *Mad About You*, launched *Chinese Restaurant*, a sitcom filmed and shown only in China. Universal and HBO have also got in on the act by setting up new television production businesses in Germany and Japan.[20]

Finally, some companies adopt a truly global structure in which they acquire resources (including capital), produce goods and services, engage in research and development, and sell products in whatever local market is appropriate, without any consideration of national boundaries. Until a few years ago, for example, General Electric kept its international business operations as separate divisions. Now, however, the company functions as one integrated global organization. GE businesses around the world connect and interact with each other constantly, and managers freely move back and forth among them. This integration is also reflected in the top management team: The head of its audit team is French, the head of quality control is Dutch, and a German runs one of GE's core business groups.[21]

Another kind of "structure" is described in the boxed insert entitled "Green Structures."

Organizational Design for the Twenty-first Century

As the world grows increasingly complex and fast paced, companies continue to seek new forms of organization that permit them to compete effectively. Among the most popular of these new forms are the boundaryless organization, the team organization, the virtual organization, and the learning organization.

Boundaryless Organization

boundaryless organization Traditional boundaries and structures are minimized or eliminated altogether.

The **boundaryless organization** is one in which traditional boundaries and structures are minimized or eliminated altogether. For example, General Electric's fluid organization structure, in which people, ideas, and information flow freely between businesses and business groups, approximates this concept. Similarly, as firms partner with their suppliers in more efficient ways, external boundaries disappear. Some of Wal-Mart's key suppliers are tied directly into the retailer's vaunted information system. As a result, when Wal-Mart distribution centres start running low on, say, Wrangler blue jeans, the

The Greening of Business

Green Structures

The term *organizational structure* is commonly used to explain theoretical concepts like departmentalization, authority, responsibility, and the hierarchical patterns within organizations. But businesses (and cities) also need physical structures like offices and factories to do their work, and managers in both the public and private sector are beginning to realize that their physical structures present significant opportunities to be eco-friendly. In Charlottetown, P.E.I., for example, a federal government office building is being constructed with photovoltaic panels that will produce 8 to 10 percent of the building's power needs. At the University of Toronto, over 90 percent of the heating requirements for the engineering and computer science building are being recovered from a nearby boiler plant. And Masdar City, Abu Dhabi—which is scheduled for completion in 2016—will be the world's first zero-carbon, zero-waste city that is fully powered by renewable energy.

Some architects think that over the next decade, it may be possible to have buildings that require no energy at all from public utilities. Birgit Siber, an architect at Toronto-based Diamond and Schmitt Architects, says that big box stores are good candidates because they already have relatively low energy requirements. Wal-Mart, for example, has started to open high-efficiency supercentres, which consume 20 percent less energy than their regular supercentres. Gerrit de Boer, president of Toronto-based Idomo Furniture Co., says that his firm will be "off the grid" within 10 years as a result of the geothermal heating system and the photovoltaic solar array that are being installed in the company's 200 000-square-foot building.

Many other organizations are also introducing eco-friendly technologies. When a hybrid heating system was installed at Delta Whistler Village Suites, greenhouse gases were reduced by 45 percent, and the hotel saved $70 000 in energy costs. The hybrid heating system alternates between electricity and fossil fuels, depending on whichever is cheaper at the moment. Manitoba Hydro's new building in Winnipeg contains a geothermal heating and air-conditioning system that provides 100 percent of the energy needed to air condition the building in the summer and 60 percent of the energy needed to heat the building in winter. The building is so energy efficient that it uses just 91 kilowatt hours of energy per square metre of floor space (the Model National Energy Code standards say that a building should not use more than 295 kilowatt hours).

Sunova Credit Union's branch in Oak Bank, Manitoba, became the greenest building in the province when it was completed in the summer of 2009. The building meets the platinum (highest) rating of the Leadership in Energy and Environmental Design (LEED) organization. Very few buildings in Canada have this designation. The building uses recycled building materials and has energy-efficient windows, a solar energy panel, a geothermal heating and cooling system, and a water retention and treatment system. Some automobile dealers are also seeking certification from LEED for buildings at their dealerships. LEED standards are also important in the planning of the facilities and venues for the 2010 Winter Olympics in British Columbia.

Even more innovative ideas are likely to emerge in the future. In Britain, for example, engineers are experimenting with a "heel-strike" technology that harnesses pedestrian footsteps. When people walk around in a building, power is generated each time their heels hit the floor. Pretty clever, but at the moment it appears that not enough energy is generated by heel strikes. Future research will no doubt improve this technology.

The movement toward greener buildings is not limited to commercial buildings. A survey by realtor Royal LePage found that 72 percent of Canadians would look for a greener home when they make their next purchase. Green realtors are now emerging that specialize in finding green homes for clients who are environmentally conscious, and there is even a Green Realty Association in British Columbia. Home buyers have two basic options: they can purchase a home that has been built to be eco-friendly; or they can renovate an older home by improving insulation, replacing windows, installing solar panels, and installing energy efficient appliances and showers.

Critical Thinking Questions

1. What are the advantages of "green" buildings? Are there any disadvantages? Explain.
2. Consider the following statement: *It's a very good idea for companies to build eco-friendly buildings, but it is very expensive to do so, and expenditures like these should not be made. Rather, the focus should be on upgrading their production facilities so that companies can make higher-quality products for consumers and more profits for their shareholders.* Do you agree or disagree with the statement? Explain your reasoning.

manufacturer receives the information as soon as the retailer does. Wrangler proceeds to manufacture new inventory and restock the distribution centre without Wal-Mart having to place a new order.

Team Organization

team organization Relies almost exclusively on project-type teams, with little or no underlying functional hierarchy.

Team organization relies almost exclusively on project-type teams, with little or no underlying functional hierarchy. People "float" from project to project as dictated by their skills and the demands of those projects. At Cypress Semiconductor, units or groups that become large are simply split into smaller units. Not surprisingly, the organization is composed entirely of small units. This strategy allows each unit to change direction, explore new ideas, and try new methods without having to deal with a rigid bureaucratic superstructure. Although few large organizations have actually reached this level of adaptability, Apple Computer and Xerox are among those moving toward it.

Virtual Organization

virtual organization A company with little or no formal structure, which exists only in response to its own needs.

A **virtual organization** has little or no formal structure. Typically, it has only a handful of permanent employees, a very small staff, and a modest administrative facility. As the needs of the organization change, managers bring in temporary workers, lease facilities, and outsource basic support services to meet the demands of each unique situation. As the situation changes, the temporary workforce changes in parallel, with some people leaving the organization and others entering it. Facilities and subcontracted services also change. In other words, the virtual organization exists only in response to its own needs.

Global Research Consortium (GRC) is a virtual organization that offers research and consulting services to firms doing business in Asia. As clients request various services, GRC's staff of three permanent employees subcontracts the work to an appropriate set of several dozen independent consultants and/or researchers with whom it has relationships. At any given time, therefore, GRC may have several projects underway and 20 or 30 people working on various projects. As the projects change, so too does the composition of the organization. Figure 7.7 illustrates a hypothetical virtual organization.

Learning Organization

learning organization Works to integrate continuous improvement with continuous employee learning and development.

The so-called **learning organization** works to integrate continuous improvement with continuous employee learning and development. Specifically, a learning organization works to facilitate the lifelong learning and personal development of all of its employees while continually transforming itself to respond to changing demands and needs.

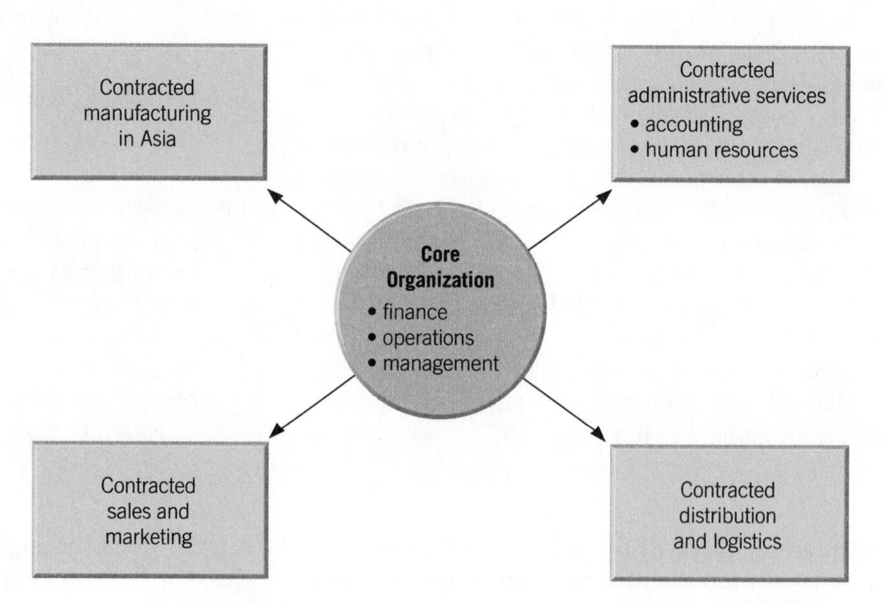

Figure 7.7 A virtual organization.

The most frequent goals of a learning organization are improved quality, continuous improvement, and performance measurement. The idea is that the most consistent and logical strategy for achieving continuous improvement is constantly upgrading employee talent, skill, and knowledge. For example, if each employee in an organization learns one new thing each day and can translate that knowledge into work-related practice, continuous improvement will logically follow. Indeed, organizations that wholeheartedly embrace this approach believe that only through constant employee learning can continuous improvement really occur.

In recent years, many different organizations have implemented this approach on various levels. Shell Oil Co., for example, recently purchased an executive conference centre called the Shell Learning Center. The facility boasts state-of-the-art classrooms and instructional technology, lodging facilities, a restaurant, and recreational amenities such as a golf course, swimming pool, and tennis courts. Line managers at the firm rotate through the centre and serve as teaching faculty. Teaching assignments last anywhere from a few days to several months. At the same time, all Shell employees routinely attend training programs, seminars, and related activities, all the while gathering the latest information they need to contribute more effectively to the firm. Seminar topics have included time management, balancing work and family demands, and international trade theory.

The Informal Organization

Explain the idea of the *informal organization.* 5

The formal organization of a business is the part that can be seen and represented on the organization chart. The structure of a company, however, is by no means limited to the organization chart and the formal assignment of authority. Frequently, the **informal organization**—the everyday social interactions among employees that transcend formal jobs and job interrelationships—effectively alters a company's formal structure. Indeed, this level of organization is sometimes more powerful than the formal structure. The Exercising Your Ethics boxed insert at the end of the chapter presents an interesting situation that illustrates the informal organization.

informal organization The everyday social interactions among employees that transcend formal jobs and job interrelationships.

Is the informal organization good or bad? On the positive side, the informal organization can help employees feel that they "belong," and it gives them an outlet for "letting off steam" in a safe environment. It also provides information that employees are interested in hearing. On the negative side, the informal organization can reinforce office politics that put the interests of individuals ahead of those of the firm. Likewise, a great deal of harm can be caused by distorted or inaccurate information communicated without management input or review. For example, if the informal organization is generating false information about impending layoffs, valuable employees may act quickly (and unnecessarily) to seek other employment. Among the more important elements of the informal organization are informal groups and the organizational grapevine.

Informal Groups

Informal groups are simply groups of people who decide to interact among themselves even though they may not be required to do so by the formal organization. They may be people who work together or who simply get together for lunch, during breaks, or after work. They may talk about business, the boss, or non-work-related topics such as families, movies, or sports. For example, at the New York Metropolitan Opera, musicians and singers play poker during the intermissions. Most pots are in the $30 to $40 range. Luciano Pavarotti, the famed tenor, once played and lost big.

The impact of informal groups on the organization may be positive (if they work together to support the organization), negative (if they work together in ways that run counter to the organization's interests), or neutral (if what they do is unrelated to the organization).

Organizational Grapevine

grapevine The informal communication network that runs through the entire organization.

The **grapevine** is the informal communication network that runs through the entire organization.[22] The grapevine is found in all organizations except the very smallest, but it does not always follow the same patterns as formal channels of authority and communication, nor does it necessarily coincide with them. Because the grapevine typically passes information orally, messages often become distorted in the process, but most office gossip has at least some kernel of truth to it. Those passing on news may deliberately alter it, either to advance their own goals or to submarine someone else's chances. Listening to and passing on information damaging to someone's reputation can backfire, harming your credibility and making you a target for similar gossip.

In general, the more detailed the information, the less likely it is to be true. Likewise, beware the hush-hush "don't quote me on this" rumour. (Cynics claim that the better the news, the less likely it is to be true.) The higher the source, the greater the likelihood that the grapevine has the real story. Don't reject information from "lower" sources, however. Many an executive assistant can provide valuable insights into a corporation's plans.

Attempts to eliminate the grapevine are fruitless, but managers do have some control over it. By maintaining open channels of communication and responding vigorously to inaccurate information, they can minimize the damage the grapevine can do. In fact, the grapevine can actually be an asset. By getting to know the key people in the grapevine, for example, the manager can partially control the information received and use the grapevine to determine employee reactions to new ideas (e.g., a change in human resource policies or benefit packages). The manager can also receive valuable information from the grapevine and use it to improve decision making.

Wise managers will tune in to the grapevine's message because it is often a corporate early warning system. Ignoring this valuable source of information

The grapevine is a powerful communications network in most organizations. These workers may be talking about any number of things—an upcoming deadline on an important project, tonight's football game, the stock market, rumours about an impending takeover, gossip about forthcoming promotions, or the weather.

can cause managers to be the last to know that they are about to get a new boss or that they have a potentially fatal image problem. The grapevine is not infallible, however. In addition to miscommunication and attempts by some people to manipulate it for their own ends, it may carry rumours with absolutely no basis in fact. Such rumours are most common when there is a complete lack of information (apparently, human nature abhors a vacuum and seeks to fill it with something, even if it is made-up information).

Test yourself on the material for this chapter at **www.pearsoned.ca/mybusinesslab.**

Summary of Learning Objectives

1. **Discuss the elements that influence a firm's *organizational structure*.** Every business needs structure to operate. *Organizational structure* varies according to a firm's mission, purpose, and strategy. Size, technology, and changes in environmental circumstances also influence structure. In general, while all organizations have the same basic elements, each develops the structure that contributes to the most efficient operations.

2. **Explain how *specialization* and *departmentalization* are the building blocks of organizational structure.** The building blocks of organizational structure are job specialization and *departmentalization.* As a firm grows, it usually has a greater need for people to perform specialized tasks (specialization). It also has a greater need to group types of work into logical units (departmentalization). Common forms of departmentalization are *customer, product, process, geographic,* and *functional.* Large businesses often use more than one form of departmentalization.

3. **Distinguish between *responsibility* and *authority* and explain the differences in decision making in *centralized* and *decentralized* organizations.** *Responsibility* is the duty to perform a task; *authority* is the power to make the decisions necessary to complete tasks. *Delegation* begins when a manager assigns a task to a subordinate; *accountability* means that the subordinate must complete the task. *Span of control* refers to the number of people who work for any individual manager. The more people supervised by a manager, the wider his or her span of control. Wide spans are usually desirable when employees perform simple or unrelated tasks. When jobs are diversified or prone to change, a narrower span is generally preferable.

   In a *centralized organization*, only a few individuals in top management have real decision-making authority. In a *decentralized organization*, much authority is delegated to lower-level management. Where both line and line-and-staff systems are involved, *line departments* generally have authority to make decisions while staff departments have a responsibility to advise. A relatively new concept, *committee and team authority*, empowers committees or work teams involved in a firm's daily operations.

4. **Explain the differences between *functional, divisional, project,* and *international organizational structures* and describe the most popular new forms of organizational design.** In a *functional organization*, authority is usually distributed among such basic functions as marketing and finance. In a *divisional organization*, the various divisions of a larger company, which may be related or unrelated, operate in a relatively autonomous fashion. In *project organization*, in which individuals report to more than one manager, a company creates teams to address specific problems or to conduct specific projects. A company that has divisions in many countries may require an additional level of *international organization* to coordinate those operations. Four of the most popular new forms of organizational design are (1) *boundaryless organizations* (traditional boundaries and structures are minimized or eliminated), (2) *team organizations* (rely on project-type teams, with little or no functional hierarchy), (3) *virtual organizations* (have little formal structure and only a handful of permanent employees, a small staff, and a modest administrative facility), and (4) *learning organizations* (work to facilitate employees' lifelong learning and personal development while transforming the organization to meet changing demands and needs).

5. **Explain the idea of the *informal organization*.** The *informal organization* consists of the everyday social interactions among employees that transcend formal jobs and job interrelationships. The informal organization exists within the formal structure of every organization and cannot be suppressed. Effective managers work with the informal organization and try to harness it for the good of the formal organization.

Key Terms

accountability (p. 219)
authority (p. 219)
boundaryless organization (p. 228)
centralized organization (p. 220)
chain of command (p. 214)
committee and team authority (p. 223)
customer departmentalization (p. 216)
decentralized organization (p. 220)
delegation (p. 219)
departmentalization (p. 215)
divisional structure (p. 224)
downsizing (p. 222)
flat organizational structure (p. 221)
functional departmentalization (p. 215)
functional structure (p. 224)
geographic departmentalization (p. 216)
grapevine (p. 232)
informal organization (p. 231)
international organizational structure (p. 227)
job specialization (p. 214)
learning organization (p. 230)
line authority (p. 223)
line departments (p. 223)
matrix organization (p. 226)
organization chart (p. 213)
organizational structure (p. 212)
process departmentalization (p. 216)
product departmentalization (p. 216)
profit centre (p. 215)
project organization (p. 225)
responsibility (p. 219)
span of control (p. 221)
staff authority (p. 223)
tall organizational structure (p. 221)
team organization (p. 230)
virtual organization (p. 230)

Questions for Analysis

1. Explain the significance of size as it relates to organizational structure. Describe the changes that are likely to occur as an organization grows.
2. Why do some managers have difficulties in delegating authority? Why does this problem tend to plague smaller businesses?
3. Draw up an organization chart for your college or university.
4. Describe a hypothetical organizational structure for a small printing firm. Describe changes that might be necessary as the business grows.
5. Compare and contrast the matrix and divisional approaches to organizational structure. How would you feel personally about working in a matrix organization in which you were assigned simultaneously to multiple units and multiple bosses?
6. If a company has a formal organizational structure, why should managers pay attention to the informal organization?
7. Consider the organization where you currently work (or one where you have previously worked). Which of the four basic structural types was it most consistent with? What was the basis of departmentalization in the company? Why was that particular basis of departmentalization used?
8. What kinds of problems might develop in a matrix organization? Why would these problems develop?

Application Exercises

1. Interview the manager of a local service business—a fast-food restaurant. What types of tasks does this manager typically delegate? Is the appropriate authority also delegated in each case?
2. Interview a manager and ask about the informal organization in his or her place of business. What advantages and disadvantages does the manager see with respect to the informal organization? What is the manager's strategy in dealing with the informal organization?

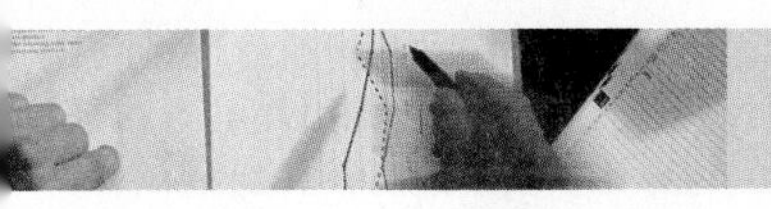

Building Your Business Skills

Getting with the Program

The Purpose of This Assignment

To encourage students to understand the relationship between organizational structure and a company's ability to attract and keep valued employees.

The Situation

You are the founder of a small but growing high-technology company that develops new computer software. With your current workload and new contracts in the pipeline, your business is thriving except for one problem: You cannot find computer programmers for product development. Worse yet, current staff members are being lured away by other high-tech firms. After suffering a particularly discouraging personnel raid in which competitors captured three of your most valued employees, you schedule a meeting with your director of human resources to plan organizational changes designed to encourage worker loyalty. You already pay top dollar, but the continuing exodus tells you that programmers are looking for something more.

Method

Working with three or four classmates, identify some ways in which specific organizational changes might improve the working environment and encourage employee loyalty. As you analyze the following factors, ask yourself the obvious question: If I were a programmer, what organizational changes would encourage me to stay?

Level of job specialization. With many programmers describing their jobs as tedious because of the focus on detail in a narrow work area, what changes, if any, would you make in job specialization? Right now, for instance, few of your programmers have any say in product design.

Decision-making hierarchy. What decision-making authority would encourage people to stay? Is expanding employee authority likely to work better in a centralized or decentralized organization?

Team authority. Can team empowerment make a difference? Taking the point of view of the worker, describe the ideal team.

Intrapreneuring. What can your company do to encourage and reward innovation? (Review the material in Chapter 4 on intrapreneuring before analyzing this factor.)

Questions for Discussion

1. With the average computer programmer earning nearly $70 000 per year and with all competitive firms paying top dollar, why might organizational issues be critical in determining employee loyalty?
2. If you were a programmer, what organizational factors would make a difference to you? Why?
3. As the company founder, how willing would you be to make major organizational changes in light of the shortage of qualified programmers?

Exercising Your Ethics: Team Exercise

To Poach or Not to Poach

The Situation

The Hails Corporation, a manufacturing plant, has recently moved toward an all team-based organization structure. That is, all workers are divided into teams. Each team has the autonomy to divide up the work assigned to it among its individual members. In addition, each team handles its own scheduling for members to take vacations and other time off. The teams also handle the interviews and hiring of new team members when the need arises. Team A has just lost one of its members who moved to another city to be closer to his ailing parents.

The Dilemma

Since moving to the team structure, every time a team has needed new members, it has advertised in the local newspaper and hired someone from outside the company. However, Team A is considering a different approach to fill its opening. Specifically, a key member of another team (Team B) has made it known that she would like to join Team A. She likes the team members, sees the team's work as being enjoyable, and is somewhat bored with her team's current assignment.

The concern is that if Team A chooses this individual to join the team, several problems may occur. For one thing, her current team will clearly be angry with the members of Team A. Further, "poaching" new team members from other teams inside the plant is likely to become a common occurrence. On the other hand, it seems reasonable that she should have the same opportunity to join Team A as an outsider would. Team A needs to decide how to proceed.

Team Activity

Assemble a group of four students and assign each group member to one of the following roles:

- member of Team A
- member of Team B
- manager of both teams
- investor in Hails Corporation

Action Steps

1. Before discussing the situation with your group, and from the perspective of your assigned role, do you think that the member of Team B should be allowed to join Team A? Write down the reasons for your position.
2. Before discussing the situation with your group, and from the perspective of your assigned role, what are the underlying ethical issues, if any, in this situation? Write down the issues.
3. Gather your group together and reveal, in turn, each member's comments on the situation. Next, reveal the ethical issues listed by each member.
4. Appoint someone to record the main points of agreement and disagreement within the group. How do you explain the results? What accounts for any disagreement?
5. From an ethical standpoint, what does your group conclude is the most appropriate action that should be taken by Hails in this situation? Should Team B's member be allowed to join Team A?
6. Develop a group response to the following questions: Assuming Team A asks the Team B member to join its team, how might it go about minimizing repercussions? Assuming Team A does not ask the Team B member to join its team, how might it go about minimizing repercussions?

For additional cases and exercise material, go to **www.pearsoned.ca/mybusinesslab**.

Concluding Case 7-1

Structure Evolves at Frantic Films

Frantic Films is a Winnipeg-based film and TV production company. Shortly after its founding in 1997, the company was named one of Canada's Hottest 50 Start-Ups by Profit Magazine. By 2004, it ranked #23 on the list of Canada's fastest-growing companies, and in 2005 it ranked #5 on the list of Manitoba's fastest-growing companies. Frantic has also received numerous awards, including the following:

- National Research Council recognition as a Canadian innovation leader
- Lions Gate Innovative Producers Award
- nomination for New Media Visionary Award
- Blizzard Award (for the documentary series *Quest for the Bay*)
- finalist in the Ernst & Young Entrepreneur of the Year award competition (multiple years)

Frantic Films started as a private corporation that was owned and managed by three principal shareholders—Jamie Brown (chief executive officer), Chris Bond (president), and Ken Zorniak (chief operating officer). It originally had three divisions—visual effects, live action, and TV commercials (see Figure 7.8)—but the visual effects division was sold in 2007.

The TV commercial division (Frantic Films Commercial Projects Inc.) produces television commercials for local Winnipeg companies, as well as for national and international clients. It also provides visual effects for commercials produced by other companies. The writers, producers, designers, compositors, animators, and editors create award-winning spots for local, national, and international companies as diverse as the Royal Winnipeg Ballet, the Disney Channel, and Procter & Gamble Canada.

The live action division (Frantic Films Live Action Productions Inc.) produces and owns programs that are broadcast around the world in over 40 countries. The division first develops the ideas for a program, then promotes the idea to broadcasters and financiers. If there is a strong interest, a budget is provided and the division produces the program. Frantic has produced documentary programs such as *Pioneer Quest* (one of the highest-rated documentary series ever broadcast on a Canadian specialty channel), lifestyle series (*'Til Debt Do Us Part*), television movies (*Zeyda and the Hitman*), and feature films (*Lucid*). Once a program is completed, rights are transferred to the releasing company and the individual, single-purpose production companies created for each show are wound up.

Until 2007, the visual effects division (Frantic Films VFX Services Inc.) produced visual effects for TV and movies. Using visual effects software packages such as Maya, Houdini, Digital Fusion, and 3Dstudio Max, the division established a reputation as one of the top visual effects

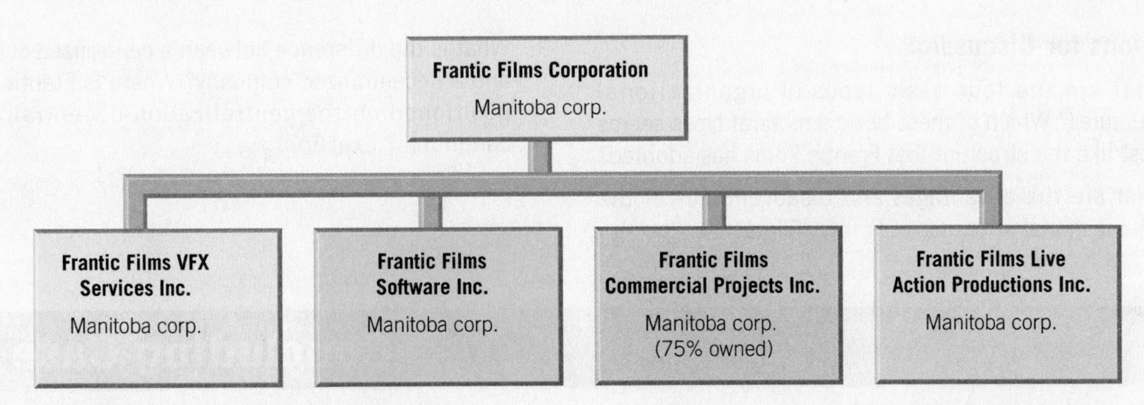

Figure 7.8 Organization chart for Frantic Films.

providers in North America. The majority of the employees at Frantic were in this division. Its output included visual effects for films like *Superman Returns, Stay, X-Men 3, The Italian Job, Catwoman, The Core, Swordfish, Mr. Magorium's Wonder Emporium*, and *Across the Universe*. The division used a matrix structure to complete film projects. This meant that a project team, made up of specialists in areas like 3D animation, 2D animation, compositing, and hardware/software support, was put together. When the project was completed, the team disbanded and its members were assigned to other projects. These teams were typically given specific goals to achieve, and then the team members used their technical expertise to decide how they could best achieve the goal.

Recently, a software division has been created (Frantic Films Software Inc.). It employs seven individuals with specialized expertise, some of whom are computer science grads. When software division employees discovered that off-the-shelf software did not meet their needs, they began creating their own new, stand-alone software to enhance certain visual effects like virtual water and smoke. This software was used to create the fluid-based character Tar Monster in the movie *Scooby-Doo II*.

Each of the divisions at Frantic Films operates fairly independently, but the company is still small enough that individuals from one division sometimes get involved in decisions in other divisions. For example, since the company does not have a marketing vice-president, marketing decisions are often made jointly by Brown, Bond, and Zorniak for each of the divisions.

In 2007, the visual effects division was sold to Prime Focus Ltd., a leader in India's post-production and visual effects services. Office space and a receptionist are now shared with Prime Focus. Jamie Brown says the change will allow the company to get a larger slice of the visual effects pie by pooling its resources with those of Prime Focus. At about the same time as the visual effects division was sold, it was announced that COO Ken Zorniak and President Chris Bond would remain with the company as employees, not owners.

When the company was first formed, the authority structure of the company was quite centralized because the principal shareholders had both the expertise to make decisions and the motivation to do so. But Brown thinks it is important to increase the involvement of lower-level workers in decisions, so he is trying to delegate more authority to them. Some progress has been made in this area. For example, managers in some of the divisions were given the authority to spend up to $5000 without having to get the approval of top management. This change was made because the top managers found that they were spending too much time discussing whether to approve requests for relatively small amounts of money, so they essentially delegated more authority to division managers by giving them the discretion. Brown also encourages employees to make recommendations on various issues to top management. He recognizes that giving employees more discretion can sometimes lead to less-than-optimal decisions, but he also wants to give people more experience in making decisions that affect the company.

Like all rapidly growing companies, Frantic Films has experienced certain "growing pains" with regard to its organizational structure. For example, offices were set up in California and British Columbia to get more visual effects business in those local areas, but until recently, there have not been dedicated salespeople responsible for generating work there. While employees in those offices have been fully employed, they are more costly. The original idea was to have them obtain work that could be sent to the lower-cost Winnipeg office, but more work is being done by a growing workforce in the satellite offices. Top management is now in the process of determining the changes that are needed to make the organization's structure more effective.

Another structural issue is the division of duties between Brown, Bond, and Zorniak. When the company first formed, all three principals were involved in decision making for all the divisions. But as the company grew, each individual gradually became more focussed. For example, Brown had primary responsibility for the live action division, while Zorniak and Bond had primary responsibility for the visual effects division.

Questions for Discussion

1. What are the four basic types of organizational structures? Which of these basic structural types seems most like the structure that Frantic Films has adopted?
2. What are the advantages and disadvantages of the organizational structure at Frantic Films?
3. What is the difference between a centralized company and a decentralized company? Where is Frantic Films positioned on the centralization-decentralization continuum? Explain.

Concluding Case 7-2

Cooking Up a New Structure

A few years ago, Sara Lee CEO John H. Bryan realized that he had a problem. During the 25 years of his tenure, the firm had grown beyond its foundation in food products to encompass dozens of lines of business—everything from cake mixes to insecticide to lingerie. The new businesses were acquisitions, and the original managers controlled each one as if it were a separate company. Calculating the cost of all this duplication, Bryan reached the conclusion that the company could not afford high costs at a time when price competition was heating up.

In an effort to fix things, starting in 1997 Bryan sold or eliminated about one-quarter of the firm's 200 products. He cut redundant factories and the workforce, reduced the number of products, and standardized company-wide processes. He called his extensive restructuring program "deverticalization," and his goal was to remove Sara Lee from manufacturing while strengthening its focus and effectiveness as a marketer. In the meantime, however, he continued to acquire rival firms to sustain the company's growth. Despite Bryan's efforts, Sara Lee continued to suffer from high costs and remained unfocussed and inefficient. Said one industry analyst about Bryan's strategy: "Sometimes, the more chairs you move around, the more dust you see behind the chairs."

In 2000, C. Steven McMillan took over from Bryan at Sara Lee, and in the immortal words of Yogi Berra, "It was déjà vu all over again." McMillan quickly realized that Bryan's moves had had little impact on the firm's performance and that he himself would need to start making some big changes. Borrowing a page from rival Kraft Foods, he began by merging the sales forces that specialized in various brands to create smaller, customer-focussed teams. In meats alone, for instance, Sara Lee had 10 different brands, including Ball Park, Hillshire Farms, Bryan, and Jimmy Dean. "So if you're a Safeway," explained McMillan, "you've got to deal with 10 different organizations and multiple invoices." Teams reduced duplication and were more convenient for buyers—a win-win situation. National retailers like Wal-Mart responded by increasing their orders for Sara Lee products.

McMillan centralized decision making at the firm by shutting down 50 weaker regional brands and reorganizing the firm into three broad product categories: Food and Beverage, Intimates and Underwear, and Household Products. He abolished several layers of corporate hierarchy, including many of the middle managers the firm had inherited from its acquisitions. He created category managers to oversee related lines of business, and the flattened organizational structure led to improved accountability and more centralized control over Sara Lee's far-flung operations.

McMillan also borrowed some tactics from his predecessor, divesting 15 businesses, including Coach leather goods, and laying off 10 percent of his workers. In another move that was widely questioned by industry observers, he paid $2.8 billion for breadmaker Earthgrains. The move increased Sara Lee's market share in baked goods, but many observers felt that McMillan paid too much for a small potential return.

McMillan still had a few tricks up his sleeves. One bold move was developing a chain of retail stores named Inner Self. Each store features a spa-like atmosphere in which to sell Sara Lee's Hanes, Playtex, Bali, and Wonderbra products. Susan Nedved, head of development for Inner Self, thinks that the company-owned stores provide a more realistic and comforting environment for making underwear purchases than do some specialty outlets. "There seems to be an open void for another specialty concept that complements Victoria's Secret," says Nedved. "There was a need for shopping alternatives that really cater to the aging population."

McMillan remains confident that his strategy—more centralization, coordination, and focus—will do the trick at Sara Lee. "I do believe the things we're doing will enhance the growth rate of our company," he says. But many observers are less optimistic. As for Inner Self and underwear, one analyst points out that "even if you fix that business, it's still apparel, and it's not really viewed as a high-value-added business."

Even if McMillan's strategy does manage to cut costs and increase market share, skeptics point out that there is no logic behind the idea of housing baked goods, meats, coffee, underwear, shoe polish, and household cleaners under one corporate roof. Unless McMillan can find some as-yet-undiscovered synergy among such disparate units, Sara Lee is probably headed for a breakup into several smaller, more focussed, more profitable companies.

Questions for Discussion

1. Describe the basic structural components at Sara Lee.
2. What role does specialization play at Sara Lee?
3. What kinds of authority are reflected in this case?
4. What kind of organizational structure does Sara Lee seem to have?
5. What role has the informal organization played in Sara Lee's various acquisitions and divestitures?

apter 8

Managing Human Resources

After reading this chapter, you should be able to:

1. Define *human resource management*, discuss its strategic significance, and explain how managers plan for human resources.
2. Identify the issues involved in *staffing* a company, including *internal* and *external recruiting* and *selection*.
3. Discuss different ways in which organizations go about developing the capabilities of employees and managers.
4. Explain ways in which organizations evaluate employee performance.
5. Discuss the importance of *wages* and *salaries*, *incentives*, and *benefit programs* in attracting and keeping skilled workers.
6. Describe some of the key *legal issues* involved in *hiring*, *compensating*, and *managing* workers.
7. Discuss *workforce diversity*, the management of *knowledge workers*, and the use of *contingent and temporary workers* as important changes in the contemporary workplace.

Are More Cracks Appearing in the Glass Ceiling?

During the 1990s, much was written about how a "glass ceiling"—the invisible barrier that prevents women from moving into the very top jobs in business firms—was starting to break down. Some dramatic changes actually did occur. In the automobile business, for example, Maureen Kempston-Darkes was appointed CEO of General Motors of Canada, Bobbie Gaunt became CEO of Ford Motor of Canada, and Cynthia Trudell became president of Saturn Corp., a subsidiary of GM. These were major changes in an industry that had been very male dominated since its beginning early in the twentieth century. Other high-profile appointments have continued to be evident. For example, in 2008, Monique Leroux (pictured) was appointed CEO of Desjardins Group, Quebec's largest financial institution. She is the first woman to lead a top 10 financial institution in Canada.

So progress is evident. But it is also slow. A 2008 Statistics Canada report showed that women aged 25–29 who worked full-time earned only 85 percent of what men earned. That gap is the same size it was five years earlier. During the last few years, other studies have revealed some other interesting statistics:

- Women with advanced degrees earn 96 percent of what men earn; women with bachelor's degrees earn 89 percent; and at the trades certificate level, women earn just 65 percent of what men earn.
- The average single woman earns 99 percent of what the average man earns.
- In law firms, women comprise 50 percent of associates but only 16 percent of partners. Women also drop out of practice at two or three times the rate of men. In contrast, more than half of all senior management positions at Vancouver City Savings Credit Union and Coast Capital Savings Credit Union are occupied by women.
- No member state in the Organisation for Economic Co-operation and Development (OECD) has been able to erase the wage gap; in the OECD as a whole, the difference is about 15 percent.
- For men aged 55–64, the proportion of potential years of work spent actually working is 92.3 percent, but for women 55–64, the ratio is only 64.2 percent.
- Compared to men, the average woman has less labour market experience, is less likely to work full-time, and is more likely to leave the labour force for long periods of time.

A study that analyzed the pay earned by males and females at equivalent levels of responsibility found that base pay rates were not much different, but men received bonuses that often doubled their total pay while women received bonuses that only slightly increased their total pay.

Various reasons have been proposed for pay inequity and the under-representation of women in the top ranks of management. They include simple male bias against promoting women, the old boys network, women dropping out of the workforce to have children, lack of organizational support and role models for women, stereotyping, partners who don't help at home, and a work culture that's not compatible with family life. Researchers say that both men and women are ambitious, competent, and competitive, but men carry everything to an extreme. For men, winning is everything and they feel the need to decisively defeat their opponents (think sports). This line of thinking says that male hormones (notably testosterone) cause men to have an extremely strong drive for dominance, status, power, and control, and that kind of behaviour is rewarded in organizations. Most women don't have strong drives for dominance and control, so they are less likely to get promoted into top management positions.

In this same vein, another study found that women don't aspire to top management positions like men do. About one-third of men surveyed said they aspired to positions like chief executive officer or chief operations officer, but only about one-fifth of women wanted such a job title. Age was also a factor: 89 percent of women aged 25–34 aspired to top positions, but only 58 percent of women aged 45–55 had such aspirations. This suggests that the issue is generational, and that more and more women are going to be appointed to top jobs as time passes because they have different attitudes about the desirability of top management jobs. ◆

How will this help me?

Effectively managing human resources is critical to the success of organizations. A firm that handles this activity well has a much better chance for success than does a firm that simply goes through the motions. After reading the material in this chapter, you'll be better able to understand—from the perspective of a manager—the importance of properly managing human resources in a department where you supervise or in a business you own. You'll also understand—from the perspective of an employee—why your employer has adopted certain approaches to dealing with issues like hiring, training, compensation, and benefits.

We start this chapter by explaining how managers plan for their organization's human resource needs. We then discuss ways in which organizations select, develop, appraise, and compensate employees. We also look at some key legal issues involved in managing workers, and we pay special attention to managing workforce diversity. Let's start with some basic concepts of human resource management.

The Foundations of Human Resource Management

1 Define *human resource management*, discuss its strategic significance, and explain how managers plan for human resources.

human resource management Set of organizational activities directed at attracting, developing, and maintaining an effective workforce.

Human resource management (HRM) is the set of organizational activities directed at attracting, developing, and maintaining an effective workforce. Human resource management takes place within a complex and ever-changing environmental context and is increasingly being recognized for its strategic importance.[1]

The Strategic Importance of HRM

Human resources are critical for effective organizational functioning. HRM (or personnel, as it is sometimes called) was once relegated to second-class status in many organizations, but its importance has grown dramatically in the last two decades. This new importance stems from increased legal complexities, the recognition that human resources are a valuable means for improving productivity, and the awareness of the costs associated with poor human resource management.

Managers realize that the effectiveness of their HR function has a substantial impact on a firm's bottom-line performance. Poor human resource planning can result in spurts of hiring followed by layoffs—costly in terms of unemployment compensation payments, training expenses, and morale. Haphazard compensation systems do not attract, keep, and motivate good employees, and outmoded recruitment practices can expose the firm to expensive and embarrassing legal action. Consequently, the chief human resource executive of most large businesses is a vice-president directly accountable to the CEO, and many firms are developing strategic HR plans that are integrated with other strategic planning activities.

Human Resource Planning

The starting point in attracting qualified human resources is HR planning, which involves job analysis and forecasting the demand for and supply of labour (see Figure 8.1).

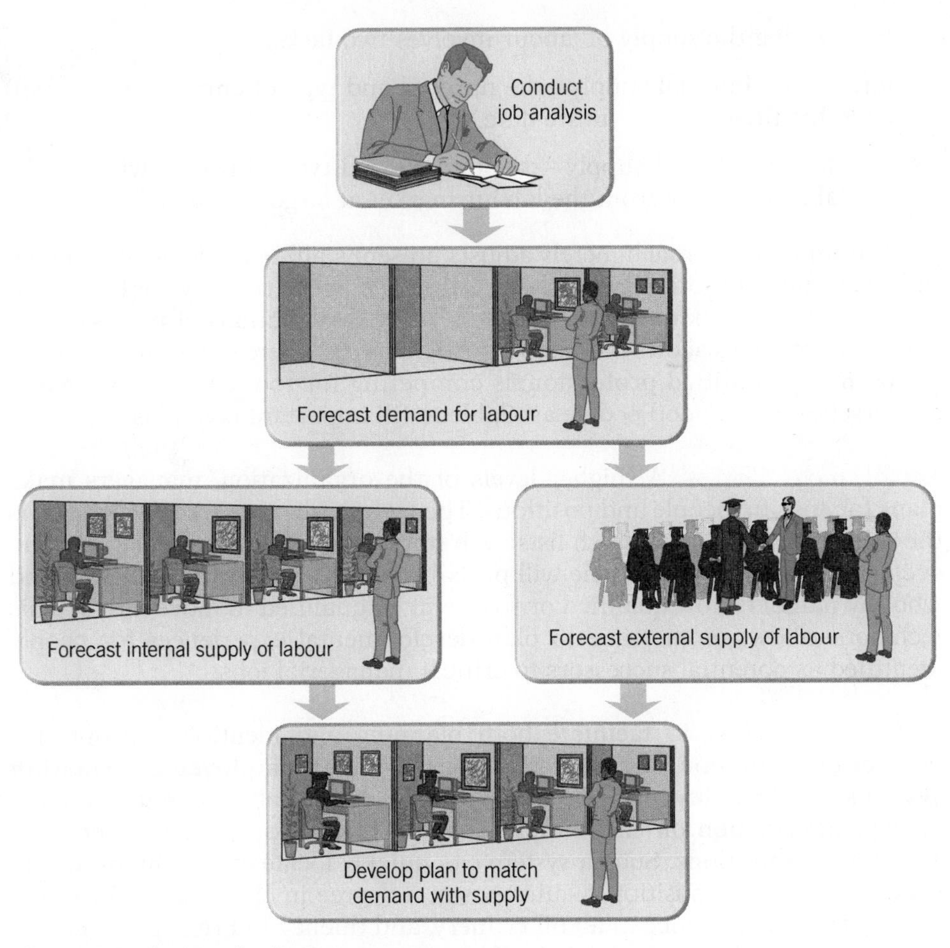

Figure 8.1 Planning for human resources.

Job Analysis

As the term implies, **job analysis** means analyzing the nature of jobs. It requires assessment of two items:

- The **job description** lists the duties of a job, its working conditions, and the tools, materials, and equipment used to perform it.
- The **job specification** lists the skills, abilities, and other credentials needed to do the job.

Job analysis information is used in many HR activities. For instance, knowing about job content and job requirements is necessary to develop appropriate selection methods and job-relevant performance appraisal systems and to set equitable compensation rates.

job analysis A detailed study of the specific duties in a particular job and the human qualities required for that job.

job description The duties of a job, its working conditions, and the tools, materials, and equipment used to perform it.

job specification The skills, abilities, and other credentials needed to do the job.

Forecasting HR Demand and Supply

After managers have analyzed the jobs that must be performed within an organization, they can start planning for the organization's future HR needs. The manager starts by assessing trends in past HR usage, future organizational plans, and general economic trends. A good sales forecast is often the foundation, especially for smaller organizations. Historical data can then be used to predict demand for different types of employees, such as operating employees and sales representatives. Large organizations use more complicated models to predict HR needs.

Forecasting the supply of labour involves two tasks:

- forecasting internal supply—the number and type of employees who will be in the firm at some future date
- forecasting external supply—the number and type of people who will be available for hiring from the labour market at large

The simplest approach merely adjusts present staffing levels for anticipated turnover and promotions. Large organizations use extremely sophisticated models to keep track of the present and future distributions of professionals and managers. This allows the company to spot areas where there will eventually be too many qualified professionals competing for too few promotions or, conversely, too few good people available to fill important positions.

Replacement Charts. At higher levels of the organization, managers make plans for specific people and positions. The technique most commonly used is the **replacement chart**, which lists each important managerial position, who occupies it, how long he or she will probably stay in it before moving on, and who (by name) is now qualified or soon will be qualified to move into it. This technique allows ample time to plan developmental experiences for people identified as potential successors to critical managerial jobs.

replacement chart An HR technique that lists each important managerial position, who occupies it, how long he or she will probably stay in it before moving on, and who (by name) is now qualified or soon will be qualified to move into it.

employee information systems (or skills inventories) Computerized systems that contain information on each employee's education, skills, work experience, and career aspirations.

Skills Inventories. To facilitate both planning and identifying people for transfer or promotion, some organizations also have **employee information systems, or skills inventories**. These systems are usually computerized and contain information on each employee's education, skills, work experience, and career aspirations. Such a system can quickly locate every employee who is qualified to fill a position requiring, say, a degree in chemical engineering, three years of experience in an oil refinery, and fluency in French.

Forecasting the external supply of labour is a different problem altogether. For example, how does a manager predict how many electrical engineers will be seeking work in Ontario or British Columbia three years from now? To get an idea of the future availability of labour, planners must rely on information from outside sources, such as government reports and figures supplied by colleges and universities on the number of students in major fields. These statistics show that Canada is likely to face a severe labour shortage within the next 10 years. The problem is already evident in Alberta, but labour shortages are likely to appear in almost all provinces over the next few years as thousands of "baby boomers" approach retirement age.[2] The worst shortages are in the construction, retail, and transportation industries.[3]

Matching HR Supply and Demand

After comparing future demand and internal supply, managers can make plans to manage predicted shortfalls or overstaffing. If a shortfall is predicted, new employees can be hired, present employees can be retrained and transferred into understaffed areas, individuals approaching retirement can be convinced to stay on, or labour-saving or productivity-enhancing systems can be installed.

If the organization needs to hire, the external labour-supply forecast helps managers plan how to recruit according to whether the type of person needed is readily available or scarce in the labour market. The use of temporary workers also helps managers in staffing by giving them extra flexibility. If overstaffing is expected to be a problem, the main options are transferring the extra employees, not replacing individuals who quit, encouraging early retirement, and laying people off.

Staffing the Organization

Identify the issues involved in *staffing* a company, including *internal* and *external recruiting* and *selection*. 2

Once managers have decided what positions they need to fill, they must find and hire individuals who meet the job requirements. A study by the Canadian Federation of Independent Business found that the top three characteristics employers are looking for when they hire people are a good work ethic, reliability, and willingness to stay on the job.[4] Staffing of the business is one of the most complex and important aspects of good human resource management. The top 10 employers by number of employees in Canada are listed in Table 8.1.

In this section, we will describe both the process of acquiring staff from outside the company (external staffing) and the process of promoting staff from within (internal staffing). Both external and internal staffing start with effective recruiting.

Recruiting Human Resources

recruiting The process of attracting qualified persons to apply for the jobs that are open.

Recruiting is the process of attracting qualified persons to apply for the jobs that are open. Some recruits are found internally while others come from outside the organization.

Internal Recruiting

internal recruiting Considering present employees as candidates for openings.

Internal recruiting means considering present employees as candidates for openings. Promotion from within can help build morale and keep high-quality employees from leaving. In unionized firms, the procedures for notifying employees of internal job-change opportunities are usually spelled out in the union contract. For higher-level positions, a skills inventory system may be used to identify internal candidates, or managers may be asked to recommend individuals who should be considered.

External Recruiting

external recruiting Attracting people outside the organization to apply for jobs.

External recruiting involves attracting people outside the organization to apply for jobs. External recruiting methods include newspaper and internet advertising, campus interviews, employment agencies, executive search firms, union hiring halls, referrals by present employees, and hiring "walk-ins" (people who show

Table 8.1 Top 10 Employers in Canada, 2008

Company	Number of Employees
1. Onex Corp.	233 000
2. George Weston Ltd.	145 000
3. Magna International Inc.	74 350
4. Royal Bank of Canada	73 323
5. Canada Post Corp.	72 500
6. The Bank of Nova Scotia	69 049
7. Bombardier Inc.	66 870
8. Metro Inc.	65 000
9. The Toronto-Dominion Bank	58 792
10. Canadian Tire Corp. Ltd.	57 000

Note: The number of employees for some large U.S.-based companies like McDonald's Restaurants of Canada Ltd. and Wal-Mart Canada Ltd. is not included here, but these companies would each have more than 75 000 employees.

At job fairs, students and recruiters can talk face to face about jobs that are available. Here, recruiters talk to students about the opportunities at the company.

up without being solicited). Private employment agencies can be a good source of clerical and technical employees, and executive search firms specialize in locating top-management talent. Newspaper and internet ads reach a wide audience and thus allow minorities equal opportunity to learn about and apply for job openings.

At a job fair, candidates browse through the positions available and talk face to face with recruiters. Job fairs are cheaper than posting jobs with an employment agency or headhunter. **Internships**—short-term paid positions where students focus on a specific project—are increasingly popular. If the individual works out well, the company often hires the student full-time after graduation. At Bayer Inc. in Toronto, interns are paid at about the same level as full-time employees.[5]

internships Short-term paid positions where students focus on a specific project.

The biggest change in recent years has been the advent of internet recruiting. Companies post positions on websites like Monster.com or Workopolis.com, and interested applicants respond. Internet recruiting gives employers and those seeking employment a fast, easy, and inexpensive way of interacting. But there are drawbacks. For example, employers often receive applications from unqualified people, and those seeking a job often find that they receive no response to their application.

The boxed insert entitled "Green Recruiting" illustrates the increasing importance of environmental considerations in recruiting.

Selecting Human Resources

Once the recruiting process has attracted a pool of applicants, the next step is to select someone to hire. The intent of the selection process is to gather information from applicants that will predict their job performance and job success and then to hire the candidates likely to be most successful. The process of determining the predictive value of information is called **validation**.

validation The process of determining the predictive value of information.

To reduce the element of uncertainty, managers use a variety of selection techniques, the most common of which are shown in Figure 8.2. Each organization develops its own mix of selection techniques and may use them in almost any order.

Application Forms

The first step in selection is usually asking the candidate to fill out an application form, which is an efficient method of gathering information about the applicant's previous work history, educational background, and other job-related

The Greening of Business

Green Recruiting

More and more graduates say they want to work for a company with a commitment to the environment. Consider just three stories:

- When Chad Hunt went looking for a job after graduating from university, one key criterion he used was the prospective employer's environmental impact. He eventually took a job with Husky Injection Molding Systems because of the company's emphasis on protecting the environment. Dirk Schlimm, vice-president of corporate affairs for Husky, says that when prospective hires are asked during job interviews why they want to work for Husky, they often mention the company's environmental responsibility program. Current employees who fill out the employee satisfaction survey also give high marks to the company on questions relating to the environmental responsibility program.
- Mike Johnson used to work as a custom framer at a Toronto art gallery, but he wanted to do something different, so he enrolled in the two-year landscape management program at Seneca College. Now he works for Green Gardeners, a small organic landscaping company that bans gasoline-powered tools and uses bike-powered trailers. Andrew Roy, the president of Green Gardeners, says that many people are looking for green jobs, so the company has a great pool of talent to recruit from.
- Sara Wong said it was the zero waste program at Hudson's Bay Company (HBC) that caught her attention when she was job-hunting. She is concerned about the environment, and she liked the focus that HBC had on recycling office waste. Bob Kolida, the senior vice-president for human resources at HBC, says workers today are more vocal about their desire to work for a green employer. When they visit the company's website, they often click on the corporate social responsibility report. HBC is also getting feedback from recruiters saying that HBC's position on the environment is attractive to job applicants.

In a survey conducted by Monster.ca, 78 percent of respondents said they would quit their current job if they could get one at a company that had an environmentally friendly focus. In a second survey, 81 percent of the respondents said that their current employer was not environmentally friendly, and only 18 percent said the employer was "extremely green."

A Sirota Survey Intelligence survey showed that 82 percent of employees who were satisfied with their employer's environmental practices also felt proud working for their company. Just 55 percent of those who were dissatisfied with the company's environmental practices were proud to work for the company.

Gabriel Bouchard, Monster.ca's vice-president and general manager, says that employers need to recognize that an environmentally friendly workplace is important to both current employees and job candidates. Bob Willard, whose has written books about how businesses can benefit by going green, says that Canadians in general have become more concerned about the environment, and they want to work for companies that share their concerns. So there is a connection between being green and being a desired employer.

Over half a million Canadians are now employed in environmentally related jobs, and many of these didn't even exist a generation ago (e.g., consultants who assess homes to see how energy efficient they are). According to the Environmental Careers Organization of Canada, the top five green careers are environmental engineer, environmental technologist, conservation biologist, geographic information system analyst, and environmental communications officer. A study by the United Nations Environment Program noted that, worldwide, 2.3 million people now work in alternative energy jobs. It predicted that 12 million new jobs could be created by 2030 in environmentally related areas like the biofuel industry, 6.3 million jobs in manufacturing (e.g., the making of solar panels), and 2 million jobs in wind power.

Germany has made a big move toward environmental jobs. It has created 250 000 jobs in areas such as electric cars, wind power, fuel cells, and energy efficient housing. A study by the German Environment Ministry says 150 000 new green jobs will be created by 2020 as a result of strong government policies and industry grants.

Ontario has set up a new $650-million fund to secure the next generation of high-paying jobs. Ontario's premier said the money will be used to develop clean and green technologies and businesses. The world is looking for innovative ways to conserve energy and to fight global warming, and some place is going to secure thousands of new jobs by developing new solutions. Ontario wants to be that place.

Critical Thinking Questions

1. What are the advantages of working for an environmentally friendly company? Are there any disadvantages? Explain.
2. Consider the following statement: *All this publicity about graduates looking for jobs at environmentally friendly companies is overblown. Graduates want to look like they are marketable in a tough job market, and since being green is the thing to do, many graduates are saying they want to work for environmentally friendly companies, even though they don't really care that much about the environment.* Do you agree or disagree with the statement? Explain your reasoning.

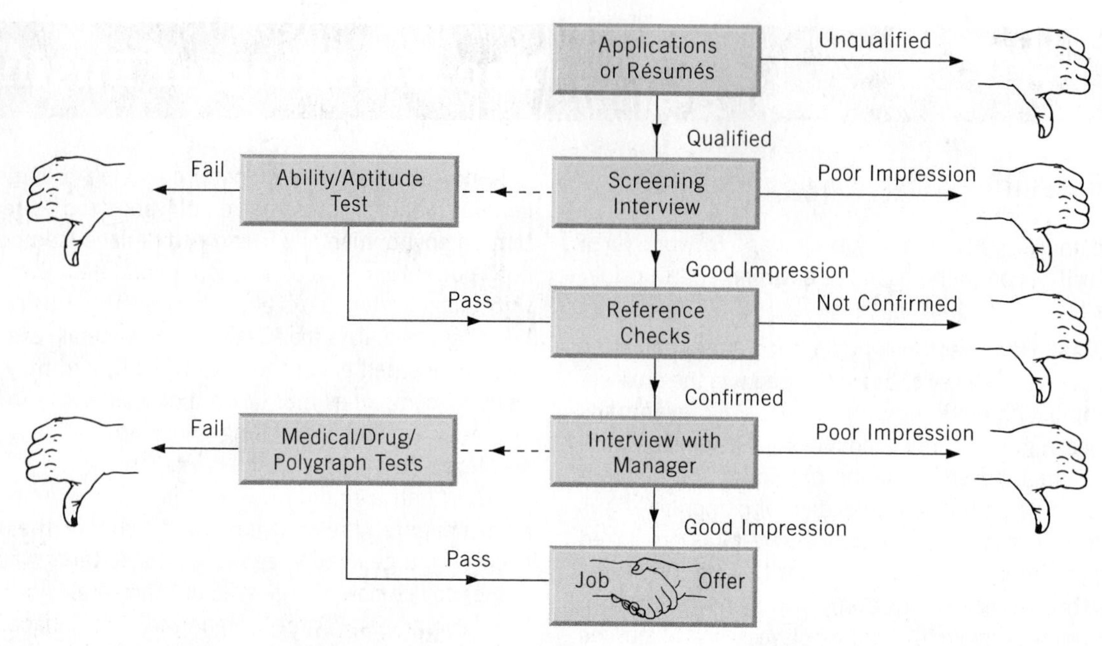

Figure 8.2 General steps in the selection process.

the job, such as gender, religion, or national origin. Application-form data are generally used informally to decide whether a candidate merits further evaluation, and interviewers use application forms to familiarize themselves with candidates before interviewing them.

Tests

Tests of ability, skill, aptitude, or knowledge relevant to a particular job are usually the best predictors of job success, although tests of general intelligence or personality are occasionally useful as well. Some companies administer tests to determine how well applicants score on the "big five" personality dimensions (see Chapter 10). These scores are used to help make hiring decisions. Regardless of the type of test that is used, it must be job related (that is, it must not serve as a basis for discriminating against anyone for reasons unrelated to the job). It must also be a valid predictor of performance (that is, it must provide evidence that people who score well on it are more likely to perform well in the job than are people who score poorly on it). Tests should be administered and scored consistently, and all candidates should be given the same directions, allowed the same amount of time, and offered the same testing environment.

A survey conducted by Development Dimensions International found that 83 percent of hiring managers use some sort of testing as part of the hiring process. At Astral Media Inc. in Montreal, for example, job candidates are required to take a series of tests that measure verbal and numerical skills, as well as psychological traits. This testing increases the chance that Astral will hire high-performing employees who will fit in with the company's culture.[6]

assessment centre A series of exercises in which candidates perform realistic management tasks under the watchful eye of expert appraisers.

video assessment Potential hires are shown videos of realistic work situations and are then asked to choose a course of action to deal with the situation.

An **assessment centre** is a series of exercises in which candidates perform realistic management tasks under the watchful eye of expert appraisers. A typical assessment centre might be set up in a large conference room and go on for two or three days. During this time, potential managers might take selection tests, engage in management simulations, make individual presentations, and conduct group discussions. Assessors check to see how each participant reacts to stress or to criticism by colleagues. A relatively new type of test that has evolved from assessment centres is **video assessment**. Here, potential hires are shown videos of realistic work situations and then asked to choose a course of action to deal with the situation. Video assessment is fast, reliable, cheap, and versatile.

Interviews

The interview is a popular selection device, but it is sometimes a poor predictor of job success because biases that are inherent in the way people perceive and judge others on first meeting affect subsequent evaluations. Interview validity can be improved by training interviewers to be aware of potential biases and by increasing the structure of the interview. In a structured interview, questions are written in advance and each interviewer asks the same questions of each candidate. Such structure introduces consistency into the interview procedure and allows the organization to validate the content of the questions. For interviewing managerial or professional candidates, a somewhat less structured approach is typically used.

Interviewers can also increase interview validity by asking "curveball" questions—that is, questions that job applicants would never expect to be asked—to see how well they think on their feet. Questions such as "How would you move Mount Fuji?" or "How would you sell me a glass of water?" are examples of curveball questions.[7]

Another approach to improving interview validity is **behaviour-based interviewing**. Instead of asking a traditional interview question like "Do you often take the initiative?" behaviour-based interviewing asks "Tell me about a situation where you became aware of a problem. What did you do?" Asking questions like this focuses the interview much more on behaviour than on what a person says. This approach can be used to test for technical skills (e.g., accounting, welding, or computer programming), management skills (e.g., organizing, motivating others, or communicating), and individual skills (e.g., dependability, discipline, or the ability to work on a team). Behaviour-based interviewing is becoming more common because companies are facing increasingly competitive environments.

behaviour-based interviewing An approach to improving interview validity by asking questions which focus the interview much more on *behaviour* than on what a person says.

Other Techniques

Organizations also use other selection techniques that vary with the circumstances. A manufacturer afraid of injuries to workers on the job might require new employees to have a physical examination. This gives the company some information about whether the potential employee is physically able to do the work and what (if any) pre-existing injuries the person might have.

Polygraph (lie detector) tests are largely illegal now, and drug tests are also coming under fire. In 1998, for example, the Ontario Divisional Court decided that Imperial Oil Ltd.'s drug policy (which included pre-employment drug testing that made offers of work conditional on a negative result) was unlawful because Imperial Oil failed to prove that a positive drug test would indicate a failure to perform essential duties. Imperial Oil's policy also required random drug and alcohol testing, but that was also judged to be discriminatory because the company could not prove that such testing was necessary to deter alcohol or drug impairment on the job.[8] The Toronto-Dominion Bank wanted to give drug tests to all new employees because it wanted to have the public's trust. However, a federal court ruled that the bank's policy was discriminatory and that it wasn't related closely enough to job performance.[9]

Developing Human Resources

Regardless of how effective a selection system is, most employees need additional training if they are to grow and develop in their jobs. This process begins with orientation and then proceeds to the assessment of training and development needs (including the performance of a needs analysis) and the selection of the best training techniques and methods.

Discuss different ways in which organizations go about developing the capabilities of employees and managers. **3**

New Employee Orientation

An Ipsos Reid survey of over 1000 workers revealed that 50 percent of them felt that they didn't always fit in well at work.[10] Jennifer Cayer, a partner with the HR consulting firm PeopleSavvy, says that a new employee's first 30 days on the job have a big influence on whether the person will stay with the company.[11] Both these findings suggest that orientation of new workers is a very important activity. **Orientation** is the process of introducing new employees to the company's policies and programs, the co-workers and supervisors they will interact with, and the nature of their job. Orientation allows new employees to feel like part of a team and to become effective contributors to the organization more rapidly. It also plays a key role in job satisfaction, performance, and retention. Overall, orientation eases the transition from outsider to insider. Poor orientation, on the other hand, can result in disenchantment, dissatisfaction, anxiety, and turnover.

orientation The process of introducing new employees to the company's policies and programs, the co-workers and supervisors they will interact with, and the nature of their job.

To help with orientation, Toronto-based Bayer Inc. has created a website where newly hired employees can get a virtual tour of the facility before they show up for their first day at work. It also provides detailed information on practical matters like parking spaces and security passes. At another Toronto company—I Love Rewards Inc.—new employees attend a company "university" for five full days, where they learn about everything from dress codes to how to make the company drink (called RedPoint). They are also tested on the material and have a graduation ceremony.[12]

Training and Development

Beyond orientation, employees must be continually trained and developed to improve the quality of the contributions they make to the organization. The starting point in assessing training and development needs is conducting a needs analysis—determining the organization's true needs and the training programs necessary to meet them. This analysis generally focuses on two things: the organization's job-related needs and the capabilities of the current workforce. The organization's needs are determined by the nature of the work that the organization needs to have done. That is, what knowledge, skills, and abilities does the organization need in order to compete? What skills must its workforce possess to perform the organization's work effectively?

Depending on both the content of the program and the instructors selected to present it, a number of techniques and methods can be used for the actual delivery of information. Some of the more popular techniques and methods are described below.

Work-Based Programs (On-the-Job Training)

Work-based programs tie training and development activities directly to task performance. The most common method of work-based training is **on-the-job training**. The employee is placed in the actual work situation and is shown how to perform a task by a supervisor or an experienced employee. Much on-the-job training is informal, as when one employee shows another how to operate the photocopy machine.

work-based program A technique that ties training and development activities directly to task performance.

on-the-job training Those development programs in which employees gain new skills while performing them at work.

Another method of work-based training is **systematic job rotations and transfers**. This method is most likely to be used for lower-level managers or for operating employees being groomed for promotions to supervisory management positions. As the term suggests, the employee is systematically rotated or transferred from one job to another. The employee thus learns a wider array of tasks, acquires more abilities, and develops a more comprehensive view of the work of an organization or a particular sub-unit.

systematic job rotations and transfers A technique in which an employee is systematically rotated or transferred from one job to another.

Instructional-Based Programs (Off-the-Job Training)

Off-the-job training is performed at a location away from the work site. It may be at a classroom within the same facility or at a different location altogether. For example, refresher courses are offered to managers of McDonald's Canadian restaurants at the Canadian Institute of Hamburgerology; in addition, training videotapes are shown to restaurant workers.[13] Coffee College is a two-week cram course run by Second Cup Ltd., Canada's largest retailer of specialty coffee. During their stay at Coffee College, franchisees and managers learn how to hire workers, keep the books, detect employee theft, and boost Christmas sales.[14]

off-the-job training Those development programs in which employees learn new skills at a location away from the normal work site.

Management development programs try to enhance conceptual, analytical, and problem-solving skills. In these programs, the **lecture or discussion approach** is normally used. A company trainer presents material to attendees just as a professor would lecture to students. Depending on the situation and the size of the training class, the trainer may opt for a pure lecture method or may include discussion with trainees. Sometimes lectures are on video or audio tapes so that various individuals in the organization can receive the same training at different times and/or at different locations.

management development programs Programs that try to enhance conceptual, analytical, and problem-solving skills.

lecture or discussion approach An instructional-based program in which a trainer presents material in a descriptive fashion to those attending a trainee program.

Most large companies run formal in-house management development programs or send managers to programs on university campuses. Some management development takes place informally, often through processes such as networking and mentoring. **Networking** refers to informal interactions among managers for the purpose of discussing mutual problems, solutions, and opportunities. Networking takes place in a variety of settings, both inside and outside the office. **Mentoring** means having a more experienced manager sponsor and teach a less experienced manager.

networking Informal interactions among managers for the purpose of discussing mutual problems, solutions, and opportunities.

mentoring Having a more experienced manager sponsor and teach a less experienced manager.

A more technically oriented type of off-the-job training is computer-assisted instruction. A trainee sits at a computer and uses software that has been specifically developed to teach certain material. The actual training materials are stored on the computer's hard drive, a CD-ROM, or a website. One major advantage of this method is that it allows self-paced learning and immediate feedback. A related training method is **vestibule training**, which takes place under conditions closely simulating the actual work environment. At Montreal-based CAE Inc., engineers built a simulator for the world's largest passenger jet, the Airbus A380. Pilots use the simulator to learn how to fly the new jet without ever leaving the ground.[15]

vestibule training A work simulation in which the job is performed under conditions closely simulating the actual work environment.

Videoconferencing has become an important part of the training function. Travel costs are reduced, and interactions between the trainer and the trainees are facilitated.

Team Building and Group-Based Training

Since more and more organizations are using teams as a basis for doing their jobs, it should not be surprising that many of the same companies are developing training programs specifically designed to facilitate co-operation among team members.

One popular method involves various outdoor training exercises. Some programs, for example, involve a group going through a physical obstacle course that requires climbing, crawling, and other physical activities. Outward Bound and several other independent companies specialize in offering these kinds of programs, and their clients include such firms as General Foods, Xerox, and Burger King. Participants, of course, must see the relevance of such programs if they are to be successful. Firms don't want employees returning from team-building programs to report merely that the experience "was childlike and fun and fairly inoffensive."[16]

Evaluating Employee Performance

4 Explain ways in which organizations evaluate employee performance.

performance appraisal The specific and formal evaluation of employees to determine the degree to which they are performing effectively.

Performance appraisal refers to the specific and formal evaluation of employees to determine the degree to which they are performing effectively. Performance appraisals help managers assess the extent to which they are recruiting and selecting the best employees. They also contribute to effective training, development, and compensation.

The Performance Appraisal Process

Several questions must be answered as part of the performance appraisal process. These questions generally relate to who conducts the performance appraisal and provides feedback to the individual whose performance is being evaluated.

Conducting the Performance Appraisal

Since managers are responsible for employees' performance, they are the most likely ones to conduct a performance appraisal. Supervisors also know the requirements of the job and have the most opportunity to observe employees as they perform their jobs.

If the person being appraised is a manager, one important source of information is the manager's subordinates, particularly when the performance appraisal focuses on the manager's leadership potential. Another source of information is self-evaluation. In many professional and managerial situations, individuals are asked to evaluate their own performance. Another source of information is customers. Restaurants such as Red Lobster ask customers to evaluate their experience at the restaurant in terms of the service they received and the quality of the food.

360-degree feedback Gathering information from a manager's subordinates, peers, and superiors when assessing the manager's performance.

It is best to rely on several information sources when conducting appraisals. A system called **360-degree feedback** gathers information from supervisors, subordinates, and co-workers. The most accurate information comes from individuals who have known the person being appraised for one to three years. Eight or ten individuals should take part in the evaluation.[17]

Providing Performance Feedback

After the performance appraisal, the next major activity is providing feedback, coaching, and counselling. Many managers do a poor job in this area, in part because they don't understand how to do it properly and in part because they don't enjoy it. Almost by definition, performance appraisal in many organizations tends to focus on negatives. As a result, managers may have a tendency to avoid giving feedback because they know that an employee who receives negative feedback may be angry, hurt, discouraged, or argumentative. But if employees are not told about their shortcomings, they will have no concrete reason to try to improve and will receive no guidance as to how to improve. It is critical, therefore, that managers follow up on appraisals by providing feedback.

Methods for Appraising Performance

Because of the nature of many jobs today, especially managerial work, most methods for appraising performance rely on judgments and ratings. A great deal of effort has been expended on trying to make relatively subjective evaluations as meaningful and useful as they can be. Both ranking and rating methods are popular.

Ranking Methods

The **simple ranking method** requires a manager to rank-order, from top to bottom or from best to worst, each member of a particular work group or department. The individual ranked first is the top performer, the individual ranked second is the second-best performer, and so forth. The basis for the ranking is generally global or overall performance. Another ranking method, the **forced distribution method**, involves grouping employees into predefined frequencies of performance ratings. Those frequencies are determined in advance and are imposed on the rater. A decision might be made, for instance, that 10 percent of the employees in a work group will be grouped as "outstanding," 20 percent as "very good," 40 percent as "average," 20 percent as "below average," and the remaining 10 percent as "poor." The forced distribution method is familiar to many students because it is the principle used by professors who "grade on the curve."

simple ranking method A method of performance appraisal that requires a manager to rank-order from top to bottom or from best to worst each member of a particular work group or department.

forced distribution method A method of performance appraisal that involves grouping employees into predefined frequencies of performance ratings.

Rating Methods

One of the most popular and widely used methods is the **graphic rating scale**, which consists of a statement or question about some aspect of an individual's job performance. Following the statement or question is a series of answers or possible responses from which the rater must select the one that fits best. For example, one common set of responses to a graphic rating scale with five possible alternatives is strongly agree, agree, neither agree nor disagree, disagree, and strongly disagree. These responses, or "descriptors," are usually arrayed along a bar, line, or similar visual representation marked with numbers or letters corresponding to each descriptor. Figure 8.3 shows a sample graphic rating scale.

graphic rating scale A method of performance appraisal that involves a statement or question about some aspect of an individual's job performance for which the rater must select the response that fits best.

Graphic rating scales are appealing because they are relatively easy to develop. A manager simply "brainstorms" a list of statements or questions that are presumably related to relevant indicators of performance. Moreover, a wide array of performance dimensions can be tapped with various rating scales on the same form. As we noted, a number or a letter accompanies each descriptor on the rating form. To develop a performance measure, the manager simply adds up the "points" for a particular employee's responses to obtain an overall index of performance.

The **critical incident method** requires the employee to give an example of especially good or poor performance. Organizations that rely on this method often require raters to recall such instances and then describe what the employee did (or did not do) that led to success or failure. This technique not only provides information for feedback but also defines performance in clear behavioural terms. In other cases, managers keep logs or diaries in which they record examples of critical incidents.

critical incident method A technique of performance appraisal in which raters recall examples of especially good or poor performance by an employee and then describe what the employee did (or did not do) that led to success or failure.

VM Variety Manufacturing

Employee Name: ______________________

Supervisor's Name: ______________________

Part 1. *Circle the most appropriate point on each scale.*

INITIATIVE

1	2	3	4	5
Never Does Anything Without Being Told		Handles Simple Matters Alone		Handles All Functions Without Help

PUNCTUALITY

1	2	3	4	5
Is Almost Always Late		Is Seldom Late		Is Never Late

CLEANLINESS

1	2	3	4	5
Work Area Is Always Dirty and Messy		Work Area Is Generally Clean and Orderly		Work Area Is Always Clean and Orderly

Please complete the separate evaluation form on page two.

Figure 8.3 Performance rating scale.

Providing Compensation and Benefits

5 Discuss the importance of *wages and salaries, incentives,* and *benefit programs* in attracting and keeping skilled workers.

compensation The set of rewards that organizations provide to individuals in return for their willingness to perform various jobs and tasks within the organization.

Compensation refers to the set of rewards that organizations provide to individuals in return for their willingness to perform various jobs and tasks within the organization. Compensation includes a number of different elements, including base salary, incentives, bonuses, benefits, and other rewards. Compensation amounts paid to employees should be the result of a careful and systematic strategic process.

The compensation received by CEOs can be extremely large, especially when bonuses and options are included. The most highly paid managers in the 2008 Financial Post Magazine survey were William Doyle of PotashCorp. of Saskatchewan ($320 million), James Balsillie and Michael Lazardis of Research In Motion ($178.5 million), and Gerald Schwartz of Onex Corp. ($61.7 million).[18] Critics have frequently questioned the wisdom of giving executives such large amounts of money, but most attempts to rein in executive salaries have failed. One study showed that the average CEO's pay in 1976 was about 36 times as much as that of the average worker, but by 2005, it was 369 times as much.[19] In 2009, there was a huge outcry in the United States about bonuses that were paid to executives of AIG, a company that was in deep financial trouble and had been bailed out by U.S. taxpayers.

In an attempt to introduce some accountability into executive compensation, Aflac Inc. (the company with the quacking duck on TV commercials) gives investors a non-binding vote on executive compensation. In 2009, shareholders at CIBC and the Royal Bank of Canada passed motions demanding that the companies give them a voice in executive compensation through non-binding shareholder votes.[20] In Sweden, Norway, and the Netherlands, shareholders have a binding vote on executive pay packages. Whether binding or non-binding, investor feedback may help boards of directors rein in executive compensation that is perceived as too high.[21]

Determining Basic Compensation

Basic compensation means the base level of wages or salary paid to an employee. **Wages** generally refer to hourly compensation paid to operating employees. Most of the jobs that are paid on an hourly wage basis are lower-level and/or operating-level jobs. In 2008, the average hourly wage in manufacturing was $21.66, while in retailing it was only $14.87. The manufacturing sector is shrinking, and retailers are now the biggest employers in Canada.[22]

wages Hourly compensation paid to operating employees.

Rather than expressing compensation on an hourly basis, the organization may instead state compensation on an annual or monthly basis. Many college and university graduates, for example, compare job offers on the basis of annual **salary** (for example, $36 000 versus $38 000 a year). Some legal issues regarding salaries are described in Concluding Case 8-1.

salary Dollars paid at regular intervals in return for doing a job, regardless of the amount of time or output involved.

Merit pay plans are compensation plans that base a portion of compensation on merit. Employees who make greater contributions receive higher pay than those who make lesser contributions. The most general form of a merit pay plan is the raise—an annual salary increase granted to employees because of their relative merit. Merit is usually defined in terms of individual performance and contribution to the organization.

merit pay plans Compensation plans that formally base some portion of compensation on merit.

Pay Surveys in Compensation

One common source of information that many organizations use to determine base compensation is **pay surveys**—surveys of compensation paid to employees by other employers in a particular geographic area, an industry, or an occupational group. Pay surveys provide the information that an organization needs to avoid an imbalance between its own pay scale and those of comparable organizations. Some pay surveys are conducted by professional associations. For example, the Canadian Federation of Business School Deans publishes an annual summary of salaries for professors teaching in business schools in Canadian universities.

pay survey A survey of compensation paid to employees by other employers in a particular geographic area, an industry, or an occupational group.

In general, a pay survey simply asks other organizations what they pay people to perform various jobs. Most organizations participate in such surveys because they will have access to the resulting data. There is, for example, a consortium of eight large electronics companies in the United States that routinely survey one another to determine what each pays new engineers and other professional employees who are hired directly out of college or university. The companies alternate the responsibility for conducting surveys from year to year, with the responsible organization sharing its results with the other members.

Job Evaluation

Another means of determining basic compensation is job evaluation, which should not be confused with job analysis. Recall that managers use job analysis to understand the requirements and nature of a job and its performance so that appropriate individuals can be recruited and selected. **Job evaluation** is a method for determining the relative value or worth of a job to the organization so that individuals who perform it can be appropriately compensated. It is mostly concerned with establishing internal pay equity.

job evaluation A method for determining the relative value or worth of a job to the organization so that individuals who perform it can be appropriately compensated.

Establishing a Pay Structure

A third method for determining basic compensation is establishing a pay structure. Compensation for different jobs is based on the organization's assessment of the relative value to the organization of each job class. Thus, there should be a logical ranking of compensation levels from the most valuable to the least valuable jobs throughout the organization. In addition, the organization decides on minimum and maximum pay ranges for each job or job class. These ranges may be decided on the basis of job performance, seniority, or a combination of the two to determine how much a person can be paid within the pay range for doing a particular job.

The internet allows job seekers and current employees to get a sense of what their true market value is more easily. If they can document the claim that their value is higher than what their current employer now pays, they may be in a position to demand higher salaries. One manager who met with a subordinate to discuss her raise was surprised when she produced data from five different websites to support her request for a bigger raise than he had intended to offer.

Performance-Based Compensation

Employees feel better about themselves and their company when they believe that they are being fairly compensated. Money motivates employees if it is tied directly to performance, and the most common method of establishing this link is the use of **incentive programs**—special pay programs designed to motivate high performance. Some programs are available to individuals, whereas others are distributed on a team or group basis.

incentive programs Special pay programs designed to motivate high performance.

Individual Incentives

Individual incentive plans reward individual performance on a real-time basis. That is, rather than increasing a person's base salary at the end of the year, an employer gives an individual a salary increase or some other financial reward for outstanding performance immediately or shortly after the performance occurs. Individual incentive systems are most common where performance can be assessed objectively (for example, by the number of units of output) rather than subjectively.

individual incentive plans A Compensation systems in which an employer gives an individual a salary increase or some other financial reward for outstanding performance immediately or shortly after the performance occurs.

Under a **piece-rate incentive plan**, an employee receives a certain amount of money for every unit produced. An assembly-line worker, for example, might be paid $0.10 for every unit produced. Critics of piece-rate pay systems argue that piece-rate systems rely on two questionable assumptions: (1) that performance is totally under an individual's control, and (2) that the individual employee does a single task continuously during the course of his or her work time. Today, therefore, incentive compensation systems tend to be much more sophisticated.

piece-rate incentive plan A compensation system in which an organization pays an employee a certain amount of money for every unit produced.

Sales employees are often paid a **sales commission** based on the number of units they sell or the dollar value of sales they generate for the company. **Bonuses**—cash payments—may also be given to employees who exceed a certain level of performance. For example, many baseball players have contract clauses that pay them bonuses for hitting over .300, making the All-Star team, or being named Most Valuable Player.

sales commission Payment to salespeople based on the number of units they sell or the dollar value of sales they generate for the company.

bonuses Cash payments given to employees who exceed a certain level of performance.

Pay-for-knowledge systems encourage individual workers to learn new skills and to become proficient at different jobs. Workers receive additional pay for each new skill or job that they master.

pay-for-knowledge Systems that encourage individual workers to learn new skills and to become proficient at different jobs.

With **pay-for-performance (or variable pay)** schemes, managers are rewarded for especially productive output—for producing earnings that significantly exceed the cost of bonuses. Such incentives go to middle managers on the basis of companywide performance, business unit performance, personal record, or all three factors. Eligible managers must often forgo merit or

pay-for-performance (or variable pay) Rewards paid to managers for especially productive output—for producing earnings that significantly exceed the cost of bonuses.

Individual incentive plans have been a big part of professional sports for many years. Players receive multimillion-dollar annual compensation for outstanding individual performance.

entitlement raises (increases for staying on and reporting to work every day), but many firms say that variable pay is a better motivator because the range between generous and mediocre merit raises is usually quite small anyway.

Other forms of individual incentives are also used; these include additional time off or special recognition in the form of points that are awarded on the recommendation of a supervisor. Recipients can convert their points into money or they can use them to buy merchandise or trips from a special online catalogue.[23] Retailers are beginning to adopt **workforce management systems**, which schedule the most productive staff to work at the store's busiest times. When employees type their code into the cash register, it displays their "performance metrics" such as average sales per hour and dollars per transaction. Less productive employees are given fewer hours or less desirable hours.[24] Not surprisingly, this system is disliked by many workers. At one store where it was implemented, the atmosphere changed from collegial to competitive.

workforce management systems Systems whereby the most productive retail staff are scheduled to work at the store's busiest times.

Team and Group Incentives

Given the increasing emphasis on team- and group-based methods of work, team and group incentives are growing in importance. One long-standing type of team incentive is **profit-sharing**, where some portion of the company's profit is paid into a profit-sharing pool that is then distributed to all employees. Walkerton, Ontario–based Larsen & Shaw Ltd., a hinge-making company, distributes 11 percent of pre-tax profits to employees twice a year. All employees receive payments, but the amount they receive depends on their seniority and performance evaluations.[25] At the Great Little Box Company Ltd. in Richmond, B.C., 15 percent of company profits are split evenly among staff. The company also has an "open book" policy of providing financial information to employees so they can relate financial performance of the company to their share of the profits.[26] At Ottawa-based Eagle Professional Resources Inc., a high-tech recruiting company, the profit-sharing plan is based on gross margin rather than profit. This prevents large fluctuations in payouts in years

profit-sharing System whereby some portion of the company's profit is paid into a profit-sharing pool that is then distributed to all employees.

when profits are low and gives employees more certainty about what they will receive.[27]

gain-sharing plans Plans that distribute bonuses to employees when a company's costs are reduced through greater work efficiency.

Gain-sharing plans distribute bonuses to employees when a company's costs are reduced through greater work efficiency. Palliser Furniture Ltd., for example, introduced a gain-sharing plan that rewarded employees for increasing production. Any profit resulting from production above a certain level is split 50–50 between the company and the employees.[28] The underlying assumption is that employees and the employer have the same goals and should therefore share in incremental economic gains.

Benefits

benefits What a firm offers its workers other than wages and salaries in return for their labour.

In addition to financial compensation, most organizations provide employees with indirect compensation in the form of benefits. **Benefits** generally refer to various rewards, incentives, and other things of value that an organization gives employees in addition to wages, salaries, and other forms of direct financial compensation. Because these benefits have tangible value, they represent a meaningful form of compensation even though they are not generally expressed in financial terms.

Canada's universal health care system is a real advantage for businesses because they do not have to pay to provide this coverage. Rather, its cost is supported largely from general tax revenues. A study of the cost of employee benefits as a percentage of wages and salaries in nine industrialized countries found that Canada's percentage (25 percent) was the lowest, and Germany's was the highest (70 percent). The other seven countries (United States, United Kingdom, Japan, the Netherlands, Austria, Italy, and France) were somewhere between these two extremes.[29]

Mandated Protection Plans

protection plans Plans that protect employees when their income is threatened or reduced by illness, disability, death, unemployment, or retirement.

employment insurance Provides a basic subsistence payment to employees who are between jobs.

Protection plans protect employees when their income is threatened or reduced by illness, disability, death, unemployment, or retirement. A number of these plans are required by law, but others are optional. One mandated benefit is **employment insurance**, which provides a basic subsistence payment to employees who are between jobs. It is intended for people who have stopped working for one organization but who are assumed to be actively seeking employment with another. Both employers and employees pay premiums to an employment insurance fund. As of 2007, employee premiums were $1.80 per hundred dollars of earnings, and employer premiums were $2.52.[30]

Canada Pension Plan Provides income to retired individuals to help them supplement personal savings, private pensions, part-time work, and so forth.

The **Canada Pension Plan** provides income to retired individuals to help them supplement personal savings, private pensions, part-time work, and so forth. It is funded through employee and employer taxes that are withheld from payroll. In 2006, the Canada Pension Plan had a surplus of almost $100 billion.[31]

workers' compensation Mandated insurance that covers individuals who suffer a job-related illness or accident.

Workers' compensation covers individuals who suffer a job-related illness or accident. Employers bear the cost of workers' compensation insurance. The exact premium is related to each employer's past experience with job-related accidents and illnesses. For example, a steel company might pay $20 per $100 of wages, while an accounting firm might pay only 10 cents per $100 of wages.

Optional Protection Plans

Another major category of employee benefits consists of various optional protection plans. Health insurance has become the most important type of coverage and has expanded in recent years to include vision care, mental health services, dental care, and prescription drugs. Employee prescription drug plan costs are doubling about every five years, and companies are increasingly concerned about their ability to offer this kind of coverage.[32]

Pension liabilities are also a problem. A study by the Certified General Accountants of Canada found that the shortfall in pension funding at Canada's largest corporate defined-benefit plans was $29 billion. A shortfall means that the assets in the pension plan are not sufficient to meet future pension promises.[33] In recent years, the majority of all federally regulated pension plans have had a shortfall.[34] Employers also face mounting liabilities for benefits for retired workers. A study of 71 of Canada's largest companies showed that their liabilities for retiree benefits (not pensions) amounted to $16 billion. In one recent year at Suncor Energy Inc., for example, the company's benefits liability was $98 million (almost as much as its pension liability of $99 million).[35]

Paid Time Off

Paid vacations are usually periods of one, two, or more weeks during which an employee can take time off from work and continue to be paid. Most organizations vary the amount of paid vacation with an individual's seniority, but some companies are reducing the time required to qualify for paid vacations. At Carlson Wagonlit Travel Canada, employees get four weeks of paid vacation after working at the company for just five years. Formerly, 10 years of service was required.[36]

Another common paid time off plan is sick leave. This benefit is provided when an individual is sick or otherwise physically unable to perform his or her job. Most organizations allow an individual to accumulate sick time according to a schedule, such as one sick day per month. Sometimes an organization will allow an employee to take off a small number of days simply for "personal business." This benefit is usually called personal leave. Occasions might include funerals, religious observances, weddings, birthdays, or simply personal holidays. The Catholic Children's Aid Society, for example, provides its child protection workers with time off when they need it because the workers face high-stress situations.[37]

Some companies go even further and offer their employees paid or unpaid sabbaticals to help them rejuvenate themselves and increase their enthusiasm for their job. At Bertelsmann AG, for example, full-time employees who have 20 years of service get a 5-week, full-pay sabbatical, while employees who have 10 years get 4 weeks. Employees at Procter & Gamble are eligible for a 12-week unpaid sabbatical after they have worked for the company for 1 year.[38]

Other Types of Benefits

There are many other benefits (often called perquisites, or perks) that companies can offer to employees. The range and significance of these perks is evident in the boxed insert entitled "The Importance of Perks."

Cafeteria-Style Benefit Plans

Most benefit programs are designed for all employees in an organization. Although the exact benefits may vary according to the employee's level in the organization, within those levels plans are generally "one size fits all." In contrast, **cafeteria-style benefit plans** allow employees to choose the benefits they really want. Under these plans, the organization typically establishes a budget, indicating how much it is willing to spend, per employee, on benefits. Employees are then presented with a list of possible benefits and the cost of each. They are free to put the benefits together in any combination they wish. Employees at Toyota's Cambridge, Ontario, plant are given the opportunity once each year to restructure their benefit packages. They can give more weight to dental coverage if they have young children, or to life insurance or disability coverage, depending on their circumstances.[39]

cafeteria-style benefit plans A flexible approach to providing benefits in which employees are allocated a certain sum to cover benefits and can "spend" this allocation on the specific benefits they prefer.

Business Accountability

The Importance of Perks

The list of perks that Canadian companies might offer to employees is very long. It includes things like unlimited sick days, on-site childcare, eldercare benefits, counselling, flexible work schedules, free beverages, concierge services, laundry pickup and delivery, training and development opportunities, discounts on company products, exercise facilities, on-site pet care, and wellness programs, to name just a few. The extent of these perks varies widely across companies.

Giving discounts to employees is a long-standing practice at some firms. Consider the following examples:

- Lululemon Athletica Ltd. gives employees a 60 percent discount on high-end clothing plus two free weekly yoga lessons.
- Starbucks employees receive free beverages during their work shifts plus one pound of coffee or one box of tea each week.
- Employees at Toronto-Dominion Bank can get fixed-rate mortgages for 1.5 percentage points below the posted rate. They can also get a Visa card with an interest rate as low as 5 percent.
- Fairmont Hotels & Resorts gives its employee deep discounts on rooms, food, and drink.
- Loblaw Companies Ltd. offers employees a 10 percent discount on store purchases. This is very uncommon in the grocery business.

Other perks have been introduced in recent years. Wellness programs concentrate on preventing illness in employees rather than simply paying their expenses when they become sick. These programs include things like exercise groups, smoking cessation, blood pressure and cholesterol screening, and stress management. Some organizations maintain full-fledged health clubs on-site and provide counselling and programs for fitness and weight loss. Labatt Brewing Co. Ltd. employs a full-time fitness coordinator who schedules appointments with nutritionists and massage therapists for employees. Kraft Ltd. also offers on-site fitness facilities. Trimark Investment Management Inc. built the Energy Zone, an on-site facility that offers aerobics, self-defence, and yoga classes. It also includes a weight room, massage room, pool tables, a big-screen TV, and an internet café.

Childcare and eldercare perks are also being more frequently offered to employees. Any organization that wants to be considered "family friendly" must have some type of childcare benefits, and being a family-friendly company is increasingly becoming a competitive advantage. These plans might include scheduling help, referrals to various types of services, or reimbursement accounts for childcare expenses. Over 300 Canadian companies sponsor childcare centres at the work site. The childcare centre run by Husky Injection Molding Systems in Bolton, Ontario, provides on-site haircuts, music lessons, and a pyjama party on Valentine's Day so parents can spend time together. If an employee has to work late, the childcare staff will feed the employee's children at no cost.

A study by Hewitt Associates showed that companies that are recognized on lists such as "The 100 Best Companies to Work For" have almost twice the number of job applications and half the annual turnover of non-ranked companies. A study done for *Report on Business Magazine* found that many of the traditional things that managers have assumed are important to employees—for example, fair pay, financial incentives like share ownership plans, and the opportunity for further training and education—are, in fact, important. However, employees also want to balance work and personal activities. Employers are increasingly willing to accommodate these wishes because employee commitment and retention rise when a company recognizes that employees have a life outside work. If a company does nothing to help employees balance work and life concerns, and if it simply assumes that people are going to be totally devoted to the company, the bottom line is negatively affected because of the stress that employees experience.

A Canada@Work study done by Aon Consulting found that when employers recognize employee needs outside the workplace, the company's employees are more likely to stay with the company and are more likely to recommend the company as a good place to work. Overall, companies need to have a "people-first" attitude about their employees, and perks play a significant role in this.

But what about companies that are struggling financially? Can they afford to give perks? The good news is that there are still effective perks that can be used. The most powerful perk—and least expensive—can be time off. Experts suggest, for example, that up to 20 percent of workers would be willing to work fewer hours for lower pay. Siemens, a German electronics firm, is offering workers a year-long "time-out" with reduced pay and a guaranteed job when they return.

Critical Thinking Questions

1. What are the advantages of perks? What are the disadvantages?
2. What other incentives might a company be able to offer its best workers to retain them?

The Legal Context of HRM

Describe some of the key *legal issues* involved in *hiring, compensating,* and *managing* workers. 6

As much as or more than any area of business, HRM is heavily influenced by federal law, provincial law, and judicial review. In this section, we summarize some of the most important and far-reaching areas of HR regulation. These include equal employment opportunity, comparable worth, sexual harassment, employee safety and health, and retirement.

Equal Employment Opportunity

The basic goal of all **equal employment opportunity regulations** is to protect people from unfair or inappropriate discrimination in the workplace. Note that discrimination in itself is not illegal. Whenever one person is given a pay raise and another is not, or when one person is hired and another is not, the organization has made a decision to discriminate. As long as the basis for this discrimination is purely job related (made, for instance, on the basis of performance or qualifications) and is applied objectively and consistently, the action is legal and appropriate. Problems arise when distinctions among people are not job related. In such cases, the resulting discrimination is illegal.

equal employment opportunity regulations Regulations to protect people from unfair or inappropriate discrimination in the workplace.

Anti-discrimination Laws

When recruiting, firms must be careful not to violate anti-discrimination laws. The key federal anti-discrimination legislation is the **Canadian Human Rights Act** of 1977. The goal of this act is to ensure that any individual who wishes to obtain a job has an equal opportunity to compete for it. The act applies to all federal agencies, federal Crown corporations, any employee of the federal government, and business firms that do business interprovincially. Thus, it applies to such firms as the Bank of Montreal, Air Canada, Canadian National Railways, and many other public and private sector organizations that operate across Canada. Even with such wide application, the act affects only about 10 percent of Canadian workers; the rest are covered under provincial human rights acts.

Canadian Human Rights Act (1977) Ensures that any individual who wishes to obtain a job has an equal opportunity to apply for it.

The Canadian Human Rights Act prohibits a wide variety of practices in recruiting, selecting, promoting, and dismissing personnel. The act specifically prohibits discrimination on the basis of age, race and colour, national and ethnic origin, physical handicap, religion, gender, marital status, or prison record (if pardoned). Some exceptions to these blanket prohibitions are permitted. For example, discrimination will not be charged if a blind person is refused a position as a train engineer, bus driver, or crane operator. Likewise, a firm will not be charged with discrimination if it does not hire a deaf person as a telephone operator or as an audio engineer.

These situations are clear-cut, but many others are not. For example, is it discriminatory to refuse women employment in a job that routinely requires carrying objects that weigh more than 50 kilograms? Difficulties in determining whether discrimination has occurred are sometimes dealt with by using the concept of **bona fide occupational requirement**. This means that an employer may choose one person over another based on overriding characteristics of the job in question. If a fitness centre wants to hire only women to supervise its women's locker room and sauna, it can do so without being discriminatory because it has established a bona fide occupational requirement.

bona fide occupational requirement When an employer may choose one applicant over another based on overriding characteristics of the job.

The Canadian Human Rights Commission carries out enforcement of the federal act. The commission can either respond to complaints from individuals who believe they have been discriminated against, or it can launch an investigation on its own if it has reason to believe that discrimination has occurred. During an investigation, data are gathered about the alleged discriminatory behaviour, and if the claim of discrimination is substantiated, the offending organization or individual may be ordered to compensate the victim.

Each province has also enacted human rights legislation to regulate organizations and businesses operating in that province. These provincial regulations are similar in spirit to the federal legislation, but there are many minor variations from province to province. All provinces prohibit discrimination on the basis of race, national or ethnic origin, colour, religion, sex, and marital status, but some do not address such issues as physical handicaps, criminal record, or age. Provincial human rights commissions enforce provincial legislation.

Employment Equity Act (1986) Federal legislation that designates four groups as employment disadvantaged—women, visible minorities, Aboriginal people, and people with disabilities.

The **Employment Equity Act** of 1986 addresses the issue of discrimination in employment by designating four groups as employment disadvantaged—women, visible minorities, Aboriginal people, and people with disabilities. These four groups contain six of every 10 individuals in the Canadian workforce, and it is estimated that their underemployment costs the Canadian economy around $50 billion each year.[40] Companies covered by the Employment Equity Act are required to publish statistics on their employment of people in the four designated groups.

In 2007, the Bank of Nova Scotia received an award from Catalyst recognizing the bank's success in promoting women to higher management levels. Women now occupy 31 percent of senior management positions, up from 19 percent in 2003. The bank also has set targets for other traditionally disadvantaged groups.[41] The Bank of Montreal (BMO) is the first company outside the United States to win a prestigious award for promoting women's careers. BMO has introduced initiatives such as flexible working hours, a mentoring program, a national career information network, and a gender awareness workshop series.[42] Companies are increasingly making provisions for disabled employees. At Rogers Cablevision, a large workplace area was completely redesigned to accommodate workers who were either visually disabled or in wheelchairs. Special equipment was also installed—a large-print computer for workers with partial sight, and a device that allows blind workers to read printed materials.[43]

Comparable Worth

comparable worth A legal concept that aims to pay equal wages for work of equal value.

Comparable worth is a legal concept that means paying equal wages for jobs that are of comparable value to the employer. This might mean comparing dissimilar jobs, such as those of nurses and mechanics or secretaries and electricians. Proponents of comparable worth say that all the jobs in a company must be evaluated and then rated in terms of basic dimensions such as the level of skill they require. All jobs could then be compared based on a common index. People in different jobs that rate the same on this index would be paid the same. Experts hope that this will help to reduce the gap between men's and women's pay. In a long-standing comparable worth dispute, the Supreme Court of Canada ruled in 2006 that flight attendants at Air Canada—who have been trying for years to achieve pay equity with male-dominated groups of employees—could compare their pay with the pay of ground crews and pilots because all these employees work for the same company.[44]

Critics of comparable worth object on the grounds that it ignores the supply and demand aspects of labour. They say, for example, that legislation forcing a company to pay people more than the open market price for their labour (which may happen in jobs where there is a surplus of workers) is another example of unreasonable government interference in business activities. They also say that implementing comparable worth will cost business firms too much money. A study prepared for the Ontario Ministry of Labour estimated that it would cost approximately $10 billion for the public and private sectors in Ontario to establish equitable payment for jobs of equal value. Yet the cost defence cannot be easily

The idea behind the concept of comparable worth is to pay equal wages for jobs that are of comparable value to the employer. This may require a comparison of jobs that are quite different.

used. In 2005, the Canadian Human Rights Tribunal ruled that a wage gap between male and female clerical workers at Canada Post was the result of systemic sex discrimination. It ordered the company to pay a total of $150 million in back pay to 6000 female clerical workers.[45] In an earlier case, the tribunal ruled that the federal government must pay a total of more than $3 billion to thousands of civil servants because it discriminated against workers in female-dominated job classifications. About 85 percent of these workers were women.

Sexual Harassment

Within the job context, **sexual harassment** refers to requests for sexual favours, unwelcome sexual advances, or verbal or physical conduct of a sexual nature that creates an intimidating or hostile environment for a given employee. The Canadian Human Rights Act takes precedence over any policies that a company might have developed on its own to deal with sexual harassment problems.

sexual harassment Requests for sexual favours, unwelcome sexual advances, or verbal or physical conduct of a sexual nature that creates an intimidating or hostile environment for a given employee.

Quid pro quo harassment is the most blatant form of sexual harassment. It occurs when the harasser offers to exchange something of value for sexual favours. A male supervisor, for example, might tell a female subordinate that he will recommend her for promotion or give her a raise in exchange for sexual favours. The creation of a **hostile work environment** is a subtler form of sexual harassment. A group of male employees who continually make off-colour jokes and lewd comments and perhaps decorate the work environment with questionable photographs may create a hostile work environment for a female colleague. Regardless of the pattern, the same rules apply: Sexual harassment is illegal, and the organization is responsible for controlling it.

quid pro quo harassment Form of sexual harassment in which sexual favours are requested in return for job-related benefits.

hostile work environment Form of sexual harassment deriving from off-colour jokes, lewd comments, and so forth.

Verbal comments by prominent managers can be problematic. For example, when Neil French, a legendary advertising executive and the creative director of WPP Group PLC, gave a speech in Toronto in 2005, he was asked why there were so few women who were creative advertising directors. He replied that women focus too much on their family duties and this usually prevents them from succeeding in management. His comments caused quite a stir, and French soon resigned from his position. It is interesting to note that the Toronto office of Ogilvy & Mather (a subsidiary of WPP) is headed by two creative directors, both of whom are women.[46]

If a manager is found guilty of sexual harassment, the company is also liable because the manager is an agent of the company. To deal with the potential for sexual harassment, managers should

- develop clear and enforceable policies dealing with sexual harassment
- inform all employees about the existence of these policies
- train employees to recognize and refrain from sexual harassment
- take complaints about sexual harassment seriously
- establish a procedure for dealing with harassment complaints
- take action against those who are involved in sexual harassment

Employee Safety and Health

Safety and health laws ensure that employees do not have to work in dangerous conditions. These laws are the direct result of undesirable conditions that existed in many Canadian businesses at the close of the nineteenth century. While dramatic improvements occurred in the twentieth century, Canada still has problems with workplace health and safety. In one study of six Western industrialized nations, Canada had the worst safety record in mining and construction and the second-worst record in manufacturing and railways.

Employee safety and health programs help to reduce absenteeism and turnover, raise productivity, and boost morale by making jobs safer and more healthful. Each province has developed its own workplace safety and health regulations, and in most of them, the Ministry of Labour appoints inspectors to enforce health and safety regulations. If the inspector finds a sufficient hazard, he or she has the authority to clear the workplace. Inspectors can usually arrive at a firm unannounced to conduct an inspection.

The Ontario Occupational Health and Safety Act is typical of safety and health laws in Canada. It requires all employers to ensure that equipment and safety devices are used properly. Employers must also show workers the proper way to operate machinery. At the job site, supervisors are charged with the responsibility of ensuring that workers use equipment properly. The act also requires workers to behave appropriately on the job. Employees have the right to refuse to work on a job if they believe it is unsafe; a legal procedure exists for resolving any disputes in this area. Directors of companies are personally responsible for workplace health and safety, and companies that permit unsafe working conditions can be fined.[47]

repetitive strain injuries (RSIs) Injuries that occur when workers perform the same functions over and over again.

Some industrial work—logging, construction, fishing, and mining—can put workers at risk of injury in obvious ways. But other types of work—such as typing or lifting—can also cause painful injuries. **Repetitive strain injuries (RSIs)** occur when workers perform the same functions over and over again. These injuries disable more than 200 000 Canadians each year and account for nearly half of all work-related time-loss claims.

Retirement

Until the 1990s, Canadian courts generally upheld 65 as the mandatory retirement age, but most Canadian provinces have now abolished mandatory retirement. The average retirement age in Canada dropped from 65 in the late 1970s to 62 in 2003.[48] However, many people "un-retire" and return to work at least part-time to keep their minds engaged. The average retirement age may begin increasing again, partly because of the financial insecurity created by the worldwide recession that began in 2008. Some managers fear that the abolition of mandatory retirement will result in less productive employees remaining at work after age 65, but research shows that employees who stay on the job past 65 are usually the most productive ones. However, workers over age 65 are nearly four times as likely to die from work-related causes as younger workers, and the health-care costs for older workers are double those for workers in their forties.[49]

New Challenges in the Changing Workplace

Discuss *workforce diversity*, the management of *knowledge workers*, and the use of *contingent and temporary workers* as important changes in the contemporary workplace. 7

As we have seen throughout this chapter, HR managers face ongoing challenges in their efforts to keep their organizations staffed with effective workers. To complicate matters, new challenges arise as the economic and social environments of business change. We conclude this chapter with a discussion of several of the most important HRM issues facing business today: managing workforce diversity, managing knowledge workers, and managing contingent and temporary workers.

Managing Workforce Diversity

One extremely important human resource challenge is the management of **workforce diversity**—the range of workers' attitudes, values, beliefs, and behaviours that differ by gender, race, age, ethnicity, physical ability, and other relevant characteristics. The situation for visible minorities is currently one of the most publicized aspects of diversity. Consider these facts:

workforce diversity The range of workers' attitudes, values, beliefs, and behaviours that differ by gender, race, age, ethnicity, physical ability, and other relevant characteristics.

- Seventy-three percent of the people who immigrated to Canada during the 1990s were visible minorities.
- By 2015, 20 percent of Saskatchewan's population will be Aboriginal.
- In 2001, approximately four million Canadians were visible minorities; by 2017, that number could increase to as much as 8.5 million.
- Visible minorities currently make up more than 40 percent of the population of Vancouver.
- By 2017, visible minorities will form more than 50 percent of the populations of Toronto and Vancouver.
- By 2017, 22 percent of the total Canadian population will be visible minorities.[50]

Procter & Gamble Canada is one of many Canadian businesses that are taking steps to capitalize on the opportunities that come with a rapidly changing population demographic. Because P&G knows that employees are more productive when their differences are respected in the work environment, a major social gathering was organized at the Toronto office to celebrate the diverse nature of the P&G workforce. (Employees come from 40 different countries and speak at least 30 different languages.) Diversity is also recognized at P&G through "affinity groups" such as the Women's Leadership Council, the French Canadian Network, the Asian Professional Network, the Christian Network, and the Jewish Network. The goal of these networks is to help employees feel comfortable about participating in corporate life and to act as a resource for employees who want insights about how to target specific markets.[51]

Western Union is another company that is focusing on diversity, and it may be further along than most, given the nature of its business—moving money overseas to the families of new Canadians who are working here and want to help their families back in their home country. The potential customers of Western Union are not easily reached by traditional marketing methods, so the company hires people who speak the language of their target market and who know what it feels like to be an immigrant in Canada. This approach has yielded some interesting benefits. In one area of Toronto, for example, customers who wanted to transfer money back to the Philippines got a free loaf of Pan de Sal bread from a local Filipino baker.[52]

Organizations that are doing a particularly good job of responding to the shifting demographics of the Canadian scene are recognized by Mediacorp in its annual listing of the top diversity employers in Canada. The listing assesses the extent to which companies have employment initiatives that address the needs of five groups: women, Aboriginal people, people with disabilities, gays/lesbians, and visible minorities. The 2009 list shows which organizations scored well in helping members of the five groups (the list below is illustrative, not exhaustive).[53]

- women: Blake, Cassels & Graydon, Corus Entertainment, KPMG Canada
- Aboriginal people: Alberta-Pacific Forest Industries, Assiniboine Credit Union, Boeing Canada, Canada Post
- people with disabilities: Canada Mortgage and Housing, Canadian Pacific Railway, HSBC Bank Canada
- gays/lesbians: Hewlett-Packard Canada, Intuit Canada
- visible minorities: WorkSafeBC, Toronto Police Service

Organizations are increasingly recognizing that diversity can be a competitive advantage. By hiring the best people available from every group—rather than hiring from just one or a few groups—a firm can develop a higher-quality workforce. A diverse workforce can bring a wider array of information to bear on problems and can provide insights on marketing products to a wider range of consumers. The head of workforce diversity at IBM thinks that "it is important for our customers to look inside and see people like them. If they can't . . . the prospect of them becoming or staying our customers declines."

Managing Knowledge Workers

knowledge workers Workers who are experts in specific fields like computer technology and engineering and who add value because of what they know, rather than how long they have worked or the job they do.

Knowledge workers add value to a company because of the knowledge they possess.[54] Knowledge workers—for example, computer scientists, engineers, professors, and physical scientists—provide special challenges for the HR manager. They are usually experts in some abstract knowledge base, and they often prefer to work independently. They identify strongly with their professional peers and may even define their performance in terms of their professions, rather than the organization they work for.

As the importance of information-driven jobs grows, the need for knowledge workers continues to grow as well. But these employees require extensive and highly specialized training, and even after knowledge workers are on the job, training updates are critical to prevent their skills from becoming obsolete. It has been suggested, for example, that the "half-life" of a technical education in engineering is about three years. The failure to update such skills will not only result in the loss of competitive advantage, but it will also increase the likelihood that the knowledge worker will move to another firm that is more committed to updating his or her knowledge.

Knowledge Worker Management and Labour Markets

Because the demand for knowledge workers has been growing, organizations that need these workers must provide regular upward market adjustments to

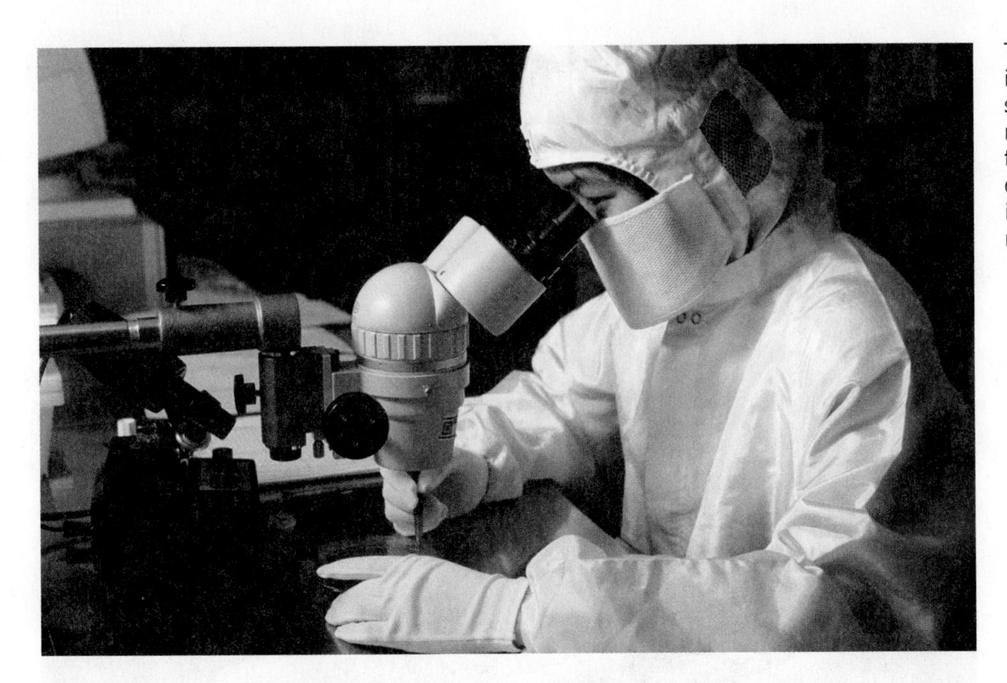

This worker has extensive training and possesses the highly specialized skills that are needed for high-tech manufacturing processes. Management of such knowledge workers is increasingly important for business success.

keep them. This is especially critical in areas in which demand is growing, as even entry-level salaries for these employees are skyrocketing. Once an employee accepts a job with a firm, the employer faces yet another dilemma. Once hired, workers are subject to the company's internal labour market, which is not likely to be growing as quickly as the external market for knowledge workers as a whole. Consequently, the longer an employee remains with a firm, the further behind the market his or her pay falls—unless, of course, it is regularly adjusted upward.

Prior to the start of the worldwide recession in 2008, some companies had to take extreme measures to attract and keep knowledge workers.[55] BP, for example, was paying starting petroleum engineers with undersea platform-drilling knowledge—not experience, just knowledge—salaries in the six figures, plus sign-on bonuses of over US$50 000. Even with these incentives, HR managers complained that they could not retain specialists because young engineers soon left to accept sign-on bonuses from competitors. The recession has reduced these extremes, but growth in demand for knowledge workers will continue.

Managing Contingent Workers

A **contingent worker** is a person who works for an organization on something other than a permanent or full-time basis. Categories of contingent workers include part-time workers, independent contractors (freelancers), on-call workers, temporary employees (usually hired through outside "temp" agencies), contract workers, and guest workers (foreigners who work in Canada for a limited time period).

contingent worker A person who works for an organization on something other than a permanent or full-time basis.

Trends in Contingent Employment

Contingent employment is on the rise in Canada. In 2007, part-time employment in all categories grew 4.7 percent, while full-time employment grew just 1.1 percent.[56] This trend became more pronounced as the recession deepened. In the boom times before the recession of 2008, companies in Italy, France, and Germany hired many temporary workers from Eastern European countries like Romania. But when the economic downturn hit, those workers were usually

This young woman is one of 1500 temporary workers at Sola Optical. Sola uses temporary workers because doing so gives human resource managers both scheduling flexibility and the opportunity to try potential permanent employees.

the first to be let go.[57] In Canada, there is increasing demand for temporary workers in top management because the economic downturn has created a lot of turnover in top management. These "temps at the top" usually stay for a year or less until a permanent person is found.[58]

The number of guest workers in Canada—one category of contingent workers—is increasing. They work in all kinds of industries, including agriculture, manufacturing, and services. In agriculture, for example, the number of documented guest workers increased from just 203 in 1974 to over 14 000 in 2007. The number is predicted to rise even further in the future.[59]

Management of Contingent Workers

The effective management of contingent workers requires consideration of three issues. First, careful planning must be done so the organization brings in contingent workers only when they are actually needed and only in the quantity they are needed to complete necessary tasks. Second, the costs and benefits of using contingent workers must be understood. Many firms bring in contingent workers in order to reduce labour costs, but if contingent workers are less productive than permanent workers, there may be no gain for the organization. Third, contingent workers should be integrated into the mainstream activities of the organization as much as possible. This involves deciding how contingent workers will be treated relative to permanent workers. For example, should contingent workers be invited to the company holiday party? Should they have the same access to employee benefits as full-time workers do? Managers must develop a strategy for integrating contingent workers according to some sound logic and then follow that strategy consistently over time.[60]

Test yourself on the material for this chapter at **www.pearsoned.ca/mybusinesslab**.

Summary of Learning Objectives

1. **Define *human resource management*, discuss its strategic significance, and explain how managers plan for human resources.** *Human resource management, or HRM*, is the set of organizational activities directed at attracting, developing, and maintaining an effective workforce. HRM plays a key strategic role in organizational performance. Planning for human resource needs entails several steps. Conducting a *job analysis* enables managers to create detailed, accurate *job descriptions* and *specifications*. After the analysis is complete, managers must forecast demand and supply for both the numbers and types of workers they will need. Then they consider steps to match supply with demand.

2. **Identify the issues involved in *staffing* a company, including *internal* and *external recruiting* and *selection*.** *Recruiting* is the process of attracting qualified persons to apply for jobs that an organization has open. *Internal recruiting* involves considering present employees for new jobs. This approach helps build morale and rewards an organization's best employees. *External recruiting* means attracting people from outside the organization to apply for openings. When organizations are actually selecting people for jobs, they generally use such selection techniques as application forms, tests, interviews, and other techniques. Regardless of what selection techniques are used, they must be valid predictors of an individual's expected performance on the job.

3. **Discuss different ways in which organizations go about developing the capabilities of employees and managers.** If a company is to get the most out of its workers, it must develop both those workers and their skills. Nearly all employees undergo some initial *orientation* process that introduces them to the company and to their new jobs. Many employees are given the opportunity to acquire new skills through various work-based and/or instructional-based programs.

4. **Explain ways in which organizations evaluate employee performance.** *Performance appraisals* help managers decide who needs training and who should be promoted. Appraisals also tell employees how well they are meeting expectations. Although a variety of alternatives are available for appraising performance, supervisors are most commonly involved. No matter who does the evaluation, however, feedback to the employee is very important. Managers can select from a variety of ranking and rating methods for use in performance appraisal.

5. **Discuss the importance of *wages* and *salaries*, *incentives*, and *benefit programs* in attracting and keeping skilled workers.** *Wages and salaries*, incentives, and *benefit* packages may all be parts of a company's *compensation* program. By paying its workers as well as or better than competitors, a business can attract and keep qualified personnel. *Incentive programs* can also motivate people to work more productively. Indirect compensation also plays a major role in effective and well-designed compensation systems.

6. **Describe some of the key *legal issues* involved in *hiring*, *compensating*, and *managing* workers.** In hiring, compensating, and managing workers, managers must obey a variety of federal and provincial laws. *Equal employment opportunity* and equal pay laws forbid discrimination other than action based on legitimate job requirements. The concept of *comparable worth* states that equal wages should be paid for jobs that are of comparable value to the employer. Firms are also required to provide employees with safe working environments, as set down by the guidelines of provincial occupational health and safety acts. *Sexual harassment* is another key contemporary legal issue in business.

7. **Discuss *workforce diversity*, the management of *knowledge workers*, and the use of *contingent* and *temporary workers* as important changes in the contemporary workplace.** *Workforce diversity* refers to the range of workers' attitudes, values, beliefs, and behaviours that differ by gender, race, ethnicity, age, physical ability, and other relevant characteristics. Many firms think that having a diverse workforce creates a competitive advantage, so they have set a goal to have a workforce that reflects the growing diversity of the population as it enters the labour pool.

   Many firms today also face challenges in managing *knowledge workers*. The recent boom in high-tech companies has led to rapidly increasing salaries and high turnover among the workers who are best prepared to work in those companies. *Contingent workers* are temporary and part-time employees hired to supplement an organization's permanent workforce. Their numbers have grown significantly since the early 1980s and are expected to rise further. The practice of hiring contingent workers is gaining in popularity because it gives managers more flexibility and because temps are usually not covered by employers' benefit programs.

Key Terms

360-degree feedback (p. 252)
assessment centre (p. 248)
behaviour-based interviewing (p. 249)
benefits (p. 258)
bona fide occupational requirement (p. 261)
bonuses (p. 256)
cafeteria-style benefit plans (p. 259)
Canada Pension Plan (p. 258)
Canadian Human Rights Act (1977) (p. 261)
comparable worth (p. 262)
compensation (p. 254)
contingent worker (p. 267)
critical incident method (p. 253)
employee information systems (skills inventories) (p. 244)
Employment Equity Act (1986) (p. 262)
employment insurance (p. 258)
equal employment opportunity regulations (p. 261)
external recruiting (p. 245)
forced distribution method (p. 253)
gain-sharing plans (p. 258)
graphic rating scale (p. 253)
hostile work environment (p. 263)
human resource management (HRM) (p. 242)
incentive programs (p. 256)
individual incentive plans (p. 256)
internal recruiting (p. 245)
internships (p. 246)
job analysis (p. 243)
job description (p. 243)
job evaluation (p. 255)
job specification (p. 243)
knowledge workers (p. 266)
lecture or discussion approach (p. 251)
management development programs (p. 251)
mentoring (p. 251)
merit pay plans (p. 255)
networking (p. 251)
off-the-job training (p. 251)
on-the-job training (p. 250)
orientation (p. 250)
pay survey (p. 255)
pay-for-knowledge (p. 256)
pay-for-performance (p. 256)
performance appraisal (p. 252)
piece-rate incentive plan (p. 256)
profit-sharing (p. 257)
protection plans (p. 258)
quid pro quo harassment (p. 263)
recruiting (p. 245)
repetitive strain injuries (RSIs) (p. 264)
replacement chart (p. 244)
salary (p. 255)
sales commission (p. 256)
sexual harassment (p. 263)
simple ranking method (p. 253)
systematic job rotations and transfers (p. 250)
validation (p. 246)
vestibule training (p. 251)
video assessment (p. 248)
wages (p. 255)
work-based program (p. 250)
workers' compensation (p. 258)
workforce diversity (p. 265)
workforce management systems (p. 257)

Questions for Analysis

1. Why is a good employee-job match important? Who benefits more, the organization or the employee? Explain.
2. Why is the formal training of workers so important to most employers? Why don't employers simply let people learn about their jobs as they perform them?
3. What are your views on drug testing in the workplace? What would you do if your employer asked you to submit to a drug test?
4. Have you or anyone you know ever suffered discrimination in a hiring decision? Did you or the person you know do anything about it?
5. What training do you think you are most likely to need when you finish school and start your career?
6. What benefits do you consider most and least important in attracting workers? In keeping workers? In motivating workers to perform their jobs well?
7. Select a job currently held by you or a friend. Draw up a job description and job specification for the position.
8. How much will benefit considerations (as opposed to salary) affect your choice of an employer after graduation?

Application Exercises

1. Interview an HR manager at a local company. Focus on a position for which the firm is currently recruiting applicants and identify the steps in the selection process.
2. Obtain a copy of an employment application. Examine it carefully and determine how useful it might be in making a hiring decision.

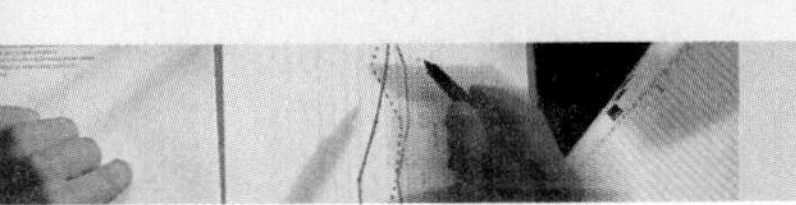

Building Your Business Skills

Getting Online for a Job

The Purpose of the Assignment

To introduce students to career-search resources available on the internet.

The Situation

If companies are on one side of the external staffing process, people looking for work are on the other. Companies need qualified candidates to fill job openings and candidates need jobs that are right for them. The challenge, of course, is to make successful matches. Increasingly, this matchmaking is being conducted on the internet. Companies are posting jobs in cyberspace, and job seekers are posting résumés in response. The number of job postings has grown dramatically in recent years. On a typical Sunday, you might find as many as 50 000 postings on the Monster Board, a leading job site. With so many companies looking for qualified candidates online, it makes good business sense to learn how to use the system.

Assignment

Using internet career resources means locating job databases and preparing and posting a résumé. (You will therefore need access to the internet to complete this exercise.)

Step 1

Team up with three classmates to investigate and analyze specific job databases. In each case, write a short report describing the database (which you and other group members may use during an actual job search). Summarize the site and its features as well as its advantages, disadvantages, and costs. Start with the following sites and add others you may find on your own:

The Monster Board, www.monster.com
Careerbuilder.com, www.careerbuilder.ca
College Grad Job Hunter, www.collegegrad.com

Step 2

Investigate the job opportunities listed on the home pages of various companies. Consider trying the following companies:

Air Canada, www.aircanada.com
Dofasco, www.dofasco.ca
Royal Bank, www.rbcroyalbank.com
IBM, www.ibm.com/ca
Wal-Mart, www.walmartstores.com
McDonald's, www.mcdonalds.com
Bombardier, www.bombardier.com

Write a summary of the specific career-related information you find on each site.

Step 3

Working with group members, research strategies for composing effective cyber résumés. The following websites provide some helpful information on formats and personal and job-related information that should be included in your résumé. They also offer hints on the art of creating a scannable résumé:

Workopolis, www.workopolis.com
Career Magazine, www.careermag.com

Two books by Joyce Lain Kennedy, *Electronic Job Search Revolution* and *Electronic Résumé Revolution*, also contain valuable information.

Step 4

Working as a group, create an effective electronic résumé for a fictitious college or university graduate looking for a first job. Pay attention to format, language, style, and the effective communication of background and goals.

Step 5

Working as a group, learn how to post your résumé online. (Do not submit the résumé you created for this exercise, which is, after all, fictitious.) The databases provided will guide you in this process.

Questions for Discussion

1. Why is it necessary to learn how to conduct an electronic job search? Do you think it will be more or less necessary in the years ahead?
2. Why do you think more computer-related jobs than non-technical jobs are posted online? Do you think this situation will change?
3. Why is it a waste of time to stylize your résumé with different fonts, point sizes, and centred headings?
4. What is the advantage of emailing your résumé directly to a company rather than applying for the same job through an online databank?

Exercising Your Ethics: Team Exercise

Handling the Layoffs

The Situation

The CEO of a moderate-sized company is developing a plan to lay off some members of the company's workforce. He wants each manager to rank his or her employees according to the order in which they should be laid off, from first to last.

The Dilemma

One manager has just asked for help. He is new to his position and has little experience to draw from. The members of the manager's team are as follows:

Tony Jones: white male, 10 years with the company, average performer, reportedly drinks a lot after work

Amanda Wiggens: white female, very ambitious, 3 years with company, above-average performer, puts in extra time at work, is known to be abrasive when dealing with others

George Sinclair: Aboriginal, 20 years with the company, average performer, was previously laid off but called back when business picked up

Dorothy Henderson: white female, 25 years with company, below-average performer, has filed five sexual harassment complaints in last 10 years

Wanda Jackson: black female, 8 years with company, outstanding performer, is rumoured to be looking for another job

Jerry Loudder: white male, single parent, 5 years with company, average performer

Martha Strawser: white female, 6 years with company, excellent performer but spotty attendance, is putting husband through university

Team Activity

Assemble a group of four students. Your group has agreed to provide the manager with a suggested rank ordering of the manager's employees.

Action Steps

1. Working together, prepare this list, ranking the manager's employees according to the order in which they should be laid off, from first to last. Identify any disagreements that occurred along the way and indicate how they were resolved.
2. As a group, discuss the underlying ethical issues in this situation and write them down.
3. As a group, brainstorm any legal issues involved in this situation and write them down.
4. Do the ethical and legal implications of your choices always align?
5. Do the ethical and performance implications of your choices always align?

For additional cases and exercise material, go to **www.pearsoned.ca/mybusinesslab.**

Concluding Case 8-1

Who Should Get Overtime Pay?

On October 28, 2008, a $360-million class-action lawsuit was filed against CIBC World Markets Inc. by a salaried group of stock analysts, financial advisors, and investment bankers. The employees claimed they had not been compensated for overtime work they had done. The lead plaintiff in the case was Michael Brown, formerly a senior analyst at CIBC. His salary was $50 000, and his employment contract required that he work 40–45 hours per week to earn that salary. But he claimed he actually had to work 60–70 hours each week in order to achieve the goals that management set for him. He was never paid any overtime. CIBC vigorously defended itself and said that its overtime policy was clear and exceeded legislative requirements. When that class-action suit was filed, CIBC was already defending itself against another overtime suit that was filed by bank tellers.

CIBC is not alone in having to defend itself against overtime lawsuits. Scotiabank and CN Rail are also having to cope with overtime lawsuits, and the "big four" accounting firms have already settled overtime claims by their employees. KPMG, for example, was hit with a class-action lawsuit alleging that the company forced some employees to work as much as 90 hours a week to complete assignments and that many employees were forced to work several hours of unpaid overtime each week to keep clients happy. While the lawsuit was still before the courts, KPMG agreed to fix the problem, and it may have to spend up to $10 million to do so. The CEO of KPMG said the company regretted not paying overtime when it should have.

Lawsuits against companies for failure to pay overtime first came to prominence in 2003, when Sharon Michalowski, formerly a manager at Nygard International Ltd., filed a complaint with the Manitoba Labour Board arguing that she should have been compensated for unpaid overtime. Nygard took the position that since Michalowski was a manager, she was required to work whatever hours were required to do the job. The Board ruled in Michalowski's favour, and so did the Manitoba Court of Appeal. Nygard then took the case all the way to the Supreme Court of Canada but lost. Michalowski was awarded $10 000 in overtime pay.

Some observers thought that this would usher in a new era of employee rights, but it hasn't worked out that way. The Supreme Court decision made many Manitoba employers nervous. They observed that since managers are generally paid better than other employees and they have greater power to set their own working conditions, they should not be paid for overtime. The province of Manitoba soon fell into line with other provinces and passed legislation that exempted managers from overtime pay rules in its labour laws.

Questions for Discussion

1. Are there positive implications of not paying managers for overtime? What are they? Are there negative implications? What are they?
2. Consider the following statement: *Managers should not expect to be paid overtime. They are highly paid, and they should focus on getting the job done, rather than on how many hours it takes to complete the job. People who don't have a "work-hard" attitude shouldn't be managers.* Do you agree or disagree with the statement? Defend your answer.

Concluding Case 8-2

Galt Contracting

Galt Contracting is a small B.C.–based company that plants trees for lumber companies like Canfor, Gorman Brothers, and Riverside. In the spring of each year, Donald Galt, the owner-manager of Galt Contracting, bids on tree-planting contracts that will be available during the upcoming summer. He visits the block of land that is up for bid and looks it over with a lumber company representative. He then develops a bid and submits it to the lumber company. If he is awarded the job, Galt's profit is determined by the amount of the lumber company contract minus the amount he pays his workers.

The Business of Tree Planting

Once Galt knows that he has got a contract, he hires tree planters to do the actual tree planting. Galt usually hires university students who are looking for good-paying summer jobs. The work is hard, but tree planters can make very good money because they are paid on a piece-rate system, that is, they are paid a certain amount of money for each tree that they plant. The amount usually varies between 16 and 32 cents per tree, depending on the terrain and the kind of tree that is being planted. The more difficult the terrain is, the higher the piece rate that planters receive.

A tree planter may plant as few as 1000 trees or as many as 2500 each day, depending on the terrain and the planter's skill. On an average day, a reasonably experienced planter can put 1300 seedlings in the ground. Planters don't have a set lunch break but eat on the run. They usually leave their lunch boxes at the main cache and eat about halfway through the day on one of their return trips to the cache to pick up more seedlings.

Each planter is assigned a "piece" to plant for the day, usually an area equal in size to a football field, but not necessarily symmetrical. The limits of each planter's area are marked with flags by the planters as they begin planting in the morning. Planters leave the main cache and begin planting trees in a straight line. As they plant, they "flag a line" which indicates the boundaries of their piece. This involves staking out strips of brightly coloured tape close to the line of trees. This line helps each planter determine where their piece begins and ends. Planting is then done in a back-and-forth pattern within each piece as planters work back toward the main cache as their bag gradually empties. They monitor the number of trees left in their planting bags so they can end up near the main cache when they run out of trees.

Trees must be planted in different concentrations on different pieces, and a certain jargon has arisen to describe this activity. For example, if spacing is "2.9," this means that trees must be planted 2.9 metres apart; if spacing is "3.1," this means that trees must be planted 3.1 metres apart. Planters prefer "2.9" days over "3.1" days because they don't have to cover as much ground and can therefore plant more trees and make more money.

Quality Control

A checker—who works for the lumber company—inspects the work of the planters to ensure that they are planting properly. Checkers use a cord to inscribe a circle on a randomly chosen part of a piece. On "2.9" days, the checker will ensure that seven trees are contained in the circle within the cord. The checker also determines whether the trees are planted properly. Trees must not have any air pockets around the roots, there must be no "j-rooted" (crooked) roots, and trees must be planted on the south (sunny) side of any obstacles on the piece. Trees must also be planted close to obstacles so that they are not trampled by the cattle that sometimes graze in the area. If a planter consistently plants too many or too few trees on a piece, the checker can demand that the piece be replanted. This happens infrequently, but when it does, the planter's pay is sharply reduced.

Galt sometimes checks workers himself, especially if he has reason to believe that they are doing a sloppy job. The biggest problem he has encountered is workers who plant large numbers of trees but do so very poorly. Planters know that, if Galt is following them around for any significant period of time, he is suspicious about the quality of their planting. Planters are very hard on each other in terms of quality. They become very upset if one of their group tries to make more money planting large numbers of trees by cutting corners. Planters put pressure on each other to do a good job because the reputation of the whole group suffers if one or two planters do poor-quality work. As well, planters resent those among them who make more money simply by planting large numbers of trees in a poor-quality way. A planter who is known to do a sloppy job or who is forced to replant an area might, for example, be nicknamed "j-root."

Planters don't know when the checker will come by. If a planter "gets in good" with a checker, the checker may go easy when checking the planter's work. The checkers are themselves checked by other lumber company employees to ensure that they are doing reasonable quality control work. In turn, the lumber company is checked by the provincial government to see that trees are planted properly.

The Problem

Galt has been paying planters on a piece-rate basis for many years, but recently he has become very concerned about it because too many trees are improperly planted and die soon after planting. Galt thinks this is happening because planters are focussing on quantity at the expense of quality (they are so motivated by the money they can earn if they plant a lot of trees that they are doing sloppy work). At the end of last year's planting season, Galt was told in no uncertain terms by one lumber company that if he did not improve the quality of his tree planting, he would not get any more jobs.

The problem is significant enough that Galt has been thinking about dropping the piece-rate system and moving toward a "flat rate" system that would give planters a fixed amount of pay for each day's work. Galt thinks that this would cause planters to take more time and care when planting each tree since they would not have to worry about how much money they were going to make for the day. In the past, Galt has occasionally paid workers on a flat rate, particularly when the terrain was uneven. But this system is not problem free either. For example, Galt gets the impression that when he pays on a flat-rate basis, planters don't work as hard, and they take more breaks. Galt also knows that planters like the piece-rate system because they can make good money. The piece-rate system generates friendly competition among planters to see who can be the most productive. Those who plant the most trees have higher status among their peers, and they also earn more money. Overall, Galt thinks that this friendly competition increases the number of trees that are planted.

When the piece-rate system is used, there is not much socializing among workers on the site, except when they are bagging up at the main cache at various times throughout the day. Socializing is generally seen as counterproductive because workers who stand around and talk aren't planting trees, and this reduces their pay.

As Galt considered all these facts, he wondered what he should do regarding the payment system he uses for planters.

Questions for Discussion

1. What are the advantages and disadvantages of paying tree planters on a piece-rate system? On a flat-rate system?
2. Look at the motivation theories in Chapter 10. What does each of those theories say (or imply) about Galt's idea of dropping the piece-rate system and paying planters a flat rate for each day of work?
3. Devise a payment system for tree planters that minimizes negative consequences. Describe the impact of your proposal on each of the following factors:
   - the motivation levels of the planters
   - the activities of the quality control checkers
   - the level of quality needed in tree planting
   - the needs of the lumber companies
   - Donald Galt's need to run a profitable company
4. What should Donald Galt do? Be specific.

apter 9

Understanding Labour–Management Relations

After reading this chapter, you should be able to:

1. Explain why workers organize into *labour unions*.
2. Trace the evolution of unions and discuss *trends in unionism* in Canada.
3. Describe the major *laws governing labour–management relations*.
4. Describe the union *certification* and *decertification* processes.
5. Identify the steps in the *collective bargaining process*.

Reports from the Battlefield

In 2009, an arbitrator ruled that workers in the United Food and Commercial Workers (UFCW) in Saint-Hyacinthe, Quebec, would not receive the wage and benefits increase they had hoped to get from Wal-Mart. In rejecting the union's demands, the arbitrator portrayed Wal-Mart as a good employer and concluded that Wal-Mart's performance-based compensation system had to be retained because it was part of the culture of the company. The arbitrator also noted that Wal-Mart sometimes paid its employees more than competitors like Zellers did. The arbitrator's ruling is the latest round in the intense battle that is taking place between the UFCW and Wal-Mart. The UFCW is committed to organizing Wal-Mart's employees, while Wal-Mart's management aggressively fights every UFCW attempt. The fight has been bitter at times, and the eventual outcome is not yet clear. Each side has had both victories and defeats. In the photo, the United Food and Commercial Workers union, which is affiliated with the Quebec Federation of Labour, reacts after the rejection of a certification bid by employees at a Wal-Mart store in Saguenay, Quebec.

In December 2008, the Quebec Labour Relations Board certified the UFCW as the sole bargaining agent for about 150 workers at a Wal-Mart store in Gatineau. That required Wal-Mart to negotiate with the union regarding a collective agreement. If the past is any indication, the negotiations are going to be very difficult. Here's why.

In August 2005, the UFCW was certified as the sole bargaining agent for nine tire and lubrication workers at another Wal-Mart in Gatineau. The UFCW and Wal-Mart then tried to negotiate a collective agreement but failed. In August 2008, an arbitrator imposed an agreement that, among other things, raised workers' wages from $9.25 an hour to $11.54 an hour over three years. In October 2008, Wal-Mart closed the shop.

Until the mid-1990s, Wal-Mart had never had a union in any of its stores in the United States, Canada, Puerto Rico, Argentina, Brazil, or Mexico. It had been able to resist unions partly by promoting its family-like culture. The company argued that forcing employees to work under a collective agreement would reduce their motivation and damage the company's successful formula for keeping customers happy. In 1996, management first began hearing rumours that the Canadian Auto Workers (CAW) union was approaching employees at the Windsor, Ontario, store about unionizing. During the organizing drive, there was much squabbling among employees, and when the certification vote was held, the workers voted 151–43 against joining the union. In spite of this, the Ontario Labour Relations Board (OLRB) certified the union as the employees' bargaining agent on the grounds that the company had intimidated employees during the membership drive. A first collective agreement was approved, but in April 2000, the union was officially decertified.

In 2003, the Labour Relations Board of British Columbia found Wal-Mart guilty of an unfair labour practice, namely, that it undermined a union-organizing drive at the Wal-Mart store in Quesnel, British Columbia. As part of their decision, the board required Wal-Mart management to schedule an employee meeting and read aloud the board's decision to employees.

During 2003 and 2004, the UFCW made efforts to organize Wal-Mart stores in Saskatchewan, British Columbia, and Manitoba. Wal-Mart won a victory in Saskatchewan when it successfully challenged the constitutionality of that province's labour law, which restricts employer-employee communication during an organizing drive. Wal-Mart argued that workers should hear the whole story before deciding whether to join a union.

The UFCW's strategy has been to organize stores in Canada because labour laws are stronger here than they are in the United States. In Quebec, for example, the card-based certification system allows workers to unionize by signing cards rather than having an actual vote. UFCW president Wayne Hanley calls this a "luxury" that does not now exist for unions in the United States (but the U.S. Congress is considering passage of such a bill). The UFCW is particularly interested in unionizing Wal-Mart's Supercentres in Alberta, British Columbia, and Ontario. That battle will be intense because Wal-Mart is deeply committed to its strategy of providing customers with very low prices.

There is also a lot at stake for the UFCW. Food workers make up about 60 percent of UFCW membership, and 40 percent of those work for Loblaw. But Loblaw management has become more aggressive in dealing with unions because its market share is under attack from Wal-Mart. When 800 workers went on strike in Quebec, Loblaw closed 13 Maxi outlets there until the strike was resolved. The UFCW also has to cope with declining unionization rates in the retail food industry. In the 1980s, 60–70 percent of food workers were unionized, but now only 40–50 percent are unionized.

Wal-Mart is not the only company where unions are trying to gain a foothold. In September 2008, Ken Lewenza, the new president of the Canadian Auto Workers (CAW), said that employees at WestJet, the discount air carrier, are "ripe" for organizing. The CAW already represents call-centre workers and customer service agents at Air Canada, and the CAW wants to organize the same types of workers at WestJet. The idea is being played down by WestJet, which says that it has a very positive corporate culture, a profit-sharing plan, and a share purchase program in which 80 percent of its employees take part. The Pro-Active Communication Team (PACT)—a non-union group that represents about 6300 WestJet workers—also represents workers' concerns, and the president of PACT sits on WestJet's board of directors. ◆

How will this help me?

By reading and understanding the material in this chapter, you'll gain insights into why employees at some companies decide to join a union, why conflict sometimes exists between managers and unions, and the influence that unions have on the operations of unionized companies. As an employee, you'll find useful information that will help you decide whether or not you wish to join a union, and as a manager you'll understand your responsibilities in dealing with unionized employees.

In this chapter, we begin by looking at the development of labour unions, their importance in the Canadian economic system, and the laws that govern labour–management relations. We then describe how unions are certified as the bargaining agents for groups of employees. Next, we explain the collective bargaining process and the major issues that are part of the process. We conclude with a discussion of what happens when labour and management have difficulty reaching an agreement on important issues.

Why Do Workers Unionize?

1 Explain why workers organize into *labour unions*.

labour union A group of individuals working together to achieve shared job-related goals, such as higher pay, shorter working hours, more job security, greater benefits, or better working conditions.

labour relations The overall process of dealing with employees who are represented by a union.

collective bargaining The process by which union leaders and managers negotiate specific terms and conditions of employment for workers who are represented by unions.

Over 2000 years ago, the Greek poet Homer wrote, "There is a strength in the union even of very sorry men." There were no labour unions in Homer's time, but his comment is a particularly effective expression of the rationale for unions. A **labour union** is a group of individuals working together to achieve shared job-related goals, such as higher pay, shorter working hours, more job security, greater benefits, or better working conditions.[1] **Labour relations** describes the overall process of dealing with employees who are represented by a union. **Collective bargaining** is the process by which union leaders and managers negotiate specific terms and conditions of employment for workers who are represented by unions.

The labour movement was born with the Industrial Revolution, which also gave birth to a factory-based production system that carried with it enormous economic benefits. Job specialization and mass production allowed businesses to create ever-greater quantities of goods at ever-lower costs. But there was also a dark side to this era. Workers became more dependent on their factory jobs. Eager for greater profits, some owners treated their workers simply as resources to be deployed, with little or no regard for the individual worker's well-being. Many businesses forced employees to work long hours; sixty-hour weeks were common, and some workers were routinely forced to work 12 to 16 hours per day.

With no minimum-wage laws or other controls, pay was also minimal, and safety standards were virtually non-existent. Workers enjoyed no job security and received few benefits. Many companies, especially textile mills, employed large numbers of children at poverty wages. If people complained, nothing prevented employers from firing and replacing them at will. Unions developed because they forced management to listen to the complaints of all their workers rather than to just the few who were brave (or foolish) enough to speak out. The power of unions comes from collective action.

The Development of Canadian Labour Unions

2 Trace the evolution of unions and discuss *trends in unionism* in Canada.

The earliest evidence of labour unions in Canada comes from the Maritime provinces early in the nineteenth century. Generally, these unions were composed of individuals with a specific craft (e.g., printers, shoemakers, barrel makers). Most of these unions were small and had only limited success. However, they laid the foundation for the rapid increase in union activity that occurred during the late nineteenth and early twentieth centuries.

A succession of labour organizations sprang up and just as quickly faded away during the years 1840–70. In 1873, the first national labour organization was formed—the Canadian Labour Union. By 1886, the Knights of Labour (a U.S.-based union) had over 10 000 members in Canada. The Canadian labour movement began to mature with the formation of the Trades and Labour Congress (TLC) in 1886. The TLC's purpose was to unite all labour organizations and to work for the passage of laws that would ensure the well-being of the working class.

The growth of labour unions began in earnest early in the twentieth century as the concept of organized labour gradually came to be accepted. Various disputes arose that resulted in numerous splits in labour's ranks. For example, there was concern that U.S.-based unions would have a detrimental effect on Canadian unions. The Canadian Federation of Labour was formed in 1908 to promote national (Canadian) unions over U.S. unions. These and other disputes—such as how communists in the movement should be handled—often led to the creation of rival union organizations that competed for membership. By 1956, these disputes had been largely resolved, and the two largest congresses of affiliated unions—the Trades and Labour Congress

The Canadian Labour Congress (CLC), which was formed in 1956, brought the majority of unionized workers in Canada into one organization.

and the Canadian Congress of Labour—merged to form the Canadian Labour Congress. This amalgamation brought approximately 80 percent of all unionized workers into one organization. Table 9.1 highlights some of the important events in Canadian labour history.

Unionism Today

Unions in Canada today face both opportunities and potentially serious threats. This is evident when we look at trends in union membership, trends in union-management relations, trends in bargaining perspectives, and the future of unions.

Trends in Union Membership

During the last 40 years, unions have experienced difficulties in attracting new members. Although 4.5 million workers belonged to unions in 2008, union membership as a proportion of the non-agricultural workforce (called *union density*) has stagnated, and less than one-third of Canadian workers belong to unions. As shown in Figure 9.1, during the period 1970–2008, union density has ranged from 25.8 percent to 30.5 percent. In the United States, union density is even lower (12.1 percent).[2]

Women are now a more important part of the union movement than in earlier years. In 1967, women accounted for less than 20 percent of union membership in Canada, but now they represent about half of all union workers. Unionized women are highly concentrated in the public sector, which provides jobs for only 19 percent of the workforce but accounts for 43 percent of all union members.[3]

Table 9.1 Some Important Dates in Canadian Labour History

1827	First union formed: boot and shoemakers in Quebec City
1873	Canadian Labour Union formed; objective was to unite unions across Canada
1879	First coal miners union in North America formed in Nova Scotia
1902	Formation of the National Trades and Labour Congress (became the Canadian Federation of Labour [CFL] in 1908); purpose was to promote national unions instead of international ones
1919	Winnipeg General Strike
1921	Confédération des Travailleurs Catholiques du Canada (CTCC) organized by the Roman Catholic clergy in Quebec; goal was to keep French-Canadian workers from being unduly influenced by English-speaking and American trade unions
1927	All-Canadian Congress of Labour (ACCL) formed; objective was to achieve independence of the Canadian labour movement from foreign control
1939	TLC expels industrial unions; Canadian Congress of Industrial Organization (CIO) Committee formed
1940	ACCL and the Canadian CIO Committee unite to form the Canadian Congress of Labour (CCL)
1956	TLC and CCL merge to form the Canadian Labour Congress (CLC)
1982	Founding convention of Canadian Federation of Labour (CFL)
1985	Formation of United Auto Workers of Canada; formerly part of international UAW
1994	Major league baseball players strike; no World Series played
1997	Strike of primary and secondary school teachers in Ontario
1999	Quebec nurses strike
2004–05	NHL players locked out; entire season lost
2005–09	United Food and Commercial Workers union tries to organize workers at various Wal-Mart locations across Canada; Wal-Mart aggressively resists; each group wins some battles and loses others
2009	Members of the Canadian Auto Workers union agree to significant wages cuts as part of an overall package designed to keep Chrysler and General Motors in business

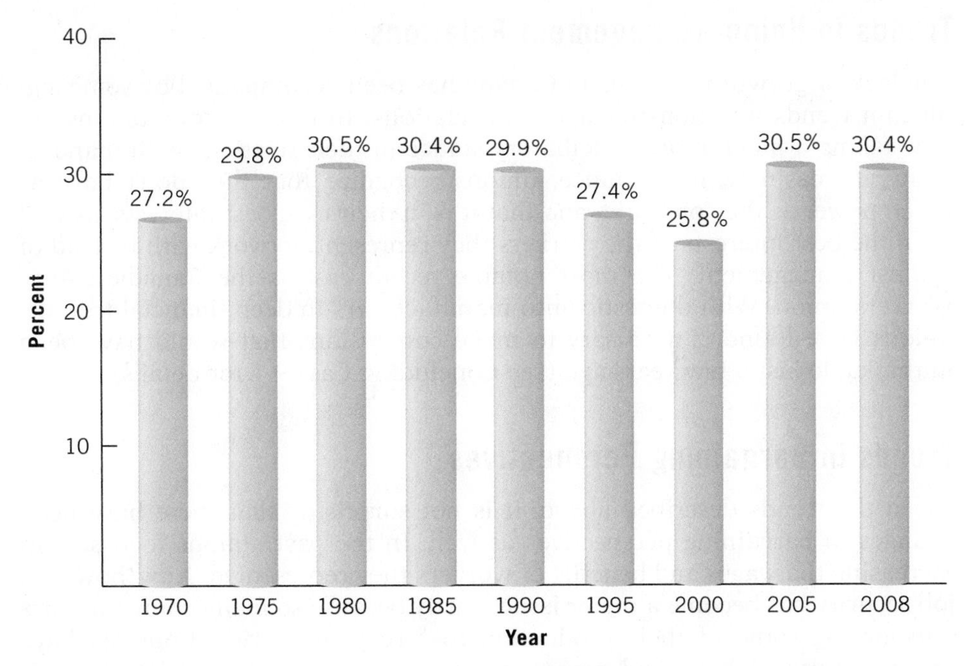

Figure 9.1 Union members as a proportion of the non-agricultural workforce.

The highest rates of unionization are found in Newfoundland (37.7 percent) and Quebec (37.5 percent). The lowest rates are found in Alberta (23.0 percent) and New Brunswick (26.4 percent). The public sector is quite heavily unionized (72.7 percent), but the private sector is not (18.1 percent).[4] In some occupations—for example, teaching and nursing—over 80 percent of workers are unionized. In other occupations—for example, management and food and beverage workers—less than 10 percent of the workers belong to unions.[5]

Over the years, unions have experienced ups and downs in terms of their success at becoming certified at new locations. Many years ago, unions routinely won certification votes. But in recent years, they have encountered increasing opposition from companies that are trying to survive in a fiercely competitive global environment. Two factors help explain the difficulties that unions have faced in recent years.

Composition of the Workforce

Traditionally, union members have been predominantly white males in blue-collar jobs, but today's workforce is increasingly composed of women and ethnic minorities. Because these groups have much weaker traditions of union affiliation, their members are less likely to join unions when they enter the workforce. In a related trend, the workforce is increasingly employed in the service sector, which traditionally has been less heavily unionized.

Anti-unionization Activities

Employers have become much more aggressive in pursuing anti-unionization. Federal and provincial labour legislation restricts what management of a company can do to keep out a union, but companies are free to pursue certain strategies to minimize unionization. For example, Japanese auto manufacturers who have set up shop in North America have avoided unionization efforts by the United Auto Workers (UAW) by providing job security and a work environment in which employees are allowed to participate and be actively involved in plant management. The Toyota plant in Cambridge, Ontario, is just one example.

Trends in Union–Management Relations

The lack of growth in unions in Canada has been accompanied by some significant trends in union–management relations. In most sectors, unions are now taking a much more conciliatory stance in their relations with management; increasingly, for instance, unions recognize that they don't have as much power as they once did, and that it is in their own best interests, as well as in the best interests of the workers they represent, to work with instead of against management. The most notable recent case is the Canadian Auto Workers union. With domestic auto manufacturers in deep financial trouble, unions have found it necessary to make concessions that would have been unthinkable just a few years ago (see Concluding Case 9-1 for details).

Trends in Bargaining Perspectives

Given the trends described above, it is not surprising that there have been changes in bargaining perspectives as well. In the past, unions focussed on increasing the wages and benefits of workers they represented. Now, however, job security has become a major issue, partly because so many companies are outsourcing some of their production to foreign countries. Conflicts have arisen between labour and management as unions try to restrict management's freedom to outsource. But unions have had limited success in achieving job security for their members.

Bargaining perspectives have also been influenced by organizational downsizing, low inflation, and the recession that began in 2008. All of these factors have made it more difficult for unions to bargain for big wage increases for their members. Most unions now have adopted the strategy of preserving what they have won in the past. They are also focussing more on pensions since those have also become an area of concern given the financial difficulties many companies are facing. (More detail on the pension crisis is presented in Chapter 14.)

The Future of Unions

Despite stagnant membership and loss of power, labour unions remain a significant factor in Canadian business. The labour organizations in the Canadian Labour Congress and large independent unions such as the International Brotherhood of Teamsters and the Canadian Union of Public Employees can disrupt the economy by refusing to work. The votes of their members are still sought by politicians at all levels. In addition, the concessions they have won for their members—better pay, shorter working hours, and safer working conditions—now benefit many non-unionized workers as well.

The challenges facing unions are many:

- the continuing decline of the so-called "smokestack industries" (for example, automobile manufacturing), where union power has traditionally been very strong
- employment growth in service industries, where union power has traditionally not been strong
- deregulation, which has led to mergers and layoffs and to the emergence of new, non-unionized companies
- free trade and the globalization of business, which has resulted in many jobs being moved to areas of the world with lower labour costs
- technological change, which increases the difficulty of organizing workers and threatens existing unionized jobs

Unions are increasingly aware that they must co-operate with employers if both companies and unions are to survive and prosper. The goal is to create effective partnerships in which managers and workers share the same goals: profitability, growth, and effectiveness, with equitable rewards for everyone. The big question is this: Will unions be able to cope with the many challenges that are currently facing them, or will their power continue to dwindle? Some experts think that a new wave of unionism may be about to sweep across Canada. This movement may be fuelled by young people (including college and university graduates) who fear they will be stuck in low-wage jobs and who hope unions can help them avoid that fate.

The Legal Environment for Unions in Canada

Describe the major *laws governing labour–management relations.* 3

In the early twentieth century, there were many political and legal barriers to unionism, and the balance of bargaining power was very much in favour of the employer. Courts often held that unions were conspiring to restrain business activities, and employers viewed their employees' efforts to unionize as attempts to deprive the employers of their private property. Employers also felt that the employment contract should be between individual workers and the employer—not between the employer and employees as a group. As firms grew in size, the employer–employee relationship became much less direct and communication among owners, managers, and workers became more distant and formalized. These trends, together with mounting public concern about worker safety and health issues, resulted in several laws being passed that were designed to place the worker on a more even footing with the employer.

In 1900, government concern about labour disputes resulted in the passage of the Conciliation Act. The act was designed to help settle labour disputes through voluntary conciliation and was a first step in creating an environment more favourable to labour. A more comprehensive law, the 1907 **Industrial Disputes Investigation Act**, provided for compulsory investigation of labour disputes by a government-appointed board before a strike was allowed. However, this act was later found to violate a fundamental provision of the British North America Act (BNA Act, see below).

Industrial Disputes Investigation Act (1907) Provided for compulsory investigation of labour disputes by a government-appointed board before a strike was allowed.

The current environment for unions did not come into being until 1943 when **Privy Council Order 1003** was issued. This order recognized the right of employees to bargain collectively, prohibited unfair labour practices on the part of management, established a labour board to certify bargaining authority, and prohibited strikes and lockouts except in the course of negotiating collective agreements.

Privy Council Order 1003 (1943) Recognized the right of employees to bargain collectively.

The **Constitution Act** (originally the BNA Act), passed in 1867, has also affected labour legislation. This act allocates certain activities to the federal government (e.g., labour legislation for companies operating interprovincially) and other activities to individual provinces (labour relations regulations in general). Thus, labour legislation emanates from both the federal and provincial governments but is basically a provincial matter. That is why certain groups of similar employees might be allowed to go on strike in one province but not in another.

Constitution Act (1867) Divided authority over labour regulations between the federal and provincial governments.

Federal Legislation: The Canada Labour Code

The **Canada Labour Code** regulates the labour practices of firms operating under the legislative authority of parliament. The code is composed of three main sections.

Canada Labour Code Legislation that applies to the labour practices of firms operating under the legislative authority of parliament.

Industrial Relations

Part I of the Canada Labour Code deals with all matters related to collective bargaining. It is subdivided into seven divisions:

- Division I—gives employees the right to join a trade union and gives employers the right to join an employers association.
- Division II—establishes the Canada Labour Relations Board, whose role is to make decisions on a number of important issues (e.g., certification of trade unions).
- Division III—stipulates the procedures required to acquire or terminate bargaining rights.
- Division IV—establishes the rules and regulations that must be adhered to during bargaining; also presents guidelines for the content and interpretation of collective agreements.
- Division V—states the requirement that the Minister of Labour must appoint a conciliation officer if the parties in the dispute cannot reach a collective agreement.
- Division VI—stipulates the conditions under which strikes and lockouts are permitted.
- Division VII—is a general conclusion that states methods that might be used to promote industrial peace.

Occupational Health and Safety

This section of the code describes the responsibilities of both employers and employees in maintaining a safe workplace. Every person running a federal work project must do so in a way that will not endanger the health or safety of any employee. Appropriate safety procedures and techniques must be implemented to reduce the risk of employment injury. Employees are required to exercise care to ensure their own safety; however, even if it can be shown that the employee did not exercise proper care, compensation must still be paid if an injury occurs. This section also makes provisions for a safety officer, whose overall duty is to ensure that the code is being honoured. The safety officer has the right to enter any federal project "at any reasonable time."

Standard Hours, Wages, Vacations, and Holidays

This section—which contains 16 major divisions—covers non-managerial workers and deals with issues such as standard hours of work (8-hour days and 40-hour weeks), maximum hours of work per week (48), overtime pay (at least one and a half times the regular pay), minimum wages, equal wages for men and women doing the same jobs, vacations, general holidays, sick leave, and maternity leave. The specific provisions are changed frequently to take into account changes in the economic and social structure of Canada, but their basic goal is to ensure consistent treatment of employees in these areas.

In 2005, a review of the Canada Labour Code was announced by the federal minister of labour. One of the issues that the review focussed on was whether managers and supervisors should also be protected by labour code restrictions on the number of hours they work each week, and whether they should receive overtime pay. The issue came to the forefront after the Manitoba Labour Board ruled that Sharon Michalowski, a manager at Nygard International, was entitled to overtime pay, even though she was a manager and had signed a contract stipulating that she would work whatever hours were required to earn her annual salary of $42 000.[6] As of 2009, managers were still not covered by the provisions of the Canada Labour Code.

Provincial Labour Legislation

Each province has enacted legislation to deal with the personnel practices covered in the Canada Labour Code. These laws vary across provinces and are frequently revised; however, their basic approach and substance is the same as that of the Canada Labour Code. Certain provinces may exceed the minimum code requirements on some issues (e.g., minimum wage). Each province also has a labour relations act. To give an indication of what these acts cover, the Ontario Labour Relations Act is briefly described below.

The Ontario Labour Relations Act

The Ontario Labour Relations Act is a comprehensive document dealing with the conduct of labour relations in that province. Some illustrative provisions of the Ontario law are noted below.

- A trade union may apply at any time to the Ontario Labour Relations Board (OLRB) for certification as the sole bargaining agent for employees in a company.
- The OLRB has the right to call for a certification vote. If more than 50 percent of those voting are in favour of the trade union, the board certifies the union as the bargaining agent.
- Following certification, the union gives the employer written notification of its desire to bargain, with the goal being the signing of a collective agreement. The parties are required to begin bargaining within 15 days of the written notice.
- On request by either party, the minister of labour appoints a conciliation officer to confer with the parties and to help achieve a collective agreement. On joint request, the minister of labour can appoint a mediator.
- The parties may jointly agree to submit unresolved differences to voluntary binding arbitration. The decision of the arbitrator is final.
- Employers are required to deduct union dues from the union members and remit these dues directly to the union.
- Every agreement must include a mechanism for settling grievances—differences between the parties arising from interpretation, application, or administration of the collective agreement.
- If a person objects to belonging to a labour union because of religious beliefs, he or she is allowed to make a contribution equal to the amount of the union dues to a charitable organization.
- If a trade union is not able to negotiate a collective agreement with management within one year of being certified, any of the employees in the union can apply to the OLRB for decertification of the union.
- No employer can interfere with the formation of a union. The employer is, however, free to express an opinion about the matter.
- No employer shall refuse to employ an individual because he or she is a member of a trade union.

The basic provisions of the Ontario Labour Relations Act are found in one form or another in the labour relations acts of all provinces, but the details and procedures vary from province to province. Administering labour relations activity is complex and time-consuming, and company management, the union, and the government all expend much time and energy in an attempt to ensure reasonable relations between management and labour.

Union Organizing Strategy

4 Describe the union *certification* and *decertification* processes.

A union might try to organize workers when a firm is trying to move into a new geographical area, or when some workers in a firm are members and the union wants to represent other workers, or when it is attempting to outdo a rival union. Management often becomes aware of a union organizing effort through gossip from the company grapevine. For example, management at Honda and Toyota plants in Ontario learned that the CAW had launched organizing drives at their plants. The CAW distributed leaflets at plant gates and contacted groups of workers inside the plant as part of its organizing drive.[7] As we saw in the opening case, WestJet also became aware of union plans to unionize WestJet's workers.

When management discovers that an organizing drive is underway, it may try to counteract it. However, management must know what it can legally do to discourage the union. In Quebec, McDonald's has been the target of union organizing drives at several of its restaurants. After a McDonald's restaurant in Saint-Hubert closed (when it appeared that the Teamsters union might be successful in getting certified as the bargaining agent for the employees), critics called for a government investigation into the possibility of unfair labour practices on the part of the company.[8]

bargaining unit Individuals grouped together for purposes of collective bargaining.

certification vote A vote supervised by a government representative to determine whether a union will be certified as the sole bargaining agent for the unit.

decertification The process by which employees legally terminate their union's right to represent them.

craft unions Unions organized by trades; usually composed of skilled workers.

Certifying a Union: An Example

Suppose that a union is trying to organize employees of a Manitoba company. If it can show that at least 50 percent of the employees are members of the union, it can apply to the Manitoba Labour Board (MLB) for certification as the sole bargaining agent for the employees. During the process, there may be an issue regarding the right of different types of workers to join or not join the union. For example, supervisors may or may not be included in a bargaining unit along with non-management workers. The **bargaining unit** includes those individuals deemed appropriate by the province, and the MLB has final authority in determining the appropriateness of the bargaining unit. Professional and non-professional employees are generally not included in the same bargaining unit unless a majority of the professional employees wish to be included. Once the MLB has determined that the unit is appropriate, it may order a **certification vote**. If a majority of those voting are in favour of the union, it is certified as the sole bargaining agent for the unit.

The outcome of this certification vote will determine whether these workers at Michelin will be represented by a union.

The same law that grants employees the right to unionize also allows them to cease being represented by a union. **Decertification** is the process by which employees legally terminate their union's right to represent them. A labour dispute over job security and safety that arose at Goldcorp Inc.'s gold mine near Red Lake, Ontario, led to a strike involving 100 workers. The strike was settled when workers agreed to decertify their union in return for severance pay that was four times the rate mandated by Ontario law.[9] In another case, the Manitoba Labour Board decertified Local 832 of the United Food and Commercial Workers for workers at the Hampton Inn & Suites in Winnipeg. The workers said they weren't getting value for the dues they were paying to the union.[10]

Types of Unions

The two basic types of union are craft and industrial unions. **Craft unions** are organized by crafts or trades—

plumbers, barbers, airline pilots, and so forth. Craft unions restrict membership to workers with specific skills. In many cases, members of craft unions work for several different employers during the course of a year. For example, many construction workers are hired by their employers at union hiring halls. When the particular job for which they are hired is finished, these workers return to the hall to be hired by another employer.

Craft unions have a lot of power over the supply of skilled workers because they have apprenticeship programs. A person who wants to become a member of a plumbers union, for example, must go through a training program. He or she starts out as an apprentice. After the training, the apprentice is qualified as a journeyman plumber.

Industrial unions are organized according to industries, for example, steel, auto, and clothing. Industrial unions include semi-skilled and unskilled workers and were originally started because industrial workers were not eligible to join craft unions. Industrial union members typically work for a particular employer for a much longer period of time than do craft union members. An industrial union has a lot of say regarding pay and human resource practices within unionized firms.

industrial unions Unions organized by industry; usually composed of semi-skilled and unskilled workers.

The **local union** (or local) is the basic unit of union organization. A local of a craft union is made up of artisans in the same craft in a relatively small geographical area. A local of an industrial union is made up of workers in a given industry or plant in a relatively small geographical area. Thus, plumbers in a local labour market may be members of the local plumbers union. Truck drivers and warehouse workers in that same area may be members of a Teamsters local.

local union (or local) The basic unit of union organization.

The functions of locals vary, depending not only on governance arrangements but also on bargaining patterns in particular industries. Some local unions bargain directly with management regarding wages, hours, and other terms and conditions of employment. Many local unions are also active in disciplining members for violations of contract standards and in pressing management to consider worker complaints.

A **national union** has members across Canada. These members belong to locals that are affiliated with the national union. There are many national unions in Canada, including the Canadian Union of Public Employees, the National Railway Union, and the Canadian Airline Pilots Union. About two-thirds of unionized Canadian workers belong to national unions.

national union A union with members across Canada.

An **international union** is a union with members in more than one country. One example is the United Steelworkers of America, made up of locals in the United States and Canada. About 30 percent of unionized workers in Canada belong to international unions.

international union A union with members in more than one country.

An **independent local union** is one that is not formally affiliated with any labour organization. It conducts negotiations with management at a local level, and the collective agreement is binding at that location only. The University of Manitoba Faculty Association is an independent local union. Less than 5 percent of unionized workers in Canada belong to independent local unions. Table 9.2 lists the 10 largest unions in Canada.

independent local union One not formally affiliated with any labour organization.

Union Security

The growing job security consciousness of Canadian workers is reflected in union goals. The seniority provision in most contracts spells out the workers' rights when layoffs, transfers, and promotions occur. Employees are ranked by length of service, and those with longer service receive better treatment. Much conflict exists regarding seniority. For example, women and members of minority groups typically have less seniority and are the first to be laid off and the last to move up to higher jobs. These workers tend to oppose the tradition of seniority.

Table 9.2 The Top 10 Unions in Canada, 2008

Union	Membership
1. Canadian Union of Public Employees (CLC)	570 000
2. National Union of Public and General Employees (CLC)	340 000
3. United Steel, Paper and Forestry, Rubber, Manufacturing, Energy, Allied Industrial and Service Workers International Union (AFL-CIO/CLC)	280 000
4. National Automobile, Aerospace, Transportation and General Workers Union of Canada (CAW Canada) (CLC)	255 000
5. United Food and Commercial Workers Canada (CtW/CLC)	245 327
6. Public Service Alliance of Canada (CLC)	173 686
7. Communications, Energy, and Paperworkers Union of Canada (CLC)	142 592
8. Fédération de la santé et des services sociaux (CSN)	122 193
9. Teamsters Canada (CtW/CLC)	108 516
10. Service Employees International Union (CtW/CLC)	92 781

union security The means of ensuring the union's continued existence and the maintenance of its membership so that it can continue to meet the criteria for certification.

closed shop An employer can hire only union members.

union shop An employer can hire non-unionized workers, but they must join the union within a certain period.

agency shop All employees for whom the union bargains must pay dues, but they are not required to join the union.

open shop An employer may hire union or non-union workers.

Union security refers to the means of ensuring the union's continued existence and the maintenance of its membership so that it can continue to meet the criteria for certification. The greatest union security is found in the **closed shop**, where an employer can hire only union members. For example, a plumbing or electrical contractor who hires workers through a union hiring hall can hire only union members. In a **union shop**, an employer may hire non-union workers even if the employer's current employees are unionized. New workers, however, must join the union within a stipulated period of time (usually 30 days). In an **agency shop**, all employees for whom the union bargains must pay dues, but they need not join the union. This compromise between the union shop and the open shop is called the Rand formula after the judge who proposed it. In the Quebec Labour Code, the Rand formula applies to all unions certified under this code. In an **open shop**, an employer may hire union and/or non-union labour. Employees need not join or pay dues to a union in an open shop.

Collective Bargaining

5 Identify the steps in the *collective bargaining* process.

When people think about collective bargaining, they usually think about the point at which a formal contract is signed between a union and a company. But collective bargaining is an ongoing process, and includes all of the time that is spent on drafting the agreement *before* it is signed, as well as all the time required to administer the contract *after* it has been signed.

Reaching Agreement on the Contract's Terms

The collective bargaining process begins with the recognition of the union as the sole bargaining agent for its members. The bargaining cycle begins when union leaders meet with management representatives to agree on a new contract. By law, both parties must negotiate "in good faith." When each side has presented its demands, the focus is on identifying the *bargaining zone*. This process is shown in Figure 9.2. For example, although an employer may initially offer no pay raise, it may expect to grant a raise of up to 6 percent. Likewise, the union may initially *demand* a 10 percent pay raise while *expecting* to accept a raise as low as 4 percent. The bargaining zone, then, is a raise between 4 and 6 percent.

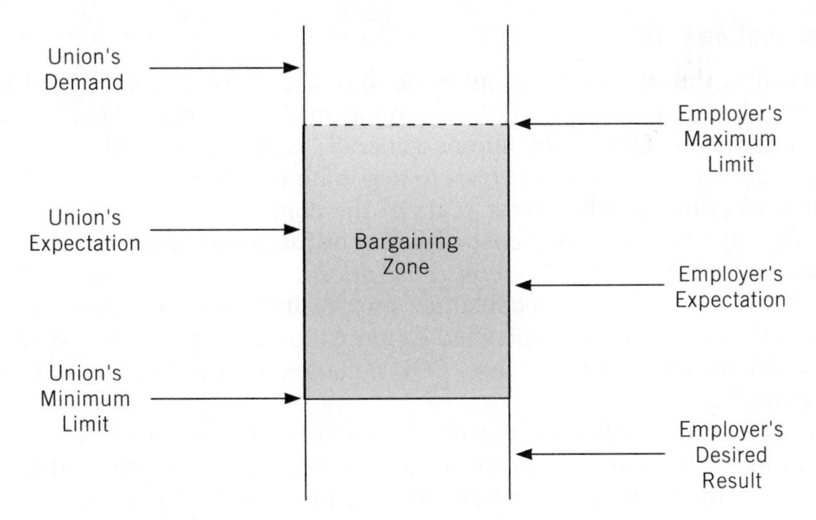

Figure 9.2 The bargaining zone.

Some compromise is usually reached between these levels, and the new agreement is submitted for a ratification vote by union membership.

Sometimes, this process goes quite smoothly. At other times, however, the two sides cannot—or will not—agree. The speed and ease with which such an impasse is resolved depend in part on the nature of the contract issues, the willingness of each side to use certain tactics, and the prospects for mediation or arbitration.

Contract Issues

The labour contract can address an array of different issues. *Mandatory items* are matters over which both parties must negotiate if either wants to. This category includes wages, working hours, and benefits. *Permissive items* may be negotiated if both parties agree. For example, a union demand for veto power over the promotion of managerial personnel would be a permissive bargaining item. Most contract issues arise from demands that unions make on behalf of their members. The main issues that typically are evident during labour–management negotiations are compensation, benefits, and job security.

Representatives of labour and management negotiate in an attempt to reach an agreement on a labour contract. Here, members of the Canadian Auto Workers and managers representing Ford Canada are negotiating the terms of a collective agreement. These negotiations have become very difficult as the automobile industry has experienced significant financial problems in the last few years.

Compensation

Historically, the most common issue has been compensation (although recently job security has become very important). One aspect of compensation is current wages. Obviously, unions generally want their employees to earn higher wages and so the union tries to negotiate increases in hourly wages for all members during subsequent years of the contract. One common tool for securing wage increases is a **cost-of-living adjustment (COLA)**. Most COLA clauses tie future raises to the *consumer price index (CPI)*, a government statistic that reflects changes in consumer purchasing power. The premise is that as the CPI increases by a specified amount during a given period of time, wages will automatically increase. COLA clauses are not as common as they used to be.

cost-of-living adjustment (COLA) A contract clause specifying that wages will increase automatically with the rate of inflation.

Wage reopener clauses may also be included. Such a clause allows wage rates to be renegotiated at preset times during the life of the contract. For example, a long-term agreement will be more acceptable to a union if management agrees to renegotiate the wage component every two years.

wage reopener clause A contract clause that allows wage rates to be renegotiated at preset times during the life of the contract.

Benefits

Unions typically want employers to pay all or most of the costs of various kinds of insurance for employees. Other benefits commonly addressed during negotiations include retirement benefits, working conditions, and the cost of supplementary health care (prescription drugs, eye care, dental care, etc.). The health-care issue is becomingly increasingly contentious during negotiations because the cost of health care is rapidly increasing. In one recent year, for example, General Motors spent more on health-care benefits for its 1.1 million workers than it did on steel. And insurance premiums for drug plans are doubling every five years.[11]

Job Security

Job security is an increasingly important agenda item in bargaining sessions. In some cases, demands for job security result in a promise by the company that it will not move to another location. In others, a contract may dictate that if the workforce is reduced, seniority will be used to determine which employees keep their jobs. The recession that started in 2008 meant that unions had to pay more attention to saving jobs than to getting big wage increases. Unions are also concerned about preserving jobs because so many businesses are outsourcing production to countries where labour costs are cheaper. For example, Gildan Activewear outsources much of its production to low-wage countries in the Caribbean.

Other Issues

Other possible issues might include such things as working hours, overtime policies, rest period arrangements, differential pay plans for shift employees, the use of temporary workers, grievance procedures, and allowable union activities (dues collection, union bulletin boards, and so forth).

Management wants as much control as possible over hiring policies, work assignments, and so forth. Unions, meanwhile, often try to limit management rights by specifying hiring, assignment, and other policies. At one Chrysler plant, for example, the contract stipulated that three workers were needed to change fuses in robots: a machinist to open the robot, an electrician to change the fuse, and a supervisor to oversee the process. Labour contracts often bar workers in one job category from performing work that falls within the domain of another. Unions try to secure jobs by defining as many different categories as possible (the Chrysler plant had over 100). Management resists this practice, which limits flexibility and makes it difficult to reassign workers.

During collective bargaining, it is not uncommon for intense conflicts to develop. The boxed insert entitled "Butting Heads Around the World" identifies several issues that are currently important.

Business Accountability

Butting Heads Around the World

The world has become a very complicated place for unions as international competitiveness becomes a key issue for business firms. In their drive to increase efficiency and cut costs, unionized businesses have come into conflict with the unions that represent their workers. Some typical examples of problems are described below.

The United States

Some creative (and controversial) tactics are being used by unions in the United States as they attempt to cope with declining membership. Two large unions—the Service Employees International Union and Unite Here—signed deals with several large employers giving those employers the right to designate which of their locations they will allow the unions to try to organize. If enough workers sign cards indicating a desire to join the union, the union will be certified as the bargaining agent. There are no secret-ballot elections as there normally are during an organizing campaign. The unions agree that if they are certified, they will not go on strike at these locations, and they will not make derogatory comments about the company. The company sites where these arrangements will be put in place are selected jointly by union and management. Union members have not been allowed to see the details of these agreements.

Critics have expressed concern that these deals are undemocratic and non-transparent. They also violate long-standing union traditions. The unions defend their actions, saying that they are succeeding in adding more workers to union rolls at a time when union membership is declining (in 2007, just 7.5 percent of private sector workers belonged to unions in the United States; in 1982, the figure was 17 percent). The unions also point out that traditional organizing campaigns have been ineffective and new approaches are needed.

Controversy has also developed over outsourcing. In 2008, about 27 000 members of the International Association of Machinists went on strike at Boeing Co. after negotiations broke down. The machinists at Boeing have gone on strike about once every 10 years since the 1960s. The latest strike was primarily about outsourcing, with Boeing saying it needs the flexibility that outsourcing gives and the union expressing concern about lost jobs. Workers point to the problems with the new 787 Dreamliner as proof that outsourcing is unwise (see the boxed insert Business Accountability in Chapter 2 for more details). In an embarrassing development, Boeing had to ask its own workers to help put the first few outsourced subassemblies together after they arrived with lots of parts missing. Union members said if the company had let them do the work in the first place, production delays would not have occurred. Boeing counters that outsourcing has helped it reduce the time it takes to build an airplane by 50 percent. Boeing has increasingly relied on outsourcing since the mid-1990s.

Canada

The Mississaugas of Scugog Island First Nation operate the Great Blue Heron Charity Casino in Port Perry, Ontario. A collective agreement was in place with the Canadian Auto Workers that covered 1000 casino workers (very few of whom were band members). The band wanted to replace the collective agreement with its own labour agreement, which contained the following provisions: employees would not have the right to strike, the union would have to pay $3000 to speak with the workers, and employees would be required to pay $12 000 to file an unfair labour practice complaint. The band felt that it could drop the collective agreement with the CAW because the band had Aboriginal treaty and self-government rights. When the band tried to implement the new labour agreement, the CAW filed a grievance. Eventually, the Ontario Court of Appeal rejected the band's arguments on the grounds that the band had not proven that a labour code was part of its tradition, nor that it was integral to its ancestral culture.

In the summer of 2008, members of the International Association of Machinists and Aerospace Workers (IAMAW) began wearing buttons with the message "Prepare to walk the line in '09" as the expiry date of their collective agreement neared. Air Canada management accused the union of trying to prejudice the bargaining process and ordered workers to stop wearing the buttons when they were in view of Air Canada's customers. The union then filed a grievance, saying that the buttons were simply an attempt to promote solidarity among union members. The union also created a combative song, which is sung to the tune of Johnny Cash's famous hit "I Walk the Line."

Germany

Deutsche Telekom AG is Europe's largest telecommunications company, but it is trying to become much more efficient so it can cope with increased competition from smaller rivals.

It is therefore planning to downsize its labour force. The company points out that two-thirds of Deutsche Telekom's employees are in Germany, but they generate less than one-half of the company's total revenue. This does not sit well with the union, partly because forced layoffs are rare in Germany. The plan is to reduce the number of call centres from 63 to 24, shift fixed-line service technicians into lower-paying jobs, and lay off thousands of other workers in the IT unit. These plans have been made by the company at the same time that other German unions are aggressively seeking higher wages, so the negotiations are going to be difficult.

After a bitter strike in 2007, the company gained the right to shift a large number of employees from fixed-line jobs into lower-paying jobs. But it says it has to do even more to remain competitive. Investors agree. The stock price has been stagnant, and analysts say the company needs to cut its fixed-line work force in half. The company wants to achieve competitive personnel costs by 2010.

Critical Thinking Questions

1. Why would the Service International Union and Unite Here sign collective agreements that don't allow their members to strike? Doesn't this put the union at a disadvantage when dealing with management?
2. What are the advantages and disadvantages of labour unions? At the present time, do you think the advantages outweigh the disadvantages? Explain.
3. Consider the following statement: *The interconnectedness of the global economy means that companies have no choice but to be cost competitive on an international level. That means that labour unions in Europe and North America are going to have to agree to significant wage concessions or they will be unable to compete with low-cost Asian companies. If unions don't agree to wage concessions, the companies that employ unionized workers will go bankrupt, and workers will have no job instead of one with reduced wages.* Do you agree or disagree with the statement? Explain your reasoning.

When Bargaining Fails

impasse Occurs when, after a series of bargaining sessions, management and labour are unable to agree on a first-time contract or a contract to replace an agreement that is about to expire.

An **impasse** occurs when, after a series of bargaining sessions, management and labour are unable to agree on a first-time contract or a contract to replace an agreement that is about to expire. Although it is generally agreed that both parties suffer when an impasse is reached, each side can employ several tactics to support its cause until the impasse is resolved.

Union Tactics

Unions can take a variety of actions when their demands are not met. Chief among these are *strikes*, *picketing*, *boycotts*, and *work slowdowns*.

strike Employees temporarily walk off the job and refuse to work.

Strikes. A **strike** occurs when employees temporarily walk off the job and refuse to work. During 2008, 500 workers at PotashCorp. of Saskatchewan were on strike for 99 days. They eventually agreed to a new contract that was not much different than the one management had offered during negotiations.[12] In 2007, nearly 2800 workers at Canadian National Railway went on strike. The strike caused major disruptions in the movement of raw materials and finished goods, and Ford closed its auto assembly plant at St. Thomas, Ontario, because it couldn't get enough supplies by rail to keep running.[13]

During the period 1996–2005, OECD countries averaged 42 working days lost as a result of strikes. The United Kingdom averaged just 23 days lost, France 53, Italy 99, and Canada 208.[14] The most strike-prone sectors in Canada were mining and transport/communication.[15]

Strikes triggered by impasses over mandatory bargaining items are called *economic strikes*, even if they occur over non-economic issues such as working hours. Most strikes in Canada are economic strikes. The strike by PotashCorp workers in 2008, the CN Rail strike in 2007, and the NHL players strike in 2004–05 were largely over economic issues.

During a strike, workers are not paid and the business is usually unable to produce its normal range of products and services. After a strike is over, employees may exhibit low morale, anger, increased absenteeism, and decreased productivity. In these situations, care must be taken to improve communications between management and workers.[16] If a strike goes on for a long time, it can create very negative outcomes for both the company and its workers. In 2000, production workers at the Versatile tractor plant in Winnipeg went on strike. After many months with no settlement in sight, the union offered to go back to work, but management locked the workers out. The union then filed an unfair labour practices claim against the company, saying that management never intended to re-start production at the Winnipeg plant because it was planning to move operations to North Dakota. Eventually, the Manitoba Labour Relations Board fined Versatile $6 million for bargaining in bad faith. The union finally agreed to a deal that paid the workers for the entire period they were on strike, but the deal also involved closing the plant, and all the workers lost their jobs.[17]

Not all strikes are legal. The Ontario primary and secondary school teachers strike against the province of Ontario in 1997 was illegal because the teachers had not gone through the necessary steps prior to going out on strike. The teachers voluntarily returned to work after striking for only two weeks. Nurses in Quebec and Saskatchewan also carried out illegal strikes. **Sympathy strikes** (also called **secondary strikes**), where one union strikes in sympathy with strikes initiated by another labour organization, may violate the sympathetic union's contract. **Wildcat strikes**—those that are not authorized by the union that occur during the life of a contract—deprive strikers of their status as employees and thus of the protection of labour laws.

sympathy strikes (also secondary strikes) ikes initiated by another labour organization.

wildcat strikes Strikes that are not authorized by the union and that occur during the life of a contract.

Unions are more reluctant to use the strike weapon than they used to be. One reason is that more and more workers are in profit-sharing plans, meaning that they receive a portion of company profits. Going on strike has a negative effect on profits, so workers are hurting themselves if they go on strike. Other reasons are the decline in union power, the bad publicity generated by strikes, and the fact that technology and globalization mean that companies can easily displace highly paid but low-skilled workers.[18]

Picketing. As part of or instead of a strike, unions faced with an impasse may picket their employer. **Picketing** involves having workers march at the entrance to the company with signs explaining their reasons for striking. During the

picketing A tactic of labour unions in which members march at the entrance to the company with signs explaining their reasons for striking.

Pilots who belong to the Air Canada Pilots Association walk the picket line during a strike.

labour dispute between the Telecommunications Workers Union (TWU) and Telus Corp., for example, union workers picketed the company. Telus responded by getting an injunction to prevent picketers from blocking access to the property.[19]

boycott Union members agree not to buy the product of the firm that employs them.

Boycotts. A **boycott** occurs when union members agree not to buy the product of the firm that employs them. Workers may also urge other consumers to shun their firm's product.

work slowdown Workers perform their jobs at a much slower pace than normal.

Work Slowdowns. In a **work slowdown**, workers perform their jobs at a much slower pace than normal. A variation is the "sickout," during which large numbers of workers call in sick.

Management Tactics

Management can respond to an impasse using a variety of tactics, including *lockouts, strikebreakers, plant closures, contracting out,* and forming *employers' associations*.

lockout A tactic of management in which the firm physically denies employees access to the workplace to pressure workers to agree to the company's latest contract offer.

Lockouts. **Lockouts** occur when employers physically deny employees access to the workplace. Management might lock workers out, for example, if they fear that workers will damage expensive equipment. In 2007, Petro-Canada workers were locked out of the Montreal refinery for more than a year. The company kept the refinery running by using replacement workers.[20] The lockout is illegal if it is used as an offensive weapon to give the firm an economic advantage in the bargaining process (for example, if sales are poor and management wants to avoid a buildup of inventory).

strikebreaker An individual hired by a firm to replace a worker on strike.

Strikebreakers. Firms faced with a strike can hire temporary or permanent replacements (**strikebreakers**) to replace the striking employees. The National Football League used replacement players during a strike in 1987, and National Hockey League owners planned to use minor league hockey players if they could not reach an agreement with striking NHL players in 1992.

Plant Closures. In extreme cases, management may simply close down a plant if they cannot reach agreement with the union. For example, Maple Leaf Foods closed its Edmonton hog processing plant when the workers went on strike there. That cost 850 workers their jobs. In 2009—when GM and Chrysler were thinking of declaring bankruptcy—there was speculation that they would be able to dissolve high-cost union collective agreements ("union busting") as part of the bankruptcy plan. But Canadian laws are different than U.S. laws, and collective agreements are not necessarily negated when a bankruptcy occurs.[21]

Contracting Out. Some firms *contract out* work as a way to blunt the effect of the union. Instead of doing all the assembly work they used to do themselves, many firms now contract out work to non-union contractors. This lessens the impact the unions can have because it results in fewer union workers.

employers' associations Groups of companies that get together to plan strategies and exchange information about how to manage their relations with unions.

Employers' Associations. **Employers' associations** are groups of companies that get together to plan strategies and exchange information about how to manage their relations with unions. They are especially important in industries that have many small firms and one large union that represents all workers. Member firms sometimes contribute to a strike insurance fund. Such a fund could be used to help members whose workers have struck. They are similar in purpose to the strike funds built up by unions.

Mediation and Arbitration

Rather than using their "weapons" on one another, labour and management can agree to call in a third party to help resolve the dispute. In **mediation**, the neutral third party (a mediator) is called in to advise the disputing parties about how they might reach a settlement. The mediator cannot impose a settlement. In 2008, when the United Steelworkers union and PotashCorp. of Saskatchewan were initially unable to reach a collective agreement, both parties asked for a mediator to help them with their contract talks.[22] Postal workers did the same in 2008, when they had difficulty reaching agreement with management about a new collective agreement.[23]

mediation A method of settling a contract dispute in which a neutral third party is asked to hear arguments from both the union and management and offer a suggested resolution.

In **voluntary arbitration**, the neutral third party (an arbitrator) dictates a settlement between two sides that have agreed to submit to outside judgment. In 2008, for example, Air Canada and the Canadian Union of Public Employees requested that an arbitrator decide on an exit package for Air Canada employees who lost their job when the company cut 2000 jobs.[24] In some cases, arbitration is legally required to settle bargaining disputes. Such **compulsory arbitration** is used to settle disputes between government and public employees such as firefighters and police officers.

voluntary arbitration A method of settling a contract dispute in which the union and management ask a neutral third party to hear their arguments and issue a binding resolution.

compulsory arbitration A method of settling a contract dispute in which the union and management are forced to explain their positions to a neutral third party who issues a binding resolution.

Administering a Labour Agreement

Once a labour agreement has been reached, its details are written down in the form of a contract that is legally enforceable in the courts. Labour contracts almost always have precise wording as to how the agreement will be enforced. In some cases, enforcement is quite clear. If the two sides agree that the company will increase wages by 2 percent per year over the next three years according to a prescribed schedule, then there is little opportunity for disagreement because wage increases can be mathematically calculated and union members will see the effects in their paycheques. However, other provisions may be much more prone to misinterpretation and conflicting perceptions.

Suppose, for example, that a labour contract specifies the process for allocating overtime assignments. Such strategies are often complex, and the employer may have to take into account a variety of factors, such as seniority, previous overtime allocations, the hours or days in which the overtime work is needed, and so forth. Now suppose that a factory supervisor is trying to follow the labour contract and offers overtime to a certain employee. This employee, however, indicates that before he or she can accept the overtime, it may be necessary to check with the individual's spouse or partner about other obligations and commitments. The supervisor may feel the pressure of a deadline and instead award the overtime opportunity to someone else. If the first employee objects to this course of action, he or she may file a complaint with the union.

When such differences of opinion arise, the union member takes the complaint to the **shop steward** (a regular employee who acts as a liaison between union members and supervisors). The shop steward may advise the employee that the supervisor handled things properly, but there are other appeal mechanisms, and the employee, even if refused by the shop steward, still has channels for appeal.

shop steward A regular employee who acts as a liaison between union members and supervisors.

If the shop steward agrees with the employee, prescribed methods for pursuing the complaint are followed. The prescribed methods might include talking with the supervisor to hear the other side of the story and then providing for an appeal further up the hierarchy of both the union and the company. In some cases, mediation or arbitration may be tried, as may other efforts to resolve the dispute. The overtime, for example, may be reassigned to the employee to whom it was first offered. Or the overtime may remain with the second employee while the first employee is also paid.

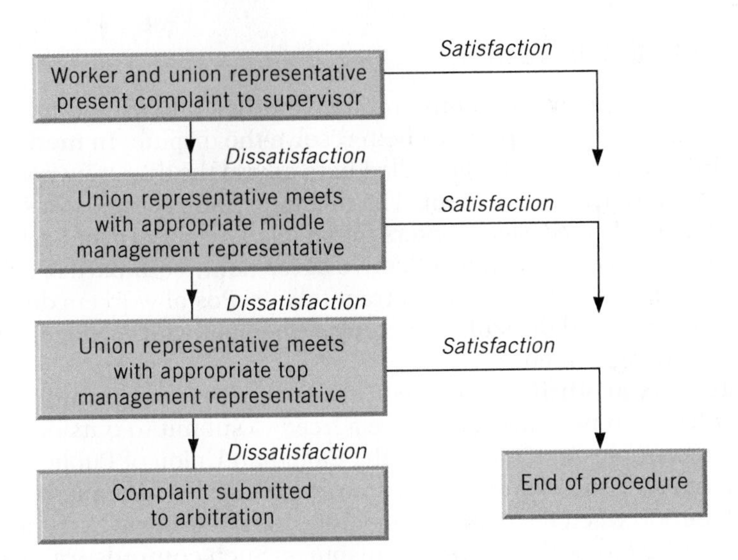

Figure 9.3 A typical grievance procedure.

grievance A complaint by a worker that a manager is violating the terms of the collective agreement.

A **grievance** is a complaint by a worker that a manager is violating the terms of the collective agreement. Figure 9.3 traces a typical grievance procedure. The union generally promises not to strike over disputes about contract interpretation. In return, unions get the right to file grievances in a formal procedure that culminates in binding arbitration. Most grievance arbitrations are about disputes regarding the discipline or discharge of employees, but safety issues are a cause for arbitration in some industries.

Test yourself on the material for this chapter at **www.pearsoned.ca/mybusinesslab**.

Summary of Learning Objectives

1. **Explain why workers organize into *labour unions*.** The Industrial Revolution and the emergence of a factory-based production system made many workers dependent on continuing factory employment, where abuses such as minimal pay, long workdays and workweeks, unsafe working conditions, and even child labour were common. Individuals had little recourse in rectifying problems. By organizing into *labour unions*, however, workers were able to act collectively to improve work conditions. Most importantly, acting as a group, they can engage in *collective bargaining* for higher wages, greater benefits, or better working conditions.

2. **Trace the evolution of unions and discuss *trends in unionism* in Canada.** The first unions in Canada were formed in the early nineteenth century in the Maritime provinces. Many labour organizations sprang up and then faded away during the nineteenth century. In the twentieth century, unions began to develop in earnest. In 1943, *Privy Council Order 1003* gave unions the right to bargain collectively with employers.

   Since the mid-1970s, labour unions in Canada have experienced increasing difficulties in attracting new members. While millions of workers still belong to labour unions, union membership as a percentage of the total workforce has been stagnant for many years. Unions recognize that they do not have as much power as they once held and that it is in their own best interests, as well as the best interests of the workers they represent, to work with management instead of against it. Bargaining perspectives have also altered in recent years.

3. **Describe the major *laws governing labour–management relations*.** Privy Council Order 1003 gave unions the right to collectively bargain in Canada. The *Constitution Act of 1867* allows the federal government to pass labour legislation (such as the *Canada Labour Code*) for companies that operate interprovincially and allows the

provincial governments to pass legislation (such as the Ontario Labour Relations Act) for companies that operate in only one province.

4. **Describe the union *certification* and *decertification* processes.** If a union can show that a certain percentage (usually 50 percent) of employees of a company are members of the union, it can apply to a provincial labour relations board for *certification* as the sole bargaining agent for the employees. A certification vote is then held. If a majority of the employees are in favour of the union, it is certified. To *decertify* a union, employees must vote to do so.

5. **Identify the steps in the *collective bargaining process.*** Once certified, the union engages in *collective bargaining* with the organization. The initial step in collective bargaining is reaching agreement on a *labour contract.* Contract demands usually involve wages, job security, or management rights.

   Both labour and management have several tactics that can be used against the other if negotiations break down. Unions may attempt a *strike* or a *boycott* of the firm or may engage in a *work slowdown.* Companies may hire replacement workers (*strikebreakers*) or *lock out* all workers. In extreme cases, *mediation* or *arbitration* may be used to settle disputes. Once a contract has been agreed upon, union and management representatives continue to interact to settle worker *grievances* and interpret the contract.

Key Terms

agency shop (p. 288)
bargaining unit (p. 286)
boycott (p. 294)
Canada Labour Code (p. 283)
certification vote (p. 286)
closed shop (p. 288)
collective bargaining (p. 278)
compulsory arbitration (p. 295)
Constitution Act (1867) (p. 283)
cost-of-living adjustment (COLA) (p. 290)
craft unions (p. 286)
decertification (p. 286)
employers' associations (p. 294)
grievance (p. 296)
impasse (p. 292)
independent local union (p. 287)
Industrial Disputes Investigation Act (1907) (p. 283)
industrial unions (p. 287)
international union (p. 287)
labour relations (p. 278)
labour union (p. 278)
local union (or local) (p. 287)
lockout (p. 294)
mediation (p. 295)
national union (p. 287)
open shop (p. 288)
picketing (p. 293)
Privy Council Order 1003 (1943) (p. 283)
shop steward (p. 295)
strike (p. 292)
strikebreaker (p. 294)
sympathy strikes (secondary strikes) (p. 293)
union security (p. 288)
union shop (p. 288)
voluntary arbitration (p. 295)
wage reopener clause (p. 290)
wildcat strikes (p. 293)
work slowdown (p. 294)

Questions for Analysis

1. Why do workers in some companies unionize while workers in other companies do not?
2. Why did it take so many years for the union movement to mature in Canada?
3. The proportion of the Canadian workforce that is unionized has been nearly constant for more than 15 years. Why hasn't the proportion increased or decreased?
4. Workers at the Canadian plants of Ford, General Motors, and Chrysler are represented by the Canadian Auto Workers. Why are automobile workers at Toyota and Honda—who are doing exactly the same kind of work—not unionized?
5. Suppose that you are a manager in a non-unionized company. You have just heard a rumour that some of your workers are discussing forming a union. What would you do? Be specific.
6. What are the implications for management of a closed shop, a union shop, and an agency shop?
7. What impact will trends like globalization, intense global competition, and consumer interest in low prices have on the future viability of unions?

Application Exercises

1. Consider the following statement: *Many years ago, workers were treated very badly by management compared to the way they are treated now. Since unions exist largely to protect workers from unreasonable behaviour by management, the need for unions has disappeared.* Do you agree or disagree with this statement? Explain your position.
2. Interview the managers of two local companies, one unionized and one non-unionized. Compare the wage and salary levels, benefits, and working conditions of workers at the two firms.
3. With your instructor playing the role of management and a student playing the role of a union organizer, role-play the processes involved in trying to form a union.

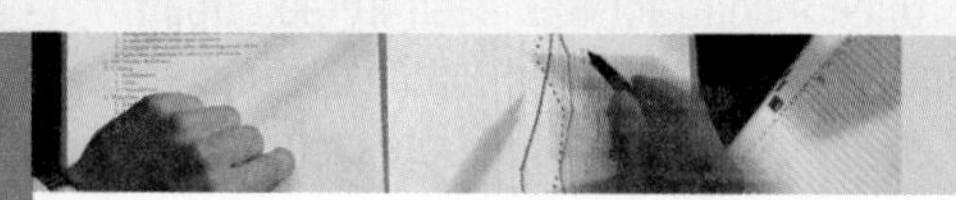

Building Your Business Skills

A Little Collective Bargaining

The Purpose of the Assignment

To encourage students to understand why some companies unionize and others do not.

The Situation

You've been working for the same non-union company for five years. Although there are problems in the company, you like your job and have confidence in your ability to get ahead. Recently, you've heard rumblings that a large group of workers want to call for a union election. You're not sure how you feel about this, because none of your friends or family members are union members.

Assignment

Step 1

Come together with three other "co-workers" who have the same questions as you do. Each person should target four companies to learn their union status. Avoid small businesses; choose large corporations such as Canadian National Railways, General Motors, and Wal-Mart. As you investigate, answer the following questions:

- Is the company unionized?
- Is every worker in the company unionized or only selected groups of workers? Describe the groups.
- If a company is unionized, what is the union's history in that company?
- If a company is unionized, what are the main labour–management issues?
- If a company is unionized, how would you describe the current status of labour–management relations? For example, is it cordial or strained?
- If a company is not unionized, what factors are responsible for its non-union status?

To learn the answers to these questions, contact the company, read corporate annual reports, search the company's website, contact union representatives, or do research on a computerized database.

Step 2

Go to the website of CUPE (www.cupe.ca) to learn more about the current status of the union movement. Then, with your co-workers, write a short report about the advantages of union membership.

Step 3

Research the disadvantages of unionization. A key issue to address is whether unions make it harder for companies to compete in the global marketplace.

Questions for Discussion

1. Based on everything you have learned, are you sympathetic to the union movement? Would you want to be a union member?
2. Are the union members you spoke with satisfied or dissatisfied with their union's efforts to achieve better working conditions, higher wages, and improved benefits?
3. What is the union's role when layoffs occur?
4. Based on what you have learned, do you think the union movement in Canada will stagnate or thrive in the years ahead?

Exercising Your Ethics: Team Exercise

What Should We Do?

The Situation

Danielle Yu works for a manager at a medium-sized, non-union company that is facing a serious union organizing campaign. Her boss, Curt Yaeger, who is determined to keep the union out, has just given Yu a list of things to do to thwart the efforts of the organizers. For example, he has strongly suggested that Yu do the following:

- Whenever Yu learns about a scheduled union meeting, she should schedule a "worker appreciation" event at the same time. He wants Yu to offer free pizza and hold a barbecue and to give cash prizes (winners have to be present to receive the prize).
- Look at the most recent performance evaluations of the key union organizers and terminate any of them who may have a low performance evaluation.
- Make an announcement that the firm is seriously considering new benefits such as on-site childcare, flexible work schedules, telecommuting options, and exercise facilities. Yu knows that the firm is indeed looking into these benefits, but she also knows that the boss is really not that enthusiastic about these ideas.

The Dilemma

When Yu questioned the ethics—and even the legality—of some of these tactics, Yaeger responded by saying, "Look, this is war." He went on to explain that he was seriously concerned that a union victory might lead to increased wages for employees which would, in turn, increase the company's cost structure and reduce its competitiveness. That could force the company to outsource production activities and, in the extreme, lead to a shutdown of the company's entire Canadian operation. He noted that a number of Canadian companies have been outsourcing significant amounts of work in the last few years. Yaeger concluded by saying that he was really looking out for the employees, even if he had to play hardball to help them. Yu realizes that there is some truth to what Yaeger says about job losses, but she is not convinced that this is the way to proceed.

Team Activity

Assemble a group of four students and assign each group member to one of the following roles:

- Danielle Yu
- Curt Yaeger
- A worker who is thinking about joining the union
- A stockholder of the company

Action Steps

1. Before discussing the situation with your group, and from the perspective of your assigned role, what do you think should be done in this situation?
2. Before discussing the situation with your group, and from the perspective of your assigned role, what are the underlying ethical issues in this situation? Write down the issues.
3. Gather the group together and reveal, in turn, each member's ideas regarding the situation.
4. Appoint someone to record the main points of agreement and disagreement within the group. How do you explain the results? What accounts for the disagreements?
5. From an ethical standpoint, what does your group conclude is the most appropriate action that should be taken? (Note: You may find that the concepts of utility, rights, justice, and caring that were discussed in Chapter 3 are helpful in making your decision.)

For additional cases and exercise material, go to **www.pearsoned.ca/mybusinesslab.**

Concluding Case 9-1

It's the Latest Crisis in the Automobile Business

During the last few decades, trends such as the globalization of business, free trade, and intense cost competition have affected all types of Canadian businesses. As managers try to achieve greater cost efficiencies, they have put increased pressure on unions and the workers they represent. These pressures are nowhere more evident than they are in automobile manufacturing

There has been a rapid decline in the number of Canadians employed in high-paying jobs in automobile assembly and automobile parts. In 2007, there were 20 000 fewer jobs in the industry than there were in 2002, and the recession that began in 2008 meant that many more jobs will likely be lost. Soon, the total number of cars made in the four so-called BRIC economies—Brazil, Russia, India, and China—may exceed the number of cars made in North America. Those four countries had the capacity to produce about 20 million cars in 2008, compared to the capacity of 17.4 million cars in North America.

In 2007, the Big Three (Ford, GM, and Chrysler) signed a new collective agreement with the UAW in the United States, which included a two-tiered wage system and a provision that new hires would get paid about half of what longer-term employees earn. The agreement also allowed car manufacturers to shift the cost of UAW retirees' medical costs off their balance sheets, and this further reduced their labour costs. The agreement meant that the Big Three manufacturers had less incentive to continue manufacturing automobiles in Canada unless the Canadian Auto Workers (CAW) union agreed to similar wage cuts.

When initially confronted with this idea, Buzz Hargrove, then president of the Canadian Auto Workers (CAW), flatly rejected the idea. But in the spring of 2008, he reached a surprisingly swift agreement with Ford Canada on a new collective agreement that included a provision that newly hired workers would receive just 70 percent of what existing workers were being paid. He said this did not mean that he had accepted the two-tiered wage idea because the new workers would move to wage parity with long-standing workers after three years. He also noted that the deal would keep labour costs level.

This development looked promising for Canadian workers, but a few months later events in the United States dashed this optimism. The CEOs of the Big Three went to the U.S. government to ask for a large bailout package and said if they didn't get it, Chrysler and GM might have to declare bankruptcy in 2009. The U.S. government essentially told them they had to reduce their labour costs to those of their Japanese competitors in the United States if they wanted bailout money. But that meant even further reductions in pay and benefits for auto workers. If the CAW did not also agree to wage cuts, 30 000 auto jobs could be lost in Canada. In 2009, GM got further concessions from the CAW in order to satisfy the conditions laid down by the Canadian government before it would agree to give GM a $3-billion emergency loan. Ford Canada also said in 2009 that it would have to renegotiate its deal to get more concessions from the CAW in order to remain competitive.

In 2009, the CAW published a report showing that it took CAW workers only 20.36 hours on average to assemble a car in Canada, while it took 21.66 hours at non-unionized Toyota. These numbers were used to support the argument that Canadian labour productivity more than compensated for the higher wages being paid to Canadian auto workers. But skeptics say that at some point higher labour costs overwhelm any advantage that is gained by producing cars more efficiently. For example, a plant that makes 25 cars per hour and has labour costs of $50/hour is less competitive than a plant that makes only 20 cars per hour but has labour costs of only $25/hour. Critics also claim that the CAW has been the victim of its own success in extracting large wage increases from Ford, GM, and Chrysler over the years. They point to the fact that CAW workers made more money than workers at non-unionized auto plants and more money than workers in many other types of businesses.

Movement toward pay reductions is already clear. In 2008, workers at a Magna auto parts plant in New York voted on a proposed agreement that would see wages cut by 25 percent, but with a promise that the plant would remain in operation. Management made it clear to the UAW that it couldn't continue to operate the plant unless workers' hourly wages were reduced.

Another problem facing unions is their persistent inability to organize auto workers at companies like Honda, Nissan, and Toyota. Those companies have used a variety of tactics to avoid unionization of their workers. For example, when Honda Motor Co. announced that it was going to build a new assembly plant in Indiana, it also stipulated that only people living within a certain distance of the plant could apply. Since many of the unionized laid-off auto workers from other plants in Indiana didn't live in the stipulated area, they weren't allowed to apply. (Note: Companies cannot refuse to hire workers based on union affiliation, but they can do so based on geographical location.) Honda says its approach is not designed to prevent unionization of the plant. Instead, it wants workers to be close to the plant so they can get to work when the weather is bad in the winter. The union doesn't believe this explanation. Wages at the new plant will be $15–$18 per hour, which is noticeably lower than the $26 per hour that unionized workers are paid in other car manufacturing plants in the region.

In 2007, there were 33 foreign automobile, engine, and transmission plants in the United States and not one of them was unionized by the UAW in spite of repeated attempts. In Canada, foreign car makers have also been successful at fending off organizing attempts by unions. Workers at Toyota Motor Corp. have refused to join the CAW on several different occasions. In 2008, another union—the International Association of Machinists—tried to organize workers, but just hours before a vote was to be held, the union withdrew its certification application and the vote was cancelled. Labour leaders say they will keep trying to organize the workers.

Questions for Discussion

1. In your own words, explain the problem facing Canadian car makers. What caused this problem to develop?
2. Consider the following statement: *Competitive and cost pressures from non-union automobile makers, as well as government demands that GM Canada and Chrysler reduce their cost structures, have forced the CAW to accept lower wages and benefits for their workers. This shows that unions no longer have the power to protect their members.* Do you agree or disagree with the statement? Explain your reasoning.
3. Why do you think workers who are given the chance to join a union often don't do so?
4. There has been much debate over the years about the pros and cons of unions. Develop a list of arguments (both pro and con) regarding the union movement.

Concluding Case 9-2

Labour Relations in Hollywood

In the fall of 2007, members of the Writers Guild of America (WGA) were involved in intense negotiations with the Alliance of Motion Picture and Television Producers (AMPTP), which is the organization that represents nearly 400 film and television production firms like NBC, ABC, CBS, Fox, MGM, Paramount, and Sony. The WGA members are the creative people who write the material for popular TV shows like *CSI*, *House*, *Jay Leno*, and *Grey's Anatomy*.

A key issue in the negotiations was the WGA's determination to get a bigger piece of the revenue pie from network shows that are eventually shown on so-called "new media" like smart phones and the internet. The two sides were unable to reach agreement on this issue, and 12 000 members of WGA went on strike on November 5, 2007. During the strike, no new episodes were written, so the major U.S. television networks had to put reruns on the air. The strike also caused the cancellation of the Golden Globe awards (the organizers of the awards feared that members of the WGA would set up picket lines).

The networks responded to the strike by airing some new reality shows and contest programs because those didn't require as much script-writing work. The networks lost millions of dollars of advertising revenues because advertisers didn't think that viewers would be very interested in watching reruns. A bigger long-term concern was that the strike would cause viewers to desert the networks altogether. The networks knew that even before the strike started, cable channels were already taking away viewers. The three long-time networks (ABC, CBS, and NBC) all lost 5 to 10 percent of their viewers during the strike. Jay Leno and Conan O'Brien—both of whom were WGA members—said they supported the strike, but both went back on the air without writers in January 2008. They said they didn't want to lay off their other staff just because the writers were on strike.

Negotiators for both sides continued meeting during December 2007 and January 2008, and finally reached a tentative agreement on February 8, 2008. WGA members then voted 92.5 percent in favour of ending the strike. The new contract was ratified by a 93.6 percent vote on February 26, 2008. As part of the deal, the networks agreed to writers' demands for a piece of the revenues generated by TV shows that are downloaded on the internet. The studios agreed to pay writers $1200 a year for two years for any show that runs online and 2 percent of any revenue beyond two years.

Some Canadian firms hoped to benefit from the strike, but problems were created for others. On the positive side, the CEO of Corus Entertainment said that viewers who were frustrated with reruns might turn to Corus' pay-TV service for on-demand HBO shows such as *Entourage* and *The Wire*. The strike might also cause advertising revenue to flow to other media such as radio since advertisers would be looking for someplace other than TV to put their advertising dollars. Corus might have benefitted here too, since it is Canada's second largest radio operator, with 52 stations.

On the negative side, the strike and its fallout affected the CBC, which normally is able to rake in advertising revenue by televising the NHL playoffs. The spring is normally a good time because there is not much competition from the United States, but in 2008 all the U.S. networks were in the process of trying to get new shows on the air and win back viewers. So, Canada's networks faced a lot of competition in the spring of 2008 that they didn't normally have to cope with.

The strike may have been about compensation from new methods of distribution, but it also motivated the networks to think of ways to rein in what they saw as the writers' gravy train. The networks therefore started rethinking the way TV programs are made. In the past, networks gave writer-producers a big chunk of money to develop ideas for new shows. Some of those ideas would be made into pilot series, but only a handful of them would actually be aired. Development costs could reach $10 million for a one-hour show. The networks also took advantage of a legal notion called *force majeure*, which allows networks to cancel deals if the writers go on strike. On January 14, 2008, nearly 100 development deals were cancelled by the networks, which planned instead to spend a lot less money and be much more efficient by not doing pilots. Instead, they will simply put shows on the air and see how they do.

The networks are also saving money by cancelling extravagant social bashes where they preview and promote their fall schedules to advertisers. In tandem with this, they are placing less emphasis on the new fall shows and instead emphasizing year-round programming strategies to increase advertising dollars. They are doing this in part because they have come to realize that the reality shows that run in the summer attract a lot of viewers.

Questions for Discussion

1. Explain how the writers' strike demonstrates the key elements in labour–management relations.
2. Why would the networks have been concerned about the possibility that WGA members would set up a picket line at the Golden Globe awards?
3. When the WGA members went on strike, why didn't the networks simply hire new writers so the network schedule wouldn't be disrupted?
4. Do you think there was a clear winner in this dispute? Explain.

apter 10

Motivating and Leading Employees

After reading this chapter, you should be able to:

1. Identify and discuss the basic *forms of behaviour* that employees exhibit in organizations.
2. Describe the nature and importance of *individual differences* among employees.
3. Explain the meaning and importance of *psychological contracts* and the *person-job fit* in the workplace.
4. Identify and summarize the most important *models of employee motivation.*
5. Describe the *strategies* used by organizations to improve job satisfaction and employee motivation.
6. Define *leadership* and distinguish it from *management.*
7. Summarize the *approaches to leadership* that developed in the twentieth century.
8. Describe the most recent ideas about effective leadership.

What Do Employees Want?

Every manager wants to have employees who are satisfied and highly motivated; such employees exhibit positive behaviours like persisting even in the face of difficulties, being involved in continuous learning and improvement, and constantly finding ways to improve quality and productivity. These behaviours, in turn, lead to several positive outcomes for the organi-zation: higher customer satisfaction, greater profits, higher quality, and lower employee turnover. But how do managers achieve the goal of having highly motivated and satisfied workers? The most general answer is this: Give employees what they want (within reason, of course).

But what do employees want? Managers often assume that they know the answer to this question, but consider the results of two surveys. The Canadian Payroll Association analyzed the frequency with which 39 specific benefits were provided by companies to their employees. The top five items were term life insurance, car allowances, tuition fees, disability-related employment benefits, and professional membership dues. But another survey of worker opinions found that they rated flexible working hours, casual dress, unlimited internet access, opportunities to telecommute, and nap time as the most desirable. There are obviously major differences in these two lists, so managers are having some difficulty assessing what employees want.

Several other studies are consistent with this conclusion. For example, a Sirota Survey Intelligence study assessed employee satisfaction levels at 237 different companies during the period 1994–2003 and found that only 14 percent of these companies had workforces that could be classified as "enthusiastic." When the stock prices of 28 companies with enthusiastic workforces were compared to the average for publicly traded companies, it was found that they outperformed the average prices by more than two and a half times, while companies with unenthusiastic workforces lagged far behind the average stock prices. Companies with enthusiastic workforces also had fewer customer complaints, lower employee turnover, and higher quality in their products.

Another study of more than 3000 Canadian employees that was conducted by Watson Wyatt Canada revealed the following:

- Forty-six percent would consider changing jobs if a comparable job became available.
- Only 40 percent of employees believe they have real opportunities for advancement with their current employer.
- Only 27 percent of employees see any connection between their job performance and their pay.

In yet another study, the Gallup Organization focussed on the attitudes of 7200 workers in Canada, the United States, and Great Britain. The survey revealed that on most measures of job satisfaction, Canadian workplaces ranked behind those of the United States. For example, only 47 percent of Canadian workers were completely satisfied with their boss, while 60 percent of American workers were. Only 29 percent of Canadian workers were completely satisfied with their opportunities for promotion, while 40 percent of Americans were. And 37 percent of Canadian workers were completely satisfied with the recognition they received, while 48 percent of Americans were. Canadian workers were also less satisfied than American workers on several other issues, including the flexibility of their work hours, workplace safety, relationships with co-workers, and the amount of vacation time they received (even though they usually received more than Americans).

Most employees start work with considerable enthusiasm, but they often lose it. Much of the blame is laid at the feet of managers whose attitudes and behaviours depress employee enthusiasm. These include failing to express appreciation to employees for a job well done, assuming that they are lazy and irresponsible, treating them as disposable objects, failing to build trust with them, and quickly laying them off when the business gets in trouble. Managerial assumptions about employee satisfaction with pay can be particularly problematic. For example, many managers assume that workers will never be satisfied with their pay. But only a minority of workers rate their pay as poor or very poor, and many rate it as good or very good. A Kelly Workforce Index study showed that 58 percent of Canadian workers would be willing to accept a lower wage if they felt their work contributed something important to their organization. A poll by the staffing firm Randstad USA found that 57 percent of workers would be willing to work overtime without pay to impress their boss so that they would be less likely to be laid off as a result of an economic downturn.

One of the simplest ways for managers to motivate workers is to praise them. Yet this occurs far less often than it should. A *Globe and Mail* web poll showed that 27 percent of the 2331 respondents had never received a compliment from their boss. Another 10 percent had not received a compliment in the last year, and 18 percent had not received a compliment in the last month. This result is disturbing, since another survey showed that 89 percent of employees rate recognition of their work as "very important" or "extremely important."

When there is a disconnect between what companies provide for workers and what they really want, we should not be surprised if motivation and satisfaction levels of workers are not high. The real question is this: In the most general sense, what can be done to make worker and company needs more consistent? Part of the answer is provided in yet another survey, this one based on responses by 8000 Canadians. That survey found that the three most important things (for employees of all ages) were to be treated with respect, to be dealt with fairly, and to feel a sense of "connection" with the organization they worked for. Managers can have a very positive influence on all of these things. And that is what this chapter is all about. ◆

How will this help me?

Some people love their jobs, while others hate them. Most people, however, fall somewhere in between. Some of these feelings are caused by the type of leadership employees are experiencing, and some are caused by the type of work that the employees do. After studying the information in this chapter, you'll be better able to understand (1) your own feelings toward your work from the perspective of an employee, (2) the feelings of others toward their work from the perspective of a boss or owner, (3) how you can more effectively function as a leader, and (4) how your manager or boss strives to motivate you through his or her leadership style.

In this chapter, we describe the different forms of behaviour that employees can exhibit at work and how employee attitudes and personality influence their work. Then we look at some important ideas about employee motivation, some strategies and techniques used by organizations to improve employee motivation, and how leadership facilitates employee motivation and performance.

Forms of Employee Behaviour

1 Identify and discuss the basic *forms of behaviour* that employees exhibit in organizations.

Employee behaviour is the pattern of actions by the members of an organization that directly or indirectly influences the organization's effectiveness. **Performance behaviours** are the behaviours directly targeted at performing a job. An assembly line worker who sits by a moving conveyor and attaches parts to a product as it passes by has relatively simple performance behaviours. By contrast, a research-and-development scientist who works in a lab trying to find new scientific breakthroughs that have commercial potential has much more complex performance behaviours.

Other behaviours—called **organizational citizenship**—provide positive benefits to the organization but in more indirect ways. An employee who does satisfactory work in terms of quantity and quality but refuses to work overtime, won't help newcomers learn the ropes, and is generally unwilling to make any contribution beyond the strict performance requirements of the job is not a good organizational citizen. By contrast, an employee with a satisfactory level of performance who works late when the boss asks and takes time to help newcomers learn their way around is a good organizational citizen.

Counterproductive behaviours are those that detract from organizational performance. **Absenteeism** occurs when an employee does not show up for work. When an employee is absent, legitimately or not, that person's work does not get done and a substitute must be hired to do it, or others in the organization must pick up the slack.

Turnover refers to the percentage of an organization's workforce that leaves and must be replaced. Some turnover is natural and healthy, but high turnover

employee behaviour The pattern of actions by the members of an organization that directly or indirectly influence the organization's effectiveness.

performance behaviours The behaviours directly targeted at performing a job.

organizational citizenship Behaviours that provide positive benefits to the organization in indirect ways.

counterproductive behaviours Behaviours that detract from organizational performance.

absenteeism Occurs when an employee does not show up for work.

turnover The percentage of an organization's workforce that leaves and must be replaced.

has many negative consequences, including numerous vacancies, disruption in production, decreased productivity, and increased retraining costs. Turnover results from a number of factors, including aspects of the job, the organization, the individual, a poor person-job fit, the labour market, and family influences. One survey of 660 workers showed that 84 percent who worked for a "kind" manager planned to stay with their company a long time, while only 47 percent of those who worked for a "bully" said they planned to stay.[1]

Other forms of counterproductive behaviour may be even more costly for an organization. *Theft and sabotage*, for example, result in direct financial costs for an organization. *Sexual and racial harassment* also cost an organization, both directly (through financial liability if the organization responds inappropriately) and indirectly (by lowering morale, producing fear, and driving off valuable employees). *Workplace aggression and violence* are also counterproductive.

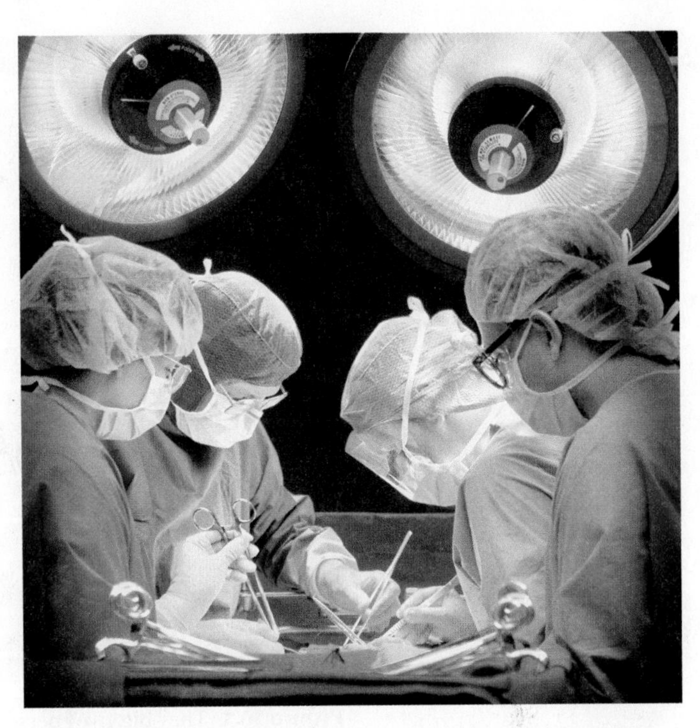

For some jobs, performance behaviours can be narrowly defined and easily measured. But for many other jobs, such as those held by scientists or doctors, performance behaviours are less objective, more diverse, and more difficult to assess.

Individual Differences Among Employees

Describe the nature and importance of *individual differences* among employees. **2**

Individual differences are physical, psychological, and emotional attributes that vary from one person to another. The individual differences that characterize a specific person make that person unique. *Personality* and *attitudes* are two main categories of individual differences.

individual differences Physical, psychological, and emotional attributes that vary from one person to another and that make each person unique.

Personality

Personality is the relatively stable set of psychological attributes that distinguishes one person from another. Researchers have identified five fundamental traits (the "big five") that are especially relevant to organizations (see Figure 10.1).

personality The relatively stable set of psychological attributes that distinguishes one person from another.

- *Agreeableness* is a person's ability to get along with others. A person with a *high* level of agreeableness is gentle, co-operative, forgiving, understanding, and good-natured in their dealings with others. A person with a *low* level of agreeableness is often irritable, short-tempered, uncooperative, and generally antagonistic toward other people. Highly agreeable people are better at developing good working relationships with co-workers, whereas less agreeable people are not likely to have particularly good working relationships.

- *Conscientiousness* refers to the number of things a person tries to accomplish. *Highly conscientious* people tend to focus on relatively few tasks at one time; as a result, they are likely to be organized, systematic, careful, thorough, responsible, and self-disciplined. *Less conscientious* people tend to pursue a wider array of tasks; as a result, they are often more disorganized and irresponsible, as well as less thorough and self-disciplined. Highly conscientious people tend to be relatively higher performers in a variety of different jobs.

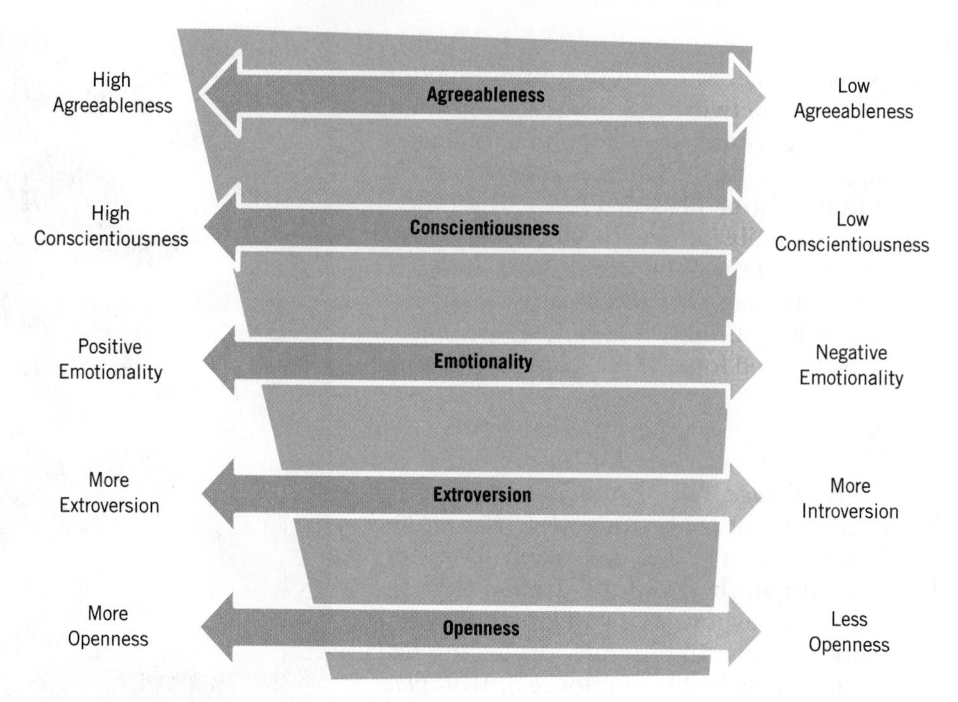

Figure 10.1 The "big five" personality traits.

- *Emotionality* refers to the degree to which people tend to be positive or negative in their outlook and behaviours toward others. People with *positive* emotionality are relatively poised, calm, resilient, and secure; people with *negative* emotionality are more excitable, insecure, reactive, and subject to mood swings. People with positive emotionality are better able to handle job stress, pressure, and tension. Their stability might also cause them to be seen as more reliable than their less-stable counterparts.
- *Extroversion* refers to a person's comfort level with relationships. *Extroverts* are sociable, talkative, assertive, and open to establishing new relationships, while *introverts* are much less sociable, less talkative, less assertive, and more reluctant to begin new relationships. Extroverts tend to be higher overall job performers than introverts and are more likely to be attracted to jobs based on personal relationships, such as sales and marketing positions.
- *Openness* reflects how open or rigid a person is in terms of his or her beliefs. People with *high* levels of openness are curious and willing to listen to new ideas and to change their own ideas, beliefs, and attitudes in response to new information. People with *low* levels of openness tend to be less receptive to new ideas and less willing to change their minds. People with more openness are often better performers due to their flexibility and the likelihood that they will be better accepted by others in the organization.

Emotional Intelligence

emotional intelligence (or emotional quotient [EQ]) The extent to which people possess social skills, are self-aware, can manage their emotions, can motivate themselves, and can express empathy for others.

Emotional intelligence, or emotional quotient (EQ), refers to the extent to which people possess social skills, are self-aware, can manage their emotions, can motivate themselves, and can express empathy for others.[2] Research suggests that people with high EQs may perform better than others, especially in jobs that require a high degree of interpersonal interaction and that involve influencing or directing the work of others. EQ appears to be something that isn't biologically based but that can be developed.[3]

Attitudes

Attitudes reflect our beliefs and feelings about specific ideas, situations, or other people. People in organizations have attitudes about many different things: their salary, their promotion possibilities, their boss, their employee benefits, and so on. People's attitudes also affect their behaviour in organizations. Especially important attitudes are *job satisfaction* and *organizational commitment*.

attitude A reflection of our beliefs and feelings about specific ideas, situations, or other people.

- **Job satisfaction** is the degree of enjoyment that people derive from performing their jobs. (A related concept—*morale*—refers to the overall attitude people have toward their workplace.) A satisfied employee tends to be absent less often, to be a good organizational citizen, and to stay with the organization. Dissatisfied employees tend to be absent more often, may experience stress that disrupts co-workers, and may be continually looking for another job. But a word of caution: Contrary to what a lot of managers believe, high levels of job satisfaction do not *automatically* lead to higher levels of productivity.

job satisfaction The degree of enjoyment that people derive from performing their jobs.

- **Organizational commitment** (sometimes called *job commitment*) reflects an individual's identification with the organization and its mission. Highly committed employees see themselves as true members of the firm, overlook minor sources of dissatisfaction, and see themselves remaining as members of the organization. Less committed employees are more likely to see themselves as outsiders, to express more dissatisfaction about the work situation, and to not see themselves as long-term members of the organization.

organizational commitment (or job commitment) An individual's identification with the organization and its mission.

One way to increase employee commitment is to give employees a voice. BBVA, Spain's second-largest bank, accomplishes this by including employees in the performance evaluation process. Not only is one's own self-evaluation considered, but co-workers also answer questions about each employee's performance. Infosys Technologies in Bangalore, India, started a Voice of Youth program, which gives top-performing young employees a seat on its management council.[4]

Matching People and Jobs

Explain the meaning and importance of *psychological contracts* and the *person-job fit* in the workplace. **3**

Given the array of individual differences that exist in people and the many different forms of employee behaviour that can occur in organizations, it is important to have a good match between people and the jobs they are performing. Two key concepts for facilitating this match are *psychological contracts* and the *person-job fit*.

Psychological Contracts

A **psychological contract** is the set of expectations held by an employee concerning what he or she will contribute to an organization (referred to as *contributions*) and what the organization will provide the employee in return (referred to as *inducements*). If either party perceives an inequity in the contract, that party may seek a change. The employee, for example, might ask for a pay raise, promotion, or bigger office, or might put forth less effort or look for a better job elsewhere. The organization can also initiate change by training workers to improve their skills, transferring them to new jobs, or terminating them. Unlike a business contract, a psychological contract is not written on paper, nor are all of its terms explicitly negotiated. Figure 10.2 illustrates the essential features of a psychological contract.

psychological contract The set of expectations held by an employee concerning what he or she will contribute to an organization (referred to as contributions) and what the organization will provide the employee in return (referred to as inducements).

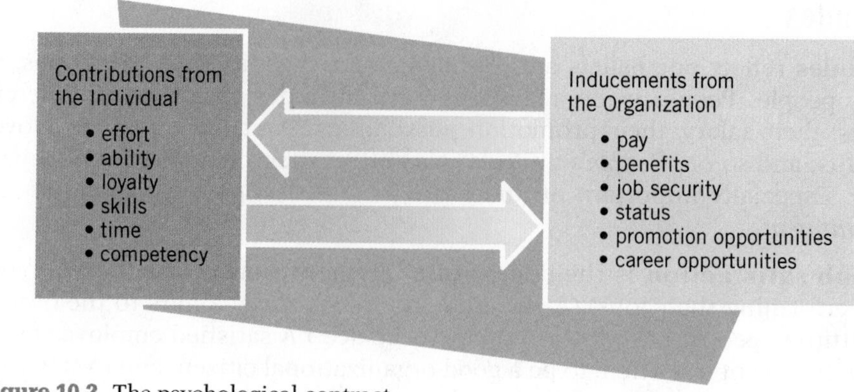

Figure 10.2 The psychological contract.

The downsizing and cutbacks that have occurred in Canadian businesses in recent years have complicated the process of managing psychological contracts. Many organizations, for example, used to offer at least reasonable assurances of job security as a fundamental inducement to employees. Now, however, because job security is less likely, alternative inducements—such as improved benefits packages or more flexible working hours—may be needed instead.

The Person-Job Fit

person-job fit The extent to which a person's contributions and the organization's inducements match one another.

The **person-job fit** refers to the extent to which a person's contributions and the organization's inducements match one another. Each employee has a specific set of needs that he or she wants fulfilled and a set of job-related behaviours and abilities to contribute. If the organization can take perfect advantage of those behaviours and abilities and exactly fulfill those needs, it will have achieved a perfect person-job fit. A good person-job fit, in turn, can result in higher performance and more positive attitudes. A poor person-job fit can have just the opposite effect.

Motivation in the Workplace

4 Identify and summarize the most important *models of employee motivation.*

motivation The set of forces that cause, focus, and sustain workers' behaviour.

Motivation is the set of forces that cause, focus, and sustain workers' behaviour. One worker may be motivated to work hard to produce as much as possible, while another may be motivated to do just enough to get by. As we saw in the opening case, effective managers recognize that because today's workers have diverse and complex needs, they must be motivated in increasingly complex ways. As well, the varying lifestyles of a diverse workforce mean that managers must pay close attention to what their employees expect to receive for their efforts and then try to link rewards with job performance.

Over the years, many theories have been proposed to address the issues of motivation. Three major approaches to motivation in the workplace have been evident—these approaches reflect a chronology of thinking about motivation: *classical theory and scientific management, behaviour theory,* and *contemporary motivation theories*.

Classical Theory and Scientific Management

classical theory of motivation Workers are motivated solely by money.

According to the so-called **classical theory of motivation**, workers are motivated solely by money. In his book *The Principles of Scientific Management* (1911), industrial engineer Frederick Taylor proposed a way for both companies and workers to benefit from this widely accepted view of life in the workplace.[5] If workers are motivated by money, Taylor reasoned, then paying them more would prompt them to produce more. Meanwhile, the firm that analyzed jobs and found better ways to perform them would be able to produce goods more cheaply, make higher profits, and thus pay—and motivate—workers better than its competitors.

Taylor's approach—known as **scientific management**—captured the imagination of many managers in the early twentieth century. Companies across Canada and the United States hired experts to perform *time-and-motion studies*—pioneered by Frank and Lillian Gilbreth—in order to discover the "one best way" of doing a job. Industrial-engineering techniques were applied to each facet of a job to determine how to perform it most efficiently. These studies were the first "scientific" attempts to break down jobs into easily repeated components and to devise more efficient tools and machines for performing them.[6] The results were impressive. For example, studies of workers loading iron on rail cars showed that productivity tripled.

The ideas of Frederick Taylor, the founder of scientific management, had a profound impact on the way manufacturing activities were carried out in the early twentieth century. His basic ideas are still used today.

Early Behavioural Theory

In 1925, a group of Harvard researchers began a study at the Hawthorne Works of the Western Electric Company. Their intent was to examine the relationship between changes in the physical environment and worker output, with an eye to increasing productivity. The results of the experiment at first confused, then amazed, the scientists. Increasing lighting levels improved productivity, but so did lowering lighting levels. And against all expectations, raising the pay of workers failed to increase their productivity. Gradually they pieced together the puzzle. The explanation for the lighting phenomenon lay in workers' response to the attention they were receiving. In essence, they determined that almost any action on the part of management that made workers believe they were receiving special attention caused worker productivity to rise. This result, known as the **Hawthorne effect**, convinced many managers that paying attention to employees is indeed good for business.

Following the Hawthorne studies, managers and researchers alike focussed more attention on how good **human relations**—the interactions

scientific management Analyzing jobs in order to find better, more efficient ways to perform them.

Hawthorne effect The tendency for workers' productivity to increase when they feel they are receiving special attention from management.

human relations The interactions between employers and employees and their attitudes toward one another.

The Hawthorne studies were an important step in developing an appreciation for the human factor at work. These women worked under different lighting conditions as researchers monitored their productivity. The researchers were amazed to find that productivity increased regardless of whether lighting levels increased or decreased.

between employers and employees and their attitudes toward one another—help in motivating employees. As they focussed on the ways in which management thinks about and treats employees, these researchers developed several now-classic motivation theories, including the *human resources model*, the *hierarchy of needs model*, and *two-factor theory*.

The Human-Resources Model: Theories X and Y

Theory X A management approach based on the belief that people must be forced to be productive because they are naturally lazy, irresponsible, and uncooperative.

Theory Y A management approach based on the belief that people want to be productive because they are naturally energetic, responsible, and co-operative.

Behavioural scientist Douglas McGregor concluded that managers had radically different beliefs about how best to use the human resources at a firm's disposal. He classified these beliefs into sets of assumptions that he labelled "Theory X" and "Theory Y."[7] Managers who subscribe to **Theory X** tend to believe that people are naturally lazy and uncooperative and must therefore be either punished or rewarded to be made productive. By contrast, managers who subscribe to **Theory Y** tend to believe that people are naturally energetic, growth oriented, self-motivated, and interested in being productive.

McGregor generally favoured Theory Y beliefs, and he argued that Theory Y managers are more likely to have satisfied, motivated employees. Of course, the Theory X and Theory Y distinctions are somewhat simplistic and offer little concrete basis for action. Their value lies primarily in their ability to highlight and analyze the behaviour of managers in light of their attitudes toward employees.

Maslow's Hierarchy of Needs Model

hierarchy of human needs model Theory of motivation describing five levels of human needs and arguing that basic needs must be fulfilled before people will work to satisfy higher-level needs.

Psychologist Abraham Maslow's **hierarchy of human needs model** proposed that people have five basic needs, which are arranged in a hierarchy of importance (see Figure 10.3). According to Maslow, lower-level needs must be largely satisfied before a person will be motivated to satisfy higher-level needs.[8]

- *Physiological needs* are survival oriented; they include food, water, shelter, and sleep. Businesses address these needs by providing both comfortable working environments and salaries sufficient to buy food and shelter.
- *Security needs* include the needs for stability and protection from the unknown. These needs are satisfied when employers offer pension plans and job security.

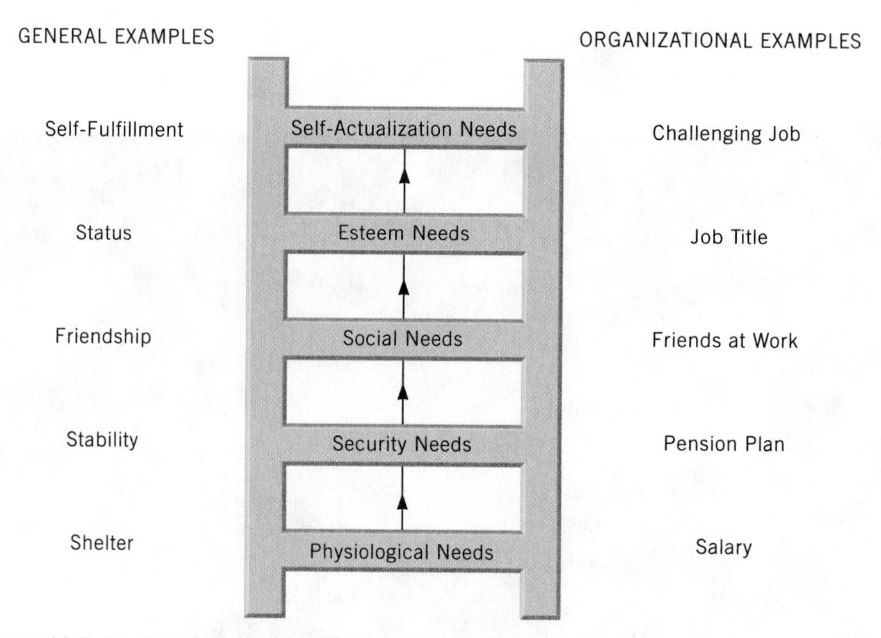

Figure 10.3 Maslow's hierarchy of human needs provides a useful categorization of the different needs people have.

- *Social needs* include the needs for friendship and companionship. Making friends at work can help to satisfy social needs, as can the feeling that you "belong" in a company.
- *Esteem needs* include the need for status and recognition as well as the need for self-respect. Job titles and large offices are among the things that businesses can provide to address these needs.
- Finally, *self-actualization needs* are needs for self-fulfillment. They include the needs to grow and develop one's capabilities and to achieve new and meaningful goals. Challenging job assignments can help satisfy these needs.

According to Maslow, once one set of needs has been satisfied, it ceases to motivate behaviour. For example, if you feel secure in your job, a new pension plan will probably be less important to you than the chance to make new friends and join an informal network among your co-workers. If, however, a lower-level need suddenly becomes unfulfilled, most people immediately refocus on that lower level. Suppose, for example, that you are seeking to meet your esteem needs by working as a divisional manager at a major company. If you learn that your division—and consequently your job—may be eliminated, you might very well find the promise of job security at a new firm as motivating as a promotion once would have been in your old company.

Two-Factor (Motivation-Hygiene) Theory

After studying a group of accountants and engineers, psychologist Frederick Herzberg proposed the **two-factor theory**, which says that job satisfaction and dissatisfaction depend on two factors: *hygiene factors* (such as working conditions, quality of supervision, interpersonal relations, pay, and job security) and *motivating factors* (such as recognition, responsibility, advancement, and achievement).[9] Motivation factors cause movement along a continuum from *no satisfaction* to *satisfaction*. For example, if workers receive no recognition for successful work, they may not be satisfied, but neither will they be dissatisfied. If recognition is provided, they will likely become more satisfied. Hygiene factors cause movement along a different continuum, one from *no dissatisfaction* to *dissatisfaction*. For example, workers will be dissatisfied if they feel that working conditions are poor, but if working conditions are improved, workers will not become *satisfied*; rather, they will no longer be *dissatisfied*. Overall, motivation factors are directly related to the *work* that employees actually perform, while hygiene factors refer to the *environment* in which they perform it (see Figure 10.4).

two-factor theory A theory of human relations developed by Frederick Herzberg that identifies factors that must be present for employees to be satisfied with their jobs and factors that, if increased, lead employees to work harder.

This theory thus suggests that managers follow a two-step approach to enhancing motivation. First, they must ensure that hygiene factors are acceptable. This practice will result in an absence of dissatisfaction. Then they must offer motivating factors as means of improving satisfaction and motivation.

Contemporary Motivation Theory

Recently, more complex models of employee behaviour and motivation have been developed. Two of the most interesting and useful ones are *expectancy theory* and *equity theory*.

Expectancy Theory

Expectancy theory suggests that people are motivated to work toward rewards that they want *and* that they believe they have a reasonable chance of obtaining.[10] A reward that seems out of reach, for example, is not likely to be motivating

expectancy theory The theory that people are motivated to work toward rewards that they want and that they believe they have a reasonable chance of obtaining.

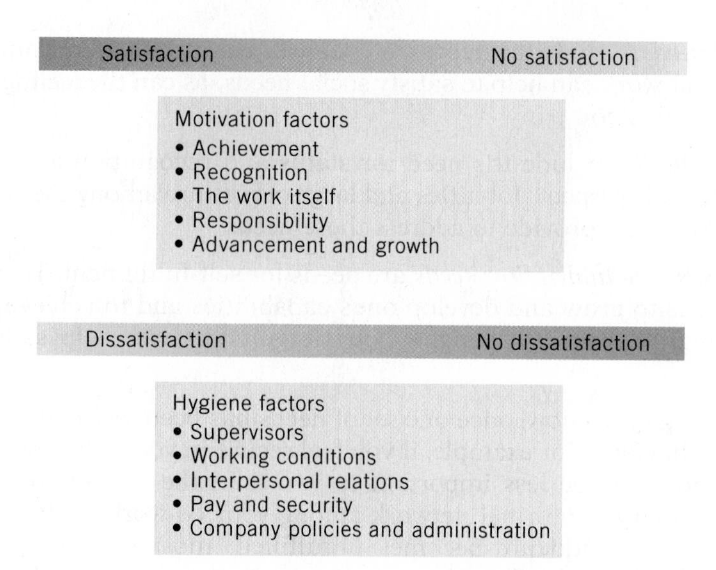

Figure 10.4 According to two-factor theory, job satisfaction depends on two factors.

even if it is very desirable. Figure 10.5 illustrates expectancy theory in terms of issues that are likely to be considered by an individual employee. Consider the case of an assistant department manager who learns that her firm needs to replace a retiring division manager two levels above her in the organization. Even though she wants that job, she does not apply because she doubts that she will be selected. In this case, she is being influenced by the *performance-reward link*. For whatever reason, she believes that her performance will not get her the position. Note that she may think that her performance merits the new job but that performance alone will not be enough. Perhaps she assumes that the reward will go to someone with more seniority.

Now assume that our employee learns that the firm is looking for a production manager on a later shift. She thinks that she could get this job but does not apply because she does not want to change shifts. In this instance, she is being influenced by the *rewards–personal goals link*. Finally, she learns of an opening one level higher—department manager—in her own division. She may well apply for this job because she wants it and because she thinks she has a good chance of getting it. In this case, her consideration of all the links has led to an expectancy that she can reach a desirable outcome.

Expectancy theory helps explain why some people do not work as hard as they can when their salaries are based purely on seniority. Paying employees the same whether they work very hard or just hard enough to get by removes the financial incentive for them to work harder. In other words, they ask themselves, "If I work harder, will I get a pay raise?" and conclude that the answer is no. Similarly, if hard work will result in one or more *undesirable* outcomes—say, a transfer to another location or a promotion to a job that requires unpleasant travel—employees will not be motivated to work hard.

Equity Theory

equity theory The theory that people compare (1) what they contribute to their job with what they get in return, and (2) their input/output ratio with that of other employees.

Equity theory focuses on social comparisons and assumes that people evaluate their treatment in an organization relative to the treatment that others receive. This approach says that people begin by analyzing *inputs* (what they contribute to their jobs in terms of time, effort, education, experience, and so on) relative to *outputs* (what they receive in return in terms of salary, benefits, recognition, security, and so on). The result is a ratio of contribution to return. Then they compare their own ratios with those of other employees and ask whether their ratios are *equal to, greater than,* or *less than* those of the people with whom they

Individual effort	→	Individual performance	→	Organizational rewards	→	Personal goals
	Effort-performance issue		Performance-reward issue		Rewards-personal goals issue	

Figure 10.5 Expectancy theory model.

are comparing themselves. Depending on the outcome of their assessments, they experience feelings of equity or inequity.[11]

Suppose that a new graduate gets a starting job at a large manufacturing firm. His starting salary is $30 000 per year, he gets a compact company car, and he shares an office with another employee. If he later learns that another new employee has received the same salary, car, and office arrangement, he will feel equitably treated. If the other newcomer, however, has received $35 000, a full-size company car, and a private office, he is likely to experience feelings of inequity.

Note, however, that the two ratios do not have to be equal—they only need to be *equitable*. Let's assume, for instance, that our new employee has a bachelor's degree and two years of work experience. Perhaps he learns subsequently that the other new employee has an advanced degree and 10 years of work experience. After first feeling inequity, our new employee may now conclude that his comparison person is actually contributing more to the organization. The other employee is therefore entitled to receive more.

When people feel that they are being inequitably treated, they are motivated to do something to restore equity. For example, they may ask for raises, reduce their effort, work shorter hours, or just complain to their bosses. They may also rationalize their situation, find different people with whom to compare themselves, or leave their jobs altogether.

Strategies for Enhancing Motivation

5

Describe the *strategies* used by organizations to improve job satisfaction and employee motivation.

Deciding what motivates workers and provides job satisfaction is only part of the manager's challenge. The other part is to apply that knowledge. Experts have suggested—and many companies have instituted—a wide range of programs designed to make jobs more interesting and rewarding and the work environment more pleasant. Six of the most popular types of programs are *reinforcement/behaviour modification theory, goal setting theory, participative management, team management, job enrichment and job redesign,* and *modified work schedules*.

Reinforcement/Behaviour Modification Theory

Many managers try to control or modify workers' behaviour through systematic rewards. The first step is to define the specific behaviours that managers want their employees to exhibit (working hard, being courteous to customers, stressing quality) and the specific behaviours they want to eliminate (wasting time, being rude to customers, ignoring quality). The next step is to "shape" employee behaviour by using reinforcement.

reinforcement Controlling and modifying employee behaviour through the use of systematic rewards and punishments for specific behaviours.

Reinforcement means applying (or withholding) positive (or negative) consequences in an attempt to motivate employees to exhibit behaviour the manager wants. A manager has four basic reinforcement options: (1) *positive reinforcement* (apply positive consequences when employees exhibit desired behaviours), (2) *punishment* (apply negative consequences when employees exhibit undesirable behaviours), (3) *omission* (withhold positive consequences when employees exhibit undesirable behaviours), and (4) *negative reinforcement* (withhold negative consequences when employees exhibit desired behaviours).

Positive reinforcement is the strategy most frequently used. For example, workers at Maple Leaf Sports & Entertainment receive "good job" cards when they do outstanding work. These cards can be redeemed for prizes.[12] WestJet rewarded its employees with a $500 travel credit when they helped deal with major flight disruptions caused by bad weather during December 2008.[13] Positive reinforcement need not be monetary to be effective. Calgary-based Pacesetter Directional and Performance Drilling rewards top employees with time off from work, and Markham, Ontario–based Nobis, a manufacturer of hats and apparel, rewards employees by allowing them to name hats after family and friends.[14] The boxed insert entitled "Employee Engagement" provides further information about rewards.

Rewards work best when people are learning new behaviours, new skills, or new jobs. As workers become more adept, rewards can be used less frequently.

Entrepreneurship and New Ventures

Employee Engagement: The Ultimate Win-Win

"The best way to engage and align employees is to promote transparency, accountability and recognition across all levels of a company," according to I Love Rewards CEO Razor Suleman. I Love Rewards sells solutions for businesses wishing to improve corporate culture, employee engagement, and motivation, and they do this primarily through the development of web-based employee rewards- or incentive-based systems that are customized to suit their clients' needs. Client employees are awarded points for performance, and these points can be redeemed for rewards, including brand name merchandise and travel, which have been carefully selected with the employee demographic in mind.

If companies can motivate their customers with rewards-based systems, why can't it work for employees? Well, companies like Microsoft, Rogers Communications, and Marriott have bought in to the concept and have contracted I Love Rewards to develop incentive-based packages for their employees. News of the successes of this high-growth company is travelling quickly. In the first quarter of 2009, the company reported a 187 percent increase in gross billings year over year. But the future didn't always look so bright for Suleman's agency.

In 2005, Suleman found himself wrestling with his own employee morale and motivation issues. In a span of six months, his company experienced almost 50 percent employee turnover. The solution? Suleman decided to incorporate his marketing expertise into his HR practices. One technique was to introduce group interviews. Suleman decided to directly involve as many as 10 to 12 current employees of his company to interview prospective employees. Employees "sell" the company to the applicant, and by doing so, the company brand is reinforced internally. Further, having so many staff members directly involved in hiring helps ensure the candidate will be a fit with the company culture. Other newly introduced incentives include flextime and at least four weeks vacation for new hires. Employee involvement extends as well to participation in objective setting, reinforced by an employee share-ownership program. Employees are also privy to the company's financial statements and can query management on any budget line expense. Amidst the hard times, Suleman had been somewhat disenchanted with his business, but his new strategy has paid off. In addition to reduced turnover and increased morale, his fresh approach has earned some other kinds of rewards.

For two years, Suleman's Toronto-based company has been named on Canada's Top 100 Employers list produced by *Maclean's* magazine. *Profit* magazine has included the business on their list of Fastest Growing Companies, and, more recently, WorldBlu, a U.S.-based social enterprise, has included the company on their list of the Most Democratic Workplaces. According to WorldBlu, the current economic crisis has dictated the need for a new business model that promotes transparency and accountability. I Love Rewards' new business model is built on these principles. These characteristics, combined with I Love Rewards' authentic democratic practices, emphasis on culture, and focus on people and recognition, have created a winning combination.

Suleman is now excited about the future of his business. His new strategies for employee engagement may have been just the competitive advantage and vehicle for growth his company was looking for.

Critical Thinking Question

1. Which of the strategies for enhancing job satisfaction and morale has Razor Suleman employed?

Because such actions contribute to positive employer-employee relationships, managers generally prefer giving rewards. They generally dislike punishing employees, partly because workers may respond with anger, resentment, hostility, or even retaliation.

Goal Setting Theory

Goal setting theory focuses on setting goals in order to motivate employees. Research has shown that **SMART goals** (*Specific*, *Measurable*, *Agreed-upon*, *Realistic*, and *Time-framed*) are most likely to result in increased employee performance. On occasion, goal setting may lead to bad behaviour on the part of managers. For example, if managers are told they will receive a bonus if they achieve a certain level of sales revenue, they may focus all their attention on generating sales *revenue*, and not pay any attention to *profits*. At Enron, managers received large bonuses for achieving revenue goals even though the company was failing.[15]

goal setting theory The theory that people perform better when they set specific, quantified, time-framed goals.

SMART goals Goals that are specific, measurable, agreed upon, realistic, and time framed and which are most likely to result in increased employee performance.

One of the most popular methods for setting performance goals is called **management by objectives (MBO),** which involves managers and subordinates in setting goals and evaluating progress (see Figure 10.6). It is an effort to apply goal setting theory throughout the organization. The motivational impact is perhaps the biggest advantage of MBO. When employees sit down with managers to set goals, they learn more about company-wide objectives, feel that they are an important part of a team, and see how they can improve company-wide performance by achieving their own goals.

management by objectives (MBO) A system of collaborative goal setting that extends from the top of an organization to its bottom.

Investors Group Financial Services has used MBO for many years to motivate its sales force in selling financial services. The MBO process begins when the vice-president of sales develops general goals for the entire sales force. This sets the stage for Planning Week, which is held annually in various regional centres across Canada. Sales reps review their financial accomplishments and think through their personal and financial goals for the coming year. During Planning Week, they meet with their division managers and reach a consensus about the specific goals the sales reps will pursue during the next year. Each division manager then forwards the proposed objectives for his or her division to the appropriate regional manager. This process continues all the way up to the vice-president of sales, who gives final approval to the overall sales objectives of the company for the coming year.[16]

Research has shown that goals that are specific, measurable, agreed upon, realistic, and time framed generate high performance in employees.

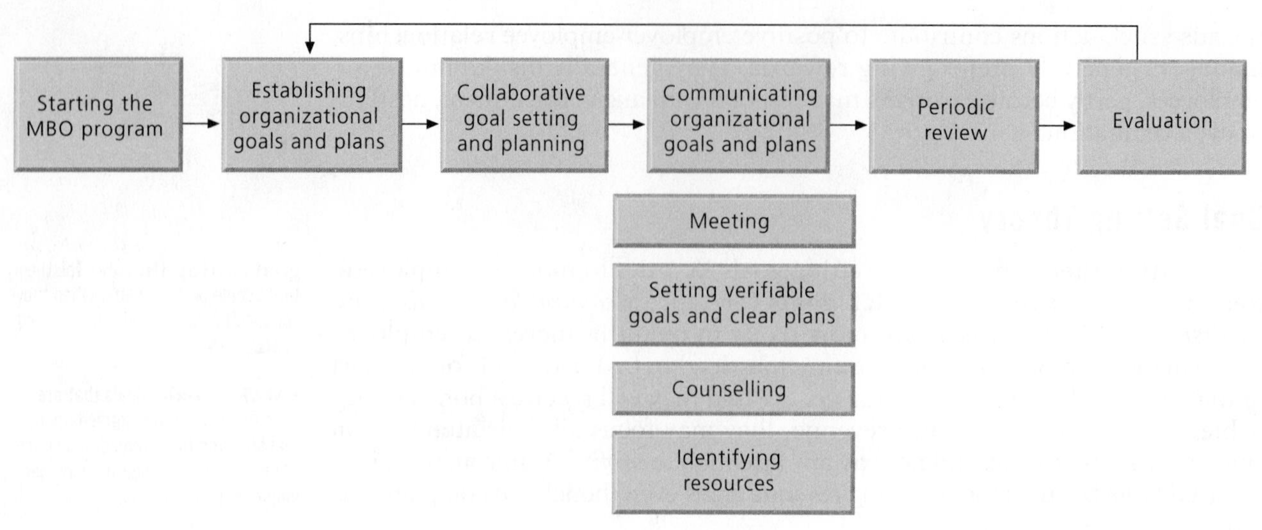

Figure 10.6 Management by objectives.

Participative Management and Empowerment

participative management and empowerment A method of increasing employees' job satisfaction by giving them a voice in how they do their jobs and how the company is managed.

Participative management and empowerment involves tapping in to workers' knowledge about the job, encouraging them to be self-motivated and to make suggestions for improvements, and giving them more authority and responsibility so that they feel they are a real part of the company's success. The South Bend, Indiana, manufacturing plant of the Eaton Corporation illustrates empowerment in practice. The traditional factory hierarchy is avoided, and everyone wears the same blue uniforms. There are no time clocks, and workers report their hours on an honour system. Production statistics for each work team are posted where everyone can see them. Each work team is responsible for keeping its own members productive and motivated. Empowerment has meant more authority and more responsibility for workers.

There are many other examples of empowerment:

- At WestJet, front-line staff have the right to issue travel credits to customers they feel have not been treated properly. WestJet thinks that the goodwill generated by the practice will increase repeat business.[17]
- At Toronto's Delta Chelsea Hotel, employees noticed that in the summer months there were fewer business guests and more vacationers' children in the hotel. As a result of employee suggestions, the hotel installed a waterslide, appointed a "kids' concierge," and set up a game room for teens to better serve this market segment.[18]
- AES Corporation is a large energy company where multifunctional teams manage themselves without the assistance of any legal, human resources, or other functional department or any written policies or procedures. No one person is in charge of the teams. As a result of this structure (some call it "empowerment gone mad"), employees exhibit flexibility and continuous learning.[19]

wikis Websites that allow employees to add content whenever they want on issues that are of interest to the business.

quality circle A technique used to encourage participative management, whereby a group of employees meet regularly to consider solutions for problems in their work area.

To enhance employee productivity, some companies are now using **wikis**—websites that allow employees to add content whenever they want on issues that are of interest to the business. This is part of a move to "mass collaboration" that is going on in business.[20] Another technique to encourage participative management is the **quality circle**, a group of employees who meet regularly to consider solutions for problems in their work area. The Great-West Life Assurance Company, for example, has reported success with its quality circle program.

Empowerment is not desired by all employees. Some will be frustrated by responsibilities they are not equipped to handle, and others will be dissatisfied if they see the invitation to participate as more symbolic than real. A good approach is to invite participation only if employees want to have input, and only if participation will have real value for an organization. The boxed insert entitled "Encouraging Employees to Share Ideas" describes some of the problems that can arise with empowerment.

Business Accountability

Encouraging Employees to Share Ideas

Empowerment can be a tricky process, particularly in an era when layoffs are common and employees may not trust management. The empowerment process typically requires workers to share their job knowledge with other workers or with management. But some workers fear that such sharing will allow others to take credit for their hard-earned knowledge or that sharing their knowledge will weaken their position in the company. So managers who assume that all workers want to be empowered may be in for a rude shock. The following examples demonstrate this difficulty:

- One employee who cut metal shafts for industrial pumps at Blackmer/Dover Resources Inc. in Grand Rapids, Michigan, had a reputation for being both fast and accurate in his work. He refused to share his knowledge with management (or his fellow workers), because he feared that management would use the knowledge to speed up the workflow and that he would then have to work faster. He is not alone. Many workers have developed extra-fast ways of doing their work, but are reluctant to share those ideas with management. Since managers are always under pressure to improve productivity, the refusal of these workers to share information is frustrating.
- A long-time employee at a small Canadian manufacturing plant taught a younger replacement worker how to run a complicated machine. Shortly thereafter, the older worker became ill and was off work for several weeks. When he returned, he found that the younger worker had essentially taken over his job. The older worker had this to say: "To pass on your experience or your knowledge to others, or to pass on to your fellow workers your secrets, how you assemble it faster, better, or more efficiently for the company, be careful; tomorrow you might have lost your job."
- Robin Miller, the executive director of the Winnipeg-based Centre for Education and Work, says that there is a lot of "informal learning" that goes on in companies, but it is not generally recognized or rewarded in Canadian workplaces. If informal learning is not rewarded, we should not be surprised if employees do not share with management the efficient shortcuts they have discovered that allow them to work faster.

The main reason workers conceal knowledge seems to be related to job security. Workers fear that if they share their knowledge, management will use that knowledge to increase output. The increased output will mean that management can get by with fewer workers, so some people will lose their jobs.

In some companies, workers don't share their knowledge because they have become convinced that management doesn't think they have anything to contribute. At the Blackmer/Dover plant, for example, a new plant manager was trying to resolve some production problems that had developed under his predecessor. He asked for worker participation so that he could understand what was wrong in the plant and how things might be improved. Workers were surprised they were being asked for their ideas, because previous management had not solicited worker input. But in this case the workers agreed to help, and the story eventually had a happy ending.

The culture of a country may also moderate the positive effects of empowerment initiatives. One study of a company with operations in the United States, Mexico, Poland, and India found that empowerment was negatively related to job satisfaction in India, but positively related to job satisfaction in the United States, Poland, and Mexico.

Critical Thinking Questions

1. Consider the following statement: *Companies provide jobs for people, so they have every right to expect that employees will do things like sharing their job knowledge with their co-workers because this will make the company more successful and allow it to continue to provide jobs.* Do you agree or disagree with the statement? Explain your reasoning.
2. Why do some workers refuse to share their job knowledge with either their co-workers or with management? What can management do to encourage workers to share their job knowledge?

Team Management

Individual employees are usually given decision-making responsibility for certain narrow activities, such as when to take lunch breaks or how to divide assignments with co-workers. But teams of employees are also being consulted on such decisions as production scheduling, work procedures and schedules, and the hiring of new employees.

Like participation and empowerment, teams are not for everyone. Levi Strauss, for example, encountered major problems when it tried to use teams. Individual workers previously performed repetitive, highly specialized tasks, such as sewing zippers into jeans, and were paid according to the number of parts they completed each day. In an attempt to boost productivity, company management reorganized everyone into teams of 10 to 35 workers and assigned tasks to the entire group. Each team member's pay was determined by the team's level of productivity. In practice, however, faster workers became resentful of slower workers because they reduced the group's total output. Slower workers, meanwhile, resented the pressure put on them by faster-working co-workers. As a result, motivation, satisfaction, and morale all dropped, and Levi's eventually abandoned the teamwork plan altogether.[21]

Team management is widely used to enhance employee motivation and company performance. Although teams are often less effective in traditional and rigidly structured bureaucratic organizations, they do help smaller, more flexible organizations make decisions more quickly and effectively, enhance company-wide communication, and encourage organizational members to feel more like a part of an organization.[22]

Job Enrichment and Job Redesign

Job enrichment and job redesign programs are generally used to increase satisfaction in jobs that are significantly lacking in motivating factors.[23]

Job Enrichment Programs

job enrichment A method of increasing employees' job satisfaction by extending or adding motivating factors such as responsibility or growth.

Job enrichment means adding one or more motivating factors to a job. At one company, a group of eight typists worked in separate cubicles. Their job involved taking calls from dozens of field sales representatives and typing up service orders. They had no client contact; if they had a question about the order, they had to call the sales representative. They also received little performance feedback. Interviews with these workers suggested that they were bored with their

This team of workers at Germany's Apollo car production plant work together to design and manufacture the Apollo sports car. Such teams often help firms make decisions more effectively, enhance communication, and lead to increased employee motivation and satisfaction.

jobs and did not feel valued. As part of a job enrichment program, each typist was paired with a small group of designated sales representatives and became a part of their team. Typists were also given permission to call clients directly if they had questions about the order. Finally, a new feedback system was installed to give the typists more information about their performance. As a result, their performance improved and absenteeism decreased markedly.[24]

Job Redesign Programs

Job redesign acknowledges that different people want different things from their jobs. By restructuring work to achieve a more satisfactory fit between workers and their jobs, **job redesign** can motivate individuals with strong needs for career growth or achievement. Job redesign is usually implemented in one of three ways: through *combining tasks, forming natural work groups,* or *establishing client relationships*.

job redesign A method of increasing employees' job satisfaction by improving the worker-job fit through combining tasks, creating natural work groups, and/or establishing client relationships.

Combining Tasks. The job of combining tasks involves enlarging jobs and increasing their variety to make employees feel that their work is more meaningful. In turn, employees become more motivated. For example, the job done by a programmer who maintains computer systems might be redesigned to include some system design and system development work. While developing additional skills, the programmer also becomes involved in the overall system package.

Forming Natural Work Groups. People who do different jobs on the same projects are candidates for natural work groups. These groups are formed to help employees see the place and importance of their jobs in the total structure of the firm. Such groups are valuable to management because the people working on a project are usually the most knowledgeable about it and thus the most capable problem solvers. To see how natural workgroups affect motivation, consider a group where each employee does a small part of the job of assembling radios. One person attaches red wires, while another attaches control knobs. The jobs could be redesigned to allow the group to decide who does what and in what order. The workers can exchange jobs and plan their work schedules. Now they all see themselves as part of a team that assembles radios.

Establishing Client Relationships. A third way of redesigning a job is to establish client relationships by letting employees interact with customers. This approach increases the variety of a job. It also gives workers greater feelings of control over their jobs and more feedback about their performance. Lotus Software uses this approach as a means of giving necessary independence to creative employees. Instead of responding to instructions from marketing managers on how to develop new products, software writers are encouraged to work directly with customers. Similarly, software writers at Microsoft observe how test users work with programs and discuss problems with them directly rather than receiving feedback from third-party researchers.

Modified Work Schedules

As another way of increasing job satisfaction, many companies are trying out different approaches to working hours and the workweek. Several types of modified work schedules have been tried, including *flextime,* the *compressed workweek, telecommuting,* and *workshare programs*.

Flextime

Flextime allows people to pick their working hours. Figure 10.7 illustrates how a flextime system might be arranged and how different people might use it.

flextime A method of increasing employees' job satisfaction by allowing them some choice in the hours they work.

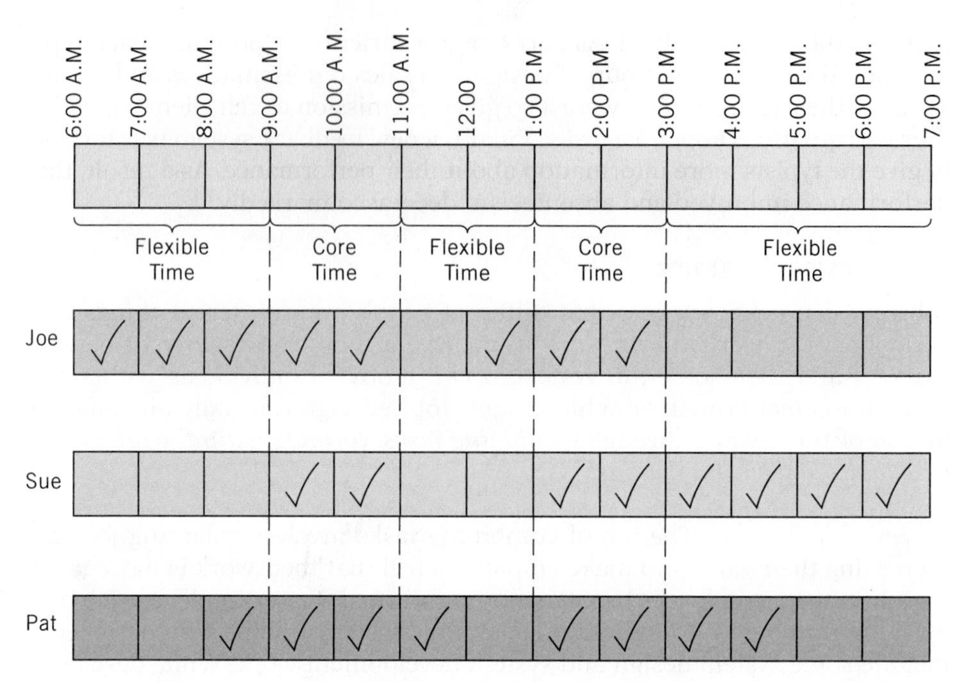

Figure 10.7 Flextime schedules include core time, when everyone must be at work, and flexible time, during which employees can set their own working hours.

The office is open from 6 a.m. until 7 p.m. Each employee works for eight hours each day. Core time is 9 a.m. until 11 a.m. and 1 p.m. until 3 p.m. Joe, being an early riser, comes in at 6 a.m., takes an hour lunch between 11 a.m. and noon, and finishes his day by 3 p.m. Sue, on the other hand, prefers a later day. She comes in at 9 a.m., takes a long lunch from 11 a.m. to 1 p.m., and then works until 7 p.m. Pat works a more traditional day, from 8 a.m. until 5 p.m.

About 70 percent of North American firms offer some variation of flextime.[25] Flextime programs give employees more freedom in their professional and personal lives and allow workers to plan around the work schedules of spouses and the school schedules of young children. The increased feeling of freedom and control over their work life also reduces individuals' levels of stress. Flextime also offers advantages to the company. For example, a Toronto company doing business in Vancouver will benefit if some employees come in at 10 a.m. and work until 7 p.m. to account for the time difference between the two cities. Companies can also benefit from the higher levels of commitment and job satisfaction among flextime workers. In large urban areas, flextime programs reduce traffic congestion that contributes to lost work time.

The Compressed Workweek

compressed workweek Employees work fewer days per week, but more hours on the days they do work.

In the **compressed workweek**, employees work fewer days per week but more hours on the days they do work. The most popular compressed workweek is four days, 10 hours per day, which is used in many companies and municipalities. In 2008, Chrysler began talking with the Canadian Auto Workers Union about instituting the practice because it would cut energy costs and give employees an additional day off each week. Workers at Babcock & Wilcox Canada also negotiated a four-day, 10-hour-day contract.[26]

Telecommuting

telecommuting Allowing employees to do all or some of their work away from the office.

A third variation in work design is **telecommuting**, which allows people to do some or all of their work away from their office. The availability of networked computers, fax machines, cellphones, email, and overnight delivery services makes it possible for many independent professionals to work at home or while travelling. A 2008 survey conducted by WorldatWork found that 40 percent of Canadian businesses offer some form of telecommuting for their employees.[27] In some business functions like customer service and telemarketing, most employees are telecommuters.[28]

When telecommuting was introduced, some managers were concerned that employees would not work as hard at home as they would in the office, but that fear has gradually diminished. When Ikon Office Solutions Inc. implemented a telecommuting program for 250 of its sales staff, the president of the company said there were some initial concerns that telecommuters might not work as hard when they were at home, but they are actually very productive.[29]

Best Buy is taking modified schedules and alternative workplaces to new extremes with its corporate "results-only-work environment" or ROWE. Under ROWE, Best Buy employees can work anytime, anywhere, as long as they achieve results. The program has been so successful that Best Buy has begun introducing the program into its retail stores.

Employees like telecommuting because it saves them time and money, and companies like it because it boosts productivity and saves them money as well. A survey by the Computing Technology Industry Association found that two-thirds of employers felt that telecommuting boosted employee productivity and saved the company money.[30] Bell Canada, for example, has reduced its real estate expenses by having 2000 of its workers work at home.[31] Some workers do report feeling isolated and "out of the loop," when they do not see co-workers very often. To avoid this problem, B.C. Tel and Bentall Development Inc. jointly developed a satellite telecommuting office in Langley, British Columbia. It allows workers who used to commute to Burnaby or Vancouver to reduce their travel time considerably and still be able to interact with other workers.[32]

Would-be telecommuters must ask themselves several important questions: Can I meet deadlines even when I'm not being closely supervised? What will it be like to be away from the social context of the office five days a week? Can I renegotiate family rules so my spouse doesn't come home expecting to see dinner on the table just because I've been home all day?

Additional information on telecommuting is provided in Concluding Case 10-1. The boxed insert entitled "The Four-Day Workweek and Telecommuting: Are They Really Green?" raises some interesting issues.

Workshare Programs

A fourth type of modified work schedule, **worksharing** (also called **job sharing**), benefits both employee and employer. This approach allows two people to share one full-time job. For example, two people might share a position advising the human resources department. One person works Mondays through Wednesdays, and the other works Wednesdays through Fridays. A Statistics Canada survey showed that 8 percent of all part-time workers in Canada share a job with someone. People who share jobs are more likely to be women, to be university educated, and to have professional occupations such as teaching and nursing. In addition, job sharers earned more than regular part-time workers.[33]

worksharing (or job sharing) A method of increasing employee job satisfaction by allowing two people to share one job.

Short-run worksharing programs can help ease experienced workers into retirement while training their replacements. Worksharing can also allow students in university co-op programs to combine academic learning with practical experience.

Long-run worksharing programs have proven a good solution for people who want only part-time work. For example, five people might decide to share one reservationist's job at Air Canada with each working one day a week. Each person earns some money, remains in the job market, and enjoys some travel benefits.

The Greening of Business

The Four-Day Workweek and Telecommuting: Are They Really Green?

For most people, the four-day workweek is attractive because it means they have to work only four days each week instead of five. Most people have lots of leisure-time activities they want to pursue, and the four-day workweek gives them more time to do that.

Recently, the four-day workweek has been touted as good not only for employee morale and satisfaction, but also for the environment. There are two main points that are usually made in support of the argument. First, since workers will be driving to work only four days each week instead of five, they will be using less gas and therefore reducing the amount of greenhouse gases that they put into the atmosphere. Whether the four-day workweek really saves gas obviously depends on what workers do on the fifth day. If they drive their SUV 400 kilometres to go visit relatives, they will burn more gas than they would have by simply driving to and from work. On the other hand, maybe they would have taken such a trip on the weekend if they had to work a traditional five-day workweek.

Second, a four-day workweek should mean that less electricity will be used by businesses because machines, computers, and heating systems will be running at very low levels on the fifth day. While it is true that factory machines will not be running on the fifth day, there may be no actual savings because those machines have already run for 40 hours as a result of the four previous days at 10 hours. Other electricity savings may also be elusive unless the company is committed to turning down the heat and turning off the lights on the fifth day. But that may be impossible, because there always seems to be office staff that needs to be at work on the fifth day. Even if workers do stay at home on the fifth day, they may do other tasks that require the equivalent amount of electricity or gas that they would have consumed at work (e.g., renovating their home).

These observations show that it may be difficult to determine if the four-day workweek is better for the environment than the five-day workweek is. But telecommuting may be a more effective strategy because workers who telecommute don't come in to the office very much. If they are at home working, they will not be driving their car, so that should save gas. As well, companies that encourage telecommuting may save considerable money on real estate and other operating costs. But even here, we need to analyze what individual workers do as alternate activities before we can conclude that telecommuting is good for the environment.

Critical Thinking Questions

1. Using material contained in this insert as well as other material that you find, develop a list of arguments that the four-day workweek is better for the environment than the five-day workweek. Then develop a list of arguments that the four-day workweek is no better for the environment than the five-day workweek. Which list is most persuasive?
2. Using material contained in this insert as well as other material you can find, develop a list of arguments that telecommuting is better for the environment than the four-day workweek. Then develop a list of arguments that telecommuting is not better than the four-day workweek. Which list is most persuasive?

Leadership and Motivation

6 Define *leadership* and distinguish it from *management.*

leadership The processes and behaviours used by managers to motivate, inspire, and influence subordinates to work toward certain goals.

Leadership refers to the processes and behaviours used by managers to motivate, inspire, and influence subordinates to work toward certain goals. People often assume that "leadership" and "management" mean the same thing, but they are really different concepts. A person can be a manager, a leader, or both.[34] Consider a hospital setting. The chief of staff (chief physician) of a large hospital is clearly a manager by virtue of the position the person occupies. But this individual may or may not be respected or trusted by others and may have to rely solely on the authority vested in the position to get people to do things. Thus, being a manager does not ensure that a person is also a leader. By contrast, an emergency-room nurse with no formal authority may be quite effective at taking charge of a chaotic situation and directing others in how to deal with specific patient problems. Others in the emergency room may respond because they trust the nurse's judgment and have confidence in the nurse's decision-making skills. In this case, the emergency-room nurse is a leader but not a manager.

Finally, the head of pediatrics, supervising a staff of 20 other doctors, nurses, and attendants, may also enjoy the staff's complete respect, confidence, and trust. The staff readily take the head's advice, follow directives without question, and often go far beyond what is necessary to help carry out the unit's mission. Thus, the head of pediatrics is both a manager and a leader. The key distinctions between leadership and management are summarized in Table 10.1.

Organizations need both management *and* leadership if they are to be effective. Leadership is necessary to create and direct change and to help the organization get through tough times, and management is necessary to achieve coordination and to complete administrative activities during times of stability and predictability.[35] Management—in conjunction with leadership—can help achieve planned orderly change. Leadership—in conjunction with management—can keep the organization properly aligned with its environment. In addition, managers and leaders also play a major role in establishing the moral climate of the organization and in determining the role of ethics in its culture.[36]

Approaches to Leadership

Political, religious, and business leaders have profoundly influenced the course of human events throughout history, but careful scientific study of leadership began only about a century ago. In the following paragraphs, we briefly summarize the development of this research.

Summarize the *approaches to leadership* that developed in the twentieth century. 7

The Trait Approach

In the first two decades of the twentieth century, researchers believed that leaders had unique traits that distinguished them from non-leaders. The **trait approach** therefore focussed on identifying the traits that would differentiate leaders from non-leaders. Many traits were proposed as important, including intelligence, dominance, self-confidence, energy, height, and knowledge about the job. As time passed, the list became so long that it lost any practical value. The trait approach was all but abandoned by the middle of the twentieth century, but in recent years it has resurfaced once again. Some researchers now argue that certain traits (for example, intelligence, drive, motivation, honesty, integrity,

trait approach An approach that focuses on identifying the traits that would differentiate leaders from non-leaders.

Table 10.1 Kotter's Distinctions Between Management and Leadership

Activity	Management	Leadership
Creating an Agenda	Planning and budgeting. Establishing detailed steps and timetables for achieving needed results; allocating the resources necessary to make those needed results happen.	Establishing direction. Developing a vision of the future, often the distant future, and strategies for producing the changes needed to achieve that vision.
Developing a Human Network for Achieving the Agenda	Organizing and staffing. Establishing some structure for accomplishing plan requirements, staffing that structure with individuals, delegating responsibility and authority for carrying out the plan, providing policies and procedures to help guide people, and creating methods or systems to monitor implementation.	Aligning people. Communicating the direction by words and deeds to all those whose co-operation may be needed to influence the creation of teams and coalitions that understand the vision and strategies and accept their validity.
Executing Plans	Controlling and problem solving. Monitoring results vs. plan in some detail, identifying deviations, and then planning and organizing to solve these problems.	Motivating and inspiring. Energizing people to overcome major political, bureaucratic, and resource barriers to change, by satisfying very basic, but often unfulfilled, human needs.
Outcomes	Produces a degree of predictability and order and has the potential to consistently produce major results expected by various shareholders (e.g., for customers, always being on time; for stockholders, being on budget).	Produces change, often to a dramatic degree, and has the potential to produce extremely useful change (e.g., new products that customers want, new approaches to labour relations that help make a firm more competitive).

and self-confidence) provide the *potential* for effective leadership, but only if the person is really motivated to be a leader. The implication is that people without these traits are not likely to be successful leaders even if they try.

The *emotional intelligence* idea that was mentioned earlier in this chapter suggests that successful leaders possess five basic traits: *self-awareness* (the ability to understand your mood), *self-regulation* (the ability to control disruptive impulses), *motivation* (a passion for work), *empathy* (the ability to understand the emotional makeup of others), and *social skill* (proficiency in managing relationships). Managers who do not have these traits, it is argued, will not be successful regardless of how intelligent or highly trained they are.[37]

The Behavioural Approach

behavioural approach Determines how the behaviours of effective leaders differ from the behaviours of less effective leaders.

task-oriented A form of leader behaviour in which the manager focuses on how tasks should be performed in order to achieve important goals.

employee-oriented A form of leader behaviour in which the manager focuses on the satisfaction, motivation, and well-being of employees.

autocratic style A form of leader behaviour in which the manager issues orders and expects them to be obeyed without question.

democratic style A form of leader behaviour in which the manager requests input from subordinates before making decisions but retains final decision-making power.

free-rein style A form of leader behaviour in which the manager serves as an adviser to subordinates who are given a lot of discretion when making decisions.

Because the trait approach was a poor predictor of leadership success, attention shifted from managers' *traits* to their *behaviours*. The goal of the **behavioural approach** was to determine how the behaviours of effective leaders differed from the behaviours of less effective leaders. This research led to the identification of two basic forms of leader behaviour: **task-oriented** (the manager focuses on how tasks should be performed in order to achieve important goals) and **employee-oriented** (the manager focuses on the satisfaction, motivation, and well-being of employees). Task-oriented managers tend to have higher-performing subordinates, but employee-oriented managers have more satisfied subordinates. Researchers have also identified three main leadership styles: the **autocratic style** (the manager issues orders and expects them to be obeyed without question), the **democratic style** (the manager requests input from subordinates before making decisions but retains final decision-making power), and the **free-rein style** (the manager serves as an adviser to subordinates who are given a lot of discretion when making decisions).

Most leaders tend to regularly use one style and may in fact find it difficult to change from one style to another. But some leaders do manage to change their style. For example, Andrall (Andy) Pearson was abrasive, numbers-oriented, and hard to please when he was president and COO of PepsiCo. But now, as director of Yum Brands, he has softened and transformed and seems to truly care about employees.[38]

The Situational (Contingency) Approach

As time passed, researchers began to realize that different situations might demand different leader behaviours. For instance, suppose a new manager takes over a work site where workers are satisfied but not very motivated to work hard. The leader should most likely exhibit task-oriented behaviours in

"I like to think of myself as a nice guy. Naturally, sometimes you have to step on a few faces."

order to improve productivity. But suppose a new manager faces a situation where productivity is high but workers are stressed out about their jobs and therefore have low levels of job satisfaction. In this instance, the manager should most likely exhibit employee-oriented behaviours to help improve job satisfaction. This line of thinking led to the development of the *situational approach to leadership*.

The **situational (or contingency) approach** emerged during the 1960s and assumed that appropriate leader behaviour varied from one situation to another. This approach was first proposed as a continuum of leadership behaviour (see Figure 10.8). At one extreme, the leader makes decisions alone; at the other extreme, the leader has employees make decisions with only minimal guidance from the leader. Each point on the continuum is influenced by *characteristics of* the leader (including the leader's value system, confidence in subordinates, personal inclinations, and feelings of security), *characteristics of the subordinates* (including the subordinates' need for independence, readiness to assume responsibility, tolerance for ambiguity, interest in the problem, understanding of goals, knowledge, experience, and expectations), and the *characteristics of the situation* (including the type of organization, group effectiveness, the problem itself, and time pressures).

situational (contingency) approach An approach that emerged during the 1960s and assumed that appropriate leader behaviour varied from one situation to another.

The leadership continuum focussed attention on leader behaviours as a continuum instead of being two simple alternatives and pointed out that various elements of any given situation affect the success of any given leadership style. Although this framework proposed the importance of certain situational factors, it was only speculative. Later models have developed more detailed and specific predictions of how different forms of leader behaviour influence subordinate satisfaction and productivity.

Recent Trends in Leadership

During the last couple of decades, many new ideas about leadership have been developed. We conclude this chapter with a brief discussion of several of these ideas.

8 Describe the most recent ideas about effective leadership.

Transformational Leadership

Transformational leadership refers to the set of abilities that allows a leader to recognize the need for change, to create a vision to guide that change, and to

transformational leadership The set of abilities that allows a leader to recognize the need for change, to create a vision to guide that change, and to execute the change effectively.

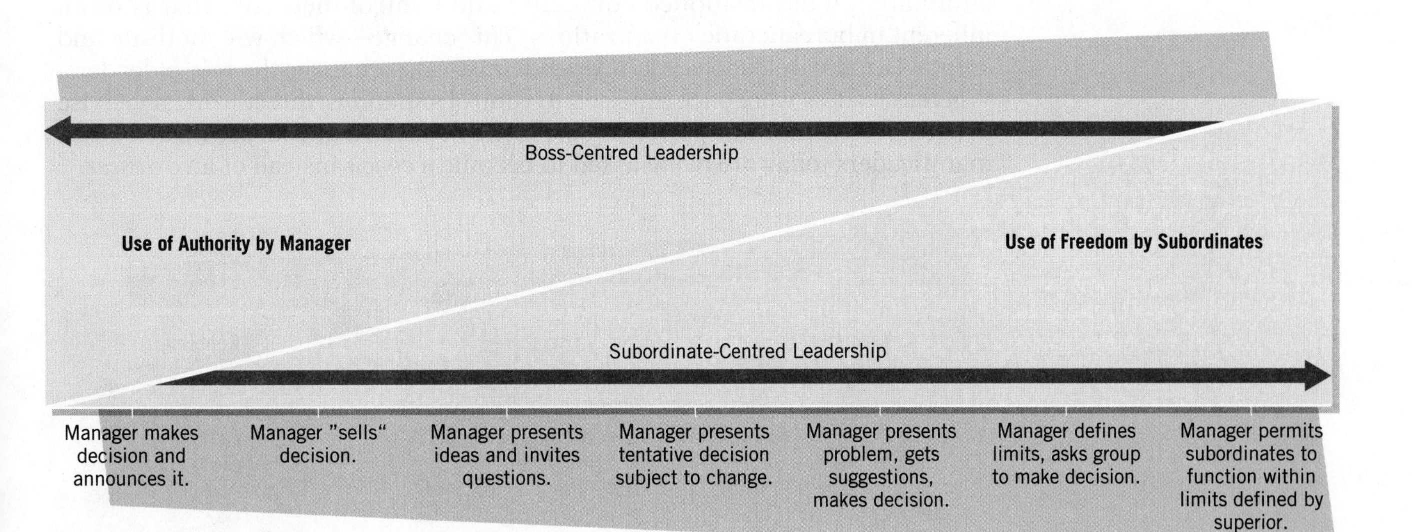

Figure 10.8 The leadership continuum.

transactional leadership Routine, regimented activities that focus on maintaining stability of operations.

execute the change effectively. By contrast, **transactional leadership** involves routine, regimented activities that focus on maintaining stability of operations.

Many leaders may find it difficult to exercise both types of leadership. For example, when Michael Eisner took over the Walt Disney organization, the company was stagnant and was heading into decline. Relying on his transformational skills, Eisner turned things around in dramatic fashion. He expanded the company's theme parks, built new hotels, improved Disney's movie business, created a successful Disney cruise line, launched several other major initiatives, and changed the company into a global media powerhouse. But when the firm began to plateau and needed some time to let the changes all settle in, Eisner was unsuccessful at changing his own approach from transformational leadership to transactional leadership and was pressured into retiring.

Charismatic Leadership

charismatic leadership A type of influence based on the leader's personal charisma.

Charismatic leadership is a type of influence based on the leader's personal charisma. Figure 10.9 portrays the three key elements of charismatic leadership that most experts acknowledge today.[39]

A highly charismatic supervisor will generally be more successful in influencing a subordinate's behaviour than a supervisor who lacks charisma. Charismatic leaders have a high level of self-confidence and a strong need to influence others. They also communicate high expectations about follower performance and express confidence in their followers. Steve Jobs, the legendary CEO of Apple Inc., commands a cult-like following from both employees and consumers. He exhibits charisma, confidence, originality, brilliance, and vision. He is clearly a leader who can deliver success in businesses that are evolving, highly technical, and demanding. Yet he has also been portrayed as an intimidating, power-hungry, aggressive egotist.[40]

Charismatic leadership ideas are popular among managers today and are the subject of numerous books and articles.[41] One concern is that some charismatic leaders will inspire such blind faith in their followers that the followers may engage in inappropriate, unethical, or even illegal behaviours simply because the leader instructs them to do so. This tendency likely played a role in the collapse of both Enron and Arthur Andersen, as people followed orders from their charismatic bosses to hide information, shred documents, and mislead investigators.

Leaders as Coaches

Many organizations are now attempting to become less hierarchical and to eliminate the old-fashioned command-and-control mentality that is often inherent in bureaucratic organizations. This change—which will motivate and empower individuals to work independently—also changes the role of leaders. Whereas leaders were once expected to control situations, direct work, supervise people, closely monitor performance, make decisions, and structure activities, many leaders today are being asked to become a *coach* instead of an *overseer*.[42]

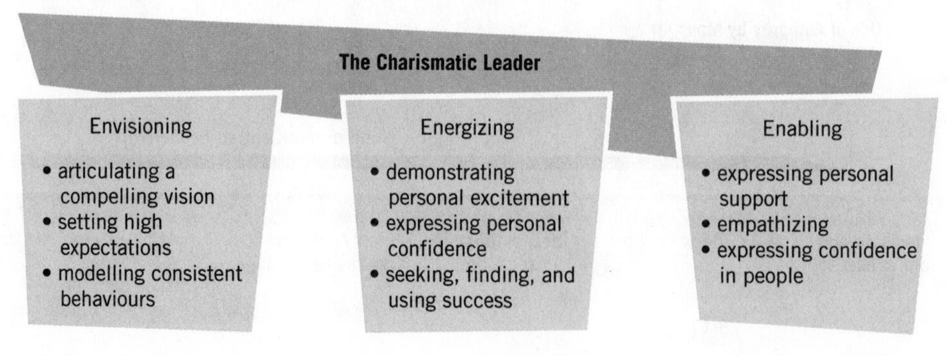

Figure 10.9 Charismatic leadership.

Consider the parallel with an athletic team. The coach selects the players for the team and decides on the general direction to take (such as emphasizing offence versus defence). The coach also helps develop player talent and teaches team members how to execute specific plays. But at game time, it's up to the players to execute plays and get the job done. While the coach may get some of the credit for the victory, he or she didn't actually score any of the points.

For business leaders, a coaching perspective calls for the leader to help select team members and other new employees, to provide some general direction, to help train and develop the team and the skills of its members, and to help the team get the information and other resources it needs. The leader may also have to help resolve conflict among team members and mediate other disputes that arise. And coaches from different teams need to link the activities and functions of their respective teams. Beyond these activities, the leader is expected to keep a low profile and let the group get its work done, with little or no direct oversight from the leader.

Gender and Leadership

Another factor that is altering the face of leadership is the growing number of women advancing to the highest levels in organizations. Given that most leadership theories and research studies have focussed on male leaders, developing a better understanding of how women lead is clearly an important next step. The key question is this: Do women and men lead differently? Some early observers predicted that (consistent with prevailing stereotypes) female leaders would be relatively warm, supportive, and nurturing compared to their male counterparts. But in reality, research suggests that female leaders are not necessarily more nurturing or supportive than male leaders. Likewise, male leaders are not systematically more harsh, controlling, or task focussed than female leaders. Women do seem to have a tendency to be more democratic when making decisions, whereas men have a tendency to be somewhat more autocratic.[43]

Cross-Cultural Leadership

Culture is a broad concept that encompasses both international differences and diversity-based differences within one culture. For instance, when a Japanese firm sends an executive to head up the firm's operation in Canada, that person will need to be sensitive to the cultural differences that exist between the two countries and consider changing his or her leadership style accordingly. Japan is generally characterized by *collectivism* (group before individual), whereas Canada is based more on *individualism* (individual before group). The Japanese

Andrea Jung (left), CEO of Avon Products, and Angela Merkel (right), chancellor of Germany, are exceptional leaders. Jung has transformed Avon and made it a powerhouse in its industry, and Merkel was recently named to *TIME* magazine's list of "people who shape our world."

executive, then, will find it necessary to recognize the importance of individual contributions and rewards and the differences in individual and group roles that exist in Japanese and Canadian businesses.

Cross-cultural factors also play a growing role in organizations as their workforces become more diverse. Most leadership research has analyzed white male leaders, because those individuals have historically dominated leadership positions in North America. But as Asians, blacks, Aboriginals, and Hispanics achieve leadership positions, it will be necessary to reassess how applicable current models of leadership are when applied to the increasingly diverse pool of leaders. (For more information on diversity, see Chapter 8.)

Canadian Versus American Management Styles. The management style of Canadian managers might look a lot like that of Americans, but there are several notable differences. Most fundamentally, Canadian managers are more subtle and subdued than American managers. Canadian managers also seem more committed to their companies, less willing to mindlessly follow the latest management fad, and more open to different cultures because of the multicultural nature of Canada. All of these characteristics are advantageous for Canadian companies that will increasingly be competing in global markets.[44]

Many Canadian-born managers have achieved significant success in companies that operate outside of Canada. For example, Bob Kelly was appointed CEO of the Bank of New York Mellon Corp., the eleventh largest financial services firm in the United States.[45] Other Canadians who have achieved high positions are Henry McKinnell (CEO of Pfizer, the world's largest pharmaceutical company), Steven McArthur (president of online travel company Expedia), Patricia Arnold (vice-president of Credit Suisse First Boston), Clara Furse (CEO of the London Stock Exchange), Simon Cooper (CEO of The Ritz-Carlton Hotel Company), and Dominic Barton (chair of McKinsey & Company's Asia Region), to name just a few.[46]

Strategic Leadership

strategic leadership A leader's ability to understand the complexities of both the organization and its environment in order to lead change in the organization, which will enhance its competitiveness.

Strategic leadership—which focuses on leadership in top management—is a leader's ability to understand the complexities of both the organization and its environment in order to lead change in the organization, which will enhance its competitiveness. Steve Jobs, CEO of Apple Inc., is an effective strategic leader who recognized the potential growth of MP3 players and the fact that those devices used technology that is similar to that found in computers. He therefore directed the development of the Apple iPod, which has become an enormously successful and profitable product. When he temporarily stepped down as CEO in 2009 because of concerns about his health, observers worried that Apple would lose its competitive advantage.

Ethical Leadership

In the wake of recent corporate scandals at firms like AIG, Enron, and WorldCom, faith in business leaders has been shaken. High standards of ethical conduct are therefore being held up as a prerequisite for effective leadership. More specifically, business leaders are being called on to maintain high ethical standards for their own conduct, to unfailingly exhibit ethical behaviour, and to hold others in their organizations to the same standards—in short, to practise **ethical leadership**.

ethical leadership Leader behaviours that reflect high ethical standards.

Virtual Leadership

virtual leadership The carrying out of leadership activities when the leader does not have regular personal contact with followers.

Virtual leadership involves carrying out leadership activities when the leader does not have regular personal contact with followers. In earlier times, leaders and their employees worked together in the same physical location and engaged in personal (i.e., face-to-face) interactions on a regular basis. But in today's world, leaders and their employees may work in locations that are far from one another. Such arrangements might include people telecommuting from a home office one or two days a week or people actually living and working far from company headquarters and seeing one another in person only very infrequently.

Under virtual leadership, communication between leaders and their subordinates will still occur, but it may be largely by telephone and email. In the future, leaders will have to work harder at creating and maintaining relationships with their employees that go beyond words on a computer screen. Nonverbal communication is not possible with email, so managers will have to work harder to convey appreciation, reinforcement, or constructive feedback to subordinates. Managers should also take advantage of every opportunity whenever they are in face-to-face situations to go further than they might have under different circumstances to develop a strong relationship.

Test yourself on the material for this chapter at **www.pearsoned.ca/mybusinesslab**.

Summary of Learning Objectives

1. **Identify and discuss the basic *forms of behaviour* that employees exhibit in organizations.** *Employee behaviour* is the pattern of actions by the members of an organization that directly or indirectly influences the organization's effectiveness. *Performance behaviours* are the total set of work-related behaviours that the organization expects employees to display. *Organizational citizenship* refers to the behaviour of individuals who make a positive overall contribution to the organization. *Counterproductive behaviours* are those that detract from, rather than contribute to, organizational performance.

2. **Describe the nature and importance of *individual differences* among employees.** Individual differences are personal attributes that vary from one person to another. *Personality* is the relatively stable set of psychological attributes that distinguish one person from another. The "big five" personality traits are agreeableness, conscientiousness, emotionality, extraversion, and openness. *Emotional intelligence, or emotional quotient (EQ)*, refers to the extent to which people are self-aware, can manage their emotions, can motivate themselves, express empathy for others, and possess social skills. Attitudes reflect our beliefs and feelings about specific ideas, situations, or other people. Especially important attitudes are *job satisfaction* and *organizational commitment*.

3. **Explain the meaning and importance of *psychological contracts* and the *person-job fit* in the workplace.** A *psychological contract* is the overall set of expectations held by employees and the organization regarding what employees will contribute to the organization and what the organization will provide in return. A good *person-job fit* is achieved when the employee's contributions match the inducements the organization offers. Having a good match between people and their jobs can help enhance performance, job satisfaction, and motivation.

4. **Identify and summarize the most important *models of employee motivation*.** *Motivation* is the set of forces that cause people to behave in certain ways. Early approaches to motivation were based first on the assumption that people work only for money and then on the assumption that social needs are the primary way to motivate people. The *hierarchy of human needs model* holds that people at work try to satisfy one or more of five different needs. The *two-factor theory* argues that satisfaction and dissatisfaction depend on hygiene factors, such as working conditions, and motivation factors, such as recognition for a job well done. *Expectancy theory* suggests that people are motivated to work toward rewards that they have a reasonable expectancy of obtaining. *Equity theory* focuses on social comparisons—people evaluating their treatment by the organization relative to the treatment of others.

5. **Describe the *strategies* used by organizations to improve employee motivation.** There are several major strategies and techniques often used to make jobs more interesting and rewarding. When using *reinforcement* theory, a manager has four basic strategies: (1) positive

reinforcement (apply desirable consequences when employees exhibit positive behaviour), (2) punishment (apply undesirable consequences when employees exhibit negative behaviour), (3) omission (withhold desirable consequences when employees exhibit undesirable behaviour), and (4) negative reinforcement (withhold undesirable consequences when employees exhibit positive behaviour).

Management by objectives (MBO) is a system of collaborative goal setting that extends from the top of an organization to the bottom. In *participative management and empowerment*, employees are given a voice in how they do their jobs and in how the company is managed. Using teams can also enhance motivation. *Job enrichment* adds motivating factors to job activities. *Job redesign* is a method of increasing job satisfaction by designing a more satisfactory fit between workers and their jobs. Some companies also use modified work schedules—different approaches to working hours. Common options include *worksharing (job sharing), flextime programs*, and *telecommuting*.

6. **Define *leadership* and distinguish it from *management*.** *Leadership* refers to the processes and behaviours used by someone to motivate, inspire, and influence the behaviours of others. While leadership and management are related concepts, they are not the same thing. Leadership involves such things as developing a vision, communicating that vision, and directing change. Management, meanwhile, focuses more on outlining procedures, monitoring results, and working toward outcomes.

7. **Summarize the *approaches to leadership* that developed in the twentieth century.** The *trait approach* to leadership focussed on identifying the traits of successful leaders. The earliest researchers believed that important leadership traits included intelligence, dominance, self-confidence, energy, activity (versus passivity), and knowledge about the job. More recent researchers have started to focus on traits such as emotional intelligence, drive, honesty and integrity, self-confidence, and charisma. The *behavioural approach* identified two basic and common leader behaviours: *task-focussed* and *employee-focussed* behaviours. The *situational approach* to leadership proposes that there is no single best approach to leadership. Instead, situational factors influence the approach to leadership that is most effective. This approach was proposed as a continuum of leadership behaviour, ranging from having the leader make decisions alone to having employees make decisions with minimal guidance from the leader. Each point on the continuum is influenced by characteristics of the leader, his or her subordinates, and the situation.

8. **Describe the most recent ideas about effective leadership.** *Transformational leadership* (as distinguished from *transactional leadership*) focuses on the set of abilities that allows a leader to recognize the need for change, to create a vision to guide that change, and to execute the change effectively. *Charismatic leadership* is influence based on the leader's personal charisma. The basic concept of charisma suggests that charismatic leaders are likely to have self-confidence, confidence in their beliefs and ideals, and a need to influence people. They also tend to communicate high expectations about follower performance and to express confidence in their followers.

Many organizations expect their leaders to play the role of coach—to select team members, to provide direction, and to train and develop, but otherwise allow the group to function autonomously. Another factor that is altering the face of leadership is the number of women advancing to higher levels. While there appear to be few differences between men and women leaders, the growing number of women leaders suggests a need for more study. Another changing perspective on leadership relates to cross-cultural issues. In this context, culture encompasses international differences and diversity-based differences within one culture.

Strategic leadership is the leader's ability to lead change in the organization so as to enhance its competitiveness. Business leaders are also being called on to practice *ethical leadership*—that is, to maintain high ethical standards for their own conduct and to hold others in their organizations to the same standards. As more leaders and employees work in different settings, a better understanding of *virtual leadership* is also becoming more important.

Key Terms

absenteeism (p. 304)
attitude (p. 307)
autocratic style (p. 324)
behavioural approach (p. 324)
charismatic leadership (p. 326)
classical theory of motivation (p. 308)
compressed workweek (p. 320)
counterproductive behaviours (p. 304)
democratic style (p. 324)
emotional intelligence (emotional quotient [EQ]) (p. 306)
employee behaviour (p.304)
employee-oriented (p. 324)
equity theory (p. 312)
ethical leadership (p. 328)
expectancy theory (p. 311)
flextime (p. 319)
free-rein style (p. 324)
goal setting theory (p. 315)
Hawthorne effect (p. 309)
hierarchy of human needs model (p. 310)
human relations (p. 309)
individual differences (p. 305)
job enrichment (p. 318)
job redesign (p. 319)
job satisfaction (p. 307)
leadership (p. 322)
management by objectives (MBO) (p. 315)
motivation (p. 308)
organizational citizenship (p. 304)
organizational commitment (p. 307)
participative management and empowerment (p. 316)
performance behaviours (p. 304)
personality (p. 305)
person-job fit (p. 308)
psychological contract (p. 307)
quality circle (p. 316)
reinforcement (p. 313)
scientific management (p. 309)
situational (contingency) approach (p. 325)
SMART goals (p. 315)
strategic leadership (p. 328)
task-oriented (p. 324)
telecommuting (p. 320)
Theory X (p. 310)
Theory Y (p. 310)
trait approach (p. 323)
transactional leadership (p. 326)
transformational leadership (p. 325)
turnover (p. 304)
two-factor theory (p. 311)
virtual leadership (p. 328)
wikis (p. 316)
worksharing (job sharing) (p. 321)

Questions for Analysis

1. Describe the psychological contract you currently have or have had in the past with an employer. If you have never worked, describe the psychological contract that you have with the instructor in this class.
2. Explain how each of the "big five" personality traits influence leadership effectiveness.
3. Compare and contrast the needs-based theories of Maslow and Herzberg with expectancy theory and equity theory.
4. How can participative management programs enhance employee satisfaction and motivation? Why do some employees not want to get involved in participative management?
5. What is the relationship between performance behaviours and organizational citizenship behaviours? Which are more important to an organization?
6. As a manager, under what sort of circumstances might you apply each of the theories of motivation discussed in this chapter? Which would be easiest to use? Which would be hardest? Why?
7. Suppose you realize one day that you are dissatisfied with your job. Short of quitting, what might you do to improve your situation?
8. List two Canadian and two U.S. managers who you think would also qualify as great leaders. Explain your choices.

Application Exercises

1. Ask a manager what traits the manager thinks are necessary for success. How does the manager's list compare with the "big five" list in this chapter? How many differences are there? Why would these differences exist?
2. Interview the manager of a local company and ask what strategies the company uses to enhance employee job satisfaction. Also ask the manager whether he or she believes that leadership can be taught. What are the implications of the manager's answer?

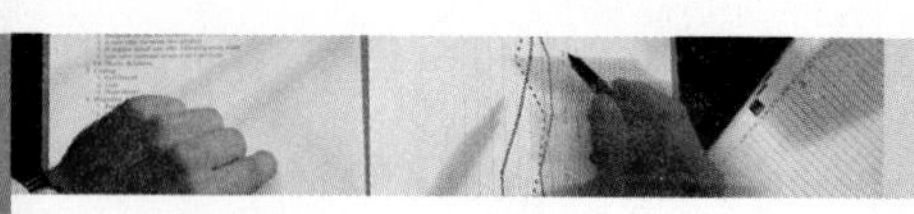

Building Your Business Skills

Too Much of a Good Thing

The Purpose of the Assignment

To encourage students to apply different motivational theories to a workplace problem involving poor productivity.

The Situation

Consider a small company that makes its employees feel as if they are members of a large family. Unfortunately, this company is going broke because too few members are working hard enough to make money for it. They are happy, comfortable, complacent—and lazy. With sales dropping, the company brings in management consultants to analyze the situation and make recommendations. The outsiders quickly identify a motivational problem affecting the sales force: Sales reps are paid a handsome salary and receive automatic year-end bonuses regardless of performance. They are also treated to bagels every Friday and regular group birthday lunches that cost as much as $200 each. Employees feel satisfied but have little incentive to work very hard. Eager to return to profitability, the company's owners wait to hear your recommendations.

Assignment

Step 1

In groups of four, step into the role of management consultants. Start by analyzing your client's workforce motivation problems from the following perspectives (the questions focus on key motivational issues):

Job satisfaction and morale. As part of a long-standing family-owned business, employees are happy and loyal, in part because they are treated so well. Can high morale have a downside? How can it breed stagnation, and what can managers do to prevent stagnation from taking hold?

Theory X versus Theory Y. Although the behaviour of these workers seems to make a case for Theory X, why is it difficult to draw this conclusion about a company that focuses more on satisfaction than on sales and profits?

Two-factor theory. Analyze the various ways in which improving such motivational factors as recognition, added responsibility, advancement, and growth might reduce the importance of hygiene factors, including pay and security.

Expectancy theory. Analyze the effect on productivity of redesigning the company's sales force compensation structure, namely, by paying lower base salaries while offering greater earnings potential through a sales-based incentive system. How would linking performance with increased pay that is achievable through hard work motivate employees? How would the threat of job loss motivate greater effort?

Step 2

Write a short report based on your analysis and make recommendations to the company's owners. The goal of your report is to change the working environment in ways that will motivate greater effort and generate greater productivity.

Questions for Discussion

1. What is your group's most important recommendation? Why do you think it is likely to succeed?
2. Changing the corporate culture to make it less paternalistic may reduce employees' sense of belonging to a family. If you were an employee, would you consider a greater focus on profits to be an improvement or a problem? How would it affect your motivation and productivity?
3. What steps would you take to improve the attitude and productivity of long-time employees who resist change?

Exercising Your Ethics: Team Exercise

Taking One for the Team

The Situation

You are a skilled technician who has worked for a major electronics firm for the past 10 years. You love your job—it is interesting, stimulating, and enjoyable, and you are well-paid for what you do. The plant where you work is one of five manufacturing centres your firm operates in a major metropolitan area. The firm is currently developing a new prototype for one of its next-generation products. To ensure that all perspectives are reflected, the company has identified a set of technicians from each plant who will work together as a team for the next two months.

The Dilemma

You have just met with your new teammates and are quite confused about what you might do next. As it turns out, the technicians from two of the manufacturing centres have heard rumours that your company is planning to close at least three of the centres and move production to a lower-cost factory in another country. These individuals are very upset. Moreover, they have made it clear that they (1) do not intend to put forth much extra effort on this project, and (2) are all looking for new jobs. You and the other technicians, though, have heard none of these rumours. Moreover, these individuals seem as excited as you are about their jobs.

Team Activity

First, working alone, write a brief summary of how you would handle this situation. For instance, would you seek more information or just go about your work? Would you start looking for another job, would you try to form a subgroup with just those technicians who share your views, or would you try to work with everyone?

Second, form a small group with some of your classmates. Share with each other the various ideas you each identified. Then, formulate a group description of what you think most people in your situation would do and share your description with the rest of the class.

For additional cases and exercise material, go to **www.pearsoned.ca/mybusinesslab**.

Concluding Case 10-1

What About Telecommuting?

On any given day, many business offices are vacant because employees are either at off-site meetings, travelling, on vacation, out sick, or attending training sessions. Many companies now recognize that there are advantages for both employees and for the company if they allow employees to work from home and "telecommute." About 1.5 million Canadians work at home at least one or two days a week, and some work from home almost all the time. Consider three fairly typical stories.

Edward Moffat works for Sun Microsystems of Canada. He signed up for the company's "open work" program, which allowed him to work largely from home (or anywhere for that matter). He wasn't in the office much anyway, because he travelled a lot. Now Ed works out of his Brampton, Ontario home 9 days out of 10. He doesn't have to pay $300 per month in highway tolls, his gas costs and car maintenance costs have gone way down, and he spends less on lunch. He thinks all those things combined save him about $50 per day. He also gets to see his wife and children more frequently. The company estimates that telecommuting saved it $71 million in real estate costs alone (because fewer employee offices are needed), and the turnover rate is half what it is for non-telecommuters.

Sylvie Bolduc decided to take advantage of Bell Canada's telework option, partly because she was sick of the 90-minute drive to work every day. She says she is a disciplined person and doesn't feel the need to constantly interact with co-workers. She has online meetings with staff on a regular basis and makes trips to the office every two weeks to catch up on other developments. She says she wants to work like this the rest of her life. Bell's program means that 11 000 tonnes of greenhouse gases are not being put into the atmosphere, because fewer employees are driving to and from work.

Deborah Corber started telecommuting at her job when her family relocated to her hometown of Montreal. Later, she worked out of her home after she started her own consulting firm. She says the biggest challenge was isolation, because she likes bouncing ideas off colleagues. She also had trouble separating her personal and professional life and felt that she was spending way too much time in her office in her home. In 2007, she decided to stop working at home, and she now shares space with several colleagues in an office close to her home.

These three stories show how varied employee experiences are with the idea of telecommuting. They also show that there are advantages and disadvantages associated with telecommuting.

Advantages for employees

- health benefits (for example, lower stress levels)
- lower costs (reduced car expenses)
- better use of time (no commuting long distances, no interruptions)

Disadvantages for employees

- feeling "out of the loop" (not being knowledgeable about important business issues or interesting personal gossip)
- having difficulty separating personal and professional life (work intrudes at home)
- feeling ill-suited for telework (lack of discipline and feeling lonely)
- finding it difficult to work closely with colleagues when necessary
- fear of career derailment

Advantages for the Employer

- increased productivity (two-thirds of employers surveyed said that employee productivity went up)
- cost savings (fewer offices and office supplies are needed; lower vehicle expenses)
- lower electric bills (fewer lights and computers are turned on in offices)
- access to qualified staff (who otherwise wouldn't be available because they don't live in the area or don't want to drive so far to work)
- lower travel expenses (teleconferencing, email, networking systems take the place of travel)
- lower employee turnover

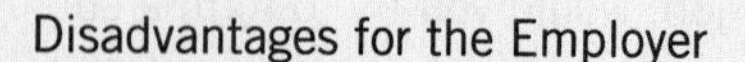

Disadvantages for the Employer

- requires a change in management thinking (forces managers to adopt an attitude of trust regarding employees)
- bosses have to spend more time with subordinates on the phone or other media (they may prefer face-to-face communication)
- bosses don't know when employees are actually working (may threaten the control of bosses who are used to having employees in sight)
- telecommuting may not work well for companies where customers are frequently in the office
- telecommuting may not work well if colleagues frequently need intense face-to-face collaboration to complete rush jobs on time

These advantages and disadvantages mean that telecommuting must be carefully thought through so that it is beneficial to both employees and to the company. It does not mean simply telling workers that they can now work at home. Rather, there must be a clear understanding between the bosses and workers about things like the nature of the arrangement, the type of tasks that can be completed away from the office, maintaining safety and confidentiality in the employee's home office, what telecommuting might mean for the employee's career path, and so on.

Questions for Discussion

1. How is telecommuting different from other forms of modified work schedules? How is it similar?
2. Do you think that telecommuting will become more prominent in the future? Explain the reasons for your position.
3. Interview a friend or relative who telecommutes in their job. What advantages and disadvantages do they see in such an arrangement? Compare their responses with the advantages and disadvantages listed above. If there are major differences, try to explain them.

Concluding Case 10-2

Leadership and Management

We generally think of leadership and management as being important mainly in business firms, but leadership and management are relevant in many different contexts. Consider the activity of polar exploration. In the nineteenth century, much time, money, and effort was spent by English, Norwegian, and American explorers as they tried to reach the North and South Poles. To achieve their goals, explorers first had to secure financial support to pay for their expeditions. But that was only the beginning. Ships and personnel had to be acquired, and tonnes of supplies and animals had to be taken across the ocean to the starting point for the expedition. All of this required a great deal of planning and organizing, both of which are key functions of management. But leadership was also crucial because these expeditions were attempting to achieve goals that were at the very edge of human capability. They were also very dangerous, and many men died on these expeditions. Leaders who could generate high motivation and commitment among their followers were therefore critical to the success of their expeditions. John Franklin, Ernest Shackleton, Roald Amundsen, and Robert Scott were particularly notable.

John Franklin (1786–1847)

John Franklin was an English explorer who hungered for fame and promotion through the ranks of the English navy. Franklin has been described as recklessly ambitious, humourless, sensitive, unimaginative, dogged, brave, indecisive, calm when danger threatened, courageous, charming, humble, and easygoing. In 1845, he led a group of 129 men in an attempt to discover the Northwest Passage. Critics of Franklin noted that he ignored the harsh environment he was entering and simply tried to transport the "civilized" English environment with him rather than adapting to the Arctic environment as the Inuit did. His expedition was last seen by a whaling ship in Baffin Bay in June 1845. His group was never seen again by white people, but his expedition may have encountered Inuit hunters somewhere in their travels. His ships were crushed by the ice and eventually all 129 members of the expedition died as they tried to find their way home.

Ernest Shackleton (1874–1922)

Ernest Shackleton was an Anglo-Irish explorer who became famous for his dramatic expeditions to the Antarctic as he tried to reach the South Pole. Shackleton has been described as quick tempered, impatient, self-confident, ruthless, egotistical, moody, optimistic, persuasive, restless, and ambitious. He was a strong leader who made things happen. His followers did whatever he ordered because they had complete faith in him. They affectionately called him "The Boss." Shackleton showed great concern for the men under his command, and he put his followers' welfare ahead of his own. His inspirational leadership motivated his men to give that extra ounce of effort in life-and-death situations.

In 1914, Shackleton decided to trek across the Antarctic, but his ship, the *Endurance*, became locked in the ice and he never even reached the continent. After the ship was crushed by the ice and sank, his party camped out for some weeks until the ice broke up. They then took to small boats and made their way to nearby Elephant Island, a desolate, isolated, and windswept speck of land in the South Atlantic Ocean. Knowing that rescue would never come there, Shackleton and a small group of men then sailed a tiny open boat across almost 1300 kilometres of ocean to South Georgia, where they organized a relief party for the men back on Elephant Island. In the end, not a man was lost and Shackleton's leadership reputation became legendary.

Robert Scott (1868–1912) and Roald Amundsen (1872–1928)

In 1911–12, the Englishman Robert Scott and the Norwegian Roald Amundsen became involved in a race to see who would be the first human being to reach the South Pole. The trip to the Pole was made in conditions that are hard to imagine. On foot or on skis, the explorers made their way across 1200 kilometres of ice and snow, through –40°C temperatures and over mountains nearly 3000 metres high. Once at the Pole, they had to turn around and fight their way back to the coast through the same conditions.

Roald Amundsen was very successful because he learned to adapt his behaviour to the environment in which he was working. He avoided almost all of the mistakes that other explorers made. For example, he learned that most expeditions actually had two leaders: the expedition commander (who typically had no navigation experience) and the ship's captain. This could lead to dissension. He also learned that there was typically conflict between the scientific staff and the sailors on the expedition. Amundsen therefore studied science and navigation and became an expert at both, so there was no divided command on his expeditions. He also took only small numbers of men so there were fewer people to feed. In sharp contrast to most other explorers, he adopted the successful strategies of the Inuit to survive in polar climates.

Amundsen was a meticulous planner because he realized that planning was absolutely essential for a successful expedition to the Pole. In the crucial areas of food and fuel, Amundsen developed a system for laying out supply depots so that they could be found even in a raging blizzard. This ensured that the Norwegians had enough supplies to make it safely back to their base camp after they had reached the Pole. By studying polar conditions, he knew that sled dogs were the best animals to haul supplies. He also knew that going to the Pole on skis was far superior to walking. Amundsen carefully selected the four men who would accompany him and who would live in very close quarters during the three-month trip to the Pole and back. Amundsen's men had complete confidence in his abilities, and he, in turn, allowed them to participate in many of the important decisions that had to be made during the expedition.

Robert Scott was a sharp contrast to Amundsen. Because he left the planning of important details of the expedition to the last minute, major mistakes were made in decisions about animals and equipment. For example, Scott decided to rely on ponies for hauling supplies, but this decision ignored the obvious fact that ponies were inferior to huskies for hauling supplies in bitterly cold weather. Scott did take skis along, but few people in his party knew how to use them properly. They therefore wasted precious energy and covered fewer kilometres each day than they might have. Scott's planning of supply depots was also haphazard, and insufficient care was taken in the storage of fuel. In the extreme cold of the Antarctic, much of the fuel that Scott had stored in supply depots evaporated. On his return trip, therefore, he consistently ran short of fuel. (Amundsen had no such problems because he had designed an airtight seal for his fuel containers.) Scott's leadership ability was also questionable. There was dissension in the ranks because of poor communication, conflicting orders, and interpersonal disagreements. Scott did not inspire confidence in his men, and he did not allow them to participate in important decisions.

Who won the race? Although both men managed to reach the South Pole, Amundsen beat Scott to the prize by a full month. In the end, Scott's men paid dearly for their leader's shortcomings: They all died of starvation and exposure as they attempted to get back to their base camp on the coast.

Questions for Discussion

1. What is the difference between leaders and managers? Were the explorers described above leaders? Were they managers?
2. Compare the leadership ability of each of the polar explorers in terms of the five traits that are thought to predict effective leadership.
3. What is emotional intelligence? To what extent did the polar explorers exhibit emotional intelligence?
4. Use any one of the contingency leadership theories discussed in the chapter to analyze the appropriateness of the leadership styles used by Scott and Amundsen. Were they using the right style? Explain.
5. What makes a leader charismatic? Which of the polar explorers do you think was the most charismatic? Explain.

CBC Video Case 2-1

Flair Bartending

Remember the movie in which Tom Cruise played a flashy bartender? That style of bartending actually has a name. It's called "flair bartending." Gavin MacMillan is the top-ranked Canadian flair bartender and second-ranked in the world. He's also an author and the owner of a bartender-for-hire business called Movers and Shakers. Now he's developing a brand-new idea for a bartender school called Bartender 1. Eventually, he wants to franchise the idea across Canada, the United States, and the world.

Potential franchisees will like his idea to use an actual bar to teach students flair bartending. Gavin doesn't rent space; rather, he borrows a bar for an evening to hold his classes. On one Monday evening, he is at a Toronto bar that is closed, but he has talked the owner into letting him run his class there for free. In return, the bar gets first pick of the graduates of Gavin's bartending school. In his first class of 12 students, Gavin has incurred $11 000 of expenses but receives only $6000 in revenues. He hopes to reduce the cost of running future classes by reusing demonstration equipment. He needs to prove this concept will really work before trying to franchise it.

Later, a Mississauga bar owner lets Gavin hold a class at his establishment. Gavin doesn't have a problem finding students who want to be bartenders, but he does have a problem finding people who can be instructors. There are only about 10 flair bartenders in Toronto and 40 in all of Canada. Finding teachers is not Gavin's only problem. He is a perfectionist who is always fussing over the little things. Sometimes he focuses so much on the details that he doesn't see the big picture. A third problem is his lack of time to do all the things he wants to do.

He has designed, built, and financed a portable bar that he hopes to sell to golf courses and hotels. He brings his idea to an entrepreneurial self-help session run by a business group that he joined. He says that he wants to make 10 of the portable bars in order to be more cost-effective, and he wants the other participants in the group to help him with ideas to market the bar. But one of the group members questions whether Gavin should even pursue the idea, because he already has too many balls in the air. He needs to prioritize.

Two months later, Gavin is conducting a two-day bartending course at the University of Guelph. His school is now making money, and everything is going well because he listened to the advice to focus on just a few projects. He has stopped putting energy into his portable bar for the moment and has begun delegating duties to others.

Gavin says he wants to make his business a great success. He is thinking big. He wants to earn enough money to buy a yacht with a helicopter pad on it.

Questions for Discussion

1. What are the big-five personality traits? How do you think Gavin MacMillan would score on each of these five traits? What might this imply for his success as an entrepreneur?
2. Do a little research and find out what the difference is between *extrinsic motivation* and *intrinsic motivation*. Do you think Gavin is extrinsically or intrinsically motivated?
3. Gavin says that he wants to eventually have a yacht with a helicopter pad on it. How does setting a goal like this motivate a person?
4. What recommendations would you have for Gavin in the area of being more focussed in his goal setting?

Video Resource: "Flair Bartending," *Dreamers and Schemers* (November 8, 2006).

CBC Video Case 2-2

Clash of the Co-workers

Venture conducted a survey to determine workers' perceptions of the main causes of conflict in the workplace. Respondents were presented with a list of 10 common worker complaints and asked to list their top three. The top three vote-getters were (1) people who talk too loudly on the phone, (2) office gossip, and (3) co-workers who waste your time. *Venture* further examined the impact of office gossip. It also looked at the issues of co-workers who don't pull their weight and clashes between older and younger workers.

Office Gossip

Office gossip can poison a workplace. A tanning salon owner who had worked hard to build her company encountered big problems when employees started spreading rumours about one another. After one salon manager disciplined a worker, other workers began spreading rumours that the salon manager was incompetent. When the owner became aware of the excessive gossip that was evident at the company, she called all employees into the head office and asked them to sign a contract that prohibited gossip. One behaviour that is prohibited is talking about a co-worker when that co-worker isn't present. A year after introducing the contract idea, the salon owner is getting calls from other companies asking about the policy.

Bob Summerhurst, a human resources specialist, says that gossip occurs when bosses play favourites or when they don't communicate properly. Any information void will be filled with gossip, and that gossip is often negative. His solution is not a ban on gossip but rather regular meetings of managers and employees.

Co-workers Who Don't Pull Their Weight

Jerry Steinberg, a Vancouver teacher, says that workers with children are often treated as "special" and he thinks it's unfair. He says an extra burden is being borne by people like himself when they are asked to work a few extra hours a week to cover for parents who are tending to their children. The problem is worst during the holiday season because people with no children are asked to work holidays so that workers with children can spend time with their kids.

Steinberg is speaking up about his concerns. He has started a website called No Kidding where child-free members can vent their frustrations about the unfair treatment they are receiving at their workplace. But Steinberg says it is hard to stand up for yourself because you don't want to rock the boat or be a whiner. He recognizes that it sounds heartless to be unsympathetic to parents' wishes to spend time with their children. But he also observes that these people made a choice to have children, and they shouldn't expect to have an advantage because they made that choice. He is also unhappy about the extra benefits that parents get. He has a simple solution for that problem: Give each employee a certain dollar amount that they can spend on whatever benefits they want.

The Generation Gap

Young people in their 20s have generally grown up in an environment where their baby-boomer parents gave them lots of things. Now those young people are entering the workforce, and they want more things—benefits, money, authority, and free time. And they want them right now.

Consider John and Ryan, who are recent college grads. They are part of a generation that is a problem for business. They feel that they work very hard, but they don't necessarily want to do what their predecessors did (like wearing a suit and tie to work, or working from 9 to 5). Mike Farrell, who researches attitudes of young people, notes that most young people are plugged in and well-informed, and these are qualities that employers crave. Theresa Williams, who hires workers for the Halifax *Chronicle-Herald*, recognizes that young people today are different from their predecessors. For example, they don't seem grateful to be offered a job like people in her generation were. She tries to overcome the difficulties in recruiting young people by emphasizing the good working conditions at the *Chronicle-Herald*.

The way students look for jobs is also changing. The job fair approach is still used, but some companies find it doesn't attract the kind of employees they want. One company therefore came up with a gimmick: They posted a job competition on the internet, with the prize being a job for a year, a free apartment, and a trip home for the holidays. The two winners—John and Ryan—moved to Halifax. A year later, they moved out of their free apartment but stayed on with the company. Now they are helping to design this year's job competition, and they're on board with "the old guys."

Questions for Discussion

1. What are the various forms of employee behaviour that can be observed in organizations, and what is the impact of the various forms on organizations? Identify the forms of employee behaviour that are evident in each of the three situations described above and how they affected the organization in which they occurred.
2. What is the difference between *management* and *leadership*? What is the relevance of management and leadership in each of the situations described above?
3. What is the difference between the *formal organization* and the *informal organization*? How is the distinction relevant for each of the three situations described above?
4. Consider the following statement with respect to the first incident described above (office gossip): *The grapevine carries a lot of inaccurate information that prevents employees from doing their jobs well. To overcome this problem, managers should provide accurate information through formal communication channels, and that will negate the need for the grapevine.* Do you agree or disagree with the statement? Explain your reasoning.

Video Resource: "Clash of the Co-workers," *Venture* (March 26, 2006).

Crafting a Business Plan

Part 2(a): The Business of Managing

Goal of the Exercise

In Part 1 of the business plan project, you formulated a basic identity for your business. Part 2(a) of the business plan project asks you to think about the goals of your business, some internal and external factors affecting the business, and the organizational structure of the business.

Exercise Background: Part 2(a) of the Business Plan

As you learned in Chapter 6, every business sets goals. In this part of the plan, you'll define some of the goals for your business. Part 2(a) of the business plan also asks you to perform a basic SWOT analysis for your business. As you'll recall from Chapter 6, a SWOT analysis looks at the business's *strengths, weaknesses, opportunities,* and *threats.* The strengths and weaknesses are internal factors—things that the business can control. The opportunities and threats are generally external factors that affect the business, such as the following:

Socio-cultural forces—Will changes in population or culture help your business or hurt it?

Economic forces—Will changes in the economy help your business or hurt it?

Technological forces—Will changes in technology help your business or hurt it?

Competitive forces—Does your business face much competition or very little?

Political-legal forces—Will changes in laws help your business or hurt it?

Each of these forces will affect different businesses in different ways, and some of these may not apply to your business at all.

Part 2(a) of the business plan also asks you to determine how the business is to be run. One thing you'll need to do is create an organizational chart to get you thinking about the different tasks needed for a successful business.

Your Assignment

Step 1

Open the saved *Business Plan* file you began working on in Part 1. You will continue to work from the same file you started working on in Part 1.

Step 2

For the purposes of this assignment, you will answer the questions in "Part 2(a): The Business of Managing."

1. Provide a brief mission statement for your business.

Hint: Refer to the discussion of mission statements in Chapter 6. Be sure to include the name of your business, how you will stand out from your competition, and why a customer will buy from you.

2. Consider the goals for your business. What are three of your business goals for the first year? What are two intermediate-to-long-term goals?

Hint: Refer to the discussion of goal setting in Chapter 6. Be as specific and realistic as possible with the goals you set. For example, if you plan on selling a service, how many customers do you want by the end of the first year, and how much do you want each customer to spend?

3. Perform a basic SWOT analysis for your business, listing its main strengths, weaknesses, opportunities, and threats.

Hint: We explained previously what factors you should consider in your basic SWOT analysis. Look around at your world, talk to classmates, or talk to your instructor for other ideas in performing your SWOT analysis.

4. Who will manage the business?

Hint: Refer to the discussion of managers in Chapter 6. Think about how many levels of management as well as what kinds of managers your business needs.

5. Show how the "team" fits together by creating a simple organizational chart for your business. Your chart should indicate who will work for each manager as well as each person's job title.

Hint: As you create your organizational chart, consider the different tasks involved in the business. Whom will each person report to? Refer to the discussion of organizational structure in Chapter 7 for information to get you started.

Note: Once you have answered the questions, save your Word document. You'll be answering additional questions in later chapters

Crafting a Business Plan

Part 2(b): The Business of Managing

Goal of the Exercise

At this point, your business has an identity and you've described the factors that will affect your business and how you will operate it. Part 2(b) of the business plan project asks you to think about your employees, the jobs they will be performing, and the ways in which you can lead and motivate them.

Exercise Background: Part 2(b) of the Business Plan

To complete this part of the plan, you need to refer back to the organizational chart that you created in Part 2(a). In this part of the business plan exercise, you'll take the different job titles you created in the organizational chart and give thought to the *skills* that employees will need to bring to the job *before* they begin. You'll also consider the *training* you'll need to provide *after* they are hired, as well as how you'll compensate your employees. Part 2(b) of the business plan also asks you to consider how you'll lead your employees and keep them happy and motivated.

Your Assignment

Step 1

Open the *Business Plan* file you have been working on.

Step 2

For the purposes of this assignment, you will answer the questions in "Part 2(b): The Business of Managing."

1. What do you see as the "corporate culture" of your business? What types of employee behaviours, such as organizational citizenship, will you expect?

Hint: Will your business demand a casual environment or a more professional environment? Refer to the discussion on employee behaviour in Chapter 10 for information on organizational citizenship and other employee behaviours.

2. What is your philosophy on leadership? How will you manage your employees day-to-day?

Hint: Refer to the discussion on leadership in Chapter 10 to help you formulate your thoughts.

3. Looking back at your organizational chart in Part 2(a), briefly create a job description for each team member.

Hint: As you learned in Chapter 8, a job description lists the duties and responsibilities of a job; its working conditions; and the tools, materials, equipment, and information used to perform it. Imagine your business on a typical day. Who is working and what are each person's responsibilities?

4. Next, create a job specification for each job, listing the skills and other credentials and qualifications needed to perform the job effectively.

Hint: As you write your job specifications, consider what you would write if you were making an ad for the position. What would the new employee need to bring to the job in order to qualify for the position?

5. What sort of training, if any, will your employees need once they are hired? How will you provide this training?

Hint: Refer to the discussion of training in Chapter 8. Will you offer your employees on-the-job training? Off-the-job training? Vestibule training?

6. A major factor in retaining skilled workers is a company's compensation system—the total package of rewards that it offers employees in return for their labour. Part of this compensation system includes wages/salaries. What wages or salaries will you offer for each job? Why did you decide on that pay rate?

Hint: Refer to Chapter 8 for more information on forms of compensation.

7. As you learned in Chapter 8, incentive programs are special programs designed to motivate high performance. What incentives will you use to motivate your workforce?

Hint: Be creative and look beyond a simple answer, such as giving pay increases. Ask yourself, who are my employees and what is important to them? Refer to Chapter 8 for more information on the types of incentives you may want to consider.

Note: Once you have answered the questions, save your Word document. You'll be answering additional questions in later chapters.

Part Three

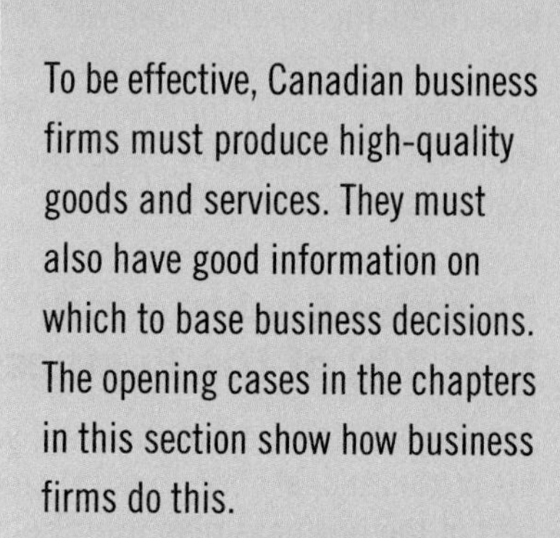

Managing Operations and Information

To be effective, Canadian business firms must produce high-quality goods and services. They must also have good information on which to base business decisions. The opening cases in the chapters in this section show how business firms do this.

Part Three, Managing Operations and Information, provides an overview of four aspects of business that are important to a firm's survival: efficiently producing goods and services, increasing productivity and quality, managing information systems, and understanding principles of accounting.

- We begin in **Chapter 11, Producing Goods and Services**, by examining how firms manage the production of goods and services and how they control both the cost and the quality of their output.
- Then, in **Chapter 12, Increasing Productivity and Quality**, we consider the various approaches companies take to improve the productivity and the quality of their output and thus their competitive position.
- Next, in **Chapter 13, Managing Information Systems and Communication Technology**, we describe the concept of management information systems and how modern electronic technologies have revolutionized the work of managers.
- Finally, in **Chapter 14, Understanding Accounting Issues**, we examine the role of accountants in gathering, assembling, and presenting financial information about a firm. We also look at the tools accountants use and the statements they prepare to report a firm's financial standing.

Chapter 11

Producing Goods and Services

After reading this chapter, you should be able to:

1. Explain the meaning of the terms *production* and *operations*.
2. Describe the four kinds of *utility* provided by production and explain the two classifications of *operations processes*.
3. Identify the characteristics that distinguish *service operations* from *goods production* and explain the main differences in the service focus.
4. Describe the factors involved in *operations planning*.
5. Explain some factors in *operations scheduling* and describe some activities involved in *operations control*, including materials management and the use of certain operations control tools.

Mattel: Getting a Toy Recall Right

Mattel began as a small toy manufacturer in 1945 in Southern California. The Barbie doll was introduced in 1959, followed in 1968 by the now-famous line of Hot Wheels cars. Millions of children grew up with the Mattel brand, and many enthusiasts continue to be loyal collectors as adults.

In the 1990s, Mattel began contracting out its manufacturing activities to companies in China in an effort to reduce costs and to remain competitive. Before long, however, the company had to recall some toys because of safety concerns. During the past few years, these recalls have increased substantially, and millions of toys that were made in China have been recalled. For example, Mattel products like Barbie doll accessories and small cars—totaling 11.5 million pieces—were recalled in 2007 because they contained lead paint and small magnets that could be easily removed and possibly swallowed by children.

How could a large and trusted company like Mattel have so many problems with toy recalls? The answer to this question requires an understanding of the difference between toy *design* and toy *manufacturing*. Toy design occurs at toy companies like Mattel. Design problems can be things like sharp edges on a toy that could lead to a cut, small detachable parts (balls and beads), open tubes and spaces, long strings that could cause strangulation, and buttons (choking hazard). It is important to design products that are safe to use because a design problem will result in an unsafe toy regardless of where it is manufactured. Only toy companies can prevent problems that are caused by faulty designs. The problem of the small magnets in the recalled toys was Mattel's design flaw, and this accounted for 90 percent of the recalled toys.

By contrast, toy *manufacturing* is carried out by overseas manufacturers. Manufacturing problems include the use of substandard material (which causes parts to break), faulty electrical circuits, and the use of lead paint that is not approved. Manufacturing defects occur because of errors or negligence, and manufacturers can prevent defects with proper attention to quality control. Ten percent of the recalled toys were the result of a manufacturing flaw (excess lead in the surface paint).

Toys are recalled when there is a fault in either design or manufacturing. A successful recall is measured by the proportion of products that are returned. When child safety is at risk, anything less than a 90 percent return rate within the first three months is deemed a failure. Designers and manufacturers both should be accountable for product safety, but when recalls are announced, the offshore manufacturers are usually blamed. Mattel initially blamed the Chinese manufacturers, but when independent researchers looked at the situation—and concluded that most of the problems were design problems, not manufacturing problems—Mattel had to backpedal. The Chinese manufacturer did use lead paint in the toys, but that did not relieve Mattel of the responsibility for its presence in the toys. Mattel needed to develop proper systems to engage more directly and closely with their overseas manufacturers.

Mattel does deserve credit for later publicly admitting that it was their design flaw that caused the problem and for taking steps to ensure that all of the affected products were recalled. The company announced the recall by placing ads on high-traffic internet sites, creating a website that clearly outlined the recall, and also providing consumers with downloadable application forms and paid shipping mailers. In addition, Mattel's CEO took responsibility for the recall and, in a prepared public apology, stated that the company "takes full responsibility for these recalls and apologizes personally to you, the Chinese people, and all of our customers who received the toys." This type of public admission of guilt was unprecedented in recall history. For their efforts in ensuring that all of the affected toys were safely removed from stores and homes, Mattel was named one of the "World's Most Ethical Companies" in 2009.

Other companies who find themselves in a recall situation can learn from the Mattel recall. Designers and manufacturers can reduce the likelihood of recalls by using effective quality control and inspection mechanisms. More robust systems for quality control and testing are also needed at the overseas factories. Unfortunately, the issue of global standards is problematic because different countries have different standards. If globalized partnering relations are to continue and be successful, an increased level of understanding and communication is necessary. The issue of recalls is larger than simply "Mattel vs. China," but rather includes the entire supply chain of suppliers, designers, manufacturers, and marketers. Each member of the supply chain must be involved in monitoring product quality and ensuring that safety standards are being applied. For that to happen, there must be a collective effort on the part of governments, corporations, industry associations, and consumers. ◆

How will this help me?

By reading and understanding methods that managers use for producing goods and services, you will benefit in two ways: (1) As an employee, you'll have a clearer picture of who your customers are, what they want, and how your job depends on the goods and services your company provides, and (2) you'll better understand how all companies—even successful ones—remain competitive by continually analyzing their production methods so they can efficiently produce high-quality products and services that consumers will want. Furthermore, you'll look at how businesses create value through production operations and at the many facets of operations, including planning, scheduling, and controlling.

1 Explain the meaning of the terms *production* and *operations*.

service operations Production activities that yield tangible and intangible service products.

goods production Production activities that yield tangible products.

Everywhere you go today, you encounter business activities that provide goods and services to their customers. You wake up in the morning, for example, to the sound of your favourite radio station. You stop at the corner newsstand for a newspaper on your way to the bus stop, where you catch the bus to work or school. Your instructors, the bus driver, the clerk at the corner store, and the morning radio announcer are all examples of people who work in **service operations**. They provide you with tangible and intangible service products, such as entertainment, transportation, education, and food preparation. Firms that make tangible products—radios, newspapers, buses, and textbooks—are engaged in **goods production**.

What Does "Production" Mean Today?

Although the term *production* has historically referred to the making of physical goods like automobiles, toothpaste, televisions, toys, and so forth, the concept as we now use it also means services. Many of the things that we need or want, from health care to fast food, are produced by service operations. As a rule, service sector managers focus less on equipment and technology than on the human element in operations. Why? Because success or failure may depend on provider-customer contact. Employees who deal directly with customers affect customer feelings about the service, and as we will see, a key difference between production and service operations is the customer's involvement in the latter.

Today, however, customers are increasingly involved in all kinds of production because electronic communications are key components in winning and keeping customers in a huge range of competitive industries. Orders are placed faster, schedules are accelerated, and delivery times are shrinking. Internet buyers can be linked to the production floor itself, where their orders for products ranging from cellphones to automobiles are launched and filled in real time. B2B (business to business) customers also expect real-time response and online delivery.

While companies are typically classified as either goods producers or service providers, the distinction is often blurred. All businesses are service operations to some extent. When you think of General Electric, for example, you most likely think of appliances and jet engines. However, GE is not just a goods producer. According to its annual report, GE's "growth engines"—its most vibrant business activities—are service operations, including media and entertainment (NBC-Universal), consumer and commercial finance, invest-

This new plant just outside of Bangalore, India, supplies transmission systems to Toyota plants all over the world. Making auto parts is a rapidly growing business in India, and there are nearly 400 parts makers in the Bangalore area alone. Exports in the industry have skyrocketed, with industry numbers targeted to grow four times, to US$40 billion, by 2015. That's only about one-tenth of what the country's software industry brings in, but the auto parts industry surge has resulted from the same factors: low labour costs and a very large, technically competent workforce.

ment, transportation services, health-care information, and real estate, which account for over 80 percent of the company's revenues.[1]

The Growth of Global Operations

Many countries have recently joined the global competition that has reshaped production into a faster-paced, more complex business activity. Although the factory remains the centrepiece for manufacturing, it bears little resemblance to its counterpart of a decade ago. The smoke, grease, and danger have been replaced in many companies by glistening high-tech machines, computers, and "clean rooms" that are contaminant free and climate controlled.

Production operations have also become much more environmentally friendly. Interface Inc., a Belleville, Ontario, carpet manufacturer, used to produce 500 000 litres of waste water every month. They solved that problem by eliminating a printing process that used a lot of water—and saved $15 000 a month as an added benefit. They also reduced carpet remnant waste from 474 tonnes per year to 39 tonnes by making some design changes in the product. Several other innovations, such as using smaller motors, reduced the company's utility bills by 70 percent. The plant became so efficient that it exported 60 percent of its production to the United States.[2] The boxed insert entitled "Move Over, George Jetson" describes one entrepreneur's efforts to build an environmentally friendly product.

Instead of needing to maintain continuous mass production, firms today face constant change. New technologies allow machines to run more cleanly, quickly, and safely, and to operate on a global scale. In a modern factory with online manufacturing, machines can log on to the internet, adjust their own settings, and make minor decisions without human help. They can communicate with other machines in the company (via an intranet) and with other companies' machines (via the internet). So-called "smart" equipment stores performance data that become available on desktops around the world, where designers can click

Entrepreneurship and New Ventures

Move Over, George Jetson

Well, this vehicle may not be able to fly, but it sure looks like it could. The Uno, touted as the world's first unicycle motorbike, was invented by Ben Gulak, a 19-year-old MIT student from Milton, Ontario. Eye-catching because of its space-age design and reminiscent of something you may have seen on the once-popular TV cartoon show *The Jetsons*, the Uno is an electric-powered motorcycle that uses gyroscope technology. It's kind of like the Segway (an electric scooter) in that it's controlled completely through body movements.

Gulak made a conscious decision to ensure that his invention provided more than just transportation; it had to possess the cool factor because "... if something doesn't look cool, people just won't be interested." Gulak got the idea for the bike when on a family vacation in China in 2006. Struck by the unbelievable pollution, he saw the need to come up with a clean, environmentally friendly, alternative vehicle for densely populated urban centres. He believed a small easily transported electric motorcycle could be the answer, but it also needed to have the right look. Back home in Milton, Gulak went to work on developing a prototype.

His first test run resulted in a chipped kneecap, but he didn't let that slow him down. The gyro control system needed some fine tuning so the machine would move more smoothly. He also had a custom motorcycle manufacturer build the body parts out of foam and fibreglass, based on Gulak's drawings. The Uno can travel up to 24 kilometres per hour, but Gulak is aiming to reach 60 kilometres per hour. It also can run for about 2.5 hours on a single charge.

So far, his parents have bankrolled his research efforts to the tune of $50 000. But that money is now gone, and the bike is not quite ready for production yet. So, how does a 19-year-old fellow get the money to advance his prototype development?

He applies to CBC's *Dragon's Den*, of course! In November 2008, Gulak wowed the Dragons with his Uno prototype, and on-air he landed a $1.25 million investment to be used for research purposes. In exchange, the Dragons demanded a 20 percent stake in his business. Since the show, however, four of the Dragons reneged on their offers and Dragon Brett Wilson is the only investor remaining. According to Wilson, "Now it's just me and I'm in for $250 000." However, Gulak has not let this setback dampen his enthusiasm. "I really believe in this product and would really like to see it to production," he says.

His ultramodern design is garnering attention and raising eyebrows in media circles. *Popular Science* magazine listed the Uno among the top 10 inventions for 2008. And a profile on the Discovery Channel and a request to do an appearance on the *Tonight Show*, with motorcycle fan and host Jay Leno, haven't been bad for publicity either. Who knows? With the right combination of engineering and business skills, Gulak just might be able to make this machine fly someday!

Critical Thinking Question

1. Explore and discuss the concepts of production value, transformation, and operations planning as they apply now, or may in the future, to the production of Gulak's Uno. Could any of these factors be reasons why the Dragons backed out of the deal?

on machine data, simulate machine action, and evaluate performance before machines themselves ever swing into action. With the internet, producers of both services and goods are integrating their production activities with those of far-off suppliers and customers.

Creating Value Through Production

2 Describe the four kinds of *utility* provided by production and explain the two classifications of *operations processes.*

utility The power of a product to satisfy a human want; something of value.

time utility That quality of a product satisfying a human want because of the time at which it is made available.

To understand the production processes of a firm, you need to understand the importance of products—both goods and services. Products provide businesses with both economic results (profits, wages, goods purchased from other companies) and non-economic results (new technology, innovations, pollution). And they provide consumers with what economists call **utility**—the power of a product to satisfy a human want.

Four basic kinds of utility would not be possible without production. By making a product available at a time when consumers want it, production creates **time utility**, as when a company turns out ornaments in time for Christmas. By making a product available in a place convenient for consumers, production creates **place utility**, as when a local department store creates a "Trim-a-Tree" section. By making a product that consumers can take pleasure in owning, production creates **ownership (possession) utility**, as when you take a box of ornaments home and decorate your tree. But above all, production makes products available in the first place. By turning raw materials into finished goods, production creates **form utility**, as when an ornament maker combines glass, plastic, and other materials to create tree decorations.

place utility That quality of a product satisfying a human want because of where it is made available.

ownership (possession) utility That quality of a product satisfying a human want during its consumption or use.

form utility That quality of a product satisfying a human want because of its form; requires raw materials to be transformed into a finished product.

Because the term *production* has historically been associated with manufacturing, it has been replaced in recent years by *operations*, a term that reflects both services and goods production. **Operations (or production) management** is the systematic direction and control of the processes that transform resources into finished goods and services. Thus production managers are ultimately responsible for creating utility for customers.

operations (or production) management The systematic direction and control of the processes that transform resources into finished goods.

As Figure 11.1 shows, **production managers** must bring raw materials, equipment, and labour together under a production plan that effectively uses all the resources available in the production facility. As demand for a good increases, they must schedule and control work to produce the amount required. Meanwhile, they must control costs, quality levels, inventory, and plant and equipment.

production managers Managers responsible for ensuring that operations processes create value and provide benefits.

Not all production managers work in factories. Farmers are also production managers. They create form utility by converting soil, seeds, sweat, gas, and other inputs into beef cattle, tobacco, heat, milk, cash, and other outputs. As production managers, farmers have the option of employing many workers to plant and harvest their crops. Or they may decide to use automated machinery or some combination of workers and machinery. These decisions affect farmers' costs, the buildings and equipment they own, and the quality and quantity of goods they produce. Table 11.1 shows examples of different types of production management.

Operations Processes

An **operations process** is a set of methods and technologies used in the production of a good or a service. We classify various types of production according to differences in their operations processes. In other words, we can describe goods according to the kind of transformation technology they require, or according to whether their operations process combines resources

operations process A set of methods and technologies used in the production of a good or a service.

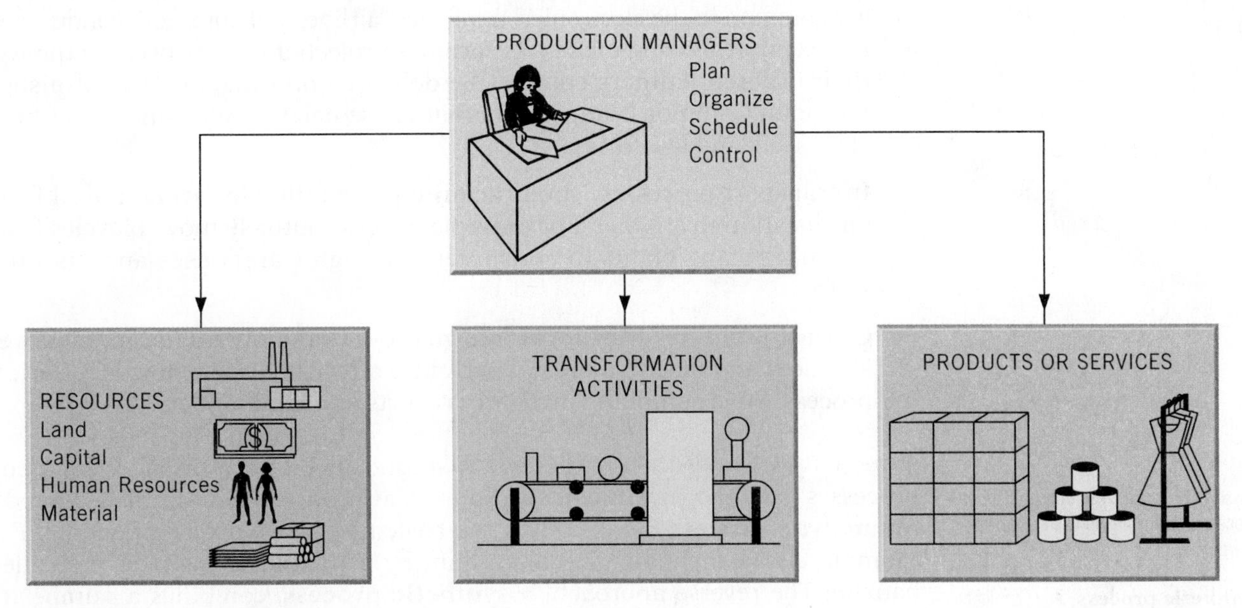

Figure 11.1 The transformation system.

Table 11.1 Inputs, Transformation, and Outputs in Production Systems

Production System	Inputs	Transformation	Outputs
Farm	Land, tractors and equipment, labour, buildings, fertilizer, farmer's management skills	Cultivation of plants and livestock	Food products, profit for owner, jobs for farmer's family
Jewellery store	Fashion-conscious customers, merchandise, sales clerks, showroom, fixtures, and equipment	Exchange of merchandise between buyer and seller	Satisfied jewellery customers
Tire producer	Rubber and chemical compounds, blending equipment, tire moulds, factory, and human skills	Chemical reactions of raw materials	Tires for autos, airplanes, trucks, trailers, and other vehicles
Furniture manufacturer	Woodworking equipment fabrics, wood, nails and screws, factory, woodworking skills	Fabrication and assembly of materials	Furniture for homes and offices

or breaks them into component parts. We can describe services according to the extent of customer contact required.

Goods-Producing Processes

All goods-manufacturing processes can be classified in two different ways: by the type of transformation technology that transforms raw materials into finished goods and by the analytic or synthetic nature of the transformation process.

Types of Transformation Technology. Manufacturers use the following types of transformation processes to turn raw materials into finished goods:

- In chemical processes, raw materials are chemically altered. Such techniques are common in the aluminum, steel, fertilizer, petroleum, and paint industries.
- Fabrication processes mechanically alter the basic shape or form of a product. Fabrication occurs in the metal forming, woodworking, and textile industries.
- Assembly processes put together various components. These techniques are common in the electronics, appliance, airline, and automotive industries. For example, Boeing missed its earnings projections partly because three of their ordered jetliners couldn't be delivered on time, due to unfinished interiors. Common components that cause delays are business and first-class seats and lavatories.[3]
- In transport processes, goods acquire place utility by being moved from one location to another. For example, trucks routinely move bicycles from manufacturing plants to consumers through warehouses and discount stores.
- Clerical processes transform information. Combining data on employee absences and machine breakdowns into a productivity report is a clerical process. So is compiling inventory reports at a retail outlet.

Analytic vs. Synthetic Processes. A second way of classifying production processes is by the way in which resources are converted into finished goods. An **analytic process** breaks down the basic resources into components. For example, Alcan manufactures aluminum by extracting it from an ore called bauxite. The reverse approach, a **synthetic process**, combines a number of raw materials to produce a finished product such as fertilizer or paint.

analytic process Any production process in which resources are broken down.

synthetic process Any production process in which resources are combined.

As this picture illustrates, many industries use transport as their primary transformation technique.

Service-Producing Processes

One way of classifying services is to ask whether a given service can be provided without the customer being part of the production system. Services are then classified according to the extent of customer contact.

High-Contact Processes. Think for a moment about the service provided by your local public transit system. When you purchase transportation, you must board a bus or train, so public transit is a **high-contact system**. For this reason, transit managers must worry about the cleanliness of the trains and buses and the appearance of the stations. This is usually not the case in low-contact systems. Large industrial companies that ship coal in freight trains, for example, are generally not concerned with the appearance inside those trains.

high-contact system A system in which the service cannot be provided without the customer being physically in the system (e.g., transit systems).

Low-Contact Processes. Consider the cheque-processing operations at your bank. Workers sort the cheques that have been cashed that day and dispatch them to the banks on which they were drawn. This operation is a **low-contact system** because customers are not in contact with the bank while the service is performed. They receive the service—their funds are transferred to cover their cheques—without ever setting foot in the cheque-processing centre. Gas and electric utilities, auto repair shops, and lawn care services are also low-contact systems.

low-contact system A system in which the service can be provided without the customer being physically in the system (e.g., lawn care services).

Business Strategy as the Driver of Operations

There is no one standard way for doing production. Rather, it is a flexible activity that can be moulded into many shapes to give quite different production (or operations) capabilities for different purposes. How, then, do companies go about selecting the kind of production that is best for their company? Its design is best driven from above by the firm's larger business strategy.

In this section we present examples of four firms—two in goods production and two in services—that have contrasting business strategies and, as we shall see, have chosen different operations capabilities. All four firms are

Table 11.2 Business Strategies That Win Customers for Four Companies

Company	Strategy for Attracting Customers	What the Company Does to Implement Its Strategy
Toyota	Quality	Cars perform reliably, have an appealing fit and finish, and consistently meet or exceed customer expectations at a competitive price
Save-A-Lot	Low Price	Foods and everyday items offered at savings up to 40 percent less than conventional food chains
3M	Flexibility	Innovation, with more than 55 000 products in a constantly changing line of convenience items for home and office
FedEx	Dependability	Every delivery is fast and on time, as promised

successful, but they've taken quite different operations paths to get there. As shown in Table 11.2, each company has identified a business strategy that it can use for attracting customers in its industry. For Toyota, quality was chosen as the strategy for competing in selling autos. Save-a-Lot grocery stores, in contrast to others in the grocery industry, offer customers lower prices. The flexibility strategy at 3M emphasizes new product development in an ever-changing line of products for home and office. FedEx captures the overnight delivery market by emphasizing delivery dependability.

Business Strategy Determines Operations Capabilities

operations capability (production capability) The activity or process that production must do especially well, with high proficiency.

Successful firms design their operations to support the company's business strategy.[4] In other words, production operations are adjusted to support the firms' target markets. Since our four firms use different business strategies, we should expect to see differences in their operations. The top-priority **operations capability (production capability)**—the activity or process that production must do especially well, with high proficiency—is listed for each firm in Table 11.3, along with key operations characteristics for implementing that capability. Each company's operations capability matches up with its business strategy so that the firm's activities—from top to bottom—are focussed in a particular direction.

As you can see in Table 11.3, Toyota's top priority focuses on quality, so its operations—inputs, transformation activities, and outputs—are devoted first and foremost to quality. Its car designs emphasize appearance, reliable performance, and desirable features at a reasonable price. All production processes, equipment, and training are designed to build better cars. The entire culture supports a quality emphasis among employees, suppliers, and dealerships. Had Toyota instead chosen to compete as the low-price car in the industry, as some successful car companies do, then a cost-minimization focus would have been appropriate, giving Toyota's operations an altogether different form. Toyota's operations support its chosen business strategy, and do it successfully.

Expanding into Additional Capabilities

Over time, excellent firms learn how to achieve more than just one competence. Our four example firms eventually became excellent in several capabilities. FedEx, in addition to dependability, is noted for world-class service quality and cost containment. But in its earlier years, its primary and distinguishing capability—that set it apart from the competition—was dependability, the foundation upon which future success was built.

Table 11.3 Operations Capabilities and Characteristics for Four Companies

Operations Capability	Key Operations Characteristics
Quality (Toyota)	• High-quality standards for materials suppliers • Just-in-time materials flow for lean manufacturing • Specialized, automated equipment for consistent product build up • Operations personnel are experts on continuous improvement of product, work methods, and materials
Low Cost (Save-A-Lot)	• Avoids excessive overhead and costly inventory (no floral departments, sushi bars, or banks that drive up costs) • Limited assortment of products, staples, in one size only for low-cost restocking, lower inventories, and less paperwork • Many locations; small stores—less than half the size of conventional grocery stores—for low construction and maintenance costs • Reduces labour and shelving costs by receiving and selling merchandise out of custom shipping cartons
Flexibility (3M)	• Maintains some excess (expensive) production capacity available for fast start-up on new products • Adaptable equipment/facilities for production changeovers from old to new products • Hires operations personnel who thrive on change • Many medium- to small-sized facilities in diverse locations, which enhances creativity
Dependability (FedEx)	• Customer automation: uses electronic and online tools with customers to shorten shipping time • Wireless information system for package scanning by courier, updating of package movement, and package tracking by customer • Maintains a company air force, global weather forecasting centre, and ground transportation for pickup and delivery, with backup vehicles for emergencies • Each of 30 automated regional distribution hubs processes up to 45 000 packages per hour for next-day deliveries

Differences Between Service and Manufacturing Operations

3 Identify the characteristics that distinguish *service operations* from *goods production* and explain the main differences in the service focus.

Service and manufacturing operations both transform raw materials into finished products. In service production, however, the raw materials, or inputs, are not glass or steel. Rather, they are people who choose among sellers because they have either unsatisfied needs or possessions for which they require some form of care or alteration. In service operations, then, "finished products" or "outputs" are people with needs met and possessions serviced. There are several key areas where service operations differ from production operations.

Focus on Performance

One very obvious difference exists between service and manufacturing operations: Whereas goods are produced, services are performed. Therefore, customer-oriented performance is a key factor in measuring the effectiveness of a service company. Wal-Mart, for example, sells to millions of people from California to China to Canada to Chile. Its superstar status stems from an obsession with speedy product delivery that it measures not in days, or even in hours, but in minutes and seconds. Wal-Mart's keen customer focus emphasizes avoiding unnecessary inventories, getting fast responses from suppliers, streamlining transaction processes, and knowing accurately the sales and restocking requirements for keeping the right merchandise moving from warehouses to store shelves. To implement this strategy, Wal-Mart has made technology—namely, its vaunted computer and telecommunications system—a core competency.[5]

In many ways, the focus of service operations is more complex than that of goods production. First, service operations feature a unique link between production and consumption—between process and outcome. Second, services are more intangible and more customized and less storable than most products. Finally, quality considerations must be defined and managed differently in the service sector than in manufacturing operations.

Focus on Process and Outcome

Manufacturing operations emphasize outcomes in terms of physical goods—for example, a new jacket. But the products of most service operations are really combinations of goods and services—both making a pizza and delivering (serving) it. Service operations thus require different skills from manufacturing operations. For example, local gas company employees may need the interpersonal skills necessary to calm and reassure frightened customers who have reported gas leaks. The job, therefore, can mean more than just repairing defective pipes. Factory workers who install gas pipes while assembling mobile homes are far less likely to need such skills.

Focus on Service Characteristics

Service companies' transactions always reflect the fact that service products are characterized by three key qualities: intangibility, customization, and unstorability.

Intangibility. Often services cannot be touched, tasted, smelled, or seen. An important value, therefore, is the intangible value that the customer experiences in the form of pleasure, satisfaction, or a feeling of safety. For example, when you hire an attorney to resolve a problem, you purchase not only the intangible quality of legal expertise but also the equally intangible reassurance that help is at hand. Although all services have some degree of intangibility, some provide tangible elements as well. Your attorney, for example, can draw up the living will that you want to keep in your safe deposit box.

Customization. When you visit a physician, you expect to be examined for your symptoms. Likewise, when you purchase insurance, have your pet groomed, or have your hair cut, you expect these services to be designed for your needs. Typically, therefore, services are customized.

The hairstyling service being provided to this customer illustrates the three key features of services operations: intangibility (customer pleasure or satisfaction with the service), customization (the service each person gets is customized for them), and unstorability (the service cannot be produced ahead of time).

Unstorability. Services such as rubbish collection, transportation, childcare, and house cleaning cannot be produced ahead of time and then stored. If a service is not used when it is available, it is usually wasted. Services, then, are typically characterized by a high degree of unstorability.

Focus on the Customer-Service Link

Because service operations transform customers or their possessions, the customer is often present in the operations process. To get a haircut, for example, most of us have to go to the barbershop or hair salon.

As physical participants in the operations process, consumers can affect it. As a customer, you expect the salon to be conveniently located (place utility), to be open for business at convenient times (time utility), to provide safe and comfortable facilities, and to offer quality grooming (form utility) at reasonable prices (value for money spent). Accordingly, the manager sets hours of operation, available services, and an appropriate number of employees to meet customer requirements. But what happens if a customer scheduled to receive a haircut also asks for additional services, such as highlights or a shave, when they arrive? In this case, the service provider must balance customer satisfaction with a tight schedule. High customer contact has the potential to significantly affect the process.

Ecommerce: The "Virtual Presence" of the Customer. The growth of ecommerce has introduced a "virtual presence," as opposed to a physical presence, of customers in the service system. Consumers interact electronically, in real time, with sellers, collecting information about product features, delivery availability, and after-sales service. They have around-the-clock access to information via automated call centres, and those who want human interaction can talk with live respondents or enter chat rooms. Many companies have invited "the virtual customer" into their service systems by building customer-communications relationships. The online travel agency Expedia.ca responds to your personalized profile with a welcome email letter, presents you with a tailor-made webpage the next time you sign in, offers chat rooms in which you can compare notes with other customers, and notifies you of upcoming special travel opportunities.

Internet technology also enables firms to build relationships with industrial customers. Electronic Data Systems (EDS), for example, helps client firms develop networks among their many desktop computers. In managing more than 700 000 desktops for clients throughout the world, EDS has created a special service called Renascence, which links clients, suppliers, and employees in a private, 500 000-computer electronic marketplace. Some 2000 software products can be viewed, purchased, tracked, and delivered if you are a member of the network.[6]

Focus on Service Quality Considerations

Consumers use different criteria to judge services and goods. Service managers must understand that quality of work and quality of service are not necessarily synonymous. For example, although your car may have been flawlessly repaired, you might feel dissatisfied with the service if you were forced to pick it up a day later than promised.

Operations Planning

Describe the factors involved in *operations planning.* **4**

Now that we've contrasted goods and services we can return to a more general consideration of production that encompasses both goods and services. Like all good managers, we start with planning. Managers from many departments contribute to the firm's decisions about operations management. As Figure 11.2 shows, however, no matter how many decision makers are involved, the process can be described as a series of logical steps. The success of any firm depends on the final result of this logical sequence of decisions.

The business plan and **forecasts** developed by top managers guide operations planning. The business plan outlines goals and objectives, including the specific goods and services that the firm will offer. Managers also develop a long-range production plan through forecasts of future demand for both new and existing products. Covering a two- to five-year period, the production plan specifies the number of plants or service facilities and the amount of labour, equipment,

forecast Estimate of future demand for both new and existing products.

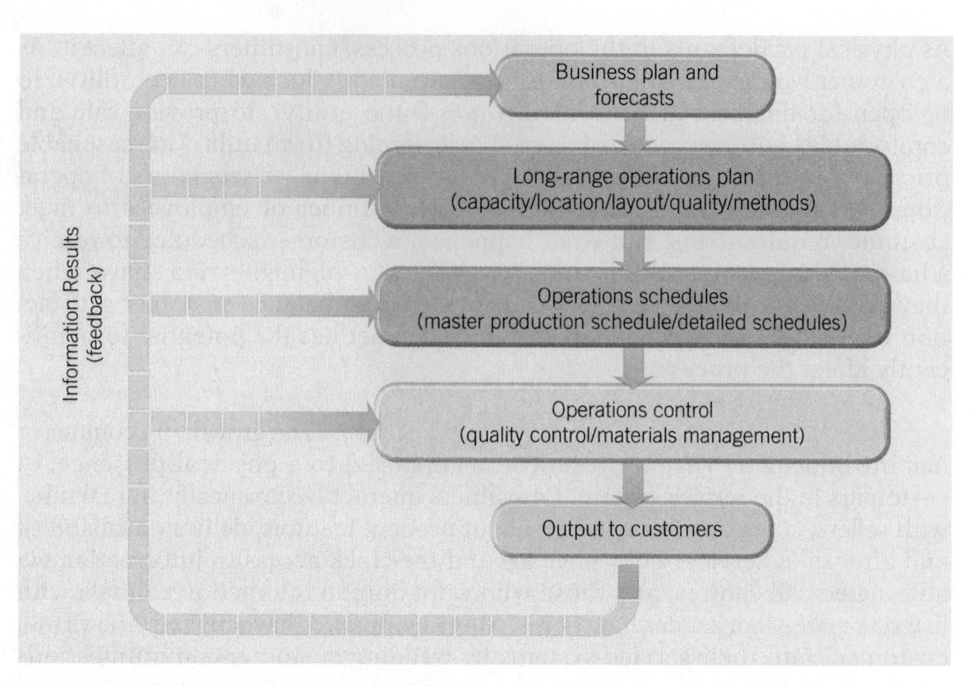

Figure 11.2 Operations planning and control.

transportation, and storage that will be needed to meet demand. It also specifies how resources will be obtained.

In the following section, we survey the main elements of operations planning, discussing the planning activities that fall into one of five categories: *capacity*, *location*, *layout*, *quality*, and *methods planning*.

Capacity Planning

capacity The amount of a good that a firm can produce under normal working conditions.

The amount of a product that a company can produce under normal working conditions is its **capacity**. The capacity of a goods or service firm depends on how many people it employs and the number and size of its facilities. Long-range planning must take into account both current and future capacity.

Capacity Planning for Producing Goods

Capacity planning for goods means ensuring that a manufacturing firm's capacity slightly exceeds the normal demand for its product. To see why this policy is best, consider the alternatives. If capacity is too small to meet demand, the company must turn away customers—a situation that not only cuts into profits but also alienates both customers and salespeople. If capacity greatly exceeds demand, the firm is wasting money by maintaining a plant that is too large, by keeping excess machinery online, or by employing too many workers.

The stakes are high in the company's capacity decisions. While expanding fast enough to meet future demand and to protect market share from competitors, it must also weigh the increased costs of expanding. The owner of Thunder Oak Cheese, Walter Shep, has been turning down orders for the Ontario-produced Gouda on a weekly basis. His facility is at full capacity and the production is tied to his family business, which produces the milk for the cheese. The decision facing many businesses, like Thunder Oak Cheese, is whether to move to a larger facility and find additional sources of inputs. Will demand for specialty cheeses continue to grow even further? With so much invested thus far, Shep must decide whether the risks of additional capacity are worth the potential gains.[7]

Capacity Planning for Producing Services

In low-contact processes, maintaining inventory allows managers to set capacity at the level of average demand. For example, a catalogue sales warehouse may hire enough order fillers to handle 1000 orders per day. When daily orders exceed this average demand, some orders are placed in inventory—set aside in a "to-be-done" file—to be processed on a day when fewer than 1000 orders are received.

In high-contact processes, managers must plan capacity to meet peak demand. A supermarket, for instance, has far more cash registers than it needs on an average day; but on a Saturday morning or during the three days before Thanksgiving, all registers will be running at full speed. Here is another example: When the Anchorage International Airport was planning a new concourse, prime tenant Alaska Airlines insisted on not having a traditional ticket counter. This unconventional, yet tested, approach uses self-service check-in machines and manned "bag drop" stations. Even during peak season, Alaska Airlines doubled its capacity, halved its staffing needs, and cut costs, all while speeding travellers through the check-in process.[8]

Location Planning

Because the location of a factory, office, or store affects its production costs and flexibility, sound location planning is crucial. Depending on the site of its facility, a company may be capable of producing a low-cost product or may find itself at an extreme cost disadvantage relative to its competitors.

Location Planning for Producing Goods

In goods-producing operations, location decisions are influenced by proximity to raw materials and markets, availability of labour, energy and transportation costs, local and provincial regulations and taxes, and community living conditions. Slovakia, for example, is fast becoming the "Detroit" of Europe. With an existing Volkswagen plant producing 850 000 cars a year, two more giant carmakers—Peugeot Citroën (French) and Hyundai Motor Company (Korean)—opened new plants in 2006. Skilled workers, a good work ethic, and wages below those of the surrounding countries aren't the only reasons. Located in Central Europe, Slovakia has a good railroad system and nearby access to the Danube River, meaning economical transportation for incoming materials and outgoing cars.[9]

Some location decisions are now being simplified by the rise of industrial parks. Created by cities interested in attracting new industry, these planned sites come with necessary zoning, land, shipping facilities, utilities, and waste disposal outlets already in place. Such sites offer flexibility, often allowing firms to open new facilities before competitors can get started in the same area. The ready-made site also provides faster construction start-ups because it entails no lead time in preparing the chosen site.

Location Planning for Producing Services

In planning low-contact services, companies have some options. Services can be located near resource supplies, labour, customers, or transportation outlets. For example, the typical Wal-Mart distribution centre is located near the hundreds of Wal-Mart stores it supplies, not near the companies that supply the distribution centre. Distribution managers regard Wal-Mart stores as their customers. To better serve them, distribution centres are located so that truckloads of merchandise flow quickly to the stores.

On the other hand, high-contact services are more restricted, because they must locate near the customers who are a part of the system. Accordingly, fast-food restaurants such as Taco Bell, McDonald's, and Burger King have begun moving into non-traditional locations with high traffic—dormitories, hospital cafeterias, museums, and shopping malls.

Layout Planning

Once a site has been selected, managers must decide on plant layout. Layout of machinery, equipment, and supplies determines whether a company can respond quickly and efficiently to customer requests for more and different products or finds itself unable to match competitors' production speed or convenience of service.

Layout Planning for Producing Goods

In facilities that produce goods, layout must be planned for three different types of space:

- Productive facilities: workstations and equipment for transforming raw materials (for example)
- Non-productive facilities: storage and maintenance areas
- Support facilities: offices, restrooms, parking lots, cafeterias, and so forth

In this section, we focus on productive facilities. Alternatives for layout planning include process, cellular, and product layouts.

process layout A way of organizing production activities such that equipment and people are grouped together according to their function.

Process Layouts. In a **process layout**, which is well suited to job shops specializing in custom work, equipment and people are grouped according to function. In a woodworking shop, for example, machines cut the wood in an area devoted to sawing, sanding occurs in a dedicated area, and jobs that need painting are taken to a dust-free area where all the painting equipment is located. The various tasks are each performed in specialized locations.

The job shop produces many one-of-a-kind products, and each product, as you can see in Figure 11.3(a), requires different kinds of work. Whereas Product X needs only three production steps prior to packaging, Product Y needs four. When there is a large variety of products, there will be many flow paths through the shop and potentially much congestion. Machine shops, custom bakeries, and dry cleaning shops often feature process layouts.

cellular layout A layout used to produce goods when families of products can follow similar flow paths.

Cellular Layouts. Another workplace arrangement for some applications is called the **cellular layout**, which is used when a family of products (a group of similar products) follows a fixed flow path. A clothing manufacturer, for example, may establish a cell, or designated area, dedicated to making a family of pockets—for example, pockets for shirts, coats, blouses, trousers, and slacks. Although each type of pocket is unique in shape, size, and style, all go through the same production steps. Within the cell, therefore, various types of equipment (for cutting, trimming, and sewing) are arranged close together in the appropriate sequence. All pockets pass stage by stage through the cell from beginning to end, in a nearly continuous flow.

In plants that produce a variety of products, there may be one or two high-volume products that justify separate manufacturing cells. Figure 11.3(b) shows two production cells, one each for Products X and Y, while all other smaller-volume products are produced elsewhere in the plant.

Cellular layouts have several advantages. Because similar products require less machine adjustment, equipment set-up time in the cell is reduced as compared with set-up times in process layouts. Because flow distances are usually shorter, there is less material handling and transit time. Finally, inventories of goods in progress are lower and paperwork is simpler because

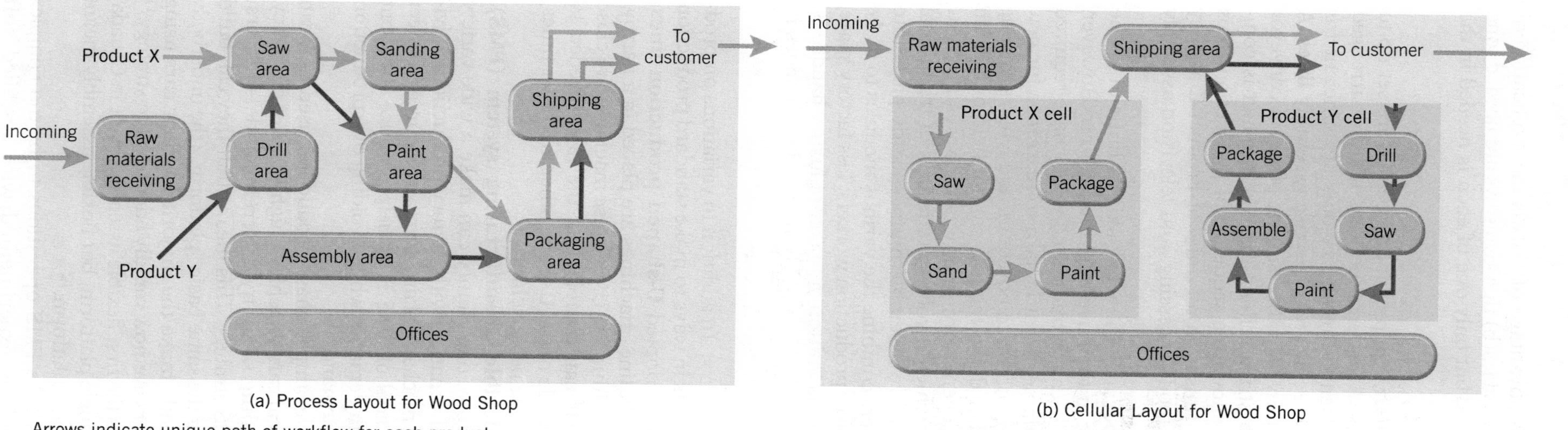

(a) Process Layout for Wood Shop

Arrows indicate unique path of workflow for each product.
Orange = Product X; Blue = Product Y

(b) Cellular Layout for Wood Shop

Arrows indicate unique path of workflow for each product.
Orange = Product X; Blue = Product Y

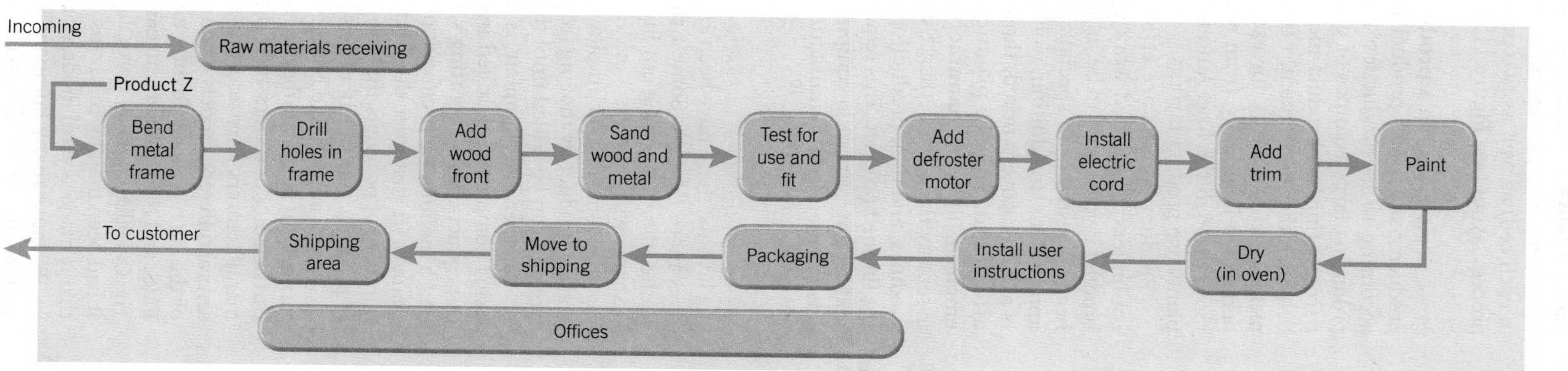

(c) Product Layout—Assembly Line

Arrows indicate the fixed path of workflow for all units of Product Z

Figure 11.3 Layouts for producing goods.

material flows are more orderly. A disadvantage of cells is the duplication of equipment. Note, for example, in Figure 11.3(b) that two saws are needed (one in each cell) as well as two paint areas, but only one of each is needed in the process layout (see Figure 11.3(a)).

product layout A way of organizing production activities such that equipment and people are set up to produce only one type of good.

assembly line A type of product layout in which a partially finished product moves through a plant on a conveyor belt or other equipment.

Product Layouts. In a **product layout**, equipment and people are set up to produce one type of product in a fixed sequence of steps and are arranged according to its production requirements. Product layouts are efficient for producing large volumes of product quickly and often use **assembly lines**. A partially finished product moves step by step through the plant on conveyor belts or other equipment, often in a straight line, until the product is completed. Figure 11.3(c), for example, shows the sequence of production steps performed identically, from start to finish, on all units of Product Z as they move through the line. Automobile, food processing, and television assembly plants use product layouts.

Product layouts are efficient because the work skill is built in to the equipment; simplified work tasks can then use unskilled labour. However, product layouts tend to be inflexible because, traditionally, they have required heavy investment in specialized equipment that is hard to rearrange for new applications. In addition, workers are subject to boredom, and when someone is absent or overworked, those farther down the line cannot help out. In an attempt to improve productivity even more, many companies are now emphasizing **lean manufacturing**, which involves getting rid of traditional assembly lines altogether. Suppliers pre-assemble many specific parts into modules, and then production workers combine the various modules to make the finished product. This requires fewer production workers, less factory space, and less investment in equipment. Louis Vuitton, a maker of luxury handbags, has adopted lean manufacturing in order to quickly respond to changes in customer preferences.[10]

lean manufacturing Manufacturing that involves getting rid of traditional assembly lines altogether. Suppliers pre-assemble many specific parts into modules, and then production workers combine the various modules to make the finished product.

Other Developments in Layout Flexibility. In addition to variations on product layouts, there have been experiments in ways to make standard production lines more flexible. Some firms have adopted **U-shaped production lines**. Rather than stretching out in a straight line, machines are placed in a narrow U shape, with workers working from within the U. Because machines are close together, one worker in slow periods can complete all the tasks needed to make a product by moving from one side of the U to the other. In busier times, workers can be added until there is one per machine.

U-shaped production lines Production layout in which machines are placed in a narrow U shape rather than a straight line.

Another development is the **flexible manufacturing system (FMS)**. Using computer-controlled instructions, one factory can make a wide variety of products. By integrating sales information with factory production activities, a manufacturer can adapt both mechanical and human resources to meet changes in customer demand. The goal of FMS is to help produce sufficient numbers of products that are in high demand, while avoiding overproduction of products that are not in as high demand.

flexible manufacturing system (FMS) A production system that allows a single factory to produce small batches of different goods on the same production line.

In the automobile business, for example, mass production used to mean turning out large numbers of identical cars to achieve high levels of efficiency. But with consumers now demanding so many different models of cars, manufacturers have adopted an FMS strategy. This means that they can build several different models of cars using the same basic "platform" (the underbody of the car). Nissan, Toyota, and Honda make the majority of their cars using FMS, and North American car makers are now rapidly adopting the strategy.[11] The Oakville, Ontario, Ford plant was the first flexible assembly plant in Canada. It had been making minivans on a single platform, but flexible assembly meant that it made several models on a single platform.[12]

Because many companies find large FMS operations to be too complex and prone to breakdowns, some have experimented with so-called **soft**

soft manufacturing Reducing huge FMS operations to smaller, more manageable groups of machines.

Business Accountability

The People's Car

It all started one rainy day in Bangalore, India. Ratan Tata was returning to the airport from a business trip when he and his driver nearly ran over a family of four whose scooter had tipped over in front of them. Mr. Tata, chair of the Tata Group and Tata Motors, decided that he needed to develop a car that would bring the comfort and safety of an automobile within the reach of thousands of families in India. The "People's Car" was unveiled and launched in 2008. Tata Motors made headlines not only when it announced it was selling the car for just $2500 but that the finished product also met safety requirements and emission norms. "We are happy to present the People's Car to India and we hope it brings the joy, pride and utility of owning a car to many families who need personal mobility," said Mr. Tata at the unveiling ceremony.

Right from the start, the development process for the Nano was very different than the traditional approach. Billionaire Baba Kalyani, head of auto parts maker Bharat Forge, said that before the Nano, if a company wanted to make a car, they would "set up a big factory, cut a lot of metal and off you went," charging customers enough to cover the cost and make a profit. Mr. Tata did the exact opposite, setting the price first and then adapting the product accordingly. Tremendous attention to detail was paid to the little car not only to ensure that costs remained at a minimum, but also because Mr. Tata's reputation was on the line. "A lot of personal success or failure revolved around what happened on a project that, rightly or wrongly, was connected with me," Mr. Tata stated. "There would have been a great deal of attention if we'd fallen on our face."

Having taken a personal interest in the project, Mr. Tata spoke to every person who worked on the project. He welcomed and listened to all of their ideas and suggestions. And they delivered. After many prototypes, the final model was developed. It has a rear-mounted, 33-horsepower, twin-cylinder engine; no air bags; no air conditioning; no radio; no power steering; and a top speed of 150 kilometres per hour. But the innovative thinking doesn't stop there. In the future, Mr. Tata envisions an entirely different manufacturing process, whereby Tata Motors will produce a ready-to-build version of the car that can be delivered in kits. With proper training, people in India can buy the kits, assemble the cars themselves, and sell to their local market. Mr. Tata stated that it's "my idea of dispersing wealth" across India.

The Nano has made headlines around the world by being the first family vehicle for $2500. Mr. Tata's actions are consistent with the idea that, if you are in a position of wealth and power, it is important to give back to the people in your community. He wanted to provide an opportunity for struggling families to feel the pride of ownership from a safe and reliable vehicle. Not bad for only $2500. Tata has created a business model to show companies the value of pitching products to the lower end of the market. More importantly, he has demonstrated how bold, innovative thinking (not just cheap goods from cheap labour) can come out of emerging economies like India's. Evidence of the impact of the Nano's success is already evident in India's used car market. Autocar is reporting that sales for India's current most popular and cheapest car (a used Maruti 800) have already dropped 30 percent. The current model sells for nearly 200 000 rupees, while the new Nano sells for about half of that. Only time will tell if the used car market will rebound once the Nano is fully integrated into the market. But one thing is certain: India's car buyers can't wait to get their hands on a new Nano.

Critical Thinking Questions

1. What is the relationship between mass production and the quality level of the Nano?
2. What are the advantages of a car like the Nano? Are there disadvantages? Explain.
3. Do you think the Nano would satisfy consumers in markets in other countries? Explain your reasoning.

manufacturing—reducing huge FMS operations to smaller, more manageable groups of machines. Automation is less likely to fail when relegated to jobs it does best, while human workers perform those assembly-line jobs that require dexterity and decision making. Both are supported by networks of computers programmed to assist in all sorts of tasks.

The very latest development is the disposable and movable factory. Because FMS is so expensive, some developing countries with lots of labour but little capital are buying up still-modern equipment from industrialized countries and then using it to produce new and untested products in their own country. For example, an unused press from upstate New York, which is capable of shaping steel with its 14 000 tonnes of pressure per square inch, will be used to manufacture the internal workings of new Chinese nuclear power plants. Areas with long-standing history in the industrial sector in North America have been recycling their old machinery to overseas companies that may not have the capital to buy new or the time to wait while the equipment is being made.[13]

Layout Planning for Producing Services

Service firms use some of the same layouts as goods-producing firms. In a low-contact system, for instance, the facility should be arranged to enhance the production of the service. A mail-processing facility at UPS or Federal Express, therefore, looks very much like a product layout in a factory: Machines and people are arranged in the order in which they are used in the mass processing of mail. In contrast, FedEx Kinko's copy centres use process layouts for different custom jobs: Specific functions such as photocopying, computing, binding, photography, and laminating are performed in specialized areas of the store.

High-contact systems should be arranged to meet customer needs and expectations. For example, Piccadilly Restaurants in the U.S. focuses both layout and services on the groups that constitute its primary market: families and elderly people. As you can see in Figure 11.4, families enter to find an array of high chairs and rolling baby beds that make it convenient to wheel children through the lineup. Servers willingly carry trays for elderly people and for those pushing strollers. Note, too, that customers must pass by the entire serving line before making selections. Not only does this layout help them make up their minds, it also tempts them to select more.

Quality Planning

In planning production systems and facilities, managers must keep in mind the firm's quality goals.[14] Thus any complete production plan includes systems for ensuring that goods are produced to meet the firm's quality standards. The issue of quality is discussed in detail in Chapter 12.

Methods Planning

In designing operations systems, managers must clearly identify every production step and the specific methods for performing them. They can then work to reduce waste, inefficiency, and poor performance by examining procedures on a step-by-step basis—an approach sometimes called methods improvement.

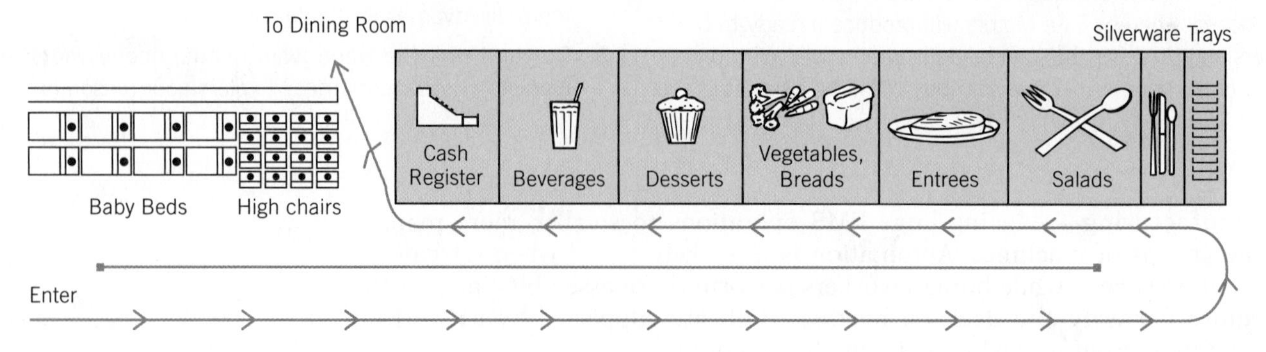

Figure 11.4 Layout of a typical Piccadilly cafeteria.

Employees at the Toyota manufacturing plant in Cambridge, Ontario, discuss a production problem. At this plant, employees are responsible not only for making automobiles but also for monitoring quality control and for maintaining a clean work area.

Methods Improvement in Goods

Improvement of production for goods begins when a manager documents the current method. A detailed description, often using a diagram called the *process flow chart*, is usually helpful for organizing and recording all information. The process flow chart identifies the sequence of production activities, movements of materials, and work performed at each stage as the product flows through production. The flow can then be analyzed to identify wasteful activities, sources of delay in production flows, and other inefficiencies. The final step is implementing improvements.

Mercury Marine, for example, used methods improvement to streamline the production of stern-drive units for powerboats. Examination of the process flow from raw materials to assembly (the final production step) revealed numerous instances of waste and inefficiency. Each product passed through 122 steps, travelled nearly sevem kilometres in the factory, and was handled by 106 people. Analysis revealed that only 27 steps actually added value to the product (for example, drilling or painting). Work methods were revised to eliminate non-productive activities. Mercury ultimately identified potential savings in labour, inventory, paperwork, and space requirements. Because production lead time was also reduced, customer orders were filled more quickly.

Methods Improvement in Services

In a low-contact process, managers can use methods improvements to speed services ranging from mowing lawns to filling prescriptions and drawing up legal documents. At a bank, for example, the cash-management unit collects accounts receivable for corporate clients; the sooner cheques are collected and deposited, the sooner the client begins collecting interest.

In high-contact services, the demands of systems analysis are somewhat different. Here, for example, the steps to be analyzed include such operations as exchanging information or money, delivering and receiving materials, and even making physical contact.

Service Flow Analysis. By showing the flow of processes that make up a given service, **service flow analysis** helps managers decide whether all those processes are necessary. Moreover, because each process is a potential contributor to good or bad service, analysis also helps identify and isolate potential problems

service flow analysis An analysis that shows the process flows that are necessary to provide a service to customers; it allows managers to determine which processes are necessary.

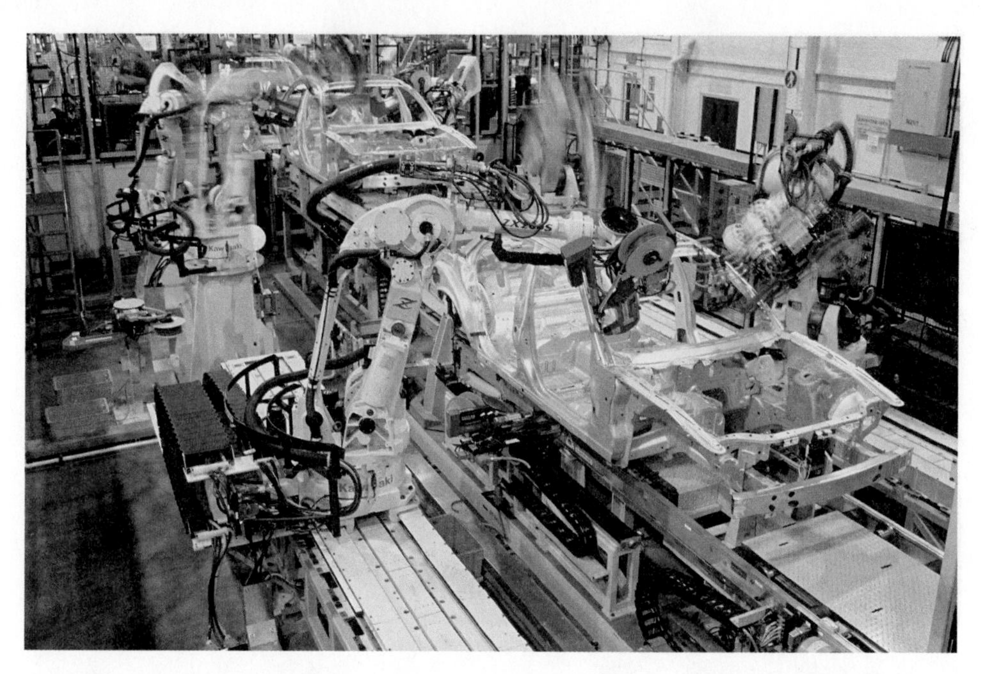

For its new XJ sedan, Jaguar wanted to use an aluminum unibody construction because it's lighter and more efficient than a steel-built body. For the same reasons, aluminum conveys a sense of high-tech design, and the company thought it was a better fit with Jaguar's elegant high-end image. But the usual method of constructing car bodies from steel—spot welding—weakens aluminum. So, at its factory in Castle Bromwich in the United Kingdom, engineers built an assembly line of 88 robots equipped with tools to drive more than 3000 rivets into each unit.

(known as fail points). In Figure 11.5, for instance, the manager of a photo-finishing shop has determined that the standard execution time for developing a roll of film is 48.5 minutes. She has also found that the "develop film" stage is the one most likely to delay service because it is the most complex. Thus, she has marked it as a potential fail point, as a reminder to give special attention to this stage of operations.

Designing to Control Employee Discretion in Services. Thus far, we have stressed the importance of the human factor in service activities—that is, the direct contact of server and customer. In some cases, however, the purpose of service design is to limit the range of activities of both employees and customers. By careful planning—and sometimes even by automating to control human discretion—managers can make services more customer-oriented because they can ensure product consistency.

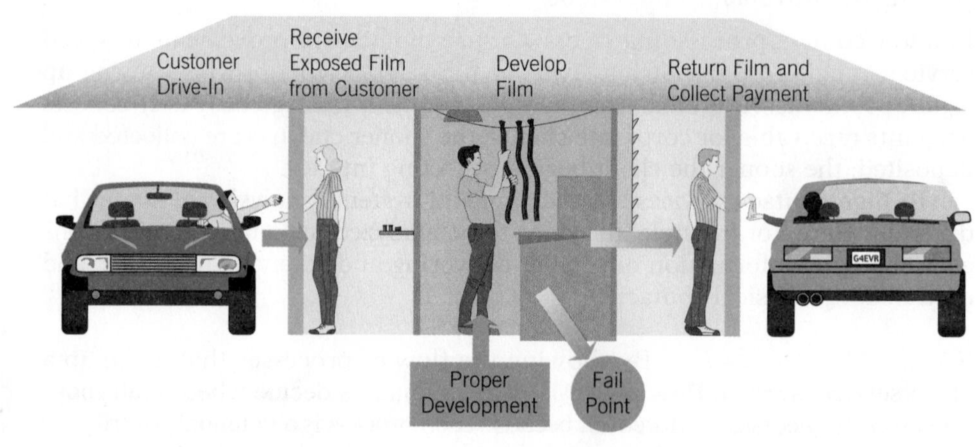

Figure 11.5 Service flow analysis.

McDonald's, for example, has done an outstanding job of designing the fast-food business as a mass-production system. By automating processes that would otherwise rely on judgment, McDonald's has been able to provide consistent service from a staff with little specialized training. At a central supply house, for instance, hamburger patties are automatically measured and packed. Specially designed scoops measure the same amount of french fries and other items into standard-sized containers. In addition, all drawers, shelves, and bins are designed to hold the ingredients for McDonald's standard product mixes only.

Design for Customer Contact in Services. In a high-contact service, the demands on system designs are somewhat different. Here, managers must develop procedures that clearly spell out the ways in which workers interact with customers. These procedures must cover such activities as exchanging information or money, delivering and receiving materials, and even making physical contact. The next time you visit your dentist's office, for instance, notice the way dental hygienists scrub up and wear disposable gloves. They also scrub after patient contact, even if they intend to work on equipment or do paperwork, and they rescrub before working on the next patient. The high-contact system in a dental office consists of very strict procedures designed to avoid contact that can transmit disease.

Operations Scheduling

Once plans identify needed resources and how they will be used to reach a firm's goals, managers must develop timetables for acquiring resources for production. This aspect of operations is called *scheduling*.

5

Explain some factors in *operations scheduling* and describe some activities involved in *operations control*, including materials management and the use of certain operations control tools.

Scheduling Goods Operations

Scheduling of goods production occurs on different levels within the firm. First, a top-level or **master production schedule** shows which products will be produced, when production will occur, and what resources will be used during specified time periods.

master production schedule
Schedule showing which products will be produced, when production will take place, and what resources will be used.

Consider the case of Logan Aluminum Inc., for example. Logan produces coils of aluminum that its main customers, Atlantic Richfield and Alcan Aluminum, use to produce aluminum cans. Logan's master schedule extends out to 60 weeks and shows how many coils will be made during each week. For various types of coils, the master schedule specifies how many of each will be produced. This type of planning and scheduling system is required to determine how much of each product is needed.

This information, however, is not complete. For example, manufacturing personnel must also know the location of all coils on the plant floor and their various stages of production. Start and stop times must be assigned, and employees must be given scheduled work assignments. Short-term detailed schedules fill in these blanks on a daily basis. These schedules use incoming customer orders and information about current machine conditions to update the sizes and variety of coils to make each day. A classic dilemma in production scheduling is described in "Exercising Your Ethics: Team Exercise" at the end of the chapter.

Scheduling Service Operations

Service scheduling may involve both work and workers. In a low-contact service, work scheduling may be based either on desired completion dates or on the time of order arrivals. For example, several cars may be scheduled for repairs at a local garage. Thus, if your car is not scheduled for work until 3:30 p.m., it may sit idle for several hours even if it was the first to be dropped off. In such businesses, reservations and appointments systems can help smooth ups and downs in demand.

In contrast, if a hospital emergency room is overloaded, patients cannot be asked to make appointments and come back later. As we have seen, in high-contact services, the customer is part of the system and must be accommodated. Thus, precise scheduling of services may not be possible in high-contact systems. A 24-hour-a-day service operation, such as a hospital, can be an even greater scheduling challenge. Nurses, for example, must be on duty around the clock, seven days a week. Few nurses, however, want to work on weekends or during the early hours of the morning. Similarly, although enough nurses must be scheduled to meet emergencies, most hospitals are on tight budgets and cannot afford to have too many on-duty nurses. Thus, incentives are often used to entice nurses to work at times they might not otherwise choose. For example, would you choose to work 12 hours per day, seven days a week? Probably not, but what if you were entitled to have every other week off in exchange for working such a schedule? A number of hospitals use just such a plan to attract nurses.

In scheduling workers, managers must also consider efficiency and costs. McDonald's, for example, guarantees workers that they will be scheduled for at least four hours at a time. To accomplish this goal without having workers be idle, McDonald's uses overlapping shifts—the ending hours for some employees overlap the beginning hours for others. The overlap provides maximum coverage during peak periods. McDonald's also trains employees to put off minor tasks, such as refilling napkin dispensers, until slow periods.

Tools for Scheduling

Special projects, such as plant renovations or relocations, often require close coordination and precise timing. In these cases, special tools, such as Gantt and PERT charts, facilitate scheduling.

Gantt chart Scheduling tool that diagrams steps to be performed and specifies the time required to complete each step.

Gantt Charts. A **Gantt chart** diagrams steps to be performed and specifies the time required to complete each step. The manager lists all activities needed to complete the work, estimates the time required for each step, and checks the progress of the project against the chart. If it's ahead of schedule, some workers may be shifted to another project. If it's behind schedule, workers may be added or completion delayed.[15]

Figure 11.6 shows a Gantt chart for the renovation of a college classroom. It shows progress to date and schedules for the remaining work. The current date is 5/11. Note that workers are about one-half week behind in removing old floor tiles and reworking tables and chairs.

PERT chart Production schedule specifying the sequence and critical path for performing the steps in a project.

PERT Charts. PERT—short for Program Evaluation and Review Technique—is useful for customized projects in which numerous activities must be coordinated. Like Gantt charts, **PERT charts** break down large projects into steps and specify the time required to perform each one. Unlike Gantt charts, however, PERT charts not only show the necessary sequence of activities but identify the critical path for meeting project goals.[16]

Figure 11.7 shows a PERT chart for the classroom renovation that we visited above. The critical path consists of activities A, B, D, G, H, and I. It's critical because any delay in completing any activity will cause workers to miss the completion deadline (nine and one-half weeks after start-up). No activity along the critical path can be started until all preceding activities are done. Chairs and tables can't be returned to the classroom (H) until after they've been reworked (G) and after new tiles are installed (F). The chart also identifies

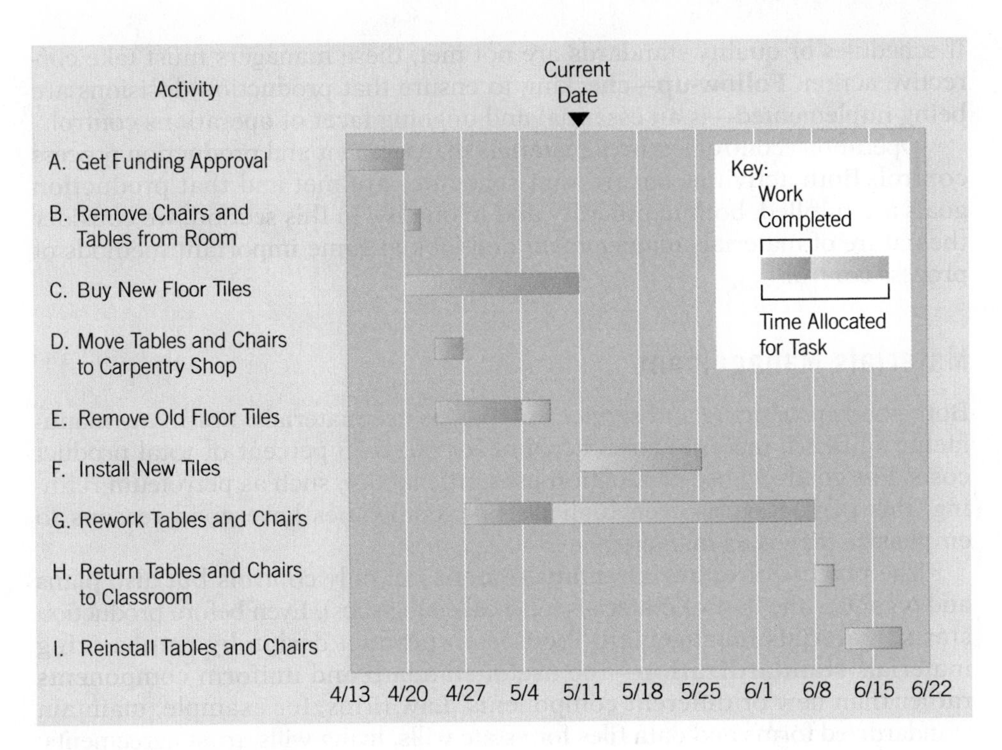

Figure 11.6 Gantt chart.

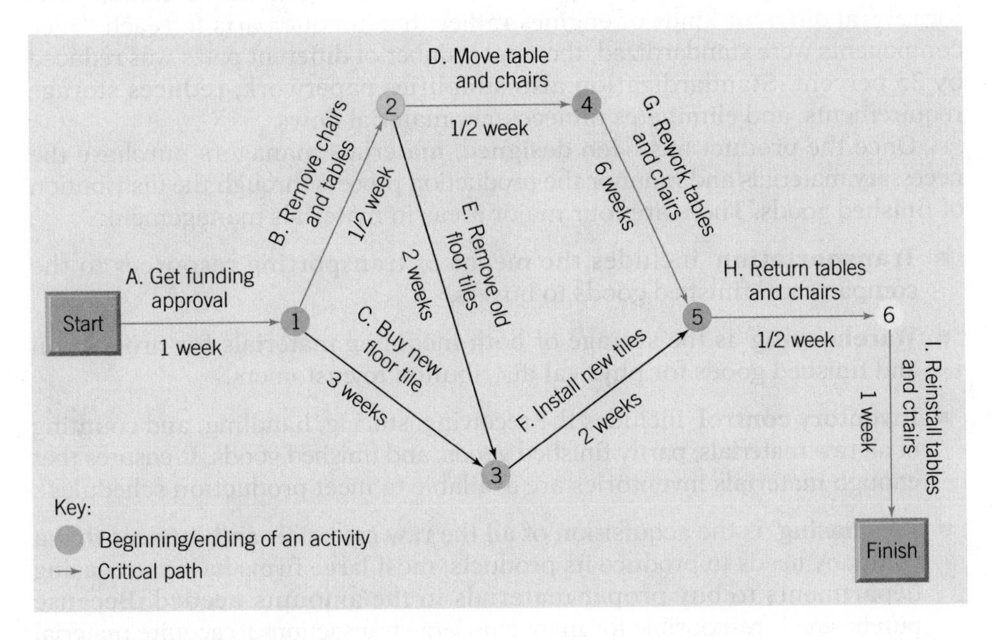

Figure 11.7 PERT chart.

activities that will cause delays unless special action is taken at the right time. By reassigning workers and equipment, managers can speed up potentially late activities and keep on schedule.

Operations Control

Once long-range plans have been put into action and schedules have been drawn up, **operations control** requires production managers to monitor production performance by comparing results with detailed plans and schedules.

operations control Managers monitor production performance by comparing results with plans and schedules.

follow-up Checking to ensure that production decisions are being implemented.

If schedules or quality standards are not met, these managers must take corrective action. **Follow-up**—checking to ensure that production decisions are being implemented—is an essential and ongoing facet of operations control.

Operations control features materials management and production process control. Both activities ensure that schedules are met and that production goals are fulfilled, both in quantity and in quality. In this section, we consider the nature of materials management and look at some important methods of process control.

Materials Management

Both goods-producing and service companies use materials. For many manufacturing firms, material costs account for 50 to 75 percent of total product costs. For goods whose production uses little labour, such as petroleum refining, this percentage is even higher. Thus, companies have good reasons to emphasize materials management.

materials management Planning, organizing, and controlling the flow of materials from purchase through distribution of finished goods.

standardization Using standard and uniform components in the production process.

The process of **materials management** not only controls but also plans and organizes the flow of materials (also called logistics). Even before production starts, materials management focuses on product design by emphasizing materials **standardization**—the use of standard and uniform components rather than new or different components. Law firms, for example, maintain standardized forms and data files for estate wills, living wills, trust agreements, and various contracts that can be adjusted easily to meet your individual needs. In manufacturing, Ford's engine plant in Romeo, Michigan, uses common parts for several different kinds of engines rather than unique parts for each. Once components were standardized, the total number of different parts was reduced by 25 percent. Standardization also simplifies paperwork, reduces storage requirements, and eliminates unnecessary material flows.

Once the product has been designed, materials managers purchase the necessary materials and monitor the production process through the distribution of finished goods. There are four major areas in materials management:

transportation The means of transporting resources to the company and finished goods to buyers.

warehousing The storage of both incoming materials for production and finished goods for physical distribution to customers.

inventory control The receiving, storing, handling, and counting of all raw materials, partly finished goods, and finished goods.

purchasing The acquisition of all the raw materials and services that a company needs to produce its products.

- **Transportation** includes the means of transporting resources to the company and finished goods to buyers.
- **Warehousing** is the storage of both incoming materials for production and finished goods for physical distribution to customers.
- **Inventory control** includes the receiving, storing, handling, and counting of all raw materials, partly finished goods, and finished goods. It ensures that enough materials inventories are available to meet production schedules.
- **Purchasing** is the acquisition of all the raw materials and services that a company needs to produce its products; most large firms have purchasing departments to buy proper materials in the amounts needed. Because purchasing is responsible for managing large transactions to acquire material resources, we will explain its activities in more detail.

Purchasing Processes

Purchasing is the acquisition of all the raw materials and services needed to make products and to conduct daily operations. Most companies have purchasing departments to buy, at reasonable prices and at the right time, proper materials in required amounts. For many years, purchasing departments practised forward buying—they routinely bought quantities of materials large enough to fill long-term needs. The practice was popular because it allowed a firm to buy materials at quantity discounts.

holding costs Costs of keeping extra supplies or inventory on hand.

But purchasing agents must balance the need for adequate inventory with the need to avoid excess supplies, which drive up **holding costs**—the costs of keeping inventory on hand.[17] These include the real costs of storage, handling, and insurance as well as opportunity costs—additional earnings that the company must pass up because funds are tied up in inventory.

Today, many purchasing departments have opted for the so-called hand-to-mouth pattern—placing small orders frequently. It requires fast delivery **lead times**—the gaps between the customer's order placement and the seller's shipment and delivery reliability. A radio maker that uses thousands of standard components may significantly reduce holding costs by ordering only what it needs for a coming day or week.

lead times In purchasing control, the gap between the customer's placement of an order and the seller's shipment of merchandise.

Supplier Selection. Purchasing departments also handle **supplier selection**—deciding which suppliers to buy from. The process typically has four stages:

supplier selection Finding and determining suppliers to buy from.

1. Investigating possible suppliers
2. Evaluating and isolating the best candidates
3. Negotiating terms of service with a final choice
4. Maintaining a positive buyer-seller relationship

Maintaining multiple supplier relationships is expensive. It takes time to survey, contact, and evaluate potential suppliers and build good relationships. In addition, fewer suppliers means stronger, mutually dependent purchaser-supplier relationships. Today, therefore, most purchasers try to reduce their number of suppliers. In the first year of a supplier-reduction program, one 3M factory trimmed its supplier list from 2800 to 600—and then reduced it to 300 the following year. Dana Corp., one of the world's largest suppliers of automobile components, is dropping half of its 86 000 suppliers.[18] The boxed insert entitled "For the Greener Good" describes the purchasing strategies of Wal-Mart as it tries to improve its environmental footprint.

Tools for Operations Process Control

Numerous tools assist managers in controlling operations. Chief among these are *worker training*, *just-in-time production systems*, *material requirements planning*, and *quality control*.

Worker Training

Customer satisfaction is closely linked to the employees who provide the service. Human relations skills are vital in anyone who has contact with the public. More and more human resource experts now realize that in businesses such as airlines, employment agencies, and hotels, employees without training in relationship skills can lose customers to better-prepared competitors. The Walt Disney Co. does an excellent job of remembering that, no matter what their jobs, service employees are links to the public. For example, Disney World has a team of sweepers constantly at work picking up bits of trash as soon as they fall to the ground. When visitors have questions about directions or time, they often ask one of the sweepers. Because their responses affect visitors' overall impressions of Disney World, sweepers are trained to respond in appropriate ways. Their work is evaluated and rewarded based on strict performance appraisal standards.[19]

Just-in-Time Production Systems

To minimize manufacturing inventory costs, many companies use **just-in-time (JIT) production systems**. JIT brings together all the needed materials and parts at the precise moment they are required for each production stage, not before. All resources are continuously flowing, from their arrival as raw materials

just-in-time (JIT) production system A method of inventory control in which materials are acquired and put into production just as they are needed.

The Greening of Business

For the Greener Good

When Wal-Mart, the retail giant, decided to make changes to the way it conducts business in an effort to be more environmentally friendly, critics and supporters alike could not have fathomed the effect it would have on suppliers, employees, and consumers. In 2005, Wal-Mart Stores Inc. unveiled an environmental plan that would boost energy efficiency, cut down on waste, and reduce greenhouse gases tied to global warming. The decision to be environmentally friendly throws the burden back onto their suppliers, where Wal-Mart has stipulated close monitoring of its overseas suppliers to make sure they meet social and environmental standards. More specifically, Wal-Mart announced it would evaluate the suppliers not only on price but also on environmental sustainability of their packaging.

The result? Wal-Mart saw unprecedented amounts of innovation in packaging in the first six months of 2007, more than in the previous five years combined. It might seem that so much change so fast would be disruptive to operations. But according to Wal-Mart, it was business as usual. It used the same tactics it uses to show its commitment to low prices, but the environmental message was different.

Skeptics have been pleasantly surprised by the shift in focus, but some are concerned about the success and sustainability of the suppliers. Historically, Wal-Mart's aggressive approach has been criticized for pushing some companies toward drastic changes in the name of cost savings and in some cases for driving some companies out of business. Even with all this negativity, critics are now conceding that Wal-Mart has the potential to use its power for good and persuade suppliers to make the necessary changes that will reduce greenhouse gas emissions and battle global warming.

Making changes to packaging could, in some cases, lead to production changes to the product itself. Wal-Mart believes that there are financial incentives for every company that makes environmentally friendly changes. These changes have affected Wal-Mart's bottom line by lowering shipping costs and reducing waste, which in turn reduces expenses. Wal-Mart says its goal is to reduce packaging by 5 percent by 2013, and, if everyone complies, this is a very attainable target.

Critical Thinking Questions

1. Wal-Mart has mandated very strict policies regarding packaging. Explain the consequences of these policies for Wal-Mart's suppliers.
2. Can the lessons learned at Wal-Mart be applied to other businesses? Explain.
3. As a consumer, would you make a conscious choice to shop only at stores that sell environmentally friendly products? Why or why not?

to subassembly, final completion, and shipment of finished products. JIT reduces to practically nothing the number of goods in process (that is, goods not yet finished) and saves money by replacing stop-and-go production with smooth movement. Once smooth movements become the norm, disruptions become more visible and thus are resolved more quickly. Finding and eliminating disruptions by continuous improvement of production is a major objective of JIT. Here are just two examples:

- Mount Sinai Hospital uses JIT. Individual suppliers no longer go to Mount Sinai to deliver the items they have sold to the hospital. Rather, all suppliers deliver their products to Livingston Healthcare Services Inc., which stores these items and fills Mount Sinai's order once each day; therefore, Mount Sinai no longer keeps any inventory. Once the goods are delivered, they are sent directly to the various departments in the hospital; the former centralized storeroom at the hospital no longer exists. In the first year using the new system, the hospital saved about \$200 000.[20]
- At Toyota's Cambridge, Ontario plant, delivery trucks constantly pull in to unload tires, batteries, steering wheels, seats, and many other items needed in the JIT production system.[21] And when General Motors of Canada's Oshawa assembly plant needs seats for cars, it sends the order electronically to a local supplier. The supplier has four hours to make the seats and ship them to the plant. The supplier loads the truck in reverse order so that the

last seat loaded is the first one that will be used on the assembly line. The supplier knows, for example, that the plant will be making a certain number of one model and then a certain number of another model of car.[22]

JIT can cause some unexpected problems. As more and more companies adopt the philosophy that they will carry only minimal inventories, the ordering of supplies has become much more last-minute and frantic. By definition, this makes supply systems more volatile, and it has been one of the reasons why economic indicators like capital goods orders have been swinging so wildly. This, in turn, makes it hard to know what shape the overall economy is in. The more uncertainty there is about the economy, the less investor enthusiasm there is.[23]

Material Requirements Planning

Like JIT, **material requirements planning (MRP)** seeks to deliver the right amount of materials at the right place and the right time for goods production. MRP uses a **bill of materials** that is basically a recipe for the finished product. It specifies the necessary ingredients (raw materials and components), the order in which they should be combined, and the quantity of each ingredient needed to make one batch of the product (say, 2000 finished telephones). The recipe is fed in to a computer that controls inventory and schedules each stage of production. The result is fewer early arrivals, less frequent stock shortages, and lower storage costs. MRP is most popular among companies whose products require complicated assembly and fabrication activities, such as automobile manufacturers, appliance makers, and furniture companies.

material requirements planning (MRP) A method of inventory control in which a computerized bill of materials is used to estimate production needs so that resources are acquired and put into production only as needed.

bill of materials Basically a recipe for the finished product.

Manufacturing resource planning (MRP II) is an advanced version of MRP that ties all parts of the organization into the company's production activities. For example, MRP inventory and production schedules are translated into cost requirements for the financial management department and into personnel requirements for the human resources department; information about available capacity for new orders goes to the marketing department.

manufacturing resource planning (MRP II) An advanced version of MRP that ties together all parts of the organization into the company's production activities.

Quality Control

Another operation control tool is **quality control**—the management of the production process to manufacture goods or supply services that meet specific quality standards. McDonald's, for example, is a pioneer in quality control in the restaurant industry. The company oversees everything from the farming of

quality control The management of the production process to manufacture goods or supply services that meet specific quality standards.

This Delphi Automotive Systems plant makes plastic housings for electrical connectors in cars and telecom equipment. Quality checkers are important members of the production team. Delphi's defect rate is only 14 parts per million. The company has spent millions of dollars on new production equipment, computers, software, and an emanufacturing network that is so efficient that the plant superintendent can work at home from his own PC.

potatoes for french fries to the packing of meat for Big Macs. Quality-assurance staffers even check standards for ketchup sweetness and french fry length. We discuss quality control in more detail in the following chapter, where we focus on the connection between productivity and quality.

Test yourself on the material for this chapter at **www.pearsoned.ca/mybusinesslab**.

Summary of Learning Objectives

1. **Explain the meaning of the terms *production* and *operations*.** *Service operations* provide intangible and tangible service products, such as entertainment, transportation, education, and food preparation. Firms that make tangible products—radios, newspapers, buses, and textbooks—are engaged in *goods production*. Because the term *production* is associated just with manufacturing, we now use *operations* to refer to both service and goods production. *Operations (or production) management* is the systematic direction and control of the processes that transform resources into finished services and goods that create value for and provide benefits to customers. In overseeing production, *inventory*, and *quality control*, operations (or production) managers are responsible for ensuring that operations processes create value and provide benefits.

2. **Describe the four kinds of *utility* provided by production and explain the two classifications of *operations processes*.** Products provide businesses with economic results—profits, wages, and goods purchased from other companies. They also provide consumers with *utility*—the ability of a product to satisfy a human want. There are four kinds of production-based utility: (1) *Time utility*—production makes products available when consumers want them; (2) *Place utility*—production makes products available where they are convenient for consumers; (3) *Ownership (or possession) utility*—production makes products available for consumers to own and use; and (4) *Form utility*—by turning raw materials into finished goods, production makes products available in the first place. An *operations process* is a set of methods and technologies used in the production of a good or a service. There are two types of operations processes for goods: (1) An *analytic process* breaks down resources into components, and (2) A *synthetic process* combines raw materials to produce a finished product. Services are classified as *high-contact processes* and *low-contact processes*, according to the extent of customer contact. To receive the service in a high-contact system, the customer must be a part of the system. In a low-contact system, customers are not in contact with the provider while the service is performed.

3. **Identify the characteristics that distinguish *service operations* from *goods production* and explain the main differences in the service focus.** Both service and manufacturing operations transform raw materials into finished products. In service production, the raw materials are people who have either unsatisfied needs or possessions needing some form of care or alteration; "finished products" are people with needs met and possessions serviced. The focus of service operations differs from that of goods production in five ways: (1) Focus on performance—because goods are produced and services performed, customer-oriented performance is crucial to a service company; (2) Focus on process and outcome—because most service products are combinations of goods and services, services focus on both the transformation process and its outcome; (3) Focus on service characteristics—service transactions reflect the three key qualities of service products: (i) Intangibility: Because services usually can't be touched, tasted, smelled, or seen, they provide intangible value experienced as pleasure, satisfaction, or a feeling of safety. (ii) Customization: Each customer expects a service to be designed (customized) for his or her specific needs. (iii) Unstorability: Because many services can't be produced ahead of time and then stored, they have a high degree of unstorability; (4) Focus on the customer-service link—because service operations often acknowledge the customer as part of the process, consumers can directly affect that process; (5) Focus on service quality considerations—service providers know that quality of work and quality of service are not necessarily the same thing (a properly repaired car is one thing, but getting it back when you need it is another).

4. **Describe the factors involved in *operations planning*.** The operations-management process is a series of logical steps. Whereas the business plan outlines goals and

objectives, managers also develop long-range production plans through forecasts of future demand for both new and existing products. Operations planning then focuses on five major categories: (1) Capacity planning—the amount of a product that a company can produce under normal working conditions is its *capacity*. The capacity of a goods or service firm depends on how many people it employs and the number and size of its facilities; (2) Location planning—in location planning, managers in goods-producing operations consider such factors as proximity to raw materials and markets, availability of labour, energy and transportation costs, regulations and taxes, and community living conditions; (3) Layout planning—layout of machinery, equipment, and supplies determines how quickly a company can respond to customer demand for more and different products. In a *process layout*, which is well-suited to job shops specializing in custom work, equipment and people are grouped according to function. *Cellular layouts* take groups of similar products through fixed flow paths. Equipment set-up is easier, flow distances are shorter, and material handling and transit time are reduced. In a *product layout*, equipment and people are set up to produce one type of product in a fixed sequence; (4) Quality planning—products must meet standards of quality. Such standards may include reasonable price and consistent performance; (5) Methods planning—when managers reduce waste and inefficiency by identifying every production stage and the specific methods for performing it, they are practising methods improvement. A process flow chart can identify the sequence of production activities, movements of materials, and work performed at each stage. The flow can then be analyzed to identify wasteful activities, sources of delay, and other inefficiencies. *Service flow analysis* helps managers decide which processes in a service are necessary. It also helps isolate potential problems known as fail points.

5. Explain some factors in *operations scheduling* and describe some activities involved in *operations control*, including materials management and the use of certain operations control tools. *A master production schedule* shows which products will be produced, when production will take place, and what resources will be used during specified periods. For scheduling special projects, two tools—*Gantt charts* and *PERT charts*—assist managers in maintaining close coordination and timing. *Operations control* requires managers to monitor performance by comparing results with detailed plans and schedules. If schedules or quality standards are not met, managers take corrective action. *Follow-up*—checking to ensure that decisions are being implemented—is an essential facet of operations control. There are four areas in materials management: (1) *Transportation* includes the means of transporting resources to the company and finished goods to buyers; (2) *Warehousing* is the storage of incoming materials and finished goods for distribution to customers; (3) *Inventory control* includes the receiving, storing, handling, and counting of all raw materials, partly finished goods, and finished goods. It ensures that enough materials inventories are available to meet production schedules; (4) *Purchasing* is the acquisition of all the raw materials and services that a company needs for production.

Key Terms

analytic process (p. 348)
assembly line (p. 358)
bill of materials (p. 369)
capacity (p. 354)
cellular layout (p. 356)
flexible manufacturing system (FMS) (p. 358)
follow-up (p. 366)
forecast (p. 353)
form utility (p. 347)
Gantt chart (p. 364)
goods production (p. 344)
high-contact system (p. 349)
holding costs (p. 366)
inventory control (p. 366)
just-in-time (JIT) production system (p. 367)
lead times (p. 367)
lean manufacturing (p. 358)
low-contact system (p. 349)
manufacturing resource planning (MRP II) (p. 369)
master production schedule (p. 363)
material requirements planning (MRP) (p. 369)
materials management (p. 366)
operations capability (production capability) (p. 347)
operations control (p. 365)
operations process (p. 348)

operations (production) management (p. 347)
ownership (possession) utility (p. 347)
PERT chart (p. 364)
place utility (p. 347)
process layout (p. 356)
product layout (p. 358)
production managers (p. 347)
purchasing (p. 366)
quality control (p. 369)
service flow analysis (p. 361)
service operations (p. 344)
soft manufacturing (p. 358)
standardization (p. 366)
supplier selection (p. 367)
synthetic process (p. 348)
time utility (p. 346)
transportation (p. 366)
U-shaped production lines (p. 358)
utility (p. 346)
warehousing (p. 366)

Questions for Analysis

1. What are the major differences between goods-production operations and service operations?
2. What are the major differences between high-contact and low-contact service systems?
3. What are the resources and finished products in the following services?
   - real estate firm
   - childcare facility
   - bank
   - city water and electric department
   - hotel
4. Analyze the location of a local firm where you do business (perhaps a restaurant, a supermarket, or a manufacturing firm). What problems do you see with this location? What recommendations would you make to management?
5. Pick three products (not services) that you regularly use. Then do some research to determine which of the basic production processes are used to produce these products (chemical, fabrication, assembly, transport, or clerical processes). To what extent are multiple processes used in the production of the product?
6. Develop a service flow analysis for some service that you use frequently, such as buying lunch at a cafeteria, having your hair cut, or riding a bus. Identify areas of potential quality or productivity failures in the process.
7. Pick three services (not products) that you regularly use. Explain what customization, unstorability, and intangibility mean for each of the services. How do these factors influence the way the service is delivered to customers?

Application Exercises

1. Find two examples of a synthetic production process and two examples of an analytic production process. Explain why you categorized them as you did.
2. Interview the manager of a local service business, such as a laundry or dry cleaning shop. Identify the major decisions involved in planning its service operations. Prepare a class report suggesting areas for improvement.
3. Select a high-contact industry. Write an advertisement seeking workers for a company in this industry. Draw up a plan for motivating workers to produce high-quality services.

Building Your Business Skills

The One-on-One Entrepreneur

The Purpose of the Assignment

To encourage students to apply the concept of customization to an entrepreneurial idea.

The Situation

You are an entrepreneur who wants to start your own service business. You are intrigued with the idea of creating some kind of customized one-on-one service that would appeal to baby boomers, who traditionally have been pampered, and working women, who have little time to get things done.

Assignment

Step 1

Get together with three or four other students to brainstorm ideas for services that would appeal to harried working people. Here are just a few:

- A concierge service in office buildings that would handle such personal and business services as arranging children's birthday parties and booking guest speakers for business luncheons.
- A personal-image consultation service aimed at helping clients improve appearance, etiquette, and presentation style.

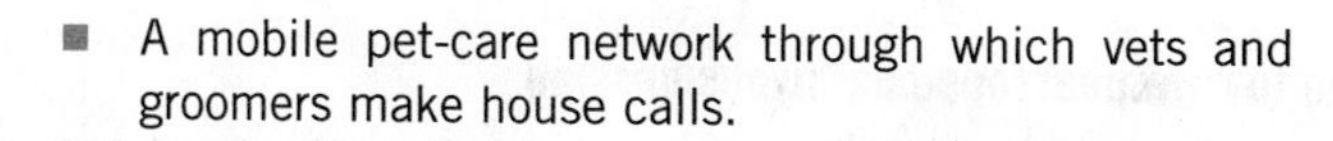

- A mobile pet-care network through which vets and groomers make house calls.

Step 2

Choose one of these ideas or one that your team thinks of. Then write a memo explaining why you think your idea will succeed. Research may be necessary as you target any of the following:

- a specific demographic group or groups (Who are your customers, and why would they buy your service?)
- the features that make your service attractive to this group
- the social factors in your local community that would contribute to success

Questions for Discussion

1. Why is the customization of and easy access to personal services so desirable in the twenty-first century?
2. As services are personalized, do you think quality will become more or less important? Why?
3. Why does the trend toward personalized, one-on-one service present unique opportunities for entrepreneurs?
4. In a personal one-on-one business, how important are the human relations skills of those delivering the service? Can you make an argument that they are more important than the service itself?

Exercising Your Ethics: Team Exercise

Promises, Promises

The Situation

Unfortunately, false promises are not uncommon when managers feel pressure to pump up profits. Many operations managers no doubt recall times when excited marketing colleagues asked for unrealistic commitments from production to get a new customer contract. This exercise will introduce you to some ethical considerations pertaining to such promises and commitments.

The Dilemma

You are the operations manager for a factory that makes replacement car mufflers and tailpipes. Your plant produces these items for all makes and models and sells them throughout Canada to muffler-repair shops that install them on used vehicles. After several years of modest but steady growth, your company has recently suffered a downturn and must shut down 5 percent of the factory's production capacity. Two supervisors and 70 production workers have been laid off. All of the company's stakeholders—employees, managers, the union, suppliers, and owners—are concerned about prospects for the immediate future.

After returning from lunch you receive a phone call from the general manager of one of the nation's top three muffler-repair chains. He says the following: "I suppose you know that we're about to sign a contract under which your firm will supply us with replacement parts in large volumes, beginning two months from now. Your sales manager has assured me that you can reliably meet my needs, and I just want to confirm that promise with you before I sign the contract."

This is the first you've heard about this contract. While your potential customer is talking, you realize that meeting his needs will involve a 20 percent increase in your current production capacity. Two months, however, isn't enough time to add more equipment, acquire tools, hire and train workers, and contract for supplies. In fact, an increase this large might even require a bigger building (which would, of course, take considerably more than two months to arrange). On the other hand, you also know how much your firm needs the business. Your thoughts are interrupted when the caller says, "So what's your production situation insofar as meeting our needs?" The caller waits in silence while you gather your thoughts.

Team Activity

Assemble a group of four students and assign each group member to one of the following roles:

- the operations manager of the factory
- the general manager of the muffler-repair chain
- the sales manager of your company
- an employee in the factory

Questions for Discussion

1. Before discussing the situation with your group, and from the perspective of your assigned role, what are the underlying ethical issues, if any, in this situation? Write down the issues.
2. Gather your group together and reveal, in turn, each member's list of ethical issues.
3. From an ethical standpoint, what does your group conclude is the most appropriate action that should be taken by the company in this situation?
4. Develop a group response to the following question: How would you handle this situation?

For additional cases and exercise material, go to **www.pearsoned.ca/mybusinesslab**.

Concluding Case 11-1

How to Keep a Project Afloat

For football fans, the Pasadena Tournament of Roses Parade is a major New Year's event. With elegant floral floats, spirited marching bands, colourful costuming, and high-stepping equestrian units, it's one of the world's premier entertainment events for more than a million streetside onlookers and a TV audience of 400 million in more than 100 countries. Hidden beneath the glamour, however, is a complicated maze of behind-the-scenes project management activity. The year-long planning is coordinated as expertly as the parade itself and includes arrangements for logistics (housing, parking, seating, food vending, toilet facilities), TV programming, moving a million visitors in and out of Pasadena on parade day, receiving applications and selecting participants, building floats, and after-parade clean-up. Without project management, the parade couldn't keep its lofty position among the world's best.

The challenges in just one activity—building a float—involve seemingly endless details. Consider, for example, the City of Burbank's 2004 float entry, "Moosic, Moosic, Moosic." First, its designers focussed on the concept that music has always been part of herd tending, so it tied in to the Tournament of Roses theme: Music, Music, Music. The float's drawings featured a bronco-riding balladeer perched atop a steep mesa keeping his eye on the herd while filling the valley with Gene Autry's "Back in the Saddle Again," as cows munch and chew and prairie dogs keep a watchful eye on a nearby dog. Its finished dimensions were 25 feet high, 18 feet wide, and a hefty 48 feet long. First, however, the year's activities had to be coordinated, from final drawings and instructions to ordering flower blossoms and paste to training volunteer workers to final construction.

Activities are scheduled in phases so that preliminary steps are completed before follow-on activities are attempted. They had to be completed neither too early (lest completed work fall apart or deteriorate from sitting too long) nor too late (causing slowdowns or lateness in project completion). For six months, volunteers—many from outside the community—worked on building the float's frame, then shaping the cartoon-like cowboy, horse, dog, cows, and prairie dogs. Then they rushed frantically into last-minute painting and gluing of the finishing seeds, barks, and grasses. Various skill levels ranging from novice to expert were used for developing scale drawings and for construction, metal bending, welding, hydraulics, flower cutting, electrical work, painting, gluing, dry material preparation, and merchandising.

The construction site—a warehouse building in the Burbank Water and Power Department yard—had to be large enough, initially, to accommodate a relatively few activities, workstations, and trainers, as well as materials, tools, and supplies. More capacity was needed, however, with the passage of time: The volunteer supervisors' workload grew when as many as 800 newcomers a day showed up in late December to apply last-minute finishing touches, accompanied by surging inflows of supplies and materials. Every inch of the float was covered with flowers—brought in from as far away as Venezuela, Colombia, and Trinidad—or other natural materials such as seeds, fruit rinds, and leaves. All of this had to be accomplished within the $125 000 budget and under close supervision so the float would be structurally safe, beautifully decorated, and finished on time. Although the pace got hectic, the all-volunteer project was a source of pride for the community.

Preparation for next year's Rose Parade float begins right after New Year's Day, as soon as the parade theme has been announced. The Burbank Tournament of Roses Association solicits ideas and drawings from the general public in a design contest. From the 72 drawings submitted for 2004, the association's board of directors selected six designs and presented them to the general membership for the final choice. This one activity involved six time-phased steps:

1. January 2: Design contest entry form and post rules on association website.
2. January 28: Deadline for receiving design submissions (drawings).
3. January 31: Board meets to review submissions and narrow down to top six.
4. February 5: Full membership of association meets to rank the six drawings.
5. February 11: Drawings taken to Pasadena for theme draft among all float builders (lottery determines the order that drawings are approved if floats are too similar).
6. February 12: Board meets to announce winning design. Work can start.

Additional activities are triggered once the design is approved. By March, final drawings and plans are under examination by the construction and decoration committees. Actual physical construction of the float begins in May. Decoration materials are ordered in July and the ensuing months. Orders for live flowers are placed with various growers in September and October. Actual decoration of the float begins December 26 and continues until December 31. On New Year's Eve, a contingent of City of Burbank motorcycle police escorts the float, via surface streets, to Pasadena. The project ends in the second week of January with float deconstruction.

Throughout the year, major activities consist of substeps that are coordinated with other major activities. Consider, for example, planning for the flowers and vegetation that elaborately decorate the entire float. The cowpoke and cartoon cow heads are sculpted from foam before flowers are added. The three cows are then covered in white cushion poms with spots made of 2500 Terra Cotta roses. The cows stand on plateaus while munching on landscaping made of native grasses, sunflowers, kangaroo paws, gerbera daisies, and stargazer lilies. The towering sides of the butte are formed of red lentil, safflower, annatto seed, yellow peas, millet, purple statice, and over 15 000 various roses (Gipsy Curiosa, Tequila, Orange Unique, Blue Curiosa, and Corvette). The bronco-riding, guitar-playing cowboy atop the butte is clad in silverleaf hat, marigold bandana, and statice blue jeans, on a horse of butterscotch strawflower with a white pampas grass mane and tail. All these materials have to be purchased and received on time and in good condition, then mounted securely on the frame covering two main engines, one for driving the float and one for running the animation and sound system.

Among the 49 floats for 2004, Burbank's is one of only six "self-built" floats (other floats are contracted out to professional float-building companies). It is designed, constructed, and decorated entirely by volunteers including Scout groups, high school clubs, community service groups, and Burbank residents and visitors, some as young as five years old. So skilfully was it completed that Burbank's entry was an award winner, receiving the Queen's Trophy for most effective use and display of roses in concept, design, and presentation.

Questions for Discussion

1. What other activities, in addition to building floats for the Tournament of Roses Parade, might benefit from project management methods? Explain your reasoning.
2. Suppose you are responsible for planning the City of Burbank's float for next year's Tournament of Roses Parade. You are concerned about the number of purchased items and suppliers scattered around the globe. What are some of the major project planning problems posed by the suppliers' geographic dispersion?
3. Consider the diversity of human skills needed at various stages throughout Burbank's preparations for the Tournament of Roses Parade. What are the various required skills and what problems do they present for planning the project?
4. Suppose you are involved in planning for accommodating the million streetside onlookers in Pasadena next New Year's Day. What are the main activities that should be considered in your project planning efforts? Which of those activities must be started early in the project and which can be delayed until later?
5. How might PERT charts be used for scheduling major activities for the Tournament of Roses Parade? In what ways can PERT be of assistance to project managers in such projects?

Concluding Case 11-2

Bailout or Bust?

After years of struggling, the automobile manufacturing industry took a significant hit in 2009. The media headlines and industry analysts spoke only of government bailouts, divesting options, bankruptcy, and restructuring plans. The "big three" in the North American auto industry—General Motors Corp., Ford Motor Co., and Chrysler—have been steadily losing market share, profits, employees, and their reputations. When such large numbers of people and communities rely on the auto industry for their livelihood, what are governments to do? Bail the companies out? While this seems like an easy and logical decision for the short-term, what sort of message does it send to the auto manufacturing industry about taking responsibility for their past actions that got them into this trouble?

Knowing that providing additional funds may be simply throwing good money after bad, the Canadian and U.S. governments have made restructuring demands that require the domestic auto companies to make deep cuts to bring their cost structures down to that of their Japanese rivals. If the companies don't make the cuts, government bailout money will not be forthcoming. These demands by government have been hard to swallow, both for the auto companies (who have long been "the big boys in town") and for auto employees (who have enjoyed high wages and benefits). But the auto companies have no choice but to start making some hard decisions. In May 2009, for example, GM announced the closure of its Oshawa, Ontario, manufacturing plant (putting 2600 workers out of a job). And both GM and Chrysler announced that they would close hundreds of dealerships across North America. So, big changes are starting to happen, and thousands more jobs are going to be lost (the number of Canadian Auto Workers members working for GM, Chrysler, and Ford has declined from 65 000 in 1990 to just 30 000 in 2008).

The current situation is different from the one in 1979, when Chrysler was on the brink of bankruptcy. Today, the auto industry is saturated. "The U.S. car market has gone bonkers in the last 10 years," says Dimitry Anastakis,

professor of automotive history at Trent University. "We have way more operational cars sitting in lots and rolling off the assembly lines than we need." According to Statistics Canada, at the time of the Chrysler bailout in 1979, there were 1.2 cars for every family; today there are 2.1 cars.

Many people feel that government bailouts are necessary, given the size and possible impact such a loss would have on the economy. Others argue that these companies are simply too big to fail. But governments are cautious about bailing out Chrysler and GM, given what they know about the performance of Japan's big three—Toyota Motor Corp., Nissan Motor Co. Ltd., and Honda Motor Co. Ltd. In one recent year, GM and Chrysler lost an average $1448 per vehicle, while Toyota's profit per vehicle was $1977. Japan's big three have to cope with the same saturated auto industry, high fuel costs, and problem economy that GM and Chrysler do. So why are they not asking for government bailouts?

Honda, for example, has not been immune to the troubles plaguing the global auto industry as a result of the credit crisis of 2008 and the subsequent downturn in consumer confidence. In 2009, Honda announced it was replacing its chief executive and making changes to its board of directors in an effort to bring fresh leadership to the company. It is also cut workers' pay and mandated 13 non-production days at its North American plants in an effort to reduce its output in summer 2009 by 62 000 vehicles. "There is a continuing need to reduce our inventory," says Honda spokesperson Ron Lietzke. "Regardless of job title or level within our organization, each Honda associate will share the responsibility of doing what we must do to remain competitive."

Toyota has also initiated change to its infrastructure by announcing production cuts and reductions in executive compensation and offering buyouts to almost 18 000 workers. These changes made by the Japanese auto companies seem drastic, but they are all trying to avoid layoffs, because their corporate cultures emphasize lifetime employment.

In addition to cutting costs at their Canadian manufacturing plants, Japan's Big Three are relocating their manufacturing facilities to countries with low land taxes, low wage rates, and weaker union laws. One popular place is the southern United States, where "right-to-work" laws are common (this means that no worker can be forced to join a union or pay union dues). The movement to the southern United States isn't the only move south that is evident. Automakers have also set up assembly plants in South Africa, Brazil, and Thailand. The cars produced in these plants have supplied markets in Japan, Europe, and North America. Until now, automakers thought that cars produced in these areas would not be well received by consumers in industrialized countries, but that is changing. BMW, for example, has poured hundreds of millions of dollars into its South African production facility. It says the cost of land, electricity, and labour is much lower there than in industrialized countries. A survey by J.D. Power & Associates found that the quality of cars produced at BMW's South African plant beats the quality of their cars produced in Germany and the United States.

Because the wages paid to workers in these overseas locations can be as little as one-tenth of those paid to North American workers, the automakers have a strong incentive to move their operations. The low wages more than make up for the cost of shipping parts to these plants and then shipping the finished cars back to North America, Japan, or Europe. Unions in North America and Europe are increasingly concerned that this trend will mean fewer high-paying jobs for their members. The CAW, for example, is angry that Ford is planning to import the Fusion from Brazil when it is also planning to close a pickup truck plant in Canada. Ford says the numbers are so small that they won't reduce the number of union jobs. But Ford also notes that its plant in Brazil is its lowest-cost plant and its quality is high; that could mean much higher production and export of vehicles in the future.

Another problem for auto manufacturers is the increasing emphasis on environmental protection, and the industry has been put under the microscope to ensure that the industry is putting forth sufficient effort to address this issue. Anastakis says that "emissions and fuel economy are issues [the big three] have dealt with in a haphazard way." The fault lies with both manufacturers and consumers (who have been, until recently, very keen about SUVs and other gas guzzlers). But the auto industry has not had the insight or the drive required to change with the times. Now that environmentalism is trendy, the pressure is on to alter production methods and redesign models to meet consumer expectations and demands.

Even in the midst of this crisis, Anastakis sees hope and growth potential. "This is an opportunity to move the companies in the direction that people have been telling them to move but the way they've been having trouble moving for the past 30 years."

Questions for Discussion

1. Explain in your own words how trends in the global automotive market are causing employment problems in automotive manufacturing in Ontario. Can anything be done to reverse the trend? If not, explain why not. If something can be done, explain what that might be.
2. Explain how problems at companies like GM and Chrysler have influenced the operations of parts suppliers in Canada.
3. What do the problems in the automotive business (for both manufacturers and parts suppliers) imply for other parts of the economy that are not directly related to the automobile business? Explain.

4. Southern U.S. states like Alabama have given hundreds of millions of dollars in incentives to companies that agree to set up manufacturing plants there. Should the provinces of Ontario and Quebec be more active in giving the same type of incentives to maintain employment in automobile manufacturing in Canada? Defend your answer.

Chapter 12

Increasing Productivity and Quality

After reading this chapter, you should be able to:

1. Describe the connection between *productivity* and *quality*.
2. Understand the importance of increasing productivity.
3. Identify the activities involved in *total quality management* and describe six tools that companies can use to achieve it.
4. Identify three trends in productivity and quality management, including *supply chain management*.
5. Explain how a *supply chain strategy* differs from traditional strategies for coordinating operations among firms.
6. Discuss four strategies that companies use to improve productivity and quality.

Quality Problems in Service Businesses

In September 2006, the U.S. Federal Aviation Administration (FAA) gave airlines until March 2008 to inspect a certain bundle of wires located near the main landing gear in all MD-80 airliners, and, if the bundle was improperly secured, to repair it. Eighteen months later, some 250 000 travellers found themselves stranded as American Airlines grounded its fleet of MD-80s and cancelled nearly 3300 flights in a hurried effort to comply with the FAA directive.

How could the United States' largest carrier make such a costly and seemingly avoidable mistake? Shortly before the deadline to repair the wiring passed, the FAA was embarrassed by revelations that another carrier, Southwest Airlines, had also violated federal regulations by flying planes that had missed their scheduled inspections. Suddenly, the FAA found itself under fire from the U.S. Congress for failing to keep closer tabs on airlines. It is not surprising, then, that the FAA became extra vigilant in inspecting the MD-80s—more vigilant, it seems, than carriers such as American had come to expect.

None of this may be much consolation to frustrated travellers. According to Bren Bowen, co-author of the *2008 Airline Quality Rating (AQR)*, 2007 "was the worst year ever for the U.S. airlines." The *AQR* measures such performance indicators as the percentage of flights arriving on time, the amount of mishandled baggage, and the number of complaints, ranging from high fares to misleading advertising to discriminatory practices. Such a varied list of concerns is a reminder that the fundamental service an airline provides—getting people from point A to point B—is only the beginning of operational performance and quality. As the American Airlines incident illustrates, however, even this fundamental service is impossible to provide without a strong emphasis on quality practices.

A different part of the travel industry in Canada is also under scrutiny—travel companies and booking agents. When Conquest Vacations suddenly ceased operations in April 2009, many travellers were stranded in hotels in Mexico, the Dominican Republic, and Cuba. Many of these Canadians were told by hotel officials that they had to pay for their room after Conquest folded because their bill had not been paid by the travel company.

The Ontario government established the Travel Industry Council of Ontario (TICO) to ensure that (1) fair business practices and ethical behaviour are adhered to, and (2) Canadian travellers are not scammed or taken advantage of. But Conquest's sudden shutdown meant that TICO was not given proper notice and therefore could not provide sufficient information to travellers. The outcome has left many critics questioning the usefulness of the travel council. There is now concern about the travel industry in general, and many people are asking if there are going to be additional travel businesses that suddenly cease operations.

These problems have arisen at a time when the travel business is hurting because of the recession. Intense competition has driven down vacation prices, and consumers are looking for the lowest all-inclusive deals. In an effort to remain competitive, tour companies are laying off staff and reducing their prices to below cost. Transat A.T. Inc. cut 53 administrative jobs at their Montreal, Toronto, and Vancouver office locations, while U.S. airline subsidiary Air Transat cut about 30 administrative positions. Analyst David Newman of National Bank Financial indicated that the restructuring efforts will eliminate duplicate functions, merge divisions, and centralize administrative and support operations in a bid to "flatten the management structure." Travel companies have assured consumers that the changes they are making will strengthen their service offering, but many customers are feeling uncertain about the level of service quality they can expect.

Customer complaints about poor service quality are obviously not limited to the travel business. To observe consumer unhappiness in action, go to Complaints.com, a forum for people who have had bad consumer experiences. Enter "missed appointment" or "late repairman" in the search engine and you will get pages of hits. Typical is this complaint about a failed window installation: "I then made an appointment for [an] employee to come to my house the next day between 2 p.m. and 4 p.m.... I took a day off from work and stayed home to wait for the [company] truck. Four p.m. came and went. No one from [the company] showed up or called."

ConsumerAffairs.com, an advocacy group for customers who have received poor service or purchased shoddy merchandise, also details numerous incidents in which people were left waiting helplessly for repair technicians who were late for scheduled appointments. Part of the problem is that the company that manufactures a product may not be the same company that provides service for that product. This is often the case with mass-produced products purchased in department stores or wholesale outlets. General Electric may make a refrigerator, but a GE repair technician is not located in every town where that refrigerator is sold. Outside contractors must then be hired to perform repairs, and they may lack the specific expertise required to do the job in a timely manner.

It's not only products in need of installation or repair that can cause customers frustrations over missed appointments. How many hours have you spent waiting in crowded doctors' offices, overbooked salons, and slow-service restaurants? In each case, even if the quality of the product or service turns out to be excellent, you may still feel dissatisfied with the overall quality of the experience. For service providers in particular, that failure can be as costly as producing a defective product. ◆

How will this help me?

You will benefit in three ways by reading and understanding important productivity and quality concepts: (1) As an employee, you'll gain a better understanding of why every employee in a business should be concerned about productivity and quality; (2) as a manager, you'll understand that in order to remain competitive, your business must continually analyze its production methods so that high-quality products and services are efficiently produced; and (3) as a consumer, you'll gain insights into how much attention companies must pay to productivity and quality issues if they hope to produce products and services that consumers will want.

In this chapter, we'll talk about productivity (how businesses can increase the efficiency of their operations) and quality (how businesses can improve and manage product quality, and why it's important that they do so).

It is no secret that *productivity* and *quality* are watchwords in today's business. Companies are not only measuring productivity and insisting on improvements but also insisting on quality so they can bring to market products that satisfy customers, improve sales, and boost profits. By focussing on the learning objectives of this chapter, you will better understand the increasingly important concepts of productivity and quality.

The Productivity–Quality Connection

1 Describe the connection between *productivity* and *quality*.

productivity A measure of economic performance that measures how much is produced relative to the resources used to produce it.

quality A product's fitness for use in terms of offering the features that consumers want.

Productivity is a measure of economic performance. It measures how much is produced relative to the resources used to produce it. The more we are able to produce the right things while using fewer resources, the more productivity grows and everyone—the economy, businesses, and workers—benefits.

Productivity considers both the amounts and the quality of what is produced. By using resources more efficiently, the quantity of output will be greater. But unless the resulting goods and services are of satisfactory quality (the "right things"), consumers will not want them. **Quality**, then, means fitness for use—offering features that consumers want.

Responding to the Productivity Challenge

Productivity has both international and domestic ramifications. When one country is more productive than another, it will accumulate more wealth. Similarly, a nation whose productivity fails to increase as rapidly as that of competitor nations will see its standard of living fall.

It is important to understand the true meaning of *productivity* and to devise ways to measure it. Since *quality* must be defined in terms of value to the

Workers at this call centre in Bangalore, India, operated by ICICI OneSource, field calls from the customers of multinational firms headquartered in North America and Europe. Global broadband makes this business model possible, so many of these jobs (30 000 in Canada) are outsourced to Indian service suppliers because workers get paid only a fraction of what Canadian workers would get. Even then, they earn eight times as much as the average Indian earns per year ($450).

customer, companies must design their marketing efforts to cultivate a more customer-oriented focus. As quality-improvement practices are implemented, more and more firms will receive payoffs from these efforts. Four factors interact in this process: *customers*, *quality*, *productivity*, and *profits*.

Measuring Productivity

How do we know how productive a country is? Most countries use **labour productivity** to measure their level of productivity:

labour productivity Partial productivity ratio calculated by dividing gross domestic product by total number of workers.

$$\text{labour productivity of a country} = \frac{\text{gross domestic product}}{\text{total number of workers}}$$

This equation reflects the general idea of productivity. It compares a country's total annual output of goods and services with the resources used to produce that output. The focus on labour, rather than on other resources (such as capital or energy), is preferred because most countries keep accurate records on employment and hours worked.

A Statistics Canada report showed that foreign-controlled manufacturing plants in Canada accounted for two-thirds of the growth in labour productivity during one recent period. But the study emphasized that it wasn't the fact that the plants were foreign controlled that led to higher productivity; rather, it was the extent to which the companies had an international orientation. In other words, Canadian producers that had foreign units were just as productive as foreign-owned plants. It seems that firms that compete internationally have more incentive to be more productive.[1]

Productivity Among Global Competitors

A study by the Organisation for Economic Co-operation and Development (OECD) reported on productivity levels in various participating countries (see Figure 12.1). As you can see, output per hour worked in Belgium is about 28 percent higher than the average for OECD members. At 31 percent below average, output in New Zealand is lowest among the nations listed in Figure 12.1.

Why such differences from nation to nation? The answer lies in many factors: technologies, human skills, economic policies, natural resources, and even in traditions. Consider, for example, just one industrial sector—food production. In Japan, the food-production industry employs more workers than

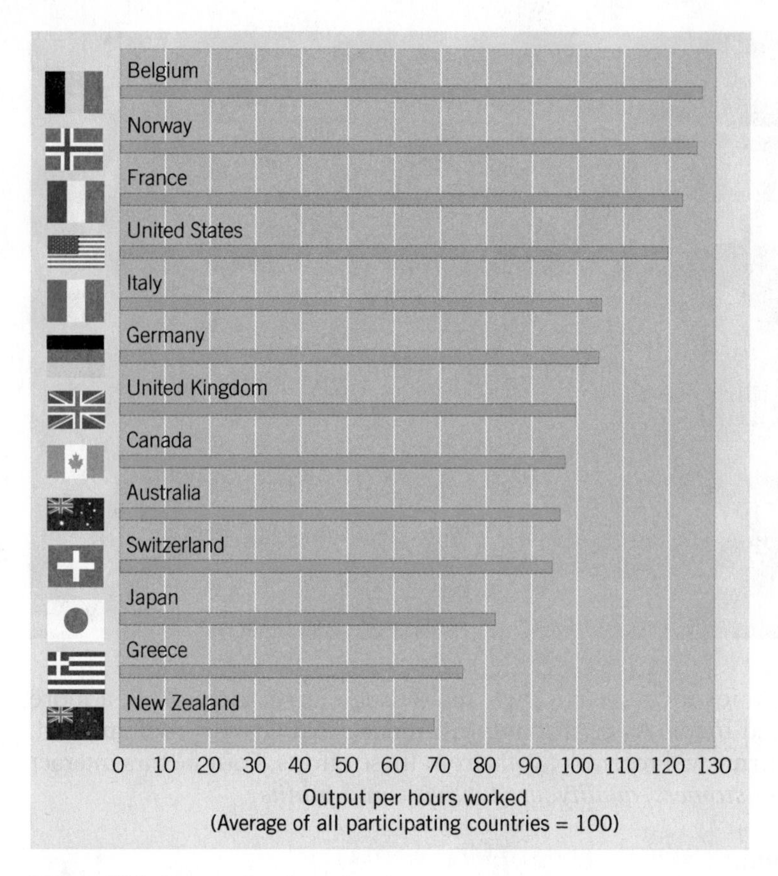

Figure 12.1 International productivity comparisons.

the automotive, computer, consumer electronics, and machine-tool industries combined. It is a fragmented, highly protected industry and, compared with U.S. food production, it is extremely inefficient. The average U.S. worker produces 3.5 times as much food as his or her Japanese counterpart. Overall, data show that in the time it takes a U.S. worker to produce $100 worth of goods, Japanese workers produce about $68 worth. Belgian workers, on the other hand, produce $107 worth.[2]

According to Michael Porter, a Harvard University expert on international competitiveness, Canada's competitiveness is a concern because we have been living off our rich diet of natural resources. In Porter's view, Canada will have to start emphasizing innovation and develop a more sophisticated mix of products if it hopes to be successful in international markets. Porter criticizes Canadian business, government, and labour for failing to abandon outdated ways of thinking regarding productivity and innovation.[3]

Domestic Productivity

Nations must be concerned about domestic productivity regardless of their global standing. A country that improves its ability to make something out of its existing resources can increase the wealth of all its inhabitants. Conversely, a decline in productivity shrinks a nation's total wealth. When that happens, an increase in one person's wealth comes only at the expense of others with whom he or she shares an economic system.

For example, additional wealth from higher productivity can be shared among workers (as higher wages), investors (as higher profits), and customers (as stable prices). When productivity drops, however, wages can be increased only by reducing profits (penalizing investors) or by increasing prices (penalizing customers). It is understandable, then, that investors, suppliers, managers, and workers are all concerned about the productivity of specific industries and companies.

Manufacturing vs. Service Productivity

Understand the importance of increasing productivity. 2

Manufacturing productivity is higher than service productivity. For many years, it was widely believed that the service sector suffered from "Baumol's disease," named after economist William Baumol who argued that since the service sector focussed more on hands-on activity that machines couldn't replace, it would be more difficult to increase productivity in services. Baumol noted, for example, that it would always require four musicians to play a Mozart quartet. But the Opera Company of Brooklyn is challenging Baumol's basic assumption. It now puts on Mozart's opera *The Marriage of Figaro* without the usual full orchestra. Instead, it uses just 12 musicians and a technician who oversees a computer program that plays all the other musical parts. The orchestra's productivity has increased sharply because it does not have to pay for the usual complement of musicians.[4]

Productivity gains are starting to appear among a wide array of service providers such as airlines, pet stores, package delivery companies, providers of financial services, and retail establishments. Many of these organizations have increased their productivity by becoming more like factories, and they use modern information technology to eliminate inefficiencies. Automated check-in kiosks in airports are a good example. Two-thirds of Northwest's passengers now check in using the kiosks.

Industry Productivity

In addition to differences between the manufacturing and service sectors, industries within these sectors differ vastly in terms of productivity. Agriculture is more productive in Canada than in many other nations because we use more sophisticated technology and superior natural resources. Technological advances have also given the computer industry a productivity edge in many areas. The productivity of the steel industry has also increased (in the early 1980s, about

On the left, workers assemble a truck the old way, manually lowering and bolting frames onto axles. On the right, the process is highly automated (and safer), with robotic grippers to flip and align the bulky frames.

10 hours of labour were required to produce a tonne of steel, but now only about four hours of labour are needed).

POSCO, a Korean steel giant, has focussed on improving customer-related services, including product quality, prices, and on-time delivery. The company changed their production methods and developed Finex, a furnace that can prepare cheaper types of coal and iron ore to be converted into pig iron. This process maintains quality, reduces costs, and reduces environmental impact.[5] In an effort to increase productivity, Canfor Corp. developed a system called Genus, which it is using to manage its forestry operations. Genus, a computerized database containing geographic information and other essential data about Canfor's vast lumber and pulp operations in British Columbia and Alberta, will be used as a strategic planning tool to determine how the company should adjust its logging plans to reflect both market demand and logging regulations laid down by the Forest Practices Code of British Columbia Act.[6]

The productivity of specific industries concerns many people for different reasons. Labour unions need to take it into account in negotiating contracts, since highly productive industries can give raises more easily than can less productive industries. Investors and suppliers consider industry productivity when making loans, buying securities, and planning their own future production.

Company Productivity

High productivity gives a company a competitive edge because its costs are lower. As a result, it can offer its product at a lower price (and gain more customers), or it can make a greater profit on each item sold. Increased productivity also allows companies to pay workers higher wages without raising prices.

The productivity of individual companies is also important to investors, workers, and managers. Comparing the productivity of several companies in the same industry helps investors in buying and selling stocks. Employee profit-sharing plans are often based on the company's productivity improvements each year. And managers use information about productivity trends to plan for new products, factories, and funds to stay competitive in the years ahead.

Total Quality Management

3 Identify the activities involved in *total quality management* and describe six tools that companies can use to achieve it.

It is no longer enough for businesses to simply measure productivity in terms of the numbers of items produced. They must also take quality into account. In the decades after the Second World War, business consultant W. Edwards Deming tried to persuade firms in North America that they needed to improve quality at least as much as quantity. He wasn't very successful, but his arguments won over the Japanese. Through years of meticulous hard work, Japan's manufacturers have changed "Made in Japan" from a synonym for cheap, shoddy merchandise into a hallmark of reliability. In 2008, for example, Toyota's Fujimatsu, Japan plant won the Gold Plant Quality Award from J.D. Power & Associates.[7] On several occasions, GM's Oshawa No. 2 plant has achieved the highest quality rating out of 80 assembly plants in North America. Another example of an attempt to convey quality and accountability to consumers is described in the Business Accountability box.

Quality advocates such as Joseph Juran and Kaoru Ishikawa introduced methods and tools for implementing quality. Juran's "Quality Trilogy"—*quality planning*, *quality control*, and *quality improvement*—was the first structured process for managing quality, and it identifies several management steps. In addition to management actions, Juran, like Deming and Ishikawa, championed the idea of company-wide employee participation. These theorists also developed quality tools for day-to-day work activities because they knew that, without

Business Accountability

Rating the Quality of Diamonds

How do you rate the quality of diamonds? Historically, diamond quality has been assessed by reference to four *Cs*: *cut*, *colour*, *clarity*, and *carat*. But perhaps a fifth *C* is emerging, and that is "country of origin." Better yet, the fifth *C* may also stand for "Canada."

Until just a few years ago, Canada was not even a player in the international diamond business. But in 1991, a promising diamond field was located in the Northwest Territories and the race was on to exploit the possibilities. Skeptics said that even if diamonds were found in commercial quantities in Canada, the diamonds would have to be sold to De Beers, the company that controlled the world diamond trade. But once diamond wholesalers were shown the first Canadian diamonds, they realized that the quality was as high as that from the best diamond mines in the world, and they eagerly bought them. The myth of De Beers control soon evaporated.

In the early 1990s, the gold mines of Yellowknife were aging and, with public concern about the environment running high, support for mining was waning. At that time, Yellowknife resident Tom Hoefer was a geologist attempting to buck the trend; working for the then NWT Chamber of Mines, he was trying to reinvigorate interest in mining and promoting the benefits that it could bring. During his term, diamonds were discovered, which fuelled a whole new life for mining in the region.

The first Canadian diamond mine was opened in the Northwest Territories in 1998; by 2003 it was already producing 6 percent of the total world's supply of rough diamonds. A second mine opened in 2003, and yet another opened in 2006. Today, Canada produces 12 percent of the world's diamonds. There are also promising developments in diamond mining in Saskatchewan, where core samples drilled by Shore Gold show that high-quality diamonds exist there.

In recent years, there has been much negative press about so-called "blood diamonds," that is, diamonds that were mined by armed workers in war-torn African countries like Angola. These diamonds were exported, and the money was used to support further military campaigns. The developing Canadian diamond industry has no such image problems. Diamonds in Canada are mined under very ethical and environmentally strict conditions. And there's one added advantage: The quality of Canadian diamonds is very high. Canadian rough diamonds average US$170 per carat in value, far above the US$100 level at which diamonds are considered precious. The samples from Saskatchewan are valued at about US$135 per carat.

The discovery of Canadian diamonds has also had a positive impact on the local communities. The cluster of three producing diamond mines—BHP Billiton's Ekati mine, De Beers Canada's Snap Lake mine, and Diavik Diamond Mines Inc.—have had a tremendous impact on the local community, with average wages pushing $100 000 per year. They are offering many local people on-the-job training and long-term stability for the first time in their lives.

But is country of origin important enough to influence consumers when they purchase a diamond? In the minds of many consumers, the quality of certain products *is* associated with the product's country of origin. Think, for example, of Swiss watches, Italian leather, and French wines. Oren Sofer, CEO of diamond wholesaler Beny Sofer & Sons LLC, says that if you can brand water, you certainly should be able to brand diamonds. He wants consumers to eventually recognize "Canadian diamonds" as an important brand name.

This is not an impossible goal. The move is already underway to establish a high-quality reputation for Canadian diamonds. Sirius Diamond Inc., a Vancouver diamond wholesaler, engraves a tiny polar bear on the Canadian diamonds it sells, and Birks & Sons Inc. engraves a maple leaf on its diamonds. The government of the Northwest Territories provides a certificate for each diamond that has come from its mines. This ensures that diamonds from other countries cannot be passed off as Canadian stones.

Critical Thinking Questions

1. How can business firms be made accountable for the conditions under which they produce diamonds? Be specific and practical in your suggestions.
2. Read the arguments of critics who say that the "blood diamonds" issue is phony and that there really aren't any "blood diamonds." Who do you think has the better arguments? Explain your reasoning.

employee participation, real quality improvement would never happen. Ishikawa, for example, developed so-called fishbone diagrams, also known as cause-and-effect diagrams or Ishikawa diagrams, which help teams of employees investigate and track down causes of quality problems in their work areas. The diagram in Figure 12.2, for instance, was designed to help an airport manager find out why his facility had so many delayed departures. Focussing on five major categories of possible causes, he then noted several potential causes of the

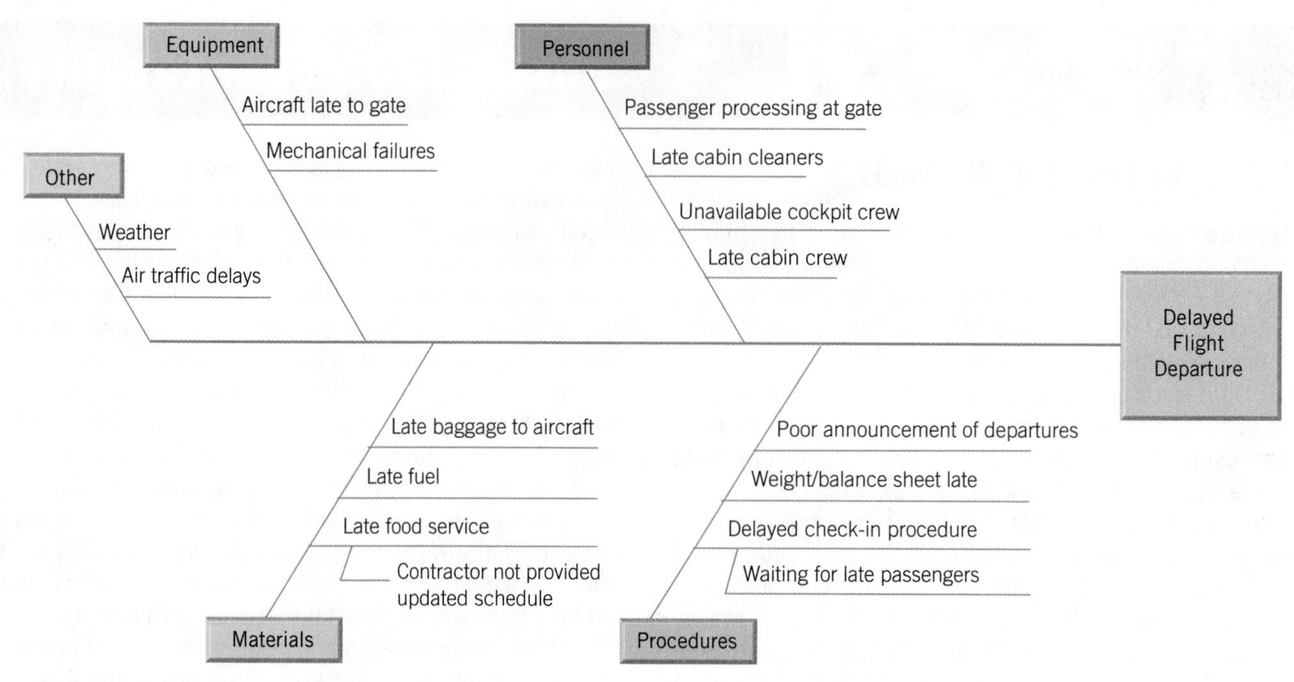

Figure 12.2 Fishbone or cause-and-effect diagram.

problem in each. (It turns out that there weren't enough tow trucks to handle baggage transfers.)[8]

Managing for Quality

total quality management (TQM) All the activities necessary for getting high-quality goods and services into the marketplace.

Total quality management (TQM) (sometimes called *quality assurance*) includes all the activities necessary for getting high-quality goods and services into the marketplace. It must consider all parts of the business, including customers, suppliers, and employees. TQM emphasizes that no defects are tolerable and that employees are responsible for maintaining quality standards. At Toyota's Cambridge, Ontario, plant, for example, workers can push a button or pull a rope to stop the production line when something is not up to standard.[9]

The strategic approach to TQM begins with leadership and the desire for TQM. This approach involves getting people's attention, getting them to think in an entirely new way about what they do, and then getting them to improve both processes and products.[10]

Customer focus is the starting point. Companies must develop methods for determining what customers want and then direct all their resources toward fulfillment of those needs to gain greater customer satisfaction. Total participation is mandatory. Unless all employees are working toward improved quality, the firm is wasting potential contributions from its human resources and is missing a chance to become a stronger competitor in the marketplace. TQM in today's competitive markets demands unending and continuous improvement of products; after-sales services; and all of the company's internal processes, such as accounting, delivery, billing, and information flow. To bring the interests of all these stakeholders together, TQM involves planning, organizing, directing, and controlling.

Successful use of TQM requires a high level of commitment from all members of the organization. Consider the case of Standard Aero in Winnipeg, which is in the business of aircraft overhaul. When the company instituted TQM, the process began with the formation of a "change council" consisting of the CEO and five senior managers. This council ensured that the TQM initiative received the money, equipment, and support it needed for success.

Next, a nine-person task force was formed that consisted of employees who had done the full range of jobs on one of Standard's major overhaul contracts. Its first job was to find out what the customer wanted. It did this by designing a questionnaire and visiting customer plants around the world to gather information. The task force also worked within Standard Aero to determine exactly how the company did its aircraft overhaul work. After weeks of analysis, the task force was able to significantly reduce the time required for overhaul work. For example, the number of times a certain gearbox was handled as it moved through the repair process was reduced by 84 percent.[11]

Another example of the importance of managing for quality is presented in the boxed insert entitled "A Cut Above."

Planning for Quality

Planning for quality should begin before products are designed or redesigned. Managers need to set goals for both quality levels and quality reliability in the beginning. **Performance quality** refers to the features of a product and how well it performs. For example, Maytag gets a price premium because its

performance quality The features of a product and how well it performs.

Entrepreneurship and New Ventures

A Cut Above

Baljit Gill likes a challenge, and she certainly demonstrated this when she took over Kitwanga Mills Ltd. in 2004, just as the company was on the verge of bankruptcy. However, through her visionary leadership and determination she has turned this business around to become one of the largest exporters of British Columbia wood products. Part of Gill's restructuring plan involved adding a timber line, which has proved to be profitable for the company, and making efforts to diversify markets. The company currently supplies premium grade lumber to the United States, China, Korea, Taiwan, and Panama. Gill knew that to succeed, it was necessary to expand beyond the traditional U.S. market, most often relied upon by the Canadian lumber industry. Gill says, "I made sure we were exploring opportunities outside of North America and that has proven to be the right step for my business." Kitwanga's ability to expand globally has been partly due to its positioning as a quality provider of lumber products.

According to Mark Starlund, mill manager at Kitwanga, "Our facility has a global reputation for quality operation." The company understands that quality is an internationally understood concept, and they decided to use this as their method of competitive positioning. To ensure provision of a high-quality product, the company made a deliberate decision to focus on two species: hemlock and cedar. In addition, the mill is located adjacent to the harvest area; therefore, milling can occur quickly in order to meet customer demands. Kitwanga has also established an exceptional grading system, and it is this high regard for quality control that has enabled the company to consistently meet customer expectations. Gill plans to gain formal recognition of her company's quality standards by pursuing ISO 14001 certification in the near future. Other plans include exploring bio-energy opportunities with waste residual product. Finally, the company also meets or exceeds provincial and federal environmental standards, while at the same time consulting with local First Nations communities to ensure that their values are met.

Gill has been pleased with the results of her diversification and positioning strategies, and she is also very proud of the fact that she has been able to achieve this while positively influencing the community. Her company is the largest employer in northwest British Columbia, and 70 percent of its workforce are First Nations people. Kitwanga is an important force in this B.C. community, and Gill was recently acknowledged for her entrepreneurial efforts as one of six Canadian women to receive an award from the Royal Bank of Canada. Her company won the HKMB Hub International Impact award, which recognizes a business that has made a significant impact on the local economy through jobs and/or citizen development. Since assuming her role as chairperson of Kitwanga in 2004, Gill has instituted corporate social responsibility efforts that include education scholarships for local youth, business development with local small manufacturers, and sponsorship of special community events. Gill is also a strong advocate of entrepreneurship and she "hopes to share [her] experiences with young entrepreneurs and motivate them to be proactive and build career paths."

Critical Thinking Question

1. Using the fishbone diagram as a guide, analyze the various ways quality at Kitwanga can be managed.

washers and dryers offer a high level of performance quality. Customers perceive Maytag as having more advanced features and being more durable than other brands. (Everyone knows that the Maytag repair technician is a lonely and idle person.)

quality reliability The consistency or repeatability of performance.

Performance quality may or may not be related to quality reliability in a product. **Quality reliability** refers to the consistency or repeatability of performance. Toyota's small cars may not equal the overall quality level or have the luxury features of Rolls Royce; consequently, Toyota's prices are much lower. But Toyotas have high-quality reliability. The firm has a reputation for producing very few "lemons."

Organizing for Quality

Perhaps most important to the quality concept is the belief that producing quality goods and services requires an effort from all parts of the organization. The old idea of a separate "quality control" department is no longer enough. Everyone—from the chairperson of the board to the part-time clerk, purchasers, engineers, janitors, marketers, machinists, and other personnel—must work to ensure quality. In Germany's Messerschmitt-Boelkow-Blohm aerospace company, for example, all employees are responsible for inspecting their own work. The overall goal is to reduce eventual problems to a minimum by making the product correctly from the beginning. The same principle extends to teamwork practice at Heinz Co., where teams of workers are assigned to inspect virtually every activity in the company. Heinz has realized substantial cost savings by eliminating waste and rework.

At Motorola, the concept of teamwork as a key to organizational quality has resulted in an international event called the Total Customer Satisfaction Team Competition. Teams are composed of Motorola employees and also include customers and outside suppliers. Teams are judged on their success not only in promoting productivity but also in sharing innovative ideas with people both inside and outside the company.

Although everyone in a company contributes to product quality, responsibility for specific aspects of total quality management is often assigned to specific departments and jobs. In fact, many companies have quality assurance, or quality control, departments staffed by quality experts. These people may be called in to help solve quality-related problems in any of the firm's other departments. They keep other departments informed of the latest developments in equipment and methods for maintaining quality. In addition, they monitor all quality control activities to identify areas for improvement.

Leading for Quality

Too often, firms fail to take the initiative to make quality happen. Leading for quality means that managers must inspire and motivate employees throughout the company to achieve quality goals. They need to help employees see how they affect quality and how quality affects their jobs and their company. Leaders must continually find ways to foster a quality orientation by training employees, encouraging their involvement, and tying wages to quality of work. If managers succeed, employees will ultimately accept **quality ownership**—the idea that quality belongs to each person who creates or destroys it while performing a job.

quality ownership The idea that quality belongs to each person who creates or destroys it while performing a job.

Controlling for Quality

By monitoring its products and services, a company can detect mistakes and make corrections. To do so, however, managers must first establish specific quality standards and measurements. Consider the following control system for a bank's teller services: Observant supervisors periodically evaluate trans-

In the auto industry, a key measure of quality is the number of recalls. By this standard, there's room for improvement in total quality management at General Motors, which recalled 7.5 million vehicles in the first quarter of 2004 alone. GM says that it is being proactive and dealing with potential problems to build consumer confidence.

actions against a checklist. Specific aspects of each teller's work—appearance, courtesy, efficiency, and so on—are recorded. The results, reviewed with employees, either confirm proper performance or indicate changes that are needed to bring performance up to standards.

In some firms, when safety and quality procedures are not regularly monitored, potential health issues can result. For example, Hallmark/Westland, a meat supplier to school lunch programs, was shut down in 2008 after an undercover Humane Society worker reported unacceptable practices in the company's cattle pens.[12]

Tools for Total Quality Management

In managing for quality, many leading companies rely on assistance from proven tools. Often, ideas for improving both the product and the production process come from **competitive product analysis**. For example, Toshiba will take apart a Xerox photocopier and test each component. Test results help Toshiba's managers decide which Toshiba product features are satisfactory (in comparison to the competition), which product features need to be upgraded, or whether Toshiba's production processes need improvement.

competitive product analysis Process by which a company analyzes a competitor's products to identify desirable improvements.

There are many specific tools that can be used to achieve TQM. Here, we briefly describe the following: value-added analysis, statistical process control, quality/cost studies, quality improvement teams, benchmarking, getting closer to the customer, ISO 9000 and ISO 14000, re-engineering, and adding value through supply chains.

Value-Added Analysis

Value-added analysis refers to the evaluation of all work activities, material flows, and paperwork to determine the value that they add for customers. It often reveals wasteful or unnecessary activities that can be eliminated without jeopardizing customer service. For example, when Hewlett-Packard reduced

value-added analysis The evaluation of all work activities, material flows, and paperwork to determine the value that they add for customers.

its customer contracts from 20 pages to as few as two, computer sales rose by more than 18 percent.

Statistical Process Control

Although every company would like complete uniformity in its outputs, all firms experience unit-to-unit variations in their products. Companies can gain better control, however, by understanding the sources of variation. **Statistical process control (SPC)** methods—especially process variation studies and control charts—allow managers to analyze variations in production data.

Process Variation

Variations in a firm's products may arise from the inputs in its production process. As people, materials, work methods, and equipment change, so do production outputs. While some amount of **process variation** is acceptable, too much can result in poor quality and excessive operating costs. Consider the box-filling operation for Honey Nuggets cereal. Each automated machine fills two 400-gram boxes per second. Even under proper conditions, slight variations in cereal weight from box to box are normal. Equipment and tools wear out, the cereal may be overly moist, and machinists make occasional adjustments. But how much variation is occurring? How much is acceptable?

statistical process control (SPC) Statistical analysis techniques that allow managers to analyze variations in production data and to detect when adjustments are needed to create products with high-quality reliability.

process variation Any change in employees, materials, work methods, or equipment that affects output quality.

Information about variation in a process can be obtained from a *process capability study*. Boxes are taken from the filling machines and weighed. The results are plotted, as in Figure 12.3, and compared with the upper and lower specification limits (quality limits) for weight. These limits define good and bad quality for box filling. Boxes with more than 410 grams are a wasteful "giveaway." Underfilling has a cost because it is unlawful.

The chart in Figure 12.3 reveals that Machine A's output is acceptable because none of its boxes violate the quality limits. Machine A, then, is fully capable of meeting the company's quality standards. Machines B and C, however, have problems. In their present condition, they are not "capable" because they cannot reliably meet Honey Nuggets' quality standards. The company must take special—and costly—actions to sort the good from the bad boxes before releasing the cereal for shipment. Unless Machines B and C are renovated, substandard production quality will plague Honey Nuggets.

Control Charts

Knowing that a process is capable of meeting quality standards is not enough. Managers must still monitor the process to prevent its drifting astray during production. To detect the beginning of bad conditions, managers can check production periodically and plot the results on a **control chart**. For example, several times a day a machine operator at Honey Nuggets might weigh several boxes of cereal together to ascertain the average weight.

control chart A statistical process control method in which results of test sampling of a product are plotted on a diagram that reveals when the process is beginning to depart from normal operating conditions.

Figure 12.4 shows the control chart for Machine A, in which the first five points are randomly scattered around the centre line, indicating that the machine was operating well. However, the points for samples 5 through 8 are all above the centre line, indicating that something was causing the boxes to overfill. The last point falls outside the upper *control limit*, confirming that the process is out of control.

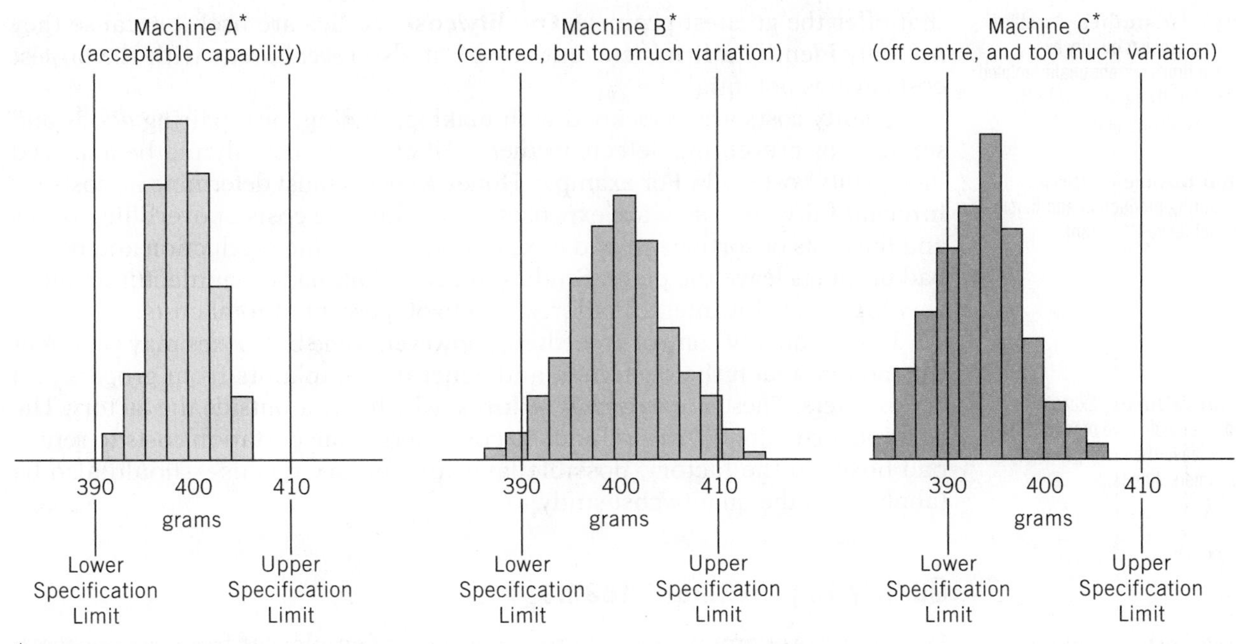

Figure 12.3 Process variation in box filling for Honey Nuggets cereal.

At this point, the machine must be shut down so that a manager and/or the operator can investigate what is causing the problem—equipment, people, materials, or work methods. Control is completed by correcting the problem and restoring the process to normal.

Quality/Cost Studies

Statistical process controls help keep operations up to existing capabilities, but in today's competitive environment, firms must consistently raise quality capabilities. However, any improvement in products or production processes means additional costs, whether for new facilities, equipment, training, or other changes. Managers thus face the challenge of identifying those improvements

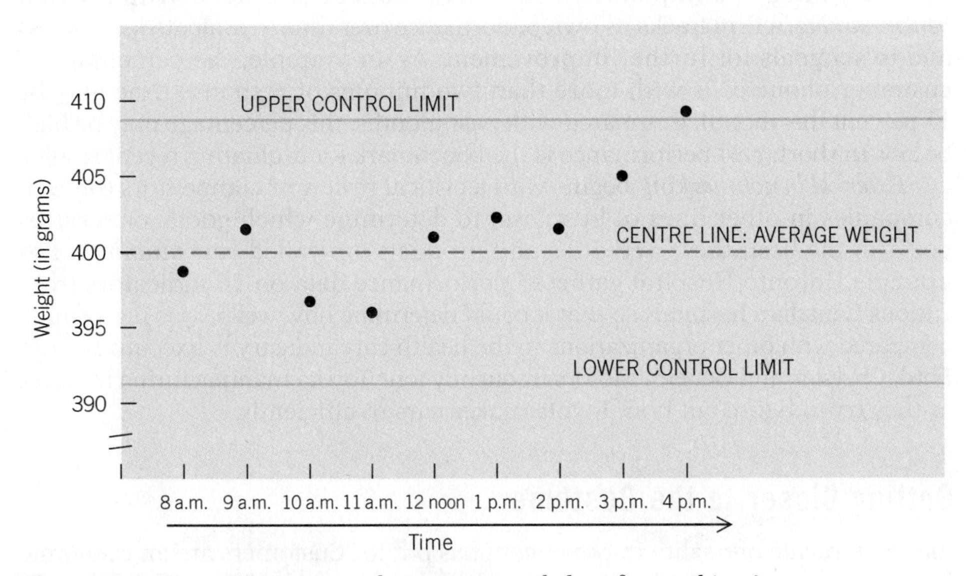

Figure 12.4 Honey Nuggets cereal process control chart for machine A.

quality/cost studies A method of improving product quality by assessing a firm's current quality-related costs and identifying areas with the greatest cost-saving potential.

internal failures Expenses incurred during production and before bad product leaves the plant.

external failures Expenses incurred when defective products are allowed to leave the factory and get into consumers' hands.

that offer the greatest promise. **Quality/cost studies** are useful because they not only identify a firm's current costs but also reveal areas with the largest cost-savings potential.[13]

Quality costs are associated with making, finding, or repairing goods and services, or preventing defects in them. All of these costs should be analyzed in a quality/cost study. For example, Honey Nuggets must determine its costs for **internal failures**. These are expenses—including the costs of overfilling boxes and the costs of sorting out bad boxes—incurred during production and before bad products leave the plant. Studies indicate that many manufacturers incur very high costs for internal failures—up to 50 percent of total costs.

Despite quality control procedures, however, some bad boxes may get out of the factory, reach the customer, and generate complaints from grocers and cereal eaters. These are **external failures,** which occur outside the factory. The costs of correcting them—refunds to customers, transportation costs to return bad boxes to the factory, possible lawsuits, factory recalls—should also be tabulated in the quality/cost study.

Quality Improvement Teams

quality improvement (QI) teams TQM tool in which groups of employees work together to improve quality.

Quality improvement (QI) teams are groups of employees from various work areas who meet regularly to define, analyze, and solve common production problems. Their goal is to improve both their own work methods and the products they make.[14] Many QI teams organize their own work, select leaders, and address problems in the workplace. Motorola sponsors company-wide team competitions to emphasize the value of the team approach, to recognize outstanding team performance, and to reaffirm the team's role in the company's continuous-improvement culture. Teams get higher marks for dealing with projects closely tied to Motorola's key initiatives. Over the years, competing teams have increased cellphone production by 50 percent and cut electronic-circuit defects by 85 percent (for a one-year savings of $1.8 million).[15]

Benchmarking

benchmarking Comparing the quality of the firm's output with the quality of the output of the industry's leaders.

A powerful TQM tool that has been effective for some firms is called **benchmarking**. To improve its own products or its business procedures, a company compares its current performance against its own past performance, or one company finds and implements the best practices of others. With *internal benchmarking*, a firm tracks its own performance over time to evaluate its progress and to set goals for further improvement. As an example, the percentage of customer phone calls with more than two minutes of response time may be 15 percent this month. Compared with past months, this percentage may be high or low. In short, past performance is the benchmark for evaluating recent results.

External benchmarking begins with a critical review of competitors (or even companies in other lines of business) to determine which goods or services perform the best; these activities and products are called *best practices*. For example, Toronto Hospital gathered performance data on 26 indicators from various Canadian hospitals so that it could determine how well it was performing compared with other organizations in the health-care industry.[16] Executives from Ford, Chrysler, and General Motors frequently tour Toyota manufacturing facilities as they try to figure out how Toyota makes cars so efficiently.

Getting Closer to the Customer

As one advocate of quality improvement has put it, "Customers are an economic asset. They're not on the balance sheet, but they should be." One of the themes of this chapter has been that struggling companies have often lost sight of customers as the driving force for all business activity. Perhaps they waste resources designing products that customers do not want. Sometimes they ignore customer reactions to existing products or fail to keep up with changing consumer tastes. By contrast, the most successful businesses keep close to their customers and know what they want in the products they consume.

At Hewlett-Packard, testing machines use tiny probes to ensure that the electronic characteristics of every semiconductor are correct. Such systems are designed to check primarily for so-called "class defects"—problems that can affect a whole range of products on the assembly line. One bad wafer at the end of the line can represent a waste of $10 000 in costs, and its commercial value is zero.

Some years ago at Greyhound Lines of Canada, the marketing and operations vice-president wanted to drive home the point to managers that clean restrooms were important to customers. He warned regional managers that he would visit bus depots on one hour's notice to see if the restrooms were clean enough to eat dinner in. Within weeks, photos of regional managers having dinner in spotless restrooms began pouring in to the vice-president's office.[17]

Cargill Corn Milling North America (CCM) was granted the 2008 Malcolm Baldridge National Quality Award by its customers. CCM maintained an error-free delivery rate of about 99 percent from their fiscal years 2005–08. Furthermore, the company's team-based culture and matrix organization foster an environment of co-operation, skill sharing, and leveraging of diverse ideas. Employees are encouraged to take ownership of their ideas and apply them to design and innovation changes. Close monitoring of these initiatives has led to establishing best practices that can be applied throughout Cargill's other business units.[18]

ISO 9000:2000 and ISO 14000

Identify three trends in productivity and quality management, including *supply chain management*. **4**

DuPont Co. had a problem: A moulding press used to make plastic connectors for computers had a 30 percent defect rate. Efforts to solve the problem went nowhere until, as part of a plant-wide quality program, press operators were asked to submit detailed written reports describing how they did their jobs. After comparing notes, operators realized that they were incorrectly measuring the temperature of the moulding press; as a result, temperature adjustments were often wrong. With the mystery solved, the defect rate dropped to 8 percent.

The quality program that led to this solution is called **ISO 9000**—a certification program attesting to the fact that a factory, a laboratory, or an office has met the rigorous quality management requirements set by the International Organization for Standardization. ISO 9000 (pronounced *ICE-o nine thousand*) originated in Europe to standardize materials received from suppliers in such high-technology industries as electronics, chemicals, and aviation. Today, more than 140 countries have adopted ISO 9000 as a national standard. More than 400 000 certificates have been issued in 160 countries.[19]

ISO 9000 A certification program attesting to the fact that a factory, a laboratory, or an office has met the rigorous quality management requirements set by the International Organization for Standardization.

The name of the latest version, ISO 9000:2000, indicates that it was revised in 2000. Revised standards allow firms to show that they follow documented procedures for testing products, training workers, keeping records, and fixing defects. To become certified, companies must document the procedures followed by workers during every stage of production. The purpose is to ensure that a manufacturer's product is exactly the same today as it was yesterday and as it will be tomorrow. Ideally, standardized processes would ensure that goods are produced at the same level of quality even if all employees were replaced by a new set of workers.

The **ISO 14000** program certifies improvements in *environmental* performance. Extending the ISO approach into the arena of environmental protection and hazardous waste management, ISO 14000 requires a firm to develop an *environmental management system (EMS)*—a plan documenting

ISO 14000 Certification program attesting to the fact that a factory, laboratory, or office has improved environmental performance.

how the company has acted to improve its performance in using resources (such as raw materials) and in managing pollution. A company must not only identify hazardous wastes that it expects to create; it must also stipulate plans for treatment and disposal. ISO 14000 covers practices in environmental labelling—the use of such terms as *energy efficient* and *recyclable*—and assesses the total environmental impact of the firm's products, not just from manufacturing, but also from use and disposal.

Process Re-engineering

Every business consists of *processes*—activities that it performs regularly and routinely in conducting business. Examples abound: receiving and storing materials from suppliers, billing patients for medical treatment, filing insurance claims for auto accidents, inspecting property for termite infestation, opening chequing accounts for new customers, and filling customer orders from internet sales. Any business process can add value and customer satisfaction by performing processes well. By the same token, any business can disappoint customers and irritate business partners by managing them poorly.

business process re-engineering Redesigning of business processes to improve performance, quality, and productivity.

Business process re-engineering focuses on improving both the productivity and quality of business processes—rethinking each step of an organization's operations by starting from scratch. *Re-engineering* is the fundamental rethinking and radical redesign of business processes to achieve dramatic improvements in measures of performance, such as cost, quality, service, and speed.[20] The example given above of Cargill's employee involvement is an example of process re-engineering. CCM measured workforce engagement and satisfaction through a nationally administered employee survey. CCM learned from the results and was able to increase its overall score from 37 percent to 65 percent.

The Re-engineering Process

Figure 12.5 shows the six steps involved in the re-engineering process. It starts with a statement of the benefits envisioned for customers and the company and then flows logically through the next five steps:

1. Identify the business activity that will be changed.
2. Evaluate information and human resources to see if they can meet the requirements for change.
3. Diagnose the current process to identify its strengths and weaknesses.
4. Create the new process design.
5. Implement the new design.

As you can see, re-engineering is a broad undertaking that requires know-how in technical matters, depends on leadership and management skills, and calls upon knowledge about customer needs and how well they are being met by the company and its competition. The bottom line in every re-engineering process is adopting a company-wide, customer-first philosophy. Redesign is guided by a desire to improve operations so that goods and services are produced at the lowest possible cost and at the highest value for the customer.

Adding Value Through Supply Chains

supply chain The flow of information, materials, and services that starts with raw-materials suppliers and continues through other stages in the operations process until the product reaches the end customer.

Managers sometimes forget that a company belongs to a network of firms that must coordinate their activities. The term *supply chain* refers to the group of companies and stream of activities that work together to create a product. A **supply chain** for any product is the flow of information, materials, and services

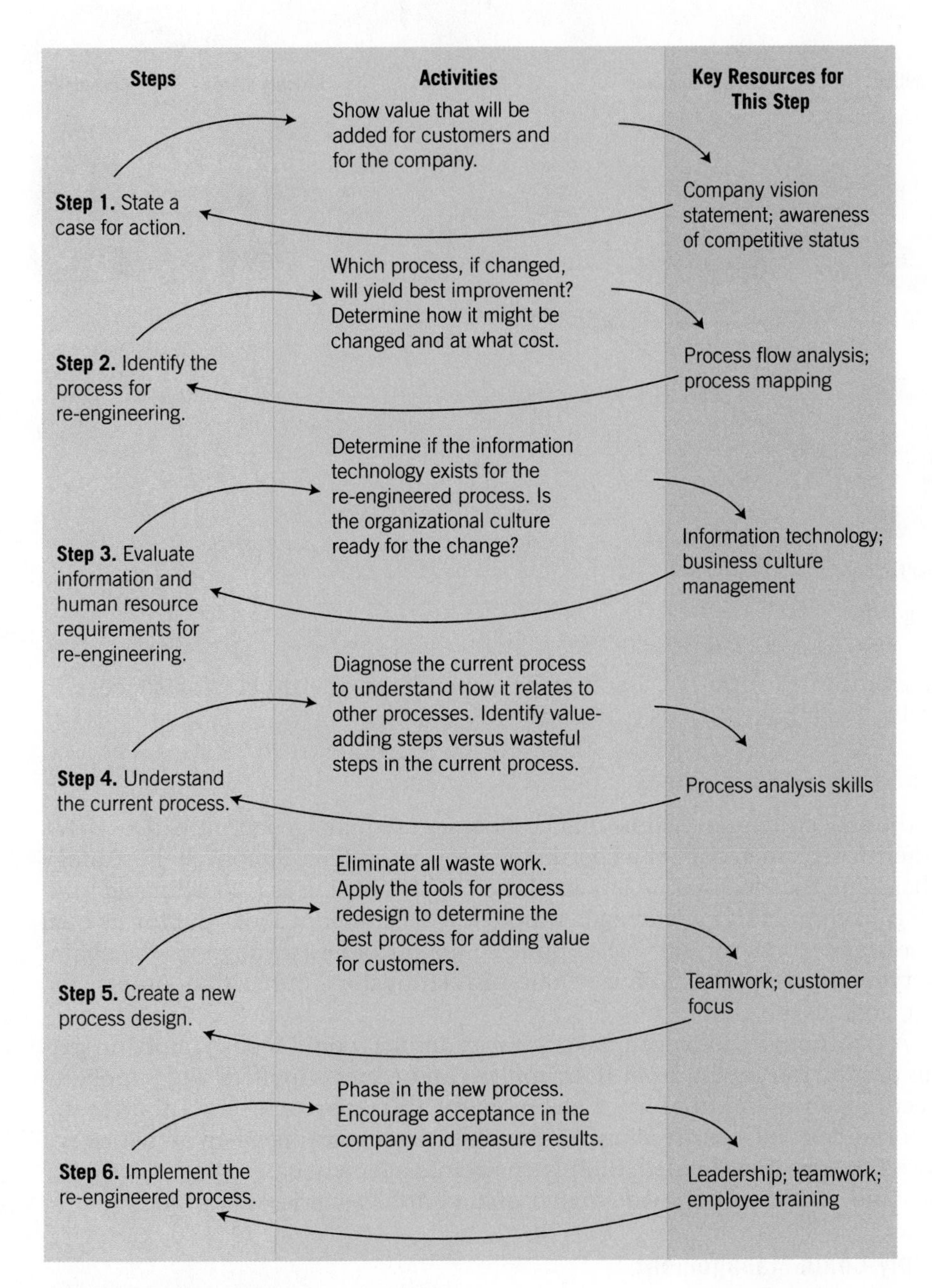

Steps
Activities
Key Resources for This Step
Show value that will be added for customers and for the company.
Company vision statement; awareness of competitive status
Step 1. State a case for action.
Which process, if changed, will yield best improvement? Determine how it might be changed and at what cost.
Process flow analysis; process mapping
Step 2. Identify the process for re-engineering.
Determine if the information technology exists for the re-engineered process. Is the organizational culture ready for the change?
Information technology; business culture management
Step 3. Evaluate information and human resource requirements for re-engineering.
Diagnose the current process to understand how it relates to other processes. Identify value-adding steps versus wasteful steps in the current process.
Process analysis skills
Step 4. Understand the current process.
Eliminate all waste work. Apply the tools for process redesign to determine the best process for adding value for customers.
Teamwork; customer focus
Step 5. Create a new process design.
Phase in the new process. Encourage acceptance in the company and measure results.
Leadership; teamwork; employee training
Step 6. Implement the re-engineered process.

Figure 12.5 Re-engineering process.

that starts with raw-materials suppliers and continues through other stages in the operations process until the product reaches the end customer.[21]

Seagate Technology, a maker of computer hard drives, used to build everything itself—disks, motors for spinning disks, and tracking mechanisms for reading and writing on disks. But it needed factories in Malaysia, Ireland, and the United States, each with its own supplies of inventory. Seagate wasn't flexible enough to respond to changes required by customers until it teamed up with a consulting firm called DesignShop and figured out how to reorganize itself. Now, company-wide operations are run by a computer-based planning system, the supplier list has been slashed, and even important components are being outsourced.

Figure 12.6 shows the supply chain activities involved in supplying baked goods to consumers. Each stage adds value for the final customer. Although a typical beginning stage is product design, our bakery example begins with raw materials (grain harvested from the farm). It also includes additional storage and transportation activities, factory operations for baking and wrapping, and

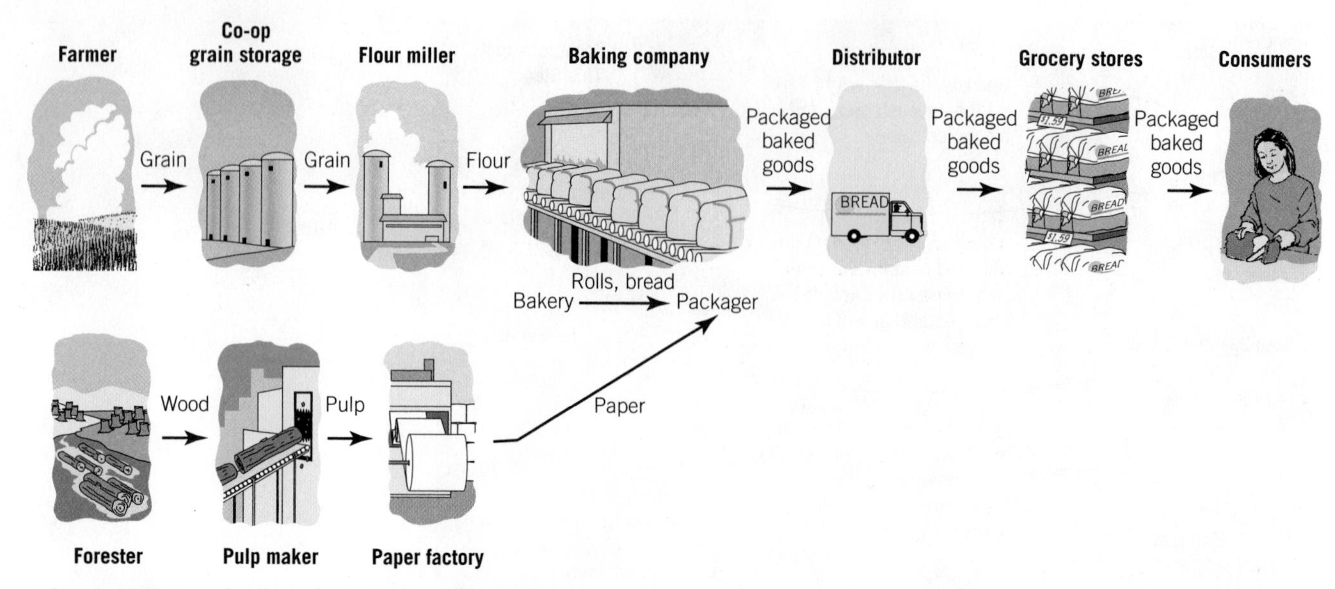

Figure 12.6 Supply chain for baked goods.

distribution to retailers. Each stage depends on the others for success in getting fresh-baked goods to consumers.

The Supply Chain Strategy

5 Explain how a *supply chain strategy* differs from traditional strategies for coordinating operations among firms.

Traditional strategies assume that companies are managed as individual firms rather than as members of a coordinated supply system. Supply chain strategy is based on the idea that members of the chain, working as a coordinated unit, will gain competitive advantage. Although each company looks out for its own interests, it works closely with suppliers and customers throughout the chain. Everyone focuses on the entire chain of relationships rather than on just the next stage in the chain.[22]

A traditionally managed bakery, for example, would focus simply on getting production inputs from flour millers and paper suppliers and supplying baked goods to distributors. Unfortunately, this approach limits the chain's performance and doesn't allow for possible improvements when activities are more carefully coordinated. Supply chain management can improve performance and, as a result, provide higher quality at lower prices.

Supply Chain Management

supply chain management (SCM) Principle of looking at the chain as a whole to improve the overall flow through the system.

Supply chain management (SCM) looks at the chain as a whole to improve the overall flow through a system composed of companies working together. Because customers ultimately get better value, SCM gains competitive advantage for each supply chain member.[23] Dell Computer's supply chain, for example, improves performance by allowing people to share information. Dell shares long-term production plans and up-to-the-minute sales data with suppliers via the internet. The process starts when customer orders are automatically translated into updated production schedules on the factory floor. These schedules are used not only by operations managers at Dell but also by such parts suppliers as Sony, which adjust their own production and shipping activities to better meet Dell's production needs. In turn, parts suppliers' updated schedules are transmitted to their materials suppliers, and so on. As Dell's requirements change, suppliers synchronize their schedules to produce the right materials and parts efficiently. As a result, Dell's prices are low and turnaround time for shipping PCs to customers is reduced to a matter of hours instead of days.

Fashion house Louis Vuitton, which produces upscale products like its Reade tote bag, used to focus mainly on product image and product design.

The Greening of Business

Green Changes in Steel Making

To be competitive, companies need to embrace change, and the steel industry is no exception. One area of change facing steel companies is the need to improve their environmental record. The iron and steel industry has been one of the most polluting ones in the world. The industry has a reputation for air, water, and noise pollution; for its negative effect on flora and fauna; and for its disturbing of the ecological balance. In order to compete in today's international business environment, the steel industry must demonstrate its environmental responsibility to legislators, employees, investors, and customers.

Knowing that change needs to happen is one thing, but successfully implementing change is quite another. One overriding consideration in any contemplated change is cost. With the worldwide economic problems that developed in 2008, it's no wonder companies are now reluctant to spend money to change their business practices. But companies need to understand that having an effective environment management system in place may actually improve operational efficiency and reduce costs.

There are some promising developments. Companies in Europe, Australia, and North America have developed processes that allow them to skip a high-polluting step in the manufacturing of iron, and they are actively wooing steel-makers in Asia and Africa that are willing to gamble on the innovation. The Pohang Steel and Iron Corporation (POSCO) has taken it one step further, spending more than $2 billion on research to create a new environmentally friendly steel-making process. The new manufacturing process eliminates the need for separate material processing and uses cheaper inputs, thus resulting in a more cost-effective operation. Chung Joon-yang, POSCO's president, said, "We could go two ways. One was to look for a totally new business. The second one was to go for new technology. We decided to look at alternative processes."

Over the years, cost pressures have grown for steelmakers as they have been forced to accept huge price increases for coal and iron inputs. They need to keep quality high and costs down (in order to be competitive), and they need to control environmental pollutants (in order to meet strict government standards designed to protect the environment).

Regardless of the type of business and its need to retain customers and market share, there are unbelievable pressures to reduce hazards and become environmentally responsible.

Improving energy efficiency is a basic yet significant way of addressing both energy security concerns and environmental concerns. While upgrades can be costly, particularly for old steel plants, promoters for new projects are working to initiate sweeping changes, from the initial design stage to the final stage of site selection and plant equipment. All of these drivers together are what is needed to foster green improvements.

Critical Thinking Questions

1. In addition to changing processing technologies, what are some other ways that steel manufacturers can help protect the environment?
2. Research the different ways to measure energy efficiency performance (MEEP) and discuss how each would apply to the steel industry.
3. From the information you have found on MEEP, what do you think are some possible next steps for improvement?

When an item became a hot seller, retailers often ran out of product because the company's production system and supply chain was not responsive to increased consumer demand. Vuitton has revamped its systems in order to ensure that retailers always have a supply of in-demand Vuitton products on their shelves. Other luxury-goods manufacturers, like Armani, Gucci, and Versace, are doing the same thing.[24]

Because the smooth flow of accurate information along the chain reduces unwanted inventories, avoids delays, and cuts supply times, materials move faster to business customers and individual consumers. For both, the efficiency of SCM means faster deliveries and lower costs than customers could get if each member acted only according to its own operations requirements.

Re-engineering Supply Chains for Better Results

By lowering costs, speeding up service, or coordinating flows of information and materials, process improvements and re-engineering often improve supply chains. Process improvements and re-engineering often are applied in supply

Before too long, you will be able to pick up an item from a Wal-Mart shelf and scan it automatically onto your debit card, skipping the checkout line altogether. The same technology—called radio frequency identification (RFID)—will signal the Wal-Mart storeroom to restock the item you bought.

chains to lower costs, speed up services, and coordinate flows of information and materials. Because the smoother flow of accurate information along the chain reduces unwanted inventories and transportation, avoids delays, and cuts supply times, materials move faster to business customers and industrial consumers. Faster deliveries result in lower costs than customers could get if each member acted only according to its own operations requirements.

Heightened concerns about supply chain risks and costs are the result of soaring energy prices and volatile financial markets, according to a report by McKinsey & Company. Businesses are responding by managing complex products and services closer to home. The study found that 56 percent of executives at large global companies have employed centralized supply chain management over the past five years, "not only to take advantage of synergies, but also to strengthen their operational expertise."[25]

Productivity and Quality as Competitive Tools

6 Discuss four strategies that companies use to improve productivity and quality.

A company's ability to compete by improving productivity and quality depends on participation by all parts of the firm. Total firm involvement stems from having company-wide strategies that we consider in this section: the company's willingness to invest in innovation, its long-run perspective on its goals, its concern for the quality of work life, and its improvement of service operations.

Invest in Innovation and Technology

Many firms that have continued to invest in innovative technology have enjoyed rising productivity and rising incomes. For example, while Steinway & Sons' piano factory is just as concerned as ever about maintaining the highest quality in its products, it's using newer technology to help the woodworkers do their jobs more efficiently and precisely. "It still takes us a year to craft one of these things," says Steinway president Bruce Stevens, "but technology is assisting us in making more precise parts that our people can assemble. It's helping us create a better instrument."[26]

Adopt a Long-Run Perspective

Instead of emphasizing short-run results, many quality-oriented firms are committed to a long-run perspective for **continuous improvement**—the ongoing commitment to improving products and processes, step by step, in pursuit of ever-increasing customer satisfaction. Motorola is a good example. In 1996, its Six Sigma program set a target of 3.4 defects per million parts. By 2003, the company's production-monitoring software—Manufacturing Intellitrak—had helped to reduce errors in some applications to two defects per *billion* parts.[27]

continuous improvement The ongoing commitment to improving products and processes, step by step, in pursuit of ever-increasing customer satisfaction.

The Six Sigma program, which is used by many other companies besides Motorola, continuously captures, measures, and eliminates defects in every company-wide process, from financial transactions and accounting practices, to R&D (research and development) and production processes, to marketing and human resources activities. The earliest adopters of Six Sigma in Canada have been full-service brokerages such as Royal LePage Commercial, which have international clients.[28] A consulting firm like Global Training Systems—which prepares corporate professionals for global business success and trains employees in other companies to use Six Sigma programs—also uses the program in its own activities.[29]

Emphasize Quality of Work Life

The products and services of businesses represent such a large part of total national output that the well-being and participation of their workers is central to improving national productivity. How can firms make their employees' jobs more challenging and interesting? Many companies are enhancing workers' physical and mental health through recreational facilities, counselling services, and other programs. In addition, more and more firms have started programs to empower and train employees.

Employee Empowerment

Many firms are replacing the work environments of yesterday, based on the principle of management-directed mass production, with worker-oriented environments that foster loyalty, teamwork, and commitment. Trident Precision Manufacturing has a program for full employee involvement. Over 95 percent of employee recommendations for process improvements have been accepted since the program started. As a result, employee turnover has fallen from 41 percent to less than 5 percent. Sales per employee have more than doubled.

As we saw in Chapter 10, firms using this approach have found success in the concept of *employee empowerment*—the principle that all employees are valuable contributors to a business and should be entrusted with certain decisions regarding their work. The Hampton Inns motel chain, for example, initiated a program of refunds to customers who were dissatisfied with their stays for any reason. Managers were pleased, and the refund policy created far more additional business than it cost. A surprise bonus was the increased morale when employees—everyone from front-desk personnel to cleaning staff—were empowered to grant refunds. With greater participation and job satisfaction, employee turnover was reduced to less than one-half its previous level. Such confidence in employee involvement contrasts sharply with the traditional belief that managers are the primary source of decision making and problem solving.

Employee Training

Employee involvement is effective when it is implemented with preparation and intelligence. *Training* is a key method of preparing employees for productivity-improvement programs. In fact, a recent American Management

Association survey found a direct relationship between training and greater productivity and profitability. Firms that increased training activities were 66 percent more likely to report improved productivity and three times more likely to report increased profits. Moreover, after training, waste diminishes and quality increases. Finally, team training not only teaches employees to work in groups, but it also acquaints them more fully with the company's markets and operations.[30]

Improve the Service Sector

As important as employee attitudes are to goods production, they are even more crucial to service production, since employees often *are* the service. The service sector has grown rapidly, but this growth has often come at a cost of high inefficiency. Many newly created service jobs have not been streamlined. Some companies operate effectively, but many others are very inefficient, dragging down overall productivity. As new companies enter these markets, however, the increased need to compete should eventually force service producers to operate more productively.

Quality begins with listening to customers to determine what services they want. Companies in the temporary-services industry, for example, have long emphasized the needs of clients for clerical and light-industrial employees. More recently, however, temp services have realized the need for highly skilled, specialized temps such as nurses, accountants, and scientists.

In trying to offer more satisfactory services, many providers have discovered five criteria that customers use to judge service quality.[31]

- *Reliability*: Perform the service as promised, both accurately and on time.
- *Responsiveness*: Be willing to help customers promptly.
- *Assurance*: Maintain knowledgeable and courteous employees who will earn the trust and confidence of customers.
- *Empathy*: Provide caring, individualized attention to customers.
- *Tangibles*: Maintain a pleasing appearance of personnel, materials, and facilities.

Test yourself on the material for this chapter at **www.pearsoned.ca/mybusinesslab**.

Summary of Learning Objectives

1. **Describe the connection between *productivity* and *quality*.** *Productivity* is a measure of economic performance; it compares how much is produced with the resources used to produce it. *Quality* is a product's fitness for use. However, an emphasis solely on productivity or solely on quality is not enough. Profitable competition in today's business world demands high levels of both productivity and quality.
2. **Understand the importance of increasing productivity.** It is important that Canadian business firms increase their rate of productivity growth so that they can be competitive in world markets. As Canadian business firms increase productivity, they will be able to produce a greater quantity of goods without using more resources.
3. **Identify the activities involved in *total quality management*, and describe six tools that companies can use to achieve it.** *Total quality management (TQM)* (sometimes called *quality assurance*) includes all the activities necessary for getting high-quality goods and

services into the marketplace. The strategic approach to TQM begins with customer focus. This includes methods for determining what customers want and then directing all the company's resources toward satisfying those wants and needs. Total participation is mandatory, and TQM is more than part-time. It demands continuous improvement of products and services, and improvement in all of the company's internal processes, such as accounting, delivery, billing, and information flows. Six tools that are used to achieve TQM: (1) *Value-added analysis* (the evaluation of all work activities, material flows, and paperwork to determine the value that they add for customers); (2) *Statistical process control* (SPC) (methods by which employees can gather data and analyze variations in production activities to determine when adjustments are needed); (3) *Quality/cost* studies (studies that identify a firm's current costs but also reveal areas with the largest cost-savings potential); (4) *Quality improvement (QI) teams* (groups of employees from various work areas who meet regularly to define, analyze, and solve common production problems); (5) *Benchmarking* (improving business products or procedures by comparing them to either the firm's own past performance or the best practices of others); and (6) *Getting closer to the customer* (know what customers want in the products they consume).

4. **Identify three trends in productivity and quality management, including *supply chain management*.** (1) *ISO 9000* is a certification program attesting to the fact that a factory, a laboratory, or an office has met the rigorous quality management requirements set by the International Organization for Standardization. It allows firms to show that they follow documented procedures for testing products, training workers, keeping records, and fixing product defects. *ISO 14000* certifies improvements in environmental performance. (2) *Business process re-engineering* focuses on improving both the productivity and quality of business processes—rethinking each step of an organization's operations by starting from scratch. *Re-engineering* is the fundamental rethinking and redesign of processes to achieve dramatic improvements in measures of performance. (3) The *supply chain* refers to the group of companies and stream of activities that operate together to create a product. Traditional strategies assume that companies are managed as individual firms rather than as members of a coordinated supply chain. *Supply chain management (SCM)* looks at the chain as a whole to improve the overall flow through a system composed of companies working together. Because customers ultimately get better value, SCM gives chain members a competitive advantage.

5. **Explain how a *supply chain strategy* differs from traditional strategies for coordinating operations among firms.** The supply chain strategy is based on the idea that members of the supply chain can gain competitive advantage by working together as a coordinated system of units. For example, sharing information allows companies to reduce inventories, improve quality, and speed delivery of products to consumers. In contrast, traditional strategies assume that companies are managed as individual firms, with each one acting in its own interest.

6. **Discuss four strategies that companies use to improve productivity and quality.** (1) *Invest in innovation and technology*: Many firms that have continued to invest in innovative technology have enjoyed rising productivity and rising incomes. Increasingly, investments in the internet and information technology are rising, with new applications in every major industry. (2) *Adopt a long-run perspective*: Many quality-oriented firms are committed to long-term efforts at continuous improvement—the ongoing commitment to improving products and processes, step by step, in pursuit of ever-increasing customer satisfaction. (3) *Emphasize quality of work life*: Business products and services represent such a large part of total national output that the well-being and participation of workers is crucial to improving national productivity. (4) *Improve the service sector*: As important as employee attitude is to goods production, it is even more crucial to service production, where employees often are the service. In trying to offer more satisfactory services, many companies have discovered five criteria that customers use to judge service quality: reliability, responsiveness, assurance, empathy, and tangibles.

Key Terms

benchmarking (p. 392)
business process re-engineering (p. 394)
competitive product analysis (p. 389)
continuous improvement (p. 399)
control chart (p. 390)
external failures (p. 392)
internal failures (p. 392)
ISO 14000 (p. 393)
ISO 9000 (p. 393)
labour productivity (p. 381)
performance quality (p. 387)
process variation (p. 390)
productivity (p. 380)
quality (p. 380)
quality improvement (QI) teams (p. 392)
quality ownership (p. 388)
quality reliability (p. 388)
quality/cost studies (p. 392)
statistical process control (SPC) (p. 390)
supply chain (p. 394)
supply chain management (SCM) (p. 396)
total quality management (TQM) (p. 386)
value-added analysis (p. 389)

Questions for Analysis

1. What is the relationship between productivity and quality?
2. High productivity in the service sector has historically been difficult to achieve. Why was this so? What might be changing in this area that will cause service productivity to increase during the next decade?
3. Explain how inputs and outputs relate to each other in the basic equation for measuring labour productivity.
4. What are the costs and benefits for a company that is in the process of deciding to pursue quality and productivity as competitive tools?
5. Explain how the functions of management (planning, organizing, leading, and controlling) relate to one another in the pursuit of quality.
6. How might benchmarking be used to increase productivity in the service sector?
7. Why is employee empowerment essential to the success of quality improvement teams?

Application Exercises

1. Interview a production manager in a local firm and determine which of the tools for total quality management the company is currently using. Also determine why the company has chosen not to use some of the tools.
2. Using a local company as an example, show how you would conduct a quality/cost study. Identify the cost categories and give some examples of the costs in each category. Which categories do you expect to have the highest and lowest costs? Why?
3. Select a company of interest to you and consider the suggestions for competing that are detailed in this chapter. Which of these suggestions apply to this company? What additional suggestions would you make to help this company improve its overall quality and productivity?

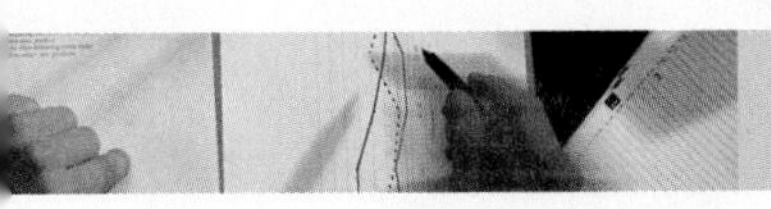

Building Your Business Skills

Making Your Benchmark in the Business World

The Purpose of the Assignment

To encourage students to understand ways in which benchmarking can improve quality and productivity.

The Situation

As the director of maintenance for a regional airline, you are disturbed to learn that the cost of maintaining your 100-plane fleet is skyrocketing. A major factor is repair time; when maintenance or repairs are required, work often proceeds slowly. As a result, additional aircraft must be pressed into service to meet the schedule. To address the problem, you decide to use a powerful total quality management tool called *benchmarking*. You will approach your problem by studying ways in which other companies have successfully managed similar problems. Your goal is to apply the best practices to your own maintenance and repair operation.

Assignment

Step 1

Working with three or four other students, choose your benchmarking target from among the following choices:

- the maintenance and repair operations of a competing airline
- the pit crew operations of an Indianapolis 500 race car team
- the maintenance and repair operations of a nationwide trucking company

Write a memo explaining the reasons for your choice.

Step 2

Write a list of benchmarking questions that will help you learn the best practices of your targeted company. Your goal is to ask questions that will help you improve your own operation. These questions will be asked during on-site visits.

Step 3

As part of a benchmarking project, you will be dealing with your counterparts in other companies. You have a responsibility to prepare for these encounters, and you must remember that what you learn during the exchange process is privileged information. Given these requirements, describe the steps that you would take before your first on-site visit and outline your benchmarking code of ethics.

Questions for Discussion

1. Why is benchmarking an important method for improving quality?
2. Why did you make your benchmarking choice? Explain why the company you selected holds more promise than other companies in helping you solve your internal maintenance problems.
3. What kind of information would help you improve the efficiency of your operations? Are you interested in management information, technical information, or both?
4. In an age of heightened competition, why do you think companies are willing to benchmark with each other?

Exercising Your Ethics: Team Exercise

Calculating the Cost of Conscience

The Situation

Product quality and cost affect every firm's reputation and profitability as well as the satisfaction of customers. This exercise will expose you to some ethical considerations that pertain to certain cost and service decisions that must be made by operations managers.

The Dilemma

As director of quality for a major appliance manufacturer, Ruth was reporting to the executive committee on the results of a recent program for correcting problems with a newly redesigned rotary compressor that the company had recently begun putting in its refrigerators. After receiving several customer complaints, the quality lab and the engineering department had determined that some of the new compressor

units ran more loudly than expected. Some remedial action was needed. One option was simply waiting until customers complained and responding to each complaint if and when it occurred. Ruth, however, had decided that this approach was inconsistent with the company's policy of offering the highest quality in the industry. Deciding that the firm's reputation called for a proactive, "pro-quality" approach, Ruth had initiated a program for contacting all customers who had purchased refrigerators containing the new compressor.

Unfortunately, her "quality-and-customers-first" policy was expensive. Local service representatives had to phone every customer in each area of the country, make appointments for home visits, and replace original compressors with a newer model. But because replacement time was only one-half hour, customers were hardly inconvenienced, and food stayed refrigerated without interruption. Customer response to the replacement program was overwhelmingly favourable.

Near the end of Ruth's report, an executive vice-president was overheard to comment, "Ruth's program has cost this company $400 million in service expenses." Two weeks later, Ruth was fired.

Team Activity

Assemble a group of four students and assign each group member to one of the following roles:

- Ruth
- Ruth's boss
- a customer
- a company investor

Action Steps

1. Before discussing the situation with your group, and from the perspective of your assigned role, do you think that Ruth's firing is consistent with the company's desire for industry leadership in quality? Write down the reasons for your position.
2. Before discussing the situation with your group, and from the perspective of your assigned role, what are the underlying ethical issues, if any, in this situation? Write down the issues.
3. Gather your group together and reveal, in turn, each member's comments on Ruth's firing. Next, reveal the ethical issues listed by each member.
4. Appoint someone to record the main points of agreement and disagreement within the group. How do you explain the results? What accounts for any disagreement?
5. From an ethical standpoint, what does your group conclude is the most appropriate action that should have been taken by the company in this situation?
6. Develop a group response to the following question: What are the respective roles of profits, obligations to customers, and employee considerations for the firm in this situation?

For additional cases and exercise material, go to **www.pearsoned.ca/mybusinesslab**.

Concluding Case 12-1

Poor Productivity: Canada's Biggest Problem?

During the past few years, considerable publicity has been given to the economic revolution that is taking place in China. With wage rates that are far below those in Canada, China has become a formidable competitor because it is such a low-cost producer of goods. The most obvious way to cope with this competitive threat is to reduce the number of hours of labour that are required to make a product and thereby reduce the product's cost. This is another way of saying that Canadian companies must increase labour productivity.

Growth rates in labour productivity (GDP per hour worked) vary across countries, and Canada has not fared well in recent years. In 2008, for example, Statistics Canada reported that Canadian labour productivity did not increase at all. In fact, it fell 0.2 percent in the second quarter of 2008, after declines of 0.6 percent in each of the previous two quarters. A spokesperson at StatsCan stated that "this is the longest series of consecutive quarterly declines since 1990."

The productivity news is not all bad. In some industries—primary metals, wood products, construction, transport equipment, paper, and chemicals—Canadian productivity actually exceeds that of the United States. But in many other industries—including computers and electronics, fabricated metal products, textiles, furniture, retail trade, financial services, and electrical equipment—Canadian productivity lags far behind the United States.

Consider the case of the automobile industry. In 2007, Harbour Consulting ranked GM Canada's Oshawa No. 1 plant at the top of its list of most productive mid-size car plants in North America. The plant, which makes Chevrolet Impalas and Monte Carlos, takes 15.15 hours to produce one car. The second most productive mid-size car plant is GM Canada's Oshawa No. 2 plant, which takes 99 seconds longer. This looked like promising news before the recession of 2008 hit, but many things have changed since then. As well, since car manufacturing is a worldwide phenomenon, Canadian automobile manufacturers must focus on quality and premium positioning on a wide range of features. Manufacturers from emerging markets, by contrast, emphasize basic mobility at the lowest price. The Nano from India's Tata Motors was brought to the Indian market for approximately $2500. In this market, small and micro cars are the largest and fastest-growing market segment, with more than a two-thirds share of total annual vehicle production. How does Canada compete in this market? The question ought to be "How can it not?" Productivity growth has been crushed as Canadian GDP grew only an annualized 0.3 percent in the second quarter and declined 0.8 percent in the first quarter of 2008.

How can labour productivity be increased? A variety of approaches have been suggested, including changes in tax policies that would encourage manufacturers to invest in more productive equipment. Consider the issue of capital cost allowance (CCA). In the United States, manufacturers are allowed to write off equipment much faster than in Canada. This means that U.S. companies pay less tax than Canadian companies. In Canada, Standen's Ltd. is a clear example of the disincentive that tax policy can create. The company, which produces truck springs, was considering buying an automotive springs plant in Wallaceburg, Ontario, but eventually decided it wouldn't make the purchase because the after-tax cost of the investment was too high. If Canadian tax laws allowed greater deductions for investment in machinery, the purchase would have been feasible.

But these suggestions are not without controversy. The Canadian Labour Congress, for example, accepts the importance of productivity and the need to increase it but says there are good and bad ways to do that. A bad way, in their view, is to cut jobs, while a good way is to invest in innovation and employee training. The Information Technology Association of Canada says that U.S. companies in the information and communications technology sector spend more than twice as much per worker as Canadian companies do.

There is also debate about the role that managers play in this problem. Some people argue that Canadian managers are not expending enough energy or do not have enough imagination, and that is why Canadian productivity is lagging. In a brief published by the C.D. Howe Institute, Jack Mintz explains that Canada has made variable progress on its tax competitiveness. Canada has reduced the burden on certain industries (manufacturing), while levying very high tax rates on others (services). In 2008, Canada ranked eleventh highest among 80 countries in terms of its tax burden on business investment.

Of particular importance to Canadian businesses is the productivity comparison with their U.S. counterparts. While productivity comparisons with the much larger U.S. economy may seem unfair, Canada's immense trade with the United States makes such comparisons important. Output per hour in Canadian manufacturing fell about 1.4 percent, compared with growth of 3.2 percent year-over-year in the United States. This poor productivity growth has helped keep labour costs higher for Canadian firms.

To catch up to the United States, Canada will have to exceed the rate of productivity growth in the United States each year by about one percentage point for the next 15 years. One percentage point might not sound like much, but it would require Canadian industry to achieve an annual productivity growth rate of over 3 percent. That rate of productivity growth has been achieved only twice in Canada in the last 25 years.

When making productivity comparisons, we must be careful that we consider certain factors that may give one country an inherent advantage over another. For example, Canadian oil and gas producers are less productive than their U.S. counterparts. This is so partly because Canadian companies are spending large amounts of money developing expensive offshore and non-conventional oil sands deposits, while U.S. oil and gas producers continue to extract energy from wells that use technology that was developed long ago. Another example: Canadian retailers are less productive than U.S. retailers, partly because Wal-Mart has forced its U.S. competitors to cut costs to survive. This cost cutting does raise productivity and benefits for *consumers*, but *employees* often suffer. One study showed that Wal-Mart workers earned 31 percent less than the average wage paid by large retailers, and that less than half of Wal-Mart's workers had health insurance.

A delicate balancing act is required to achieve higher productivity while not reducing worker well-being. Companies need to foster a competitive climate (which drives productivity growth) and at the same time promote social, environmental, and employee welfare.

Questions for Discussion

1. Weak productivity growth means that the speed at which the economy can expand without generating inflation is lower. What are some suggestions to alleviate this problem?
2. Identify several challenges that North American auto manufacturers need to be aware of.
3. What is the impact of a high tax burden on Canada's struggling manufacturing sector?

Concluding Case 12-2

Supply Chain Management at Loblaw

Loblaw Companies Limited is one of Canada's biggest sellers of groceries, and its Real Canadian Superstores—which sell both groceries and general merchandise—are a prominent feature on the Canadian retail scene. Loblaw also operates stores under the Provigo, Fortinos, and No Frills names. Because price-conscious consumers are always looking for the best prices, in 2005 Loblaw embarked on an ambitious plan to improve its supply chain system in order to compete with Wal-Mart (which by 2007 had seven Supercentres with a full range of food and non-food merchandise). But Loblaw's aggressive strategy has run into problems, and it has now decided to close some of its stores, lay off 1000 head office staff, and cut back on the number of non-food items it carries in an attempt to regain its former market position.

In 2005, Loblaw came to the conclusion that it was taking too long for its products to get from its warehouses to its retail grocery stores. To fight off Wal-Mart and to better serve customers, Loblaw embarked on a $62-million restructuring project, which involved improving its supply chain network; reorganizing grocery merchandising, procurement, and operations groups; updating its information technology systems; consolidating work formerly done in regional offices into its new Ontario head office building; reducing the number of warehouses from 32 to 26; consolidating operations in state-of-the-art facilities; and cutting 1400 jobs.

But problems developed as system implementation began, and Loblaw president John Lederer admitted to financial analysts that the company had moved too fast in trying to implement too many changes. For example, too many distribution facilities were closed before the newer, high-tech ones were ready to cope with increased volume. One supplier shipped merchandise to the Calgary warehouse, but the shipment was refused. Many weeks passed before the shipment was finally accepted and the supplier was paid. These distribution problems forced Loblaw to pull back on marketing its general merchandise offerings. Since it is well known in the retail business that customers get very unhappy when advertised items are not on the shelf, it made little sense to spend money on marketing if the company couldn't guarantee product availability.

Loblaw also incurred some other not-so-obvious costs because of distribution problems. For example, it had to mark down many toys because they were received too late for the Christmas season. Loblaw discovered that it isn't only groceries that are perishable. There was another problem: Since customers don't know all the products that the superstores carry, there are often noticeably fewer people in the non-grocery sections. The retailer has also made efforts to revive its core business of food, including its house brand, President's Choice. Despite these efforts, Loblaw has failed to increase profit in nine of the past 12 quarters.

The company also experienced problems as it tried to move 2000 administrative employees to the company's new headquarters in Brampton, Ontario. When about 75 general merchandise product buyers decided to quit the company rather than move, this turnover made it difficult to maintain continuity with suppliers. These missteps not only cost the company millions, they set back its plans for implementation by at least a year. If Loblaw cannot effectively sell both groceries and general merchandise, they will be at a disadvantage compared to Wal-Mart.

Loblaw must compete with Wal-Mart's legendary supply chain management system. To do so, it must develop its own system for keeping in-demand products on its shelves. Such a system will also allow Loblaw to lower its prices and compete with Wal-Mart. Loblaw has hired a supply chain expert from Wal-Mart to spearhead the resolution of its distribution problems. Loblaw is wise to not underestimate the Wal-Mart threat. In the United States, Wal-Mart went from having a zero share in groceries to that country's largest grocer in less than a decade. If Wal-Mart has that kind of success in Canada, it will obviously have a detrimental effect on Canadian retailers like Loblaw and Sobey's.

Not all of Loblaw's problems are logistical. In an attempt to compete with Wal-Mart—which is also well-known for its anti-union stance—Loblaw is trying to reduce labour costs by getting the union to agree to wage cuts. Its employees are represented by the United Food and Commercial Workers union, and the union is likely to put up significant resistance to wage cuts. In addition to wage cuts, Loblaw is requiring their suppliers to buy an additional 1 percent of sales (either through discounts or rebates). These food suppliers and manufacturers are facing unparalleled challenges. The market is experiencing fluctuating commodity costs, and many grocery products are manufactured or partially sourced in the United States. The decline of the Canadian dollar in 2008 made these products more expensive and reduced already slim margins. As a result, there is often nothing left over to offer as promotional rebates or discounts.

Questions for Discussion

1. What is a supply chain? Why is efficiency in its supply chain so important to Loblaw?

2. What is supply chain management? How is it relevant for Loblaw?
3. What is the relationship between supply chain management, productivity, and quality?
4. What options do retailers like Loblaw have in difficult economic times like those that were evident in 2008–09?

apter 13

Understanding Information Systems and Communication Technology

After reading this chapter, you should be able to:

1. Explain the importance of *information management* to business firms.
2. Understand what an *information system* is, who the key users of information systems are, and the most widely used types of information systems.
3. Explain how the rapid growth of information technologies has affected *organizational processes and operations*.
4. Describe the building blocks of *information technology.*
5. Identify the *threats and risks* that are associated with the use of information technology by businesses.
6. Describe the ways in which businesses protect themselves from the threats and risks posed by information technology.

The Instapreneur

Have you ever had an idea for a great new product but lacked the resources and specialized knowledge necessary to make it a reality? Did you ever wish that your ideas and designs could be magically transformed into finished products without having to manufacture them on your own? Well, a web-based production company called Ponoko is helping to make this fantasy a reality for customers worldwide.

Launched in 2007, Ponoko is a personal manufacturing service that allows users to upload designs for anything from jewellery to furniture. The designer needs only to upload a blueprint of their idea to the Ponoko website. The design information is then transferred to a computer-directed laser cutter, which cuts each product exactly as the designer specified. Ponoko also maintains an online storefront so that users can sell their designs directly on the website. The website administrators pick featured products, free of charge to the designer, and display them on the main page of Ponoko.com. Designers can also mingle on the site's forums, where they can share their designs and receive valuable feedback and advice.

The Ponoko service is uniquely tailored to each customer's demands, and there are no minimum orders or warehousing fees since users pay for materials and cutting fees only on an as-needed basis. Therefore, there is very little risk involved for entrepreneurs interested in selling their designs. Designers can set the price for their products and decide whether they want to sell them on the Ponoko website or independently. Ponoko, and other services like it, help entrepreneurs with an idea and an internet connection to instantly start their own business and become what *Wired* magazine has dubbed an instapreneur.

The internet is providing more and more entrepreneurs with business opportunities, and there is more potential for growth as unrealized markets become evident. Google, for example, is developing software as an online service, rather than a physical good, and that approach is changing the way consumers and businesses work. Google Docs offers (for free) much of the same functionality as Microsoft's pricey Office suite, and Docs is usable from any computer that has internet access, without software disks. Services like this are driving traditionally offline firms online in order to compete. In late 2007, Microsoft introduced Office Live Workspace, a companion service to its Office 2007 suite that allows users to store documents online and work on them with other users. Analysts predict that, by 2010, software as a service (SaaS) will make up over 40 percent of the software market.

The virtual worlds of online games like Second Life and World of Warcraft have created many new opportunities for virtual entrepreneurs to make real-world profits. For example, Second Life has its own currency, the Linden (L$), which can be bought and sold for U.S. dollars on the game's online currency exchange, the LindeX. The Linden averages about L$265 per US$, and in 2006 Second Life's virtual world was estimated to have a gross domestic product of US$150 million. Entrepreneurs can also earn real money in Second Life from the sale of a wide variety of goods and services. In 2006, Ailin Graef was the first person to become a millionaire from business conducted in Second Life, buying and selling virtual real estate.

Unfortunately, not all entrepreneurs take advantage of the potential of virtual worlds in ethical ways. World of Warcraft requires a substantial time investment to make the richest and most powerful characters, but there are many players who are willing to pay to enjoy the benefits of high-level play instead of earning them. This demand has created a huge business in developing countries like China, where gamers work in sweatshop-like conditions for low wages to slay monsters and earn virtual gold. Though this practice, known as gold farming, is a violation of the game's terms of service, there were an estimated 100 000 gold farmers operating in 2005 in China alone.

Given that we are becoming dependent on technology to function in both our business and personal lives, it is no wonder that many people are taking advantage of the timing to open innovative and technology-driven businesses. Gone are the days when entrepreneurs needed major investments just to get their business ideas off the ground. Today, all one needs is a little determination, some creativity, and some technological know-how. ◆

How will this help me?

Services such as those offered by Ponoko are examples of the way the internet and related technologies are reshaping the business landscape. But even the most traditional businesses must change with the times, whether those times are defined by paper and pencil, telephone and fax machine, or smartphone and Wi-Fi. Indeed, it may seem like the times are changing more rapidly with each passing year, and it is in this context that our discussion of the various kinds of information technologies, their functions, and the benefits and risks associated with each assumes particular importance. By understanding the material in this chapter, you'll have a clearer picture of how technology is used by businesses, how it affects businesses, and how you can use it to your best advantage.

Information Management

1 Explain the importance of *information management* to business firms.

information manager The manager responsible for the activities needed to generate, analyze, and disseminate information that a company needs to make good decisions.

information management An internal operation that arranges the firm's information resources to support business performance and outcomes.

data Raw facts and figures.

information A meaningful, useful interpretation of data.

The activities of business firms—for example, designing products and services, ensuring product delivery and cash flow, evaluating personnel, and creating advertising—require information. Because information is so important, companies have **information managers**, just as they have production, marketing, and finance managers. The goal of **information management** is to organize the firm's information resources to support business performance and outcomes.

The question that faces so many businesses today is how to get useful information to the right people at the right time. Although managers often complain that they receive too much information, they usually mean that they get too much **data**—raw facts and figures. **Information** refers to data that have been interpreted so they are useful (see Figure 13.1). Consider the modern grocery store. The checkout scanner reads the bar code on the product you buy. Data are then transmitted to the store's inventory-control system, which updates the number of available units. If inventory falls below a given level, more product is ordered electronically. Meanwhile, the correct price is added to your bill and checkout coupons are printed automatically according to the specific product you bought. Your debit card transfers funds, sales reports are

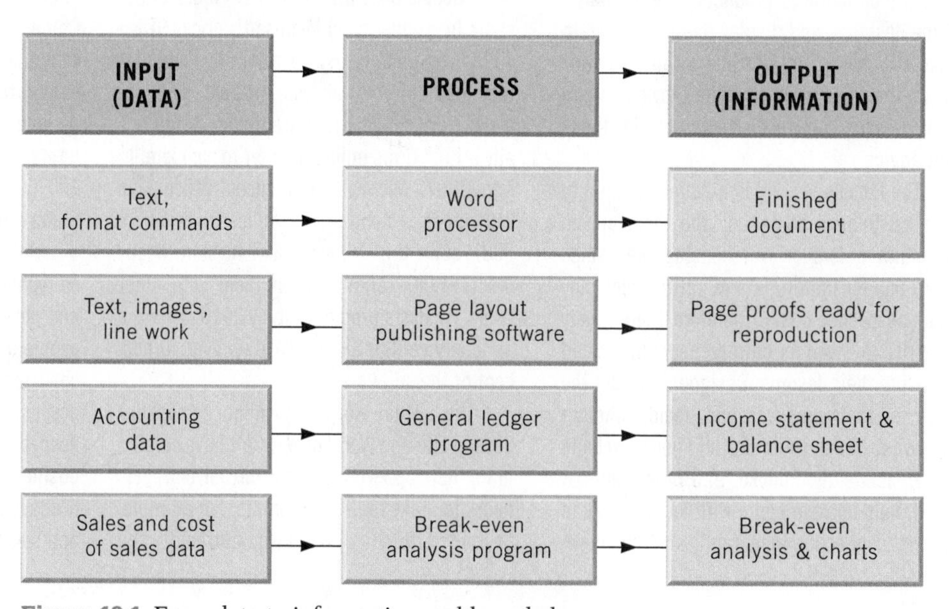

Figure 13.1 From data to information and knowledge.

generated for the store's management, and all the while, satellite transmissions are dispatching a truck to begin loading replacement supplies for the store. This entire process extracts useful information from raw data.

Information Systems

Understand what an *information system* is, who the key users of information systems are, and the most widely used types of information systems. 2

information system (IS) An organized method of transforming data into information that can be used for decision making.

An **information system (IS)** transforms raw data into information and transmits it for use in decision making. IS managers must first determine what information is needed, gather the relevant data, convert that data into information, and finally see that the information goes to those people who need it.[1] The information that is supplied varies according to such factors as the functional areas in which people work (say, accounting or marketing) and their management levels.

At one time, IS applications were quite narrow and technically focussed—processing payroll data, simulating new engineering designs, compiling advertising expenditures. But managers now use IS not merely to solve technical problems but also to analyze management control and planning problems (e.g., applying quality control standards to production, comparing costs against budgeted amounts, keeping records on employee absences and turnover, and making decisions on a firm's products and markets for the next five to 10 years). There is also increased interdependence between a company's business strategy and its IS. The choice of a business strategy—say, to be the low-cost provider or the most flexible provider or the highest-quality provider—requires an information system that can support that strategy.

Wal-Mart's information system gathers data on the billions of sales transactions—time, date, place—at the company's locations around the world. Keeping track of nearly 700 million stock-keeping units (SKUs) weekly, the information system enforces uniform reordering and delivery procedures—on packaging, timing, and quantities—for more than 30 000 suppliers. It also regulates the flow of the more than five billion cases through its distribution centres and deliveries by nearly 8000 Wal-Mart truck drivers to its stores.

The top priority for Wal-Mart's IS—improving in-stock reliability—requires integration of Wal-Mart's and suppliers' activities with store sales. That's why Proctor & Gamble, Johnson & Johnson, and other suppliers connect into Wal-Mart's information system to observe up-to-the-minute sales data on individual items, by store. They can use the system's computer-based tools—spreadsheets, sales forecasting, weather information—to forecast sales demand and plan delivery schedules. Coordinated planning avoids excessive inventories, speeds up deliveries, and holds down costs throughout the supply chain while keeping shelves stocked for retail customers.

Information systems are becoming increasingly important as managers try to cope with the flood of data they are confronted with each day.

Key Users of Information Systems

Four different groups—top, middle, and first-line managers and knowledge workers (see Chapter 8)—have different information needs. *Top managers* need information to carry out long-range planning for the entire organization, to assess the business environment, and to improve overall company performance. *Middle managers* need summaries and analyses for setting intermediate and long-range goals for the departments or projects under their supervision. *First-line managers* need information to oversee the day-to-day details of their departments or projects. *Knowledge workers* need special information for conducting technical projects.

Consider how these different needs for information are evident in a flooring manufacturer. Knowledge workers who are developing new flooring materials need information on the chemical properties of adhesives and compression strengths for floor structures. Sales managers (first-level managers) supervise salespeople, assign territories to the sales force, and handle customer service and delivery problems; they need current information on the sales and delivery of products—lists of incoming customer orders and daily delivery schedules to customers in their territories. Regional managers (middle managers) set sales quotas for each sales manager, prepare budgets, and plan staffing needs for the upcoming year; they need information on monthly sales by product and region. Finally, top managers need both internal information (e.g., sales data summarized by product, customer type, and geographic region, along with comparisons to previous years) and external information (e.g., consumer behaviour patterns, the performance of competitors, and economic forecasts).

Types of Information Systems

The term *information system* is something of a misnomer because it suggests that there is just one system. In reality, "the information system" is several systems that share information while serving different levels of the organization, different departments, and different operations. Several of the most well-known and highly developed information systems are discussed below.

Transaction Processing Systems

transaction processing systems (TPS) Applications of information processing for basic day-to-day business transactions.

Transaction processing systems (TPS) are applications of information processing for basic day-to-day business transactions. Customer order-taking by online retailers, approval of claims at insurance companies, receiving and confirming reservations by airlines, payroll processing and bill payment at almost every company—all are routine business processes. Typically, the TPS for first-level (operational) activities is well defined with predetermined data requirements and follows the same steps to complete all transactions in the system.

Systems for Knowledge Workers and Office Applications

Systems for knowledge workers and office applications support the activities of both knowledge workers and employees in clerical positions. IS knowledge workers include both systems analysts (who design systems that meet users' requirements) and systems programmers (who write the software instructions that tell computers what to do). People who run the company's computer equipment are called **system operations personnel**. They ensure that the right programs are run in the correct sequence, and they monitor equipment to ensure that it is operating properly. Many organizations also have personnel for entering data into the system for processing.

system operations personnel People who run a company's computer equipment.

Support systems like word processing, document imaging, desktop publishing, computer-aided design, and simulation modelling have increased the productivity of both office and knowledge workers. **Computer-aided design (CAD)** assists in designing products by simulating the real product and displaying it in three-dimensional graphics. Immersion's MicroScribe-3D software, for example, uses a pen-like tool to scan the surface of any three-dimensional object, such as a football helmet, and electronically transforms

computer-aided design (CAD) Computer analysis and graphics programs that are used to create new products.

it into a 3-D graphic. The helmet designer can then try different shapes and surfaces in the computer and analyze the new designs on a video monitor.[2] Products ranging from cellphones to auto parts are created using CAD because it creates faster designs at lower cost than manual modelling methods.

Computer-aided manufacturing (CAM) is used to design the manufacturing equipment, facilities, and plant layouts for better product flows and productivity. *Computer operations control* refers to any system for managing the day-to-day production activities for either goods or service production. Hospitals, for instance, use computer-based scheduling for preparing patients' meals, just as manufacturers do for making cars, clocks, and paper products.

computer-aided manufacturing (CAM) Computer systems used to design and control all the equipment and tools for producing goods.

Management Information Systems

Management information systems (MIS) support an organization's managers by providing reports, schedules, plans, and budgets. Each manager's information activities vary according to his or her functional area (say, accounting or marketing) and management level. Whereas mid-level managers focus mostly on internal activities and information, higher-level managers are also engaged in external activities. Middle managers, the largest MIS user group, need information to plan such upcoming activities as personnel training, materials movements, and cash flows. They also need to know the current status of the jobs and projects being carried out in their departments: What stage is it at now? When will it be finished? Is there an opening so the next job can be started? Many of a firm's management information systems—cash flow, sales, production scheduling, and shipping—are indispensable for helping managers find answers to such questions.

management information systems (MIS) Systems that support an organization's managers by providing reports, schedules, plans, and budgets.

Decision Support Systems

Middle- and top-level managers receive decision-making assistance from a **decision support system (DSS)**—an interactive system that locates and presents information needed to support the decision-making process. Whereas some DSSs are devoted to specific problems, others serve more general purposes, allowing managers to analyze different types of problems. Thus a firm that often faces decisions on plant capacity, for example, may have a *capacity DSS* in which the manager inputs data on anticipated levels of sales, working capital, and customer-delivery requirements. Then the system's built-in transaction processors manipulate the data and make recommendations on the best levels of plant capacity for each future time period.

decision support system (DSS) An interactive system that locates and presents information needed to support the decision-making process.

The 3-D computer model of this dinosaur is constructed from digital scans of fossilized tissue.

Robotics is a category of artificial intelligence. Robots can "learn" repetitive tasks and "remember" the causes of past mistakes.

executive support system (ESS) A quick-reference, easy-access application of information systems specially designed for upper-level managers.

artificial intelligence (AI) The development of computer systems to imitate human thought and behaviour.

expert system A form of artificial intelligence in which a program draws on the rules an expert in a given field has laid out to arrive at a solution for a problem.

Executive Support Systems

An **executive support system (ESS)** is designed to assist with executive-level decisions and problems, ranging from "What lines of business should we be in five years from now?" to "Based on forecasted developments in electronic technologies, to what extent should our firm be globalized in five (or 10) years?" An ESS uses a wide range of internal information and external sources, such as industry reports, global economic forecasts, and reports on competitors.

Artificial Intelligence

Artificial intelligence (AI) refers to the development of computer systems to imitate human thought and behaviour—in other words, systems that perform physical tasks, use thought processes, and learn. For example, a credit-evaluation system may decide which loan applicants are creditworthy and which are too risky, and it may then compose acceptance and rejection letters accordingly.

Some AI systems possess sensory capabilities, such as lasers that "see," "hear," and "feel." Toronto-based AND Corp. has developed a software program—called Hnet—that can learn to recognize faces. This may seem like a simple thing, but millions of dollars had been spent on this problem without success until AND Corp. developed the software. The system can be used to improve airport security and to track terrorists.[3]

A special form of AI, the **expert system**, is designed to imitate the thought processes of human experts in a particular field.[4] For example, the Campbell Soup Co. developed an expert system to mimic complex decision processes and save the expert knowledge that was going to be lost when a long-time expert soup maker announced his intention to retire.[5]

Information Technology

information technology (IT) The various devices for creating, storing, exchanging, and using information in diverse modes, including visual images, voice, multimedia, and business data.

No matter where we go, we can't escape the impact of **information technology (IT)**—the various devices for creating, storing, exchanging, and using information in diverse modes, including visual images, voice, multimedia, and business data. We see ads all the time for the latest cellphones, MP3 players, laptops, and software products, and most of us connect daily to the internet. Email has become a staple in business, and even such traditionally "low-tech" businesses as hair salons and garbage collection companies are becoming dependent on the internet, computers, and networks. As consumers, we interact with databases every time we withdraw money from an ATM, order food at McDonald's, or check on the status of a package at UPS or FedEx. The top 10 information technology companies in Canada are listed in Table 13.1.

IT developments have also had a major impact on how individual managers do their jobs. For example, the packing list for Barry Martin's upcoming fishing trip reflects his new outlook on where, when, and how he gets his work done. It reads, in part, as follows: (1) fly rod, (2) dry-pack food, (3) tent, and (4) BlackBerry. Five years ago, his list would have included a cellphone, road and area maps, phone directory, appointments calendar, office files, and client project folders, all of which are replaced now by just one item—his

Table 13.1 Top 10 Information Technology Companies in Canada, 2008

Company	Annual Revenues (in billions of $)
1. CGI Group Inc.	$3.7
2. Microsoft Canada Co.	2.2
3. MacDonald, Dettwiler and Associates	1.1
4. SXC Health Solutions Corp.	0.92
5. Accenture Inc.	0.77
6. Oracle Corp. Canada Inc.	0.74
7. Open Text Corp.	0.73
8. SAP Canada Inc.	0.58
9. Hartco Income Fund	0.46
10. (No information available—only 9 companies listed in original source)	

BlackBerry—a wireless handheld messaging device that allows him to take the office with him wherever he goes.

For a project manager like Martin, the BlackBerry is more than just a cellphone. With its continuous connection, there's no dialing in, and his email is displayed the same moment it arrives on his PC back at the office. Even in the Canadian wilderness, Martin can place phone calls and read new email messages. Along with internet browsing, there's access to desktop tools—such as an organizer and an address book—for managing work and staying in touch with customers, suppliers, and employees from any location.

The mobile messaging capabilities of devices like the BlackBerry offer businesses powerful tools that save time and travel expenses. They also mean that employees no longer work only at the office or the factory and that not all of a company's operations are performed at one place. When using such devices, offsite employees have continuous access to information instead of being forced to be at a desk to access their files and the internet. Such benefits have attracted several million enthusiastic subscribers, making BlackBerry the leader in the handheld wireless industry.[6]

The BlackBerry wireless handheld messaging device allows employees to take the office with them.

Information Technology and Organizational Processes

The rapid growth of new information technologies has changed organizational processes and operations in many different ways, some of which are discussed below.

3 Explain how the rapid growth of information technologies has affected *organizational processes and operations.*

Better Service Through Coordination of Remote Deliveries

With access to the internet, company activities may be geographically scattered but remain coordinated through a networked system that provides better service for customers. Many businesses, for example, coordinate activities from one centralized location, but their deliveries flow from several remote locations, often at lower cost. When you order furniture from an internet storefront—for example, a chair, a sofa, a table, and two lamps—the chair may come from a warehouse in Toronto, the lamps from a manufacturer in China, and the sofa and table from a supplier in North Carolina. Beginning with the customer's order, activities are coordinated through the company's network, as if the whole order were being processed at one place. This avoids the expensive in-between step of first shipping all the items to a central location.

Leaner, More Efficient Organizations

Networks and technology are also leading to leaner companies with fewer employees and simpler structures. Because networks enable firms to maintain information linkages between employees and customers, more work and customer satisfaction can be accomplished with fewer people. Bank customers can access 24-hour information systems and monitor their accounts without employee assistance. Instructions that once were given to assembly workers by supervisors are now delivered to workstations electronically. Truck drivers delivering freight used to return to the trucking terminal to receive instructions from supervisors on reloading for the next delivery, but now instructions arrive on electronic screens in the trucks so drivers know in advance what will be happening next.

Increased Collaboration

Collaboration among internal units and with outside firms is greater when firms use collaboration software and other IT communications devices. Companies are learning that complex problems can be solved better through IT-supported collaboration, either with formal teams or through spontaneous interaction among people and departments. The design of new products, for example, was once largely an engineering responsibility. Now it is a shared activity using information from people in marketing, finance, production, engineering, and purchasing who collectively determine the best design. When Boeing designed its new 777 aircraft, information came not just from engineers, but also from passengers (who said they wanted electronic outlets to recharge personal electronic devices), cabin crews (who wanted more bathrooms and wider aisles), and air-traffic controllers (who wanted larger, safer airbrakes).

Improved Global Exchange

The global reach of IT is enabling business collaboration on a scale that was unheard of just a few years ago. Consider Lockheed Martin's contract for designing the Joint Strike Fighter and supplying thousands of the planes in different versions for Canada, the United States, the United Kingdom, Italy, Denmark, and Norway. Lockheed can't do the job alone, so it is collaborating with the United Kingdom's BAE Systems and more than 70 U.S. and 18 international subcontractors at some 190 locations. An Australian manufacturer of aviation communications and a Turkish electronics supplier entered the project in 2005, joining seven other Australian and two other Turkish firms that were already involved. Over the project's 20-year life, more than 1500 firms will supply everything from radar systems to engines to bolts. Collaboration on this massive scale is essential for coordinating design, testing, and construction while avoiding delays, holding down costs, and maintaining quality.[7]

Greater Independence of Company and Workplace

Many employees no longer work only at the office or the factory, and not all of a company's operations are performed at one location. The sales manager for an advertising agency may visit the company office in Toronto once every two weeks, preferring instead to work over the firm's electronic network from her home office in Montreal. A medical researcher for a Calgary clinic may work at a home office networked into the clinic's system. With new developments in IT, a company's activities may also be geographically scattered but still highly coordinated. Many ebusinesses, for example, do not conduct any activities at one centralized location; all of their activities are launched instantaneously by the customer's order and coordinated through the network, just as if all of them were being processed at one location.

Improved Management Processes

IT has also changed the nature of the management process. At one time, upper-level managers didn't concern themselves with all of the detailed information filtering upward from the workplace, because it was expensive to gather, slow in coming, and quick to become out of date; rather, workplace management was delegated to middle and first-line managers. Now, instantaneous information is accessible and useful to all levels of management. A good example of this change is enterprise resource planning (ERP), which we discussed in Chapter 2.

Improved Flexibility for Customization

IT has also created new manufacturing capabilities that enable businesses to offer customers greater variety and faster delivery cycles. Whether it's a personal computer from Dell, one of Nokia's cellphones, or a Rawlings baseball glove, today's design-it-yourself world has become possible through fast, flexible manufacturing using IT networks. At Timbuk2's website, for example, you can "build your own" custom messenger bag at different price levels with choices of size, fabric, colour combinations, accessories, liner material, strap, and even left- or right-hand access.[8] The principle is called **mass-customization**: Although companies produce in large volumes, each unit features the unique options the customer prefers. As shown in Figure 13.2, flexible production and speedy delivery depend on an integrated network of information to coordinate all the activities among customers, manufacturers, suppliers, and shippers.

mass-customization Producing large volumes of products or services, but giving customers the choice of features and options they want.

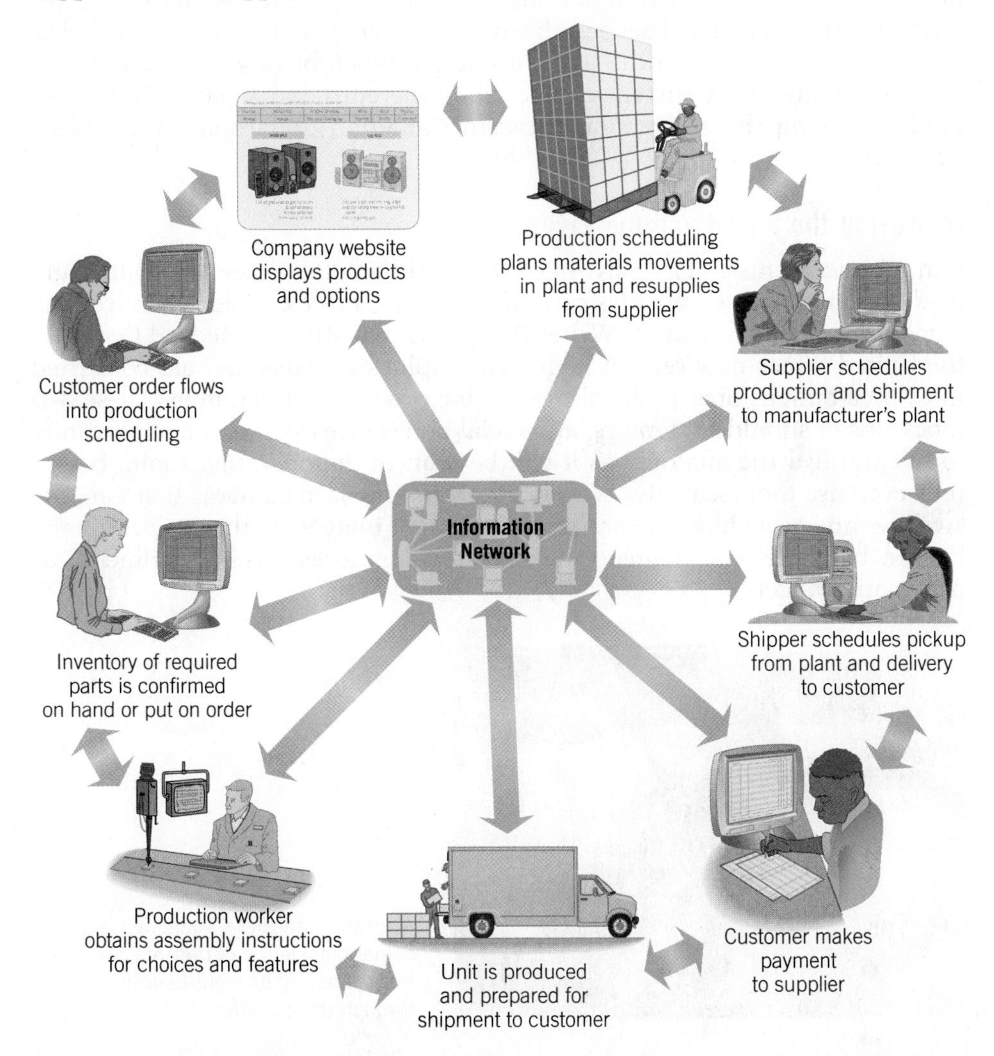
Company website displays products and options
Production scheduling plans materials movements in plant and resupplies from supplier
Customer order flows into production scheduling
Supplier schedules production and shipment to manufacturer's plant
Information Network
Inventory of required parts is confirmed on hand or put on order
Shipper schedules pickup from plant and delivery to customer
Production worker obtains assembly instructions for choices and features
Unit is produced and prepared for shipment to customer
Customer makes payment to supplier

Figure 13.2 Networking for mass-customization.

Providing New Business Opportunities

Not only is IT improving existing businesses, it is creating entirely new businesses where none existed before. For big businesses, this means developing new products, offering new services, and reaching new clients. Only a few years ago, the multibillion-dollar behemoth known as Google was a fledgling search engine. Today, that company boasts not just a search engine but instant messaging, email, and auction features, as well as the online software Google Docs, mentioned earlier.

The IT landscape has also presented small business owners with new ebusiness opportunities. Consider Richard Smith, who began collecting stamps at age seven. Now, some 40 years later, he's turned his hobby into a profitable eBay business. Each day begins at the PC in his home office, scanning eBay's listings for items available and items wanted by sellers and buyers around the world. With more than 3000 sales transactions to date, Richard maintains a perfect customer rating and recently earned more than $4000 on a single eBay transaction.

To assist start-up businesses, eBay's services network is a ready-made online business model, not just an auction market. Services range from credit financing to protection from fraud and misrepresentation, information security, international currency exchanges, and post-sales management. These activities enable users like Richard to complete sales transactions, deliver merchandise, and get new merchandise for future resale, all from the comfort of their own homes.

Meanwhile, eBay's PayPal system—an online financial institution—processes $20 billion in transactions annually. As a seller, Richard receives payments into his PayPal account from buyers using credit cards, debit cards, bank accounts, or their own PayPal accounts. When buying merchandise, he can pay in any of six currencies, including the euro and Japanese yen, with PayPal making the conversion between Canadian dollars and the seller's currency.

Improving the World and Our Lives

Can advancements in IT really make the world a better place? Hospitals and medical equipment companies certainly think so. For example, when treating combat injuries, surgeons at Walter Reed National Military Medical Center in the United States now rely on high-tech graphics displays that are converted into three-dimensional physical models for pre-surgical planning. These 3-D mock-ups of shoulders, femurs, and facial bones give doctors the opportunity to see and feel the anatomy as it will be seen in the operating room, before they even use their scalpels.[9] Meanwhile, vitamin-sized cameras that patients swallow are providing doctors with computer images of the insides of the human body, helping them to make better diagnoses for such ailments as ulcers and cancer.[10]

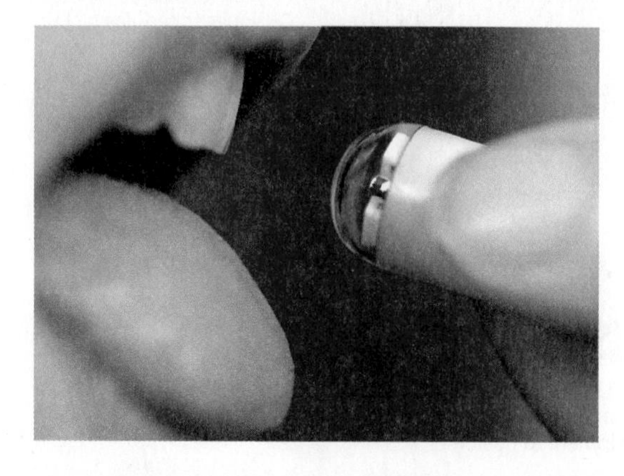

After this capsule is swallowed, the camera inside it can transmit 50 000 images during its eight-hour journey through the digestive tract.

IT Building Blocks

Describe the building blocks of *information technology.* 4

We have already seen how dramatically IT is affecting the business landscape. The *tools* that make it work are things like the *internet*, *email* and other communications technologies, *networks*, *hardware devices*, and *software*.

The Internet and Other Communication Technologies

The internet—and its companion system, the World Wide Web—are today among the world's most powerful communication technologies. The **internet** is a system of more than 100 million interconnected computers in over 100 countries around the world. Canadians spend more time each month on the internet (45.5 hours) than people in any other country.[11] The **World Wide Web** is a standardized code for accessing information and transmitting data over the internet. It provides the common language that allows information sharing on the internet. For thousands of businesses, the internet is replacing the telephone, fax machine, and standard mail as the primary communication tool.

internet The gigantic network of networks that serves millions of computers; offers information on business, science, and government; and provides communication flows among more than 170 000 separate networks around the world.

World Wide Web A standardized code for accessing information and transmitting data over the internet, which provides the common language that allows information sharing on the internet.

The internet has spawned a number of other business communications technologies, including *intranets*, *extranets*, *electronic conferencing*, and *VSAT satellite communications*.

Intranets. Many companies maintain internal websites linked throughout the firm. These private networks, or **intranets**, are accessible only to employees. For example, Ford Motor Company's intranet connects 175 000 workstations in Asia, Europe, and North America to thousands of Ford websites containing private information on Ford's employee benefits, production management tools, and product design resources. Sharing information on engineering, distribution, and marketing has reduced the lead time for getting new models into production and has shortened customer delivery times.[12]

intranet A company's private network that is accessible only to employees via entry through electronic firewalls.

Extranets. **Extranets** allow outsiders limited access to a firm's internal information network. The most common application allows buyers to enter a system to see which products are available for sale and delivery, thus providing convenient product availability information. Industrial suppliers are often linked into customers' information networks so that they can see planned production schedules and prepare supplies for customers' upcoming operations. The extranet at Chaparral Steel, for example, lets customers shop electronically through its storage yards and gives them electronic access to Chaparral's planned inventory of industrial steel products.

extranet A network that allows outsiders limited access to a firm's internal information system.

Electronic Conferencing. **Electronic conferencing** allows groups of people to communicate simultaneously from various locations via email, phone, or video. One form, called *data conferencing*, allows people in remote locations to work simultaneously on one document. Working as a team, they can revise a marketing plan or draft a press release. *Video conferencing* allows participants to see one another on video screens while the conference is in progress. For example, Lockheed Martin's Joint Strike Fighter project, discussed earlier, uses internet collaboration systems with both voice and video capabilities. Although separated by oceans, partners can communicate as if they were in the same room as they redesign components and alter production schedules. Electronic conferencing is attractive to many businesses because it eliminates travel and saves money. Recent improvements in video technology mean sharper pictures and better voice coordination than that found in the older video conferencing systems.[13]

electronic conferencing Allows people to communicate simultaneously from different locations via telephone, video, or mail group software.

VSAT satellite communications A transmitter-receiver (transceiver) that sits outdoors with a direct line of sight to a satellite. The hub—a ground station computer at the company's headquarters—sends signals to and receives signals from the satellite, exchanging voice, video, and data transmissions.

VSAT Satellite Communications. Another internet technology businesses use to communicate is **VSAT satellite communications**. VSAT (short for *Very*

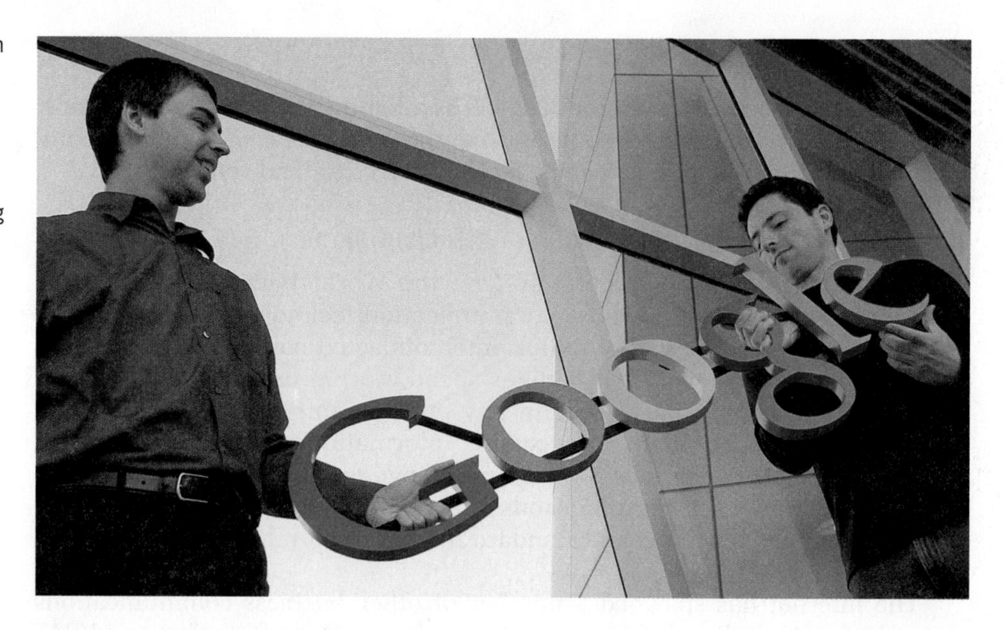

Larry Page (left) and Sergey Brin started the search engine Google when both were graduate students in the mid-1990s. They originally called their program "BackRub" because it was good at analyzing the "back links" from one website to another. Raising money primarily from Silicon Valley venture capitalists, they incorporated Google in 1998. When the six-year-old company went public in 2004, its founders, each of whom held 38 million shares, cleared $3 billion apiece.

Small Aperture Terminal) systems have a transmitter-receiver (*transceiver*) that sits outdoors with a direct line of sight to a satellite. The hub—a ground station computer at the company's headquarters—sends signals to and receives signals from the satellite, exchanging voice, video, and data transmissions. An advantage of VSAT is privacy. A company that operates its own VSAT system has total control over its communications without dependence on other companies. A firm might use VSAT to exchange sales and inventory information, advertising messages, and visual presentations between headquarters and store managers at remote sites.

Networks: System Architecture

computer network A group of two or more computers linked together by some form of cable (fibre-optic, coaxial, or twisted wire) or by wireless technology to share data or resources.

client-server network A network composed of both clients (users) and servers that allows the clients to access various services without costly and unnecessary duplication.

A **computer network** is a group of two or more computers linked together by some form of cable (fibre-optic, coaxial, or twisted wire) or by wireless technology to share data or resources, such as a printer. The most common type of network used in businesses is a client-server network. In **client-server networks**, *clients* are usually the laptop or desktop computers through which users make requests for information or resources. *Servers* are the computers that provide the services shared by users. In big organizations, servers are usually assigned a specific task. For example, in a local university or college network, an *application server* stores the word-processing, spreadsheet, and other programs used by all computers connected to the network. A *print server* controls the printer, stores printing requests from client computers, and routes jobs as the printer becomes available. An *email server* handles all incoming and outgoing email. With a client-server system, users can share resources and internet connections—and avoid costly duplication.

wide area networks (WANs) Computers that are linked over long distances—province-wide or even nationwide—through telephone lines, microwave signals, or satellite communications.

local area networks (LANs) Computers that are linked in a smaller area, such as all of a firm's computers within a single building.

Wide Area Networks (WANs). Computers that are linked over long distances—province-wide or even nationwide—through telephone lines, microwave signals, or satellite communications make up what are called **wide area networks (WANs)**. Firms can lease lines from communications vendors or maintain private WANs. Wal-Mart, for example, depends on a private satellite network that links 5000 retail stores to its Bentonville, Arkansas, headquarters.

Local Area Networks (LANs). In **local area networks (LANs)**, computers are linked in a smaller area, such as all of a firm's computers within a single building. On cable TV's Home Shopping Network (HSN), for example, hundreds of operators at the HSN facility are united by a LAN for entering call-in orders.

The arrangement requires only one computer system with one database and one software system.

Wireless Networks. Wireless networks use airborne electronic signals to link network computers and devices. Like wired networks, wireless networks can reach across long distances or exist within a single building or small area. For example, the BlackBerry system shown in Figure 13.3 consists of devices that send and receive transmissions on **wireless wide area networks (WWANS)** of more than 100 service providers in over 40 countries. The wireless format that the system relies on to control wireless messaging is supplied by Research In Motion (RIM), the Canadian company that makes the BlackBerry, and is installed on the user company's computer. The *firewall* provides privacy protection (we discuss firewalls in more detail later).

wireless wide area networks (WWANs) Networks that use airborne electronic signals instead of wires to link computers and electronic devices over long distances.

Wi-Fi. Hotspots are specific locations such as coffee shops, hotels, and airport terminals that provide wireless internet connections for people on the go. Each hotspot, or **Wi-Fi** (short for *wi*reless *fi*delity) access point, is actually its own small network, called a **wireless local area network (wireless LAN or WLAN)**.

Wi-Fi (wireless fidelity) An access point in a specific location, such as a coffee shop, hotel, or airport terminal, that provides wireless internet connections for people on the go.

wireless local area network (wireless LAN or WLAN) The individual network that provides Wi-Fi.

The benefit of Wi-Fi is that you're not tethered to a wire for accessing the internet. Employees can wait for a delayed plane in the airport and still be connected to the internet through their wireless-enabled laptop. However, as with every technology, Wi-Fi has limitations, including a short range of distance. This means that your laptop's internet connection can be severed if you move farther than about 90 metres from the hotspot. So, while a city may have hundreds of hotspots, your laptop must remain near one to stay connected. This distance limitation is expected to be improved soon by *WiMax* (*Worldwide Interoperability for Microwave Access*), the next step in wireless advancements, with its wireless range of 48 kilometres.

Hardware and Software

Any computer network or system needs **hardware**—the physical components, such as keyboards, monitors, system units, and printers. In addition to the laptops, desktop computers, and BlackBerrys mentioned earlier, *handheld computers* are also used in businesses. For example, Wal-Mart employees roam store aisles using handhelds to identify, count, and order items; track deliveries; and update backup stock at distribution centres to keep store shelves replenished with merchandise.

hardware The physical components of a computer, such as keyboards, monitors, system units, and printers.

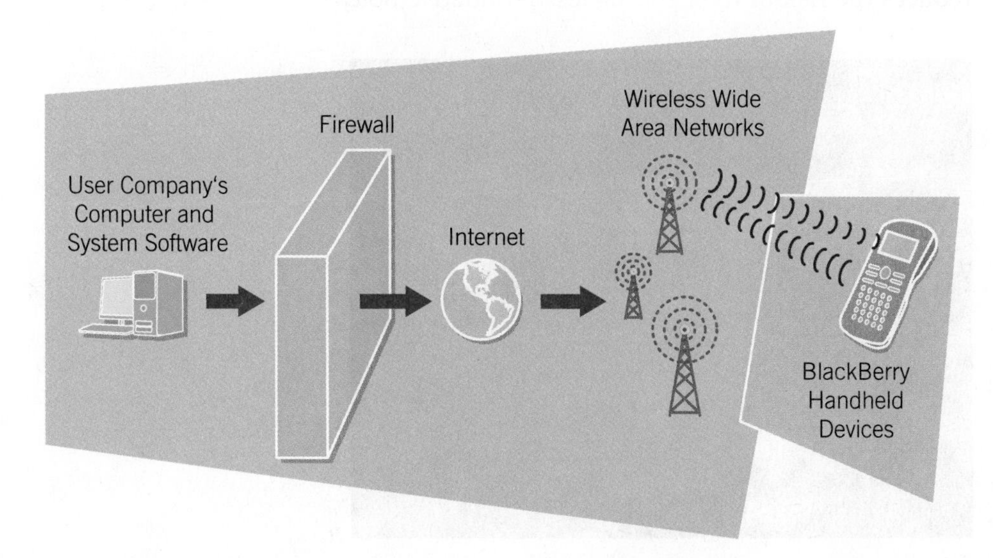

Figure 13.3 BlackBerry wireless internet architecture.

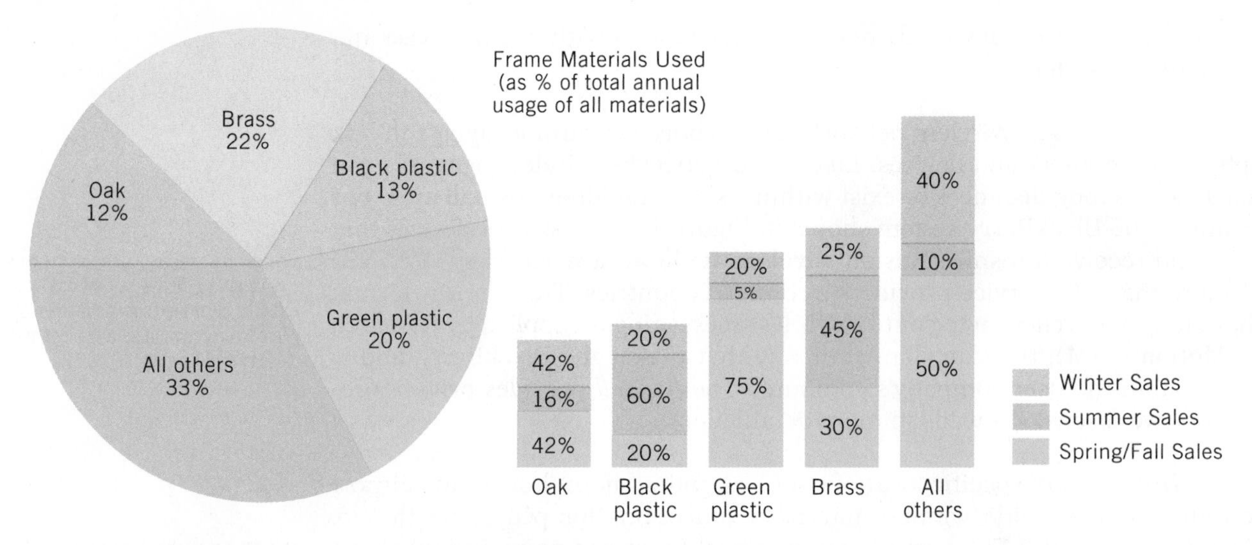

Figure 13.4 Both the pie chart and the bar graph show that four frame materials are the most used, but the bar graph also shows that brass and oak are the most popular materials in winter.

software Programs that tell the computer how to function.

The other essential in any computer system is **software**—programs that tell the computer how to function. Software includes *system software*, such as Microsoft Windows, which tells the computer's hardware how to interact with the software, as well as *application software*, which meets the needs of specific users. Examples of application software include word-processing programs like Microsoft Word, spreadsheet programs like Lotus 1-2-3, graphics programs like Corel Draw, message centre software like WinFax Pro, integrated programs like Quicken, and database programs like Access. Brief descriptions of several different types of software are presented in the following paragraphs.

computer graphics programs Programs that convert numeric and character data into pictorial information like charts and graphs.

Computer Graphics. One example of a software program is **computer graphics**, which converts numeric and character data into pictorial information like charts and graphs. These allow managers to see relationships more easily and generate clearer and more persuasive reports and presentations. As Figure 13.4 shows, both types of graphics can convey different kinds of information—in this case, the types of materials that should be ordered by a picture framing shop like Artists' Frame Service.

IBM's Visualization Data Explorer software uses data from field samples to model the underground structure of an oil field. The imagery in Figure 13.5, for example, provides engineers with better information on oil location and reduces the risk of their hitting less productive holes.

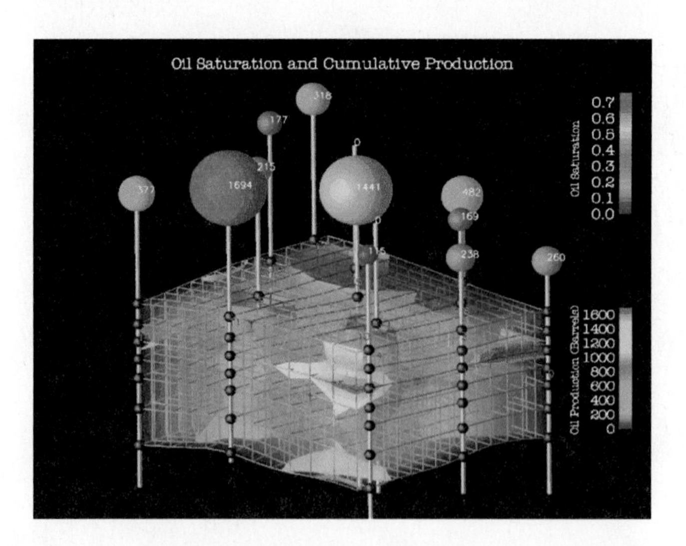

Figure 13.5 3-D computer modelling software gives engineers a better idea of where oil might be located.

Groupware. Collaboration between a firm's internal units and outside firms (remote collaboration) is made possible with **groupware**—software that connects group members for email distribution, electronic meetings, message storing, appointments and schedules, and group writing. Linked by groupware, people can collaborate from their own desktop PCs, even if they're remotely located. Groupware systems include IBM Lotus Domino 6.5, Microsoft Exchange Server 2007, and Novell GroupWise 6.(5).

groupware Software that connects group members for email distribution, electronic meetings, message storing, appointments and schedules, and group writing.

Electronic Spreadsheets. **Electronic spreadsheets** arrange data across and down the page in rows and columns. Users enter data, including formulas, at row and column intersections, and the computer automatically performs the necessary calculations. Payroll records, sales projections, and a host of other financial reports can be prepared in this manner.

electronic spreadsheets Arrange data across and down the page in rows and columns.

Business Accountability

Social Matters

The term *social marketing* refers to the use of marketing techniques to achieve a particular "social good" (for example, encouraging people to wear seat belts or to volunteer their time for good causes). This activity is known for tight budgets, large audiences, and limited investors. To try to overcome the stress and pressures of this field, businesses are moving toward the use of new social networking technologies that offer venues with more immediate feedback and measurable results.

Katie Delahaye Paine, the founder and CEO of KDPaine & Partners, has discovered that venues like social blogs, podcasts, and Facebook are opening up many new ways for marketers to reach and interact with their target audience. She says that most companies become involved in social marketing not because they are interested in large sales numbers but because they want to cultivate "reputation, relationships, customer satisfaction, and employee engagement." When there is limited money to invest in a new campaign or in fancy promotional materials, marketers have difficulty predicting what their return on investment (ROI) will be. New thinking suggests that the focus should be on the "return" and not on the "investment" needed to obtain success. Many businesses are afraid to participate in social marketing efforts because the pressure to succeed is intense, but with the aid of new internet communication technologies, this fear should be reduced.

An example of a company created specifically to advance social marketing is Social Networks for Everything, created by Marc Andreessen (who built Netscape) and Gina Bianchini. Users of this network post comments, questions, photos, and videos regarding a multitude of topics, and the company has recorded more than 230 000 networks. All of their created networks serve as a platform for an entire business and represent an ever-expanding commercial universe. One of the most popular network sites belongs to hip-hop mogul 50 Cent; it has over 170 000 members. Chris Romero, the creative director of new media for 50 Cent's site, describes it as "an entertainment-industry news/rumour/editorial blog in the vein of TMZ.com, combined with unparalleled access and interaction with the celebrity." Network sites have a multitude of uses, although Romero hopes to release music and video directly to the public one day, bypassing record companies altogether. The viral expansion loops have long existed in the "real world," with Tupperware parties being a classic example of the cyclical effect networking has on a business. The most interesting part of the online community concept is how each network is created and targeted to a very specific group of users. Show My Pony is for horse enthusiasts, GAX for gamers, and GYNite for "gay guys and their friends." The cost associated with starting a social network is minimal, but the results are unparalleled. YouTube started a viral loop by allowing anyone to embed a video link in their blog or MySpace page. The more who saw it, the more links were embedded, and soon, millions of users were funnelled directly to YouTube.

We are starting to see more instances where advances in information technologies have significant impact on other areas of business. People are turning to the internet to satisfy all of their informational needs; businesses would be crazy not to follow suit. This new social networking technology can easily be applied to social marketing and media efforts where exposure is critical and precision is vital. By allowing marketers the power to attract and connect with virtual tools, the emphasis can be placed on the "return" and less stress needs to be placed on the required "investment."

Critical Thinking Questions

1. What is the difference between social marketing and social networking?
2. Why does the use of the social networking technology look promising for the field of social marketing?

The realism of the space creatures and alien environments in *Star Wars* is due to special effects created with computer graphics.

Spreadsheets are good planning tools because they let managers see how making a change in one item affects related items. For example, you can insert operating-cost percentages, tax rates, or sales revenues into the spreadsheet. The computer will automatically recalculate all the other figures and determine net profit. Popular spreadsheet packages include Lotus 1-2-3, Quattro Pro, and Microsoft Excel for Windows.[14]

IT Risks and Threats

5 Identify the *threats and risks* that are associated with the use of information technology by businesses.

Unfortunately, IT has attracted abusers who are intent on doing mischief, with severity ranging from mere nuisance to outright destruction. In this section, we look at various IT threats, and in the next section, we describe steps that businesses have taken to protect themselves.

Hackers

hackers Cyber-criminals who gain unauthorized access to a computer or network, either to steal information, money, or property or to tamper with data.

Hackers are cyber-criminals who gain unauthorized access to a computer or network, either to steal information, money, or property or to tamper with data. For example, one 16-year-old British hacker got into the U.S. Air Force's top command-and-control facility 150 different times. From there, he got into the computers of several defence contractors and the South Korean Atomic Research Institute.

At Equifax Canada, computer hackers breached its system and gained access to personal information on hundreds of Canadians.[15] In the United States, a computer hacker was charged with stealing more than one billion records from Acxiom, a data-selling company. The company admitted that the stolen data could include information about millions of people. It also admitted that it didn't even know its system had been hacked into until it was contacted by investigators in the case. Since then, Acxiom has beefed up its password protocols and its encryption and has also conducted many security audits.

One common reason hackers break into a computer network is to launch *denial of service (DOS) attacks*. DOS attacks flood networks or websites with bogus requests for information and resources, thereby shutting down the networks or websites and making it impossible for legitimate users to access them. Such attacks cost companies millions in lost productive time and revenue.

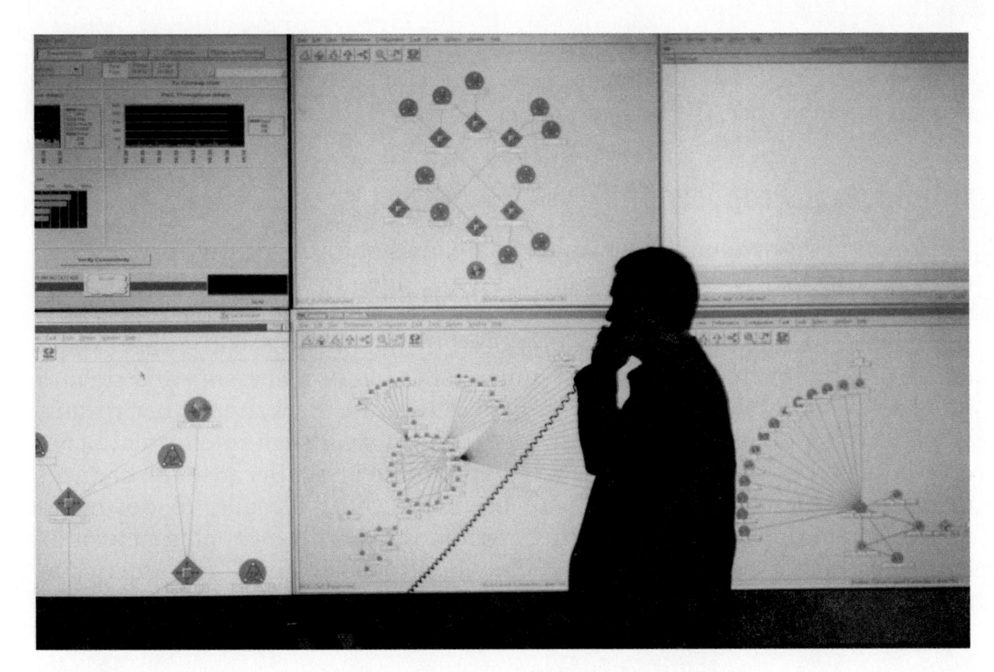

At Acxiom, computer systems track consumer data provided by nearly every credit-card issuer, bank, and insurance company in North America. The company is currently improving its computer-security models, but many people who worry about the potential for abuse point out that Acxiom itself has been successfully "hacked" more than once in the past couple of years.

Wireless mooching is also a growing problem. Once hackers get inside an unsecured wireless network, they use it to commit identity theft and to steal credit card numbers, among other activities. When police try to track down these criminals, they're long gone, leaving the network host exposed to criminal prosecution.

Software Piracy

Software piracy—the unauthorized use of software such as word processing and spreadsheets—is a worldwide problem. The Canadian Alliance Against Software Theft (CAAST) estimates that about one-third of software that is installed on computers in Canada is pirated. The piracy rate in countries like Vietnam and China is over 90 percent. CAAST estimates that software piracy has resulted in sales losses of $41 billion worldwide for companies that sell software.[16]

software piracy The unauthorized use of software such as word processing and spreadsheets.

Identity Theft

Identity theft refers to the unauthorized stealing of personal information (such as social insurance numbers and addresses) to get loans, credit cards, or other monetary benefits by impersonating the victim. Clever crooks get information on unsuspecting victims by digging in trash, luring internet users to bogus websites, and stealing mail. Some America Online customers, for example, received an email notifying them of a billing problem with their AOL accounts. The email, displaying AOL logos and legitimate-looking links, requested personal information like credit-card numbers, social security numbers, and banking accounts with passwords and PINs. When the customers clicked on the AOL Billing Center link, they were transferred to a spoofed (falsified) AOL-looking webpage, where they submitted the requested information—into the hands of the thief. The accounts were soon empty. The thieves in this case used *phishing* or *pharming*—emailing a deceptive, real-looking imitation of a popular website (e.g., AOL, PayPal, or your local bank) as bait, to masses of recipients, tricking them into giving up personal information.

identity theft The unauthorized stealing of personal information (such as social insurance numbers and addresses) to get loans, credit cards, or other monetary benefits by impersonating the victim.

Identity theft is rapidly becoming a major problem. Identity thieves are not often caught, but when they are, they may receive stiff penalties. One hacker was sentenced to nine years in prison for breaking into a computer system and stealing credit-card account numbers of customers of a Lowe's home improvement store.[17]

Intellectual Property Theft

intellectual property A product of the mind—something produced by the intellect, with great expenditure of human effort—that has commercial value.

Information is so valuable that most companies enforce security precautions to protect it. Nearly every company faces the dilemma of protecting product plans, new inventions, and industrial processes. **Intellectual property** is a product of the mind—something produced by the intellect, with great expenditure of human effort—that has commercial value. Its ownership and right to its use may be protected by patent, copyright, trademark, and other means. Hackers often break in to company networks to steal such intellectual property, but it's not just hackers who are doing the stealing. Because the chances of getting caught seem slim, home users continue, illegally, to download unpaid-for movies, music, and other resources from file-swapping networks. Recent estimates conservatively indicate industry losses in North America at more than $5 billion for music, $13 billion for software, and $4 billion for movies each year.[18]

Computer Viruses, Worms, and Trojan Horses

Another IT risk facing businesses is rogue programmers who disrupt IT operations by contaminating and destroying software, hardware, or data files. Viruses, worms, and Trojan horses are three kinds of malicious programs that, once installed, can shut down any computer system. A *computer virus* exists in a file that attaches itself to a program and migrates from computer to computer as a shared program or as an email attachment. It does not infect the system unless the user opens the contaminated file, and users typically are unaware they are spreading the virus by file-sharing. It can, for example, quickly copy itself over and over again, using up all available memory and effectively shutting down the computer.

Worms are a particular kind of virus that travel from computer to computer within networked computer systems without your needing to open any software to spread the contaminated file. In a matter of days, the notorious Blaster Worm infected some 400 000 computer networks, destroying files and even allowing outsiders to take over computers remotely. The worm replicates itself rapidly, sending out thousands of copies to other computers in the network. Travelling through internet connections and email address books in the network's computers, it absorbs system memory and shuts down network servers, web servers, and individual computers.

Unlike a virus, a *Trojan horse* does not replicate itself. Instead, it most often comes into the computer at your request, masquerading as a harmless, legitimate software product or data file. Once installed, the damage begins. For instance, it may simply redesign desktop icons or, more maliciously, delete files and destroy information.

Spyware

spyware Software masquerading as a friendly file available as a "giveaway" or shared among individual users on their PCs that monitors the host computer's activities.

As if forced intrusion isn't bad enough, internet users unwittingly invite spies masquerading as a friendly file available as a "giveaway" or shared among individual users on their PCs. This so-called **spyware** is downloaded by users who are lured by "free" software. Once installed, it crawls around to monitor the host computer's activities, gathering email addresses, credit-card numbers, passwords, and other inside information that it transmits back to someone outside the host system. Spyware authors assemble incoming stolen information to create their own "intellectual property" that they then sell to other parties to use for marketing or advertising purposes or for identity theft.[19]

Spam

Spam is junk email sent to a mailing list or a newsgroup (an online discussion group).[20] Spam is a greater nuisance than postal junk mail because the internet is open to the public, email costs are negligible, and massive mailing lists are accessible through file-sharing or by theft. Spam operators send unwanted messages ranging from explicit pornography to hate mail to advertisements and even destructive computer viruses. In addition to wasting users' time, spam also consumes a network's bandwidth, thereby reducing the amount of data that can be transmitted in a fixed amount of time for useful purposes. Industry experts estimate spam's damage in lost time and productivity at more than $9 billion annually.[21]

spam Junk email sent to a mailing list or a newsgroup.

IT Protection Measures

Describe the ways in which businesses protect themselves from the threats and risks posed by information technology. 6

Security measures against intrusion and viruses are a constant challenge. Businesses guard themselves against intrusion, identity theft, and viruses by using *firewalls*, *special software*, and *encryption*.

Firewalls

Many systems guard against unauthorized access by requiring users to have protected passwords. This helps ensure that intruders are unable to access your computer or the data on it. However, many firms rely on additional safeguards, such as **firewalls**, which are security systems with special software or hardware devices designed to keep computers safe from hackers. Figure 13.6 shows how a firewall works. The firewall is located where the two networks—

firewall Security system with special software or hardware devices designed to keep computers safe from hackers.

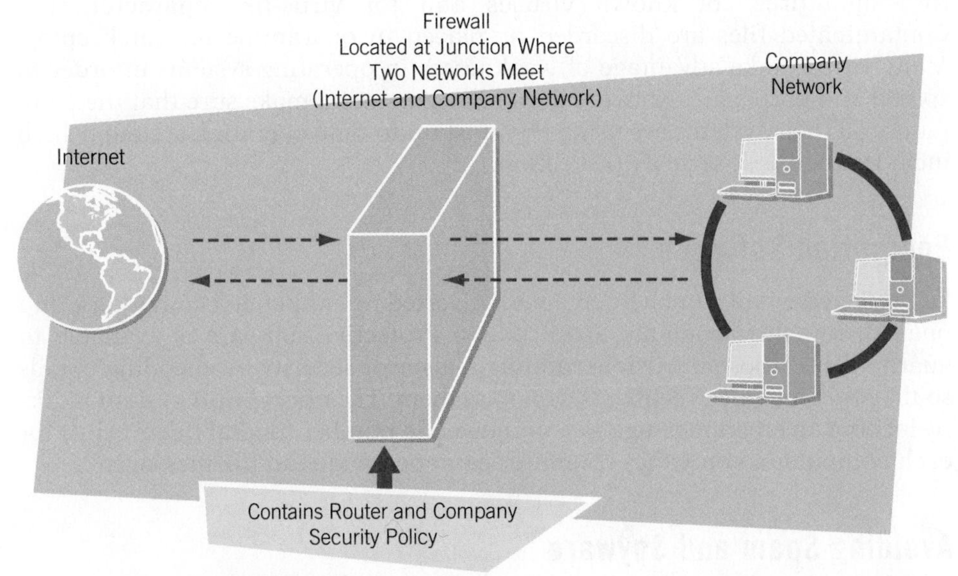
Firewall
Located at Junction Where
Two Networks Meet
(Internet and Company Network)
Company
Network
Internet
Contains Router and Company
Security Policy
What Happens Inside
1. Message enters firewall.
2. Message source is compared against security policy.
3. If message passes security policy, router sends the message to the other network.
Otherwise, router closes the gate to prevent entry.

Figure 13.6 How a firewall works.

the internet and the company's internal network—meet. It contains two components for filtering each incoming message:

- The company's *security policy*—Access rules that identify every type of message that the company doesn't want to have pass through the firewall.
- A *router*—A table of available routes or paths, a "traffic switch" that determines which routes or paths on the network to send each message through after it is tested against the security policy.

Only those messages that meet the conditions of the user's security policy are routed through the firewall and permitted to flow between the two networks. Messages that fail the access test are blocked and cannot flow between the two networks. As mentioned earlier, a firewall is used for protecting the BlackBerry wireless system from intrusion.

Preventing Identity Theft

Internet privacy experts say that a completely new identity verification system is needed to stop the rising tide of internet identity theft. One possibility is an "infocard," which would act like a credit card and would allow websites to verify a customer's identity without keeping personal information on the customer.[22] While foolproof prevention is impossible, steps can be taken to reduce the chance that you will be victimized. A visit to the Identity Theft Resource Center (www.idtheftcenter.org) is a valuable first step to get information on everything from scam alerts to victim issues—including assistance on lost and stolen wallets—to media resources, current laws, and prevention of identity theft in the workplace.

Preventing Viruses: Anti-virus Software

anti-virus software Products that protect systems by searching incoming email and data files for "signatures" of known viruses and for virus-like characteristics.

Combatting viruses, worms, and Trojan horses has become a major industry for systems designers and software developers. Installation of **anti-virus software** products protects systems by searching incoming email and data files for "signatures" of known viruses and for virus-like characteristics. Contaminated files are discarded or placed in quarantine for safekeeping. Many viruses take advantage of weaknesses in operating systems in order to spread and propagate. Network administrators must make sure that the computers on their systems are using the most up-to-date operating system, which includes the latest security protection.

Encryption Software

encryption system The use of a secret numerical code to scramble characters in a message, so that the message is not understandable during transmission.

Unprotected email can be intercepted, diverted to unintended computers, and opened, revealing contents to intruders. Protective software is available to guard against those intrusions, adding a layer of security by encoding emails so that only intended recipients can open them. The **encryption system** works by locking an email message to a unique code number (digital fingerprint) for each computer so only that computer can open and read the message.[23]

Avoiding Spam and Spyware

To help their employees avoid privacy invasion and to improve productivity, businesses often install anti-spyware and spam filtering software on their systems. Dozens of anti-spyware products provide protection—software such as Webroot's Spy Sweeper and the Microsoft AntiSpyware Beta—but they must be continually updated to keep pace with new spyware techniques.

While it cannot be prevented entirely, spam is abated by many **internet service providers (ISPs)** that ban the spamming of ISP subscribers. One ISP was recently awarded $1 billion in a lawsuit against 300 spammers that jammed the ISP system with an astounding 10 million emails a day. Anti-spam groups, too, promote the public's awareness of known spammers. The Spamhaus Project (www.spamhaus.org), for example, maintains a list—Register of Known Spam Operators (ROKSO)—of over 200 professional spammers who are responsible for over 80 percent of spam traffic in North America and Europe.

internet service providers (ISPs) Commercial firms that maintain a permanent connection to the internet and sell temporary connections to subscribers.

Test yourself on the material for this chapter at **www.pearsoned.ca/mybusinesslab.**

Summary of Learning Objectives

1. **Explain the importance of *information management* to business firms. Businesses possess a large amount of data—raw facts and figures—about their customers, competitors, and their own operations.** Converting this *data* into *information*—usefully interpreted data—is necessary for business success. The activities of business firms—for example, designing products and services, ensuring product delivery and cash flow, evaluating personnel, and creating advertising—require information. Because information is so important, companies have *information managers*, just as they have production, marketing, and finance managers. The goal of *information management* is to organize the firm's information resources to support business performance and outcomes.

2. **Understand what an *information system* is, who the key users of information systems are, and the most widely used types of information systems.** *An information system (IS)* transforms raw data into information and transmits it for use in decision making. IS managers must determine what information is needed, gather data and convert it into information, and see that the information goes to those people who need it. Control is important to ensure not only that the system operates correctly but also that data and information are transmitted through secure channels to people who really need them.

   The key users of information systems are top managers (who need information to carry out long-range planning for the entire organization), middle managers (who need summaries and analyses for setting intermediate and long-range goals for the departments or projects under their supervision), first-line managers (who need information to oversee the day-to-day details of their departments or projects), and knowledge workers (who need special information for conducting technical projects). Widely used types of information systems include *transaction processing systems (TPS)*, which are useful for routine transactions such as taking reservations and meeting payrolls); systems for knowledge workers, which include personal productivity tools such as word processing, document imaging, desktop publishing, and *computer-aided design (CAD)*; *management information systems (MIS)*, which support an organization's managers by providing daily reports, schedules, plans, and budgets; *decision support systems (DSSs)*, which assist the decision-making processes of middle and top-level managers; *executive support systems (ESSs)*, which are quick-reference, easy-to-access programs to assist upper-level managers; and *artificial intelligence (AI)* and *expert systems*, which are designed to imitate human thinking and behaviour and provide computer-based assistance in performing certain business activities.

3. **Explain how the rapid growth of information technologies has affected *organizational processes and operations*.** Information networks are leading to leaner organizations—businesses with fewer employees and simpler organizational structures—because networked firms can maintain electronic, rather than human, information links among employees and customers. Operations are more flexible because electronic networks allow businesses to offer greater product variety and faster delivery cycles. Aided by *intranets* and the *internet*, greater collaboration is possible, both among internal units and with outside firms. With access to the internet, company activities may be geographically scattered but remain coordinated through a networked system that provides better service for customers. Many businesses, for example, coordinate activities from one centralized location, but their deliveries

flow from several remote locations, often at lower cost. The global reach of *IT* is enabling business collaboration on a scale that was unheard of just a few years ago. Separation of the workplace and the company is more common because electronic links are replacing the need for physical proximity between the company and its workstations. Improved management processes are evident because managers have rapid access to more information about the current status of company activities and easier access to electronic tools for planning and decision making. Not only is IT improving existing businesses, it is helping to create entirely new businesses where none existed before. For existing large businesses, IT helps with the development of new products, new services, and reaching new clients.

4. **Describe the building blocks of *information technology*.** The building blocks of IT include the internet (the system of more than 100 million interconnected computers in over 100 countries around the world), the *World Wide Web* (the standardized code for accessing information and transmitting data over the internet), intranets (company-maintained internal websites linked throughout the firm), *extranets* (which allow outsiders limited access to a firm's internal information network), *electronic conferencing* (which allows groups of people to communicate simultaneously from various locations via email, phone, or video), *VSAT satellite communications* (sending and receiving signals from a satellite, exchanging voice, video, and data transmissions), *computer networks* (a group of two or more computers linked together by some form of cable or by wireless technology to share data or resources, such as a printer), *wide-area networks* (computers that are linked over long distances—province-wide or even nationwide—through telephone lines, microwave signals, or satellite communications), *local area networks* (computers that are linked in a smaller area, such as all of a firm's computers within a single building), *wireless networks* (which use airborne electronic signals to link network computers and devices), *Wi-Fi* (specific locations—called hotspots—such as coffee shops, hotels, and airport terminals that provide wireless internet connections for people on the go), *hardware* (the physical devices and components, including the computer), and *software* (the computer's operating system and application programs like computer graphics, *groupware*, spreadsheets, and word processing).

5. **Identify the *threats and risks* that are associated with the use of information technology by businesses.** The following threats and risks exist: (1) *Hackers* are cyber-criminals who gain unauthorized access to a computer or network, either to steal information, money, or property or to tamper with data. (2) *Software piracy* is the unauthorized use of software such as word processing and spreadsheets. (3) *Identity theft* refers to the unauthorized stealing of personal information (such as social insurance number and addresses) to get loans, credit cards, or other monetary benefits by impersonating the victim. (4) *Intellectual property* is a product of the mind—something produced by the intellect, with great expenditure of human effort—that has commercial value. Intellectual property theft includes the theft of things like a company's new product plans, new inventions, and new industrial processes, as well as illegal downloading of unpaid-for movies, music, and other resources from file-swapping networks. (5) A *computer virus* exists in a file that attaches itself to a program and migrates from computer to computer as a shared program or as an email attachment. Worms are a particular kind of virus that travel from computer to computer within networked computer systems without your needing to open any software to spread the contaminated file. (6) *Spyware* is downloaded by users who are lured by "free" software. (7) *Spam* is junk email sent to a mailing list or a newsgroup (an online discussion group).

6. **Describe the ways in which businesses protect themselves from the threats and risks posed by information technology.** Businesses guard against intrusion with a variety of tactics, including the following: (1) *Firewalls* are security systems with special software or hardware devices designed to keep computers safe from hackers. One possibility is an *"infocard,"* which acts like a credit card and allows websites to verify a customer's identity without keeping personal information on the customer. (2) Installation of *anti-virus software* products protects systems by searching incoming email and data files for "signatures" of known viruses and virus-like characteristics. Contaminated files are discarded or placed in quarantine for safekeeping. (3) An *encryption system* works by locking an email message to a unique code number (digital fingerprint) for each computer so only that computer can open and read the message. (4) To help their employees avoid privacy invasion and to improve productivity, businesses often install anti-spyware and spam filtering software on their systems. Dozens of anti-spyware products provide protection, but they must be continually updated to keep pace with new spyware techniques.

Key Terms

anti-virus software (p. 428)
artificial intelligence (AI) (p. 414)
client-server network (p. 420)
computer graphics programs (p. 422)
computer network (p. 420)
computer-aided design (CAD) (p. 412)
computer-aided manufacturing (CAM) (p. 413)
data (p. 410)
decision support system (DSS) (p. 413)
electronic conferencing (p. 419)
electronic spreadsheets (p. 423)
encryption system (p. 428)
executive support system (ESS) (p. 414)
expert system (p. 414)
extranet (p. 419)
firewall (p. 427)
groupware (p. 423)
hackers (p. 424)
hardware (p. 421)
identity theft (p. 425)
information (p. 410)
information management (p. 410)
information manager (p. 410)
information system (IS) (p. 411)
information technology (IT) (p. 414)
intellectual property (p. 426)
internet (p. 419)
internet service providers (ISPs) (p. 429)
intranet (p. 419)
local area networks (LANs) (p. 420)
management information systems (MIS) (p. 413)
mass-customization (p. 417)
software (p. 422)
software piracy (p. 425)
spam (p. 427)
spyware (p. 426)
system operations personnel (p. 412)
transaction processing systems (TPS) (p. 412)
VSAT satellite communications (p. 419)
wide area networks (WANs) (p. 420)
Wi-Fi (wireless fidelity) (p. 421)
wireless local area network (wireless LAN or WLAN) (p. 421)
wireless wide area networks (WWANs) (p. 421)
World Wide Web (p. 419)

Questions for Analysis

1. Why must a business manage information as a resource?
2. How can an electronic conferencing system increase productivity and efficiency?
3. Why do the four levels of user groups in an organization need different kinds of information from the IS?
4. In what ways are local area networks (LANs) different from or similar to wide area networks (WANs)?
5. Give two examples (other than those in this chapter) of each of the major types of business application programs.
6. Describe three or four activities in which you regularly engage that might be made easier by technology like that found in a global positioning system (GPS) or a personal digital assistant (PDA).
7. Give three examples (other than those in this chapter) of how a company can become leaner by adopting a networked IS.

Application Exercises

1. Visit a company and interview an individual who is knowledgeable about the firm's management information system. Determine what problems and opportunities exist because of the system.
2. Describe the IS at your school. Identify its components and architecture. What features either promote or inhibit collaboration?
3. Visit a small business in your community to investigate the ways it's using communication technologies and the ways it plans to use them in the future. Prepare a report for class presentation.

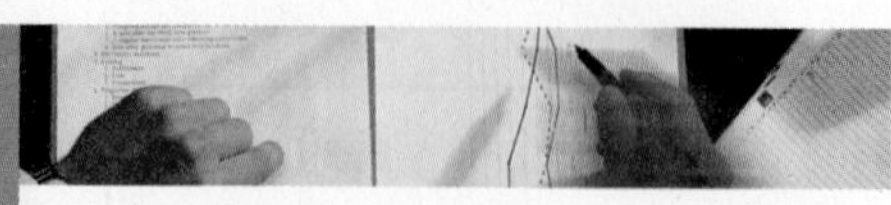

Building Your Business Skills

The Art and Science of Point-and-Click Research

The Purpose of the Assignment

To introduce students to internet search sites.

Background

In a recent survey of nearly 2000 web users, two-thirds said they used the web to obtain work-related information. With an estimated 320 million pages of information on the web, the challenge for business users is fairly obvious—how to find what they're looking for.

Assignment

You'll need a computer and access to the internet to complete this exercise.

Step 1

Get together with three classmates and decide on a business-related research topic. Choose a topic that interests you—for example, "Business Implications of the Most Recent Census," "Labour Disputes in Professional Sports," or "Marketing Music Lessons and Instruments to Parents of Young Children."

Step 2

Search the following sites for information on your topic, dividing them among group members to speed the process:

Alta Vista www.altavista.com
Ask.com www.ask.com
Dogpile www.dogpile.com
Excite www.excite.com
Google www.google.ca
Hotbot www.hotbot.com
Go www.go.com
Lycos www.lycos.com
Metacrawler www.metacrawler.com
Northern Light www.northernlight.com
Yahoo! www.yahoo.com

Take notes as you search so that you can explain your findings to other group members.

Step 3

Working as a group, answer the following questions about your collective search.

1. Which sites were the easiest to use?
2. Which sites offered the most helpful results? What specific factors made these sites better than the others?
3. Which sites offered the least helpful results? What were the problems?
4. Why is it important to learn the special code words or symbols—called operators—that target a search? (Operators are words like AND, OR, and NOT that narrow search queries. For example, using AND in a search tells the system that all words must appear in the results—for example, American AND Management AND Association.)

Questions for Discussion

1. Research the differences between search engines and search directories. Then place the sites listed in Step 2 in the proper category. Which did you find more helpful in this exercise, search engines or search directories?
2. Why is it important to learn how to use the search site "Help" function?
3. Based on your personal career goals, how do you think that mastering web research techniques might help you in the future?
4. How has the web changed the nature of business research?

Exercising Your Ethics: Team Exercise

Supplying the Right Answers

The Situation

Networked systems facilitate information sharing among companies and often involve sensitive customer data. This exercise asks you to consider ethical issues that might arise when firms are developing information technologies for use in networked systems.

The Dilemma

Home Sweet Home-e (HSH-e) was an ebusiness start-up that sold virtually everything in home furnishings—from linens and towels to cleaning supplies and furniture. From home computers, HSH-e members could shop in virtual storefronts, chat online with other shoppers, talk live with virtual store clerks, and pay electronically at a one-stop website. In reality, HSH-e was a virtual store: a network of numerous suppliers located around the country, each specializing in a particular line of goods. The network was connected by a centrally controlled information technology that HSH-e developed, owned, and operated. Once a customer's order was placed, suppliers instantaneously received information on what to ship, where to ship it, and how much to charge.

HSH-e chose only suppliers who guaranteed fast, reliable deliveries and promised to supply HSH-e exclusively. The linen supplier, for example, could not supply products to other home-furnishings ebusinesses. In return, the supplier was guaranteed all HSH-e orders for linen products. As HSH-e grew, suppliers stood to gain more business and to prosper in an expanding etail industry. As it turns out, some prospective suppliers refused to join the network and others in the network were discontinued by HSH-e for failing to expand fast enough to keep up with demand.

Team Activity

Assemble a group of four students and assign each group member to one of the following roles:

- customer of HSH-e
- employee of HSH-e
- supplier of HSH-e
- owner of HSH-e

Questions for Discussion

1. Before discussing the situation with your group, and from the perspective of your assigned role, what are the underlying ethical issues, if any, in this situation?
2. Assemble the group and have each member list the ethical issues that he or she identified. Did the different roles result in different kinds of ethical issues being identified? If so, why might role differences result in dissimilar priorities on ethical issues?
3. For the various ethical issues that were identified, decide as a group which one is second most important for HSH-e to resolve. Which is second most important? Explain your group's reasoning.
4. What does your group finally recommend be done to resolve the most important ethical issue? And to resolve the second most important ethical issue?
5. Consider past suppliers who have been discontinued or have withdrawn from the HSH-e network. Do they face any ethical issues involving HSH-e customers? Involving HSH-e operations? Involving other HSH-e suppliers?
6. Suppose you work at HSH-e and discover a non-network supplier that is more attractive than one of the company's existing suppliers. What ethical considerations do you face in deciding whether or not to replace an existing supplier?

For additional cases and exercise material, go to www.pearsoned.ca/mybusinesslab.

Concluding Case 13-1

Sharing the Wealth

Janus Friis and Niklas Zennström are the Baltic programmers who invented Kazaa—the most downloaded file-sharing program in the world—which provides a free market for videos, music, and porn. With lawyers tracking them, these elusive internet pirates moved quietly into London, then secretly to a favourite hangout—the NoKu bar—in Tallinn (Estonia's capital) for a moment of relaxation, and farther to Sweden under cover of darkness for secret strategy meetings. "They've resulted in significant damage to the record industry," says Matt Oppenheim, head legal officer for the Recording Industry Association of America (RIAA). While Oppenheim—the chief Kazaa hunter—doggedly tried to serve them legal papers, Friis and Zennström launched an even grander software application called Skype, which is revolutionizing telephoning.

Skype—Zennström's unique version of what the industry calls Voice Over Internet Protocol (VOIP)—is software that provides nearly costless PC-to-PC telephoning. Once it's downloaded onto your computer, a window pops up so you can search the directory for other registered users. Crystal-clear calls are possible so long as both parties have microphones and are connected to the internet. In a recent six-month period more than six million users in 170 countries downloaded Skype. Zennström hopes for and—frighteningly for competitors—is likely to get another 25 million downloads very soon. Why? The download is free and Skype's cost to add a new user is just one-tenth of a cent, compared to $400 to add a new customer at Vonage—the biggest independent VOIP service provider in the United States. Skype's cost advantage stems from tricks Friis and Zennström learned while experimenting with Kazaa. It uses peer-to-peer technology, in which digital files are stored on subscribers' computers rather than on the company's central computer, allowing Skype to grow without adding much infrastructure to deal with the millions of files.

What impact, then, is in store for the telecom industry? "I knew it was over when I downloaded Skype," says Michael Powell, chairman of the U.S. Federal Communications Commission. "When the inventors of Kazaa are distributing for free a little program that you can use to talk to anybody else, and the quality is fantastic, and it's free—it's over. The world will change now inevitably." Once millions of callers get used to the idea of free phone calling, it will be a hard habit to reverse. So, Friis and Zennström's business plan has a global reach with a system capable of handling six billion customers. "We're building the next great communications platform," says Skype's product manager, Andreas Sjolund.

Consumers are not the only ones seeing the massive cost advantage of using Skype technology. As we saw in the Business Accountability box, social networking is a very cost-effective way for companies to reach their target markets. Companies are also turning to social networking technologies to communicate with their employees and to ensure that all employees are aware of the company's efforts, mission, and objectives. For example, Steve Mandel—who started a management training and consulting company—says that his 65 employees use Skype to stay connected to the office as well as their clients. "If Skype didn't exist, our phone bills would be, I'm guessing, 50 percent to 100 percent higher than they are now," says Mandel.

Skype has allowed small- and medium-sized companies to expand nationally without the added burden of phone costs. The new use of the software is expected to allow employees to make domestic and international calls using regular office telephones instead of a headset plugged in to a personal computer. In 2009, Skype announced a version of its internet software that connects to corporate phone systems. The company used to charge about 2.1 cents per minute for calls to cellphones and fixed lines, but calls from computers to phone systems using the Skype software will be free (similar to what it now charges for its consumer service).

Addressing the change in user rates is simply acknowledgement of the fact that about 35 percent of Skype customers already use the service for business purposes. Skype is hoping to take advantage of the downturn in the economy by targeting small- and medium-sized companies that would be most interested in reducing their phone bills. This new shift in focus comes in response to eBay's purchase of Skype in 2005 for $2.6 billion in cash and stock. In 2008, eBay reported $550 million in revenue from the uses of Skype technology, but investors are pressuring the company to make more money or sell the Skype part of the business.

The $200-billion business communications market is extremely competitive, but Skype, with its 405 million users, has a competitive advantage. Being first to market has allowed the company to establish itself as a brand leader, which has also created consumer perceptions that the service is reliable, of high quality, and secure. It is important to ensure that security problems (such as system hackers) will not breach consumer confidentiality. Lawrence Orans, a Gartner analyst, warns of the potential risk to businesses that make use of the software. Because the software involves the internet and requires frequent updates, it is always beneficial to invest in "operational and support costs" to offset the possible risks. However, even with security measures in place, there is always the risk of someone hacking into the system and gaining access to confidential information or injecting a virus into the company's system.

Questions for Discussion

1. With no geographic or political boundaries, who is accountable for how the Skype system is used, its growth, its impact on competition, and regulation of the technology?
2. In the absence of uniform international regulations, does accountability reside with the technology's users or the service providers?
3. Given what you know of Skype and its competitive environment, what industries, in addition to those mentioned in the case, might be good prospects for adopting Skype technologies? Support your answer.
4. When Michael Powell, chairman of the U.S. Federal Communications Commission, saw how Skype worked, he said, "I knew it was over when I downloaded Skype." What do you think he meant?

Concluding Case 13-2

Internet Wars

There is an international drug war going on. No, not the one against heroin and cocaine. This drug war pits manufacturers of cigarettes and prescription drugs against internet companies that sell these products at cut-rate prices. Here's the story, first for cigarettes, and then for prescription drugs.

Cigarettes

During the last few years, many companies have begun selling cigarettes on the internet. Italian brothers Gianpaolo and Carlo Messina, who operate Yesmoke.ch in a duty-free customs location in Balerna, Switzerland, near the Swiss-Italian border, are typical. They buy name-brand cigarettes like Camels and Marlboros from duty-free airport retailers for less than $1 a pack, then ship them to customers (mostly in the United States) who have placed orders on their internet site. Although it is illegal for U.S. citizens to buy cigarettes without paying taxes, anyone with a credit card can buy these cigarettes. Customers get their cigarettes at far below normal retail costs because the Messinas don't pay any cigarette taxes to U.S. jurisdictions and can therefore charge much lower prices than retailers do.

In an attempt to stop Yesmoke's activities, Philip Morris filed a lawsuit against the company, charging unfair business practices and patent infringement. Yesmoke ignored the suit and a judge ruled against Yesmoke in a default judgment. But Yesmoke says it is not breaking Swiss law by simply exporting cigarettes, and since it does not operate in the United States, it is not bound by U.S. law. An interesting twist to the story is Yesmoke's claim that Philip Morris is actually selling cigarettes to Yesmoke from one of its factories in the Philippines that produces too much for the local market there. Yesmoke claims it buys the excess cigarettes at a deep discount. Philip Morris denies that it is selling cigarettes to Yesmoke, but the European Union recently charged Philip Morris with complicity in smuggling by intentionally overproducing cigarettes at some of its European factories. As part of a larger anti-smuggling agreement with the EU, Philip Morris agreed to pay $1.25 billion (over 12 years), and the charges were dropped.

In 2004, New York City also filed a lawsuit against Yesmoke, saying that the company owed the city $17 million in back taxes on sales to residents of New York. Whether the city will ever be able to collect those back taxes is doubtful. U.S. states are very concerned that internet sales of cigarettes will prevent them from collecting millions of dollars in cigarette taxes, money that they badly need. Traditional retailers are also concerned, since internet retailers will cut into their business.

Prescription Drugs

For many years, Americans who live in border cities have been coming to Canada to purchase prescription drugs because these drugs are cheaper in Canada. When only a

relatively small number of Americans came across the border to buy drugs, not much of a fuss was made. But the internet has made it possible for Americans living anywhere in the United States to purchase Canadian drugs without even coming to Canada. Instead, they can simply go online and order the drugs (they must provide a U.S. doctor's prescription).

In 2003, the U.S. House of Representatives approved a bill that allowed Americans to import drugs from 25 different nations (including Canada). This gave a big boost to Canadian internet pharmacies. All this demand for Canadian drugs has created a group of Canadian entrepreneurs who want to satisfy it (and, of course, make a profit doing so). Both the big drug companies and the Canadian Pharmacists Association (CPhA) oppose internet pharmacies. Depending on who you talk to, their reasons are either selfish (they fear loss of profit) or caring (they are concerned about the health and safety of others).

The big drug companies say that there are several problems with respect to internet pharmacies:

- The safety of drugs is compromised when they are sold over the internet because the internet pharmacist doesn't know if the patient is taking other drugs that might interfere with the patient's prescription request.
- The internet system can't easily verify that the person wanting the prescription filled hasn't already had it filled from some other internet pharmacy as well.
- The internet system can't verify whether the prescription is authentic.
- When drugs are shipped, they can be exposed to various hazards that might reduce their effectiveness.

The internet pharmacies respond to these claims with several counter-arguments:

- The drug companies won't sell to Canadian-based internet pharmacies because the drug companies will make lower profit margins than if they sold to U.S. pharmacies.
- Internet pharmacies are providing patients with more affordable prescription drugs; without these drugs, the quality of life of these patients would be much lower.
- Traditional pharmacists oppose internet pharmacies simply because they are resisting new ways of doing things.

Most of the big drug companies now refuse to sell any of their products to internet pharmacies, and the Canadian Competition Bureau concluded that no laws were violated by this decision. When the drug companies refused to ship their products to internet pharmacies or to the wholesalers who were supplying them, it was assumed that internet pharmacies would have great trouble getting supplies of prescription drugs. But they have continued to get access to drugs and sell those drugs to people in the United States.

How do they do it? By being very entrepreneurial and establishing elaborate supply networks, that's how. More specifically, internet pharmacies are getting their supplies from hundreds of traditional neighbourhood Canadian pharmacies. But since the big drug companies carefully examine orders from pharmacies looking for suspicious "spikes" in demand, the internet pharmacies are very careful about ordering only small amounts from traditional pharmacies. They also pay these traditional pharmacies a "commission" to supply them. These commissions range from 5 to 15 percent.

Late in 2004, Health Minister Ujjal Dosanjh announced that the government was considering shutting down internet pharmacies to protect both the pricing regime and the supply of prescription drugs for Canadians. If the internet pharmacies were shut down, it would cause the loss of thousands of jobs that were created in the industry. In June 2005, however, Dosanjh backed off from his earlier threats and instead announced that legislation would be introduced to protect Canada's drug supply by allowing the government to shut down bulk exports of prescription medicines from internet pharmacies. The legislation would allow Canadian internet pharmacies to continue to fill prescriptions from individuals in the United States. The internet pharmacies breathed a sigh of relief upon hearing this announcement, because it was a much less threatening decision than the one that Dosanjh had been considering in late 2004.

Questions for Discussion

1. Explain how the internet has facilitated the growth of companies selling cigarettes and prescription drugs.
2. Should internet cigarette sellers and internet pharmacies be allowed to operate? What regulations, if any, should the Canadian government put on these companies?
3. Would you buy cigarettes from an internet seller? Would you buy prescription drugs from an internet pharmacy? Why or why not?

4. Critique each of the arguments that are being made by the drug companies and the Canadian Pharmacists Association. Then do the same for each of the arguments being made by the internet pharmacies. On balance, which arguments do you think are the most compelling? Explain.
5. Develop arguments for and against selling cigarettes on the internet.

apter 14

Understanding Accounting Issues

After reading this chapter, you should be able to:

1. Explain the role of *accountants* and distinguish among the three types of professional accountants in Canada.
2. Describe how the *accounting equation* is used.
3. Describe three basic *financial statements* and show how they reflect the activity and financial condition of a business.
4. Explain the key standards and principles for reporting financial statements.
5. Explain how computing *financial ratios* can help in analyzing the financial strengths of a business.
6. Explain some of the special issues that arise in *international accounting.*

Accounting for Pensions

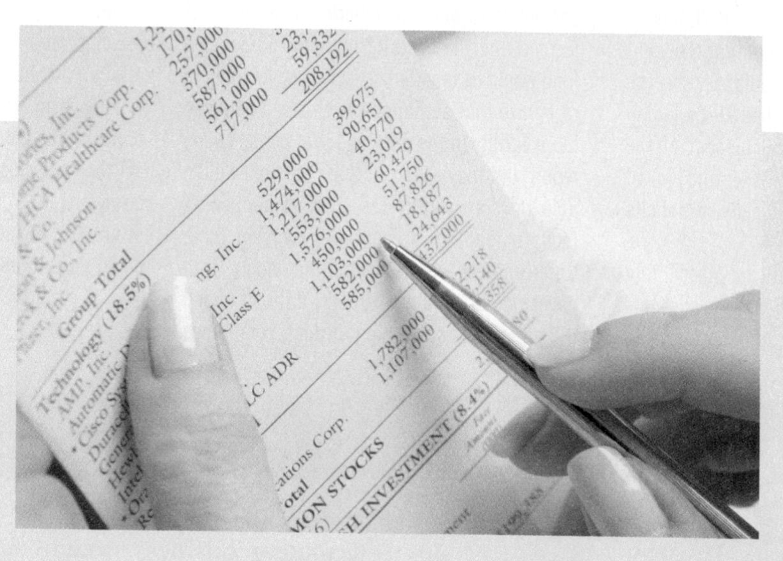

Traditional pension plans have historically been defined benefit plans, that is, the company promises to pay a certain defined amount of money to employees when they retire. But the dramatic decline of the stock market in 2008 created large pension shortfalls because the market value of the assets that pension plans held declined sharply. The Ontario Teachers' Pension Plan, for example, posted an 18 percent loss in 2008 (the fund's value declined by $21 billion). As of 2008, GM Canada's pension plan was underfunded by more than $6 billion, which means that workers would receive only 50 percent of what they thought they were going to get. The Canada Pension Plan has also been hard hit; during the second quarter of fiscal 2009, the CPP fund declined in value by 6.7 percent ($7.9 billion).

Watson Wyatt Worldwide reported that in 2007 the typical pension plan was 96 percent funded (that is, the market value of a pension plan's assets nearly equalled its liabilities), but in 2008 the typical pension plan was only 69 percent funded. There were predictions that 2009 would be better and that pension fund returns would be about 7.5 percent, but even if that rate of return could be sustained, it would take 15 years for pension funds to return to fully funded status.

There are also problems in funding retiree *benefits* (not pensions). A study of 71 of Canada's largest companies showed that their liabilities for retiree benefits amounted to $16 billion. In one recent year at Suncor Energy Inc., for example, the company's benefits liability was $98 million (almost as much as its pension liability of $99 million). With baby boomers living longer and with large numbers of them heading into retirement, the situation for both retiree pensions and retiree benefits is likely to get worse before it gets better.

The problems in pension plans have been caused by a variety of factors, but two stand out. First, recent returns on investments held by pension plans have been much lower than anticipated. In the 1990s, returns on pension plan investments averaged 11 percent (higher than the 7.5 percent that had been predicted). But during the economic downturn of 2001–03, the average rate of return for pension plan investments was just 3.1 percent, well below the 7 percent that had been assumed. And during 2008, pension funds *lost* 15 to 30 percent of their value. This situation was made even worse because companies began to invest more heavily in equities as a result of their positive experience in the stock market boom of the 1990s. In 1990, 64 percent of pension assets were invested in fixed-income securities and only 36 percent in the riskier equities. By 2004, however, 56 percent of pension assets were invested in equities and only 37 percent in fixed-income securities.

Second, because pension plan investments had achieved such high returns in the 1990s, many companies took pension plan contribution "holidays" and did not contribute anything to the plans they were sponsoring. When the lower investment returns of the twenty-first century started showing up, pension surpluses quickly became pension deficits. In retrospect, companies realize they should not have taken contribution holidays.

The crisis in defined benefit pension plans has caused employers to examine alternative ways to deal with pensions. The simplest solution is to drop defined *benefit* pension plans and instead offer employees defined *contribution pension* plans. When the latter is used, the company's liability is known, but the value of the pension plan when a person retires is unknown (its value is determined solely by the rate of return that the investments in the plan have achieved). Defined contribution plans reduce uncertainty for the company, but they create more uncertainty for retirees.

Companies are increasingly shifting to defined contribution pension plans. In the United States, for example, there were 112 000 defined benefit plans in 1985, but now there are only about 29 000. The move away from defined benefit plans is also occurring in Canada, although at a slower rate. But that is likely to change, since Canadian legislation requires companies to bear the full financial burden of pension deficits. The current crisis in defined benefit plans means that, over the next five years, billions of extra dollars will have to be put in to those plans to make up for past investment losses. Companies therefore have an incentive to move away from defined benefit plans and toward defined contribution plans, because with the latter they at least know what their contribution requirements are.

Canadian accounting rules may also need to be re-examined. Under current rules, companies can delay recognizing changes in the value of their pension plans. Using a practice called "smoothing," companies can

▶

spread the reporting of changes over several years. When stock markets were booming, no one scrutinized pension plans much because their value was going up. But when stock markets started dropping, large liabilities began building up (but companies kept that information off their balance sheets). National Bank Financial studied 79 Canadian companies—representing 80 percent of the capitalization of the S&P/TSX—and found that their off-balance sheet pension deficits totalled $21 billion.

Canadian and international accounting regulators are working on changes to accounting rules that will bring more realism to pension reporting. The most obvious change involves ending the practice of smoothing and reporting pension fund returns as they actually take place. This means that income from the pension fund would be reported as investment income and the costs of running the pension fund would be reported as expenses. Regulators recognize that a change like this will increase the volatility in the earnings that corporations report, but they point out that investors will be able to more clearly see what is happening (good or bad) in a company's pension fund. Unfortunately, the economic problems that developed in 2008 made it very difficult to end the practice of smoothing. In fact, companies were given even more time (10 years) to make up for pension shortfalls.

For long-term investors such as the Canada Pension Plan (CPP) Investment Board, understanding how changing regulatory regimes and disruptive technologies could affect a business is critical to the assessment of long-term risk and return. Companies and boards that have yet to examine the quality of their disclosures should undertake this analysis. In a risk-constrained world, their ability to attract stable, long-term capital could depend on it. ◆

How will this help me?

By understanding the material presented in this chapter, you'll benefit in three ways: (1) If you're an *entrepreneur* thinking about starting your own business, you'll discover your obligations for reporting your firm's financial status; (2) as an *employee*, you'll learn how to evaluate your company's financial condition and its prospects for the future; and (3) as an interested *citizen*, you'll learn about accounting ethics and the regulatory requirements for maintaining the public's trust in the Canadian business system.

In this chapter, we focus on the development and use of accounting information. We begin by looking at the role of accountants in providing information. We examine how the accounting equation is used in accounting and describe the three basic financial statements. We conclude the chapter with an explanation of the key standards and principles for reporting financial information.

What Is Accounting?

accounting A comprehensive system for collecting, analyzing, and communicating financial information.

bookkeeping Recording accounting transactions.

Accounting is a comprehensive information system for collecting, analyzing, and communicating financial information. As such, it is a system for measuring business performance and translating those measures into information for management decisions. **Bookkeeping** is just one phase of accounting—the recording of accounting transactions. Clearly, accounting is much more comprehensive than bookkeeping because accounting involves more than just the recording of information.

Accounting also uses performance measures to prepare performance reports for owners, the public, and regulatory agencies. To meet these objectives, accountants keep records of such transactions as taxes paid, income received, and expenses incurred, and they analyze the effects of these transactions on particular business activities. By sorting, analyzing, and recording thousands of transactions, accountants can determine how well a business is being managed and how financially strong it is. As the opening case shows, the accounting system can produce distorted results that, in turn, can create huge problems for both owners and managers.

Because businesses engage in many thousands of transactions, ensuring consistent, dependable financial information is mandatory. This is the job of the **accounting information system (AIS)**—an organized procedure for identifying, measuring, recording, and retaining financial information so that it can be used in accounting statements and management reports. The system includes all the people, reports, computers, procedures, and resources for compiling financial transactions.[1]

accounting information system (AIS) An organized procedure for identifying, measuring, recording, and retaining financial information so that it can be used in accounting statements and management reports.

There are numerous users of accounting information:

- *Business managers* use accounting information to set goals, develop plans, set budgets, and evaluate future prospects.
- *Employees and unions* use accounting information to get paid and to plan for and receive such benefits as health care, insurance, vacation time, and retirement pay.
- *Investors and creditors* use accounting information to estimate returns to stockholders, to determine a company's growth prospects, and to decide if the company is a good credit risk before investing or lending.
- *Tax authorities* use accounting information to plan for tax inflows, to determine the tax liabilities of individuals and businesses, and to ensure that correct amounts are paid in a timely fashion.
- *Government regulatory agencies* rely on accounting information to fulfill their duties; the provincial securities commissions, for example, require firms to file financial disclosures so that potential investors have valid information about a company's financial status.

Who Are Accountants and What Do They Do?

At the head of the AIS is the **controller**, who manages all the firm's accounting activities. As chief accounting officer, the controller ensures that the accounting system provides the reports and statements needed for planning, controlling, and decision-making activities. This broad range of activities requires different types of accounting specialists. In this section, we will begin by distinguishing between the two main fields of accounting, *financial* and *managerial.* Then we will discuss the different functions and activities of the three professional accounting groups in Canada.

controller The individual who manages all the firm's accounting activities.

Financial and Managerial Accounting

In any company, two fields of accounting—financial and managerial—can be distinguished by the different users they serve. As we have just seen, it is both convenient and accurate to classify users of accounting information as users outside the company and users inside the company. This same distinction allows us to categorize accounting systems as either *financial* or *managerial.*

Explain the role of *accountants* and distinguish among the three types of professional accountants in Canada. 1

Financial Accounting

A firm's **financial accounting system** is concerned with external users of information—consumer groups, unions, shareholders, and government agencies. It prepares and publishes income statements and balance sheets at regular intervals. All of these documents focus on the activities of *the company as a whole*, rather than on individual departments or divisions.

financial accounting system The process whereby interested groups are kept informed about the financial condition of a firm.

In reporting data, financial accountants must conform to standard reporting formats and procedures imposed by both the accounting profession and government regulatory agencies. This requirement helps ensure that users can clearly compare information, whether from many different companies or from the same company at different times. The information in such reports is mostly *historical*, that is, it summarizes financial transactions that have occurred during past accounting periods.

Managerial Accounting

managerial (or management) accounting Internal procedures that alert managers to problems and aid them in planning and decision making.

In contrast, **managerial (or management) accounting** serves internal users. Managers at all levels need information to make decisions for their departments, to monitor current projects, and to plan for future activities. Other employees, too, need accounting information. Engineers, for instance, want to know costs for materials and production so they can make product or operations improvements. To set performance goals, salespeople need data on past sales by geographic region. Purchasing agents use information on materials costs to negotiate terms with suppliers.

Reports to these users serve *the company's individual units*, whether departments, projects, plants, or divisions. Internal reports may be designed in any form that will assist internal users in planning, decision making, and controlling. Furthermore, as *projections* and *forecasts* of both financial data and business activities, internal reports are an extremely important part of the management accounting system: They are forward-looking rather than historical in nature.

Professional Accountants

Users of financial statements want to be confident that the accountants who have prepared them have a high level of expertise and credibility. Three professional accounting organizations have developed in Canada to certify accounting expertise.

Chartered Accountants

chartered accountant (CA) An individual who has met certain experience and education requirements and has passed a licensing examination; acts as an outside accountant for other firms.

The Canadian Institute of Chartered Accountants (CICA) grants the **chartered accountant (CA)** designation. To achieve this designation, a person must earn a university degree, then complete an educational program and pass a national exam. About half of all CAs work in CA firms that offer accounting services to the public; the other half work in government or industry. CA firms typically provide audit, tax, and management services (see Table 14.1 for a list of the top 10 CA firms in Canada). CAs focus on external financial reporting, that is, certifying for various interested parties (shareholders, lenders, Canada Customs and Revenue Agency, and so on) that the financial records of a company accurately reflect the true financial condition of the firm. In 2008, there were about 74 000 CAs in Canada.[2]

Certified General Accountants

certified general accountant (CGA) An individual who has completed an education program and passed a national exam; works in private industry or a CGA firm.

The Certified General Accountants Association of Canada grants the **certified general accountant (CGA)** designation. To become a CGA, a person must complete an education program and pass a national exam; to be eligible, a person must have an accounting job with a company. Formerly, CGAs were not allowed to audit the financial statements of publicly held companies, but this is rapidly changing, and now CGAs can audit corporate financial statements in most provinces. Most CGAs work in private companies, but there are a few CGA firms. Some CGAs also work in CA firms. CGAs also focus on external financial reporting and emphasize the use of the computer as a management accounting tool. From time to time, CGA Canada commissions reports on important issues such as pensions (see the opening case). In 2008, there were about 71 000 CGAs in Canada, the Caribbean, and China.[3]

Table 14.1 Top 10 Chartered Accountant Firms in Canada, 2008

Company	Annual Revenues (in millions of $)
1. Deloitte & Touche LLP	$1419
2. KPMG LLP	1122
3. PricewaterhouseCoopers LLP	1062
4. Ernst & Young LLP	856
5. Grant Thornton Canada	442
6. BDO Dunwoody LLP	343
7. Meyers Norris Penhy LLP	260
8. Collins Barrow National Cooperative Inc.	126
9. RSM Richter LLP	117
10. HLB/Schwartz Levitsky Feldman	48

Certified Management Accountants

The Society of Management Accountants of Canada grants the **certified management accountant (CMA)** designation. To achieve the designation, a person must a have university degree, pass a two-part national entrance examination, and complete a strategic leadership program while gaining practical experience in a management accounting environment. CMAs work in organizations of all sizes and focus on applying best management practices in all the operations of a business. CMAs bring a strong market-focus to strategic management and resource deployment, synthesizing and analyzing financial and non-financial information to help organizations maintain a competitive advantage. CMAs emphasize the role of accountants in the planning and overall strategy of the firm in which they work. In 2008, there were about 40 000 CMAs in Canada, with an additional 10 000 students in the program.[4]

certified management accountant (CMA) An individual who has completed a university degree, passed a national examination, and completed a strategic leadership program; works in industry and focuses on internal management accounting.

Accounting Services

CAs and CGAs usually perform several accounting services for their clients. The most common of these are auditing, tax services, and management services.

Auditing

In an **audit**, the accountant examines a company's AIS to determine whether the company's financial reports fairly present its financial operations. Companies normally must provide audited financial reports when applying for loans or when selling stock. The audit will determine whether the firm has controls to prevent errors or fraud from going undetected. Auditors also examine receipts such as shipping documents, cancelled cheques, payroll records, and cash receipts records. In some cases, an auditor may physically check inventories, equipment, or other assets, even if it means descending 200 metres underground in a lead mine.

audit An accountant's examination of a company's financial records to determine whether it used proper procedures to prepare its financial reports.

Detecting fraud is not the primary purpose of audits, but in recent years there has been much publicity about the alleged failure of auditors to detect fraud. Therefore, when audits are being conducted, sometimes **forensic accountants** are used to track down hidden funds in business firms. Because white-collar crime is on the increase, the number of forensic accountants has increased in recent years. Forensic accountants were used to examine Swiss bank accounts for assets deposited by victims of Nazi persecution during the

forensic accountant An accountant who tracks down hidden funds in business firms, usually as part of a criminal investigation.

Business Accountability

Who's Accountable for Offshore Oversight?

Planning on an accounting career for job security? If so, you may want to take a second look at what's happening with business process outsourcing (BPO), which is the use of third parties to perform services that a company would otherwise do internally. As we saw in Chapter 2, outsourcing is an increasingly popular option for businesses. Universities and hospitals outsource cafeteria operations to food service firms, retailers outsource human resources activities to HR firms, and manufacturing companies outsource shipping and delivery activities to companies like UPS and FedEx. Offshoring is also popular for professional services that have low customer contact and require little customization, such as radiology analysis (e.g., x-rays, CT scans, MRIs), computer software development, and engineering (e.g., product design, testing, and analysis). Worldwide, the outsourcing of finance and accounting services exceeds $40 billion.

The basic philosophy of outsourcing is that businesses do best when they focus on their core activities rather than getting sidetracked into non-core activities. John Gillespie, a partner at Accenture, says that outsourcing of accounting services makes sense because there are a lot of people involved in accounting activities, and there is much routine work that doesn't need to be done by highly paid executives. Accounting's basic number-crunching activities—payroll, accounts receivable, accounts payable, cash accounting, and inventory valuation—are easily outsourced because once the overseas outsourcing provider learns Canadian or U.S. accounting rules, they apply equally to all customers. Data for these activities are transmitted for offshore processing, and results are then transmitted back to the outsourcer.

In addition to cost savings, clients also expect more accurate and faster reporting from outsourcing. On the downside, however, outsourcing increases the risk to data security. Placing private information in faraway hands, especially in the absence of clear-cut legislation on data privacy and security (as in India), increases the chance of violating the client's trust in accounting integrity. In determining what practices to employ for protecting clients, some advocates suggest that, at the very least, accountants seek clients' permission for using offshore outsourcing. While the accounting profession searches for answers to these outsourcing-related issues, one principle remains clear: The use of third parties in no way diminishes the accountants' accountability for privacy, confidentiality, and security to their clients.

India, with its abundance of well-educated and highly skilled employees, has become the back office of the world. Accounting skills are plentiful, and salaries average just one-fifth of those in Western countries. With over one-third of its university graduates speaking more than two languages fluently, and many speaking as many as six, India is well positioned as an international outsourcing provider. Its Chartered Accountant designation for ensuring professionalism is similar in rigour and esteem to the CPA certification in the United States. The accounting firm Deloitte Touche Tohmatsu forecasts that by 2008 India's financial and accounting services will be boosted by some one million new back-office jobs and technology-related positions, moved there by the world's top 100 financial companies.

While India holds the premier position today in offshore work, other countries—Australia, Ireland, Malaysia, the Philippines, and South Africa—are gearing up with low-cost, high-technology expertise in the battle of accounting outsourcing destinations. Among the brightest contenders, if it can overcome a non-English-speaking tradition, is China, with its population of one billion, rapid economic growth, low-cost labour, and heavy investment in technical education. Its stated goal is to become the world's top outsourcing destination for accounting.

Critical Thinking Questions

1. What factors do you think are most important to consider in deciding which parts of a firm's accounting system, if any, are appropriate for outsourcing?
2. Suppose the accounting firm that prepares your income tax return outsources the work to a third-party tax-service provider overseas. Do you think the accounting firm should get your permission before outsourcing the work? Explain why or why not.
3. What ethical issues, if any, are involved in a decision about outsourcing a firm's accounting activities? Explain.

Second World War.[5] Al Rosen, who writes articles about accounting practices, is a well-known Canadian forensic accountant.

generally accepted accounting principles (GAAP) Standard rules and methods used by accountants in preparing financial reports.

One of the auditor's responsibilities is to ensure that the client's accounting system adheres to **generally accepted accounting principles (GAAP)**, a body of theory and procedure developed and monitored by the CICA. At the end of an audit, the auditor will certify whether the client's financial reports

A financial report is an integral component of the financial accounting system.

comply with GAAP. By 2011, Canadian companies will adopt the International Financial Reporting Standards.[6] This will make it easier for investors in other countries to understand the financial statements of Canadian companies, thus making for improved access to global capital markets.

Tax Services

Tax services include helping clients not only with preparing their tax returns but also with their tax planning. Tax laws are complex. A CA's advice can help a business structure (or restructure) its operations and investments and save millions of dollars in taxes. To serve their clients best, of course, accountants must stay abreast of changes in tax laws—no simple matter.

Management Consulting Services

Management consulting services range from personal financial planning to the planning of corporate mergers. Other services include plant layout and design, marketing studies, production scheduling, computer feasibility studies, and design and implementation of accounting systems. Some accounting firms even assist in executive recruitment. Small wonder that the staffs of accounting firms may include engineers, architects, mathematicians, and even psychologists.

management consulting services Specialized accounting services to help managers resolve a variety of problems in finance, production scheduling, and other areas.

Private Accountants

To ensure the fairness of their reports, CAs and CGAs must be independent of the firms they audit. They are employees of accounting firms and provide services for many clients. But businesses also hire their own **private accountants** as salaried employees to deal with the company's day-to-day accounting needs.

private accountant An accountant hired as a salaried employee to deal with a company's day-to-day accounting needs.

Private accountants perform a variety of accounting jobs. An internal auditor at Petro-Canada, for example, might fly to the Hibernia site to confirm the accuracy of oil-flow meters on the offshore drilling platform. But a supervisor responsible for $200 million in monthly accounts payable to vendors and employees may travel no further than the executive suite. The nature of the accounting job thus depends on the specific business and the activities needed to make that business a success. Large businesses employ specialized account-

Entrepreneurship and New Ventures

New Opportunities in Forensic Accounting

Anyone who watches television knows about the forensic investigations that police officers conduct as they try to catch the bad guys (think *CSI: Miami*). It's pretty interesting stuff. But did you know that forensics is also very relevant to the field of accounting? The numerous corporate financial scandals of the past few years have caused an increase in demand for forensic accountants—individuals who investigate the financial transactions of companies in order to determine whether something fishy is going on. Forensic accountants are also proactive in helping to develop strategies that prevent fraudulent activity from occurring in the first place. In fact, prevention has taken on much greater significance since the Sarbanes-Oxley Act was passed in the United States in 2002. This act requires U.S.-listed companies to analyze their reporting controls and to make any improvements that are necessary. There is also wide speculation that these regulations will soon become mandated in Canada, an effort widely viewed as having major implications for institutions with accounting specializations. This new act will undoubtedly contribute to an increase in demand for specific areas of emphasis within the accounting field.

The CA-designated specialist in investigative and forensic accounting (CA IFA) combines the well-recognized and respected attributes of the CA with an in-depth knowledge and experience in investigative and forensic accounting. This is accomplished through a profession-endorsed certification process that has ongoing experience and education requirements. Individuals who pursue a career in IFA are well positioned to practise in areas such as fraud and economic loss quantification. Some of the responsibilities include testifying as an expert witness, investigating and analyzing financial evidence, and becoming involved in criminal investigations, as well as the rapidly evolving area of computer and internet fraud. If you think that accounting is a less-than-exciting field of study, you may have to rethink your position, given recent developments in forensic accounting. While the work of some accountants is repetitive and routine, the work of forensic accountants is quite varied and compelling.

It is estimated that the number of chartered accountants in Canada who specialize in forensic accounting is rising by as much as 10 percent per year. Exposure to white-collar crime, corporate fraud, and accounting inquiries has escalated for corporations worldwide. In this high-risk business climate, the need for experienced and objective financial and business investigations is critical. According to the latest Kroll Global Fraud Report, companies lost an average of $8.2 million to fraud in the past three years, largely because of the credit crunch and tough economic climate. Blake Coppotelli, senior managing director in Kroll's Business Intelligence & Investigations division, said, "The findings show that fraud is not only widespread but also growing, and we expect to see this increase further as conditions become tougher for business and the full impact of the credit crunch unfolds."

Most of the publicity about financial scandals focuses on large companies, but forensic investigation is needed in businesses of all shapes and sizes. The Atlantic Lottery Corp., for example, hired a forensic accounting firm to review the operations of its small, individually owned lottery retail outlets when reported winnings were higher than statistically possible. That led to widespread concerns that some retailers were cheating by pocketing prizes won by other players, who weren't properly notified of their winnings.

At the other end of the size scale, a major multinational consumer-goods producer became concerned when one of its best-known products began to lose market share in Europe because a competitor was selling its brand at a substantially lower price. Kroll was asked to determine whether the competitor's actions were legitimately supported by lower production costs or whether they reflected unfair market practices. After considerable research, Kroll discovered that the competitor had found a novel means of production that sharply reduced its costs without reducing the quality of its product. Kroll recommended that the company license the technology so that it could also achieve lower costs.

Critical Thinking Questions

1. Visit the Canadian Institute of Chartered Accountants website (www.cica.ca). How much emphasis is placed on forensic accounting? How does a person become a forensic accountant?
2. Interview a forensic accountant and ask the following questions: (a) What general approach do forensic accountants take when investigating the financial statements of companies? (b) What specific techniques are used to determine whether accounting fraud has occurred?

ants in such areas as budgets, financial planning, internal auditing, payroll, and taxation. Each accounting area has its own challenges and excitement. In small businesses, a single individual may handle all accounting tasks.

The Accounting Equation

All accountants, whether public or private, rely on record keeping. Underlying all record-keeping procedures is the most basic tool of accounting: the **accounting equation**. At various points in the year, accountants use the following equation to balance the data pertaining to financial transactions:

Assets = Liabilities + Owners' equity

After each transaction (e.g., payments to suppliers, sales to customers, wages to employees, and so on), the accounting equation must be in balance. To understand the importance of this equation, we must first understand the terms *assets, liabilities,* and *owners' equity*.[7]

accounting equation The most basic tool of accounting, used to balance the data pertaining to financial transactions: assets = liabilities + owners' equity.

Assets and Liabilities

An **asset** is any economic resource that is expected to benefit a firm or an individual who owns it. Assets include land, buildings, equipment, inventory, and payments due the company (accounts receivable). A **liability** is a debt that the firm owes to an outside party.

Describe how the *accounting equation* is used. 2

asset Any economic resource that is expected to benefit a firm or an individual who owns it.

liability A debt that the firm owes to an outside party.

Owners' Equity

You may have heard of the equity that a homeowner has in a house—that is, the amount of money that could be made by selling the house and paying off the mortgage. Similarly, **owners' equity** is the amount of money that owners would receive if they sold all of a company's assets and paid all of its liabilities. We can rewrite the accounting equation to highlight this definition:

Assets − Liabilities = Owners' equity

owners' equity The amount of money that owners would receive if they sold all of a company's assets and paid all of its liabilities.

If a company's assets exceed its liabilities, owners' equity is *positive*; if the company goes out of business, the owners will receive some cash (a gain) after selling assets and paying off liabilities. If liabilities outweigh assets, owners' equity is *negative*; assets are insufficient to pay off all debts. If the company goes out of business, the owners will get no cash and some creditors won't be paid. Owners' equity is meaningful for both investors and lenders. Before lending money to owners, for example, lenders want to know the amount of owners' equity in a business. Owners' equity consists of two sources of capital:

1. The amount that the owners originally invested
2. Profits earned by and reinvested in the company

When a company operates profitably, its assets increase faster than its liabilities. Owners' equity, therefore, will increase if profits are retained in the business instead of paid out as dividends to stockholders. Owners' equity also increases if owners invest more of their own money to increase assets. However, owners' equity can shrink if the company operates at a loss or if owners withdraw assets.

Describe three basic *financial statements* and show how they reflect the activity and financial condition of a business. 3

Financial Statements

If your business purchases inventory with cash, you do two things: (1) decrease your cash, and (2) increase your inventory. Similarly, if you purchase supplies on credit, you (1) increase your supplies, and (2) increase your accounts payable. If you invest more money in your business, you (1) increase the company's cash, and (2) increase your owners' equity. In other words, *every transaction affects two accounts*. Accountants thus use a **double-entry accounting system** to record the *dual effects* of financial transactions.

double-entry accounting system A bookkeeping system, developed in the fifteenth century and still in use, that requires every transaction to be entered in two ways—how it affects assets and how it affects liabilities and owners' equity—so that the accounting equation is always in balance.

As we noted earlier, the job of accounting is to summarize the results of a firm's transactions and to issue reports to help managers make informed decisions. Among the most important reports are **financial statements**, which fall into three broad categories—*balance sheets*, *income statements*, and *statements of cash flows*.[8]

financial statement Any of several types of broad reports regarding a company's financial status; most often used in reference to balance sheets, income statements, and/or statements of cash flows.

Balance Sheets

balance sheets Supply detailed information about the accounting equation factors: assets, liabilities, and owners' equity.

Balance sheets supply detailed information about the accounting equation factors: assets, liabilities, and owners' equity. Because they also show a firm's financial condition at one point in time, balance sheets are sometimes called *statements of financial position*. Figure 14.1 shows the balance sheet for Perfect Posters.

Assets

As we have seen, an asset is any economic resource that a company owns and from which it can expect to derive some future benefit. From an accounting standpoint, most companies have three types of assets: *current*, *fixed*, and *intangible*.

current assets Cash and other assets that can be converted into cash within a year.

liquidity The ease with which assets can be converted into cash.

Current Assets. **Current assets** include cash and assets that can be converted into cash within a year. They are normally listed in order of **liquidity**—the ease with which they can be converted into cash. Business debts, for example,

Perfect Posters, Inc.
555 Riverview, Toronto, Ontario

Perfect Posters, Inc.
Balance Sheet
As of December 31, 2009

Assets			
Current Assets:			
Cash		$7,050	
Marketable securities		2,300	
Accounts receivable	$26,210		
Less: Allowance of doubtful accounts	(650)	25,560	
Merchandise inventory		21,250	
Prepaid expenses		1,050	
Total current assets			**$57,210**
Fixed Assets:			
Land		18,000	
Building	65,000		
Less: Accumulated depreciation	(22,500)	42,500	
Equipment	72,195		
Less: Accumulated depreciation	(24,815)	47,380	
Total fixed assets			**107,880**
Intangible Assets:			
Patents	7,100		
Trademarks	900		
Total intangible assets			**8,000**
Total assets			**$173,090**

Liabilities and Owners' Equity		
Current liabilities:		
Accounts payable	$16,315	
Wages payable	3,700	
Taxes payable	1,920	
Total current liabilities		**$21,935**
Long-term liabilities:		
Notes payable, 8% due 2010	10,000	
Bonds payable, 9% due 2012	30,000	
Total long-term liabilities		**40,000**
Total liabilities		**$61,935**
Owners' Equity		
Common stock, $5 par	40,000	
Additional paid-in capital	15,000	
Retained earnings	56,155	
Total owners' equity		**111,155**
Total liabilities and owners' equity		**$173,090**

Figure 14.1 Perfect Posters' balance sheet shows clearly that the firm's total assets equal its total liabilities and owners' equity.

can usually be satisfied only through payments of cash. A company that needs but cannot generate cash (in other words, a company that is not liquid) may thus be forced to sell assets at sacrifice prices or even go out of business.

By definition, cash is completely liquid. *Marketable securities* purchased as short-term investments are slightly less liquid but can be sold quickly if necessary. Marketable securities include stocks or bonds of other companies, government securities, and money market certificates. There are three other important non-liquid assets held by many companies: *accounts receivable, merchandise inventory*, and *prepaid expenses.*

Accounts receivable are amounts due from customers who have purchased goods on credit. Most businesses expect to receive payment within 30 days of a sale. In our hypothetical example, the entry labelled *Less: Allowance of doubtful accounts* in Figure 14.1 indicates $650 in receivables that Perfect Posters does not expect to collect. Total accounts receivable assets are decreased accordingly.

accounts receivable Amounts due from customers who have purchased goods on credit.

Following accounts receivable on the Perfect Posters balance sheet is **merchandise inventory**—the cost of merchandise that has been acquired for sale to customers and is still on hand. Accounting for the value of inventories on the balance sheet is difficult because inventories are flowing in and out throughout the year. Therefore, assumptions must be made about which ones were sold and which ones remain in storage.

merchandise inventory The cost of merchandise that has been acquired for sale to customers and is still on hand.

Prepaid expenses include supplies on hand and rent paid for the period to come. They are assets because they have been paid for and are available to the company. In all, Perfect Posters' current assets as of December 31, 2009, totalled $57 210.

prepaid expenses include supplies on hand and rent paid for the period to come.

Fixed Assets. **Fixed assets** (for example, land, buildings, and equipment) have long-term use or value. But as buildings and equipment wear out or become obsolete, their value decreases. To reflect decreasing value, accountants use **depreciation** to spread the cost of an asset over the years of its useful life. Depreciation means calculating an asset's useful life in years, dividing its worth by that many years, and subtracting the resulting amount each year. Each year, therefore, the asset's remaining value decreases on the books. In Figure 14.1, Perfect Posters shows fixed assets of $107 880 after depreciation.

fixed assets Assets that have long-term use or value to the firm, such as land, buildings, and machinery.

depreciation Distributing the cost of a major asset over the years in which it produces revenues; calculated by each year subtracting the asset's original value divided by the number of years in its productive life.

Intangible Assets. Although their worth is hard to set, intangible assets have monetary value. **Intangible assets** usually include the cost of obtaining rights or privileges such as patents, trademarks, copyrights, and franchise fees. **Goodwill** is the amount paid for an existing business beyond the value of its

intangible assets Non-physical assets, such as patents, trademarks, copyrights, and franchise fees, that have economic value but the precise value of which is difficult to calculate.

goodwill The amount paid for an existing business beyond the value of its other assets.

The inventory at this car dealership is part of the company's assets. The cars constitute an economic resource because the firm will benefit financially as it sells them. When they are sold, at the end of the company's accounting period, the dealership will convert the cost of the cars as expenses and show them as costs of goods sold.

other assets. Perfect Posters has no goodwill assets; however, it does own trademarks and patents for specialized storage equipment. These are intangible assets worth $8000. Larger companies, of course, have intangible assets that are worth much more.

Liabilities

current liabilities Debts that must be paid within one year.

accounts payable Unpaid bills to suppliers for materials, as well as wages and taxes that must be paid in the coming year.

long-term liabilities Debts that are not due for at least one year.

Like assets, liabilities are often separated into different categories. **Current liabilities** are debts that must be paid within one year. These include **accounts payable**—unpaid bills to suppliers for materials, as well as wages and taxes that must be paid in the coming year. Perfect Posters has current liabilities of $21 935.

Long-term liabilities are debts that are not due for at least one year. These normally represent borrowed funds on which the company must pay interest. Perfect Posters' long-term liabilities are $40 000.

Owners' Equity

The final section of the balance sheet in Figure 14.1 shows owners' equity broken down into *common stock, paid-in capital*, and *retained earnings*. When Perfect Posters was formed, the declared legal value of its common stock was $5 per share. By law, this $40 000 ($5 × 8000 shares) cannot be distributed as dividends. **Paid-in capital** is additional money invested in the firm by its owners. Perfect Posters has $15 000 in paid-in capital.

paid-in capital Additional money invested in the firm by its owners.

retained earnings Net profits minus dividend payments to stockholders.

Retained earnings are net profits minus dividend payments to stockholders. Retained earnings accumulate when profits, which could have been distributed to stockholders, are kept instead for use by the company. At the close of 2009, Perfect Posters had retained earnings of $56 155.

Income Statements

income (profit-and-loss) statement A description of revenues and expenses in a figure showing the firm's annual profit or loss.

The **income statement** is sometimes called a **profit-and-loss statement** because its description of revenues and expenses results in a figure showing the firm's annual profit or loss. In other words,

$$\text{Revenues} - \text{Expenses} = \text{Profit (or loss)}$$

Popularly known as "the bottom line," profit or loss is probably the most important figure in any business enterprise. Figure 14.2 shows the 2009 income statement for Perfect Posters, whose bottom line that year was $12 585. The income statement is divided into three major categories: *revenues, cost of goods sold*, and *operating expenses*.

Revenues

revenues The funds that flow into a business from the sale of goods or services.

When a law firm receives $250 for preparing a will or when a supermarket collects $65 from a customer buying groceries, both are receiving **revenues**—the funds that flow in to a business from the sale of goods or services. In 2009, Perfect Posters reported revenues of $256 425 from the sale of art prints and other posters.

Cost of Goods Sold

cost of goods sold Any expenses directly involved in producing or selling a good or service during a given time period.

In Perfect Posters' income statement, the **cost of goods sold** category shows the costs of obtaining materials to make the products sold during the year. Perfect Posters began 2009 with posters valued at $22 380. Over the year, it spent $103 635 to purchase posters. During 2009, then, the company had $126 015 worth of merchandise available to sell. By the end of the year, it had sold all but $21 250 of those posters, which remained as merchandise inventory. The cost of obtaining the goods sold by the firm was thus $104 765.

o o o o o o o o o o o o o			**Perfect Posters, Inc.** 555 Riverview, Toronto, Ontario
Perfect Posters, Inc.			
Income Statement			
Year ended December 31, 2009			
Revenues (gross sales)			**$256,425**
Costs of goods sold:			
Merchandise inventory, January 1, 2009	$22,380		
Merchandise purchases during year	103,635		
Goods available for sale		$126,015	
Less: Merchandise inventory, December 31, 2009		21,250	
Cost of goods sold			**104,765**
Gross profit			**151,660**
Operating expenses:			
Selling and repackaging expenses:			
Salaries and wages	49,750		
Advertising	6,380		
Depreciation—warehouse and repackaging equipment	3,350		
Total selling and repackaging expenses		59,480	
Administrative expenses:			
Salaries and wages	55,100		
Supplies	4,150		
Utilities	3,800		
Depreciation—office equipment	3,420		
Interest expense	2,900		
Miscellaneous expenses	1,835		
Total administration expenses		71,205	
Total operating expenses			**130,685**
Operating income (income before taxes)			20,975
Income taxes			8,390
Net income			**$12,585**

Figure 14.2 Perfect Posters' income statement. The final entry on the income statement, the bottom line, reports the firm's profit or loss.

Gross Profit (or Gross Margin). To calculate **gross profit (or gross margin)**, subtract the cost of goods sold from the revenues obtained from goods sold. Perfect Posters' gross profit in 2009 was $151 660 ($256 425 − $104 765). Expressed as a percentage of sales, gross profit is 59.1 percent ($151 660 = $256 425).

gross profit (or gross margin) A firm's revenues (gross sales) less its cost of goods sold.

Gross profit percentages vary widely across industries. In retailing, Home Depot reports 30 percent; in manufacturing, Harley-Davidson reports 34 percent; and in pharmaceuticals, Wyeth reports 75 percent. For companies with low gross margins, product costs are a big expense. If a company has a high gross margin, it probably has low cost-of-goods-sold but high selling and administrative expenses.

Operating Expenses

In addition to costs directly related to acquiring goods, every company has general expenses ranging from erasers to the president's salary. Like cost of goods sold, **operating expenses** are resources that must flow out of a company for it to earn revenues. As you can see in Figure 14.2, Perfect Posters had operating expenses of $130 685 in 2009. This figure consists of $59 480 in selling and repackaging expenses and $71 205 in administrative expenses.

operating expenses Resources that must flow out of a company for it to earn revenues.

Selling expenses result from activities related to selling the firm's goods or services. These may include salaries for the sales force, delivery costs, and advertising expenses. General and administrative expenses, such as management salaries, insurance expenses, and maintenance costs, are expenses related to the general management of the company.

operating income Compares the gross profit from business operations against operating expenses.

net income (or net profit or net earnings) A firm's gross profit less its operating expenses and income taxes.

Operating Income and Net Income. Sometimes managers must determine **operating income**, which compares the gross profit from business operations against operating expenses. This calculation for Perfect Posters ($151 660 – $130 685) reveals an operating income, or income before taxes, of $20 975. Subtracting income taxes from operating income ($20 975 – $8390) reveals **net income** (also called **net profit** or **net earnings**). In 2009, Perfect Posters' net income was $12 585.

Statement of Cash Flows

statement of cash flows A financial statement that describes a firm's generation and use of cash during a given period.

Some companies prepare only balance sheets and income statements. However, many firms also report a **statement of cash flows**. This statement describes a company's yearly cash receipts and cash payments. It shows the effects on cash of three business activities:

- *Cash flows from operations.* This part of the statement is concerned with the firm's main operating activities: the cash transactions involved in buying and selling goods and services. It reveals how much of the year's profits result from the firm's main line of business (for example, Jaguar's sales of automobiles) rather than from secondary activities (for example, licensing fees a clothing firm paid to Jaguar for using the Jaguar logo on shirts).
- *Cash flows from investing.* This section reports net cash used in or provided by investing. It includes cash receipts and payments from buying and selling stocks, bonds, property, equipment, and other productive assets.
- *Cash flows from financing.* The final section reports net cash from all financing activities. It includes cash inflows from borrowing or issuing stock as well as outflows for payment of dividends and repayment of borrowed money.

The overall change in cash from these three sources provides information to lenders and investors. When creditors and stockholders know how firms

At the end of its accounting period, this pharmaceuticals company will subtract the cost of making the goods that it sold from the revenues received from sales. The difference will be its gross profit (or gross margin). Cost of goods sold does not include the firm's operating expenses, including such selling expenses as advertising and sales commissions. In part, gross margins in the pharmaceuticals industry are high because they do not account for high selling expenses.

obtained and used their funds during the course of a year, it is easier for them to interpret the year-to-year changes in the firm's balance sheet and income statement.

The Budget: An Internal Financial Statement

For planning, controlling, and decision making, the most important internal financial statement is the **budget**—a detailed statement of estimated receipts and expenditures for a period of time in the future. Although that period is usually one year, some companies also prepare budgets for three- or five-year periods, especially when considering major capital expenditures.

budget A detailed financial plan for estimated receipts and expenditures for a period of time in the future, usually one year.

Budgets are also useful for keeping track of weekly or monthly performance. Procter & Gamble, for example, evaluates all of its business units monthly by comparing actual financial results with monthly budgeted amounts. Discrepancies in "actual vs. budget" totals signal potential problems and initiate action to get financial performance back on track.

Although the accounting staff coordinates the budget process, it requires input from many people in the company regarding proposed activities, needed resources, and input sources.[9] Figure 14.3 shows a sample sales budget. In preparing such a budget, the accounting department must obtain from the sales group its projections for units to be sold and expected expenses for each quarter of the coming year. Accountants then draw up the final budget, and throughout the year, the accounting department compares the budget with actual expenditures and revenues.

Reporting Standards and Practices

Accountants follow numerous standard reporting practices and principles when they prepare external reports, including financial statements. The common language dictated by standard practices is designed to give external users confidence in the accuracy and meaning of the information in any financial

Perfect Posters, Inc.
555 Riverview, Toronto, Ontario

Perfect Posters, Inc.
Sales Budget
First Quarter, 2010

	January	**February**	**March**	**Quarter**
Budgeted sales (units)	7,500	6,000	6,500	20,000
Budgeted selling price per unit	$3.50	$3.50	$3.50	$3.50
Budgeted sales revenue	**$26,250**	**$21,000**	**$22,750**	**$70,000**
Expected cash receipts:				
From December sales	$26,210[a]			$26,210
From January sales	17,500[b]	$8,750		26,250
From February sales		14,000	$7,000	21,000
From March sales			15,200	15,200
Total cash receipts:	**$43,710**	**$22,750**	**$22,200**	**$88,660**

[a] This cash from December sales represents a collection of the Account Receivable appearing on the December 31, 2009 Balance Sheet.
[b] The company estimates that two-thirds of each month's sales revenues will result in cash receipts during the same month. The remaining one-third is collected during the following month.

Figure 14.3 Perfect Posters, Inc. sales budget, First Quarter, 2010.

statement. Spelled out in great detail in GAAP, these principles cover a wide range of issues, such as when to recognize revenues from operations, the so-called "matching" of revenues and expenses, and full public disclosure of financial information to the public. Without agreed-upon practices in these and many other accounting categories, users of financial statements would be unable to compare financial information from different companies and thus misunderstand—or be led to misconstrue—a given company's true financial status.

Revenue Recognition

4 Explain the key standards and principles for reporting financial statements.

As we noted earlier, revenues are funds that flow in to a business as a result of its operating activities during the accounting period. *Revenue recognition* is the formal recording and reporting of revenues in the financial statements. Although any firm earns revenues continuously as it makes sales, earnings are not reported until the earnings cycle is completed. This cycle is complete under two conditions:

1. The sale is complete and the product has been delivered.
2. The sale price to the customer has been collected or is collectible (accounts receivable).

The completion of the earning cycle, then, determines the timing for revenue recognition in the firm's financial statements. Revenues are recorded for the accounting period in which sales are completed and collectible (or collected). This practice assures the reader that the statement gives a fair comparison of what was gained for the resources that were given up.

Matching

Net income is calculated by subtracting expenses from revenues. The *matching principle* states that expenses will be matched with revenues to determine net income for an accounting period.[10] Why is this principle important? It permits the user of the statement to see how much net gain resulted from the assets that had to be given up to generate revenues during the period covered in the statement. Consequently, when we match revenue recognition with expense recognition, we get net income for the period.

Consider the hypothetical case of Little Red Wagon Co. Let's see what happens when the books are kept in two different ways:

1. Correct Method: Revenue recognition is matched with expense recognition to determine net income when the earnings cycle is *completed*.
2. Incorrect Method: Revenue recognition occurs *before* the earnings cycle is completed.

Suppose that 500 red wagons are produced and delivered to customers at a sales price of $20 each during 2007. In 2008, 600 red wagons are produced and delivered. In part (A) of Table 14.2, the correct matching method has been used: Revenues are recorded for the accounting period in which sales are completed and collectible from customers, as are the expenses of producing and delivering them. The revenues from sales are matched against the expenses of completing them. By using the matching principle, we see clearly how much better off the company is at the end of each accounting period as a result of that period's operations: It earned $2000 net income for 2007 and $3000 for 2008.

In part (B) of Table 14.2, revenue recognition and the matching principle have been violated. Certain activities of the two accounting periods are disguised and mixed together rather than separated for each period. The result is

Table 14.2 Revenue Recognition and the Matching Principle

(A) The correct method reveals each accounting period's activities and results

	Year ended December 31, 2007	Year ended December 31, 2008
Revenues	$10,000	$12,000
Expenses	8,000	9,000
Net income	2,000	3,000

(B) The incorrect method disguises each accounting period's activities and results

	Year ended December 31, 2007	Year ended December 31, 2008
Revenues	$14,000	$8,000
Expenses	8,000	9,000
Net income	6,000	(1,000)

a distorted performance report that incorrectly shows that 2007 was a better year than 2008. Here's what Little Red Wagon's accountants did wrong: The sales department sold 200 red wagons (with revenues of $4000) to a customer late in 2007. Those *revenues* are included in the $14 000 for 2007. But because the 200 wagons were produced and delivered to the customer in 2008, the *expenses* are recorded, as in (A), for 2008. The result is a distorted picture of operations. It looks as if expenses for 2008 are out of line for such a low sales level, and it looks as if expenses (as compared with revenues) were kept under better control during 2007.

The firm's accountants violated the matching principle by ignoring *the period during which the earnings cycle was completed.* Although $4000 in sales of wagons occurred in 2007, the earnings cycle for those wagons was not completed until they were produced and delivered, which occurred in 2008. Accordingly, both the revenues and expenses for those 200 wagons should have been reported in the same period—namely, in 2008, as was reported in part (A). There, we can see clearly what was gained and what was lost on activities that were completed *in an accounting period.* By requiring this practice, the matching principle provides consistency in reporting and avoids financial distortions.

Full Disclosure

Full disclosure means that financial statements should include not just numbers but also interpretations and explanations by management so that external users can better understand information contained in the statements. Because management knows more about inside events than outsiders, management prepares additional useful information that explains certain events or transactions or discloses the circumstances underlying certain financial results.

Analyzing Financial Statements

Financial statements present a great deal of information, but what does it all mean? How, for example, can statements help investors decide what stock to buy or help managers decide whether to extend credit? Statements provide data, which in turn can be applied to various ratios (comparative numbers). These ratios can then be used to analyze the financial health of one or more companies. They can also be used to check a firm's progress by comparing current and past statements.

Explain how computing *financial ratios* can help in analyzing the financial strengths of a business.

5

Ratios are normally grouped into three major classifications:

- **Solvency ratios**, both short-term and long-term, estimate risk.
- **Profitability ratios** measure potential earnings.
- **Activity ratios** reflect management's use of assets.

solvency ratios Ratios that estimate the financial risk that is evident in a company.

profitability ratios Measures of a firm's overall financial performance in terms of its likely profits; used by investors to assess their probable returns.

activity ratios Measures of how efficiently a firm uses its resources; used by investors to assess their probable returns.

Depending on the decisions to be made, a user may apply none, some, or all the ratios in a particular classification.

Solvency Ratios

What are the chances that a borrower will be able to repay a loan and the interest due? This question is first and foremost in the minds of bank lending officers, managers of pension funds and other investors, suppliers, and the borrowing company's own financial managers. Solvency ratios provide measures of the firm's ability to meet its debt obligations.

Short-Term Solvency Ratios

short-term solvency ratios Measure a company's liquidity and its ability to pay immediate debts.

current ratio A form of liquidity ratio calculated as current assets divided by current liabilities.

Short-term solvency ratios measure a company's liquidity and its ability to pay immediate debts. The most commonly used ratio is the **current ratio**, which reflects a firm's ability to generate cash to meet obligations through the normal, orderly process of selling inventories and collecting revenues from customers. It is calculated by dividing current assets by current liabilities. The higher a firm's current ratio, the lower the risk to investors. For many years, the guideline was a current ratio of 2:1 or higher—which meant that current assets were at least double current liabilities. More recently, many firms that are financially strong operate with current ratios of less than 2:1.

How does Perfect Posters measure up? Look again at the balance sheet in Figure 14.1. Judging from its current assets and current liabilities at the end of 2009, we see that the company looks like a good credit risk:

$$\frac{\text{Current assets}}{\text{Current liabilities}} - \frac{\$57\ 210}{\$21\ 935} = 2.61$$

Long-Term Solvency

Stakeholders are also concerned about long-term solvency. Has a company been overextended by borrowing so much that it will be unable to repay debts in future years? A firm that can't meet its long-term debt obligations is in danger of collapse or takeover—a risk that makes creditors and investors quite cautious. To evaluate a company's risk of running into this problem, creditors turn to the balance sheet to see the extent to which a firm is financed through borrowed money. Long-term solvency is calculated by dividing **debt**—total liabilities—by owners' equity. The lower a firm's debt, the lower the risk to investors and creditors. Companies with **debt-to-owners'-equity ratios** above 1.0 may be relying too much on debt. In the case of Perfect Posters, we can see from the balance sheet in Figure 14.1 that the debt-to-equity ratio calculates as follows:

debt A company's total liabilities.

debt-to-owners'-equity ratio A form of debt ratio calculated as total liabilities divided by owner's equity.

$$\frac{\text{Debt}}{\text{Owners' equity}} = \frac{\$61\ 935}{\$111\ 155} = \$0.56$$

Sometimes, high debt can be not only acceptable but also desirable. Borrowing funds gives a firm **leverage**—the ability to make otherwise unaffordable investments. In *leveraged buyouts*, firms have sometimes taken on huge debt in order to get the money to buy out other companies. If owning the purchased company generates profits above the cost of borrowing the

leverage Using borrowed funds to make purchases, thus increasing the user's purchasing power, potential rate of return, and risk of loss.

purchase price, leveraging makes sense. Unfortunately, many buyouts have caused problems because profits fell short of expected levels or because rising interest rates increased payments on the buyer's debt.

Profitability Ratios

Although it is important to know that a company is solvent in both the long term and the short term, safety or risk alone is not an adequate basis for investment decisions. Investors also want some measure of the returns they can expect. Return on equity and earnings per share are two commonly used profitability ratios. (Sometimes these are called *shareholder return ratios* or *performance ratios.*)

Return on Equity

Owners are interested in the net income earned by a business for each dollar invested. **Return on equity** measures this performance by dividing net income (recorded in the income statement, Figure 14.2) by total owners' equity (recorded in the balance sheet, Figure 14.1).[11] For Perfect Posters, the return-on-equity ratio in 2009 can be calculated as follows:

return on equity A form of profitability ratio calculated as net income divided by total owners' equity.

$$\frac{\text{Net income}}{\text{Total owners' equity}} = \frac{\$12\ 585}{\$111\ 155} = 11.3\%$$

Is this figure good or bad? There is no set answer. If Perfect Posters' ratio for 2009 is higher than in previous years, owners and investors should be encouraged. But if 11.3 percent is lower than the ratios of other companies in the same industry, they should be concerned.

Return on Sales

Companies want to generate as much profit as they can from each dollar of sales revenue they receive. The **return on sales** ratio is calculated by dividing net income by sales revenue (see Figure 14.2). For Perfect Posters, the return on sales ratio for 2009 is as follows:

return on sales Calculated by dividing net income by sales revenue.

$$\frac{\text{Net income}}{\text{Sales revenue}} = \frac{\$12\ 585}{\$256\ 425} \times 100 = 4.9\%$$

Is this figure good or bad? Once again, there is no set answer. If Perfect Posters' ratio for 2009 is higher than in previous years, owners and investors should be encouraged, but if 4.9 percent is lower than the ratios of other companies in the same industry, they will likely be concerned.

Earnings per Share

Defined as net income divided by the number of shares of common stock outstanding, **earnings per share** determines the size of the dividend a company can pay to its shareholders. Investors use this ratio to decide whether to buy or sell a company's stock. As the ratio gets higher, the stock value increases, because investors know that the firm can better afford to pay dividends. Naturally, stock will lose market value if the latest financial statements report a decline in earnings per share. For Perfect Posters, we can use the net income total from the income statement in Figure 14.2 to calculate earnings per share as follows:

earnings per share A form of profitability ratio calculated as net income divided by the number of common shares outstanding.

$$\frac{\text{Net income}}{\text{Number of common shares outstanding}} = \frac{\$12\ 585}{\$8\ 000} = \$1.57 \text{ per share}$$

Activity Ratios

The efficiency with which a firm uses resources is linked to profitability. As a potential investor, then, you want to know which company gets more mileage from its resources. Activity ratios measure this efficiency. For example, suppose that two firms use the same amount of resources or assets. If Firm A generates greater profits or sales, it is more efficient and thus has a better activity ratio.

Inventory Turnover Ratio

inventory turnover ratio An activity ratio that measures the average number of times inventory is sold and restocked during the year.

Certain specific measures can be used to explain how one firm earns greater profits than another. One of the most important measures is the **inventory turnover ratio**, which calculates the average number of times that inventory is sold and restocked during the year—that is, how quickly inventory is produced and sold.[12] First, a company needs to know its average inventory—the typical amount of inventory on hand during the year. Average inventory can be calculated by adding end-of-year inventory to beginning-of-year inventory and dividing by two. The company can then calculate the inventory turnover ratio, which is expressed as the cost of goods sold divided by average inventory:

$$\frac{\text{Cost of goods sold}}{\text{Average inventory}} = \frac{\text{Cost of goods sold}}{\text{Beginning inventory} + \text{Ending inventory} \div 2}$$

High inventory turnover ratio means efficient operations. Because a smaller amount of investment is tied up in inventory, the company's funds can be put to work elsewhere to earn greater returns. However, inventory turnover must be compared with both prior years and industry averages. An inventory turnover rate of 5, for example, might be excellent for an auto supply store, but it would be disastrous for a supermarket, where a rate of about 15 is common. Rates can also vary within a company that markets a variety of products. To calculate Perfect Posters' inventory turnover ratio for 2009, we take the merchandise inventory figures for the income statement in Figure 14.2. The ratio can be expressed as follows:

$$\frac{\$104\ 765}{(\$22\ 380 + \$21\ 250) \div 2} = 4.8 \text{ times}$$

The inventory turnover ratio measures the average number of times that a store sells and restocks its inventory in one year. The higher the ratio, the more products that get sold and the more revenue that comes in. Supermarkets must have a higher turnover ratio than, say, auto supply or toy stores. In almost all retail stores, products with the highest ratios get the shelf spaces that generate the most customer traffic and sales.

In other words, new merchandise replaces old merchandise every 76 days (365 days divided by 4.8). The 4.8 ratio is below the average of 7.0 for comparable wholesaling operations, indicating that the business is slightly inefficient.

International Accounting

Explain some of the special issues that arise in *international accounting*. **6**

As we saw in Chapter 5, many companies, such as McCain Foods, Sabian Cymbals, and Electrovert Ltd., receive large portions of their operating revenues from foreign sales. As well, Canadian companies purchase components from foreign countries. Retailers such as Sears buy merchandise from other countries for sale in Canada. In addition, more and more companies own subsidiaries in foreign countries. With all this international activity, there is obviously a need to keep track of foreign transactions. One of the most basic accounting needs is translating the values of the currencies of different countries.

Foreign Currency Exchange

A unique consideration in international accounting is the value of currencies and their exchange rates. As we saw in Chapter 5, the value of any country's currency is subject to occasional change. Political and economic conditions, for instance, affect the stability of a nation's currency and its value relative to the currencies of other countries.

As the currency is traded around the world, market forces determine the currency's value—what buyers are willing to pay for it. The resulting values are called **foreign currency exchange rates**. When a currency becomes unstable—that is, when its value changes frequently—it is regarded as a *weak currency*. The value of the Brazilian real, for example, fluctuated between 0.416 and 0.957—a variation of 130 percent in U.S. dollars—during the period from 1997 to 2002. On the other hand, a *strong currency* historically rises or holds steady in comparison to other currencies.

foreign currency exchange rates What buyers are willing to pay for a given currency.

As changes in exchange rates occur, they must be considered by accountants when recording international transactions. They will affect, perhaps profoundly, the amount that a firm pays for foreign purchases and the amount it gains from sales to foreign buyers.

International Transactions

International purchases, credit sales, and accounting for foreign subsidiaries all involve transactions affected by exchange rates. When a Canadian company imports Bordeaux wine from the French company Pierre Bourgeois, the Canadian company's accountant must be sure that the company's books reflect its true costs. The amount owed to Pierre Bourgeois changes daily along with the exchange rate between euros and Canadian dollars. Thus, the accountant must identify the actual rate *on the day that payment in euros is made* so that the correct Canadian-dollar cost of the purchase is recorded.

"It's up to you now, Miller. The only thing that can save us is an accounting breakthrough."

International Accounting Standards

Professional accounting groups from about 80 countries are members of the International Accounting Standards Board (IASB), which is trying to eliminate national differences in financial reporting procedures.[13] Bankers, investors, and managers want procedures that are comparable from country to country and applicable to all firms regardless of home nation. Standardization is occurring in some areas but is far from universal. IASB financial statements include an income statement, balance sheet, and statement of cash flows similar to those issued by Canadian and U.S. accountants. International standards, however, do not require a uniform format, and variety abounds.

The Greening of Business

The Green Revolution Hits Accounting

If you are asked to think about ways that business firms can reduce the negative impact of their activities on the environment, you're probably most likely to think about changes that companies could make to their production processes that would reduce water or air pollution. But changes can be made in all areas of a business, including the accounting area. In accounting, for example, there is at least one important activity that affects the environment, and that is the use of paper for all those financial statements. The electronic revolution has provided the opportunity to substantially reduce the use of paper, while at the same time making it easier for clients and managers to deal with accounting information. A paperless system not only reduces waste and allows accountants to quickly respond to clients, but it also reduces the overhead of storage, tracking, and accessing documents. With the flexibility of an electronic system, accountants can work virtually anywhere in the world, as long as there is an internet connection available.

For example, traditional accounting firms are spending increasing amounts of valuable time on handling paperwork, such as invoices. The paperless system solution eliminates the need to store paper invoices, by storing their digital images and retrieving the images as needed. Now the firm has easier access to more data, facilitating analyses that save it thousands of dollars.

There are real incentives for companies to embrace environmentally friendly business practices like saving paper. But careful thought has to be given to how this will be done because of the well-known tendency of human beings to resist change. To resolve any resistance that is based on *technical* concerns, management must ensure that the IT infrastructure is working properly and that there is an adequate storage and security system. To deal with resistance that is based on *emotional* concerns, management needs to provide incentives to motivate people to change to the new system. In the accounting area, one incentive is the potential flexibility that the electronic revolution brings. Having digital images of files reduces the need to travel in order to share documents with clients and other associates. This also enables a company to reduce its dependency on a traditional work environment; now, more employees can choose to work flexible hours and have a more balanced work and family life. Being technically and digitally connected allows for enhanced productivity.

Another incentive is the increased efficiency that will be evident with the use of electronic technology. Increased efficiency means that a given amount of work can be done with fewer people than were previously needed, and this will increase competitiveness. A large number of accountants are expected to retire within the next few years, and increased efficiency means that companies will not have to look for as many people as they would have otherwise. This will save money and simplify recruiting efforts.

It is anticipated that accounting firms increasingly will train their clients to perform more of the initial data entry to allow for the electronic exchange of information. Firms will not be limited by geographic boundaries. They can also bill for higher-level accounting tasks, and the firm can be much more selective about which clients they accept. These new methods will help eliminate the bottom 10 to 20 percent of unproductive clients and allow more time to cultivate the profitable files.

Critical Thinking Questions

1. What other methods can firms use to have a greener accounting system?
2. There are clearly benefits for firms that embrace green accounting practices, but are there also benefits to clients? If so, describe them.
3. Why might there be reluctance on the part of accounting firms or their clients to embrace green initiatives like paperless systems?

Test yourself on the material for this chapter at **www.pearsoned.ca/mybusinesslab**.

Summary of Learning Objectives

1. **Explain the role of *accountants* and distinguish among the three types of professional accountants in Canada.** By collecting, analyzing, and communicating financial information, accountants provide business managers and investors with an accurate picture of a firm's financial health. *Chartered Accountants (CAs)* and *Certified General Accountants (CGAs)* provide accounting expertise for client organizations who must report their financial condition to external stakeholders. *Certified Management Accountants (CMAs)* provide accounting expertise for the firms that employ them.

2. **Describe how the *accounting equation* is used.** Accountants use the following equation to balance the data pertaining to financial transactions:

   Assets – Liabilities = Owners' equity

   After each financial transaction (e.g., payments to suppliers, sales to customers, wage payments to employees), the accounting equation must be in balance. If it isn't, then an accounting error has occurred. The equation also provides an indication of the firm's financial health. If *assets* exceed *liabilities, owners' equity* is positive; if the firm goes out of business, owners will receive some cash (a gain) after selling assets and paying off liabilities. If liabilities outweigh assets, owners' equity is negative; assets aren't enough to pay off debts. If the company goes under, owners will get no cash and some creditors won't be paid, thus losing their remaining investments in the company.

3. **Describe three basic *financial statements* and show how they reflect the activity and financial condition of a business.** The *balance sheet* summarizes a company's assets, liabilities, and owners' equity at a given point in time. The *income statement* details revenues and expenses for a given period of time and identifies any profit or loss. The *statement of cash flows* reports cash receipts and payment from operating, investing, and financial activities.

4. **Explain the key standards and principles for reporting financial statements.** Accountants follow standard reporting practices and principles when they prepare financial statements. Otherwise, users wouldn't be able to compare information from different companies, and they might misunderstand—or be led to misconstrue—a company's true financial status. Revenue recognition is the formal recording and reporting of revenues in financial statements. All firms earn revenues continuously as they make sales, but earnings are not reported until the earnings cycle is completed. This cycle is complete under two conditions: (a) The sale is complete and the product delivered, and (b) the sale price has been collected or is collectible. This practice assures interested parties that the statement gives a fair comparison of what was gained for the resources that were given up.

5. **Explain how computing *financial ratios* can help in analyzing the financial strengths of a business.** Drawing upon data from financial statements, ratios can help creditors, investors, and managers assess a firm's finances. The *current, liquidity,* and *debt-to-owners'-equity ratios* all measure solvency, a firm's ability to pay its debt in both the short and long runs. *Return on sales, return on equity,* and *earnings per share* are all ratios that measure profitability. The *inventory turnover ratio* shows how efficiently a firm is using its funds.

6. **Explain some of the special issues that arise in *international accounting.*** Accounting for foreign transactions involves special procedures, such as translating the values of different countries' currencies and accounting for the effects of exchange rates. Moreover, currencies are subject to change; as they're traded each day around the world, their values are determined by market forces—what buyers are willing to pay for them. The resulting values are *foreign currency exchange rates*, which can be fairly volatile. When a currency becomes unstable—when its value changes frequently—it is called a weak currency. The value of a strong currency historically rises or holds steady in comparison with the U.S. dollar.

   International purchases, sales on credit, and accounting for foreign subsidiaries all involve transactions affected by exchange rates. When a Canadian company imports a French product, its accountant must be sure that its books reflect its true costs. The amount owed to the French seller changes daily along with the exchange rate between euros and dollars. The Canadian accountant must therefore identify the actual rate on the day that payment in euros is made so that the correct Canadian-dollar cost of the product is recorded.

With accounting groups from about 80 countries, the International Accounting Standards Board (IASB) is trying to eliminate national differences in financial reporting. Bankers, investors, and managers want financial reporting that is comparable from country to country and across all firms regardless of home nation. Standardization governs some areas but is far from universal.

Key Terms

accounting (p. 440)
accounting equation (p. 447)
accounting information system (AIS) (p. 441)
accounts payable (p. 450)
accounts receivable (p. 449)
activity ratios (p. 456)
asset (p. 447)
audit (p. 443)
balance sheets (p. 448)
bookkeeping (p. 440)
budget (p. 453)
certified general accountant (CGA) (p. 442)
certified management accountant (CMA) (p. 443)
chartered accountant (CA) (p. 442)
controller (p. 441)
cost of goods sold (p. 450)
current assets (p. 448)
current liabilities (p. 450)
current ratio (p. 456)
debt (p. 456)
debt-to-owners'-equity ratio (p. 456)
depreciation (p. 449)
double-entry accounting system (p. 447)
earnings per share (p. 457)
financial accounting system (p. 441)
financial statement (p. 448)
fixed assets (p. 449)
foreign currency exchange rates (p. 459)
forensic accountant (p. 443)
generally accepted accounting principles (GAAP) (p. 444)
goodwill (p. 449)
gross profit (gross margin) (p. 451)
income (profit-and-loss) statement (p. 450)
intangible assets (p. 449)
inventory turnover ratio (p. 458)
leverage (p. 456)
liability (p. 447)
liquidity (p. 448)
long-term liabilities (p. 450)
management consulting services (p. 445)
managerial (management) accounting (p. 442)
merchandise inventory (p. 449)
net income (net profit or net earnings) (p. 452)
operating expenses (p. 451)
operating income (p. 452)
owners' equity (p. 447)
paid-in capital (p. 450)
prepaid expenses (p. 449)
private accountant (p. 445)
profitability ratios (p. 456)
retained earnings (p. 450)
return on equity (p. 457)
return on sales (p. 457)
revenues (p. 450)
short-term solvency ratios (p. 456)
solvency ratios (p. 456)
statement of cash flows (p. 452)

Questions for Analysis

1. Balance sheets and income statements are supposed to be objective assessments of the financial condition of a company. But the accounting scandals of the last few years show that certain pressures may be put on accountants as they audit a company's financial statements. Describe these pressures. To what extent do these pressures make the audit more subjective?
2. If you were planning to invest in a company, which of the three types of financial statements would you want most to see? Why?
3. A business hires a professional accountant like a CA or CGA to assess the financial condition of the company. Why would the business also employ a private accountant?
4. How does the double-entry system reduce the chances of mistakes or fraud in accounting?
5. Explain how financial ratios allow managers to monitor their own efficiency and effectiveness.
6. The "credit crunch" of 2008 was highlighted by the inability of banks to convert customers' investments

back to cash when requested, as the investments lacked liquidity. Explain what liquidity is, how it is measured, and why it is important to any company.

7. Suppose that Inflatables Inc., makers of air mattresses for swimming pools, has the following transactions in one week:
   - sold three deluxe mattresses to Al Wett (paid cash $50, remaining $25 on credit) on 7/16
   - received cheque from Ima Flote in payment for mattresses bought on credit ($120) on 7/13
   - received new shipment of 200 mattresses from Airheads Mfg. (total cost $3000, paying 50 percent cash on delivery) on 7/17

   Construct a journal for Inflatables Inc.

8. Dasar Company reports the following data in its September 30, 2009, financial statements:

   Gross sales $225 000

   Current assets $50 000

   Long-term assets $130 000

   Current liabilities $33 000

   Long-term liabilities $52 000

   Net income $11 250

   a. Compute the owners' equity.
   b. Compute the current ratio.
   c. Compute the debt-to-equity ratio.
   d. Compute the return on sales.
   e. Compute the return on owners' equity.

Application Exercises

1. Interview an accountant at a local manufacturing firm. Trace the process by which budgets are developed in that company. How does the firm use budgets? How does budgeting help its managers plan business activities? How does budgeting help them control business activities? Give examples.
2. Interview the manager of a local retail or wholesale business about taking inventory. What is the firm's primary purpose in taking inventory? How often is it done?
3. Interview the manager of a local business and ask about the role of ethics in the company's accounting practices. Is ethics in accounting an important issue to the manager? What steps are taken to ensure ethical practices internally?

Building Your Business Skills

Putting the Buzz in Billing

The Purpose of the Assignment

To encourage students to think about the advantages and disadvantages of using an electronic system for handling accounts receivable and accounts payable.

Assignment

Step 1

Study Figure 14.4. The outside cycle depicts the seven steps involved in issuing paper bills to customers, payment of these bills by customers, and handling by banks of debits and credits for the two accounts. The inside cycle shows the same bill issuance and payment process handled electronically.

Step 2

As the chief financial officer of a provincial hydroelectric utility, you are analyzing the feasibility of switching from a paper to an electronic system of billing and bill payment. You decide to discuss the ramifications of the choice with three business associates (choose three classmates to take on these roles). Your discussion requires that you research electronic payment systems now being developed. Specifically, using online and library research, you must find out as much as you can about the electronic bill-paying systems being developed by Visa International, Intuit, IBM, and the Checkfree Corp. After you have researched this information, brainstorm the advantages and disadvantages of using an electronic bill-paying system in your company.

Questions for Discussion

1. What cost savings are inherent in the electronic system for both your company and its customers? In your answer, consider such costs as handling, postage, and paper.
2. What consequences would your decision to adopt an electronic system have on others with whom you do business, including manufacturers of cheque-sorting equipment, Canada Post, and banks?
3. Switching to an electronic bill-paying system would require a large capital expenditure for new computers and computer software. How could analyzing the company's income statement help you justify this expenditure?
4. How are consumers likely to respond to paying bills electronically? Are you likely to get a different response from individuals than you get from business customers?

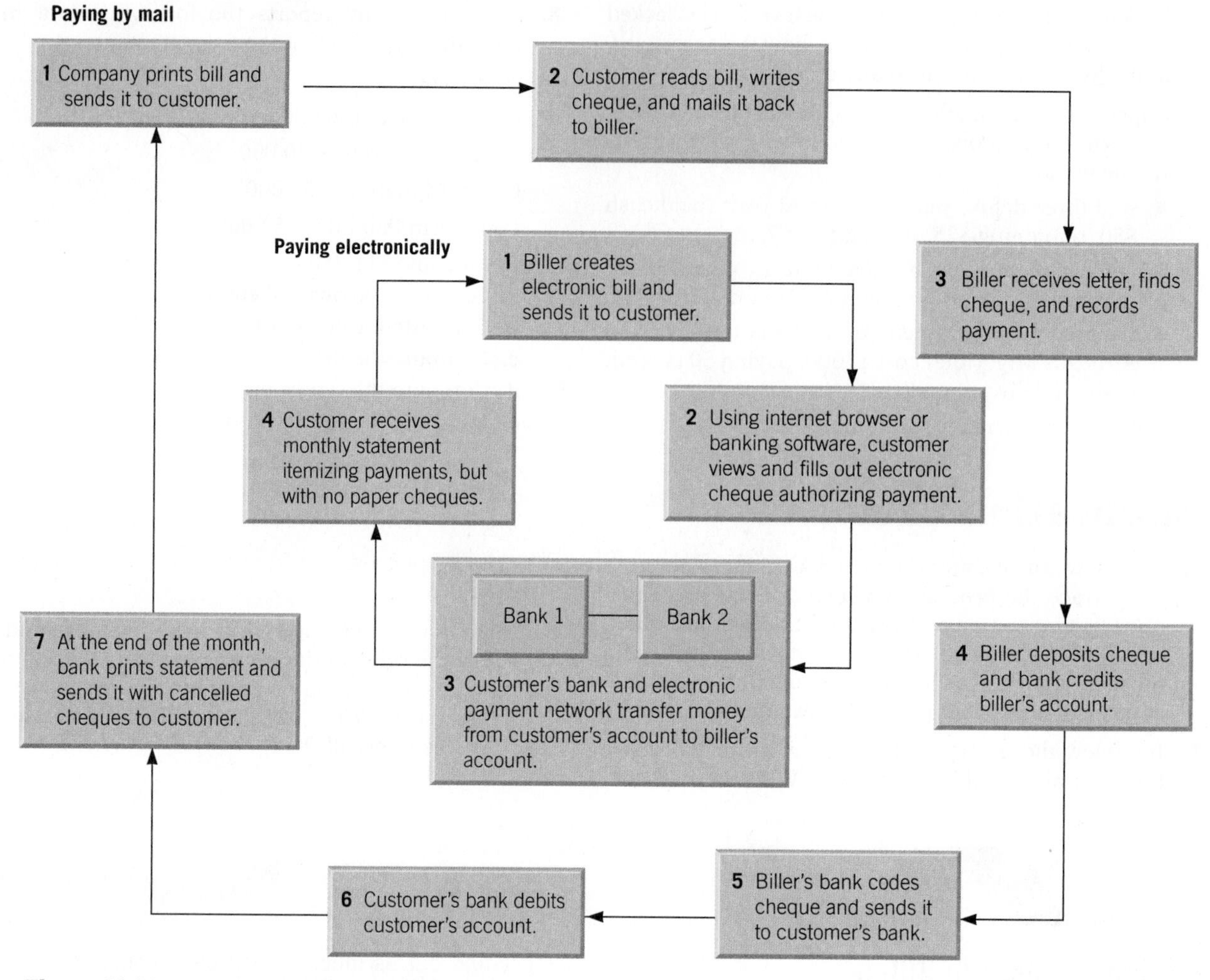

Figure 14.4 Managing operations and information.

Exercising Your Ethics: Team Exercise

Confidentially Yours

The Situation

Accountants are often entrusted with private, sensitive information that should be used confidentially. In this exercise, you're encouraged to think about ethical considerations that might arise when an accountant's career choices come up against a professional obligation to maintain confidentiality.

The Dilemma

Assume that you're the head accountant in Turbatron, a large electronics firm that makes components for other manufacturing firms. Your responsibilities include preparing Turbatron's financial statements that are then audited for financial reporting to shareholders. In addition, you regularly prepare confidential budgets for internal use by managers responsible for planning departmental activities, including future investments in new assets. You've also worked with auditors and CA consultants who assess financial problems and suggest solutions.

Now let's suppose that you're approached by another company, Electrolast, one of the electronics industry's most successful firms, and offered a higher-level position. If you accept, your new job will include developing Electrolast's financial plans and serving on the strategic planning committee. Thus, you'd be involved not only in developing strategy but also in evaluating the competition, perhaps even using your knowledge of Turbatron's competitive strengths and weaknesses.

Your contractual commitments with Turbatron do not bar you from employment with other electronics firms.

Team Activity

Assemble a group of four to five students and assign each group member to one of the following roles:

- head accountant (leaving Turbatron)
- general manager of Turbatron

- shareholder of Turbatron
- customer of Turbatron
- general manager of Electrolast (if your team has five members)

Questions for Discussion

1. Before discussing the situation with your group, and from the perspective of your assigned role, are any ethical issues confronting the head accountant in this situation? If so, write them down.
2. Return to your group and reveal the ethical issues identified by each member. Were the issues the same among all roles or did differences in roles result in different issues?
3. Among the ethical issues that were identified, decide as a group which one is most important for the head accountant. Which is most important for Turbatron?
4. What does your group finally recommend be done to resolve the most important ethical issue(s)?
5. What steps do you think Turbatron might take in advance of such a situation to avoid any difficulties it now faces?

For additional cases and exercise material, go to **www.pearsoned.ca/mybusinesslab**.

Concluding Case 14-1

Do We Need to Audit the Auditors?

The large amount of negative publicity that has been given to firms like Enron and WorldCom during the last few years makes for very interesting reading, but it is also making accountants very nervous. More and more investors are asking questions like "How much confidence can I really have when I read in an auditor's statement that a company's practices adhere to generally accepted accounting principles?" or "How can a company go bankrupt shortly after having their books audited by an independent auditor?" In 2002, NFO WorldGroup, a market research firm, gave outside auditors a D grade for their overall performance.

The case of Livent Inc., a live theatre company that formerly had theatres in Vancouver, Toronto, and New York, illustrates the problems that the auditing profession is facing. Livent went bankrupt in the late 1990s amid charges of questionable accounting practices, and in 2009, two of its executives—Garth Drabinsky and Myron Gottlieb—were found guilty of defrauding investors and creditors out of $500 million. Investors lost 95 percent of their investment after Livent first disclosed accounting irregularities in 1998.

In 2000, the Institute of Chartered Accountants of Ontario (ICAO) took disciplinary action against Livent's senior vice-president of finance, who was a chartered accountant. He was fined $25 000 and expelled from the ICAO after admitting that he had filed false financial statements and fraudulently manipulated Livent's books. After that, the ICAO began investigating the role of Deloitte & Touche, the accounting firm that was Livent's auditors, and in 2004, the ICAO laid charges of professional misconduct against four partners at Deloitte & Touche. (A few years earlier, in a U.S. court, a judge concluded that Deloitte had not participated in the fraud.) Deloitte is also facing several other lawsuits, including one resulting from the collapse of the Italian dairy firm Parmalat. In that case, investors are suing Parmalat executives and two partners in Deloitte's Italian branch for allegedly conspiring to hide nearly $17 billion of debt.

At a disciplinary hearing in April 2004, Deloitte's lawyer argued that the ICAO charges were "rubbish" and that the allegations were simply differences of opinion regarding the application of generally accepted accounting principles. He pointed out that Livent managers had admitted lying to Deloitte auditors to prevent them from finding out about Livent's real financial condition. The lawyer indicated that his clients were angry that they had been charged and criticized the long delay in bringing the ICAO charges forward. He also filed an application with the Ontario Superior Court to drop the charges and prevent the ICAO from pursuing the case further.

William Parrett, the CEO of Deloitte, says that there is an "expectation gap" between what the investing public expects and what external auditors can possibly deliver. While auditors simply certify the accuracy of a company's financial statements (based on information provided by the company), investors want auditors to certify that a company is actually financially healthy. Parrett also says that it is not reasonable to hold auditing firms accountable for the illegal and secretive behaviour of corporate executives. Parrett does agree that auditing firms will have to improve the rigour of their audits, and he said that Deloitte has been working hard to overcome any existing deficiencies. The company has appointed an ethics officer in each of its national companies, has added more resources to audit teams, and rechecks initial audit results.

Parrett's explanation sounds pretty reasonable, but people still want to know how cases like Livent, Parmalat, and Enron happen even after the companies' financial statements have been audited by an independent accounting firm. One answer is that auditors are sometimes tempted to "look the other way" when they encounter questionable practices. But *why* would accounting firms not point out questionable accounting practices when they find them? One reason is that many accounting firms have historically also done management consulting for the firms they are auditing. The fees generated from this management consulting can be very lucrative, and often exceed the auditing fees the accounting firm receives. Accountants are human beings, so we should not be surprised if they worry that their clients will be upset if auditors question certain accounting practices. And if clients get upset enough, they may not give the accounting firm any more management consulting contracts. The obvious solution to this problem is to prohibit accounting firms from doing both auditing and management consulting for a given client. The Canadian Imperial Bank of Commerce no longer allows its auditors to do any management consulting for CIBC.

One very specific Canadian response so far is the establishment of a new Canadian Public Accountability Board (CPAB), which will oversee supervision, inspection, and discipline of Canada's largest accounting firms. The accounting firms will have to get CPAB clearance before their clients' financial statements are accepted. In short, the auditors are going to be audited.

We should not conclude from all of this that doom and gloom reigns in the auditing business. In fact, things are looking up, partly because the Sarbanes-Oxley Act was passed in 2002 by the U.S. Congress. Section 404 of the act requires U.S.-listed companies to analyze their reporting controls and to make any improvements that are necessary. At each year-end, auditors must certify these controls. Many people in the accounting field believe that Canadian legislators will soon introduce similar legislation. And guess what? That will affect over 4000 Canadian corporations, which in turn will create a substantial increase in demand for the services of auditors. Canadian public accounting firms have already begun recruiting more staff. The increased demand for accountants who are knowledgeable about Sarbanes-Oxley is particularly evident in places like Calgary, the home of many Canadian companies that are listed on U.S. stock exchanges.

Questions for Discussion

1. What role does the Institute of Chartered Accountants of Ontario (ICAO) play in ensuring full disclosure on the part of accountants and auditors? How does the ICAO monitor auditor activity and maintain integrity within the accounting profession? What is the ICAO's relationship to the CPAB?
2. What are some ways to ensure that an auditing firm does not find itself in the position that Deloitte & Touche did in the Livent case?
3. Do you think business practices like disclosure and auditing proceedings are changing as a result of the Sarbanes-Oxley Act? Do you think the number of fraud allegations will decline? Explain your answers.
4. There has been much publicity during the last few years about white-collar fraud. Give some examples of fraud that you are familiar with. What role, if any, did accounting fraud play in these cases?

Concluding Case 14-2

Continuing Concerns in the Accounting Profession

The corporate accounting and insider trading scandals of a few years ago have caused users of financial data to be increasingly concerned that the balance sheets and income statements of corporations may not be exactly what they seem. Those concerns prompted the Canadian Senate Banking Committee to analyze ways to restore investor confidence in financial data. The committee made several recommendations, including forcing CEOs to vouch for the truthfulness of their financial statements, passing new legislation governing the conflicts of interest faced by investment analysts, and requiring companies to have only independent directors on their audit committees.

Most of the really dramatic cases of corporate fraud have occurred in the United States, but Canada has the dubious distinction of having one of its own in the limelight. Canadian-born Bernard Ebbers had risen from Alberta milkman and nightclub bouncer to become CEO of WorldCom Inc., one of the largest companies in the United States. It was alleged that Ebbers conspired with subordinates to "cook the books" when a business downturn occurred. These actions wiped out $100 billion of the company's market value, cost 17 000 people their jobs, and wiped out the life savings of investors. Scott Sullivan, one of Ebbers's subordinates, pled guilty and testified that Ebbers had ordered him to cook the books to hit earnings targets. In 2005, Ebbers was found guilty on nine charges of securities fraud and filing false documents. He was sentenced to 25 years in prison for his role in the collapse of WorldCom.

In addition to outright accounting fraud, concerns have been expressed about the difficulty investors have in understanding what accounting statements really mean. In recent years, two issues in this area have received attention: overstating sales revenue and understating pension liabilities. The problem of overstating sales revenue is discussed below.

Overstating Sales Revenue

Sometimes companies are tempted to use "creative accounting" to inflate sales revenue, and this yields a distorted picture of how much product or service a company is actually selling. This is done so that the company will not disappoint the expectations of the stock market and then see its stock price drop. There are different ways that sales revenue can be overstated. For example, some software makers sell a lot of product at the end of a quarter and then count all those sales as revenue without taking into account the future costs the firm will incur to support the software or to provide the free upgrades they promised. Or a company that acts as a sales agent for an airline might include the ticket price, plus the commission it earns, as revenue. When the airline firm is paid, the cost goes on the expense line. This approach vastly overstates revenue (but not profit). The company should have included only its sales commissions as revenue.

High-tech firms in particular are seen as too liberal in recording revenues on their financial statements. Because of this, the Ontario Securities Commission is shifting its emphasis from examining prospectuses to analyzing the way companies report income. It has set up a continuous disclosure team to review the financial reports of corporations in a systematic manner. To get a better understanding of the revenue problem, the OSC is also asking companies how they account for revenue from things like service contracts and whether they benchmark their accounting practices against those used by other firms in their industry.

Other Concerns

A variety of other concerns have also been raised during recent years, including the following:

- There is sometimes a "chummy" relationship between auditors and their clients; this makes it more difficult for auditors to be completely objective.
- There is considerable "elasticity" in the application of generally accepted accounting principles; thus, companies have a lot of leeway in their accounting practices.
- If a person from an accounting firm takes a management position with a firm that is a client, future audits may be too "cozy" and fail to be objective.
- Self-regulation by the accounting industry doesn't work.
- There has been much fruitless debate in accounting firms about how to deal with stock options that are given to executives (if these are shown as expenses, they depress corporation earnings and lower the stock price).
- The accounting profession has moved away from establishing broad accounting principles and instead spent much of its time drafting detailed rules; even if these detailed rules are followed, the financial statements that are produced can present a distorted picture of a company's financial condition.

What should be done to resolve these problems? A few of the more commonly heard solutions are as follows:

- Auditors should clarify their language so that readers of financial statements will have a better idea of how a company is doing before they invest in it.
- Auditors should give more consideration to the users of financial statements, perhaps emphasizing different data for different user groups.
- Auditors should be charged with detecting fraud and reporting it when they find it.
- Firms should be required to change their auditors on a regular basis (for example, once every five years) to prevent "chummy" relationships from developing.
- Auditors should not be allowed to take jobs with former clients until after a specified time period has passed (say, three to five years).
- A truly independent monitoring group should be formed that would assess the extent to which companies are meeting standards in their financial reporting.
- Stock options should be shown as expenses.
- When earnings forecasts are made, there must be a clear statement of how the forecasted numbers were arrived at.
- Companies should be required to show how much they paid for auditing services and how much they paid for management consulting from the same auditor.
- Auditors should be required to rank a company's accounting practices in terms of how "aggressive" they are, rather than just saying the books are okay or not okay.

Questions for Discussion

1. Who are the various users of accounting information? How will each of these users be influenced if sales revenues are overstated and pension liabilities are understated?
2. What are the three basic financial statements that accountants generate for business firms? What does each one show? How will overstating sales revenue and understating pension liabilities affect each of these statements?
3. Read the sections in this chapter on revenue recognition and matching. How is the material in those sections helpful in dealing with the "overstating of sales revenue" problem noted in the case?
4. Consider the following statement: *Since sales revenues and pension returns are measured in dollars, and since dollars are easy to quantify, it should be very clear what sales revenues and investment income a firm had in a given period. It is therefore unnecessary to have policies about how sales revenues and pension returns should be reported.* Do you agree or disagree? Explain.

CBC Video Case 3-1

Tree Planters

At Touchwood Lake, Alberta, 36 rookie tree planters (as well as a group of veteran planters) meet Cal Dyck, who has contracts to plant seven million white and black spruce seedlings in Alberta and Saskatchewan. The trees won't be ready to harvest for 90 years. The tree planting industry was born in the 1970s when the idea of sustainable forestry caught on. Originally, convicts were used, but then forestry companies found out that hippies were cheaper.

During a two-day orientation session, Cal gives the workers a lot of information about tree planting. He knows most of them want to make a lot of money in a short period of time, and he tells them they can do that if they are highly motivated and committed to working hard (planters can burn up to 7000 calories per day). Workers are paid between 10 and 25 cents per tree, depending on the terrain. For a $30 per day charge, Cal will feed the tree planters and move them around to various planting sites. He also provides hot showers.

Among the rookies at the orientation are three friends: Misha (who is studying journalism at Concordia), Megan (a student at the Emily Carr Institute in Vancouver), and Lianne (also a student at the Emily Carr Institute). They will soon learn about the frailty of the human body in the business of tree planting (blisters, tendonitis, twisted ankles, and so on). The orientation also includes all-important demonstrations about how to properly plant a seedling. Spacing the seedlings, planting them at the right depth, choosing the right type of soil, and having the seedlings at the right temperature are all important considerations. The rookies train as a group, but then they're on their own and can work at their own pace. Their work is constantly checked for quality. If planting is not done right, it must be redone.

The rookies plant for just four hours during their first day on the job. While rookies are learning how to plant, they may plant fewer than 100 trees a day, but an experienced veteran can plant 3000 trees in a day. These high-volume planters—called "pounders" because of their intense work ethic—can earn $15 000 during the summer season. They set their own high production goals to motivate themselves to work hard.

For the rookies, the first week is already starting to blur. They eat, sleep, and plant. The work cycle is four days on and one day off. Within just a few weeks, some rookies are already starting to wonder why they are in the bush, especially on days when the rain is pouring down and they are soaked through and through. At Kananaskis, Alberta, work slows down because the terrain is rough and steep. It's only halfway through the season, but some planters already have bad cases of tendonitis from the repeated motions of jamming their shovel into the ground as they plant seedlings. Already eight of the 36 rookies have quit.

Lianne has made $2500 so far, and she is one of the top rookie planters. By season's end, Lianne will have planted more than 98 000 trees. Megan (Lianne's school buddy) is starting to waver. She is fighting a sinus infection and is not even making minimum wage. Misha has decided to quit. A friend of hers is getting married back east and she will not return after the wedding. A week later, Megan quits as well.

At Candle Lake, Saskatchewan, the planting crews are behind schedule as the season nears its end. They still have 1.2 million trees to plant, and the ranks of rookie planters are thinning fast. Only 14 of 36 rookies are still on the job. Smaller work crews mean more work for those who are left, and the opportunity to make more money. After more than three months in the bush, each rookie who is still on the job has planted thousands of trees. Lianne has learned to stop calculating her daily earnings. Brad, a veteran planter, says that he admires the rookies who have pulled through. He says that it's amazing that people can be brought into the bush from the city to do this kind of work.

Questions for Discussion

(Note: Consider the information here and in Concluding Case 8-2 when answering the questions below.)

1. Explain what the terms *productivity* and *quality* mean. How are they related in the actual practice of tree planting?
2. Consider the following statement: *The productivity and quality of rookie tree planters is very low, and the turnover rate is very high. Tree planting companies should therefore hire only experienced tree planters.* Do you agree or disagree with the statement? Defend your answer.
3. Why do you think tree planters are paid on a piece-rate basis? What are the advantages and disadvantages of paying tree planters this way? (Review the relevant material in Chapter 8 before answering this question.)
4. Explain the various forms of employee behaviour. How does each one of these forms of behaviour influence the productivity and quality of tree planters? (Review the relevant material in Chapter 10 before answering this question.)

Video Resource: "Tree Planters," *The National* (May 25, 2007).

CBC **Video Case 3–2**

African Accountants

In Canada's business jungle, all tracks lead to Bay Street, where lions of modern industry reign. Accountants keep Bay Street's books, but the heat is on for individual business owners to keep better books. Accountants don't like people who bring in shoeboxes full of receipts and then ask the accountant to organize them. Instead, accountants want the material organized before they try to do any calculations. But all this organizing costs money, and small- and mid-sized businesses don't usually have the money to pay for it.

For George Wall, of Wall & Associates, finding enough casual workers to do data organization and entry was a big challenge. He had to pay them up to $20 an hour, and that service was way too pricey for many of his clients. But what if Wall could find workers who would do this work for one-tenth the hourly wage that he had to pay people in Toronto? He found the solution by adopting global outsourcing. It works like this: When that shoebox arrives, each piece of paper is first fed into a high-speed scanner and then stored on a server. While Bay Street sleeps, the material is sent to Kampala, Uganda, over the internet, where the data are keyed in by African accountants who are paid only about $1 a day.

In a freshly painted office in Kampala, a dozen computers have just been taken out of their boxes and a dozen workers have just been hired. Their boss is "20-something" Abu Luaga, a Ugandan with a commerce degree who has the contract to do accounting work for Wall & Associates. He teaches the new hires what to do. His start-up funds came from his family, and he got involved with Wall & Associates through his connections with a Canadian business consultant.

There is much competition from other developing countries to get this kind of business, but Luaga's workers are keen and already trained as bookkeepers. They're eager to see what the developed world has to offer, but many have never had a computer before and need training so that they can recognize various financial documents and learn Canadian accounting jargon. They're also being trained to think the way Canadian businesses do. As well, Luaga reminds them about deadlines and privacy. Because these workers are dealing with sensitive information, no cellphones are allowed in the office and the copying or saving of files or images is prohibited.

What are the implications of all this information flowing from the First World to the Third World and back again? It may be just the kind of miracle Uganda needs. The telecommunications industry has been a bright spot in the Ugandan economy, but Ugandans still make only about $1 a day. The country still relies on money earned by exporting coffee, and the government is dependent on foreign donors for part of its budget. Officials admit that the technical skills of workers aren't as good as those of people in some Asian countries, but this system allows educated Ugandans to work in their home country.

Luaga's workers say the work has already changed their career prospects. But not all Canadian clients have jumped at the chance to zip their documents to Africa. George Wall is convinced they will eventually be comfortable with the idea, and Luaga is banking on it. He's leasing bigger and better office space because he thinks that a new office and clients in Canada will impress other potential clients in Africa.

Questions for Discussion

1. What is the difference between *financial* and *managerial* accounting? Is the work that the African accountants are doing financial or managerial accounting? Explain.
2. Why might Canadian clients be reluctant to have Wall & Associates send their data to Africa for organizing? What can George Wall do to respond to their concerns?
3. Suppose that you read a newspaper editorial condemning the practice of sending documents to Africa on the grounds that this was yet another example of exporting Canadian jobs overseas to low-wage countries. How would you respond?

Video Resource: "African Accountants," *Venture* (February 16, 2003).

Crafting a Business Plan

Part 3: Managing Operations and Information

Goal of the Exercise

This part of the business plan project asks you to think about your business in terms of operations, accounting concepts, and information technology (IT) needs and costs. (Review Chapter 13 for material on IT.)

Exercise Background: Part 3 of the Business Plan

An increasingly important part of a business plan is a consideration of how IT—computers, the internet, software, and so on—influences businesses. This part of the business plan asks you to assess how you will use technology to improve your business. Will you, for example, use a database to keep track of your customers? How will you protect your business from hackers and other IT security risks?

This part of the business plan also asks you to consider the costs of doing business, such as salaries, rent, and utilities. You'll also be asked to complete the following financial statements:

- *Balance Sheet.* The balance sheet is a foundation for financial reporting. This report identifies the valued items of the business (its *assets*) as well as the debts that it owes (its *liabilities*). This information gives the owner and potential investors a "snapshot" view of the health of the business.
- *Income Statement (or Profit-and-Loss Statement).* This is the focus of the financial plan. This document will show you what it takes to be profitable and successful as a business owner for your first year. You'll also be asked to consider various factors relating to operating your business.

Your Assignment

Step 1

Open the saved *Business Plan* file you have been working on.

Step 2

For the purposes of this assignment, you will answer the following questions in "Part 3: Managing Operations and Information":

1. What kinds of IT resources will your business require?

Hint: Think about the employees in your business and what they will need in order to do their jobs. What computer hardware and software will they need? Will your business need a network and an internet connection? What type of network? Refer to Chapter 13 for a discussion on IT resources you may want to consider.

2. How will you use IT to keep track of your customers and potential customers?

Hint: Many businesses—even small businesses—use databases to keep track of their customers. Will your business require a database? What about other information systems? Refer to Chapter 13 for more information on these topics.

3. What are the *costs* of doing business? Equipment, supplies, salaries, rent, utilities, and insurance are just some of these expenses. Estimate what it will cost to do business for one year.

Hint: The Business Plan Student Template provides a table for you to insert the costs associated with doing business. Note that these are just estimates—just try your best to include accurate costs for the expenses you think will be a part of doing business.

4. How much will you charge for your product? How many products do you believe you can sell in one year (or how many customers do you think your business can attract)? Multiply the price that you will charge by the number of products that you hope to sell or the amount you hope each customer will spend. This will give you an estimate of your *revenues* for one year.

Hint: You will use the amounts you calculate in the costs and revenues questions in this part of the plan in the accounting statements, so be as realistic as you can.

5. Create a balance sheet and an income statement (profit-and-loss statement) for your business.

Hint: You will have two options for creating these reports. The first option is to use the Microsoft Word versions that are found within the Business Plan Student Template itself. The second option is to use the specific Microsoft Excel templates created for each statement, which are found on the book's MyBusinessLab. These Excel files are handy to use because they already have the worksheet calculations preset—all you have to do is "plug in" the numbers and the calculations will be performed automatically for you. If you make adjustments to the different values in the Excel worksheets, you'll automatically see how changes to expenses, for example, can improve the "bottom line."

6. Create a floor plan of the business. What does it look like when you walk through the door?

Hint: When sketching your floor plan, consider where equipment, supplies, and furniture will be located.

7. Explain what types of raw materials and supplies you will need to run your business. How will you produce your good or service? What equipment do you need? What hours will you operate?

Hint: Refer to the discussion of operations in Chapter 11 for information to get you started.

8. What steps will you take to ensure that the quality of the product or service stays at a high level? Who will be responsible for maintaining quality standards?

Hint: Refer to the discussion of quality improvement and TQM in Chapter 12 for information to get you started.

Note: Once you have answered the questions, save your Word document. You'll be answering additional questions in later chapters.

Part Four

Managing Marketing

What is the first thing you think of when you hear the names Coffee Crisp, Post-It, Crest, and Eno? If you grew up in Canada, you probably didn't hesitate at all before picturing candy, little slips of paper with one sticky edge, toothpaste, and something to calm your stomach. Your rapid association of company names and the goods or services they provide is a tribute to the effectiveness of the marketing managers of the firms that produce these goods. These and many other names have become household words because companies have developed the right products to meet customers' needs, have priced those products appropriately, have made prospective customers aware of the products' existence and qualities, and have made the products readily available.

Part Four, Managing Marketing, provides an overview of the many elements of marketing, including developing, pricing, promoting, and distributing various types of goods and services.

- We begin in **Chapter 15, Understanding Marketing Processes and Consumer Behaviour**, by examining the ways in which companies distinguish their products, determine customer needs, and otherwise address consumer buying preferences.
- Then, in **Chapter 16, Developing and Promoting Goods and Services**, we explore the development of different types of products, the effect of brand names and packaging, how promotion strategies help a firm meet its objectives, and the advantages and disadvantages of several promotional tools.
- Finally, in **Chapter 17, Pricing and Distributing Goods and Services,** we look at the strategies firms use to price their products. We also consider the various outlets business firms use to distribute their products, and we discuss the problems of storing goods and transporting them to distributors.

apter 15

Understanding Marketing Processes and Consumer Behaviour

After reading this chapter, you should be able to:

1. Explain the concept of *marketing* and describe the five forces that constitute the *external marketing environment.*
2. Explain the purpose of a *marketing plan* and identify the four components of the *marketing mix.*
3. Explain *market segmentation* and show how it is used in *target marketing.*
4. Explain the purpose and value of *market research.*
5. Describe the key factors that influence the *consumer buying process.*
6. Discuss the three categories of *organizational markets* and explain how *organizational buying behaviour* differs from consumer buying behaviour.
7. Describe the *international* and *small business marketing mixes.*

Why So Serious?

The five Batman movies released between 1989 and 2008 grossed more than $1.6 billion worldwide. It would be understandable, then, if the producers decided to skimp on the marketing budget for film #6. If ever a movie could be expected to market itself, it would be *The Dark Knight.* Instead, the producers teamed with 42 Entertainment, a California-based creator of alternate reality games, to immerse fans in one of the most elaborate viral marketing campaigns ever conceived. The fun began over a year before the movie opened, with the appearance of posters and a website "supporting" one of the film's characters, Harvey Dent, in his campaign for district attorney of Gotham City. Visitors to the website quickly discovered a link to a similar site—www.whysoserious.com—that appeared to have been vandalized by the movie's main villain, the Joker.

The emergence of the Joker set in motion a series of games in which fans vied with one another to solve puzzles. The fastest fans received cellphones that let them access information that led them deeper into the puzzle. Meanwhile, the websites multiplied: fake newspapers with articles like "Batman Stops Mob Melee"; safety tips from the Gotham Police Department; even a link to Betty's House of Pies, a restaurant that plays a small but crucial role in the movie's plot.

The appeal of viral marketing, according to Jonathan Waite, owner of the Alternate Reality Gaming Network, is that "you're not a passive onlooker; you're taking an active role. And any time you take an active role, you're emotionally connecting." Or, as one blogger put it, "I've never been a fan of the Batman series, but this sort of thing makes me want to go see it."

The Dark Knight's innovative marketing campaign helped catapult the movie to a record-breaking box office debut, earning over $158 million in its opening weekend. Domestically and internationally, the film was a great success, earning more than $873 million worldwide. That was more than half the money earned by the previous five Batman movies combined. Was it the innovative marketing tactics or the captivating line-up of stars that contributed to the film's success? We may never know. ◆

How will this help me?

Marketing is a business activity that focuses on providing value to customers so they will want to purchase goods and services that companies offer for sale. If you understand the marketing methods and ideas that are presented in this chapter, you will benefit in two ways: (1) You'll be better prepared to enhance your career by using effective marketing ideas, both as an employee and as a manager; and (2) you'll be a more informed consumer, with greater awareness of how businesses use marketing to influence your purchases.

We start this chapter by looking at how marketing provides value, satisfaction, and utility to customers in order to motivate them to purchase goods and services. We then look at the marketing plan and the components of the marketing mix and discuss market segmentation and how it is used in target marketing. Next, we look at the idea of market research and how this activity helps companies develop and sell goods and services. The chapter concludes with a discussion of the key factors that influence the buying processes of consumers and organizational buyers.

What Is Marketing?

1 Explain the concept of *marketing* and describe the five forces that constitute the *external marketing environment.*

marketing Planning and executing the development, pricing, promotion, and distribution of ideas, goods, and services to create exchanges that satisfy both buyers' and sellers' objectives.

marketing concept The idea that the whole firm is directed toward serving present and potential customers at a profit.

What do you think of when you hear the word **marketing**? If you are like most people, you probably think of advertising for something like detergent or soft drinks. But marketing is more than just advertising. Marketing is "the process of planning and executing the conception, pricing, promotion, and distribution of ideas, goods, and services to create exchanges that satisfy individual and organizational goals."[1]

Because we are all consumers and because we all buy goods and services, we are influenced by the marketing activities of companies that want us to buy their products. But as consumers, we are in fact the essential ingredients in the marketing process. Every day, we express needs for such essentials as food, clothing, and shelter and wants for such non-essentials as entertainment and leisure activities. Our needs and wants are the forces that drive marketing.

The **marketing concept** means that the whole firm is coordinated to achieve one goal—to serve its present and potential customers and to do so at a profit. This concept means that a firm must get to know what customers really want and follow closely the changes in tastes that occur. The various departments of the firm—marketing, production, finance, and human resources—must operate as a system, well coordinated and unified in the pursuit of a common goal—customer satisfaction.

We begin our study of marketing by looking at how marketing focuses on providing value and utility for consumers. We then explore the marketing environment and the development of marketing strategy. Finally, we focus on the four activities that compose the marketing mix: *developing*, *pricing*, *promoting*, and *placing products*.

Providing Value and Satisfaction

What attracts buyers to one product instead of another? While our desires for the many goods and services available to us may be unbounded, limited financial resources force most of us to be selective. Accordingly, consumers buy products that offer the best value when it comes to meeting their needs and wants.

Value and Benefits

Value compares a product's benefits with its costs. The benefits of a high-value product are much greater than its costs. Benefits include not only the functions of the product but also the emotional satisfactions associated with owning, experiencing, or possessing it. Every product has costs, including sales price, the expenditure of the buyer's time, and the emotional costs of making a purchase decision. The satisfied buyer perceives the benefits derived from the purchase to be greater than its costs.

value Relative comparison of a product's benefits vs. its costs.

Thus the simple but important ratio for value:

$$\text{Value} = \frac{\text{Benefits}}{\text{Costs}}$$

Marketing strategies focus on increasing value for customers. Marketing resources are deployed to add value to products to satisfy customers' needs and wants. Satisfying customers may mean developing an entirely new product that performs better (provides greater benefits) than existing products. Or it may mean keeping a store open extra hours during a busy season (adding the benefit of greater shopping convenience). Some companies simply offer price reductions (the benefit of lower cost). Customers may also gain benefits from an informational promotion that explains how a product can be used in new ways.

Value and Utility

To understand how marketing creates value for customers, we need to know the kind of benefits that buyers get from a firm's goods or services. Products provide consumers with **utility**—the ability of a product to satisfy a human want or need. Marketing strives to provide four kinds of utility.

utility Ability of a product to satisfy a human want or need.

- When a company turns out ornaments in time for Christmas, it creates time utility: It makes products available when consumers want them.
- When a department store opens its annual Christmas department, it creates place utility: It makes products available where customers can conveniently purchase them.
- When the store sells ornaments, it provides ownership utility by conveniently transferring ownership from store to customer.
- By making products available in the first place—by turning raw materials into finished ornaments—the ornament maker creates form utility.

Marketing plays a role in all four areas—determining the timing, place, terms of sale, and product features that provide utility and add value for customers. Marketers, therefore, must begin with an understanding of customers' wants and needs. Their methods for creating utility are described in this and the following two chapters.

Goods, Services, and Ideas

The marketing of tangible goods is obvious in everyday life. You walk into a department store and are given a free scented paper strip as an initial product sample of a new perfume. A pharmaceutical company proclaims the virtues of its new cold medicine. Your local auto dealer offers to sell you an automobile with no interest charges for four years. These products—the perfume, the cold medicine, and the car—are all **consumer goods**: products that you, the consumer, buy for personal use. Firms that sell products to consumers for personal consumption are engaged in consumer marketing.

consumer goods Products purchased by individuals for their personal use.

Business Accountability

When Smoke Gets in Your Eyes

In Canada, government restriction on the advertising of cigarettes has a long history. Television advertising of cigarettes has been prohibited since 1971, and various other restrictions (including some rather dramatic label requirements) have come into force since then. Recent legislation discourages tobacco companies from sponsoring sports and cultural events so that they can get their brands prominently displayed to consumers. At a charity dinner in Toronto in 2004, for example, the Rothmans, Benson & Hedges table simply said "anonymous" in spite of the fact that the company had paid thousands of dollars to sponsor the table. Tobacco companies are still allowed to advertise in magazines and newspapers, but the rules are so restrictive they generally don't try anymore. Yves-Thomas Dorval, a spokesman for Imperial Tobacco Canada Ltd., says that since "promotion" is essentially prohibited by law, tobacco companies are focussing on the three other *P*s of marketing (price, place, and product).

Clashes between stop-smoking groups and tobacco companies are common, particularly when tobacco companies appear to be ignoring the spirit of the restrictions that have been placed on them. For example, as part of the TD Canada Trust Toronto Jazz Festival, Imperial Tobacco set up an outdoor smoking lounge in Nathan Phillips Square. The lounge was criticized by the Ontario Tobacco-Free Network, which called on the mayor of Toronto to stop Imperial from using "scantily clad girls" to promote cigarettes on city property.

All of these situations are interesting, but an important question remains: Who is accountable for the negative effects of tobacco use? Government agencies in both Canada and the United States (Health Canada and the American Public Health Association, respectively) seem to take the position that it is the companies who sell cigarettes that bear most of the responsibility. Not surprisingly, cigarette companies argue that because tobacco use is an individual behaviour choice for which potential health risks are well-known, accountability falls to the consumer instead of the producer of the product.

Coalitions of health advocacy groups—including the World Health Organization and other grassroots public health organizations—are insisting that corporate accountability be formally acknowledged. In the United States, the $39 billion in settlement revenues that was given to states during a recent five-year period is cited as tangible recognition of the industry's accountability, but only for after-effects. Not far enough, insist the health advocates, arguing that the more than 400 000 tobacco-related deaths each year in North America are preventable: Companies should also be accountable for effective preventive measures that are absent now and are likely to remain so until more regulation is imposed on them. Tobacco firms, in response, point to several recent court rulings in the United States that denied more than $50 billion in claims brought by health maintenance organizations (HMOs) and insurance companies for reimbursement of tobacco-related health expenses. They point to these cases as supportive of the industry's argument that it is not accountable.

While the issue of accountability simmers, marketing finds itself on both sides of the controversy. Advertising expenditures by Canadian and U.S. tobacco companies have soared to more than $11 billion each year. Health advocates cite "predatory marketing practices" as the industry advertises in youth magazines and develops advertising campaigns targeted at Hispanic, Asian, and other population groups that as yet may not be fully aware of health risks from smoking. Young adults with low incomes and lower education levels are representative of the target-market demographics of smoking. Consider the following statistics:

- The rate of smoking among people who did not complete high school is three times the rate for those with an undergraduate university degree.
- Smoking among pregnant women is 15 times greater for those who did not graduate from high school than it is for those with a university education.
- About one-third of people living below the poverty line are smokers, compared with only one-quarter of those above the poverty line.
- Low-wage workers smoke more than those with high wages.

Health advocates say that tobacco companies have increasingly paid retailers to display tobacco advertising, have used "buy one, get one free" promotions, and have set up promotional racks and giveaways that make cigarettes easier to buy among these targeted smokers.

Marketing by health advocacy groups has embraced "idea-and-information" messages to promote the stop-smoking idea and to appeal for more corporate accountability. The American Legacy Foundation's award-winning TV "truth" campaign debunks the idea that smoking is glamorous and features information about the social costs and health consequences of tobacco. A report by the U.S. National Cancer Institute publicized the idea that "light" cigarettes don't reduce health risks and often simply lead to brand switching rather than quitting. Community-based and grassroots efforts include counter-marketing campaigns to educate higher risk groups—targeted by the tobacco industry—about tobacco's harmful effects. Media ads and promotional materials targeted at

legislators and regulators are appealing for more regulation and explicit acknowledgement of industry's accountability for reducing the ill effects from tobacco. Meanwhile, both sides know that each day brings with it hundreds of new smokers, quitters, and tobacco-related deaths.

Critical Thinking Questions

1. Who is more accountable for the health risks associated with smoking, the tobacco companies or the people who decide to smoke cigarettes? Explain your reasoning.
2. Should tobacco companies be held more accountable for the health problems of low-income, low-education smokers than for the health problems of high-income, high-education smokers?
3. Consider the following statement: *There is overwhelming evidence that cigarettes cause a variety of serious health problems. The Canadian government, in its role of protecting consumers, should therefore ban the sale of cigarettes.* Do you agree or disagree with this statement? Explain your reasoning.

Marketing is also important for **industrial goods**, which are products used by companies to produce other products. Surgical instruments and earth movers are industrial goods, as are such components and raw materials as integrated circuits, steel, and unformed plastic. Firms that sell products to other manufacturers are engaged in industrial marketing.

industrial goods Products purchased by companies to use directly or indirectly to produce other products.

Marketing is also relevant for **services**—intangible products such as time, expertise, or some activity that you can purchase. Service marketing has become a major growth area in Canada. Insurance companies, airlines, investment counsellors, health clinics, and accountants all engage in service marketing, both to individuals and to other companies.

services Intangible products, such as time, expertise, or an activity that can be purchased.

Finally, marketers also promote ideas. Television ads, for example, can remind us that teaching is an honourable profession and that teachers are "heroes." Other ads stress the importance of driving only when sober and the advantages of not smoking.

Relationship Marketing

Although marketing often focuses on single transactions for products, services, or ideas, marketers also take a longer-term perspective. Thus, **relationship marketing** emphasizes lasting relationships with customers and suppliers. Stronger relationships—including stronger economic and social ties—can result in greater long-term satisfaction and customer loyalty.[2]

relationship marketing A type of marketing that emphasizes lasting relationships with customers and suppliers.

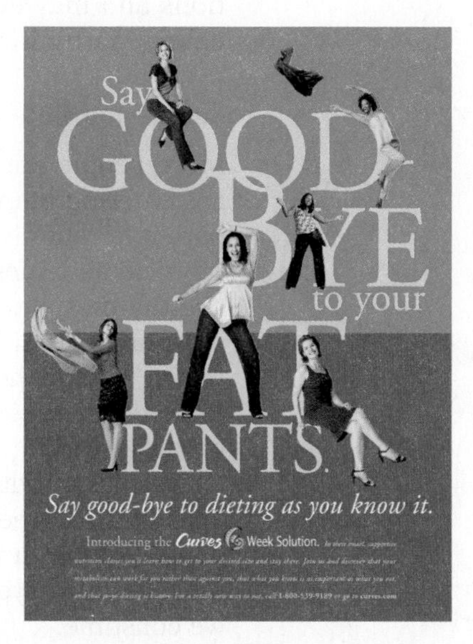

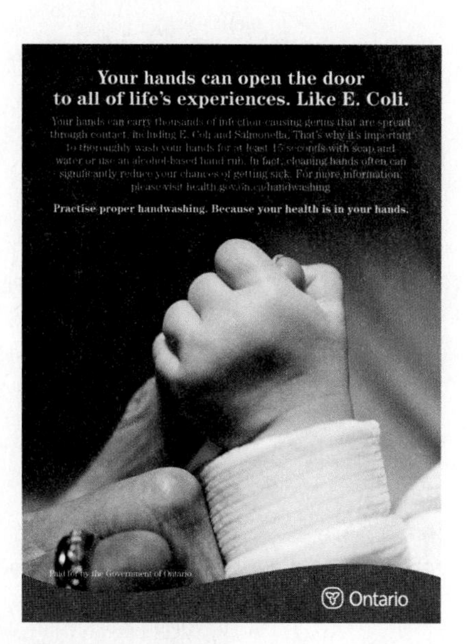

Each of these advertisements provides information about a specific product, service, or idea. The soy milk, for example, is a tangible consumer product. The advertisement for the fitness club promotes a service that can be enjoyed. The public service ad promotes the idea of healthy behaviour.

Banks, for example, offer economic incentives to encourage longer-lasting relationships. Customers who purchase more of the bank's products (for example, chequing accounts, savings accounts, and loans) accumulate credits toward free or reduced-price services, such as unlimited monthly transactions. Motorcycle manufacturer Harley-Davidson offers social incentives through the Harley Owners Group (H.O.G.), which gives motorcyclists the opportunity to bond with other riders and to develop long-term friendships. For companies needing assistance and ideas, Loyalty Works designs and manages incentive and loyalty marketing programs. Their programs focus not only on building loyal customers but also on aligning channel partners and employees for an integrated approach to improving relationship marketing.

The Marketing Environment

Marketing plans, decisions, and strategies are not determined unilaterally by any business—not even by marketers as experienced and influential as Coca-Cola and Procter & Gamble. Rather, they are strongly influenced by powerful outside forces. As you can see in Figure 15.1, any marketing program must recognize the outside factors that compose a company's **external environment**. In this section, we will describe five of these environmental factors: the political/legal, social/cultural, technological, economic, and competitive environments.

external environment Outside factors that influence marketing programs by posing opportunities or threats.

Political and Legal Environment

Political activities, both foreign and domestic, have profound effects on business (refer back to Chapter 1 for a discussion of how government influences business). Legislation on the use of cellphones in cars and legislation on pollution can determine the destinies of entire industries. Marketing managers therefore try to maintain favourable political/legal environments in several ways. For example, to gain public support for their products and activities, marketing uses advertising campaigns for public awareness on issues of local, regional, or national importance. They also lobby and contribute to political candidates (although there are legal restrictions on how much they can contribute). Such activities sometimes result in favourable laws and regulations and may even open new international business opportunities.

Figure 15.1 The external marketing environment.

Social and Cultural Environment

More people are working at home, more women are entering the workforce, the number of single-parent families is increasing, food preferences and physical activities reflect the growing concern for healthy lifestyles, and the growing recognition of cultural diversity continues. These and other issues reflect the values, beliefs, and ideas that form the fabric of Canadian society today. These broad attitudes toward issues have direct effects on business. Today, for example, as we continue to insist on a "greener" Canada, we have seen the demise of Freon in air conditioners and increased reliance on recycling materials in the goods that we consume.

Changing social values force companies to develop and promote new products for both individual consumers and industrial customers. For example, although most of us value privacy, web surfers are discovering that a loss of privacy is often a price for the convenience of internet shopping. Dot-com sites regularly collect personal information that they use for marketing purposes and which they often sell to other firms. Responding to the growing demand for better privacy protection, firms like iNetPrivacy offer such products as Anonymity 4 Proxy software, which allows you to surf the internet anonymously.

Technological Environment

New technologies affect marketing in several ways. Obviously, they create new goods (say, the satellite dish) and services (home television shopping). New products make some existing products obsolete (for example, music downloads are replacing compact discs), and many of them change our values and lifestyles. In turn, they often stimulate new goods and services not directly related to the new technology itself. Cellphones, for example, not only facilitate business communication but also free up time for recreation and leisure.

Consider the phenomenon of DNA "fingerprinting": The O.J. Simpson trial (United States), the Guy Paul Morin case (Canada), and the television show *CSI: Crime Scene Investigation* have made just about everyone aware of its availability to law-enforcement officials. Bear in mind, however, that it is also the focal point of a new industry—one that involves biological science and laboratory analysis and instrumentation as well as criminology. DNA fingerprinting, then, is a product. Along with its technical developments, therefore, it involves marketing decisions—such as pricing and promotion. This has been the case with literally thousands of technological breakthroughs in such fields as genetics, electronics, aeronautics, medicine, information sciences, communications systems, transportation, the internet, and emarketing.

Marketing strategies are strongly influenced by powerful outside forces. For example, new technologies create new products, such as the Chinese cellphone "filling station" kiosk shown here. Called *shouji jiayouzhan* in Chinese, these kiosks enable customers to recharge their cellphones as they would refuel their cars. The screens on the kiosks also provide marketers with a new way to display ads to waiting customers.

Economic Environment

Economic conditions determine spending patterns by consumers, businesses, and governments. Thus they influence every marketer's plans for product offerings, pricing, and promotional strategies. Among the more significant economic variables, marketers are concerned with inflation, interest rates, recession, and recovery. In other words, they must monitor the general business cycle, which typically features a pattern of transition from periods of prosperity to recession to recovery (return to prosperity). Not surprisingly, consumer spending increases as consumer confidence in economic conditions grows during periods of prosperity. Conversely, spending decreases during low-growth periods, when unemployment rises and purchasing power declines.

Traditionally, analysis of economic conditions focussed on the national economy and the government's policies for controlling or moderating it. Increasingly, however, as nations form more and more economic connections, the global economy is becoming more prominent in the thinking of marketers everywhere.[3]

At U.S.-based Wal-Mart, for example, more than 18 percent of all sales revenue comes from the retailer's international division. International sales were up 9.9 percent for 2009, which suggests that some U.S. companies can remain profitable from strong international sales despite a U.S. economic slowdown.

Competitive Environment

In a competitive environment, marketers must convince buyers that they should purchase their products rather than those of some other seller. In a broad sense, because both consumers and commercial buyers have limited

The Greening of Business

Guelph Thinks Green

The first important plastic, celluloid, was discovered in 1869 by the American inventor John W. Hyatt and manufactured by him in 1872. However, plastics did not come into modern industrial use until 1909, after the production of bakelite by the American chemist L.H. Baekeland. The majority of plastics that have been manufactured since then are still in existence. As little as 4 percent of plastics produced have been recycled, and only 2 percent have been incinerated. The remaining masses are either buried, blowing around, sitting in a landfill, or floating in our oceans. Larger populations, continuous consumption, and increased demand for products have taken a terrible toll on our environment. Today's consumers are becoming more aware of their impact on the environment and are starting to look for ways to reduce waste.

A group of University of Guelph students decided to look more closely at a niche market to try to address waste issues. Green World Solutions (GWS) was created by Kwasi Danso, Jonathan Wolff, and Ashley van Herten. This ambitious group recognized that, in order to make a difference to the environment, consumers must become collectively accountable for their actions. Their research brought GWS in contact with the patent holder of a revolutionary additive that makes plastic biodegradable. GWS has aligned itself with the Canadian exclusive holder of this additive and has begun discussions and developing pricing strategies for manufacturing a variety of household items.

One product idea was a pet waste bag but, before the idea could be launched, GWS needed to conduct significant market research to determine competitiveness and product feasibility. What they found was surprising: Most of the biodegradable bags for pet waste were currently on the market were not biodegradable in a landfill. The ideal environment for the breakdown of the materials could only be found in commercial composts. This new revelation did not make sense to GWS, as consumers were led to believe the products currently on the market would compost when left in a garbage can. This new information—showing that current product offerings needed to be improved—gave GWS the basis for demonstrating to consumers that their product was superior to others already on the market.

GWS is constantly testing this biodegradable additive with additional products in order to help all industries make an easy environmental choice. As this is a new market and environmental interest is at an all-time high, GWS is also spending considerable time and effort in creating a strong, recognizable brand image as an environmentally conscious company. Their name is descriptive and appealing to the targeted audience, and the logo shows imagery of a clean blue and green earth.

Green World Solutions has now incorporated and will shortly be commencing production on biodegradable waste bags. The next steps for GWS are to actively promote environmental consumerism and to spread awareness of the importance of taking action for one's own footprint. Green World Solutions foresees tremendous opportunity in the biodegradable retail plastic industry and has future goals for the consumer household market.

Neil Seldman is a waste recycling expert and president of the Institute for Local Self-Reliance, an organization with a long track record of promoting sustainable communities. He explains that saving money by altering plastic consumption is not limited to supermarkets and retailers through the elimination of plastic bags. According to Seldman, "There is a lot of money to be made in alternative plastics and in managing refillable reusables."

Critical Thinking Questions

1. Research some other plastics products that might benefit from having a biodegradability additive. What do you think would be the biggest barrier to getting the new product in the mainstream market?
2. What are some of the concerns that businesses would have when undertaking new initiatives like those at GWS? What concerns might consumers have?
3. Research the waste management industry. What can you learn from their websites about the benefits of new biodegradable plastics?

resources to spend, every dollar spent to buy one product is no longer available for other purchases. Each marketing program, therefore, seeks to make its product the most attractive; theoretically, a failed program loses the buyer's dollar forever (or at least until it is time for the next purchase decision).

By studying the competition, marketers determine how best to position their own products for three specific types of competition:

- **Substitute products** are dissimilar from those of competitors but can fulfill the same need. For example, your cholesterol level may be controlled with either a physical-fitness program or a drug regimen; the fitness program and the drugs compete as substitute products.
- **Brand competition** occurs between similar products, such as the auditing services provided by large accounting firms like Ernst & Young and KPMG. The competition is based on buyers' perceptions of the benefits of products offered by particular companies.
- **International competition** matches the products of domestic marketers against those of foreign competitors—say, a flight on Swiss International Air Lines vs. Air Canada. The intensity of international competition has been heightened by the formation of alliances such as the European Union and NAFTA.

substitute product A product that is dissimilar from those of competitors but that can fulfill the same need.

brand competition Competitive marketing that appeals to consumer perceptions of similar products.

international competition Competitive marketing of domestic against foreign products.

Strategy: The Marketing Mix

Explain the purpose of a *marketing plan* and identify the four components of the *marketing mix*. **2**

As a business activity, marketing requires management. Although many individuals also contribute to the marketing of a product, a company's **marketing managers** are typically responsible for planning and implementing all the marketing-mix activities that result in the transfer of goods or services to its customers. These activities culminate in the **marketing plan**—a detailed and focussed strategy for gearing marketing activities to meet consumer needs and wants. Marketing, therefore, begins when a company identifies a consumer need and develops a product to meet it.

In planning and implementing strategies, marketing managers develop the four basic components (often called the "four Ps") of the **marketing mix** (see Figure 15.2). In this section, we briefly describe each of those components: *product*, *price*, *place*, and *promotion*.

The importance of these four elements varies, depending on the product that is being sold. Price might play a large role in selling fresh meat but a very small role in selling newspapers. Distribution might be crucial in marketing gasoline but not so important for lumber. Promotion is vital in toy marketing but of little consequence in marketing nails. The product is important in every case, but probably less so for toothpaste than for cars.

marketing managers Managers responsible for planning and implementing all the marketing-mix activities that result in the transfer of goods or services to customers.

marketing plan A detailed strategy for gearing the marketing mix to meet consumer needs and wants.

marketing mix The combination of product, pricing, promotion, and distribution strategies used in marketing a product.

Product

Marketing begins with a **product**—a good, a service, or an idea designed to fill a consumer need or want. Conceiving and developing new products is a constant

product A good, service, or idea that satisfies buyers' needs and demands.

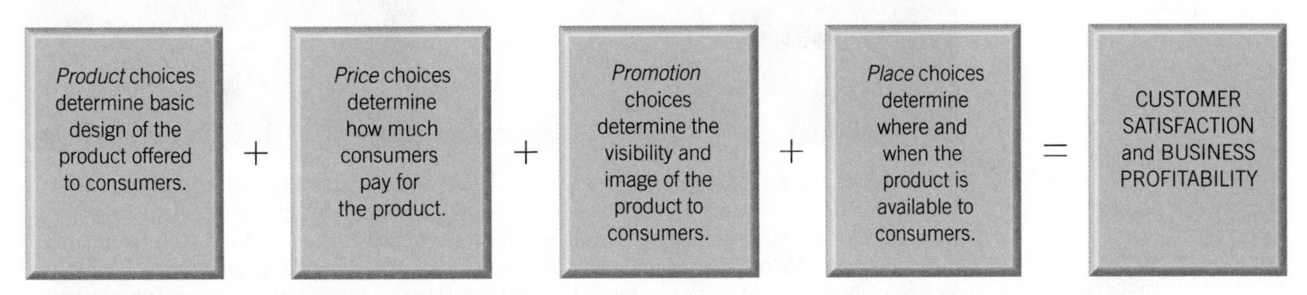

Figure 15.2 Choosing the marketing mix for a business.

challenge for marketers, who must always consider the factor of change—changing technology, changing consumer wants and needs, and changing economic conditions. Meeting consumer needs, then, often means changing existing products to keep pace with emerging markets and competitors. Mass-customization, which was explained in Chapter 13, allows marketers to provide products that satisfy very specific needs of consumers.

product differentiation The creation of a product or product image that differs enough from existing products to attract consumers.

Producers often promote particular features of products to distinguish them in the marketplace. **Product differentiation** is the creation of a feature or image that makes a product differ enough from existing products to attract consumers. For example, Crest toothpaste has nine different products for different consumer needs. People looking for alternatives in a car might consider an electric vehicle (EV); GM's EV1 used the slogan "A different driving experience," which appealed to early users looking for a unique driving technology that also helps the environment.

Price

price That part of the marketing mix concerned with choosing the appropriate price for a product to meet the firm's profit objectives and buyers' purchasing objectives.

Price refers not only to the actual amount of money that consumers must pay for a product or service but also to the total value of things that consumers are willing to give up in return for being able to have the benefits of the product or service. For example, if a person wants to own a Chrysler 300, that person may have to take money out of a savings account to pay for the car. The value of the interest that would have been earned on the savings account is part of the value that the customer gives up to own the car. From the seller's perspective, determining the best price at which to sell a product is often a balancing act. On the one hand, prices must support a variety of costs—operating, administrative, research, and marketing costs. On the other hand, prices can't be so high that consumers turn to competitors' products. Successful pricing means finding a profitable middle ground between these two requirements.

Both low- and high-price strategies can be effective in different situations. Low prices, for example, generally lead to larger sales volumes. High prices usually limit market size but increase profits per unit. High prices may also

Jann Wenner started *Rolling Stone* magazine in 1967, and it's been the cash cow of Wenner Media ever since. In 1985, Wenner bought *Us* magazine and set out to compete with *People*, perhaps the most successful magazine ever published. Wenner's latest strategy calls for greater differentiation between the two products. *People* is news driven, reporting on ordinary people as well as celebrities, and Wenner intends to punch up *Us* with more coverage of celebrity sex and glitter. So far, he hasn't been successful. *People* reaches 3.7 million readers, *Us* about 900 000.

attract customers by implying that a product is of high quality. We discuss pricing in more detail in Chapter 17.

Place (Distribution)

In the marketing mix, place refers to **distribution**. Placing a product in the proper outlet—say, a retail store—requires decisions about several activities, all of which are concerned with getting the product from the producer to the consumer. Decisions about warehousing and inventory control are distribution decisions, as are decisions about transportation options.

Firms must also make decisions about the channels through which they distribute products. Many manufacturers, for instance, sell goods to other companies that, in turn, distribute them to retailers. Others sell directly to major retailers such as Sears, Wal-Mart, or Safeway. Still others sell directly to final consumers. We explain distribution decisions further in Chapter 17.

Apple's latest iPhone features an application that allows travellers to wirelessly map an entire city layout.

Promotion

The most highly visible component of the marketing mix is **promotion**, which refers to techniques for communicating information about products. The most important promotional tools include advertising, personal selling, sales promotions, and public relations. One example of a promotional tactic used to entice consumers is the loyalty program. Rupert Duchesne, CEO of Group Aeroplan Inc., is convinced that loyalty marketing is boundaryless, and he has identified four components of loyalty: travel loyalty, financial services loyalty, retail loyalty, and data analytics (getting information on where consumers travel, how much they spend, and which stores they frequent).[4] We describe promotional activities more fully in Chapter 16.

distribution That part of the marketing mix concerned with getting products from the producer to the buyer, including physical transportation and choice of sales outlets.

promotion Techniques for communicating information about products.

Product, price, place, and promotion focus on the seller's perspective. From the buyer's perspective, each of the four Ps provides a certain benefit. In effect, the seller's four Ps are a mirror image of the buyer's four Cs: customer solution (product), customer cost (price), customer convenience (place), and customer communication (promotion).[5]

Target Marketing and Market Segmentation

3 Explain *market segmentation* and show how it is used in *target marketing.*

Marketing managers long ago recognized that they cannot be "all things to all people." People have different tastes, different interests, different goals, different lifestyles, and so on. The marketing concept's recognition of consumers' various needs and wants has led marketing managers to think in terms of target marketing. **Target markets** are groups of people with similar wants and needs.

target market Any group of people who have similar wants and needs and may be expected to show interest in the same product(s).

market segmentation Dividing a market into categories according to traits customers have in common.

Target marketing clearly requires **market segmentation**, dividing a market into categories of customer types or "segments." For example, Mr. Big & Tall sells to men who are taller and heavier than average. Certain special interest magazines are oriented toward people with specific interests (see Table 15.1). Once they have identified market segments, companies may adopt a variety of product strategies. Some firms decide to provide a range of products to the market in an attempt to market their products to more than one segment. For example, General Motors of Canada offers compact cars, vans, trucks, luxury cars, and sports cars with various features and prices. Its strategy is to provide an automobile for nearly every segment of the market.

In contrast, some businesses restrict production to one market segment. Rolls-Royce understands that only a relatively small number of people are

Table 15.1 Magazines with Specific Target Audiences

Accounting	**Fishing/Hunting**
CAmagazine	*Canadian Fly Fisher*
CGA Magazine	*Outdoor Canada*
CMA Management	*B.C. Outdoors Sport Fishing*
Agriculture	**Automotive**
Agro-Nouvelles	*Aftermarket Canada*
Meat & Poultry Magazine	*Bodyshop*
Country Life in B.C.	*World of Wheels*
Sports	**Boating**
Cycle Canada	*Boating Business*
Chalk and Cue	*Canadian Boating*
Athletics Canada	*Porthole Magazine*
Gardening	**Music**
Canadian Gardening	*CHART Magazine*
The Gardener for the Prairies	*CODA Magazine*
Gardening Life	*Opus*

willing to pay $310 000 for exclusive touring limousines. Rolls, therefore, makes no attempt to cover the entire range of possible products; instead, it markets to only a very small segment of the total automobile buyers market. In contrast, U.S. retailer Target has deals with Mossimo Giannulli and Isaac Mizrahi. Through these partnerships, says Target vice-president Trish Adams, "our guests have learned, and come to expect, that high fashion doesn't have to mean high prices." The key to luxury today lies in creating an emotional rapport between the consumer and the product.[6]

Table 15.2 shows how a marketer of home electronics equipment might segment the radio market. Note that segmentation is a strategy for analyzing consumers, not products. The analysis in Table 15.2, for example, identifies consumer users—joggers, commuters, and travellers. Only indirectly, then, does it focus on the uses of the product itself. In marketing, the process of fixing, adapting, and communicating the nature of the product itself is called positioning.

Table 15.2 Possible Segmentation of the Radio Market

Segmentation	Product/Target Market
Age	Inexpensive, unbreakable, portable models for young children
	Inexpensive equipment—possibly portable—for teens
	Moderate-to-expensive equipment for adults
Consumer attitude	Sophisticated components for audio buffs
	All-in-one units in furniture cabinets for those concerned with room appearance
Product use	Miniature models for joggers and commuters
	"Boom box" portables for taking outdoors
	Car stereo systems for travelling
	Components and all-in-one units for home use
Location	Battery-powered models for use where electricity is unavailable
	AC current for North American users
	DC current for other users

Identifying Market Segments

By definition, the members of a market segment must share some common traits or behaviours that will affect their purchasing decisions. In identifying market segments, researchers look at geographic, demographic, psychographic, and product-use variables.

Geographic Variables

In some cases, where people live affects their buying decisions. The heavy rainfall in British Columbia prompts its inhabitants to purchase more umbrellas than does the climate in Arizona's desert. Urban residents have less demand for pickup trucks than do their rural counterparts. Sailboats sell better along both coasts than they do in the prairie provinces. **Geographic variables** are the geographical units, from countries to neighbourhoods, that may be considered in a segmentation strategy.

geographic variables Geographical units that may be considered in a segmentation strategy.

These patterns affect marketing decisions about what products to offer, at what price to sell them, how to promote them, and how to distribute them. For example, consider the marketing of down parkas in rural Saskatchewan. Demand will be high, price competition may be limited, local newspaper advertising may be very effective, and the best location may be one easily reached from several small towns.

Although the marketability of some products is geographically sensitive, others enjoy nearly universal acceptance. Coca-Cola, for example, gets more than 70 percent of its sales from markets outside the United States. It is the market leader in Great Britain, China, Germany, Japan, Brazil, and Spain. By contrast, Pepsi earns 78 percent of its income from the United States. Coke's chief competitor in most countries is not Pepsi but a local soft drink.

Demographic Variables

Demographic variables describe populations by identifying characteristics such as age, income, gender, ethnic background, marital status, race, religion, and social class. These are objective criteria that cannot be altered. Marketers must work with or around them. Table 15.3 lists some demographic market

demographic variables Characteristics of populations that may be considered in developing a segmentation strategy.

Table 15.3 Demographic Market Segmentation

Age	Under 5; 5–11; 12–19; 20–34; 35–49; 50–64; 65+
Education	Grade school or less; some high school; graduated high school; some college or university; college diploma or university degree; advanced degree
Family life cycle	Young single; young married without children; young married with children; older married with children under 18; older married without children under 18; older single; other
Family size	1, 2–3, 4–5, 6+
Income	Under $9000; $9000–$14 999; $15 000–$25 000; over $25 000
Nationality	Including but not limited to African, Asian, British, Eastern European, French, German, Irish, Italian, Latin American, Middle Eastern, and Scandinavian
Race	Including but not limited to Inuit, Asian, black, and white
Religion	Including but not limited to Buddhist, Catholic, Hindu, Jewish, Muslim, and Protestant
Sex	Male, female
Language	Including but not limited to English, French, Inuktitut, Italian, Ukrainian, and German

"I'd get out of children and into older people."

segments. Depending on the marketer's purpose, a segment can be a single classification (aged 20–34) or a combination of categories (aged 20–34, married with children, earning $25 000–$34 999). Foreign competitors, for example, are gaining market share in auto sales by appealing to young buyers (under age 30) with limited incomes (under $30 000). While companies such as Hyundai, Kia, and Daewoo are winning entry-level customers with high-quality vehicles and generous warranties, Volkswagen targets under-35 buyers with its entertainment-styled VW Jetta.[7]

Another important demographic variable is ethnicity. Canada's great ethnic diversity requires companies to pay close attention to ethnicity as a segmentation variable. For example, Rogers Communication Inc.'s television advertising campaign for its Bollywood Oye! video-on-demand service is designed to promote its business to South Asian communities in Canada. Rogers currently has 78 multicultural channels in more than 20 languages and wants to be a leader in customizing services to suit specific ethnic groups. Visible minorities in Canada control $76 billion in annual buying power, and to be effective in multicultural marketing, companies must really understand the underlying values that ethnic minority customers hold.[8]

Psychographic Variables

psychographic variables Psychological traits that a group has in common, including motives, attitudes, activities, interests, and opinions.

Members of a market can also be segmented according to such **psychographic variables** as lifestyle, opinions, interests, and attitudes. One company that is using psychographic variables to revive its brand is Burberry, whose plaid-lined gabardine raincoats have been a symbol of British tradition since 1856. After a recent downturn in sales, Burberry is repositioning itself as a global luxury brand, like Gucci and Louis Vuitton. The strategy calls for luring top-of-the-line, fashion-conscious customers. Burberry pictures today's luxury-product shopper as a world traveller who identifies with prestige fashion brands and monitors social and fashion trends in *Harper's Bazaar*.[9] Robert Polet, chief executive of the Gucci Group, agrees with this strategy. "We're not in the business of selling handbags. We are in the business of selling dreams."[10]

Psychographics are particularly important to marketers because, unlike demographics and geographics, they can sometimes be changed by marketing efforts. Many companies have succeeded in changing at least some consumers' opinions by running ads highlighting products that have been improved directly in response to consumer desires. For example, Las Vegas began courting the gay community a few years ago as part of a broader effort to target a range of minority audiences. Studies showed that the gay and lesbian travel market was among the most lucrative. According to research from Community Marketing Inc., a gay and lesbian market research company, gay and lesbian travel accounts for $55 billion of the overall U.S. travel market.[11]

Product-Use Variables

product-use variables The ways in which consumers use a product, the benefits they expect from it, their reasons for purchasing it, and their loyalty to it.

The term **product-use variables** refers to the ways in which consumers use a product, the benefits they expect from it, their reasons for purchasing it, and

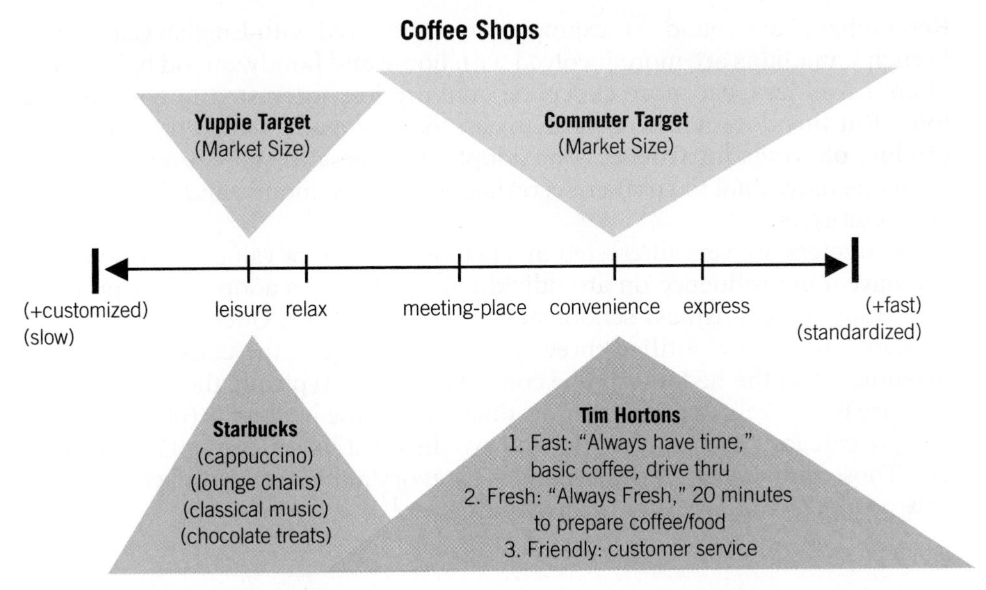

Figure 15.3 Product positioning.

their loyalty to it.[12] A women's shoemaker might identify three segments—wearers of athletic, casual, and dress shoes. Each segment is looking for different benefits in a shoe. A woman buying an athletic shoe may not care about its appearance but may care a great deal about arch support and traction in the sole. A woman buying a casual shoe will want it to look good and feel comfortable. A woman buying a dress shoe may require a specific colour or style and may even accept some discomfort. Speaking of shoes, when Nike—the leader in the $15.5 billion athletic footwear industry—found that women's footwear accounted for about one-third of industry sales but generated only about one-fifth of Nike's business, they changed their strategy and introduced a marketing campaign that focussed on differences between the way men and women think about sports and the way they shop for clothing. According to Nike marketers, women are more interested in image trends and active lifestyles than in athletic competition and sports celebrities.

Whatever basis is used for segmenting a market, care must be taken to position the product correctly. A product's position refers to the important attributes that consumers use to assess the product. For example, a low-priced car like the Ford Focus tends to be positioned on the basis of economy, while a Porsche is positioned in terms of high performance. In Figure 15.3, the product positioning chart shows that Tim Hortons emphasizes a standardized product and provides fast service to people in a hurry, while Starbucks provides more customized products in more leisurely surroundings.

Market Segmentation: A Caution

Segmentation must be done carefully. A group of people may share an age category, income level, or some other segmentation variable, but their spending habits may be quite different. Look at your friends in school. You may all be approximately the same age, but you have different needs and wants. Some of you may wear cashmere sweaters, while others wear sweatshirts. The same holds true for income. University professors and truck drivers frequently have about the same level of income. However, their spending patterns, values, tastes, and wants are generally quite different.

In Canada, the two dominant cultures—English and French—have historically shown significant differences in consumer attitudes and behaviour.

Researchers have found, for example, that compared with English Canadians, French Canadians are more involved with home and family, attend ballet more often, travel less, eat more chocolate, and are less interested in convenience food. But this does not necessarily mean that companies must have different product offerings for Quebec. The adoption process for new products varies from one individual to another according to socio-economic and demographic characteristics.

Marketers are very interested in a person's system of values because values can have a big influence on an individual's tendency to adopt a new product. One study using business school students from France, Quebec, and the rest of North America identified three types of consumers: the conservatives, the dynamics, and the hedonists. The conservatives are typically those consumers who are least likely to adopt new products, while the hedonists (pleasure seekers) are categorized as innovators and are the most likely to adopt a new product. Those individuals in the dynamics category are somewhat likely to adopt new products, but are often seen as imitators.[13]

Market Research

4 Explain the purpose and value of *market research.*

market research The systematic study of what buyers need and how best to meet those needs.

Market research—the study of what buyers need and how best to meet those needs—can address any element in the marketing mix. Business firms spend millions of dollars each year as they try to figure out their customers' habits and preferences. Market research can greatly improve the accuracy and effectiveness of market segmentation.[14] For example, comic books have historically not been of much interest to girls, but DC Comics and Marvel Entertainment are convinced they can change that after observing the success of upstart companies like Tokyopop and Viz Media, who produce translated Japanese comics called *manga*. These companies have succeeded in attracting female readers by having "girl-friendly" content and by distributing their products in both comic book shops and mainstream bookstores. The total comics and graphic novel market was $640 million in 2007, and manga comics accounted for $200 million of that total.[15]

The place of market research in the overall marketing process is shown in Figure 15.4. Ultimately, its role is to increase the firm's competitiveness by understanding the relationship among the firm's customers, its marketing variables, and its marketing decisions. Market researchers use a variety of methods to obtain, interpret, and use information about customers. They determine the kinds of information that are needed for decisions on marketing strategy, goal setting, and target-market selection. In doing so, they may conduct studies on how customers will respond to proposed changes in the current marketing mix. One researcher, for example, might study consumer response to an experimental paint formula (new product). Another might explore the response to a price reduction (new price) on calculators. A third might check response to a proposed advertising campaign (new promotion). Marketers can also try to learn whether customers are more likely to purchase a given product in a specialty shop or on the internet (new place).

Most companies will benefit from market research, but they need not do the research themselves. Using a new tool and a virtual store developed by Kimberly-Clark Corp., Safeway stores asked participants to walk through the "store" and shop for items. The shoppers were actually in a virtual store and were surrounded by three screens showing a typical store aisle. A retina-tracking device recorded their every glance. When Safeway tested the display inside its stores, sales of items in that section increased.[16]

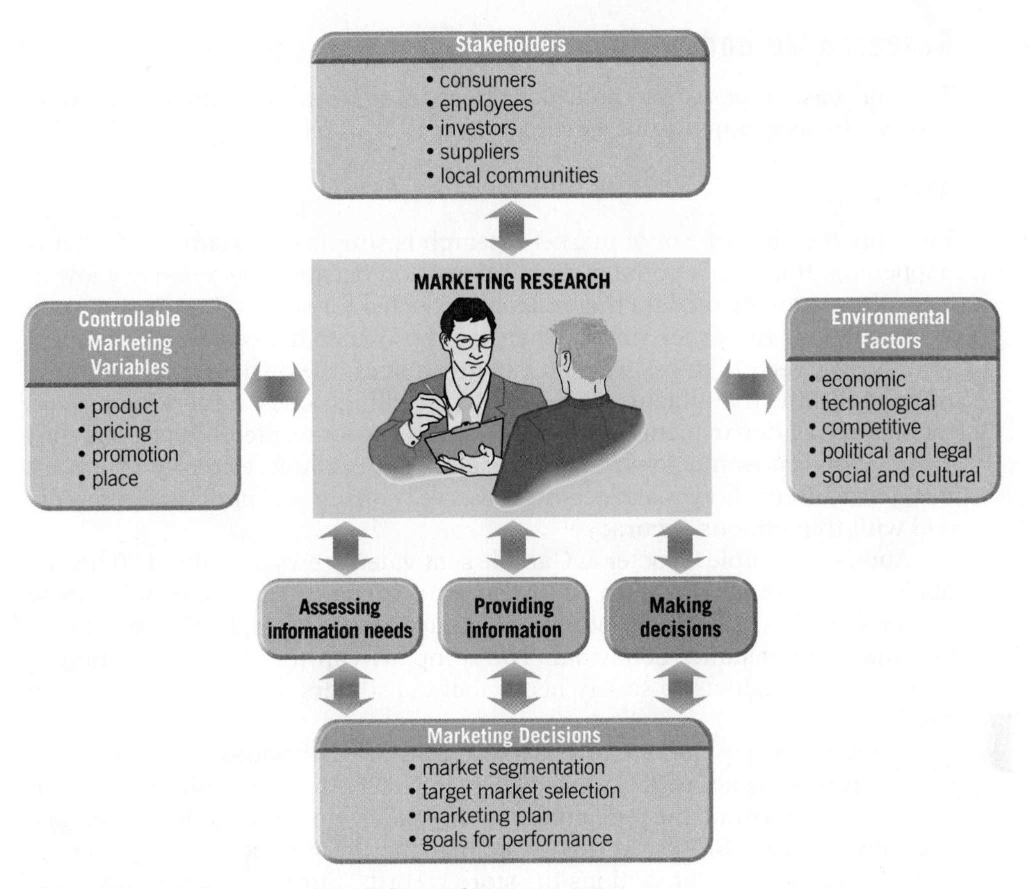

Figure 15.4 Market research and the marketing process.

The Research Process

Market research can occur at almost any point in a product's existence. Most commonly, however, it is used when a new or altered product is being considered. These are the five steps in performing market research:[17]

1. Study the current situation. What is the need and what is being done to meet it at this point?
2. Select a research method. In choosing a method, marketers must bear in mind the effectiveness and costs of different methods.
3. Collect data. **Secondary data** is information already available as a result of previous research by the firm or other agencies. For example, Statistics Canada publishes a great deal of data that is useful for business firms. Using secondary data can save time, effort, and money. But in some cases secondary data are unavailable or inadequate, so **primary data**—new research by the firm or its agents—must be obtained. Hostess Frito-Lay, the maker of Doritos, spent a year studying how to best reach its target market—teenagers. The researchers hung around shopping malls, schools, and fast-food outlets to watch teens.[18]
4. Analyze the data. Data are not useful until they have been organized into information.
5. Prepare a report. This report should include a summary of the study's methodology and findings. It should also identify alternative solutions (where appropriate) and make recommendations for the appropriate course of action.

secondary data Information already available to market researchers as a result of previous research by the firm or other agencies.

primary data Information developed through new research by the firm or its agents.

Research Methods

The four basic types of methods used by market researchers are observation, surveys, focus groups, and experimentation.

Observation

observation A market research technique involving viewing or otherwise monitoring consumer buying patterns.

Probably the oldest form of market research is simple **observation** of what is happening. It is also a popular research method because it is relatively low in cost, often drawing on data that must be collected for some other reason, such as reordering. In earlier times, when a store owner noticed that customers were buying red children's wagons, not green ones, the owner reordered more red wagons, the manufacturer's records showed high sales of red wagons, and the marketing department concluded that customers wanted red wagons. But observation is now much more sophisticated. For example, electronic scanners in supermarkets allow marketers to "observe" consumers' preferences rapidly and with tremendous accuracy.

Another example: Procter & Gamble sent video crews into about 80 households in the United Kingdom, Germany, and China to capture people's daily routines and how they use products. By analyzing the tapes, P&G hoped to get insights into consumer behaviour. The company can use this information to develop new products to satisfy needs that consumers didn't even know they had.[19]

Using video equipment to observe consumer behaviour is called video mining. It is being adopted by many stores in North America, which use hidden cameras to determine the percentage of shoppers who buy and the percentage who only browse. Stores do this by comparing the number of people taped with the number of transactions the store records. Some consumer organizations are raising privacy concerns, since shoppers are unaware that they are being taped.[20]

Surveys

survey A market research technique based on questioning a representative sample of consumers about purchasing attitudes and practices.

Sometimes marketers need to ask questions about new marketing ideas or about how well the firm is doing its marketing tasks. One way to get answers is by conducting a **survey**. When Sara Lee Corp. acquired Kiwi shoe polish, they surveyed 3500 people in eight countries about shoe care needs. They learned that people do not care as much about the shine on their shoes as they do about how fresh and comfortable they are on the inside. The firm has since unveiled several new products under the Kiwi name and is doing quite well.[21]

Because no firm can afford to survey everyone, marketers must be careful to get a representative group of respondents when they do surveys. They must also construct the survey questions so that they get honest answers that address the specific issue being researched. Surveys can be expensive to carry out and may vary widely in their accuracy.

In the past, surveys have been mailed to individuals for their completion, but online surveys are now gaining in popularity because the company gets immediate results and because the process is a less intrusive way of gathering data. At Hudson's Bay Co., customers can use online surveys to tell the company how happy or unhappy they are about the service they received at any of the Bay's department stores. The company can then make any changes that are needed to keep customers happy. The Bay used to hire mystery shoppers to find out how well it was serving the public, but that program ended when the online survey system was adopted.[22]

Focus Groups

focus group A market research technique involving a small group of people brought together and allowed to discuss selected issues in depth.

Many firms also use **focus groups**, where six to 15 people are brought together to talk about a product or service. A moderator leads the group's discussion, and employees from the sponsoring company may observe the proceedings from behind a one-way mirror. The people in the focus group are not usually told which company is sponsoring the research. The comments of people in the focus group are taped, and then researchers go through the data looking for common themes.

When Procter & Gamble was developing a new air freshener, it asked people in focus groups to describe their "desired scent experience." They discovered that people get used to a scent after about half an hour and no longer notice it. P&G used this information to develop a "scent player," called Febreze Scentstories, which gives off one of five different scents every 30 minutes.[23] Focus groups at farm implement manufacturer John Deere have suggested many improvements in farm tractors, including different ways to change the oil filter and making the steps to the tractor cab wider.[24]

Consumers don't necessarily express their real feelings when participating in focus groups or when filling out surveys. They may say one thing and think something else. This has led marketers to look at other ways of gathering information. Sensory Logic Inc., for example, studies facial expressions and eye movements to determine what consumers really think of a product.[25]

Experimentation

The last major form of market research, **experimentation**, also tries to get answers to questions that surveys cannot address. As in science, experimentation in market research attempts to compare the responses of the same or similar individuals under different circumstances. For example, a firm trying to decide whether to include walnuts in a new candy bar probably would not learn much by asking people what they thought of the idea. But if it made some bars with nuts and some without and then asked people to try both, the responses could be very helpful.[26]

experimentation A market research technique in which the reactions of similar people are compared under different circumstances.

Data Warehousing and Data Mining

Almost everything you do leaves a trail of information about you. Your preferences in movie rentals, television viewing, internet sites, and groceries; the destinations of your phone calls, your credit-card charges, your financial status; personal information about age, gender, marital status, and even health—these are just some of the items in a huge cache of data that are stored about

As they watch a sitcom with six commercial breaks, these women are participating in a marketing research experiment. The researchers think that their results will be more accurate than questionnaire and focus group responses because they're getting them straight from the subjects' brains. A spike in a subject's left prefrontal cortex means that she probably likes a product or an ad. A spike in the right prefrontal cortex is bad news for the advertiser. Using machines designed to detect brain tumours, researchers can even tell which part of an ad makes a dent in the subject's long-term memory.

Retailers such as Wal-Mart rely on data warehousing and mining to keep shelves stocked with in-demand merchandise.

data warehousing Process of collecting, storing, and retrieving data in electronic form.

each of us. The collection, storage, and retrieval of such data in electronic files is called **data warehousing**. For marketing researchers, the data warehouse is a gold mine of clues about consumer behaviour.[27]

The Uses of Data Mining

data mining Application of electronic technologies for searching, sifting, and reorganizing data to collect marketing information and target products in the marketplace.

After collecting information, marketers use **data mining**—the application of electronic technologies for searching, sifting, and reorganizing pools of data—to uncover useful marketing information and to plan for new products that will appeal to target segments in the marketplace.[28] Using data mining, for example, the insurance company Farmers Group discovered that a sports car is not an exceptionally high insurance risk if it's not the only family car. The company thus issued more liberal policies on Corvettes and Porsches and so generated more revenue without significantly increasing payout claims. Among retailers, Wal-Mart has long been a data-mining pioneer, maintaining perhaps the world's largest privately held data warehouse. Data include demographics, markdowns, returns, inventory, and other data for forecasting sales and the effects of marketing promotions.[29]

Understanding Consumer Behaviour

consumer behaviour The study of the process by which customers come to purchase and consume a product or service.

Market research in its many forms can be of great help to marketing managers in understanding how the common traits of a market segment affect consumers' purchasing decisions. Why do people buy DVDs? What desire are they fulfilling? Is there a psychological or sociological explanation for why consumers purchase one product and not another? These questions and many others are addressed in the area of marketing known as **consumer behaviour**, which focuses on the decision process by which customers come to purchase and consume a product or service.

Influences on Consumer Behaviour

To understand consumer behaviour, marketers draw heavily on the fields of psychology and sociology. The result is a focus on four major influences on consumer behaviour: psychological, personal, social, and cultural. By identifying the four influences that are most active, marketers try to explain consumer choices and predict future purchasing behaviour.

- Psychological influences include an individual's motivations, perceptions, ability to learn, and attitudes.
- Personal influences include lifestyle, personality, economic status, and life-cycle stage.
- Social influences include family; opinion leaders (people whose opinions are sought by others); and reference groups such as friends, co-workers, and professional associates.
- Cultural influences include culture (the "way of living" that distinguishes one large group from another), subculture (smaller groups, such as ethnic groups, with shared values), and social class (the cultural ranking of groups according to criteria such as background, occupation, and income).

Although these factors can have a strong impact on a consumer's choices, their effect on actual purchases is sometimes weak or negligible. Some consumers, for example, regularly purchase certain products because they are satisfied with their performance. Such people (for example, users of Craftsman tools) are less subject to influence and stick with preferred brand names. On the other hand, the clothes you wear and the food you eat often reflect social and psychological influences on your consuming behaviour.

The Consumer Buying Process

Describe the key factors that influence the *consumer buying process.* 5

Researchers who have studied consumer behaviour have constructed models that help marketing managers understand how consumers come to purchase products. Figure 15.5 presents one such model. At the heart of this and similar models is an awareness of the psychosocial influences that lead to consumption. Ultimately, marketing managers use this information to develop marketing plans.

Problem/Need Recognition

The buying process begins when a consumer becomes aware of a problem or need. After strenuous exercise, you may recognize that you are thirsty and need refreshment. After the birth of twins, you may find your one-bedroom

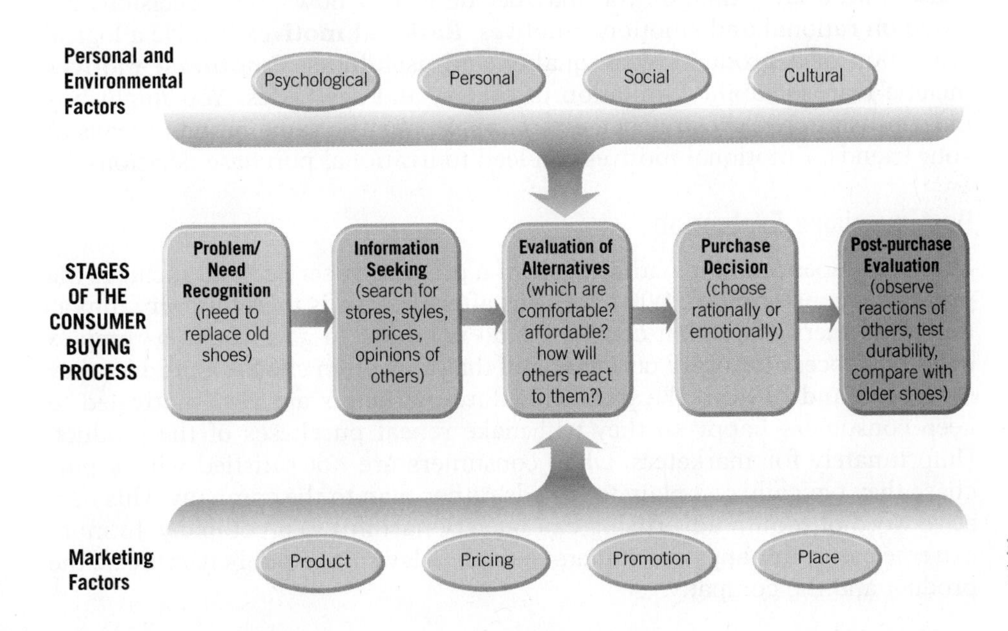

Figure 15.5 Consumer buying process.

apartment too small for comfort. After standing in the rain to buy movie tickets, you may decide to buy an umbrella. Need recognition also occurs when you have a chance to change your purchasing habits. For example, the income from your first job after graduation will allow you to purchase items that were too expensive when you were a student. You may also discover a need for professional clothing, apartment furnishings, and a car. Credit cards and credit issuing companies recognize this shift and market their credit cards to graduates.

Information Seeking

Having recognized a need, consumers seek information. This search is not always extensive. If you are thirsty, you may ask where the pop machine is, but that may be the extent of your information search. Other times you simply rely on your memory for information. Before making major purchases, most people seek information from personal sources, marketing sources, public sources, and experience. For example, if you move to a new town, you will want to find out who is the best local dentist, physician, hair stylist, butcher, or pizza maker. To get this information, you may check with personal sources such as acquaintances, co-workers, and relatives. Before buying an exercise bike, you may read the latest issue of *Consumer Reports*—a public source of consumer ratings—on such equipment. You may also ask market sources such as the sales clerk or rely on direct experience. For example, you might test ride the bike to learn more before you buy. The internet has become an important source of information; almost three quarters (73 percent) of Canadians aged 16 and older rely on the internet to gather information.[30]

Evaluation of Alternatives

If you are in the market for a set of golf clubs, you probably have some idea of who produces clubs and how they differ. You may have accumulated some of this knowledge during the information-seeking stage and combined it with what you knew before. Based on product attributes such as colour, taste, price, prestige, quality, and service record, you will decide which product best meets your needs.

Purchase Decisions

rational motives Those reasons for purchasing a product that involve a logical evaluation of product attributes such as cost, quality, and usefulness.

emotional motives Those reasons for purchasing a product that involve non-objective factors.

Ultimately, you make a purchase decision. You may decide to defer the purchase until a later time or you may decide to buy now. "Buy" decisions are based on rational and emotional motives. **Rational motives** involve a logical evaluation of a product's cost, quality, and usefulness. **Emotional motives** include fear, sociability, imitation of others, and aesthetics. You might buy mouthwash to avoid ostracism, or you might buy the same brand of jeans as your friends. Emotional motives can lead to irrational purchase decisions.

Post-purchase Evaluations

Marketing does not stop with the sale of a product or service, but includes the process of consumption. What happens after the sale is therefore very important. Marketers know that consumers do not want to go through a complex decision process for every purchase and that they often choose a product they have used and liked in the past. Therefore marketers are very motivated to keep consumers happy so they will make repeat purchases of the product. Unfortunately for marketers, when consumers are not satisfied with a purchase they typically complain to friends rather than to the company. This negative word-of-mouth advertising can be very harmful to a company. In more extreme cases, unhappy consumers may file a lawsuit or publicly criticize the product and the company.

People can complain about products or services at www.complaints.com. Dissatisfied customers can have a very negative impact on a company's marketing effort. **Word-of-mouth marketing (also known as buzz marketing)** is therefore a very powerful marketing tool. It can, however, be the most devastating, since businesses cannot control it.[31]

word-of-mouth marketing (also buzz marketing) Opinions about the value of products, passed among consumers in informal discussions.

Organizational Marketing and Buying Behaviour

Discuss the three categories of *organizational markets* and explain how *organizational buying behaviour* differs from consumer buying behaviour. 6

Buying behaviour is observable daily in the consumer market, where marketing activities, including buying-selling transactions, are visible to the public. Equally important, however, but far less visible, are organizational (or commercial) markets—organizations that buy goods and services to be used in creating and delivering consumer products. Marketing to these buyers involves different kinds of organizational markets, and buying behaviours that are quite different from those found in consumer markets.

Organizational Markets

Organizational or commercial markets fall into three categories: *industrial*, *reseller*, and *government/institutional markets*.

Industrial Market

The **industrial market** includes businesses that buy goods falling into one of two categories—goods to be converted into other products and goods that are used up during production. This market includes farmers, manufacturers, and some retailers. For example, Seth Thomas purchases electronics, metal components, and glass to make clocks for the consumer market. The company also buys office supplies, tools, and factory equipment—items never seen by clock buyers—to be used during production.

industrial market Businesses that buy goods to be converted into other products that will be sold to ultimate consumers.

Reseller Market

Before products reach consumers, they pass through a **reseller market** consisting of intermediaries, including wholesalers and retailers, who buy the finished goods and resell them (wholesalers and retailers are discussed in Chapter 17). Retailers like department stores, drugstores, and supermarkets buy clothing, appliances, foods, medicines, and other merchandise for resale to the consumer market. Retailers also buy such services as maintenance, housekeeping, and communications.

reseller market Intermediaries like wholesalers and retailers who buy finished products and resell them.

Government and Institutional Market

Federal, provincial, and municipal governments purchase millions of dollars worth of computer equipment, buildings, paper clips, and other items. The **institutional market** consists of non-governmental organizations, such as hospitals, churches, museums, and charitable organizations, which also compose a substantial market for goods and services. Like organizations in other commercial markets, these institutions use supplies and equipment, as well as legal, accounting, and transportation services.

institutional market Non-government organizations such as hospitals, churches, and schools.

Organizational Buying Behaviour

In some respects, industrial buying behaviour bears little resemblance to consumer buying practices. Differences include the buyers' purchasing skills and an emphasis on buyer-seller relationships.

Differences in Buyers

Unlike most consumers, organizational buyers are professional, specialized, and expert (or at least well-informed).

- As professionals, organizational buyers are trained in methods for negotiating purchase terms. Once buyer-seller agreements have been reached, buyers also arrange for formal contracts.
- As a rule, industrial buyers are company specialists in a line of items. As one of several buyers for a large bakery, for example, you may specialize in food ingredients. Another buyer may specialize in baking equipment (industrial ovens and mixers), while a third may buy office equipment and supplies.
- Industrial buyers are often experts about the products they buy. On a regular basis, organizational buyers study competing products and alternative suppliers by attending trade shows, by reading trade magazines, and by conducting technical discussions with sellers' representatives.

Differences in the Buyer-Seller Relationship

Consumer-seller relationships are often impersonal, short-lived, one-time interactions. In contrast, industrial situations often involve frequent and enduring buyer-seller relationships. The development of a long-term relationship provides each party with access to the technical strengths of the other as well as the security of knowing what future business to expect. Thus, a buyer and a supplier may form a design team to create products of benefit to both. Accordingly, industrial sellers emphasize personal selling by trained representatives who understand the needs of each customer.

The International Marketing Mix

7 Describe the *international* and *small business marketing mixes.*

Marketing products internationally means mounting a strategy to support global business operations. This is no easy task, since foreign customers may differ from domestic buyers in language, customs, business practices, and consumer behaviour. When companies decide to go global, marketers must consider how each element of the marketing mix might be affected.

International Products

Some products (for example, Budweiser, Coca-Cola, and Marlboro) can be sold in many different countries with virtually no changes, but often only a redesigned (or completely different) product will meet the needs of foreign buyers. To sell its computers in Japan, for example, Apple had to develop a Japanese-language operating system.

Mattel, the maker of Barbie dolls, is just one company that has learned some interesting lessons about the international market. When it conducted focus groups with kids in dozens of countries, it found that worldwide demand existed for many of the same products. Mattel discovered, in essence, that children have similar tastes no matter where they live. Mattel's experience with its famous Barbie doll is illustrative. The dolls sold in Japan, for example, had always had black hair and Asian features, not the blonde, blue-eyed appearance of Barbie dolls sold in North America. This seemed to make intuitive sense, but now Mattel is finding that the original Barbie doll is selling just as well in Asia as in North America.

Mattel's experience is not unique. Various other companies that sell products to international consumers have found the same phenomenon:

- The Harry Potter book series already had a global following when the first Harry Potter movie was released.
- Harlequin Enterprises, which sells millions of romance novels in many different countries, uses the same book covers around the world. The pictures of Caucasians on the book covers do not seem to deter customers in other countries from buying Harlequin romance novels.
- Sports is another universal language. Basketball stars like Michael Jordan and Shaquille O'Neal have high name recognition overseas. In a poll of Chinese students in rural Shaanxi province, Michael Jordan tied with former Chinese premier Zhou En-lai for the title "World's Greatest Man."

But there are still important differences between countries, and these cannot be ignored. For example, German children aren't attracted to action toys the way Canadian and American children are. There are also differences even within basic product lines. American kids, for example, want NASCAR toy cars, while European children want Formula One models.

International Pricing

When pricing for international markets, marketers must handle all the considerations of domestic pricing while also considering the higher costs of transporting and selling products abroad. Some products cost more overseas than in Canada because of the added costs of delivery. Due to the higher costs of buildings, rent, equipment, and imported meat, a McDonald's Big Mac that sells for C$2.99 in Canada has a price tag of over C$10 in Japan. In contrast, products like jet airplanes are priced the same worldwide because delivery costs are incidental; the huge development and production costs are the major considerations regardless of customer location.

International Promotion

Some standard Canadian promotional techniques do not always succeed in other countries. In fact, many Europeans believe that a product must be inherently shoddy if a company does any hard-sell advertising. International marketers must also be aware that cultural differences can cause negative reactions to products that are advertised improperly. Some Europeans, for example, are offended by television commercials that show weapons or violence. Advertising practices are regulated accordingly. Quebec is the only province, and in fact the only jurisdiction in North America, in which commercial advertising to persons under 13 is generally prohibited. Meanwhile, liquor and cigarette commercials that are banned from Canadian and U.S. television are thriving in many Asian and European markets.

Symbolism, too, is a sometimes-surprising consideration. In France, for instance, yellow flowers suggest infidelity. In Mexico, they are signs of death—an association made in Brazil with the colour purple. Clearly, product promotions must be carefully matched to the customs and cultural values of each country.

International Distribution

In some industries, delays in starting new distribution networks can be costly. Therefore, companies with existing distribution systems often enjoy an advantage over new businesses. Several companies have gained advantages in

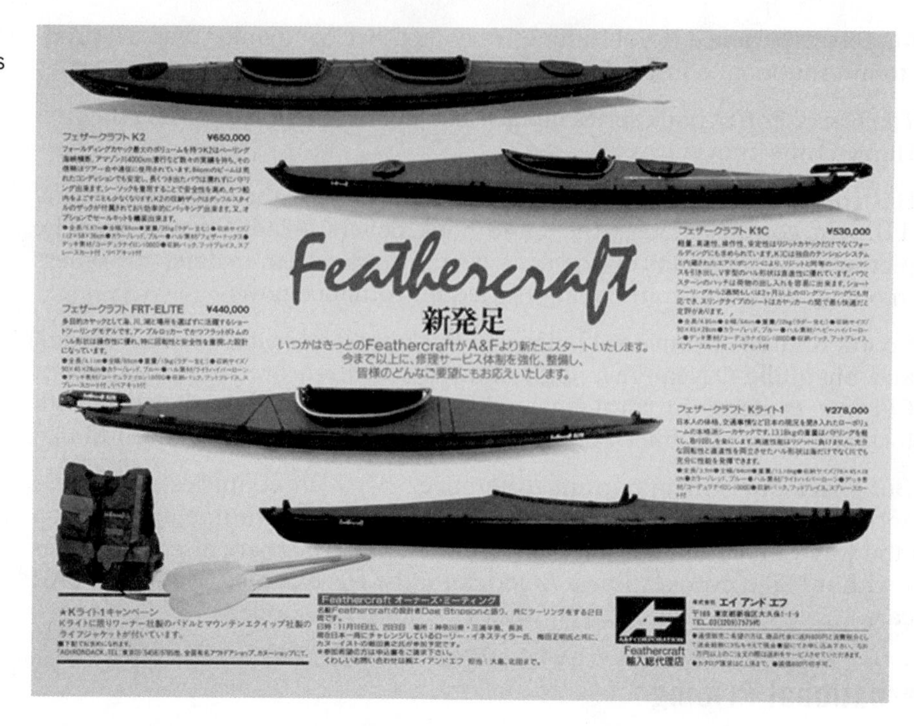

Feathercraft is a small British Columbia manufacturer that has been successful selling kayaks in the Japanese market.

time-based competition by buying existing businesses. Procter & Gamble, for example, saved three years of start-up time by buying Revlon's Max Factor and Betrix cosmetics, both of which are well-established in foreign markets. P&G can thus immediately use these companies' distribution and marketing networks for selling its own brands in the United Kingdom, Germany, and Japan.

Other companies contract with foreign firms or individuals to distribute and sell their products abroad. Foreign agents may perform personal selling and advertising, provide information about local markets, or serve as exporters' representatives. But having to manage interactions with foreign personnel complicates a marketing manager's responsibilities. In addition, packaging practices in Canada must sometimes be adapted to withstand the rigours of transport to foreign ports and storage under conditions that differ radically from domestic conditions.

Small Business and the Marketing Mix

As we noted in Chapter 4, far more small businesses fail than succeed, yet many of today's largest firms were yesterday's small businesses. McDonald's began with one restaurant, a concept, and one individual (Ray Kroc) who had tremendous foresight. Behind the success of many small firms lies a skilful application of the marketing concept and careful consideration of each element in the marketing mix.

Small Business Products

Some new products—and firms—are doomed at the start simply because few consumers want or need what they have to offer. Too often, enthusiastic entrepreneurs introduce products that they and their friends like, but they fail to estimate realistic market potential. Other small businesses offer new products before they have clear pictures of their target segments and how to reach them. They try to be everything to everyone, and they end up serving no one well. In contrast, sound product planning has paid off for many small firms.

"Keep it simple" is a familiar key to success—that is, fulfill a specific need and do it efficiently.

Small Business Pricing

Haphazard pricing that is often little more than guesswork can sink even a firm with a good product. Most often, small business pricing errors result from a failure to project operating expenses accurately. Owners of failing businesses have often been heard to utter statements like "I didn't realize how much it costs to run the business!" and "If I price the product high enough to cover my expenses, no one will buy it!" But when small businesses set prices by carefully assessing costs, many earn very satisfactory profits—sometimes enough to expand or diversify.

Small Business Promotion

Successful small businesses plan for promotional expenses as part of start-up costs. Some hold down costs by taking advantage of less expensive promotional methods. Local newspapers, for example, are sources of publicity when they publish articles about new or unique businesses. Other small businesses have succeeded by identifying themselves and their products with associated groups, organizations, and events. Thus a custom-crafts gallery might join with a local art league and local artists to organize public showings of their combined products.

Small Business Distribution

Problems in arranging distribution can make or break small businesses. Perhaps the most critical aspect of distribution is facility location, especially for new service businesses. The ability of many small businesses—retailers, veterinary clinics, and gourmet coffee shops—to attract and retain customers depends partly on the choice of location.

In distribution, as in other aspects of the marketing mix, however, smaller companies may have advantages over larger competitors, even in highly complex industries. They may be quicker, for example, in applying service technologies. Everex Systems Inc. sells personal computers to wholesalers and dealers through a system the company calls "Zero Response Time." Phone orders are reviewed every two hours so that the factory can adjust assembly to match demand.

Test yourself on the material for this chapter at **www.pearsoned.ca/mybusinesslab**.

Summary of Learning Objectives

1. **Explain the concept of *marketing* and describe the five forces that constitute the *external marketing environment*.** *Marketing* is the process of planning and executing the conception, pricing, promotion, and distribution of ideas, goods, and services to create exchanges that satisfy individual and organizational goals. Products provide consumers with *utility*—the ability of a product to satisfy a human want or need. Marketing can be used to promote consumer and industrial goods and services, as well as ideas. The *external environment* consists of the outside

forces that influence marketing strategy and decision making. The *political/legal environment* includes laws and regulations, both domestic and foreign, that may define or constrain business activities. The *social and cultural environment* is the context within which people's values, beliefs, and ideas affect marketing decisions. The *technological environment* includes the technological developments that affect existing and new products. The *economic environment* consists of the conditions—such as inflation, recession, and interest rates—that influence both consumer and organizational spending patterns. Finally, the *competitive environment* is the environment in which marketers must persuade buyers to purchase their product rather than that of their competitors.

2. **Explain the purpose of a *marketing plan* and identify the four components of the *marketing mix*.** Marketing managers plan and implement all the marketing activities that result in the transfer of products to customers. These activities culminate in the *marketing plan*—a detailed strategy for focussing the effort to meet consumer needs and wants. Marketing managers rely on the four Ps of marketing, or the *marketing mix:* (1) *Product:* Marketing begins with a product, a good, a service, or an idea designed to fill a consumer need or want. Product differentiation is the creation of a feature or image that makes a product differ from competitors. (2) *Pricing:* Pricing is the strategy of selecting the most appropriate price at which to sell a product. (3) *Place* (Distribution): All distribution activities are concerned with getting a product from the producer to the consumer. (4) *Promotion:* Promotion refers to techniques for communicating information about products and includes advertising.

3. **Explain *market segmentation* and show how it is used in *target marketing*.** Marketers think in terms of *target markets*—groups of people who have similar wants and needs and who can be expected to show interest in the same products. Target marketing requires *market segmentation*—dividing a market into customer types or "segments." Four of the most important influences are (1) *geographic variables* (the geographical units that may be considered in developing a segmentation strategy); (2) *demographic variables* (population traits such as age, income, gender, ethnic background, marital status, race, religion, and social class); (3) *psychographic variables* (such as lifestyles, interests, and attitudes); and (4) *product-use variables* (the ways in which consumers use a product, the benefits they expect from it, their reasons for purchasing it, and their loyalty to it).

4. **Explain the purpose and value of *market research*.** *Market research* is the study of what buyers need and of the best ways to meet those needs. This process involves a study of the current situation, the selection of a research method, the collection of data, the analysis of data, and the preparation of a report that may include recommendations for action. The four most common research methods are *observation, surveys, focus groups,* and *experimentation.*

5. **Describe the key factors that influence the *consumer buying process*.** *Consumer behaviour* is the study of the process by which customers decide to purchase products. The result is a focus on four major influences on consumer behaviour: (1) *Psychological influences* include motivations, perceptions, ability to learn, and attitudes; (2) *Personal influences* include lifestyle, personality, and economic status; (3) *Social influences* include family, opinion leaders, and such reference groups as friends, co-workers, and professional associates; (4) *Cultural influences* include culture, subculture, and social class. By identifying which influences are most active in certain circumstances, marketers try to explain consumer choices and predict future purchasing behaviour.

6. **Discuss the three categories of *organizational markets* and explain how *organizational buying behaviour* differs from *consumer buying behaviour*.** *Organizational (or commercial)* markets, in which organizations buy goods and services to be used in creating and delivering consumer products, fall into three categories: (1) *The industrial market* consists of businesses that buy goods to be converted into other products or goods that are used during production. (2) Before products reach consumers, they pass through a *reseller market* consisting of intermediaries that buy finished goods and resell them. (3) The third category is *government and institutional markets.* Federal, provincial, and local governments buy durable and nondurable products. The institutional market consists of non-governmental buyers such as hospitals, churches, museums, and charities. Organizational buying behaviour differs from consumer buyer behaviour in two major ways: (1) *Differences in buyers:* Organizational buyers are professionals trained in arranging buyer-seller relationships and negotiating purchase terms. They are usually specialists in a line of items and are often experts about the products they are buying. (2) *Differences in the buyer-seller relationship:* Whereas consumer-seller relationships are often fleeting, one-time interactions, industrial situations often involve frequent, enduring buyer-seller relationships.

7. **Describe the *international* and *small business marketing mixes*.** When they decide to go global, marketers must reconsider each element of the marketing mix. (1) *International products:* Whereas some products can be sold abroad with virtually no changes, sometimes only a

redesigned product will meet the needs of foreign buyers. (2) *International pricing:* When pricing for international markets, marketers must consider the higher costs of transporting and selling products abroad. (3) *International distribution:* In some industries, companies have gained advantages by buying businesses already established in foreign markets. (4) *International promotion:* Occasionally, a good ad campaign can be transported to another country virtually intact. Quite often, however, standard Canadian promotional tactics do not succeed in other countries.

Behind the success of many small firms lies an understanding of each element in the marketing mix. (1) *Small business products:* Understanding of what customers need and want has paid off for many small firms. (2) *Small business pricing:* Haphazard pricing can sink even a firm with a good product. Small business pricing errors usually result from failure to project operating expenses accurately. But when small businesses set prices by carefully assessing costs, many earn satisfactory profits. (3) *Small business distribution:* Perhaps the most critical aspect of distribution is facility location. The ability of many small businesses to attract and retain customers depends partly on the choice of location. (4) *Small business promotion:* Successful small businesses plan for promotional expenses as part of start-up costs. Some take advantage of less expensive promotional methods.

PEARSON mybusinesslab To improve your grade, visit the MyBusinessLab website at www.pearsoned.ca/mybusinesslab. This online homework and tutorial system allows you to test your understanding and generates a personalized study plan just for you. It provides you with study and practice tools directly related to this chapter's content. MyBusinessLab puts you in control of your own learning!

Key Terms

brand competition (p. 483)
consumer behaviour (p. 494)
consumer goods (p. 477)
data mining (p. 494)
data warehousing (p. 494)
demographic variables (p. 487)
distribution (p. 485)
emotional motives (p. 496)
experimentation (p. 493)
external environment (p. 480)
focus group (p. 492)
geographic variables (p. 487)
industrial goods (p. 479)
industrial market (p. 497)
institutional market (p. 497)
international competition (p. 483)
market research (p. 490)
market segmentation (p. 485)
marketing (p. 476)
marketing concept (p. 476)
marketing managers (p. 483)
marketing mix (p. 483)
marketing plan (p. 483)
observation (p. 492)
price (p. 484)
primary data (p. 491)
product (p. 483)
product differentiation (p. 484)
product-use variables (p. 488)
promotion (p. 485)
psychographic variables (p. 488)
rational motives (p. 496)
relationship marketing (p. 479)
reseller market (p. 497)
secondary data (p. 491)
services (p. 479)
substitute product (p. 483)
survey (p. 492)
target market (p. 485)
utility (p. 477)
value (p. 477)
word-of-mouth (buzz) marketing (p. 497)

Questions for Analysis

1. Why and how is market segmentation used in target marketing?
2. Select an everyday product (books, CDs, skateboards, dog food, or shoes, for example). Show how different versions of your product are aimed toward different market segments. Explain how the marketing mix differs for each segment.
3. Select another product and describe the consumer buying process that likely occurs before it is purchased.
4. Explain the key differences between consumer buying behaviour and organizational buying behaviour.
5. What is the value to consumers of things like loyalty cards and discount cards? Why would companies offer consumers such cards?
6. Why has the in-store use of hidden cameras become so popular? Is this "video mining" ethical? If not, how could it be made more acceptable?

7. If you were starting your own small business, what are the key marketing pitfalls you would try to avoid?
8. Select a product or service that you regularly use. Explain the relative importance of each of the four elements in the marketing mix (product, price, promotion, and place). Then select another product and determine the extent to which the relative emphasis changes. If it changed, why did it change?

Application Exercises

1. Interview the marketing manager of a local business. Identify the degree to which this person's job is focussed on each element in the marketing mix.
2. Select a product made by a foreign company and sold in Canada. What is the product's target market? What is the basis on which the target market is segmented? Do you think that this basis is appropriate? How might another approach, if any, be beneficial? Why?

Building Your Business Skills

Dealing in Segments and Variables

The Purpose of the Assignment

To encourage students to analyze the ways in which various market segmentation variables affect business success.

The Situation

You and four partners are thinking of purchasing a heating and air conditioning (H/AC) dealership that specializes in residential applications priced between $2000 and $40 000. You are now in the process of deciding where that dealership should be. You are considering four locations: Miami, Florida; Toronto, Ontario; Vancouver, British Columbia; and Dallas, Texas.

Assignment

Step 1

Working with four classmates (your partnership group), do library research to learn how H/AC makers market their residential products. Check for articles in *The Globe and Mail, Canadian Business, The Wall Street Journal*, and other business publications.

Step 2

Continue your research. This time, focus on the specific marketing variables that define each prospective location. Check Statistics Canada data at your library and on the internet and contact local chambers of commerce (by phone and via the internet) to learn about the following factors for each location:

- geography
- demography (especially age, income, gender, family status, and social class)
- psychographic variables (lifestyles, interests, and attitudes)

Step 3

Meet with group members to analyze which location holds the greatest promise as a dealership site. Base your decision on your analysis of market segment variables and their effects on H/AC sales.

Questions for Discussion

1. Which location did you choose? Describe the market segmentation factors that influenced your decision.
2. Identify the two most important variables you believe will have the greatest impact on the dealership's success. Why are these factors so important?
3. Which factors were least important in your decision? Why?
4. When equipment manufacturers advertise residential H/AC products, they often show them in different climate situations (in winter, summer, or high-humidity conditions). Which market segments are these ads targeting? Describe these segments in terms of demographic and psychographic characteristics.

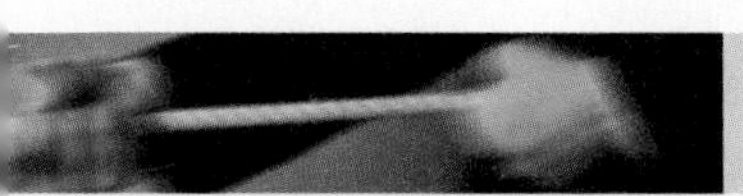

Exercising Your Ethics: Team Exercise

A Big Push for Publicity

The Situation

Marsden Corp. is known as a "good citizen" and prides itself on the publicity it receives from sponsoring civic programs and other community projects. The company's executive vice-president, Jane Martin, has just been named chairperson of annual fundraising for the Coalition for Community Services (CCS), which is a group of community services organizations that depend on voluntary donations. In the highly visible chairperson's role, Martin has organized the support of officials at other firms to ensure that the fundraising target is met or surpassed.

The Dilemma

Martin began a meeting of 30 department managers to appeal for 100 percent employee participation in CCS giving in the fundraising drive. As follow-up the week before the drive officially started, she met with each manager, saying "I expect you to give your fair share and for you to ensure that all your employees do likewise. I don't care what it takes, just do it. Make it clear that employees will at least donate cash. Even better, get them to sign up for weekly payroll deductions to the CCS fund because it nets more money than one-time cash donations."

An hour after meeting with Martin, Nathan Smith was both surprised and confused. As a newly appointed department manager, he was unsure how to go about soliciting donations from his 25 subordinates. Remembering Martin's comment, "I don't care what it takes, just do it," Nathan wondered what to do if someone did not give. Personally, too, he was feeling uneasy. How much should he give? With his family's pressing financial needs, he would rather not give money to CCS. He began to wonder if his donation to CCS would affect his career at Marsden.

Team Activity

Assemble a group of four to five students and assign each group member to one of the following roles:

- Nathan Smith (employee)
- Jane Martin (employer)
- director of CCS (customer)
- Marsden stockholder (investor)
- Marsden CEO (use this role only if your group has five members)

Questions for Discussion

1. Before discussing the situation with your group, and from the perspective of your assigned role, do you think there are any ethical issues with Marsden's fundraising program? If so, write them down.
2. Before discussing the situation with your group, and from the perspective of your assigned role, are any problems likely to arise from Marsden's fundraising program? If so, write them down.
3. Together with your group, share the ethical issues you identified. Then share the potential problems you listed. Did the different roles you were assigned result in different ethical issues and problems?
4. For the various ethical issues that were identified, decide as a group which one is the most important for Marsden to resolve. Likewise, for potential problems that were identified, which is the most important one for Marsden?
5. From an ethical standpoint, what does your group recommend be done to resolve the most important ethical issue? How should the most important problem be resolved? Identify the advantages and drawbacks of your recommendations.

For additional cases and exercise material, go to **www.pearsoned.ca/mybusinesslab**.

Concluding Case 15-1

Dell-ivering on Consumer Electronics

There's a good reason why competitors don't match Dell's success in selling computers. From the outset, Michael Dell's vision recognized a market with different kinds of potential users—the business sector, non-business organizations such as schools and other institutions, as well as the growing segment of PC users in homes—each with different needs and resources. Choosing to focus more on the business and institutional segments, Dell envisioned an unheard-of combination of service features for PC customers: high-quality products, lowest cost, ease in ordering and receiving products, live interaction with expert technical assistance for building a PC "the way you like it," super-fast deliveries, and after-the-sale communications to ensure product performance and keep users informed about upgrades to enhance their PCs.

The market response has been overwhelming, resulting in Dell's dominant position as industry leader. Dell's unique vision for integrating all stages of marketing—developing the product and related services, pricing it, selling to consumers directly via telephone or the internet, delivering directly to customers from efficient manufacturing plants, and using promotional messages for product awareness and use—are unmatched by competitors that are struggling to copy Dell's way of doing business.

As if that were not enough to cause headaches in the PC industry, Dell recently launched itself into the broader consumer electronics market for even greater revenue growth. Giant electronics retailers like Best Buy may soon be looking over their shoulders if Dell's customer-friendly business model is successfully carried over into flat-panel TVs, DVD recorders, MP3 players, and digital cameras. Plans even call for opening an online music-downloading store on the same popular website where PC users buy other Dell products. The potential range of products is enormous because music, movies, photos, and other entertainment are increasingly digital and, thus, are becoming compatible extensions of PCs. Commenting on the company's new thrust, chairman Michael Dell states, "The whole new ballgame is these worlds [computing and consumer electronics] converging, and that's a world we're comfortable in."

But will they necessarily succeed? Some experts think the crossover into consumer products could be a problem because, unlike Gateway's and Hewlett-Packard's focus on the consumer segment, Dell's primary PC focus has been on business and institutional markets. A classic example of a failed crossover is IBM's ill-fated attempt in the 1980s to woo consumers with its downsized PC Jr. With hugely successful sales and technical support for business customers, IBM never understood the consumer market, and Big Blue's efforts proved a mismatch that ended with the withdrawal of the PC Jr. from the marketplace in the late 1990s. But Dell CEO Kevin Rollins says such risks are largely offset by Dell's brand familiarity in both business and consumer markets.

Price is equally important to consumers, says industry analyst Peter Kastner. "Dell's no-middleman model almost guarantees a value-based price," and that means more intense price-for-performance competition than exists now in consumer electronics. The bottom line for consumers will be lower prices while other firms in the industry try to imitate Dell's low-price, high-value business model.

For masses of electronics lovers, Dell's entry comes as welcome news. Consumers will see prices fall as competition drives down profit margins and prices. Retailers and etailers, in contrast, will experience what might be called "reverse sticker shock." Sellers currently enjoying net profit margins of 25 to 40 percent on consumer electronics may have to survive on the modest 10 percent margin to which PC sellers are accustomed. That leaves lots of room for Dell to push electronics prices down, gain large volume sales, and reap high total profits while competing firms in the industry try to imitate its low-price, high-value business model.

Dell's promotional efforts first are aimed at building brand familiarity by dramatically increasing daily interaction with consumers. Electronics lovers from Canada, Japan, the United States, and Brazil who are accustomed to such brands as Sony and Samsung may be surprised to see the Dell name on TVs, pocket PCs, MP3 players, and the Digital Jukebox, among its upcoming line of products. Winning this massive customer base is essential for high-volume sales, and Dell plans to attract consumers to its new Dell.com website with Music Store, an online music-downloading service that will include the major labels and performers. Unlike Apple's iTunes service, which is available only to users of Apple products, Dell's downloading version is open to the public, not just to Dell PC users. It has the additional advantage of working with Microsoft Windows and, promises CEO Kevin Rollins, at prices below those of competitors.

The new Dell.com is reportedly designed to appeal to consumers and to set it apart from Dell's business products. Its main screen will provide easy ways to find not only electronics equipment but also music, radio stations, photos, and other media, all of which capitalize on the logical linkages between home computers and consumer electronics. More and more consumers in the "digital home" are viewing DVDs, video clips, games, and photos through their computers. So Dell plans to sell related media products the same way it sells other PC peripherals such as printers.

Because consumer buying habits don't change overnight, no one at Dell expects to dominate the electronics market the way it does in PCs, where it leads with a 31.4 percent market share and 21.8 percent growth rate in sales worldwide (while Hewlett-Packard's market share decreased to 25 percent). Before buying an expensive flat-screen TV, for example, most consumers want to see the quality of its picture first-hand rather than buying through catalogues or a website. As Forrester Research analyst Jed Kolko notes, "With video products it's harder to demonstrate value online." Consumers hold similar reservations about the sound quality of audio products. Only with the passage of time can Dell establish relationships with consumers by informing them, by convincing them to switch over from an already-crowded list of competing sellers—including newcomers such as Apex Digital, which is already underpricing more established brands—and by demonstrating superior product value in the Dell brand. Both industry experts and electronics consumers will soon witness Dell's bottom-line results in this new venture.

Questions for Discussion

1. What social and technological factors have influenced the growth of the consumer electronics market?
2. What demographics would you use to define the flat-screen TV target market? How about the target market for home PCs?
3. Identify the main factors favouring success for Dell's crossover into consumer electronics. What prominent factors suggest major problems or even failure for this crossover attempt?
4. Applying the textbook's definition for product value to Dell's plans, what are the "benefits" in Dell's consumer electronics offerings? What are the "costs"?
5. Applying the textbook's definition for product value to electronics retailers such as Best Buy, what are the "benefits" and "costs"? How well or poorly does Dell's product value ratio stack up against its competitors' ratios?

Concluding Case 15-2

An Old Company with New Potential

Bell Canada is Canada's largest communications company and offers consumers solutions to all of their communication needs. Bell has responded to the ever-changing needs of consumers by providing telephone services, wireless communications, high-speed internet, digital television, and VOIP. It is no surprise, then, that with the changing scale of entertainment technologies Bell would open an online video store.

The idea behind this is not new, but the new service offering at Bell Canada certainly is. Currently, iTunes offers the same service, but at present the service rights do not extend into Canada. Bell believes that an online video store is another way to offer affordable convenience to consumers looking for entertainment options, and the corporation is looking at ways to expand their entertainment categories. At this time, the Bell Video Store offers approximately 1500 movies, TV shows, documentaries, and music videos available for download at any time on any day of the week. Part of the success can be attributed to partnership agreements with Paramount Digital Entertainment for first-time release of its digital content in Canada and with Canadian broadcaster Corus Entertainment for its animated content. Collectively, this team of entertainment and communication experts may change the way consumers enjoy video entertainment.

Not everyone is overjoyed with Bell's announcement to launch an online video store, and most of the skepticism surrounds the untimely launch of the store in the midst of a legal battle that involves one of Bell's competitors in the United States. While Bell has been working on the development of the new service offering for quite some time, the choice to open the online store now poses unavoidable comparisons to the FCC investigation of Comcast in the United States, where a company called Vuze accused Comcast of inhibiting its legal P2P (peer-to-peer) video sales, while at the same time offering their own video-on-demand through its cable system. To counteract such a comparison, Bell claims that 5 percent of its users generate 60 percent of its total traffic and that 60 percent of this total traffic is P2P that is negatively affecting 95 percent of all customers. The Canadian Radio-television and Telecommunications Commission (CRTC) wants to see the calculations, and it has requested that Bell Canada provide full disclosure. "Provide full rationale and evidence in support of Bell Canada's view that 95 percent of its customers were being negatively affected," says the first of the CRTC interrogatories. Bell believes that this is simply procedural and that soon everyone, including the critics, will see the full benefit this new service has to offer.

Bell is the first online service in Canada to offer download-to-own movies the same day they become available in retail stores and download-to-rent shortly thereafter. Kevin Crull, president of Bell Residential Services, explains that "the Video Store is another first for Bell, offering 24/7 access to the most hit videos in Canada without ever having to leave the comfort and convenience of home." The actual benefit will be experienced by the consumer, who will have the opportunity to enjoy a wide selection of entertainment options. Bell currently provides a download-to-own service starting at $4.99 and a download-to-rent service starting at $1.99. With download-to-rent, customers have access to their movie for 30 days after they have downloaded it, but once they hit play, they have just 24 hours to view the film (as many times as they like). This service also offers consumers the opportunity to use the Bell Video Store media player on a PC or laptop and to be able to begin viewing their video only a few moments after purchasing it. Also, consumers with a Media Center PC will be able to use their remote to watch Bell Video Store content right on their TV.

While this feature sounds advantageous for consumers, what are the implications for those who use a Mac? Similar to all new offerings, this new launch has certain product limitations that will inhibit full market integration. Bell Video Store does not work with Macs or Linux machines because the site uses Windows Media DRM, and, surprisingly, not even the creators of the store are happy with this situation.

One interesting and amusing comment made on the FAQ page of the Bell Video Store explicitly states that while the two systems are not compatible, "We're hoping that one day Microsoft, Apple, the content owners, and video sites like ours will have a big group hug and we can all share content... Please share any ideas on how we can get MAC and PC to play nice together." While these limitations seem large, the software does work with all XP or Vista software, and the content can also be used with Xbox 360 or be downloaded to other portable devices. Because iTunes is not currently being offered in Canada, consumers will have more options when choosing online video content. There is tremendous added value to consumers because "the Bell Video Store will also bring additional value to Bell digital TV subscribers," explains Crull. New experiences will be created through heightened product delivery options of online viewing.

When any company updates its product offerings, there are bound to be comments and criticisms, but what Bell has demonstrated is a keen desire to offer its consumers a vast array of entertainment options in a highly competitive atmosphere. Some critics argue that Bell is using its significant size to gain a foothold in this new market. Only time will tell whether this new launch is a smart move for Bell, or if the old saying holds any truth—the bigger they are, the harder they fall.

Questions for Discussion

1. Assess the relative importance of the four Ps in Bell's new venture.
2. What are market strengths and weaknesses of Bell's new venture? Create a SWOT analysis and explain your findings. (Review the SWOT material in Chapter 6 before answering this question.)
3. Are there any product limitations that might affect consumer willingness to adopt the new technology?
4. How important is timing and PR with this type of new product launch?

apter 16

Developing and Promoting Goods and Services

After reading this chapter, you should be able to:

1. Explain the definition of a product as a *value package*.
2. Describe the new product development process and trace the stages of the *product life cycle*.
3. Explain the importance of *branding, packaging,* and *labelling*.
4. Identify the important objectives of *promotion* and discuss the considerations in selecting a *promotional mix*.
5. Discuss the most important *advertising* strategies and describe the key *advertising media*.
6. Outline the tasks involved in *personal selling* and list the steps in the personal selling process.
7. Describe the various types of *sales promotions*, and distinguish between *publicity* and *public relations*.
8. Describe the development of international and small business *promotion* strategies.

Psst! Did You Hear the Latest?

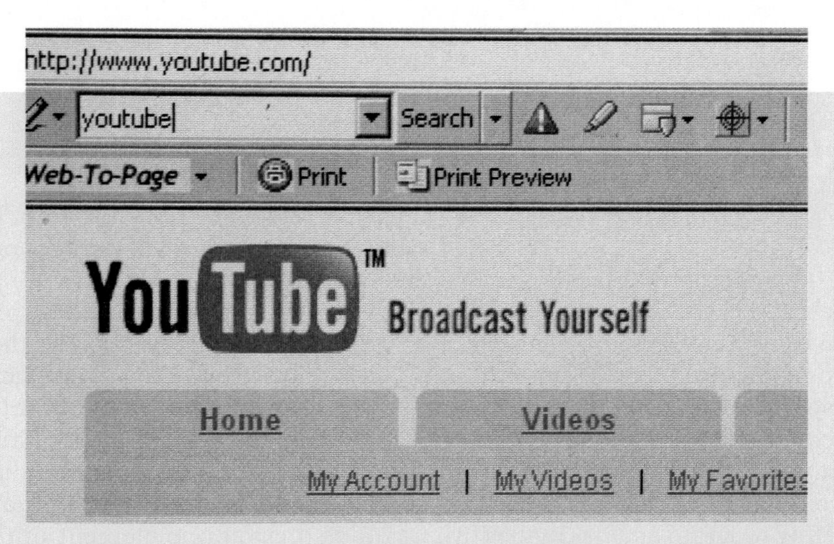

Word-of-mouth advertising is probably the oldest form of advertising. Ever since the first brand names developed hundreds of years ago, consumers have been exchanging information with each other about the positive and negative features of the products they buy. In the eighteenth and nineteenth centuries, marketing was very fragmented and most products were promoted only in local areas at retailers like the general store. Word-of-mouth advertising was therefore mostly confined to local or regional markets because existing technology did not allow consumers to be well connected.

By the 1930s, the development of radio, and later television, allowed businesses to market their products nationwide. Word of mouth did not disappear, but it was overshadowed by mass marketing. More recently, word-of-mouth advertising has again gained prominence, partly because of the internet. PQ Media predicts that spending in the United States on word-of-mouth advertising will reach $3.7 billion by 2011 because companies recognize the emerging importance of social networking sites like YouTube and Facebook and of personal blogs.

Word-of-mouth advertising is relatively cheap, and the messages that it carries are trusted by those who hear them. A Nielsen study showed that 78 percent of consumers trust word-of-mouth messages. Newspapers were trusted by 63 percent of consumers, television by 56 percent, and text ads on cellphones by only 18 percent.

Word of mouth is a double-edged sword. If consumers are spreading positive messages about a product, sales will likely soar. For example, Nike spent very little money advertising its Presto line of stretchy sneakers, but kids and teens spread the word to each other about the shoes and the fashion statement they could make by having them. If, however, consumers are spreading negative messages, sales will suffer. The movie *Snakes on a Plane*, which starred Samuel L. Jackson, bombed at the box office because most of the word of mouth focussed on how bad the film was. And when Pontiac gave away one of its new G6 models on the Oprah Winfrey show, the company hoped that the publicity would generate significant word of mouth among potential customers. But sales did not materialize.

Procter & Gamble—which is famous for its television commercials—is very active in word-of-mouth advertising. When the company introduced a new cleaning product called Dawn Direct Foam, it provided information about the product to Vocalpoint, a group of 450 000 brand "evangelists" who talk up P&G products. The new product launch was a success. P&G has another word-of-mouth unit called Tremors, which includes over 200 000 teenagers who are active on social networks. These individuals are often early adopters of new products. P&G is planning to use Canada as a testing ground for online advertising spending, especially in light of the fact that an Ipsos Reid survey showed that Canadian consumers spend 39 percent of their media consumption time on the internet, 26 percent on TV, and 11 percent on print media. This large percentage of media consumption time spent on the internet means great opportunities for word of mouth.

Many other companies also recognize the importance of word-of-mouth advertising:

- The Sprinkles Cupcake chain is expanding even during a recession by choosing locations in affluent areas and then relying on word of mouth to bring customers in.
- Lee Jeans recruited 1000 "agents" who each received a pair of One True Fit jeans and a promotional kit that included a list of people to target with information about the Lee brand.
- Algordonza is a Swiss-based company that makes artificial diamonds from the carbon found in the ashes of people who have been cremated. It sells about 700 diamonds each year to friends and relatives of the deceased. The company does not advertise but relies on word of mouth to make people aware of its product.
- Volkswagen Canada cancelled a scheduled advertising campaign for its new Eos automobile because the cars were rapidly being sold due to positive word of mouth about the car among consumers.
- Google did no marketing of its Gmail; instead they gave out Gmail accounts to only certain "power users" and the resulting word of mouth increased demand for the service.

A group called The Influencers is Canada's first word-of-mouth community. It has created its own word-of-mouth campaign for promoting word-of-mouth advertising and cites various interesting statistics:

- The average person has 56 word-of-mouth conversations each week.
- Ninety-three percent of customers say word of mouth is the most trustworthy source of product information.
- Word of mouth is rated as the most reliable of 15 different marketing influences.
- Seventy-seven percent of word-of-mouth advertising is face to face.
- Forty-four percent of Canadians avoid buying products that overwhelm them with advertising. ◆

How will this help me?

By understanding the material in this chapter, you can benefit in three ways: (1) As an employee and as a manager, you'll be better able to use the concepts of developing and promoting products in your career; (2) as a consumer, you'll have a clearer picture of how the complex process of new product development and promotion leads to more consumer choice; and (3) as an investor, you'll be better prepared to evaluate a company's marketing program and its competitive potential before buying the company's stock.

In Chapter 15, we introduced the four basic elements in the marketing mix: product, promotion, price, and place (distribution). In this chapter, we focus on two of these components—products and how they are promoted. We begin by looking at the different classifications of products, the new product development process, the product life-cycle idea, and the branding of products. We then discuss the various aspects of promotion—advertising, personal selling, sales promotion, and publicity. As you read this chapter and the one that follows, keep in mind that it is virtually impossible to focus on just one element of the marketing mix (for example, the product) without having to also deal with the others (price, promotion, and distribution).

What Is a Product?

1 Explain the definition of a product as a *value package.*

In developing the marketing mix for any product—whether ideas, goods, or services—marketers must consider what consumers really buy when they purchase products. Only then can they plan their strategies effectively. In this section we look first at product features and benefits, then explain the major classifications of products, then discuss the product mix.

Product Features and Benefits

features Qualities—tangible and intangible—that a company builds in to its products.

Product **features** are the qualities—tangible and intangible—that a company builds in to its products, such as a 12-horsepower motor on a lawn mower. Products are therefore much more than just visible features. In buying a product, consumers are also buying an image and a reputation. The marketers of Swatch Chrono watches, for example, are well aware that the brand name, packaging, labelling, and after-the-purchase service are also indispensable parts of their product. Advertisements remind consumers that they don't just get "real" features like shock and water resistance, quartz precision, and Swiss manufacture. They also get Swatch's commitment that its products will be young and trendy, active and sporty, and stylistically cool and clean.

value package Product marketed as a bundle of value-adding attributes, including reasonable cost.

To attract buyers, product features must also provide benefits. The lawn mower, for example, must produce an important intangible benefit—an attractive lawn. Today's consumers regard a product as a bundle of attributes, which, taken together, marketers call the **value package**. Increasingly, buyers expect to receive products with greater value—with more benefits at reasonable costs. For example, the possible attributes in a personal computer value package are things like easy access to understandable pre-purchase information, choices of colour, attractive software packages, fast ordering via the internet, speedy delivery, and internet chat room capability. Although the computer includes physical features—like processing devices and other hardware—most items in the value package are services or intangibles that, collectively, add value by providing benefits that increase the customer's satisfaction.

Look carefully at the ad in Figure 16.1 for SAS Institute (www.sas.com), a designer of statistical software. In this ad, SAS does not emphasize the technical features of its products, nor even the criteria that companies use in selecting software—efficiency, compatibility, support. Rather, the ad focuses on the customer-oriented benefits that a buyer of SAS software can expect from using the firm's products. These benefits are being marketed as part of a complete value package.

Figure 16.1 SAS ad.

Classifying Goods and Services

Buyers fall into two basic groups, consumer and industrial. Marketing products and services to consumers is vastly different from marketing them to companies.

Classifying Consumer Products

Consumer products are commonly divided into three categories that reflect buyers' behaviour: convenience, shopping, and specialty products.

- **Convenience goods** (such as milk and newspapers) and **convenience services** (such as those offered by fast-food restaurants) are consumed rapidly and regularly. They are relatively inexpensive and are purchased frequently and with little expenditure of time and effort.
- **Shopping goods** (such as stereos and tires) and **shopping services** (such as insurance) are more expensive and are purchased less frequently than convenience goods and services. Consumers often compare brands, sometimes in different stores. They may also evaluate alternatives in terms of style, performance, colour, price, and other criteria.
- **Specialty goods** (such as wedding gowns) and **specialty services** (such as catering for wedding receptions) are extremely important and expensive purchases. Consumers usually have strong preferences, will accept no substitutes, and will often spend a great deal of time and money to get a specific product or service.

convenience goods/services Relatively inexpensive consumer goods or services that are bought and used rapidly and regularly, causing consumers to spend little time looking for them or comparing their prices.

shopping goods/services Moderately expensive consumer goods or services that are purchased infrequently, causing consumers to spend some time comparing their prices.

specialty goods/services Very expensive consumer goods or services that are purchased rarely, causing consumers to spend a great deal of time locating the exact item desired.

Classifying Industrial Products

Industrial products are usually divided into two categories, based on how much they cost and how they will be used.

- **Expense items** are materials and services that are consumed within a year by firms producing other goods or services. The most obvious expense items are industrial goods used directly in the production process, for example, bulk loads of tea processed into tea bags.
- **Capital items** are permanent—that is, expensive and long-lasting—goods and services. All these items have expected lives of more than a year. Buildings (offices, factories), fixed equipment (water towers, baking ovens), and accessory equipment (computers, airplanes) are capital goods. **Capital services** are those for which long-term commitments are made. These may include

expense items Relatively inexpensive industrial goods that are consumed rapidly and regularly.

capital items Expensive, long-lasting industrial goods that are used in producing other goods or services and have a long life.

capital services Services for which long-term commitments are made.

purchases for employee food services, building and equipment maintenance, or legal services.

The Product Mix

product mix The group of products a company has available for sale.

The group of consumer or industrial products a company has available for sale is known as the firm's **product mix**. Black & Decker, for example, makes toasters, vacuum cleaners, electric drills, and a variety of other appliances and tools. 3M makes everything from Post-it Notes to laser optics.

Product Lines

product line A group of similar products intended for a similar group of buyers who will use them in a similar fashion.

A **product line** is a group of products that are closely related because they function in a similar manner or are sold to the same customer group, who will use them in similar ways. Many companies that begin with a single product find that, over time, the initial product fails to suit every consumer shopping for the product type. To meet market demand, they introduce similar products designed to reach more customers. For example, ServiceMaster originally offered mothproofing and carpet cleaning, then subsequently expanded into other closely related services for homeowners—lawn care (TruGreen, ChemLawn), pest control (Terminix), and cleaning (Merry Maids).

Companies may also introduce multiple product lines that go well beyond their existing product line. After years of serving residential customers, ServiceMaster added business and industry services (landscaping and janitorial), education services (management of schools and institutions, including physical facilities and financial and personnel resources), and health-care services (management of support services like plant operations, asset management, and laundry/linen supply for long-term care facilities).

Developing New Products

All products and services—including once-popular TV shows like *Seinfeld, Everybody Loves Raymond, Friends,* and *Frasier*—eventually fall out of favour with consumers. Firms must therefore develop and introduce new products. Levi's jeans, for example, was once one of Canada's most popular brands, but the company failed to keep pace with changing tastes and lost market share. The company got back on track when it introduced the new Signature brand of casual clothing. The brand has become very popular, and Levi's has opened Signature stores in several countries.

While new product development is critical, it is also very risky. Consider the battle between Toshiba (HD DVD) and Sony (Blu-ray) for global dominance in the format of high-definition DVDs. Both companies invested millions of dollars in their respective products, and experts predicted that there would be a prolonged fight between the two companies. But in less than two years, Toshiba gave up the fight and stopped producing its product. Why? Because Sony was successful in convincing movie studios like Warner to release movies only in the Blu-ray format. Major retail outlets like Wal-Mart and Netflix also announced they would sell only the Blu-ray format. Sony's success with Blu-ray is in marked contrast to its failure in the 1980s to get its Betamax format adopted for VCRs. In that earlier fight, Sony lost out when consumers preferred the VHS format.[1]

The Time Frame of New Product Development

2 Describe the new product development process and trace the stages of the *product life cycle.*

Companies often face multi-year time horizons, high risks, and lots of uncertainty when developing new products. In 2004, Montreal-based Bombardier announced that it would build a new C-series line of regional passenger jets. In 2006, it shelved the project, but it restarted it in 2007. In 2008, Bombardier announced that it had received the first orders for the new plane, which will not enter service until 2013.[2] Two other commercial airplane manufacturers have also had delays with their new planes. Boeing's 787 Dreamliner was originally supposed to be available to buyers in 2008, but a strike by machinists and incomplete work by suppliers will delay the introduction of the new plane until 2010. Boeing's main competitor, Airbus, has experienced its own problems. It had to redesign its A350, which pushed back the planned start of production by nearly three years.[3] Other products that have experienced delays are high-definition television and the hydrogen fuel cell.

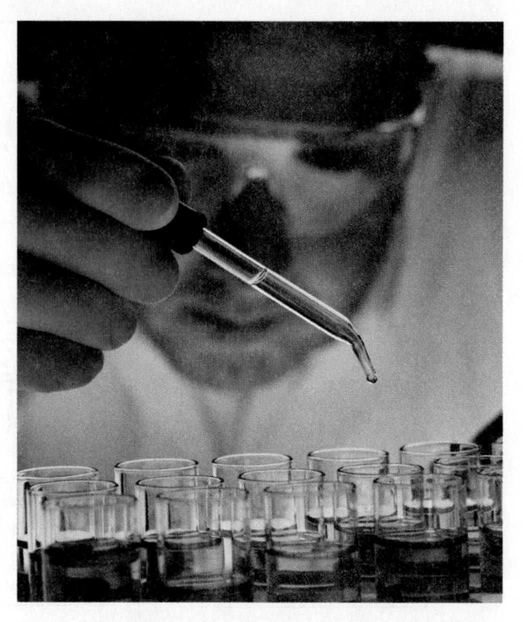

Pharmaceutical companies spend large amounts of money on research and development, yet bring relatively few new products to market each year.

Product Mortality Rates

It takes about 50 new product ideas to generate one product that finally reaches the market, and then only 10 percent of these products become successful. Creating a successful new product has become increasingly difficult, even for the most experienced marketers, because the number of new products hitting the market each year has increased dramatically.

Speed to Market

The more rapidly a product moves from the laboratory to the marketplace, the more likely it is to survive. By introducing new products ahead of competitors, companies establish market leadership and become entrenched in the market before being challenged by newer competitors. The importance of **speed to market**—a firm's success in responding to customer demand or market changes—can be seen in this statistic: A product that is only three months late to market (three months behind the leader) loses 12 percent of its lifetime profit potential. A product that is six months late will lose 33 percent.[4]

speed to market Strategy of introducing new products to respond quickly to customer and/or market changes.

The Seven-Step Development Process

To increase their chances of developing successful new products or services, many firms use a basic seven-step process (see Figure 16.2). Steps 2, 3, 4, 6, and 7 are the same for both products and services, but there are some differences in Steps 1 and 5.

1. *Product ideas.* Product development begins with a search for ideas for new products. Product ideas can come from consumers, the sales force, research and development, or engineering. Developing services ideas includes a task called defining the **service package**, which involves identification of the tangible and intangible features that define the service and state service specifications.

service package Identification of the tangible and intangible features that define the service.

2. *Screening.* This stage is an attempt to eliminate all product ideas that do not mesh with the firm's abilities, expertise, or objectives. Representatives from marketing, engineering, and production must have input at this stage.
3. *Concept testing.* Once ideas have been culled, companies use market research to solicit consumers' input. Firms can identify benefits that the product must provide as well as an appropriate price level for the product.
4. *Business analysis.* This involves developing a comparison of costs and benefits for the proposed product. Preliminary sales projections are compared with cost projections from finance and production to determine whether the product can meet minimum profitability goals.

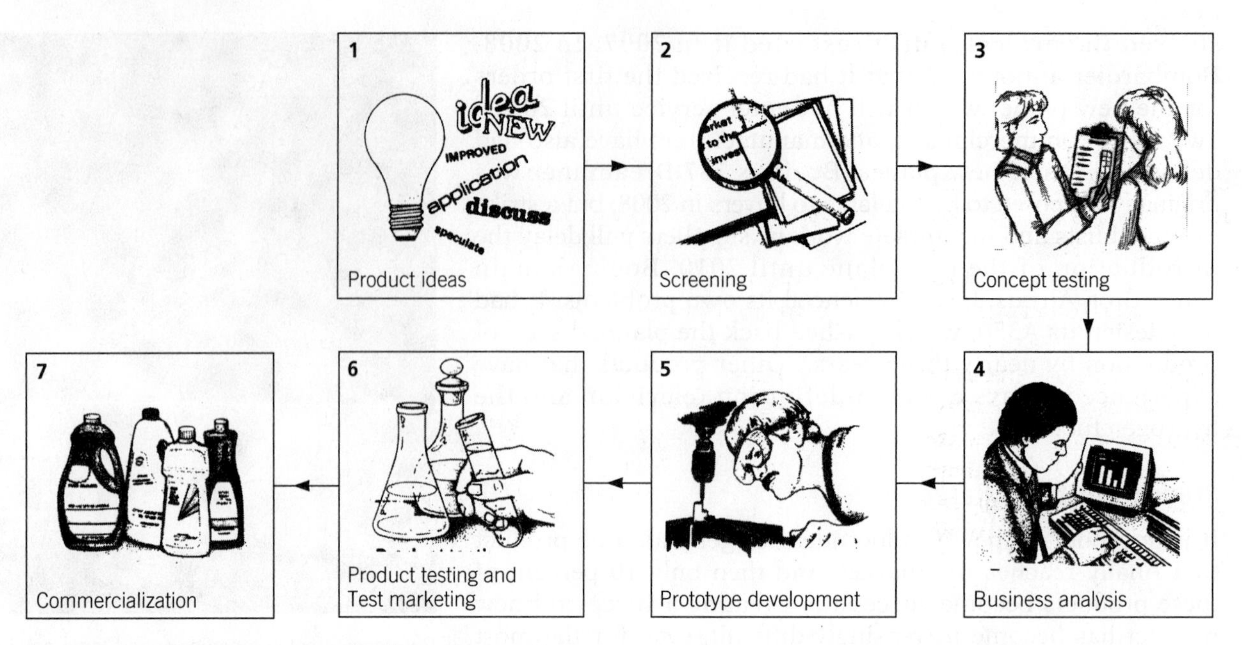

Figure 16.2 The new product development process.

5. *Prototype development.* Using input from the concept-testing phase, engineering and/or research and development produce a preliminary version of the product. Prototypes can be extremely expensive, often requiring extensive hand crafting, tooling, and development of components, but this phase can help identify potential production problems. **Service process design** involves selecting the process (identifying each step in the service, including the sequence and the timing), identifying worker requirements (specifying employee behaviours, skills, capabilities, and interactions with customers), and determining facilities requirements (designating all of the equipment that supports delivery of the service).

service process design Selecting the process, identifying worker requirements, and determining facilities requirements so that the service can be effectively provided.

6. *Product testing and test marketing.* The company begins limited production of the item. If the product meets performance requirements, it is made available for sale in limited areas (test markets). This stage is very costly, since promotional campaigns and distribution channels must be established. Test marketing gives a company its first information on how consumers will respond to a product under real market conditions.

7. *Commercialization.* If test-marketing results are positive, the company will begin full-scale production and marketing of the product. Gradual commercialization, with the firm providing the product to more and more areas over time, prevents undue strain on the firm's initial production capabilities, but delays in commercialization may give competitors a chance to bring out their own version.

The Product Life Cycle

product life cycle (PLC) The concept that the profit-producing life of any product goes through a cycle of introduction, growth, maturity (levelling off), and decline.

The concept of the **product life cycle (PLC)** is based on the idea that products have a limited profit-producing life. This life may be a matter of months, years, or decades, depending on the ability of the product to attract customers over time. Products such as Kellogg's Corn Flakes, Coca-Cola, Ivory soap, Argo cornstarch, and Caramilk candy bars have had extremely long product life cycles.

Stages in the Product Life Cycle (PLC)

The life cycle for both goods and services is a natural process in which products are born, grow in stature, mature, and finally decline and die.[5] In Figure 16.3(a), the four phases of the PLC are applied to several products with which you are familiar.

1. *Introduction.* The introduction stage begins when the product reaches the marketplace. During this stage, marketers focus on making potential consumers aware of the product and its benefits. Because of extensive promotional and development costs, profits are non-existent.
2. *Growth.* If the new product attracts and satisfies enough consumers, sales begin to climb rapidly. During this stage, the product begins to show a profit. Other firms in the industry move speedily to introduce their own versions.
3. *Maturity.* Sales growth begins to slow. Although the product earns its highest profit level early in this stage, increased competition eventually leads to price cutting and lower profits. Toward the end of the stage, sales start to fall.
4. *Decline.* During this final stage, sales and profits continue to fall. New products in the introduction stage take away sales. Companies remove or reduce promotional support (ads and salespeople) but may let the product linger to provide some profits.

Figure 16.3(b) plots the relationship of the PLC to a product's typical sales, costs, and profits. Although the early stages of the PLC often show negative cash flows, successful products usually recover those losses and, in fact, continue

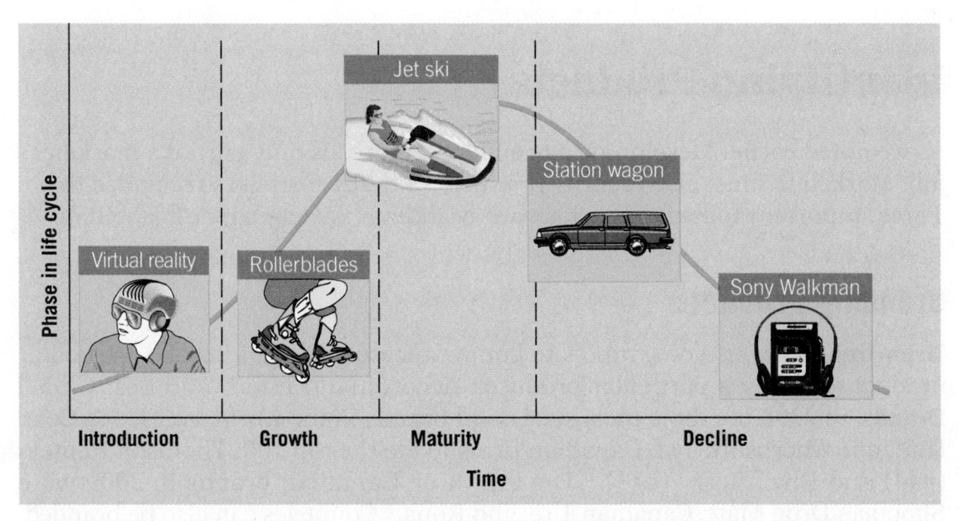

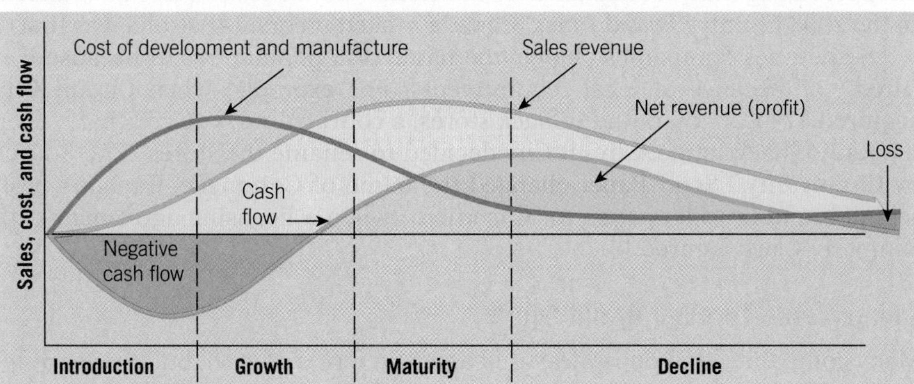

Figure 16.3 The product life cycle: stages, sales, cost, and profit.

to generate profits until the decline stage. For most products, profitable life spans are short—thus, the importance placed by so many firms on the constant replenishment of product lines. In the pension industry, for example, "defined benefit" programs are approaching the end of their life cycle, while "defined contribution" plans are in the growth stage.

Extending Product Life: An Alternative to New Products

Companies try to keep products in the maturity stage as long as they can. Sales of TV sets, for example, have been revitalized by such feature changes as colour, portability, miniaturization, stereo capability, and high definition. Companies can extend product life through a number of creative means. Foreign markets, for example, offer three possibilities for lengthening product life cycles:

product extension The process of marketing an existing, unmodified product globally.

1. In **product extension**, an existing product is marketed globally instead of just domestically. Coca-Cola and Levi's 501 jeans are prime examples of international product extensions.

product adaptation The process of modifying a product to have greater appeal in foreign markets.

2. With **product adaptation**, the product is modified for greater appeal in different countries. In Germany, a McDonald's meal includes beer, and in Japan, Ford puts the steering wheel on the right side. After Kraft Foods changed the shape of the traditional round Oreo Cookie to be long and thin (and coated the cookie in chocolate), it became the best-selling cookie in China. The new shape is also sold in Canada.[6]

reintroduction The process of reviving for new markets products that are obsolete in older ones.

3. **Reintroduction** means reviving, for new markets, products that are becoming obsolete in older ones. NCR, for instance, has reintroduced manually operated cash registers in Latin America.

Identifying Products

As we noted earlier, developing a product's features is only part of a marketer's job. Marketers must also identify products so that consumers recognize them. Three important tools for this task are branding, packaging, and labelling.

Branding Products

3 Explain the importance of *branding, packaging,* and *labelling.*

branding The use of symbols to communicate the qualities of a particular product made by a particular producer.

Branding is the use of symbols to communicate the qualities of a particular product made by a particular producer. According to Interbrand Best Global Brands, in 2008 the three most successful brands in the world were Coca-Cola, IBM, and Microsoft. Two Canadian firms made the top 100: Thomson Reuters (#44) and BlackBerry (#73).[7] The top three Canadian brands in 2009 were Shoppers Drug Mart, Canadian Tire, and Rona.[8] Countries can also be branded. In the 2008 Country Brand Index, Canada ranked second (Australia was first).[9]

Sometimes companies change the name of a popular brand because it is "tired," or because of legal requirements. For example, when Circuit City acquired 874 Canadian RadioShack stores, a court ruling required that it drop the RadioShack name. Circuit City decided to rename the stores "The Source by Circuit City." Scott Paper changed the name of Cottonelle, Canada's best-selling brand of toilet paper, to "Cashmere" when a licensing agreement with Kimberly-Clark expired.[10]

Adding Value Through Brand Equity

Many companies that once measured assets in terms of cash, buildings, equipment, and inventories now realize that a strong brand is an equally important asset. Widely known and admired brands are valuable because of their power to attract customers. Those with higher **brand equity** generate greater brand awareness and loyalty on the part of consumers, have larger market shares than competing brands, and are perceived to have greater quality. In the 2009 survey of Canadian brand equity, the top three companies were the Royal Bank of Canada (whose brand equity was valued at $5.3 billion), BlackBerry ($4.6 billion), and TD Canada Trust ($4.0 billion).[11]

brand equity Degree of consumers' loyalty to and awareness of a brand and its resultant market share.

Ebusiness and International Branding

The expensive and fierce struggle for brand recognition is very evident in the branding battles among dot-com firms. Collectively, the top internet brands—Google, America Online, Yahoo!, and Amazon.com—spend billions each year. Cisco Systems Inc., the network-equipment manufacturer, developed a successful promotional campaign that increased its brand awareness by 80 percent. The campaign also lifted Cisco's reputation as an internet expert above that of Microsoft, IBM, and Lucent.[12]

Firms that sell products internationally must consider how product names will translate in various languages. In Spanish, for example, the name of Chevrolet's now-defunct Nova simply became no va—"it does not go." Not surprisingly, sales were poor in South America. Similarly, Rolls-Royce was once going to name a new touring car Silver Mist, but changed the name to Silver Shadow when it discovered that *mist* is German for *manure*.[13]

Differences in approaches to brand names are evident even within countries. When Headspace Marketing Inc. asked 1000 Quebecers to rate how well 12 different brands had adapted to the needs and expectations of Quebecers, they found that the top three brands were Tim Hortons, Canadian Tire, and Bureau en gros (in that order). Tim Hortons ranked much higher than Starbucks (which ranked last) even though Tim Hortons did very little to adapt its product line to the Quebec market and Starbucks did a lot. However, Tim Hortons got involved with community charities and activities and used Quebec actors in their ad campaigns. This apparently made the Tim Hortons brand "resonate" better with Quebecers.[14]

The experience of Tim Hortons is not unusual. Consider the "brand wars" between Coke and Pepsi in Quebec. Coke sells better than Pepsi in most places in the world, but not in Quebec. Why is that? Perhaps it's because Pepsi customizes its advertisements to meet distinct Quebecois tastes. One now-famous ad shows what happens when a European tourist orders a Coke in Quebec: a hush comes over the restaurant, wildlife stops in the forest, and traffic comes to a halt. The waiter finally opens a Pepsi for the tourist, who then says, "Ah! Ici, c'est Pepsi."[15] Bombardier's national ad campaign uses the slogan "Planes. Trains. Canadian Spirit" except in Quebec, where the slogan is "Planes. Trains. A Source of Pride."[16]

Types of Brand Names

Virtually every product has a brand name of some form. However, different types of brand names tell consumers something about the product's origin.

National Brands. Brand name products that are produced and distributed by the manufacturer are called **national brands**. These brands, such as Scotch tape, are often widely recognized by consumers because of large national advertising campaigns. The costs of developing a positive image for a national brand are high, so some companies use their national brand on several related products. Procter & Gamble markets Ivory shampoo, capitalizing on the widely recognized name of its soaps.

national brands Products distributed by and carrying a name associated with the manufacturer.

Licensed Brands. More and more nationally recognized companies and personalities have sold other companies the right to place their names on

SpongeBob macaroni and cheese is Kraft Foods' top-selling licensed pasta product, and SpongeBob Band-Aids now outsell Scooby Doo bandages. There are SpongeBob dolls and bowling balls, and the brand also appears on toothpaste and underwear. SpongeBob belongs to Nickelodeon Enterprises, a children's TV programmer that's been the highest-rated basic cable network since 1995. Product licensing is worth about $2.5 billion to Nickelodeon each year.

licensed brands Products for which the right to use a brand name, a celebrity's name, or some other well-known identification mark was sold to another company to use on a product.

products, which are **licensed brands**. The Olympic logo generates millions in revenues for the International Olympic Committee, which licenses its name on clothing, tableware, coins, licence plates, and countless other merchandise items. Harley-Davidson's famous logo—emblazoned on boots, eyewear, gloves, purses, lighters, and watches—brings the motorcycle maker more than $210 million annually. Licensing for character-based brands—Punisher, Spider-Man, and Pokémon—is equally lucrative. Nelvana and U.S.-based Sears signed a licensing agreement allowing Sears to set up Franklin the Turtle boutiques at its stores. These boutiques market Franklin clothing and accessories that are available exclusively at Sears.[17]

private brands Products promoted by and carrying a name associated with the retailer or wholesaler, not the manufacturer.

Private Brands. When a wholesaler or retailer develops a brand and has the manufacturer place that brand name on the product, the resulting product name is a **private brand**. Sears has two well-known private brands—Craftsman tools and Kenmore appliances. J. Sainsbury PLC, the largest supermarket chain in Britain, introduced its own private brand of cola in a can that looks strikingly like the one used by Coke. The product is made by Cott Corp. of Toronto, which also makes the "American Choice" label for Wal-Mart. Loblaw Companies Ltd. created a line of upscale products under the private brand President's Choice. Shoppers Drug Mart produces a line of products under the Life label.[18] E.D. Smith, a maker of jams and pie fillings, makes private label items for retailers like Wal-Mart and Pizza Pizza Ltd.[19]

Brand Loyalty

brand loyalty Customers' recognition of, preference for, and insistence on buying a product with a certain brand name.

Brand loyalty means that when customers need a particular item, they will go back to the same brand and buy the company's products. Brand loyalty exists at three levels: *brand awareness* (customers recognize the brand name), *brand preference* (consumers have a favourable attitude toward the product), and *brand insistence* (consumers demand the product and are willing to go out of their way to get it). Brand insistence implies a lot of consumer trust in a brand. Canadians have less trust in brands than they did 20 years ago, but some well-known brands like Becel margarine, Robin Hood flour, Wal-Mart, and Black & Decker are still viewed positively.[20]

Brand loyalty is strong in several sports, including baseball, basketball, and soccer, and fans respond to marketing efforts by companies like Nike and

Adidas. But in some other sports (for example, skateboarding) brand loyalty is difficult to develop. Because skateboarders go through a lot of boards each year, they are reluctant to buy brand name boards, which cost three to five times what "blank" boards cost. The International Association of Skateboard Companies estimates that 50 to 70 percent of all boards sold are blank, not branded.[21]

Brand loyalty can have a major impact on a company's profits. In the beer industry, for example, each market share point is worth about $25 million in profit. This is why companies like Labatt and Molson have such fierce competitive battles for market share.[22]

Trademarks, Patents, and Copyrights

Because brand development is very expensive, a company does not want another company using its name and confusing consumers. Companies can apply to the Canadian government and receive a **trademark**, the exclusive legal right to use a brand name. Trademarks are granted for 15 years and may be renewed for further periods of 15 years, but only if the company continues to protect its brand name. In 2008, a European court ruled that the construction toys made by Lego AS can no longer be protected by trademark law. Montreal-based Mega Brands Inc., which makes a competitive product called Mega Bloks, had challenged Lego's trademark.[23]

trademark The exclusive legal right to use a brand name.

Exactly what can be trademarked is not always clear. If the company allows the name to lapse into common usage, the courts may take away protection. Common usage occurs when the company fails to use the ® symbol for its brand. It also occurs if the company fails to correct those who do not acknowledge the brand as a trademark. Windsurfer (a popular brand of sailboards by WSI Inc.) lost its trademark. Like the trampoline, yo-yo, and thermos, the brand name has become the common term for the product and can now be used by any sailboard company. But companies owning brands like Xerox, Coke, Jell-O, and Scotch tape have successfully defended their brand names.

Companies want to be sure that both product brands and new product ideas are protected. A **patent** protects an invention or idea for a period of 20 years. The cost is $1000 to $1500; it takes from nine months to three years to secure a patent from the Canadian Patent Office.[24] Patents can be very valuable. In 2006, Research In Motion (RIM), maker of the immensely popular BlackBerry device, agreed to pay $612.5 million to NTP Inc., a U.S. firm that claimed RIM was infringing on some patents it held.[25] Two months later, RIM was sued by another U.S. company claiming that RIM had also infringed on its patents.[26] In yet another patent dispute, Pfizer Inc. reached an agreement in 2008 with an Indian generic drug maker that will keep a cheaper version of the cholesterol-lowering drug Lipitor out of the U.S. market until 2011. Sales revenues of Lipitor are about US$13 billion annually, so this is a very important deal for Pfizer.[27]

patent Exclusive legal right to use and license a manufactured item or substance, manufacturing process, or object design.

Copyrights give exclusive ownership rights to the creators of books, articles, designs, illustrations, photos, films, and music. Computer programs and even semiconductor chips are also protected. In Canada, the copyright process is relatively simple, requiring only the use of the copyright symbol © and the date. Copyrights extend to creators for their entire lives and to their estates for 50 years thereafter in Canada (70 years in the United States). Copyrights apply to the tangible expressions of an idea, not to the idea itself. For example, the idea of cloning dinosaurs from fossil DNA cannot be copyrighted, but Michael Crichton, the author of *Jurassic Park*, had a copyright for his novel (which is now held by his estate) because it is the tangible result of the basic idea.

copyright Exclusive ownership rights belonging to the creators of books, articles, designs, illustrations, photos, films, and music.

There is much debate about how copyrights apply to material that appears on the internet. In 2005, the Author's Guild and several publishers sued Google, claiming that its book-scanning project was infringing on their copyrights.

In 2008, Google agreed to pay US$125 million to settle the lawsuits. Google can now make available millions of books online.[28]

Packaging Products

packaging Physical container in which a product is sold, advertised, or protected.

Except for products like fresh fruits and vegetables and structural steel, almost all products need some form of **packaging** so they can be transported to the market. Packaging also serves several other functions: It is an in-store advertisement that makes the product attractive; it clearly displays the brand; it identifies product features and benefits; and it reduces the risk of damage, breakage, or spoilage. The package is the marketer's last chance to say "buy me" to the consumer.

Companies are paying close attention to consumer concerns about packaging. Beyond concerns about product tampering, packaging must be tight enough to withstand shipping but not so tight that it frustrates consumers when they try to open the package. Nestlé—which spends more than $6 billion annually on packaging—spent nine months coming up with a new, easier-to-open lid and an easier-to-grip container for its Country Creamery ice cream. In general, companies have found that packaging costs can be as high as 15 percent of the total cost to make a product, and features like zip-lock tops can add 20 percent to the price that is charged.[29]

Labelling Products

label That part of a product's packaging that identifies the product's name and contents and sometimes its benefits.

Every product has a **label** on its package. Like packaging, labelling can help market the product. First, it identifies the product or the brand, such as the name Campbell on a can of soup or Chiquita on a banana. Labels also promote products by getting consumers' attention. Attractive colours and graphics provide visual cues to products that otherwise might be overlooked on the shelf. Finally, the label describes the product by providing information about nutritional content, directions for use, proper disposal, and safety.

Consumer Packaging and Labelling Act A federal law that provides comprehensive rules for packaging and labelling of consumer products.

The federal government regulates the information on package labels. The **Consumer Packaging and Labelling Act** has two main purposes: The first is to provide a comprehensive set of rules for packaging and labelling of consumer products, and the second is to ensure that manufacturers provide full and factual information on labels. All pre-packaged products must state in French and English the quantity enclosed in metric units, as well as the name and description of the product.

Sellers are very sensitive to what is on the label of the products they sell. For example, the Maple Leaf is on all beer that Labatt Brewing Co. Ltd. sells in Canada—except in Quebec. There, the label has a stylized sheaf of wheat instead of the Maple Leaf. Interestingly, the Maple Leaf is much more prominent on Labatt's beer sold in the United States.[30] Many companies use different labels for their products in Quebec than they do for products sold elsewhere in Canada.

Promoting Products and Services

4 Identify the important objectives of *promotion* and discuss the considerations in selecting a *promotional mix.*

promotion Any technique designed to sell a product.

As we noted in Chapter 15, **promotion** is any technique designed to sell a product. It is part of the *communication mix*: the total message a company sends to consumers about its product. Promotional techniques, especially advertising, must communicate the uses, features, and benefits of products. Sales promotions also include various programs that add value beyond the benefits inherent in the product. For example, it is nice to get a high-quality product at a reasonable price, but it is even better when the seller offers a rebate or a bonus pack with "20 percent more *free*."

Information and Exchange Values

In free market systems, businesses use promotional methods to accomplish four objectives with potential customers:

- make them aware of products
- make them knowledgeable about products
- persuade them to like products
- persuade them to purchase products

Successful promotions provide communication about the product and create exchanges that satisfy the objectives of customers (who get a desired product) and sellers (who get sales and profits). The promotion program can determine the success or failure of any business or product, whether it is in the introduction stage (promoting for new product awareness) or the maturity stage (promoting brand benefits and customer loyalty).

Promotional Objectives

The ultimate objective of any promotion is to increase sales. However, marketers also use promotion to *communicate information, position products, add value,* and *control sales volume*.[31]

Communicating Information

Consumers cannot buy a product unless they have been informed about it. Information can advise customers about the availability of a product, educate them on the latest technological advances, or announce the candidacy of someone running for a government office. Information may be communicated in writing (newspapers and magazines), verbally (radio, in person, or over the telephone), or visually (television, the internet, a matchbook cover, or a billboard). Today, the communication of information regarding a company's products or services is so important that marketers try to place it wherever consumers may be. The average Canadian sees about 3000 marketing messages every day, much more than the average consumer saw 30 years ago.[32] The boxed insert entitled "Promoting a Green Business Image" describes how companies communicate information about their green initiatives to consumers.

Positioning Products

As we saw in Chapter 15, **product positioning** establishes an easily identifiable image of a product in the minds of consumers. For example, by selling only in department stores, Estée Lauder products are positioned as more upscale than cosmetics sold in drugstores. With product positioning, the company is trying to appeal to a specific segment of the market rather than to the market as a whole.

product positioning The establishment of an easily identifiable image of a product in the minds of consumers.

Adding Value

Today's value-conscious customers gain benefits when the promotional mix is shifted so that it communicates value-added benefits in its products. Burger King, for instance, shifted its promotional mix by cutting back on advertising dollars and using those funds for customer discounts. Receiving the same food at a lower price is added value for Burger King's customers.

The Greening of Business

Promoting a Green Business Image

In addition to their traditional role of promoting their products and services, Canadian businesses are also promoting themselves as "green" enterprises. They are doing this because the market for green products has increased rapidly during the last few years as consumers have become more concerned about the environment. For example, the image of Canada's oil sands producers is that of environmental "bad boys," so the companies have banded together to get out the word that they are investing in new technology that will reduce the impact of oil sands activity on the air, land, and water. The campaign includes a new website and a national advertising campaign that is designed to provide information and correct misperceptions that consumers may have about oil sands development.

Even companies that have a good reputation for being green are stepping up their efforts. The Body Shop unveiled a major advertising campaign in 2008 that aggressively touted its long-standing commitment to having a corporate culture of concern for the environment. The company is advertising because its competitors are touting their own commitment to the environment, and The Body Shop wants to stand out from the crowd.

Convincing customers that a business is green is becoming increasingly difficult because consumers have become quite cynical and because watchdog groups carefully scrutinize green claims. A Gandalf Group survey of 1500 Canadians found that the majority of consumers think that (a) environmental claims by businesses are just a marketing ploy, and (b) labelling regulations are needed so buyers can understand what terms like *eco-friendly* mean. These consumer attitudes have developed partly because some companies have tried to claim that their products are more eco-friendly than they really are. The term *greenwashing* has been coined to describe the practice of exaggerating or making false claims about the environmental impact of a product or service (it is a modern variation of the older term *whitewashing*, which means making things look better than they actually are). EnviroMedia publishes a Greenwashing Index that ranks the eco-friendly advertising claims of various companies.

Charges of greenwashing can create very negative publicity for a company. A case in point—World Wildlife Fund (WWF) accused Shell Oil of greenwashing after Shell advertised that its Alberta oil sands operations were "sustainable." WWF filed a complaint with the U.K. Advertising Standards Authority, and in 2008 the authority ruled that the advertisement was misleading and confusing to consumers. WWF publicized the ruling—and made critical comments about Shell—on a large digital billboard in central London.

Another oil company that has had difficulties is BP. Its slogan "Beyond Petroleum" promotes its green image, and the company has been praised by the Natural Resource Defense Council in the United States as a leader in the industry's move toward renewable energy. But BP is involved in extracting oil from the Alberta oil sands, which Greenpeace has called "the greatest climate crime in history." BP has also been cited for environmental offences several times during the last decade.

Some green advertising campaigns may strike consumers as downright audacious. Much to the dismay of animal rights activists, the Fur Council of Canada—which emphasizes its ties with Aboriginal Canadians and its made-in-Canada attributes—is now promoting itself as a green industry. Its billboard and print advertisements stress the sustainability of the fur industry and point out that trappers are the first to sound the alarm when wildlife habitats are threatened. The trapping industry has endured much negative publicity during the last couple of decades, so this advertising campaign will likely make consumers sit up and take notice.

In response to concerns about greenwashing, the Canadian Competition Bureau, in co-operation with the Canadian Standards Association, has drafted industry guidelines that will require companies to back up their environmental claims with scientific evidence. Laws prohibiting misleading advertising already exist, but environmental claims are difficult to assess since there are no consistent definitions and standards that can be used to judge whether a product is really eco-friendly. The new guidelines will create national definitions for terms like *recyclable* and will also prohibit vague claims about products (for example, "our product is non-toxic"). In 2008, Lululemon Athletics Inc. was required to remove its unsubstantiated claims about the health benefits of seaweed from one of its clothing lines.

Critical Thinking Questions

1. What is your reaction to the Fur Council of Canada's green advertising campaign? What would you say to an animal rights activist who is outraged at the claims the Fur Council is making?
2. Consider the following statement: *The Competition Bureau's plan to create national guidelines to define terms like "recyclable" is well intentioned, but it will not work in practice, because companies will figure out ways to get around the rules and still make unwarranted claims about how "green" they are.* Do you agree or disagree with the statement? Explain your reasoning.

Controlling Sales Volume

Many companies, such as Hallmark Cards, experience seasonal sales patterns. By increasing promotional activities in slow periods, these firms can achieve more stable sales volume throughout the year. They can thus keep production and distribution systems running evenly. Promotions can even turn slow seasons into peak sales periods. For example, greeting card companies and florists together have done much to create Grandparents Day. The result has been increased consumer demand for cards and flowers in the middle of what was once a slow season for both industries.

Promotional Strategies

Once a firm's promotional objectives are clear, it must develop a promotional strategy to achieve these objectives. A company using a **push strategy** will aggressively "push" its product through wholesalers and retailers, who in turn persuade customers to buy the product. In contrast, a company using a **pull strategy** appeals directly to customers, who then demand the product from retailers, who in turn demand the product from wholesalers. Generally speaking, makers of industrial products use a push strategy, and makers of consumer products use a pull strategy, but many large firms use a combination of the two. For example, General Foods uses advertising to create consumer demand (pull) for its cereals, but it also pushes wholesalers and retailers to stock these products (push).

push strategy A promotional strategy whereby a company aggressively pushes its product through wholesalers and retailers, who persuade customers to buy it.

pull strategy A promotional strategy in which a company appeals directly to customers, who demand the product from retailers, who demand the product from wholesalers.

In rare cases, a company may purposely avoid both strategies. For example, Langlitz Leathers makes leather jackets that cost as much as $800. They are worn by rebels like Hells Angels, musicians like Bruce Springsteen, and actors like Sylvester Stallone. Even though the company does virtually no advertising, customers who want a Langlitz have to wait several months to get one after they place their order.[33]

The Promotional Mix

As we noted in Chapter 15, there are four types of promotional tools: advertising, personal selling, sales promotions, and publicity/public relations. The best combination of these tools—the **promotional mix**—depends on many factors, with the most important being the target audience. In establishing a promotional mix, marketers match promotional tools with the five stages in the buyer decision process we described in Chapter 15:

promotional mix That portion of marketing concerned with choosing the best combination of advertising, personal selling, sales promotions, and publicity to sell a product.

1. *Buyers recognize the need to make a purchase.* At this stage, marketers must make sure that buyers are aware of their products. Advertising and publicity, which can reach many people quickly, are important.

2. *Buyers seek information about available products.* Advertising and personal selling are important because both can be used to educate consumers.

3. *Buyers compare competing products.* Personal selling can be vital. Sales representatives can demonstrate product quality and performance in comparison with competitors' products.

4. *Buyers purchase products.* Sales promotion is effective because it can give consumers an incentive to buy. Personal selling can help by bringing products to convenient purchase locations.

5. *Buyers evaluate products after purchase.* Advertising, or even personal selling, is sometimes used to remind consumers that they made wise purchases.[34]

Figure 16.4 summarizes the effective promotional tools for each stage of the consumer buying process, and Figure 16.5 shows different combinations of products, promotional tools, and target consumers.

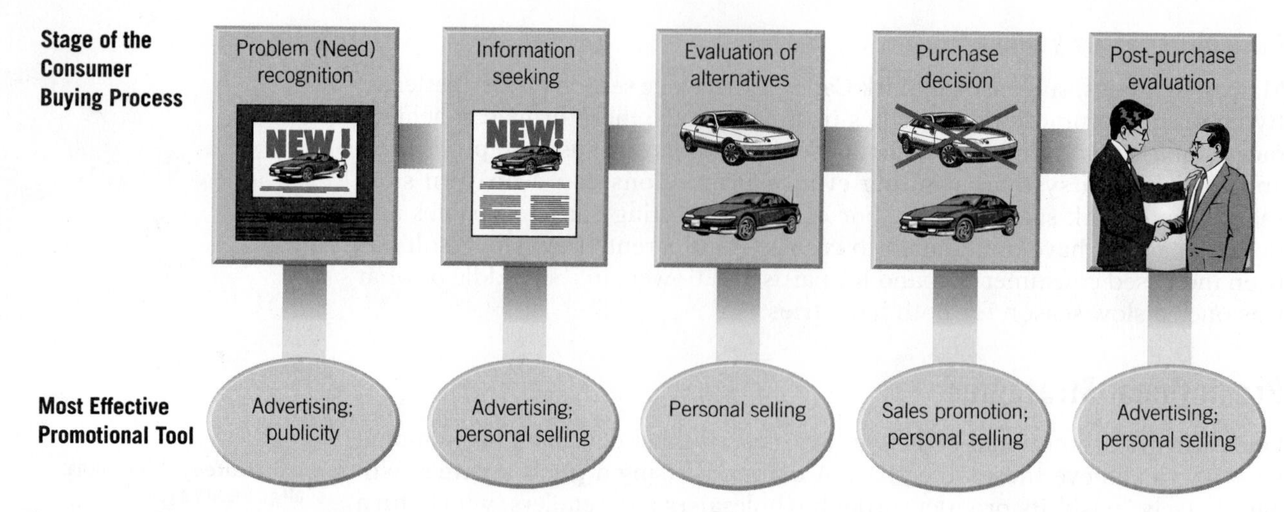

Figure 16.4 The consumer buying process and promotional mix.

Goods Promotion: House (real estate)
Tool: Personal selling
Consumer: House buyer

Service Promotion:
Weight-loss program
Tool: Sales promotion (coupon)
Consumer: Overweight person

You loved it as a girl...
Come back as a leader
Girl greatness starts here.
Girl Guides of Canada
Guides du Canada
Join today!
1-800-565-8111
girlguides.ca

Organizational Promotion: Scouts Canada
Tool: Publicity
Consumer: Young men and women

Event Promotion: Rock concert
Tool: Advertising
Consumer: Cheering fan

Person or Idea Promotion:
Candidate for prime minister
Tool: Publicity/advertising/personal sales
Consumer: Voter

Figure 16.5 Each promotional tool should be properly matched with the product being promoted and the target consumer.

Advertising Promotions

Discuss the most important *advertising* strategies and describe the key *advertising media.* 5

What candy bar is "one of life's sweet mysteries"? What soap is "99 and 44/100% pure"? What is the store where "the lowest price is the law"? What product is "only available in Canada—pity"? If you are like most Canadians, you can answer these questions because of **advertising**, which is a promotional tool consisting of paid, non-personal communication used by an identified sponsor to inform an audience about a product. (The answers are Caramilk, Ivory soap, Zellers, and Red Rose tea, respectively.) Consumers remember brand names more easily if the company has a catchy advertising slogan. Buckley's Mixture, a well-known product in Canada, is also sold in the United States. In one television advertisement, the announcer intones, "Buckley's Mixture, the famous Canadian cough remedy, is now available here. It tastes awful, and it works."[35]

advertising A promotional tool consisting of paid, non-personal communication used by an identified sponsor to inform an audience about a product.

Advertising Strategies

Advertising strategies depend on which stage of the product life cycle the product is in. During the introduction stage, **informative advertising** can help develop an awareness of the company and its product among buyers and can establish a primary demand for the product. For example, before a new textbook is published, instructors receive direct-mail advertisements notifying them of the book's contents and availability. During the growth stage, **persuasive advertising** can influence a larger number of consumers to buy the company's products. During the maturity stage, **comparative advertising**—which involves comparing the company's brand name with a competitor's brand name in such a way that the competitor's brand looks inferior—is often used. When Procter & Gamble aired advertisements claiming that its Bounty brand had more absorbency than Scott Paper's competing product, Scott retaliated by producing an advertisement that said that Scott Clean Ultra was 60 percent more absorbent than P&G's Bounty.[36] During the latter part of the maturity stage and all of the decline stage, **reminder advertising** keeps the product's name in front of the consumer.

informative advertising An advertising strategy, appropriate to the introduction stage of the product life cycle, in which the goal is to make potential customers aware that a product exists.

persuasive advertising An advertising strategy, appropriate to the growth stage of the product life cycle, in which the goal is to influence the customer to buy the firm's product rather than the similar product of a competitor.

comparative advertising An advertising strategy, appropriate to the maturity stage of the product life cycle, in which the goal is to influence the customer to switch from a competitor's similar product to the firm's product by directly comparing the two products.

reminder advertising An advertising strategy, appropriate to the latter part of the maturity stage of the product life cycle, in which the goal is to keep the product's name in the minds of customers.

Advertising Media

Consumers tend to ignore the bulk of advertising messages that bombard them. Marketers must therefore find out who their customers are, which media they pay attention to, what messages appeal to them, and how to get their attention. Thus, marketers use several different **advertising media**—specific communication outlets for carrying a seller's message to potential customers. For example, IBM uses television ads to keep its name fresh in the minds of consumers, newspaper and magazine ads to educate them about product features, and trade publications to introduce new software. Often marketers turn to a multimedia company so that the seller's message is the same across the different advertising media. The combination of media through which a company chooses to advertise its products is called its **media mix**. Although different industries use different mixes, most depend on multiple media to advertise their products and services. The top 10 multimedia companies in Canada are listed in Table 16.1.

An advertiser selects media with a number of factors in mind. The marketer must first ask: Which medium will reach the people I want to reach? If a firm is selling hog breeding equipment, it might choose a business magazine read mostly by hog farmers. If it is selling silverware, it might choose a magazine for brides. If it is selling toothpaste, the choice might be a general audience television program or a general audience magazine such as Reader's Digest (or Sélection du Reader's Digest, for exposure to a similar audience of francophones).

advertising media The specific communication devices—television, radio, newspapers, direct mail, magazines, billboards, the internet—used to carry a firm's advertising message to potential customers.

media mix The combination of media through which a company chooses to advertise its products.

Table 16.1 Top 10 Multimedia Companies in Canada, 2008

Company	Annual Revenues (in billions of $)
1. Rogers Cable Inc.	$3.8
2. CanWest Global Communications Corp.	3.1
3. Shaw Communications Inc.	3.1
4. Vidéotron Ltée	1.8
5. Rogers Media Inc.	1.4
6. Bell ExpressVu LP	1.3
7. Cogeco Inc.	1.1
8. Astral Media Inc.	0.8
9. Corus Entertainment Inc.	0.7
10. Canadian Broadcasting Corp.	0.5

Newspapers

Newspapers offer excellent coverage. Most local markets have at least one daily newspaper, and many people read the paper every day. This medium offers flexible, rapid coverage since ads can change from day to day. It also offers believable coverage since ads are presented side by side with news. However, newspapers are generally thrown out after one day, they often are not printed in colour, they have poor reproduction quality, and they do not usually allow advertisers to target their audience. Advertisers spent $1.7 billion on newspaper advertising in Canada in 2007.[37]

In recent years the volume of classified ads placed in newspapers has declined as advertisers have shifted their emphasis to the internet. The *Toronto Star* has tried to counter this trend by giving a free internet posting to anyone who buys a classified ad in the newspaper.[38]

Television

Television allows advertisers to combine sight, sound, and motion, thus appealing to almost all of the viewer's senses. Information on viewer demographics for a particular program allows advertisers to promote to their target audiences. One disadvantage of television is that too many commercials cause viewers to confuse products. In addition, viewers who record programs on DVRs (digital video recorders) often fast-forward through the ads appearing on the TV shows they have recorded. The brevity of TV ads also makes television a poor medium in which to educate viewers about complex products.

Television is the most expensive medium in which to advertise. Worldwide, advertisers spent US$146.8 billion on television advertising in 2005.[39] Spending on television advertising in Canada totalled $3.3 billion in 2007.[40] A 30-second commercial during the NFL Super Bowl costs about US$2.4 million.[41]

Direct Mail

direct mail Printed advertisements, such as flyers, mailed or faxed directly to consumers' homes or places of business.

Direct mail involves flyers or other types of printed advertisements that are mailed directly to consumers' homes or places of business. Direct mail allows the company to select its audience and personalize its message. Although many people discard "junk mail," targeted recipients with stronger-than-average interest are more likely to buy. Direct mail involves the largest advance costs of any advertising technique, but it appears to have the highest cost-effectiveness. Particularly effective have been "fax attacks," in which advertisers send their "mail" messages electronically via fax machines and get higher response rates than they would if they used Canada Post. Advertisers spent $1.7 billion on direct mail promotion in 2007.[42]

Radio

A tremendous number of people listen to the radio each day, and radio ads are inexpensive. In addition, since most radio is programmed locally, this medium gives advertisers a high degree of customer selectivity. For example, radio stations are segmented into listening categories such as rock and roll, country and western, jazz, talk shows, news, and religious programming. Like television, however, radio ads are very short, and radio permits only an audio presentation. People tend to use the radio as "background" while they are doing other things, and this means they may pay little attention to advertisements. Spending on radio advertisements totalled $1.4 billion in Canada in 2007.[43]

Magazines

The many different magazines on the market provide a high level of consumer selectivity. The person who reads *Popular Photography* is more likely to be interested in the latest specialized lenses from Canon than is a *Gourmet* magazine subscriber. Magazine advertising allows for excellent reproduction of photographs and artwork that not only grab buyers' attention but also may convince them of the product's value. And magazines allow advertisers plenty of space for detailed product information. Magazines have a long life and tend to be passed from person to person, thus doubling and tripling the number of exposures. The Canadian magazine with the largest readership is *Reader's Digest*, followed by *Canadian Living* (*Chatelaine* and *Canadian Geographic* are tied for third).[44] Spending on magazine advertisements totalled $718 million in Canada in 2007.[45]

Outdoor Advertising

Outdoor advertising—billboards; signs; and advertisements on buses, taxis, and subways—is relatively inexpensive, faces little competition for customers' attention, and is subject to high repeat exposure. Like many other areas of advertising, outdoor advertising has gone high-tech. Winnipeg-based Sidetrack Technologies Inc., for example, has developed a system of 360 digital strips that are placed at intervals along subway walls. When a train passes by, the strips blend together, creating the impression of an artificial video. The strips can be changed remotely, thus allowing a company like McDonald's to

Speed and creativity have given billboards like these a new prominence in the world of advertising media. Instead of relying on highly skilled human artists, outdoor ad sellers can now commission digital creations that not only turn heads but cost less than most other media. Whereas it used to take a month to launch a billboard-based campaign, it now takes just days.

advertise Egg McMuffins during the morning commute and Big Macs during the afternoon commute.[46]

Titan Worldwide has developed an LED display that shows commercials on New York City buses. The display contains GPS technology, so it can target audiences based on the time of day and postal code where the bus is located. The technology will also be introduced to Canada and Ireland.[47] Many billboards now feature animation and changing images, and today's billboard messages are cheaper because they can be digitally printed in colour in large quantities. On the downside, outdoor ads can present only limited information, and sellers have little control over who sees their advertisements. Worldwide spending on outdoor advertising in 2005 totalled $23.2 billion, while in Canada the total was $422 million in 2007.[48]

Word-of-Mouth Advertising

word-of-mouth advertising Opinions about the value of products passed among consumers in informal discussions.

As noted in the opening case, **word-of-mouth advertising** occurs when consumers talk to each other about products they are using. According to the Word of Mouth Marketing Association, there are several varieties of word-of-mouth advertising. These include buzz marketing (using high-profile news to get consumers talking about a product), viral marketing (consumers passing product information around on the internet), product seeding (providing free product samples to influential consumers), and cause marketing (involving consumers who feel strongly about a cause such as reducing poverty).[49]

Consumers form very strong opinions about products as a result of conversations with friends and acquaintances, so when consumers start talking about a new product or idea, the information can build momentum and spread like wildfire. This "spreading the word" can happen without any expenditure of money by the company selling the product in question. But companies do spend money developing formal word-of-mouth advertising campaigns because they recognize how powerful they are. The now-famous "Evolution" ad for Dove soap (which showed an "ordinary" girl being transformed into a goddess) was posted on YouTube instead of the traditional places. It was eventually viewed by 300 million people and generated huge publicity for the brand. The only cost to the company was that incurred in making the video.[50]

The Internet

ecommerce Buying and selling processes that make use of electronic technology.

internet marketing The promotional efforts of companies to sell their products and services to consumers over the internet.

Ecommerce refers to buying and selling processes that make use of electronic technology, while **internet marketing** refers to the promotional efforts of companies to sell their products and services to consumers over the internet.[51] The internet is the most recent advertising medium to arise, and thousands of well-known and lesser-known firms have placed ads there. Online ad sales were valued at $1.2 billion in 2007, more than double the amount for 2006.[52] Craigslist.org offers free local classified advertising on over 200 websites around the world. More information about internet marketing is provided in Chapter 17.

MySpace is using a "hypertargeting" system to categorize its users into different categories like "rodeo watcher" or "scrapbook enthusiast." Live Nation, a concert promoter, saw increased traffic on its Coldplay page after it placed ads on MySpace that were directed at fans of Coldplay and other similar bands. This sounds very positive for marketers, but privacy concerns have arisen about technologies that track consumers as they surf the web. For example, a company called NebuAd has developed ad-tracking software that has gotten the attention of critics who claim that it violates wiretap laws.[53]

Online marketing can be profitable for companies, but what happens when consumers turn against them? With so many individuals participating in social networking sites like Facebook or MySpace and keeping personal blogs, it's increasingly common for a single unhappy customer to wage war against a company for selling faulty products or providing poor service. Individuals may post negative reviews of products on blogs, upload angry videos outlining complaints on YouTube, or join public discussion forums where they can voice their opinion. While companies benefit from the viral spread of good news, they must also be on guard for an online backlash that can damage their reputation.[54]

YouTube—the most popular online video site—began selling ads within videos in 2007. The ads appear on the bottom 20 percent of the screen; if the consumer doesn't click on the ad within 10 seconds, it disappears. YouTube found that 75 percent of viewers clicked on the ad and watched it in its entirety. The ads also had higher click-through rates than standard display ads that appear on websites.[55] Changes are occurring in the way consumers navigate the web, and more online searches now take place on YouTube than on Yahoo. Companies are therefore changing their advertising strategies. Pizza Hut, for example, started buying mobile search ads and buying ads through Facebook.[56]

Internet advertising offers advantages for both buyers and sellers. For buyers, advantages include convenience (websites can be accessed 24 hours a day, and there is no need to fight traffic at shopping malls), privacy (no face-to-face high-pressure sales tactics are possible), selection (the products and services that are available are almost unlimited), useful information (about competing products and services), and control (consumers can "build" custom products for themselves).

For sellers, advantages include reach (access to consumers around the world), direct distribution (eliminating intermediaries), reduced expenses (which would normally be incurred when owning "bricks-and-mortar" outlets), relationship building (with customers on interactive websites), flexibility (sellers can quickly change prices or the terms of sale based on market developments), and feedback (sellers can measure the success of messages by counting how many people see each ad and tracking the number of click-throughs to their own website).[57]

While internet marketing has some obvious advantages for both buyers and sellers, it also has weaknesses, including profitability problems (many internet marketers are unprofitable and the failure rate is high), information overload (consumers may not know what to do with all the information available to them), and limited markets (consumers who use the web are typically more highly educated).

In addition to these weaknesses, internet marketers must also cope with consumer concerns about two security-related issues. An Angus Reid/Globe and Mail poll of 1500 Canadians found that their main concern about internet marketing was security. People who had made at least one purchase on the internet were more likely to list security as their top concern than were those who had never purchased anything on the internet. In particular, people were concerned that their credit-card number might end up in the wrong hands, and that their privacy would be invaded if they purchased on the internet.[58]

Consumers also object to "spyware" software, which monitors websites they visit and observes their shopping habits. This software is often implanted on their personal computers as they wander the web. It then generates "pop-up" advertisements that are targeted to that particular consumer. Because people are often unaware that such spyware is on their computer, the technique has generated a lot of anger among consumers. Consumers can, however, get free anti-spyware software that removes spyware from their computer. Spyware is also a concern for companies that sell from their own websites because the pop-ups are designed to divert web surfers from the products offered by the website.[59] If it going to reach its full potential, internet marketing is going to have to improve its image.

Virtual Advertising

virtual advertising A technique that uses digital implants of brands or products onto live or taped programming, giving the illusion that the product is part of the show.

Virtual advertising uses digital implants of brands or products onto live or taped programming, giving the illusion that the product is part of the show. With this technique, an advertiser's product can appear as part of the television show—when viewers are paying more attention—instead of during commercial breaks. In a televised basketball game, for example, the digital image of a brand—for example, the round face of a Rolex watch or an Acura hubcap—can be electronically enlarged and superimposed on centre court without physically changing the playing floor. For videotaped movies, digital images can be inserted easily. A Kmart shopping bag can be digitally added to the table in a kitchen scene, or a Philips Flat TV can be superimposed on the wall for display during a dramatic scene.[60]

A variation of virtual advertising is described in the boxed insert entitled "Fuelling the World of Branded Entertainment."

Other Advertising Media

A combination of many additional media, including catalogues, sidewalk handouts, Yellow Pages, skywriting, telephone calls, special events, and door-to-

Entrepreneurship and New Ventures

Fuelling the World of Branded Entertainment

The casual gaming industry develops non-violent, easy-to-play video games that appeal to a wide variety of users. Industry sales are $2.3 billion worldwide, expected annual growth is 20 percent, and the market is about 200 million people.

Fuel Industries of Ottawa, Ontario, founded in 1999, has positioned itself as an up-and-comer in this industry by winning contracts that typically would be awarded to big-name companies like DreamWorks Animation and Pixar Animation Studios. The company's success has not gone unnoticed. In 2008, *Canadian Business* magazine recognized Fuel as one of the country's fastest growing businesses in Canada.

Fuel doesn't just develop online video games. Rather, it is pioneering a new model of branded online entertainment (referred to as "advergames"). Essentially, an advergame is an online video game and advertising rolled into one. The theory behind the concept is simple: If consumers are having fun while interacting with the entertainment, they are more likely to remember and feel positive toward the brand. Instead of trying to make an impression during a traditional 60-second commercial, advergames keep consumers engaged for as long as 600 seconds! Many companies are beginning to see the benefits of this market-ing strategy.

Fuel was launched into the branded digital promotion business when it created an advergame called Fairies and Dragons that helped McDonald's promote its Happy Meal in 40 European countries. With every Happy Meal, kids received a fairy or dragon toy along with a CD-ROM that contained three games and 10 hours of game play. That approach differed noticeably from the usual tactic of licensing characters from established entertainment companies like Disney. Plans are underway to launch the same concept for McDonald's in other regions, including Australia, Japan, and North America.

Since their success with McDonald's, Fuel has done similar work for U.S. toy company JAKKS Pacific's branded game Girl Gourmet Cupcake Maker. The company is also behind the development of Spark City, an online game targeted to tween girl gamers. This virtual world is part of the All Girl Arcade website. The branded element appears through the integration with television and retail. As an example, Fuel is adding a movie theatre to Spark City and the "agency is in talks with broadcasters and film companies looking to run trailers in the theatre."

So, what's the cost to get your brand into Spark City? It could be anywhere between $25 000 and $200 000. But is there a risk of virtual world burnout among customers as branded sites flourish? According to Virtual Worlds Management, a Texas-based company, the future looks good, but "the cream will definitely rise to the top." Therefore, if a company chooses this strategy, as with any product, branded sites need to be developed to address the needs and wants of the selected target market.

Critical Thinking Questions

1. Discuss how marketers can build relationships with customers through newer methods of virtual advertising like advergames.
2. What are the advantages and disadvantages of internet advertising?

Once the master of mass-marketing (especially the 30-second TV spot), Coca-Cola has bowed to audience fragmentation and the advent of devices like TiVo, which allow people to skip TV ads altogether. Coke has begun experimenting with alternative approaches to promotion, focussing on events and activities that can be integrated into the daily routines of targeted consumers. In Europe, the company posts interactive websites built around music, and in the United States it has installed Coke Red Lounges in a few select malls, offering teenagers exclusive piped-in music, movies, and videos.

door communications, make up the remaining advertisements to which Canadians are exposed.

Types of Advertising

Regardless of the media used, advertisements fall into one of several categories. **Brand advertising** promotes a specific brand, such as the Canon Rebel digital camera, Air Canada, or Nike Air Jordan basketball shoes. A variation on brand advertising, **product advertising,** promotes a general type of product or service such as dental services and milk. The "Got Milk?" advertisements are an example of product advertising. **Advocacy advertising** promotes a particular candidate or viewpoint, as in ads for political candidates at election time and anti-drug commercials. **Institutional advertising** promotes a firm's long-term image rather than a specific product.

In consumer markets, local stores usually sponsor **retail advertising** to encourage consumers to visit the store and buy its products and services. Larger retailers, such as Kmart and The Bay, use retail advertising both locally and nationally. Often retail advertising is actually **co-operative advertising**, with the cost of the advertising shared by the retailer and the manufacturer.

In industrial markets, to communicate with companies that distribute its products, some firms use **trade advertising** publications. For example, a firm that makes plumbing fixtures might advertise in Hardware Retailer to persuade large hardware stores to carry its products. And to reach the professional purchasing agent and managers at firms buying raw materials or components, companies use **industrial advertising**.

brand advertising Advertising that promotes a specific brand-name product.

product advertising A variation on brand advertising that promotes a general type of product or service.

advocacy advertising Advertising that promotes a particular viewpoint or candidate.

institutional advertising Advertising that promotes a firm's long-term image, not a specific product.

retail advertising Advertising by retailers designed to reach end-users of a consumer product.

co-operative advertising Advertising in which a manufacturer together with a retailer or a wholesaler advertise to reach customers.

trade advertising Advertising by manufacturers designed to reach potential wholesalers and retailers.

industrial advertising Advertising by manufacturers designed to reach other manufacturers' professional purchasing agents and managers of firms buying raw materials or components.

Preparing an Advertising Campaign

An **advertising campaign** is the arrangement of ads in selected media to reach target audiences. It includes several activities that, taken together, constitute a program for meeting a marketing objective, such as introducing a new product or changing a company's image in the public mind. A campaign typically includes six steps:

1. Identifying the target audience
2. Defining the objectives of the advertising messages
3. Establishing the advertising budget

advertising campaign The arrangement of ads in selected media to reach target audiences.

4. Creating the advertising messages
5. Selecting the appropriate media
6. Evaluating advertising effectiveness

advertising agencies Firms that specialize in creating and placing advertisements in the media for clients.

Advertising agencies—independent companies that provide some or all of their clients' advertising needs—help in the development of advertising campaigns by providing specialized services. The agency works together with the client company to determine the campaign's central message, create detailed message content, identify advertising media, and negotiate media purchases.[61] The advantage offered by agencies is expertise in developing advertising themes, message content, and artwork, as well as in coordinating advertising production and advising on relevant legal matters. As payment for its services, the agency usually receives a percentage, traditionally 15 percent of the media purchase cost. For example, if an agency purchases a $1-million television commitment for a client's campaign, it would receive $150 000 for its services.

The globalization of business has affected advertising agencies, both in Canada and elsewhere. Increasingly, large U.S. companies are using one single agency (often headquartered somewhere other than Canada). The Association of Quebec Advertising Agencies says that big U.S. companies often bypass Montreal-based advertising agencies when they are developing advertising campaigns for Quebec. The group says that it is pointless to try to simply translate into French a campaign that is developed by a New York or Toronto agency for the rest of Canada.[62]

Personal Selling

6 Outline the tasks involved in *personal selling* and list the steps in the personal selling process.

Virtually everyone has done some personal selling. Perhaps as a child you had a lemonade stand or sold candy for the drama club. Or you may have gone on a job interview, selling your abilities as an employee to the interviewer's company. In personal selling, a salesperson communicates one-on-one with a potential customer to identify the customer's need and match that need with the seller's product.

personal selling Promotional tool in which a salesperson communicates one-on-one with potential customers.

Personal selling—the oldest form of selling—provides the personal link between seller and buyer. It adds to a firm's credibility because it provides buyers with someone to interact with and to answer their questions. Because it involves personal interaction, personal selling requires a level of trust between the buyer and the seller. When a buyer feels cheated by the seller, that trust has been broken and a negative attitude toward salespeople in general can develop.

Personal selling is the most expensive form of promotion per contact because presentations are generally made to one or two individuals at a time. Personal selling expenses include salespeople's compensation and their overhead, usually travel, food, and lodging. The average cost of each industrial sales call has been estimated at nearly $300.[63]

Costs have prompted many companies to turn to telemarketing—using telephone solicitations to conduct the personal selling process. Telemarketing is useful in handling any stage of this process and in arranging appointments for salespeople. It cuts the cost of personal sales visits to industrial customers, each of whom requires about four visits to complete a sale. Such savings are stimulating the growth of telemarketing, which provides 150 000 jobs in Canada and generates $25 billion in annual sales. Telemarketing returns $6.25 for every dollar that is spent.[64]

Because many consumers are annoyed by telemarketing pitches, a do-not-call registry was set up in Canada in 2008, and six million people quickly registered. Heavy fines can be levied on companies that ignore the new rules.

A survey by VoxPop showed that 80 percent of Canadians who registered now receive fewer telemarketing calls than they used to,[65] but in 2009, it was discovered that some unscrupulous marketers were actually using the registry to call people. Michael Geist, a Canada Research Chair in Internet and E-commerce Law at the University of Ottawa, says the government's registry is flawed.[66]

In personal selling, the salesperson has the opportunity to explain in detail the benefits of the product or service, and can also respond to concerns that the customer may express regarding the product or service.

Sales Force Management

Sales force management means setting goals at top levels of the organization, setting specific objectives for individual salespeople, organizing the sales force to meet those objectives, and implementing and evaluating the success of the overall sales plan.

sales force management Setting goals at top levels of an organization; setting practical objectives for salespeople; organizing a sales force to meet those objectives; implementing and evaluating the success of a sales plan.

Personal Selling Situations

Managers of both telemarketers and traditional salespeople must consider the ways in which personal sales activities are affected by the differences between consumer and industrial products:

- **Retail selling** is selling a consumer product for the buyer's personal or household use.
- **Industrial selling** is selling products to other businesses, either for the purpose of manufacturing other products or or resale.

retail selling Selling a consumer product for the buyer's own personal or household use.

industrial selling Selling products to other businesses, either for manufacturing other products or for resale.

Levi's, for instance, sells jeans to the retail clothing chain Gap Inc. (industrial selling). In turn, consumers purchase Levi's jeans at one of Gap's stores (retail selling). Each of these situations has distinct characteristics. In retail selling, the buyer usually comes to the seller, but in industrial selling, the salesperson comes to the buyer.

Personal Selling Tasks

Improving sales efficiency requires marketers to consider salespeople's tasks. Three basic tasks are generally associated with selling: order processing, creative selling, and missionary selling. Sales jobs usually require salespeople to perform all three tasks to some degree, depending on the product and the company.

Order Processing. In **order processing**, a salesperson receives an order and oversees the handling and delivery of that order. Route salespeople are often order processors. They call on regular customers to check the customer's supply of bread, milk, snack foods, or soft drinks. Then, with the customer's consent, they determine the size of the reorder, fill the order from their trucks, and stack the customer's shelves.

order processing In personal sales, the receiving and follow-through on handling and delivery of an order by a salesperson.

Creative Selling. When the benefits of a product are not clear, **creative selling** may persuade buyers that they have a need for it. Most industrial products involve creative selling because the buyer has not used the product before or may not be familiar with its features and uses. Creative selling is also crucial for high-priced consumer products, such as homes, where buyers comparison shop. Any new product can benefit from creative selling that differentiates it from other products.

creative selling In personal sales, the use of techniques designed to persuade a customer to buy a product when the benefits of the product are not readily apparent or the item is very expensive.

missionary selling In personal sales, the indirect promotion of a product by offering technical assistance and/or promoting the company's image.

Missionary Selling. The goal of **missionary selling** is to promote the company and its products over the long term, rather than to make a quick sale. Drug company representatives promote their companies' drugs to doctors who, in turn, may eventually prescribe them to their patients. The sale is actually made at the drugstore.

The Personal Selling Process

Although all three sales tasks are important to an organization using personal selling, perhaps the most complicated is creative selling. It is the creative salesperson who is responsible for most of the steps in the personal selling process described below.

prospecting In personal sales, the process of identifying potential customers.

qualifying In personal sales, the process of determining whether potential customers have the authority to buy and the ability to pay for a product.

Prospecting and Qualifying. **Prospecting** is the process of identifying potential customers. Salespeople find prospects through past company records, existing customers, friends, relatives, company personnel, and business associates. **Qualifying** means determining whether prospects have the authority to buy and the ability to pay.

Approaching. The *approach* refers to the first few minutes that a salesperson has contact with a qualified prospect. The success of later stages depends on the prospect's first impression of the salesperson, since this impression affects the salesperson's credibility. Salespeople need to present a neat, professional appearance and to greet prospects in a strong, confident manner.

Presenting and Demonstrating. Presenting involves a full explanation of the product, its features, and its uses. It links the product's benefits to the prospect's needs. A presentation may or may not include a demonstration of the product, but it is wise to demonstrate a product whenever possible, since most people have trouble visualizing what they have been told.

Handling Objections. Prospects may have objections to various aspects of the product, including its price. Objections show the salesperson that the buyer is interested in the presentation and which parts of the presentation the buyer is unsure of or has a problem with. They tell the salesperson what customers feel is important and, essentially, how to sell to them.

closing In personal sales, the process of asking the customer to buy the product.

Closing. The most critical part of the selling process is the **closing**, in which the salesperson asks the prospective customer to buy the product. Successful salespeople recognize the signs that a customer is ready to buy. For example, prospects who start to figure out monthly payments for the product are clearly indicating that they are ready to buy. Salespeople can ask directly for the sale or they can indirectly imply a close.

Following Up. The sales process does not end with the close of the sale. Sales follow-up activities include fast processing of the customer's order and on-time delivery. Training in the proper care and use of the product and speedy service if repairs are needed may also be part of the follow-up.

Sales Promotions

sales promotions Short-term promotional activities designed to stimulate consumer buying or co-operation from distributors and other members of the trade.

Sales promotions are short-term promotional activities designed to stimulate consumer buying or co-operation from distributors, sales agents, or other members of the trade. For example, soap may be bound into packages of four with the promotion. "Buy three and get one free." Sales promotions are important because they enhance product recognition and increase the likelihood that buyers will try products. To be successful, sales promotions must be convenient and accessible when the decision to purchase occurs. If Harley-Davidson has a one-week motorcycle promotion and there is no dealer in your area, the promotion is neither convenient nor accessible to you, and you will not buy. But if the Bay offers a 20 percent off coupon that you can save for later use, the promotion is convenient and accessible.

Describe the various types of *sales promotions*, and distinguish between *publicity* and *public relations*. 7

Types of Sales Promotions

The best-known sales promotions are coupons, point-of-purchase displays, purchasing incentives (such as free samples, trading stamps, and premiums), trade shows, and contests and sweepstakes.

- Certificates entitling the bearer to stated savings off a product's regular price are **coupons**. Coupons may be used to encourage customers to try new products, to attract customers away from competitors, or to induce current customers to buy more of a product. They appear in newspapers and magazines and are often sent through direct mail.
- To grab customers' attention as they walk through a store, some companies use **point-of-purchase (POP) displays**, which often coincide with a sale on the item(s) being displayed. Displays are located at the end of an aisle or near the checkout in supermarkets to make it easier for customers to find a product and easier for manufacturers to eliminate competitors from consideration.
- Free samples and premiums are purchasing incentives. **Free samples** allow customers to try a product for a few days at no cost. They may be given out at local retail outlets or sent by manufacturers to consumers via direct mail. **Premiums** are free or reduced-price items, such as pens, pencils, calendars, and coffee mugs, given to consumers in return for buying a specified product. For example, in one sales promotion, Molson Canadian included a free T-shirt with certain packages of its beer.[67] Premiums may not work as well as originally hoped, since customers may switch to a new brand just to get the premiums that company is offering and then return to their customary brand.

coupon A method of sales promotion featuring a certificate that entitles the bearer to stated savings off a product's regular price.

point-of-purchase (POP) displays A method of sales promotion in which a product display is so located in a retail store as to encourage consumers to buy the product.

free samples A method of sales promotion in which a small sample of product is offered free, allowing customers to try a product for a few days at no cost.

premium A method of sales promotion in which some item is offered free or at a bargain price to customers in return for buying a specified product.

Best Buy, a chain once known for consumer electronics and appliances, is now the biggest retailer of CDs and DVDs. To promote its entertainment products, Best Buy uses promotional tie-ins, such as a deal to become the exclusive retailer of a U2 DVD. Meanwhile, CEO Brian Dunn has continued to pursue a strategy of putting electronics and entertainment under one roof.

trade shows A method of sales promotion in which members of a particular industry gather for displays and product demonstrations designed to sell products to customers.

- **Trade shows** allow companies to rent booths to display and demonstrate their products to customers who have a special interest or who are ready to buy. Trade shows are relatively inexpensive and are very effective, since the buyer comes to the seller already interested in a given type of product.
- Customers, distributors, and sales representatives may all be persuaded to increase sales of a product through the use of contests and sweepstakes. For example, distributors and sales agents may win a trip to Hawaii for selling the most pillows in the month of February, or customers may win $1 million in a magazine sweepstake.

Publicity and Public Relations

publicity Information about a company that is made available to consumers by the news media; it is not controlled by the company, but it does not cost the company any money.

Much to the delight of marketing managers with tight budgets, **publicity** is free. Moreover, because it is presented in a news format, consumers see publicity as objective and highly believable. However, marketers often have little control over publicity, and that can have a very negative effect on the company. For example, a YouTube video showing what appeared to be a Guinness beer commercial portrayed several people in a suggestive sexual arrangement with the title "Share One with a Friend." Guinness was quick to distance itself from the fake advertisement, saying that was not how they wanted their product portrayed. In another case, the restaurant chain Olive Garden was placed in a difficult position when it received favourable publicity from Playboy Playmate Kendra Wilkinson, who at that time was one of Hugh Hefner's three live-in girlfriends and who was featured in the E! series *The Girls Next Door*. She gave several on-air plugs for the restaurant chain, but the restaurant is concerned because Wilkinson's reputation is not consistent with the company's wholesome, family-friendly image.[68]

public relations A company-influenced activity that attempts to establish a sense of goodwill between the company and its customers through public-service announcements that enhance the company's image.

Public relations is company-influenced activity that attempts to establish a sense of goodwill between the company and its customers through public-service announcements that enhance the company's image. For example, a bank may announce that senior citizens' groups can have free use of one of the bank's meeting rooms for their social activities. Corporate sponsorships of athletic events also help promote a company's image. Organizers of the 2012 Olympic Games announced in 2008 that Cadbury PLC had paid approximately $40 million to be a sponsor of the Games. It will be the sole supplier of confectionery sold in the Olympic Park.[69]

International Promotion Strategies

8 Describe the development of international and small business *promotion* strategies.

As we saw in Chapter 5, recent decades have witnessed a profound shift from "home-country" marketing to "multi-country" marketing and now to "global" marketing. Nowhere is this rapidly growing global orientation more evident than in marketing promotions, especially advertising.

Emergence of the Global Perspective

global perspective A company's approach to directing its marketing toward worldwide rather than local or regional markets.

Every company that markets products in several countries faces a basic choice—use a decentralized approach (maintaining separate marketing for each country) or adopt a global perspective (directing a coordinated marketing program at one worldwide audience). The **global perspective** is a philosophy that directs marketing toward worldwide rather than toward local or regional markets.

Before creating an international advertisement like this Chinese ad for Coca-Cola, it is crucial to research what differences—such as meaning of words, traditions, and taboos—exist between different societies. For example, German manufacturers of backpacks label them as "body bags," which is not terribly enticing to the Canadian consumer. Gerber baby food is not sold in France because the French translation of gerber is "to vomit."

The Movement Toward Global Advertising

A truly global perspective means designing products for multinational appeal—that is, genuinely global products.[70] A few brands, such as Coca-Cola, McDonald's, Mercedes-Benz, Rolex, and Xerox, enjoy global recognition and have become truly global brands. One universal advertising program would obviously be more efficient and cost-effective than developing different programs for each of many countries. For several reasons, however, global advertising is not feasible for many companies. Four factors make global advertising a challenging proposition:

- *Product variations.* Even if a product has universal appeal, some variations (slightly different products) are usually preferred in different cultures. In the magazine business, Hearst Corp. has expanded to 33 editions of *Cosmopolitan* magazine, including one for Central America; English and Spanish editions for the United States; and local editions for Italy, Turkey, Russia, Hong Kong, and Japan. *Reader's Digest* has 48 editions in 19 languages. Many companies have found that without a local or national identity, universal ads don't cause consumers to buy. Coca-Cola's "think global, act local" strategy and Nestlé's approach to small-scale local advertising call for ads tailored to different areas. Such ads are designed to produce variations on a universal theme while appealing to local emotions, ideas, and values. Advertising agencies have set up worldwide agency networks that can coordinate a campaign's central theme while allowing regional variations.
- *Language differences.* Compared with those in other languages, ads in English require less print space and airtime because English is a more efficient and precise language than most others. But translations can be inexact and confusing. When Coke first went to China many years ago, the direct translation of *Coca-Cola* came out "Bite the wax tadpole" in Chinese.
- *Cultural receptiveness.* There are differences across nations regarding the mass advertising of sensitive products (such as birth control or personal

hygiene products), not to mention those for which advertising may be legally restricted (alcohol, cigarettes). A Canadian in Paris may be surprised to see nudity in billboard ads and even more surprised to find that France is the only country in the European Union (EU) that bans advertising or selling wine on the internet. In the EU and through much of Asia, comparative advertising is considered distasteful or even illegal.

- *Image differences.* Any company's image can vary from nation to nation, regardless of advertising appeals for universal recognition. American Express, IBM, and Nestlé have better images in the United States than in the United Kingdom, where Heinz, Coca-Cola, and Ford have better images.

Promotional Practices in Small Business

Although small businesses generally have fewer resources, cost-effective promotions can improve sales and enable small firms to compete with much larger firms.

Small Business Advertising

Few developments in history have provided more advertising opportunities than the internet. Cheaper access to computing equipment, to online services, and to website expertise puts cyberspace within the grasp of nearly every firm. Still, owners must decide which audiences to target and what messages to send. And even though the web can instantaneously reach distant customers, other methods depend on the market that the small business is trying to reach—local, national, or international.

Non-primetime ads on local or cable TV have good impact at costs within the reach of many small firms. More often, however, small firms use newspaper, radio, and, increasingly, direct mail to reach local markets. For year-round advertising, the Yellow Pages is popular for both industrial and consumer products. However, many small businesses, especially those selling to consumer markets, rely more on seasonal advertising.

Many small businesses have grown by using direct mail, particularly catalogues. By purchasing mailing lists from other companies, small firms can cut costs with targeted mailings. The ability to target an audience also makes specialized magazines attractive to small businesses. When it comes to international markets, television, radio, and newspapers are too expensive for small businesses. Most small firms find direct mail and carefully targeted magazine ads the most effective tools.

The Role of Personal Selling in Small Business

As with advertising, small business personal selling strategies depend on intended markets. Some small firms maintain sales forces, especially in local markets, where clients can be quickly visited. But most small companies cannot afford to establish international offices, although some entrepreneurs do visit prospective customers in other countries. For most small businesses, even sending sales representatives abroad is too expensive. Some contract with sales agencies—companies that act on behalf of several clients. Because the costs of a national sales force are high, small companies prefer sales agencies and such methods as telemarketing. By combining telemarketing with catalogues or other print media, small businesses can sometimes compete with larger companies on a national scale. Syncsort Inc. combined a telemarketing staff with eight national sales reps to become the number-one developer of computer software for sorting data into convenient formats (IBM is number two).

Small Business Promotions

Small companies also use sales promotions to market their products. Large firms tend to rely on coupons, POP displays, and sales contests, but small firms prefer premiums and special sales because they are less expensive.[71] An automobile dealership, for example, might offer you a fishing reel if you come in to road test a new car. Service companies ranging from martial arts centres to dry cleaners frequently feature special sale prices.

Test yourself on the material for this chapter at **www.pearsoned.ca/mybusinesslab**.

Summary of Learning Objectives

1. **Explain the definition of a product as a *value package*.** A *product* is a good, service, or idea that is marketed to satisfy consumer needs and wants. Consumers regard a product as a bundle of attributes that, taken together, constitute the *value package*. Consumers expect to receive products with greater value, that is, products with more benefits at a reasonable price. A successful product is a value package that provides the right *features* and offers the right benefits. Features are the qualities, tangible and intangible, that a company builds into its products.

2. **Describe the new *product development process* and trace the stages of the *product life cycle*.** Many firms adopt some version of a basic seven-step new product development process: (1) *Product ideas:* searching for ideas for new products; (2) *Screening:* eliminating all product ideas that do not mesh with the firm's abilities or objectives; (3) *Concept testing:* using market research to get consumers' input about product benefits and prices; (4) *Business analysis:* comparing manufacturing costs and benefits to see whether a product meets minimum profitability goals; (5) *Prototype development:* producing a preliminary version of a product; (6) *Product testing* and *test marketing:* going into limited production, testing the product to see if it meets performance requirements, and, if so, selling it on a limited basis; and (7) *Commercialization:* beginning full-scale production and marketing.

   The *product life cycle (PLC)* is a series of four stages or phases characterizing a product's profit-producing life: (1) *Introduction:* Marketers focus on making potential consumers aware of the product and its benefits; (2) *Growth:* Sales begin to climb and the product begins to show a profit; (3) *Maturity:* Although the product earns its highest profit level, increased competition eventually leads to price cutting and lower profits, and sales start to fall; (4) *Decline:* Sales and profits are further lost to new products in the introduction stage.

3. **Explain the importance of *branding, packaging,* and *labelling*.** *Branding* is a process of using symbols to communicate the qualities of a particular product made by a particular producer. Brands are designed to signal uniform quality. *Packaging* refers to the physical container in which a product is sold, advertised, or protected. A package makes the product attractive, displays the brand name, and identifies features and benefits. It also reduces the risk of damage, breakage, or spoilage, and it lessens the likelihood of theft. Every product has a *label* on its package that identifies its name, manufacturer, and contents. Like packaging, labelling can help market a product.

4. **Identify the important objectives of *promotion* and discuss the considerations in selecting a *promotional mix*.** *Promotion* is any technique designed to sell a product. Besides the ultimate objective of increasing sales, marketers may use promotion to accomplish any of the following four goals: (1) *communicating information*, (2) *positioning products*, (3) *adding value*, and (4) *controlling sales volume*.

   There are four types of promotional tools: *advertising, personal selling, sales promotions,* and *publicity* and *public relations*. The best combination of these tools—the best *promotional mix*—depends on several factors, the most important of which is the target audience and buyer decision process. Marketers try to match promotional tools with stages in the buyer decision process.

5. **Discuss the most important *advertising* strategies and describe the key *advertising media*.** The advertising strategies used for a product most often depend on the stage of the product life cycle the product is in. As products become established and competition increases, advertisers may choose one of three strategies: (1) *persuasive advertising*, (2) *comparative advertising*, and (3) *reminder advertising*.

   Marketers use several different advertising media-specific communication devices for conveying a seller's message to potential customers: (1) *television*, (2) *newspapers*, (3) *direct mail*, (4) *radio*, (5) *magazines*, (6) *outdoor advertising*, (7) *internet advertising*, and (8) *virtual advertising*.

6. **Outline the tasks involved in *personal selling* and list the steps in the personal selling process.** There are three basic tasks in personal selling: (1) *order processing*, (2) *creative selling*, and (3) *missionary selling*. The creative salesperson goes through most of the following six steps in the personal selling process: (1) *Prospecting* and *qualifying*: Prospecting identifies potential customers, who are then qualified to determine whether they have the authority to buy and ability to pay. (2) *Approaching:* The first few minutes of contact with a qualified prospect make up the approach. (3) *Presenting* and *demonstrating:* After the approach, the salesperson makes a presentation. (4) *Handling objections:* Objections pinpoint the parts of the presentation with which the buyer has a problem and which the salesperson must overcome. (5) *Closing:* In the closing, the salesperson asks the prospective customer to buy the product. (6) *Following up:* To cement lasting relationships with buyers, sellers supply additional after-sale services.

7. **Describe the various types of *sales promotions*, and distinguish between *publicity* and *public relations*.** Sales promotions are short-term promotional activities designed to stimulate consumer buying or co-operation from members of the trade. The following are the best-known forms of promotions: (1) *Coupons* are certificates entitling bearers to savings off regular prices. (2) *Point-of-purchase (POP) displays* are used by companies to grab customers' attention as they move through stores. (3) *Free samples* are purchasing incentives that allow customers to try products without risk. (4) *Premiums* are gifts to consumers in return for buying certain products. (5) Industries sponsor *trade shows*, at which companies rent booths to display and demonstrate products to customers with a special interest in them. (6) *Contests* are a means to persuade customers, distributors, and sales reps to increase sales.

   Publicity is a promotional tool in which information about a company or product is created and transmitted by general mass media. It is free, and because it is presented in a news format, consumers often see it as objective and credible. However, marketers often have little control over it, and it can be as easily detrimental as beneficial. *Public relations* is company-influenced publicity that seeks to build good relations with the public and to deal with unfavourable events.

8. **Describe the development of *international and small business promotion* strategies.** Recent decades have witnessed a profound shift from home-country marketing to global marketing. Every company that markets its products in several countries faces a basic choice: Use a *decentralized approach*, with separate marketing management for each country, or adopt a *global perspective*, directing marketing toward a worldwide rather than a local or regional market. There are four factors that determine whether global advertising is feasible: (1) *product variations*, (2) *language differences*, (3) *cultural receptiveness*, and (4) *image differences*. In recognizing national differences, many global marketers try to build on a universal advertising theme that nevertheless allows for variations. In doing so, they rely on help from different advertising agencies in various geographic regions.

Key Terms

advertising (p. 527)
advertising agencies (p. 534)
advertising campaign (p. 533)
advertising media (p. 527)
advocacy advertising (p. 533)
brand advertising (p. 533)
brand equity (p. 519)
brand loyalty (p. 520)
branding (p. 518)
capital items (p. 513)
capital services (p. 513)
closing (p. 536)
comparative advertising (p. 527)
Consumer Packaging and Labelling Act (p. 522)
convenience goods/services (p. 513)
co-operative advertising (p. 533)
copyright (p. 521)
coupon (p. 537)
creative selling (p. 535)
direct mail (p. 528)
ecommerce (p. 530)
expense items (p. 513)
features (p. 512)
free samples (p. 537)
global perspective (p. 538)
industrial advertising (p. 533)
industrial selling (p. 535)
informative advertising (p. 527)
institutional advertising (p. 533)
internet marketing (p. 530)
label (p. 522)
licensed brands (p. 520)
media mix (p. 527)
missionary selling (p. 536)
national brands (p. 519)
order processing (p. 535)
packaging (p. 522)
patent (p. 521)
personal selling (p. 534)
persuasive advertising (p. 527)
point-of-purchase (POP) displays (p. 537)
premium (p. 537)
private brands (p. 520)
product adaptation (p. 518)
product advertising (p. 533)
product extension (p. 518)
product life cycle (PLC) (p. 516)
product line (p. 514)
product mix (p. 514)
product positioning (p. 523)
promotion (p. 522)
promotional mix (p. 525)
prospecting (p. 536)
public relations (p. 538)
publicity (p. 538)
pull strategy (p. 525)
push strategy (p. 525)
qualifying (p. 536)
reintroduction (p. 518)
reminder advertising (p. 527)
retail advertising (p. 533)
retail selling (p. 535)
sales force management (p. 535)
sales promotions (p. 536)
service package (p. 515)
service process design (p. 516)
shopping goods/services (p. 513)
specialty goods/services (p. 513)
speed to market (p. 515)
trade advertising (p. 533)
trade shows (p. 538)
trademark (p. 521)
value package (p. 512)
virtual advertising (p. 532)
word-of-mouth advertising (p. 530)

Questions for Analysis

1. What impact do the different levels of brand loyalty (recognition, preference, insistence) have on the consumer buying process that was described in Chapter 15?
2. Why would a business use a push strategy rather than a pull strategy?
3. Analyze several advertisements that use comparative advertising. Do these advertisements leave you with a positive or negative image of the company? Also, analyze differences in the comparative advertisements that are shown on U.S. and Canadian television networks. Do these differences affect your opinion of the advertiser?
4. How would you expect the branding, packaging, and labelling of convenience, shopping, and specialty goods to differ? Why? Give examples to illustrate your answers.
5. Choose two advertising campaigns that have recently been conducted by business firms in your area. Choose one that you think is effective and one that you think is ineffective. What differences in the campaigns make one better than the other?
6. Select a good or service that you have purchased recently. Try to retrace the relevant steps in the buyer decision process as you experienced it. Which steps were most important to you? Which steps were least important?
7. Find examples of publicity about some business, either a local firm or a national firm. Did the publicity have, or is it likely to have, positive or negative consequences for the business? Why?

Application Exercises

1. Interview the manager of a local manufacturing firm. Identify the company's different products according to their positions in the product life cycle.
2. Select a product that is sold nationally. Identify as many media used in its promotion as you can. Which medium is used most often? On the whole, do you think the campaign is effective? What criteria did you use to make your judgment about effectiveness?
3. Interview the owner of a local small business. Identify the company's promotional objectives and strategies, and the elements in its promotional mix. What, if any, changes would you suggest? Why?
4. Check out your college's or university's website and determine how effective it is as a tool for promoting your school.

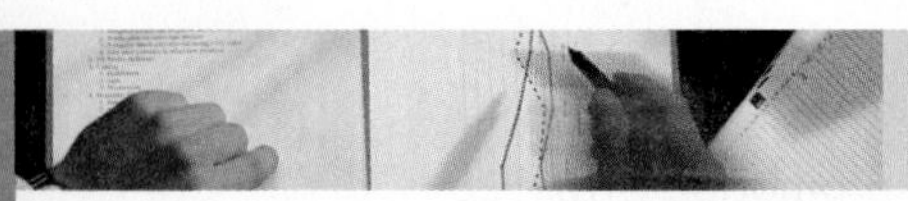

Building Your Business Skills

Greeting Start-up Decisions

The Purpose of the Assignment

To encourage students to analyze the potential usefulness of two promotional methods—personal selling and direct mail—for a start-up greeting card company.

Assignment

You are the marketing adviser for a local start-up company that makes and sells specialty greeting cards in a city of 400 000. Last year's sales totalled 14 000 cards, including personalized holiday cards, birthday cards, and special-events cards for individuals. Although revenues increased last year, you see a way of further boosting sales by expanding into card shops, grocery stores, and gift shops. You see two alternatives for entering these outlets:

1. Use direct mail to reach more individual customers for specialty cards
2. Use personal selling to gain display space in retail stores

Your challenge is to convince the owner of the start-up company which alternative is the more financially sound decision.

Step 1

Get together with four or five classmates to research the two kinds of product segments, personalized cards and retail store cards. Find out which of the two kinds of marketing promotions will be more effective for each of the two segments. What will be the reaction to each method from customers, retailers, and card company owners?

Step 2

Draft a proposal to the company owner. Leaving budget and production details to other staffers, list as many reasons as possible for adopting direct mail. Then list as many reasons as possible for adopting personal selling. Defend each reason. Consider the following reasons in your argument:

- Competitive environment: Analyze the impact of other card suppliers that offer personalized cards and cards for sale in retail stores.
- Expectations of target markets: Who buys personalized cards, and who buys ready-made cards from retail stores?
- Overall cost of the promotional effort: Which method—direct mail or personal selling—will be more costly?
- Marketing effectiveness: Which promotional method will result in greater consumer response?

Now respond to the following items:

1. Why do you think some buyers want personalized cards? Why do some consumers want ready-made cards from retail stores?
2. Today's computer operating systems provide easy access to software for designing and making cards on home PCs. How does the availability of this product affect your recommendation?
3. What was your most convincing argument for using direct mail? And for using personal selling?
4. Can a start-up company compete in retail stores against industry giants such as Hallmark?

The use of DVRs has led to a sharp drop in "live" television viewing, and people who are watching a DVR program may not even be watching the ads. Not surprisingly, TV companies disagree with that assessment. They argue that ad rates should be determined by the total viewership an ad gets.

Measuring Internet Viewership

Two web measurement services—comScore and Nielsen Online—gather data on internet use by getting people to agree to let their online surfing and purchasing patterns be monitored. The behaviour of these individuals is then extrapolated to the larger population. Since this method is similar to the traditional assessment method that Nielsen used to measure television viewing habits, there are also concerns about its accuracy. To overcome these concerns, Google Inc. introduced a new service designed to more accurately measure internet use. Because it shows which websites various target audiences visit, the new system should help advertisers figure out which are the best places to buy online ads. Google's system uses data from web servers, and this should allow for a better understanding of how the internet is used by consumers. Both comScore and Nielsen Online charge advertisers for the data they provide, but Google will provide the information free of charge. Google also introduced a new system to help advertisers determine how web surfers respond to the ads they see on the various sites they visit. The system works by comparing people who have seen the ads with people who haven't.

No system is perfect, and it is clear that using web servers to gather data has some problems of its own. For example, measurement is based on "cookies" (tracking data), but some users delete cookies and then another cookie is attached when they later revisit a website. This can lead to overstatement of the number of website visits. As well, the system has trouble telling whether a website visit is from an actual consumer or from a technology that visits different websites.

One of the potentially serious problems with gathering data about consumer behaviour is "click fraud." It can occur in several ways, such as when a web developer repeatedly clicks on a website in order to make it seem like there is a great deal of interest in it. Or computers can be programmed to repeatedly click on ads to simulate a real consumer clicking on ads on a webpage. When this happens, advertisers get a bigger bill but no extra sales revenue. When click fraud occurs, the money spent on advertising is obviously wasted. Click Forensics Inc., a click fraud reporting service, reports that the click fraud rate is about 16 percent. But Google claims that only 2 out of 10 000 clicks are fraudulent.

Questions for Discussion

1. The viewership data that Nielsen develops is important in determining how much advertisers pay to place their ads on TV. What are the advantages and disadvantages of the system? Are there alternative systems that might work better? Explain.
2. The argument has been made that counting DVR viewing isn't useful, because people don't watch program advertisements when using a DVR and because advertisements simply don't have the same urgency as they do when the program actually airs. Do you agree or disagree with this argument? Give reasons. Whatever your position, how do you think uncertainty over issues like this influences the value of the data that are produced? What could be done to improve the data?
3. Suppose that you are buying advertising space on TV. Would you be more likely to accept Nielsen data for, say, sports programs than you would for dramas? Explain. What kind of biases might you have and why?
4. What are the strong and weak points of measuring viewership for internet advertisements?

Concluding Case 16 -2

The Changing Face of Advertising

A long time ago (in the 1960s and 1970s), advertising was simple. Sellers of products paid for radio, TV, and newspaper advertisements to get the attention of prospective customers. Consumers basically put up with advertisements because they knew that advertisers were providing radio, TV, or newspaper content in return for their advertisements being shown. But consumers have never liked most advertisements, and when they are given an opportunity to avoid them, they take it. And that opportunity has increasingly been provided as consumers are given the tools to help them avoid advertisements.

In TV, the problem (from the advertisers' perspective) is caused by VCRs and digital video recorders like TiVo. Although these devices were primarily designed to allow consumers to record TV shows when they had other commitments, consumers quickly discovered that they could fast-forward through those annoying advertisements.

This obviously defeated the purpose for which TV advertisements were produced. It is estimated that by 2010 almost half of all television programming will be watched this way and that consumers will fast-forward through 80 percent of the advertisements they might otherwise have seen.

In radio, the development of satellite radio poses another threat to advertisers. Earth-based radio stations beam their signal to orbiting satellites, which in turn beam the signal to a satellite radio company such as Sirius Satellite. These companies then make the signal available to consumers who pay a monthly fee for the service. In 2005, the Canadian Radio-television and Telecommunications Commission approved licences for Canadian companies to start providing ad-free satellite radio service. In addition to allowing listeners to avoid advertisements, satellite radio may threaten the competitive position of existing AM radio stations because the satellite radio companies are required to have only 10 percent Canadian content, while existing AM radio stations are required to have 35 percent Canadian content. However, consumer interest in satellite radio has to date been much higher in the United States than in Canada.

Advertisers are not sitting idly by as these trends unfold. Instead, they are using several new tactics to reach consumers. These include stealth advertising, product placement, cellphone advertising, and interactive television advertising.

Stealth Advertising

As the name implies, stealth advertising is designed to advertise a company's product without consumers knowing that they are the target of an actual advertisement. (For more information on stealth advertising, see Chapter 3.)

Product Placement

Product placement (also called embedded advertising) involves using brand name products as part of the actual storyline of TV shows. For example, Home Depot has been able to embed its brand name into shows like *Trading Spaces*, *Survivor*, and *The Apprentice*. In one installment of *Canadian Idol*, the Subway logo was clearly displayed on water bottles in front of the judges. Other products either mentioned or displayed during the program were sponsored by Disney World, Coca-Cola, and Nokia. Many companies are using product placement, including Bell Canada (on CBC's *Making the Cut*) and Buick (on *Desperate Housewives*).

Product placement is not limited to TV advertising; it can also be found in movies, novels, video games, pop songs, music videos, and Broadway plays. It is also rapidly increasing in importance. PQ Media estimated that spending in the United States on product placements in all media was $2.9 billion in 2007, with television accounting for $2 billion. In Canada, $32 million was spent on product placement in 2007, with television accounting for $26 million. More and more time is being devoted to product placement on prime-time television shows. On the big U.S. networks, nine minutes of each hour is devoted to showing products as part of the program's storyline. There are also nearly 14 minutes of traditional commercials each hour, so nearly 23 minutes (37 percent of each hour) is taken up with advertisements of one sort or another.

Product placement must be done carefully because it is a complex type of advertising. Pat Wilkinson, director of marketing for Home Depot Canada, says that for every dollar the company spends on branded entertainment, it must spend an additional $3–$5 to make it deliver further results. And Michael Beckerman, the chief marketing officer for the Bank of Montreal, says that product placements must be "natural." He says that if a person is watching, say, *Desperate Housewives* and the characters started talking about BMO mutual funds, viewers would see it as a blatant advertisement, and it would not likely be effective.

Cellphone Advertising

Capitalizing on new technology and the popularity of cellphones, Maiden Group PLC and Filter UK Ltd. have developed a system where transmitters detect cellphones that are equipped with Bluetooth, a short-range wireless technology, and then the transmitters beam out text messages to these cellphones. For example, passengers in the first-class lounge who were waiting to board a Virgin Atlantic Airways flight at London's Heathrow airport were asked if they would like to watch a video-clip about a new SUV on their phone. The transmitters are also installed in billboards in train stations in the United Kingdom. In one test, the transmitters discovered 87 000 Bluetooth-equipped phones at the railway station; 13 000 of the cellphone users agreed to view the advertisement when asked. Cellphone advertising is important to advertisers because people are spending less time watching TV or reading newspapers.

Interactive Television Advertising

Interactive television advertising allows viewers of advertisements to opt for more information about products if they are interested. Consider this example: Sony Corp. produced a TV advertisement for the action movie *XXX: State of the Union* that included an icon that appeared on TV screens. The icon invited viewers to press a button on their remote to learn more about the movie. If they pushed the button, they got access to a 30-minute program that included 10 minutes of the actual movie as well as interviews with the stars. A unit of Chrysler also developed an interactive ad that lets viewers go to a special screen where they can customize a car.

One new variation of interactive advertising is nanogaming, which is a blend of trivia games and social networking that allows television viewers to use their knowledge to predict what will happen next on a program. For example, viewers might guess who will score on the next play in a football game, or predict who will be the next person to be kicked off a show like *Big Brother*. Viewers who make correct predictions earn points that can be redeemed for merchandise. Advertisers like nanogaming because it can only be done if the viewer is actually tuned in to the live broadcast of the program (not just watching it on a DVR). This prevents viewers from fast-forwarding through advertisements.

The idea of giving consumers an opportunity to interact with advertisers is also evident on the internet. Procter & Gamble developed an online contest for its Crest Whitening Expressions brand where internet users voted for their favourite potential new flavour. Crest promised to make a product based on the winning flavour. Over 785 000 votes were recorded over a three-month period. To promote its Malibu Maxx vehicle, GM Canada ran an online search for the Canadian couple with the greatest height difference. Contestants logged on to www.LongandShort.gmcanada.com and completed a survey.

Questions for Discussion

1. Consumers are taking advantage of ways to avoid seeing advertisements, but companies are also developing new techniques to increase the visibility of their products. What do you think will be the eventual outcome in this "contest"? Give examples to demonstrate your reasoning.
2. Will the emphasis on each of the four Ps of marketing (product, price, promotion, and place) change in importance as consumers get more opportunities to avoid viewing advertisements? Why or why not?
3. To what extent will the changes that are occurring in advertising affect the new product development process in companies?
4. Does the value of brand names increase or decrease when consumers are able to take advantage of ways to avoid seeing advertisements?

apter 17

Pricing and Distributing Goods and Services

After reading this chapter, you should be able to:

1. Identify the various *pricing objectives* that govern pricing decisions and describe the price-setting tools used in making these decisions.
2. Discuss *pricing strategies* and tactics for existing and new products.
3. Explain the distribution mix, the different *channels of distribution,* and different *distribution strategies.*
4. Explain the differences between *merchant wholesalers* and *agents/brokers,* and describe the activities of e-intermediaries.
5. Identify the different types of *retailing* and *retail stores.*
6. Define *physical distribution* and describe the major activities in *warehousing* operations.
7. Compare the five basic forms of *transportation* and explain how distribution can be used as a marketing strategy.

Buyers and Sellers Jockey for Position

Retail shoppers want to get the lowest price possible, and retailer sellers want to get the highest price possible to protect their profit margins. As a result, there is always a certain level of tension between sellers of goods and the customers who buy them. As a result of the recession that started in 2008, this tension has reached a new level.

Stores continue to trumpet low prices as they always have, but they don't want to attract just the "cherry-picking" customers (those who go from store to store buying only on-sale items). Rather, retailers want customers who buy a variety of products, because this allows the retailer to keep profit margins higher. When you go into a Zellers store, for example, you might see boxes of canned Coca-Cola near the entrance with a bargain price of three for $9.99. But you'll have to look harder to find the discount price of $58.97 on Sesame Street's Elmo. As you are looking for Elmo, the store hopes you will find some other item that you need that is not on sale.

Wal-Mart tries to cope with cherry-picking consumers by placing products that customers might overlook close to high-demand items (e.g., placing reduced-priced slippers next to higher-priced boots). Canadian Tire and Loblaw Companies Ltd. have also noted the cherry-picking trend. In addition to strategically placing sale items, retailers can cope with cherry-pickers by limiting quantities (e.g., "one per customer"), advertising higher-margin items, and developing promotional programs that encourage shoppers to buy a broad range of products.

Retailers aren't the only ones struggling with low margins. Manufacturers are also faced with pricing dilemmas. For example, when Unilever Canada Ltd. was faced with big cost increases in the price of soybean oil used in Hellmann's mayonnaise, it debated about whether it should increase the price or simply absorb the cost increase. It finally decided to do neither. Instead, it kept the price the same but decreased the size of the mayonnaise jar from 950 mL to 890 mL and changed the container from glass to plastic (which cut manufacturing costs).

This practice has become very common because marketers believe that people don't notice the change in quantity like they do the change in price. Other examples of this strategy are as follows:

- General Motors started charging extra for antilock brakes instead of including them at no charge as it used to (this also constituted a price increase).
- Juicy Fruit gum reduced the number of pieces in a pack from 17 to 15 while keeping the price the same.
- Tropicana orange juice reduced its container size from 2.84 litres to 2.63 litres.
- General Mills introduced smaller boxes for Cheerios and Wheaties, and Kellogg Co. did the same with many of its cereals.

Here is an interesting statistic that is relevant for the issue of prices: In November 2008, only two of the 30 companies that make up the Dow Jones Industrial Average had higher stock prices than they did in November 2007 before the recession hit. Those two companies—McDonald's and Wal-Mart—are legendary for their low prices, and both of them benefited as consumers "traded down" to cheaper meals and consumer products as a result of the recession. There are many other examples as well. Consider the recent success of so-called dollar stores—retailers that offer ultra-cheap prices on a limited selection of goods. These include stores like The Silver Dollar, Dollarama, and Buck or Two. Sales revenues for this type of retail outlet have doubled in the last five years, and the number of stores has tripled. While dollar stores originally targeted low-income shoppers, they now are appealing to buyers at all income levels, and they are gaining the attention of companies that once ignored them. Procter & Gamble, for example, created a special version of Dawn dish soap that sells for $1, and Kraft Foods sells boxes of macaroni and cheese in dollar stores.

Pricing issues are very significant in the cigarette industry. For many years, the North American cigarette market has been an oligopoly that is dominated by a few very large tobacco companies like Imperial Tobacco, R.J. Reynolds, Philip Morris, Brown & Williamson, and Lorillard Tobacco. The pricing strategy that has historically been used by these companies is to increase prices to maintain (or increase) profits. This strategy worked for decades because customers were very loyal to their favourite brand. But now, some new cigarette manufacturing companies have started up and are pricing their cigarettes as much as 50 percent lower than the "majors." The majors are likely to have less control over the market than they used to, and they are going to have much more difficulty simply raising prices in the future. ◆

How will this help me?

By understanding the material presented in this chapter, you will benefit in three ways: (1) As a consumer, you will have a better understanding of how a product's development, promotion, and distribution affect its selling price; (2) as an investor, you'll be better prepared to evaluate a company's marketing program and its competitive potential before buying the company's stock; and (3) as an employee and/or manager, you'll be able to use your knowledge about product pricing and distribution to further your career.

In this chapter, we continue with our analysis of the four Ps of marketing by looking first at price and then at place (channels of distribution). As the opening case shows, the price element of the marketing mix has become intensely competitive during the last few years. But price is not the only important element. We analyze the distribution function of marketing as well, because consumers also want products and services to be available in the right place at the right time.

Pricing Objectives and Tools

1 Identify the various *pricing objectives* that govern pricing decisions and describe the price-setting tools used in making these decisions.

In **pricing**, managers decide what the company will receive in exchange for its products. In this section, we first discuss the objectives that influence a firm's pricing decisions. Then we describe the major tools that companies use to achieve those objectives.

pricing Deciding what the company will receive in exchange for its product.

pricing objectives Goals that producers hope to attain in pricing products for sale.

Pricing to Meet Business Objectives

Different companies have different **pricing objectives**. Some firms want to maximize profit, while others try to achieve a high market share. Pricing decisions are also influenced by the need to survive in the marketplace, by social and ethical concerns, and even by corporate image.

Profit-Maximizing Objectives

Pricing to maximize profits is tricky. If prices are set too low, the company will probably sell many units of its product, but it may miss the opportunity to make additional profit on each unit—and may in fact lose money on each exchange. Conversely, if prices are set too high, the company will make a large profit on each item but will sell fewer units, resulting in excess inventory and a need to reduce production operations. Again, the firm loses money. To avoid these problems, companies try to set prices to sell the number of units that will generate the highest possible total profits.

The strategy of charging prices based on market conditions is increasingly evident. For example, Coca-Cola tested a vending machine that automatically raised the price of a Coke as the temperature climbed. It also tried setting prices at different vending machines at different levels, depending on how many customers used the machine.[1] The Ottawa Senators increased prices 20 percent for games against the Toronto Maple Leafs and the Detroit Red Wings.[2]

In the public sector, governments are also using prices, not to maximize profit, but to manage traffic patterns. An experimental dynamic-pricing system of toll-road fees has been introduced in Stockholm, Sweden, in an attempt to reduce traffic congestion. In the busiest time of the day, road users must pay fees that are double those charged during lighter traffic times. During the trial period, declines were evident in the number of vehicles using the roads, the number of personal injuries, and the amount of emissions from motor vehicles.[3] In the United Kingdom, one auto insurer has introduced a system where car insurance premiums vary depending on how much, where, and when a person drives. For example, a 40-year-old driver who is driving on a divided highway at 2 p.m. might pay only one pence per mile to drive, but a teenager driving at 1 a.m. would pay dramatically more (about one *pound* per mile).[4] In Canada, Skymeter Corp. is developing a technology that tracks how far a car travels and where it parks. It does away with the need for highway toll booths and parking attendants. A GPS unit on the car's dashboard makes the measurements and calculations.[5]

"O.K., who can put a price on love? Jim?"

Managers in business firms calculate profits by comparing revenues against costs for materials and labour to create the product. But they also consider the capital resources (plant and equipment) that the company must tie up to generate that level of profit. The costs of marketing (such as maintaining a large sales staff) can also be substantial. Concern over the efficient use of these resources has led many firms to set prices so as to achieve a targeted level of return on sales or capital investment.[6]

Market Share Objectives

In the long run, a business must make a profit to survive. Nevertheless, many companies initially set low prices for new products. They are willing to accept minimal profits—even losses—to get buyers to try products. In other words, they use pricing to establish **market share**—a company's percentage of the total market sales for a specific product. Even with established products, market share may outweigh profits as a pricing objective. For a product like Philadelphia brand cream cheese, dominating a market means that consumers are more likely to buy it because they are familiar with a well-known, highly visible product.

market share A company's percentage of the total market sales for a specific product.

Other Pricing Objectives

In some instances, neither profit maximizing nor market share is the best objective. During difficult economic times, for instance, loss containment and survival may become a company's main objectives. Not long after the recession began in 2008, for example, retailers began cutting prices in an attempt to attract customers. A few years earlier, Universal cut the price it charged for CDs by one-third as a response to consumer complaints about high CD prices.[7]

Price-Setting Tools

Whatever a company's objectives, managers must measure the potential impact before deciding on final prices. Two basic tools are often used for this purpose: *cost-oriented pricing* and *break-even analysis*. These tools are often combined to identify prices that will allow the company to reach its objectives.

Cost-Oriented Pricing

Cost-oriented pricing considers the firm's desire to make a profit and takes into account the need to cover production costs. A music store manager, for instance, would price CDs by calculating the cost of making them available to shoppers. Included in this figure would be store rent, employee wages, utilities, product displays, insurance, and, of course, the cost of buying CDs from the manufacturer.

Let's assume that the cost from the manufacturer is \$8 per CD. If the store sells CDs for this price, it will not make any profit. Nor will it make a profit if it sells CDs for \$8.50 each or even for \$10 or \$11. The manager must account for product and other costs and set a figure for profit. Together, these figures constitute markup. In this case, a reasonable markup of \$7 over costs would result in a \$15 selling price. Markup is usually stated as a percentage of selling price. Markup percentage is thus calculated as follows:

$$\text{Markup percentage} = \frac{\text{Markup}}{\text{Sales price}}$$

In the case of our CD retailer, the markup percentage is 46.7:

$$\text{Markup percentage} = \frac{\$7}{\$15} = 46.7\%$$

In other words, out of every dollar taken in, 46.7 cents will be gross profit for the store. From this profit the store must still pay rent, utilities, insurance, and all other costs. Markup can also be expressed as a percentage of cost: The \$7 markup is 87.5 percent of the \$8 cost of a CD (\$7 ÷ \$8).

In some industries, cost-oriented pricing doesn't seem to be used. When you go to a first-run movie theatre, for example, you pay the same price for each film you see. But it may cost as little as \$2 million or as much as \$200 million to make a film. Shouldn't the admission price be based on how much the film cost to make? After all, you pay a lot more for a Lincoln Continental than you do for a Ford because the Lincoln costs more to make. Shouldn't the same pricing system apply to Hollywood? Apparently not. Consumers are simply not willing to pay more than a certain amount to see a movie. The boxed insert entitled "Men and Cars: Unrequited Love" describes a situation where, unlike the movie example, the price of a service may not be a big concern for customers.

Break-Even Analysis: Cost-Volume-Profit Relationships

variable costs Those costs that change with the number of goods or services produced or sold.

fixed costs Those costs unaffected by the number of goods or services produced or sold.

break-even analysis An assessment of how many units must be sold at a given price before the company begins to make a profit.

Using cost-oriented pricing, a firm will cover its **variable costs**—costs that change with the number of goods or services produced or sold. It will also make some money toward paying its **fixed costs**—costs that are unaffected by the number of goods or services produced or sold. But how many units must the company sell before all of its fixed costs are covered and it begins to make a profit? To determine this figure, it needs a **break-even analysis.**[8]

To continue our music store example, suppose again that the variable cost for each CD (in this case, the cost of buying the CD from the producer) is \$8. This means that the store's annual variable costs depend on how many CDs are sold—the number of CDs sold multiplied by \$8 cost per CD. Say that fixed costs for keeping the store open for one year are \$100 000. These costs are unaffected by the number of CDs sold; costs for lighting, rent, insurance, and salaries are steady however many CDs the store sells. Therefore, how many CDs must be sold to cover both fixed and variable costs and to start to generate some profit? The answer is the **break-even point**, which is 14 286 CDs. We arrive at this number through the following equation:

break-even point The number of units that must be sold at a given price before the company covers all of its variable and fixed costs.

$$\text{Break-even point (in units)} = \frac{\text{Total fixed costs}}{\text{Price} - \text{Variable cost}}$$

$$= \frac{\$100\ 000}{\$15 - \$8} = 14\ 286 \text{ CDs}$$

Entrepreneurship and New Ventures

Men and Cars: Unrequited Love

Men have always had a bit of a love affair with their cars, but the customers of Auto Vault are downright obsessive. You would be too if you had $500 000 invested in a Lamborghini, or some other exotic coupe. Auto Vault, a Toronto-based secure car-storage facility for luxury automobiles and motorcycles, is owned and operated by Gary Shapiro. Shapiro got the idea for Auto Vault when working in sales at a high-end auto dealership. Potential customers complained that money wasn't the issue when it came to making a purchase; rather, the problem was where they would store the vehicle. Shapiro's company was launched in 2004, and it has been experiencing steady growth since inception, expanding from 80 customers at the end of its first year of operations to 400 in 2008.

For a $229 monthly fee, customers can purchase Auto Vault's Gold Package, which includes an exterior dust cover, interior mats and steering wheel cover, access to dedicated staff, secure parking, security monitoring, valet delivery, and detailing. But if you think your "baby" deserves more than that, then sign up for the Platinum Package. For $299 per month, you can get all the features of the Gold Package, plus tire pressure monitoring, battery and fluid checks, scheduled vehicle start-ups, and visual inspections.

Aside from the storage and services, Auto Vault's customers are purchasing peace of mind. They trust Shapiro and they like him. "I was once called 'likeable' in a newspaper article.... I hope I am, it would make it easier to convince someone to hand over the keys to a $500 000 car and their American Express card," said Shapiro. Shapiro is also known for his discretion; people are not told who owns which car and some of his customers even have cars that are unknown to their families. Finally, the location is secret and disclosed to customers only after Shapiro meets with them.

As part of his service offering, Shapiro also likes to maintain personal contact with his clients, and this is done through his handling of all incoming calls. "Word spread that I take good care of people," he said. This has helped him to get referrals, and according to Shapiro, he doesn't have to push his product; customers come to him. Gary Shapiro thinks he can extend his business to another level, however.

His next venture is a $15-million storage facility to be converted into parking condos. For $40 000, plus monthly maintenance fees, prestige car owners can purchase their own customized unit (average size is 400 square feet) and Shapiro's imagination for what his car condo can offer has no boundaries. He's talking about such features as decor to match your car's colour, 24-hour concierge service, a detailing service, and common areas with large-screen TVs, among other things. This romance between men and cars . . . it must be true love! And price is no object.

Critical Thinking Question

1. Review the various types of pricing strategies and distribution options and identify the choices made by Auto Vault. Do you think Shapiro's pricing reflected the market he was targeting? Why or why not?

Figure 17.1 shows the break-even point graphically. If the store sells fewer than 14 286 CDs, it loses money for the year. If sales exceed 14 286 CDs, profits grow by $7 for each CD sold. If the store sells exactly 14 286 CDs, it

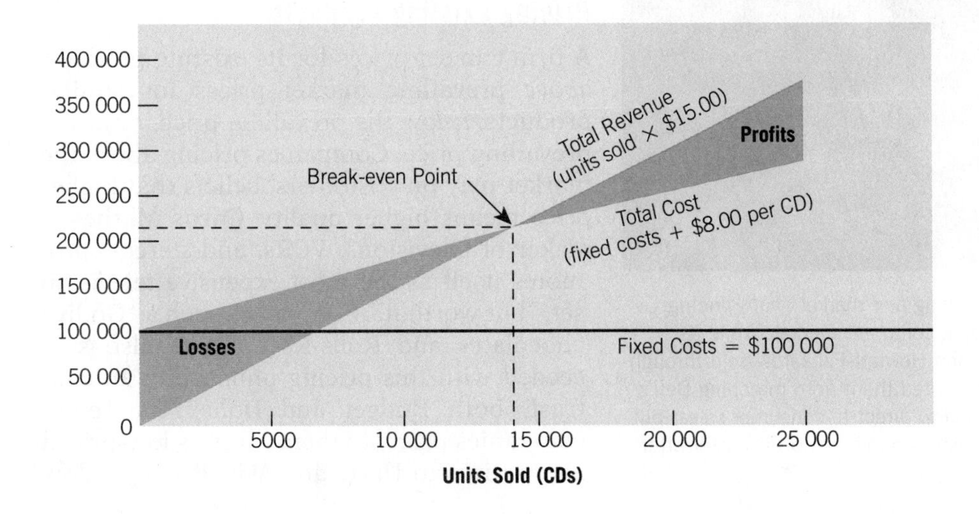

Figure 17.1 Break-even analysis.

will cover all of its costs but will earn zero profit. Zero profitability at the break-even point can also be seen by using the following profit equation:

$$\text{Profit} = \text{total revenue} - (\text{total fixed costs} + \text{total variable costs})$$
$$= (14\,286 \text{ CDs} \times \$15) - (\$100\,000 \text{ fixed costs} + [14\,286 \text{ CDs} \times \$8 \text{ variable costs}])$$

The music store owner would certainly like to hit the break-even quantity as early as possible so that profits will start rolling in. Why not charge $20 per CD and reach the break-even point earlier? The answer lies in the downward-sloping demand curve we discussed in Chapter 1. At a price of $20 per CD, sales at the store would drop. In setting a price, the manager must consider how much CD buyers will pay and what the store's local competitors charge.

Pricing Strategies and Tactics

2 Discuss *pricing strategies* and tactics for existing and new products.

The pricing tools discussed in the previous section provide guidance for managers trying to set prices on specific goods. But they do not provide general direction for managers trying to decide on a pricing philosophy for their company. In this section, we discuss *pricing strategy*—that is, pricing as a planning activity that affects the marketing mix. We then describe some basic *pricing tactics*—ways in which managers implement a firm's pricing strategies.

Pricing Strategies

Let's begin this section by asking two questions. First, can a manager really identify a single "best" price for a product? Probably not. One study of prices for popular non-aspirin pain relievers (such as Tylenol and Advil) found variations of 100 percent.[9] Such large price differences may reflect some differences in product costs, but the bigger issue is likely differing brand images that attract different types of customers. In turn, these images reflect vastly different pricing philosophies and strategies. Second, just how important is pricing as an element in the marketing mix? As we have already seen, it is a mistake to try to isolate any element in the marketing mix from the others. Nevertheless, pricing is a critical variable because it has a major impact on company revenues, and it is extremely important to consumers.

Using low-cost direct-to-consumer selling and market share pricing, Dell profitably dominated the personal computer market, while its competitors—Apple IBM, Compaq, and Hewlett-Packard—sold through retailers, adding extra costs that prevented them from matching Dell's low prices. Competitors have switched to direct-to-consumer sales, but Dell is strongly anchored as the industry's number-two PC maker after Hewlett-Packard.

Pricing Existing Products

A firm can set prices for its existing products *above* prevailing market prices for similar products, *below* the prevailing price, or *at* the prevailing price. Companies pricing above the market play on customers' beliefs that higher price means higher quality. Curtis Mathes, a maker of televisions, VCRs, and stereos, promotes itself as the most expensive television set, "but worth it." Companies such as Godiva chocolates and Rolls-Royce have also succeeded with this pricing philosophy. In contrast, both Budget and Dollar car rental companies promote themselves as low-priced alternatives to Hertz and Avis. Pricing below the prevailing market price can succeed if the firm can offer a product of acceptable quality while keeping costs below those of higher-priced options.

In some industries, a dominant firm establishes product prices and other companies follow along. This is called **price leadership**. (Don't confuse this approach with *price fixing*, the illegal process of producers agreeing among themselves what prices will be charged.) Price leadership is often evident in products such as structural steel, gasoline, and many processed foods because these products differ little in quality from one firm to another. Companies compete through advertising campaigns, personal selling, and service, not price.

price leadership The dominant firm in the industry establishes product prices and other companies follow suit.

Pricing New Products

Companies introducing new products into the market have to consider two contrasting pricing policy options—coming in with either a very high price or a very low one. **Price skimming**—setting an initially high price to cover costs and generate a profit—may generate a large profit on each item sold. The revenue is often needed to cover development and introduction costs. Skimming works only if marketers can convince consumers that a product is truly different from those already on the market. High-definition TVs, microwave ovens, electronic calculators, video games, and video cameras were all introduced at high skimming prices. In contrast, **penetration pricing**—setting an initially low price to establish a new product in the market—seeks to create consumer interest and stimulate trial purchases.

price skimming The decision to price a new product as high as possible to earn the maximum profit on each unit sold.

penetration pricing The decision to price a new product very low to sell the most units possible and to build customer loyalty.

Whatever price strategy a company is using, it must be communicated to buyers. Wal-Mart consistently communicates a low-price strategy to consumers, but some other retailers do not. Zellers, for example, tried to compete with Wal-Mart by adopting an "everyday low prices" (EDLP) policy a few years ago but abandoned it and returned to its former practice of promotional markdowns on some products to attract customers to its stores.[10]

Fixed vs. Dynamic Pricing for Ebusiness

The electronic marketplace has introduced a highly variable pricing system as an alternative to more conventional—and more stable—pricing structures for both consumer and business-to-business (B2B) products. *Dynamic pricing* works because information flows on the web notify millions of buyers of instantaneous changes in product availability. To attract sales that might be lost under traditional fixed-price structures, sellers can alter prices privately, on a one-to-one, customer-to-customer basis.[11]

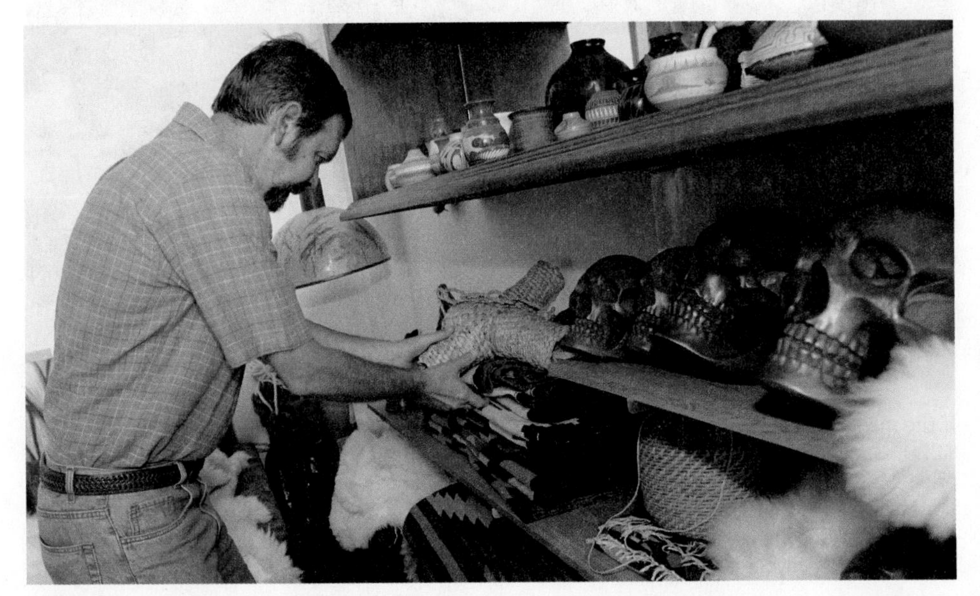

Roy Cooper scours the markets of Quito, Ecuador, for tapestries, baskets, and religious relics. He pays $10 to $15 for selected items and then posts them on eBay, where they usually sell at substantial markups. His online enterprise nets Cooper about $1300 a month ($2500 in November and December). His Ecuadorian suppliers, whose average income is $1460 per year, seem happy with their share. In a country where only 2.7 percent of the population has ever been online, very few people have heard of dynamic pricing.

Pricing Tactics

Regardless of its general pricing strategy, a company may adopt one or more specific pricing tactics, such as *price lining* or *psychological pricing*. Managers must also decide whether to use *discounting* tactics.

Price Lining

price lining The practice of offering all items in certain categories at a limited number of predetermined price points.

Companies selling multiple items in a product category often use **price lining**—offering all items in certain categories at a limited number of prices. Three or four *price points* are set at which a particular product will be sold. For example, all men's suits might be priced at $175, $250, or $400. The store's buyers select suits that can be purchased and sold profitably at one of these three prices.

Psychological Pricing

psychological pricing The practice of setting prices to take advantage of the nonlogical reactions of consumers to certain types of prices.

odd-even pricing A form of psychological pricing in which prices are not stated in even dollar amounts.

Psychological pricing is based on the idea that customers are not completely rational when making buying decisions. One type of psychological pricing, **odd-even pricing**, assumes that customers prefer prices that are not stated in even dollar amounts. Thus, customers may regard a price of $99.95 as significantly lower than a price of $100.00. But Wal-Mart is going against this trend. In an attempt to make it easier for money-conscious customers to calculate their bill before they get to the cash register, Wal-Mart is rounding prices to the nearest dollar on many products.[12]

Discounting

discount Any price reduction offered by the seller to persuade customers to purchase a product.

cash discount A form of discount in which customers paying cash, rather than buying on credit, pay lower prices.

seasonal discount A form of discount in which lower prices are offered to customers making a purchase at a time of year when sales are traditionally slow.

trade discount A discount given to firms involved in a product's distribution.

The price that is set for a product is not always the price at which all items are actually sold. Many times a company offers a price reduction—a **discount**—to stimulate sales. In recent years, **cash discounts** have become popular. Stores may also offer **seasonal discounts** to stimulate the sales of products during times of the year when most customers do not normally buy the product. **Trade discounts** are available to companies or individuals in a product's distribution channel (for example, wholesalers, retailers, and interior designers

If the manufacturer says a product should retail for $349, why does every retailer sell it for, say, $229? Such discrepancies between a manufacturer's suggested retail price and the actual retail price are the norm in the electronics industry, and consumers have come to expect discounted prices. "You can't have a discount until there's a price to discount it from," explains an editor at Consumer Reports, but the practice raises an interesting question: If no one charges suggested retail prices, is anyone really getting a discount?

pay less for fabric than the typical consumer does). **Quantity discounts** involve lower prices for purchases in large quantities. Discounts for cases of motor oil or soft drinks at retail stores are examples of quantity discounts.

quantity discount A form of discount in which customers buying large amounts of a product pay lower prices.

International Pricing

When Procter & Gamble reviewed its prospects for marketing products in new overseas markets, it encountered an unsettling fact: Because it typically priced products to cover hefty R&D costs, profitably priced items were out of reach for too many foreign consumers. The solution was, in effect, to reverse the process. Now P&G conducts research to find out what foreign buyers can afford and then develops products that they can buy. P&G penetrates markets with lower-priced items and encourages customers to trade up as they become able to afford higher-quality products.

As P&G's experience shows, pricing products for other countries is complicated because additional factors are involved. Income and spending trends must be analyzed. In addition, the number of intermediaries varies from country to country, as does their effect on a product's cost. Exchange rates change daily, there may be shipping costs, import tariffs must be considered (Chapter 5), and different types of pricing agreements may be permitted.

The Distribution Mix

The success of any product depends in part on its **distribution mix**—the combination of distribution channels a firm uses to get a product to end-users. In this section, we explain the need for *intermediaries*, then discuss the basic *distribution strategies*, and then consider some special issues in channel relationships.

Explain the distribution mix, the different *channels of distribution*, and different *distribution strategies*. 3

distribution mix The combination of distribution channels a firm selects to get a product to end-users.

Intermediaries and Distribution Channels

Once called *middlemen*, **intermediaries** are the individuals and firms who help distribute a producer's goods. **Wholesalers** sell products to other businesses, which resell them to final consumers. **Retailers** sell products directly to consumers. While some firms rely on independent intermediaries, others employ their own distribution networks and sales forces. Intermediaries are appearing in places where most people might think they aren't needed. A Canadian company called Imagine This Sold Ltd. began operating in 2004. For a percentage of the selling price, it provides expertise to people who are trying to sell items on eBay. This company exists because trading has become so competitive on eBay that more expertise is needed to succeed than a lot of people thought.[13]

intermediary Any individual or firm other than the producer who participates in a product's distribution.

wholesalers Intermediaries who sell products to other businesses, which in turn resell them to the end-users.

retailers Intermediaries who sell products to end-users.

Distribution of Consumer Products

A **distribution channel** is the path that a product follows from producer to end-user. Figure 17.2 shows how eight primary distribution channels can be identified according to the kinds of channel members involved in getting products to buyers. Note that all channels must begin with a producer and end with a consumer or an industrial user. Channels 1 through 4 are most often used for the distribution of consumer goods and services.

distribution channel The path a product follows from the producer to the end-user.

Channel 1: Direct Distribution of Consumer Products. In a **direct channel**, the product travels from the producer to the consumer without intermediaries. Using their own sales forces, companies such as Avon, Fuller Brush, and

direct channel A distribution channel in which the product travels from the producer to the consumer without passing through any intermediary.

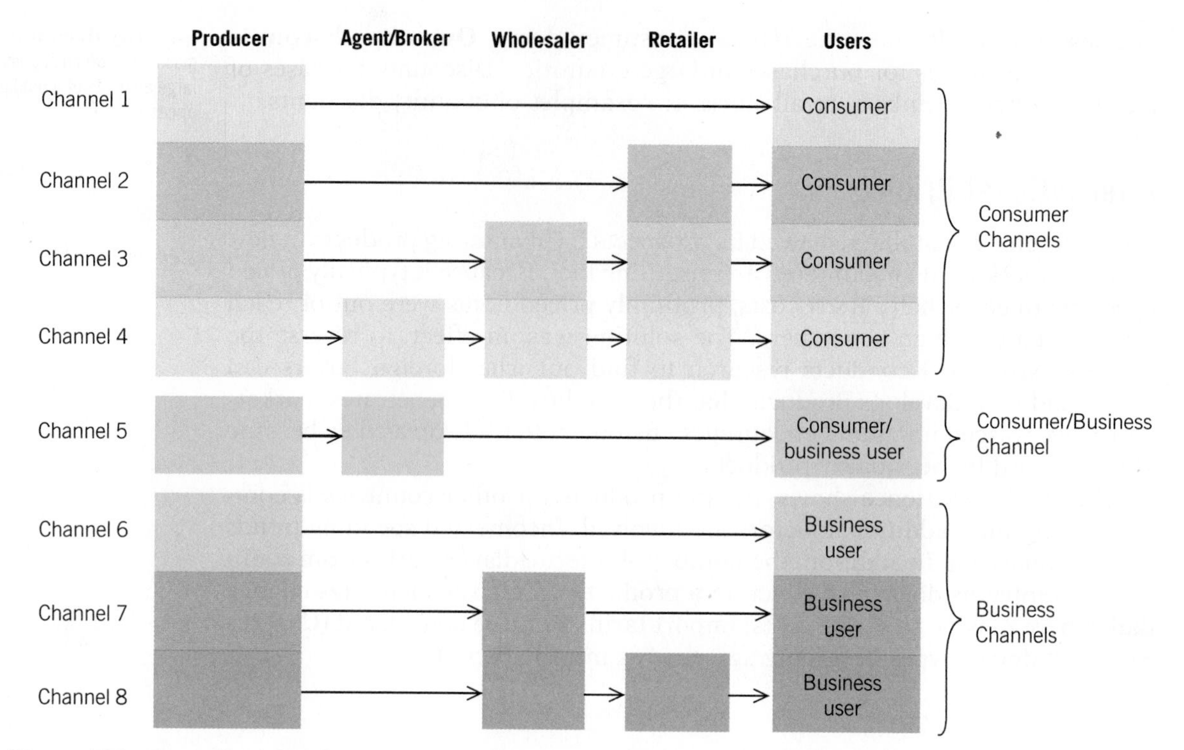

Figure 17.2 Channels of distribution: How the product travels from producer to consumer or user.

Tupperware use this channel. The direct channel is also prominent on the internet, where consumers can purchase airline reservations (and thousands of other products and services) directly from internet sites.

Channel 2: Retail Distribution of Consumer Products. In Channel 2, producers distribute products through retailers. Goodyear, for example, maintains its own system of retail outlets. Levi's has its own outlets but also produces jeans for other retailers such as Gap Inc.

Channel 3: Wholesale Distribution of Consumer Products. Faced with the rising cost of store space, many retailers found that they could not afford both retail and storage space. Thus, wholesalers entered the distribution network to perform the storage function. The combination convenience store/gas station is an example of Channel 3. With approximately 90 percent of the space used to display merchandise, only 10 percent is left for storage and office facilities. Wholesalers store merchandise and restock it frequently. Wholesalers are prominent in ecommerce because internet stores give customers access to information and product displays 24 hours a day. Buyers can also place orders electronically and confirm delivery almost instantaneously. In the diamond industry, retail companies can access wholesalers such as Diasqua Group, visually examine diamonds, place orders, and receive delivery dates, all over the internet.

sales agents (or brokers) Independent business people who represent a business and receive a commission in return, but never take legal possession of the product.

Channel 4: Distribution Through Sales Agents or Brokers. **Sales agents (or brokers)** represent producers and sell to wholesalers, retailers, or both. They receive commissions based on the prices of the goods they sell. Lafferty and Co. Food Brokers Inc. represents several prominent food manufacturers—Pillsbury, Old El Paso, and Sunkist. To relieve manufacturers of sales activities, Lafferty arranges sales of their products to other companies, allowing manufacturers to do what they do best—produce food products—rather than divert resources to sales and distribution. Agents generally deal in the related product lines of a few producers and work on a long-term basis. Travel agents,

"On the one hand, eliminating the middleman would result in lower costs, increased sales, and greater consumer satisfaction; on the other hand, we're the middleman."

for example, represent airlines, car-rental companies, and hotels. In contrast, brokers match sellers and buyers as needed. The real estate industry relies on brokers to match buyers and sellers of property.

The Pros and Cons of Non-direct Distribution

Each link in the distribution chain makes a profit by charging a markup or commission. Thus, non-direct distribution means higher prices. The more intermediaries in the channel, the higher the final price will be. Calculated as a percentage of cost, *markups* are applied each time a product is sold. They may range from 10 to 40 percent for manufacturers, from 2 to 25 percent for wholesalers, and from 5 to 100 percent for retailers. *E-intermediaries*—wholesalers and agents who use internet channels—also charge markups. In general, markup levels depend on competitive conditions and practices in a particular industry.

Intermediaries provide *added value* by saving consumers both time and money. Moreover, the value accumulates with each link in the supply chain. Intermediaries provide time-saving information and make the right quantities of products available where and when consumers need them. Figure 17.3 illustrates the problem of making chili without benefit of a common intermediary—the supermarket. As a consumer/buyer, you would obviously spend a lot more time, money, and energy if you tried to gather all the ingredients from one retailer at a time.

Even if intermediaries are eliminated, the costs associated with their functions are not. Intermediaries exist because they do necessary jobs in cost-efficient ways. For example, in this do-it-yourself era, more and more people are trying to save money by opting to sell their homes without using the services of a real estate agent. Since the agent's fee is normally between 5 and 6 percent of the purchase price of the house, the savings can be substantial. But the seller has to do all the work that brokers would normally do to earn their fee.

Remember this: Although intermediaries like real estate agents provide an essential service, this does not mean that they necessarily provide a *low-cost* service. Ebrokers have emerged who charge a flat rate for selling a home, and that rate is far below what traditional real estate brokers charge. It is not surprising that this development has been viewed with some alarm by traditional

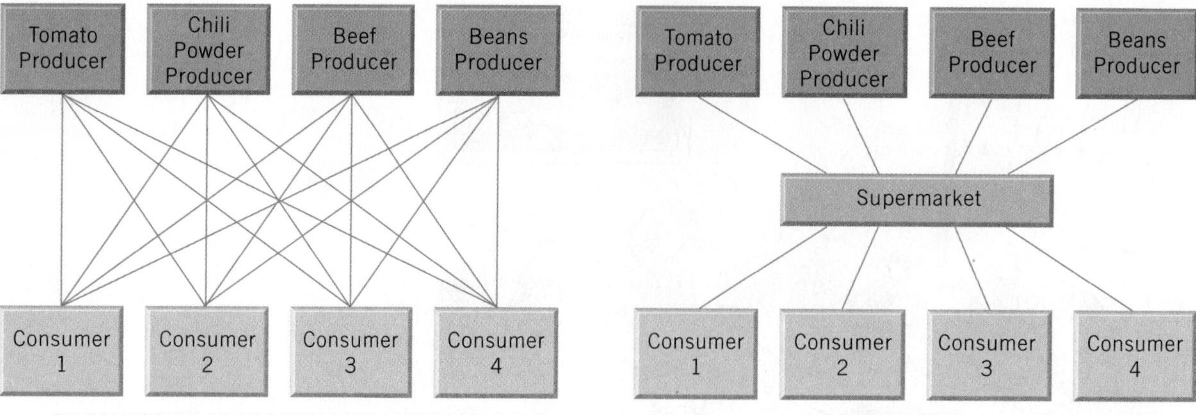

Figure 17.3 Advantages of intermediaries.

real estate agents. What's worse, in 2007 the Canadian Competition Bureau launched an inquiry into changes the Canadian Real Estate Association (CREA) made to its operating procedures. Ebrokers claimed these changes were designed to maintain high fees for traditional real estate brokers by cutting ebrokers out of the CREAs Multiple Listing Service.[14]

Channel 5: Distribution by Agents to Consumers and Businesses. Channel 5 differs from previous channels in two ways: (1) An agent functions as the sole intermediary, and (2) the agent distributes to both consumers and business customers. Consider Vancouver-based Uniglobe Travel International, a travel agent representing airlines, car-rental companies, and hotels. Uniglobe books flight reservations and arranges complete recreational-travel services for consumers. The firm also services companies whose employees need lodging and transportation for business travel.

Ecommerce works well in this channel because it directly informs more people about products. At Uniglobe, for instance, an online subsidiary combines a high-tech website with an old-fashioned human touch in a specialty market—booking cruises. Customers can scan for destinations, cruise lines, restaurants, and cabin locations for many different ships. Using Uniglobe's online chat function, travellers can simply open a window to speak in real time with one of 75 cruise specialists. The strategy has paid off: Uniglobe.com leads the market in online cruise bookings.[15]

Distribution of Business Products

Industrial channels are important because every company is also a customer that buys other companies' products. The Kellogg Co., for example, buys grain to make breakfast cereals, and Imperial Tobacco buys tobacco to make cigarettes. **Industrial (business) distribution** is the network of channel members involved in the flow of manufactured goods to business customers. Business products are traditionally distributed through Channels 6, 7, and 8 (refer back to Figure 17.2).

industrial (business) distribution The network of channel members involved in the flow of manufactured goods to business customers.

Channel 6: Direct Distribution of Business Products. Most business goods are sold directly by the manufacturer to the industrial buyer. Lawless Container Corp., for instance, produces packaging containers for direct sale to Fisher-Price (toys), Dirt Devil (vacuum cleaners), and Mr. Coffee (coffee makers). Many manufacturers maintain **sales offices** as contact points with customers and headquarters for salespeople. Ecommerce technologies have popularized channel 6. Dell Computer Corp., a pioneer in direct internet sales, now gets about two-thirds of its sales from other businesses, governments, and schools.[16]

sales offices Offices maintained by sellers of industrial goods to provide points of contact with their customers.

Channel 7: Wholesale Distribution of Industrial Products. Channel 7 mostly handles accessory equipment (computers, fax machines, and other office equipment) and supplies (USB memory sticks, pencils, and copier paper). Manufacturers produce these items in large quantities, but companies buy them in small quantities. For example, few companies order truckloads of paper clips, so intermediaries help end-users by breaking down large quantities into smaller sales units.

Channel 8: Wholesale Distribution to Business Retailers. In the office-products industry, channel 7 is being displaced by a channel that looks very much like channel 3 for consumer products. Instead of buying office supplies from wholesalers (channel 7), many businesses are now shopping at office discount stores such as Staples, Office Depot, and Office Max. Before selling to large companies, these warehouse-like superstores originally targeted retail consumers and small businesses that bought supplies at retail stores (and at retail prices). Today, however, small business buyers shop at discount stores designed for industrial users, selecting from 7000 items at prices 20 to 75 percent lower than retail.

Distribution Strategies

Three strategies—*intensive*, *exclusive*, and *selective distribution*—provide different degrees of market coverage for products. **Intensive distribution** means distributing a product through as many channels and channel members (using both wholesalers and retailers) as possible. For example, as Figure 17.4 shows, Caramilk bars flood the market through all suitable outlets. Intensive distribution is normally used for low-cost consumer goods such as candy and magazines.

intensive distribution A distribution strategy in which a product is distributed in nearly every possible outlet, using many channels and channel members.

In contrast, **exclusive distribution** occurs when a manufacturer grants the exclusive right to distribute or sell a product to one wholesaler or retailer in a given geographic area. Exclusive distribution agreements are most common for high-cost prestige products. For example, Jaguar or Rolls-Royce automobiles are typically sold by only one dealer in a large metropolitan area.

exclusive distribution A distribution strategy in which a product's distribution is limited to only one wholesaler or retailer in a given geographic area.

Selective distribution falls between intensive and exclusive distribution. A company that uses this strategy selects only wholesalers and retailers who will give special attention to the product in terms of sales efforts, display position,

selective distribution A distribution strategy that falls between intensive and exclusive distribution, calling for the use of a limited number of outlets for a product.

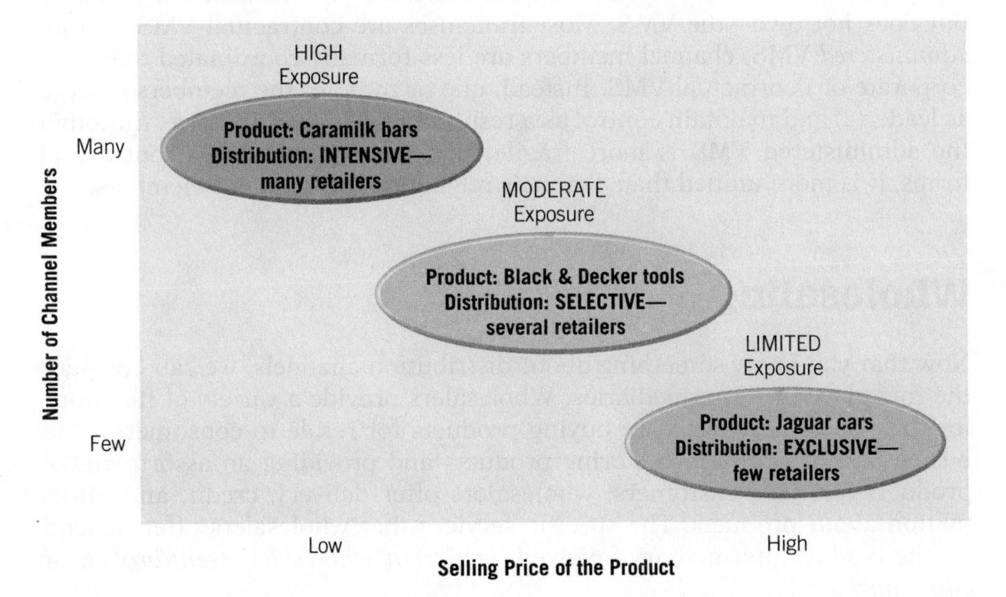

Figure 17.4 Amounts of market exposure from the three kinds of distribution.

and so on. Selective distribution policies have been applied to virtually every type of consumer product. They are often used by companies like Black & Decker, whose product lines do not require intense market exposure to increase sales. Para Paints uses a selective distribution policy because it keeps its high-end paint products out of the "big-box" stores such as Canadian Tire and Home Depot. Doing so has increased Para's margins (because big-box stores demand steep discounts), and has also increased sales by 15 to 20 percent because the independent stores that sell Para paint have remained loyal to Para.[17]

Channel Conflict and Channel Leadership

channel conflict Conflict arising when the members of a distribution channel disagree over the roles they should play or the rewards they should receive.

Channel conflict occurs when members of the distribution channel disagree over the roles they should play or the rewards they should receive. John Deere, for example, would object if its dealers began distributing Russian and Japanese tractors. Similarly, when a manufacturer-owned factory outlet store discounts the company's apparel or housewares, it runs the risk of alienating the independent retailers who also sell the manufacturer's products. Channel conflict may also arise if one member has more power than others or is viewed as receiving preferential treatment. Such conflicts defeat the purpose of the system by disrupting the flow of goods to their destinations.

channel captain The channel member that is the most powerful in determining the roles and rewards of organizations involved in a given channel of distribution.

Conflicts are resolved when members' efforts are better coordinated. A key factor in coordinating the activities of independent organizations is channel leadership. Usually, one channel member—the **channel captain**—can determine the roles and rewards of other members. Often, the channel captain is a manufacturer, particularly if the manufacturer's product is in high demand. In some industries, an influential wholesaler or a large retailer such as Wal-Mart may emerge as the channel captain because of its large sales volumes.

vertical marketing system (VMS) A system in which there is a high degree of coordination among all the units in the distribution channel so that a product moves efficiently from manufacturer to consumer.

To overcome problems posed by channel conflict and issues of channel leadership, the **vertical marketing system (VMS)** has emerged. In a VMS, separate businesses join to form a unified distribution channel, with one member coordinating the activities of the whole channel. There are three main types of VMS arrangements. In a *corporate* VMS, all stages in the channel are under single ownership. The Limited, for example, owns both the production facilities that manufacture its apparel and the retail stores that sell it. In a *contractual* VMS, channel members sign contracts agreeing to specific duties and rewards. The Independent Grocers' Alliance (IGA), for example, consists of independent retail grocers joined with a wholesaler who contractually leads—but does not own—the VMS. Most franchises are contractual VMSs. In an *administered* VMS, channel members are less formally coordinated than in a corporate or contractual VMS. Instead, one or more of the members emerge as leader(s) and maintain control as a result of power and influence. Although the administered VMS is more fragile than the corporate and contractual forms, it is more unified than channels relying on independent members.

Wholesaling

4 Explain the differences between *merchant wholesalers* and *agents/brokers*, and describe the activities of e-intermediaries.

Now that you know something about distribution channels, we can consider the role played by intermediaries. Wholesalers provide a variety of functions for their customers, who are buying products for resale to consumers or to businesses. In addition to storing products and providing an assortment of products for their customers, wholesalers offer delivery, credit, and information about products. The specific services that wholesalers offer depend on the type of intermediary involved: *merchant wholesaler, agent/broker,* or *e-intermediary*.

Merchant Wholesalers

Most wholesalers are independent operators who derive their income from sales of goods produced by a variety of manufacturers. All **merchant wholesalers** take title to merchandise, that is, they buy and own the goods they resell to other businesses. They usually provide storage and a means of delivery.

merchant wholesaler An independent wholesaler that buys and takes legal possession of goods before selling them to customers.

A **full-service merchant wholesaler** provides credit, marketing, and merchandising services. Approximately 80 percent of all merchant wholesalers are full-service wholesalers. **Limited-function merchant wholesalers** provide only a few services, sometimes merely storage. Their customers are normally small operations that pay cash and pick up their own goods. One such wholesaler, the **drop shipper**, receives orders from customers, negotiates with producers to supply goods, takes title to them, and arranges for shipment to customers.

full-service merchant wholesaler A merchant wholesaler that provides storage and delivery in addition to wholesaling services.

limited-function merchant wholesaler An independent wholesaler that provides only wholesaling—not warehousing or transportation—services.

drop shipper A type of wholesaler that does not carry inventory or handle the product.

Other limited-function wholesalers, known as **rack jobbers**, market consumer goods—mostly non-food items—directly to retail stores.[18] Procter & Gamble, for example, uses rack jobbers to distribute products like Pampers diapers. After marking prices, setting up display racks, and displaying diapers in one store, the rack jobber moves on to another outlet to check inventories and shelve products.

rack jobber A limited-function merchant wholesaler specializing in non-food merchandise that sets up and maintains display racks of some products in retail stores.

Agents and Brokers

Agents and brokers, including internet e-agents, serve as the sales and merchandising arms of manufacturers that do not have their own sales forces. They work on commissions, usually about 4 to 5 percent of net sales. Unlike merchant wholesalers, they do not take title to the merchandise they sell. The value of agents and brokers lies primarily in their knowledge of markets and their merchandising expertise. They also provide a wide range of services, including shelf and display merchandising and advertising layout. Finally, they maintain product saleability by removing open, torn, or dirty packages; arranging products neatly; and generally keeping them attractively displayed. Many supermarket products are handled through brokers.

Retailing

Identify the different types of *retailing* and *retail stores*. **5**

If you are like most Canadians, you buy nearly all the goods and services you consume from retailers. Most retailers are small operations, often consisting of just the owners and part-time help. But there are a few very large retailers, and these account for billions of dollars of sales each year in Canada (see Table 17.1).

Types of Retail Outlets

Retail operations in Canada vary as widely by type as they do by size. They can be classified in various ways—by pricing strategies, location, range of services, or range of product lines. Choosing the right types of retail outlets is a crucial aspect of every seller's distribution strategy. There are two basic categories of retail stores: *product line retailers* and *bargain retailers*.

Product Line Retailers

Retailers that feature broad product lines include **department stores**, which are organized into specialized departments such as shoes, furniture, women's clothing, and so forth. Stores are usually large and handle a wide range of

department stores Large retail stores that offer a wide variety of high-quality items divided into specialized departments.

Table 17.1 Top 10 Retailers in Canada, 2008

Company	Annual Revenues (in billions of $)
1. Wal-Mart Canada Corp.	$16.6
2. Costco Wholesale Canada Ltd.	10.1
3. Canadian Tire Corp. Ltd.	9.1
4. Home Depot Canada	6.1
5. Sears Canada Inc.	5.7
6. Best Buy Canada Ltd.	5.5
7. Rona Inc.	4.8
8. Home Hardware Stores Ltd.	4.8
9. Liquor Control Board of Ontario	4.1
10. B.C. Liquor Distribution Branch	2.6

goods. In addition, they usually offer a variety of services, such as generous return policies, credit plans, and delivery. Similarly, **supermarkets** are divided into departments of related products—food products, household products, and so on. The emphasis is on wide selection and self-service.

supermarkets Large retail stores that offer a variety of food and food-related items divided into specialized departments.

In contrast, **specialty stores** are small stores that carry one line of related products. They serve specific market segments with full product lines in narrow product fields and often feature knowledgeable sales personnel. Sunglass Hut International, for instance, has 1600 outlets in Canada, the United States, Europe, and Australia that carry a deep selection of competitively priced sunglasses. Retailers who carry an extremely deep selection of goods in a relatively narrow product line and who hire technical experts to give customers advice are called **category killers**. Home Depot and Staples are examples of category killers.

specialty stores Small retail stores that carry one line of related products.

category killers Retailers who carry a deep selection of goods in a narrow product line.

Bargain Retailers

Bargain retailers carry wide ranges of products and come in many forms. The first **discount houses** sold large numbers of items (such as televisions and other appliances) at substantial price reductions to certain customers. As name-brand items became more common, they offered better product assortments while still transacting cash-only sales in low-rent facilities. As they became firmly entrenched, they began moving to better locations, improving decor, and selling better-quality merchandise at higher prices. They also began offering a few department store services, such as credit plans and non-cash sales. Wal-Mart and Zellers are bargain retailers.

bargain retailers Retail outlets that emphasize low prices as a means of attracting consumers.

discount houses Bargain retail stores that offer major items such as televisions and large appliances at discount prices.

catalogue showroom A bargain retail store in which customers place orders for items described in a catalogue and pick up those items from an on-premises warehouse.

Catalogue showrooms use mail catalogues to attract customers into showrooms to view display samples, place orders, and wait briefly while clerks retrieve orders from attached warehouses. **Factory outlets** are manufacturer-owned stores that avoid wholesalers and retailers by selling merchandise directly from factory to consumer. The **warehouse club (or wholesale club)** offers large discounts on a wide range of brand name merchandise to customers who pay annual membership fees. **Convenience stores** such as 7-Eleven and Circle K offer ease of purchase, easily accessible locations, extended store hours, and speedy service. They differ from most bargain retailers in that they do not feature low prices. Like bargain retailers, they control prices by keeping in-store service to a minimum.

factory outlets Bargain retail stores that are owned by the manufacturers whose products they sell.

warehouse club (or wholesale club) Huge, membership-only, combined retail–wholesale operations that sell brand-name merchandise.

convenience stores Retail stores that offer high accessibility, extended hours, and fast service on selected items.

The boxed insert entitled "Green Retailing" describes how retailers are joining the green movement.

The Greening of Business

Green Retailing

When people think about green practices in business, the first thing they typically think about is factories doing something to reduce air and water pollution. But the green movement has become active in both manufacturing and service companies, including the retailing sector. Here are some examples of the green movement in retailing:

- Nature's Path Foods reduced packaging sizes by 10 percent, and this meant a 20 percent reduction in transportation emissions.
- Cities as different as San Francisco, California, and Leaf Rapids, Manitoba, have banned the use of plastic bags; several grocers in Nova Scotia are also considering the move.
- Wal-Mart and other retailers are training their cashiers to ask customers if they even need a bag of any kind.
- In 2007, Loblaw opened four Superstores where customers have to use reusable bags; more than 14 million reusable bags have been sold by Loblaw, and the number of plastic bags given to customers has been reduced by 20 percent.
- Many stores, including IKEA and No Frills, charge customers for plastic bags and try to encourage consumers to stop using the bags.

Canadians use 55 million plastic bags each week. While they are convenient, they also cause problems. Because they are derived from oil, they can take up to 1000 years to degrade. Even when they do degrade, the toxins they contain get into the soil. They are also an eyesore when they blow around landfills and elsewhere.

Mountain Equipment Co-op (MEC) wants to convince customers to stop using disposable bags altogether, so it makes a five-cent donation to environmental groups each time a customer declines to take a plastic bag. Between 2006 and 2008, MEC contributed $207 000 to environmental groups as a result of the program. MEC also offers compostable bags to its customers. These bags, which are eaten by micro-organisms and become compost, are even more environmentally friendly than biodegradable bags (which are still out there in the environment even after they degrade).

Reusable cloth bags and collapsible plastic crates are increasing in popularity as substitutes for plastic bags. Most major retailers sell them. One really green alternative is reusable bags that are themselves made from recycled plastic bottles.

It is not just retailers who are trying to change consumer behaviour. Consumers are also starting to demand that retailers provide more eco-friendly packaging that is biodegradable, recycled, or reusable. One alternative to traditional plastic bottles is corn-derived PLA polymer. Another is polyethylene terephthalate plastic bottles, which can be produced from recycled material. And remember that old-fashioned glass is 100 percent recyclable. Consumers want less packaging overall, whatever type it is.

Critical Thinking Questions

1. All things considered, which type of shopping bag is best: plastic, paper, or reusable cloth?

Non-store Retailing

Not all goods and services are sold in stores. In fact, some retailers sell all or most of their products without bricks-and-mortar stores. For example, certain types of consumer goods—soft drinks, candy, and cigarettes—lend themselves to distribution in *vending machines*. Non-store retailing also includes **direct-response retailing**, in which firms contact customers directly to inform them about products and to take sales orders. **Mail order (or catalogue marketing)** is a popular form of direct-response retailing. So is **telemarketing**—the use of the telephone to sell directly.

The oldest form of direct-response retailing is **direct selling**, which is still used by companies that sell door-to-door or through home-selling parties. Avon Products has more than four million sales reps in 100 different countries[19], and Tupperware has more than 60 000 salespeople in Russia alone.[20] The Fuller Brush Company, which was started in 1906 by Arthur Fuller, a self-described

direct-response retailing A type of retailing in which firms make direct contact with customers both to inform them about products and to receive sales orders.

mail order (or catalogue marketing) A form of non-store retailing in which customers place orders for merchandise shown in catalogues and receive their orders via mail.

telemarketing Use of the telephone to sell directly to consumers.

direct selling Form of non-store retailing typified by door-to-door sales.

"country bumpkin" from Nova Scotia, used to be well-known in door-to-door selling. But sweeping changes in North American society—women leaving the home to work, mass retailing, and the globalization of business—caused the company to fall on hard times. Two of its most famous salespeople were the Reverend Billy Graham and disc jockey Dick Clark.

e-intermediaries Internet-based distribution-channel members that collect information about sellers and present it in convenient form to consumers and/or help deliver internet products to consumers.

An increasingly important category of non-store retailing includes **e-intermediaries**—internet-based channel members who perform one or both of the following functions: (1) They collect information about sellers and provide it for consumers, or (2) they help deliver internet products to buyers. We will examine three types of e-intermediaries—*syndicated sellers, shopping agents*, and *eretailers*.

Syndicated Sellers

syndicated selling Occurs when a website offers other websites a commission for referring customers.

Syndicated selling occurs when one website offers another a commission for referring customers. For example, Expedia's webpage shows a list of car rental companies, and when Expedia customers click on, say, the Dollar banner for a car rental, they are transferred from the Expedia site to the Dollar site. Dollar pays Expedia a fee for each booking that comes through this channel. Although the new intermediary increases the cost of Dollar's supply chain, it adds value for customers because they are efficiently guided to a car-rental agency.[21]

Shopping Agents

shopping agent (e-agent) A type of intermediary that helps internet consumers by gathering and sorting information they need to make purchases.

Shopping agents (e-agents) help internet consumers by gathering and sorting information. Although they don't take possession of products, they know which websites and stores to visit, give accurate comparison prices, identify product features, and help consumers complete transactions by presenting information in a usable format—all in a matter of seconds. PriceScan.com is a well-known cyber-shopping agent. Since e-agents have become so plentiful, unsure shoppers are turning to rating sites, such as eSmarts.com, that evaluate and compare e-agents.

Ecommerce intermediaries called *business-to-business (B2B) brokers* have also emerged for business customers. The pricing process between B2B buyers and sellers of commodities can be outsourced, for example, to an internet company like FreeMarkets Inc. (which merged with Ariba). As a pricing broker, FreeMarkets links any large-volume buyer with potential suppliers that bid to become the supplier for the industrial customer. Client companies (the commodity buyers), such as Quaker Oats or Emerson Electric, pay FreeMarkets a fixed annual subscription fee and receive networking into FreeMarkets's auction headquarters, where real-time bids come in from suppliers at remote locations. The website (www.freemarkets.com) provides up-to-date information until the bidding ends with the low-price supplier. In conducting the pricing transactions electronically, FreeMarkets doesn't take possession of any products. Rather, it brings together timely information and links businesses to one another.[22]

Electronic Retailing

electronic retailing (etailing) Allows consumers to shop from home using the internet.

Electronic retailing (also called *etailing*) allows consumers to shop from home using the internet. Sears Canada, one of the most popular etailers in Canada, offers more than 10 000 items for sale on its website.[23] Etailing is made possible by communications networks that let sellers post product information on consumers' PCs. Electronic retailing includes *electronic catalogues, internet-based stores, electronic storefronts and cybermalls*, and *interactive and video marketing*.

Electronic Catalogues. **Ecatalogues** use the internet to display products for both retail and business customers. Using electronic displays (instead of traditional mail catalogues), firms give millions of users instant access to pages of product information. The seller avoids mail-distribution and printing costs, and once an online catalogue is in place, there is little cost in maintaining and accessing it. Popular consumer ecatalogues include JCPenney, L.L.Bean, and Victoria's Secret. Top B2B ecatalogues include Dell Computer and Office Depot.[24]

ecatalogues Non-store retailing that uses the internet to display products and services for both retail shoppers and business customers.

Internet-Based Stores. In 2007, Canadians bought $12.8 billion worth of goods and services over the internet. That was up 61 percent from just two years earlier. As large as these numbers seem, they still represent only about 1.5 percent of the $853 billion that consumers spent on goods and services in 2007.[25] Ice.com, a Montreal-based company, is a typical internet-based store. It sells mid- and low-priced jewellery over the internet to mostly U.S. customers. The company is profitable because it deals in products that are high value, high margin, small size, and easy to ship to customers.[26] Using the internet to do *comparison shopping* is increasing rapidly. Internet sites like Ask Jeeves Inc., Google Inc., and Yahoo! Inc. allow consumers to compare prices and products before making a purchase.

Approximately 32 000 Canadians make a significant portion of their annual income by selling goods and services on eBay alone. These "small retailers" who use sites like eBay, Kijiji, and Craigslist often do not pay income tax or sales tax on their sales, so both the Canada Revenue Agency and the federal government are losing millions of dollars in tax revenues each year. The Federal Court of Appeal has ordered eBay to provide information on people who sell more than $1000 per month on its site.[27] eBay is also planning to retreat from its recently adopted strategy of selling new goods over the internet and will return to its original strategy of being the web's flea market.[28]

Electronic Storefronts and Cybermalls. Today, a seller's website is an **electronic storefront** (or *virtual storefront*) from which consumers collect information about products and buying opportunities, place orders, and pay for purchases. Producers of large product lines, such as Dell Computer, dedicate storefronts to their own product lines. Other sites, such as CDNOW, which offers CDs and audio and videotapes, are category sellers whose storefronts feature products from many manufacturers.

electronic storefront A seller's website in which consumers collect information about products and buying opportunities, place sales orders, and pay for their purchases.

Search engines like Yahoo! serve as **cybermalls**—collections of virtual storefronts representing diverse products. After entering a cybermall, shoppers can navigate by choosing from a list of stores (L.L.Bean or Lands' End), product listings (computers or MP3 players), or departments (apparel or bath/beauty). When your virtual shopping cart is full, you check out and pay your bill. The value-added properties of cybermalls are obvious—speed, convenience, 24-hour access, and efficient searching.

cybermalls Collections of virtual storefronts representing diverse products.

From Door-to-Door to Esales? Not surprisingly, cyberspace is encroaching on door-to-door distribution. Amway is famous for a **multilevel marketing** channel in which self-employed distributors get commissions for recruiting new customers and new Amway reps. Now Amway is expanding this system to the internet with a spinoff called Quixstar. With help from Quixstar, you can start your own at-home internet business. You will be paid for directing new customers to the Quixstar site and for encouraging others to become Quixstar reps. The internet's huge at-home sales potential is also luring other famous door-to-door names—Tupperware, Avon, and Mary Kay. Such firms are racing to board the internet train even though they are courting potential channel conflict. Thousands of loyal door-to-door sales reps stand to lose customers to their own companies' internet outlets.[29]

multilevel marketing A system in which salespeople earn a commission on their own sales and on the sales of any other salespeople they recruit.

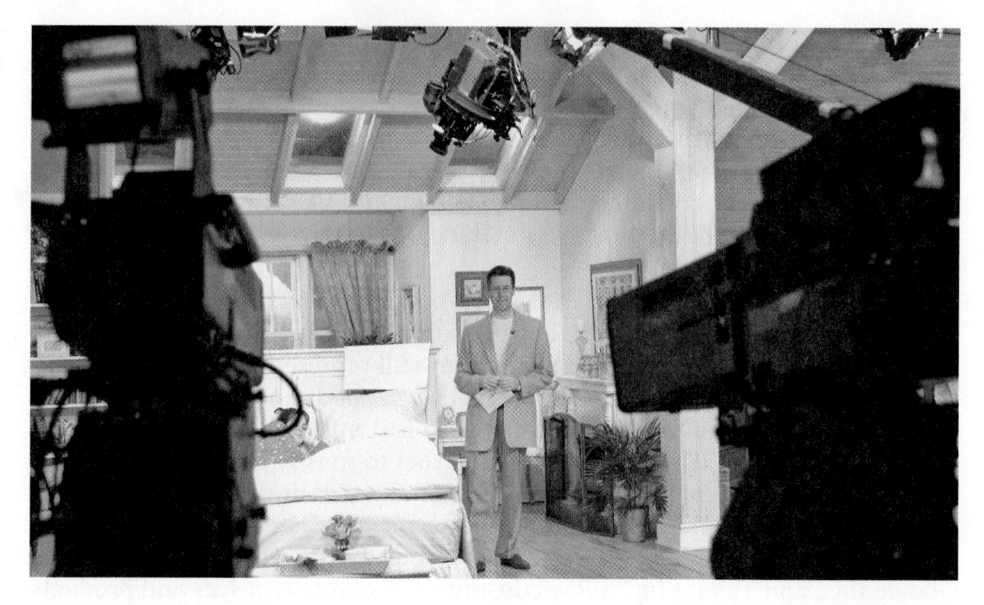

Veteran QVC host Bob Bowersox is getting ready to offer bedding made by a company called Northern Lights, which distributes regularly through the TV home-shopping channel. Northern Lights, which sells sheets, pillows, and other bedding products, markets through such electronic retailing outlets as eBay and Shopping.com, as well as QVC.

interactive marketing Selling products and services by allowing customers to interact with multimedia websites using voice, graphics, animation, film clips, and access to live human advice.

video marketing Selling to consumers by showing products on television that consumers can buy by telephone or mail.

Interactive and Video Marketing. Both retail and B2B customers interact with multimedia sites using voice, graphics, animation, film clips, and access to live human advice. One good example of **interactive marketing** is LivePerson.com, a leading provider of real-time sales and customer service for over 3000 websites. When customers log on to the sites of Toyota, Earthlink, Hewlett-Packard, Verizon, Microsoft—all of which are LivePerson clients—they can enter a live chat room where a service operator initiates a secure one-on-one text chat. Questions and answers go back and forth to help customers get answers to specific questions before deciding on a product. Another form of interaction is the so-called banner ad that changes as the user's mouse moves about the page, revealing new drop-down, check, and search boxes.[30]

Video marketing, a long-established form of interactive marketing, lets viewers shop at home from TV screens by phoning in or emailing orders. Most cable systems offer video marketing through home-shopping channels that display and demonstrate products and allow viewers to phone in or email orders. One U.S. network, QVC, also operates in the United Kingdom, Germany, Mexico, and South America.

Physical Distribution

6 Define *physical distribution* and describe the major activities in *warehousing* operations.

physical distribution Those activities needed to move a product from the manufacturer to the end-consumer.

warehousing That part of the distribution process concerned with storing goods.

Physical distribution refers to the activities needed to move products efficiently from manufacturer to consumer. The goals of physical distribution are to keep customers satisfied, to make goods available when and where consumers want them, and to keep costs low. Physical distribution includes *warehousing* and *transportation operations*, as well as *distribution for ecustomers*.

Warehousing Operations

Storing, or **warehousing**, is a major part of distribution management. In selecting a strategy, managers must keep in mind both the different characteristics and costs of warehousing operations.

Types of Warehouses

There are two basic types of warehouses—*private* and *public*. Facilities can be further divided according to use as *storage warehouses* or *distribution centres*.

Public and Private Warehouses. **Public warehouses** are independently owned and operated. Because companies rent only the space they need, they are popular with firms needing storage only during peak periods. Manufacturers who need multiple storage locations to get products to multiple markets also use public warehouses. **Private warehouses** are owned by a single manufacturer, wholesaler, or retailer. Most are run by large firms that deal in mass quantities and need regular storage.

public warehouse An independently owned and operated warehouse that stores the goods of many firms.

private warehouse A warehouse owned and used by just one company.

Storage Warehouses and Distribution Centres. **Storage warehouses** provide storage for extended periods. Producers of seasonal items, such as agricultural crops, use this type of warehouse. **Distribution centres** provide short-term storage of products whose demand is both constant and high. Retail chains, wholesalers, and manufacturers who need to break down large quantities of merchandise into the smaller quantities that stores or customers demand also use them. Distribution centres are common in the grocery and food industry. Kellogg's, for example, stores virtually no products at its plants. Instead, it ships cereals from factories to regional distribution centres.

storage warehouse A warehouse used to provide storage of goods for extended periods of time.

distribution centre A warehouse used to provide storage of goods for only short periods before they are shipped to retail stores.

Warehousing Costs

Typical warehouse costs include such obvious expenses as storage-space rental or mortgage payments (usually computed on a square-foot basis), insurance, and wages. They also include the costs of *inventory control and materials handling*.

Inventory Control. **Inventory control** means ensuring that an adequate supply of a product is in stock at all times, while avoiding an excessive inventory of supplies.

inventory control The part of warehouse operations that keeps track of what is on hand and ensures adequate supplies of products are in stock at all times.

Materials Handling. Most warehouse personnel are involved in **materials handling**—the transportation, arrangement, and orderly retrieval of inventoried goods. Holding down materials-handling costs requires making decisions about product placement within the warehouse as well as decisions about whether to store products as individual units, in multiple packages, or in sealed containers. A **unitization** strategy calls for standardizing the weight and form of materials. A GE warehouse, for example, receives apartment-size refrigerators from Europe in containers of 56 refrigerators each. Dealing with the huge containers rather than individual boxes not only makes handling easier but also reduces theft and damage. It also optimizes shipping space and makes restocking easier.

materials handling The transportation and arrangement of goods within a warehouse and orderly retrieval of goods from inventory.

unitization Standardizing the weight and form of materials.

Transportation Operations

The major transportation modes are rail, water, truck, air, and pipeline. In the early part of the twentieth century, railroads dominated the Canadian transportation system, but by the 1970s, truck and air transportation had become important as well. Using operating revenue as the criterion, the most important modes of transportation in Canada are now trucks, air, and rail.

Compare the five basic forms of *transportation* and explain how distribution can be used as a marketing strategy. **7**

Cost is a major factor when a company chooses a transportation method, but it is not the only consideration. A company must also consider the nature of its products, the distance the product must travel, timeliness, and customers' needs. A company shipping orchids or other perishable goods will probably use air transport, while a company shipping sand or coal will use rail or water transport.

Transportation Modes

Each of the major transportation modes has advantages and disadvantages. Key differences in cost are most directly related to delivery speed.

Trucks. The advantages of trucks include flexibility, fast service, and dependability. All sections of Canada except the Far North can be reached by truck. Trucks are a particularly good choice for short-distance distribution and more expensive products. Large furniture and appliance retailers in major cities, for example, use trucks to shuttle merchandise between their stores and to make deliveries to customers. Trucks can, however, be delayed by bad weather. They also are limited in the volume they can carry in a single load.

Planes. Air is the fastest available transportation mode, and in Canada's Far North, it may be the *only* available transportation. Other advantages include greatly reduced costs in packing, handling, unpacking, and final preparations necessary for sale to the consumer. Also, eliminating the need to store certain commodities can reduce inventory-carrying costs. Fresh fish, for example, can be flown to restaurants each day, avoiding the risk of spoilage that comes with packaging and storing. However, air freight is the most expensive form of transportation.

Railroads. Railroads have been the backbone of the Canadian transportation system since the late 1800s. Until the 1960s, when trucking firms lowered their rates and attracted many customers, railroads carried a wide variety of products. Railroads are now used primarily to transport heavy, bulky items such as cars, steel, and coal.

Water Carriers. Of all the transportation modes, transportation by water is the least expensive. Unfortunately, it is also the slowest. Boats and barges are mainly used for extremely heavy, bulky materials and products (like sand, gravel, oil, and steel) for which transit times are relatively unimportant. The St. Lawrence Seaway is a vital link in Canada's domestic water transportation system. Water transportation is also important in Canada's Far North, where barges deliver commodities such as fuel oil to isolated hamlets along the western edge of Hudson's Bay during the summer months. Northern Transportation Company Ltd. moves freight on the Athabasca River because of demand created by the oil sands projects in Northern Alberta.[31] In international trade, manufacturers often use water carriers for long distance ocean transportation because many ships are now specially constructed to load and store large standardized containers.

Pipelines. Traditionally, pipelines have transported liquids and gases, and they provide a constant flow of these products and are unaffected by weather conditions. Like water transportation, pipelines are slow in terms of overall delivery time. They also have a lack of adaptability to other products, and limited routes make pipelines a relatively unimportant transportation method for most industries.

Changes in Transportation Operations

For many years, transport companies specialized in one mode or another. With deregulation, however, this pattern has changed. New developments in cost-efficiency and competitiveness include *intermodal transportation*, *containerization*, and *order fulfillment through ecommerce channels*.

intermodal transportation The combined use of different modes of transportation.

Intermodal Transportation. The combined use of different modes of transportation—**intermodal transportation**—has come into widespread use. For example, shipping by a combination of truck and rail ("piggyback"), water and rail ("fishyback"), or air and rail ("birdyback") has improved flexibility and reduced costs.

A container train crosses the Salmon River bridge in New Brunswick.

Containerization. To make intermodal transport more efficient, **containerization** uses standardized heavy-duty containers into which many items are sealed at point of shipment; the containers are opened only at their final destination. Containers may be stowed on ships for ocean transit, transferred to trucks, loaded onto railcars, and delivered to final destinations by other trucks. Unloaded containers are then returned for future use.

containerization The use of standardized heavy-duty containers in which many items are sealed at the point of shipment; they are opened only at the final destination.

Order Fulfillment Through Ecommerce Channels. New ecommerce companies often focus on sales, only to discover that delays in after-sale distribution cause customer dissatisfaction. **Order fulfillment** begins when the sale is made and involves getting the product to each customer in good condition and on time. But the volume of a firm's transactions can be huge, and fulfillment performance—in terms of timing, content, and terms of payment—has been disappointing for many ebusinesses.

order fulfillment All activities involved in completing a sales transaction, beginning with making the sale and ending with on-time delivery to the customer.

To improve on-time deliveries, many businesses, such as Amazon.com, maintain distribution centres and ship from their own warehouses. Other etailers, however, entrust order-filling to distribution specialists such as UPS. The clients of Atomic Box, a much smaller company, range from manufacturers to dot-coms that prefer to concentrate on selling while outsourcing logistics and storage activities. The company maintains 325 000 square feet of warehousing through which it annually delivers products worth more than $200 million. It handles the flow of goods and information in both B2B and business-to-consumer transactions.

Companies like Atomic Box and UPS process customer orders, ship goods, provide information about product availability, inform customers about the real-time status of their orders, and handle returns. To perform these tasks, the client's computer system must be integrated with that of the distribution specialist. In deciding whether to build their own distribution centres or to use third-party distributors, clients must consider fixed costs as well as the need for shipping expertise. Because the capital investment required for a 1-million-square-foot distribution centre is $60 to $80 million, only high-volume companies can afford it. The alternative is paying a third-party distributor about 10 percent of each sale to fulfill orders.[32]

Companies Specializing in Transportation

The major modes of transportation are available from one or more of four types of transporting companies: *common carriers*, *freight forwarders*, *contract carriers*, and *private carriers*.

common carriers Transportation companies that transport goods for any firm or individual wishing to make a shipment.

Common carriers transport merchandise for any shipper—manufacturers, wholesalers, retailers, and even individual consumers. They maintain regular schedules and charge competitive prices. The best examples of common carriers are truck lines and railroads.

freight forwarders Common carriers that lease bulk space from other carriers and resell that space to firms making small shipments.

Not all transportation companies own their own vehicles. A **freight forwarder** is a common carrier that leases bulk space from other carriers, such as railroads or airlines. It then resells parts of that space to smaller shippers. Once it has enough contracts to fill the bulk space, the freight forwarder picks up whatever merchandise is to be shipped. It then transports the goods to the bulk carrier, which makes delivery to an agreed-on destination and handles billing and any inquiries concerning the shipment.

contract carriers Independent transporters who contract to serve as transporters for industrial customers only.

Some transportation companies will transport products for any firm for a contracted amount and time period. These **contract carriers** are usually self-employed operators who own the vehicle that transports the products. When they have delivered a contracted load to its destination, they generally try to locate another contract shipment (often with a different manufacturer) for the return trip.

private carriers Transportation systems owned by the shipper.

A few manufacturers and retailers maintain their own transportation systems (usually a fleet of trucks) to carry their own products. The use of such **private carriers** is generally limited to very large manufacturers such as Kraft Foods and Canada Safeway.

Distribution as a Marketing Strategy

Distribution is an increasingly important way of competing for sales. Instead of just offering advantages in product features and quality, price, and promotion, many firms have turned to distribution as a cornerstone of their business strategies. This approach means assessing and improving the entire stream of activities—wholesaling, warehousing, and transportation—involved in getting products to customers.

The Use of Hubs

hubs Central distribution outlets that control all or most of a firm's distribution activities.

One approach to streamlining is the use of **hubs**—central distribution outlets that control all or most of a firm's distribution activities. Two contrasting strategies have emerged from this approach: *supply-side and "pre-staging" hubs* on the one hand and *distribution-side hubs* on the other.

Supply-Side and "Pre-staging" Hubs. *Supply-side hubs* are located at the same site where production activities take place. They make sense when large shipments flow regularly to a single industrial user, such as an automobile manufacturer. But these incoming shipments can create a lot of congestion, so some firms use *pre-staging hubs*, which are located near the factory. For example, Saturn maintains a pre-staging hub—managed by Ryder System—where all incoming material is organized to ensure that Saturn's production schedule at the factory is not disrupted. At the hub, long-haul tractors are disconnected from trailers and sent on return trips to any of 339 suppliers in many different geographical areas. Responding to Saturn's up-to-the-minute needs, hub headquarters arranges transport for pre-sorted and pre-inspected materials to the factory by loading them onto specially designed tractors.

The chief job of the hub, then, is to coordinate the customer's materials needs with supply-chain transportation. If the hub is successful, factory inventories are virtually eliminated, storage-space requirements are reduced, and long-haul trucks are kept moving instead of being queued up at the unloading dock. By outsourcing distribution activities to its hub, Saturn can focus on what it does best—manufacturing. Meanwhile, Ryder is paid for its special skills in handling transportation flows.

Distribution-Side Hubs. Whereas supply-side hubs are located near industrial customers, *distribution-side hubs* may be located much farther away, especially if customers are geographically dispersed. UPS, for example, has a large distribution-side hub at Burlington, Ontario.[33] National Semiconductor, one of the world's largest chip makers, airfreights chips worldwide from a single centre in Singapore.

Test yourself on the material for this chapter at **www.pearsoned.ca/mybusinesslab**.

Summary of Learning Objectives

1. **Identify the various *pricing objectives* that govern pricing decisions and describe the price-setting tools used in making these decisions.** *Pricing objectives* are the goals that producers hope to achieve as a result of pricing decisions. These objectives may include (1) pricing to maximize profits, and (2) pricing to achieve *market share* objectives. Sometimes, neither profit maximizing nor market share is the best objective. During difficult economic times, loss containment and survival may be the main objectives. Managers use two basic pricing tools, which are often combined: (1) *cost-oriented pricing,* and (2) *break-even analysis.* Break-even analysis assesses total costs versus revenues for various sales volumes. It shows, at any particular sales price, the financial result—the amount of loss or profit—for each possible sales volume.

2. **Discuss *pricing strategies* and tactics for existing and new products.** There are three *strategies* for pricing existing products: (1) pricing above the market, (2) pricing below the market, (3) and pricing at or near the market. Companies pricing new products must often choose between two pricing policy options: (1) *price skimming* (setting an initially high price), or (2) *penetration pricing* (setting an initially low price).

   Regardless of its pricing strategy, a company may adopt various *pricing tactics,* including *price lining* (offering all items in certain categories at a limited number of prices), *psychological pricing* (taking advantage of the fact that customers are not completely rational when making buying decisions), and using *discounts* to stimulate sales.

3. **Explain the distribution mix, the different *channels of distribution,* and different *distribution strategies.*** The *distribution mix* refers to the combination of distribution channels a firm selects to get a product to end-users. In selecting a distribution mix, a firm may use all or any of eight distribution channels. The first four are aimed at getting products to consumers, the fifth is for consumers or business customers, and the last three are aimed at getting products to business customers (see Figure 17.2). There are three basic *distribution strategies:* (1) *intensive* (make products available in as many outlets as possible), (2) *selective* (make products available in a few outlets), and (3) *exclusive* (make products available in only one outlet in a geographic area).

4. **Explain the differences between *merchant wholesalers* and *agents/brokers,* and describe the activities of e-intermediaries.** *Merchant wholesalers* buy products from manufacturers (i.e., they take title to the products) and sell them to other businesses, usually providing storage and delivery. A *full-service merchant wholesaler* also provides credit, marketing, and merchandising. *Limited-function merchant wholesalers* provide only a few services, sometimes merely storage. *Agents and brokers* are independent representatives of many companies and work on commissions. They serve as sales and merchandising arms of producers that don't have sales forces.

   E-intermediaries are internet-based channel members who perform one or both of two functions: (1) They collect information about sellers and present it to consumers; (2) they help deliver internet products. There are three types of e-intermediaries: *syndicated sellers, shopping agents,* and *business-to-business brokers.*

5. **Identify the different types of *retailing* and *retail stores.*** Retail operations fall under two classifications. (1) *Product line retailers* feature broad product lines. Types of stores

include *department stores* and *supermarkets*, which are divided into departments of related products. Small *specialty stores* serve clearly defined market segments by offering full product lines in narrow product fields. (2) *Bargain retailers* carry wide ranges of products and come in many forms, such as *discount houses, catalogue showrooms, factory outlets, warehouse clubs* (*or wholesale clubs*), and *convenience stores.*

Important forms of non-store retailing include *direct-response retailing, mail order (or catalogue marketing), telemarketing,* and *direct selling. Electronic retailing* uses communications networks that allow sellers to connect to consumers' computers. Sellers provide members with internet access to product displays. Buyers can examine detailed descriptions, compare brands, send for free information, or purchase by credit card. *Ecatalogues* use the internet to display products for both retail and business customers. A seller's website is an *electronic storefront* in which consumers collect information about products, place orders, and pay for purchases. Search engines such as Yahoo! serve as *cybermalls*. In a *multilevel marketing channel,* self-employed distributors get commissions for recruiting new customers and reps. Both retail and B2B customers participate in *interactive marketing. Video marketing* lets viewers shop at home from television screens.

6. **Define *physical distribution* and describe the major activities in *warehousing* operations.** *Physical distribution* (which includes *warehousing*) refers to the activities needed to move products from manufacturer to consumer. These activities make goods available when and where consumers want them, keep costs low, and provide customer services. There are two types of warehouses: *private warehouses* are owned and used by a single manufacturer, wholesaler, or retailer; while *public warehouses* are independently owned and operated and permit companies to rent only the space they need. *Storage warehouses* provide storage for extended periods. *Distribution centres* store products whose market demand is constant and high. Retail chains, wholesalers, and manufacturers use them to break down large quantities of merchandise into the smaller quantities that stores or customers demand. In addition to keeping track of what is on hand at any time, *inventory control* involves the balancing act of ensuring that an adequate supply of a product is in stock at all times and avoiding excessive supplies of inventory. *Materials handling* refers to the transportation, arrangement, and orderly retrieval of inventoried goods.

7. **Compare the five basic forms of *transportation* and explain how distribution can be used as a marketing strategy.** The advantages of trucks include flexibility, fast service, and dependability. Railroads are now used primarily to transport heavy, bulky items such as cars and steel. Air transport is the fastest available mode of transportation but also the most expensive. Transportation by water is the least expensive but the slowest. Pipelines are slow and inflexible, but do provide a constant flow of products and are unaffected by weather. Many firms regard distribution as a cornerstone of business strategy. One approach to streamlining distribution is the use of *hubs*. Supply-side hubs make the most sense when large shipments flow regularly to a single industrial user. To clear congestion, some firms operate pre-staging hubs, at which all incoming supplies are managed to meet production schedules. Whereas supply-side hubs are located near industrial customers, distribution-side hubs may be located much farther away, especially if customers are geographically dispersed. From these facilities, finished products, which may be produced in plants throughout the world, can be shipped to customer locations around the globe.

Key Terms

bargain retailers (p. 566)
break-even analysis (p. 554)
break-even point (p. 554)
cash discount (p. 558)
catalogue showroom (p. 566)
category killers (p. 566)
channel captain (p. 564)
channel conflict (p. 564)
common carriers (p. 574)
containerization (p. 573)
contract carriers (p. 574)
convenience stores (p. 566)
cybermalls (p. 569)
department stores (p. 565)
direct channel (p. 559)
direct selling (p. 567)
direct-response retailing (p. 567)
discount (p. 558)
discount houses (p. 566)
distribution centre (p. 571)
distribution channel (p. 559)
distribution mix (p. 559)
drop shipper (p. 565)
ecatalogues (p. 569)
e-intermediaries (p. 568)
electronic retailing (etailing) (p. 568)
electronic storefront (p. 569)
exclusive distribution (p. 563)
factory outlets (p. 566)
fixed costs (p. 554)
freight forwarders (p. 574)
full-service merchant wholesaler (p. 565)
hubs (p. 574)
industrial (business) distribution (p. 562)
intensive distribution (p. 563)
interactive marketing (p. 570)
intermediary (p. 559)
intermodal transportation (p. 572)
inventory control (p. 571)
limited-function merchant wholesaler (p. 565)
mail order (catalogue marketing) (p. 567)
market share (p. 553)
materials handling (p. 571)
merchant wholesaler (p. 565)
multilevel marketing (p. 569)
odd-even pricing (p. 558)
order fulfillment (p. 573)
penetration pricing (p. 557)
physical distribution (p. 570)
price leadership (p. 557)
price lining (p. 558)
price skimming (p. 557)
pricing (p. 552)
pricing objectives (p. 552)
private carriers (p. 574)
private warehouse (p. 571)
psychological pricing (p. 558)
public warehouse (p. 571)
quantity discount (p. 559)
rack jobber (p. 565)
retailers (p. 559)
sales agents (or brokers) (p. 560)
sales offices (p. 562)
seasonal discount (p. 558)
selective distribution (p. 563)
shopping agent (e-agent) (p. 568)
specialty stores (p. 566)
storage warehouse (p. 571)
supermarkets (p. 566)
syndicated selling (p. 568)
telemarketing (p. 567)
trade discount (p. 558)
unitization (p. 571)
variable costs (p. 554)
vertical marketing system (VMS) (p. 564)
video marketing (p. 570)
warehouse club (wholesale club) (p. 566)
warehousing (p. 570)
wholesalers (p. 559)

Questions for Analysis

1. How do cost-oriented pricing and break-even analysis help managers measure the potential impact of prices?
2. From the manufacturer's point of view, what are the advantages and disadvantages of using intermediaries to distribute products? From the end-user's point of view?
3. In what key ways do the four channels used only for consumer products differ from the channels used only for industrial products?
4. Explain how the activities of e-agents (internet shopping agents) or brokers differ from those of traditional agents/brokers.
5. Suppose that a small publisher selling to book distributors has fixed operating costs of $600 000 each year and variable costs of $3 per book. How many books must the firm sell to break even if the selling price is $6? If the company expects to sell 50 000 books next year and decides on a 40 percent markup, what will the selling price be?
6. Novelties Ltd. produces miniature Canadian flag decals. The fixed costs for their latest project are $5000. The variable costs are $0.70/flag, and the company should be able to sell them for $2 apiece. How many flags must Novelties Ltd. sell to break even? How many flags must the company sell to make a profit of $2000? If the maximum number of flags the company can sell is 5000, should it get involved in this project?
7. Consider the various kinds of non-store retailing. Give examples of two products that typify the kinds of products sold to at-home shoppers through each form of non-store retailing. Are different products best suited to each form of non-store retailing? Explain.
8. A retailer buys a product from a manufacturer for $25 and sells it for $45. What is the markup percentage? Explain what the term *markup percentage* means.
9. Suppose that your company produces industrial products for other firms. How would you go about determining the prices of your products? Describe the method you would use to arrive at a pricing decision.
10. Give three examples (other than those provided in the chapter) of products that use intensive distribution. Do the same for products that use exclusive distribution and selective distribution. For which category was it easiest to find examples? Why?
11. If you could own a firm that transports products, would you prefer to operate an intermodal transportation business or one that specializes in a single mode of transportation (say, truck or air)? Explain your choice.

Application Exercises

1. Select a product with which you are familiar and analyze various possible pricing objectives for it. What information would you want to have if you were to adopt a profit-maximizing objective? A market-share objective? An image objective?
2. Interview the manager of a local manufacturing firm. Identify the firm's distribution strategy and the channels of distribution that it uses. Where applicable, describe the types of wholesalers or retail stores used to distribute the firm's products.
3. Choose any consumer item at your local supermarket and trace the chain of physical distribution activities that brought it to the store shelf.

Building Your Business Skills

Are You Sold on the Net?

The Purpose of the Assignment

To encourage students to consider the value of online retailing as an element in a company's distribution system.

The Situation

As the distribution manager of a privately owned clothing manufacturer specializing in camping gear and outdoor clothing, you are convinced that your product line is perfect for online distribution. However, the owner of the company is reluctant to expand distribution from a successful network of retail stores and a catalogue operation. Your challenge is to convince the boss that retailing via the internet can boost sales.

Assignment

Step 1

Join together with four or five classmates to research the advantages and disadvantages of an online distribution system for your company. Among the factors to consider are the following:

- The likelihood that target consumers are internet shoppers. Young, affluent consumers who are comfortable with the web generally purchase camping gear.
- The industry trend to online distribution. Are similar companies doing it? Have they been successful?
- The opportunity to expand inventory without increasing the cost of retail space or catalogue production and mailing charges.
- The opportunity to have a store that never closes.
- The lack of trust many people have about doing business on the web. Many consumers are reluctant to provide credit-card data over the web.
- The difficulty that electronic shoppers have in finding a website when they do not know the store's name.
- The frustration and waiting time involved in web searches.
- The certainty that the site will not reach consumers who do not use computers or who are uncomfortable with the web.

Step 2

Based on your findings, write a persuasive memo to the company's owner stating your position about expanding to an online distribution system. Include information that will counter expected objections.

Questions for Discussion

1. What place does online distribution have in the distribution network of this company?
2. In your view, is online distribution the wave of the future? Is it likely to increase in importance as a distribution system for apparel companies? Why or why not?

Exercising Your Ethics: Team Exercise

The Chain of Responsibility

The Situation

Because several stages are involved when distribution chains move products from supply sources to end-consumers, the process offers ample opportunity for ethical issues to arise. This exercise encourages you to examine some of the ethical issues that can emerge during transactions among suppliers and customers.

The Dilemma

A customer bought an expensive wedding gift at a local store and asked that it be shipped to the bride in another province. Several weeks after the wedding, the customer

contacted the bride, who had not confirmed the arrival of the gift. It hadn't arrived. Charging that the merchandise had not been delivered, the customer requested a refund from the retailer. The store manager uncovered the following facts:

- All shipments from the store are handled by a well-known national delivery firm.
- The delivery firm verified that the package had been delivered to the designated address two days after the sale.
- Normally, the delivery firm does not obtain recipient signatures; deliveries are made to the address of record, regardless of the name on the package.

The gift giver argued that even though the package had been delivered to the right address, it had not been delivered to the named recipient. It turns out that, unbeknownst to the gift giver, the bride had moved. It stood to reason, then, that the gift was in the hands of the new occupant at the bride's former address. The manager informed the gift giver that the store had fulfilled its obligation. The cause of the problem, she explained, was the incorrect address given by the customer. She refused to refund the customer's money and suggested that the customer might want to recover the gift by contacting the stranger who received it at the bride's old address.

Team Activity

Assemble a group of four students and assign each group member to one of the following roles:

- customer (the person who had originally purchased the gift)
- employee (of the store where the gift was purchased)
- bride (the person who was supposed to receive the gift)
- customer service manager (of the delivery company)

Questions for Discussion

1. Before discussing the situation with your group, and from the perspective of your assigned role, do you think there are any ethical issues in this situation? If so, write them down.
2. Before discussing the situation with your group, and from the perspective of your assigned role, decide how this dispute should be resolved.
3. Together with your group, share the ethical issues that were identified. What responsibilities does each party—the customer, the store, and the delivery company—have in this situation?
4. What does your group recommend be done to resolve this dispute? What are the advantages and disadvantages of your recommendations?

For additional cases and exercise material, go to **www.pearsoned.ca/mybusinesslab.**

Concluding Case 17-1

This Distribution Net's for You

For many years, two Canadian beer brands—Molson Canadian and Labatt's Blue—have been locked in an intense battle for market share dominance in the Canadian market. But now there is a new brand that just may be the top-selling beer in Canada. That beer is Budweiser, which is brewed by Labatt as part of an agreement with Anheuser-Busch (AB) of St. Louis, Missouri. Those familiar with the beer industry estimate that Molson has about 11 percent of the Canadian market, and Labatt has about 20 percent (11 percent from Budweiser and about 9 percent from Blue). The talk in the industry is that Molson Canadian is a brand in crisis because of competition from various sources, including American beers, cheap discount beers, chic micro-breweries, and trendy imports.

This development may come as an unpleasant surprise to Canadians, but if you ask beer connoisseurs to name the world's largest-selling brand, they'll likely say Budweiser. The secret to AB's market leadership is a combination of factors: good-tasting products, four generations of brand development and recognition, and a superior distribution system that has become a formidable competitive weapon. AB's state-of-the-art distribution system is a cornerstone in Budweiser's marketing strategy.

BudNet, AB's nationwide data network, is a space-age information technology that's integrated into AB's long-established distribution channel. The information technology and the distribution network, working together, are part and parcel of a strategy for moving product to more consumers. While sales reps from AB's 700 beer distributors continue with traditional services—convincing retailers to put more Bud products on the shelf, order taking, rearranging displays, restocking shelves, and installing promotional materials and displays—they also gather real-time data that AB uses for product promotions and sales strategies.

Here's how they do it. First, the several thousand sales reps and drivers for AB wholesalers are the eyes and ears of the system. When reps visit customer stores, they bring book-size, hand-held PCs and scanners for gathering retail sales data. Commenting on using the PC in a customer's store, sales rep Derek Gurden says, "First I'll scroll through and check accounts receivable, make sure everything's current. Then it'll show me an inventory screen with a four-week history. I get past sales, package placements—facts and numbers on how much of the sales they did when they had a display in a certain location." But information doesn't stop with just AB products: Gurden walks through the store noting what competitors are doing—product displays, shelf space, packaging—inputting what he sees in painstaking detail. "Honestly? I think I know more about these guys' businesses than they do. At least in the beer section," says Gurden.

Connecting their PCs to a cellphone, the reps transmit marketing data along with new sales orders to the warehouse, where the distributor compiles the data, then transmits it daily to AB corporate headquarters, where marketing specialists analyze it to see what beer lovers are buying. They know how much the consumer pays, time of sales, whether it's in bottles or cans, cold or warm, and the kind of store, all correlated with recent sales promotions for each sale. The accumulated data are stored in a digital "data warehouse" for fast retrieval and scientific analysis of consumer behaviour. Using the detailed analysis possible with data mining, computers comb through possible matchups between different sales promotions and consumer buying patterns, along with competitors' marketing actions, so brand managers can design marketing promotions to suit the ethnic makeup of various markets. The resulting new promotional plans are entered into BudNet, where distributors log on daily to get the latest recommendations for store displays and stock rotations. The results—AB's steadily increasing market share—seem to confirm what August Busch IV, president for domestic operations, told a recent gathering of distributors: "Brewers and wholesalers with a clear, data-driven focus will have a distinct competitive advantage."

In 2004, AB reached its highest domestic market share ever in the United States: 50.1 percent—more than two and a half times the volume of Miller Brewing Company, the second largest U.S. brewer. And, as noted earlier, AB is also doing very well in Canada. This lofty market position in both countries stems from BudNet's technology, with up-to-the-minute information on consumer buying patterns and competitors' distribution and sales activities. It replaces slow-moving weekly or monthly written reports that once flowed from retailer to wholesaler to brewer, a practice that still exists at some of AB's competitors. By providing current field intelligence to its marketing specialists, wholesaler reps are essential in AB's "Seamless Selling" program, a strategy for removing barriers between brewer, wholesalers, and retailers.

Seamless Selling energizes the entire supply chain for fast reaction in moving millions of barrels of brew annually in the right varieties of customer-ready packages from brewer to consumer. Using product managers' overnight analysis of what products consumers will buy in different kinds of stores—convenience stores, supermarkets, spirits shops, restaurants—and in various geographic regions and neighbourhoods, AB's distribution network responds with next-day deliveries.

BudNet's evolution is no accident. In 1997, chairman August Busch III announced AB's commitment to industry leadership in mining customers' buying patterns, with a technology investment costing $100 million. Since then, comments Joe Patti, vice-president for retail planning, "Wholesaler and store-level data have become the lifeblood of our organization."

The introduction of hand-held PCs provides greater efficiencies at the distributor level, too, for day-to-day scheduling of deliveries to retail stores. Before PCs, sales orders were accumulated from store to store throughout the day and delivered at day's end from sales reps to the warehouse. Sorting through large batches of orders presented a huge surge in evening workload and warehouse congestion, causing excessive time to pick products from storage, load them into delivery trucks, maintain accurate warehouse records, and have trucks loaded for delivery starting early the next morning. Even worse, when sales reps were late getting back at day's end, the evening's warehousing activities were delayed, causing costly overtime to load trucks for morning deliveries. With hand-held PCs, congestion has all but vanished. Sales reps communicate in real time with the warehouse, so sales orders flow in throughout the day. In addition to savings on costly overtime, it reduces administrative time in the warehouse and, even more importantly, gives sales reps more time with customers. The resulting increase in distributors' sales improves AB's chances for even greater gains in market share.

Questions for Discussion

1. In what ways has BudNet changed the wholesaler rep's job, as compared to pre-BudNet days?
2. Among the eight channels of distribution described in the text, which channel is used for distributing Anheuser-Busch products? Do you think another channel might be better?
3. Considering the roles and activities of each member in the distribution channel, which channel member is the channel captain? Explain your reasoning.
4. What are the warehousing activities performed by AB wholesalers? What are their transportation activities?
5. In what specific ways does BudNet remove barriers between brewer, wholesalers, and retailers so that the supply chain is more effective than before?

Concluding Case 17-2

Changing Distribution Channels in the Music Business

Physical distribution of music in the form of CDs is rapidly declining, and digital distribution of music is rapidly increasing. A 2008 report by PricewaterhouseCoopers LLP predicts that by 2011 physical music sales in Canada will decline to just $275 million. That's down from $572 million in 2007. The study also predicts that by 2011 digital sales from sites such as iTunes will increase to $366 million. Thus, sometime in 2010 more music will be distributed digitally than physically.

The increase in digital music delivery has been dramatic. In 2007, digital music sales were just $122 million in Canada. That was only one-quarter of the volume of physical music sales. Music piracy is getting worse as consumers share music on the internet, and this is hastening the decline of physical music sales (which declined 11.9 percent in 2006 and 19.8 percent in 2007). In response to these declines, record stores have shifted their emphasis away from CDs and toward DVDs and video games.

The evolution of retail music sales shows how dramatically changes in technology can influence channels of distribution. For decades, consumers visited music stores, looked over the merchandise, and then decided what to buy (originally breakable records, then vinyl records, then eight-track tapes, then cassettes, and finally CDs). Then came internet stores offering thousands of titles among CDs and cassettes. Customers searched the lists, placed orders electronically or over the phone, and then received their music by mail.

Then came an online music service called Napster, where customers downloaded free software onto their computers that allowed them to put their music on Napster's website and trade with anyone else who was live on the internet at the same time. Not surprisingly, recording industry executives were not impressed with this new channel of distribution. They argued that file-sharing denied music artists the royalties they were due. The threat from Napster was seen as so great that the Recording Industry Association of America (RIAA) decided to prosecute. The courts soon shut Napster down for copyright infringement. But the victory was short-lived, and other file-sharing services like Morpheus, Kazaa, and Grokster popped up.

To combat illegal downloading, the recording industry launched two online music services—MusicNet and Pressplay. If customers used MusicNet, they paid $9.95 a month and got 100 downloads (but they couldn't copy them, and the deal expired at the end of the month). If they used Pressplay, they got 100 downloads for $24.95 per month (and the right to burn 20 tracks to a CD). Other similar services are offered by iTunes (the industry leader), Microsoft, Yahoo!, and a rejuvenated Napster.

The recording industry also filed lawsuits against Grokster and StreamCast Networks (the makers of Morpheus), and in 2005 the U.S. Supreme Court ruled that the entertainment industry could sue companies like Grokster and Morpheus. A few months later, Grokster agreed to shut down and pay $50 million to settle piracy complaints by the music industry. Grokster then announced plans to launch a legal service called 3G, which would require customers to pay a fee to get access to songs that could be downloaded.

In 2009, a Swedish court delivered another blow to illegal file-sharing when it found four men guilty of illegally posting online a pirated copy of the film *X-Men Origins: Wolverine*. Their website—called Pirate Bay—indexed songs, movies, and TV shows. It is visited by more than 22 million people each day. The men were sentenced to one year in jail and ordered to pay $3.6 million in damages to various entertainment companies.

But will the Swedish court ruling stop the illegal downloading of music? Grokster and Morpheus software is in the hands of millions of consumers who can still engage in illegal downloading, and more file-sharing software becomes available all the time. Overseas programmers also offer new software to consumers and they are beyond the reach of the law in North America. A survey by Forrester Research found that 80 percent of consumers who were surveyed said they were not going to stop free downloading.

Music companies should never underestimate how clever consumers can be when they are highly motivated to get something for free. Consider what happened with Apple's iTunes software. There is an option on the software called "share my music," which allows users to make their library of songs available to any other computer running iTunes. The software allows people to listen to other peoples' collection of music but not to copy it. Or so Apple thought when it developed the software. Then, some clever programmers figured out a way to get around the restriction and they started using iTunes software to facilitate illegal downloading.

It is hard to predict how this story will end, but for related developments, see Concluding Case 6-2.

Questions for Discussion

1. Consider the traditional channels of distribution for music albums. Which channel elements are most affected by the presence of services like Grokster, Kazaa, and Morpheus? Explain how those elements are affected.

2. Why is the music industry so concerned about internet distribution? Are there any opportunities for the recording industry in internet distribution?
3. Develop arguments opposing the legality of services offered by Grokster and Morpheus. Then take the reverse position and develop an argument in favour of these services.
4. What types of ethical or social responsibility issues does file-sharing raise?
5. What other products, besides music albums, are the most likely candidates for distribution on the internet, now and in the future?

CBC Video Case 4–1

The "Feel-Better" Bracelet

Q-Ray advertisements say that its "Serious Performance Bracelet is designed to help people play, work, and live better." According to the ads, the $200 bracelet—which makes people feel better by balancing natural positive and negative forces—is ionized using a special secret process. Golfers claim that the bracelet reduces their pain, so *Marketplace* went looking for answers at the golf course. Sandra Post, a champion golfer, is a paid spokesperson for the bracelet. When Wendy Mesley of *Marketplace* interviews her, Post emphasizes the jewellery aspect of the Q-Ray, not its pain-relief qualities. Mesley also interviews golfers Frank and Sam. Frank tells her that the bracelet has reduced his arthritis pain, but Sam (who also wears one of the bracelets) thinks the pain relief is mostly in people's heads.

Advertising that a product provides pain relief is a tricky business. Even though a lot of people wear the Q-Ray for pain relief, the company cannot advertise that its product relieves pain unless there are medical studies that clearly show this. And there are no such studies. Until 2006, people in Q-Ray ads said that the bracelet had cured their pain. But now they can't say that, because the U.S. Federal Trade Commission ruled that such advertising is deceptive.

Andrew Park brought the Q-Ray to North America, and now his son Charles is marketing the product in Canada. Park says that 150 000 Q-Rays have been sold in Canada at a price of $200 each. In an interview with Mesley, Park says that the company does not make pain-relief claims for the product in its advertisements. But then Mesley shows a hidden camera film clip to Park in which he is making a pain-relief claim during the shooting of an infomercial. Park says that he believes that the product reduces pain, and that if you believe the bracelet will relieve your pain, it will. Mesley also plays a hidden camera clip showing retail salespeople telling customers that the Q-Ray reduces the pain of arthritis. Park says he can't control what retailers tell their customers.

Marketplace also asks Christopher Yip, an engineer at the University of Toronto, to test a Q-Ray bracelet to determine if it is ionized. Yip finds that the bracelet does not hold an electrical charge and is therefore not ionized. When Park is confronted with this evidence, he says that he never claimed that the bracelet would hold an electrical charge. Rather, he simply says that the bracelet is ionized using an "exclusive ionization process." Hidden camera film of retail salespeople shows them explaining ionization by saying things like "it picks up the iron in your blood and speeds up circulation" and "negative ions are collected in the ends of the bracelet." Retail salespeople say they aren't sure what ionization is.

Mesley also shows Park a hidden camera interview with the Q-Ray sales coordinator. The coordinator mentions several types of pain that Q-Ray bracelets relieve—migraine, carpal tunnel, and arthritis. Park says that he will have to meet with the sales coordinator and inform her that she cannot make these pain-relief claims.

Questions for Discussion

1. Is the Q-Ray bracelet a convenience, shopping, or specialty good? Explain your reasoning. Also analyze the "value package" provided by the Q-Ray bracelet.
2. Briefly describe the variables that are typically used to segment markets and what each involves. Which variable is Q-Ray using?
3. Consider the following statement: *People suffering from chronic pain need hope, and a product like Q-Ray provides hope. Even though it might be scientifically difficult to prove that the bracelet relieves pain, if people believe the product will reduce their pain, that might become a self-fulfilling prophecy and the person's pain will be relieved. So companies like Q-Ray should not be prohibited from advertising that their product has pain-relieving qualities.* Do you agree or disagree with this statement? Defend your answer.
4. Which of the four Ps is most important in the marketing of the Q-Ray bracelet? Explain your reasoning.

Video Resource: "Buyer Belief," *Marketplace* (November 14, 2007).

CBC Video Case 4–2

Shall We Dance?

Baby boomers (those born between 1946 and 1964) now make up one-third of Canada's population, and they control 55 percent of the disposable income in Canada. The needs and wants of this demographic group have created many new business opportunities in the health, leisure, and security industries. Many entrepreneurs are now chasing "boomer bucks."

Consider Beverly and Robert Tang, who are former North American dance champions. They want to capitalize on boomers' love of dancing. Their timing is good, since television has boosted interest in ballroom dancing with immensely popular shows like *Dancing with the Stars*. The Tangs want to cash in on the dance craze by targeting baby boomers (mostly women) because boomers have the money to spend on dancing lessons. And they want their company—Dancescape—to be a world-class dance lifestyle company that is the basis for a global dance brand.

It's Thursday night at a Ukrainian church hall, and baby boomers are dancing under the instruction of the Tangs. The Tangs spend a lot of time giving instruction, but they have also invested $20 000 to make a learn-to-dance video. It's already selling in the United States and they're working on Canadian and British distribution. A key element of their plan is three websites where dancers can shop, socialize, and download dance videos. The Tangs hope their website will be the new "Facebook for dancers." But to build their brand and build their business, they need $1.4 million. They manage to get an audience with Tim Draper, a venture capitalist who has made millions on the internet. He likes karaoke, and he invested in Hotmail, so they know he's open to new ideas. To prepare for their meeting with him, they hire a brand coach to help them prepare their sales pitch. Unfortunately, after working with them, the coach thinks they aren't ready to meet with Draper. The coach thinks they are spending so much time running the business that they don't have time to refine and polish their sales pitch.

On pitch day, Tim Draper gets an impromptu lesson from Beverly and also listens to Robert's sales pitch. The sales pitch gets off to a rocky start when Robert calls Tim "Steve" on two different occasions. That is very embarrassing. Draper listens carefully to Robert's sales pitch but makes no commitment. But he doesn't give them a flat "No" either. They're still hopeful he may come through.

Marketplace talks with two experts about the prospects of success for Dancescape. Lina Ko works for National Public Relations, a company that does surveys with boomers. She also has a blog that provides insights into Canadian consumers' needs and wants. The other expert is Robert Herjavec, who owns a computer company. He says it's good that the Tangs are doing something they love, because "you should love what you do and you'll never work a day in your life." But, he observes, that doesn't automatically mean that you'll have a viable business doing what you love. He notes that the Tangs are promoting dancing to the boomer generation, but they are trying to do it using the technology of the Facebook generation. He is not convinced that boomers are technologically savvy enough for this to work. He also has concerns because he wants to see young people dancing, not boomer-age people. He thinks the Tangs need a viral marketing idea that will have broad appeal. Selling their videos through niche stores limits their market and is inconsistent with their goal of being a global brand.

Ko disagrees with Herjavec and says that the perception that boomers are not technically savvy is incorrect. She also notes that the dancing concept is good because boomers are interested in exercising and dancing is good exercise. Dancing also makes people feel younger than they really are. The targeting of women is also a good idea because women have a big influence on family purchase decisions. But Ko thinks that the Tangs should revamp their language. Boomers don't want to hear the word *retirement*. Rather, they want to reinvent themselves. Ko also says that the Tangs need to further segment the boomer market because boomers in their 40s are quite different than boomers in their 60s.

Questions for Discussion

1. What is the difference between *goods*, *services*, and *ideas*? Are the Tangs marketing a good, a service, or an idea? Explain your reasoning.
2. Which of the four Ps of marketing do you think is most important in the case of dancing lessons? Explain your reasoning.
3. Which variables do marketers generally use to identify market segments? Which variables are being used by the Tangs? Be specific.

Video Resource: "Boomer Bonanza," *Fortune Hunters* (March 8, 2008).

Crafting a Business Plan

Part 4: Principles of Marketing

Goal of the Exercise

So far, your business has an identity; you've described the factors that will affect your business; and you've examined your employees, the jobs they'll be performing, and the ways in which you can motivate them. Part 4 of the business plan project asks you to think about marketing's four Ps—product, price, place (distribution), and promotion—and how they apply to your business. You'll also examine how you might target your marketing toward a certain group of consumers.

Exercise Background: Part 4 of the Business Plan

In Part 1, you briefly described what your business will do. The first step in Part 4 of the plan is to more fully describe the product (good or service) you are planning to sell. Once you have a clear picture of the product, you'll need to describe how this product will "stand out" in the marketplace—that is, how will it differentiate itself from other products?

In Part 1, you also briefly described who your customers would be. The first step in Part 4 of the plan is to describe your ideal buyer, or target market, in more detail, listing their income level, educational level, lifestyle, age, and so forth. This part of the business plan project also asks you to discuss the price of your products, as well as where the buyer can find your product.

Finally, you'll examine how your business will get the attention and interest of the buyer through its promotional mix—advertising, personal selling, sales promotions, and publicity and public relations.

This part of the business plan encourages you to be creative. Have fun! Provide as many details as you possibly can, as this reflects an understanding of your product and your buyer. Marketing is all about finding a need and filling it. Does your product fill a need in the marketplace?

Your Assignment

Step 1

Open the saved *Business Plan* file you have been working on.

Step 2

For the purposes of this assignment, you will answer the following questions in "Part 4: Principles of Marketing":

1. Describe your target market in terms of age, education level, income, and other demographic variables.

Hint: Refer to Chapter 15 for more information on the aspects of target marketing and market segmentation that you may want to consider. Be as detailed as possible about who you think your customers will be.

2. Describe the features and benefits of your product or service.

Hint: As you learned in Chapter 16, a product is a bundle of attributes—features and benefits. What features does your product have—what does it look like and what does it do? How will the product benefit the buyer?

3. How will you make your product stand out in the crowd?

Hint: There are many ways to stand out in the crowd, such as a unique product, outstanding service, or a great location. What makes your great idea special? Does it fill an unmet need in the marketplace? How will you differentiate your product to make sure that it succeeds?

4. What pricing strategy will you choose for your product, and what are the reasons for this strategy?

Hint: Refer to this chapter for more information on pricing strategies and tactics. Since your business is new, so is the product. Therefore, you probably want to choose between price skimming and penetration pricing. Which will you choose, and why?

5. Where will customers find your product or service? (That is, what issues of the distribution mix should you consider?)

Hint: If your business does not sell its product directly to consumers, what types of retail stores will sell your product? If your product will be sold to another business, which channel of distribution will you use? Refer to Chapter 17 for more information on aspects of distribution you may want to consider.

6. How will you advertise to your target market? Why have you chosen these forms of advertisement?

Hint: Marketers use several different advertising media—specific communication devices for carrying a seller's message to potential customers—each having its advantages and drawbacks. Refer to Chapter 16 for a discussion of the types of advertising media you may wish to consider here.

7. What other methods of promotion will you use, and why?

Hint: There's more to promotion than simple advertising. Other methods include personal selling, sales promotions, and publicity and public relations. Refer to the discussion of promotion in this chapter for ideas on how to promote your product that go beyond just advertising.

Note: Once you have answered the questions, save your Word document. You'll be answering additional questions in later chapters.

Part Five

Managing Financial Issues

The opening cases in each of the chapters in this part of the text deal with some aspect of the critical area of financial management. As the financial crisis of 2008 clearly showed, management of the financial transactions of a business firm is critical to its survival. Whether it involves raising money to start a new firm, assessing the riskiness of the firm's investments, managing the firm's cash, or monitoring the firm's activities in securities markets, financial management is a key business activity.

Part Five, Managing Financial Issues, provides an overview of business finance, including how firms raise and manage money, how they define and manage risk, and how they use Canadian and international securities markets to meet their financial needs.

- We begin in **Chapter 18, Understanding Money and Banking**, by exploring the nature of money, its creation through the banking system, and the role of the Bank of Canada in the nation's financial system. We also describe other important financial services organizations.
- Next, in **Chapter 19, Understanding Securities and Investments**, we consider the securities markets in which firms raise long-term funds by examining how these markets operate and how they are regulated.
- Finally, in **Chapter 20, Financial Decisions and Risk Management**, we look at three reasons businesses need funds and how financial managers raise both long- and short-term funds. We also examine the kinds of risks businesses encounter and the ways in which they deal with such risks.

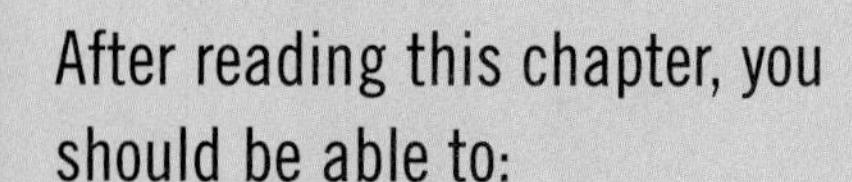

Chapter 18
Understanding Money and Banking

After reading this chapter, you should be able to:

1. Define *money* and identify the different forms it takes in the nation's money supply.
2. Understand the different kinds of *financial institutions* in the Canadian financial system, including the *Bank of Canada*.
3. Explain the role of *chartered banks* in the Canadian financial system.
4. Explain the role of *alternate banks*, *specialized lending and savings intermediaries*, and *investment dealers* in the Canadian financial system.
5. Understand the key concepts and activities in *international banking and finance*.

Money, Money, Money

Money has been important in business (and family) transactions for thousands of years. Various objects have served as money, including pig tusks (New Guinea), whale teeth (Fiji Islands), large stones (Islands of Yap in the western Pacific Ocean), cows (Ireland), and cowrie shells (China). Objects that have been used as money typically have one (or more) of the following characteristics: They are rare (for example, gold or silver), hard to get (for example, whale teeth), or have some intrinsic beauty that makes them desirable (for example, feathers from a beautiful bird).

Some items that we would consider odd are still used for money. For example, the teeth of spinner dolphins are used as money in the Solomon Islands of the South Pacific. One dolphin tooth is equal to about two Solomon Islands dollars (a dollar was worth about US$0.26 in 2008). The governor of the Central Bank of the Solomon Islands says people keep dolphin teeth as a "store of wealth" in much the same way that people in most countries put money in the bank. A pig costs about 50 dolphin teeth, while just a handful of dolphin teeth are needed to buy some yams and cassava. Counterfeiting is an issue in the Solomon Islands just as it is in industrialized societies (counterfeiters try to pass off the teeth of fruit bats as dolphin teeth).

The demand for dolphin teeth as currency is driven by a couple of unique aspects of Solomon Island society. First, tribal disputes that result in the loss of property or human life are often settled by paying compensation, in teeth, rather than in dollars. Second, teeth are the currency of choice when young men pay a dowry for a bride (one bride costs at least 1000 teeth). Each dolphin yields only about 20 teeth, so many dolphins need to be killed each year to balance supply and demand. Henry Sukufatu is a dolphin hunter who sells about 1000 teeth a month. He says he can't keep up with demand, which is why the exchange value of teeth is rising.

In most societies today, metal coins and paper money predominate. But have you ever wondered how a country decides what denominations of coins and paper money it should have? One model—called D-metric—uses the average day's net pay to make suggestions about the denomination structure of a country's currency. For example, if the average day's pay in a country is $100, the D-metric model recommends that the lowest denomination be the nickel, and that a $500 bill be introduced. The model also recommends introducing a $5 coin when the average day's net pay reaches $150. Another model looks at other factors, including cultural preferences, the impact of other methods of paying for things (credit and debit cards), and the average size of exchange transactions. It provides similar recommendations.

A Bank of Canada study in 2005 suggested that Canada drop the penny because it is more trouble than it is worth, and it is costing Canadian society about $130 million each year. New Zealand stopped making the penny in 1987 and Australia in 1990. France, Norway, and Britain have also eliminated low-denomination coins. But in Canada, there is still a lot of demand for pennies. The production of pennies has actually increased in recent years because people are not recirculating them. In 2006 alone, the Royal Canadian mint produced 1.4 billion pennies. In 2008, a report from the Desjardins Group proposed eliminating the nickel, replacing the $5 bill with a coin, adding a 20-cent piece, making the 25-cent piece smaller, and introducing a $200 bill.

The United States is also dealing with the question of denominations for its currency. Many people wonder why the United States is still using a $1 bill and note that it is out of step with many other industrialized countries. For example, the smallest bill used in the 15 countries in the euro zone is the five-euro note (worth US$7.83 in 2008). In Britain, the smallest bill is the five-pound note (worth US$9.85 in 2008), and in Japan, it's the 1000-yen note (worth about US$9.30 in 2008). It is estimated that if the United States switched to a $1 coin like Canada has done, it would save taxpayers there about $522 million a year in production expenses. Each dollar bill costs about four cents to produce, and it has a life span of only about 21 months. By contrast, a coin costs more to produce (about 20 cents), but lasts 30 years or more. The United States has tried on a couple of occasions to introduce a $1 coin but has not succeeded. But now the government is getting serious. The Presidential $1 Coin Act of 2005 directs the U.S. Treasury and the Federal Reserve to make sure there is extensive circulation of a new series of $1 coins depicting past presidents. From early 2007 to mid-2008, more than a billion of these new $1 coins were minted.

The use of coins and paper money dominate in modern society. But the barter system—exchanging goods and services instead of paying money for them—is still evident. For example, a painter might agree to paint a plumber's house if the plumber will fix the painter's leaky pipes. Barter was common in ancient societies, and it is making something of a comeback. In the 1990s, when Russia was trying to move away from a command economy and toward a market-based economy, barter accounted for more than half of the business transactions. When the recession began in 2008, barter exchanges reported a big jump in the number of transactions that were taking place. Barter became more important even in North America because during an economic downturn participants want to conserve cash.

High-tech barter organizations like International Monetary Systems and U-Exchange.com make it possible for people from around the world to get involved in the barter economy. For example, Rich Rowley of Tacoma, Washington, offered to provide new home construction, remodelling, home repairs, home maintenance, and commercial improvements in return for things like tickets to sporting events, vacations, land, medical and dental care, a boat, and a motor home. Participants can build up credits that they can use for future transactions. The trade publication Barternew.com estimates that in the United States, bartering is worth more than $3 billion annually. ◆

How will this help me?

By understanding the material in this chapter, you will benefit in two ways: (1) As a consumer, you'll learn what money is, where it comes from, how the supply of money grows, and the kinds of services that are available to you from the financial services industry; and (2) as a manager, you will have a greater understanding of the various financial institutions in Canada and how the activities of these financial institutions influence business firms.

In this chapter, we note the different forms that money takes and the different kinds of financial institutions that make up the Canadian financial system. We also examine how financial institutions create money and the means by which these institutions are regulated. We discuss the role of the Bank of Canada and ways in which the money and banking system is changing. We conclude with a discussion of the key concepts and activities in international banking and finance.

What Is Money?

1 Define *money* and identify the different forms it takes in the nation's money supply.

When someone asks you how much money you have, what do you say? Do you count the bills and coins in your pockets? Do you include the funds in your chequing and savings accounts? What about stocks, bonds, or your car? Taken together, the value of everything you own is your personal *wealth*. Not all of it, however, is *money*. In this section, we will consider the characteristics of money, the functions of money, and the supply of money.

The Characteristics of Money

As we saw in the opening case, many different objects have been used as money in different societies. Modern money usually takes the form of stamped metal or printed paper—Canadian dollars, U.S. dollars, British pounds, Japanese yen—that is issued by governments. The Chinese were using metal money as early as 1100 BCE to represent the objects they were exchanging (for example, bronze spades and knives). Coins probably came into use in China sometime around 600 BCE and paper money around 1200 CE. Just about any object can serve as **money** if it is portable, divisible, durable, and stable. To understand why these qualities are important, imagine using as money something that lacks these features—a 35-kilogram salmon, for example.

money Any portable, divisible, durable, and stable object generally accepted by people as payment for goods and services.

- *Portability*. If you wanted to use the salmon to buy goods and services, you would have to lug a 35-kilogram fish from shop to shop. Modern currency, by contrast, is lightweight and easy to handle.

This 100-kilogram gold coin—produced by the Royal Canadian Mint—is the largest gold coin ever produced. It is 99.999 percent pure gold, and sells for $3 million. The coin won the Most Innovative Circulation Coin award at the Mint Directors' Conference in Paris in 2006.

- *Divisibility*. Suppose you wanted to buy a hat, a book, and some milk from three different stores—all using the salmon as money. How would you divide the fish? First, out comes a cleaver at each store. Then, you would have to determine whether a kilogram of its head is worth as much as a kilogram from its middle. Modern currency is easily divisible into smaller parts with fixed values for each unit. In Canada, for example, a dollar can be exchanged for four quarters, 10 dimes, 20 nickels, 100 pennies, or any combination of these coins. It is easy to match units of money with the value of all goods.
- *Durability*. Fish seriously fail the durability test. Each day, whether or not you "spend" it, the salmon will be losing value (and gaining scents). Modern currency, on the other hand, does not spoil, it does not die, and, if it wears out, it can be replaced with new coins or paper money.
- *Stability*. If salmon were in short supply, you might be able to make quite a deal for yourself. But in the middle of a salmon run, the market would be flooded with fish. Since sellers would have many opportunities to exchange their wares for salmon, they would soon have enough fish and refuse to trade for salmon. While the value of the paper money we use today has fluctuated over the years, it is considerably more stable than salmon.

The Functions of Money

Imagine a successful fisherman who needs a new sail for his boat. In a *barter economy*—one in which goods are exchanged directly for one another—he would have to find someone who not only needs fish but who is willing to exchange a sail for it. If no sailmaker wants fish, the fisherman must find someone else—say, a shoemaker—who wants fish and will trade for it. Then the fisherman must hope that the sailmaker will trade for his new shoes. In a *money economy*, the fisherman would simply sell his catch, receive money, and exchange the money for such goods as a new sail. Thus, the barter econ-

In the modern world, we've become used to highly structured monetary systems. But in some places, centuries-old systems still survive. In Quetta, Pakistan, for example, traders like Mohammad Essa transfer funds through handshakes and code words. The system is called *hawala*, which means "trust" in Arabic. The worldwide hawala system, though illegal in most countries, moves billions of dollars past regulators annually and is alleged to be the system of choice for terrorists because it leaves no paper trail.

omy is relatively inefficient compared to the money economy. This example clearly demonstrates the three functions of money:

- *Medium of exchange.* We use money as a way of buying and selling things. Without money, we would be bogged down in a system of barter.
- *Store of value.* Pity the fisherman who catches a fish on Monday and wants to buy a few bars of candy on, say, the following Saturday. By then, the fish would have spoiled and be of no value. By contrast, money can be used for future purchases and therefore "stores" value.
- *Unit of account.* Money lets us measure the relative values of goods and services. It acts as a unit of account because all products can be valued and accounted for in terms of money. For example, the concepts of "$1000 worth of clothes" or "$500 in labour costs" have universal meaning because everyone deals with money every day.

The Spendable Money Supply: M-1

For money to serve as a medium of exchange, a store of value, or a unit of account, buyers and sellers must agree on its value. The value of money, in turn, depends in part on its supply, that is, how much money is in circulation. When the money supply is high, the value of money drops. When the money supply is low, the value of money increases.

Unfortunately, it is not easy to measure the supply of money, nor is there complete agreement on exactly how it should be measured. The "narrow" definition of the money supply is called M-1. **M-1** counts only the most liquid forms of money—currency and demand deposits (chequing accounts) in banks. **Currency** is paper money and coins issued by the government. It is widely used to pay small bills. The phrase "This note is legal tender," which appears on Canadian paper money, means that the law requires a creditor to accept it in payment of a debt. Illegal tender (counterfeiting) has been a problem for many years. It is now a worldwide problem, partly because new technologies like scanners and colour copiers allow counterfeiters to make

M-1 Only the most liquid forms of money (currency and demand deposits).

currency Paper money and coins issued by the government.

real-looking bills rather easily. In 2008, there were over 1.4 billion Bank of Canada notes in circulation; over 107 000 counterfeit bills were detected, with a value exceeding $6 million.[1] A survey conducted by SES Canada Research Inc. found that 18 percent of Canadians have received a counterfeit bill, and 39 percent felt that it was likely that they would receive a counterfeit bill at some point.[2] In an attempt to reduce counterfeiting, the Bank of Canada has issued new $20 and $5 bills with more sophisticated security features.[3]

The majority of Canadian households have chequing accounts, against which millions of cheques are written each year. A **cheque** is an order instructing the bank to pay a given sum to a specified person or firm. Cheques enable buyers to make large purchases without having to carry large amounts of cash. Sellers gain a measure of safety because the cheques they receive are valuable only to them and can later be exchanged for cash. Money in chequing accounts, known as **demand deposits**, is counted in M-1 because such funds may be withdrawn at any time without notice.

cheque An order instructing the bank to pay a given sum to a specified person or firm.

demand deposits Money in chequing accounts; counted as M-1 because such funds may be withdrawn at any time without notice.

M-1 Plus the Convertible Money Supply: M-2

M-2 includes everything in M-1 plus items that cannot be spent directly but that are easily converted to spendable forms: *time deposits*, *money market mutual funds*, and *savings deposits*. M-2 accounts for nearly all of the nation's money supply. It thus measures the store of monetary value that is available for financial transactions. As this overall level of money increases, more is available for consumer purchases and business investment. When the supply is tightened, less money is available; financial transactions, spending, and business activity thus slow down. As of February 2009, M-2 totalled $896.3 billion in Canada.[4]

M-2 Everything in the M-1 money supply plus savings deposits, time deposits, and money market mutual funds.

Unlike demand deposits, **time deposits** require prior notice of withdrawal and cannot be transferred by cheque. On the other hand, time deposits pay higher interest rates. The supply of money in time deposits—such as *certificates of deposit (CDs)* and *savings certificates*—grew rapidly in the 1970s and 1980s as interest rates rose to 15 percent. But when interest rates dropped in the late 1990s, consumers began putting more of their money into mutual funds.

time deposits A deposit that requires prior notice to make a withdrawal; cannot be transferred to others by cheque.

Money market mutual funds are operated by investment companies that bring together pools of assets from many investors. The fund buys a collection of short-term, low-risk financial securities. Ownership of and profits (or losses) from the sale of these securities are shared among the fund's investors. These funds attracted many investors in the 1980s and 1990s because of high payoffs. But the sharp decline in the stock market in 2001–02 and again in 2008 meant reduced consumer interest in mutual funds.

money market mutual funds Funds operated by investment companies that bring together pools of assets from many investors.

Credit Cards: Plastic Money?

Although not included in M-1 or M-2, credit—especially credit cards—has become a major factor in the purchase of consumer goods in Canada. The use of MasterCard, Visa, American Express, Discover, and credit cards issued by individual businesses has become so widespread that many people refer to credit cards as "plastic money." Credit cards are actually a *money substitute*; they serve as a temporary medium of exchange but are not a store of value. More detail about credit cards is provided in Appendix B.

In 2007, Canadians held 71 million credit cards; that was 9.2 percent more than in 2006. The number of credit-card transactions rose more than 11 percent from 2006, and the value of goods and services bought with credit cards was US$261 billion.[5] Visa is the world's biggest credit-card company, with 44 billion transactions in 2007, more than MasterCard and American Express combined. Worldwide, the total value of goods purchased with Visa cards was $3.2 trillion.[6]

The hub of operations at Amazon.com is this 840 000-square-foot warehouse, where workers can ship as many as 11 000 boxes an hour. The key to the efficiency of the facility is technology—all orders are processed electronically. The most important technology of all may be the credit card. If you had nothing but cash, you'd find it hard to shop on the internet, and internet retailers who depend on credit-card transactions (like Amazon, Dell, and eBay) couldn't exist in a cash-only world.

Credit cards are big business for two reasons. First, they are quite convenient for consumers. Second, credit cards are extremely profitable for issuing companies because of fees they collect. Some cards charge annual fees to holders, and all of them charge interest on unpaid balances. Depending on the issuer, cardholders pay interest rates ranging from 11 to 20 percent. Merchants who accept credit cards also pay fees to card issuers.

Banks like the Bank of Montreal, the Canadian Imperial Bank of Commerce, the Bank of Nova Scotia, and the TD Canada Trust are the biggest issuers of Visa cards in Canada. Each time a card is used, the banks receive an "interchange" fee, which is a percentage of the purchase value of the transaction. The banks use these fees to offset costs they incur with loyalty and points programs.

There is an ongoing battle for market share among Canada's major banks as they issue credit cards, so banks are continually offering more perks. Consumers regularly switch cards as they attempt to get better rates and more perks. However, as the perks get better for consumers, banks pass on their costs to retailers in the form of higher interchange fees. For example, the fees paid by the owner of the Bloor Street Diner in Toronto on Visa transactions increased from 1.51 percent to 1.86 percent, including interchange fees (the annual payout of credit-card fees is about $120 000). The owner feels that he simply has to take Visa credit cards or he will lose business.[7] Credit card companies collected $4.5 billion in fees in 2008.[8]

Credit-card fraud is an increasing concern for both consumers and retailers. The Interac Association estimated that credit- and debit card fraud cost financial institutions over $100 million in 2007.[9] Sometimes criminals pay retail workers to steal information from customers' credit cards. Then that information is used to quickly purchase thousands of dollars worth of goods over the internet or through mail-order houses. By the time the credit-card holder gets his or her next bill, the thieves are long gone. Another approach is to use a card reader. When a credit card is swiped through the reader, key information about the cardholder is produced. Then a counterfeit card is made and used.[10]

To deal with these problems, credit-card companies have developed a new encryption technology. In 2008, holders of CIBC Visa, Royal Bank Visa, and BMO MasterCard began receiving new high-tech, crime-fighting credit cards with a computer chip embedded in them. Two million of the new cards were sent to customers, and millions more will be sent out in the next couple of years. Royal Bank said its customers will receive the new chip cards when their old ones expire. With the new system, consumers won't swipe their cards as they used to. Rather, they will insert the credit card in a reader, then punch in a personal identification number (PIN) just as they do with their debit card. They will then remove the card from the reader once it is approved. There is no signature required. A pilot project in Kitchener-Waterloo, Ontario, involved the use of more than 170 000 chip cards and 3500 reading devices at various retailers. There was an 80 percent decrease in fraudulent activity in areas where the new cards were being used.[11]

The Canadian Financial System

Understand the different kinds of *financial institutions* in the Canadian financial system, including the *Bank of Canada*. **2**

Many forms of money, especially demand deposits and time deposits, depend on the existence of financial institutions to provide a broad spectrum of services to both individuals and businesses. In the sections that follow, we describe the major types of financial institutions found in Canada, explain how they work, and describe the services they offer.

Financial Institutions

There are several different types of financial institutions in Canada, but their main function is to facilitate the flow of money from sectors with surpluses to those with deficits by attracting funds into chequing and savings accounts. Incoming funds will be loaned to individuals and businesses and perhaps invested in government securities.

For many years, the financial community in Canada was divided rather clearly into four distinct legal areas. Often called the "four financial pillars," they were (1) chartered banks; (2) alternate banks, such as trust companies and credit unions (or *caisses populaires*); (3) life insurance companies and other specialized lending and saving intermediaries, such as factors, finance companies, venture capital firms, mutual funds, and pension funds; and (4) investment dealers. We will discuss each of these financial institutions in detail a bit later in this chapter, but it is important to understand that so many changes have taken place in the financial services industry in the last couple of decades that the differences across the four divisions have become very blurred.

Changes Affecting Financial Institutions

The crumbling of the four financial pillars began in 1980 when several changes were made to the Bank Act. In the years since then, many other changes have been made as well. For example, banks are now permitted to own securities dealers, to establish subsidiaries to sell mutual funds, and to sell commercial paper (see Chapter 20). Trust companies have declined in importance, and many trust companies have been bought by banks or insurance companies. The largest trust company—Canada Trust—merged with the Toronto-Dominion Bank and is now called TD Canada Trust. Additional changes are evident as a result of *deregulation*, *changing consumer demands*, and *changes in international banking*.

Deregulation

Deregulation has allowed banks to shift away from their historical role as intermediaries between depositors and borrowers. As we shall see, Canada's banks are diversifying to provide a wider array of financial products to their clients. Training bankers to be effective in this environment is necessary. For example, over 100 executives at TD Canada Trust attended a Harvard University course that taught them to think like investment bankers. The Bank of Montreal conducted a similar course for over 400 executives.

Changing Consumer Demands

Consumers are no longer content to simply keep money in a bank when they can get more for it elsewhere. They are increasingly turning to electronic banks like ING Direct and President's Choice Financial that pay higher interest on savings accounts. Those companies can pay higher interest rates because they don't incur the costs associated with having branches like traditional banks do. Competition is also coming from retailers like Sears, Loblaw, Wal-Mart, and Canadian Tire who are developing financial services products. Canadian Tire Corp., for example, was granted a bank licence in 2003, and in 2007 the company began offering combined mortgage, chequing, and savings accounts in three test markets in Canada. Even though the provision of financial services is a recent development at Canadian Tire (it constituted just 9 percent of the company's revenues in 2006), financial services generated nearly one-third of the company's total profits.[12]

Traditional banks are responding to this new competition by selling a growing array of services in their branches. For example, the Bank of Montreal started providing bereavement services in 2007. If a customer's mother dies, for example, BMO offers a service that takes care of everything from the funeral planning to having Canada Post redirect the deceased person's mail.[13]

Banks also want to get much more involved in selling insurance in their branches, but as of 2009, the Bank Act still prohibited banks from selling insurance *in their branch offices* (they are allowed to sell insurance at other locations). Canadian banks are being "creative" in keeping insurance and banking activities separate (but not too separate). In Oakville, Ontario, Royal Bank of Canada consumers who enter the branch will notice the RBC bank on the right and RBC Insurance on the left. The two operations are separated by only a glass wall. Dan Danyluk, the CEO of the Insurance Brokers Association of Canada, says that RBC's strategy is flouting the intent of the law. He argues that credit-granting institutions like banks should not be allowed to sell insurance in their branches because they may try to tie the buying of, say, car insurance to the approval of the loan to buy the car.[14]

All of this activity is transforming the profit base of banks. In the past, they made most of their money from the spread between interest rates paid to depositors and the rates charged on loans. Investment banking, on the other hand, is fee-based. Banks are making a larger proportion of their profits from fees, and this is blurring the traditional boundary between banks and securities firms.

Changes in International Banking

Because U.S. and other foreign banks are now allowed to do business in Canada, Canada's banks are going to experience increased competition. They are responding to this threat with a variety of tactics, including attempts to merge with one another so they can afford the millions of dollars in technology investment that will be needed to remain competitive. But bank mergers have been blocked by the federal government because it feared the mergers would reduce competition and harm consumers. As we saw earlier, however, the government did allow Canada Trust and Toronto-Dominion Bank to merge. Banks are also trying other things to be more competitive, like co-operating to spread their fixed costs. Syncor Services, for example, is a joint venture between three of the "big six" banks that provides cheque-clearing services across Canada.[15]

The Bank of Canada

The **Bank of Canada**, formed in 1935, is Canada's central bank. It has a crucial role to play in managing the Canadian economy and in regulating certain aspects of chartered bank operations. The Bank of Canada is managed by a board of governors composed of a governor, a deputy governor, and 12 directors appointed from different regions of Canada. The directors, with cabinet approval, appoint the governor and deputy governor. The deputy minister of finance is also a non-voting member of the board. Between meetings of the board, normally held eight times per year, an executive committee acts for the board. This committee is composed of the governor, the deputy governor, two directors, and the deputy minister of finance. The executive committee meets at least once a week.

Bank of Canada Canada's central bank; formed in 1935.

Operation of the Bank of Canada

The Bank of Canada plays an important role in managing the money supply in Canada. (See Figure 18.1.) If the Bank of Canada wants to *increase* the money supply, it can buy government securities. The people selling these bonds deposit the proceeds in their banks, and these deposits increase banks' reserves and their willingness to make loans. The Bank of Canada can also lower the bank rate; this action will cause increased demand for loans from businesses and households because these customers borrow more money when interest rates drop.

If the Bank of Canada wants to *decrease* the money supply, it can sell government securities. People spend money to buy bonds, and these withdrawals bring down banks' reserves and reduce their ability to make loans. The Bank of Canada can also raise the bank rate; this action will cause decreased demand for loans from businesses and households because these customers borrow less money when interest rates rise.

Member Bank Borrowing from the Bank of Canada

The Bank of Canada is the lender of last resort for chartered banks. The rate at which chartered banks can borrow from the Bank of Canada is called the **bank rate, or rediscount rate**. It serves as the basis for establishing the chartered banks' prime interest rates. By raising the bank rate, the Bank of Canada depresses the demand for money; by lowering it, the demand for money increases. In practice, chartered banks seldom have to borrow from the Bank of Canada. However, the bank rate is an important instrument of monetary policy as a determinant of interest rates.

bank rate (rediscount rate) The rate at which chartered banks can borrow from the Bank of Canada.

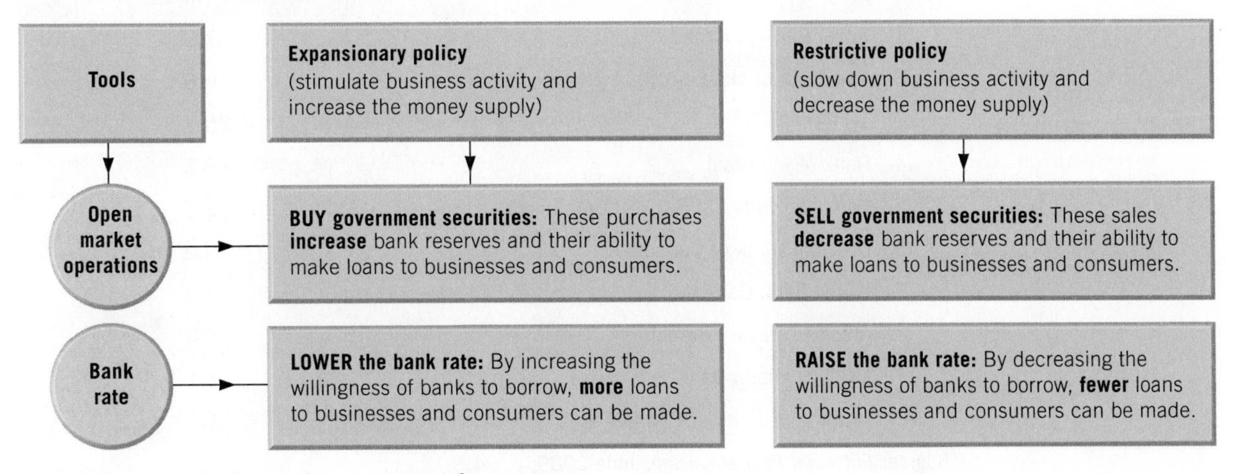

Figure 18.1 Bank of Canada monetary policy actions.

Financial Pillar #1—Chartered Banks

3 Explain the role of *chartered banks* in the Canadian financial system.

chartered bank A privately owned, profit-seeking firm that serves individuals, non-business organizations, and businesses as a financial intermediary.

A **chartered bank** is a privately owned, profit-seeking firm that serves individuals, non-business organizations, and businesses as a financial intermediary. Chartered banks offer chequing and savings accounts, make loans, and provide many other services to their customers. They are the main source of short-term loans for business firms.

Chartered banks are the largest and most important financial institutions in Canada. In February 2009, Canadian chartered banks had assets totalling $1.8 trillion.[16] They offer a unique service. Their liability instruments (the claims against their assets) are generally accepted by the public and by business as money or as legal tender. Initially, these liability instruments took the form of bank notes issued by individual banks. The Bank Act amendments of 1944 removed the right to issue bank notes.

The 1980 Bank Act requires Schedule A banks to be Canadian owned and to have no more than 10 percent of their voting shares controlled by a single interest. The five largest Schedule A banks account for about 90 percent of total bank assets. There are thousands of bank branch offices in Canada, about one for every 3300 people. The Bank Act also permits Schedule B banks, which may be domestically owned banks that do not meet the 10 percent limit or may be foreign controlled. Schedule B banks are initially limited to one main office and one branch. Since the passing of the Act, several foreign banks have set up Schedule B subsidiaries. The act limits foreign-controlled banks to deposits that do not exceed 8 percent of the total domestic assets of all banks in Canada. The largest chartered banks in Canada are shown in Table 18.1.

Services Offered by Banks

The banking business today is a highly competitive industry. No longer is it enough for banks to accept deposits and make loans. Most, for example, now offer many other services, such as pension services, trust services, international services, financial advice, and electronic money transfer.

Pension Services

Most banks help customers establish savings plans for retirement. Banks serve as financial intermediaries by receiving funds and investing them as directed

Table 18.1 Top 10 Banks in Canada, 2008

Company	Annual Revenues (in billions of $)
1. Royal Bank of Canada	$37.5
2. The Bank of Nova Scotia	26.6
3. TD Canada Trust	25.7
4. Bank of Montreal	19.8
5. Canadian Imperial Bank of Commerce	12.6
6. National Bank of Canada	6.0
7. HSBC Bank Canada	4.2
8. Alberta Treasury Branches	1.4
9. MBNA Canada Bank	1.1
10. Laurentian Bank of Canada	1.1

Source: *Financial Post Magazine*, June 2009, p. 94.

by customers. They also provide customers with information on investment possibilities.

"And, hey, don't kill yourself trying to pay it back. You know our motto—'What the hell, it's only money.'"

Trust Services

Many banks offer **trust services**—the management of funds left "in the bank's trust." In return for a fee, the trust department will perform such tasks as making your monthly bill payments and managing your investment portfolio. Trust departments also manage the estates of deceased persons.

trust services The management of funds left "in the bank's trust."

International Services

The three main international services offered by banks are *currency exchange*, *letters of credit*, and *banker's acceptances*. Suppose, for example, that a Canadian company wants to buy a product from a French supplier. For a fee, it can use one or more of three services offered by its bank:

1. It can exchange Canadian dollars for euros at a Canadian bank and then pay the French supplier in euros.
2. It can pay its bank to issue a **letter of credit**—a promise by the bank to pay the French firm a certain amount if specified conditions are met.
3. It can pay its bank to draw up a **banker's acceptance**, which promises that the bank will pay some specified amount at a future date.

letter of credit A promise by a bank to pay money to a business firm if certain conditions are met.

banker's acceptance A promise that the bank will pay a specified amount of money at a future date.

Financial Advice

Many banks, both large and small, help their customers manage their money. Depending on the customer's situation, the bank may recommend different investment opportunities. The recommended mix might include guaranteed investment certificates, mutual funds, stocks, and bonds. Today, bank advertisements often stress the role of banks as financial advisers. Banks are also becoming involved in the green movement, as described in the boxed insert entitled "Ebanking: Easy and Eco-friendly."

Electronic Funds Transfer

Electronic funds transfer (EFT) combines computer and communication technology to transfer funds or information into, from, within, and among financial institutions. Examples include the following:

electronic funds transfer (EFT) Combines computer and communication technology to transfer funds or information into, from, within, and among financial institutions.

Automated Banking Machines (ABMs). **ABMs**, or 24-hour tellers (called automated teller machines—ATMs—in the United States), are electronic terminals that let you bank at almost any time of the day or night. They also allow transfers of funds between accounts and provide information on account status. Some banks offer cards that can be used in affiliated nationwide systems. Machines are now located at bank buildings, grocery stores, airports, shopping malls, and other locations around the world. Among the world's nearly one million ABMs, 32 percent are located in Asia, 31 percent are located in North America, 25 percent in Western Europe, and 8 percent in Latin America. Many banks now offer international ABM services. Citicorp, for example, installed Shanghai's first 24-hour ABM and is the first foreign bank to receive approval from the People's Bank of China to issue local currency through ABMs.

automated banking machines (ABMs) Automated machines that allow bank customers to conduct account-related activities 24 hours a day, 7 days a week.

The Greening of Business

Ebanking: Easy and Eco-friendly

Online banking has seen growing popularity in recent years largely because of the convenience it offers customers. A 2007 internet use survey conducted by Statistics Canada revealed that 63 percent of Canadians used the internet for electronic banking or paying bills. Paperless banking saves banks and consumers money and has the added advantage of being environmentally friendly. As banks see the benefits of these eco-friendly efforts, they are increasingly willing to adopt measures to support movement in this direction.

Banks continue to improve and expand their online services, and customers are increasingly comfortable using them. With electronic chequing, banks save on cheque-clearing costs, and with paperless statements and online bill paying, they save on printing and mailing. Staffing costs are also reduced as brick-and-mortar branch traffic slows. Corporate clients save on file-storage costs, and individuals reduce clutter in their homes. The immediacy of online banking transactions may also prevent customers from running out of paper cheques or accruing late fees.

These endeavours may have their roots in speed and convenience, but they're also good for the environment. Less paper translates into saving trees and reducing wastewater and greenhouse gas emissions. Several banks have pushed these efforts even further. TD Canada Trust, through partnerships with Bullfrog Power and the Pembina Institute, has created a network of Green Machines. These ATMs are powered by clean sources, such as wind and low-impact water power. TD Canada Trust considers itself to be a leader in the Canadian banking system when it comes to efforts to reduce its carbon footprint. Its goal is to become carbon neutral by 2010. Similarly, Scotiabank is becoming more environmentally friendly through advancements that will track and improve performance related to paper consumption, recycling efforts, energy consumption, sustainable real estate practices, and environmentally conscious procurement processes.

These endeavours are not only socially responsible and cost-effective, but they also serve as a powerful marketing strategy to attract an increasingly eco-conscious public.

Critical Thinking Question

1. What forces are behind the changes in the banking system, demonstrated by TD Canada Trust and Scotiabank? What future changes do you predict for the industry?

To use an ABM, you insert a special card and enter your own identification number to withdraw cash, make deposits, or transfer funds between accounts. Banks typically charge about $1.50 per transaction, but at the Dragonfly Nightclub in the Niagara Fallsview Casino Resort, the ABM surcharge is $2.99. In terms of consumer access, Canada ranks first in the world in ABMs. Only one-third of ABMs are owned by banks; the other two-thirds—so-called "white label" machines—are owned by private companies.[17]

Pay-by-Phone. These systems let you telephone your financial institution and instruct it, by pushing the proper buttons on your phone, to pay certain bills or to transfer funds between accounts.

Direct Deposits and Withdrawals. This system allows you to authorize in advance specific, regular deposits and withdrawals. You can arrange to have paycheques and social assistance cheques automatically deposited and recurring expenses, such as insurance premiums and utility bills, automatically paid.

debit card A type of plastic money that immediately on use reduces the balance in the user's bank account and transfers it to the store's account.

Point-of-Sale Transfers. These let you pay for retail purchases with your **debit card**, a type of plastic money that immediately reduces the balance in your bank account when it is used. For example, if you use a debit card at a grocery store, the clerk simply runs the card through the machine and asks you to punch in a personal identification number on a keypad next to the cash register. The price of the groceries is then deducted electronically from your chequing account, and money moves from your chequing account to the grocery store's account.

The average Canadian uses his or her debit card 76 times each year; this rate of usage is the highest in the world.[18] Interac, which processes debit card transactions in Canada, reported that on just one day in December 2008, there were 15.9 million debit card transactions.[19] And Visa, which has 844 million debit card holders in 170 different countries, reported that debit card transactions exceeded its credit-card transactions for the first time ever in 2008.[20]

Smart Cards. **Smart cards**—also known as "electronic purses" or "stored-value cards"—can be programmed with "electronic money" at ABMs or, with special telephone hookups, even at home. After using your card to purchase an item, you can then check an electronic display to see how much money is left on your card. Phone callers and shoppers in Europe and Asia are the most avid users. In North America, smart cards are most popular in gas pump payments, followed by prepaid phone service, ABMs, self-operated checkouts, and automated banking services.[21] Analysts predict that, in the near future, smart cards will function as much more than electronic purses. For example, travel industry experts predict that people will soon book travel plans at home on personal computers and then transfer their reservations onto their smart cards. The cards will then serve as airline tickets and boarding passes.

smart card A credit-card-sized computer that can be programmed with "electronic money."

Ecash. Electronic money, known as **ecash**, is money that moves along multiple channels of consumers and businesses via digital electronic transmissions. Ecash moves outside the established network of banks, cheques, and paper currency. How does ecash work? Traditional currency is used to buy electronic funds, which are downloaded over phone lines into a PC or a portable "electronic wallet" that can store and transmit ecash. Ecash is purchased from any company that sells it, including banks. When shopping online—say, to purchase jewellery—a shopper sends digital money to the merchant instead of using traditional cash, cheques, or credit cards. Businesses can purchase supplies and services electronically from any merchant that accepts ecash. The money flows from the buyer to the seller's ecash funds, which are instantaneously updated and stored on a microchip.

ecash Money that moves among consumers and businesses via digital electronic transmissions.

Although ecash transactions are cheaper than handling cheques and the paper records involved with conventional money, there are some potential problems. Hackers, for example, may break into ecash systems and drain them instantaneously. Moreover, if the issuer's computer system crashes, it is conceivable that money "banked" in memory may be lost forever. Finally, regulation and control of ecash systems remains largely non-existent; there is virtually none of the protection that covers government-controlled money systems.

Figure 18.2 summarizes the services that chartered banks offer. Banks are chartered by the federal government and are closely regulated when they provide these services.

Bank Deposits

Chartered banks provide a financial intermediary service by accepting deposits and making loans with this money. One type of deposit a customer can make in a bank is a chequable, or demand, deposit. A **chequable deposit** is a chequing account. Customers who deposit coins, paper currency, or other cheques in their chequing accounts can write cheques against the balance in their accounts. Their banks must honour these cheques immediately; this is why chequing accounts are also called demand deposits.

chequable deposit A chequing account.

Long- and short-term loans
Automated teller machines
Safeguard property entrusted to it
Debit and credit cards
Savings accounts
Guaranteed investment certificates
DRIVE-THRU
TD Canada Trust
Chequing accounts
Buy and sell securities for customer accounts
Exchange Canadian dollars for foreign currencies
Exchange foreign currencies for Canadian dollars
Advise customers on financial matters

Figure 18.2 Examples of services offered by many chartered banks and trust companies.

term deposit Money that remains with the bank for a period of time with interest paid to the depositor.

The other type of deposit a customer can make in a chartered bank is a **term deposit**, one that remains with the bank for a period of time. Interest is paid to depositors for the use of their funds. There are two types of term deposits—the regular passbook savings account (intended primarily for small individual savers and non-profit organizations) and guaranteed investment certificates (a deposit made for a specified period of time ranging from 28 days to several years that normally pays higher rates of interest than regular savings accounts).

Bank Loans

Banks are the major source of short-term loans for business. Although banks make long-term loans to some firms, they prefer to specialize in providing short-term funds to finance inventories and accounts receivable. A *secured* loan is backed by collateral such as accounts receivable or a life insurance policy. If the borrower cannot repay the loan, the bank sells the collateral. An *unsecured* loan is backed only by the borrower's promise to repay it. Only the most creditworthy borrowers can get unsecured loans.

prime rate of interest The lowest rate charged to borrowers.

Borrowers pay interest on their loans. Large firms with excellent credit records pay the prime rate of interest. The **prime rate of interest** is the lowest rate charged to borrowers. This rate changes constantly owing to changes in the demand for and supply of loanable funds as well as to policies of the Bank of Canada. The so-called "big six" Canadian banks (Royal Bank, CIBC, Bank of Montreal, Bank of Nova Scotia, TD Canada Trust, and National Bank of Canada) typically act in concert with respect to the prime rate.

People who want to start their own small business but who have no real assets are typically turned away by banks. Muhammad Yunus thought that wasn't right, so he started the Grameen Bank in Bangladesh, which loans money to women who wouldn't otherwise qualify for a loan. Small loans—typically $100 to $500—have been made to thousands of women in the last few years, and they almost always pay them back. Yunus won the Nobel Peace Prize for his microfinance idea in 2006. The Grameen Bank has given women an opportunity for personal growth and business success that traditional banks will not give them. Now Yunus is making the same kinds of loans to low-income Latin American immigrants in New York.[22]

Banks as Creators of Money

In the course of their activities, banks provide a special service to the economy—they create money. This is not to say that they mint bills and coins. Rather, by

Devout Muslims can't pay or receive interest, a fact that complicates banking operations. Because money has to work in order to earn a return, institutions like the Shamil Bank in Bahrain invest deposits directly in such ventures as real estate and then pay back profit shares rather than interest. Buying a car is possible through a complex arrangement in which the bank takes temporary ownership and then sells the car to the individual at a profit. Mortgage arrangements are similar but even more complicated.

taking in deposits and making loans, they expand the money supply. We will first look at how this expansion process used to work when banks had a **reserve requirement**, that is, that they had to keep a portion of their chequable deposits in vault cash or as deposits with the Bank of Canada (the reserve requirement was dropped in 1991).

reserve requirement The requirement (until 1991) that banks keep a portion of their chequable deposits in vault cash or as deposits with the Bank of Canada.

Suppose that you saved \$100, took it to a bank, and opened a chequing account. Let's assume that there is a reserve requirement, and that it is 10 percent. Your bank must therefore keep \$10 of your \$100 deposit in reserve, so it has only \$90 to lend. Now suppose that a person named Jennifer Leclerc borrows \$90 from your bank. She now has \$90 added to her chequing account. Assume that she writes a cheque for \$90 payable to Canadian Tire. Canadian Tire's bank ends up with a \$90 deposit, and that bank is also required to keep 10 percent in reserve. It therefore has \$81 to lend out to someone else. This process of deposit expansion is shown in abbreviated form in Figure 18.3. As you can see, your original deposit of \$100 increases the total supply of money.

What happens if there is no reserve requirement? At the extreme, it means that banks could (theoretically) create infinite amounts of money because they don't have to keep any in reserve. But banks will not do this because it is risky. So, in practice, the dropping of the reserve requirement simply means that banks will be able to create more money than they did when there was a reserve requirement.

Deposit	Money Held in Reserve by Bank	Money to Lend	Total Supply
\$100.00	\$10.00	\$90.00	**\$190.00**
90.00	9.00	81.00	**271.00**
81.00	8.10	72.90	**343.90**
72.90	7.29	65.61	**409.51**
65.61	6.56	59.05	**468.56**

Figure 18.3 How the chartered banking system creates money.

The boxed insert entitled "Canadian vs. U.S. Banks: Quite a Difference" provides information on some key differences between banks in Canada and the United States.

Business Accountability

Canadian vs. U.S. Banks: Quite a Difference

In 2008 and 2009, as the worldwide recession deepened, increasing concern was being expressed that many U.S. banks were in financial trouble. It was feared that at least 100 U.S. banks, and possibly more, would fail by the end of 2009. There was also talk that the United States might have to nationalize some banks. That news was in sharp contrast to the situation in Canada, where the top five Canadian banks earned $18.9 billion in profits (the top five U.S. banks lost $37 billion). A 2009 World Economic Forum report ranked the Canadian banking system as the soundest in the world (the U.S. ranked fortieth).

Why are there such big differences between the U.S. and Canadian banking systems? One reason is that the accountability of Canadian banks is higher because regulation of Canadian banks is much more stringent than the regulation of U.S. banks. The Office of the Superintendent of Financial Institutions, Canada's banking regulator, gets credit for being very conservative and keeping a close watch on the activities of Canadian banks. There is a bit of irony here, because the characteristics of the Canadian banking system that have worked well in the financial crisis are the same characteristics that Canadian consumers have complained about for years.

Another reason is that there are differences in the structures of the banking industries in the two countries. In the United States, there are thousands of banks, and most of them have just one (or a few) branches. By contrast, in Canada there are very few banks, but each one has hundreds of branches. In an ironic twist, the structure of the Canadian banking system is much like that envisioned by Alexander Hamilton, the first American Secretary of the Treasury. He thought it was best to have just a few large national banks, with each one having branches from coast to coast. But by the mid-1800s, opposition to large banks in the United States led to the formation of many state-chartered banks and a very free market mentality about the banking system. Regulations across states were not consistent, and whenever economic troubles arose, there would be lots of bank failures. In the Great Depression of the 1930s, hundreds of banks failed in the United States.

In the recession that began in 2008, it became clear that the regulation of U.S. banks left a lot to be desired. Put simply, there were so many banks that it was difficult to know how big the problems were. By the time it became clear that there were major problems, drastic action was needed to fix them. In 2008–09, multibillion-dollar bailouts for financial institutions were prominent as the United States tried to cope with bank problems. President Obama admitted that the Canadian banking system was managed much better than the U.S. banking system. Canadian banks in the United States—Royal Bank's RBC Bank, Bank of Montreal's Harris Bank, and Toronto Dominion's TD Bank—have all noted a surge in deposits as their U.S. rivals struggle with financial problems.

All Canadian banks are regulated by the federal government, and they have strict rules they must adhere to. For example, Canadian banks must maintain a bigger cushion to absorb potential losses, and their shares must be widely held. Canadian laws also place limits on the amount of foreign competition that Canadian banks have. That may lead Canadian banks to be less responsive to competitive pressures at any given point in time, but it also means that Canadian banks do not feel compelled to take on the kinds of risks that got U.S. banks into trouble.

Canadian banks have a reputation for being risk-averse, and that serves them well when the economy is in trouble. During 2006 and 2007, U.S. banks became deeply involved in risky mortgages, but Canadian banks largely avoided that problem because of their conservative nature. When they did get involved, they showed the risky mortgages on their balance sheets so the public knew exactly what their financial condition was. The Canadian government may end up buying about $125 billion in questionable mortgages, but that is a small fraction of what the U.S. government is buying.

The eventual outcome of the current crisis in the United States may be a consolidation of the banking industry. For example, the United States may end up with just 50 or 60 large banking institutions as a result of the current financial crisis. The U.S. federal government may also take over licensing of banks from the individual states or at least impose stricter regulations on the largest U.S. banks.

Critical Thinking Questions

1. Is there a trade-off between bank accountability to customers and customer satisfaction with banks?
2. Consider the following statement: *Governments around the world should continuously apply very strict standards for banks, even in good economic times, so that the kinds of financial problems that developed in the United States will not happen again.* Do you agree with the statement? Explain your reasoning.

Financial Pillar #2—Alternate Banks

Trust Companies

Explain the role of *alternate banks, specialized lending and savings intermediaries*, and *investment dealers* in the Canadian financial system. 4

One type of so-called alternate bank that serves individuals and businesses is the trust company. A **trust company** safeguards property—funds and estates—entrusted to it. For example, a corporation selling bonds to investors appoints a trustee, usually a trust company, to protect the bondholders' interests. A trust company can also serve as a transfer agent and registrar for corporations. A transfer agent records changes in ownership of a corporation's shares of stock. A registrar certifies to the investing public that stock issues are correctly stated and comply with the corporate charter. Other services include preparing and issuing dividend cheques to shareholders and serving as trustee for employee profit sharing funds. Trust companies also accept deposits and pay interest on them. As noted previously, trust companies have declined in importance during the last couple of decades.

trust company Safeguards funds and estates entrusted to it; may also serve as trustee, transfer agent, and registrar for corporations.

Credit Unions/Caisses Populaires

Credit unions (called *caisses populaires* in Quebec) are also alternate banks. **Credit unions** and *caisses populaires* are co-operative savings and lending associations formed by a group with common interests. They are important to businesses because they lend money to consumers to buy durable goods such as cars and furniture. They lend money to businesses as well. Members (owners) can add to their savings accounts by authorizing deductions from their paycheques or by making direct deposits. They can borrow short-term, long-term, or mortgage funds from the credit union. Credit unions pay somewhat higher interest rates than chartered banks on money that is invested in financial instruments like GICs. Credit unions also invest substantial amounts of money in corporate and government securities. The largest credit unions in Canada are listed in Table 18.2.

credit union Co-operative savings and lending association formed by a group with common interests.

Each year, the market research firm Synovate ranks Canadian financial institutions in 11 areas of service provided to customers. In the 2008 survey, credit unions ranked ahead of all banks and other financial institutions in overall customer service excellence, financial planning and advice, and branch service excellence.[23]

Table 18.2 Top 10 Credit Unions in Canada, 2008

Company	Annual Revenues (in millions of $)
1. Mouvement des Caisses Desjardins	$8373
2. Vancouver City Savings Credit Union	906
3. Caisse Centrale Desjardins	717
4. Servus Credit Union Ltd.	583
5. Coast Capital Savings Credit Union	581
6. Central 1 Credit Union	326
7. Meridian Credit Union Ltd.	292
8. Credit Union Central of Saskatchewan	236
9. Conexus Credit Union	229
10. Envision Financial	218

Financial Pillar #3—Specialized Lending and Savings Intermediaries

Life Insurance Companies

life insurance company A mutual or stock company that shares risk with its policyholders for payment of premiums.

An important source of funds for individuals, non-business organizations, and businesses is the life insurance company. A **life insurance company** shares risk with its policyholders in return for payment of a premium and lends some of the money it collects from premiums to borrowers. Life insurance companies are substantial investors in real estate mortgages and in corporate and government bonds. Next to chartered banks, they are the largest financial intermediaries in Canada. We discuss insurance companies in more detail in Chapter 20.

Factoring Companies

factoring company Buys accounts receivable from a firm for less than their face value, and then collects the face value of the receivables.

An important source of short-term funds for many firms is factoring companies. A **factoring company** (or factor) buys accounts receivable (amounts due from credit customers) from a firm. It pays less than the face value of the accounts but collects the face value of the accounts. The difference, minus the cost of doing business, is the factor's profit.

A firm that sells its accounts receivable to a factor without recourse shifts the risk of credit loss to the factor. If an account turns out to be uncollectible, the factor suffers the loss. However, a factor is a specialist in credit and collection activities. Using a factor may enable a business firm to expand sales beyond what would be practical without the factor. The firm trades accounts receivable for cash. The factor then notifies the firm's customers to make their overdue payments to the factor.

Financial Corporations

sales finance company Specializes in financing instalment purchases made by individuals or firms.

consumer finance company Makes personal loans to consumers.

There are two types of financial corporations—sales finance companies and consumer finance companies. A **sales finance company** specializes in financing instalment purchases made by individuals and firms. When you buy durable goods from a retailer on an instalment plan with a sales finance company, the loan is made directly to you. The item you purchased serves as security for the loan. Sales finance companies enable many firms to sell on credit, even though the firms could not afford to finance credit sales on their own. General Motors Acceptance Corporation (GMAC) is a sales finance company. It is a captive company because it exists to finance instalment contracts resulting from sales made by General Motors. Industrial Acceptance Corporation is a large Canadian sales finance company.

A **consumer finance company** makes personal loans to consumers. Often the borrower pledges no security (collateral) for the loan. For larger loans, collateral may be required, such as a car or furniture.

Venture Capital Firms

venture capital firm Provides funds for new or expanding firms thought to have significant potential.

A **venture capital firm** provides funds for new or expanding firms that have significant potential. For example, Google announced in 2009 that it had started a venture capital fund to support "young companies with awesome potential."[24] Venture capital firms prefer a situation where the company they have invested in becomes very successful and experiences substantial increases in its stock price. Venture capital firms may provide either equity or debt funds to businesses, but they typically buy shares in companies they are interested in. They may demand an ownership stake of 50 percent or more before they will buy in to a company. Because financing new, untested businesses is so risky, venture capital firms want to earn a higher-than-normal return on their investment. They may insist that they be given at least one seat on the board of directors so they can observe first-hand how their investment is faring.

Venture capital firms obtain their funds from initial capital subscriptions, from loans from other financial intermediaries, and from retained earnings. The amount of venture capital that is raised varies according to economic conditions. In 2008, venture capital firms raised a total of $1.5 billion, but that was down 25 percent from 2007 and was the lowest level of fundraising in 13 years. Canada's venture capital industry has been experiencing serious problems during the past few years, so many Canadian entrepreneurs have turned to U.S.-based venture capital companies for funding.[25] Between 2003 and 2008, venture capital investment dropped 35 percent in Canada (from 0.13 percent of GDP to 0.08 percent), but in the United States during the same period, it rose 17 percent (from 0.18 percent of GDP to 0.21).[26] In the first quarter of 2009, venture capital investment was down 47 percent from the fourth quarter of 2008.[27] The average investment per firm was $2.7 million.[28]

Pension Funds

A **pension fund** accumulates money that will be paid out to plan subscribers at some time in the future. The money collected is invested in corporate stocks and bonds, government bonds, or mortgages until it is to be paid out.

pension fund Accumulates money that will be paid out to plan subscribers in the future.

Financial Pillar #4—Investment Dealers

Investment dealers (called stockbrokers or underwriters) perform two important financial functions. First, they are the primary distributors of new stock and bond issues (underwriting). Second, investment dealers facilitate secondary trading of stocks and bonds, both on stock exchanges and on over-the-counter stock and bond markets (the brokerage function). These two functions are discussed in more detail in Chapter 19.

Other Sources of Funds

In Canada, a number of different government suppliers of funds are important to business. In general, they supply funds to new and/or growing companies. However, established firms can also use some of them.

The Business Development Bank of Canada (BDC) makes term loans, primarily to smaller firms judged to have growth potential but unable to secure funds with reasonable terms from traditional sources. It provides proportionally more equity financing and more management counselling services. A variety of provincial industrial development corporations also provide funds to developing business firms in the hope that they will provide jobs in the province. A number of federal and provincial programs are specifically designed to provide loans to agricultural operators. Most of these are long-term loans for land purchase.

The federal government's Export Development Corporation finances and insures export sales for Canadian companies. The Canada Mortgage and Housing Corporation (CMHC) is involved in providing and guaranteeing mortgages. The CMHC is particularly important to the construction industry.

In addition to these activities, governments are involved in providing grants to business operations. For example, the federal government, through the Department of Regional Industrial Expansion (DRIE), gives grants for certain types of business expansion in designated areas of the country. Other federal government grants are available for activities such as new product development.

International Banking and Finance

5 Understand the key concepts and activities in *international banking and finance*.

International banking networks and electronic technologies now permit nearly instantaneous financial transactions around the globe. The economic importance of international finance is evident from both the presence of foreign banks in the Canadian market and the sizes of certain banks around the world. In addition, each nation tries to influence its currency exchange rates for economic advantage in international trade. The subsequent country-to-country transactions result in an *international payments process* that moves money between buyers and sellers on different continents.

Exchange Rates and International Trade

As we saw in Chapter 5, a country's currency exchange rate affects its ability to buy and sell on the global market. The value of a given currency, say, the Canadian dollar, reflects the overall supply and demand for Canadian dollars both at home and abroad. This value changes with economic conditions. Around the world, therefore, firms will watch those trends, and decisions about doing business in Canada will be affected by more or less favourable exchange rates. At one point, in 2009, for example, the Canadian dollar was valued at US$0.97. This was up sharply from its 2002 value of US$0.63, but lower than its value in 2007, when the Canadian dollar was worth more than the U.S. dollar. When the Canadian dollar trades for less than the U.S. dollar, American companies are more interested in buying Canadian companies.

The Law of One Price

How do firms determine when exchange rates are favourable? When a country's currency becomes overvalued, its exchange rate is higher than warranted by its economic conditions. Its high costs make it less competitive. Because its

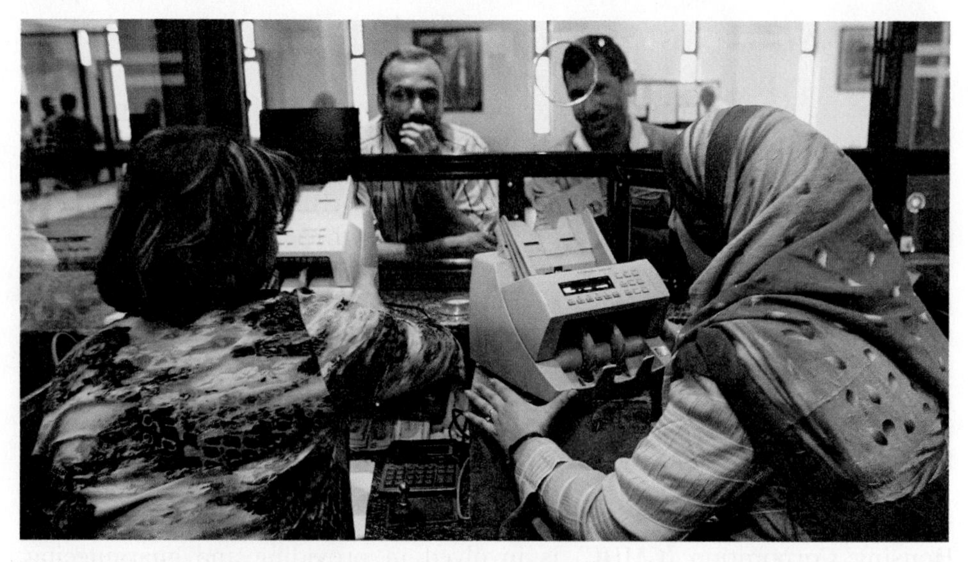

Tellers at the Bank of Baghdad in the capital's Karrada neighbourhood work with customers to convert Iraqi dollars into euros for sending payments from Iraq to a French seller.

products are too expensive to make and buy, fewer are purchased by other countries. The likely result is a trade deficit (see Chapter 5). In contrast, an undervalued currency means low costs and low prices. It attracts purchases by other countries, usually leading to a trade surplus.

How do we know whether a currency is overvalued or undervalued? One method involves a simple concept called the **law of one price**—the principle that identical products should sell for the same price in all countries. In other words, if the different prices of a Rolex watch in different countries were converted into a common currency, the price should be the same everywhere.

law of one price The principle that identical products should sell for the same price in all countries.

But what if prices are not equal? In theory, the pursuit of profits should equalize them. Sellers in high-priced countries will have to reduce prices if they are to compete successfully and make profits. As prices adjust, so should the exchange rates between different currencies until the Rolex can be purchased for the same price everywhere.

A simple example that illustrates over- and undervalued currencies is the Big Mac Index, which is published by the British magazine *The Economist*. The index lists a variety of countries and their Big Mac prices in terms of U.S. dollars. In July 2009, for example, a Big Mac cost $3.57 in the United States. If a Big Mac in another country costs more than $3.57, that means the currency is overvalued; if it costs less than $3.57, the currency is undervalued. In 2009, the most overvalued currencies were those of Norway, Switzerland, Denmark, Sweden, and Brazil. The most undervalued currencies were those of Hong Kong, China, Thailand, and Russia (the Canadian dollar was slightly undervalued). These different values mean that in theory, you could buy Big Macs in Hong Kong and sell them in Norway at a handsome profit. If you did that, the demand for burgers would increase in Hong Kong, driving up the price toward the higher prices in the other countries. In other words, the law of one price would set it. [29]

Government Influence on Exchange Rates

What happens when a currency becomes overvalued or undervalued? A nation's economic authorities may take action to correct its balance-of-payments conditions. Typically, they will devalue or revalue the nation's currency. The purpose of *devaluing* is to cause a decrease in the home country's exchange value. It will then be less expensive for other countries to buy the home country's products. As more of its products are purchased, the home country's payment deficit goes down. The purpose of *revaluation* is the reverse—to increase the exchange value and reduce the home country's payment surplus.

The International Payments Process

Now we know why a nation tries to control its balance of payments and what, at least in part, it can do about an unfavourable balance. Exactly how are payments made? Transactions among buyers and sellers in different countries are simplified through the services provided by their banks. For example, payments from buyers flow through a local bank that converts them from the local currency into the foreign currency of the seller. Likewise, the local bank receives and converts incoming money from the banks of foreign buyers. The payments process is shown in Figure 18.4.[30]

Step 1. A Canadian olive importer withdraws $1000 from its chequing account to buy olives from a Greek exporter. The local Canadian bank converts those dollars into Greek drachmas at the current exchange rate (230 drachmas per dollar).

Step 2. The Canadian bank sends the cheque for 230 000 drachmas (230 × 1000) to the exporter in Greece.

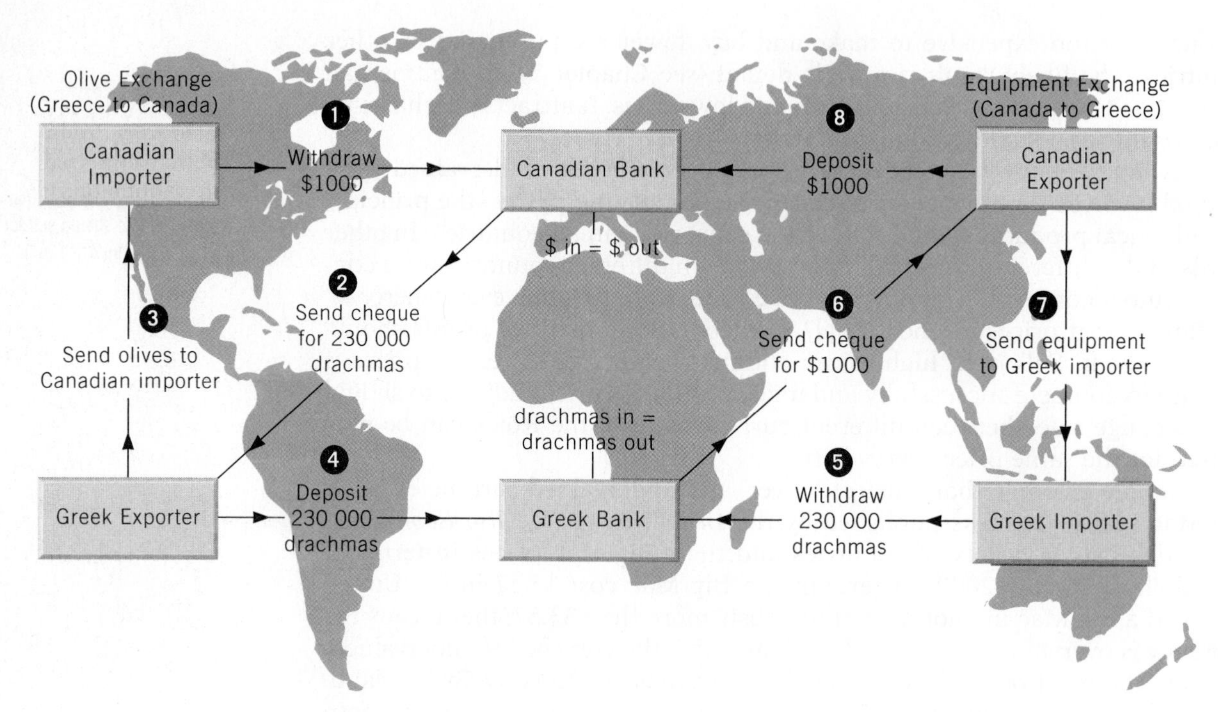

Figure 18.4 The international payments process.

Steps 3 and 4. The exporter sends olives to its Canadian customer and deposits the cheque in its local Greek bank. While the exporter now has drachmas that can be spent in Greece, the importer has olives to sell in Canada. At the same time, a separate transaction is being made between a Canadian machine exporter and a Greek olive oil producer. This time, the importer/exporter roles are reversed between the two countries: The Greek firm needs to import a $1000 olive oil press from Canada.

Steps 5 and 6. Drachmas (230 000) withdrawn from a local Greek bank account are converted into $1000 Canadian and sent via cheque to the Canadian exporter.

Steps 7 and 8. The olive oil press is sent to the Greek importer, and the importer's cheque is deposited in the Canadian exporter's local bank account.

In this example, trade between the two countries is *in balance*: Money inflows and outflows are equal for both countries. When such a balance occurs, *money does not actually have to flow between the two countries*. Within each bank, the dollars spent by local importers offset the dollars received by local exporters. In effect, therefore, the dollars have simply flowed from Canadian importers to Canadian exporters. Likewise, the drachmas have moved from Greek exporters to Greek importers.

The International Bank Structure

There is no worldwide banking system that is comparable—in terms of policy making and regulatory power—to the system of any single industrialized nation. Rather, worldwide banking stability relies on a loose structure of agreements among individual countries or groups of countries.

The World Bank and the IMF

Two United Nations agencies, the World Bank and the International Monetary Fund (IMF), help to finance international trade. Unlike true banks, the **World Bank** (technically the International Bank for Reconstruction and Development) provides only a very limited scope of services. For instance, it funds national improvements by making loans to build roads, schools, power plants, and hospitals. The resulting improvements eventually enable borrowing countries to increase productive capacity and international trade.

World Bank A United Nations agency that provides a limited scope of financial services, such as funding national improvements in underdeveloped countries.

The **International Monetary Fund** is a group of 186 nations that have combined their resources for the following purposes:

International Monetary Fund A United Nations agency consisting of about 186 nations that have combined resources to promote stable exchange rates, provide temporary short-term loans, and serve other purposes.

- to promote the stability of exchange rates
- to provide temporary, short-term loans to member countries
- to encourage members to co-operate on international monetary issues
- to encourage development of a system for international payments

The IMF collects money—called *quotas*—from member nations, with the amount being proportional to each country's size and strength (Canada's quota is about $10 billion).[31] The IMF then makes loans to nations suffering from temporary negative trade balances. By making it possible for these countries to continue buying products from other countries, the IMF facilitates international trade. In 2008, the IMF had about $350 billion available for loans. That seemed like a lot of money, but when the worldwide recession hit, it became clear that $350 billion wasn't going to be nearly enough (remember that in 2009 the U.S. developed a stimulus bill for its own economy that exceeded $800 billion). Thus, the IMF may not be able to help several countries that are on the verge of bankruptcy, because of the worldwide recession.[32] Another problem is the IMF's credibility. Its largest shareholder is the United States, which is mistrusted by many nations, and the United States has been taking actions to cope with its own economic problems that the IMF has always told other countries not to take.[33]

Test yourself on the material for this chapter at **www.pearsoned.ca/mybusinesslab**.

Summary of Learning Objectives

1. **Define *money* and identify the different forms it takes in the nation's money supply.** Any item that is portable, divisible, durable, and stable satisfies the four basic characteristics of *money*. Money also serves three functions: It is a medium of exchange, a store of value, and a unit of account. The nation's money supply is often determined by two measures. *M-1* includes liquid (or spendable) forms of money—*currency* (bills and coins), *demand deposits*, and other *"chequable" deposits* (such as chequing accounts and *ABM* withdrawals). *M-2* includes M-1 plus items that cannot be directly spent but which can be easily converted to spendable forms—*time deposits, money market funds*, and savings deposits. Credit must also be considered as a factor in the money supply.
2. **Describe the different kinds of *financial institutions* that make up the Canadian financial system, including the *Bank of Canada*.** The financial intermediaries in Canada are *chartered banks*, alternate banks, specialized lending and savings intermediaries, and investment dealers. The chartered banks, which are at the heart of our financial system, are the most important source of short-term funds for business firms. The chartered banking system creates

money in the form of expanding demand deposits. The four kinds of financial institutions offer services like financial advice and brokerage services, *electronic funds transfer*, pension and trust services, and lending of money. They also expand the money supply by taking in deposits and making loans. The *Bank of Canada* manages the Canadian economy, controls the money supply, and regulates certain aspects of chartered banking operations. If the Bank of Canada wants to increase the money supply, it can buy government securities or lower the *bank rate*. If it wants to decrease the money supply, it can sell government securities or increase the bank rate.

3. **Explain the role of *chartered banks* in the Canadian financial system.** A chartered bank is a privately owned, profit-seeking firm that serves individuals, businesses, and non-business organizations as a financial intermediary. Chartered banks are the largest and most important financial institutions in Canada. Banks offer a wide variety of services, including chequing and savings accounts, pension services, trust services, international services, loans, financial advice, and various electronic funds transfer services. They are the main source of short-term loans for businesses.

4. **Explain the role of *alternate banks, specialized lending and savings intermediaries,* and *investment dealers* in the Canadian financial system.** *Alternate banks* include trust companies and credit unions. *Trust companies* safeguard property that is entrusted to them. *Credit unions* are co-operative savings and lending associations formed by a group with common interests. They lend money both to businesses and to consumers. *Specialized lending and savings intermediaries* include life insurance companies, (which share risks with their policyholders in return for payment of a premium), *factoring companies* (which buy accounts receivable from businesses at a discount and then collect the face value of the account receivable), financial corporations (which specialize in financing instalment purchases made by businesses and individuals), *venture capital firms* (which provide funds for new or expanding businesses), and *pension funds* (which accumulate and invest money that will be paid out to plan subscribers at some time in the future).

5. **Understand the key concepts and activities in *international banking and finance.*** Electronic technologies now permit speedy global financial transactions to support the growing importance of international finance. Country-to-country transactions are conducted according to an *international payment process* that moves money among buyers and sellers in different nations. Each nation tries to influence its currency *exchange rates* to gain advantage in international trade. For example, if a currency is overvalued, a higher exchange rate usually results in a trade deficit. Conversely, undervalued currencies can attract buyers and create trade surpluses. Governments may act to influence exchange rates by *devaluing* or *revaluing* their national currencies (that is, by decreasing or increasing them). Devalued currencies make it less expensive for other countries to buy the home country's products.

Key Terms

automated banking machines (ABMs) (p. 599)
Bank of Canada (p. 597)
bank rate (rediscount rate) (p. 597)
banker's acceptance (p. 599)
chartered bank (p. 598)
chequable deposit (p. 601)
cheque (p. 593)
consumer finance company (p. 606)
credit union (p. 605)
currency (p. 592)
debit card (p. 600)
demand deposits (p. 593)
ecash (p. 601)
electronic funds transfer (EFT) (p. 599)
factoring company (p. 606)
International Monetary Fund (p. 611)
law of one price (p. 609)
letter of credit (p. 599)
life insurance company (p. 606)
M-1 (p. 592)
M-2 (p. 593)
money (p. 590)
money market mutual funds (p. 593)
pension fund (p. 607)
prime rate of interest (p. 602)
reserve requirement (p. 603)
sales finance company (p. 606)
smart card (p. 601)
term deposit (p. 602)
time deposits (p. 593)
trust company (p. 605)
trust services (p. 599)
venture capital firm (p. 606)
World Bank (p. 611)

Questions for Analysis

1. What kinds of changes in banking are shifting banks away from their historical role?
2. Do we really need all the different types of financial institutions we have in Canada? Could we make do with just chartered banks? Why or why not?
3. Should credit cards be counted in the money supply? Why or why not? Support your view by using the definition of money.
4. Should chartered banks be regulated or should market forces be allowed to set the money supply? Defend your answer.
5. If the Bank of Canada wants to increase the money supply, what options does it have? Explain how each of these options work to increase the money supply.
6. Explain the difference between factoring companies and financial corporations.
7. What is the logic behind the "law of one price" concept? Give an example using Switzerland and China.

Application Exercises

1. Start with a $1000 deposit and assume a reserve requirement of 15 percent. Now trace the amount of money created by the banking system after five lending cycles.
2. Interview several consumers to determine which banking services and products they use (debit cards, ABMs, smart cards, and so on). If interviewees are using these services, determine the reasons. If they are not, find out why not.
3. Interview the manager of a local chartered bank. Identify the ways in which the Bank of Canada helps the bank and the ways in which it limits the bank.

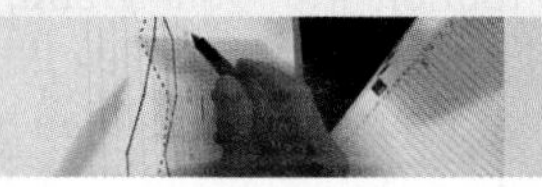

Building Your Business Skills

The Risks and Rewards of Credit Cards

The Purpose of the Assignment

To help students evaluate the risks and rewards associated with excessive credit-card use.

The Situation

Suppose that you've been out of school for a year and are now working in your first job. Your annual $30 000 salary is enough to support your apartment, car, and the basic necessities of life, but the luxuries are still out of reach. You pay cash for everything until one day you get a pre-approved credit-card solicitation in the mail, which offers you a $1500 line of credit. You decide to take the offer and begin charging purchases. Within a year, five other credit-card companies have contacted you, and you accumulate a total credit card debt of $12 000.

Assignment

Step 1

Working with three or four classmates, evaluate the advantages and dangers inherent in this situation, both to

the consumer and to credit-card issuers. To address this issue, research the current percentage of credit-card delinquencies and rate of personal bankruptcies. Find out, for example, how these rates compare with those in previous years. In addition, research the profitability of the credit-card business.

Step 2

Evaluate the different methods that credit-card companies use to attract new customers. Specifically, look at the following practices:

- sending unsolicited, pre-approved credit-card applications to consumers with questionable and even poor credit
- offering large credit lines to consumers who pay only monthly minimums
- lowering interest rates on accounts as a way of encouraging revolving payments
- charging penalties on accounts that are paid in full at the end of every billing cycle (research the GE Rewards MasterCard)
- sending cardholders catalogues of discounted gifts that can be purchased with their charge cards
- linking credit-card use to a program of rewards—say, frequent flyer miles linked to amounts charged

Step 3

Compile your findings in the form of a set of guidelines designed for consumers receiving unsolicited credit-card offers. Your guidelines should analyze the advantages and disadvantages of excessive credit-card use.

Questions for Discussion

1. If you were the person in our hypothetical example, how would you handle your credit situation?
2. Why do you think credit-card companies continue to offer cards to people who are financially overextended?
3. What criteria can you suggest to evaluate different credit-card offers?
4. How do you know when you have enough credit?

Exercising Your Ethics: Team Exercise

Telling the Ethical from the Strictly Legal

The Situation

When upgrading services for convenience to customers, chartered banks are concerned about setting prices that cover all costs so that, ultimately, they make a profit. This exercise challenges you to evaluate one banking service—ABM transactions—to determine if there are also ethical issues that should be considered in a bank's pricing decisions.

The Dilemma

Assume that a bank has more than 300 ABMs serving the nearly 400 000 chequing and savings accounts of its customers. Customers are not charged a fee for their 30 million ABM transactions each year, so long as they use their bank's ABMs. For issuing cash to non-customers, however, the bank charges a $2 ABM fee. The bank's officers are re-examining their policies on ABM surcharges because of public protests.

In considering its current policies, the bank's vice-president for community relations is concerned about more than mere legalities. She wants to ensure that her company is "being a good citizen and doing the right thing." Any decision on ABM fees will ultimately affect the bank's customers, its image in the community and industry, and its profitability for its owners.

Team Activity

Assemble a group of four students and assign each group member to one of the following roles:

- a bank customer
- the bank's vice-president for community relations
- a bank stockholder
- the bank's CEO

Questions for Discussion

1. Before discussing the situation with your group, and from the perspective of your assigned role, do you think there are any ethical issues in this situation? If so, write them down.
2. Before discussing the situation with your group, and from the perspective of your assigned role, decide how this dispute should be resolved.
3. For the various ethical issues that were identified, decide as a group which one is the most important for the bank to resolve. Which issue is second in importance?
4. From an ethical standpoint, what does your group recommend be done to resolve the most important ethical issue? To resolve the second most important ethical issue? What are the advantages and disadvantages of your recommendations?

For additional cases and exercise material, go to **www.pearsoned.ca/mybusinesslab**.

Concluding Case 18-1

Coping with Currency Fluctuations

After decades of being valued at far less than the U.S. dollar, the Canadian dollar began dramatically appreciating in value during 2007. It reached par with the U.S. dollar on September 20, 2007, and then soared as high as US$1.10. The rise of the Canadian dollar was caused by many factors, including a high level of mergers and acquisitions in Canada, high oil prices, large U.S. budget deficits, lower interest rates in the United States than in Canada, problems in the U.S. economy, and the strength of the Canadian economy.

By mid-2009, the Canadian dollar had once again declined to US$0.80. One reason was the dramatic decline in the price of oil, which went from $147 per barrel to less than $35 per barrel in the space of just a few months in 2008. Another reason is the recession that started in 2008. The Canadian dollar (like most other currencies) declined against the U.S. dollar because investors wanted a secure haven for their money during the recession. In spite of the fact that the United States was facing hard economic times of its own, investors still saw it as a safe haven for money. The increased demand for U.S. dollars drove up their value.

Currency fluctuations like we have seen in the last couple of years are interesting (and unnerving). When the Canadian dollar rises like it did in 2007, there are winners and losers. Winners include Canadian consumers (because retail prices tend to go down), Canadian professional sports teams (who pay their players in U.S. dollars), and Canadians travelling to the United States (because the Canadian dollar is worth more). Losers include the domestic Canadian tourist industry (because fewer U.S. tourists visit Canada), Canadian farmers who export grain (the product becomes more expensive in foreign markets), Canadian manufacturers who export to the United States (the prices of their products increase), Canadian railroads (whose revenue is in U.S. dollars), and Canadians who keep U.S. dollar savings accounts (their U.S. dollars decline in value). Here are some specific examples:

- Sherbrooke, Quebec–based furniture maker Shermag Inc. closed four of its eight plants in 2007 and cut 320 jobs because demand for its furniture in the United States had declined. The company experienced a 51 percent drop in export sales between 2006 and 2007.
- Windsor, Ontario–based Cunningham Sheet Metal—which fabricates products like railings, furniture, and canopies—survived the rise in the Canadian dollar by concentrating on the high-quality niche market for its products. But if other companies start doing the same thing (because they have lost customers in the declining automobile manufacturing industry), further problems will develop for the company.
- Canadian oil and gas companies don't like a high Canadian dollar, because their revenues come in U.S. dollars but their expenses come in Canadian dollars. So, when the Canadian dollar increases in value, the value of the U.S. dollars they receive for it is relatively less than it was when the Canadian dollar was lower in value. For example, a US$80 barrel of oil in 2008 was worth the same as a US$52 barrel of oil in 2002 (when the Canadian dollar was worth US$0.65).

When the Canadian dollar rises, Canadian manufacturers can no longer get by with low productivity as they could when the Canadian dollar was low. They need to buy productivity-enhancing machinery, but Canadian capital investment per worker continues to lag behind the United States and the OECD average.

If companies focus on improving productivity, they can cope with a higher value of the Canadian dollar. Mike Keilhauer, a veteran furniture manufacturer, says his company is now doing as much business as it did in 2000, even though it is using only half the space it formerly needed and has only 60 percent of the employees it formerly had. The company has also focussed on reducing manufacturing, shipping, and inventory costs.

There are also winners and losers when the Canadian dollar declines in value (the categories noted above are basically reversed). For example, Canadian exporters benefit because their products become cheaper in the United States and so there is more demand for their products.

It's not just Canadians who have to cope with the uncertainties caused by fluctuating currencies. European companies that do business with the United States had the same kinds of problems that Canadian firms had because the euro also rose in value against the U.S. dollar in 2007. Consider the case of Airbus, a European manufacturer of commercial airplanes. If the U.S. dollar falls, say, 10 cents against the euro, Airbus loses a billion euros in foreign exchange because the majority of the company's expenses are in euros, but its aircraft are sold in U.S. dollars (this is the same problem that Canadian oil and gas companies are faced with).

In 2007, the decline of the U.S. dollar resulted in some rather notable symbolic changes around the world. For example, India announced that visitors to the Taj Mahal would now have to pay in Indian rupees, not U.S. dollars.

Iran, Venezuela, and Russia now demand payment for their oil in euros, not U.S. dollars. And rapper Jay-Z is shown flashing a wad of euros, not dollars, in a 2007 video.

The decline in the value of the U.S. dollar also affected other countries, particularly those that peg their currency to the value of the U.S. dollar. In Saudi Arabia, for example, the riyal has been pegged to the U.S. dollar since 1986. Saudi Arabia has typically followed trends in U.S. interest rates. But when the U.S. Federal Reserve cut interest rates in the United States in the fall of 2007, Saudi Arabia didn't want to follow suit because that would increase inflation rates in Saudi Arabia (the rate was already at 4 percent, up from 0.3 percent in 2003). In May 2007, Kuwait unpegged its currency from the United States because it was also concerned about inflation.

Some financial experts are calling for rather dramatic action to reduce the uncertainty caused by currency fluctuations. One solution that has been proposed is to have just three world currency zones—the dollar, the euro, and the yen (for North America, Europe, and Asia, respectively). Stephen Jarislowsky, a renowned Canadian money manager, says that Canada should either replace its dollar with a new North American currency (patterned after the euro) or it should peg the Canadian dollar to the U.S. dollar to reduce dollar gyrations. While life would be simpler with one North American currency because there would be no exchange rate risk, the Canadian government opposes this idea because it fears Canada's sovereignty would be threatened and the government would give up its right to control inflation and interest rates.

Questions for Discussion

1. Several factors caused the Canadian dollar to rise in value against the U.S. dollar in 2007. Explain how each of the factors mentioned above influenced the upward movement of the Canadian dollar. Then explain why the Canadian dollar dropped so sharply in 2008.
2. Have Canadian professional sports teams been helped or hurt by the rise in the Canadian dollar? Explain.
3. Consider the following statement: *The Canadian dollar is going to continue to experience wide fluctuations in value compared to the U.S. dollar.* Do you agree or disagree with this statement? Explain your answer.
4. Explain how increasing productivity would help Canadian companies cope with a higher Canadian dollar. What would be the effect of increasing productivity if the Canadian dollar dropped?

Concluding Case 18-2

The Struggle to Finance Fish Farming

In Vancouver's Middle Island Bay, about 70 000 captive salmon are swimming around in a big plastic pen. They are part of the struggling fish farming industry in Canada. But these B.C. salmon may be different because they are owned by Richard Buchanan, a man who thinks he has solved one of the big problems plaguing fish farming: salmon poop. In traditional fish farming, the approach is to simply allow salmon waste to drop to the bottom of the ocean below the cages and then let it be eventually dispersed by ocean currents. Environmentalists have long expressed outrage at this practice, and charge that fish farming damages the marine ecosystem and spreads diseases to wild salmon. But Buchanan—the CEO of AgriMarine Industries Ltd.—has invented a system for filtering salmon waste that he says could dramatically reduce the problems of fish farming. Buchanan's idea could be very important, because in 2008 the provincial government of B.C. announced a moratorium on salmon fish farms on B.C.'s north coast. This decision was made partly because public opinion about fish farming is very negative.

The problems of farming salmon are very similar to those encountered when farming cod. During the heyday of cod fishing in the 1980s, commercial fishing operators from Newfoundland harvested more than 220 000 tonnes of wild cod each year. But by 1992, cod stocks had declined sharply, and the federal fisheries minister drastically reduced the number of fish that could be harvested. Thousands of people involved in fish catching and fish processing lost their jobs, and the industry has never recovered.

In 1997, the federal government suggested that Newfoundland become a pioneer in cod aquaculture. By 1999, 18 cod aquaculture operations had started. Newfoundland did manage to produce 227 tonnes of cod in 2002, but big problems developed in the industry in 2003. The market price of cod declined sharply and that led to much lower sales revenue. But the biggest factor was the industry's inventory problem—fish farmers couldn't get young cod (called fry), because financial and other problems had forced two large hatcheries out of business. By 2006, there was not a single cod farm in operation in Newfoundland. What happened?

One answer is the high cost of feed, which constitutes about 80 percent of total expenses in cod farming. Most Newfoundland fish farmers were able to get credit from the companies they purchased their feed from. These feed companies were essentially acting as bankers for the cod farmers, but there were only three of them in Atlantic Canada, and fish farmers found they were paying interest rates of more than 25 percent on their loans. The cod farmers couldn't get lower-cost bank loans because Canadian banks would not loan them any money. The banks were not interested in making loans to cod farmers because it is a risky business and the time frame for getting revenue from sales is long (it takes three years to raise cod fry to a size where they can be sold to consumers). Some foreign banks—in Iceland and Norway—have funded other, more traditional seafood industries in Canada, but none appeared interested in fish farming.

There are several factors that make fish farming a risky business. First, factors like bad weather and fish diseases can wipe out a whole year's work in short order. Second, if a fish farming operation does go bankrupt, there are very few assets that can be sold to help investors recoup their money. Third, the fluctuating value of the Canadian dollar means that Canadian seafood products that are exported to the United States (where most of Canada's seafood is sold) are sometimes very competitively priced and sometimes not. It is difficult to plan under these circumstances.

In an attempt to solve the financing problems of fish farmers, the government of Newfoundland developed a provincial loan guarantee program that guarantees 80 percent of any debt owed if a fish farming company needs to be liquidated. But the program requires that at least one bank participate, and so far only one company has gotten bank approval.

In terms of the supply of fry, most people seem to agree that the Newfoundland fish farming industry can move forward only if there is a local hatchery to provide cod fry to the fish farmers. There is a cod farming research facility in Pool's Cove. It has been supported by a $12.4 million grant provided by several different organizations, including the provincial and federal governments, the Canadian Foundation for Innovation, and the Atlantic Innovation Fund. But there are no cod farming operations.

The difficulties in Newfoundland are a bit perplexing, since cod farming has been working elsewhere. Cod cages are in the water in the Bay of Fundy, and the cod grown there have been featured on the menus of some high-end restaurants in the northeastern United States. In Scotland, Johnson Seafarms has raised more than $48 million to pursue organic cod farming. Investors became interested after they were informed that 20 percent of their initial investment would be tax-free; also, if they hold their stock for at least three years, they won't have to pay any capital gains tax. Norway has had even more success in cod farming. In 2006, it produced 40 000 tonnes of cod. By 2010, the Norwegian industry is expected to be producing 225 000 tonnes of cod.

In 2006, the Newfoundland minister of Fisheries and Aquaculture announced that $33 450 worth of funding had been approved to help the Newfoundland Aquaculture Industry Association (NAIA) develop a business plan for a demonstration cod farm. The funding will help the NAIA identify what will be required to develop commercial cod farming operations. The minister acknowledged that cod farming is still in the development stage in Newfoundland, but thought that it was a promising industry that would benefit rural communities.

In addition to the problems of financing and the supply of fry, there are environmental concerns. In 2006, there were 96 salmon farming sites in New Brunswick, and each of these sites had between 200 000 and 300 000 fish. Waste from these fish collects on the sea floor, and studies have shown that the sea floor under fish cages is not normal. Oxygen levels are low, and a layer of sludge up to 20 centimetres deep exists. The water simply can't neutralize the large amount of waste that is concentrated in a relatively small area, so other marine life is harmed. These problems are particularly evident in Passamaquoddy Bay, where there are many salmon farms. It doesn't matter which fish species is involved—it is the technology of fish farming that causes the problem.

The dilemma is that wild stocks of most fish species are declining because of overfishing. Consumer demand for fish is high, so aquaculture is a tempting solution. Experts say that ocean stocks are going to keep declining, so aquaculture may be the thing of the future. If the experimental cod farms can show a profit, a new era will dawn. But large investments are needed to secure the future of aquaculture.

Questions for Discussion

1. Why did feed companies charge such high interest rates to cod farmers?
2. Why were banks not interested in providing loans to cod farmers?
3. Which source of funds were cod farmers using? Why were they using that source? What other sources of funding might be possible for this type of business? (Read the material in Chapter 20 on sources of funds for businesses before answering this question.)
4. Do you think that provincial government financing will move the cod farming industry toward real commercial success? Defend your answer.

Chapter 19

Understanding Securities and Investments

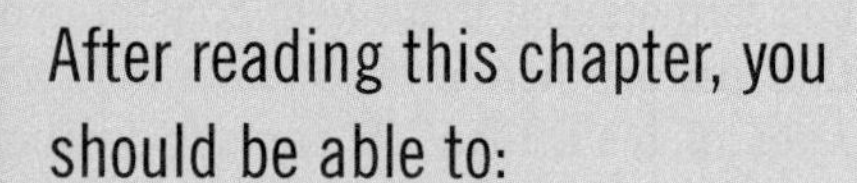

After reading this chapter, you should be able to:

1. Explain the difference between *primary* and *secondary securities markets.*
2. Discuss the value of *common stock* and *preferred stock* to shareholders and describe the secondary market for each type of security.
3. Distinguish among various types of *bonds* in terms of their issuers, safety, and retirement.
4. Describe the investment opportunities offered by *mutual funds* and *commodities.*
5. Explain the process by which securities are bought and sold.
6. Explain how securities markets are regulated.

And the Markets Came Tumbling Down—Again

From 2000 to 2010, stock markets in Canada and the United States have been extremely volatile, with stock prices soaring during some time periods and dropping dramatically in others. What was causing this volatility? Here is the story.

In the late 1990s, thousands of Canadian and American investors became paper millionaires in a booming economy spurred by a vibrant stock market. Annual returns of 15 to 25 percent were commonplace as investors pumped money into the market at a record pace. Major market indexes—the Toronto Stock Exchange (S&P/TSX), the Dow Jones Industrial Average (DJIA), and the NASDAQ Composite—climbed to record highs. Dot-coms and other beneficiaries of the new economy led a parade toward record levels of wealth and prosperity. Government revenues grew so fast that legislators struggled to figure out how to spend the nation's newfound wealth. As investor assets rapidly accumulated, older workers began planning for early retirement.

Then something happened. A slowdown that had first surfaced in late 1999 gradually gained momentum and began to dampen stock prices in 2000. Soon the slowdown became an unmistakable retreat, particularly after it became apparent that many dot-com companies were simply grand-sounding ideas that were never going to be profitable. The stock market was also negatively affected by a series of corporate scandals involving well-known firms—RT Capital Management, Global Crossings, Enron, Arthur Andersen, ImClone, WorldCom, and a host of others—that caused both fear and anger in retirees, employees, and investors. The public's trust dwindled until, by the fall of 2002, the market had tumbled to its lowest level in years as wary investors pulled money out of stocks and went looking for safer investments. In 2000, the S&P/TSX was at 11 000, but it fell to 7000 by the summer of 2002. The NASDAQ Composite fell from a record high 5100 in 2000 to just above 1300 in mid-July 2002, losing 74 percent of its value. In that same period, the DJIA fell 32 percent. Some individual companies fared even worse. Nortel Networks fell from $124 per share in 2000 to less than $1 per share in 2002.

To respond to the crisis of confidence and to get economies moving again, the Bank of Canada, the U.S. Federal Reserve, and other central banks around the world cut interest rates. This strategy worked. By mid-2003, markets were recovering, and there were positive economic signs—increases in sales and industrial production, low inflation, and strong consumer spending. But low interest rates eventually caused even bigger problems, especially in the United States. Why? One of the reasons was home mortgages, which could now be obtained with very low interest rates. People who had previously not been able to get a mortgage suddenly found that banks were willing to lend them money. With more people looking to buy a house, it was not surprising that house prices soared. (More detail on the role that home mortgages played in the overall financial meltdown of 2008 is found in the opening case in Chapter 20.)

So another bubble was forming, this one caused not by dot-com companies but by housing. And, like all bubbles, it eventually burst. When it did (in 2006), house prices started dropping, and many people found that they owed more on their mortgage than their house was worth. This led to a wider financial crisis as banks and other financial institutions discovered that they had on their books literally trillions of dollars in mortgage loans that would likely never be repaid. Once this became clear to investors, they lost confidence in the stock prices of these (and other) companies, and stock markets plunged once again. As confidence eroded, companies began laying off employees in anticipation of tough times ahead. Consumers started spending less freely, and this worsened the problem.

The DJIA reached a peak of 14 000 in the fall of 2007, and then started dropping. In Canada, where there was no housing crisis, markets kept rising a bit longer. The S&P/TSX index reached 15 000 in June 2008, but as the problems in the U.S. economy spread around the world, all stock markets began to drop dramatically. By September 2008, the S&P/TSX had dropped to 12 000 and by late October it was down to 9200. By February 2009, the index had dropped to 7500, meaning that it had lost half its value. Stunned investors realized that this drop was even worse than the one that had occurred in 2000–02. Stock market declines were not limited to Canada and the United States. Indexes in China, India, and Russia declined by 40 to 70 percent.

By early 2009, most economists were predicting a deep and lengthy recession for the world economy. This meant that stock prices were going to be depressed for some time, perhaps years. Inevitably, there were comparisons to the great stock market crash that occurred in 1929. There is an old saying about the stock market that "there is greed on the way up and fear on the way down." And that is exactly what has been evident during the past decade. In both of the big run-ups, all sorts of people eagerly bought stocks in an attempt to cash in on the boom. But when the big declines started, everyone looked around in desperation for a way out.

By the fall of 2009, the S&P/TSX had once again risen to 11 500 but it continued to be quite volatile. This volatility was evidence that investors were jumpy and were responding to any data that suggested that the economic problems were (or were not) being resolved.

How long will it take the S&P/TSX to get back to 15 000? Well, after the stock market crashed in 1929, it took 25 years for the DJIA to get back to the high point it reached in 1929. Could that happen this time? Everyone hopes not, but investors now have some tough questions to answer. Should they stay in the market or get out (and take big losses if they sell)? Should they put their money in money market mutual funds? Should they gamble on further downfalls by selling short? How about buying more stock because current prices are so low? ◆

How will this help me?

By understanding the material in this chapter, you will benefit in two ways: (1) As an investor, you'll be better prepared to evaluate investment opportunities that will improve your personal financial situation in both the short and long term; (2) as a manager, you'll be able to more clearly understand how securities markets affect the firm you work for and the various alternative sources of funds that are available to your company.

In this chapter, we describe the role of securities markets and securities as a stimulus for business. We discuss common stock, preferred stock, and the various types of bonds, the markets where they are bought and sold, and the regulation of securities markets.

Securities Markets

1 Explain the difference between *primary* and *secondary securities markets.*

securities Stocks and bonds (which represent a secured-asset-based claim on the part of investors) that can be bought and sold.

Stocks and bonds are known as **securities** because they represent *secured*, or *asset-based*, claims on the part of investors. In other words, holders of stocks and bonds have a stake in the business that issued them. As we saw in Chapter 4, stockholders have claims on some of a corporation's assets (and a say in how the company is run) because each share of stock represents part-ownership. In contrast, *bonds* represent strictly financial claims for money owed to bondholders by a company. Companies sell bonds to raise long-term funds. The markets in which stocks and bonds are sold are called *securities markets*.

Primary and Secondary Markets for Securities

primary securities market The sale and purchase of newly issued stocks and bonds by firms or governments.

Primary securities markets handle the buying and selling of new stocks and bonds by firms or governments. New securities are sometimes sold to one buyer or a small group of buyers. These so-called *private placements* allow the businesses that use them to keep their plans confidential.

Investment Banking

investment banker Any financial institution engaged in purchasing and reselling new stocks and bonds.

Most new stocks and some bonds are sold to the wider public market. To bring a new security to market, the issuing corporation must obtain approval from a provincial securities commission. It also needs the services of an **investment banker**, who serves as a financial specialist in issuing new securities. Such well-known firms as RBC Dominion Securities and TD Securities provide three types of investment banking services:

1. They advise the company on the timing and financial terms for the new issue.
2. By *underwriting* (buying) the new securities, investment bankers bear some of the risk of issuing the new security.
3. They create the distribution network that moves the new securities through groups of other banks and brokers into the hands of individual investors.

New securities represent only a small portion of securities traded, however. The market for existing stocks and bonds, the **secondary securities market**, is handled by organizations such as the Toronto Stock Exchange. We will consider the activities of these markets in a moment.

secondary securities market The sale and purchase of previously issued stocks and bonds.

Stocks

Discuss the value of *common stock* and *preferred stock* to shareholders and describe the secondary market for each type of security. 2

Each year, financial managers, along with millions of individual investors, buy and sell the stocks of thousands of companies. This widespread ownership has become possible because of the availability of different types of stocks and because markets have been established for conveniently buying and selling them. In this section, we will focus on the value of *common* and *preferred stock* as securities. We will also describe the *stock exchanges* where they are bought and sold.

Common Stock

Individuals and other companies buy a firm's common stock in the hope that the stock will increase in value, affording them a capital gain, and/or will provide dividend income. But what is the value of a common stock? Stock values are expressed in three different ways—as *par value*, as *market value*, and as *book value*.

Par Value

The face value of a share of stock—its **par value**—is set by the issuing company's board of directors. Each company must preserve the par value money in its retained earnings, and it cannot be distributed as dividends.

par value The arbitrary value of a stock set by the issuing company's board of directors and stated on stock certificates; used by accountants but of little significance to investors.

Market Value

A stock's real value is its **market value**—the current price of a share on the stock market. Market value reflects buyers' willingness to invest in a company. The market price of a stock can be influenced by both objective factors (e.g., a company's profits) and subjective factors, like *rumours* (unverified information such as a claim that a company has made a big gold strike), *investor relations* (playing up the positive aspects of a company's financial condition to financial analysts and financial institutions), and *stockbroker recommendations* (a recommendation to buy a stock may increase demand for the stock and cause its price to increase, while a recommendation to sell can decrease demand and cause the price to fall).

market value The current price of one share of a stock in the secondary securities market; the real value of a stock.

Book Value

Recall from Chapter 14 our definition of *owners' equity*—the sum of a company's common stock par value, retained earnings, and additional paid-in capital. The **book value** of common stock represents owners' equity divided by the

book value Value of a common stock expressed as total stockholders' equity divided by the number of shares of stock.

number of shares. Book value is used as a comparison indicator because, for successful companies, the market value is usually greater than the book value. Thus, when market price falls to near book value, some investors buy the stock on the principle that it is underpriced and will increase in value in the future.

Investment Traits of Common Stock

As the opening case shows, common stocks are among the riskiest of all securities. Uncertainties about the stock market can quickly change a given stock's value. Furthermore, when companies have unprofitable years, they often cannot pay dividends. Shareholder income—and perhaps share price—may both drop as a result. At the same time, however, common stocks offer high growth potential. The prospects for growth in various industries change from time to time, but the blue-chip stocks of well-established, financially sound firms such as IBM and Imperial Oil have historically provided investors with steady income through consistent dividend payouts.

What Is a Blue-Chip Stock?

blue-chip stocks Stocks from well-established, financially sound firms.

A **blue-chip stock** is one that has been issued by a well-established, financially sound firm.[1] With the proliferation of internet and start-up dot-coms about a decade ago, some people started to think that perhaps many of the old performance guidelines for assigning blue-chip status to a stock had changed. Guidelines such as a company's history of dividend payouts, steady growth in earnings per share, and a low price-earnings ratio (current stock price divided by annual earnings per share) didn't seem to matter anymore because the market prices of start-ups that hadn't ever earned a profit were soaring.

Consider this example: If you had invested $10 000 in Wal-Mart stock in July 1997, the peak value of this blue-chip stock during 1997–2000 would have been about $40 000, but the same $10 000 investment in start-up Yahoo! would have surged to nearly $600 000. This huge difference could not have been predicted using traditional indicators. Investors were betting that it would become a profitable business in the future. But that bet was extremely risky because during that time period, Yahoo! had zero or negative earnings per share, whereas Wal-Mart's net earnings had grown steadily during the previous 10 years. Wal-Mart also had a steady history of payouts to stockholders, but Yahoo! had never paid a cash dividend. Reality returned when the price of Yahoo! dropped sharply in late 2000. (In May 2009, one share of Wal-Mart stock was worth about $50, while one share of Yahoo was worth about $15.)

market capitalization The dollar value (market value) of stocks listed on a stock exchange.

Market Capitalization. The market value of a company's stock is known as its **market capitalization**. It is computed by multiplying the number of a company's outstanding shares times the value of each share. The top 10 Canadian companies in terms of market capitalization are shown in Table 19.1. There are three points of interest here: First, almost all of the companies in the top 10 are either financial institutions or natural resource companies. Second, the rankings have changed dramatically during the last decade (for example, the market capitalization of Nortel Networks was $221.9 billion in 2000, but the company is now bankrupt). Third, the market capitalization of most companies has declined as a result of the recession that began in 2008 (for example, Royal Bank of Canada's market capitalization was $61.3 billion in 2005, but only $55.4 billion in 2008).

Preferred Stock

preferred stock Stock that pays dividends that are expressed as a percentage of par value.

Preferred stock is usually issued with a stated par value, such as $100. Dividends paid on preferred stock are usually expressed as a percentage of

Table 19.1 Top 10 Canadian Companies, 2005 and 2008 (as measured by market capitalization)

Corporation	Market Capitalization (in billions of $)	
	2005	2008
1. Royal Bank of Canada	$61.3	$55.4
2. Toronto-Dominion Bank	46.8	40.2
3. Imperial Oil Ltd.	36.4	39.1
4. EnCana Corp.	40.0	38.7
5. Barrick Gold Corp.	—	35.6
6. The Bank of Nova Scotia	47.1	34.6
7. Goldcorp Inc.	—	30.9
8. Research In Motion Ltd.	—	30.8
9. PotashCorp. of Saskatchewan	—	30.0
10. Canadian Natural Resources Ltd.	33.3	26.4

the par value. For example, if a preferred stock with a $100 par value pays a 6 percent dividend, shareholders would receive an annual dividend of $6 on each share.

Some preferred stock is *callable*. The issuing firm can require the preferred shareholders to surrender their shares in exchange for a cash payment. The amount of this cash payment, known as the *call price*, is specified in the agreement between the preferred shareholders and the firm.

Investment Traits of Preferred Stock

Because of its preference on dividends, preferred stock is less risky than the common stock of the same company. Moreover, most preferred stock is cumulative. With **cumulative preferred stock**, any dividend payments the firm misses must be paid later, as soon as the firm is able. Typically, the firm cannot pay any dividends to its common shareholders until it has made up all late payments to preferred shareholders. If a firm with preferred stock having a $100 par value and paying a 6 percent dividend fails to pay that dividend for two years, it must make up the arrears of $12 per share before it can pay dividends to common shareholders.

cumulative preferred stock Preferred stock on which dividends not paid in the past must first be paid up before the firm may pay dividends to common shareholders.

The income from cumulative preferred stock is not as certain as the corporate bonds of the same company. The company cannot pay dividends if it does not make a profit. The purchase price of the preferred stock can also fluctuate, leading to a capital gain or loss for the shareholder. And the growth potential of preferred stock is limited due to its fixed dividend.

Stock Exchanges

Most of the secondary market for stocks is handled by organized stock exchanges. In addition to stock markets, a so-called "dealer," or the over-the-counter market, handles the exchange of some stocks. A **stock exchange** is an organization of individuals formed to provide an institutional setting in which shares of stock can be bought and sold. The exchange enforces certain rules to govern its members' trading activities. Most exchanges are non-profit corporations established to serve their members.

stock exchange An organization of individuals formed to provide an institutional setting in which shares of stock can be bought and sold.

To become a member, an individual must purchase one of a limited number of memberships—called "seats"—on the exchange. Only members (or their representatives) are allowed to trade on the exchange. In this sense, because all orders to buy or sell must flow through members, they have a legal monopoly. Memberships can be bought and sold like other assets.

The Trading Floor

Each exchange regulates the places and times at which trading may occur. Trading used to take place only at an actual physical location called the *trading floor*, where specialists matched buy and sell orders they received from brokers. Over 400 traders worked on the trading floor of the Toronto Stock Exchange in the 1980s, but the floor was closed in 1997. Now, alternative trading systems (ATSs) like Pure Trading, Alpha, and Chi-X Canada use computers to match buy and sell orders. These ATSs have lowered the cost and increased the speed of stock trading.[2]

Brokers

broker An individual licensed to buy and sell securities for customers in the secondary market; may also provide other financial services.

A **broker** receives buy and sell orders from those who are not members of the exchange and executes the orders. In return, the broker earns a commission from the order placer. Brokerage assistance can be purchased at either discount or full-service prices.

Discount Brokers. Discount brokers offer well-informed individual investors a fast, low-cost way to participate in the market. For example, you can buy shares of stock and pay brokers' fees of less than $10, depending on how often you trade, how large your account is, and which firm you use; if you are an experienced trader, you could buy 100 shares of a $50 stock and pay just $4.95 in brokers' commissions if you use Questrade. The same purchase might cost you $50 or more at a full-service brokerage firm.[3]

Discount brokerage services cost less because sales personnel receive fees or salaries, not commissions. Discount brokers generally do not offer investment advice or person-to-person sales consultations. They do, however, offer automated online services, such as stock research, industry analysis, and screening for specific types of stocks.

Online trading is becoming increasingly popular among investors because it allows for convenient access to the internet; fast, no-nonsense transactions; and the opportunity for investors to manage their own portfolios while paying low fees for trading. But online traders must still use a broker. Using costs and fees as key criteria, a 2008 survey of online brokers rated Qtrade Investor, BMO InvestorLine, and E*Trade Canada as the top three online brokers.[4]

Full-Service Brokers. Despite the emergence of discount brokers and online investing, there is still demand for full-service brokerages, which help both new, uninformed investors and experienced investors who don't have time to keep up with all the latest developments. Full-service brokers offer clients suggestions on investments that clients might overlook when trying to sift through an avalanche of online financial data. They also provide estate planning, tax strategies, and a wider range of investment products. Initial public offerings (IPOs) of stock, for example, are generally not available to the public through online retail brokers. But a full-service broker, who is also the investment banker who sells the IPO shares, can sell IPO shares to his or her clients. The Business Accountability box provides information on the financial advisers who help investors.

Canadian Stock Exchanges

The *Toronto Stock Exchange (TSX)* is the largest stock exchange in Canada. It is made up of about 100 individual members who hold seats. The securities of most major corporations are listed there. A company must pay a fee before it

Business Accountability

Accountability Goes Professional

Investment recommendations by financial advisers offer clients possibilities of both losses and gains. As professionals, advisers should be, but sometimes haven't been, trustworthy stewards of clients' private information. That's why the financial industry, as early as 1947, began establishing societies that later merged to become the Association for Investment Management and Research (AIMR). Today, its members include more than 60 000 investment practitioners—securities analysts, portfolio managers, financial strategists—and educators in more than 100 countries. AIMR serves three broad areas for which members are accountable—continuing education, conduct and ethics, and standards of practice—to maintain high standards of professionalism in their field.

The association's flagship activity is the Chartered Financial Analyst (CFA) program. Regarded as the industry's premier certification, the CFA designation has been earned by more than 55 000 investment professionals, from among some 480 000 CFA exam-takers, since 1963. Industry giants such as Citigroup, Prudential Financial, Morgan Stanley, and Deutsche Bank encourage and compete for CFA professionals in banking, investments, mutual funds, insurance, and consulting.

Earning a charter involves a progression of post-graduate tests and three years of professional experience. The program's three levels of study each require 250 hours of preparation and an examination covering a broad-based "Body of Knowledge" for the investment community. Level 1 includes tools and concepts for determining the value of investments, portfolio management, and AIMR's code of ethics and professional conduct. Level 2 applies the tools from Level 1 in analyzing investments and applies the code of ethics and conduct in practical situations. Level 3 explores the portfolio management process, including ethics and conduct, in thorough detail. After meeting these requirements and signing a professional conduct statement, the AIMR member has the right to use the CFA designation.

While the testing hurdle is a one-time requirement, professional accountability is a never-ending obligation. Every year, members must disclose any customer complaints or disciplinary procedures about their professional conduct. The public, too, may file complaints against an AIMR member for unethical behaviour, misconduct, or incompetence. Officials review each disclosure or complaint and conduct inquiries that could lead to disciplinary actions. Punishments range from letters of caution to public censure and even removal from membership or revocation of the CFA charter. Continuous accountability is a cornerstone for maintaining ethical and professional standards.

Critical Thinking Questions

1. What are the advantages of having the CFA designation? Are there any disadvantages? If so, describe them.
2. Consider the following statement: *The CFA designation is very popular, but it will not prevent some financial professionals from behaving unethically or from taking actions that are detrimental to their clients. Something else needs to be done to restore consumer confidence in financial advisors.* Do you agree or disagree with the statement? Explain your reasoning.

The Toronto Stock Exchange is one of several in Canada where shares of stock in Canadian companies are bought and sold.

can list its security on the exchange. Formerly, there were also stock exchanges in Calgary, Vancouver, and Montreal, but in 1999 an agreement was reached that created the new Canadian Venture Exchange (CDNX) from the Vancouver and Calgary stock exchanges. The CDNX focuses on junior companies.

Foreign Stock Exchanges

Many foreign countries also have active stock exchanges. In fact, several foreign stock exchanges—most notably those in the United States and England—trade far more shares each day than the TSX does.

The New York Stock Exchange. For many people, "the stock market" means the *New York Stock Exchange (NYSE)*, which was founded in 1792 and is the largest of all U.S. exchanges. In January 2009, the market value of shares traded on the NYSE was US$9.3 billion. Only firms meeting certain minimum requirements—earning power, total value of outstanding stock, and number of shareholders—are eligible for listing on the NYSE.[5]

The American Stock Exchange. The second largest U.S. exchange, the *American Stock Exchange (AMEX)*, is also located in New York City. It accounts for about 2 percent of all shares traded on U.S. exchanges and, like the NYSE, has minimum requirements for listings. They are, however, less stringent.

U.S. Regional Stock Exchanges. Regional stock exchanges were established in the United States long before the advent of modern communications in order to serve investors in places other than New York. The largest regional exchanges are the Chicago (formerly the Midwest) Stock Exchange and the Pacific Stock Exchange in Los Angeles and San Francisco. Many corporations list their stocks both regionally and on either the NYSE or the AMEX.

Other Foreign Stock Exchanges. As recently as 1980, the U.S. market accounted for more than half the value of the world market in traded stocks, and as late as 1975, the equity of IBM alone was greater than the national market equities of all but four countries. Market activities, however, have shifted dramatically as the value of shares listed on foreign exchanges continues to grow. The annual dollar value of trades on exchanges in London, Tokyo, and other cities is in the trillions, and there are actually more stocks listed on the

Government agencies and religious organizations control about 50 percent of all economic activity in Iran. IPOs of newly privatized automakers, shipping companies, and banks have attracted more and more budding capitalists to the stock market floor.

London exchange than there are on the NYSE. In market value, however, transactions on U.S. exchanges remain larger than those in any other country. Relatively new stock exchanges are also flourishing in cities from Shanghai to Warsaw.

The Over-the-Counter Market. The **over-the-counter (OTC) market** is so called because its original traders were somewhat like retailers. They kept supplies of shares on hand and, as opportunities arose, sold them over the office counter to interested buyers. Even today, the OTC market has no trading floor. Rather, it consists of many people in different locations who hold an inventory of securities that are not listed on any of the major exchanges. The over-the-counter market consists of independent dealers who own the securities that they buy and sell at their own risk. Although OTC activities are of interest from a historical perspective, trading volume is small in comparison with other markets.[6]

over-the-counter (OTC) market Organization of securities dealers formed to trade stock outside the formal institutional setting of the organized stock exchanges.

NASDAQ and NASD. In the 1960s, a study by the U.S.-based Securities and Exchange Commission recommended automation of the OTC, calling for a new system to be implemented by the National Association of Securities Dealers Inc. (NASD). The resulting automated OTC system, launched in 1971, is known as the **National Association of Securities Dealers Automated Quotation (NASDAQ)** system, the world's first electronic stock market.[7] The NASDAQ telecommunications system operates the NASDAQ Stock Market by broadcasting trading information on an intranet to over 350 000 terminals worldwide. Whereas orders at the NYSE are paired on the trading floor, NASDAQ orders are paired and executed on a computer network. Current listings include Starbucks and such well-known technology stocks as Intel, Dell, Oracle Technology, and Microsoft. In January 2009, the market value of shares traded on NASDAQ was US$2.2 billion.

National Association of Securities Dealers Automated Quotation (NASDAQ) A stock market implemented by NASD that operates by broadcasting trading information on an intranet to more than 350 000 terminals worldwide.

Bonds

3 Distinguish among various types of *bonds* in terms of their issuers, safety, and retirement.

A **bond** is an IOU—a written promise that the borrower will pay the lender, at some stated future date, a sum of money (the principal) plus an additional amount (the interest). Bondholders have a claim on a corporation's assets and earnings that comes before the claims of common and preferred shareholders. Bonds differ from one another in terms of maturity, tax status, and level of risk vs. potential yield. Investors must take these factors into consideration when deciding which particular bond to buy.

bond A written promise that the borrower will pay the lender, at a stated future date, the principal plus a stated rate of interest.

To help bond investors make assessments, several services rate the quality of bonds from different issuers. Table 19.2 shows ratings by two principal rating services, Moody's and Standard & Poor's. The rating measures the bond's default risk—the chance that one or more promised payments will be deferred or missed altogether. The financial crisis of 2008 revealed some significant problems with bond rating agencies. The credibility of companies like Moody's and Standard & Poor's has declined because they gave overly favourable ratings

Table 19.2 Bond Ratings

	High Grade	Medium Grade (Investment Grade)	Speculative	Poor Grade
Moody's	Aaa Aa	A Baa	Ba B	Caa to C
Standard & Poor's	AAA AA	A BBB	BB B	CCC to D

to mortgage-backed securities that were actually very risky investments. People who made investments based on the ratings lost billions of dollars when bonds they thought were safe turned out not to be.[8] Standard & Poor's is revamping its procedures to help investors understand the difference between traditional corporate bonds and the so-called *structured securities* that turned out to be much riskier than anyone thought.[9]

Although all corporations issue common stock, not all of them issue bonds. Shareholders provide equity (ownership) capital, while bondholders are lenders (although they are also considered "investors" as far as the securities market is concerned). Stock certificates represent ownership, while bond certificates represent indebtedness.

corporate bonds Bonds issued by a company as a source of long-term funding.

registered bonds Bonds where the names of holders are registered with the company.

bearer (or coupon) bonds Bonds that require bondholders to clip coupons from certificates and send them to the issuer to receive interest payments.

secured bonds Bonds issued by borrowers who pledge assets as collateral in the event of non-payment.

debentures Unsecured bonds.

Corporate Bonds

Corporate bonds are a major source of long-term financing for Canadian corporations. They have traditionally been issued with maturities ranging from 20 to 30 years, but in the past few years, 10-year maturities have come into wider use. Longer-term corporate bonds are somewhat riskier than shorter-term bonds. Bond ratings of new and proposed corporate issues are published to keep investors informed of the latest risk evaluations on many bonds. Negative ratings do not preclude a bond's success, but they do raise the interest rate that issuers must offer. Corporate bonds may be categorized in one of two ways: (1) according to methods of interest payment, and (2) according to whether they are *secured* or *unsecured*.

More choices and more options than ever before
Perfect for the secure part of your RRSP
NEW CANADA SAVINGS BONDS
YOU'RE ON SOLID GROUND.
Canada
7/00

Private corporations are not the only organizations that issue bonds. The government of Canada issues Canada Savings Bonds to finance its debt.

Interest Payment: Registered and Bearer Bonds

Registered bonds register the names of holders with the company, which simply mails out cheques to the bondholders. **Bearer (or coupon) bonds** require bondholders to clip coupons from certificates and send them to the issuer to receive payment. Coupons can be redeemed by anyone, regardless of ownership.

Secured and Unsecured Bonds

With **secured bonds**, borrowers can reduce the risk of their bonds by pledging assets to bondholders in the event of default. First mortgages, other mortgages, or other specific assets may back secured bonds. If the corporation does not pay interest when it is due, the firm's assets can be sold and the proceeds used to pay the bondholders.

Unsecured bonds are called **debentures**. No specific property is pledged as security for these bonds. Holders of unsecured bonds generally have claims against property not otherwise pledged in the company's other bonds. Accordingly, debentures have inferior claims on the corporation's assets. Financially strong corporations often use debentures.

The Retirement of Bonds

Maturity dates on bonds of all kinds may be very long. Of course, all bonds must be paid off, or retired, at some point. With regard to maturity dates, there are three types of bonds: *callable*, *serial*, and *convertible*.

Callable Bonds

The issuer of **callable bonds** may call them in and pay them off at a price stipulated in the indenture, or contract, before the maturity date. Usually the issuer cannot call the bond for a certain period of time after issue, often within the first five years. Issuers usually call in existing bonds when prevailing interest rates are lower than the rate being paid on the bond. The issuer must still pay a *call* price to call in the bond. The call price usually gives a premium to the bondholder. The premium is merely the difference between the face value and call price. For example, a bond that bears a $100 face value might be callable by the firm for $108.67 any time during the first year after issue. The call price (and therefore the premium) decreases annually as the bonds approach maturity.

callable bonds Bonds that may be paid off by the issuer before the maturity date.

Sinking Funds. Callable bonds are often retired by the use of **sinking fund provisions**. The issuing company is required to put a certain amount of money into a special bank account annually. At the end of a certain number of years, the money (including interest) will be sufficient to redeem the bonds. Failure to meet the sinking fund provision places the issue in default. Such bonds are generally regarded as safer investments than many other bonds.

sinking fund provision A clause in the bond indenture (contract) that requires the issuing company to put enough money into a special bank account each year to cover the retirement of the bond issue on schedule.

Serial Bonds

Some corporations issue serial or convertible bonds. With a **serial bond**, the firm retires portions of the bond issue in a series of different preset dates. For example, a company with a $100-million issue maturing in 20 years may retire $5 million each year.

serial bond A bond issue in which redemption dates are staggered so that a firm pays off portions of the issue at different predetermined dates.

Convertible Bonds

Convertible bonds can be converted into the common stock of the issuing company. At the option of the holder, payment is made in stock instead of in cash. Because holders are given such flexibility and because there are potential benefits of converting bonds into stock, firms can offer lower interest rates when the bonds are issued. However, because holders cannot be forced to accept stock instead of cash, conversion works only when the bond buyer also regards the issuing corporation as a good investment.

convertible bonds Any bonds that offer bondholders the option of accepting common stock instead of cash in repayment.

Suppose that Canadian Arctic Explorations sold a $100-million issue of 4.5 percent convertible bonds in 2000. The bonds were issued in $1000 denominations, and they mature in 2010. At any time before maturity, each debenture of $1000 is convertible into 19.125 shares of the company's common stock. Suppose that between October 2000 and March 2007, the stock price ranged from a low of $28 to a high of $67. In that time, then, 19.125 common shares had a market value ranging from $535 to $1281. The bondholder could have exchanged the $1000 bond in return for stock to be kept or sold at a possible profit (or loss).

Government Bonds

Government bonds—for example, Canada Savings Bonds—are among the safest investments available because the Canadian government backs all federal bonds. Government securities are sold in large blocks to institutional investors who buy them to ensure desired levels of safety in portfolios. As their needs change, they may buy or sell government securities to other investors. As with corporate bonds, government bonds with longer maturities are somewhat riskier than short-term issues because their longer lives expose them to more political, social, and economic changes.

government bonds Bonds issued by the federal government.

municipal bonds Bonds issued by provincial or local government.

Provincial and local governments also issue bonds (called **municipal bonds**) to finance school and transportation systems and a variety of other projects. Banks invest in bonds nearing maturity because they are relatively safe, liquid investments. Pension funds, insurance companies, and private citizens also make longer-term investments in municipal bonds.

Secondary Markets for Bonds

Nearly all secondary trading in bonds occurs in the OTC market rather than on organized exchanges. Thus, precise statistics about annual trading volumes are not recorded. As with stocks, however, market values and prices change daily. As interest rates go up, bond prices tend to go down. The prices of riskier bonds fluctuate more widely than those of higher-grade bonds.

Other Investments

4 Describe the investment opportunities offered by *mutual funds* and *commodities*.

Stocks and bonds are very important, but they are not the only marketable securities for businesses. Financial managers are also concerned with investment opportunities in *mutual funds*, *hedge funds*, *commodities*, and *stock options*. In striking the right balance for risk among investment alternatives, financial managers use *diversification* and *asset allocation*.

Mutual Funds

mutual fund Any company that pools the resources of many investors and uses those funds to purchase various types of financial securities, depending on the fund's financial goals.

no-load fund A mutual fund in which investors are not charged a sales commission when they buy in to or sell out of the fund.

load fund A mutual fund in which investors are charged a sales commission when they buy in to or sell out of the fund.

Companies called **mutual funds** pool investments from individuals and other firms to purchase a portfolio of stocks, bonds, and short-term securities. Investors are part-owners of this portfolio. For example, if you invest $1000 in a mutual fund that has a portfolio worth $100 000, you own 1 percent of the portfolio. Mutual funds usually have portfolios worth many millions of dollars. Investors in **no-load funds** are not charged a sales commission when they buy in to or sell out of the mutual fund. **Load funds** levy a charge of between 2 and 8 percent of the invested funds.

Mutual funds vary by the investment goals they stress. The portfolios of mutual funds that emphasize safety include treasury bills and other safe issues that offer immediate income (liquidity). Other funds seek higher returns and are willing to sacrifice some safety. They invest in long-term municipal bonds, corporate bonds, and in common stocks with good dividend-paying records. Mutual funds that stress growth take on even more risk and hold a mixture of bonds, preferred stocks, and common stocks. Aggressive growth mutual funds seek maximum capital appreciation. To get it, these funds sacrifice current income and safety. They invest in stocks of new companies, troubled companies, and other high-risk securities. Table 19.3 lists the top 10 mutual funds in Canada.

ethical funds Mutual funds that focus on investing in companies that produce safe and useful products and do good in terms of employee relations, environmental practices, and human rights.

Mutual funds that stress socially responsible investing are called **ethical funds**. They avoid investing in companies that make products like cigarettes or weapons and instead focus on investing in companies that produce safe and useful products and do good in terms of employee relations, environmental practices, and human rights. Clean Environment Equity, Summa Investors, and Ethical Growth are examples of ethical funds. In spite of the many corporate scandals in recent years, ethical funds have not attracted as much interest in Canada as they have in the United States and Europe. They have also not performed as well as other mutual funds.[10]

Mutual funds give small investors access to professional financial management. Their managers have up-to-date information about market conditions

Table 19.3 Top 10 Mutual Funds in Canada, 2008

Company	Assets (in billions of $)
1. RBC Asset Management	$92.3
2. IGM Financial Inc.	84.5
3. CI Financial Corp.	64.2
4. TD Asset Management	46.9
5. CIBC Asset Management	41.9
6. Fidelity Investments Canada ULC	33.6
7. BMO Financial Group	29.5
8. Invesco Trimark Ltd.	28.6
9. AGF Funds Inc.	19.9
10. Franklin Templeton	18.4

and the best large-scale investment opportunities. But there are no guarantees of good returns, and in the difficult market conditions that prevailed in 2001–03 and in 2008–09, many people pulled their money out of mutual funds. Some estimates indicate that up to 80 percent of mutual funds do not perform as well as the average return of the overall stock market.[11] This under-performance has resulted in the emergence of *index mutual funds*, which hold many of the same stocks as the market they track. This requires little human input and reduces management expenses.

Like an index mutual fund, an **exchange-traded fund (ETF)** is a bundle of stocks (or bonds) that are in an index that tracks the overall movement of a market. But ETFs can be traded throughout the day, much like a stock. Unlike mutual funds—which are priced only at the end of each day—you can buy or sell ETFs at any time during the day when the market reaches your target price. Also unlike mutual funds—which incur the costs of active management—ETFs have lower operating expenses because they are bound by rules that specify what stocks will be purchased and when. Once the rule is established, little human action is needed, and this reduces management expenses. Annual fees for mutual funds average 1.4 percent of assets, but for ETFs the rate is as low as 0.09 percent.[12]

exchange-traded fund (ETF) A bundle of stocks (or bonds) that are in an index that tracks the overall movement of a market.

Hedge Funds

Hedge funds are private pools of money that try to give investors a positive return regardless of stock market performance. Hedge funds often engage in risky practices like *short-selling* (essentially betting that a company's stock price will go down) and *leveraging* (borrowing money against principal). Historically, interest in hedge funds has been limited to wealthy people (called "accredited investors") who are assumed to be very knowledgeable about financial matters and are able to weigh the risks of investing. But recently, hedge funds have begun marketing their products to the average investor with something called "principal-protected notes." These guarantee that investors will get their original investment back at a certain time, but they do not guarantee that any additional returns will be forthcoming.

hedge funds Private pools of money that try to give investors a positive return regardless of stock market performance.

The number of hedge funds has increased rapidly in recent years, and the majority of money invested in hedge funds is now in the form of principal-protected notes.[13] Hedge funds are not as closely regulated as mutual funds and are not required to report management fees. But these management fees can be higher than those charged by mutual funds, so there are concerns that

Traders deal in futures contracts—agreements to buy or sell commodities for certain prices at a future time.

investors will be shortchanged. As a result, there are now calls for increased regulation of hedge funds.[14]

Commodities

Commodities are products ranging from coffee beans and hogs to propane and platinum. **Futures contracts**—agreements to purchase specified amounts of commodities at given prices on set dates—can be bought and sold in the **commodities market**. These contracts are available not only for commodities but also for stocks. Because selling prices reflect traders' *estimates* of future events and values, futures prices are quite volatile, and trading is risky.

Let's look at an example. On November 1, 2003, the price of gold on the open market was $387 per ounce. Futures contracts for June 2004 gold were selling for $385 per ounce. This price reflected investors' judgment that gold prices would be slightly lower the following June. Now suppose that you purchased a 100-ounce gold futures contract in November for $38 500 ($385 × 100). If in January 2004 the June gold futures sold for $418 (which they really did), you could sell your contract for $41 800. Your profit after the two months would be $3300.

futures contract Agreement to purchase specified amounts of a commodity (or stock) at a given price on a set future date.

commodities market Market in which futures contracts are traded.

margin The percentage of the total sales price that a buyer must put up to place an order for stock or a futures contract.

Margins

Usually, buyers of futures contracts need not put up the full purchase amount. Rather, the buyer posts a smaller amount—the **margin**—that may be as little as $3000 for contracts up to $100 000. Let us look again at our gold futures example. If you had posted a $3000 margin for your June 2004 gold contract, you would have earned a $3300 profit on that investment of $3000 in only two months.

However, you also took a big risk involving two big *ifs*: If you had held on to your contract until June *and* if gold had dropped to, say, $340, you would have lost $4500 ($38 500 − $34 000). If you had posted a $3000 margin to buy the contract, you would have lost all of that margin and would owe an additional $1500. As it turns out, June gold prices increased to $394, so your investment of $38 500 would have gained $900 in June. However, between 75 and 90 percent of all small-time investors lose money in the futures market. The action is fast and furious, with small investors trying to keep up with professionals. As one veteran financial planner said, "After trading commodities, trading stocks is like watching the grass grow."

Stock Options

stock option The purchased right to buy or sell a stock.

call option The purchased right to buy a particular stock at a certain price until a specified date.

put option The purchased right to sell a particular stock at a certain price until a specified date.

A **stock option** is the right to buy or sell a stock. A **call option** gives its owner the right to buy a particular stock at a certain price, with that right lasting until a particular date. A **put option** gives its owner the right to sell a particular stock at a specified price, with that right lasting until a particular date. These options are traded on several stock exchanges.

Suppose that you thought the price of BSX Ltd. (which sold for $49.10 per share on August 15, 2009) was going to go up. You might buy a call option giving you the right to buy 100 shares of BSX any time in the next two months at a so-called strike price of $65. If the stock rose to $75 before October 2009, you would exercise your call option. Your profit would be $10 per share ($75 − $65) less the price you paid to buy the option. However, if the stock price fell instead of rose, you would not exercise your call option because BSX would be available on the open market for less than $65 per share. (Your stock option would be "under water," that is, it would be worthless.) You would lose whatever you paid for the option.

In contrast, if you thought the price of BSX would fall below $49.10 sometime during the two months after August 15, 2009, you might buy a put option. Assume that this option gave you the right to sell 100 shares for $54.10 per share any time before October 2009. If the stock price fell to $44.10, your profit would be $10 per share ($54.10 − $44.10), less whatever you paid for the option. Assume that the price of a put option was $3 per share at that time. If the stock price increased, you would not exercise your option to sell, and you would lose what you paid for the put option. The daily prices of put and call options are listed in the financial press.

Making Choices for Diversification, Asset Allocation, and Risk Reduction

Investors seldom take an extreme approach—total risk-seeking or total risk avoidance—in selecting their investments. Extreme positions cause extreme results, and while most investors have a preference toward either risk or risk avoidance, they are not totally oriented to either end of the risk spectrum. Instead, they select a mixture, or *portfolio*, of investments—some riskier and some more conservative—that provides the level of risk and financial stability at which they are comfortable. They do this in two ways—through *diversification* and through *asset allocation*.

Diversification

Diversification means buying several different kinds of investments rather than just one. Diversification as applied to common stocks means, for example, that you invest in stocks of several different companies, such as Vale Inco, IBM, Cisco Systems, and Bombardier, rather than putting all your money into just one of them. The risk of loss is reduced by spreading the total investment across more stocks because, while any one stock may tumble, there is less chance that all of them will fall, especially if the companies are from different industries. Even more diversification is gained when funds are spread across more kinds of investment alternatives—stocks, bonds, mutual funds, real estate, and so on.

diversification Purchase of several different kinds of investments rather than just one.

But these are only general principles, and they will not always apply. This was demonstrated when the financial crisis hit in 2008 and the value of most investments dropped sharply. Think for a moment about the difference between insurance and investments. An insurance company diversifies its risks by selling, say, homeowner's insurance in different geographic areas because a house fire in Saskatoon will not spread to Toronto. But the same logic does not necessarily apply to financial investments. If a problem develops in one area (for example, subprime mortgages), investors may panic and conclude that all investments are at risk (this is called *contagion*). This contagion drives down the value of all investments, so even people who had diversified portfolios in 2008 saw the value of most of their investments decline.[15]

Asset Allocation

Asset allocation is the proportion of funds invested in each of the investment alternatives. You may decide, for example, to allocate $20 000 to common stocks, $10 000 to a money market mutual fund, and $10 000 to a Canada Savings Bond. Ten years later, you may decide on a less risky asset allocation of $10 000, $15 000, and $15 000 in the same investment categories, respectively. As your investment objectives change (in this example from moderate risk to

asset allocation The relative amount of funds invested in (or allocated to) each of several investment alternatives.

lower risk for capital preservation), your asset allocation must be changed accordingly.

Buying and Selling Securities

5 Explain the process by which securities are bought and sold.

The process of buying and selling stocks, bonds, and other financial instruments is complex. To start, you need to find out about possible investments and match them to your investment objectives. Then you must decide whether you want to get advice from experts or whether you want to make decisions on your own.

Using Financial Information Services

Have you ever looked at the financial section of your daily newspaper and found yourself wondering what all those tables and numbers mean? If you cannot read stock and bond quotations, you probably should not invest in these issues. Fortunately, this skill is easily mastered.

Stock Quotations

Figure 19.1 shows the type of information newspapers provide about daily market transactions of individual stocks. The corporation's name (for example, Vale Inco) is shown along with the number of shares sold, the high and low prices of the stock for that trading day, the closing price of the stock, and the change from the closing price on the previous day.

Bond Quotations

Bond prices also change from day to day. These changes form the *coupon rate*, which provides information for firms about the cost of borrowing funds. Prices of domestic corporation bonds, Canadian government bonds, and foreign bonds are reported separately. Bond prices are expressed in terms of 100, even though most have a face value of $1000. Thus, a quote of 85 means that the bond's price is 85 percent of its face value, or $850.

A corporation bond selling at 155¼ would cost a buyer $1552.50 ($1000 face value × 1.5525), plus commission. The interest rate on bonds is also

Company	Volume	High	Low	Close	Change
Four Seasons	633	67.49	65.27	66.15	−1.13
Goldcorp	35 233	31.99	30.65	31.15	+0.83
GW Life	54	25.80	25.57	25.80	−0.22
Hudson Bay	32 376	15.06	15.00	15.04	−0.02
Vale Inco	**18 640**	**58.82**	**57.01**	**58.05**	**+0.84**
Ipsco	4341	106.40	104.09	105.75	−0.25
Jean Cou	6918	14.56	14.31	14.31	−0.06
Kinross	72 321	13.68	12.92	13.10	+0.27

- *Stock*
  Vale Inco (Name of Company).
- *Volume*
  18 640 (total number of shares traded on this date [in 100's).
- *High and Low*
  During the trading day, the highest price was $58.82 and the lowest price was $57.01.
- *Close*
  At the close of trading on this date, the last price paid per share was $58.05.
- *Net Change*
  Difference between today's closing price and the previous day's closing price. Price increased by 84 cents per share.

Figure 19.1 How to read a daily stock quotation.

Issuer	Coupon	Maturity	Price	Yield
		GOVERNMENT OF CANADA		
Canada	5.00	June 1, 14	103.71	4.45
Canada	8.00	June 1, 27	145.92	4.58
		PROVINCIALS		
Hy Que	6.50	Feb. 15, 11	108.55	4.50
Man	7.75	Dec. 22, 25	135.19	4.93
		CORPORATE		
BC Tel	**9.65**	**Apr 8, 22**	**138.49**	**6.48**
Loblaw	6.65	Nov. 8, 27	107.91	5.99

- *Issuer*
  Company name is British Columbia Telephone.
- *Coupon*
  The annual rate of interest at face value is 9.65 percent.
- *Maturity*
  The maturity date is April 8, 2022.
- *Price*
  On this date, $138.9 was the price of the last transaction.
- *Yield*
  The yield is computed by dividing the annual interest paid by the current market price.

Figure 19.2 How to read a bond quotation.

quoted as a percentage of par, or face, value. Thus "$6^1/_2$ s" pays 6.5 percent of par value per year. Typically, interest is paid semi-annually at half of the stated interest or coupon rate.

The market value (selling price) of a bond at any given time depends on its stated interest rate, the "going rate" of interest in the market, and its redemption or maturity date. A bond with a higher stated interest rate than the going rate on similar quality bonds will probably sell at a premium above its face value—its selling price will be above its redemption price. A bond with a lower stated interest rate than the going rate on similar-quality bonds will probably sell at a discount—its selling price will be below its redemption price. How much the premium or discount is depends largely on how far in the future the maturity date is. The maturity date is shown after the interest rate. Figure 19.2 shows the type of information daily newspapers provide about bond transactions.

Bond Yield. Suppose you bought a $1000 par-value bond in 1989 for $650. Its stated interest rate is 6 percent, and its maturity or redemption date was 2009. You therefore received $60 per year in interest. Based on your actual investment of $650, your yield is 9.2 percent. If you held it to maturity, you got $1000 for a bond that originally cost you only $650. This extra $350 increased your true, or effective, yield.

Mutual Funds Quotations

Selling prices for mutual funds are reported daily or weekly in most newspapers. Additional investor information is also available in the financial press. Figure 19.3 shows a partial listing of T. Rowe Price funds from *Barron's Mutual Funds*, a prominent weekly financial newspaper. Three funds are listed in the figure—Balanced, Science and Technology, and Short-Term Bond—but the published list would include all of Price's more than 90 different funds.

The fund's net asset value (NAV), the current market value of one share, is perhaps the key term for understanding the quotations. The fund managers calculate NAV at day's end by taking the fund's net assets—securities it owns, plus cash and any accumulated earnings, minus liabilities—and dividing the remainder by the number of shares outstanding. Let's focus on the first fund listed, the Balanced fund:

- Column 1 shows the fund's highest net asset value (NAV)—$19.04—during the past 52 weeks.
- Column 2 shows the 52-week low NAV ($16.51).

① 52 Week High	② Low	③ Fund Name	④ Close NAV	⑤ Wk's Chg	⑥ % Return 1-Wk	⑦ YTD	⑧ 3-Yrs
		Price Funds:					
19.04	16.51	Balanced *n*	18.37	–0.01	–0.1	+0.4	+7.8
20.00	15.03	SciTec *n*	18.29	–0.21	–1.1	–2.7	–33.4
4.90	4.75	Sht-Bd *n*	4.75	–0.01	–0.2	–0.3	+13.5

Figure 19.3 How to read a mutual fund quotation.

- Column 3 lists the company name (Price Funds) at the top and the individual fund names beneath the company name. The "n" code indicates no front-end or back-end sales charge (a *no-load* fund)
- Column 4 lists the NAV ($18.37) at the close of the most recent week.
- Column 5 shows the net asset value change, that is, the dollar gain or loss based on the previous week's NAV. The Balanced fund closed $0.01 lower this week than in the previous week.
- The next three columns report each fund's recent and longer-term performance. These numbers reflect the percentage change in NAV. These three columns show the percentage return of the fund for the most recent past week (column 6), current year to date (column 7), and the last three years (column 8).

Market Indexes

market index A measure of the market value of stocks; provides a summary of price trends in a specific industry or of the stock market as a whole.

bull market A period of rising stock prices; a period in which investors act on a belief that stock prices will rise.

bear market A period of falling stock prices; a period in which investors act on a belief that stock prices will fall.

Dow Jones Industrial Average (DJIA) Market index based on the prices of 30 of the largest firms listed on NYSE and NASDAQ.

Although they do not indicate how specific securities are performing, **market indexes** provide a useful summary of trends in specific industries and the stock market as a whole. Market indexes reveal bull and bear market trends. **Bull markets** are periods of upward-moving stock prices. The years 1981–90, 1993–99, and 2004–06 featured strong bull markets. Periods of falling stock prices are called **bear markets**. The years 1991–92, 2000–02, and 2008–09 were bear markets.

The Dow Jones Industrial Average. The most widely cited market index is the **Dow Jones Industrial Average (DJIA)**, which measures the performance of U.S. financial markets by focussing on 30 blue-chip companies as reflectors of economic health. The Dow is the average of the stock prices for these 30 large firms. The Dow increased sharply during the late 1990s and reached 11 000 early in 2000. But after the dot-com bubble burst, it dropped to below 8000 in 2002. By the fall of 2007, it had risen again to about 14 000, but a deep recession began in 2008, and by early 2009, the Dow had dropped all the way down to 7000. Because of the small number of firms it considers, the DJIA is a limited gauge of the overall stock market.

Standard & Poor's Composite Index (S&P 500) Market index based on the performance of 400 industrial firms, 40 utilities, 40 financial institutions, and 20 transportation companies.

The S&P 500. **Standard & Poor's Composite Index (S&P 500)** is a broader report than the Dow. It consists of 500 stocks, including 400 industrial firms, 40 utilities, 40 financial institutions, and 20 transportation companies. Because the index average is weighted according to market capitalization of each stock, the more highly valued companies exercise a greater influence on the index.

S&P/TSX index An average computed from 225 different large Canadian stocks from various industry groups.

The S&P/TSX Index. The **S&P/TSX index** is an average computed from 225 large Canadian stocks from various industry groups.[16] Like the Dow, the

S&P/TSX (formerly called the TSE 300) has been very volatile during the last few years. It moved sharply upward during the bull market of the late 1990s and topped 11 000 in the summer of 2000. It then dropped to 6500 by the end of 2000, but by mid-2008, the index had risen to 15 000. By January 2009, the index had dropped to just 7500, but by October 2009 it had risen again to 11 500.

The NASDAQ Composite Index. Because it considers more stocks, some financial observers regard the **NASDAQ Composite Index** as the most important of all market indexes. Unlike the Dow, the S&P 500, and the S&P/TSX, all NASDAQ-listed companies are included in the index. The popularity of the NASDAQ index goes hand in hand with investors' growing interest in technology and small-company stocks. The NASDAQ index has also been very volatile. In early 2000, it reached 5000, but by 2001 it had dropped to just 1300. By 2006, it had increased again to 2400, but by early 2009 it had dropped once again to just 1300.

NASDAQ Composite Index Value-weighted market index that includes all NASDAQ-listed companies, both domestic and foreign.

Stock indexes in all countries suffered large declines as a result of the recession that began in 2008. Several indexes (for example, in Russia, India, and China) declined even more than North American indexes.

Buying and Selling Stocks

Based on your own investigations and/or recommendations from your broker, you can place many types of orders. A **market order** authorizes the broker to buy or sell a certain stock at the prevailing market price. A **limit buy order** authorizes the broker to purchase a stock if its price is less than or equal to a given limit. For example, a limit buy order at $80 per share means that the broker is to buy it if and only if the stock price is $80 or less. A **limit sell order** authorizes the sale of a stock when its price is equal to or greater than a given limit. For example, a limit sell order at $80 per share means that the broker is to sell it if and only if the stock price is $80 or more. A **stop order** instructs the broker to sell a stock if its price falls to a certain level. For example, a stop order of $80 on a particular stock means that the broker is to sell it if and only if its price falls to $80 or below.

market order An order to a broker to buy or sell a certain security at the current market price.

limit buy order An order to a broker to buy a certain security only if its price is less than or equal to a given limit.

limit sell order An order to a broker to sell a certain security only if its price is equal to or greater than a given limit.

stop order An order to a broker to sell a certain security if its price falls to a certain level or below.

You can also place orders of different sizes. A **round lot** order requests 100 shares or some multiple thereof. Fractions of a round lot are called **odd lots**. Trading odd lots is usually more expensive than trading round lots because an intermediary called an odd-lot broker is often involved, which increases brokerage fees.

round lot The purchase or sale of stock in units of 100 shares.

odd lots The purchase or sale of stock in units other than 100 shares.

The business of buying and selling stocks is changing rapidly. More and more individuals are buying and selling stocks on the internet, and traditional brokers are worried that before long customers will avoid using their services altogether. To make matters worse for brokers, it will soon be possible for Canadians to purchase shares of stock directly from the companies that issue them instead of having to go through a broker or the internet. The fees that customers will have to pay for these direct purchases will be even lower than the fees currently charged by discount brokers. Thus, customers will be able to "cut out the middleman."[17]

Financing Securities Purchases

When you place a buy order of any kind, you must tell your broker how you will pay for the purchase. You might maintain a cash account with your broker. Then, as stocks are bought and sold, proceeds are added to the account and the broker subtracts commissions and costs of purchases. In addition, as with almost every good in today's economy, you can buy shares on credit.

Margin Trading

As with futures contracts, you can buy stocks on margin—putting down only a portion of the stock's price. You borrow the rest from your broker, who, in turn, borrows from the banks at a special rate and secures the loans with stock.

Margin trading offers several advantages. Suppose you purchased $100 000 worth of stock in WestJet. Let's also say that you paid $50 000 of your own money and borrowed the other $50 000 from your broker at 10 percent interest. Valued at its market price, your stock serves as your collateral. If shares have risen in value to $115 000 after one year, you can sell them and pay your broker $55 000 ($50 000 principal plus $5000 interest). You will have $60 000 left over. Your original investment of $50 000 will have earned a 20 percent profit of $10 000. If you had paid the entire price out of your own pocket, you would have earned only a 15 percent return.

Although investors often recognize possible profits to be made in margin trading, they sometimes fail to consider that losses, too, can be amplified. Suppose, for example, that you decided on January 4, 2007, to buy 1000 shares of Canadian Petroleum for $53 per share. You put up $26 500 of your own money and borrow $26 500 from your broker. As the stock rises, you reason, the loan will enable you to profit from twice as many shares. Now let us say that shortly after you purchase your stock, its market price begins to fall. You decide to hold on until it recovers, but by January 4, 2009, when the price has fallen to $23 per share, you give up hope and sell.

Now let us see how margin trading has amplified your losses. If you had invested your own $26 500 instead of borrowing it, you would recover $23 000 of your $53 000 investment (excluding commissions). Your loss, therefore, would be nearly 57 percent ($30 000 loss divided by $53 000 invested). By trading on margin, however, even though you still recover $23 000 of your $26 500 investment, you must repay the $26 500 that you borrowed, plus $2 650 in loan interest (at a 10 percent annual rate). In this case, your losses total $32 650 ($55 650 in outlays less $23 000 recovered). The percentage loss is 123 percent of your investment ($32 650 loss divided by $26 500 investment)—much greater than the 57 percent loss you would have suffered without margin trading.

If you're a day trader, are volatile markets good or bad? When the market's volatile, there are often wider spreads between bid prices (what traders pay for a share of stock) and ask prices (what they charge for it). The difference isn't necessarily large, but if you can make a number of quick hits during the day, you can make a dime here and a dollar there. That strategy appeals to traders at large firms but also to individual traders working on their own.

The rising use of margin credit by investors was a growing concern during the bull market of 2004–06. Investors focussed on the upside benefits but were not sensitive enough to the downside risks of margin trading. Especially at online brokerages, inexperienced traders were borrowing at an alarming rate, and some were using the borrowed funds for risky and speculative day trading. So-called *day traders* visited websites online to buy and sell a stock in the same day (so-called *intraday trades*), seeking quick in-and-out fractional gains on large volumes (many shares) of each stock. While some day traders were successful, most ended up as financial losers.

The boxed insert entitled "Green Trading" describes a different kind of trading that is being increasingly debated.

Short Sales

A **short sale** occurs when you borrow a security from your broker and sell it (one of the few times it is legal to sell what you do not own). At a given time in the future, you must restore an equal number of shares of that issue to the brokerage, along with a fee. For example, suppose that in June you believe the price of a certain company's stock will soon fall. You order your broker to sell short 100 shares at the market price of $38 per share. Your broker will make the sale and credit $3800 to your account. If the company's price falls to $32 per share in July, you can buy 100 shares for $3200 and give them to your broker, leaving you with a $600 profit (before commissions). The risk is that the price will not fall but will hold steady or rise, leaving you with a loss.

short sale Selling borrowed shares of stock in the expectation that their price will fall before they must be replaced, so that replacement shares can be bought for less than the original shares were sold for.

The Greening of Business

Green Trading

Traders are accustomed to using financial markets for investing in just about everything—ranging from pork bellies to movie production—in the hope of gaining a profit. However, new financial markets for commodities known as carbon credits are driven not just by the profit motive but by a sense of social responsibility. The economic incentives of emissions trading (ET) bring together both environmental polluters and green companies in an effort to save the planet and turn a profit.

Here's how it works. Regulators in various countries are setting limits on the amounts of several industrial pollutants that can be released into the atmosphere, including carbon dioxide (CO_2), sulfur dioxide, and mercury. A leading example is the European Union's Emissions Trading Scheme (ETS), which was started by the European Commission in 2005 to meet the EU's obligations for carbon reductions in accordance with the Kyoto Protocol on Climate Change. The ETS annually sets a cap for the total amount of CO_2 emission allowed for each EU country and for each business in that country. The country totals and the EU total cannot exceed the caps.

Individual companies are issued a permit containing a number of "credits," which represent the right to emit a certain amount of CO_2. Any company producing below its CO_2 cap can sell its surplus credits to other, more pollution-prone companies that need more credits to keep operating so they won't go over their cap. This is where the trading opportunities arise. It's like a stock exchange that quickly matches up buyers and sellers, in this case buyers and sellers of emissions credits.

With emissions trading, environmentally oriented companies sell unneeded emissions allowances and gain a financial return on their past investment for reducing pollution. Such companies view environmental clean-up not as an expense but as a responsible investment. Other companies, who have previously avoided making such investments, face higher costs as they bid for others' unused carbon credits. The trading scheme has created a new financial incentive for the development of cleaner industries that reduce carbon emissions and other greenhouse gases.

Critical Thinking Questions

1. What are the advantages of emissions trading? What are the disadvantages?
2. What has been the experience of the European Union to date with emissions trading?
3. What is the Canadian government doing about introducing emissions trading?

Securities Regulation

6 Explain how securities markets are regulated.

The buying and selling of securities is regulated in both Canada and the United States. There are both similarities and differences in the way the two countries regulate securities.

Canadian Securities Regulations

Canada, unlike the United States, does not have comprehensive federal securities legislation or a federal regulatory body. Government regulation is primarily provincial and emphasizes self-regulation through the various provincial securities exchanges. A 2003 report by a government-appointed committee that studied Canada's system of securities regulation concluded that it is in dire need of reform. The committee noted that Canada is the only country in the industrialized world with a patchwork of provincial regulations. It recommended a single regulator for Canada. The main complaints the committee noted were lack of meaningful enforcement of securities laws and unnecessary costs and time delays that make Canada's capital markets uncompetitive internationally. As of 2009, changes had still not been made.

Ontario is generally regarded as having the most progressive securities legislation in Canada. The Ontario Securities Act contains disclosure provisions for new and existing issues, prevention of fraud, regulation of the Toronto Stock Exchange, and takeover bids. It also prohibits insider trading. The Toronto Stock Exchange provides an example of self-regulation by the industry. The TSX has regulations concerning listing and delisting of securities, disclosure requirements, and issuing of prospectuses for new securities.

In 1912, the Manitoba government pioneered in Canada laws applying mainly to the sale of new securities. Under these **blue-sky laws**, corporations issuing securities must back them up with something more than the "blue sky." Similar laws were passed in other provinces. Provincial laws also generally require that stockbrokers be licensed and securities be registered before they can be sold. In each province, issuers of proposed new securities must file a prospectus with the provincial securities exchange. The prospectus must be made available to prospective investors.

blue-sky laws Laws regulating how corporations must back up securities.

When the American and Canadian stock markets declined sharply during 2000–01 and again in 2008–09, there was a public outcry for more regulation of securities markets. Both countries are in the process of developing tougher legislation in the hope of restoring public trust in the stock market.

U.S. Securities Regulation

To protect the investing public and to maintain smoothly functioning markets, the Securities and Exchange Commission (SEC) oversees many phases of the process through which securities are issued. The SEC regulates the public offering of new securities by requiring that all companies file a prospectus before a proposed offering can go forward. A **prospectus** contains pertinent information about both the offered security and the issuing company. False statements are subject to criminal penalties.

prospectus A detailed registration statement about a new stock filed with a provincial securities exchange; must include any data helpful to a potential buyer.

The SEC has been criticized for failing to protect investors from various other financial manipulation schemes. The most prominent recent case is that of Bernie Madoff, who operated a Ponzi scheme that defrauded investors of $50 *billion*. In spite of being warned on multiple occasions by an independent researcher that Madoff's operation was a Ponzi scheme, the SEC did nothing and investors lost everything.[18]

In addition to regulation by government agencies, both the NASD and the NYSE exercise self-regulation in an attempt to maintain the public trust and to ensure professionalism in the financial industry. A visible example is the NYSE's actions in establishing so-called *circuit breakers*—trading rules for reducing excessive market volatility and promoting investor confidence—that suspend trading for a preset length of time. For example, if the DJIA drops more than 1050 points before 2 p.m., trading is halted for an hour. The interruption provides a "cooling off" period that slows trading activity, gives investors time to reconsider their trading positions, and allows computer programs to be revised or shut down.[19] Bigger drops lead to longer "cooling off" periods.

One oft-cited cause of sudden market fluctuations is **program trading**—the portfolio trading strategy involving the sale or purchase of a group of stocks valued at $1 million or more. It is often triggered by computerized trading programs that can be launched without human supervision or control. As market values change and economic events transpire during the course of a day, computer programs are busy recalculating the future values of stocks. Once a calculated value reaches a critical point, the program automatically signals a buy or sell order. Because electronic trading can cause the market to spiral out of control, it has led to the establishment of circuit breakers.

program trading Large purchase or sale of a group of stocks, often triggered by computerized trading programs that can be launched without human supervision or control.

Test yourself on the material for this chapter at **www.pearsoned.ca/mybusinesslab**.

Summary of Learning Objectives

1. **Explain the difference between *primary* and *secondary securities markets*.** *Primary securities markets* involve the buying and selling of new *securities*, either in public offerings or through private placements (sales to single buyers or small groups of buyers). *Investment bankers* specialize in trading securities in primary markets. *Secondary securities markets* involve the trading of existing stocks and *bonds* through such groups as the New York Stock Exchange and the Toronto Stock Exchange.

2. **Discuss the value of *common stock* and *preferred stock* to shareholders and describe the secondary market for each type of security.** *Common stock* affords investors the prospect of capital gains, dividend income, or both. Common stock values are expressed in three ways—as *par value* (the face value of a share when it is issued), *market value* (the current market price of a share), and *book value* (the value of shareholders' equity compared with that of other stocks). Market value is the most important value to investors. *Preferred stock* is less risky than common stock; for example, cumulative preferred stock entitles holders to receive missed dividends when the company is financially capable of paying. It also offers the prospect of steadier income than common stock. Shareholders of preferred stock must be paid dividends before shareholders of common stock.

   Both common and preferred stock are traded on *stock exchanges* (institutions formed to conduct the trading of existing securities) and in *over-the-counter (OTC) markets* (dealer organizations formed to trade securities outside stock exchange settings). "Members" who hold seats on stock exchanges act as *brokers*—agents who execute buy-and-sell orders—for non-members. Exchanges include the New York Stock Exchange, the Toronto Stock Exchange, and regional and foreign exchanges.

3. **Distinguish among various types of *bonds* in terms of their issuers, safety, and retirement.** The safety of bonds issued by various borrowers is rated by such services as Moody's and Standard & Poor's. *Government bonds* are the safest investment because the federal government backs them. *Municipal bonds*, which are offered by provincial and local governments to finance a variety of projects, are also usually safe. *Corporate bonds* are issued by businesses to gain long-term funding. They may be *secured* (backed by pledges of the issuer's assets) or unsecured (*debentures*), and they offer varying degrees of safety. *Serial bonds* are retired as portions are redeemed at preset dates; *convertible bonds* may be retired by conversion into the issuer's common stock or by cash. Some government and corporate bonds are *callable*; that is, they can be paid off by the issuer prior to their maturity dates.

4. **Describe the investment opportunities offered by *mutual funds* and *commodities*.** Like stocks and bonds, *mutual funds*—companies that pool investments to purchase portfolios of financial instruments—offer investors different levels of risk and growth potential. *Load funds* require investors to pay commissions of 2 to 8 percent; *no-load funds* do not charge commissions when investors buy in or sell out. *Futures contracts*—agreements to buy specified amounts of commodities at given prices on preset dates—are traded in the *commodities market*. Commodities traders often buy on *margin*—the percentage of the total sales price that must be put up to order futures contracts.

5. **Explain the process by which securities are bought and sold.** Investors generally use such financial information services as newspaper and online stock, bond, and OTC quotations to learn about possible investments. Market indexes such as the *S&P/TSX index, the Dow Jones Industrial Average, Standard & Poor's Composite Index*, and the *NASDAQ Composite Index* provide useful summaries of trends, both in specific industries and in the market as a whole. Investors can then place different types of orders. *Market orders* are orders to buy or sell at current prevailing prices. Because investors do not know exactly what prices will be when market orders are executed, they may issue *limit* or *stop* orders that are to be executed only if prices rise to or fall below specified levels. *Round lots* are purchased in multiples of 100 shares. *Odd lots* are purchased in fractions of round lots. Securities can be bought on margin or as part of *short sales* (investors sell securities that are borrowed from brokers and returned at a later date).

6. **Explain how securities markets are regulated.** To protect investors, provincial securities commissions regulate the public offering of new securities and enforce laws against such practices as insider trading (using special knowledge about a firm for profit or gain). Many provincial governments prosecute the sale of fraudulent securities and enforce *blue-sky laws* that require corporations to back up securities with something more than the "blue sky." As well, stockbrokers must be licensed and securities must be registered before they can be sold.

PEARSON **mybusinesslab** To improve your grade, visit the MyBusinessLab website at **www.pearsoned.ca/mybusinesslab**. This online homework and tutorial system allows you to test your understanding and generates a personalized study plan just for you. It provides you with study and practice tools directly related to this chapter's content. MyBusinessLab puts you in control of your own learning!

Key Terms

asset allocation (p. 633)
bear market (p. 636)
bearer (coupon) bonds (p. 628)
blue-chip stocks (p. 622)
blue-sky laws (p. 640)
bond (p. 627)
book value (p. 621)
broker (p. 624)
bull market (p. 636)
call option (p. 632)
callable bonds (p. 629)
commodities market (p. 632)
convertible bonds (p. 629)
corporate bonds (p. 628)
cumulative preferred stock (p. 623)
debentures (p. 628)
diversification (p. 633)
Dow Jones Industrial Average (DJIA) (p. 636)
ethical funds (p. 630)
exchange-traded fund (ETF) (p. 631)
futures contract (p. 632)
government bonds (p. 629)
hedge funds (p. 631)
investment banker (p. 621)
limit buy order (p. 637)
limit sell order (p. 637)
load fund (p. 630)
margin (p. 632)
market capitalization (p. 622)
market index (p. 636)
market order (p. 637)
market value (p. 621)
municipal bonds (p. 630)
mutual fund (p. 630)
NASDAQ Composite Index (p. 637)
National Association of Securities Dealers Automated Quotation (NASDAQ) (p. 627)
no-load fund (p. 630)
odd lots (p. 637)
over-the-counter (OTC) market (p. 627)
par value (p. 621)
primary securities market (p. 620)
preferred stock (p. 622)
program trading (p. 641)
prospectus (p. 640)
put option (p. 632)
registered bonds (p. 628)
round lot (p. 637)
secondary securities market (p. 621)
secured bonds (p. 628)
securities (p. 620)
serial bond (p. 629)
short sale (p. 639)
sinking fund provision (p. 629)
S&P/TSX index (p. 636)
Standard & Poor's Composite Index (S&P 500) (p. 636)
stock exchange (p. 623)
stock option (p. 632)
stop order (p. 637)

Questions for Analysis

1. Assume that the price of gold on the open market was $400 per ounce on March 31, 2009. Assume also that futures contracts for June 2010 gold were selling for $428 per ounce. This price reflected investors' judgments that gold prices would be higher the following June. Now suppose that you purchased a 100-ounce gold futures contract in October 2009 for $42 800 (428 x 100). If in December 2009 the June gold futures sold for $453, what could you sell your contract for? What would your profit be after the two months?
2. Suppose you decided to invest in common stocks as a personal investment. Which kind of broker—full-service or online discount—would you use for buying and selling stock? Why?
3. Choose a stock from the TSX and find a newspaper listing of a recent day's transactions for the stock. Explain what each element in the listing means.
4. Choose a bond from the TSX and find a newspaper listing of a recent day's transactions for the bond. Explain what each element in the listing means.
5. Which of the three measures of common stock value is most important? Why?
6. Explain how an investor might make money in a commodities trade. Then explain how an investor might lose money in a commodities trade.
7. How do the provincial securities commissions regulate securities markets? Give an example of how they are doing their job well and an example of how they failed to do their job.
8. Which type of stock or bond would be most appropriate for your investment purposes at this time? Why? Which type of mutual fund would be most appropriate for your investment purposes at this time? Why?

Application Exercises

1. Interview the financial manager of a local business. What are the investment goals of the organization? What mix of securities does it use? What advantages and disadvantages do you see in its portfolio?
2. Contact a broker for information about setting up a personal account for trading securities. Prepare a report on the broker's requirements for placing buy/sell orders, credit terms, cash account requirements, services available to investors, and commissions/fees schedules.

Building Your Business Skills

Market Ups and Downs

The Purpose of the Assignment

To encourage students to understand the forces that cause fluctuations in stock prices.

Background

Investing in stocks requires an understanding of the various factors that affect stock prices. These factors may be intrinsic to the company itself or part of the external environment.

- Internal factors relate to the company itself, such as an announcement of poor or favourable earnings, earnings that are more or less than expected, major layoffs, labour problems, management issues, and mergers.
- External factors relate to world or national events, such as a threatened war in the Persian Gulf, the possibility of a bird flu epidemic, weather conditions that affect sales, the Bank of Canada's adjustment of interest rates, and employment figures that were higher or lower than expected. By analyzing these factors, you will often learn a lot about why a stock did well or why it did poorly. Being aware of these influences will help you anticipate future stock movements.

Assignment

Step 1

Working alone, choose a common stock that has experienced considerable price fluctuations in the past few years. Here are several examples (but there are many others): Nortel Networks, IBM, Amazon.com, and Apple Computer. Find the symbol for the stock and the exchange on which it is traded.

Step 2

At your library, find the *Daily Stock Price Record*, a publication that provides a historical picture of daily stock closings. There are separate copies for the various stock exchanges. Find your stock, and study its trading pattern.

Step 3

Find four or five days over a period of several months or even a year when there have been major price fluctuations in the stock. (A two- or three-point price change from one day to the next is considered major.) Then research what happened on that day that might have contributed to the fluctuation. The best place to begin is *The Globe and Mail* or *The Wall Street Journal*.

Step 4

Write a short analysis that links changes in stock price to internal and external factors. As you analyze the data, be aware that it is sometimes difficult to know why a stock price fluctuates.

Step 5

Get together with three other students who studied different stocks. As a group, discuss your findings, looking for fluctuation patterns.

Questions for Discussion

1. Do you see any similarities in the movement of the various stocks during the same period? For example, did the stocks move up or down at about the same time? If so, do you think the stocks were affected by the same factors? Explain your thinking.
2. Based on your analysis, did internal or external factors have the greater impact on stock price? Which factors had the more long-lasting effect? Which factors had the shorter effect?
3. Why do you think it is so hard to predict changes in stock price on a day-to-day basis?

Exercising Your Ethics: Team Exercise

Serving Two Masters: Torn Between Company and Client

The Situation

Employees in financial services firms are sometimes confronted by conflicting allegiances between the company and its clients. In managing customers' stock portfolios, for example, the best timing for buy and sell decisions for clients' financial positions may not be the most profitable for the financial manager's firm. Investment managers, as a result, must choose a "right" course of action for reconciling possible conflicting interests.

The Dilemma

George Michaels is a customer portfolio manager employed by Premier Power Investments. His 35 clients—individual investors—have portfolios with market values ranging from $200 000 to $2 million in stocks, bonds, and mutual funds. Clients generally rely on George's recommendations to buy, sell, or hold each security based on his knowledge of their investment goals and risk tolerance, along with his experience in keeping up with market trends and holding down transactions costs. Premier Power Investments Company earns sales commissions ranging from 2 percent to 4 percent of market value for each buy and sell transaction.

On Monday morning, George's boss, Vicky Greene, informs George that due to Premier Power Investments Company's sagging revenues, it is to everyone's benefit to increase the number of transactions in customers' portfolios. She suggests that he find some different and attractive securities to replace existing securities for his customers. As George thinks about possible ways for accelerating his buy and sell recommendations, he has qualms about the motivation behind Vicky's comments. He is unsure what to do.

Team Activity

Assemble a group of four students and assign each group member to one of the following roles:

- George Michaels (employee)
- Vicky Greene (employer)
- portfolio owner (customer)
- owner (one of many outside shareholders of Premier Power Investments Company)

Questions for Discussion

1. Before discussing the situation with your group, and from the perspective of your assigned role, do you think there are any ethical issues in this situation? If so, write them down.
2. Return to your group and reveal any ethical issues that were identified by each member. Be especially aware to see if the different roles resulted in different kinds of ethical issues. Why might role differences result in dissimilar priorities on ethical issues?
3. For the various ethical issues that were identified, decide as a group which one is the most important for Premier Power Investments to resolve. Which issue is second in importance?
4. From an ethical standpoint, what does your group finally recommend be done to resolve the most important ethical issue? To resolve the second most important ethical issue?

For additional cases and exercise material, go to **www.pearsoned.ca/mybusinesslab**.

Concluding Case 19-1

Scandal in the Mutual Fund Industry

During the past 20 years, Canadians have invested heavily in the stock market. Most of them buy shares in mutual funds. Fund managers pool the money of many individual investors and then decide which companies they will invest in and how much they will invest. Mutual funds are touted as a good deal for individual investors who do not have the time or expertise to intelligently invest in the stock market.

This sounds pretty good, but in the last five years or so, mutual funds have received some very negative publicity because their actions are not always in the best interests of the average investor. Concerns have been raised about mutual funds in three areas—management fees, market timing, and late trading.

Management Fees

It is important to investors that mutual fund managers are efficient in their work so that management costs do not unduly reduce the returns that mutual funds earn. In 2004, *The Globe and Mail* reported the results of a study that assessed the performance of 615 mutual funds during the period 1999–2004. The study used a key measure of mutual fund performance: the "Fee-to-Performance Value Indicator" (which shows how much of a fund's returns are used for fees like managers' salaries and commissions). The study found that the typical mutual fund has a score of 25 on the fee-to-performance indicator, meaning that about 25 cents out of every dollar earned goes to cover management fees. But fee-to-performance scores varied a lot. The best funds in the study were Ferique Equity (where only 6.5 cents of every dollar earned was used for management fees), PH&N Dividend Income (7.4 cents), and Sprott Canadian Equity (7.4 cents). The worst funds were Investors Canadian Enterprise (where 88.9 cents of every dollar was used for management fees), Clarica Canadian Diversified (76.9 cents), and Ethical Growth (62.7 cents).

The study also found that billions of dollars have been invested by Canadians in mutual funds that are not giving them good value for their money. During the period 1999–2004, $32.7 billion was contributed to mutual funds, like AGF American Growth Class and BMO International Equity Fund, that actually lost money. These funds delivered no value at all to investors (and because they lost money, it is not possible to calculate a negative fee-to-performance score for these funds). But these same mutual funds collected millions of dollars in fees from investors. Canadians also invested $21 billion in mutual funds where more than 50 percent of the gross revenue of the fund was used to pay management fees. These firms delivered questionable value to investors.

Ken Kivenko, a spokesperson for the Small Investor Protection Association, said that most individual investors don't even realize that they are paying fees to mutual funds. He found it surprising that some mutual funds can attract billions of dollars of investment from Canadians even though their fees are uncompetitive. Mutual funds that charge high fees counter these claims by noting that they provide better service to customers than do mutual funds that charge lower fees.

Market Timing

This refers to the practice of rapid in-and-out trading in mutual fund shares to profit from near-term price changes. While it is not technically illegal, it violates a basic principle of fairness because mutual funds typically have a strategy of long-term investing and do not normally allow people to do in-and-out trading (unless they pay a penalty). If a select few traders are allowed to engage in market timing without paying the penalty, this obviously works to the detriment of small investors who are not given this deal.

In 2004, four large Canadian mutual funds were fined a total of $156 million for allowing certain traders to engage in market timing. These traders made a total of $301 million in profits by using market timing. Three brokerages that were owned by banks were also fined a total of $46.5 million. All of the money will be used to reimburse investors who were disadvantaged by market timing. Paul Moore, the vice-chairman of the Ontario Securities Commission, said that by allowing only certain people to make market timing trades, these companies reduced returns for their long-term investors and failed in their duty to protect their interests. He also said that the fines will remind mutual fund managers that they have a responsibility to be vigilant in monitoring the activities of the people who work in their firms.

Michael Watson, the OSC's enforcement director, said he was disturbed by the fact that the problem of market timing was brought to the OSC's attention by New York Attorney General Elliot Spitzer, who was prosecuting U.S. mutual funds that allowed the practice. Watson said there must have been many people in Canada who knew that market timing was going on, but no one said anything.

In the United States, charges were filed against several firms, including Putnam Investments, which is the fifth largest mutual fund firm in the United States, with $272 billion in assets. Regulators allege that executives knew that two of the firm's managers were market timing their own funds for personal profit, told them to stop but didn't fire them, and let them keep the profits they made from market timing. After this became known, CEO Lawrence Lasser and four managers were fired.

Late Trading

Sounds incredible, doesn't it, that someone can bet on events from the past? It turns out that's what's been going on in the $7 trillion scandal-laden mutual funds industry. Some mutual fund managers have been making transactions after the market outcomes are known. It's what you might call a "sure thing"—a great way to erase market risk and take profits that are inaccessible to honest investors.

It's called "late trading"—trading in fund shares after the market closes but at the close-of-trade price—and it's illegal. After the 4:00 p.m. (Eastern Time) cut off, when the day's closing price is known, preferred customers get to trade—buy or sell—at the pre-4:00 p.m. price. It's like betting after the game is over. Late trading gives these traders an unfair information advantage over other investors because when big news breaks after the 4:00 p.m. closing—news that will almost certainly affect the next day's securities markets—late traders are nearly assured of a next-day quick profit or avoidance of a loss.

In the United States, the Securities and Exchange Commission's (SEC) enforcement director, Stephen Cutler, told a Senate hearing that about 10 percent of fund groups may have engaged in late trading and as many as one-quarter of America's largest mutual funds helped favoured clients by allowing illegal late trading. Preferential trading arrangements for big-money clients can be draining off billions of dollars from ordinary investors in mutual funds.

The SEC, the New York Attorney General's Office, and the Wisconsin Department of Financial Institutions are all looking into alleged market-timing transactions by Richard Strong, the board chairman of Strong Mutual Funds, that may have benefited him, his family, and friends. Strong Mutual Funds has policies against market timing because it hurts long-term shareholders and increases the fund's costs of operations. Under those conditions, regulators say, it's fraudulent to allow favoured people to do market timing without disclosing it to shareholders. The company confirmed that Strong invested assets in a small number of short-term, next-day transactions taking advantage of market-moving news. Strong resigned as board chair of the $42-billion fund and said he would reimburse investors for any losses they suffered because of his trading.

What should be done to reduce the problems of marketing timing and late trading? An indignant U.S. Congress proposed possible remedies and pledged that new, stiffer SEC regulations will eventually emerge. Meanwhile, the SEC and the National Association of Securities Dealers brought actions seeking injunctions, penalties, and financial relief for investors against several more illicit brokerages and mutual funds. But fixing the problem won't be easy, because each proposal seems to create new potential problems and there's no agreement on the best course of action. For example, proposals by the Investment Company Institute to outlaw all late trading could extend the time to process a trade—what now takes one day could take three or more days. That means mutual fund insiders would know about investment movements underway by big pension funds and have more time to use that information for self-gain. The trick is to fix the old problems without causing new ones.

Questions for Discussion

1. Why do you suppose the Ontario Securities Commission was slow in detecting the industry's market-timing abuses?
2. What remedies do you believe would be appropriate for fund managers who are found guilty of market timing and late trading? Defend your answer.
3. Suppose you are the manager of one of the equity funds for a large mutual funds firm. What steps would you take to ensure compliance with OSC regulations by your employees?
4. As a Chartered Financial Analyst (CFA) working at a mutual funds firm, what would you do if you suspected other employees of doing market timing or late trading?
5. Think of an after-hours news event that resulted in a next-day decline in the stock market. Then think of an after-hours news event that resulted in a next-day increase in the stock market. Why do you think the market would fall in one case and increase in the other?

Concluding Case 19-2

Stock Market Shenanigans

The stock market is supposed to be a place where you can increase your assets over time if you invest wisely and have patience. But some people don't want to trust their financial situation to unpredictable markets, so they come up with creative (often illegal) ways to manipulate the market to ensure that they will get a positive outcome. Unfortunately, it takes the bad behaviour of only a few people to make it seem like the stock market is a haven for con artists. In the following paragraphs, several classic frauds are briefly described.

Diverting Investors' Funds

Vincent Lacroix, the founder of Norbourg Asset Management Inc., was found guilty in 2008 of diverting $115 million from Norbourg into accounts that he and his wife controlled. Some investors lost their entire life savings. Lacroix was sentenced to 12 years in prison and fined $255 000, but he is appealing the sentence. The case was brought against Lacroix by the Autorité des marchés financiers (AMF), which is the securities watchdog for the province of Quebec. The AMF is itself the target of a class action suit, which claims that the AMF didn't do enough to protect small investors.

Ponzi Schemes

In 2009, Bernie Madoff confessed to running a Ponzi scheme that bilked investors out of $50 billion. A Ponzi scheme attracts investors by promising them that they will make very large returns on their money, much larger than can normally be made. Investors who join the scheme early may indeed make large returns because they are being paid with money that is being contributed by later investors. But eventually the scheme collapses, and almost everyone loses their investment. For most of the period from 1990 to 2008, Madoff reported to investors that they were making 12 percent annually on their investment. That was about double what investors could normally be expected to make. But it is alleged that Madoff never invested anyone's money in anything. Rather, he simply falsified financial reports and told people that their "investments" were doing fine. Many charitable organizations and rich individuals lost millions of dollars each as a result of their investment with Madoff.

Insider Trading

Andrew Rankin was an investment banking star with RBC Dominion Securities when he was charged with insider trading and "tipping" his friend Daniel Duic about several big corporate deals that were about to take place. Using the information provided by Rankin, Duic made over $4 million in profit by buying and selling the stocks of these companies at opportune times. When this was discovered, Duic made a deal with the Ontario Securities Commission to testify against his friend. Rankin was convicted of "tipping" and was sentenced to six months in jail. However, he appealed, and in 2008 the Ontario Securities Commission agreed to withdraw the criminal charges and he was spared jail time. Rankin was also fined $250 000 and barred for life from working in the securities industry.

In another insider trading case, Barry Landen of Agnico-Eagle Mines was found guilty after he sold shares he owned before it became publicly known that the company was going to report poor results. He was sentenced to 45 days in jail and fined $200 000.

In a third case, Glen Harper, the president of Golden Rule Resources Ltd., was found guilty of insider trading. He had sold $4 million worth of shares in his company after he found out that its supposedly huge gold find in Ghana was in doubt. When Harper sold his shares, the price of Golden Rule's stock was about $13 per share. After the bad news became public, the stock fell to 10 cents a share. Harper was sentenced to one year in prison and fined nearly $4 million.

"Wash" Trading

Visa Gold Exploration hunts for treasure found in sunken ships off the coast of Cuba. Officials at the TD Canada Trust alerted government regulators to suspicious trading patterns in the company's stock in November 2000. The alleged manipulation involved "wash trading," which occurs when the people who want to manipulate the price of a stock use several different brokerage accounts to establish an artificial price for a stock. This makes it look like there is a lot of interest in the stock by the general public, and that may cause its price to go up. The individuals who already own the stock benefit because of the increased price. In reality, very few buyers were involved in purchasing the stock of Visa Gold Exploration. The price of Visa Gold's stock declined from $1.15 per share in November 2000 to 5 cents a share by the end of 2001. Trading in the stock was suspended in 2002.

High-Closing

Several employees at RT Capital Management Inc., the investment arm of the Royal Bank of Canada, were charged with illegal trading in an attempt to manipulate stock prices. The OSC and the TSX concluded that the stock prices of many different Canadian companies were being manipulated using a practice called "high-closing." It works like this: Just before the stock exchange closes, a trader buys enough shares of a given stock so that the price of that stock rises above the price of the previous trade. This makes it look as if the stock has upward momentum. The motivation to "high-close" a stock can be strong for money managers, because they are under intense pressure to increase the value of their portfolios so they can demonstrate high performance and attract more clients. The temptation is particularly strong at year-end because money managers' annual bonuses are tied to their performance. RT Capital admitted that it had manipulated the closing price of 26 stocks over one eight-day period. The employees who were involved included a senior vice-president and two traders, all of whom were suspended, and the company was fined $3 million.

"Salting" Gold Mines

David Walsh started a small gold-mining company in Calgary that he called Bre-X. After claiming that core samples showed that the company had found a major gold deposit in Indonesia, the price of the stock rose from 27 cents a share to nearly $300 a share. But it eventually became clear that the core samples had been tampered with and that there was no gold at the site. The shares of Bre-X quickly became worthless and investors lost millions. Two other gold exploration companies—Timbuktu Gold Corp. and Delgratia Mining Corp.—also revealed that their core samples had been tampered with.

Questions for Discussion

1. What factors determine the market price of a share of stock? Which of those factors were at work in the cases described above that dealt with the issue of stock prices?
2. What is the difference between debt and equity financing? Are the situations described above examples of debt or equity issues? Explain.
3. Consider the following statement: *Insider trading should not be illegal. In a free market economy, individuals who have the motivation and intelligence to gather information that allows them to make a lot of money should not be prevented from capitalizing on the information they have collected.* Do you agree or disagree with the statement? Explain your reasoning.

apter 20

Financial Decisions and Risk Management

After reading this chapter, you should be able to:

1. Describe the responsibilities of a *financial manager.*
2. Distinguish between *short-term (operating)* and *long-term (capital) expenditures.*
3. Identify four sources of *short-term financing* for businesses.
4. Distinguish among the various sources of *long-term financing* and explain the risks involved in each.
5. Discuss some key issues in financial management for small businesses.
6. Explain how *risk* affects business operations and identify the five steps in the *risk-management process.*
7. Explain the distinction between *insurable* and *uninsurable risks,* and distinguish among the different *types of insurance* purchased by businesses.

A Financial Meltdown

In September 2008, a financial crisis started in the United States and quickly spread to the world economy. Stock markets dropped disastrously, investment banks failed, and consumer and business credit became very difficult to obtain. For most people, the crisis was sudden and unexpected, and they did not understand what had gone wrong. Overall, the cause was a combination of regulatory failure, low interest rates, and greed on the part of financial institutions and individuals. Here is what happened.

The seeds of the 2008 financial meltdown were actually sown back in 2000, when the tech bubble burst and a recession ensued. The Bank of Canada, the U.S. Federal Reserve, and other central banks around the world cut interest rates in an attempt to encourage investment and get their economies moving again. It worked, but the low interest rates caused a boom in real estate values in the United States because home mortgages could be obtained with very low interest rates. Many people who had previously not been able to get a mortgage suddenly found that banks were eager to lend them money. Not surprisingly, the increased demand for houses caused home prices to increase. Low interest rates also caused investors to look for ways to make a greater return on their money, and that often led them to higher risk investments that gave a greater return.

The increase in housing prices was very pronounced in the United States because of the activity of companies like the Federal National Mortgage Association (nicknamed Fannie Mae) and the Federal Home Mortgage Corporation (nicknamed Freddie Mac). Fannie Mae was formed during the Great Depression of the 1930s to encourage banks to extend credit to homeowners. It was privatized in 1968. Freddie Mac was formed in 1970 to prevent monopolization in the home mortgage market. As time went on, these two companies (which together guarantee nearly half the mortgages in the United States) made increasingly risky loans to homeowners, and this added to the problem. (Some of the other lesser-known players in the mortgage industry are described in the book *Chain of Blame* by Paul Muolo.)

During the period from 2003 to 2006, almost anyone in the United States could qualify for a mortgage (even though they couldn't actually make their monthly payments). These mortgages came to be called NINJA loans (because the borrower had no income, no job, and no assets). Brokers who arranged such loans had a big incentive to do so—they received from $1000 to as much as $10 000 for each loan they arranged. Investment banks and other financial institutions started borrowing money so they could lend it to all the people who wanted to buy houses. These financial institutions then issued assets (called collateralized debt obligations, or CDOs) to cover their costs. These CDOs were marketed to investors as being very safe because the collateral backing them up was the homes that had been purchased with the money. This would not have been a problem if housing prices had continued to rise, but they didn't, and here's why: The mortgages came with very low "teaser" rates for the first year or two, after which the rate of interest charged increased sharply. Once people got into the third or fourth year of their mortgage, their monthly costs went way up and they realized they couldn't make their payments. So they defaulted on their loans and the banks wound up foreclosing on the home. This caused a drop in demand for homes, which, in turn, caused housing prices to drop. As time passed, more and more people got into trouble because many of them owed more on their mortgage than the new (lower) value of their home. Many simply walked away from their homes and stopped making payments.

When housing prices dropped, financial institutions had to borrow more money to make up for the reduced value of their CDO assets. But by then investors had become aware of the problems and were reluctant to loan money to anybody. Because banks held so much bad debt, they were also unwilling to loan money (to consumers and to each other), and this caused a liquidity crisis. The London Interbank Offered Rate (LIBOR) is the rate large banks charge each other when making loans; in September 2008, the rate went as high as 6 percent, which indicated considerable mistrust between banks.

The crisis was worsened by credit default swaps. These are essentially insurance against defaults on mortgage loans, and they work like this: Let's say that an investor buys bonds from Corporation X. The investor can buy a credit default swap from a company like American International Group (AIG) that guarantees that the investor will get his or her money back if Corporation X defaults on its bond payments. The investor pays AIG a fee (the equivalent of an insurance premium). Because the aforementioned CDOs were assumed to be very safe investments, very low premiums were charged for credit default swaps. When the housing market went bust, the companies that sold credit default swaps were in big financial trouble because they had to come up with collateral for all those defaulted mortgages (which they had earlier assumed would never be in default). For example, AIG had $300 billion of credit default swaps on its books, and it charged far too little for them.

Stock markets plunged as the credit crisis worsened, and this meant huge losses for Canadians who had bought stocks. This development was particularly problematic for people who were about to retire because the value of their stocks declined by as much as 50 percent in just a few months. By the end of 2008, most economists were predicting a deep and lengthy recession for the world economy.

The financial difficulties also caused the bankruptcy of large investment banks like Bear Stearns and Lehman Brothers. Merrill Lynch & Co. was also in trouble and was taken over by Bank of America. Fannie Mae, Freddie Mac, and AIG were essentially taken over by the U.S. government (total cost: $285 billion). But the bailout of individual companies was not enough. It was becoming apparent that the entire world's financial system was getting very close to a complete meltdown. To deal with the crisis, U.S. legislators agreed to form a $700-billion bailout fund that gave the U.S. Treasury the authority to buy up so-called "toxic" mortgages and other bad debts that were held by banks. The central governments of Britain, Germany, France, and Italy also developed multibillion-dollar bailout plans. The idea was that if banks around the world were relieved of their bad debts, they would start loaning money again to people who wanted to buy houses, and that would stabilize the housing markets. Loans would also encourage consumers to start buying again, and that demand would create jobs in both goods- and service-producing companies. ◆

How will this help me?

The opening case clearly shows the importance of managing risk with respect to the financial activities of business firms. The material in this chapter will benefit you in two ways: (1) as an employee or manager, you will be better able to use your knowledge about finance to improve your career prospects; (2) as a consumer, you will have a greater awareness of how businesses use financial instruments to support their activities and how those activities affect the prices you pay for the products you buy.

In this chapter, we first describe the objectives and responsibilities of financial managers. We then identify the short-term and long-term expenditures that firms make and the short-term and long-term sources of funds that are available to support these expenditures. We conclude with a discussion of what is required to effectively manage risk in a business.

The Role of the Financial Manager

1 Describe the responsibilities of a *financial manager.*

financial managers Those managers responsible for planning and overseeing the financial resources of a firm.

finance (or corporate finance) The business function involving decisions about a firm's long-term investments and obtaining the funds to pay for those investments.

We have seen that production managers are responsible for planning and controlling the output of goods and services. We have noted that marketing managers must plan and control the development and marketing of products. Similarly, **financial managers** plan and control the acquisition and dispersal of the company's financial assets. The business activity known as **finance (or corporate finance)** typically involves four responsibilities:

- determining a firm's long-term investments
- obtaining funds to pay for those investments
- conducting the firm's everyday financial activities
- helping to manage the risks that the firm takes

Objectives of the Financial Manager

Financial managers collect funds, pay debts, establish trade credit, obtain loans, control cash balances, and plan for future financial needs. But a financial manager's overall objective is to increase a firm's value—and thus stockholders' wealth. Whereas accountants create data to reflect a firm's financial status, financial managers make decisions for improving that status. Financial managers, then, must ensure that a company's earnings exceed its costs—in other words, that it earns a profit. In sole proprietorships and partnerships, profits translate directly into increases in owners' wealth. In corporations, profits translate into an increase in the value of common stock.

Responsibilities of the Financial Manager

The responsibility of the financial manager to increase a firm's wealth falls into three general categories: *cash flow management*, *financial control*, and *financial planning*.

Cash Flow Management

To increase a firm's value, financial managers must ensure that it has enough funds on hand to purchase the materials and human resources that it needs to produce goods and services. Funds that are not needed immediately must be invested to earn more money for a firm. This activity—**cash flow management**—requires careful planning. If excess cash balances are allowed to sit idle instead of being invested, a firm loses the cash returns it could have earned. One study has revealed that companies averaging $2 million in annual sales typically hold $40 000 in non-interest-bearing accounts. Larger companies hold even larger sums. By locating idle cash and putting it to work, firms not only gain additional income, they also avoid having to borrow from outside sources. The savings on interest payments can be substantial.

cash flow management Managing the pattern in which cash flows in to the firm in the form of revenues and out of the firm in the form of debt payments.

Financial Control

Financial control is the process of checking actual performance against plans to ensure that the desired financial status occurs. For example, planned revenues based on forecasts usually turn out to be higher or lower than actual revenues because sales are unpredictable. Control involves monitoring revenue inflows and making appropriate financial adjustments. Excessively high revenues, for instance, may be deposited in short-term interest-bearing accounts, or they may be used to pay off short-term debt. Otherwise earmarked resources

financial control The process of checking actual performance against plans to ensure that the desired financial status is achieved.

Financial managers have the responsibility of ensuring that the financial assets of a company are used effectively. This includes investments it may have in other companies in the form of shares of stock. Regular assessment of how these investments are performing is an important responsibility of financial managers.

can be saved or put to better use. In contrast, lower-than-expected revenues may necessitate short-term borrowing to meet current debt obligations.

Budgets (as we saw in Chapter 14) are often the backbone of financial control. The budget provides the "measuring stick" against which performance is evaluated. The cash flows, debts, and assets of each department and the whole company are compared at regular intervals against budgeted amounts. Discrepancies indicate the need for financial adjustments so that resources are used to the best advantage.

Financial Planning

financial plan A description of how a business will reach some financial position it seeks for the future; includes projections for sources and uses of funds.

Financial planning is the cornerstone of effective financial management. A **financial plan** describes a firm's strategies for reaching some future financial position. In constructing the plan, a financial manager must ask several questions:

- What amount of funds does the company need to meet immediate plans?
- When will it need more funds?
- Where can it get the funds to meet both its short-term and its long-term needs?

To answer these questions, a financial manager must develop a clear picture of *why* a firm needs funds. Managers must also assess the relative costs and benefits of potential funding sources. In the sections that follow, we will explain why businesses need funds and identify the main sources of business funding for both the short term and the long term.

Why Do Businesses Need Funds?

2 Distinguish between *short-term (operating)* and *long-term (capital) expenditures.*

Every company needs money to survive. Failure to make a contractually obligated payment can lead to bankruptcy and the dissolution of the firm. However, the successful financial manager must distinguish between two different kinds of financial outlays—*short-term (operating) expenditures* and *long-term (capital) expenditures*.

Short-Term (Operating) Expenditures

A firm makes short-term expenditures regularly in its everyday business activities. To handle these expenditures, financial managers must pay attention to *accounts payable*, *accounts receivable*, *inventories*, and *working capital*.

Accounts Payable

In Chapter 14, we defined *accounts payable* as unpaid bills owed to suppliers plus wages and taxes due within the upcoming year. For most companies, this is the largest single category of short-term debt. To plan for funding flows, financial managers want to know *in advance* the amounts of new accounts payable as well as when they must be repaid. For information about such obligations and needs—say, the quantity of supplies required by a certain department in an upcoming period—financial managers must rely on other managers. The Exercising Your Ethics feature at the end of the chapter presents an interesting dilemma regarding accounts payable.

Accounts Receivable

Accounts receivable consist of funds due from customers who have bought on credit. A sound financial plan requires financial managers to project accurately both how much credit is advanced to buyers and when they will make payments on their accounts. For example, managers at Kraft Foods must know how many dollars' worth of cheddar cheese Safeway supermarkets will order each month; they must also know Safeway's payment schedule. Because accounts receivable represent an investment in products for which a firm has not yet received payment, they temporarily tie up its funds. Clearly, the seller wants to receive payment as quickly as possible.

Credit Policies. Predicting payment schedules is a function of **credit policy**—the rules governing a firm's extension of credit to customers. This policy sets standards as to which buyers are eligible for what type of credit. Typically, credit is extended to customers who have the ability to pay and who honour their obligations. Credit is denied to firms with poor payment histories.

credit policy Rules governing a firm's extension of credit to customers.

Credit policy also sets payment terms. For example, credit terms of "2/10, net 30" mean that the selling company offers a 2 percent discount if the customer pays within 10 days. The customer has 30 days to pay the regular price. Under these terms, the buyer would have to pay only $980 on a $1000 invoice on days one to 10, but all $1000 on days 11 to 30. The higher the discount, the more incentive buyers have to pay early. Sellers can thus adjust credit terms to influence when customers pay their bills.

Inventories

Between the time a firm buys raw materials and the time it sells finished products, it ties up funds in **inventory**—materials and goods that it will sell within the year. Failure to manage inventory can have grave financial consequences. Too little inventory of any kind can cost a firm sales, while too much inventory means that funds are tied up and cannot be used elsewhere.

There are three basic types of inventories: *raw materials*, *work-in-process*, and *finished goods*. The basic supplies a firm buys to use in its production process are its **raw materials inventory**. Levi Strauss's raw materials inventory includes huge rolls of denim. **Work-in-process inventory** consists of goods partway through the production process. Jeans that are cut out but not yet sewn are part of the work-in-process inventory. Finally, **finished goods inventory** refers to items that are ready for sale. Completed blue jeans ready for shipment to dealers are finished goods inventory.

inventory Materials and goods currently held by the company that will be sold within the year.

raw materials inventory That portion of a firm's inventory consisting of basic supplies used to manufacture products for sale.

work-in-process inventory That portion of a firm's inventory consisting of goods partway through the production process.

finished goods inventory That portion of a firm's inventory consisting of completed goods ready for sale.

Working Capital

Working capital is the difference between a firm's current assets and current liabilities. It is a liquid asset out of which current debts can be paid. A company calculates its working capital by adding up the following:

- inventories—that is, raw materials, work-in-process, and finished goods on hand
- accounts receivable (minus accounts payable)

Large companies typically devote 20 cents of every sales dollar to working capital. If companies can reduce working capital, they benefit, because every dollar that is not tied up in working capital becomes a dollar of more useful cash flow. Reducing working capital also raises earnings permanently because money costs money (in interest payments and the like). Reducing working capital means saving money.

Long-Term (Capital) Expenditures

Companies also need funds to cover long-term expenditures for fixed assets. *Fixed assets* are items that have a lasting use or value, such as land, buildings, and machinery. The Hudson's Bay Oil and Gas plant in Flin Flon, Manitoba, is a fixed asset.

Long-term expenditures are usually more carefully planned than short-term outlays because they pose special problems. They differ from short-term outlays in the following ways, all of which influence the ways that long-term outlays are funded:

- Unlike inventories and other short-term assets, they are not normally sold or converted into cash.
- Their acquisition requires a very large investment.
- They represent a binding commitment of company funds that continues long into the future.

Sources of Short-Term Funds

3 Identify four sources of *short-term financing* for businesses.

Firms can call on many sources for the funds they need to finance day-to-day operations and to implement short-term plans. These sources include *trade credit*, *secured* and *unsecured loans*, and *factoring accounts receivable*.

Trade Credit

trade credit The granting of credit by a selling firm to a buying firm.

open-book credit Form of trade credit in which sellers ship merchandise on faith that payment will be forthcoming.

promissory note Form of trade credit in which buyers sign promise-to-pay agreements before merchandise is shipped.

trade draft Form of trade credit in which buyers must sign statements of payment terms attached to merchandise by sellers.

trade acceptance Trade draft that has been signed by the buyer.

Accounts payable are not merely expenditures. They are also a source of funds to the company, which has the use of the product purchased until it pays its bill. **Trade credit**—the granting of credit by one firm to another—is effectively a short-term loan. Trade credit can take several forms.

- The most common form, **open-book credit**, is essentially a "gentlemen's agreement." Buyers receive merchandise along with invoices stating credit terms. Sellers ship products on faith that payment will be forthcoming on the due date.
- When sellers want more reassurance, they may insist that buyers sign legally binding **promissory notes** before merchandise is shipped. The agreement states when and how much money will be paid to the seller.
- The **trade draft** is attached to the merchandise shipment by the seller and states the promised date and amount of payment due. To take possession of the merchandise, the buyer must sign the draft. Once signed by the buyer, the document becomes a **trade acceptance**. Trade drafts and trade acceptances are useful forms of credit in international transactions.

Trade credit insurance is available for sellers (particularly Canadian companies that export to the United States) who are concerned that buyers may not pay their bills. Premiums are generally 1 to 2 percent of the value of the goods that are being sold (there is a 10 percent deductible provision). Montreal-based ELPRO International Inc., an exporter of luggage and handbags, is happy it bought trade credit insurance, because one of its U.S. customers suddenly went out of business and didn't pay what they owed. ELPRO received payment for the shipment from the insurance company.[1]

Secured Short-Term Loans

secured loan A short-term loan for which the borrower is required to put up collateral.

For most firms, bank loans are a vital source of short-term funding. Such loans almost always involve a promissory note in which the borrower promises to repay the loan plus interest. In **secured loans**, banks require the borrower to put up **collateral**—assets that the bank can seize if loan payments are not made as promised. Secured loans allow borrowers to get funds when they might not qualify for unsecured credit. Secured loans generally carry lower interest rates than unsecured loans. Most short-term business borrowing is secured by inventories and accounts receivable.

collateral Any asset that a lender has the right to seize if a borrower does not repay a loan.

Inventory as Collateral

When a loan is made with inventory as collateral, the lender loans the borrower some portion of the stated value of the inventory. Inventory is more attractive as collateral when it provides the lender with real security for the loan amount; for example, if the inventory can be readily converted into cash, it is more valuable as collateral. Boxes full of expensive, partially completed lenses for eyeglasses are of little value on the open market. Meanwhile, a thousand crates of boxed, safely stored canned tomatoes might well be convertible into cash.

Accounts Receivable as Collateral

When accounts receivable are used as collateral, the process is called **pledging accounts receivable**. In the event of nonpayment, the lender may seize the receivables—that is, funds owed the borrower by its customers. If these assets are not enough to cover the loan, the borrower must make up the difference. This option is especially important to service companies such as accounting firms and law offices. Because they do not maintain inventories, accounts receivable are their main source of collateral. Typically, lenders who will accept accounts receivable as collateral are financial institutions with credit departments capable of evaluating the quality of the receivables.

pledging accounts receivable Using accounts receivable as collateral for a loan.

Unsecured Short-Term Loans

With an **unsecured loan**, the borrower does not have to put up collateral. In many cases, however, the bank requires the borrower to maintain a *compensating balance*, that is, the borrower must keep a portion of the loan amount on deposit with the bank in a non-interest-bearing account.

The terms of the loan—amount, duration, interest rate, and payment schedule—are negotiated between the bank and the borrower. To receive an unsecured loan, a firm must ordinarily have a good banking relationship with the lender. Once an agreement is made, a promissory note will be executed and the funds transferred to the borrower. Although some unsecured loans are one-time-only arrangements, many take the form of *lines of credit*, *revolving credit agreements*, or *commercial paper*.

unsecured loan A short-term loan in which the borrower is not required to put up collateral.

Lines of Credit

A **line of credit** is a standing agreement with a bank to lend a firm a maximum amount of funds on request. The bank does not guarantee that the funds will be available when requested, however. For example, suppose that TD Canada Trust gives Sunshine Tanning Inc. a $100 000 line of credit for the coming year. By signing promissory notes, Sunshine's borrowings can total up to $100 000 at any time. Sunshine benefits from the arrangement by knowing in advance that the bank regards the firm as creditworthy and will loan funds to it on short notice.

line of credit A standing agreement between a bank and a firm in which the bank specifies the maximum amount it will make available to the borrower for a short-term unsecured loan; the borrower can then draw on those funds, when available.

Revolving Credit Agreements

Revolving credit agreements are similar to credit cards. Under a revolving credit agreement, a lender agrees to make some amount of funds available on demand to a firm for continuing short-term loans. The lending institution

revolving credit agreement A guaranteed line of credit for which the firm pays the bank interest on funds borrowed as well as a fee for extending the line of credit.

guarantees that funds will be available when sought by the borrower. In return, the bank charges a *commitment fee*—a charge for holding open a line of credit for a customer even if the customer does not borrow any funds. The commitment fee is often expressed as a percentage of the loan amount, usually 0.5 to 1 percent of the committed amount.

For example, suppose that TD Canada Trust agrees to lend Sunshine Tanning up to $100 000 under a revolving credit agreement. If Sunshine borrows $80 000, it still has access to $20 000. If it pays off $50 000 of the debt, reducing its debt to $30 000, then it has $70 000 available to it. Sunshine pays interest on the borrowed funds and also pays a fee on the unused funds in the line of credit.

Commercial Paper

commercial paper A method of short-run fundraising in which a firm sells unsecured notes for less than the face value and then repurchases them at the face value within 270 days; buyers' profits are the difference between the original price paid and the face value.

Some firms can raise short-term funds by issuing **commercial paper**. Since commercial paper is backed solely by the issuing firm's promise to pay, it is an option for only the largest and most creditworthy firms. Here's how it works: Corporations issue commercial paper with a face value, but buyers pay less than that value. At the end of a specified period (usually 30 to 90 days but legally up to 270 days), the issuing company buys back the paper—*at the face value*. The difference between the price the buying company paid and the face value is the buyer's profit. For example, if CN needs to borrow $10 million for 90 days, it might issue commercial paper with a face value of $10.2 million. An insurance company with excess cash might buy the paper for $10 million. After 90 days, CN would pay $10.2 million to the insurance company. In 2007, serious problems developed in the commercial paper market in Canada (see Concluding Case 20-1 for details).

Factoring Accounts Receivable

A firm can raise funds by *factoring*—selling the firm's accounts receivable. The purchaser of the receivables, usually a financial institution, is known as the factor. The factor pays some percentage of the full amount of receivables. The seller gets this money immediately. For example, a factor might buy $40 000 worth of receivables for 60 percent of that sum ($24 000). The factor profits to the extent that the money it eventually collects exceeds the amount it paid. This profit depends on the quality of the receivables, the cost of collecting them, and interest rates.

As CFO of *Nylon* magazine, which focuses on fashion and pop culture for women, Larry Rosenblum is responsible for collecting the money that advertisers owe the publication. The magazine depends on that money for its cash flow. To get the money, Rosenblum typically resorts to factors—lenders who buy the legal right to collect a company's outstanding invoices (in return for up to 3 percent of the amount due). Among Canadian and U.S. business firms, factoring accounts for more than $1 trillion in credit. The bill collecting business no longer has the unsavoury reputation that it once had.

Sources of Long-Term Funds

Distinguish among the various sources of *long-term financing* and explain the risks involved in each.

4

Firms need long-term funding to finance expenditures on fixed assets—the buildings and equipment necessary for conducting their business. They may seek long-term funds through *debt financing* (that is, from outside the firm), *equity financing* (by drawing on internal sources), or *hybrid financing* (a middle ground). In making decisions about sources of long-term funds, companies must consider the *risk-return relationship*.

Debt Financing

Long-term borrowing from outside the company—**debt financing**—is a major component of most firms' long-term financial planning. The two primary sources of such funding are *long-term loans* and the sale of *corporate bonds*.

debt financing Raising money to meet long-term expenditures by borrowing from outside the company; usually takes the form of long-term loans or the sale of corporate bonds.

Long-Term Loans

Most corporations get their long-term loans from a chartered bank, usually one with which the firm has developed a long-standing relationship. Credit companies (like Household Finance Corp.), insurance companies, and pension funds also grant long-term business loans. Long-term loans are attractive to borrowers for several reasons:

- Because the number of parties involved is limited, loans can often be arranged very quickly.
- The firm need not make public disclosure of its business plans or the purpose for which it is acquiring the loan (in contrast, the issuance of corporate bonds requires such disclosure).
- The duration of the loan can be matched to the borrower's needs.
- If the firm's needs change, the terms of the loan can usually be changed.

Long-term loans also have some disadvantages. Large borrowers may have trouble finding lenders to supply enough funds, they may have restrictions placed on them as conditions of the loan, they may have to pledge long-term assets as collateral, and they may have to agree not to take on any more debt until the borrowed funds are repaid.

Interest Rates. Interest rates are negotiated between borrower and lender. Although some bank loans have fixed rates, others have floating rates tied to the prime rate (the rate the bank charges its most creditworthy customers). A loan at 1 percent above prime, then, is payable at one percentage point higher than the prime rate. This rate may fluctuate, or float, because the prime rate itself goes up and down as market conditions change.

Corporate Bonds

A corporate *bond* is a contract—a promise by the issuing company or organization to pay the holder a certain amount of money on a specified date. Most bonds pay the bondholder a stipulated sum of interest semi-annually or annually. If it fails to make a bond payment, the company is in default. In many cases, bonds may not be redeemed for 30 years from the time of issue.

Corporate bonds are the major source of long-term debt financing for most corporations. Bonds are attractive when companies need large amounts of funds for long periods of time. The issuing company gets access to large numbers of lenders through nationwide bond markets. But bonds involve expensive administrative and selling costs. They also may require very high interest payments if the issuing company has a poor credit rating.

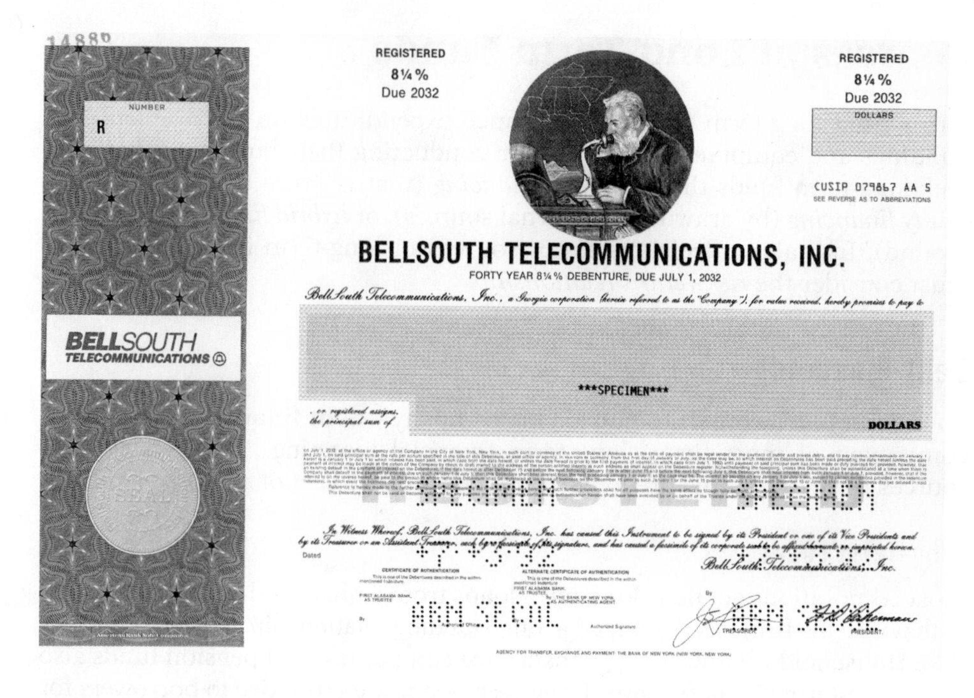

The proceeds from this corporate bond will be used to purchase fixed assets that are necessary for the production of goods or services.

bond indenture Statement of the terms of a corporate bond.

Bond Indenture. The **bond indenture** spells out the terms of a bond, including the amount to be paid, the interest rate, and the maturity (payoff) date. The indenture also identifies which of the firm's assets, if any, are pledged as collateral for the bonds.

Because of the risk of default, debt financing appeals most strongly to companies that have predictable profits and cash flow patterns. For example, demand for electric power is quite steady from year to year and predictable from month to month. Thus, provincial hydroelectric utility companies enjoy steady streams of income and can carry substantial amounts of debt.

Equity Financing

equity financing Raising money to meet long-term expenditures by issuing common stock or by retaining earnings.

Although debt financing has strong appeal in some cases, looking inside the company for long-term funding is preferable under other circumstances. In small companies, the founders may increase their personal investment in the firm. In most cases, however, **equity financing** takes the form of issuing common stock or of retaining the firm's earnings. Both options involve putting the owners' capital to work.

Issuing Common Stock

By selling shares of stock, the company gets the funds it needs for buying land, buildings, and equipment. When shareholders purchase common stock, they seek profits in the form of both dividends and increases in the price of the stock.

Suppose that Sunshine Tanning's founders invested $10 000 by buying the original 500 shares of common stock (at $20 per share) in 2003. If the company used these funds to buy equipment and succeeded financially, by 2009 it might need funds for expansion. A pattern of profitable operations and regularly paid dividends might allow Sunshine to raise $50 000 by selling 500 new shares of stock for $100 per share. This additional paid-in capital would increase the total shareholders' equity to $60 000, as shown in Table 20.1.

The use of equity financing via common stock can be expensive because paying dividends is more expensive than paying bond interest. Why? Interest paid to bondholders is a business expense and, hence, a tax deduction for the firm. Stock dividends are not tax-deductible.

Table 20.1 Stockholders' Equity for Sunshine Tanning

Common Stockholders' Equity, 2003	
Initial common stock (500 shares issued @ $20 per share, 2003)	$10 000
Total stockholders' equity	$10 000
Common Stockholders' Equity, 2009	
Initial common stock (500 shares issued @ $20 per share, 2003)	$10 000
Additional paid-in capital (500 shares issued @ $100 per share, 2009)	50 000
Total stockholders' equity	$60 000

Retained Earnings

Another approach to equity financing is to use *retained earnings*. These earnings represent profits not paid out in dividends. Using retained earnings means that the firm will not have to borrow money and pay interest on loans or bonds. A firm that has a history of eventually reaping much higher profits by successfully reinvesting retained earnings may be attractive to some investors. But the smaller dividends that can be paid to shareholders as a result of retained earnings may decrease demand for—and thus the price of—the company's stock.

For example, if Sunshine Tanning had net earnings of $50 000 in 2009, it could pay a $50-per-share dividend on its 1000 shares of common stock. But if it plans to remodel at a cost of $30 000 and retains $30 000 of earnings to finance the project, only $20 000 is left to distribute for stock dividends ($20 per share).

If equity funding can be so expensive, why don't firms rely totally on debt capital? Because long-term loans and bonds carry fixed interest rates and represent a fixed promise to pay regardless of the profitability of the firm. If the firm defaults on its obligations, it may lose its assets and even go into bankruptcy. In 2009, for example, CanWest Global announced that it was halting interest payments of $30.4 million to bondholders as it tried to recapitalize the company and avoid bankruptcy. The firm said it might replace the old debt with new debt guaranteeing that bondholders would get their money from cash that CanWest was planning to generate by selling some of its assets.[2]

Hybrid Financing: Preferred Stock

Falling somewhere between debt and equity financing is *preferred stock*. Preferred stock is a hybrid because it has some of the features of corporate bonds and some features of common stocks. As with bonds, payments on preferred stock are for fixed amounts, such as $6 per share per year. Unlike bonds, however, preferred stock never matures. It can be held indefinitely, like common stock. And dividends need not be paid if the company makes no profit. If dividends are paid, preferred shareholders receive them first, in preference to dividends on common stock.

A major advantage of preferred stock to the issuing corporation is its flexibility. It secures funds for the firm without relinquishing control, since preferred shareholders have no voting rights. And it does not require repayment of principal or payment of dividends in lean times.

Choosing Between Debt and Equity Financing

A key part of financial planning involves striking a balance between debt and equity financing to meet the firm's long-term need for funds. The mix of debt

capital structure Relative mix of a firm's debt and equity financing.

vs. equity is the firm's **capital structure**. Financial plans contain targets for the capital structure, such as 40 percent debt and 60 percent equity. But choosing a target is not easy. A wide range of debt-vs.-equity mixes is possible.

The most conservative strategy would be to use all equity financing and no debt. Under this strategy, a company has no formal obligations for financial payouts. But equity is a very expensive source of capital. At the other extreme, the strategy would be to use all debt financing. While less expensive than equity funding, indebtedness increases the risk that a firm will be unable to meet its obligations and will go bankrupt. Somewhere between the two extremes, financial planners try to find a mix that will maximize shareholders' wealth. Figure 20.1 summarizes the factors management must take into account when deciding between debt and equity financing. The boxed insert entitled "An Online Community for People 50 and Older" describes one small company's fundraising dilemma.

Indexes of Financial Risk

To help understand and measure the amount of financial risk they face, financial managers often rely on published indexes for various investments. *Financial World*, for example, publishes independent appraisals of mutual

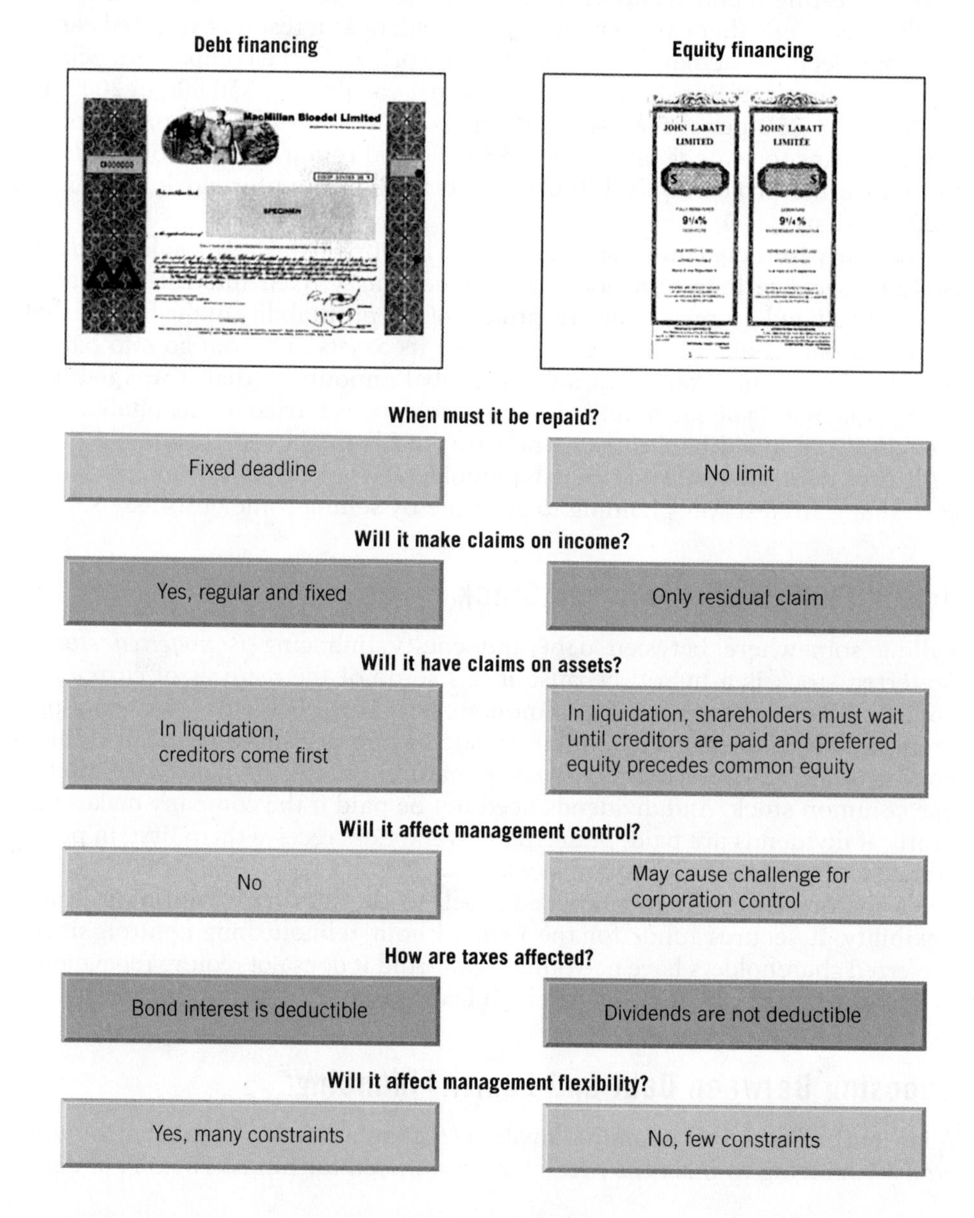

Figure 20.1 Comparing debt and equity financing.

Entrepreneurship and New Ventures

An Online Community for People 50 and Older

The social networking site Facebook began specifically for college students, and over 80 percent of its users are under the age of 35. That's one reason Kelly and Jeff Lantz founded 55-Alive!, a social networking site for users over 50 years old. Launched in 2005, the company had a meagre $5000 in revenues for 2006. The following year, revenues jumped to $30 000 as the site's activities expanded into instant messaging, blogging, and chat rooms for member-created groups. Two groups that are widely subscribed to are "Man's Best Friend" and "Widow/Widower" forums.

So what's next? To date, 55-Alive! is financed with the Lantz's own money and has just one part-time employee. Kelly and Jeff project a need for at least $250 000 of outside funding to expand the site's content and to hire someone to help with sales ads. Despite its early success, 55-Alive! still receives only 100 000 visits per month, just a small fraction of Facebook's 100 million daily users. While Facebook seems to continue to appeal largely to a younger demographic, it has been experiencing significant growth in the 35–54 age category.

Questions for Discussion

1. What possible sources of financing are available to 55-Alive!?
2. How important is it that Kelly and Jeff develop a business plan to help secure this money?

funds, using risk-reward ratings of A (very good) to E (poor) to indicate each fund's riskiness in comparison with its anticipated financial returns. An A-rated fund is judged to offer very good returns relative to the amount of risk involved. An E-rated fund carries the greatest risk with smaller returns. Similarly, Standard & Poor's publishes various indexes for numerous funds and for stocks that are available for purchase by financial managers.

By using such indexes, financial managers can determine how a particular investment compares with other opportunities in terms of its stability. A bond, for example, is considered to be "investment grade" if it qualifies for one of the top four ratings of either S&P or Moody's. Bonds below investment grade are called *junk bonds* because they have high default rates. Junk bonds appeal to some investors because they promise uncommonly high yields.

If bond rating agencies like Moody's and Standard & Poor's downgrade a company's ratings to low enough levels, its bonds become junk bonds. That's what happened to the Gap after sales at virtually every store in the chain fell every single month for nearly two years. As a result, the Gap found it harder to raise money.

The Risk-Return Relationship

While developing plans for raising capital, financial managers must be aware of the different motivations of individual investors. Why, for example, do some individuals and firms invest in stocks while others invest only in bonds? Investor motivations, of course, determine who is willing to buy a given company's stocks or bonds. Everyone who invests money is expressing a personal preference for safety vs. risk. Investors give money to firms and, in return, anticipate receiving future cash flows.

Some cash flows are more certain than others. Investors generally expect to receive higher payments for higher uncertainty. They generally do not expect large returns for secure investments such as government-insured bonds. Each type of investment, then, has a risk-return relationship. Figure 20.2 shows the general **risk-return relationship** for various financial instruments. High-grade corporate bonds, for example, rate low in terms of risk on future returns but also low on the size of expected returns. The reverse is true of junk bonds, those with a higher risk of default.

risk-return relationship Shows the amount of risk and the likely rate of return on various financial instruments.

Risk-return differences are recognized by financial managers, who try to gain access to the greatest funding at the lowest possible cost. By gauging investors' perceptions of their riskiness, a firm's managers can estimate how much it must pay to attract funds to their offerings. Over time, a company can reposition itself on the risk continuum by improving its record on dividends, interest payments, and debt repayment.

Financial Management for Small Businesses

5 Discuss some key issues in financial management for small businesses.

Most new businesses have inadequate funding. An Ontario government study found that the average investment needed to start a new enterprise was about \$58 000 but that more than half of all new companies had less than \$15 000 invested.[3] Another study of nearly 3000 new companies revealed a survival rate of 84 percent for new businesses with initial investments of at least \$50 000. Those with less funding had a much lower survival rate.[4]

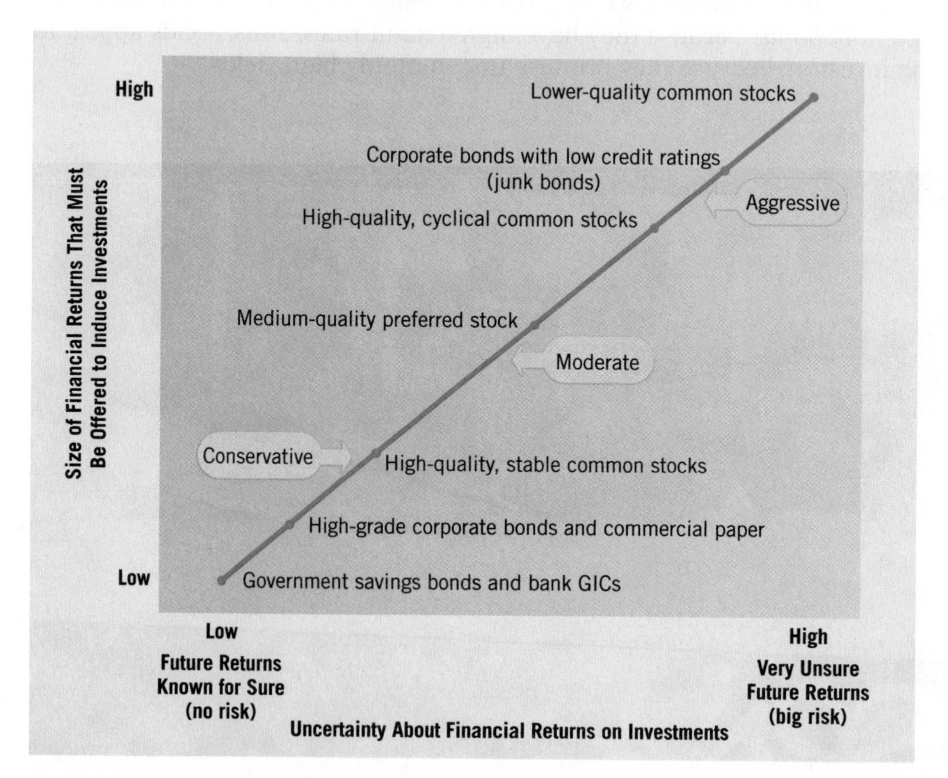

Figure 20.2 The risk-return relationship.

Why are so many start-ups underfunded? For one thing, entrepreneurs often underestimate the value of establishing *bank credit* as a source of funds and use *trade credit* ineffectively. In addition, they often fail to consider *venture capital* as a source of funding, and they are notorious for not *planning cash flow needs* properly.

Establishing Bank Credit and Trade Credit

Some banks have liberal credit policies and offer financial analysis, cash flow planning, and suggestions based on experiences with other local firms. Some provide loans to small businesses in bad times and work to keep them going. Obtaining credit, therefore, begins with finding a bank that can—and will—support a small firm's financial needs. Once a *line* of credit is obtained, the small business can seek more liberal credit policies from other businesses. Sometimes, for instance, suppliers give customers longer credit periods—say, 45 or 60 days rather than 30 days. Liberal trade credit terms with their suppliers let firms increase short-term funds and avoid additional borrowing from banks.

Start-up firms without proven financial success usually must present a business plan to demonstrate that the firm is a good credit risk.[5] As we saw in Chapter 4, a business plan is a document that tells potential lenders why the money is needed, the amount needed, how the money will be used to improve the company, and when it will be paid back.

Venture Capital

Many newer businesses—especially those undergoing rapid growth—cannot get the funds they need through borrowing alone. They may, therefore, turn to **venture capital**—outside equity funding provided in return for part-ownership of the borrowing firm. Venture capital firms actively seek opportunities to invest in new firms with rapid growth potential. Because failure rates are high, they typically demand high returns, which are often 20 to 30 percent.

venture capital Outside equity financing provided in return for part-ownership of the borrowing firm.

Planning for Cash Flow Requirements

All businesses should plan for their cash flows, but it is especially important for small businesses to do so. Success or failure may hinge on anticipating times when cash will be short and when excess cash is expected. Figure 20.3

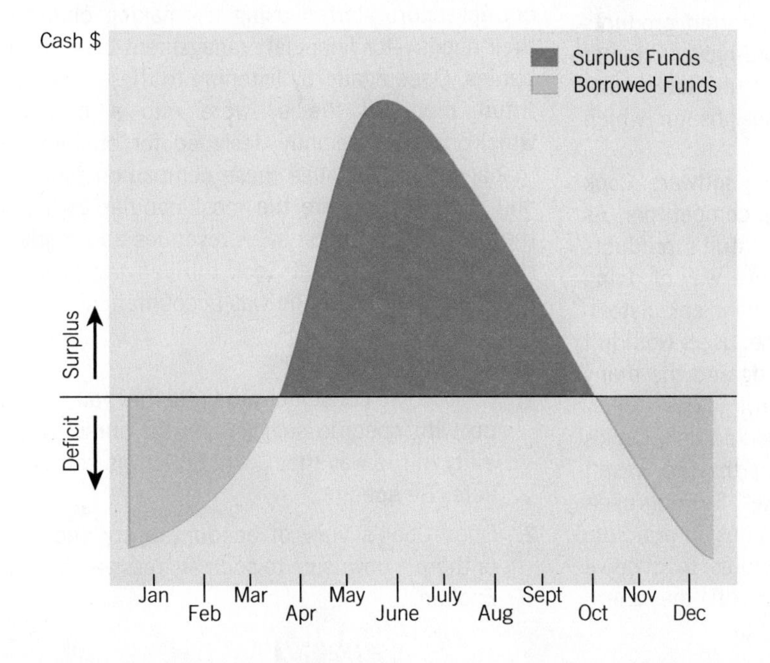

Figure 20.3 Cash flow for Slippery Fish Bait Supply Company.

shows possible cash inflows, cash outflows, and net cash position (inflows minus outflows) on a month-by-month basis for Slippery Fish Bait Supply. In this highly seasonal business, bait stores buy heavily from Slippery during the spring and summer months. Revenues outpace expenses, leaving surplus funds that can be invested. During the fall and winter, expenses exceed revenues. Slippery must borrow funds to keep going until sales revenues pick up again in the spring. Comparing predicted cash inflows from sales with outflows for expenses shows the firm's monthly cash flow position.

By anticipating shortfalls, a financial manager can seek funds in advance and minimize their cost. By anticipating excess cash, a manager can plan to put the funds to work in short-term, interest-earning investments. The Business Accountability box describes how one entrepreneur was successful by helping other individuals organize their financial activities.

Business Accountability

A Quicken Course in Accountability

After deciding to hold himself accountable for designing new products, Scott Cook created some unique methods to ensure he'd meet those design obligations when he founded a company back in 1983. Cook is the former CEO of Intuit, the $1.7 billion company whose well-known software tools—Quicken and QuickBooks—have changed the way we manage our financial lives.

Cook initially envisioned three core principles for product design that eventually led to superb commercial success. First, it's the customer that's most important; listen to the customer and design the product for customer value. Second, be open-minded in identifying all competing ways the customer could perform the task, not just the obvious ways. Third, simplify and improve the product so it provides the easiest way for the customer to complete the task to be performed.

From the beginning, Cook believed these principles would lead to superior, user-friendly, preferred products that customers would buy and use. Accordingly, customer acceptance of the products would be the ultimate measure of success or failure of product designs for which Cook was accountable.

Although the firm was selling computer software, Cook didn't restrict his vision to just software competitors. As the second design principle stipulates, Intuit's products had to perform better than any alternative way of doing the task, including competitors' software, hand calculators, and pencil-and-paper methods. Otherwise, users wouldn't prefer Intuit's products for cheque writing and the many other financial tasks they had to perform.

While the initial version of Quicken worked well, Cook's insistence on pleasing customers meant that he wasn't satisfied when it first came on the market. Seeking user-based improvements, he applied the first design principle by assigning employees in computer stores to observe consumers when they bought Quicken off the shelf. Cook's imaginative "Follow Me Home" program surprised customers when they were asked if the employee could come home with them to watch their reaction to the software. Everything about the user's experience was noted, beginning with ease or difficulty in opening the package, reading instructions, installing the software on a computer, using it, and even turning away to write with pencil and paper. Cook insisted that anything preventing ease of use, no matter how small, was Intuit's fault, not the customer's. So watching for even the tiniest display of displeasure or frustration, the employee silently observed the user's facial expressions, body language, vocal reactions, pauses, and rereading of instructions in each stage, from opening the shrink-wrapped package to using the product.

Guided by what was learned from "Follow Me Home," the company invoked the third principle for simplifying and improving Quicken. As word spread about the software's success with personal finance on PCs at home, entrepreneurs started using it—making changes to suit their needs—for financial management tasks in their companies. Once again, by listening to these new customers, Intuit modified the software into a new product—QuickBooks—especially designed for business financial management. Because these companion tools—Quicken and QuickBooks—are the most popular in the industry, the firm's $1.7 billion sales revenues and market leadership are evidence that Cook fulfilled the product-design obligations for which he was accountable.

Critical Thinking Questions

1. Choose two consumer products that you use and come up with specific suggestions for pursuing accountability in the way that Cook did for his company's products. Be specific.
2. Does Cook's view of accountability seem extreme? Is there a downside to such aggressive accountability? Explain.

Risk Management

Explain how *risk* affects business operations and identify the five steps in the *risk-management process.* 6

Risk—uncertainty about future events—is a factor in every manager's job because nearly every managerial action raises the possibility for either positive or negative outcomes. Risk management is therefore essential.[6] Firms devote considerable resources not only to recognizing potential risks but also to positioning themselves to make the most advantageous decisions regarding risk.

risk Uncertainty about future events.

The financial crisis that erupted in 2008 caused many firms to take a second look at their risk-management practices. For example, the Caisse de dépôt et placement du Québec incurred heavy losses in 2008 as a result of its involvement in currency- and stock-related derivatives and the commercial paper crisis.[7] The Bank of Montreal (BMO) also had problems and reported writedowns of $490 million in 2008. That was on top of the $850-million charge they incurred as the result of fraud committed by one of their traders (see Concluding Case 20-2 for details). As a result of the losses, BMO did a complete review of their risk-management systems and procedures. Bill Downe, the CEO, admitted that BMO got involved in some business activities that were beyond the company's risk tolerance and strategic plan.[8]

Coping with Risk

There are two basic types of risk. **Speculative risks** involve the possibility of gain or loss, while **pure risks** involve only the possibility of loss or no loss. Manufacturing and selling a new product, for example, is a speculative risk, while the chance of a warehouse fire is a pure risk.

speculative risk An event that offers the chance for either a gain or a loss.

pure risk An event that offers no possibility of gain; it offers only the chance of a loss.

For a company to survive and prosper, it must manage both types of risk in a cost-effective manner. We therefore define the process of **risk management** as "conserving the firm's earning power and assets by reducing the threat of losses due to uncontrollable events."[9] The risk-management process usually involves the five steps outlined in Figure 20.4.

risk management Conserving a firm's (or an individual's) financial power or assets by minimizing the financial effect of accidental losses.

Step 1: Identify Risks and Potential Losses

Managers analyze a firm's risks to identify potential losses. For example, a firm with a fleet of delivery trucks can expect that one of them will eventually be involved in an accident. The accident may cause bodily injury to the driver or to others, may cause physical damage to the truck or other vehicles, or both.

Step 2: Measure the Frequency and Severity of Losses and Their Impact

To measure the frequency and severity of losses, managers must consider both past history and current activities. How often can the firm expect the loss to occur? What is the likely size of the loss in dollars? For example, our firm with the fleet of delivery trucks may have had two accidents per year in the past. If it adds trucks, however, it may reasonably expect the frequency of accidents to increase.

Step 3: Evaluate Alternatives and Choose the Techniques That Will Best Handle the Losses

Having identified and measured potential losses, managers are in a better position to decide how to handle them. With this third step, they generally have four choices: *risk avoidance*, *control*, *retention*, or *transfer*.

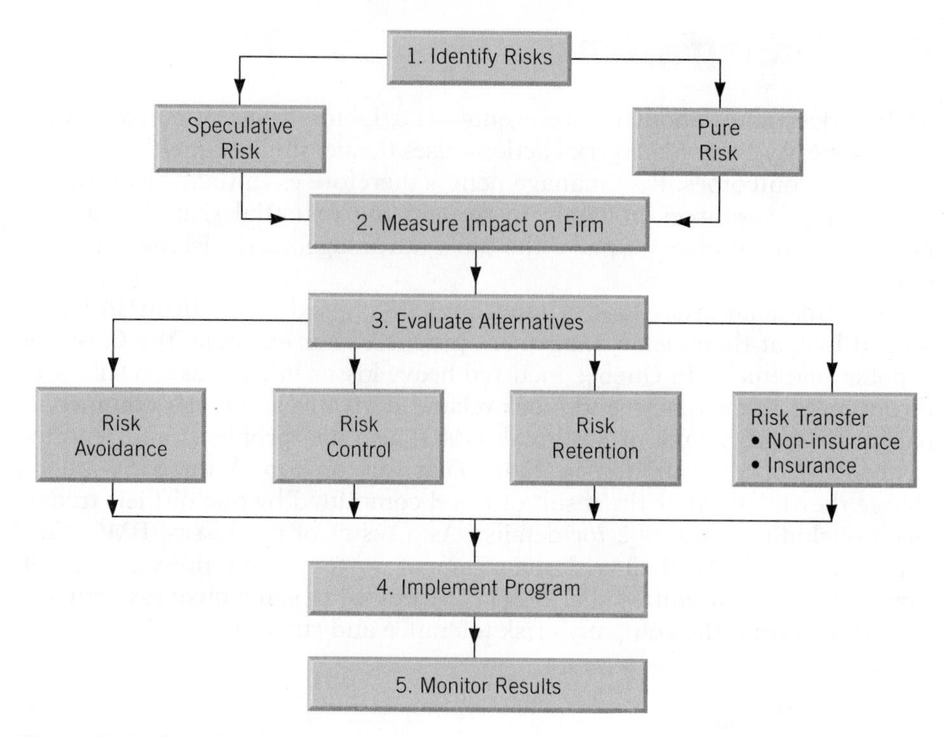

Figure 20.4 The risk-management process.

risk avoidance Stopping participation in or refusing to participate in ventures that carry any risk.

Risk Avoidance. A firm opts for **risk avoidance** by declining to enter into or by ceasing to participate in a risky activity. For example, the firm with the delivery trucks could avoid any risk of physical damage or bodily injury by closing down its delivery service. Similarly, a pharmaceutical maker may withdraw a new drug for fear of liability lawsuits.

risk control Techniques to prevent, minimize, or reduce losses or the consequences of losses.

Risk Control. When avoidance is not practical or desirable, firms can practise **risk control**—say, the use of loss-prevention techniques to minimize the frequency of losses. A delivery service, for instance, can prevent losses by training its drivers in defensive-driving techniques, mapping out safe routes, and conscientiously maintaining its trucks.

risk retention The covering of a firm's unavoidable losses with its own funds.

Risk Retention. When losses cannot be avoided or controlled, firms must cope with the consequences. When such losses are manageable and predictable, they may decide to cover them out of company funds. Since the firm "assumes" the financial consequences of the loss, the practice is known as **risk retention**. For example, the firm with the fleet of trucks may find that vehicles suffer vandalism totalling \$100 to \$500 per year. Depending on its coverage, the company may find it cheaper to pay for repairs out of pocket rather than to submit claims to its insurance company.

risk transfer The transfer of risk to another individual or firm, often by contract.

Risk Transfer. When the potential for large risks cannot be avoided or controlled, managers often opt for **risk transfer**. They transfer the risk to another firm—namely, an *insurance company*. In transferring risk to an insurance company, the firm pays a *premium*, and in return, the insurance company issues an *insurance policy*—a formal agreement to pay the policyholder a specified amount in the event of certain losses. In some cases, the insured party must also pay a *deductible*—an agreed-upon amount of the loss that the insured must absorb prior to reimbursement from the insurance company. Thus, our company with the fleet of trucks may buy insurance to protect itself against theft, physical damage to trucks, and bodily injury to drivers and others involved in an accident.

Step 4: Implement the Risk-Management Program

The means of implementing risk-management decisions depends on both the technique chosen and the activity being managed. For example, risk avoidance for certain activities can be implemented by purchasing those activities from outside providers, such as hiring delivery services instead of operating delivery vehicles. Risk control might be implemented by training employees and designing new work methods and equipment for on-the-job safety. For situations in which risk retention is preferred, reserve funds can be set aside out of revenues. When risk transfer is needed, implementation means selecting an insurance company and buying the right policies.

Step 5: Monitor Results

Because risk management is an ongoing activity, follow-up is always essential. New types of risks, for example, emerge with changes in customers, facilities, employees, and products. Insurance regulations change, and new types of insurance become available. Consequently, managers must continually monitor a company's risks, re-evaluate the methods used for handling them, and revise them as necessary.

Insurance as Risk Management

To deal with some risks, both businesses and individuals may choose to purchase one or more of the products offered by insurance companies. Buyers find insurance appealing for a very basic reason: In return for a relatively small sum of money, they are protected against specific losses, some of which are potentially devastating. In this sense, buying insurance is a function of risk management. We can now amplify our definition of *risk management* to say that it is the logical development and implementation of a plan to deal with chance losses.

With insurance, then, individuals and businesses share risks by contributing to a fund out of which those who suffer losses are paid. Insurance companies are willing to accept these risks for other companies because they make profits by taking in more **premiums** than they pay out to cover policyholders' losses. Although many policyholders are paying for protection against the

premiums Money paid to an insurance company by customers in return for being covered for certain types of losses should they occur.

Losses are reduced or prevented when this security specialist uses electronic surveillance (above), when valuables are stored under lock and key (top left), and when workers are reminded to wear safety gear at this construction site (bottom left).

same type of loss, it is highly unlikely that all of them will suffer such a loss. But it does occasionally happen, as AIG discovered (see the Opening Case).

Insurable vs. Uninsurable Risks

7 Explain the distinction between *insurable* and *uninsurable risks*, and distinguish among the different *types of insurance* purchased by businesses.

Like every other business, insurance companies must avoid certain risks. Insurers thus divide potential sources of loss into *insurable* and *uninsurable risks*.[10] Obviously, they issue policies only for insurable risks. An insurable risk must generally satisfy the four criteria of *predictability*, *casualty*, *unconnectedness*, and *verifiability*.

Predictability. The insurer must be able to use statistical tools to forecast the likelihood of a loss. For example, an auto insurer needs information about the number of car accidents in the past year to estimate the expected number of accidents for the following year. With this knowledge, the insurer can translate expected numbers and types of accidents into expected dollar losses. The same forecast also helps insurers determine premiums charged to policyholders.

Casualty. A loss must result from an accident, not from an intentional act by the policyholder. For example, an insurer does not have to cover damages if a policyholder deliberately sets fire to a business. To avoid paying in cases of fraud, insurers may refuse to cover losses when they cannot determine whether policyholders' actions contributed to them.

Unconnectedness. Potential losses must be random and must occur independently of other losses. No insurer can afford to write insurance when a large percentage of those who are exposed to a particular kind of loss are likely to suffer such a loss. One insurance company, for instance, would not want all the hail coverage in Saskatchewan or all the earthquake coverage in Vancouver. By carefully choosing the risks it will insure, an insurance company can reduce its chances of a large loss.

Verifiability. Finally, insured losses must be verifiable as to cause, time, place, and amount. Did an employee develop emphysema because of a chemical to which she was exposed or because she smoked 40 cigarettes per day for 30 years? Did the policyholder pay the renewal premium before the fire destroyed his factory? Were the goods stolen from the company's office or from the president's home? What was the insurable value of the destroyed inventory? When all these points have been verified, payment by the insurer goes more smoothly.

The Insurance Product

The types of insurance coverage they offer often distinguish insurance companies. Whereas some insurers offer only one area of coverage—life insurance, for example—others offer a broad range. In this section, we briefly describe three major categories of business insurance—*liability*, *property*, and *life*. (A more detailed description of life insurance products is presented in Appendix B, which can be found on MyBusinessLab.)

liability insurance Covers losses resulting from damage to people or property when the insured party is judged liable.

Liability Insurance. *Liability* means responsibility for damages in case of accidental or deliberate harm to individuals or property. **Liability insurance** covers losses resulting from damage to people or property when the insured party is judged liable.

Canadian exporters may have difficulty getting liability insurance at a price they can afford. Kantain Products Ltd. of Kitchener, Ontario, a maker of chemical tank liners, wanted to sell its products in the United States. When the president of the company tried to buy liability insurance, he discovered that the premiums would be at least $50 000 per year. This amount far outweighed the potential profit he thought he could make, so he abandoned his plan to sell in the United States.[11]

A business is liable for any injury to an employee when the injury arises from activities related to occupation. When workers are permanently or temporarily disabled by job-related accidents or disease, employers are required by law to provide **workers' compensation coverage** for medical expenses, loss of wages, and rehabilitation services.

workers' compensation coverage Compensation for medical expenses, loss of wages, and rehabilitation services for injuries arising from activities related to occupation.

There is growing concern about fraudulent claims submitted by people who buy liability insurance. One popular scam is the "staged accident." The swindler purposely (but carefully) runs into, say, a telephone pole, and then everyone in the car claims that they are suffering from whiplash. After the accident is reported, the insurance company contacts the car's occupants and sends them accident benefit packages. Sometimes people who aren't even insured are paid benefits because they use counterfeit "proof of insurance" cards.[12]

Every year in Canada, well over $1 billion is lost to insurance fraud. The insurance industry estimates that between $10 and $15 of every $1000 dollars you pay in premiums goes to cover fraud losses. The Insurance Bureau of Canada (IBC) is an industry association that represents Canadian companies that provide car, home, and business insurance. The IBC protects honest policyholders by monitoring insurance claims and determining which ones are fraudulent. Two areas of particular concern are organized crime rings and fraudulent injury claims. The IBC also lobbies the government to make legislative changes that will deter insurance fraud. Visit the IBC website at www.ibc.ca.

Property Insurance. Firms purchase **property insurance** to cover injuries resulting from physical damage to real estate or personal property. Property losses may result from fire, lightning, wind, hail, explosion, theft, vandalism, or other destructive forces, such as hurricanes. In 2005, insurance companies received claims exceeding $55 billion as a result of several hurricanes that hit the southern United States and flooded New Orleans. That figure was double the previous record (which was set in 2004). Canadian insurers were expected to pay out about $570 million of the 2005 total.

property insurance Covers injuries to firms resulting from physical damage to or loss of real estate or personal property.

In some cases, loss to property is minimal in comparison with loss of income. A manufacturer, for example, may have to close down for an extended

Catastrophic losses like those caused by fire are avoided when a business buys property insurance. The cost of the rebuilding will be paid by the insurance company. But interruption of the firm's normal operations will also be harmful, so many businesses buy business interruption insurance as well.

time while fire damage is being repaired. During that time, the company is not generating any income, but certain expenses—such as taxes, insurance premiums, and salaries for key personnel—may continue. To cover such losses, a firm may buy *business interruption insurance*.

life insurance Insurance that pays benefits to survivors of a policyholder.

Life Insurance. Insurance can also protect a company's human assets. As part of their benefits packages, many businesses purchase **life insurance** for employees. Life insurance companies receive premiums in return for the promise to pay beneficiaries after the death of insured parties. As with other types of insurance, a portion of the premium is used to cover the insurer's own expenses.

Life insurance can, of course, also be purchased by individuals. For many years, Canadian life insurance companies have sold insurance policies to Canadians, but now they are rapidly expanding overseas, particularly in China and India. Sun Life Financial, for example, has formed a joint venture with Aditya Birla Group to sell life insurance and mutual funds in India. As a result of this partnership, Sun Life is the second largest privately owned life insurance company in India.[13] In some areas of the world, unstable and dangerous situations have motivated entrepreneurs to sell special kinds of insurance. For example, the al Ameen Insurance Co. pays out $3500 to beneficiaries of people who are killed as a result of insurgent activity in Iraq. The annual premium is about $35.[14] The largest life insurance companies in Canada are shown in Table 20.2.

group life insurance Life insurance underwritten for a group as a whole rather than for each individual member.

Most companies buy **group life insurance**, which is underwritten for groups as a whole rather than for each individual member. The insurer's assessment of potential losses and its pricing of premiums are based on the characteristics of the entire group.

Special Forms of Business Insurance

Many forms of insurance are attractive to both businesses and individuals. For example, homeowners are as concerned about insuring property from fire and theft as businesses are. Businesses, however, have some special insurable concerns—the departure or death of key employees or owners.

Key Person Insurance. Many businesses choose to protect themselves against loss of the talents and skills of key employees. If a salesperson who brings in $2.5 million of sales revenue dies or takes a new job, the firm will suffer loss. It will also incur recruitment costs to find a replacement and training expenses

Table 20.2 Top 10 Life Insurance Companies in Canada, 2008

Company	Annual revenues (in billions of $)
1. Great-West Lifeco Inc.	$33.9
2. Manulife Financial Corp.	33.0
3. Sun Life Financial Inc.	15.5
4. Industrial Alliance Ins. and Fin. Services Inc.	4.4
5. Desjardins Financial Security Life Assurance	2.8
6. The Standard Life Assurance Co. of Canada	1.7
7. SSQ, Société d'assurance-vie Inc.	1.5
8. RBC Life Insurance Co.	1.2
9. La Capitale Civil Service Mutual	1.0
10. Co-operators Life Insurance Co.	0.7

once a replacement is hired. **Key person insurance** is designed to offset both lost income and additional expenses.[15]

key person insurance Insurance that protects a company against loss of the talents and skills of key employees.

Business Continuation Agreements. Who takes control of a business when a partner or an associate dies? Surviving partners are often faced with the possibility of having to accept an inexperienced heir as a management partner. This contingency can be handled in **business continuation agreements**, whereby owners make plans to buy the ownership interest of a deceased associate from his or her heirs. The value of the ownership interest is determined when the agreement is made. Special policies can also provide survivors with the funds needed to make the purchase.

business continuation agreement An agreement in which owners of a business make plans to buy the ownership interest of a deceased associate from his or her heirs.

Test yourself on the material for this chapter at **www.pearsoned.ca/mybusinesslab**.

Summary of Learning Objectives

1. **Describe the responsibilities of a *financial manager.*** *Finance* (or corporate finance) entails four responsibilities: (1) determining long-term investments, (2) obtaining funds to pay for those investments, (3) conducting everyday financial activities, and (4) helping to manage risks. *Financial managers* plan and control the acquisition and dispersal of financial resources. But a financial manager's overall objective is to increase a firm's value and stockholders' wealth.

   The specific responsibilities of the financial manager are (1) *cash flow management* (ensuring that the company has enough funds on hand to purchase the resources that it needs to produce products); (2) *financial control* (the process of checking actual performance against plans to ensure that desired financial results occur); and (3) *financial planning* (developing a plan that describes how a firm will reach some future financial position).

2. **Distinguish between *short-term (operating)* and *long-term (capital) expenditures.*** *Short-term (operating)* expenditures are incurred in a firm's everyday business activities. Managers must pay special attention to three areas of financial activity: (1) *accounts payable,* (2) *accounts receivable,* and (3) *inventories.* Between the time a firm buys raw materials and the time it sells finished products, it ties up funds in *inventory*—materials and goods that it will sell within the year. Too little inventory can mean lost sales; too much inventory means tied-up funds. *Working capital* is the difference between a firm's current assets and current liabilities. It is a liquid asset from which current debts can be paid. Working capital is calculated by adding up inventories (*raw materials, work-in-process,* and *finished goods* on hand) and accounts receivable (minus accounts payable).

3. **Identify four sources of *short-term financing* for businesses.** (1) *Trade credit* is really a short-term loan from one firm to another. (2) *Secured short-term loans* like bank loans usually involve *promissory notes* in which the borrower promises to repay the loan plus interest. These loans require *collateral,* which can be seized if payments are not made as promised. (3) *Factoring accounts receivable* raises funds by selling the firm's accounts receivable. (4) *Unsecured short-term loans* are those where a borrower does not have to put up collateral. The bank may, however, require the borrower to maintain a *compensating balance*—a portion of the loan amount kept on deposit with the bank.

4. **Distinguish among the various sources of *long-term financing* and explain the risks involved in each.** Firms may seek long-term funds to pay for fixed assets through two channels. (1) Long-term borrowing from sources outside the company is called *debt financing.* There are two primary sources of such funding: *long-term loans* from chartered banks, or the issuance of *corporate bonds* (a promise by the issuer to pay the holder a certain amount of money on a specified date). (2) Looking inside the company for long-term funding is sometimes preferable to debt financing. *Equity financing* usually means issuing common stock or using retained earnings for expenditures. Equity financing by means of common stock can be expensive because paying dividends is more expensive than paying bond interest. A middle ground between debt financing and equity financing is the use of *preferred stock.* As with

bonds, payments on preferred stock are fixed amounts. But like common stock, preferred stock can be held indefinitely.

5. **Discuss some key issues in financial management for small businesses.** Obtaining credit begins with finding a bank that will support a small firm's financial needs. Once *a line of credit* is obtained, the small business can seek more liberal *credit policies* from other businesses. Obtaining long-term loans is more difficult for new businesses than for established companies, and start-ups pay higher interest rates than older firms. To demonstrate that it's a good credit risk, a start-up must usually present a business plan—a document explaining why the money is needed, the amount, how it will be used to improve the company, and when it will be paid back.

   Many newer businesses can't get needed funds through borrowing alone. They may turn to *venture capital*—outside equity funding provided in return for part-ownership. But with the high failure rates of small businesses, such investors demand high returns. Planning for cash flows is especially important for small businesses. Success or failure may hinge on anticipating those times when cash will be short or when excess cash can be expected.

6. **Explain how *risk* affects business operations and identify the five steps in the *risk-management process*.** Businesses face two basic types of risk. (1) *Speculative risks,* such as financial investments, involve the possibility of gain or loss. (2) *Pure risks* (such as the chance of a warehouse fire) involve only the possibility of loss or no loss. *Risk management* means conserving earning power and assets by reducing the threat of losses due to uncontrollable events. The process has five steps: (1) identify risks and potential losses, (2) measure the frequency and severity of losses and their impact, (3) evaluate alternatives and choose the techniques that will best handle the losses (*risk avoidance, risk control, risk retention,* and *risk transfer*), (4) implement the risk-management program, and (5) monitor results.

7. **Explain the distinction between *insurable* and *uninsurable risks*, and distinguish among the different *types of insurance* purchased by businesses.** In return for a relatively small sum of money, insurance buyers are protected against certain losses. Thus, *buying insurance* is a function of risk management, which is the implementation of a plan to deal with chance losses. Insurance companies make profits by taking in more *premiums* than they pay out to cover policyholders' losses. Insurers divide potential losses into *insurable* and *uninsurable risks,* and an insurable risk must meet four criteria: (1) Predictability—the insurer must be able to use statistical tools to forecast the likelihood of a loss. (2) Casualty—a loss must result from an accident, not from an intentional act. (3) Unconnectedness—potential losses must be random and occur independently of other losses. (4) Verifiability—insured losses must be verifiable as to cause, time, place, and amount.

   There are three major categories of business insurance: (1) *Liability insurance*—liability means responsibility for damages in case of accidental or deliberate harm, and liability insurance covers losses resulting from damage to people or property when the insured party is held liable. The law requires most employers to provide employees injured on the job with *workers' compensation coverage* for medical expenses, loss of wages, and rehabilitation services. (2) *Property insurance*—firms purchase property insurance to cover injuries resulting from damage to or loss of real estate or personal property. A firm may buy *business interruption insurance* to cover expenses incurred when it is closed down and generating no income. (3) *Life insurance*—life insurance policies promise to pay beneficiaries after the death of insured parties. Most companies buy *group life insurance,* which is underwritten for groups as a whole rather than for each individual member.

   Two forms of business insurance apply to the loss of key employees or owners: (1) Many businesses protect themselves against loss of the talents and skills of key employees by buying *key person insurance.* (2) Certain contingencies are handled in *business continuation agreements,* in which owners make plans to transfer the ownership interest of a deceased associate.

Key Terms

bond indenture (p. 660)
business continuation agreement (p. 673)
capital structure (p. 662)
cash flow management (p. 653)
collateral (p. 657)
commercial paper (p. 658)
credit policy (p. 655)
debt financing (p. 659)
equity financing (p. 660)
finance (corporate finance) (p. 652)
financial control (p. 653)
financial managers (p. 652)
financial plan (p. 654)
finished goods inventory (p. 655)
group life insurance (p. 672)
inventory (p. 655)
key person insurance (p. 673)
liability insurance (p. 670)
life insurance (p. 672)
line of credit (p. 657)
open-book credit (p. 656)
pledging accounts receivable (p. 657)
premiums (p. 669)
promissory note (p. 656)
property insurance (p. 671)
pure risk (p. 667)
raw materials inventory (p. 655)
revolving credit agreement (p. 657)
risk (p. 667)
risk avoidance (p. 668)
risk control (p. 668)
risk management (p. 667)
risk retention (p. 668)
risk transfer (p. 668)
risk-return relationship (p. 664)
secured loan (p. 656)
speculative risk (p. 667)
trade acceptance (p. 656)
trade credit (p. 656)
trade draft (p. 656)
unsecured loan (p. 657)
venture capital (p. 665)
workers' compensation coverage (p. 671)
work-in-process inventory (p. 655)

Questions for Analysis

1. In what ways do the two sources of debt financing differ from each other? How do they differ from the two sources of equity financing?
2. Describe the relationship between investment risk and return. In what ways might the risk-return relationship affect a company's financial planning?
3. What is the basic relationship between the amount of risk associated with a project and the likelihood of gains (or losses) on the project? Explain how several financial instruments (GICs, common stocks, preferred stocks, corporate bonds) illustrate this basic relationship.
4. What factors would you take into account when deciding on the best mix of debt and equity for a company?
5. Why would a business "factor" its accounts receivable?
6. Give two examples of risks that are uninsurable. Why are they uninsurable?
7. Why is liability insurance important to business firms?
8. As a risk manager of a large firm, what risks do you think your firm would face? What are the risks for a small firm? What accounts for the most important differences?

Application Exercises

1. Interview the owner of a small local business. Identify the types of short-term and long-term funding that this firm typically uses. Why has the company made the financial management decisions that it has?
2. Interview the owner of a small local business. Ask this person to describe the risk-management process that he or she follows. What role, for example, is played by risk transfer? Why has the company made the risk-management decisions that it has?

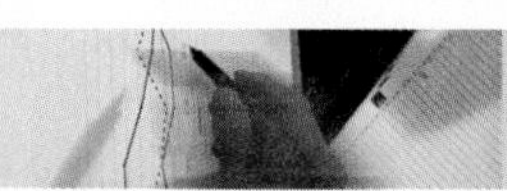

Building Your Business Skills

Understanding Risk-Management Issues

The Purpose of the Assignment

To encourage students to gain a better understanding of the major financial and risk-management issues that face large companies.

Assignment

During the last few years, all of the following companies reported financial problems relating to risk management:

- Air Canada
- Bombardier
- EarthLink Inc.
- Levi Strauss & Co.
- Nortel Networks

Step 1

Working alone, research one of the companies listed above to learn more about the financial risks that were reported in the news.

Step 2

Write a short explanation of the risks and financial management issues that were faced by the firm you researched.

Step 3

Join in teams with students who researched other companies and compare your findings.

Questions for Discussion

1. Were there common themes in the "big stories" in financial management?
2. What have the various companies done to minimize future risks and losses?

Exercising Your Ethics: Team Exercise

Doing Your Duty When Payables Come Due

The Situation

Sarah Keats is the vice-president of finance at Multiverse, a large firm that manufactures consumer products. On December 15, 2009 (two weeks before the end of the fiscal year), she attends an executive committee meeting at which Jack Malvo, the CEO, expresses concern that the firm's year-end cash position will be less favourable than projected. The firm has exceeded analysts' performance expectations in each of his eight years at the helm and Malvo is determined that stockholders will never be disappointed as long as he is CEO. The purpose of the meeting is to find solutions to the cash problem and decide on a course of action.

The Dilemma

To open the meeting, Malvo announces, "We have just two weeks to either reduce expenses or increase revenues. We need a $100-million swing to get us where market analysts predicted we'd be on cash flows for the year. Any suggestions?"

In the discussion that ensues, it is noted that Multiverse owes $150 million to about 80 different companies that supply component parts and other operating supplies to Multiverse. The money is due before year-end. Sarah Keats says, "Our cash outflows for the year will be lower if we delay paying suppliers, which will help the bottom line. And it's like getting a free loan." The procurement director, Julie Levin, expresses the following concern: "Our agreements with suppliers call for faithful payments at designated times, and many of the smaller firms depend on receiving that cash to meet their obligations. Also, we've worked hard for two years at improving relationships with all suppliers, and that effort could go down the drain if we don't meet our financial commitments as promised."

As the meeting draws to a close, Malvo announces, "Keep me posted on any unexpected developments, but if nothing helpful comes up in the next few days, let's go ahead and withhold supplier payments for three weeks."

Team Activity

Assemble a group of four students and assign each group member to one of the following roles:

- Jack Malvo (CEO of Multiverse)
- Sarah Keats (vice-president of finance)
- Julie Levin (procurement director)
- a stockholder of Multiverse

Questions for Discussion

1. Before discussing the situation with your group, and from the perspective of your assigned role, do you think there are any ethical issues here?
2. Before discussing the situation with your group, and from the perspective of your assigned role, what action do you think should be taken? Write down your recommended action.
3. Gather your group together and reveal, in turn, each member's comments and recommendations.
4. Appoint someone to record the main points of agreement and disagreement within the group. How do you explain the results? What accounts for any disagreements?
5. From an ethical standpoint, what does your group recommend?

For additional cases and exercise material, go to **www.pearsoned.ca/mybusinesslab**.

Concluding Case 20-1

The Commercial Paper Crisis

Commercial paper is sold to investors on the promise that the issuing organization will pay back the principal (plus interest) in the near future (usually 30 or 60 days). In effect, the issuer might say something like this: If you loan my company $99, in one month my company will give you $100. So, the investor earns $1 of interest in one month on a $99 loan. Both individuals and organizations buy commercial paper because they want to put their extra cash into a liquid (and safe) short-term investment that will earn interest until they need the money.

In recent years, a variation of this basic system came into being. Asset-backed commercial paper (ABCP) is issued by companies (called conduits) that sold subprime mortgages to people with poor credit ratings. They then packaged these mortgages together with other, more traditional loans (on credit cards, automobiles, and regular home mortgages) and sold them as collateralized debt obligations (CDOs) to investors. These products were much riskier than traditional commercial paper, but investors typically didn't know that.

In 2007, problems developed in the Canadian commercial paper market as a result of problems in the U.S. subprime mortgage market (where people who wouldn't usually qualify for mortgage money go to get money to buy a house). People who wanted to buy a home but had a poor credit rating got subprime mortgages with low interest "teaser" rates for the first two years. But those rates then rose to market rates for the remaining years of the mortgage. When people with subprime mortgages started defaulting in 2006 because they couldn't afford the higher interest rates, the subprime market collapsed. Foreclosures increased and the returns that normally would have been earned on these mortgages dropped sharply. And since these subprime mortgages were included in commercial paper that was sold to investors, the conduits couldn't pay their investors as they had promised. When word got out about this problem, investors refused to "roll over" their commercial paper (i.e., they wouldn't agree to keep their money in commercial paper for another 30 or 60 days) because they felt that it was too risky. The conduits thus experienced a sharp decline in the money they had available. They then went to their liquidity providers (Canadian banks) to get more money, but the banks argued that since the whole commercial paper market hadn't seized up (just the non-bank part of the market), they weren't obliged to provide the conduits with any money. The result was that many holders of commercial paper did not receive their principal and interest when they thought they would.

Many individuals who bought ABCP were assured by their financial advisers or by the Canadian bond rating firm DBRS that ABCP was AAA rated and was as safe as Guaranteed Investment Certificates (GICs). DBRS was later criticized for giving such high ratings to such risky investments. Many other investors didn't even know they owned any ABCP until they tried to get some of their money and were told it was "frozen." For example, Angela Speller, a retiree in Victoria, invested almost $1 million in ABCP and expected to be able to withdraw money as she needed it. But now she fears she will have to wait years to see her money.

Baffinland Iron Mines Corp. is typical of companies that discovered they were not going to get their money when they wanted it. The company mines iron ore deposits on Baffin Island and needs money to buy equipment of all kinds to carry on its regular operations. In July 2007, the company bought $43.8 million of ABCP to earn interest on extra cash that it had. In August 2007, some of the proceeds of the ABCP (principal plus interest) that were supposed to be paid to Baffinland were not paid, because the company Baffinland had bought the ABCP from was unable to pay. This caused a severe cash shortage at Baffinland that will hinder its future exploration activities. Another example is Petrolifera Petroleum Ltd. of

Calgary. The company invested about $37 million in ABCP, but when $31 million of the notes came due, they were not paid.

Caisse de dépôt et placement du Québec had the greatest exposure to the ABCP securities market (perhaps as much as $13 billion). Other organizations with some exposure included NAV Canada ($368 million), Ontario Power Generation Inc. ($102 million), and Canada Post ($27 million). Major Canadian banks had exposure too. In December 2007, the Canadian Imperial Bank of Commerce revealed that it lost $1 billion in the commercial paper market.

One way to solve the problem was to simply convert short-term commercial paper into longer-term debt and then gradually pay off investors. But that solution ignores the very reason that investors buy commercial paper in the first place (i.e., short-term liquidity). In 2007, a group called the Pan-Canadian Investors Committee was formed for the purpose of resolving the commercial paper mess. In April 2008, the Committee announced that noteholders had voted in favour of a plan designed to solve the problem, but in September 2008, the financial crisis hit and that further delayed settlement. Finally, in December 2008, the committee announced a formal agreement to restructure $33 billion of ABCP by exchanging short-term notes for longer-term ones. Purdy Crawford, the chair of the group, said that most individuals and companies would likely get all their money back if they held the restructured notes to maturity. The agreement requires the federal government and the provinces of Quebec, Ontario, and Alberta to provide over $4 billion to ensure that the $32 billion in ABCP is actually restructured.

Questions for Discussion

1. Why do investors buy commercial paper? Why did some investors buy non-bank commercial paper?
2. How does the commercial paper crisis demonstrate the risk-return principle?
3. Explain how problems in the U.S. subprime mortgage market caused difficulties in the Canadian commercial paper market.
4. Should Canada's federal government become more involved in regulation of the commercial paper market so problems like the one described above won't happen again? Defend your answer.

Concluding Case 20-2

Pursuing Effective Risk Management

Canadian business firms face risks in many different areas—the company's computer network may be hacked into, interest rates may change, executive talent may be raided by another company, a natural disaster or terrorist attack may occur, consumers may sue the company, a recession may occur, or all of the above may happen. How do business firms cope with these risks? There are three key actions that business firms take: (1) create a top-level executive position to oversee risk management, (2) buy insurance to shield the company from various kinds of risks, and (3) institute control systems that will reduce the risk that inappropriate employee behaviour will cause financial harm to the company.

Create a Top-Level Position to Oversee Risk Management

Companies have traditionally had a chief executive officer (CEO), a chief operating officer (COO), and a chief financial officer (CFO), but not too many of them have had chief risk officers (CRO). But that is rapidly changing, partly because of the financial crisis that developed in 2008. Businesses are realizing that they need a high-level executive who is responsible for developing and implementing plans for dealing with risk, rather than just trying to respond to risk after something unexpected happens. Rick Waugh, the CEO of the Bank of Nova Scotia, says that companies need risk officers with grey hair because those people recognize that financial crises occur more often than most people think. Executive recruiters report that top risk managers are now one of the hottest commodities in the field of finance.

Hydro One Inc. already has a CRO, partly because the deregulation of electricity means that it needs to manage the risk of price fluctuations in the new market-based pricing system. But it's not just pricing risk that Hydro One needs to deal with. John Fraser, Hydro One's CRO, has already dealt with a major risk situation that has little to do with pricing. When Hydro One offered an early retirement package to employees, 1400 people took the offer. This was far more than the company expected, so Fraser was charged with analyzing how the loss of so many people might affect the company's ability to achieve its objectives. After a department-by-department analysis, he concluded that by hiring 125 people and paying consultants to do some other critical work, Hydro One could reduce its risks to an acceptable level.

Buying Insurance

There are many different types of business insurance that are available. Risk managers must decide what kind of insurance the company needs to carry and whether it can afford to carry such insurance. Consider what happened to Kitchener, Ontario–based Kentain Products, which manufactures chemical tank liners. Its products have been very successful in Canada, so owner Glen Lippert thought it was a natural extension of the business to begin exporting the products to the United States. He was in for a rude shock. When his insurance company found out what he was planning, they would no longer sell him liability insurance, because they felt that selling to the United States was too risky. When Lippert checked around at other insurance companies, he discovered that it would cost him $50 000 in annual premiums to get liability insurance. Since that figure exceeded the profit he expected to make in the United States, he abandoned his export plans.

It's not just exporting companies that are having trouble with insurance premiums. One Waterloo, Ontario–based company that sells industrial air compressors had its premiums increased from $6500 to $40 000 in one year. A cabinetmaking firm saw its premiums double from $10 000 to $20 000 in one year, and then to $60 000 two years later. Many small businesses can't get insurance at any price. This is a big problem because banks usually demand that a company have liability insurance before they will loan it money. A survey by the Federation of Independent Business found that most small businesses have faced increases in the 30 percent range during each of the last few years. In the survey, 83 percent of the respondents said that high insurance premiums were their single biggest cost.

The insurance industry gives a variety of reasons for the rapidly escalating insurance premiums—uncertainty in the stock market (where insurance companies have much of their money invested), low interest rates, terrorist activity, natural disasters, and liability lawsuits against companies. Put simply, insurance companies are not getting enough revenue from premium payments and their investments to pay all the claims that are arising. So they increase premiums and refuse to cover some high-risk activities.

Some people think that the insurance business is not very interesting, what with all the mathematical calculations and actuarial tables that are required. But consider the following examples:

- Producers of the Broadway show *Titanic* paid about US$400 000 for insurance to cover such things as a member of the audience being hit by a flying deck chair or a cast member being injured during the performance. Interestingly, Chubb Corp., the company that covered the real *Titanic* (the one that sank on April 15, 1912, claiming 1523 lives) also covered the Broadway show. That real *Titanic* disaster cost the insurance company US$100 000, but the Broadway show was insured for US$14 million.
- Rap artists such as Snoop Doggy Dogg can earn more than US$50 000 per night on a multi-city concert tour. But national tours by rap artists have been virtually non-existent for over a decade because stabbings and gunfire were becoming all too common at these shows, making it difficult to obtain liability insurance to cover the tour.
- Diamond State Insurance Company, which issued an insurance policy to the band Limp Bizkit, claimed it had no liability for damages awarded following the death of a teenaged fan at a Limp Bizkit rock concert in Australia. The insurance company argued that singer Fred Durst "incited" the crowd and that led to the teenager's death when she was trampled.

Implement Effective Control Systems

There is always a risk that some employees will act in ways that are financially detrimental to their employer. Companies therefore institute control systems in an attempt to prevent financial losses due to fraud. But creative fraudsters find ways to circumvent these control systems. Consider the case of David Lee, a Bank of Montreal (BMO) natural gas trader who was based in New Jersey. For a while he was flying high. During the period from 2003 to 2006, his annual compensation rose from about $722 000 to $5.35 million. But in 2008, he pleaded guilty to charges of conspiracy, fraud, making false bank entries, and obstructing a U.S. regulatory investigation. He is facing up to 60 years in prison.

What exactly did Lee do? He falsified records to make it look like his natural gas trades were profitable when, in fact, they were not. But didn't BMO have controls in place to prevent this sort of thing? Yes, they did, but the system was circumvented by Lee. Here's how: BMO verified the values Lee was claiming for his portfolio, by obtaining a quote from an independent brokerage firm called Optionable Inc. But that firm has now been charged with providing phony quotes to BMO. The quotes were simply made up so that they matched the numbers Lee was claiming. The fraud was discovered when BMO also got quotes from other independent brokerages that did not match the quotes that Optionable was providing. The CEO of Optionable Inc. (who has previously spent time in prison for money laundering) has also been charged with conspiracy, fraud, and making false bank entries. By the end of 2007, BMO had incurred trading losses of $850 million as the result of Lee's activities.

A more complicated case is that of Jérôme Kerviel, a trader who worked at Société Générale SA (SocGen), a large bank in France. The bank alleged that Kerviel forged trading records and circumvented the bank's control system in a fraud that eventually cost the bank over $7 billion. Kerviel says that he actually made money with his trades in 2007, and that as long as he was making money, his bosses ignored his unauthorized trades. It was only when he started losing money on his trades in 2008 that fraud was alleged by his bosses. Other traders in the industry also expressed doubt that a person like Kerviel could conceal so much unauthorized trading for so long without being detected. Some observers say that Kerviel is guilty of a breach of trust (that is, making decisions he did not have the authority to make) but not fraud. As a result of the dispute, SocGen has come under increasing pressure to explain how its risk-management system failed to detect Kerviel's unauthorized trades. The president of France even called for the CEO of SocGen to step down.

The cases involving Jérôme Kerviel and David Lee are just the latest in a series of situations where risk controls didn't quite work. For example, John Rusnak, a currency trader at Allfirst Financial, defrauded the company of $691 million by creating phony currency trades. Stephen Humphries, a trader at Sussex Futures Ltd. in England, engaged in so much fraudulent trading activity that he destroyed the company he worked for. Sussex Futures ceased operations, and 70 people lost their jobs. Nicholas Leeson, who worked for Barings PLC, a British merchant bank, bought and sold futures contracts, particularly investments known as derivatives. Over a three-week period, Leeson managed to incur trading losses of nearly $1 billion. When losses spiralled out of control, Leeson fled, and Barings had to declare bankruptcy. Leeson was eventually convicted and sentenced to six-and-a-half years in prison.

In all of these cases, there were control systems in place to prevent fraud, but they simply were not up to the job of detecting creative and determined individuals who were engaged in fraudulent activities. There was, in effect, a failure to properly manage risk. That failure led to massive financial losses, corporate bankruptcies, and the loss of many jobs.

Questions for Discussion

1. Briefly describe the steps in the risk-management process. To what extent does the risk-management process focus on detecting employee fraud?
2. Assume for a moment that Jérôme Kerviel's bosses knew what he was doing and they went along with it as long as he was making money for SocGen. Assume also that they charged him with fraud only after he started losing money. If that were really the situation, do you think Kerviel should have been charged with breach of contract (i.e., with making decisions he was not authorized to make)? Explain your reasoning.
3. Consider the following statement: *In every company, there are likely to be at least a few people who will engage in fraudulent behaviour in order to benefit themselves at the expense of others. Therefore, all companies should have a CRO in order to eliminate the possibility of employee fraud.* Do you agree with the statement? Explain your reasoning.

CBC Video Case 5-1

Debt Nation

We are a nation in debt, so *Marketplace* examined the finances of three Canadian families. Here are their stories.

Wayne and Theresa

Wayne and Theresa earn about $85 000 a year between them, but they are struggling with a total debt of $343 000 (mortgages, taxes, and loans). Wayne finishes furniture and Theresa works 25 hours a week from home. When Wayne has lots of work, they get by, but when he doesn't, there are problems because they simply buy too many things. Theresa feels very insecure about their financial situation. When unexpected expenses come up, stress levels increase. For example, when Wayne's van broke down, he borrowed money from Household Finance at a high interest rate.

A financial adviser (John) talks to Wayne and Theresa about their debt problems. John observes that their mortgage is not getting smaller as time passes. He says they simply must make higher payments on their mortgage to reduce the amount they owe. He also notes that some of their credit-cards carry a 30 percent interest rate. He says they should cut up their credit cards because they have become addicted to credit-card debt. John says that Wayne is too easygoing about their debt level and fears that he won't follow through on plans to reduce the family's debts.

Wayne and Theresa also talk to a psychologist (Sherrell). Sherrell says they behave like ostriches and they need to get their heads out of the sand and analyze their situation. She recommends that the two of them take 30 minutes each week so that Theresa can bring Wayne up to speed about her concerns about their financial situation. They both admit that they haven't cut up their credit cards. They say they just can't give them up.

Joanne and Travis

Joanne and Travis live in a farmhouse in the country. Travis is a musician, and Joanne is often unemployed. They are trying to pay off debts of about $186 000 (credit cards, car loans, and mortgages). Joanne is a shopaholic (she likes vintage dresses), and she shops whether she's on a high or feeling low. She says she buys things she doesn't need (like a drill from Canadian Tire, which was on sale). Like Wayne and Theresa, unexpected expenses have caused Joanne and Travis additional stress. For example, their septic tank had to be drained, which cost several hundred dollars that they didn't have.

John, the financial adviser, talks to Joanne and Travis about their problems. He discovers that Travis earns between $15 000 and $25 000 each year. John tells them to pay off their high interest debt by selling part of their property, but Joanne and Travis like their country acreage.

Sherrell, the psychologist, says that Joanne's obsession with shopping must stop if they hope to get out of their financial hole. Sherrell says that the great lie of the consumer mentality is that "If I shop, I'll feel better, and the feeling will last." She tells Joanne she must take control of her debt. Sherrell tells Joanne to create a "mad money" jar that can be used when Joanne feels the urge to shop. When the jar has no money in it, Joanne is not allowed to shop.

Hannalaura

Hannalaura is a teacher who wants to retire soon but knows she can't afford to. Her total debt is about $187 000. She also wants to take her daughter on a trip to England. She initially got into trouble when a nasty marriage breakup cost her $50 000 (she added that debt to her existing mortgage). She doesn't want her children to have to look after her during her retirement.

John, the financial adviser, visits Hannalaura and tells her she won't likely be able to get out of debt before she retires. He tells her that the trip to England is out of the question and that she should finish three more university credits she needs for a degree because that will help her earn more money. But Hannalaura is reluctant.

Sherrell, the psychologist, notes that very few people can follow financial advice. She thinks that Hannalaura has a lot of unresolved anger about her past experiences and that she feels rather helpless about not being able to change things in her life. Sherrell tells her that she must spend less and save more for her retirement. Sherrell is afraid that Hannalaura will not change.

Questions for Discussion

1. Identify several reasons why people get into financial difficulty. Which reason applies to which family? Is there a common underlying reason for these three families?
2. Consider the following statement: *Credit-card companies should cancel the credit card of any consumer whose credit-card balance exceeds $10 000. This will prevent the consumer from falling more deeply into debt.* Do you agree or disagree with this statement? Explain your reasoning.
3. Sherrell, the psychologist, says that very few people follow financial advice. Why do you think that people don't follow financial advice?
4. How successful do you think each family will be as they attempt to resolve their financial problems? (After you have turned in your answers, your instructor will give you an update on the three families.)

Video Resource: "Debt Nation," *Marketplace* (January 15, 2006).

CBC **Video Case 5–2**

Card Tricks

Do you think that you're credit-card savvy? Do you know what's in the fine print in cardholders' agreements? Meet four people who got so fed up with hidden fees and rising interest rates on their credit cards that they decided to do something about it.

David Caldarelli was mistakenly charged double for a highway toll. When he sent in his monthly credit-card payment, he did not pay for the highway toll overcharge. When he got his next statement, he was shocked to discover that he had been charged $23 in interest (even on the part of the total bill he had already paid). When he inquired about the charge, he was informed that since he had not paid the entire bill, he was charged interest on his total month's charges. He discovered that if you don't pay every penny you owe on your monthly statement, the next month you will be charged interest as if you hadn't paid anything. He was therefore being charged interest on money that he had already paid back. He discovered that this provision was in his cardholder agreement, but these agreements are complex (almost as if they are written by lawyers for lawyers). David complained about this and was successful in getting the $23 charge cancelled (a one-time goodwill gesture, he was told). David learned to beware of the partial payment.

Paul Cassano got hit with a fee of a different kind. He stayed at a hotel in New York and originally left an imprint of his card. But when he checked out, he paid in cash and the hotel cancelled the charge on his credit card. When he got his Visa bill a month later, there was a charge for $42.36 that he couldn't figure out. He inquired and discovered that he had been charged an extra fee for using his credit card in the United States. It is called a currency conversion fee (this fee is on top of the usual currency exchange rate). He sued Visa on the basis that he had been charged an undisclosed 1.65 percent fee when he first charged his hotel room and then again when he had cancelled that and paid cash. That fee is now disclosed. A similar lawsuit against the Canadian Imperial Bank of Commerce cost that bank $19.5 million. After it lost, CIBC upped its conversion fee.

Victor Moge is concerned that interest rates on unpaid credit-card balances keep going up, even as interest rates on many other things are going down. His MBNA card rate used to be 15.99 percent, but now it's 19.99 percent. He discovered that credit-card companies can raise your rate whenever they want. Some companies have raised the rate by five percentage points in one jump (for example, if the person misses a payment). The prime rate would never go up that fast, but the rate charged on credit cards has nothing to do with the prime rate. The debt that consumers rack up on credit cards is unsecured, so the card providers want to reduce the risk that you will not pay your bill. If you are carrying a high balance, they get worried that you might not pay your bill. They cover that risk by charging higher interest rates (there is a legal ceiling—60 percent).

Sheri Aberback-Ptack pays her American Express monthly credit-card bill on time, but when she was charged $11 interest for a supposedly late payment, she looked into the situation. She discovered that even if you pay your bill on time, the credit-card company may not record the payment until a few days later. If that few days later is after the due date, you are charged interest. She was upset and brought in her lawyer. He says American Express should have to assume the cost of any processing delay on their part. On another occasion, Sheri paid her bill two days earlier so she wouldn't get charged interest. But she was still charged interest because the payment wasn't actually processed before the due date. She says the customer should not have to guess how many days ahead they have to pay their bill in order to avoid interest charges. So, the payment due date is an illusion. Here is the lesson: If you don't send the money before the due date (or even if you do), you might get charged a late payment fee. Sheri and her lawyer are preparing a class action suit against the company.

Since none of the credit-card companies or banks would talk to *Marketplace*, Sheri and her lawyer went to the director of public affairs for the Canadian Bankers Association. The CBA spokesperson observed that credit-card debt is unsecured, so the rates customers are charged vary quite a bit, depending on how much risk credit-card companies think they are exposed to. She also noted that credit-card interest rates have nothing to do with the prime rate, and it's up to the card user to determine whether they want to carry a balance or pay their entire bill each month.

How do you avoid losing in the credit-card game? One strategy is to talk to your bank about options like a line of credit or a low interest credit card. If you can't get either of those, you should look around for cheaper alternatives at other banks or other credit-card companies.

Questions for Discussion

1. Credit cards are often referred to as "plastic money." Explain why credit-cards do not actually qualify as money.
2. Think about the situation that was encountered by each of the four individuals profiled above. Do you think the individual or the credit-card company had the most defensible position? Explain your reasoning for each case.
3. Consider the following statement: *If consumers don't pay off their credit-card balance each month, that's their decision, and they shouldn't complain about the interest they are charged. They should just stop spending so much money and pay off their bill each month (or just stop using their credit card). Demanding more restrictive legislation on credit-card companies is not the answer. Consumers get into debt because they spend more than they can afford.* Do you agree or disagree with the statement? Explain your reasoning.

Video Resource: "Card Tricks," *Marketplace* (February 27, 2005).

Crafting a Business Plan

Part 5: Financial Issues

Goal of the Exercise

In this final part of the business plan project, you'll consider how you'll finance your business as well as create an executive summary for your plan.

Exercise Background: Part 5 of the Business Plan

In the previous part of the business plan, you discussed the costs of doing business as well as how much revenue you expect to earn in one year. It's now time to think about how to finance the business. To get a "great idea" off the ground requires money. But how will you get these funds?

You'll then conclude this project by creating an executive summary. The purpose of the executive summary is to give the reader a quick snapshot of your proposed business. Although this exercise comes at the end of the project, once you're done writing it, you'll end up placing the executive summary at the beginning of your completed business plan.

Your Assignment

Step 1

Open the saved Business Plan file you have been working on.

Step 2

For the purposes of this assignment, you will answer the following questions, based on issues discussed in "Part 5: Managing Financial Issues."

1. How much money will you need to get your business started?

Hint: Refer back to Part 3 of the plan, where you analyzed the costs involved in running your business. Approximately how much will you need to get your business started?

2. How will you finance your business? For example, will you seek out a bank loan? Borrow from friends? Sell stocks or bonds initially or as your business grows?

Hint: Refer to Chapter 19 for information on securities such as stocks and bonds. Refer also to Chapter 20 and Chapter 4 for more information on sources of short-term and long-term funds.

3. Now, create an executive summary for your business plan. The executive summary should be brief—no more than two pages long—and should cover the following points:
   - the name of your business
   - where your business will be located
   - the mission of your business
   - the product or service you are selling
   - who your ideal customers are
   - how your product or business will stand out in the crowd
   - who the owners of the business are and what experience they have
   - an overview of the future prospects for your business and industry

Hint: At this point, you've already answered all of these questions, so what you need to do here is put the ideas together into a "snapshot" format. The executive summary is really a sales pitch—it's the investor's first impression of your idea. Therefore, as with all parts of the plan, write in a clear and professional way.

Congratulations on completing the business plan project!

Appendix A
Business Law

The Role of Law in Canadian Society

law The set of rules and standards that a society agrees upon to govern the behaviour of its citizens.

Law is the set of rules and standards that a society agrees upon to govern the behaviour of its citizens. Both the British and the French influenced the development of law in Canada. In 1867, the British North America (BNA) Act created the nation of Canada. The BNA Act was "patriated" to Canada in 1982 and is now known as the Constitution Act. This act divides legislative powers in Canada between the federal and provincial governments.

Sources of Law

The law in Canada has evolved and changed in response to our norms and values. Our laws have arisen from three sources: (1) customs and judicial precedents (the source of common law), (2) the actions of provincial and federal legislatures (the source of statutory law), and (3) rulings by administrative bodies (the source of administrative law).

common law The unwritten law of England, derived from precedent and legal judgments.

Common law is the unwritten law of England, derived from ancient precedents and judges' previous legal opinions. Common law is based on the principle of equity, the provision to every person of a just and fair remedy. Canadian legal customs and traditions derive from British common law. All provinces except Quebec, which uses the French Civil Code, have laws based on British common law, and court decisions are often based on precedents from common law. That is, decisions made in earlier cases that involved the same legal point will guide the court.

statutory law Written law developed by city councils, provincial legislatures, and parliament.

Statutory law is written law developed by city councils, provincial legislatures, and parliament. Most law in Canada today is statutory law.

administrative law The rules and regulations that government agencies and commissions develop based on their interpretations of statutory laws.

Administrative law is the rules and regulations that government agencies and commissions develop based on their interpretations of statutory laws. For example, Consumer and Corporate Affairs Canada develops regulations on false advertising, using federal legislation.

The Court System

In Canada, the judiciary branch of government has the responsibility of settling disputes among organizations or individuals by applying existing laws. Both provincial and federal courts exist to hear both criminal and civil cases. The Supreme Court of Canada is the highest court in Canada. It decides whether to hear appeals from lower courts.

Business Law

business law Laws that specifically affect how business firms are managed.

Business firms, like all other organizations, are affected by the laws of the country. **Business law** refers to laws that specifically affect how business firms are managed. Some laws affect all businesses, regardless of size, industry, or location. For example, the Income Tax Act requires businesses to pay income tax. Other laws may have a greater impact on one industry than on others. For example, pollution regulations are of much greater concern to Inco than they are to Carlson Wagonlit Travel.

Business managers must have at least a basic understanding of eight important concepts in business law:

- contracts
- agency
- bailment
- property
- warranty
- torts
- negotiable instruments
- bankruptcy

Contracts

Agreements about transactions are common in a business's day-to-day activity. A **contract** is an agreement between two parties to act in a specified way or to perform certain acts. A contract might, for example, apply to a customer buying a product from a retail establishment or to two manufacturers agreeing to buy products or services from each other. A valid contract includes several elements:

contract An agreement between two parties to act in a specified way or to perform certain acts.

- *an agreement*—All parties must consciously agree about the contract.
- *consideration*—The parties must exchange something of value (e.g., time, products, services, money, and so on).
- *competence*—All parties to the contract must be legally able to enter into an agreement. Individuals who are below a certain age or who are legally insane, for example, cannot enter into legal agreements.
- *legal purpose*—What the parties agree to do for or with each other must be legal. An agreement between two manufacturers to fix prices is not legal.

The courts will enforce a contract if it meets the criteria described above. Most parties honour their contracts, but occasionally one party does not do what it was supposed to do. **Breach of contract** occurs when one party to an agreement fails, without legal reason, to live up to the agreement's provisions. The party who has not breached the contract has three alternatives under the law in Canada: (1) discharge, (2) sue for damages, or (3) require specific performance.

breach of contract When one party to an agreement fails, without legal reason, to live up to the agreement's provisions.

An example will demonstrate these three alternatives. Suppose that Barrington Farms Inc. agrees to deliver 100 dozen long-stemmed roses to the Blue Violet Flower Shop the week before Mother's Day. One week before the agreed-upon date, Barrington informs Blue Violet that it cannot make the delivery until after Mother's Day. Under the law, the owner of Blue Violet can choose among the following actions.

Discharge

Blue Violet can also ignore its obligations in the contract. That is, it can contract with another supplier.

Sue for Damages

Blue Violet can legally demand payment for losses caused by Barrington's failure to deliver the promised goods. Losses might include any increased price Blue Violet would have to pay for the roses or court costs incurred in the damage suit.

Require Specific Performance

If monetary damages are not sufficient to reimburse Blue Violet, the court can force Barrington to live up to its original contract.

Agency

agency-principal relationship Established when one party (the agent) is authorized to act on behalf of another party (the principal).

In many business situations, one person acts as an agent for another person. Well-known examples include actors and athletes represented by agents who negotiate contracts for them. An **agency-principal relationship** is established when one party (the agent) is authorized to act on behalf of another party (the principal).

The agent is under the control of the principal and must act on behalf of the principal and in the principal's best interests. The principal remains liable for the acts of the agent as long as the agent is acting within the scope of authority granted by the principal. A salesperson for IBM, for example, is an agent for IBM, the principal.

Bailment

bailor-bailee relationship In a bailor-bailee relationship, the bailor (the property owner) gives possession of his or her property to the bailee (a custodian) but retains ownership of the item.

Many business transactions are not covered by the agency-principal relationship. For example, suppose that you take your car to a mechanic to have it repaired. Because the repair shop has temporary possession of something you own, it is responsible for your car. This is a **bailor-bailee relationship**. In a bailor-bailee relationship, the bailor (the car owner) gives possession of his or her property to the bailee (the repair shop) but retains ownership of the item. A business firm that stores inventory in a public warehouse is in a bailor-bailee relationship. The business firm is the bailor and the warehouse is the bailee. The warehouse is responsible for storing the goods safely and making them available to the manufacturer upon request.

The Law of Property

property Anything of tangible or intangible value that the owner has the right to possess and use.

real property Land and any permanent buildings attached to that land.

personal property Tangible or intangible assets other than real property.

Property includes anything of tangible or intangible value that the owner has the right to possess and use. **Real property** is land and any permanent buildings attached to that land. **Personal property** is tangible or intangible assets other than real property. Personal property includes cars, clothing, furniture, money in bank accounts, stock certificates, and copyrights.

Transferring Property

deed A document that shows ownership of real property.

lease Grants the use of an asset for a specified period of time in return for payment.

title Shows legal possession of personal property.

From time to time, businesses and individuals need to transfer property to another person or business. A **deed** is a document that shows ownership of real property. It allows the transfer of title of real property.

A **lease** grants the use of an asset for a specified period of time in return for payment. The business or individual granting the lease is the lessor and the tenant is the lessee. For example, a business (the lessee) may rent space in a mall for one year from a real estate development firm (the lessor).

A **title** shows legal possession of personal property. It allows the transfer of title of personal property. When you buy a snowmobile, for example, the former owner signs the title over to you.

Warranty

warranty A promise that the product or service will perform as the seller has promised it will.

express warranty A specific claim that the manufacturer makes about a product.

When you buy a product or service, you want some assurance that it will perform satisfactorily and meet your needs. A **warranty** is a promise that the product or service will perform as the seller has promised it will.

There are two kinds of warranties—express and implied. An **express warranty** is a specific claim that the manufacturer makes about a product. For example, a warranty that a screwdriver blade is made of case-hardened steel is an express warranty. An **implied warranty** suggests that a product will perform as the manufacturer claims it will. Suppose that you buy an outboard motor for your boat and the engine burns out in one week. Because the manufacturer implies by selling the motor that it will work for a reasonable period of time, you can return it and get your money back.

implied warranty A suggestion that a product will perform as the manufacturer claims it will.

Because opinions vary on what is a "reasonable" time, most manufacturers now give limited time warranties on their products. For example, they will guarantee their products against defects in materials or manufacturing for six months or one year.

Torts

A **tort** is a wrongful civil act that one party inflicts on another and that results in injury to the person, to the person's property, or to the person's good name. An **intentional tort** is a wrongful act intentionally committed. If a security guard in a department store suspects someone of shoplifting and uses excessive force to prevent him or her from leaving the store, the guard might be guilty of an intentional tort. Other examples are libel, embezzlement, and patent infringement.

tort A wrongful civil act that one party inflicts on another and that results in injury to the person, to the person's property, or to the person's good name.

intentional tort A wrongful act intentionally committed.

Negligence is a wrongful act that inadvertently causes injury to another person. For example, if a maintenance crew in a store mops the floors without placing warning signs in the area, a customer who slips and falls might bring a negligence suit against the store.

negligence A wrongful act that inadvertently causes injury to another person.

In recent years, the most publicized area of negligence has been product liability. **Product liability** means that businesses are liable for injuries caused to product users because of negligence in design or manufacturing. **Strict product liability** means that a business is liable for injuries caused by their products even if there is no evidence of negligence in the design or manufacture of the product.

product liability The liability of businesses for injuries caused to product users because of negligence in design or manufacturing.

strict product liability The liability of businesses for injuries caused by their products even if there is no evidence of negligence in the design or manufacture of the product.

Negotiable Instruments

Negotiable instruments are types of commercial paper that can be transferred among individuals and business firms. Cheques, bank drafts, and certificates of deposit are examples of negotiable instruments.

negotiable instruments Types of commercial paper that can be transferred among individuals and business firms.

The Bills of Exchange Act specifies that a negotiable instrument must

- be written
- be signed by the person who puts it into circulation (the maker or drawer)
- contain an unconditional promise to pay a certain amount of money
- be payable on demand
- be payable to a specific person (or to the bearer of the instrument)

Negotiable instruments are transferred from one party to another through an endorsement. An **endorsement** means signing your name to a negotiable instrument; this makes it transferable to another person or organization. If you sign only your name on the back of a cheque, you are making a *blank* endorsement. If you state that the instrument is being transferred to a specific person, you are making a *special* endorsement. A *qualified* endorsement limits your liability if the instrument is not backed up by sufficient funds. For example, if you get a cheque from a friend and want to use it to buy a new stereo, you can write "without recourse" above your name. If your friend's cheque bounces, you have no liability. A *restrictive* endorsement limits the negotiability of the instrument. For example, if you write "for deposit only" on the back of a cheque and it is later stolen, no one else can cash it.

endorsement Signing your name to a negotiable instrument, making it transferable to another person or organization.

Bankruptcy

bankruptcy The court-granted permission for organizations or individuals to not pay some or all of their debts.

At one time, individuals who could not pay their debts were jailed. Today, however, both organizations and individuals can seek relief by filing for **bankruptcy**, which is the court-granted permission to not pay some or all of their debts.

Thousands of individuals and businesses file for bankruptcy each year. They do so for various reasons, including cash flow problems, reduced demand for their products, or some other problem that makes it difficult or impossible for them to resolve their financial problems. In recent years, large businesses like Eaton's, Olympia & York, and Enron have sought the protection of bankruptcy laws. Three main factors account for the increase in bankruptcy filings:

1. The increased availability of credit
2. The "fresh-start" provisions in current bankruptcy laws
3. The growing acceptance of bankruptcy as a financial tactic

insolvent person (or company) One who cannot pay current obligations to creditors as they come due, or whose debts exceed their assets.

bankrupt person (or company) One who has either made a voluntary application to start bankruptcy proceedings (voluntary bankruptcy) or has been forced by creditors into bankruptcy (involuntary bankruptcy) by a process referred to as a receiving order.

In Canada, jurisdiction over bankruptcy is provided by the Bankruptcy and Insolvency Act. An **insolvent person (or company)** is defined as one who cannot pay current obligations to creditors as they come due, or whose debts exceed their assets. A **bankrupt person (or company)** is one who has either made a voluntary application to start bankruptcy proceedings (voluntary bankruptcy) or has been forced by creditors into bankruptcy (involuntary bankruptcy) by a process referred to as a *receiving order*. A person who is insolvent may or may not be bankrupt, and a person who is bankrupt may or may not be insolvent, as there are other bases for bankruptcy under the act. Another procedure under the act is referred to as a *proposal*, which can delay or avoid liquidation by providing the debtor with time to reorganize affairs and/or propose a payment schedule to creditors.

On a practical basis, business bankruptcy under the act may be resolved or avoided by one of three methods:

- Under a *liquidation plan*, the business ceases to exist. Its assets are sold and the proceeds are used to pay creditors.
- Under a *repayment plan*, the bankrupt company works out a new payment schedule to meet its obligations. The time frame is usually extended, and payments are collected and distributed by a court-appointed trustee.
- *Reorganization* is the most complex form of business bankruptcy. The company must explain the sources of its financial difficulties and propose a new plan for remaining in business. Reorganization may include a new slate of managers and a new financial strategy. A judge may also reduce the firm's debts to ensure its survival. Although creditors naturally dislike debt reduction, they may agree to the proposal, since getting, say, 50 percent of what you are owed is better than getting nothing at all.

Appendix B

Managing Your Personal Finances

This feature presents a down-to-earth, hands-on approach that will help you manage your personal finances. The practical information found in this feature includes a worksheet for determining net worth, insightful examples demonstrating the time value of money, a method for determining how much to invest now in order to build a future nest egg of a certain size, suggestions on how to manage credit-card debt, guidelines for purchasing a house, and a personalized worksheet for setting financial goals. The information contained in this feature will be immensely useful to you.

Please visit the MyBusinessLab website at www.pearsoned.ca/mybusinesslab for practical information about managing your own financial situation.

PEARSON mybusinesslab

Appendix C

Comprehensive Cases

IVEY

Richard Ivey School of Business
The University of Western Ontario

GOOGLE'S WAY—DON'T BE EVIL[1]

On February 22, 2006, Google Inc. (Google) announced the appointment of Dr. Larry Brilliant as the executive director of the newly created Google.org. With one per cent of Google Inc.'s equity and profit as seed money, Google.org's founding mandate was to tackle global poverty, communicable diseases and climate change. Sergey Brin and Larry Page, the founders of Google and currently the presidents of Technology and Products respectively, offered the hope that someday Google.org would "exceed Google itself in terms of overall world impact by ambitiously applying innovation and significant resources to the largest of the world's problems."[2] Although charity by successful entrepreneurs was not unusual, this news release signaled a new organizational form, a for-profit philanthropic company.[3]

Dr. Brilliant's role as executive director was to work with Brin and Page to define the mission and strategic goals of Google's philanthropic efforts.[4] Brilliant's task ahead was unprecedented. How could he leverage the company's for-profit status to make the biggest impact possible with the resources entrusted to Google.org? What decision-making criteria should be used to allocate resources? How would he measure Google.org's success?

From Googol to Google

In 1996, two Stanford PhD students, Sergey Brin and Larry Page, set out to create a system for exploring the web through a ranking system for Internet sites and "accidentally" created a search engine.[5] Looking through websites and URLs for ideas for a name for their creation, Brin and Page stumbled across a list of very large numbers. The word *googol*, representing the number 1 followed by 100 zeros, was at the top. This word reflected their mission to organize the limitless amount of information on the web, but a spelling error created *Google* instead. While still housing the Google system in Page's dorm, the search engine gained in popularity among Internet users. However, because of the lack of interest from Internet companies to purchase the system, Brin and Page took leave from their studies to create their own company out of their college research project.[6]

Google Inc. was incorporated in California in September 1998 and filed its initial public offering (IPO) with the U.S. Securities and Exchange Commission (SEC) on August 18, 2004. Its mission from the outset was "to organize the world's information and make it universally accessible and

---

Marlene J. Le Ber wrote this case under the supervision of Professor Tima Bansal solely to provide material for class discussion. The authors do not intend to illustrate either effective or ineffective handling of a managerial situation. The authors may have disguised certain names and other identifying information to protect confidentiality.

useful."[7] The automated search technology was freely available to anyone with an Internet connection. This technology included *Blogger* (an automated weblog publishing tool that sent updates to a site via file transfer protocol [FTP]), *Gmail* (a web-based email service that included more than two gigabytes of storage) and many other products all available at no cost to the user (see Exhibit 1).

Business Model

From its inception, the revenue generation model was based on relevant, cost-effective online advertising.[8] Google's initial products, *AdWords* and *AdSense*, still generated 99 per cent of its revenue.[9] With *AdWords*, advertisers selected their own target keywords, which were matched to relevant search and content pages. The advertiser's website was displayed to the right of a Google user's query results. The advertiser only paid when a Google user clicked on the ad. The *AdSense* program expanded this advertising model by enabling web publishers to provide a Google web search on their own pages. The advertising click results were used to generate revenue for the publisher, and a small portion of the fee was retained by Google.

This business model was very successful financially. As can be seen in Exhibit 2, the profit curve was steep. Although Google experienced a net loss in its first two years, its net earnings increased each year, from US$7 million in 2001 to more than US$3 billion in 2006. Year-over-year growth of revenues continued to outpace the year-over-year growth of expenses, resulting in continued increasing profitability. These healthy financials allowed Google to continue to grow the business and make acquisitions without an additional infusion of capital.

Google Values

As reflected in the Google annual reports, Brin and Page took great pride in being an unconventional company. They believed that their unwavering commitment to their core values was the foundation of their success. In their initial public offering, they articulated the importance of being value driven as a company:

> Our intense and enduring interest was to objectively help people find information efficiently. We also believed that searching and organizing all the world's information was an unusually important task that should be carried out by a company that is trustworthy and interested in the public good. We believe a well functioning society should have abundant, free and unbiased access to high quality information. Google therefore has a responsibility to the world.[10]

In the IPO, they also confirmed several specific values: serving end users first, maximizing long-term value, sharing decision making, rewarding and empowering employees, living the motto "don't be evil" and making the world a better place.

Serving End Users First

Brin and Page believed that the most effective and most profitable way to accomplish their mission was to put their users first, ahead of short-term economic gain. This value was reflected in the ongoing free availability of Google products for anyone with an Internet connection. All the products and services they developed focused on creating value for the user. Even the online advertising needed to be relevant and unobtrusive to its users.

Maximizing Long-Term Value

Eschewing quarterly market expectations, Brin and Page had tried to project three- to five-year scenarios when making decisions. Using this strategy, they had realized opportunities that might have sacrificed higher quarterly financial results but were, they believed, in the best long-term interests of the shareholders. Similarly, Google had sought promising yet high-risk, high-reward projects in which to invest.

Sharing Decision Making

Dr. Eric Schmidt joined Brin and Page as the chief executive officer (CEO) in 2001. The triumvirate met daily to update each other and to collaboratively work through immediate issues. When decisions led to disagreement, differences were resolved through discussion, analysis and consensus. The company's dual-class voting structure, with 61.4 per cent of the voting power retained by executive management and directors as a group, preserved Google's core values, editorial integrity and corporate culture and insulated the company against short-term market forces.

Rewarding and Empowering Employees

Significant employee ownership had been intentional as both an incentive and a reward. The extent of employee identification with the company was evidenced by their own term for themselves — Googlers. Benefits that have saved employees time and improved their health and productivity have also attracted new Googlers. The real motivator, however, was access to Google's computational power that enabled individuals to work on self-initiated projects that would make a difference to the world.

Living the Motto "Don't Be Evil"

Described as broadly shared within the company,[11] and permeating every cell of their being,[12] the motto, "Don't be evil," reflected the desire to "be a force for good — always do the right, ethical thing."[13] Not only was it a moral imperative for Brin and Page, but they believed that in the long term, doing good was in the best interest of shareholders and all others. However, as the expansion into China with government requirements for filtering of anti-government websites demonstrated, what the right thing was in a specific situation could be ambiguous. Censorship ran counter to Google's basic values. On the other hand, at its core was the belief that expanding access to information worldwide would lead to a better and freer world. Google executives' final decision was based on a judgment that Google.cn would "make a meaningful—though imperfect — contribution to the overall expansion of access to information in China."[14]

Making the World a Better Place

The other half of the motto was to "be a force for good." At the time of the Google IPO, Brin and Page committed contributions of employee time and one per cent of Google's equity and profits to the resolution of the world's largest problems.[15] In addition, nonprofit organizations had access to free online advertising through the Google Grants program. The Google Foundation was established in October 2005 as a private foundation, in accordance with provision 501(c)(3) of the US Internal Revenue Code, with an endowment of US$90 million. The commitment of one per cent of equity amounted to three million Google shares valued at more than US$900 million at the time of the IPO.[16]

Form Follows Values

The corporate umbrella created for "making the world a better place" was Google.org. It included the Google Foundation; some of Google's projects, such as the Google Grants; as well as partnerships, grants and loans that addressed Google.org's founding goals.[17] These goals spanned three domains:

- *Global Development* (developing scalable, sustainable solutions to poverty by focusing on economic growth in the private sector and improving access to information and services for the poor);
- *Global Public Health* (enabling the world to better predict, prevent and eradicate communicable diseases through better access to and use of information); and
- *Climate Change* (mitigating the effect of climate change on the poor by reducing greenhouse gas emissions, improving energy efficiency, and supporting clean energy sources).[18]

These goals were not unlike those of other charities; however, Google.org's for-profit structure set it apart and allowed it to lobby government, form partnerships with venture capitalists and fund start-up companies.[19] This flexibility to use whatever vehicle best addressed the goals of the organization motivated the for-profit status.[20] The trade-off was that any profits within Google.org would be fully taxed.

Google Inc. felt an impact as well. Although any monies given to the Google Foundation were considered charitable, any corporate earnings used to finance Google.org were subject to the usual taxes. Similarly, the financial information of Google Foundation was publicly available, whereas the tax forms of Google.org were private and thus were included as part of the tax filings of the parent, Google Inc.[21] The ongoing commitment made by Brin and Page was that any profits made by Google.org would not be at Google Inc.'s disposal but instead would be kept within Google.org for reinvestment in its mission.[22] However, shareholders of Google Inc. could someday object and pressure the board of directors to call on these monies. The disclosure of the philanthropic intent prior to the IPO and the majority voting power retained by executive management and directors as a group, mitigated these objections. The unconventional for-profit form allowed Google maximum flexibility to accomplish its mission. Dr. Larry Brilliant, hired by Brin and Page to be the executive director of Google.org, was "every bit as iconoclastic as Google's philanthropic arm."[23]

A Life of Service—Dr. Larry Brilliant

A man with a most unusual background, Dr. Larry Brilliant had been described as a counterculture figure, a Grateful Dead intimate, a spiritual seeker, a global health warrior,[24] a hippie-turned-doctor and a tech executive.[25] And, he was a respected academic. Dr. Brilliant earned a master's degree in Public Health in health planning and economic development (University of Michigan) after receiving his MD (Wayne State Medical School).[26] He himself had confided that "my life makes no sense at all except in retrospect... this new position at Google is the first time that my life has made any sense in any direction, as if everything else led up to this."[27]

Born a Social Activist

Born in 1944,[28] Brilliant showed his interest in social activism at the age of 15 when he joined the NAACP (National Association for the Advancement of Colored People).[29] Later, while in medical school, he took a summer job in San Francisco as a civil rights specialist with the Office of Equal Health Opportunities. The experience changed him. It was 1967 — the "Summer of Love" and as Brilliant described it, "I don't think that I've ever quite recovered from that."[30] Returning to San Francisco for his medical internship two years later, he became involved with the Alcatraz Indian occupation. He went to the island to help a Lakota Sioux pregnant woman, who wanted to give birth on Indian-held land. The publicity of his role in the Alcatraz Indian occupation led to an offer to play a young doctor in a movie in exchange for funding for a medical clinic at Alcatraz. This adventure took him across the United States to Kathmandu over the course of two years.[31]

Meant to be a Global Health Warrior

Brilliant's travels led him to a Himalayan ashram where his guru told him to go work for the United Nations and help eradicate smallpox.[32] Brilliant did so, living in India for 10 years while playing a key role in the successful World Health Organization (WHO) smallpox eradication program. He returned to the United States to teach at the University of Michigan as a professor of epidemiology, global health planning and economic development.[33] His passion to eradicate blindness led to the establishment of the Seva Foundation in 1978. Through the efforts of the Seva Foundation, more than two million people in Tibet, Nepal, India, Bangladesh, Cambodia, Tanzania, Egypt and Guatemala have regained their sight.[34] Dr. Brilliant's service has been recognized through numerous awards, the most recent being the 2006 Sapling Foundation's TED Prize. Dr. Brilliant is using the US$100,000 award as seed money to build a global early warning system to find and contain new pandemics.[35]

Finally, a Tech Exec

Brilliant became interested in computer conferencing when the helicopter he was using for a research project crashed and needed a new engine. Using the experience of acquiring a new helicopter engine from the remote Himalayan Mountains through a satellite connection with his computer, he started a virtual community company, The Well, in 1985.[36] He went on to become the CEO of Cometa Networks, a joint venture of Intel, IBM and AT&T that sought to develop a national Wi-Fi system. Later, he became the CEO of an Internet service company, SoftNet.[37]

In the announcement of Dr. Brilliant's appointment as executive director of Google.org, Brin was quoted as saying that Dr. Brilliant embodied the goals of Google.org "in spirit and in accomplishments."[38]

The First Year at google.org

During the first year of his tenure, Brilliant retreated from the public eye and met with foundation leaders, activists, nongovernmental organizations (NGOs), scientists and Googlers from all over the world.[39] Brilliant's priority was to get the right people in place.

Impressive Teams

Brilliant recruited content experts in each of the domains and paired them with experienced Google managers.[40] As seen in Exhibit 3, the content experts were not only well accomplished in the fields of climate change, global public health and economic development but had relevant experience in philanthropy, government regulation and science. These teams were also supported by experienced corporate managers.

First Projects

In addition to the more than US$7 million granted to Acumen Fund, TechnoServe and several academics at Berkeley and Harvard, prior to Dr. Brilliant's appointment[41], US$6.4 million was allocated during Dr. Brilliant's first year at Google.org (see Exhibit 4). Climate change initiatives totaled US$1.2 million and consisted of several smaller grants of up to US$200,000. Global Development initiatives, the recipients of prior large grants, totaled less than US$1 million and consisted of a few smaller grants. Global Public Health initiatives totaled US$3.626 million with two main recipients, INSTEDD (International System for Total Early Disease Detection) and the Seva Foundation. Both were nonprofit organizations founded by Dr. Brilliant.

Although not yet distributed, Google.org had also committed US$10 million "to accelerate the development of battery technology, plug-in hybrids, and vehicles capable of returning stored energy to the grid."[42] This commitment was the organization's first major project initiative announcement.

The Future of google.org

With his world-class teams in place, Dr. Brilliant was now poised to move forward on the agenda of tackling global poverty, communicable diseases and climate change. He reflected:

> So where are we going now? Google.org is looking to better understand the inextricable linkages among climate change, global public health and economic development, and the impact of global warming on the poor. We want to fund projects that are making a difference and that are effective on a large scale.
>
> We live in very complicated times. Global health, poverty, and climate are inextricably interrelated, and it is the poor of the world who bear the heaviest burden. Google.org is focused on learning initiatives that simultaneously fund good organizations working in these areas and provide insights into "big ideas" that could be scalable from these pilot projects.
>
> During this year we anticipate making more significant grants and investments in support of our major initiatives. We hope to innovate both in what we do, and how we do it.[43]

The culture of the parent company, Google Inc. which included its values that drove decisions and its processes of decision making, would shape innovation at Google.org. Yet, Brilliant still had several large questions to ponder: How could he leverage the for-profit status to make the biggest impact possible with the resources entrusted to Google.org? What decision-making criteria should be used to allocate resources? How would he measure Google.org's success?

Exhibit 1 Google Products

Search Products	
Alerts	Email updates of the latest relevant Google results based on query or topic
Blog	Find blogs on favorite topics
Book	Search full text of books
Catalogs	Discover and browse catalogs online
Desktop	Search own computer
Directory	Browse the web by topic
Google Earth	Explore the world with satellite imagery, maps, terrain and 3-D buildings
Images	Search for images on the web
Local	Find local business and services
Maps	View maps and get directions
News	Search news stories
Notebook	Clip and collect information while browsing the web
Scholar	Search scholarly papers
Specialized Searches	Search within specific topics
Toolbar	Add a search box to own browser
University Search	Search a specific school's website
Video	Search videos and upload own videos
Web Search	Search more than 8 billion web pages
Communication Products	
Blogger	Express yourself online
Docs & Spreadsheets	Create and share documents online and access from anywhere
Picasa	Find, edit and share your photos
Calendar	Develop schedule and share events with friends
Gmail	Fast, searchable email with less spam
Groups	Create mailing lists and discussion groups
Talk	Call friends through a computer
Translate	View web pages in other languages
Mobile Products	
Maps	View maps and get directions on mobile phone
Mobile	Use Google on mobile phone
SMS	Use text messaging for quick info
Other Products	
Pack	A free collection of essential software selected by Google such as: Spyware Doctor, Skype, Norton Security Scan, Adobe Reader and Real Player

Source: "More Google Products," http://www.google.ca/intl/en/options/index.html, accessed August 15, 2007.

Exhibit 2 Consolidated statements of earnings

(Years ended December 31, 1999 to 2006)
(In thousands of dollars, except per share amounts)

	2006	2005	2004	2003	2002	2001	2000	1999
Income								
Google web sites	6,332,797	3,377,061	1,589,032	792,063	306,978	86,426	19,108	220
Google network web sites	4,159,831	2,687,942	1,554,256	628,600	103,937			
Interest	461,040	124,400	10,040	4,190			47	440
Licensing & other	112,289	73,558	45,935	45,271	28,593			
	11,065,957	6,262,961	3,199,263	1,470,124	439,508	86,426	19,155	660
Y/Y Growth	*73%*	*92%*	*118%*	*234%*	*409%*	*351%*	*2802%*	*NA*
Expenses								
Cost of revenues	4,225,027	2,577,088	1,468,967	634,411	132,575	15,104	6,248	908
Research & development	1,228,589	599,510	395,164	229,605	40,494	20,940	12,089	2,930
Sales & marketing	849,518	468,152	295,749	164,935	48,783	21,743	10,899	1,677
General & administrative	751,187	386,532	188,151	94,519	31,190	17,675	4,609	1,221
Settlement of dispute with Yahoo	–	–	201,000	–	–	–	–	–
Contribution to Google Foundation	–	90,000	–	–	–	–	–	–
Interest	–	–	–	–	1,551	896	–	–
	7,054,921	4,121,282	2,549,031	1,123,470	254,593	76,358	33,845	6,736
Y/Y Growth	*71%*	*62%*	*127%*	*344%*	*235%*	*126%*	*402%*	*NA*
Earnings before income taxes	4,011,035	2,141,679	650,232	346,654	184,915	10,068	–4,690	–6,076
Provision for income taxes	933,590	676,282	251,113	241,006	85,259	3,083	–	–
Net earnings (loss)	3,077,446	1,465,397	399,119	105,648	99,656	6,985	–14,690	–6,076
Earnings per share	10.21	5.31	2.07	0.77	0.86	0.07	–0.22	–0.14

Source: Financial Statements: Google Inc., http://finance.google.com/finance?fstype=ci&q=GOOG, accessed August 9, 2007; Google Inc. IPO Filed with the Securities and Exchange Commission on August 18, 2004; and "Google: Investor Relations," http://investor.google.com/fin_data.html, accessed August 14, 2007.

Exhibit 3 Individuals Hired at Google.Org as of June 4, 2007

Clean Energy and Climate Change Initiatives, Policy and Advocacy Team	
Dan Reicher	Former Assistant Secretary of Energy for Energy Efficiency and Renewable Energy, U.S. government
Aimee Christensen	Trained as a lawyer with more than a decade of designing, implementing and advising on energy and environmental strategies; former fulltime consultant to the World Bank's legal department, serving the Bank's Carbon Finance Business; former Executive Director of Environment 2004; former lawyer with Baker & McKenzie where she advised clients on energy and environmental matters and legislative strategies.[1]
Kirsten Olsen	Former consultant for Accenture and an account executive at Sterling Hager, a high-tech consulting firm. She has also held positions in the White House Office of Political Affairs and at the El Pomar Foundation.[2]
Ki Mun	Googler
Global Public Health Team	
Mark Smolinski	MD, MPH and CDC-trained epidemiologist who worked at the Institute of Medicine and was formerly a Vice President at the Nuclear Threat Initiative, where he worked on a regional disease surveillance system
Corrie Conrad	A researcher focusing on preventable diseases afflicting the poor, formerly with the Clinton Foundation, where she was working on its HIV/AIDS program in Rwanda.
Katie Wurtz	Googler
Matt Waddell	Googler
Emily Delmont	Googler
Global Economic Development Team	
Sheryl Sandberg	VP of Online Sales and Operations and Google.org board member leads this effort
Blaise Judja-Sato	Born in Cameroon, Blaise was most recently President of the Nelson Mandela Foundation USA and the founder of VillageReach, a nonprofit that brings sustainable health care and essential services to more than 3.5 million people in Mozambique
Sonal Shah	The co-founder of Indicorps, a nonprofit offering one-year fellowships for people of Indian origin to work on development projects in India, and was previously a Vice President at Goldman, Sachs & Co. developing the firm's corporate citizenship and environmental strategies
Juliette Gimon	The chair of the Global Fund for Children and a trustee of the William and Flora Hewlett Foundation. She also serves on the board of the Synergos Institute and the advisory committees of Youth Philanthropy Worldwide and the Global Philanthropy Forum.
Rachel Payne	Googler
Meryl Stone	Googler
Kim Thompson	Googler
Corporate Support to the three teams:	
Linda Segre	Responsible for managing Google.org's project initiatives and operations within Google
Gregory Miller	Responsible for Google.org's investing and grant practices, legal affairs and strategic partnerships as well as the affairs of the Google Foundation
Elliot Schrage	VP of Global Communications and Public Affairs – responsible for coordination of PR efforts, Google.org's advocacy and communications agenda, and efforts to influence public policy and media
Jacquelline Fuller	Reports to Elliot Schrage, formerly Deputy Director of the Global Health program at the Bill & Melinda Gates Foundation, where she managed Public Affairs and served as speechwriter for U.S. Secretary of Health and Human Services Dr. Louis Sullivan
Gillian Peoples	Assistant to Larry Brilliant
Chris Busselle	Investments Manager
Brad Presner	Googler
Alan Louie	Googler
Tara Canobbio	Googler
Dr. Larry Simon	On sabbatical from Brandeis University's Heller School, where he is Professor and Director of the Sustainable International Development Graduate Programs and Associate Dean for Academic Programs. A specialist on poverty and vulnerability, Larry led Oxfam America's work in Central America and the Caribbean.

[1]"NAELS Board of Directors," http://www.naels.org/about/bod/christensen.htm, accessed August 10, 2007.
[2]"Kirsten Olsen, NetImpact," http://www.nciia.org/CD/public/htmldocs/presenters/olsen.html, accessed August 10, 2007.

Source: Unless otherwise cited "New Team Members for Google.org," http://googleblog.blogspot.com/2007/04/new-team-members-for-googleorg.html, accessed June 20, 2007.

Exhibit 4 Monies Granted October 2005 to December 2006
(These monies include grants made by both Google.org and the Google Foundation.)

Climate Change–US$1.2 million

Brookings Institution	$200,000 to support a conference in spring 2008 on federal policy to promote plug-in hybrids
CalCars	$200,000 to the California Cars Initiative of the International Humanities Center to support CalCars' work educating the public about plug-in hybrid electric vehicles (PHEVs)
Electric Power Research Institute	$200,000 to support EPRI's plug-in hybrid research and development program including participating in advanced infrastructure development, vehicle-to-grid technology demonstrations, and studies of the environmental and economic benefits of plug-in hybrids
Energy Foundation	$50,000 for climate change research
NRDC	$100,000 to support the Environmental Entrepreneurs Climate Campaign to assist with the implementation of the Global Warming Solutions Act of 2006 (California's AB 32)
Plug-In America	$100,000 to support PIA's work in educating the public about plug-in transportation
Rocky Mountain Institute	$200,000 to partially fund an "Innovation Workshop" to promote new strategies for greater production and market adoption of plug-in next-generation hybrid vehicles
Dr. Willett Kempton at University of Delaware	$150,000 for megawatt plug-in to grid research and implementation planning

Global Development–US$7.67 million

Acumen Fund	$5,200,000 to support Acumen's entrepreneurial approaches to address global poverty and services for the poor (granted prior to Dr. Brilliant's appointment)
PlanetRead	$345,000 to support Same Language Subtitling (SLS) programs in India
TechnoServe	$1,500,000 to support "Believe, Begin, Become" business plan competitions in Ghana and Tanzania (granted prior to Dr. Brilliant's appointment)
Other	Over $625,000 to organizations supporting entrepreneurship and other development activities

Public Health–US$3.626 million

INSTEDD	an initial start up grant of $975,000 (through Community Foundation Silicon Valley) to establish INSTEDD as an independent nonprofit federation which aspires to build an early detection and response system for disease outbreaks and other global threats
Seva Foundation	$2,000,000 to support programs to prevent blindness and restore eyesight in India, Nepal, Tibet, Cambodia, Bangladesh, Egypt, Tanzania and Guatemala
UC Berkeley Regents	$451,000 to support research on water intervention in Kenya (granted prior to Dr. Brilliant's appointment)
UC San Francisco	$200,000 to support Dr. John Kane's malaria research

Hurricane Katrina and Rita Grants – US$0.95 million

$750,000 for job training, tutoring/educational programs, and micro-enterprise development and loan assistance given to five non-profits including:

- Accion USA
- Trickle Up Program
- City Year Louisiana
- National Urban League
- Greater New Orleans Foundation

Liberty Bank	$200,000 to provide new lending to victims of Hurricanes Katrina and Rita for home purchases and business recapitalization.

Source: "Google.org Grants,"http://www.google.org/projects.html, accessed July 20, 2007.

Endnotes

[1] This case has been written on the basis of published sources only. Consequently, the interpretation and perspectives presented in this case are not necessarily those of Google Inc. or any of its employees.

[2] "Google Names Larry Brilliant as Executive Director of Google.org," **http://www.google.com/press/pressrel/brilliant.html**, accessed July 20, 2007.

[3] Katie Hafner, "Philanthropy Google's Way: Not the Usual," *The New York Times*, September 14, 2006. **http://www.nytimes.com/2006/09/14/technology/14google.html?ei=5070&en=8e0015**, accessed September 15, 2006.

[4] "Google Names Larry Brilliant as Executive Director of Google.org," **http://www.google.com/press/pressrel/brilliant.html**, accessed July 20, 2007.

[5] Rachael Hanley, "From Googol to Google: Co-founder Returns," February 12, 2003. **http://daily.stanford.edu/article/2003/2/12/fromGoogolToGoogle**, accessed August 14, 2007.

[6] "Corporate Information," **http://www.google.com/corporate/history.html**, accessed August 14, 2007.

[7] Initial Public Offering, Google Inc., filed with the Securities and Exchange Commission on August 18, 2004. p.1. **http://www.sec.gov/Archives/edgar/data/1288776/000119312504142742/ds1a.htm**, accessed July 17, 2007.

[8] Initial Public Offering, Google Inc., filed with the Securities and Exchange Commission on August 18, 2004. **http://www.sec.gov/Archives/edgar/data/1288776/000119312504142742/ds1a.htm**, accessed July 17, 2007.

[9] "Investor Relations," **http://investor.google.com/fin_data.html**, accessed August 14, 2007.

[10] Initial Public Offering, Google Inc., filed with the Securities and Exchange Commission on August 18, 2004, p. 30. **http://www.sec.gov/Archives/edgar/data/1288776/000119312504142742/ds1a.htm**, accessed July 17, 2007.

[11] Initial Public Offering, Google Inc., filed with the Securities and Exchange Commission on August 18, 2004, p. 32. **http://www.sec.gov/Archives/edgar/data/1288776/000119312504142742/ds1a.htm**, accessed July 17, 2007.

[12] Jim Hopkins, "Google Signs on Do-good Doctor to Head Charity," *USA Today*, posted 2/21/2007. **http://www.usatoday.com/money/industries/technology/2006-02-21-google-org_x.htm**, accessed July 20, 2007.

[13] "Playboy Interview: Google Guys." Initial Public Offering, Google Inc., filed with the Securities and Exchange Commission on August 18, 2004, p. B-3. **http://www.sec.gov/Archives/edgar/data/1288776/000119312504142742/ds1a.htm**, accessed July 17, 2007.

[14] Elliot Schrage, "Testimony: The Internet in China," posted February 15, 2006. **http://googleblog.blogspot.com/search/label/Asia**, accessed August 27, 2007.

[15] Initial Public Offering, Google Inc., filed with the Securities and Exchange Commission on August 18, 2004. **http://www.sec.gov/Archives/edgar/data/1288776/000119312504142742/ds1a.htm**, accessed July 17, 2007.

[16] "Googling for Charity," *BusinessWeek*, October 20, 2005. **http://www.businessweek.com/print/technology/content/oct2005/tc20051020_721687.htm**, accessed July 20, 2007.

[17] "About Us," **http://www.google.org/about.html**, accessed July 20, 2007.

[18] Ibid.

[19] Katie Hafner, "Philanthropy Google's Way: Not the Usual," *The New York Times*, September 14, 2006, **http://www.nytimes.com/2006/09/14/technology/14google.html?ei=5070&en=8e0015**, accessed September 15, 2006.

[20] "Googling for Charity," *BusinessWeek*, October 20, 2005, **http://www.businessweek.com/print/technology/content/oct2005/tc20051020_721687.htm**, accessed July 20, 2007.

[21] Katie Hafner, "Philanthropy Google's Way: Not the Usual," *The New York Times*, September 14, 2006, **http://www.nytimes.com/2006/09/14/technology/14google.html?ei=5070&en=8e0015**, accessed September 15, 2006.

[22] Ibid.

[23] Ibid.

[24] Patrick Hoge, "Doctor Looks to Use Technology to Aid Global Health Care," San Francisco Chronicle, February 24, 2006, page A-1. **http://sfgate.com/cgi-bin/article.cgi?f=/c/a/2006/02/24/MNGKLHE6QJ1.DTL**, accessed July 20, 2007.

[25] Jim Hopkins, "Google Signs on Do-good Doctor to Head Charity," *USA Today*, posted 2/21/2007, **http://www.usatoday.com/money/industries/technology/2006-02-21-google-org_x.htm**, accessed July 20, 2007.

[26] "Corporate Information: Google Management," **http://google.com/intl/en/corporate/execs.html#brilliant**, accessed July 20, 2007.

[27] Harry Kreisler, "A Life of Service: Conversation with Larry Brilliant, M.D.," April 17, 2006, **http://globetrotter.berkeley.edu/Elberg/Brilliant/brilliant-con1.html**, accessed July 20, 2007.

[28] "Larry Brilliant," **http://en.wikipedia.org/wiki/Larry_Brilliant**, accessed July 20, 2007.

[29] Harry Kreisler, "A Life of Service: Conversation with Larry Brilliant, M.D.," April 17, 2006, **http://globetrotter.berkeley.edu/Elberg/Brilliant/brilliant-con1.html**, accessed July 20, 2007.

[30] Ibid.

[31] Ibid.

[32] Ibid.

[33] "Corporate Information: Google Management," **http://google.com/intl/en/corporate/execs.html#brilliant**. accessed July 20, 2007.

[34] "Sight Programs," **http://www.seva.org/site/PageServer?pagename=programs_sight**, accessed August 23, 2007.

[35] "Themes TED Prize Winners," **http://ted.com/index.php/themes/view/id/12**, accessed August 23, 2007.

[36] Harry Kreisler, "A Life of Service: Conversation with Larry Brilliant, M.D.," April 17, 2006, **http://globetrotter.berkeley.edu/Elberg/Brilliant/brilliant-con1.html**, accessed July 20, 2007.

[37] Jim Hopkins, "Google Signs on Do-good Doctor to Head Charity," *USA Today*, posted 2/21/2007, **http://www.usatoday.com/money/industries/technology/2006-02-21-google-org_x.htm**, accessed July 20, 2007.

[38] "Google Names Larry Brilliant as Executive Director of Google.org," **http://www.google.com/press/pressrel/brilliant.html**, accessed July 20, 2007.

[39] Larry Brilliant, "New Team Members for Google.org," June 4, 2007, **http://googleblog.blogspot.com/2007/04/new-team-members-for-googleorg.html**, accessed June 20, 2007.

[40] Ibid.

[41] Google Annual Report 2005.

[42] Felicity Barringer and Matthew Wald, "Google and Utility to Test Hybrids That Sell Back Power," *The New York Times*, June 19, 2007, **http://www.nytimes.com/2007/06/19/technology/19electric.htnl?th=&emc=th&pagewant**, accessed June 22, 2007.

[43] Larry Brilliant, "New Team Members for Google.org," June 4, 2007. **http://googleblog.blogspot.com/2007/04/new-team-members-for-googleorg.html**, accessed June 20, 2007.

A MIDSUMMER DAY'S NIGHTMARE

Discussion Questions/Objectives

1. What is the problem here? Why is it a problem?
2. To whom or to what do you have a responsibility in this situation? Why?
3. What fundamental purposes, principles, and potential consequences are relevant here? Construct consequential, principled, and purposive arguments, both for and against alternatives you consider relevant.
4. As the decision maker of this case, how would you proceed and why?

Lindsay Sawyer and John Melnyk

This case was developed for the sole purpose of providing material for class discussion. It is not intended to illustrate either effective or ineffective handling of a managerial situation. All characters and events are real, but names of people and organizations have been disguised. Any reproduction, in any form, of the material in this case is prohibited except with the written consent of the authors.

A Midsummer Day's Nightmare

I started work at a nationally known fast food restaurant when I was seventeen. I had had other jobs, but none of them was as much fun as this one. I reported for my first shift and was introduced to a new atmosphere that was unlike anything I had experienced before.

One of the first things I learned was that having fun was really encouraged. Smiles were the norm, and, in fact, expected. This friendly environment led to a lot of fast friendships with my co-workers, especially since we all went to neighbouring high schools. Our employer encouraged these ties and would organize activities for us outside of work.

We enjoyed these outings, but the best "perk" by far was the food, which was half price to employees, even outside of scheduled shifts! We could even informally extend this discount to friends once in a while, which made it an even more enviable privilege.

I loved my job and worked very hard at it. After fourteen months I got my first promotion. Six months later I was promoted again to a junior management position along with two of my co-workers.

We received very little preparation to deal with this move up to management. We were given a workbook covering topics such as food safety, employee relations, shift planning, scheduling, etc., and were supposed to get time on the job to work through it and then go to classes. But that never happened. However, we were all told immediately about the importance of management always presenting a united front. Most of our training was on the job—we were given a different colour shirt, a new nametag, and encouraged to do our best. My first shift as a manager I was left alone to supervise a busy dinner hour.

My promotions brought me into more frequent contact with Michael Roberts, area manager for the district. Michael was a scary figure to all store employees because whenever he came in he found faults. Heaven help you if your personal grooming wasn't perfect, if you didn't have your nametag on, or even if you weren't using the prescribed pattern to mop the floor!

Now that I was in a management position, Michael knew me by name, and made a point of talking to me every time he came in. I suddenly had to develop a working relationship with him and meet his high standards.

There were many benefits to this promotion though, the best of which was now, free food! The expensive items on the menu were now always available to us. We would take advantage of this whenever we could, sometimes eating three meals a day at our restaurant! We now also had the authority to reward our subordinates with free food.

Because we were a small branch, we rarely had more than one manager working at a time, which left me completely in charge during my shift. This meant that it was up to me to ensure that company standards were met and that all customers were satisfied, as well as to deal with any complaints. I also had to make sure everything was in place for the next shift; if there was something that I wasn't able to finish, I had to communicate it clearly to the manager of the next shift.

I also became privy to more knowledge about our store. I quickly learned that we had trouble making a profit because the restaurant was so small. As a result we had to be very careful about expenses, especially food wastage. We would order $5000 to $6000 of supplies every week to ten days, and try to be careful to order only what we would need. As a result sometimes we would run out of something, or several things, before the next order. I hated when that happened.

If it was just a little thing, like milk or tomatoes, we would buy some at retail to tide us over, although this was not encouraged. For more basic items, like hamburger patties and buns, I had to phone around to other outlets and "beg" to "borrow" some supplies. This was a real hassle, and irritating to the other managers too. Furthermore, we often had only two or three employees working at a time, so it was a huge inconvenience to send one to pick up supplies—that is, provided I could convince someone with a driver's licence and gas in their car to go. I once had to go myself on a busy Saturday during Christmas season to pick up eighty trays of buns. It took me three hours and my mom's SUV.

Most of the equipment in our restaurant was old and in bad repair. We couldn't get authorization to replace it, so we had to make do. When I complained, I was told to use the manuals and try to fix it myself! I had absolutely no idea how to service these temperamental machines that would often act up, especially when we were busy. I once had an ice cream machine explode goo all over me for my trouble trying to fix it.

The air conditioning didn't always work either, but the grills were by far the most troublesome. They would stop heating properly in the middle of the day and not cook the food thoroughly. I got to know several repairmen on a first-name basis; we spent many hours going over this problem together.

Nevertheless I persevered, and over the next ten months I gained valuable experience and completed all the necessary steps to be promoted again. Towards the end of this period I met with my restaurant manager several times, and she assured me that a promotion was in the works, subject to the approval of the area manager.

I was really looking forward to that... it would mean I would no longer have to wear a hat on the job!

One Summer Day...

One summer day I came in to open the restaurant after a day off. It was 6:00 a.m. and already warm outside, even more so inside the store because the air conditioning didn't work well. I started getting the computer system up and counting the cash, and sent the open staff person, Jason, to start making the muffins and getting the tables ready for our 7:00 a.m. opening.

As I was counting the cash, Jason called to me from the back. He was young and somewhat excitable, so I didn't think anything of it as I went over to see what was the matter.

Jason gestured excitedly and directed me towards the large walk-in freezer, insisting I look inside. I went into the freezer to take a look. I didn't like going in there because it was always so cold. But not today!

The freezer was room temperature! It must have been off overnight!

> *"Oh NO!"* I thought,

as I looked in an open box of chicken and picked up a piece. It was warm and squishy; the coating crumbled off on my hand. I opened a box of hamburger patties and touched one on top. It felt mushy, and was beginning to lose its shape. I leaned over and opened a box in the middle. It was cool, and the meat in the centre of the box seemed still frozen.

My mind started racing. I ran to the phone to call my restaurant manager; I knew she was opening at another location that morning. It was about 6:30 a.m. Pat picked up the phone after several rings.

> *"Hi Pat, it's me... umm... I have a really big problem. You see... uh... "*
>
> *"Jennifer, I'm really busy! Hurry up!"* she snapped.
>
> *"I came in this morning and the freezer has been off for hours. Everything is goopy and gross and I don't know what to do. It's disgusting!"*
>
> *"WHAT! You've got to be kidding. Who the hell was working yesterday? I just don't believe this. Damn! I'm too busy to deal with this now. Call Mike."* Click—she hung up.

I looked at my watch; it was 6:35 a.m. I had to call Michael at home.

> *"Hi Michael, it's Jennifer from 82nd West... Pat told me to call you!"* I blurted out. *"Sorry about this, but I have a big problem. Our freezer has been off for several hours, the food's gross and mushy. I don't know what to do."*

There was a brief pause as Michael woke up.

> *"What? Are you joking? Why is the freezer off? Is it broken? Is it unplugged?"*
>
> *"Umm... I don't really know."*

In a panic I ran to the back room to figure out why the freezer wasn't on. The answer was at the fuse box, where I discovered the freezer circuits were in the "off" position. Quickly I reset them. I knew we had received a supply order the day before. In order to save energy in the heat of the day, the freezer was likely shut off while the order was carried in. This wouldn't have been a problem... if only someone had remembered to turn it back on.

I could tell Michael was seething, but he controlled it well.

> *"OK, as long as all the cooking temperatures are met, the food will be all right. You can still use everything there."*
>
> He went on, *"It's important that we don't cause a panic about this. Don't talk about it in the restaurant and make sure food temperatures are met. Everything will be OK. Continue your shift Jennifer." "Uh... OK... umm... "*

I hung up the phone in a daze. I couldn't quite bring myself to carry out those instructions right away. I felt confused and upset, as I stood lost in my thoughts searching for some instruction or part of my training for guidance. I knew what to do if there was a bomb threat, but nothing had prepared me for this.

I had about twenty minutes worth of food in our small freezers up front. Jason was waiting for my instructions. I looked at my watch—it was 6:45 a.m.

Appendix

Exhibit 1 Excerpts from the Food and Drug Act, and Food and Drug Regulations, as Administered by Health Canada

Interpretation

"Unsanitary conditions" means such conditions or circumstances as might contaminate with dirt or filth, or render injurious to health, a food, drug or cosmetic.

Food

4. No person shall sell an article of food that
   (a) has in or on it any poisonous or harmful substance;
   (b) is unfit for human consumption;
   (c) consists in whole or in part of any filthy, putrid, disgusting, rotten, decomposed or diseased animal or vegetable substance;
   (d) is adulterated; or
   (e) was manufactured, prepared, preserved, packaged or stored under unsanitary conditions.

Sale of Barbecued, Roasted or Broiled Meat or Meat By-Products

B.14.072 No person shall sell meat or a meat by-product that has been barbecued, roasted or broiled and is ready for consumption unless the cooked meat or meat by-product
   (a) at all times
      (i) has a temperature of 40° F (4.4° C) or lower, or 140° F (60° C) or higher, or
      (ii) has been stored at an ambient temperature of 40° F (4.4° C) or lower, or 140° F (60° C) or higher
   (b) carries on the principal display panel of the label a statement to the effect that the food must be stored at a temperature of 40° F (4.4° C) or lower, or 140° F (60° C) or higher.

THE LAST RESORT RETIREMENT COMMUNITY

The Situation

On January 12, 2010, Dave Kerrigan, the Chief Executive Officer (CEO) of the Last Resort Retirement Community, returned from lunch, and glancing at the thermometer outside his office window, thought, "sixteen degrees—what a beautiful day for the middle of January, even in Vancouver. Too bad things aren't going nearly so beautifully inside the office."

As he slumped into his chair, Kerrigan wondered what he should do. Since hiring the new director of nursing last year, the situation in the nursing home had been steadily deteriorating. Several department heads were unhappy with a variety of developments in the nursing home. Two of the managers disliked each other intensely, and each accused the other of spreading false rumours. Informal alliances were developing among the managers, which threatened the cooperative attitude that had characterized the management group for the past several years. Plus, Kerrigan had just discovered that his immediate subordinate, the nursing home administrator (NHA), and her subordinate, the director of nursing, had together written a letter to the board of directors questioning his leadership.

Kerrigan had to do something. But what?

Background

The Last Resort Retirement Community was a large complex for retired people. The "campus" included duplex and quadruplex housing for independent elderly people, a large daycare centre, a school, a church, a small store, and a nursing home that provided comprehensive nursing care for aged individuals unable to care for themselves.

The nursing home was divided into two basic areas: the skilled nursing section for people who required 24-hour nursing supervision, and the assisted living section for people who could do some things for themselves. Laundry and meals were provided for residents of both sections.

As CEO of the entire complex, Dave Kerrigan had overall responsibility for its effective operation (see Figure C1-1). He coordinated information from all areas of the complex and facilitated the process of managerial decision making. He stressed planning and teamwork, used a participative management style, and usually did not impose decisions on subordinate managers. Therefore, decision making in the organization was quite decentralized. Kerrigan got along well with his subordinates, and until recently, the staff had gotten along well with each other.

Because the nursing home was such an important part of the complex, the NHA was part of top management. Doris Beck, the NHA, had five managers

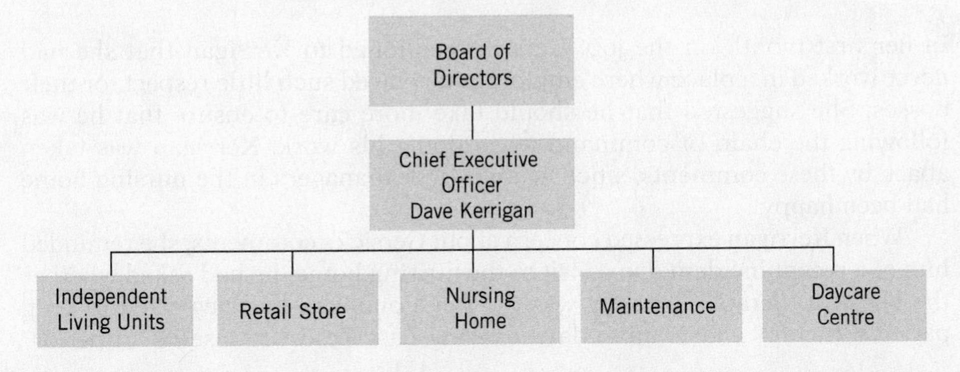

Figure C1-1 Organization Chart for the Last Resort Retirement Community

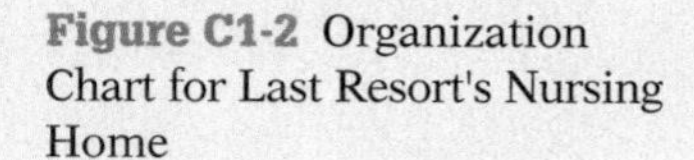

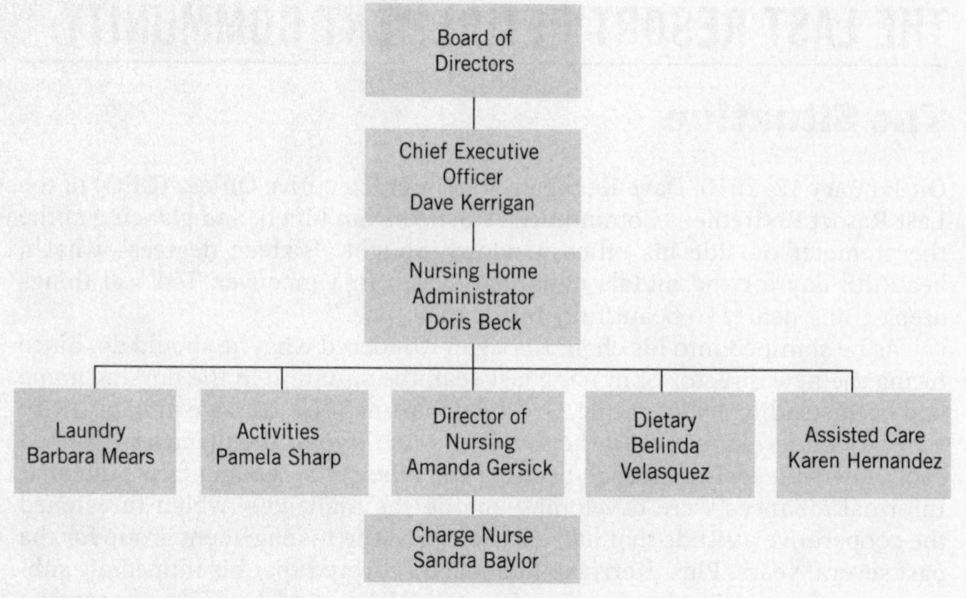

Figure C1-2 Organization Chart for Last Resort's Nursing Home

reporting to her. Each of these managers was responsible for one of the key functions in the nursing home (see Figure C1-2).

Until last year, this system had worked well. The seven managerial staff met weekly to discuss the effectiveness of nursing home operations, and to resolve any problems that arose. Morale among the managers was high, cooperation was the norm, and information sharing was constant at the weekly meetings.

In 2008, the long-time and well-liked Director of Nursing, Martha Kane, resigned to take a higher-paying position in a larger retirement facility. Kane was objective, professional, and adept at problem solving. She acted as the informal leader in the nursing home, even though she was not the NHA. Beck, the actual NHA, was not a strong leader and often acted in a laissez faire manner. While she was very effective in handling clearly specified jobs like organizing special events, Beck had difficulties conceptualizing the "big picture," handling conflicts, and managing people.

Several candidates applied for the vacant director of nursing position. One was Amanda Gersick, who was strongly recommended by a member of the board of directors. This board member had known Gersick some years earlier in another organization and was impressed with her work. When Kerrigan interviewed Gersick, he was reasonably impressed, but had some reservations, noting in his interview summary that she seemed to be rather uptight. In spite of this reservation, Kerrigan hired Gersick, and she began her new job in January 2009.

Problems Begin

In her first month on the job, Gersick mentioned to Kerrigan that she had never worked in a place where employees displayed such little respect for their bosses. She suggested that he should take more care to ensure that he was following the chain of command when doing his work. Kerrigan was taken aback by these comments, since he knew that managers in the nursing home had been happy.

When Kerrigan expressed concern about Gersick's comments, she reminded him of a recent incident. On a visit to the nursing home, he had asked whether the physical therapist on duty was the same one who had neglected to keep patients' therapy charts up-to-date, causing Last Resort to lose its "superior" rating some months earlier. When told that she was the same person, Kerrigan checked the charts of the people she had recently performed therapy on. Once again, she hadn't recorded anything. Kerrigan was amazed and informed Beck, the NHA, that she must not let this physical therapist work in the nursing home again.

After listening to Gersick's description of the incident, Kerrigan asked how he had violated the chain of command by telling Beck, his immediate subordinate, about the problem. Gersick's muddled answer gave Kerrigan the distinct impression that Gersick felt that she, not Beck, was in charge of the nursing home.

Over the next few weeks, Kerrigan heard that Gersick reminded her subordinates regularly of the importance of the chain of command and the absolute authority of bosses over subordinates. Kerrigan was concerned about this attitude because it was at odds with the team approach that had been used prior to Gersick's arrival.

Kerrigan became very concerned about Gersick's management style, particularly when he discovered the negative impact her actions had on Sandra Baylor, the charge nurse (see Figure C1-2). A long-time and loyal employee, Baylor was efficient, organized, and the "go-to" person for patient care. Kerrigan knew that in a nursing home, "the devil is in the details," meaning that if details aren't attended to, people immediately notice. For example, a woman visiting her 80-year-old father in the nursing home did not like to see him with one sock up to his knees and the other down around his ankles. Baylor was effective in attending to details, and Kerrigan didn't want to lose her.

Unfortunately, Baylor and Gersick, both strong-willed, did not get along. In March, Baylor complained to Kerrigan that Gersick's management style was very difficult to cope with, and that morale among the staff was low. Two weeks later, Baylor submitted her resignation.

The Situation Worsens

In May 2009, Gersick approached Kerrigan and said she considered it a "slap in the face" that, as the director of nursing, she did not have her own office. She also told him that she had informed the board of directors about the lack of respect accorded managers, and the poor state of interpersonal relations in the nursing home. Kerrigan was very upset after hearing this and felt Gersick's actions reflected badly on him as executive director. He also saw a great irony: While Gersick wanted everyone to observe the chain of command, she had no qualms about violating it to suit her purposes.

Other problems in the nursing home evolved by the summer of 2009. The most obvious was the conflict between the Head of Assisted Care, Karen Hernandez, and the Head of Activities, Pamela Sharp. Hernandez was very opinionated, liked to be in the centre of the action, and continually psychoanalyzed her colleagues. Sharp was a hyper, excitable person who sometimes unwittingly encroached on other people's turf in her enthusiasm to do a good job. For example, if she saw a maintenance worker vacuuming in a wrong way, she would show the person how to do it properly.

By the fall of 2009, the rift between Hernandez and Sharp had grown worse. Hernandez reported to Beck, her supervisor, that Sharp continued to "meddle in other departments." Beck decided to counsel Sharp about her behaviour. To Sharp's dismay, Hernandez, who was not her boss, attended the meeting and made critical comments.

A few weeks later Hernandez, Sharp, and Belinda Velasquez, the head of the dietary department, set up a meeting with Kerrigan to talk about ways of improving the interpersonal climate in the nursing home. Kerrigan told Beck about the meeting, but she decided not to come. At the meeting, three decisions were made:

1. Beck would be required to talk privately with any employees that she felt needed disciplining; Hernandez was not to sit in on any of these meetings.
2. When Sharp and Hernandez had a conflict, they would be expected to go to Beck together and try to resolve it, instead of Hernandez "tattling" on Sharp.
3. Beck would be expected to interact with staff more regularly and not be aloof from the day-to-day activities of her managers.

This meeting seemed to have some positive impact on the overall operations of the nursing home. However, the relationship between Hernandez and Sharp continued to be high-tension, and Kerrigan feared it could become a fight at a moment's notice.

Open Conflict Erupts

Kerrigan's worst fears were soon realized. In October, he discovered that Hernandez' lawyer had sent a letter to Sharp indicating that she would be sued for defamation if she did not stop spreading rumours about Hernandez. Sharp promptly made copies of the letter and gave them to all the staff. In addition, she consulted a lawyer on Last Resort's board of directors and had him send Hernandez a letter threatening to counter-sue for harassment.

All of these threats and counter-threats were apparently too much for Hernandez and Sharp—they both resigned shortly thereafter. Kerrigan was relieved and started thinking about finding replacements. To his dismay, however, he found that Beck had hired her sister to replace Hernandez as the head of the assisted care department. Kerrigan reminded Beck that she had no authority to hire department heads without consulting him first. However, he agreed to keep Beck's sister on as acting head until the upcoming inspection of the nursing home was completed.

Kerrigan also stressed the importance of exercising more control over Gersick. In particular, he was concerned that Gersick's hot temper and her outbursts at staff and managers were damaging morale. When Beck said she did not think the situation was that bad, Kerrigan asked how bad the tension would have to become before she would do something. He became very frustrated when she did not give a definitive answer.

At the management meeting in December, Belinda Velasquez reported that unless the managers started handling conflicts among themselves more effectively, they could not really expect their employees to work well together. She said a rumour was going around that Kerrigan intended to fire both Beck and Gersick. Kerrigan said the rumour was untrue, however, he was tired of listening to Gersick's complaints about people violating the chain of command when she didn't observe it herself. He also noted that Beck, not Gersick, was the NHA, and that Beck had to start doing her job of managing the nursing home or risk losing it. After these comments, the room was very quiet. The managers noticed that the tenor of the meeting was nothing like the good old days.

Questions

1. What problems are evident at the Last Resort Nursing Home?
2. Develop specific suggestions for resolving each of the problems you identified in question 1.

MediaSpark

Doug Lionais, Sherry Finney, and Melissa Cameron

In September of 2001, Mathew Georghiou, the President and CEO of MediaSpark (**http://www.mediaspark.com**) in Sydney, Nova Scotia, finished a phone conversation with IBM Canada. IBM had just informed Georghiou that they were interested in exclusively carrying MediaSpark's new product, GoVenture Entrepreneur (**http://www.goventure.net**) in the Canadian market. Georghiou had been researching possible distribution channels for GoVenture in North America. The phone call with IBM completed Georghiou's research and he now needed to sift through the information and decide how he was going to get his product to market.

Background

Georghiou completed a two year engineering diploma at Cape Breton University (then University College of Cape Breton), before transferring to Dalhousie University in Halifax, Nova Scotia, to complete his Electrical Engineering Degree. After Georghiou's second year at Dalhousie, IBM awarded him a sixteen month internship in Toronto, an offer which he took. In 1991, Georghiou received a national award for innovation during his internship which led IBM to guarantee him a position upon graduation. After graduating in 1993, Georghiou immediately moved back to Toronto to work for IBM. While employed at IBM, Georghiou gained much experience in the engineering field which included programming and computer product manufacturing.

Georghiou had a vision to establish his own business and left IBM in 1994. He moved back to Sydney, Nova Scotia, and with personal savings and financing from Enterprise Cape Breton Corporation (ECBC), he established MediaSpark. The business began in the basement of his home and after only two years, he needed to expand and he relocated his offices downtown. MediaSpark focused on technology and design; the business offered a wide range of services such as multi-media production, Internet development, e-learning, technology consulting, and image and print design.

GoVenture Entrepreneur

In 2000, MediaSpark launched GoVenture Entrepreneur, an educational software program which simulated establishing and running a small business (Exhibit 1). This software created a practical replication of an entrepreneur's business start-up, daily management, and personal activities. Georghiou felt GoVenture Entrepreneur would be a perfect learning tool for any business education class because it provided students the opportunity to gain experience and knowledge without risk. Georghiou described GoVenture Entrepreneur as a "flight simulator for business."

In the GoVenture Entrepreneur simulation, participants establish and manage a small business start-up. The program simulates all aspects of entrepreneurial decision making, including business and personal outcomes. Performance evaluation tools included in the simulation allow the user and/or the instructor to set goals, adjust performance evaluation weightings and measure outcomes in terms of business success and personal work-life balance. MediaSpark designed the product to be as flexible as possible for teachers.

MediaSpark identified the broader market for GoVenture Entrepreneur as middle school to adult; however, the primary target was high school classes. Georghiou saw GoVenture Entrepreneur as enhancing the existing curriculum.

MediaSpark positioned it for use in business, marketing, and entrepreneurship courses. Georghiou identified three general ways of using GoVenture Entrepreneurship in the classroom. First, educators could use GoVenture Entrepreneurship as an introduction to a course to demonstrate the purpose of learning the concepts in the course. Second, they could use it to end a course as a capstone module to apply the lessons of the course. Third, educators could use it throughout a course to complement ongoing lessons.

To serve the educational market, MediaSpark developed a number of support materials for GoVenture Entrepreneurship. For example, institutions that purchased software licenses received an "Experiencing Entrepreneurship" text. MediaSpark developed this book as an easy to use summary of the subject that educators could use either as a textbook or as a complement to existing textbooks. MediaSpark's educational bundle also included an instructor's manual, lesson plans focusing on different topics, and a test bank.

The Market

Georghiou divided the educational publishing industry between the K–12 market and the university market. Georghiou's target market fell in the K–12 category. Georghiou felt the market in the United States was much larger than the Canadian market, with more growth in the educational software sector. There were 90 000 to 100 000 elementary and secondary schools in the United States while there were only 16 500 in Canada, and Canada's K–12 enrolment

Exhibit 1 MediaSpark GoVenture Entrepreneur Website

GoVenture Entrepreneur is a highly visual and realistic business simulation that recreates the day-to-day experiences involved in starting and running a small business.

Like a flight simulator for small business, Entrepreneur engages you in realistic situations and problems. Take your own test flights, at your own speed. Within the world of Entrepreneur, the decisions and the consequences are highly realistic. So virtual entrepreneurs rapidly gain the authentic wisdom that normally only comes from on-the-job experience.

The GoVenture Experience

- **Experience** what it is like to manage numerous business and personal tasks.
- **Make** necessary compromises to reach both business and personal success.
- **Learn** what you need to know to start a business in minutes, not months.

This simulation makes learning about being an entrepreneur fun. You can run the simulation for as long as you want. You can dive in using the Quick Start feature or take the time to go through the Personal and Business Profiles to select and start a business. You can conduct business, get advice, attend training seminars, and even close or sell your company. At any point, you may save your simulation and return to it later.

There is no penalty for failure, so if your first business doesn't succeed, try another. You can even control how fast the simulation time clock runs!

You can check your own personal financial status or your company's at any time. Review the business' financial statements and charts on recent operations. If you're doing well, you can pay yourself a bonus and buy one of those items on your wish list.

Watch out for random events—you could become injured and have to stay home for a while. Or if you forget your spouse's birthday your stress level may go up. If your stress level is too high, you may have to take some time off from the company. Can your employees run it without you?

The simulation immerses you in a life-like world of entrepreneurship and small business—a world where you still have to remember to pay your bills and get enough sleep.

It is an engaging experience, which makes learning fun, as you build an understanding of what it is like to be an entrepreneur and to meet the challenges of starting and running a small business.

The Entrepreneur CD-ROM simulation can be used in schools, in self-paced home or work study, in life-long learning programs, and in corporate training initiatives for employees or customers. Never before has it been so easy to experience the life of an entrepreneur.

was 5.3 million students, approximately one-tenth the size of the United States. According to market studies that Georghiou had reviewed, U.S. schools spent $5.50 per student on software and the market for CD-ROMs in schools approximated US$300 million. Georghiou hoped to generate significant sales in both the Canadian and the U.S. market, but the focus was on the U.S. market because it was much larger than the Canadian market and it had greater access to funding.

Marketing and Pricing Strategy

Georghiou was concerned about how to sell and distribute the product. The education market was accustomed to purchasing texts rather than multimedia products. Whereas a catalogue description can describe a text fairly well, Georghiou felt that educators would need to experience GoVenture Entrepreneur before considering it for use in the classroom. Georghiou felt that it would be difficult to convince educators of the value of his product as either a text complement or as a text replacement without a hands-on trial. Georghiou commented, "To sell the product, people need to see it; they need to try it out for themselves." Thus, he was only interested in marketing channels which placed the product in educators' hands for a decision or at least provided an opportunity to demonstrate the product in action.

The price of GoVenture Entrepreneur varied depending on the user and country. Georghiou identified six user groups: individuals, educational K–12, educational post-secondary, home school, non-profit or government, and all others. He wanted his initial target market to be the educational K–12 and offered this segment a 50% price reduction for a limited time in an effort to break into the market. The regular price varied per package depending on the quantity purchased (Exhibit 2). The cost of goods sold was generally 5% to 10% of the suggested retail price.

Exhibit 2 MediaSpark GoVenture Entrepreneur Pricing

GOVENTURE ENTREPRENEUR PRODUCT PRICE

	1 SEAT*	5 SEAT*	30 Seat*	SITE**
GoVenture Entrepreneur Software License–Educational (USD)	$199	$349	$749	$1199
GoVenture Entrepreneur Software License–Educational (CAD)	$199	$499	NA	$1499

Software License Includes:

- License for a specified number of concurrent user(s). See Software License Descriptions below for important information.
- 1 CD-ROM for Windows (GoVenture Entrepreneur is also compatible with Macintosh). Program can be copied from CD to computer hard drives or network drive.
- User Guide.
- Performance Reports (built into the software).
- FREE Experiencing Book (text on Entrepreneurship).
- FREE Education Bundle (including instructor guide, lesson plans and test bank).
- FREE Value Option for 1 Year (includes additional customer service support).

*__SEAT License:__ This license allows for many people to use the software at the same organization (or school) at one physical address location. The number of seats purchased determines how many computers may run the software concurrently (at the same time). For example, a 5-Seat License allows for the software to be run on up to 5 computers at the same time. In this example, the software may be installed on a network, or installed on more than 5 computers, but the software may not be run on more than 5 computers concurrently. Individual Seats cannot be shared amongst different organizations (or schools).

**__SITE License:__ This license allows for use of the software on all your organization's (or school's) computers at one physical address location at any time. There are no limits on how many computers may run the software concurrently—as long as they are on the same site (one physical address location). A SITE License cannot be shared amongst different organizations.

Distribution Channels

Georghiou identified two basic distribution alternatives for GoVenture Entrepreneur: direct or indirect. Indirect distribution channels would include catalogue companies, textbook publishers, or software publishers. If Georghiou was to sell directly, MediaSpark would have to handle the full advertising and distributing duties.

Educational product catalogue companies sold thousands of products to educational institutions through published or on-line catalogues. The larger publishers would send out educational catalogues to most schools in North America, though Georghiou questioned how many actually got to teachers he wished to reach. Catalogue companies would typically only list a product in exchange for an exclusive deal. Thus, Georghiou would not be able to sell GoVenture Entrepreneur in the same region through any other channel. Georghiou had researched the reseller discount for all possible distribution channels. The reseller discount was the percentage of the final price that the reselling company retained. For catalogue companies, Georghiou reported the reseller discount to be between 20% and 35%.

Georghiou's second indirect option, textbook publishers, supplied most schools with their core text books. Textbook publishers differed from catalogue companies as they employed a sales force as well as a published catalogue of products. Sales representatives would travel to schools and trade shows to present the product catalogue, and potential purchasers would have a better chance of seeing a demonstration of the product. Text publishers, however, would also require an exclusive deal to carry a product and would demand a reseller discount of 40%–60%.

Georghiou had identified two main text publishers: Glencoe McGraw-Hill and Southwestern. Georghiou knew that Glencoe was already carrying a competing product: Virtual Business (**http://www.knowledgematters.com**). Georghiou had heard that Southwestern had turned down his competitor's product, but thought it would likely want to pick up a competing product since Glencoe started carrying Virtual Business. Georghiou identified Southwestern as the leading business education provider to the K–12, higher education, and professional markets in the United States. It did not, however, distribute in Canada. Its main focus was text books; however, it had distributed some interactive software in keyboarding, marketing, management, and accounting. Glencoe also focused on text books with a small amount of software titles (like Virtual Business).

Because of the technological nature of his product, Georghiou also considered software distribution companies as a third indirect distribution channel. A software distributor could give Georghiou's product more profile when compared to being "lost in the thousands of traditional text products in a publisher's catalogue." Again, software distributors would require an exclusive deal to carry a product. Georghiou found that the software distribution market was highly fragmented. There were no companies that operated in both the Canadian and the U.S. markets. Furthermore, in the United States, there were very few national distributors; many were small companies who would carry other firms' products as well as their own. The reseller discount for software distributors was comparable to that of text publishers at 40% to 60%.

One option within the United States was to distribute through a non-profit company called MarkED, a consortium of 40 state education departments and other organizations. As an industry-run organization, MarkED would lend credibility to the products it supported. MarkED sold products through a catalogue it distributed to its constituent organizations. However, it did not have a sales force to complement the catalogue and Georghiou could not be sure that the catalogue would reach the right teachers.

In Canada, the software distribution choices were much different. The most prominent distributor was IBM which operated a software distribution division in Canada.[1] Established in 1880, IBM was the world's largest and most recognizable information technology company. IBM Canada had its own sales force which was already distributing to schools. Since 1995, IBM invested $75 million in its Reinventing Education program which it established to break down barriers to academic achievement. IBM estimated that this program would reach 100 000 teachers and 10 million students in 10 countries by the end of 2004. IBM provided research and technical expertise, as well as equipment and cash contributions, to improve teaching and learning. The educational software currently available to the K–12 market focused on reading, language arts, mathematics, and science. In addition to this, IBM supplied many schools with the interface and internet software for their computers, as well as interactive white boards.

Georghiou felt that IBM was a good candidate because it was technology based, had brand recognition, and was already distributing to schools. IBM had proposed a two-year exclusive deal with MediaSpark to distribute to the K–12 educational market. Georghiou's only reservation was that he felt IBM may focus its attention on its hardware sales rather than software.

Finally, Georghiou could also consider an in-house direct distribution channel. MediaSpark currently employed only one marketing/sales person. Georghiou estimated that to effectively market GoVenture, he would have to hire 5 to 10 sales representatives and an additional 2 to 3 marketing people located in various areas throughout Canada and the United States. The majority of his sales would originate from tradeshows, events, and inside sales calls. Georghiou expected that MediaSpark would have to appear at over ten trade shows in the United States and at least two in Canada. MediaSpark's sales team would have to be responsible for inside sales calls, email campaigns, direct mail, CD demos, seminars, public speaking, and catalogue sales. Georghiou estimated that if MediaSpark did market and sell GoVenture independently, he would not be able to hire all the sales representatives he required and would have to survive with only one or two marketing/sales people. In such a situation, Georghiou himself would likely attend a number of tradeshows and make sales trips throughout the year. The advantage of selling in-house was that MediaSpark would make a much higher margin on each unit sold as there would be no reseller discount. However, tradeshows were expensive and the need to sell GoVenture Entrepreneur may distract MediaSpark from new product development.

The Decision

Georghiou struggled with the distribution decision. He first had to decide whether or not to go with a third party distributor and if he did, which one or ones to go with. Georghiou was most worried about the exclusivity required by distributors. In essence, if Georghiou went with a distributor, he was putting all his eggs in one basket; he had to have absolute confidence in the distributor he chose. If the distributor did not succeed in selling the product, Georghiou would have no other avenues to make a sale. Georghiou worried that his product would be one product among many in any distributor's product line and that they may put more focus on other products. The lack of technology knowledge of some of the potential distributors was

[1] IBM also sold software in the United States but it was in the midst of changing its strategy and moving towards only carrying a very small number of products. Because it was undergoing some changes, MediaSpark saw no real opportunity to work with them.

another worry. As Georghiou explained, "Success depended on leveraging a distributor's brand awareness and market reach to sell more units than we can on our own."

Ivey
Richard Ivey School of Business
The University of Western Ontario

SECURITY BREACH AT TJX[1]

Introduction

"The company collected too much personal information, kept it too long and relied on weak encryption technology to protect it — putting the privacy of millions of its customers at risk."

—*Jennifer Stoddart,*
Privacy Commissioner, Government of Canada,
on September, 26, 2007, in Montreal[2]

November 12, 2007, was the first day for Owen Richel as the chief security officer at the Framingham, Massachusetts, U.S., headquarters of The TJX Companies Inc. (TJX). As he was driving to work, Richel had mixed feelings. He was excited about his new role — but also apprehensive. Up before dawn, he had been reviewing some of the statements he had highlighted in the report of the Privacy Commissioner of the Government of Canada, including Stoddart's comment, above, which had been widely reported. These statements pertained to gaps in the company's systems security. The times ahead, he knew, would be troubled.

When Richel accepted the offer from TJX two months earlier, he'd been sure he was making a smart career move. As chief information officer (CIO) of a small Canadian retailer, Richel was aware of TJX as a mega retailer and a market leader in a niche category in North America. He was also aware that the company had been hit by hackers in December 2006. The management had downplayed the attack during the job interview, at which Richel could not glean any information beyond what was available in the public domain. Richel had been moved to sign with the company because the panel had expressed confidence in his background in the retail industry and his ability to manage information technology (IT) security. The position was also being newly created for him. Richel was impressed. As far as hacking was concerned, he knew from experience that all retailers, large and small, were vulnerable to attacks and that one of the best safeguards was top-level commitment to IT security.

As he started tracking the development in detail during the interim period, Richel realized the scale of intrusion had escalated. While TJX had said that the data of about 46 million credit and debit cardholders had been affected, a class action suit filed by interested financial institutions, in late October 2007, had placed the number at about 94 million. Calling it the largest breach of personal data ever reported in the history of IT security, *The Boston*

R. Chandrasekhar wrote this case under the supervision of Professor Nicole Haggerty solely to provide material for class discussion. The authors do not intend to illustrate either effective or ineffective handling of a managerial situation. The authors may have disguised certain names and other identifying information to protect confidentiality.

Globe quoted a Gartner Inc. professional as saying, "It is the biggest card heist ever. It has done considerable damage."[3] The lawsuits by affected customers and financial institutions were moving forward quickly. The Federal Bureau of Investigation (FBI) of the U.S. government was already part of the company's internal investigation.

Now, sitting in his car in traffic, minutes away from starting his position at TJX, Richel was mulling over the issues, several new to him, which he would have to deal with simultaneously and quickly.

Company Background

TJX was the largest apparel and home fashions retailer in the United States in the off-price segment. TJX ranked 138th in the Fortune 500 rankings for 2006. With US$17.4 billion in sales for the year ending January 2007, the company was more than triple the size of Ross Stores Inc., its closest competitor.

Founded in 1976, TJX operated eight independent businesses under a common umbrella—T.J. Maxx, Marshalls, HomeGoods, A.J. Wright and Bob's Stores in the United States; Winners and HomeSense in Canada; and T.K. Maxx in Europe. The group had over 2,400 stores, and about 125,000 associates.

As an off-price retailer, TJX occupied the space between deep discounters selling unbranded goods at low prices and department or specialty stores selling branded goods at premium prices. TJX sold branded apparel and home fashions at prices between 20 and 70 per cent lower than department or specialty stores. It bought merchandise directly from manufacturers at wholesale prices throughout the year, in contrast to department or specialty stores, whose buying was driven by current trends and was seasonal in nature. It also acquired merchandise from department and specialty stores themselves, who were often stuck with excess goods every season as a result of late order cancellations, missed production deadlines and scheduling changes.

Operational efficiency, vendor relationships and scale were crucial to an off-price store, whereas fashion was the most important variable for department and specialty stores. For off-price stores, the quality of internal information systems was critical to maintaining margins, among the lowest in retail, and to staying competitive. IT systems helped large retailers like TJX connect people, places and information all along the value chain. They enabled rapid delivery of data, facilitating quick decisions at different levels. Vendors, buyers, merchandisers, stores associates, customers and financial institutions were inter-connected through IT networks, thereby boosting the retailer's productivity (throughput of product from manufacturing through sales). In-store technologies (such as kiosks and hand-held price/inventory barcode scanners) helped retailers enhance customer service and differentiate their stores from competitors. Many retailers invested in customer relationship management (CRM) technologies to increase revenues by targeting the most profitable customers.

TJX had witnessed a change of guard at the top level of management in the fall of 2005. A focus on "profitable sales growth" had led to a rebound in financial results for the year ending January 2007. In a business in which margins were low, net income as percentage of sales had moved up (see Exhibit 1).

The Computer Intrusion[4]

It was on December 18, 2006, that the company learned of hacking (see Appendix 1 for a glossary of terms used in computer intrusion and detection investigations). The presence of suspicious software, altered computer files and mixed-up data were among the first evidence of the intrusion. Involving the segment of the computer network handling payment cards (both credit cards and debit cards), cheques, and merchandise return transactions for customers, it seemed to affect all the eight businesses of the company and all the stores in the United States, Puerto Rico, Canada and the United Kingdom. The company quickly started an internal investigation and called in security consultants—General Dynamics Corporation and International Business Machines (IBM) Corporation—the next day. The latter confirmed, on December 21, that the company's computer systems had been "intruded upon" and that the intruder was still on the systems. While planning to contain the intrusion and protect customer data, the company notified law enforcement officials. The U.S. Secret Service suggested that disclosure of intrusion might impede an ongoing criminal investigation and that TJX should therefore maintain confidentiality till it was advised by the Secret Service to the contrary. The company was only allowed to notify contracting banks, credit and debit card companies and cheque-processing companies of the intrusion.

On February 21, 2007, TJX made a public announcement of the timing and scope of the intrusion. It said that its computer systems were first accessed by an unauthorized intruder in July 2005, on subsequent dates in 2005 and again from mid-May 2006 to mid-January 2007. It stated that no customer data had been stolen after December 18, 2006. The company said that in trying to identify the nature of data that was stolen by the intruder, TJX had faced three hurdles. First, before it had discovered the intrusion it had deleted, in the ordinary course of business, the contents of many files that had been stolen. The files pertained to records going back as far as 2002. Second, the technology used by the intruder had made it impossible for TJX to determine the contents of most of the files stolen in 2006. Third, TJX believed some data was stolen during the payment card approval process. Thus, it was not able to precisely identify the nature of all of the data that was vulnerable to theft.[5]

The company said:

> We do not believe that customer personal identification numbers (PINs) were compromised, because, before storage on the Framingham system, they are separately encrypted in U.S., Puerto Rican and Canadian stores at the PIN pad, and because we do not store PINs on the Watford system.

The "Framingham system" processed and stored information pertaining to debit and credit card, cheque and unreceipted merchandise-return transactions for customers of T.J. Maxx, Marshalls, HomeGoods and A.J. Wright stores in the United States and Puerto Rico, and of Winners and HomeSense stores in Canada. The "Watford system" processed and stored information related to payment card transactions at T.K. Maxx in the United Kingdom and Ireland.

Until December 2006, when the intrusion was discovered, TJX was storing customer personal information on its Framingham system. The information, received from its stores in the United States, Puerto Rico and Canada, pertained to returns of merchandise without receipts and some cheque transactions. The personal information consisted of driver's license numbers and identification (ID) numbers (such as military and state ID, in some cases including social security numbers), together with names and addresses of the customers who had returned goods. Since April 7, 2004, the practice was to encrypt the information before it was stored. Actual characters were substituted by encryption, using an encryption algorithm provided by the software vendor.

TJX assured its payment card customers that their names and addresses were not included with the payment card data believed stolen for any period, because TJX did not process or store that information on either the Framingham or the Watford system in connection with payment card transactions. It also assured its customers that by April 3, 2006, the Framingham system was masking payment card PINs and some portions of cheque transaction information. For transactions after April 7, 2004, the Framingham system was encrypting all payment card and cheque transaction information. With respect to the Watford system, masking and encryption practices had been implemented at various points in time for various portions of the payment card data.

Subsequent investigations revealed that the data had been picked up by a group of East European residents (specializing in collecting stolen credit card numbers), which in turn passed them on to a group in Florida. Both the groups were part of a diversified fraud ring whose activities included manufacturing "white plastic," a plain card with a properly encoded magnetic stripe. Although it could not be used in personal encounters with retail clerks, the white plastic could be swiped, without risk of detection, during self-checkouts (at gas stations and some big-box stores). The Florida group, under observation by the Secret Service, also specialized in manufacturing bogus credit cards complete with embossing, logos, holograms and properly encoded magnetic strips. The group was said to have applied new magnetic strips containing the stolen data to generate bogus cards. Having done so, it resorted to a tactic common among fraudsters: it used the bogus credit cards to purchase gift cards (usually up to $400, before additional identification was required) and then cashed the gift cards at the stores later. The gift card float technique was attractive to fraudsters because it bought them time. When a credit card was stolen and detected by the victim, it was only a matter of hours before the card was invalidated and its spending power had expired–an outcome which the purchase of gift cards circumvented.

How Did It Happen?

Richel learned through his preparatory research that there was a widely held view among IT security professionals that TJX systems had been intruded upon at multiple points of attack. This theory could partly account for the enormity of the intrusion, which affected millions of people. These multiple points included encryption, wireless attack, USB drives at in-store kiosks, processing logs and compliance and auditing practices. Though TJX identified encryption as a particular vulnerability, Richel felt he would need to fully investigate the other reports of multiple security vulnerabilities as a first priority in his new role.

Encryption

TJX had made the following announcement of how, it thought, the intrusion had occurred.

> Despite our masking and encryption practices on our Framingham system in 2006, the technology utilized in the Computer Intrusion during 2006 could have enabled the Intruder to steal payment card data from our Framingham system during the payment card issuer's approval process, in which data is transmitted to payment card issuers without encryption. Further, we believe that the Intruder had access to the decryption tool for the encryption software utilized by TJX.[6]

Widely used in the retail industry to protect credit card information in e-commerce transactions, encryption was a process of scrambling information so as to make it unintelligible until it was unscrambled by the intended recipient. Since credit cards could not be processed when their numbers were encrypted (or scrambled), a smart crook could seek a way to get the data during that window of time when it was in a state of being "in the clear"—that is, when it was decrypted (or unscrambled)—for less than a second. Additionally, as TJX found out, the intruders had the decryption key for the encryption software (WEP) that was in use at TJX.[7]

While TJX's view of how the attack occurred seemed legitimate, Richel felt there could be other points of entry for the computer intrusion.

Wireless Attack

The *Wall Street Journal*[8] was among the first to suggest that the TJX break-in started in July 2005 with a wireless hack of a Marshalls store in St. Paul, Minnesota. Said the report:

> The thieves pointed a telescope-shaped antenna toward the store and used a laptop computer to decode data streaming through the air between hand-held price-checking devices, cash registers [point-of-sale, presumably] and the store's computers. That helped them hack into the central database of Marshalls' parent, TJX Cos. in Framingham, Mass., to repeatedly purloin information about customers.

Wireless was a popular means of attacking retail chains. "By focusing on those little handheld (price check) guns and their interactions with the database controller, you can capture IP addresses. That's your gateway," the *Journal* quoted an auditor as saying. It also reported that the attackers performed "most of their break-ins during peak sales periods to capture lots of data and used that data to crack the encryption code." It added:

> They digitally eavesdropped on employees logging into TJX's central database in Framingham and stole one or more user names and passwords. With that information, they set up their own accounts in the TJX system and collected transaction data including credit-card numbers into about 100 large files for their own access. They were able to go into the TJX system remotely from any computer on the Internet. They were so confident of being undetected that they left encrypted messages to each other on the company's network, to tell one another which files had already been copied and avoid duplicating work.

USB Drives at In-store Kiosks

An *InformationWeek* story suggested that the data breach had begun at TJX with in-store kiosks as entry points. "The people who started the breach opened up the back of those terminals and used USB drives to load software onto those terminals," said the story.

> The USB drives contained a utility program that let the intruder or intruders take control of these computer kiosks and turn them into remote terminals that connected into TJX's networks. The firewalls on TJX's main network weren't set to defend against traffic coming from the kiosks. Typically, the USB drives in the computer kiosks are used to plug in mice or printers.[9]

Processing Logs

In its filings before the U.S. Securities and Exchange Commission, TJX had put the number of cards at risk at 46 million. But in their filings in the courts, the banks had placed the number at 94 million.[10] The discrepancy suggested that TJX did not have the log data needed to do a forensic analysis. Such logs could generally provide information about files on the system—when they had been added, changed, accessed, the format of contents and so on.

Compliance Practices

The Payment Card Industry Data Security Standards (PCI DSS) were a strong security blueprint for retailers (see Exhibit 2). Court documents showed that TJX had not met nine of the dozen requirements covering encryption, access controls and firewalls.

Auditing Practices

Under PCI DSS, an approved auditor had to conduct an annual on-site audit and quarterly network scans on what were called Level 1 businesses, those that processed over six million credit card transactions per year. Level 2 and 3 companies—those that processed between 20,000 and six million credit card transactions per year—had to fill out an annual self-assessment questionnaire

EXHIBIT 1 The TJX Companies, Inc.—Consolidated Statement of Income

	(Years ending January 31, in thousands of US$)					
	2007		2006		2005	
	Amount	%	Amount	%	Amount	%
Net sales	17,404,637	100.0	15,955,943	100.0	14,860,746	100.0
Cost of sales	13,213,70	75.9	12,214,671	76.5	11,357,391	76.4
Selling, general & administration costs	2,928,520	16.8	2,703,271	16.9	2,487,804	16.7
Interest cost	15,566	0.1	29,632	0.2	25,757	0.2
Income from continuing operations	1,246,848	7.2	1,008,369	6.3	989,794	6.6

Source: Company annual reports

EXHIBIT 2 Payment Card Industry (PCI) Data Security Standards

Control Objectives	Requirements
1. Build and Maintain a Secure Network	■ Install and maintain a firewall configuration to protect cardholder data ■ Do not use vendor-supplied defaults for system passwords and other security parameters
2. Protect Cardholder Data	■ Protect stored cardholder data ■ Encrypt transmission of cardholder data across open, public networks
3. Maintain a Vulnerability Management Program	■ Use and regularly update anti-virus software ■ Develop and maintain secure systems and applications
4. Implement Strong Access Control Measures	■ Restrict access to cardholder data by business need-to-know ■ Assign a unique ID to each person with computer access ■ Restrict physical access to cardholder data
5. Regularly Monitor and Test Networks	■ Track and monitor all access to network resources and cardholder data ■ Regularly test security systems and processes
6. Maintain an Information Security Policy	■ Maintain a policy that addresses information security

Source: https://www.pcisecuritystandards.org.

and have an approved vendor conduct quarterly network scans. TJX had passed a PCI DSS check-up. The auditors had not noticed three key problems with TJX systems—the absence of network monitoring, the absence of logs and the presence of unencrypted data stored on the system. They had also not asked why TJX had retained customer data years after it should have been purged. Some of the stolen information was from transactions concluded as long ago as 2002.

The Summer of Discontent

During the summer of 2007, a number of class actions had been filed against TJX in state and federal courts in Alabama, California, Massachusetts and Puerto Rico, and in provincial Canadian courts in Alberta, British Columbia, Manitoba, Ontario, Quebec and Saskatchewan, on behalf of customers whose transaction data were allegedly compromised by the computer intrusion. An action had also been filed against TJX in federal court in Massachusetts, putatively on behalf of all financial institutions who issued credit and debit cards used at TJX stores during the period of the security breach. The actions asserted claims for negligence and related common-law and/or statutory causes of action stemming from the intrusion, and sought various forms of relief including damages, related injunctive or equitable remedies, multiple or punitive damages and attorney's fees. A number of government agencies were also conducting investigations as to whether TJX had violated laws regarding consumer protection.

Recent Developments

By August 2007, TJX had booked a cost of US$168 million for the data breach it had announced in February — $118 million in after-tax costs taken in the most recent quarter and $21 million projected as a possible hit for 2008 on top of the $29 million already reported in prior quarters. *The Boston Globe* had quoted a TJX official as saying that the US$118 million quarterly after-tax figure was about $196 million pretax, and that the $21 million for 2008 was about $35 million pretax.

On September 21, 2007, the company had entered into a settlement agreement, subject to court approvals, in regard to customer class actions. As per the agreement, customers who had returned merchandise without a receipt and to whom TJX had sent letters reporting that their driver's license or other identification information may have been compromised, were offered three years of credit monitoring, along with identity theft insurance coverage paid for by TJX. The company would also reimburse these customers for the documented cost of driver's license replacements. The company was to offer vouchers to any customers who showed they shopped at TJX stores during the relevant periods and who had incurred certain costs as a result of the intrusion. TJX would also organize a one-time, three-day customer appreciation special event, in which prices would be reduced by 15 per cent.

November 12, 2007

As the TJX headquarters sign came into view, Richel felt renewed determination to see the blossoming crisis at TJX as an opportunity. He would use his business leadership skills, combined with his abilities to work with the IT organization, to stay on top of the situation. He saw his priorities as falling into two distinct areas—short-term and long-term. The short-term priority was to understand the failure points and tighten and improve systems security at TJX. In the long term, Richel had to work on minimizing risks, so that an intrusion would not happen again. Most importantly, he needed to secure management buy-in to the fact that IT security was a business issue and not a technology issue.

The first visitor he had at his office that day was Vincent George, who introduced himself as the company's manager of customer service. "Welcome to the party," he said, giving him a copy of a letter he had received in the mail the previous day (see Appendix 2); "I will catch up with you later in the day."

Appendix 1

Glossary of Terms Used in Security and Intrusion Detection

Access Control: A mechanism that ensures that resources are only granted to those users entitled to them.

Activity Monitors: They prevent virus infection by monitoring the system for malicious activity and blocking that activity when possible.

Advanced Encryption Standard (AES): An encryption standard meant to specify an unclassified, publicly disclosed, symmetric encryption algorithm.

Algorithm: A finite set of step-by-step instructions for a problem-solving or computation procedure, especially one that can be implemented by a computer.

Asymmetric Cryptography: A modern branch of cryptography in which the algorithms employ a pair of keys (a public key and a private key) and use a different component of the pair for different steps of the algorithm.

Brute Force: A form of attack involving an exhaustive procedure trying all possibilities, one by one.

Business Continuity Plan (BCP): The plan for emergency response, backup operations and post-disaster recovery steps ensuring the availability of critical resources and facilitating continuity of operations in an emergency situation.

Covert Channels: Means by which information can be communicated between two parties in a covert fashion using normal system operations.

Data Encryption Standard (DES): A widely used method of data encryption using a private (secret) key. There are 72 quadrillion possible encryption keys that can be used. For each given message, the key is chosen at random from among this enormous number of keys. As with other private key cryptographic methods, both the sender and the receiver must know and use the same private key.

Day Zero: The day a new vulnerability is made known.

Decryption: Process of transforming an encrypted message into its original plaintext.

Defacement: The method of modifying the content of a website in such a way that it becomes vandalized, embarrassing to the website owner.

Defense In-Depth: Usage of multiple layers of security to guard against failure of a single security component.

Demilitarized Zone (DMZ): Network area that sits between an organization's internal network and an external network, usually the Internet.

Dictionary Attack: An attack that tries all of the phrases or words in a dictionary, trying to crack a password or key. A dictionary attack uses a predefined list of words, unlike a brute force attack, which tries all possible combinations.

Disaster Recovery Plan (DRP): The process of recovering IT systems in the event of a disaster.

Due Diligence: A protection plan that organizations must develop and deploy to prevent fraud and abuse.

Dumpster Diving: Obtaining passwords and corporate directories by searching through discarded media.

Encapsulation: Inclusion of one data structure within another to hide it for the time being.

Encryption: Transformation of data (called "plain text") into a form (called "cipher text") that conceals the data's original meaning to prevent it from being known or used.

Escrow Passwords: Passwords written down and stored in a secure location (like a safe) for use by emergency personnel when privileged personnel are unavailable.

Firewall: A logical or physical discontinuity in a network to prevent unauthorized access to data.

Flooding: An attack causing a systems failure by providing more input than the entity can process properly.

Fragmentation: The process of storing a data file in several "chunks" or fragments rather than in a single contiguous sequence of bits in one place on the storage medium.

Hardening: Process of identifying and fixing vulnerabilities on a system.

Hybrid Encryption: An application of cryptography combining two or more encryption algorithms.

One-Way Encryption: Irreversible transformation of plaintext to cipher text, such that the plaintext cannot be recovered from the cipher text even if the cryptographic key is known.

Scavenging: Searching through data residue in a system to gain unauthorized knowledge of sensitive data.

Shadow Password File: A system file in which encryption user passwords are stored so that they are not available to people who try to break into the system.

Spoof Attempt: An unauthorized user trying to gain access to a system by posing as an authorized user.

Steganography: Method of hiding the existence of a message or other data. This is different from cryptography, which hides the meaning of a message but does not hide the message itself. An example of a steganographic method is "invisible" ink.

Symmetric Cryptography: A branch of cryptography involving algorithms that use the same key for two different steps of the algorithm (such as encryption and decryption, or signature creation and signature verification).

Virus: A hidden, self-replicating section of computer software that propagates by inserting a copy of itself into and becoming part of another program.

Wireless Application Protocol: A specification for a set of communication protocols to standardize the way that wireless devices, such as cellular telephones and radio transceivers, can be used for Internet access.

Wireless Equivalent Privacy: A security protocol for wireless local area networks.

Source: http://www.sans.org/resources/glossary referenced January 30, 2008.

Appendix 2

Letter from a Customer

November 08, 2007

Mr Vincent George
Customer Service Manager
The TJX Companies Inc
Framingham, Massachusetts, US

Dear Mr George:

I have been a loyal shopper at Winners and HomeSense for a long time so I was deeply shocked when I heard about the computer problems which put my personal information at risk. In fact, I have stopped shopping at both stores because of the losses I have personally suffered. Let me explain.

December 05, 2006 was a horrible day for me. That was the day when I went into my bank to withdraw cash for holiday shopping and was surprised when the teller said that there was no balance in my checking account. He then turned the screen towards me and I noticed five consecutive ATM withdrawals, during the preceding six days, of $1,000 each. I knew I had not made these withdrawals because since my monthly pay arrived in late November, I had been really busy at work and basically didn't do anything other than work and go home to sleep. But, the teller and then the bank manager were categorical that I could not lodge a claim because ATM transactions were not covered by the bank's liability policy.

The next day, I faced a double whammy when I received the credit card statement for the previous month by mail. The statement showed a series of ten purchases of US $400 each, spread over a week, at a well known big box store. I had never shopped in US currency while in Toronto. I immediately called up the credit card company. The call center representative told me that he would trigger an investigation right away, assuring me that I would be fully covered for all unauthorized transactions on which my valid signature could not be found.

So after two weeks of scrambling to cover mortgage and bill payments and worrying about a huge increase in my credit card debt, I got a call from the credit card company to say that $4,000 was being returned to my account because none of the ten signatures matched mine for the gift cards that had been purchased. The company offered to cancel my card and re-issue a new one, which I'm still leery of using for fear this will happen again.

I had given up on the loss of $5,000 on my debit card till I saw a newspaper report on February 22, 2007 about your public disclosure on a hit on your computer systems. The report said that the segment of computer network hacked at TJX included "merchandise return" transactions. It was then that I recalled that I had returned two items I had purchased at your store in Toronto a few months ago – in early November 2006. One return transaction pertained to my debit card and the other to my credit card. I had to produce a lot of identification at the time of return, as required, since I could not locate the receipts. I am absolutely certain that YOUR organization is responsible for the financial loss I've suffered. I expect full compensation. If you are an honorable organization you'll take care of my concerns swiftly–otherwise, I'll see you in court.

Mary Smith

Endnotes

[1] This case has been written on the basis of published sources only. Consequently, the interpretation and perspectives presented in this case are not necessarily those of TJX Companies Inc. or any of its employees. Individuals represented in the case are fictional but represent accurate portrayals of decision-makers and customers typically involved in such situations.

[2] Quoted in Mark Jewell, "Encryption Faulted in TJX Hacking," USA Today, September 27, 2007, available online at **http://www.usatoday.com/tech/news/computersecurity/infotheft/2007-09-26-tjx-encryption-breach_N.htm**, accessed November 6, 2007.

[3] Jenn Abelson, "Breach of Data at TJX Is Called the Biggest Ever," The Boston Globe, March 29, 2007.

[4] 10-K Filings, March 28, 2007, **www.tjx.com/investorinformation/SECfilings/10-K/03/28/2007**.

[5] Frequently Asked Questions page, on company website, available at **http://www.tjx.com/tjx_faq.html**, accessed February 13, 2008.

[6] 10-K Filings, March 28, 2007, **www.tjx.com/investorinformation/SECfilings/10-K/03/28/2007.**

[7] WEP is short for wireless equivalent privacy, which is an encryption algorithm for wireless data. Information about cracking WEP is widely available online via simple Google searches.

[8] Joseph Pereira, "How Credit-Card Data Went Out Wireless Door," Wall Street Journal, May 4, 2007, available online at **http://online.wsj.com/article/SB117824446226991797.html**, accessed November 5, 2007.

[9] Larry Greenemeier, "The TJX Effect," InformationWeek, online edition August 11, 2007, at **http://www.informationweek.com/security/showArticle.jhtml?articleID=201400171&cid=RSSfeed_Tech**, accessed November 5, 2007.

[10] Jaikumar Vijayan, "Court Filing Doubles Scope of TJX Data Breach," Computer World, October 25, 2007.

Notes, Sources, and Credits

Reference Notes

Chapter 1

1. "Canada's 500 Largest Corporations," *Financial Post Magazine*, June 2009, 42–43.

2. See Robert A. Collinge and Ronald M. Ayers, *Economics by Design: Principles and Issues*, 2nd ed. (Upper Saddle River, NJ: Prentice Hall, 2000), 41–42; Michael J. Mandel, "The New Economy," *Business Week*, January 31, 2000, 73–77.

3. Karl E. Case and Ray C. Fair, *Principles of Economics*, 6th ed. (Upper Saddle River, NJ: Prentice Hall, 2003), 224–225.

4. Andres Oppenheimer, "Latin America Is Skeptical," *The Orlando Sentinel*, February 20, 2006, A19.

5. James Kynge, "Private Firms' Growth in China Striking: Report," *National Post*, May 11, 2000, C14.

6. Richard I. Kirkland, Jr., "The Death of Socialism," *Fortune*, January 4, 1988, 64–72.

7. See Karl E. Case and Ray C. Fair, *Principles of Economics*, 5th ed. (Upper Saddle River, NJ: Prentice Hall, 1999), 69–74; Robert A. Collinge and Ronald M. Ayers, *Economics by Design: Principles and Issues*, 2nd ed. (Upper Saddle River, NJ: Prentice Hall, 2000), 51–52.

8. Andres Oppenheimer, "While Latin America Nationalizes, India Opens Up," *Orlando Sentinel*, January 22, 2007, A11.

9. *Bank of Canada Banking and Financial Statistics*, Series G1, Government of Canada Fiscal Position, April 2009, S83.

10. Jim Middlemiss, "Don't Get Caught Offside in Rules Changes; Wrong Advice on Competition Act Could Be Costly," *National Post*, March 23, 2009, FP6. For an analysis of the current situation in the United States regarding resale price maintenance, see Joseph Pereira, "Price-Fixing Makes Comeback After Supreme Court Hearing," *The Wall Street Journal*, August 18, 2008, A1, A12.

11. Shirley Won and Jacquie McNish, "Antitrust Watchdog Loses Beer Battle," *The Globe and Mail*, March 29, 2007, B1, B6.

12. Steven Chase and Jacquie McNish, "Prentice Probes Watchdog's Court Conduct," *The Globe and Mail*, January 30, 2008, B1–B2.

13. John Gray, "Texas Fold 'Em," *Canadian Business*, October 9–22, 2006, 44–46.

14. Barrie McKenna, "Hyundai Gorged on Federal Funds," *The Globe and Mail*, March 25, 1994, B3.

15. Jennifer Allen, "New Lobby Rules Mean More Work for Lawyers," *The Globe and Mail*, August 13, 2008, B5.

16. See Karl E. Case and Ray C. Fair, *Principles of Economics*, 5th ed. (Upper Saddle River, NJ: Prentice Hall, 1999), 70–90; Robert A. Collinge and Ronald M. Ayers, *Economics by Design: Principles and Issues*, 2nd ed. (Upper Saddle River, NJ: Prentice Hall, 2000), 74–77.

17. Andy Hoffman, "Global Demand for Maple Syrup Keeps Rising. Sweet!," *The Globe and Mail*, March 12, 2009, B1.

18. For a detailed analysis of the rise in food prices, see Sinclair Stewart and Paul Waldie, "The Byzantine World of Food Pricing: How Big Money Is Wreaking Havoc," *The Globe and Mail*, May 31, 2008, B4–B7.

19. See Paul Heyne, Peter J. Boettke, and David L. Prychitko, *The Economic Way of Thinking*, 10th ed. (Upper Saddle River, NJ: Prentice Hall, 2003), 190, 358–359.

20. See Gina M. Larson, "bebe Bridges Style Gap," www.office.com/global/0,2724,509-10386_1,FF.html, July 10, 2001; Natural Fibers Information Center, "Ranking of Top U.S. Public Apparel Companies," www.utexas.edu/depts/bbr/natfiber, June 2001; "bebe.com Finishes #1," *Fashion Windows.com*, www.fashionwindows.com/beauty/2002/bebe.asp., January 13, 2002.

21. Karl E. Case and Ray C. Fair, *Principles of Economics*, 6th ed. (Upper Saddle River, NJ: Prentice Hall, 2003), 300–309.

22. *Hoover's Handbook of World Business 2002* (Austin, TX: Hoover's Business Press, 2002), 74–75.

23. Karl E. Case and Ray C. Fair, *Principles of Economics*, 6th ed. (Upper Saddle River, NJ: Prentice Hall, 2003), 300–309.

24. "Royal Mail's Reign Comes to an End," *The Globe and Mail*, January 2, 2006, B7.

25. Eric Bellman, "As Economy Zooms, India's Postmen Struggle to Adapt," *The Wall Street Journal*, October 3, 2006, A1, A12.

Chapter 2

1. See Jay B. Barney and William G. Ouchi, ed., *Organizational Economics* (San Francisco: Jossey-Bass, 1986), for a detailed analysis of linkages between economics and organizations.

2. Richard Blackwell, "The 'R' Word," *The Globe and Mail*, October 16, 2008, B5.

3. Karl E. Case and Ray C. Fair, *Principles of Economics*, 6th ed., updated (Upper Saddle River, NJ: Prentice Hall, 2003), 432–433.

4. Ibid., 15.

5. Ibid.

6. *Bank of Canada Banking and Financial Statistics*, Series H1, National Accounts, April 2009, S96.

7. Heather Scoffield, "Remeasuring the World's Economies," *The Globe and Mail*, December 22, 2007, B15.

8. Barry Marquardson, "GDP Fails as a Measurement," *The Globe and Mail*, July 16, 1998, B2.

9. Heather Scoffield, "Remeasuring the World's Economies," *The Globe and Mail*, December 22, 2007, B15.

10. Olivier Blanchard, *Macroeconomics*, 3rd ed. (Upper Saddle River, NJ: Prentice Hall, 2003), 24–26.

11. Jay Heizer and Barry Render, *Operations Management*, 6th ed. (Upper Saddle River, NJ: Prentice Hall, 2001), 15–16.

12. Neil Reynolds, "Stimulating Our Way Into a Crisis," *The Globe and Mail*, February 18, 2009, B2.

13. *Bank of Canada Banking and Financial Statistics*, Series G1, Government of Canada Fiscal Position, April 2009, S83; Steven Chase, "Decade of Debt Reduction in Peril," *The Globe and Mail*, January 22, 2009, B1.

14. Neil Reynolds, "U.S. Debt: Don't Worry, Be Happy (till 2017)," *The Globe and Mail*, April 3, 2009, B2.

15. This section is based on Paul Heyne, Peter J. Boettke, and David L. Prychitko, *The Economic Way of Thinking*, 10th ed. (Upper Saddle River, NJ: Prentice Hall, 2003), 491–493.

16. Celia Dugger, "Life in Zimbabwe: Wait for Useless Money, Then Scour for Food," *The New York Times*, October 2, 2008, A1, A14.

17. Geoffrey York, "How Zimbabwe Slew the Dragon of Hyperinflation," *The Globe and Mail*, March 23, 2009, B1.

18. Tavia Grant, "Lard in 1913, Plasma TV Now: CPI Tracks Changes," *The Globe and Mail*, April 21, 2005, B1, B15.

19. Bruce Little, "There's Been a Huge Shift in How Consumers Spend," *The Globe and Mail*, July 5, 2004, B4.

20. *Bank of Canada Banking and Financial Statistics*, Series H5, Labour Force Status of the Population, April 2009, S101.

21. Paul Heyne, Peter J. Boettke, and David L. Prychitko, *The Economic Way of Thinking*, 10th ed. (Upper Saddle River, NJ: Prentice Hall, 2003), 403–409, 503–504.

22. Julie Jargon, "Seeking Sweet Savings," *The Wall Street Journal*, October 2, 2007, B1–B2.

23. Sarah Efron, "Miracle Fibres," *Financial Post Business*, September 2007, 46–49.

24. Statistics Canada, *Industrial Research and Development: Intentions*, Catalogue no. 88-202-X, Table 4, Concentration of Total Intramural Research and Development Expenditures by Companies Size (Ottawa: Minister of Industry, 2009), www.statcan.gc.ca/pub/88-202-x/2008000/t050-eng.htm.

25. Statistics Canada, *Industrial Research and Development Intentions*, Catalogue no. 88-202-XIE2005000, (Ottawa: Minister of Industry, 2005), 10.

26. Statistics Canada, 2008, *Industrial Research and Development: Intentions*, Catalogue no. 88-202-X, Table 4, Concentration of Total Intramural Research and Development Expenditures by Companies Size, www.statcan.gc.ca/pub/88-202-x/2008000/t050-eng.htm.

27. Invest in Ontario, "Canadian Industrial Intramural R&D Expenditures, Selected Industries," www.investinontario.com/siteselector/bcrd_508.asp.

28. Thomas Wheelen and J. David Hunger, *Strategic Management and Business Policy* (Upper Saddle River, NJ: Pearson, 2004), 280.

29. L. G. Franko, "Global Corporate Competition: Who's Winning, Who's Losing, and the R&D Factor as One Reason Why," *Strategic Management Journal* (September–October 1989): 449–474.

30. Roberta S. Russell and Bernard W. Taylor III, *Operations Management*, 4th ed. (Upper Saddle River, NJ: Prentice Hall, 2003), Chapter 12.

31. Terrence Belford, "The Little Guys Are Getting with Big Boys' Program," *The Globe and Mail*, June 2, 2005, B16.

32. Brian Laghi, "U.S. Backlash Seen Growing," *The Globe and Mail*, March 27, 2003, B1, B10.

33. Sinclair Stewart, "CIBC's Solid Profit Overshadowed by Woes," *The Globe and Mail*, February 27, 2004, B1, B6.

34. Richard Blackwell, "The Greening of the Corner Office," *The Globe and Mail*, March 26, 2007, B1, B4.

35. Michael Porter, *Competitive Strategy: Techniques for Analyzing Industries and Competitors* (New York: The Free Press, 1980).

36. Judy Strauss and Raymond Frost, *E-Marketing* (Upper Saddle River, NJ: Prentice Hall, 2001), 245–246.

37. Tessa Wegert, "Advertisers Get Creative in Bid to Infect the Internet," *The Globe and Mail*, October 27, 2005, B13.

38. Lee J. Krajewski and Larry P. Ritzman, *Operations Management: Strategy and Analysis*, 6th ed. (Upper Saddle River, NJ: Prentice Hall, 2002), 3–4.

39. Ibid., Chapter 3.

40. Julie Jargon and Aaron Patrick, "More Sweet Deals in the Candy Aisle?" *The Globe and Mail*, April 29, 2008, B1–B2.

41. Jacquie McNish and Boyd Erman, "A Hangover After an Incredible Binge," *The Globe and Mail*, January 28, 2008, B6; Romina Maurino, "Wave of Consolidation Isn't Over Yet," *Winnipeg Free Press*, December 26, 2006, B6.

42. Lawrence Surtees, "Takeover Concern Prompts BCE Poison Pill Plan," *The Globe and Mail*, February 25, 2000, B5.

43. "Culture of Fun Benefits Clients, Staff," *National Post*, October 27, 2008, FP12.

44. "Nunavut Diamond Find Sends Shares Soaring," *Winnipeg Free Press*, February 4, 2003, B10.

Chapter 3

1. Sinclair Stewart, "CIBC Sues 6 Former Employees, Alleges They Took Confidential Data, Recruited Colleagues to Upstart Genuity," *The Globe and Mail*, January 6, 2005, B1, B4.

2. Howard Levitt, "Managers Have Duty to Remain Loyal to Employer; Court Penalizes Merrill Lynch for Taking RBC Staff," *National Post*, November 12, 2008, FP15.

3. Ronald Ebert and Ricky Griffin, *Business Essentials* (Upper Saddle River, NJ: Prentice Hall, 2009), 21.

4. Thomas Donaldson and Thomas W. Dunfee, "Toward a Unified Conception of Business Ethics: An Integrative Social Contracts Theory," *Academy of Management Review* 19, no. 2 (1994): 252–284.

5. "Drug Companies Face Assault on Prices," *The Wall Street Journal*, May 11, 2000, B1, B4.

6. John Saunders, "Bitter Air Carrier Dogfight Heads to Court," *The Globe and Mail*, July 8, 2004, B3.

7. Andrew Crane, "Spying Doesn't Pay; Intelligence Gathering is Still an Ethical and Legal Minefield," *National Post*, November 11, 2008, FP12.

8. Ann Zimmerman and Anita Raghavan, "Diamond Group Widens Probe of Bribe Charges," *The Wall Street Journal*, March 8, 2006, B1–B2.

9. This section follows the logic of Gerald F. Cavanaugh, *American Business Values with International Perspectives*, 4th ed. (Upper Saddle River, NJ: Prentice Hall, 1998), Chapter 3.

10. Steve Ladurantaye, "Maple Leaf Battered by Meat Recall Costs," *The Globe and Mail*, October 30, 2008, B3; Kristine Owram, "Maple Leaf Claims 'Progress' After Recall," *The Globe and Mail*, February 25, 2009, B5.

11. Mark Schwartz, "Heat's on to Get an Effective Code," *The Globe and Mail*, November 27, 1997, B2.

12. Julie Schmidt, "Nike's Image Problem," *USA Today*, October 4, 1999, 1B, 2B.

13. Jeffrey S. Harrison and R. Edward Freeman, "Stakeholders, Social Responsibility, and Performance: Empirical Evidence and Theoretical Perspectives," *Academy of Management Journal* 42, no. 5 (1999): 479–485. See also David P. Baron, *Business and Its Environment*, 3rd ed. (Upper Saddle River, NJ: Prentice Hall, 2000), Chapter 17.

14. Richard Blackwell, "The Double-Edged Sword of Corporate Altruism," *The Globe and Mail*, November 10, 2008, B5.

15. Jeremy Main, "Here Comes the Big New Cleanup," *Fortune*, November 21, 1988, 102–118.

16. Neil Reynolds, "The Dirty Truth of China's Energy," *The Globe and Mail*, March 28, 2007, B2.

17. Bill Curry, "Ottawa Wants Kyoto Softened," *The Globe and Mail*, May 12, 2006, A1, A7.

18. Jeffrey Ball, "U.N. Effort to Curtail Emissions in Turmoil," *The Wall Street Journal*, April 12–13, 2008, A1, A5.

19. "Going Green Losing Its Shine Among World's Citizens: Poll," *Winnipeg Free Press*, November 28, 2008, A20.

20. Catherine Collins, "The Race for Zero," *Canadian Business*, March 1991, 52–56.

21. Allan Robinson and Allan Freeman, "Mining's Dam Problem," *The Globe and Mail*, May 16, 1998, B1–B2.

22. Daniel Machalaba, "As Old Pallets Pile Up, Critics Hammer Them as New Eco-Menace," *The Wall Street Journal*, April 1, 1998, A1.

23. Egle Procuta, "One Man's Garbage is Another's Gold," *The Globe and Mail*, April 11, 2006, B7.

24. Geoffrey Scotton, "Cleanups Can Hurt, Companies Warned," *Financial Post*, June 25, 1991, 4.

25. Marc Huber, "A Double-Edged Endorsement," *Canadian Business*, January 1990, 69–71.

26. Patrick Barta, "Goro No Tropical Paradise for Inco," *The Globe and Mail*, July 12, 2006, B5.

27. Claudia Cattaneo, "Talisman Braces for Jungle Standoff; Threats of Violence," *National Post*, November 14, 2008, FP1.

28. Steve Ladurantaye, "Maple Leaf Battered by Meat Recall Costs," *The Globe and Mail*, October 30, 2008, B3.

29. Nicholas Casey, Nicholas Zamiska, and Andy Pasztor, "Mattel Seeks to Placate China With Apology on Toys," *The Wall Street Journal*, September 22–23, 2007, A1, A7.

30. John Wilke, "U.S. Probes Ice Makers Collusion Case," *The Wall Street Journal*, August 7, 2008, B1, B10.

31. Paul Waldie, "Chocolate Bar Makers Probe Over Prices," *The Globe and Mail*, November 28, 2007, B1, B10.

32. "Chocolate Makers Face Legal Challenges," *The Globe and Mail*, February 20, 2008, B9.

33. Jason Magder, Jack Branswell, and Ken Meaney, "Gas Firms Guilty of Price-Fixing," *Winnipeg Free Press*, June 13, 2008, A15.

34. Jonathan Cheng, "False Ads: Chinese Consumers Awaken to a Western Problem," *The Wall Street Journal*, July 8, 2005, B9.

35. Shawn McCarthy, "Crackdown on New York's Canal Street," *The Globe and Mail*, August 30, 2004, B1, B11.

36. Holly Shaw, "Buzzing Influencers," *National Post*, March 13, 2008, FP12.

37. Tim Barker, "Word-of-Mouth Advertising Grows in Influence, Concern," *Orlando Sentinel*, March 17, 2006, A1, A19.

38. Michael McCarthy and Lorrie Grant, "Sears Drops Benetton After Controversial Death Row Ads," *USA Today*, February 18, 2000, 2B.

39. Shona McKay, "Willing and Able," *Report on Business Magazine*, October 1991, 58–63.

40. "Why Business Is Hiring the Mentally Abled," *Canadian Business*, May 1991, 19.

41. J. Southerst, "In Pursuit of Drugs," *Canadian Transportation*, November 1989, 58–65.

42. G. Bylinsky, "How Companies Spy on Employees," *Fortune*, November 4, 1991, 131–140.

43. Jerald Greenberg and Robert A. Baron, *Behavior in Organizations: Understanding and Managing the Human Side of Work*, 7th ed. (Upper Saddle River, NJ: Prentice Hall, 2000), 374–375.

44. Brent Jang and Patrick Brethour, "This WestJet Staffer Blew the Whistle on His Employer's Corporate Spying. He's Still Waiting for Someone to Say Thanks," *The Globe and Mail*, October 18, 2006, A1, A12.

45. Cora Daniels, "'It's a Living Hell,'" *Fortune*, April 15, 2002, 367–368.

46. Janet McFarland, "Former Agnico Executive Sentenced to Jail Time," *The Globe and Mail*, January 30, 2009, B3.

47. Janet McFarland and Brent Jang, "Andrew Rankin: Barred From Trading Stocks, but Cleared of Criminal Charges," *The Globe and Mail*, February 22, 2008, B1, B4.

48. Greg Farrell, "Enron Law Firm Called Accounting Practices 'Creative'," *USA Today*, January 16, 2002, 1B.

49. Daniel Stoffman, "Good Behavior and the Bottom Line," *Canadian Business*, May 1991, 28–32.

50. "Great-West Life, London Life and Canada Life Donate $100,000 to the Salvation Army to Help Provide a Brighter Christmas for Many Across Canada," *Canada NewsWire*, December 18, 2008.

51. Diana McLaren, "Spirit of Philanthropy Is Thriving," *The Globe and Mail*, December 10, 2008, B7.

52. "Survey Shows Canadian Businesses Engaged in Meeting Community Need," *Canada NewsWire*, February 7, 2008, 1.

53. Tom Kierans, "Charity Begins at Work," *Report on Business Magazine*, June 1990, 23.

54. Theresa Ebden and Dawn Walton, "Walkerton Recipient of New-Style Corporate Giving," *The Globe and Mail*, June 3, 2000, B1, B6.

55. Alan Muller and Gail Whiteman, "Exploring the Geography of Philanthropic Disaster Response: A Study of Fortune Global 500 Firms," *Journal of Business Ethics* 84 (2009): 589–603.

56. Diane McLaren, "Doing Their Part—With Goals in Mind," *The Globe and Mail*, December 10, 2008, B7.

57. Kira Vermond, "A Great Way to Engage Your Employees," *The Globe and Mail*, July 26, 2008, B16.

58. Sandra Waddock and Neil Smith, "Corporate Responsibility Audits: Doing Well by Doing Good," *Sloan Management Review* (Winter 2000): 75–85.

59. Richard Blackwell, "The Double-Edged Sword of Corporate Altruism," *The Globe and Mail*, November 10, 2008, B5.

60. Alison Arnot, "The Triple Bottom Line," *CGA Magazine* (January–February 2004): 27–32.

Chapter 4

1. Statistics Canada, *Business Dynamics in Canada*, Catalogue no. 61-534-XIE (Ottawa: Minister of Industry, 2006).

2. P. D. Reynolds, S. M. Camp, W. D. Bygrave, E. Autio, and M. Hay, *Global Entrepreneurship Monitor: 2001 Executive Report* (Kansas City, MO: Kauffman Center for Entrepreneurial Leadership, 2001); P. D. Reynolds, M. Hay, W. D. Bygrave, S. M. Camp, and E. Autio, *Global Entrepreneurship Monitor: 2000 Executive Report* (Kansas City, MO: Kauffman Center for Entrepreneurial Leadership, 2000).

3. Monica Diochon, Teresa Menzies, and Yvon Gasse, "Exploring the Relationship Between Start-up Activities and New Venture Emergence: A Longitudinal Study of Canadian Nascent Entrepreneurs," *International Journal of Management and Enterprise Development* 2, no. 3/4 (2005): 408–426.

4. Queen's School of Business, "Queen's Centre for Business Venturing Announces Canada's Best Small and Medium Employers," January 14, 2009, www.business.queensu.ca/news/2009/01-14-09-BSME.php. Reprinted with permission of Queen's School of Business.

5. Nancy M. Carter, William B. Gartner, and Paul D. Reynolds, "Firm Founding," in *Handbook of Entrepreneurial Dynamics: The Process of Business Creation*, ed. W. B. Gartner, K. G. Shaver, N. M. Carter, and P. D. Reynolds (Thousand Oaks, CA: Sage, 2004), 311–323.

6. William D. Bygrave and C. W. Hofer, "Theorizing About Entrepreneurship," *Entrepreneurship Theory and Practice* 16, no. 2 (Winter 1991): 14; Donald Sexton and Nancy Bowman-Upton, *Entrepreneurship: Creativity and Growth* (New York, NY: MacMillan Publishing Company, 1991), 7.

7. Fred Vogelstein, "How Mark Zuckerberg Turned Facebook Into the Web's Hottest Platform," *Wired*, September 6, 2007, www.wired.com/techbiz/startups/news/2007/09/ff_facebook?currentPage=3; Ellen McGirt, "Hacker, Dropout, CEO," *Fast Company*, May 2007, www.fastcompany.com/magazine/115/open_features-hacker-dropout-ceo.html.

8. John Cooper, "A Pint of Success," *CMA Management* (December 1999–January 2000): 44–46.

9. www.heritage.org/index/ranking.aspx

10. Angela Dale, "Self-Employment and Entrepreneurship: Notes on Two Problematic Concepts," in *Deciphering the Enterprise Culture*, ed. Roger Burrows (London: Routledge, 1991), 45, 48.

11. Donald Sexton and Nancy Bowman-Upton, *Entrepreneurship: Creativity and Growth* (New York, NY: MacMillan Publishing Company, 1991), 11.

12. Allan A. Gibb, "The Enterprise Culture and Education: Understanding Enterprise Education and Its Links with Small Business, Entrepreneurship and Wider Educational Goals," *International Small Business Journal* 11 no. 3 (1993): 13–34; Donald Sexton and Nancy Bowman-Upton, *Entrepreneurship: Creativity and Growth,* (New York, NY: MacMillan Publishing Company, 1991).

13. Terrence Belford, "Intrapreneurs Combine Big-biz Clout with Entrepreneurial Style," *CanWest News*, March 23, retrieved from CBCA Current Events database. (Document ID: 1009719591).

14. Industry Canada, Small Business Research and Policy, *Key Small Business Statistics*, Table 1 (Ottawa: Public Works

and Government Services Canada, July 2008), www.ic.gc.ca/eic/site/sbrp-rppe.nsf/eng/rd02300.html.

15. Industry Canada, Small Business Research and Policy, *Key Small Business Statistics*, Table 3 (Ottawa: Public Works and Government Services Canada, July 2008), www.ic.gc.ca/eic/site/sbrp-rppe.nsf/eng/rd02300.html.

16. Industry Canada, Small Business Research and Policy, *Key Small Business Statistics* (Ottawa: Public Works and Government Services Canada, July 2008), www.ic.gc.ca/eic/site/sbrp-rppe.nsf/eng/rd02371.html.

17. Industry Canada, Small Business Research and Policy, *Key Small Business Statistics* (Ottawa: Public Works and Government Services Canada, 2006), 10.

18. Since government statistics exclude businesses without employees, a business counted as "new" could possibly have been operating for several years before being statistically counted as a new business. This can happen because an unincorporated business operated by a self-employed person (with no employees) would *not* be included in Statistics Canada's business register. If such a business operated for several years prior to hiring employees it would only be classified as a new business when the employees were first acquired.

19. William B. Gartner, Kelly G. Shaver, Nancy M. Carter, and Paul D. Reynolds, *Handbook of Entrepreneurial Dynamics* (Thousand Oaks, CA: Sage Publications, Inc., 2004), ix.

20. Industry Canada, *Key Small Business Statistics* (Ottawa: Public Works and Government Services Canada, January 2009), 3.

21. Ibid.

22. Ibid., 10.

23. Ibid., 4.

24. Richard Bloom, "Building a Future on Sweet Dreams," *The Globe and Mail*, October 21, 2004, B9.

25. Lauren McKeon, "Tied to Home," *Canadian Business*, April 14, 2008, 33.

26. Roma Luciw, "Stay-at-Home Moms Stay the Business Course," *The Globe and Mail*, March 3, 2007, B10.

27. www.rbcroyalbank.com/sme/women/top_news.html.

28. RBC Canadian Woman Entrepreneur Award, www.theawards.ca/cwea/past-winners.cfm.

29. Murray McNeill, "Patience Pays Off for Native Owner," *Winnipeg Free Press*, November 6, 2002, B3.

30. Sarah Kennedy, "Self-Styled Pioneer Aims to Alter Face of Fashion," *The Globe and Mail*, July 1, 2002, B12.

31. Geoff Kirbyson, "Market-Research Firm Lands Major Contract," *Winnipeg Free Press*, July 19, 2004, D7.

32. Dianne Rinehart, "Seed Money Gives Wing to Aboriginal Ventures," *The Globe and Mail*, October 17, 2007, E8.

33. Donald F. Kuratko and Richard M. Hodgetts, *Entrepreneurship: Theory, Process, Practice*, 7th ed. (Mason, OH: Thomson South-Western, 2007), 118–125; John A. Hornday, "Research About Living Entrepreneurs," in *Encyclopedia of Entrepreneurship*, ed. Calvin Kent, Donald Sexton, and Karl Vesper (Englewood Cliffs, NJ: Prentice Hall, 1982), 26–27; Jeffry A. Timmons and Stephen Spinelli, *New Venture Creation: Entrepreneurship for the 21st Century*, 7th ed. (Boston, MA: McGraw-Hill Irwin, 2007), 9.

34. Jeffry A. Timmons and Stephen Spinelli, *New Venture Creation: Entrepreneurship for the 21st Century*, 7th ed. (Boston, MA: McGraw-Hill Irwin, 2007), 19.

35. J. D. Kyle, R. Blais, R. Blatt, and A. J. Szonyi, "The Culture of the Entrepreneur: Fact or Fiction," *Journal of Small Business and Entrepreneurship* (1991): 3–14.

36. R. H. Brockhaus and Pam S. Horwitz, "The Psychology of the Entrepreneur," in *The Art and Science of Entrepreneurship*, ed. D. L Sexton and Raymond W. Smilor (Cambridge, MA: Ballinger Pub. Co., 1986); William B. Gartner, "What Are We Talking About When We Talk About Entrepreneurship?," *Journal of Business Venturing* 5 no. 1 (1990): 15–29; Allan A. Gibb, "The Enterprise Culture and Education: Understanding Enterprise Education and Its Links with Small Business, Entrepreneurship and Wider Educational Goals," *International Small Business Journal* 11 no. 3 (1993): 13–34; J. C. Mitchell, "Case and Situation Analysis," *Sociological Review* 31 no. 2 (1983): 187–211.

37. Donald Sexton and Nancy Bowman-Upton, *Entrepreneurship: Creativity and Growth* (New York, NY: MacMillan Publishing Company, 1991); Karl H. Vesper, *New Venture Strategies* (Englewood Cliffs, NJ: Prentice Hall, 1990); W. D. Bygrave and C. W. Hofer, "Theorizing About Entrepreneurship," *Entrepreneurship Theory and Practice* 16 no. 2 (Winter 1991): 14.

38. Walter Good, *Building a Dream* (Toronto: McGraw-Hill Ryerson, 1998), 40.

39. Ronald Ebert and Ricky Griffin, *Business Essentials* (Upper Saddle River, NJ: Prentice Hall, 2009), 137.

40. Wayne A. Long and W. Ed McMullan, *Developing New Ventures* (San Diego: Harcourt Brace Jovanovich, 1990), 374–375.

41. "Sally Fox: Innovation in the Field," www.vreseis.com/sally_fox_story.htm.

42. Michael E. Porter, "Know Your Place," *Inc.* 13 no. 9 (September 1992): 90–93.

43. Howard H. Stevenson, H. Irving Grousbeck, Michael J. Roberts, and Amarnath Bhide, *New Business Ventures and the Entrepreneur* (Boston: Irwin McGraw-Hill, 1999), 19.

44. Ibid., 21.

45. Marc J. Dollinger, *Entrepreneurship: Strategies and Resources* (Upper Saddle River, NJ: Prentice Hall, 1999), 94–101.

46. Thomas W. Zimmerer and Norman M. Scarborough, *Essentials of Entrepreneurship and Small Business Management*, 4th ed. (Upper Saddle River, NJ: Pearson Prentice Hall, 2005), 359.

47. Michael E. Porter, "Know Your Place," *Inc.* 13 no. 9 (September 1992): 90–93.

48. Dianne Rinehart, "It's Not Just Business, It's Personal," *The Globe and Mail*, October 10, 2007, B13.

49. Karl H. Vesper, *New Venture Mechanics* (Englewood Cliffs, NJ: Prentice Hall, 1993), 105.

50. Jeffry A. Timmons, *New Venture Creation* (Boston: Irwin McGraw-Hill, 1999), 277.

51. Lisa Stephens, "With Some Shape Shifting, This Company Has Legs," *The Globe and Mail*, October 5, 2005, B10.

52. George Anders, Carol Hymowitz, Joann Lublin, and Don Clark, "All in the Family," *The Wall Street Journal*, August 1, 2005, B1, B4.

53. Mary Agnes Welch, "When Name Is Everything," *Winnipeg Free Press*, May 12, 2002, B1–B2.

54. Quoted in Lowell B. Howard, *Business Law* (Woodbury, NY: Barron's Woodbury Press, 1965), 332.

55. "How They Stack Up," *The Globe and Mail*, November 10, 2008, B7.

56. "NYSE Euronext Takes Top Spot in IPOs," *The Globe and Mail*, December 29, 2007, B7.

57. "Clearwater Foods Going Private," *National Post*, August 15, 2008, www.nationalpost.com/story-printer.html?id=725985.

58. Terry Pedwell, "Income Trusts Face Tough Rules," *Winnipeg Free Press*, November 1, 2006, B7.

59. "An Overview of Available Business Structures," www.umanitoba.ca/afs/agric_economics/MRAC/structures.html#Cooperatives.

60. Industry Canada, *Key Small Business Statistics* (Ottawa: Public Works and Government Services Canada, January 2009), 12.

61. Kevin Marron, "Want to Succeed? Read This," *The Globe and Mail*, October 19, 2005, E1, E5. Several excellent articles on starting and operating a small business are found in Section E, "Report on Small Business" in *The Globe and Mail*, October 19, 2005.

62. See Norman M. Scarborough and Thomas W. Zimmerer, *Effective Small Business Management: An Entrepreneurial Approach*, 7th ed. (Upper Saddle River, NJ: Prentice Hall, 2003).

Chapter 5

1. Risha Gotlieb, "From Logs to Riches," *The Globe and Mail*, October 17, 2007, E10.

2. John Miller, "WTO Predicts Global Trade Will Slide 9% This Year," *The Wall Street Journal*, March 24, 2009, A8; "EDC Sees Exports Falling 22 Percent," *The Globe and Mail*, April 29, 2009, B13.

3. Ricky W. Griffin and Michael W. Pustay, *International Business: A Managerial Perspective*, 6th ed. (Upper Saddle River, NJ: Prentice Hall, 2009); The World Bank: Data & Statistics, www.web.worldbank.org/WBSITE/EXTERNAL/DATASTATISTICS/0,,contentMDK:20420458~pagePK:641331150~piPK:64133175~theSitePK:239419,00.html.

4. Thomas Friedman, *The World Is Flat* (New York: Farrar, Straus, and Giroux, 2005).

5. David Fairlamb and Gail Edmondson, "Work in Progress," *Business Week*, January 31, 2000, 80–81+.

6. Edmund L. Andrews, "The Metamorphosis of Germany Inc.," *The New York Times*, March 12, 2000, section 3, 1, 12.

7. Ronald Ebert and Ricky Griffin, *Business Essentials* (Upper Saddle River, NJ: Prentice Hall, 2009), 49.

8. Barrie McKenna, "China, India Crowd G7 in Driver's Seat," *The Globe and Mail*, July 19, 2006, B11; Andrew Batson, "China's Rise as Auto-Parts Power Reflects New Manufacturing Edge," *The Wall Street Journal*, August 1, 2006, A1, A6.

9. Mark Landler, "Mapping Out Silicon Valley East," *The New York Times*, April 5, 1999, C1, C10; Bruce Einhorn with Cathy Yang, "Portal Combat," *Business Week*, January 17, 2000, 96–97.

10. Ricky W. Griffin and Michael W. Pustay, *International Business: A Managerial Perspective*, 2nd ed. (Reading, MA: Addison-Wesley, 1999), Chapter 3; Dominick Salvatore, *International Economics*, 6th ed. (Upper Saddle River, NJ: Prentice Hall, 1998), 27–33; Karl E. Case and Ray C. Fair, *Principles of Economics*, 5th ed. (Upper Saddle River, NJ: Prentice Hall, 1999), 813–817.

11. This section is based on Michael Porter, *The Competitive Advantage of Nations* (Boston: Harvard Business School Press, 1990), Chapters 3 and 4; Warren J. Keegan, *Global Marketing Management*, 6th ed. (Upper Saddle River, NJ: Prentice Hall, 1999), 312–321; John J. Wild, Kenneth L. Wild, and Jerry C.Y. Han, *International Business: An Integrated Approach* (Upper Saddle River, NJ: Prentice Hall, 2000), 175–178.

12. *The Global Competitiveness Report 2008-2009* (Geneva: World Economic Forum, 2009), www.weforum.org/en/initiatives/gcp/Global%20Competitiveness%20Report/index.htm.

13. *Bank of Canada Banking and Financial Statistics*, Series J4, Commodity Classification of Merchandise Exports, April 2009, S114–S115.

14. *Bank of Canada Banking and Financial Statistics*, Series J2, Canadian Balance of International Payments, April 2009, S112.

15. Karl E. Case and Ray C. Fair, *Principles of Economics*, 5th ed. (Upper Saddle River, NJ: Prentice Hall, 1999), 818–821.

16. "Exports, Eh?," *Canadian Business*, January 1997, 21.

17. Shirley Won, "Small Firms Beating a Path to the Middle Kingdom," *The Globe and Mail*, August 31, 2004, B7.

18. "2007 Worldwide Grosses," *Box Office Mojo*, www.boxofficemojo.com/yearly/chart/?view2=worldwide&yr=2007&p=.htm; Dave McNary, "Foreign Box Office Hits Record Levels," *Variety*, January 1, 2008, www.variety.com/article/VR111798262.html?categoryid=1236&cs=1&query=%22resident+evil%22.

19. Ronald Ebert and Ricky Griffin, *Business Essentials* (Upper Saddle River, NJ: Prentice Hall, 2009), 56.

20. Ray August, *International Business Law: Text, Cases, and Readings*, 3rd ed. (Upper Saddle River, NJ: Prentice Hall, 2000), 192–197.

21. Christopher Tkaczyk and David Goldman, "Fortune 500—Big Business Battles It Out," *Fortune*, April 21, 2008, www.finance.yahoo.com/career-work/article/104864/Fortune-500-Big-Business-Battles-It-Out.

22. Warren J. Keegan, *Global Marketing Management*, 6th ed. (Upper Saddle River, NJ: Prentice Hall, 1999), 290–292; Ricky W. Griffin and Michael W. Pustay, *International Business: A Managerial Perspective*, 2nd ed. (Reading, MA: Addison-Wesley, 1999), 427–431; John J. Wild, Kenneth L. Wild, and Jerry C.Y. Han, *International Business: An Integrated Approach* (Upper Saddle River, NJ: Prentice Hall, 2000), 454–456.

23. Ricky W. Griffin and Michael W. Pustay, *International Business: A Managerial Perspective*, 2nd ed. (Reading, MA: Addison-Wesley, 1999), 431–433; John J. Wild, Kenneth L. Wild, and Jerry C.Y. Han, *International Business: An Integrated Approach* (Upper Saddle River, NJ: Prentice Hall, 2000), 456–458.

24. Shirley Won, "Small Firms Beating a Path to the Middle Kingdom," *The Globe and Mail*, August 31, 2004, B7.

25. Gordon Pitts, "Manulife's Army of Agents on the March for Middle Class," *The Globe and Mail*, October 23, 2004, B4.

26. Shirley Won, "Small Firms Beating a Path to the Middle Kingdom," *The Globe and Mail*, August 31, 2004, B7.

27. Gregory White and Guy Chazan, "BP, Russians Settle Feud over TNK-BP," *The Globe and Mail*, September 5, 2008, B9.

28. John J. Wild, Kenneth L. Wild, and Jerry C.Y. Han, *International Business: An Integrated Approach* (Upper Saddle River, NJ: Prentice Hall, 2000), Chapter 7; Ricky W. Griffin and Michael W. Pustay, *International Business: A Managerial Perspective*, 2nd ed. (Reading, MA: Addison-Wesley, 1999), 436–439.

29. Janet McFarland, "Corporate Canada Easy Prey for Foreign Buyers," *The Globe and Mail*, February 27, 2008, B1–B2.

30. Roma Luciw, "Hollowed Out Fears? Relax, Foreigners Lead on Hiring," *The Globe and Mail*, July 14, 2006, B1–B2.

31. Gordon Pitts, "Mixed Messages on Danger of Foreign Takeovers," *The Globe and Mail*, September 18, 2006, B1, B3. For an extensive analysis of the effect of foreign takeovers of Canadian business firms, see Roger Martin and Gordon Nixon, "Who, Canada," *The Globe and Mail*, July 2, 2007, B1–B3.

32. John Partridge, "Foreign Takeover Fears Played Down," *The Globe and Mail*, August 22, 2007, B3.

33. Rick Cash, "Dealing with the Dragon," *The Globe and Mail*, October 23, 2004, B3; Gordon Pitts, "Learn This Mantra: Customer Is King in China," *The Globe and Mail*, July 12, 2004, B1, B5.

34. Stephanie Nolen, "McCain Learns Tough Cultural Lesson in South Africa," *The Globe and Mail*, October 21, 2004, B1, B19; Gordon Pitts, "McCain Boss Picks Up Pace of Global French Fry Assault," *The Globe and Mail*, June 14, 2004, B1, B12.

35. Steven Chase, "Canada Slaps Duties on Chinese-made Barbecues," *The Globe and Mail*, August 28, 2004, B2.

36. Peter Kennedy, "Softwood Decision Gets Mixed Reviews," *The Globe and Mail*, December 8, 2005, B6.

37. Paul Veira, "Emerson Warns Lumber Leaders of 'Consequences'," *Financial Post*, August 1, 2006, FP1, FP5; Steve Merti, "Lumber Exporters Taste Sting of Softwood Deal," *Winnipeg Free Press*, September 22, 2006, B5.

38. Roger Thurow and Geoff Winestock, "How an Addiction to Sugar Subsidies Hurts Development," *The Wall Street Journal*, September 16, 2002, A1, A10.

39. "WTO Strikes Down U.S. Cotton Subsidy Appeal," *The Globe and Mail*, March 4, 2005, B10.

40. Scott Kilman and Roger Thurow, "To Soothe Anger Over Subsidies, U.S. Cotton Tries Wooing Africa," *The Wall Street Journal*, August 5, 2005, A1, A6.

41. Simon Tuck, "Farmers to WTO: If It Ain't Broke...," *The Globe and Mail*, August 9, 2004, B1–B2.

42. Anthony DePalma, "Chiquita Sues Europeans, Citing Banana Quota Losses,"

The New York Times, January 26, 2001, C5; Brian Lavery, "Trade Feud on Bananas Not as Clear as It Looks," *The New York Times*, February 7, 2001, W1; David E. Sanger, "Miffed at Europe, U.S. Raises Tariffs for Luxury Goods," *The New York Times*, March 4, 1999, A1, A5.

43. Wendy Stueck, "Mining Firms Hit Again by Chavez Threat," *The Globe and Mail*, September 23, 2005, B4; Barrie McKenna, "A Nation of Big Riches, Bigger Risks," *The Globe and Mail*, September 24, 2005, B4.

44. Konrad Yakabuski, "Quebec Courts Margarine War," *The Globe and Mail*, October 14, 1997, B1, B4.

45. Bertrand Marotte, "Ontario Calls for Dispute Panel in Quebec Margarine Battle," *The Globe and Mail*, March 26, 2002, B10.

46. Neville Nankivell, "Spilled Milk Over Provincial Trade," *National Post*, April 24, 2000, C9.

47. Gerry Stobo, "Cross-Border Mobility," *CGA Magazine* (May–June 2005): 13–16.

48. Gary McWilliams, "Wal-Mart Era Wanes Amid Big Shifts in Retail," *The Wall Street Journal*, October 3, 2007, A1, A17.

49. Sinclair Stewart, "Uncle Sam Nabs Net Millionaires," *The Globe and Mail*, January 17, 2007, B1, B8.

50. Dawn Walton, "Builders Most Likely to Bribe, Report Finds," *The Globe and Mail*, January 21, 2000, B5.

51. Nicholas Bray, "OECD Ministers Agree to Ban Bribery as Means for Companies to Win Business," *The Wall Street Journal*, May 27, 1997, A2.

52. "Canada Ties for First in List of Countries Resistant to Corrupt Business," *National Post*, December 10, 2008, FP2; "Russian Firms Most Prone to Bribery, Survey Finds," *The Globe and Mail*, December 10, 2008, B14.

53. Transparency International, "Corruption Perceptions Index, 2008," www.transparency.org/policy_research/surveys_indices/cpi/2008.

54. Russell Gold and David Crawford, "U.S., Other Nations Step Up Bribery Battle," *The Wall Street Journal*, September 12, 2008, B1, B6.

55. "EU Fines Banana Importers for Cartel Actions," *The Globe and Mail*, October 16, 2008, B11; "EU Imposes Highest Fine Over Auto Glass Cartel," *The Globe and Mail*, November 13, 2008, B9; "Oil Companies fined by EU over 'Paraffin Mafia' Cartel," *The Globe and Mail*, October 2, 2008, B7.

56. Steven Chase, "Canadian Bike Makers Fear Hit from Cheap Chinese Imports," *The Globe and Mail*, September 7, 2004, B4.

57. Peter Wonacott, "Downturn Heightens China-India Tension on Trade," *The Wall Street Journal*, March 20, 2009, A8.

58. "New Global Trade Regulator Starts Operations Tomorrow," *Winnipeg Free Press*, December 31, 1994, A5.

59. Helene Cooper and Bhushan Bahree, "World's Best Hope for Global Trade Topples Few Barriers," *The Wall Street Journal*, December 3, 1996, A1, A8.

60. John Miller, "Global Trade Talks Fail as New Giants Flex Muscle," *The Wall Street Journal*, July 30, 2008, A1, A12.

61. Michelle MacAfee, "Trade Protest Turns Violent," *Winnipeg Free Press*, July 29, 2003, A9.

62. "European Union Expands into 10 New Countries," *Reuters*, news release, April 30, 2004.

63. Bruce Little, "Free-Trade Pact Gets Mixed Reviews," *The Globe and Mail*, June 7, 2004, B3.

64. Barrie McKenna, "Dead End for Free Trade," *The Globe and Mail*, May 17, 2008, B4–B5.

65. Peter Cook, "Free Trade Free-for-all Causes Confusion," *The Globe and Mail*, December 5, 1994, B7.

Chapter 6

1. Grant Buckler, "Workplace Wheel of Fortune," *The Globe and Mail*, December 18, 2007, B8.

2. Peter Burrows, "The Hottest Property in the Valley?," *Business Week*, August 30, 1999, 69–74.

3. www.paultan.org/archives/2007/08/02volkswagen-experiences-the-power-of-word-of-mouth.

4. Alex Taylor III, "How a Top Boss Manages His Day," *Fortune*, June 19, 1989, 95–100.

5. "On a Roll," *Canadian Business*, October 9–22, 2006, 51.

6. Joann Lublin, "Top Brass Try Life in the Trenches," *The Wall Street Journal*, June 25, 2007, B1, B3.

7. Virginia Galt, "Lousy People Skills Are Biggest Hurdle for Leaders," *The Globe and Mail*, October 15, 2005, B11.

8. *The Leader-Post* (Regina), www.2.canada.com/reginaleaderpost/news/business_agriculture/story.html?id=cd94cd.

9. Jerry Useem, "Boeing vs. Boeing," *Fortune*, October 2, 2000, 148–160; "Airbus Prepares to 'Bet the Company' as It Builds a Huge New Jet," *The Wall Street Journal*, November 3, 1999, A1, A10.

10. Peter Tingling, "Fact or Fantasy?," *National Post*, April 21, 2009, FP12.

11. Charles P. Wallace, "Adidas—Back in the Game," *Fortune*, August 18, 1997, 176–182.

12. Barry M. Staw and Jerry Ross, "Good Money After Bad," *Psychology Today*, February 1988, 30–33.

13. Gerry McNamara and Philip Bromiley, "Risk and Return in Organizational Decision Making," *Academy of Management Journal* 42 (1999): 330–339.

14. Brian O'Reilly, "What it Takes to Start a Startup," *Fortune*, June 7, 1999, 135–140.

15. "Kodak Deems Transformation Complete," *The Globe and Mail*, January 31, 2008, B10.

16. Sinclair Stewart and Derek DeCloet, "It's Mr. Focus v. Mr. Diversification," *The Globe and Mail*, June 3, 2006, B4.

17. Gordon Pitts, "Taking a Stand: How One CEO Gained Respect," *The Globe and Mail*, January 31, 2006, B8.

18. Bertrand Marotte, "Gildan Takes T-shirt Making to the Cutting-Edge of Casual Apparel," *The Globe and Mail*, July 3, 2004, B3.

19. Amy Hoffman, "Potash Strike Leaves Slippery Side Effects," *The Globe and Mail*, November 17, 2008, B1.

20. Steve Ladurantaye, "Maple Leaf Battered by Meat Recall Costs," *The Globe and Mail*, October 30, 2008, B3.

21. Kristine Owram, "Maple Leaf Claims 'Progress' After Recall," *The Globe and Mail*, February 25, 2009, B5.

22. Richard Bloom, "How Parmalat Juggled the Struggle," *The Globe and Mail*, May 23, 2005, B3.

23. Ric Dolphin, "Magna Force," *Canadian Business*, May 1988.

24. Isadore Sharp, "Quality for All Seasons," *Canadian Business Review* (Spring 1990): 21–23.

25. Bruce McDougall, "The Thinking Man's Assembly Line," *Canadian Business*, November 1991, 40–44.

26. Peter Verburg, "Prepare for Takeoff," *Canadian Business*, December 25, 2000, 95–99.

27. Sanam Islam, "Execs See Link to Bottom Line; Gap is Closing; More Firms Keen to be Seen as Best Corporate Culture," *National Post*, November 12, 2008, FP16.

28. Wallace Immen, "Half of Workers Don't Fit In," *The Globe and Mail*, October 22, 2008, C2.

29. Derek Sankey, "Cult-Like Culture is Key," *Financial Post*, July 28, 2008, www.nationalpost.com/story-printer.html?id=684225.

30. Calvin Leung, "Culture Club," *Canadian Business*, October 9–22, 2006, 115, 116, 118, 120; "Golden Rule Is Measure of Success: 10 Most Admired Corporate Cultures," *National Post*, December 3, 2008, FP16.

31. Neal Boudette, "Nardelli Tries to Shift Chrysler's Culture," *The Wall Street Journal*, June 18, 2008, B1.

32. Gordon Pitts, "It Boiled Down to a Culture Clash," *The Globe and Mail*, June 11, 2005, B5.

Chapter 7

1. Robert L. Simison, "Ford Rolls Out New Model of Corporate Culture," *The Wall Street Journal*, January 13, 1999, B1, B4.

2. Joann Muller, "Ford: Why It's Worse Than You Think," *Business Week*, June 25, 2001, 80–84.

3. John A. Wagner and John R. Hollenbeck, *Management of Organizational Behavior* (Englewood Cliffs, NJ: Prentice Hall, 1992), 563–565.

4. Jay Diamond and Gerald Pintel, *Retailing*, 6th ed. (Upper Saddle River, NJ: Prentice Hall, 1996), 83–84.

5. "Nike Redefines Its Regions Amid Spending Pullback," *The Globe and Mail*, March 21, 2009, B7.

6. Michael E. Raynor and Joseph L. Bower, "Lead from the Center," *Harvard Business Review* (May 2001): 93–102.

7. Bruce Horovitz, "Restoring the Golden-Arch Shine," *USA Today*, June 16, 1999, 3B.

8. *Hoover's Handbook of American Business 2006* (Austin, TX: Hoover's Business Press, 2006); Brian Dumaine, "How I Delivered the Goods," *Fortune Small Business*, October 2002.

9. Lee Hawkins, "Reversing 80 Years of History, GM Is Reining in Global Fiefs," *The Wall Street Journal*, October 6, 2004, A1, A14.

10. Gary Yukl, *Leadership in Organizations*, 5th ed. (Upper Saddle River, NJ: Prentice Hall, 2002), 35–36.

11. "Multi-Tasking: Cost-Reduction Strategy at Case Corp.," *Machinery Systems Inc.*, www.machinerysystems.com/RavingFan/CaseCorp.html, July 20, 2001.

12. Donna Fenn, "The Buyers," *Inc.* (June 1996): 46–48+.

13. "Teck to Drop Cominco, Split Into Five Units," *The Globe and Mail*, October 2, 2008, B7.

14. J. Galbraith, "Matrix Organization Designs: How to Combine Functional and Project Forms," *Business Horizons* (1971): 29–40; H.F. Kolodny, "Evolution to a Matrix Organization," *Academy of Management Review* 4 (1979): 543–553.

15. Interview with Tom Ward, operations manager for Genstar Shipyards.

16. Lawton R. Burns, "Matrix Management in Hospitals: Testing Theories of Matrix Structure and Development," *Administrative Science Quarterly* 34 (1989): 48–50.

17. Diane Brady, "Martha Inc.," *Business Week*, January 17, 2000, 62–66.

18. Miguel Helft, "Yahoo Chief Rearranges Managers Once Again," *The New York Times*, February 27, 2009, B5.

19. Gail Edmondson, "Danone Hits Its Stride," *Business Week*, February 1, 1999, 52–53.

20. Frank Rose, "Think Globally, Script Locally," *Fortune*, November 8, 1999, 156–160.

21. Thomas A. Stewart, "See Jack. See Jack Run," *Fortune*, September 27, 1999, 124–127+.

22. Jerald Greenberg and Robert A. Baron, *Behavior in Organizations: Understanding and Managing the Human Side of Work*, 7th ed. (Upper Saddle River, NJ: Prentice Hall, 2000), 308–309.

Chapter 8

1. See Angelo S. DeNisi and Ricky W. Griffin, *Human Resource Management* (Boston, MA: Houghton Mifflin, 2001) for a complete overview.

2. Patrick Brethour and Heather Scoffield, "Plenty of Work, Not Enough Bodies," *The Globe and Mail*, August 21, 2006, B4.

3. Heather Scoffield, "Amid Jobs Boom, Hundreds of Thousands Left Behind," *The Globe and Mail*, August 21, 2006, B5.

4. Elizabeth Church, "Store Owners Struggle with Staffing," *The Globe and Mail*, November 25, 1996, B6.

5. Kira Vermond, "Get This: Lame Summer Internships Now Sizzle," *The Globe and Mail*, July 19, 2008, B17.

6. Wallace Immen, "Prospective Hires Put to the Test," *The Globe and Mail*, January 26, 2005, C1, C2.

7. Katie Rook, "Curveball Job Questions: How Not to Strike Out," *The Globe and Mail*, September 3, 2005, B9.

8. Malcolm MacKillop, "An Employer's Guide to Drug Testing," *The Globe and Mail*, April 9, 1998, B13.

9. Margot Gibb-Clark, "Ruling Narrows Options for Drug Testing," *The Globe and Mail*, July 28, 1998, B11.

10. Wallace Immen, "Half of Workers Don't Fit In," *The Globe and Mail*, October 22, 2008, C2.

11. Kira Vermond, "Rolling Out the Welcome Mat," *The Globe and Mail*, April 26, 2008, B19.

12. Ibid.

13. Charles Davies, "Strategy Session 1990," *Canadian Business*, January 1990, 50.

14. Scott Feschuk, "Phi Beta Cuppa," *The Globe and Mail*, March 6, 1993, B1, B4.

15. Mark Blanchard, "Pilots Enter Superjumbo Virtual Reality," *The Globe and Mail*, January 20, 2005, B8.

16. Abby Ellin, "Training Programs Often Miss the Point on the Job," *The New York Times*, March 29, 2000, C12.

17. Kira Vermond, "Taking a Full-Circle Look at Work Reviews," *The Globe and Mail*, November 24, 2007, B18.

18. "Potash Corp CEO Doyle Highest Paid in Canada," *The Leader-Post* (Regina), November 18, 2008, www.canada.com/reginaleaderpost/news/business_agriculture/story.html?id=cd94cdd8-9afa-4c3e-9549-58a9386aa4ca.

19. Joann Lublin and Scott Thrum, "Behind Soaring Executive Pay, Decades of Failed Restraints," *The Wall Street Journal*, October 12, 2006, B8.

20. Boyd Erman, "Shareholders Win Voice on CEO Pay at 3 Big Banks," *The Globe and Mail*, February 27, 2009, B1.

21. Joann Lublin, "Say on the Boss's Pay," *The Wall Street Journal*, March 7, 2008, B1–B2.

22. Heather Scoffield, "New National Refrain: Can I Help You?," *The Globe and Mail*, May 27, 2008, B1, B6.

23. Elizabeth Church, "Nortel Workers Pick Tailor-Made Perks," *The Globe and Mail*, December 8, 2000, B11.

24. Vanessa O'Connell, "Retailers Reprogram Workers in Efficiency Push," *The Wall Street Journal*, September 10, 2008, A1, A11.

25. Mary Gooderham, "A Piece of the Pie as Motivational Tool," *The Globe and Mail*, November 20, 2007, B8.

26. Cathryn Atkinson, "The Total Package: Anatomy of a Great Place to Work," *The Globe and Mail*, July 2, 2008, B6.

27. Mary Gooderham, "A Piece of the Pie as Motivational Tool," *The Globe and Mail*, November 20, 2007, B8.

28. David Roberts, "A Long Way from Cambodia," *The Globe and Mail*, July 5, 1994, B18.

29. Virginia Galt, "Medicare Cut Seen Raising Labour Costs," *The Globe and Mail*, February 12, 2002, B10.

30. "EI Premiums to Drop on Jan. 1," *Winnipeg Free Press*, November 7, 2006, B7.

31. Dale Jackson, "Pumped Up and Ready to Pay Out," *The Globe and Mail*, October 21, 2006, B13.

32. Virginia Galt, "Companies, Unions, Expect Little Relief," *The Globe and Mail*, September 15, 2004, B4.

33. Elizabeth Church, "Pension Funding Shortfall Increases Dramatically," *The Globe and Mail*, November 8, 2005, B5.

34. Elizabeth Church, "Pension Fund Shortfall Soars in First Half," *The Globe and Mail*, November 23, 2005, B1, B7.

35. Elizabeth Church, "Cost of Retiree Benefit Liabilities 'Sleeping Giant,'" *The Globe and Mail*, August 23, 2004, B4.

36. Virginia Galt, "Gift of Time Pays off for Savvy Employers," *The Globe and Mail*, December 28, 2004, B3.

37. Ibid.

38. Erin White, "Sabbaticals: The Pause That Refreshes," *The Wall Street Journal*, August 2, 2005, B1, B4.

39. Bruce McDougall, "The Thinking Man's Assembly Line," *Canadian Business*, November 1991, 40.

40. Kamal Dib, "Diversity Works," *Canadian Business*, March 29, 2004, 53–54.

41. Virginia Galt, "How to Hammer the Glass Ceiling," *The Globe and Mail*, April 5, 2007, B1, B4.

42. John Partridge, "B of M Lauded for Promoting Women's Careers," *The Globe and Mail*, January 7, 1994, B3.

43. Vivian Smith, "Breaking Down the Barriers," *The Globe and Mail*, November 17, 1992, B24.

44. Richard Blackwell and Brent Jang, "Top Court Sides with Airline Attendants," *The Globe and Mail*, January 27, 2006, B1, B6.

45. Neco Cockburn, "Clerks to Get $150 Million in Back Pay," *Winnipeg Free Press*, October 8, 2005, A3.

46. Keith McArthur, "Criticism of Women's Fitness for Top Jobs Causes International Stir," *The Globe and Mail*, October 21, 2005, A1, A14.

47. Ted Kennedy, "Beware of Health and Safety Law: It Could Bite You," *Canadian Business*, December 1990, 19.

48. Wallace Immen, "Post-65 Workers 'Productive and Engaged,'" *The Globe and Mail*, March 18, 2005, C1.

49. Michael Moss, "For Older Employees, On-the-Job Injuries Are More Often Deadly," *The Wall Street Journal*, June 17, 1997, A1, A10.

50. Jill Mahoney, "Visible Majority by 2017," *The Globe and Mail*, March 23, 2005, A1, A7.

51. Virginia Galt, "P & G Leverages Its Cultural Diversity," *The Globe and Mail*, April 7, 2005, B1, B5.

52. Virginia Galt, "Western Union Remakes 'Canadian' Image," *The Globe and Mail*, November 23, 2004, B1, B24.

53. "The Top 35 Best Diversity Employers," *TheStar.com*, February 19, 2009, www.thestar.com/Business/article/589497.

54. Max Boisot, *Knowledge Assets* (Oxford: Oxford University Press, 1998).

55. Thomas Stewart, "In Search of Elusive Tech Workers," *Fortune*, February 16, 1998, 171–172.

56. "Full-Time Jobs on the Wane," *The Globe and Mail*, July 12, 2008, B7.

57. Joellen Perry, Luca DiLeo, and Stacy Meichtry, "Mass Cuts of Temp Workers Pose a Tough Test for Europe," *The Wall Street Journal*, March 12, 2009, A1, A10.

58. Tavia Grant, "Financial Crisis sparks More Demand for Temps at the Top," *The Globe and Mail*, November 14, 2008, B16.

59. Augusta Dwyer, "Ottawa Looks to Mexico to Ease Labour Crunch," *The Globe and Mail*, May 19, 2008, B3. For a discussion of some issues related to foreign workers, see Susan Bourette, "Welcome to Canada, Hope You Aren't Planning on Staying," *Report on Business*, October 2007, 66–78.

60. Aaron Bernstein, "When Is a Temp Not a Temp?" *Business Week*, December 7, 1998, 90–92.

Chapter 9

1. David Lipsky and Clifford Donn, *Collective Bargaining in American Industry* (Lexington, MA: Lexington Books, 1981).

2. Alia McMullen, "Ottawa Targets Strikers' Impact," *National Post*, September 2, 2008, www.nationalpost.com/story-printer.html?id=76075; Human Resources and Skills Development Canada, "Union Membership in Canada—2008," www.hrsdc.gc.ca/eng/labour/labour_relations/info_analysis/union_membership/index.

3. Susan Bourette, "Organized Labour Lures Growing Number of Youth," *The Globe and Mail*, July 4, 1997, B1, B4; Susan Bourette, "Women Make Strides in Union Movement," *The Globe and Mail*, August 29, 1997, B1–B2.

4. Statistics Canada, "Perspectives in Labour and Income," Autumn 2003, 15, 3, 50.

5. Statistics Canada, "Perspectives in Labour and Income," Autumn 2003, 15, 3, 51.

6. Virginia Galt, "Worn-Out Middle Managers May Get Protection," *The Globe and Mail*, January 3, 2005, B1, B8.

7. Greg Keenan, "CAW Targets Honda, Toyota," *The Globe and Mail*, June 15, 1999, B1, B8.

8. Sarah Binder, "McDonald's Store Closes, Union Wails," *The Globe and Mail*, February 14, 1998, B23.

9. Paul McKie, "Goldcorp Workers Accept Offer, Dismantle Union," *Winnipeg Free Press*, April 22, 2000, A6.

10. Murray McNeill, "Hotel Workers Sever Relationship with Union," *Winnipeg Free Press*, July 22, 2005, B14.

11. Paul Waldie, "How Health Costs Hurt the Big Three," *The Globe and Mail*, March 22, 2005, B1–B2; Virginia Galt, "Companies, Unions Expect Little Relief," *The Globe and Mail*, September 15, 2004, B4.

12. David Ebner, "Potash Workers Ratify Deal that Changes Little," *The Globe and Mail*, November 15, 2008, B7.

13. Brent Jang, "CN Strike Takes Mounting Toll as Rail Delays Hit Manufacturers," *The Globe and Mail*, February 19, 2007, B1, B8; Brent Jang, "CN Rail Strike Ends With Fragile Truce," *The Globe and Mail*, February 26, 2007, B1, B3.

14. William Watson, "Strike Champs," *National Post*, May 24, 2007, FP15.

15. Jack Mintz, "The Perils of the Picket Line," *Canadian Business*, February 27–March 12, 2006, 15.

16. Margot Gibb-Clark, "Wounds Left by Strike Require Healing," *The Globe and Mail*, September 30, 1991, B4.

17. Martin Cash, "Tractor Plant Workers Locked Out," *Winnipeg Free Press*, March 28, 2001, B3; Paul McKie, "A Bitter End at Versatile," *Winnipeg Free Press*, August 14, 2001, A1–A2.

18. Jeffrey Ball, Glenn Burkins, and Gregory White, "Why Labor Unions Have Grown Reluctant to Use the S-word," *The Wall Street Journal*, December 16, 1999, A1, A8.

19. Patrick Brethour, "Telus Gets Injunction Against Union," *The Globe and Mail*, July 25, 2005, B1, B4.

20. "Petro-Canada Workers Locked Out Last Year Advised to Accept Contract," *National Post*, December 20, 2008, FP2.

21. Jim Middlemiss, "Can't Bust Unions Through Bankruptcy; Difference in Canadian Law Compared With U.S.," *National Post*, April 11, 2009, FP5.

22. "Potash Corp., Union Seek Mediator to Get Contract Talks Back on the Rails," *National Post*, July 31, 2008, www.nationalpost.com/story-printer.html?id=690890.

23. "Postal Workers Vote to Strike," *National Post*, October 21, 2008, www.nationalpost.com/story-printer.html?id-895040.

24. "Ottawa Names Arbitrator to Decide Exit Package Terms for Air Canada Workers," *National Post*, August 20, 2008, www.nationalpost.com/story-printer.html?id=735135.

Chapter 10

1. "Bosses: Killing Them with Kindness Pays Off," *The Globe and Mail*, October 8, 2008, C3.

2. Daniel Goleman, *Emotional Intelligence: Why It Can Matter More Than IQ* (New York: Bantam Books, 1995); also Kenneth Law, Chi-Sum Wong, and Lynda Song, "The Construct and Criterion Validity of Emotional Intelligence and Its Potential Utility for Management Studies," *Journal of Applied Psychology* 89 no. 3 (2004): 78–90.

3. Daniel Goleman, "Leadership That Gets Results," *Harvard Business Review*, March–April 2000, 78–90.

4. Doris Burke, Corey Hajim, John Elliott, Jenny Mero, and Christopher Tkaczyk, "The Top Ten Companies for Leaders," *Fortune*, October 1, 2007, http://money.cnn.com/galleries/2007/fortune/0709/gallery.leaders_global_topten.fortune/index.html.

5. Frederick W. Taylor, *Principles of Scientific Management* (New York: Harper and Brothers, 1911).

6. See Daniel Wren, *The History of Management Thought* (New York: John Wiley & Sons, 2004).

7. Douglas McGregor, *The Human Side of Enterprise* (New York: McGraw-Hill, 1960).

8. Abraham Maslow, "A Theory of Human Motivation," *Psychological Review* (July 1943): 370–396.

9. Frederick Herzberg, Bernard Mausner, and Barbara Bloch Snydeman, *The Motivation to Work* (New York: Wiley, 1959).

10. Victor Vroom, *Work and Motivation* (New York: Wiley, 1964); Craig Pinder, *Work Motivation* (Glenview, IL: Scott, Foresman, 1984).

11. J. Stacy Adams, "Toward an Understanding of Inequity," *Journal of Abnormal and Social Psychology* 75 no. 5 (1963): 422–436.

12. Andy Holloway, "How the Game Is Played," *Canadian Business*, April 2, 2001, 26–35.

13. Brent Jang, "'WestJetters' Reap Rewards for Wild-Weather Work," *The Globe and Mail*, January 8, 2009, B7.

14. Deena Waisberg, "Tip of the Hat to Excellence; Employers get Creative with Rewards to Keep Top Performers," *National Post*, November 19, 2008, FP15.

15. For more information on some of the potential problems with goal setting, see Drake Bennett, "Do Goals Undermine Good Management?," *National Post*, March 24, 2009, FP10; also Wallace Immen, "The Goal: To Set Goals That Really Can Be Met," *The Globe and Mail*, March 20, 2009, B12.

16. Interviews with Sterling McLeod and Wayne Walker, senior vice-presidents of sales for Investors Group Financial Services.

17. Brent Jang, "High-Flying WestJet Morale Gets Put to the Test," *The Globe and Mail*, November 25, 2005, B3.

18. Virginia Galt, "Change Is a Good Thing When Everyone Is Involved," *The Globe and Mail*, June 25, 2005, B11.

19. Robert Grant, "AES Corporation: Rewriting the Rules of Management," *Contemporary Strategy Analysis* (Hoboken, NJ: John Wiley & Sons, 2007), www.blackwellpublishing.com/grant/docs/17AES.pdf.

20. Patricia Kitchen, "Tap Your Employees," *Orlando Sentinel*, March 14, 2007, F1.

21. Gregory Moorhead and Ricky W. Griffin, *Organizational Behavior*, 6th ed. (Boston: Houghton Mifflin, 2001), Chapter 7.

22. Ibid.

23. Ibid.

24. Ricky Griffin, *Task Design* (Glenview, IL: Scott, Foresman, 1982).

25. Kira Vermond, "Punching In on the Variable Clock," *The Globe and Mail*, March 22, 2008, B14.

26. Tavia Grant, "Lower Costs, Higher Morale Benefits of Four-Day Work Week," *The Globe and Mail*, August 18, 2008, B4.

27. Paul Lima, "With New Advances in Technology, Why Are We Still Jumping in the Car?," *The Globe and Mail*, October 20, 2008, E9.

28. Joyce Rosenberg, "Out of Sight, On Your Mind: Learning to Trust Telecommuters," *The Globe and Mail*, September 20, 2008, B19.

29. Paul Lima, "With New Advances in Technology, Why Are We Still Jumping in the Car?," *The Globe and Mail*, October 20, 2008, E9.

30. "Productivity Rises for Teleworkers: Survey," *The Globe and Mail*, October 15, 2008, C7.

31. Randi Chapnik Myers, "The Back and Forth of Working from Home," *The Globe and Mail*, March 8, 2008, B16.

32. Margot Gibb-Clark, "Satellite Office a Hit with Staff," *The Globe and Mail*, November 18, 1991, B4.

33. Dawn Walton, "Survey Focuses on Job Sharing," *The Globe and Mail*, June 10, 1997, B4.

34. John Kotter, "What Leaders Really Do," *Harvard Business Review*, December 2001, 85–94.

35. Ronald Heifetz and Marty Linsky, "A Survival Guide for Leaders," *Harvard Business Review*, June 2002, 65–74.

36. Frederick Reichheld, "Lead for Loyalty," *Harvard Business Review*, July–August 2001, 76–83.

37. Daniel Goleman, "What Makes a Leader?" *Harvard Business Review*, November–December 1998, 93–99.

38. David Dorsey, "Andy Pearson Finds Love," *Fast Company*, August 2001, 78–86.

39. David A. Waldman and Francis J. Yammarino, "CEO Charismatic Leadership: Levels-of-Management and Levels-of-Analysis Effects," *Academy of Management Review* 24 no. 2 (1999): 266–285.

40. Ronald Ebert and Ricky Griffin, *Business Essentials* (Upper Saddle River, NJ: Prentice Hall, 2009), 129.

41. Jane Howell and Boas Shamir, "The Role of Followers in the Charismatic Leadership Process: Relationships and Their Consequences," *Academy of Management Review* 30 no. 1 (2005): 96–112.

42. J. Richard Hackman and Ruth Wageman, "A Theory of Team Coaching," *Academy of Management Review* 30 no. 2 (2005): 269–287.

43. "How Women Lead," *Newsweek*, October 24, 2005, 46-70.

44. Madelaine Drohan, "What Makes a Canadian Manager?," *The Globe and Mail*, Feburary 25, 1997, B18.

45. Sinclair Stewart, "Passed by at TD, CEO Hits Stride in New York," *The Globe and Mail*, December 5, 2006, B1, B21.

46. Zena Olijnyk, Mark Brown, Andy Holloway, Calvin Leung, Alex Mlynek, Erin Pooley, Jeff Sanford, Andrew Wahl, and Thomas Watson, "Canada's Global Leaders," *Canadian Business*, March 28–April 10, 2005, 37–43.

Chapter 11

1. *Our Time: GE Annual Report: 2004* (Fairfield, CT: General Electric Co., 2005), 4–5.

2. Andrew Nikiforuk, "Pure Profit," *Canadian Business*, April 3, 2000, 70–76.

3. Daniel Michaels and J. Lynn Lunsford, "Lack of Seats, Galleys Delays Boeing, Airbus," *The Wall Street Journal*, August 2008, B1.

4. Judy Strauss and Raymond Frost, *Marketing on the Internet* (Upper Saddle River, NJ: Prentice Hall, 1999), 266–271.

5. Eryn Brown, "America's Most Admired Companies," *Fortune*, March 1, 1999, 68, 70–73; http://walmartstores.com, April 24, 2000.

6. Judy Strauss and Raymond Frost, *Marketing on the Internet* (Upper Saddle River, NJ: Prentice Hall, 1999), 266–271.

7. Rasha Mourtada, "Building on a Gouda Reputation," *The Globe and Mail*, June 30, 2008, B4.

8. Susan Carey, "The Case of the Vanishing Airport Lines," *The Wall Street Journal*, August 9, 2007, B1.

9. Mark Lander, "Slovakia No Longer a Laggard in Automaking," *nytimes.com*, April 13, 2004, www.nytimes.com/2004/04/13/business/worldbusiness.

10. Christina Passariello, "Louis Vuitton Tries Modern Methods on Factory Lines," *The Wall Street Journal*, October 9, 2006, A1, A15.

11. Neal Boudette, "Chrysler Gains Edge by Giving New Flexibility to Its Factories,"

The Wall Street Journal, April 11, 2006, A1, A15.

12. Greg Keenan, "Ford's New Maxim: Flex Manufacturing," *The Globe and Mail*, May 10, 2006, B3.

13. Lou Michel, "WNY's Trash, China's Treasure," *The Buffalo News*, July 20, 2008.

14. Don Marshall, "Time for Just in Time," *P&IM Review*, June 1991, 20–22. See also Gregg Stocker, "Quality Function Deployment: Listening to the Voice of the Customer," *APICS: The Performance Advantage*, September 1991, 44–48.

15. Lee J. Krajewski and Larry P. Ritzman, *Operations Management: Strategy and Analysis*, 6th ed. (Upper Saddle River, NJ: Prentice Hall, 2002), 153–154, 828–829; Robert S. Russell and Bernard W. Taylor III, *Operations Management*, 4th ed. (Upper Saddle River, NJ: Prentice Hall, 2003), 221–222, 593–595.

16. Robert S. Russell and Bernard W. Taylor III, *Operations Management*, 4th ed. (Upper Saddle River, NJ: Prentice Hall, 2003), 222–224.

17. Lee J. Krajewski and Larry P. Ritzman, *Operations Management: Strategy and Analysis*, 6th ed. (Upper Saddle River, NJ: Prentice Hall, 2002), 595.

18. Tom Murphy, "E Cyber Squeeze: The Pressure Is On," *Ward's Auto World* (December 2000): 44–47.

19. The Disney Institute, www.disneyinstitute.com/DisneyInstitute/ProfessionalPrograms/DisneyDifference/index.html.

20. Bruce Little, "Stock Answers," *The Globe and Mail*, June 6, 1995, B12.

21. Bruce McDougall, "The Thinking Man's Assembly Line," *Canadian Business*, November 1991, 40.

22. Alan Freeman, "Why Firms Avoid Taking Inventory," *The Globe and Mail*, December 12, 1994, B1, B4.

23. Clare Ansberry, "A New Hazard for Recovery: Last-Minute Pace of Orders," *The Wall Street Journal*, June 25, 2002, A1, A12.

Chapter 12

1. Gordon Pitts, "Message for Manufacturers: Go Big, Don't Stay at Home," *The Globe and Mail*, December 6, 2005, B1, B7.

2. Bart VanArk and Robert McGuckin, "International Comparisons of Labor Productivity and per Capita Income," *Monthly Labor Review*, July 1999, 33–41.

3. Harvey Enchin, "Canada Urged to Stop Living Off Fat of the Land," *The Globe and Mail*, October 25, 1991, B1, B6.

4. Jon Hilsenrath, "Behind Surging Productivity: The Service Sector Delivers," *The Wall Street Journal*, November 7, 2003, A1, A8.

5. Evan Ramstad, "Steelmakers Develop New Iron Recipes," *The Wall Street Journal* (Eastern Edition), August 29, 2008, B1.

6. Peter Kennedy, "Canfor Goes High Tech to Cut Costs," *The Globe and Mail*, July 29, 2000, 3.

7. J.D. Power and Associates, *2008 Initial Quality Study*, www.jdpower.com/corporate/news/releases/pressrelease.aspx?id=2008063.

8. Lee J. Krajewski and Larry P. Ritzman, *Operations Management: Strategy and Analysis*, 5th ed. (Reading, MA: Addison-Wesley, 1999), 229–230.

9. Bruce McDougall, "The Thinking Man's Assembly Line," *Canadian Business*, November 1991, 40.

10. Thomas Foster Jr., *Managing Quality: An Integrative Approach* (Upper Saddle River, NJ: Prentice Hall, 2001), 22–23.

11. Ted Wakefield, "No Pain, No Gain," *Canadian Business*, January 1993, 50–54.

12. David Kesmodel, "Oversight 'Flaw' led to Meat Recall; Lax Monitoring Seen at Plant's Cattle Pens Before Closure," *The Wall Street Journal* (Eastern Edition), March 11, 2008, B1.

13. Thomas Foster Jr., *Managing Quality: An Integrative Approach* (Upper Saddle River, NJ: Prentice Hall, 2001), 325–339.

14. Ibid.

15. James Evans and James Dean Jr., *Total Quality: Management, Organization, and Strategy*, 2nd ed. (Cincinnati, OH: South-Western, 2000), 230.

16. Margot Gibb-Clark, "Hospital Managers Gain Tool to Compare Notes," *The Globe and Mail*, September 9, 1996, B9.

17. "Customer Service You Can Taste," *Canadian Business*, July 1991, 19–20.

18. www.nist.gov/public_affairs/releases/cargill_profile.html.

19. Roberta S. Russell and Bernard W. Taylor III, *Operations Management*, 4th ed. (Upper Saddle River, NJ: Prentice Hall, 2003), 658–662; Thomas Foster Jr., *Managing Quality: An Integrative Approach* (Upper Saddle River, NJ: Prentice Hall, 2001), 85–86.

20. Roberta S. Russell and Bernard W. Taylor III, *Operations Management*, 4th ed. (Upper Saddle River, NJ: Prentice Hall, 2003), 137–140.

21. Sunil Chopra and Peter Meindl, *Supply Chain Management: Strategy, Planning, and Operation*, 6th ed. (Upper Saddle River, NJ: Prentice Hall, 2001), 3–6; Lee J. Krajewski and Larry P. Ritzman, *Operations Management: Strategy and Analysis*, 5th ed. (Reading, MA: Addison-Wesley, 1999), Chapter 11; Roberta S. Russell and Bernard W. Taylor III, *Operations Management*, 4th ed. (Upper Saddle River, NJ: Prentice Hall, 2003), Chapter 7; Thomas Foster Jr., *Managing Quality: An Integrative Approach* (Upper Saddle River, NJ: Prentice Hall, 2001), Chapter 9.

22. Sunil Chopra and Peter Meindl, *Supply Chain Management: Strategy, Planning, and Operation*, 6th ed. (Upper Saddle River, NJ: Prentice Hall, 2001), Chapter 20.

23. Ibid., 348–349.

24. Christina Passariello, "Louis Vuitton Tries Modern Methods on Factory Lines," *The Wall Street Journal*, October 9, 2006, A1, A15.

25. Duncan Mavin, "Supply Chains Worry CEOs," *National Post*, September 11, 2008, FP3.

26. Catherine Greenman, "An Old Craft Learns New Tricks," *The New York Times*, June 10, 1999, G1, G7.

27. Gillian Babicz, "Six Sigma Software Generates Improvements," *Quality*, April 2002, 28.

28. Terrence Belford, "Real Estate Heaven Is No Mistake," *The Globe and Mail*, March 22, 2005, B9.

29. Neil Orkin, "Focus on China," *Training Magazine* 45 no. 6 (July–Aug. 2008), ABI/INFORM Global database, p.18.

30. "Evaluate the Value of Training," *Quality*, April 2002, 48.

31. Leonard L. Berry, A. Parasuraman, and Valarie A. Zeithaml, "Improving Service Quality in America: Lessons Learned," *Academy of Management Executive* 8 no. 2 (1994): 32–45.

Chapter 13

1. Kenneth C. Laudon and Jane P. Laudon, *Management Information Systems: Managing the Digital Firm*, 7th ed. (Upper Saddle River, NJ: Prentice Hall, 2002), 7–11.

2. Gene Bylinsky, "Industry's Amazing Instant Prototypes," *Fortune*, January 12, 1998, 120(B-D).

3. Geoffrey Rowan, "Unique Software Thinks Like a Human," *The Globe and Mail*, December 31, 1996, B1, B4.

4. Kenneth C. Laudon and Jane P. Laudon, *Essentials of Management Information Systems*, 3rd ed. (Upper Saddle River, NJ: Prentice Hall, 1999), 383–388; E. Wainwright Martin et al., *Managing Information Technology: What Managers Need to Know*, 3rd ed. (Upper Saddle River, NJ: Prentice Hall, 1999), 225–227.

5. Emily Smith, "Turning an Expert's Skills into Computer Software," *Business Week*, October 7, 1985, 104–107.

6. Mike Lazaridis, "Because Someone Had to Stand Up for All Those Frustrated Engineers," *Inc. Magazine*, April 2005, 98; "Blackberry Subscribers Surge to Over

Three Million," *Business Wire*, May 9, 2005.

7. "Northrup Grumman Awards International Contracts for F-35 Joint Strike Fighter," *Northrup Grumman News Release*, September 29, 2005, www.irconnect.com/noc/pages/news_printer.html?=86963&print=1; Faith Keenan and Spencer T. Ante, "The New Teamwork," *BusinessWeek Online*, February 18, 2002, www.businessweek.com/magazine/content/02_07/b3770601.htm.

8. Emily Walzer, "Have it Your Way," *Sporting Goods Business* 38 no. 1 (2005): 42.

9. "3D Systems Helps Walter Reed Army Medical Center Rebuild Lives," *3D Systems*, July 6, 2005, www.3Dsystems.com.

10. "Wireless Endoscopy—The Camera Is a Pill," *Three Rivers Endoscopy Center*, August 17, 2005, www.gihealth.com; "Expanding the Scope of GI," *Given Imaging*, July 6, 2005, www.givenimaging.com.

11. Canadian Media Directors Council, *Media Digest, 2008-2009* (Toronto: Marketing, 2008), www.cmdc.ca/pdf/2008_09_Media_Digest.pdf.

12. "An Intranet's Life Cycle," *morebusiness.com*, November 6, 2005, www.morebusiness.com/getting_started/website/d928247851.brc; "Calling All Workers," *CIO Magazine*, December 1, 2001, 222.cio.com/archive/120101/ruke_ford.html.

13. William Bulkeley, "Better Virtual Meetings," *The Wall Street Journal*, September 28, 2006, B1, B5.

14. Kenneth C. Laudon and Jane P. Laudon, *Management Information Systems: Managing the Digital Firm*, 7th ed. (Upper Saddle River, NJ: Prentice Hall, 2002), 237–244.

15. Simon Avery, "Hunting Season for Computer Attackers," *The Globe and Mail*, July 6, 2005, B1, B4.

16. "Canada's Software Piracy Rate Decreases," *Winnipeg Free Press*, May 24, 2006, B7.

17. "Hacker Sentenced to Prison for Breaking into Lowe's Companies Computers with Intent to Steal Credit Card Information," news release, Department of Justice, Western District of North Carolina, December 15, 2004.

18. Hiawatha Bray, "Music Industry Aims to Send in Radio Cops," *The Boston Globe*, November 15, 2004, www.boston.com/business/technology/articles/2004/11/15/music_industry_aims_to_send_in_radio_cops?mode=PF; "Bush Creates Intellectual Property Czar," *Patent Baristas*, July 28, 2005, www.patentbaristas.com/archives/00217.php; Howard Paul, "What You Cannot Protect, You Cannot Own," *Sai Global*, January 29, 2004, www.sai-global.com/newsroom/tgs/2004-02/digital/digital.htm.

19. For information on spyware, see www.webopedia.com/TERM/S/spyware.html.

20. www.webopedia.com.

21."ISP Wins $1 Billion in Spam Suit," *CNET News.com*, December 19, 2004, http://news.cnet.com/ISP-wins-1-billion-in-spam-suit/2100-1028_3-5497211.html; Mike Wendland, "Innocents Suffer in War on Spam," *Detroit Free Press*, July 11, 2003, www.freep.com/cgi-bin/forms/printerfriendly.pl.

22. Allison Jones, "Verification Revamp Urged vs. Net Fraud," *Winnipeg Free Press*, October 19, 2006, B10.

23. Jason Stein, "Madison, Wis., Company Offers Software that Protects Clients' Information," *The Wisconsin State Journal*, July 20, 2005, 1.

Chapter 14

1. Ronald Hilton, *Managerial Accounting*, 2nd ed. (New York: McGraw-Hill, 1994), 7.

2. "Canada's Chartered Accountants Congratulate 2,701 Candidates Who Passed the 2008 Uniform Evaluation," *CICA*, media release, www.cica.ca/news/media-centre/media-releases-and-backgrounders/2008/item8644.aspx.

3. "CGA-Canada Announces 2008 Fellowship Recipients," *Canada NewsWire*, www.newswire.ca/en/releases/archive/February2009/05/c5463.html.

4. Certified Management Accountants of Canada, www.cma-canada.org.

5. Elizabeth MacDonald, "Accounting Sleuths Ferret Hidden Assets," *The Wall Street Journal*, December 18, 1996, B1–B2.

6. Philip Mathias, "Non-Profits Fight Move to GAAP Accounting," *Financial Post*, March 5, 1994, 15.

7. Bruce Horovitz, "Restoring the Golden-Arch Shine," *USA Today*, June 16, 1999, 3B.

8. Charles T. Horngren, Walter T. Harrison Jr., and Linda Smith Bamber, *Accounting*, 5th ed. (Upper Saddle River, NJ: Prentice Hall, 2002), 17–20.

9. Ronald Hilton, *Managerial Accounting*, 2nd ed. (New York: McGraw-Hill, 1994), 402–403.

10. Billie Cunningham, Loren Nikolai, and John Bazley, *Accounting: Information for Business Decisions* (Fort Worth, TX: Dryden, 2000), 133–134.

11. Charles T. Horngren, Walter T. Harrison Jr., and Linda Smith Bamber, *Accounting*, 4th ed. (Upper Saddle River, NJ: Prentice Hall, 1999), 562–563; Arthur J. Keown et al., *The Foundations of Finance: The Logic and Practice of Financial Management*, 2nd ed. (Upper Saddle River, NJ: Prentice Hall, 1998), 89–95.

12. Charles T. Horngren, Walter T. Harrison Jr., and Linda Smith Bamber, *Accounting*, 4th ed. (Upper Saddle River, NJ: Prentice Hall, 1999), 201–202.

13. Alvin C. Burns and Ronald F. Bush, *Marketing Research*, 3rd ed. (Upper Saddle River, NJ: Prentice Hall, 2000), 70–84.

Chapter 15

1. American Marketing Association, "Marketing Services Guide," August 23, 2001, www.ama.org/about/ama/markdef.asp. 2; Philip Kotler, *Marketing Management*, 11th ed. (Upper Saddle River, NJ: Prentice Hall, 2003), 76–78.

3. Warren J. Keegan and Mark C. Green, *Global Marketing*, 3rd ed. (Upper Saddle River, NJ: Prentice Hall, 2003), 8–15.

4. Jennifer Wells, "Hoarding, Frustrating, Winning," *The Globe and Mail*, August 23, 2008, B4.

5. Philip Kotler and Peggy Cunningham, *Marketing Management* (Toronto: Prentice Hall, 2004), 18.

6. Peter Gumbel, "Mass vs. Class," *Fortune*, September 17, 2007, 82.

7. Chris Isidore, "Sweet Spot: Luxury SUV's are Hot," *CNNMoney*, January 7, 2004, http://money.cnn.com/2004/01/06/news/companies/detroit_luxury_suv/index.htm.

8. Aparita Bhandari, "Ethnic Marketing—It's More Than Skin Deep," *The Globe and Mail*, September 7, 2005, B3.

9. Lauren Goldstein, "Dressing Up an Old Brand," *Fortune*, November 9, 1998, 154–156.

10. Peter Gumbel, "Mass vs. Class," *Fortune*, September 17, 2007, 82.

11. Tamara Audi, "Las Vegas Goes All Out to Attract Gay Travelers," *The Wall Street Journal*, November 2, 2007, B1.

12. Philip Kotler, *Marketing Management*, 11th ed. (Upper Saddle River, NJ: Prentice Hall, 2003), 292–294.

13. Naoufel Daghfous, John V. Petrof, and Frank Pons, "Values and Innovations: A Cross-cultural Study," *The Journal of Consumer Marketing* 16 no. 4 (2009): 314–331.

14. John Morton, "How to Spot the Really Important Prospects," *Business Marketing* (January 1990): 62–67.

15. Matt Phillips, "Pow! Romance! Comics Court Girls," *The Wall Street Journal*, June 8, 2007, B1.

16. Ellen Byron, "A Virtual View of the Store Aisle," *The Wall Street Journal*, October 3, 2007, B1.

17. Alvin C. Burns and Ronald F. Bush, *Marketing Research*, 3rd ed. (Upper Saddle River, NJ: Prentice Hall, 2000), 70–84.

18. Marina Strauss, "First You Have to Get Their Attention," *The Globe and Mail*, July 12, 1991, B1.

19. Emily Nelson, "P&G Checks Out Real Life," *The Wall Street Journal*, May 17, 2001, B1, B4.

20. Joseph Pereira, "Spying on the Sales Floor," *The Wall Street Journal*, December 21, 2004, B1, B4.

21. Julie Jargon, "Kiwi Goes beyond Shine in Effort to Step Up Sales," *The Wall Street Journal*, December 20, 2007, B1.

22. Marina Strauss, "Mining Customer Feedback, Firms Go Undercover and Online," *The Globe and Mail*, May 13, 2004, B1, B25.

23. Deborah Ball, Sarah Ellison, and Janet Adamy, "Probing Shoppers' Psyche," *The Wall Street Journal*, October 28, 2004, B1, B8.

24. Oliver Bertin, "John Deere Reaps the Fruits of Its Labours," *The Globe and Mail*, September 2, 1991, B1, B3.

25. Peter Morton, "Marketing at Face Value," *National Post*, July 11, 2007, FP3.

26. Alvin C. Burns and Ronald F. Bush, *Marketing Research*, 3rd ed. (Upper Saddle River, NJ: Prentice Hall, 2000), 140–148.

27. Kenneth C. Laudon and Jane P. Laudon, *Management Information Systems: Managing the Digital Firm*, 7th ed. (Upper Saddle River, NJ: Prentice Hall, 2002), 221–222.

28. Ibid., 222–224.

29. Paul S. Foote and Malini Krishnamurthi, "Forecasting Using Data Warehousing Model: Wal-Mart's Experience," *The Journal of Business Forecasting Methods & Systems*, Fall 2001, 13–17.

30. www.statcan.gc.ca.

31. Thomas Russell, Glenn Verrill, and W. Ronald Lane, *Kleppner's Advertising Procedure*, 11th ed. (Englewood Cliffs, NJ: Prentice Hall, 1990); James Engel, Martin Warshaw, and Thomas Kinnear, *Promotional Strategy*, 6th ed. (Homewood, IL: Richard D. Irwin, 1987).

Chapter 16

1. Barrie McKenna and Matt Hartley, "Stringer Makes His Mark," *The Globe and Mail*, February 20, 2008, B1, B6.

2. Eric Reguly, "Beaudoin's Big, Bold Bet," *The Globe and Mail*, July 14, 2008, B1, B10.

3. Susanna Ray, "Dreamliner a Scheduling Nightmare; Delayed Yet Again; Boeing This Time Cites Strike and Fastener Problem," *National Post*, December 12, 2008, FP12.

4. James C. Anderson and James A. Narus, *Business Market Management: Understanding, Creating, and Delivering Value* (Upper Saddle River, NJ: Prentice Hall, 1999), 203–206.

5. Philip Kotler, *Marketing Management*, 11th ed. (Upper Saddle River, NJ: Prentice Hall, 2003), 328–339.

6. Julie Jargon, "The Iconic Oreo Squares Off in Kraft's Battle for Global Taste Buds," *The Globe and Mail*, May 1, 2008, B13.

7. Jennifer Wells, "Canadian Companies Hop on the Global Brand Wagon," *The Globe and Mail*, September 19, 2008, B7.

8. "30 Second Spot: Dispatches from the World of Media and Advertising," *The Globe and Mail*, January 16, 2009, B5.

9. "Australia Ranks #1 as World's Top Country Brand for Third Consecutive Year, Global Study Reveals," *Country Brand Index: 2008*, www.countrybrandindex.com/press-release.

10. Keith McArthur, "How to Survive an Identity Crisis," *The Globe and Mail*, November 14, 2005, B1, B11.

11. "Canada's Most Valuable Brands 2009," *Brand Finance Canada*, Spring 2009, www.brandfinance.com/Uploads/pdfs/BrandFinanceCanadaMostValuableBrands2009.pdf.

12. John Frook, "Cisco Scores with Its Latest Generation of Empowering Tools," *B to B*, August 20, 2001, 20.

13. Cyndee Miller, "Little Relief Seen for New Product Failure Rate," *Marketing News*, June 21, 1993, 1; Nancy J. Kim, "Back to the Drawing Board," *The Bergen Record* (New Jersey), December 4, 1994, B1, B4.

14. Marina Strauss, "The Secret to Gaining Success in Quebec," *The Globe and Mail*, September 27, 2005, B4.

15. Konrad Yakabuski, "How Pepsi Won Quebec," *The Globe and Mail*, August 28, 2008, B1-B2.

16. Bertrand Marotte, "I Am Canadian—But Not Necessarily in Quebec Marketing," *The Globe and Mail*, December 8, 2007, B8.

17. Brian Milner, "Canada's Franklin the Turtle Heads South," *The Globe and Mail*, February 14, 2000, B1, B10.

18. Marina Strauss, "Shoppers Sees Gold in Private Labels," *The Globe and Mail*, January 3, 2005, B1–B2.

19. Richard Bloom, "Taking on the World, One Jar at a Time," *The Globe and Mail*, July 4, 2005, B3.

20. Marina Strauss, "Consumers Less Trusting of Brands," *The Globe and Mail*, February 13, 2003, B3.

21. Paul Glader, "Avid Boarders Bypass Branded Gear," *The Wall Street Journal*, July 27, 2007, B1–B2.

22. Keith McArthur, "Why Molson Is Crying in Its Beer," *The Globe and Mail*, July 10, 2004, B4.

23. "Mega Brands Wins Case over Lego," *The Globe and Mail*, November 13, 2008, B3.

24. David Square, "Mouse Pad Gets Oodles of Nibbles," *Winnipeg Free Press*, July 26, 1997, B10.

25. Paul Waldie, "How RIM's Big Deal Was Done," *The Globe and Mail*, March 6, 2006, B1, B14.

26. Simon Avery, "RIM Faces New U.S. Fight Over Patents," *The Globe and Mail*, May 2, 2006, B3.

27. Avery Johnson, "Pfizer Buys More Time for Lipitor," *The Wall Street Journal*, June 19, 2008, B1.

28. "Google to Pay US$125 Million to Settle Copyright Lawsuits Over Book Project," *National Post*, October 29, 2008, FP6.

29. Deborah Ball, "The Perils of Packaging: Nestle Aims for Easier Openings," *The Wall Street Journal*, November 17, 2005, B1, B5.

30. Keith McArthur, "Oh? Canada? Ads Beg to Differ," *The Globe and Mail*, July 1, 2004, B1, B18.

31. William Pride and O.C. Ferrell, *Marketing*, 5th ed. (Boston: Houghton Mifflin, 1987).

32. Calvin Leung, "Marketing Ubiquity," *Canadian Business*, February 18, 2008, 28.

33. Robert Berner, "The Rolls-Royce of Leather Jackets Is Hard to Come By," *The Wall Street Journal*, November 22, 1996, A1, A10.

34. Kenneth E. Clow and Donald Baack, *Integrated Advertising, Promotion, and Marketing Communications* (Upper Saddle River, NJ: Prentice Hall, 2002), Chapter 5.

35. John Heinzl, "Buckley Wants U.S. to Swallow Its Bad Taste," *The Globe and Mail*, November 11, 1999, B1, B12.

36. Marina Strauss, "Towel War Turns to Name-Naming," *The Globe and Mail*, December 5, 1995, B1, B10.

37. Canadian Media Directors Council, *Media Digest, 2008-2009*, Components of Net Advertising Revenue by Medium, (Toronto: Marketing, 2008), 14, www.cmdc.ca/pdf/2008_09_Media_Digest.pdf.

38. Andrew Wahl, "Red All Over," *Canadian Business*, February 13–26, 2006, 53–54.

39. Aaron O. Patrick, "Technology Boosts Outdoor Ads as Competition Becomes Fiercer," *The Wall Street Journal*, August 23, 2006, A1, A10.

40. Canadian Media Directors Council, *Media Digest, 2008-2009*, Components of Net Advertising Revenue by Medium, (Toronto: Marketing, 2008), 14, www.cmdc.ca/pdf/2008_09_Media_Digest.pdf.

41. Allan Kreda, "Advertisers Lured by Super Bowl's Glitz, Huge Ratings," *The Globe and Mail*, December 30, 2004, B3.

42. Canadian Media Directors Council, *Media Digest, 2008-2009*, Components of Net Advertising Revenue by Medium, (Toronto: Marketing, 2008), 14, www.cmdc.ca/pdf/2008_09_Media_Digest.pdf.

43. Ibid.

44. James Adams, "*Reader's Digest* Still Rules Magazine Roost," *The Globe and Mail*, March 27, 2009, B2.

45. Canadian Media Directors Council, *Media Digest, 2008-2009*, Components of Net Advertising Revenue by Medium, (Toronto: Marketing, 2008), 14, www.cmdc.ca/pdf/2008_09_Media_Digest.pdf.

46. Matt Hartley, "Tunnel Visionaries," *The Globe and Mail*, January 31, 2008, B18.

47. "30 Second Spot: Dispatches from the World of Media and Advertising," *The Globe and Mail*, October 31, 2008, B8.

48. Aaron O. Patrick, "Technology Boosts Outdoor Ads as Competition Becomes Fiercer," *The Wall Street Journal*, August 23, 2006, A1, A10; Grant Robertson, "Growth in Internet Ads Outpaces All Others," *The Globe and Mail*, June 23, 2006, B4; Canadian Media Directors Council, *Media Digest, 2008-2009*, Components of Net Advertising Revenue by Medium, (Toronto: Marketing, 2008), 14, www.cmdc.ca/pdf/2008_09_Media_Digest.pdf.

49. Mike Blaney, "Word of Mouth Advertising," blog, www.themarketingguy.wordpress.com/2007/10/09/word-of-mouth-advertising.

50. Sarah Scott, "Ready for Their Close-Up," *Financial Post Business*, September 2007, 40–45.

51. Philip Kotler, Gary Armstrong, and Peggy H. Cunningham, *Principles of Marketing*, 6th Canadian ed. (Toronto: Pearson, 2005), 88.

52. Canadian Media Directors Council, *Media Digest, 2008-2009*, Components of Net Advertising Revenue by Medium, (Toronto: Marketing, 2008), 14, www.cmdc.ca/pdf/2008_09_Media_Digest.pdf.

53. Amol Sharma and Emily Steel, "Ads Critical to MySpace," *The Wall Street Journal*, August 4, 2008, B5.

54. Ronald Ebert and Ricky Griffin, *Business Essentials* (Upper Saddle River, NJ: Prentice Hall, 2009), 161.

55. Emily Steel, "YouTube Launches Video Ads," *The Wall Street Journal*, August 22, 2007, B9.

56. Emily Steel, "As Search Habits Change, Advertisers Look Past Google, Yahoo," *The Globe and Mail*, January 20, 2009, B10.

57. Philip Kotler, Gary Armstrong, and Peggy H. Cunningham, *Principles of Marketing*, 6th Canadian ed. (Toronto: Pearson, 2005), 89–91.

58. Simon Tuck, "Security Rated Top On-Line Fear," *The Globe and Mail*, July 5, 1999, B5.

59. James Hagerty and Dennis Berman, "New Battleground in Web Privacy War: Ads That Snoop," *The Wall Street Journal*, August 27, 2003, A1, A8.

60. Stuart Elliott, "Real or Virtual? You Call It," *The New York Times*, October 1, 1999, C1, C6.

61. William Wells, John Burnett, and Sandra Moriarty, *Advertising: Principles and Practice*, 5th ed. (Upper Saddle River, NJ: Prentice Hall, 2000), 77–83.

62. Ann Gibbon, "Ad Group Tries to Demystify Quebec," *The Globe and Mail*, November 25, 1993, B6.

63. "Regulators Wary of Ads Rapping Rivals," *The Globe and Mail*, May 23, 1991, B4.

64. Simon Avery, "Do Not Call List Could Give Boost to Direct Mail," *The Globe and Mail*, September 29, 2008, B3.

65. Hollie Shaw, "Do Not Call List a Ringing Success," *National Post*, March 13, 2009, FP12.

66. Oliver Moore, "Clement Blasts Do-Not-Call Scammers," *The Globe and Mail*, January 26, 2009, A4.

67. John Heinzl, "Beer Firms Rethink Giveaways," *The Globe and Mail*, March 3, 2003, B1, B5.

68. Grant Robertson, "Thanks, But No Thanks," *The Globe and Mail*, August 29, 2008, B5; Rebecca Dana, "When You're Here, You're Family—But What About a Playboy Model?," *The Wall Street Journal*, August 13, 2008, A1, A14.

69. "2012 Games Boost Finances with Cadbury Sponsorship," *The Globe and Mail*, October 21, 2008, B15.

70. Warren J. Keegan, *Global Marketing Management*, 7th ed. (Upper Saddle River, NJ: Prentice Hall, 2002), Chapter 14.

71. Norman M. Scarborough and Thomas W. Zimmerer, *Effective Small Business Management: An Entrepreneurial Approach*, 6th ed. (Upper Saddle River, NJ: Prentice Hall, 2000), Chapter 11.

Chapter 17

1. Constance L. Hays, "Coke Tests Weather-Linked Pricing," *The Globe and Mail*, October 29, 1999, B11.

2. Stefan Fatsis, "The Barry Bonds Tax: Teams Raise Prices for Good Games," *The Wall Street Journal*, December 3, 2002, D1, D8.

3. Leila Abboud and Jenny Clevstrom, "Swedes Try Toll Plan to Unsnarl Traffic," *The Globe and Mail*, August 29, 2006, B10; Lawrence Solomon, "Sweden Proves Congestion Tolls Work," *National Post*, August 4, 2007, FP13.

4. Lawrence Solomon, "Revolution on the Road: Pay-Per-Mile Insurance," *National Post*, October 14, 2006, FP15.

5. David George-Cosh, "Cisco Joins Skymeter to Help Unsnarl City Traffic," *National Post*, October 6, 2008, www.nationalpost.com/story-printer.html?id=862402.

6. Stephen Kindel, "Tortoise Gains on Hare," *Financial World*, February 23, 1988, 18–20.

7. Ethan Smith, "Universal Slashes CD Prices in Bid to Revive Music Industry," *The Wall Street Journal*, September 4, 2003, B1, B8.

8. Chester Zelasko, "Acesulfame-K," *Better Life Institute*, May 17, 2001, www.betterlifeunlimited.com/healthnews/health_az/display.aspx?id=69141141052.

9. Stewart A. Washburn, "Establishing Strategy and Determining Cost in the Pricing Decision," *Business Marketing*, July 1985, 64–78.

10. Marina Strauss, "Why Everyday Low Prices Failed Zellers," *The Globe and Mail*, March 22, 2005, B8.

11. Judy Strauss and Raymond Frost, *E-Marketing*, 2nd ed. (Upper Saddle River, NJ: Prentice Hall, 2001), 166–167; Eloise Coupey, *Marketing and the Internet* (Upper Saddle River, NJ: Prentice Hall, 2001), 281–283.

12. "Wal-Mart Rounds Prices to Lure Shoppers," *The Globe and Mail*, April 15, 2009, B12.

13. Marina Strauss, "Taking 'e' Out of E-commerce: Meet the eBay Middleman," *The Globe and Mail*, October 6, 2004, B1, B19.

14. Paul Waldie, "Battle over Real Estate Listings Spurs Probe," *The Globe and Mail*, March 26, 2007, B1–B2.

15. Ahmad Diba, "An Old-Line Agency Finds an Online Niche," *Fortune*, April 3, 2000, 258.

16. *Fiscal 2001 In Review,* Dell Annual Report, April 22, 2002, www.dell.com/downloads/global/corporate/annual/2001_DELL_Annual.pdf; Qiao Song, "Legend Outlines Role in China's Wireless Future," *ebn*, March 25, 2002, 3; Faith Hung, "Legend Looks to Defend Its Turf—WTO Entry Will Force China's Top PC Maker to Fend Off Unrestricted Rivals," *ebn*, December 17, 2001, 44; Neel Chowdhury, "Dell Cracks China," *Fortune*, June 21, 1999, 120–124.

17. Keith McArthur, "Para Paints' Bold Stroke," *The Globe and Mail*, October 18, 1999, M1.

18. Dale M. Lewison, *Retailing*, 5th ed. (New York: Macmillan, 1994), 454; Louis Stern and Adel I. El-Ansary, *Marketing Channels*, 4th ed. (Englewood Cliffs, NJ: Prentice Hall, 1992), 129–130.

19. Direct Selling Association, www.dsa.org.

20. Gordon Pitts, "Tupperware Shows the World How to Party," *The Globe and Mail*, February 9, 2008, B3.

21. Expedia.com, www.expedia.com.

22. Ann Bednarz, "Acquisitions Tighten Supply-Chain Market," *Network World*, February 9, 2004, 21–22.

23. Marina Strauss, "E-tailing in Age of Refinement," *The Globe and Mail*, August 3, 2005, B6.

24. "Did You Know?" *Catalog News.com*, www.catalog-news.com, April 8, 2002; Judy Strauss and Raymond Frost, *E-Marketing* (Upper Saddle River, NJ: Prentice Hall, 2001), 140.

25. "More Than 8.4 Million Canadians Spent $12.8 Billion over the Internet in 2007," *National Post*, November 18, 2008, FP6.

26. Zena Olijnyk, "Dot-Com Wonder Boys," *Canadian Business*, April 14, 2003, 30–36.

27. Vito Pilieci, "Taxman Eyes Internet Sellers," *Winnipeg Free Press*, November 18, 2008, B5.

28. Geoffrey Fowler, "EBay Retreats in Web Retailing," *The Wall Street Journal*, March 12, 2009, A1, A11.

29. Peter Elkind, "Shhhhh! Amway's on the Web," *Fortune*, March 6, 2000, 76.

30. "LivePerson.com™," www.liveperson.com, April 19, 2000.

31. Gordon Jaremko, "River Highway in Canada's North Open for Business," *Winnipeg Free Press*, July 25, 2006, B10.

32. Anne T. Coughlan et al., *Marketing Channels*, 6th ed. (Upper Saddle River, NJ: Prentice Hall, 2001), 458–462.

33. "Just One Word: Logistics," *Financial Post Business*, June 2007, 14–23.

Chapter 18

1. *Bank of Canada Banking and Financial Statistics*, Series B4, Statistics Pertaining to Counterfeit Bank of Canada Notes, April 2009, S14.

2. Dean Beeby, "Canadians Worry about Counterfeit Cash: Survey," *Winnipeg Free Press*, June 26, 2006, B8.

3. Omar El Akkad, "Canada's $5 Bill Offers New Security Features," *The Globe and Mail*, April 5, 2006, B5.

4. *Bank of Canada Banking and Financial Statistics*, Series E1, Selected Monetary Aggregates, April 2009, S50.

5. Tara Perkins, "Credit Card Perks Putting the Squeeze on Retailers," *The Globe and Mail*, June 24, 2008, B1, B5.

6. Boyd Erman, "Visa's IPO Taps into the World's Love of Plastic," *The Globe and Mail*, February 26, 2008, B1, B6.

7. Tara Perkins, "Credit Card Perks Putting the Squeeze on Retailers," *The Globe and Mail*, June 24, 2008, B1, B5.

8. "Retailers Want Ottawa to Regulate Debit and Credit Card Fees," *CBC.ca*, www.cbc.ca/consumer/story/2009/04/21/fees.html.

9. Danny Bradbury, "Better Safeguards in the Cards; Credit Card Safety," *National Post*, March 12, 2009, FP12.

10. Tom Lowry, "Thieves Swipe Credit with Card Readers," *USA Today*, June 28, 1999, 1B.

11. Geoff Kirbyson, "High-Tech Credit Cards Latest Crime-Fighting Tool," *Winnipeg Free Press*, December 23, 2008, A5.

12. Marina Strauss, "Need a Mortgage with Those Tools?," *The Globe and Mail*, September 5, 2007, B1, B4.

13. Tara Perkins, "They'll Even Plan Your Funeral," *The Globe and Mail*, September 29, 2007, B4–B6.

14. Tara Perkins, "A Piece of Drywall Away from Being Part of the Branch," *The Globe and Mail*, April 26, 2008, B6.

15. Karen Horcher, "Reconstruction Zone," *CGA Magazine*, June 1997, 19.

16. *Bank of Canada Banking and Financial Statistics*, Series C1, Chartered Bank Assets, April 2009, S16.

17. Tara Perkins and Tavia Grant, "You Can Make a Lot of Money in This Business," *The Globe and Mail*, April 23, 2007, B6.

18. Robin Arnfield, "Canada Addresses Dispute Resolution," *Cards & Payments*, April 1, 2006, www.highbeam.com/doc/1G1-145024321.html.

19. "What You Bought on the Busiest Shopping Day of the Year," *City News*, www.citynews.ca/news/news_30437.asp.

20. Seamus McFee, "Visa's Debit Card Transactions Overtake Credit Cards," www.creditcards.com/credit-card-news/credit-card-stories.php; Theresa Ebden, "Interac in a Fight for Its Life," *The Globe and Mail*, April 15, 2009.

21. "Statistics for Smart Cards," *ePaynews.com*, June 14, 2004, www.epaynews.com/statistics/scardstats.html.

22. Tavia Grant, "Yunus Sees Big Answers in Microcredit," *The Globe and Mail*, June 11, 2008, B8.

23. "Credit Unions Continue to Lead in Customer Service," September 2, 2008, www.cucentral.ca/Synovate_2sept08.

24. "Google VC Fund Looking for 'Young Companies with Awesome Potential'," *National Post*, April 1, 2009, FP2.

25. David George-Cosh, "Lean Times for Tech Startups: VC's Offer Ideas on How to Kickstart the Industry," *National Post*, January 16, 2009, FP4; Stephen Hurwitz, "Misadventure Capitalism: A Byzantine Cross-Border Investment Regime Is Killing the Canadian Venture-Capital and Technology Industries," *National Post*, May 1, 2009, FP11.

26. Matt Hartley, "Venture Capital Breakdown," *The Globe and Mail*, May 8, 2009, B1.

27. Amit Monga, "Tough Times For Entrepreneurs," *National Post*, May 5, 2009, FP6.

28. "Venture Capital Investment Weakens," *BNN*, May 12, 2009, www.bnn.ca/news/9307.html.

29. www.economist.com/daily/chartgallery/displaystory.cfm?story_id=14065333.

30. Robert J. Carbaugh, *International Economics*, 5th ed. (Cincinnati, OH: South-Western, 1995), Chapter 11.

31. "The IMF, Deficits, and Tighter Regulation," *The Globe and Mail*, October 22, 2008, B6.

32. Kevin Carmichael and Brian Milner, "Nations Near Bankruptcy, but IMF Too Poor to Help," *The Globe and Mail*, February 27, 2009, B1.

33. Barrie McKenna, "Financial Crisis Puts IMF Back in Business," *The Globe and Mail*, October 24, 2008, B3.

Chapter 19

1. Joseph Nocera, "Do You Believe? How Yahoo! Became a Blue Chip," *Fortune*, June 7, 1999, 76–81.

2. Jeffrey Macintosh, "Unfair Trade: Alternative Trading Systems Make Stock Trading Cheaper and More Efficient, but There's a Downside," *National Post*, January 13, 2009, FP13.

3. Rob Carrick, "With Online Trading, It Pays to Shop Around," *The Globe and Mail*, June 2, 2008, B14.

4. "Online Broker Survey: Qtrade Wins Again," *The Globe and Mail*, November 20, 2008, E2.

5. Gordon J. Alexander, William F. Sharpe, and Jeffery V. Bailey, *Fundamentals of Investments*, 3rd ed. (Upper Saddle River, NJ: Prentice Hall, 2001), 36–39.

6. Ibid., 44–46.

7. *NASDAQ*, www.nasdaq.com/about/timeline.stm, June 25, 2000.

8. Aaron Lucchetti, "As Housing Boomed, Moody's Opened Up," *The Wall Street Journal*, April 11, 2008, A1, A15.

9. Boyd Erman, "DBRS to Roll Out a New Road Map on Risk," *The Globe and Mail*, February 8, 2008, B1, B6.

10. Keith Damsell, "Ethical Investing Proving a Hard Sell in Canada," *The Globe and Mail*, August 12, 2004, B10.

11. "Advantages and Disadvantages of Mutual Funds," *The Motley Fool*, www.fool.com.

12. "Why Exchange-Traded Funds?," *Yahoo! Finance*, Exchange-Traded Funds Center, www.finance.yahoo.com/etf/education/02.

13. Rob Carrick, "Tread Carefully in the World of Hedge Funds," *The Globe and Mail*, May 27, 2006, B8.

14. Paul Waldie and Sinclair Stewart, "Hedge Funds in the Crosshairs," *The Globe and Mail*, May 30, 2005, B4; Sinclair Stewart and Paul Waldie,

"The New Breed of 800-Pound Gorilla," *The Globe and Mail*, May 31, 2005, B7.

15. Boyd Erman and Derek DeCloet, "The Guys Who Had a Gut Feeling for Risk," *The Globe and Mail*, February 23, 2008, B4–B5.

16. Richard Blackwell, "TSE 300 Shift Will Shrink Index," *The Globe and Mail*, January 31, 2002, B17.

17. Rob Carrick, "Direct Plans Cut Brokers Out," *The Globe and Mail*, August 21, 1999, B8.

18. John Doyle, "The Rich Get Robbed—And It's Delicious TV," *The Globe and Mail*, May 12, 2009, R3.

19. Gordon J. Alexander, William F. Sharpe, and Jeffery V. Bailey, *Fundamentals of Investments*, 3rd ed. (Upper Saddle River, NJ: Prentice Hall, 2001), 37–38.

Chapter 20

1. Denise Deveau, "No Garden Variety Insurance," *Financial Post*, October 20, 2008, www.nationalpost.com/story-printer.html?id=892400.

2. Andrew Willis, "CanWest Halts Bondholder Payments," *The Globe and Mail*, March 13, 2009, B3.

3. *The State of Small Business, 1989 Annual Report on Small Business in Ontario* (Toronto: Ministry of Industry, Trade and Technology, 1990).

4. J. W. Duncan, *D&B Reports* (September–October 1991): 8.

5. Norman M. Scarborough and Thomas W. Zimmerer, *Effective Small Business Management: An Entrepreneurial Approach*, 6th ed. (Upper Saddle River, NJ: Prentice Hall, 2000), esp. 298–300.

6. Richard S. Boulton, Barry D. Libert, and Steve M. Samek, "Managing Risk in an Uncertain World," *Upside*, June 2000, 268–278.

7. Gordon Pitts and Bertrand Marotte, "Has Sabia Jumped from the Frying Pan into the Fire?," *The Globe and Mail*, March 14, 2009, www.globeinvestor.com/servlet/story/GAM.20090314.RSABIA14/GIStory/.

8. Tara Perkins, "BMO Retreats to Its Low-Risk Roots," *The Globe and Mail*, March 5, 2008, B5.

9. Thomas Fitch, *Dictionary of Banking Terms*, 2nd ed. (Hauppauge, NY: Barron's, 1993), 531.

10. Mark S. Dorfman, *Introduction to Risk Management and Insurance*, 6th ed. (Upper Saddle River, NJ: Prentice Hall, 2000), Chapter 1.

11. Oliver Bertin, "Firms Face Major Hurdles En Route to U.S. Markets," *The Globe and Mail*, April 29, 2004, B16.

12. Denyse O'Leary, "The Scams That Drive Up Premiums," *The Globe and Mail*, May 2, 1995, B1; Denyse O'Leary, "Insurers United Against Fraud Face Serious Obstacles," *The Globe and Mail*, May 2, 1995, B1.

13. Sinclair Stewart, "Sun Life's Insurance Policy: The Great Indian Middle Class," *The Globe and Mail*, October 1, 2005, B1, B6.

14. Yochi Dreazen, "As Iraq Terror Rises, Businessmen Find Niche in Life Insurance," *The Wall Street Journal*, August 19, 2005, A1, A16.

15. Mark S. Dorfman, *Introduction to Risk Management and Insurance*, 6th ed. (Upper Saddle River, NJ: Prentice Hall, 2000), 420–421.

Appendix B

1. See Chris Arthur J. Keown, *Personal Finance*, 3rd ed. (Upper Saddle River, NJ: Pearson Prentice Hall, 2004), 600–609.

2. Christopher Farrell, "No Need to Hit the Panic Button," *Business Week*, July 26, 2004, 76–80.

Sources

Chapter 1

The Ups and Downs of Commodities Vincent Lauerman, "Either Way You Look at It, Oil Sands in for Long Slump; Environment, Economy to Limit Demand Growth," *National Post*, January 6, 2009, FP6; Claudia Cattaneo, "OPEC Oil Cut Deep, but Not Deep Enough; Markets Answer Dare by Driving Price Down," *National Post*, December 18, 2008, FP3; Jamie Sturgeon, "Auto Woes Hit Palladium Mining; Catalytic Converter; North American Palladium Halts Ontario Mine," *National Post*, October 22, 2008, FP4; Geoffrey York and Andy Hoffman, "Big Red Machine Hits Speed Bump," *The Globe and Mail*, October 13, 2008, B1, B4; Shawn McCarthy, "The Cost of the Next Barrel," *The Globe and Mail*, June 14, 2008, B4; Guy Chazan, "Oil Sands Are Shifting in Alberta," *The Wall Street Journal*, February 5, 2008, A8; Peter Tertzakian, "Canada: Energy Superpower?," *The Globe and Mail*, May 28, 2005, B6; Barrie McKenna, "Welcome to the Age of Scarcity," *The Globe and Mail*, May 21, 2005, B15; Patrick Brethour, "Alberta's Earth-Shaking Ambitions," *The Globe and Mail*, April 4, 2005, B4–B5; Gregory L. White, "How Ford's Big Batch of Rare Metal Led to $1 Billion Write-Off," *The Wall Street Journal*, February 6, 2002, A1, A6.

Table 1.1 *Financial Post Magazine*, June 2009, 82. Material reprinted with the express permission of "The National Post Company," a Canwest Partnership.

Table 1.2 *The Competition Act*, Part VI, Offences in Relation to Competition, www.laws.justice.gc.ca/en/showdoc/cs/C-34/bo-ga:1_VI//en.

Entrepreneurship and New Ventures "Alexandre Dumas," The Modern Library, www.randomhouse.com/modernlibrary/library/author.pperl?authorid=7552; "Doing Business Abroad," Foreign Affairs and International Trade, www.tradecommissioner.gc.ca/eng/home.jsp; "Genuwine Cellars Captivates Discriminating Tastes—Robb Denomme Wins BDC's Young Entrepreneur Award for Manitoba," *Canada NewsWire*, October 21, 2008, retrieved from Proquest Database; Jean-Rene Halde, "BDC's Young Entrepreneur Awards," *Canadian Business*, November 24, 2008, 19; "Savouring the Taste of Success: Meet Manitoba Winner Robbie Denomme," *BDC Etc.*, December 2008–January 2009, www.genuwinecellars.com/PDF/ETCarticle.pdf; "Uncorking Success in Foreign Markets," Foreign Affairs and International Trade, www.dfait-maeci.gc.ca/commerce/success/genuwine-en.asp; "Wine Proverbs and Quotes," *Life in Italy*, www.lifeinitaly.com/wines/wine-quotes.asp.

Business Accountability Sarah McBride, "Copper Caper: Thieves Nab Art to Sell for Scrap," *The Wall Street Journal*, May 1, 2008, A1, A14; Paul Waldie, "From Wal-Mart Quotas to a 'Frenzy' in Vancouver, Asia's Rice Crisis Goes Global," *The Globe and Mail*, April 24, 2008, B1, B8; Bob Davis and Douglas Belkin, "Food Inflation, Riots Spark Worries for World Leaders," *The Wall Street Journal*, April 14, 2008, A1, A11; Lauren Etter, "Rice Prices Are Steaming, with Many Implications," *The Wall Street Journal*, December 15–16, 2007, B1, B5; Patrick Barta and Jane Spencer, "As Alternatives Fuels Heat Up, Environmental Concerns Grow," *The Wall Street Journal*, December 5, 2006, A1, A13; Joel Millman, "Metal Is So Precious That Scrap Thieves Now Tap Beer Kegs," *The Wall Street Journal*, March 14, 2006, A1, A15.

Concluding Case 1-1 Claudia Cattaneo, "Peak Oil Demand Theory in Vogue," *National Post*, January 26, 2009, FP1; John Lyons and David Luhnow, "Brazil May Be the Globe's Next Big Spigot," *The Globe and Mail*, May 23, 2008, B8; Neil King and Peter Fritsch, "IEA Set to Lower Global Oil Supply Forecast," *The Wall Street Journal*, May 22, 2008, B11; "New Method to Extract Gas Hydrates," *Winnipeg Free Press*, April 17, 2008, A6; Neil King, "A Rosy View of Oil Supply," *The Globe and Mail*, January 17, 2008, B7; Russell Gold and Ann Davis, "Oil Officials See Limit Looming on Production," *The Wall Street Journal*, November 19, 2007, A1, A17; Judy Monchuk, "Slew of Deals Shows Oil Sands Fever Not Breaking," *The Globe and Mail*, August 6, 2007, B3; Shawn McCarthy, "Canada's Oil Boom Has Legs, IEA Says," *The Globe and Mail*, July 10, 2007, B1, B16; Neil Reynolds, "Peak Oil Doomsayers Fall Silent as Reserves Grow Ever Larger," *The Globe* *and Mail*, April 11, 2007, B2; Robert Hirsch, "Peaking of World Oil Production: Recent Forecasts," *WorldOil 228 (*April 2007*)*; Patrick Brethour, "Peak Oil Theorists Don't Know Jack," *The Globe and Mail*, September 6, 2006, B1, B6; Michael Lynch, "Oil Discovery Forecasts Doomed," *The Globe and Mail*, May 28, 2005, B6; Peter Tertzakian, "Canada: Energy Superpower?," *The Globe and Mail*, May 28, 2005, B6; Barrie McKenna, "Welcome to the Age of Scarcity," *The Globe and Mail*, May 21, 2005, B15; Haris Anwar, "Supply: Are Saudi Reserves Drying Up?," *The Globe and Mail*, May 21, 2005, B19.

Concluding Case 1-2 Martin Cash, "Wine Stores Seek $2.5 Million in Legal War with Liquor Board," *Winnipeg Free Press*, December 20, 2008, B7; Barry Critchley, "Liquor Rules Hard to Swallow," *National Post*, November 7, 2008, FP2; Dan Lett, "Wine Stores Collect $8 Million," *Winnipeg Free Press*, June 21, 2006, A3; Eric Reguly, "Ontario's Liquor Stores Look Good, but Where's the Profit?," *The Globe and Mail*, July 19, 2005, B2; Trevor Harrison, "Demon Rum and the Perils of Privatization," *Winnipeg Free Press*, June 19, 2003, A13; John Cotter, "Privatized Liquor Stores a Flop, Study Suggests," *Winnipeg Free Press*, June 6, 2003, A20; Bill Redekopp, "Private Wine Stores Cheesed with MLCC," *Winnipeg Free Press*, July 8, 2000, A6; David Menzies, "Sour Grapes," *Canadian Business*, February 26, 1999, 28–35; Brian Hutchinson, "Cheers!," *Canadian Business*, November 1994, 23–28.

Chapter 2

Inflation or Deflation? Alia McMullen, "U.S. CPI Posts First Annual Drop Since '55; Deflation Threat Persists Despite Signs of Revival," *National Post*, April 16, 2009, FP4; Allan Robinson, "Negative Inflation Rate Expected," *The Globe and Mail*, January 16, 2009, B10; Alia McMullen, "Japan Drawn Back into Vortex of Deflation," *National Post*, December 20, 2008, FP2; Eric Beauchesne, "Rising Food Prices Pack Punch," *Winnipeg Free Press*, July 24, 2008, B5; David Parkinson, "China Positioned to Unleash Global Deflation," *The Globe and Mail*, November 13, 2008, B12; George Athanassakos, "Confusion Reigns with Deflation-Inflation Conundrum," *The Globe and Mail*, November 6, 2008, B11; Anuj Chopra, "India's Growing Inflation Problem," *The Globe and Mail*, August 13, 2008, B1, B4; Heather Scoffield, "Now Canada Faces the Demons," *The Globe and Mail*, July 16, 2008, B5; Heather Scoffield, "Shock Move Sounds Inflation Alarm," *The Globe and Mail*, June 11, 2008, B1, B4; Andrew Batson, "Inflation, Spanning Globe, Is Set to Reach Decade High," *The Wall Street Journal*, April 10, 2008, A1, A12.

Figure 2.3 www.canadianeconomy.gc.ca/English/economy/inflation.cfm.

Figure 2.4 *Bank of Canada Banking and Financial Statistics*, Series H5, April 2009, S101.

Figure 2.5 *Industrial Research and Development: Intentions 2008, Catalogue No. 88-202-XWE, Table 2,* International Comparison of Business Enterprise Expenditures on Research and Development as a Percentage of Gross Domestic Product, by Selected OECD Countries (Ottawa: Minister of Industry, March 2009), www.statcan.gc.ca/pub/88-202-x/2008000/t002-eng.htm.

The Greening of Business Tomoko Hosaka, "Honda's New Fuel Cell Car Goes Hollywood," *The Globe and Mail*, June 17, 2008, B11; Yuri Kageyama, "Toyota's Hybrid Sales Top 1 Million Vehicles," *Winnipeg Free Press*, June 8, 2007, B16; Peter Kennedy, "Ballard's Celebrated Drive Hits a Bumpy Road," *The Globe and Mail*, July 17, 2004, B6; Peter Kennedy, "GM Aims to Finish First in Fuel Cell Race," *The Globe and Mail*, June 10, 2003, B5; Chris Nuttall-Smith, "Waiting for the Revolution," *Report on Business*, February 2003, 44–54; Jeffrey Ball, "Hydrogen Fuel May Be Clean, but Getting It Here Looks Messy," *The Wall Street Journal*, March 7, 2003; Rebecca Blumenstein, "Auto Industry Reaches Surprising Consensus: It Needs New Engines," *The Wall Street Journal*, January 5, 1998, A1, A10.

Entrepreneurship and New Ventures "Nothing Shady about This Glen, Court Rules," *The Globe and Mail*, January 24, 2009, B7; "Cape Breton Distillery Toasts Scotch Shortage," *CBC.ca*, November 6, 2008, www.cbc.ca/canada/nova-scotia/story/2008/11/06/glenora-scotch.html; "Cape Breton Distiller Fighting to Defend Product's Name," *CanWest News*, April 7, 2008; "Scotch Whisky Association Filing Appeal in Dispute with N.S. Distiller," *Canada NewsWire*, March 9, 2007; Keith McArthur, "Could Name Dispute put N.S. Whisky on the Rocks?," *The Globe and Mail*, December 16, 2006, B7; Brian Flinn, "Battle of the Glen Shapes up over Nova Scotia Distiller," *CanWest News*, July 9, 2004, 1; Rod Currie, "Distillery Produces Single Malt Whisky in Cape Breton Highlands," *Canada NewsWire*, April 29, 2002; Corinne McLean, "Turning Liquid Silver into Gold: Glenora Captures the Spirit of Scotland," *Plant* 59 no. 15 *(*2000*)*: 12; Allan Lynch, "Scotch on the Rocks," *Profit* 10 no. 8 *(*1991*)*: 38.

Business Accountability Susanna Ray, "Dreamliner a Scheduling Nightmare; Delayed Yet Again; Boeing This Time Cites Strike and Fastener Problem," *National Post*, December 12, 2008, FP12; Dave Carpenter, "Turbulent Time for Boeing as Jet Delayed Again," *Winnipeg Free Press*, April 10, 2008, B7; J. Lynn Lunsford, "Boeing Scrambles to Fix Problems with New 787 Jet," *The Wall Street Journal*, December 7, 2007, A1, A13; Jeff Buckstein, "Navigating the Outsourcing Minefield," *The Globe and Mail*, November 7, 2007, B10; Marcus Gee, "Moving On Up in the Outsourcing World," *The Globe and Mail*, September 26, 2007; Barrie McKenna, "Outsourcing May Not Be the Real Job Killer," *The Globe and Mail*, May 22, 2007, B8; Shane Schick, "Outsourcing Breeds Its Own Middle Management," *The Globe and Mail*, December 14, 2006, B13; John Partridge, "Agency Predicts further Outsourcing," *The Globe and Mail*, April 26, 2005, B5.

Concluding Case 2-1 "Don't Fight, Adapt," *National Post*, December 13, 2007, FP15; Ross McKitrick, "Contaminated Data," *National Post*, December 5, 2007, FP19; Diane Francis, "Be Very Afraid, Lloyd's Warns Us," *National Post*, November 29, 2007, www.nationalpost.com/story-printer.html?id=130604; Konrad Yakabuski, "Greenpeace Swinging Its Axe in the Wrong Forest," *The Globe and Mail*, November 15, 2007, B2; Tom Wright and Jim Carlton, "FSC's Green Label for Wood Product Gets Growing Pains," *The Wall Street Journal*, October 30, 2007, B1-B2; Douglas Belkin, "Northern Vintage: Canada's Wines Rise with Mercury," *The Wall Street Journal*, October 15, 2007, A1, A20; George Koch, "Careful with That Axe," *Canadian Business*, October 2007, 44–51; Nathan VanderKlippe, "Forest for the Trees," *National Post*, September 15, 2007, FP3; Barrie McKenna, "Global Warming a Farmer's Bane?," *The Globe and Mail*, September 12, 2007, B3; Sean Silcoff, "Canada's Money Trees," *National Post*, September 8, 2007, FP1, FP5; Wendy Stueck, "The Mighty Are Falling," *The Globe and Mail*, September 1, 2007, B4–B5; Kathryn Young, "Organic Wine: It's a Money Thing," *National Post*, September 1, 2007, FP3.

Concluding Case 2-2 The Reputation Institute, "Top 25 Reputation Leaders in the World," www.reputationinstitute.com/events/Global_Pulse_2008_Results.pdf; www.harrisinteractive.com; Gordon Pitts, "The RBC Dynasty Continues," *The Globe and Mail*, January 30, 2006, B1, B10.

Chapter 3

What Really Happened at Livent? Jacquie McNish, "Convictions Seen as Much-Needed Regulatory Win," *The Globe and Mail*, March 26, 2009, B4; Janet McFarland, "ICAO Appeal Panel Upholds Deloitte Decision," *The Globe and Mail*, February 19, 2009, B9; Grant McCool and John Poirier, "Madoff Mess Manoeuvres," *National Post*, December 18, 2008, FP3; Shannon Kari, "Livent Defence Calls No Witnesses; Final Arguments," *National Post*, November 4, 2008, FP5; Janet McFarland, "File Listed Livent 'Problems': Investigator," *The Globe and Mail*, October 22, 2008, B9;

Janet McFarland, "Livent Brass Pulled 'Numbers out of a Hat'," *The Globe and Mail*, September 9, 2008, B2; Janet McFarland, "Ex-Livent Official Tells of 'Absurd' Plan," *The Globe and Mail*, September 3, 2008, B5; Janet McFarland, "Livent Staff Dodged Drabinsky's Controls, Lawyer Says," *The Globe and Mail*, July 18, 2008, B2; Janet McFarland, "Livent Software Was Altered, Court Hears," *The Globe and Mail*, July 17, 2008, B9; Janet McFarland, "Ad Firms Helped Livent, Ex-Official Says," *The Globe and Mail*, July 16, 2008, B7; Janet McFarland, "All His Time Spent on Fraud: Ex-Livent Official," *The Globe and Mail*, July 15, 2008, B4; Janet McFarland, "Ex-CFO Testified She Hid Fraud at Livent," *The Globe and Mail*, June 12, 2008, B3.

The Greening of Business Hollie Shaw, "Keeping It Green; Outdoor-Recreation Retailer Finds Ways to Draw Customers," *National Post*, November 28, 2008, FP14; Laura Pratt, "Sustainability Reporting," *CGA Magazine*, September–October 2007, 18–21; Sharda Prashad, "Good Green Goals," *TheStar.com*, April 22, 2007, www.thestar.com/printArticle/205855; Ralph Shaw, "Peak Performance (Mountain Equipment Co-op)," *Alternatives Journal* 31 no. 1 (2005): 19–20.

Business Accountability "EBay Claims Court Victory in Belgium over L'Oreal in Counterfeit Goods Case," *National Post*, August 13, 2008, www.nationalpost.com/story-printer.html?id=718982; "EBay Quashes Tiffany Trademark Suit," *The Globe and Mail*, July 15, 2008, B6; "The End of Louis Vuitton on eBay?," *ETonline.com*, June 30, 2008, www.etonline.com/news/2008/06/63035; Maureen Fan, "China's Olympic Turnabout on Knockoffs," June 13, 2008, A1; Aileen McCabe, "China's Knock-Off Shops Help the Rich Scrape By," *Winnipeg Free Press*, April 19, 2008, C19; Daryl-Lynn Carlson, "The Costly Reality of Fakes," *The National Post*, December 5, 2007; Daryl-Lynn Carlson, "Canada's IP Protection Laws Soft," *The National Post*, December 5, 2007; Paul Waldie, "Court Clobbers Store for Selling Vuitton Fakes," *The Globe and Mail*, November 26, 2007, B3; Jonathan Cheng, "A Small Firm Takes on Chinese Pirates," *The Wall Street Journal*, July 5, 2007, B1–B2; Stacy Meichtry, "Swell or Swill?," *The Wall Street Journal*, August 10, 2006, B1–B2; Alessandra Galloni, "As Luxury Industry Goes Global, Knock-Off Merchants Follow," *The Wall Street Journal*, January 31, 2006, A1, A13; Alessandra Galloni, "Bagging Fakes and Sellers," *The Wall Street Journal*, January 31, 2006, B1–B2; Gordon Fairclough, "Tobacco Firms Trace Fakes to North Korea," *The Wall Street Journal*, January 27, 2006, B1–B2; Jeff Sanford, "Knock-Off Nation," *Canadian Business*, November 8–21, 2004, 67–71; Shawn McCarthy, "Crackdown on New York's Canal Street," *The Globe and Mail*, August 30, 2004, B1, B11.

Entrepreneurship and New Ventures "Frequently Asked Questions," Arthur's Juice, http://arthursjuice.ca/en_faq.asp; The Packaging Association of Canada, "Presentation Highlights and Speaker Profiles," www.pac.ca/ePromos/NA09_Walmart_Sus_Conf_3info.htm#Travis_Bell; Karen Davidson, "New Products Sport Green Nutrition," *The Grower*, May 1, 2009; Randy Ray, "Fresh Ideas for Green Manufacturing," *The Globe and Mail*, April 22, 2009, E10; Cleve Dheensaw, "100 Marathons Earn Place on Walk of Fame," *Times Colonist*, October 11, 2008; Rick Spence, "Top 100 List Reveals Healthy Economy," *Financial Post*, June 2, 2008, FP5; Ken Ramstead, "The Juices Are Flowing," *Canadian Grocer* 121 no. 3 (2007): 53.

Concluding Case 3-1 Ross McKitrick, "Contaminated Data," *National Post*, December 5, 2007; Lawrence Solomon, "Open Mind Sees Climate Clearly," *National Post*, June 29, 2007, FP15; "List of Scientists Opposing the Mainstream Scientific Assessment of Global Warming," http://en.wikipedia.org/wiki/List_of_Scientists_opposing_global_warming_consensus; Christopher Essex, "There Is No Global Temperature," *National Post*, June 23, 2007, FP15; Timothy Patterson, "Read the Sunspots," *National Post*, June 20, 2007, FP17; David Ebner, "The Greening of the Oil Sands," *The Globe and Mail*, January 6, 2007, B4; Lauren Etter, "For Icy Greenland, Global Warming Has a Bright Side," *The Wall Street Journal*, July 18, 2006, A1, A12; Patrick Brethour, "Canada's Big Emitters Brace for Investment Climate Change," *The Globe and Mail*, February 19, 2005, B4; Jared Diamond, *Collapse: How Societies Choose to Fail or Succeed* (New York: Penguin Books, 2005), 493–494; Robert Park, *Voodoo Science* (Oxford: Oxford University Press, 2000), 31–34, 43–45; James Trefil, *101 Things You Don't Know about Science and No One Else Does Either* (Boston: Houghton Mifflin, 1996), 124–126, 142.

Concluding Case 3-2 Bruce Stanley, "Ships Draw Fire for Rising Role in Air Pollution," *The Wall Street Journal*, November 27, 2007, A1, A16; Bill McAllister, "Alaska Still Out Front on Environmental Monitoring," *The Juneau Empire*, May 29, 2004; Marilyn Adams, "Former Carnival Exec Says He Was Fired for Helping Federal Inquiry," *USA Today*, November 8–10, 2003; Marilyn Adams, "Cruise-Ship Dumping Poisons Seas, Frustrates U.S. Enforcers," *USA Today*, November 8–10, 2003; Michael Connor, "Norwegian Cruise Line Pleads Guilty in Pollution Case," *Reuters*, December 7, 2002; "What Is a Dead Zone?" *Oceana Interactive*, June 10, 2004, www.oceana.org/index.cfm?sectionID511&fuseaction59#25.

Chapter 4

Family Businesses Burke Campbell, "Sisters Toast Family Roots as Business Bears Fruit," *National Post*, September 29, 2008, www.nationalpost.com/story-printer.html?id=846427; Gabriel Kahn, "A Vintage Strategy Faces Modernity," *The Wall Street Journal*, April 5–6, 2008, A6; Chris Morris, "Rumours of Irving Family Corporate Breakup Swirl," *Winnipeg Free Press*, November 23, 2007, B14; Gordon Pitts and Jacquie McNish, "Shaking the Family Tree," *The Globe and Mail*, November 22, 2007, B1, B9; Gordon Pitts and Jacquie McNish, "Irving Brothers Look to Break Up Empire," *The Globe and Mail*, November 21, 2007, B1, B6; Martin Peers, Matthew Karnitschnig, and Merissa Marr, "Shaken from the Family Tree," *The Globe and Mail*, July 20, 2007, B6; Paul Waldie, "Mitchell's Feud Goes Public," *The Globe and Mail*, November 30, 2002, B3; Gordon Pitts, "The Cuddy Situation is an Extreme Case of Family Company Dysfunctionality," *The Globe and Mail*, April 17, 2000, B9; David Berman, "Carving Up Cuddy," *Canadian Business*, March 27, 1998, 39–44.

Table 4.1
www.business.queensu.ca/news/2009/01-14-09-BSME.php.

Table 4.5 *Financial Post Magazine*, June 2009, 42. Material reprinted with the express permission of "The National Post Company," a Canwest Partnership.

The Greening of Business Laura Ramsay, "Small Firms Can Go Green Too: There's Lots of Help out There," *The Globe and Mail*, October 14, 2008, E1; Burke Campbell, "Entrepreneur's Green Inspiration from the East," *National Post*, September 22, 2008, www.nationalpost.com/story-printer.html?id=812446; Stephanie Whittaker, "Mompreneur Finds Online Niche for Organic Stock," *National Post*, March 31, 2008, www.nationalpost.com/todays_paper/story.html?id=411279.

Business Accountability Rasha Mourtada, "Help Me Get an Angel in My Underwear," *The Globe and Mail*, January 28, 2008, B13; Terrence Belford, "When Money Is the Mother of Invention," *The Globe and Mail*, October 17, 2007, E7; Marjo Johne, "Moolah from Heaven," *The Globe and Mail*, July 24, 2007, B14.

Concluding Case 4-1 Alexandra Lopez-Pacheco, "Home-Preneurs Want it All; She Said," *National Post*, December 22, 2008, FP4; David Hatton, "Home-Preneurs Want it All; He Said," *National Post*, December 22, 2008, FP4; Daryl-Lynn Carlson, "A Beautiful Balance with Help from Outsourcing," *National Post*, September 8, 2008, www.nationalpost.com/story-printer.html?id=776154; Melissa Martin, "Mompreneurial Spirit," *Winnipeg Free Press*, September 2, 2008, D1, D5; Stephanie Whittaker, "Mompreneur Finds Online Niche for

Organic Stock," *National Post*, March 31, 2008, www.nationalpost.com/todays_paper/story.html?id=411279; Robeez Footwear Ltd., www.robeez.com/en-us/about/sandra.htm?PriceCat=1&Lang=EN-US; Rebecca Gardiner, "It Pays to be Nice," *Profit* 24 no. 6 (2005): 23.

Concluding Case 4-2 Marlene Cartash, "My Best Sale: Asked to Recall the Defining Moment of Their Selling Careers, 10 Celebrated Entrepreneurs Cited Gutsy Moves That Still Fill Them with Pride," *Profit* 13 no. 4 (1995): 34–41; Bruce Erskine, "Gibson Got in on Ground Floor," *The Halifax Herald Limited*, April 26, 2006, www.thechronicleherald.ca/external/bbi/index11.html. Used with permission.

Chapter 5

Bombardier's Global Strategy: Eric Reguly, "Beaudoin's Big, Bold Bet," *The Globe and Mail*, July 14, 2008, B1, B10; Tu Thanh Ha, "A Power Plant That Is Quieter, Fuel Efficient but Still Years Away," *The Globe and Mail*, July 14, 2008, B1, B10; Shawn McCarthy and Eric Reguly, "Canadian Hopes, Global Risks," *The Globe and Mail*, July 14, 2008, A1, A6.

Figure 5.2 *Bank of Canada Banking and Financial Statistics*, Series J1, April 2009, S110.

Table 5.1 *Bank of Canada Banking and Financial Statistics*, Series J3, April 2009, S113.

Table 5.2 *Financial Post Magazine*, June 2009, 72. Material reprinted with the express permission of "The National Post Company," a Canwest Partnership.

Entrepreneurship and New Ventures "Epic Newsgroup Inc. Charts New Territory—Sabrina Heinekey and Tiffany Steeves Win BDC's Young Entrepreneur Award for British Columbia," *Canada NewsWire*, October 16, 2007, 1; Brian Morton, "Media Export: Businesswomen Built Their Empire on Faraway Places," *The Telegram*, October 22, 2007, www.thetelegram.com/index.cfm?sid=73310&sc=82; Business Development Bank of Canada, "Young Entrepreneur," *Profits* 27 no. 2 (2007): 10; "Vancouver Pair Wins B.C. Prize for Entrepreneurs," *Business Edge* 4 no. 22 (2007), www.businessedge.ca/article.cfm/newsID/16611.cfm.

Business Accountability Lauren Krugel, "Niko Confirms Probe by RCMP of Improper Payments in Bangladesh," *The Globe and Mail*, January 16, 2009, B4; "Zimbabwe Won't Pay, Metallon Shutters Mines," *The Globe and Mail*, November 7, 2008, B9; Andy Hoffman, "Congo Deals Major Blow to Miners," *The Globe and Mail*, February 6, 2008, B5; Patrick Barta, "Goro No Tropical Paradise for Inco," *The Globe and Mail*, July 12, 2006, B5; Geoffrey York, "Blowout in Bangladesh," *The Globe and Mail*, April 1, 2006, B4–B5; Celeste Mackenzie, "Rumble in the Jungle," *Canadian Business*, February 28–March 13, 2005, 57–63; "Hot Spots," *Canadian Business*, March 17, 2003, 30–31.

Concluding Case 5-1 "Siemens Pays $1.6 Billion to Settle Bribery Charges," *The Globe and Mail*, December 16, 2008, B9; David Crawford and Mike Esterl, "Siemens Prepares for Fines of $1.3 Billion," *The Globe and Mail*, November 6, 2008, B9; Mike Esterl and David Crawford, "At Siemens, a Conviction Could Trigger More Cases," *The Wall Street Journal*, July 29, 2008, B1; "Ex-Manager Details Siemens Slush Fund," *The Globe and Mail*, May 27, 2008, B9; David Crawford, Antonio Regalado, and David Gauthier-Villars, "Bribe Probe Exposes Alstom Network in Brazil," *The Wall Street Journal*, June 19, 2008, B1–B2; David Crawford, "French Firm Scrutinized in Global Bribe Probe," *The Wall Street Journal*, May 6, 2008, A1, A18; Mike Esterl and David Crawford, "Siemens Probe May Point to Board Members," *The Wall Street Journal*, January 17, 2008, B13; David Crawford and Mike Esterl, "Siemens Ruling Suggests Bribery Spanned Globe," *The Wall Street Journal*, November 16, 2007, A1, A17; David Crawford and Mike Esterl, "Siemens Fine Ends a Bribery Probe," *The Wall Street Journal*, October 5, 2007, A2.

Concluding Case 5-2 Martin Cash, "China Wins Apparel War?," *Winnipeg Free Press*, July 30, 2005, B8, B11; Gordon Pitts, "Peerless on a Mission: Stop China Now," *The Globe and Mail*, January 14, 2005, B8; Bertrand Marotte, "Gildan Takes T-Shirt Making to the Cutting-Edge of Casual Apparel," *The Globe and Mail*, July 3, 2004, B3; Gordon Pitts, "Who Will Be the Next Huntingdon?," *The Globe and Mail*, January 8, 2005, B7.

Chapter 6

Corporate Culture Carrie Tait, "CIBC Shuffles the Deck," *National Post*, January 8, 2008, www.nationalpost.com/story; Meagan Fitzpatrick, "RCMP 'Horribly Broken,' Need Fix Quickly: Report," *Winnipeg Free Press*, June 16, 2007, A9; Roma Luciw, "No. 1 Employee Not Always Your No. 1 Manager," *The Globe and Mail*, February 17, 2007, B10; Calvin Leung, "Culture Club," *Canadian Business*, October 9–22, 2006, 115–120; Andrew Wahl, "Culture Shock," *Canadian Business*, October 10–23, 2005, 115–116; Gordon Pitts, "It Boiled Down to a Culture Clash," *The Globe and Mail*, June 11, 2005, B5; Sinclair Stewart and Andrew Willis, "Hunkin Is De-Risking the Place," *The Globe and Mail*, December 11, 2004, B4; Doug Nairne, "Mounties Riding the Vision Thing," *Winnipeg Free Press*, September 16, 1996, A5.

Business Accountability Henry Mintzberg, *The Nature of Managerial Work* (New York: Harper and Row, 1973); Harvey Schachter, "Monday Morning Manager," *The Globe and Mail*, November 8, 2005, B2.

The Greening of Business "Rona Wins Kudos on Green Initiative," *The Globe and Mail*, November 22, 2008, B7; Marjo Johne, "Shoppers Get a Brand New Bag," *The Globe and Mail*, October 20, 2008, E5; John Murphy, "Honda CEO Vies for Green Mantle," *The Wall Street Journal*, June 16, 2008, B1–B2; "Deadline Set for Big Polluters," *National Post*, December 13, 2007, www.nationalpost.com/news/canada/story.html?id=164992; *Agriculture and Agri-Food Canada, Going Green: The Future of the Retail Food Industry, July 2007*, www.ats.agr.gc.ca/us/4351_e.htm; "Google Sets Goal of Making Renewables Cheaper Than Coal," *Clean Edge News*, November 28, 2007, www.cleanedge.com/story.php?nID=5036; Sharda Prashad, "Good Green Goals," *TheStar.com*, April 22, 2007, www.thestar.com/printArticle/205855.

Entrepreneurship and New Ventures *Photo-Kicks Martial Arts Photography*, http://photo-kicks.com; Inc.com 5000, www.lnc.com/inc5000/2007/company-profile.html?id+200705920; Joanne Schneider, "Action: Filmmakers Open Studios in Columbia," *Columbia Business Times*, February 20, 2009, www.columbiabusinesstimes.com/3527/2009/02/20/action-filmmakers-open-studios-in-columbia.

Concluding Case 6-1 Vanessa O'Connell, "Coach Targets China—and Queens," *The Wall Street Journal*, May 29, 2008, B1; "Coach's Drive Picks Up the Pace," *Business Week*, March 29, 2004, 98–100; Julia Boorstin, "How Coach Got Hot," *Fortune*, October 28, 2003, 131–134; Marilyn Much, "Consumer Research Is His Bag," *Investor's Business Daily*, December 16, 2003; "S&P Stock Picks and Pans: Accumulate Coach," *Business Week*, October 22, 2003.

Concluding Case 6-2 Brian Milner, "The Unmaking of a Dynasty," *Cigar Aficionado*, January 20, 2009, www.cigaraficionado.com/Cigar/CA_Profiles/People_Profile/0,2540,176,00.html; Mathew Ingram, "Nokia's Deal with Record Firms Could Have Music Fans Hanging Up," *The Globe and Mail*, July 2, 2008, R3; "Warner Music to Sell Tunes on Amazon.com," *The Globe and Mail*, December 28, 2007, B4; Simon Avery, "Music Firms Hope to Leave the Blues Behind," *The Globe and Mail*, April 5, 2007, B14; Shawn McCarthy, "Bronfman Is Eager to Gain Redemption for His Music Gambit," *The Globe and Mail*, January 4, 2005, B4; Shawn McCarthy, "Bronfman Jumps Back into Music with Winning Bid," *The Globe and Mail*, November 25, 2003; Brian Milner, "Broken Spirits," *Report on Business Magazine*, September 2002, 26–38; Brian Milner, "Seagram's Top Gun Shoots for the Stars," *The Globe and Mail*, June 6, 1998, B1, B6; Brian Milner, "Seagram Snares Polygram," *The Globe and Mail*, May 22, 1998, B1, B4; Brian Milner,

"The Selling of Edgar Bronfman Jr.," *The Globe and Mail*, February 15, 1999, B15.

Chapter 7

Reorganizing the Irving Empire Chris Morris, "Rumours of Irving Family Corporate Breakup Swirl," *Winnipeg Free Press*, November 23, 2007, B14; Gordon Pitts and Jacquie McNish, "Shaking the Family Tree," *The Globe and Mail*, November 22, 2007, B1, B9; Gordon Pitts and Jacquie McNish, "Irving Brothers Look to Break Up Empire," *The Globe and Mail*, November 21, 2007, B1, B6.

Business Accountability Betsy Morris, "The Pepsi Challenge," *Fortune*, February 19, 2008, www.money.cnn.com/2008/02/18/news/companies/morris_nooyi.fortune/index.htm; "PepsiCo Unveils New Organizations Structure, Names CEOs of Three Principal Operating Units," May 11, 2007, *FLEXNEWS*, www.flex-news-food.com/pages/12058/pepsi/pepsico-unveils-new-organizational-structure-names-ceos-three-principal-operating-units.html; Joann Lublin, "Place vs. Product: It's Tough to Choose a Management Model," *The Wall Street Journal*, June 27, 2001, A1, A4; Richard Blackwell, "New CIBC Boss Promises Shakeup," *The Globe and Mail*, April 2, 1999, B1, B4; Rekha Bach, "Heinz's Johnson to Divest Operations, Scrap Management of Firm by Region," *The Wall Street Journal*, December 1997, B10–B12; Jana Parker-Pope and Joann Lublin, "P&G Will Make Jager CEO Ahead of Schedule," *The Wall Street Journal*, September 1998, B1, B8.

The Greening of Business Gerald Flood, "At One with the World," *Winnipeg Free Press*, April 19, 2009, B1–B2; Jay Somerset, "A Building with an Energy All Its Own," *The Globe and Mail*, November 11, 2008, B9; Marta Gold, "More Realtors Turning Green," *Winnipeg Free Press*, August 24, 2008, F2; Murray McNeill, "Green Is the New Green at Credit Union Branches," *Winnipeg Free Press*, August 20, 2008, B6, B8; "Delta Hotels Expands Green Initiatives with Hybrid Heating," press release, www.sempapower.com/media/newsarticles/16.06.08%20-%20Delta%20Hotels%20Expands%20Green%20Initiatives%20with%20Hybrid%20Heating.pdf, August 15, 2008; Peter Mitham, "Going for the Gold in Green," *The Globe and Mail*, August 5, 2008, B5; John D. Stoll, "Car Dealers Set 'Green' Blueprints," *The Wall Street Journal*, May 15, 2008, B1; *Agriculture and Agri-Food Canada, Going Green: The Future of the Retail Food Industry, July 2007,* www.ats.agr.gc.ca/us/4351_e.htm.

Concluding Case 7-1 Randall King, "Frantic Films Sells Division," *Winnipeg Free Press*, November 28, 2007, B7; interviews with Jamie Brown, CEO of Frantic Films; documents provided by Frantic Films.

Concluding Case 7-2 "Our Brands," *Sara Lee*, www.saralee.com, July 3, 2002; Deborah Cohen, "Sara Lee Opens Alternative to Victoria's Secret," *The Wall Street Journal*, January 3, 2003, B4; Julie Forster, "Sara Lee: Changing the Recipe—Again," *Business Week*, September 10, 2001, 87–89: "Sara Lee: Looking Shapely," *Business Week*, October 1, 2002, 52.

Chapter 8

Are More Cracks Appearing in the Glass Ceiling? Sandra Rubin, "What Will It Take to Crack the Glass Ceiling?," *The Globe and Mail*, December 17, 2008, B8; Wallace Immen, "One More Gap in Pay Between Men and Women," *The Globe and Mail*, August 15, 2008, C1; Meagan Fitzpatrick, "Women Still Earning Less Than Men: Statistics Canada," *Winnipeg Free Press*, May 2, 2008, A5; Konrad Yakabuski, "Meet the New Leading Lady of Finance," *The Globe and Mail*, March 27, 2008, pp. B1–B2; "Women Less Likely to Aspire to Top Corporate Positions," *Hudson Canada*, March 6, 2008, http://ca.hudson.com/node.asp?kwd=03-06-08-women-survey; Rudy Mezzetta, "Banks, Credit Unions Put Women in Top Spots," *Investment Executive*, February 2008; Matthew McClearn, "Mind the Gap," *Canadian Business*, November 5, 2007, 21–22; Margaret Wente, "It's Manly at the Top," *The Globe and Mail*, May 7, 2005, A21; Janet McFarland, "Women Still Find Slow Rise to Power Positions," *The Globe and Mail*, March 13, 2003, B1, B7; Virginia Galt, "Top Women Still Finding Barriers," *The Globe and Mail*, September 25, 2002, B7; Marie Drolet, "The Male–Female Wage Gap," *Perspectives on Labour and Income, Online Edition*, December 2001, www.statcan.gc.ca/pub/75-001-x/01201/4095957-eng.html; Elizabeth Church, "Women Still Shut Out of Many Top Posts," *The Globe and Mail*, February 10, 2000, B15; Belle Rose Ragins, "Gender Gap in the Executive Suite: CEOs and Female Executives Report on Breaking the Glass Ceiling," *Academy of Management Executive*, February 1998, 28–42; Greg Keenan, "Ford Canada Gets New CEO," *The Globe and Mail*, April 9, 1997, B1; Greg Keenan and Janet McFarland, "The Boys' Club," *The Globe and Mail*, September 27, 1997, B1, B5; Greg Keenan, "Woman at the Wheel," *The Globe and Mail*, July 8, 1995, B1, B6.

Table 8.1 *Financial Post Magazine*, June 2009, 74. Material reprinted with the express permission of "The National Post Company," a Canwest Partnership.

The Greening of Business Greg McMillan, "The Greening of the Jobscape," *The Globe and Mail*, November 14, 2008, B7; Marjo Johne, "Show Us the Green, Workers Say," *The Globe and Mail*, October 10, 2007, C1; "Creating Jobs by Going Green," *Office of the Premier, news release*, June 19, 2007, www.premier.gov.on.ca/news/event.php?ItemID=3998&Lang=EN.

Business Accountability Roma Luciw and John Partridge, "How to Keep Staff? More Perks, of Course," *The Globe and Mail*, February 23, 2008, B17; Virginia Galt, "Statscan Studies Workplace Stress," *The Globe and Mail*, June 26, 2003, B3; David Leonhardt, "Did Pay Incentives Cut Both Ways?" *The New York Times*, April 7, 2002, BU1–3; Dean Foust and Michelle Conlin, "A Smarter Squeeze?," *Business Week*, December 31, 2001, 42–44; Tischelle George, "Bye-Bye Employee Perks," *Information Week*, October 15, 2001; Rick Perera, "Siemens Offers Workers 'Time-Outs' to Save Cash," *The Industry Standard*, August 31, 2001; Anne Howland, "There's No Place Like Work," *CGA Magazine*, July–August, 2000, 21–25.

Concluding Case 8-1 "CIBC Staffers Seek OK for Overtime Group Suit," *The Globe and Mail*, December 9, 2008, B10; Jim Middlemiss, "Lawsuit Seeks OT for Bankers; CIBC Targeted," *National Post*, October 29, 2008, FP1; Richard Blackwell, "KPMG to Pay Workers Overtime," *The Globe and Mail*, February 20, 2008, B8; Virginia Galt, "Managers' Overtime Victory Short-Lived," *The Globe and Mail*, April 20, 2007, B3.

Chapter 9

Reports from the Battlefield Terence Corcoran, "Wal-Mart Wins Big Union Battle," *National Post*, April 9, 2009, FP13; Marina Strauss, "UFCW Digs in Heels in Looming Retail Food Fight," *The Globe and Mail*, January 12, 2009, B1; Bert Hill, "Another Wal-Mart Unionized; Second for Quebec," *National Post*, December 20, 2008, FP6; Brent Jang, "CAW Eyes Union Drive at WestJet Airlines," *The Globe and Mail*, September 10, 2008, B3; Brent Jang, "WestJet Brushes off Potential CAW Drive," *The Globe and Mail*, September 11, 2008, B5; Allison Lampert, "Unions Want More Wal-Mart Wins," *Winnipeg Free Press*, August 22, 2008, B8; Jean-Francois Bertrand, "Union Contract Imposed on Quebec Wal-Mart Store a First," *Winnipeg Free Press*, August 16, 2008, B10; "Arbitrator Sides with Wal-Mart Workers," *The Globe and Mail*, August 16, 2008, B7; Peter Rakobowchuk, "Early Closing of Unionized Wal-Mart Called Cowardly," *Winnipeg Free Press*, April 30, 2005, C15; Marina Strauss, "Wal-Mart Faces Another Unionized Store in Quebec," *The Globe and Mail*, January 20, 2005, B4; Barrie McKenna, "Unions Starting to Make Inroads at Wal-Mart," *The Globe and Mail*, August 23, 2004, B1, B12; Aldo Santin, "Wal-Mart vs. Union Battle Now Shifts to Manitoba," *Winnipeg Free Press*, August 5, 2004, B3; Patrick Brethour, "Wal-Mart Hails Saskatchewan Court Ruling in Union Drives," *The Globe and Mail*, July 28, 2004, B1, B20; Virginia Galt, "Wal-Mart Must Give Union Access," *The Globe and Mail*, May 13, 2003, B5; "Union Is Trying to Organize

Staff at Wal-Mart," *Winnipeg Free Press*, May 13, 2003, A7; Zena Olijnyk, "CAW Walks Away from Wal-Mart," *National Post*, April 20, 2000, C5; Susan Bourettte, "Wal-Mart Staff Want Out of Union," *The Globe and Mail*, April 23, 1999, B9; John Heinzl and Marina Strauss, "Wal-Mart's Cheer Fades," *The Globe and Mail*, February 15, 1997, B1, B4; Margot Gibb-Clark, "Why Wal-Mart Lost the Case," *The Globe and Mail*, February 14, 1997, B10.

Table 9.2 Union Membership in Canada—2008, http://www.hrsdc.gc.ca/eng/labour/labour_relations/info_analysis/union_membership/index.shtml, Table 2: Unions with Largest Membership, Source: Strategic Policy, Analysis, and Workplace Information Directorate, Labour Program, Human Resources and Skills Development Canada. Reproduced with the permission of the Minister of Public Works and Government Services, 2009.

Business Accountability Mike Esterl, "Deutsche Telekom, Union Clash," *The Wall Street Journal*, September 12, 2008, B2; J. Lynn Lunsford, "Outsourcing at Crux of Boeing Strike," *The Wall Street Journal*, September 8, 2008, B1, B4; Brent Jang, "Union Buttons Cross the Line," *The Globe and Mail*, August 11, 2008, B3; Kris Maher, "Unions Forge Secret Pacts with Major Employers," *The Wall Street Journal*, May 10–11, 2008, A1, A8; Peter Brieger, "Court Rejects First Nation's Bid for Own Union Pact," *National Post*, November 29, 2007, www.nationalpost.com/story-printer.html?id=130625.

Concluding Case 9-1 "The Real Fat Cats of the Auto Industry," *The Globe and Mail*, April 24, 2009, B2; Nicolas Van Praet, "GM Seeks $150M in CAW Concessions," *National Post*, February 3, 2009, FP1; Nicolas Van Praet, "Canadian Auto Workers Most Productive," *National Post*, January 26, 2009, FP2; Greg Keenan, "Bush's Tough Auto Talk Puts CAW in Crosshairs," *The Globe and Mail*, December 23, 2008, B1; Greg Keenan, "Ford Wins Cost Cuts in Pivotal Labour Pact," *The Globe and Mail*, April 29, 2008, B1, B6; Nicolas Van Praet, "Loonie Gives Korean Autos an Advantage," *Financial Post*, April 9, 2008, www.nationalpost.com/todays_paper/story.html?id=431505; Nicolas Van Praet, "Auto Report Wake-Up Call For Canada," *Financial Post*, March 28, 2008, www.nationalpost.com/todays_paper/story.html?id=405728; "Steelworkers Drop Dofasco Union Bid," *Financial Post*, March 28, 2008, www.nationalpost.com/todays_paper/story.html?id=405721; Nicolas Van Praet, "Union Vote at Toyota Cancelled," *Financial Post*, March 20, 2008, www.nationalpost.com/todays_paper/story.html?id=386980; Greg Keenan, "CAW Leader Bucks Trend, Refuses Wage Cuts," *The Globe and Mail*, February 21, 2008, B1, B8; Omar El Akkad and Greg Keenan, "Hargrove 'Fearful' for Future of GM, Ford," *The Globe and Mail*, February 13, 2008, B1, B13; Greg Keenan, "Ford Fires Warning Shot at CAW," *The Globe and Mail*, January 10, 2008, B7; Greg Keenan, "CAW Gears Up for Toughest Fight in 2008," *The Globe and Mail*, December 31, 2007, B3; Greg Keenan, "CAW Members Approve Deal," *The Globe and Mail*, December 8, 2007, B10; Nicolas Van Praet, "Buzz Hargrove Has Some Very Big Problems," *National Post*, December 7, 2007, FP3; Jason Clemens and Keith Godin, "Unions' Democracy Talk Is Hot Air," *National Post*, November 29, 2007, FP15; Wayne Fraser, Sid Ryan, Cec Makowski, Sharleen Stewart, Dave Ritchie, and Warrant Thomas, "The Magna Sell-Out," *National Post*, November 23, 2007, www.financialpost.com/story.html?id=e9163705-0d0b-4664-bdcb-0d4c7ea5f5c8; Jeffrey McCracken, Josee Valcourt, and John D. Stoll, "UAW Shifts Its Chrysler Strategy," *The Wall Street Journal*, October 22, 2007, A3; Thomas Watson, "Car Trouble," *Canadian Business*, October 22, 2007, www.canadianbusiness.com/shared/print.jsp?content=20071017_198710_198710&; John D. Stoll and Josee Valcourt, "Chrysler, UAW Reach Agreement," *The Wall Street Journal*, October 11, 2007, A3; Jeffrey McCracken, "Deal to Help GM Cut Cost Gap with Rivals," *The Wall Street Journal*, October 11, 2007, A3; Neal Boudette, "Honda and UAW Clash over New Factory Jobs," *The Wall Street Journal*, October 10, 2007, A1, A19.

Concluding Case 9–2 "2007–2008 Writers Guild of America Strike," http://en.wikipedia.org/wiki/2007_Writers_Guild_of_America_strike; Grant Robertson, "After the Strike, It's All Changed," *The Globe and Mail*, March 13, 2008, B1, B4; Richard Siklos, "The Show Goes On, but Hollywood's Gravy Train Screeches to a Halt," *The Globe and Mail*, February 12, 2008, B11; Grant Robertson, "As the Writers Strike Ends, the Accounting Begins," *The Globe and Mail*, February 11, 2008, B1, B3; Barbara Shecter, "Hooray for Hollywood Writers' Strike," *National Post*, January 10, 2008, www.nationalpost.com/story-printer.html?id=226866.

Chapter 10

What Do Employees Want? Wallace Immen, "Meaning Means More Than Money at Work: Poll," *The Globe and Mail*, February 27, 2009, B14; Wallace Immen, "Hey, Boss, Shine Your Shoes? Keep Me Around," *The Globe and Mail*, October 22, 2008, C3; Tavia Grant, "Favourite Perk? Not a Blackberry," *The Globe and Mail*, September 10, 2008, C1; Wallace Immen, "Boomers, Gen-Yers Agree: It's All about Respect," *The Globe and Mail*, January 24, 2007, C1; Wallace Immen, "The Continuing Divide over Stress Leave," *The Globe and Mail*, June 10, 2005, C1; Jeff Buckstein, "In Praise of Praise in the Workplace," *The Globe and Mail*, June 15, 2005, C1, C5; Virginia Galt, "This Just In: Half Your Employees Ready to Jump Ship," *The Globe and Mail*, January 26, 2005, B1, B9; David Sirota, Louis Mischkind, and Michael Meltzer, "Nothing Beats an Enthusiastic Employee," *The Globe and Mail*, July 29, 2005, C1; Virginia Galt, "Business's Next Challenge: Tackling Mental Health in the Workplace," *The Globe and Mail*, April 12, 2005, B1, B20; Virginia Galt, "Canadians Take Dour View on Jobs, Bosses, Angels," *The Globe and Mail*, October 18, 2004, B1, B7; Virginia Galt, "Worker Stress Costing Economy Billions, Panel Warns," *The Globe and Mail*, July 21, 2000, B9; "A Better Workplace," *Time*, April 17, 2000, 87.

Entrepreneurship and New Ventures Leena Rao, "I Love Rewards Raises $5.9 Million For Employee Rewards Program," *TechCrunch*, www.techcrunch.com/2009/05/07/i-love-rewards-raises-59-million-for-employee-rewards-program/; Chris Atchison, "Masters of One," *Profit* 28 no. 2 (2009): 18; "I Love Rewards Reports Record Results as Demand for Rewards and Recognition Programs Grows," *Canada NewsWire*, April 24, 2009; "I Love Rewards Named One of the World's Most Democratic Workplaces," *Marketwire*, April 14, 2009; Ari Weinzweig, "Ask Inc.: Tough Questions, Smart Answers," *Inc.* 29 no. 12 (2007): 84; Ryan McCarthy, "'Help Wanted' Meets 'Buy it Now': Why More Companies Are Integrating Marketing and Recruiting," *Inc.* 29 no. 11 (2007): 50.

Business Accountability Virginia Galt, "Ideas: Employees' Best-Kept Secrets," *The Globe and Mail*, June 18, 2005, B11; Frederick A. Starke, Bruno Dyck, and Michael Mauws, "Coping with the Sudden Loss of an Indispensable Worker," *Journal of Applied Behavioural Science* 39 no. 2 (2003): 208–229; Timothy Aeppel, "On Factory Floors, Top Workers Hide Secrets to Success," *The Wall Street Journal*, July 1, 2002, A1, A10; Christopher Robert, Tahira Probst, Joseph Martocchio, Fritz Drasgow, and John Lawler, "Empowerment and Continuous Improvement in the United States, Mexico, Poland, and India: Predicting Fit on the Basis of the Dimensions of Power Distance and Individualism," *Journal of Applied Psychology*, October 2000, 643–658; Timothy Aeppel, "Not All Workers Find Idea of Empowerment as Neat as It Sounds," *The Wall Street Journal*, September 8, 1997, A1, A13.

Concluding Case 10-1 Joyce Rosenberg, "Out of Sight, On Your Mind; Learning to Trust Telecommuters," *The Globe and Mail*, September 20, 2008, B19; "Productivity Rises for Teleworkers: Survey," *The Globe and Mail*, October 15, 2008, C7; Randi Chapnik Myers, "The Back and Forth of Working from Home," *The Globe and Mail*, March 8, 2008, B16; Paul Lima, "With New Advances in Technology, Why Are We Still Jumping in the Car?," *The Globe and Mail*, October 20, 2008, E9; Kira Vermond, "In Support of Ditching the Commute," *The Globe and Mail*, November 17, 2007, B23.

Concluding Case 10-2 Roland Huntford, *The Last Place on Earth (New York: Atheneum, 1985);* Pierre Berton, *The Arctic Grail (Toronto: McClelland and Stewart, 1988),* esp. 125–196, 435–486, and 531–548; Roland Huntford, *Shackleton (London: Hodder and Stoughton, 1985).*

Chapter 11

Mattel: Getting a Toy Recall Right www.mattel.com; John Quelch, "Mattel: Getting a Toy Recall Right," *Harvard Business School,* August 27, 2007; Nicholas Casey, Nicholas Zamiska, and Andy Pasztor, "Mattel Seeks to Placate China," *The Wall Street Journal*, September 22, 2007; Hari Bapuji and Paul W. Beamish, "Toy Recalls—Is China Really the Problem?," *Canada-Asia Commentary 45 (September 2007);* Paul W. Beamish and Hari Bapuji, "Toy Recalls and China: Emotion vs. Evidence," *Management and Organization Review* 4 no. 2 (2008): 197–209.

Entrepreneurship and New Ventures "Hold on Tight! The World's First Unicycle Motorbike," *MailOnline*, April 29, 2008, www.dailymail.co.uk/news/article-562726/Hold-tight-The-worlds-unicycle-MOTORBIKE.html; James F. Quinn, "Uno and Only: Start with a Motorcycle, Add 'Star Wars' and Give the Segway a Run for Its Futuristic Money," *Chicago Tribune*, June 29, 2008, www.motorcycleenhancements.com/uno_chicago_ tribune /uno_chicago_ tribune.htm#; Mary Teresa Bitti, "The Brett Wilson Show," *Financial Post*, January 9, 2009, www.nationalpost.com/related/topics/story.html?id=1159190; Trish Crawford, "Star Power for the Uno: Milton Teen's 'Cool' Electric Bike Creates Buzz," *The Hamilton Spectator*, June 3, 2008, A01; Trish Crawford, "Teenager's Electric Unicycle Creates One Singular Sensation; Science Fair Project Getting World Attention," *The Toronto Star*, June 3, 2008, A04; "Uno Inventory Lands $1.25 Million for Research Centre," *Milton Canadian Champion*, November 21, 2008.

Business Accountability John Neff, "Tata Nano Tanking Used Car Market in India," *Autoblog*, February 8, 2008, www.autoblog.com/2008/02/08/tata-nano-tanking-used-car-market-in-india/; Alex Nunez, "What $2500 Buys in India: Tata Nano Unveiled," *Autoblog*, January 10, 2008, www.autoblog.com/2008/01/10/what-2-500-buys-in-india-tata-nano-unveiled/4; Marcus Gee, "Game Changer," *The Globe and Mail*, April 11, 2008, B1.

The Greening of Business www.walmart.ca/wms/microsite/GreenerGood/en/initiatives.html; Allison Linn, "Wal-Mart Pushes Suppliers to 'Go Green'; Company Uses Business-as-usual Tactics to Drive Environmental Agenda," *MSNBC.com*, www.msnbc.msn.com/id/18056716/; "Is Wal-Mart Going Green? CEO Vows to Be 'Good Steward for the Environment' in Announcing Goals," *MSNBC.com news services*, October 25, 2005, www.msnbc.msn.com/id/9815727/.

Concluding Case 11-1 Pasadena Convention and Visitors Bureau, "Pasadena Tournament of Roses Parade and Rose Bowl Game: A Grand Tradition," news release, March 29, 2004, www.pasadenacal.com; Burbank Tournament of Roses Association, "2004 Float Entry Fact Sheet," March 29, 2004, www.burbankrosefloat.com; Cindy Chang, "Finally, a Chance to Relax," *Pasadena Star-News*, January 1, 2004, www.pasadenastarnews.com, March 29, 2004; Bill Hetherman, "Overnighters in Partying Mood," *Pasadena Star-News*, January 1, 2004, www.pasadenastarnews.com, March 29, 2004; Naush Boghossian, "Float Volunteers Feel the Moosic of Rose Parade," *Los Angeles Daily News*, December 26, 2003, www.dailynews.com, January 6, 2004; personal observations of the author as a volunteer assembling the float on December 28, 2003.

Concluding Case 11-2 Kimberly Johnson and Tom Krisher, "Ford Loss Smaller Than Feared," *The Associated Press*, April 24, 2009; Fabrice Taylor, "When Not Failing Is Succeeding, Ford's a 'Buy'," *The Globe and Mail*, April 24, 2009; "More U.S. Cash for Auto Makers," *The Associated Press*, April 21, 2009; "Honda Offers Buyouts, Cuts Pay in North America, Cuts Production," *The Associated Press*, March 31, 2009; "Honda Canada Sales in February Fall by 42 percent from a Year Earlier," *The Canadian Press*, March 3, 2009; Brett Popplewell, "Will Another Bailout Repair Ailing Industry?," *Thestar.com*, December 13, 2008, *www.thestar.com/Article/553220*; Mike Ramsey, "Japan's Big Three Widen Their Lead," *The Globe and Mail*, August 8, 2007, B4.

Chapter 12

Quality Problems in Service Businesses Ross Marowits, "Transat Cuts 53 Administrative Jobs," *The Canadian Press*, April 21, 2009; Karen Howlett, "Ontario Launches Review of Travel Industry Watchdog Due to Conquest's Demise," *The Globe and Mail*, April 22, 2009; Keith Leslie, "Other Tour Operators 'Likely' Face Financial Problems: McGuinty," *The Globe and Mail*, April 21, 2009; Bob Cox, "FAA Knew of MD-80 Wiring Problem in 2003," *Airport Business*, April 14, 2008, www.airportbusiness.com/web/online/Top-News-Headlines/FAA-knew-of-MD-80-wiring-problem-in-2003/1$18873; "American Airlines Grounds Fleet of MD-80s," *MSNBC.com news services*, March 26, 2008, www.msnbc.msn.com/id/23808772/; "American's MD-80s Cleared to Fly Again," *MSNBC.com news services*, April 14, 2008, www.msnbc.msn.com/id/24029455; Brent D. Bowen and Dean E. Headley, *2008 Airline quality Rating, report* (AQR Aero Inc., April 2008), http://aqr.aero/aqrreports/2008aqr.pdf; "Survey: Airline Complaints Sky High," *CBS News.com*, April 7, 2008, www.cbsnews.com/stories/2008/04/07/business/main3996989.shtml.

Business Accountability Jane Werniuk, "Making Huge Strides," *Canadian Mining Journal* 129 no. 6 (2008): 34–35, from ABI/INFORM Global database (Document ID: 1559298121); Calvin Leung, "Diamonds in the Rough," *Canadian Business*, February 28–March 13, 2005, 65–67; Joel Baglole, "Political Correctness by the Carat," *The Wall Street Journal*, April 17, 2003, B1, B3; Matthew Hart, "The Ice Storm," *Canadian Business*, November 2002, 52–62.

Entrepreneurship and New Ventures www.kitwanga.ca; "Kitwanga Mills Ltd.," YouTube video, March 19, 2009, www.youtube.com/user/Baljit1006; "NRI-PIO Section," *India Empire Magazine*, www.indiaempire.com/v1/2009/April/pravasi_diaspora.asp; RBC Canadian Woman Entrepreneur Awards, www.theawards.ca/cwea/past-winners.cfm; "RBC Canadian Woman Entrepreneur Awards 2008," *Digital Pixie*, www.dpixie.com/articles/2008/cwea08/cwea_08_p1.html; "Six Women Win RBC Canadian Woman Entrepreneur Awards," *Canada NewsWire*, December 10, 2008, retrieved from Canadian Business and Current Affairs Database.

The Greening of Business Evan Ramstad, "Steelmakers Develop New Iron Recipes," *The Wall Street Journal*, August 29, 2008, B1; Chennai, "Tempering Profits with Green Logic," *Businessline*, June 25, 1998, 1; Kanako Tanaka, "Assessment of Energy Efficiency Performance Measures in Industry and Their Application for Policy," *Energy Policy* 36 no. 8 (2008): 2877; *Posco Management Innovation for Customer Satisfaction*, Business Korea, November 2001.

Concluding Case 12-1 Jacqueline Thorpe "Poor Productivity Canada's Biggest Problem", *National Post*, September 11, 2008, FP4; *The Challenge of Globalization, (Oliver Wyman, 2008)*, www.oliverwyman.com/ow/pdf_files/The_Challenge_of_Globalization.pdf; www.oliverwyman.com/content_images/ow_en_Automotive_Pres_2008_Harbour Chart08.pdf; Gordon Pitts, "Ottawa's New, Improved Mantra: Productivity," *The Globe and Mail*, October 3, 2005, B1, B6; Greg Keenan, "GM Oshawa Cranks out Productivity Award," *The Globe and Mail*, June 3, 2005, B1, B8; Grant Robertson, "In the Boardroom at the General Motors Oshawa Plant Is a Baseball Bat. Two Words are Carved on It: Beat Toyota," *The Globe and Mail*, September 15, 2005, B16; Gordon Pitts, "Manufacturers' Choice—Compete or Die," *The Globe and Mail*, October 5, 2005, B7; "Canada's Standard of Living," *National Post Business*, June 2003,

19–20; Jeffrey Bernstein, Richard Harris, and Andrew Sharpe, "The Widening Canada–US Manufacturing Productivity Gap," *International Productivity Monitor,* Fall 2002, 3–22; Pierre Fortin, "Differences in Annual Work Hours Per capita between the United States and Canada," *International Productivity Monitor,* Spring 2003, 38–46; Frank Graves and Richard Jenkins, "Canadian Attitudes towards Productivity: Balancing Standard of Living and Quality of Life," in *The Review of Economic Performance and Social Progress* (Montreal: The Institute for Research on Public Policy, 2002), 243–258; Andrew Sharpe, "Why Are Americans More Productive Than Canadians?," *International Productivity Monitor* 6 (Spring 2003): 19–37; Jason Myers, "Back to Basics: Canada's Productivity Challenge," *Canadian Manufacturers and Exporters,* April 2003, 14–18; Pierre Fortin, "Canadian Productivity: When Do We Catch Up?," *ISUMA* (Spring 2002).

Concluding Case 12–2 George Condon, "In Demand," *Canadian Grocer* 122, 10 (2008/2009), 114; Hollie Shaw, "Another Shakeup at Loblaw; Turnaround Doubts," *National Post,* April 22, 2008, FP4; Marina Strauss, "Battered Loblaw Makes Deep Job Cuts," *The Globe and Mail*, January 23, 2007, B1, B7; Marina Strauss, "New Team at Loblaw to Trim Stores, Wares," *The Globe and Mail*, November 17, 2006, B1, B6; Zena Olijnyk, "All in the Family," *Canadian Business,* September 25–October 8, 2006, 75–76; *National Post,* "Analysts Dismiss Loblaw's Woes," *Canada.com,* April 28, 2006, www.canada.com/national/nationalpost/financialpost/investing/story.html?id=971c8cd8-1a0f-4189-bf5b-8e9535ec2441; Marina Strauss, "Loblaw's Supply Chain Reaction," *The Globe and Mail*, February 25, 2006, B4; Blaise Robinson, "Bay Street Week Ahead—Food Fight in Canada Grocery Aisle," *Globe Investor.com,* January 6, 2006, www.globeinvestor.com/servlet/ArticleNews/story/ROC/20060106/2006-01-06T224057Z_01_MUN681582_RTRIDST_0_BUSINESS-COLUMN-MARKETS-COL; "Canadian Retailer Loblaw's Earnings Hit Due to Delays and Challenges in Supply Chain Network Redesign Project," *Supply Chain Digest,* November 17, 2005, www.scdigest.com/assets/newsviews/05-11-17-1.cfm?cid=158.

Chapter 13

The Instapreneur www.ponoko.com; Ian Mount, "Manufacture and Sell Anything—in Minutes," *Wired*, March 24, 2008, www.wired.com/techbiz/it/magazine/16-04/bz_instapreneur.

Table 13.1 *Financial Post Magazine*, June, 2009, 86. Material reprinted with the express permission of "The National Post Company," a Canwest Partnership.

Business Accountability Jeromy Lloyd, "Redefining Social Media Investments at Mesh," *Marketing*, May 23, 2008; Adam L. Penenberg, "Ning's Infinite Ambition," *Fast Company*, May 2008, 76–84.

Concluding Case 13-1 Geoffrey A. Fowler, "Corporate News: Skype Targets Companies to Ring up Revenue," *The Wall Street Journal*, March 23, 2009, B3; "Social Networking Is Spreading Worldwide as Facebook and Others Adapt Locally," *Winnipeg Free Press*, www.winnipegfreepress.com/historic/33000899.html; Daniel Roth, "Catch Us If You Can," *Fortune*, February 9, 2004, 64–74.

Concluding Case 13-2 Paul Samyn and Leah Janzen, "Bulk-Sale Ban Hailed by Online Drug Industry," *Winnipeg Free Press*, June 30, 2005, B15; Mia Rabson, "Feds Would Kill City Jobs to Safeguard Drug Supply," *Winnipeg Free Press*, December 16, 2004, A1, A4; Dan Lett, "Drug Pipeline Goes Underground," *Winnipeg Free Press,* July 18, 2004, B1; Marton Dunai, "Duty-Free Site's Cigarette Sales Draw Scrutiny," *The Wall Street Journal*, August 5, 2004, B1, B7; Leonard Zehr, "Net Pharmacies Cheer New U.S. Import Bill," *The Globe and Mail*, July 26, 2003, B1, B4; Leah Janzen, "Internet Pharmacy's Drug Search Denounced," *Winnipeg Free Press*, July 5, 2003, A3; David Kuxhaus, "An Internet Pharmacy Primer," *Winnipeg Free Press*, June 22, 2003, A1, A8; Carol Sanders, "Net Druggists Pen Deal," *Winnipeg Free Press*, June 3, 2003, B1; David Kuxhaus, "U.S. Drug Agency Deals Blow to Net Pharmacy Operation," *Winnipeg Free Press*, March 27, 2003, A3; Paul Samyn, "Competition Bureau Backs Drug Giant," *Winnipeg Free Press*, March 22, 2003, B3.

Chapter 14

Accounting for Pensions Boyd Erman, "Teachers' Books Worst-Ever Year after 18 Percent Plunge," *The Globe and Mail*, April 3, 2009, B4; Janet McFarland, "Who's Responsible?," *The Globe and Mail*, March 6, 2009, B1; Lori McLeod, "Pension Plans Suffer Historic Losses," *The Globe and Mail*, January 9, 2009, A1; Janet McFarland, "Returns Forecast This Year Will Do Little to Offset 2008 Shortfalls," *The Globe and Mail*, January 14, 2009, B3; Janet McFarland, "Relief Falls Short, Pension Plans Warn," *The Globe and Mail*, November 28, 2008, B1; Elizabeth Church, "Pension Funding Shortfall Increases Dramatically," *The Globe and Mail*, November 8, 2005, B5; Elizabeth Church, "Pension Fund Shortfall Soars in First Half," *The Globe and Mail*, November 23, 2005, B1, B7; Elizabeth Church, "Cost of Retiree Benefit Liabilities 'Sleeping Giant'," *The Globe and Mail*, August 23, 2004, B4; Paul Waldie and Karen Howlett, "Reports Reveal Tight Grip of Ebbers on WorldCom," *The Globe and Mail*, June 11, 2003, B1, B7; Barrie McKenna, Karen Howlett, and Paul Waldie, "Probes Cite Ebbers in 'Fraud,'" *The Globe and Mail*, June 10, 2003, B1, B16; Elizabeth Church, "Accounting Overhaul Coming," *The Globe and Mail*, December 23, 2002, B1, B6; Richard Blackwell, "OSC Targets Tech Accounting," *The Globe and Mail*, September 26, 2000, B1, B6.

Table 14.1 *Financial Post Magazine*, June 2009, 98. Material reprinted with the express permission of "The National Post Company," a Canwest Partnership.

Business Accountability Lawrence M. Gill, "Questions Loom as Accountants Outsource Work Abroad," *Chicago Lawyer,* January 26, 2004,; Jim Peterson, "Turf Battle Shows Signs of Truce," *International Herald Tribune*, November 8, 2003, 17; Beth Ellyn Rosenthal, "Deloitte Study Discovers 75 Percent of Global Financial Institutions Plan to Outsource Offshore," *BPO Outsourcing Journal,* June 2003, www.bpo-outsourcing-journal.com/jun2003-deloitte.html; Todd Furniss and Michel Janssen, "Offshore Outsourcing Part 1: The Brand of India," *BPO Outsourcing Journal*, December 2003, www.bpo-outsourcing-journal.com/dec2003-india.html; "How to Evaluate an Outsourcing Provider and Watch the Bottom Line," *The CPA Journal,* June 2002, 19; Liz Loxton, "Offshoring—Offshore Accounting," *Accountancy,* February 2004, 48; Thomas J. Smedinghoff and Creighton R. Meland, Jr., "Financial Institution Outsourcing: Managing the Risks," *Outsourcing Journal,* May 2002, www.outsourcing-journal.com/may2002-legal.html; Todd Furniss, "China: The Next Big Wave in Offshore Outsourcing," *BPO Outsourcing Journal,* June 2003, www.bpo-outsourcing-journal.com/jun2003-everest.html; "Cover Feature—Outsourcing the Finance Function—Out with the Count," *Accountancy*, September 1, 2001, 32.

Entrepreneurship and New Ventures *The Daily Gleaner*, A1, from Canadian Newsstand Core database, (Document ID: 1652944261); Randy Ray, "It Is a Sexy Environment and Ee Are the CSIs," *The Globe and Mail*, October 10, 2007, B8; Chartered Accountants of Canada, www.cica.ca; Elisabeth Bumiller, "Bush Signs Bill Aimed at Fraud in Corporations," *The New York Times*, July 31, 2007; Kroll Investigative Services, www.kroll.com; *Stephen Llewellyn,* "Some Lottery Retailers Don't Obey the Rules; Winnings 20% Failed Anti-Cheating Test," *The Daily Gleaner,* February 28, 2009.

The Greening of Business Ken Garen, "Are You Ready to Prosper?," *The Practical Accountant,* June 2008, SR29; Jeff Sanford, "The Next Pension Crisis," *Canadian Business Journal* 80 14 (August 2007): 62–63; Dom Serafini, "Regulations Are the Consumers' Best Friends," *Intermedia*, July 2004, 32, 2, ABI/INFORM Global database, 23.

Concluding Case 14-1 Jeff Buckstein, "SOX Provision Holds Management's Feet to the Fire," *The Globe and Mail*, April 19, 2006, B13; Claire Gagne, "The *Sarbanes-Oxley Act* Restores Shine to Auditors' Reputation—and Fills Their

Coffers," *Canadian Business*, September 27–October 10, 2004, 47–49; Karen Howlett, "Livent's Auditors Charged with Misconduct," *The Globe and Mail*, April 6, 2004, B1, B4; Karen Howlett, "Accounting Hearing Is Told Misconduct Charges Against Auditors Are 'Rubbish,'" *The Globe and Mail*, April 14, 2004, B3; Shawn McCarthy, "Investors Expect Too Much: Deloitte CEO," *The Globe and Mail*, October 17, 2005, B10; Elizabeth Church, "Accounting Overhaul Coming," *The Globe and Mail*, December 23, 2002, B1, B6; Richard Blackwell, "Auditing Firms Get Tighter Rules," *The Globe and Mail*, July 18, 2002, B1, B4; John Partridge and Karen Howlett, "CIBC Restricts Its Auditors," *The Globe and Mail*, March 1, 2002, B1, B4; Lily Nguyen, "Accountants Primed for Change," *The Globe and Mail*, February 4, 2002, B9; Richard Blackwell, "Accountants to Issue New Rules," *The Globe and Mail*, March 28, 2002, B1, B7; John Gray, "Hide and Seek," *Canadian Business*, April 1, 2002,28–32; Steve Liesman, Jonathan Weil, and Michael Schroeder, "Accounting Debacles Spark Calls for Change: Here's the Rundown," *The Wall Street Journal*, February 6, 2002, A1, A8; Edward Clifford, "Big Accounting Firms Face Insurance Crunch," *The Globe and Mail*, November 13, 1993, B3; Patricia Lush, "Gap Widens Between Views on Auditor's Role in Canada," *The Globe and Mail*, February 14, 1986, B3; Chris Robinson, "Auditor's Role Raises Tough Questions," *The Financial Post*, June 22, 1985.

Concluding Case 14–2 Elizabeth Church, "Pension Funding Shortfall Increases Dramatically," *The Globe and Mail*, November 8, 2005, B5; Elizabeth Church, "Pension Fund Shortfall Soars in First Half," *The Globe and Mail*, November 23, 2005, B1, B7; Elizabeth Church, "Cost of Retiree Benefit Liabilities 'Sleeping Giant,'" *The Globe and Mail*, August 23, 2004, B4; Paul Waldie and Karen Howlett, "Reports Reveal Tight Grip of Ebbers on WorldCom," *The Globe and Mail*, June 11, 2003, B1, B7; Barrie McKenna, Karen Howlett, and Paul Waldie, "Probes Cite Ebbers in 'Fraud,'" *The Globe and Mail*, June 10, 2003, B1, B16; Elizabeth Church, "Accounting Overhaul Coming," *The Globe and Mail*, December 23, 2002, B1, B6; Richard Blackwell, "OSC Targets Tech Accounting," *The Globe and Mail*, September 26, 2000, B1, B6.

Chapter 15

Why So Serious? "Batman Film Series," May 23, 2008, http://en.wikipedia.org/wiki/Batman_%28film_series%29; Claude Brodesser-Akner, "Hyping Joker-Without Exploiting Heath's Death," *Advertising Age*, May 12, 2008, http://adage.com/article.php?article_id=126981; Chungaiz, "New Batman Dark Knight Marketing Continues, Fantastic!, blog," December 13, 2007, www.altogetherdigital.com/20071213/new-batman-dark-knight-marketing-continues-fantastic; Chris Lee, "The Dark Knight Marketing Blitz," *Los Angeles Times*, March 24, 2008, articles.latimes.com/2008/mar/24/entertainment/et-batmanviral24. See also http://batman.wikibruce.com/Timeline; www.42entertainment.com; http://whysoserious.com.

Business Accountability Keith McArthur, "A Year Later: No Medium for the Message," *The Globe and Mail*, November 1, 2004, B3; Cheryl Healton and Kathleen Nelson, "Reversal of Misfortune: Viewing Tobacco as a Social Justice Issue," *American Journal of Public Health*, February 2004, 186t; *Federal Trade Commission Cigarette Report for 2001*, June 15, 2003, www.ftc.gov/os/2003/06/cigreport.pdf.

The Greening of Business Statistics Canada, "Canadian Economic Accounts," *The Daily*, March 3, 2008, www.statcan.gc.ca/daily-quotidien/080303/dq080303a-eng.htm; "Industry Statistics & Trends," *American Pet Products Manufacturing Association*, www.americanpetproducts.org/press_industrytrends.asp; Blair Coursey, "North America: Plastic Waste—More Dangerous Than Global Warming," *Ethical Corporation*, May 8, 2007; Statistics Canada, *"Canadian Economic Accounts," The Daily*, March 3, 2008, www.statcan.gc.ca/daily-quotidien/080303/dq080303a-eng.htm.

Concluding Case 15-1 Joel Hruska, "Apple, Dell Big Market Share Winners for the First Quarter," *Ars Technica*, April 17, 2008; Kevin Maney, "Dell to Dive into Consumer Electronics Market," *USA Today*, September 25, 2003, 1B–2B; David Teather, "Michael Dell Quits as Chief of His Own Company," *The Guardian*, March 5, 2004.

Concluding Case 15-2 Nate Anderson, "Bell Canada Opens Online Video Store as P2P Debate Rages On," *Ars Technica*, May 22, 2008; Etan Vlessing, "Bell Canada in Deal with Paramount," *Hollywood Reporter*, May 21, 2008; Jack Kapica, "Bell Launches Video Download Store," *The Globe and Mail*, May 21, 2008; Jason Laszlo, "New Bell Video Store Offers the Most Download-to-own and Rent Movies and TV shows in Canada," *Bell Canada Enterprises*, May 21, 2008.

Chapter 16

Psst! Did You Hear the Latest? Hollie Shaw, "Reaching Out via Web; Marketers Look for Creative Ways to Draw in Consumers," *National Post*, November 7, 2008, FP14; Nick Turner, "Cupcake Business Reaps Sweet Rewards; Location and Word of Mouth Key to Success," *National Post*, October 27, 2008, FP9; Sam Cage, "Word of Mouth Sells 'Remembrance' Gems," *National Post*, September 15, 2008; Sinclair Stewart, "Hey, Did You Hear about That Great New Toothpaste?," *The Globe and Mail*, November 20, 2007, B3; Erin White, "Word of Mouth Makes Nike Slip-On Sneakers Take Off," *The Globe and Mail*, June 7, 2001, B1, B4; Mike Blaney, *"Word of Mouth Advertising," blog*, www.themarketingguy.wordpress.com/2007/10/09/word-of-mouth-advertising; www.theinfluencers.ca/why_wom.php.

Table 16.1 *Financial Post Magazine*, June, 2009, 87. Material reprinted with the express permission of "The National Post Company," a Canwest Partnership.

The Greening of Business Hollie Shaw, "Making the Case That Wearing Fur Can Be Eco-Friendly," *Winnipeg Free Press*, December 5, 2008, B6; Daryl-Lynn Carlson, "Advertising Guidelines Target 'Greenwashing'," *Winnipeg Free Press*, November 21, 2008, B6; Marina Strauss, "Standing Out in a Sea of Green," *The Globe and Mail*, August 16, 2008, B3; Randy Boswell, "Oil Sands Ad 'Greenwash' Environment Group Crows," *The Globe and Mail*, August 14, 2008, C8; Richard Blackwell, "Eco-Friendly? Canadians Want to See the Proof," *The Globe and Mail*, July 28, 2008, B1, B3; Shawn McCarthy, "Oil Sands Tries Image Makeover," *The Globe and Mail*, June 24, 2008, B1, B7; Sharon Epperson, "BP's Fundamental but Obscured Energy Contradiction," *CNBC.com*, May 21, 2008, www.cnbc.com/id/24758394; Carly Weeks, "New Scrutiny for Green Claims," *The Globe and Mail*, March 11, 2008, B1, B6; "Oil Company BP Pleads Guilty to Environmental Crime," *International Herald Tribune*, November 29, 2007, www.iht.com/articles/ap/2007/11/30/business/NA-FIN-US-BP-Settlement-Alaska.php?page=1; Terry Macalister, "Greenpeace Calls BP's Oil Sands Plan an Environmental Crime," *Guardian.co.uk*, December 7, 2007, www.guardian.co.uk/business/2007/dec/07/bp.

Entrepreneurship and New Ventures Jonathan Paul, "RPGs look for Brands to Play With," *Strategy*, April 2009, 33; Frank Armstrong, "Fairytale Ending for Tiny Ottawa Firm," *The Globe and Mail*, November 11, 2008; Lana Castleman, "Virtual Worlds on the Menu at Kids Marketing Agencies," *KidScreen*, October 2008, 79; Lana Castleman, "McDonald's Is Lovin' Customer Content," *KidScreen*, May 2008, 26; Rob Gerlsbeck, "Fuel Industries," *Marketing* 112, 21 (2007): 22.

Concluding Case 16-1 Grant Surridge, "People, Lend Them Your Ears; More Accurate Radio Monitoring," *National Post*, November 26, 2008, FP1; Emily Steel, "Google Set to Roll Out Web-Measurement Tool," *The Wall Street Journal*, June 24, 2008, B14; Jennifer Wells, "The Brain Guy Wants to Get Inside Your Head," *The Globe and Mail*, March 15, 2008, B4–B5; "TV Networks Pay Back Advertisers," *National Post*, December 13, 2007; David George-Cosh, "Fighting Click Fraud: Is It Really Down for the Count?," *The Globe and Mail*, August 23, 2007, B7; Brooks Barnes, "New TV Ratings Will Produce Ad-Price

Fight," *The Wall Street Journal*, December 22, 2005, B1, B3; Brooks Barnes, "Where're *the* Ratings, Dude?," *The Wall Street Journal*, March 7, 2005, B1, B6; Keith McArthur, "New TV Ratings Devices Know What You're Watching," *The Globe and Mail*, November 29, 2004, B1, B12; Keith McArthur, "Advertisers Wary of Plan to Fuse TV Ratings Systems," *The Globe and Mail*, July 13, 2004, B1, B20; Brooks Barnes, "For Nielsen, Fixing Old Ratings System Causes New Static," *The Wall Street Journal*, September 16, 2004, A1, A8; Elizabeth Jensen, "Networks Blast Nielsen, Blame Faulty Ratings for Drop in Viewership," *The Wall Street Journal*, November 22, 1996, A1, A8.

Concluding Case 16-2 Jennifer Wells, "Ad Nauseam," *The Globe and Mail*, July 25, 2008, B5; "30-Second Spot: Dispatches from the World of Media and Advertising," *The Globe and Mail*, December 19, 2008, B6; Scott Valentine, "Interactive TV-Watching Had Advertisers Sitting Up," *The Globe and Mail*, January 24, 2008, B8; Grant Robertson, "Radio Rivals Resort to Merger," *The Globe and Mail*, February 20, 2007, B1, B6; Keith McArthur and Grant Robertson, "CRTC Ponders Impact of Product Placement," *The Globe and Mail*, November 21, 2005, B1, B10; Grant Robertson and Richard Blackwell, "Eased Satellite Radio Rules Could 'Shock' System," *The Globe and Mail*, September 25, 2005, B7; Tessa Wegert, "On-Line Marketing Concept Gives Consumers a Say," *The Globe and Mail*, October 13, 2005, B13; Aaron Patrick, "Commercials by Cellphone," *The Wall Street Journal*, August 22, 2005, B1, B3; Frazier Moore, "You Can't Fast-Forward Past These Commercials," *Winnipeg Free Press*, July 25, 2005, D3; Simon Tuck, "CRTC Turns Radio on Its Head with Landmark Satellite Ruling," *The Globe and Mail*, June 17, 2005, B1, B6; Eric Reguly, "Blame the *Act*, Not the Regulator," *The Globe and Mail*, June 16, 2005, B2; Joe Flint and Brian Steinberg, "Proctor & Gamble Tweaks Its Traditional TV Ad Strategy," *The Wall Street Journal*, June 13, 2005, B6; Peter Grant, "Interactive Ads Start to Click on Cable and Satellite TV," *The Wall Street Journal*, May 26, 2005, B1, B6; Keith McArthur, "Branded Content Generates Buzz," *The Globe and Mail*, April 6, 2005, B4; Keith McArthur, "A Year Later: No Medium for the Message," *The Globe and Mail*, November 1, 2004, B3.

Chapter 17

Buyers and Sellers Jockey for Position "Consumers Trade Down, McDonald's Sales Go Up," *The Globe and Mail*, December 9, 2008, B12; Marina Strauss, "Stores Aim to Convert 'Cherry Pickers'," *The Globe and Mail*, November 19, 2008, B11; Janet Adamy, "McDonald's Strategy to Take Sales from Pricier Restaurants Working," *National Post*, October 23, 2008, FP2; David Hutton, "Consumers Get Less Bang for Their Buck," *The Globe and Mail*, July 8, 2008, B2; Ann Zimmerman, "Behind the Dollar-Store Boom: A Nation of Bargain Hunters," *The Wall Street Journal*, December 13, 2004, A1, A10; Gordon Fairclough, "Four Biggest Cigarette Makers Can't Raise Prices as They Did," *The Wall Street Journal*, October 25, 2002, A1, A8; Timothy Aeppel, "After Cost Cutting, Companies Turn toward Price Increases," *The Wall Street Journal*, September 18, 2002, A1, A12.

Table 17.1 *Financial Post Magazine*, June, 2009, 86. Material reprinted with the express permission of "The National Post Company," a Canwest Partnership.

Entrepreneurship and New Ventures *Auto Vault*, www.autovaultcanada.com; Deirdre Kelly, "Nowhere to Park the Lamborghini?" *The Globe and Mail*, September 20, 2008, M3; Jerry Langton, "Driven by Love of Hot Wheels; Entrepreneur Cashes in on Need for Secure Storage for Owners' Exotic Cars with Auto Vault, Car Condo," *The Toronto Star*, May 12, 2008, B01; Joshua Knelman, "Auto Focus: This 40,000 Square-foot Car Park Protects Your Precious Ride from All the Elements—Criminal and Climactic," *Toronto Life*, May 2005, 27; "Storing Your 'Baby' for Winter," *The Expositor*, www.brantfordexpositor.ca/ArticleDisplay.aspx?archive=true&e=1283051.

The Greening of Business Marjo Johne, "Shoppers Get a Brand New Bag," *The Globe and Mail*, October 20, 2008, E5; *Agriculture and Agri-Food Canada, Going Green: The Future of the Retail Food Industry, July 2007*, www.ats.agr.gc.ca/us/4351_e.htm.

Concluding Case 17-1 Keith McArthur, "Why Molson *Is* Crying in *Its* Beer," *The Globe and Mail*, July 10, 2004, B4; Kevin Kelleher, "66,207,896 Bottles of Beer on the Wall," *Business 2.0*, January/February 2004, 47–49; Tim Davis, "Surfin' the Net, Bud Style," *Beverage World*, August 1995, 28; "This Budnet's for You," *Progressive Grocer*, May 1996, 16; *2003 Annual Report* (St. Louis: Anheuser-Busch Companies Inc., 2004).

Concluding Case 17-2 Matt Hartley, "From Pirate Bay, a Torpedo to Illegal File-Sharing," *The Globe and Mail*, April 18, 2009, B3; Grant Robertson, "Death Knell Sounds for CDs," *The Globe and Mail*, June 19, 2008, B3; Shawn McCarthy, "U.S. Court Shuts Door on Internet File-Sharing," *The Globe and Mail*, June 28, 2005, B3; "File Sharing Firm Will Shut Down," *Winnipeg Free Press*, Novermber 8, 2005, A11; Nick Wingfield, "Online Music's Latest Tune," *The Wall Street Journal*, August 27, 2004, B1, B2; Nick Wingfield, "New File-Swapping Software Limits Sharers to a Select Few," *The Wall Street Journal*, October 4, 2004, B1, B4; Sarah McBride, "Stop the Music!," *The Wall Street Journal*, August 23, 2004, B1; also Vauhini Vara, "On Campus, iTunes Finds an Illicit Groove," *The Wall Street Journal*, August 23, 2004, B1–B2; Nick Wingfield and Sarah McBride, "Green Light for Grokster," *The Wall Street Journal*, August 20, 2004, B1, B3; Nick Wingfield, "The Day the Music Died," *The Wall Street Journal*, May 2, 2003, B8; "The End of File-Shares as We Know Them," *Winnipeg Free Press*, July 4, 2003, A8; Ted Birdis, "Music Industry Escalates Net Fight," *Winnipeg Free Press*, June 26, 2003, A12; Matthew Ingram, "Digital Music Industry Gets New Spin on Napster Judge's Decision," *The Globe and Mail*, February 26, 2002; Nick Wingfield, "Napster Boy, Interrupted," *The Wall Street Journal*, October 1, 2002, B1, B3; Anna Matthews and Charles Goldsmith, "Music Industry Faces New Threats on Web," *The Wall Street Journal*, February 21, 2003, B1, B4.

Chapter 18

Money, Money, Money Jill Connelly, "SMEs Turn to Bartering, Saving Cash," *National Post*, January 5, 2009, FP8; Tom Hundley, "So Why Does the $1 Bill Still Exist?," *The Buffalo News*, July 20, 2008, D3; Yaroslav Trofimov, "Shrinking Dollar Meets Its Match in Dolphin Teeth," *The Wall Street Journal*, April 30, 2008, A1, A13; Roma Luciw, "Goodbye Penny, Hello $5 Coin?," *The Globe and Mail*, April 10, 2008, B5; Tara Perkins, "Lose the Loose Change? Bank Study Proposed Dropping Penny," *The Globe and Mail*, July 3, 2007, B3; "What Is Money?" *The British Museum*, www.britishmuseum.org/explore/themes/money/what_is_money.aspx.

Table 18.1 *Financial Post Magazine*, June, 2009, 94. Material reprinted with the express permission of "The National Post Company," a Canwest Partnership.

Table 18.2 *Financial Post Magazine*, June, 2009, 94. Material reprinted with the express permission of "The National Post Company," a Canwest Partnership.

The Greening of Business "TD Canada Trust Greens All Its Green Machines with Renewable Electricity," *Canada NewsWire*, June 17, 2008, www.cnw.ca/en/releases/ archive/June2008/17/c4777.html; Luann Lasalle, "Almost 75 Per cent of Canadians Use the Internet; Teens Drive up Its Use," *The Canadian Press*, June 12, 2008, retrieved from CBCA Current Events database; "CSR at Scotiabank: Reducing Our Impact," *Scotiabank*, www.scotiabank.com/cda/content/0,1608,CID12002_LIDen,00.html; www.payitgreen.org.

Business Accountability Konrad Yakabuski, "You May Love Canada's Banks Now, But . . .," *The Globe and Mail*, April 30, 2009, B2; Janet Whitman, "Maybe Canadian Banks Are the New Swiss Watches; Stability Played Up and Paying Off," *National Post*, April 4, 2009, FP4; Tara Perkins, "Why Canadian Banks Work," *The Globe and Mail*,

March 7, 2009, B1; Theresa Tedesco, "The Great Solvent North," *The New York Times*, February 28, 2009, A19.

Concluding Case 18-1 Jacqueline Thorpe, "Loonie Route Deepens, Commodity Pain Takes Toll around the Globe," *National Post*, October 23, 2008, FP1; John Partridge, "Loonie Tumbles Below 80 Cents US," *The Globe and Mail*, October 22, 2008, www.bnn.ca/news4290.html; Alia McMullen, "Softening Dollar Offers U.S. Exporters Some Hope," *National Post*, January 3, 2008, www.nationalpost.com/story-printer.html?id=211694; "Adapt or Perish," *National Post*, January 2, 2008, www.nationalpost.com/story-printer.html?id=209540; Kate Jaimet, "Loonie Squeezes Iconic Tool Maker," *National Post*, December 24, 2007, www.nationalpost.com/story-printer.html?id=194940; David Blanks, "Lack of Access," *National Post*, November 29, 2007, www.nationalpost.com/story-printer.html?id=130590; Gwynne Dyer, "Countries Begin to Say Farewell to Greenback," *Winnipeg Free Press*, November 28, 2007, A15; Scott Deveau, "Airbus Sales Can't Stop Tailspin," *National Post*, November 23, 2007, FP1, FP3; Steven Chase, "Consider a Continental Currency, Jarislowsky Says," *The Globe and Mail*, November 23, 2007, B3; Zena Olijnyk, "Retail: Dollar Daze," *Canadian Business*, November 19, 2007, www.canadianbusiness.com/shared/print.jsp?content=20071119_198707_198707&; Rachel Puffer, "Design'07 (Furniture): The Chair Man," *Canadian Business*, November 19, 2007, www.canadianbusiness.com/shared/print.jsp?content=20071119_198704_198704&; Robin Banerjee, "The Petroloonie," *National Post*, November 15, 2007, FP19; Greg Keenan, "Loonie Has Parts Makers Reeling," *The Globe and Mail*, November 15, 2007, B14; Jeff D. Opdyke and Jane J. Kim, "Dollar Daze: Investing with a Weak Currency," *The Wall Street Journal*, September 26, 2007, D1, D4; Jacqueline Thorpe, "Liftoff a Long Time Coming," *National Post*, September 22, 2007, FP1–FP2; Nathan VanderKlippe, "Prices Lag Dollar's 'Moonshot'," *National Post*, September 22, 2007, FP4; David Berman, "Currency Not Alone in Rise Against U.S. Dollar," *National Post*, September 21, 2007, FP1, FP3; Steven Chase, "Parity. So What?," *The Globe and Mail*, September 21, 2007, A1, A5; Claudia Cattaneo, "High Dollar a Cash Drain on Oilpatch," *National Post*, September 21, 2007, FP3; Joanna Slater, "Falling Dollar Squeezes U.S. Trade Partners," *The Wall Street Journal*, September 21, 2007, C1, C9; Michael M. Phillips, "World Economy in Flux as America Downshifts," *The Wall Street Journal*, September 20, 2007, A1, A11.

Concluding Case 18-2 Nathan Vanderklippe, "Saving Salmon Farming," *National Post*, March 29, 2008, www.nationalpost.com/todays_paper/story.html?id=407589; "Newfoundland Aquaculture Industry Association Receives Funding for Cod Aquaculture Initiative," news release, January 30, 2006, www.releases.gov.nl.ca/releases/2006/lfishaq/0130n01.htm; Lindsay Royston, "Cod Walloped," *Canadian Business*, November 21–December 4, 2005, 114; "Newfoundland Projects Work toward Cod Commercialization," *The Fish Site.com*, April 2005, www.thefishsite.com/articles/78/newfoundland-projects-work-toward-cod-commercialization; "Newfoundland Cod Comeback!," *news release*, January 16, 2004, www.releases.gov.nl.ca/releases/2004/fishaq/0116n01.htm; *Land and Sea*, TV series (CBC, May 21, 2006).

Chapter 19

And the Markets Came Tumbling Down—Again Harvey Schachter, "Market Meltdown: The Buck Starts Here," *The Globe and Mail*, October 15, 2008, C2; Richard Blackwell, "From Subprime to Stock Swoon," *The Globe and Mail*, October 13, 2008, B3; "Wall Street's Rescue," *The Globe and Mail*, October 6, 2008, B4; "Contagion," *Winnipeg Free Press*, October 3, 2008, A15; "Investors Lost Billions, Large Banks and Brokerages Failed, Wall Street's Troubles Went Global," *The Globe and Mail*, October 1, 2008, B1; Kristine Owram, "Happy Days Here Again?," *Winnipeg Free Press*, September 20, 2008, B11; Justin Lahart, "The Crash of 2002," *CNNMoney*, July 19, 2002, ; "We All Got Burned, Now What?" *CNNMoney*, July 19, 2002, http://money.cnn.com; "Dow Plunges Below Its Post-Terrorist Attack Low," *USA Today*, July 19, 2002, www.usatoday.com.

Table 19.1 *Financial Post Magazine*, June, 2009, 70. Material reprinted with the express permission of "The National Post Company," a Canwest Partnership.

Table 19.3 *Financial Post Magazine*, June, 2009, 96. Material reprinted with the express permission of "The National Post Company," a Canwest Partnership.

Business Accountability "Our True Identity Revealed: AIMR Changes Name to CFA Institute," *CFA Institute*, April 19, 2004, www.cfainstitute.org.

The Greening of Business Ronald Ebert and Ricky Griffin, *Business Essentials, 7th ed.* (Upper Saddle River, NJ: Prentice Hall, 2009), 227.

Concluding Case 19-1 Karen Howlett and John Saunders, "Fund Firms Admit Role in Market Timing Trades," *The Globe and Mail*, December 17, 2004, B1, B4; Janet McFarland and Rob Carrick, "The Fee Crunch: Not All Investors Get Value for Money," *The Globe and Mail*, June 24, 2004, B6; Christine Dugas, "Putnam Ousts CEO in Midst of Fund Probe," *USA Today*, November 3, 2003, www.usatoday.com/money/perfi/funds/2003-11-03-putnam_x.htm; John Waggoner, "Senators Blast SEC over Mutual Fund Trading Scandal," *USA Today*, November 3, 2003, www.usatoday.com/money/perfi/funds/2003-11-02-hearing_x.htm; John Waggoner, Christine Dugas, and Thomas A. Fogarty, "Scandal Outrage Keeps Growing," *USA Today*, November 3, 2003, www.usatoday.com/money/perfi/funds/2003-11-03-fund-cover_x.; "NYC Pensions Pull Assets from Putnam," *CNNMoney*, November 4, 2003, http://money.cnn.com; "Chairman of Strong Mutual Resigns," *USA Today*, November 3, 2003, www.usatoday.com/money/perfi/funds/2003-11-03-strong_x.htm.

Concluding Case 19-2 Janet McFarland, "Former Agnico Executive Sentenced to Jail Time," *The Globe and Mail*, January 30, 2009, B3; Tara Perkins, "Former Trader Pleads Guilty in Fraud That Cost BMO $850 Million," *The Globe and Mail*, November 19, 2008, B1; Janet McFarland and Brent Jang, "Andrew Rankin: Barred from Trading Stocks, but Cleared of Criminal Charges," *The Globe and Mail*, February 22, 2008, B1, B4; Bertrand Marotte, "Mutual Fund Fraudster Gets 12 Years," *The Globe and Mail*, January 29, 2008, B1, B4; Richard Blackwell, "Firm, Ex-CEO Pay Millions in Penalties," *The Globe and Mail*, December 20, 2001, B1, B6; Richard Blackwell, "OSC Scores Trading Conviction," *The Globe and Mail*, July 22, 2000, B1–B2; "CEO Jailed for Insider Trading," *Winnipeg Free Press*, September 19, 2000, B8; Karen Howlett, "Below the Decks of Treasure Ship Deals," *The Globe and Mail*, July 19, 2003, B1, B4; Karen Howlett, Sinclair Stewart, and Paul Waldie, "Brokers Caught Up in Police Probe," *The Globe and Mail*, June 20, 2003, B1, B20; David Paddon and Hollie Shaw, "Top Heads Roll at Royal after Scandal," *Winnipeg Free Press*, July 21, 2000, B7, B12; Karen Howlett, Janet McFarland, and Dawn Walton, "Stock Rigging Appears Widespread," *The Globe and Mail*, July 1, 2000, B1, B4; Richard Blackwell and Jacquie McNish, "OSC prepared to Deal with RT," *The Globe and Mail*, July 1, 2000, B5; Jacquie McNish, "How the High Closing High Fliers Got Caught," *The Globe and Mail*, July 3, 2000, B1, B3.

Chapter 20

A Financial Meltdown Terence Corcoran, "The Big Global Screw-Up," *National Post*, February 24, 2009, FP11; Harvey Schachter, "Market Meltdown: The Buck Starts Here," *The Globe and Mail*, October 15, 2008, C2; Tavia Grant, "Bailouts Tied to Curbing Executive Pay," *The Globe and Mail*, October 15, 2008, B4; Marcus Walker, Sara Schaefer-Munoz, and David Gauthier-Villars, "Bailout Price Tags Raise the Question: How?," *The Globe and Mail*, October 14, 2008, B11; Richard Blackwell, "From Subprime to Stock Swoon," *The Globe and Mail*, October 13, 2008, B3; Joel Schlesinger, "A Brief History of a Financial Meltdown," *Winnipeg Free Press*, October 12, 2008, B9; "Wall Street's

Rescue," *The Globe and Mail*, October 6, 2008, B4; "Contagion," *Winnipeg Free Press*, October 3, 2008, A15; "Investors Lost Billions, Large Banks and Brokerages Failed, Wall Street's Troubles Went Global," *The Globe and Mail*, October 1, 2008, B1; Rachel Puffer, "Easy Money," *Canadian Business*, September 29, 2008, 38; Janet Whitman, "Scramble to Start Financial Rescue," *National Post*, September 22, 2008, www.nationalpost.com; Eoin Callan, "Paulson Bailout Extended," *National Post*, September 22, 2008, www.nationalpost.com; Jeanne Aversa and Julie Davis, "U.S. Puts Taxpayer on Huge Hook," *Winnipeg Free Press*, September 20, 2008, B11; Kristine Owram, "Happy Days Here Again?," *Winnipeg Free Press*, September 20, 2008, B11; Barrie McKenna, "A Desperate Disease, a Desperate Remedy," *The Globe and Mail*, September 20, 2008, B5; Derek DeCloet, "Five Days That Shook the Financial World," *The Globe and Mail*, September 20, 2008, B2; Barrie McKenna, "Fannie, Freddie Stay in Free Fall on Bailout Talk," *The Globe and Mail*, August 21, 2008, B9.

Table 20.2 *Financial Post Magazine*, June, 2009, 96. Material reprinted with the express permission of "The National Post Company," a Canwest Partnership.

Entrepreneurship and New Ventures "Towne Square," *55-Alive!*, www.55-alive.com/index.php; Peter Corbett, "2009 Facebook Demographics and Statistics Report: 276% Growth in 35–54 Year Old Users," *iStrategyLabs*, January 5, 2009, www.istrategylabs.com/2009-facebook-demographics-and-statistics-report-276-growth-in-35-54-year-old-users/.

Business Accountability Michael S. Hopkins, "Because He Learns, and Teaches," *Inc.*, April 2004, 119–120.

Concluding Case 20-1 Philip Ling, "$4.45 Billion Fund to Ensure ABCP Solution: Backstop in Place; Major Hurdle in Process Crossed, Purdy Says," *National Post*, December 27, 2008, FP4; Boyd Erman, "A Long, Tough Struggle Ends Finally, with a Deal," *The Globe and Mail*, December 26, 2008, B4; "Strategem Issues ABCP Warning," *National Post*, www.nationalpost.com/story-printer.html?id=209530; John Greenwood, "Frustrated as Hell," *National Post*, October 21, 2008, www.nationalpost.com/story-printer.html?id=895020; Janet McFarland, Boyd Erman, Karen Howlett, and Tara Perkins, "Ordinary People, an Extraordinary Mess," *The Globe and Mail*, August 9, 2008, B4–B6; David Friend, "Investors in ABCP Approve Restructuring," *Winnipeg Free Press*, April 26, 2008, B13; Boyd Erman, "DBRS to Roll Out a New Road Map on Risk," *The Globe and Mail*, February 8, 2008, B1, B6; Gary Norris, "Financial Rescue Has Holes," *Winnipeg Free Press*, December 26, 2007, B17; Duncan Mavin, "Subprime Torpedoes CIBC," *Winnipeg Free Press*, December 7, 2007, B1; Matthew McClearn, "The Asset-Backed Commercial Paper Crunch Has Burned Investors: Now Lawyer Purdy Crawford Is Trying to Sort out the Mess," *Canadian Business*, November 5, 2007, 130–139; Thomas Watson, "Issues of Trust," *Canadian Business*, November 5, 2007, 141–147; Aaron Lucchetti and Kara Scannell, "Ratings Firms: A Dollar Short and Day Late?," *The Wall Street Journal*, September 26, 2007, C1–C2; Karen Mazurkewich and John Greenwood, "Caisse Top ABCP Holder," *National Post*, September 18, 2007, FP1, FP5; Peter Eavis, "Oh, the People You'll Blame," *Fortune*, September 17, 2007, 118–124; John Greenwood, "Banks Left on Hook in Credit Market Freeze," *National Post*, September 15, 2007, FP7; John Greenwood and Duncan Mavin, "Credit Rout far from Over," *National Post*, September 12, 2007, FP1, FP13; Jeff Sanford, "How This Happened," *Canadian Business*, September 10, 2007, 87–88; Doug Alexander, "Banks Feel Heat of ABCP Meltdown," *National Post*, September 8, 2007, FP7; Tara Perkins, "Misguided, or Misunderstood?," *The Globe and Mail*, September 8, 2007, B4–B5; John Greenwood, "ABCP Losses Could Hit 50%," *National Post*, September 5, 2007, FP1, FP5; Kara Scannell and Deborah Solomon, "Unraveling the Subprime Mess," *The Wall Street Journal*, September 4, 2007, A6; "Mortgage Mayhem," *Fortune*, September 3, 2007, 82–83; Jon Birger, "Markdown," *Fortune*, September 3, 2007, 77–78; Shawn Tully, "Risk Returns with a Vengeance," *Fortune*, September 3, 2007, 51–56; Boyd Erman, "Commercial Paper Had Never Suffered for a Lack of Buyers and Sellers—Until Recent Liquidity Concerns Sent Investors Running for the Exits," *The Globe and Mail*, August 25, 2007, B2; John Greenwood, "Legal Actions Looming," *National Post*, August 24, 2007, FP1, FP3; Barbara Shecter, "Greenspan's Rate Cuts Helped Create a Culture of Debt That Ignored Borders and Was Ultimately Shunned as Too Risky," *National Post*, August 18, 2007, FP1, FP4; Sean Silcoff, "Warnings Were Issued Well Ahead of Crisis," *National Post*, August 18, 2007,. FP1, FP3; Andrew Willis and Boyd Erman, "Credit Crunch Claims Victim in Canada," *The Globe and Mail*, August 14, 2007, B1, B4; David Wolf, "The Butterfly Market, *Canadian Business*, August 13–27, 2007, 15.

Concluding Case 20-2 Tara Perkins, "Former Trader Pleads Guilty in Fraud That Cost BMO $850 Million," *The Globe and Mail*, November 19, 2008, B1; Boyd Erman and Derek DeCloet, "The Guys Who Had a Gut Feeling for Risk," *The Globe and Mail*, February 23, 2008, B4–B6; "Defiant Kerviel Refuses to Play 'Scapegoat'," *The Globe and Mail*, February 6, 2008, B12; Paul Waldie, "Kerviel Made Millions from Mortgage Meltdown," *The Globe and Mail*, January 31, 2008, 1, B13; Eric Reguly, "Exchange Says It Questioned Kerviel's Actions," *The Globe and Mail*, January 29, 2008, B7; Harris Anwar, "Chief Risk Officer: A Valuable Addition to the C-Suite," *The Globe and Mail*, June 20, 2005, B13; Oliver Bertin, "Sector Hit Hard by Sharp Increases in Premiums," *The Globe and Mail*, April 27, 2004, B14; Oliver Bertin, "Firms Face Major Hurdles En Route to U.S. Markets," *The Globe and Mail*, April 29, 2004, B16; "Singer 'Incited' Crowd," *Winnipeg Free Press*, August 15, 2005, D2; Leslie Scism, "If Disaster Strikes This 'Titanic,' Chubb Could Lose Millions," *The Wall Street Journal*, April 9, 1997, A1, A4; Patrick Reilly, "Insurers Are Downbeat on Rap Concert Tours," *The Wall Street Journal*, March 26, 1997, B1, B12.

Image Credits

Prologue

xxv Kim Kulish/Corbis; xxvi Bill Graveland/CP Images; xxvi John M. Heller/Getty Images; xxvi Pam Francis/Getty Images; xxvii Junko Kimura/Getty Images; xxvii Paul A. Souders/Encyclopedia/Corbis; xxviii Nigel Cattlin/Alamy; xxviii George Widman/AP Images

Part One

2-3 Bill Brooks/Alamy

Chapter 1

5 Courtesy of Inco **7** The New Yorker Collection/Joseph Mirachi/CartoonBank.com; **8** (top left) Sculpies/Dreamstime.com; (top right) Tinabelle/Dreamstime.com; (bottom left) Eschcollection L/Alamy; (bottom right) Prebranac/Dreamstime.com; **12** Frederic J. Brown/AFP/Getty Images; **15** Tim Pohl/iStockphoto; **23** Masterfile (Royalty-Free Div.) www.masterfile.com; **27** Ritz Sino/The New York Times; **28** Namas Bhojani

Chapter 2

37 Chris Wattie/Reuters/Corbis; **43** Louie Psihoyos/Terra/Corbis; **47** Bettmann/Corbis; **52** Rich Pedroncelli/AP Images; **59** Fredrik Renander/Alamy

Chapter 3

71 (left & right) Toronto Star/GetStock.com; **75 L** Antony Nettle/Alamy; **R** David Osborn/Alamy; **79** Tony Karumba/Getty Images; **86** Donna Terek Photography; **89** Courtesy of Construction Association of Ontario; **91** The New Yorker Collection/Frank Cotham/CartoonBank.com; **94** McDonald's Restaurant

Chapter 4

105 David Lees/Corbis; **108** Rick Rycroft/AP Images; **110** Rob Crandall/Alamy; **118** Kelvin Jay Wakefield/iStockphoto; **123** Dick Hemingway; **129** Don Denton/CP Images

Chapter 5

141 Photo courtesy of Bombardier Inc. and used under license; **145** Index Open/Photolibrary.com; **147** Everett Collection; **158** Uriel Sinai/Getty Images; **160** Mark Gibson/Digital Vision/Getty Images; **163** Namas Bhojani

Part Two

176-177 Justin Horrocks/iStockphoto

Chapter 6

179 Greg Fulmes/CP Images; **183** Kyodo News; **185** (top) Frank Siteman/A.G.E. Foto Stock/First Light; (middle) PhotoAlto/Alamy; (bottom) ColorBlind Images/Getty Images; **191** Oliver Fantitsch/AP Images; **197** Frédéric Neema/Sygma/Corbis; **200** Matthew Mcvay/Corbis; **202** Richard Wolowicz/Getty Images

Chapter 7

211 canadabrian/Alamy; **214** Everett Collection; **216** Dick Hemingway; **220** Julio Cortez/CP Images; **224** Adamsmith/Taxi/Getty Images **226** Courtesy of Hydro-Québec **227** Chiaki Tsukumo/AP Images **232** Bob Scott/The Image Bank/Getty Images

Chapter 8

241 Clement Allard/CP Images; **246** Javier Larrea/A.G.E. Foto Stock/First Light; **251** Harry Sieplinga/HMS Images/The Image Bank/Getty Images; **257** Kathy Willens/AP/CP Images; **262** (left) Sean Locke/iStockphoto; (right) Gary Douglas-Beet/iStockphoto; **267** Chris Sattlberger/Corbis; **268** Mark Richards

Chapter 9

277 Chicoutimi Le Quotidien-Rocket Lavoie/CP Images; **279** Prentice Hall Archives; Andrew Vaughan/CP Images; **289** Kevin Frayer/CP Images; **293** Thomas Cheng/AFP/Getty Images

Chapter 10

303 Masterfile (Royalty-Free Div.) www.masterfile.com; **305** Lester Lefkowitz/Ivy/Corbis; **309** (top) Bettmann/Corbis; (bottom) Courtesy Western Electric; **315** Masterfile (Royalty-Free Div.) www.masterfile.com; **318** Jan Peter Kasper/epa/Corbis; **321** Justin Sullivan/Getty Images; **324** The New Yorker Collection/Mike Twohy/CartoonBank.com; **327** (left) Tina Fineberg/AP Images; (right) Money Sharma/epa/Corbis

Part Three

340-341 George Steinmetz/Terra/Corbis

Chapter 11

343 Alex Wong/ZUMAPRESS.com/Keystone Press; **345** Namas Bhojani; **349** Greg Smith/Corbis; **352** Masterfile (Royalty-Free Div.) www.masterfile.com; **358** © Rex Features [2005]. All rights reserved./CP Images; **361** Toyota Motor Manufacturing Canada, Inc.; **362** Jaguar Cars Limited; **369** LTI New York

Chapter 12

379 Scott Olson/Getty Images; **381** Christopher Anderson; **383** (left & right) Ted Rice; **389** Eckehard Schulz/AP Images; **390** Aaron Bacall/CartoonBank.com; **398** Scott Sady/AP Images

Chapter 13

409 Courtesy of Ponoko; **411** Steve Cole/iStockphoto; **413** Roger Harris/Photo Researchers; **414** Benelux Press/Taxi/Getty Images; **415** David McNew/Getty Images; **418** Reuters/Corbis; **420** Ben Margot/AP Images; **423** Photofest; **425** Alec Soth Photography

Chapter 14

439 kolvenbach/Alamy; **445** Damir Karan/iStockphoto; **449** Peter Lennihan/AP Images; **452** Contact Press Images, Inc.; **458** Jonathan Barth/Liaison/Planet Earth Pictures **459** The New Yorker Collection/Robert Weber/CartoonBank.com

Part Four

472-3 Bill Brooks/Alamy

Chapter 15

475 Warner Bros./DC Comics/The Kobal Collection; **476** (left) Courtesy of Nutrisoya Foods Inc.; (middle) Courtesy of Publicis USA, Dallas; (right) Text and Advertisement © Queen's Printer for Ontario, 2006. Reproduced with permission. Photograph © Philip Lee Harvey/Stone+/Getty Images; **481** Ting Shi; **484** Chester Higgins/*The New York Times*; **485** Jason DeCrow/AP Images; **492** The New Yorker Collection/Bernard Schoenbaum/CartoonBank.com; **493** David Levenson/Stockphoto.com/Black Star; **494** PorterGifford/BW/Corbis; **500** Feathercraft Products, Ltd.

Chapter 16

511 Jeff J. Mitchell/Getty Images; **513** Courtesy of SAS; **515** PhotoDisc; **520** Michelle V. Agins/*The New York Times*; **526** (top left) Fresh Meat Media LLC/Riser/Getty Images; (top right) Dave & Les Jacobs/Blend Images/Corbis; (bottom left) Courtesy of Girl Guides of Canada-Guides du Canada; (middle right) Didier Debusschere/CP Images; (bottom right) Tom Hanson/CP Images; **529** Contact Press Images, Inc.; **533** David Burtow/Redux Pictures; **535** Monkeybusinessimages/Dreamstime.com/GetStock.com; **537** (left) Jeff Haynes/AFP/Getty Images; (right) Brendan McDermid/Reuters/Corbis; **539** Todd Gipstein/Encyclopedia/Corbis

Chapter 17

551 Najlah Feanny/Corbis; **553** The New Yorker Collection/Jack Ziegler/CartoonBank.com; **556** Ed Kashi/Terra/Corbis; **557** Guillermo Granja/Corbis/Reuters America LLC; **558** Daniel Acker/Bloomberg News/Landov LLC; **561** The New Yorker Collection/Robert Mankoff/CartoonBank.com; **570** QVC, Inc.; **573** Canadian National

Part Five

586-587 Mark Blinch/Reuters/Landov LLC

Chapter 18

589 Corey Hochachka/MaXx Images; **591** Tom Hanson/CP Images; **592** Vincent Laforet/*The New York Times*; **594** Macduff Everton/Encyclopedia/Corbis; **599** The New Yorker Collection/J. B. Handelsman/CartoonBank.com; **602** Kathy deWitt/Alamy; **603** Nikolai Ignatiev/Network Photographers, Ltd.; **608** Chris Hondros/Getty Images

Chapter 19

619 Andrew Wallace/GetStock.com; **625** *Toronto Star*/Dick Loek; **626** Abbas Kowsari/Bloomberg News; **628** Reproduced with the permission of the Minister of Finance; **632** Bloomberg/Landov LLC; **638** Dan Krauss/*The New York Times*

Chapter 20

651 Andy Dean/Dreamstime.com; **653** Jim Pickerell/Stock Connection Blue/Alamy; **658** Naomi Harris; **660** Use of the BellSouth bond certificate photo is granted under permission by AT&T Intellectual Property; **663** Aileen Tat Photography; **669** (top left) Ulrich Welch/Photo Researchers; (bottom left) Eunice Harris/Photo Researchers; (right) Lawrence Migdale/Photo Researchers; **671** David Mah/*Prince George Citizen*/CP Images

Name and Organization Index

A

Ab-Original Wear, 112
ABB (Asea Brown Boveri), 144
ABC, 301
Aberback-Ptack, Sheri, 682
AbitibiBowater Inc., 67
Aboriginal Business Canada, 112
ABZ for Me, 136
Accenture Inc., 415t
Accor SA, 154
ACE Aviation Holdings Inc., 127
Acura, 532
Acxiom, 424, 425
Adams, Trish, 486
Adidas, 192, 521
Aditya Birla Group, 672
Adolph Coors Co., 61
AES Corporation, 316
AGF American Growth Class, 646
AGF Funds Inc., 631t
Agnico-Eagle Mines, 90, 648
Agricore United, 61
AgriMarine Industries Ltd., 616
Air Canada, 12, 74, 89–90, 126, 127, 182, 186, 212, 261, 262, 271, 278, 293, 295, 321, 483, 533, 676
Airbus, 23, 141, 142, 190, 191, 515, 615
al Ameen Insurance Co., 672
Alaska Airlines, 355
Alberta Gaming and Liquor Commission, 14t
Alberta-Pacific Forest Industries, 266
Alberta Treasury Branches, 598t
Alcan Aluminum, 144, 155, 363
Algoma Steel, 185
Algordonza, 511
All Nippon Airways, 60
Alliance of Motion Picture and Television Producers (AMPTP), 301
Allied Domecq PLC, 154
Alpha, 624
Alstom SA, 170
Alternative Reality Gaming Network, 475
Amazon.com, 132, 185, 594
America Online (AOL), 425, 519
American Airlines, 190, 379
American Express, 540, 555, 593
American International Group (AIG), 90, 254, 651–652
American Legacy Foundation, 478
American Management Association, 399–400
American Public Health Association, 478
American Stock Exchange (AMEX), 626
Amundsen, Roald, 334, 335
Amway, 569
Anastakis, Dimitry, 375
Anchorage International Airport, 355
AND Corp., 414
Andreesen, Marc, 114, 423
Angus Reid/*Globe and Mail*, 531
Anheuser-Busch (AB), 579, 580
Aon Consulting, 260
Apple Computer, 198, 208, 230, 326, 328, 485, 506, 508, 556, 581
Arctic Glacier Inc., 85
Argentine Oil Company, 157
Ariba, 568
Armani, 55, 396
Armour Construction, 138
Arnold, Patricia, 328
Arthur Andersen LLP, 56, 65, 326, 619
Arthur's Fresh, 95
Asia Pacific Potash Corp., 157
Asian Professional Network, 265
Ask Jeeves Inc., 569
Assiniboine Credit Union, 266
Associated Press, 181
Association for Investment Management and Research (AIMR), 625
Association of Consulting Engineers of Canada, 17
Association of Quebec Advertising Agencies, 534
Astral Media Inc., 248, 528t
Atco Ltd., 193
Atlantic, 208
Atlantic Innovation Fund, 617
Atlantic Lottery Corp., 446
Atlantic Richfield, 363
Atomic Box, 573
Atomic Research, 424
Author's Guild, 521
Auto Vault, 555
Autorité des marchés financiers (AMF), 648
Autry, Gene, 374
Avis, 556
Avon Products, 327, 559, 567, 569
Ayre, Calvin, 161

B

Babcock & Wilcox Canada, 320
BAE Systems, 416
Baekeland, L.H., 482
Baffinland Iron Mines Corp., 677
Baja Technology Inc., 60
Ballard, 50
Balsillie, James, 8, 254
Bank for Reconstruction and Development, 611
Bank of America, 652
Bank of Baghdad, 608
Bank of Canada, 37, 46, 48, 63, 589, 590, 593, 597, 597f, 602, 603, 612, 619, 651
Bank of Montreal (BMO), 53, 59, 89, 261, 262, 548, 594, 596, 598t, 602, 604, 667, 679–680
Bank of New York Mellon Corp., 328
Bank of Nova Scotia (Scotiabank), 245t, 262, 273, 594, 598t, 600, 602, 623t, 678
Barrick Gold Corp., 623t
Barron's Mutual Funds, 635
Bartelsmann AG, 259
Barternew.com, 590
Barton, Dominic, 328
Bartz, Carol, 227
Baskin-Robins, 112, 154
Bata Shoes, 127
Batson, Neal, 56
Baumol, William, 383
Bayer Inc., 250
BBVA, 307
B.C. Hydro and Power Authority, 14t
B.C. Liquor Distribution Branch, 566t
B.C. Tel, 321
BCE, 197
BDO Dunwoody LLP, 443t
Bear Stearns, 652
Beaver, Chris, 119
bebe Stores, 22
Beckerman, Michael, 548
Beddoe, Clive, 89
Beer, John, 71
Bell, Scott, 95
Bell, Travis, 95
Bell Canada Enterprises (BCE), 62, 89, 127, 193, 201, 333, 508, 548, 660
Bell ExpressVu LP, 23, 528t
Bell Residential Services, 508
Bell Video Store, 508
Ben Barry Agency, 112
Benefits by Design Inc., 107t
Benetton, 88
Benetton USA, 88
Bentall Development Inc., 321
Beny Sofer & Sons LLC, 385
Berra, Yogi, 238
Best Buy, 181, 321, 506, 537
Best Buy Canada Ltd., 566t
Betrix, 500
Better Business Bureau, 85, 95
Bettig, Lori, 136
BHP Billiton, 385
Bianchini, Gina, 114, 423
Big Blue, 506
Bijouxbead, 173
Birks & Sons Inc., 385
Black & Decker, 514
Black Oak Brewing Company, 108
Blackmer/Dover Resources Inc., 317
Blake, Cassels & Graydon, 266
Blockbuster Video, 122
Bloor Street Diner, 594
Blue Moose Clothing Company, 112
BMO Financial Group, 631t
BMO International Equity Fund, 646
BMO MasterCard, 594
BMW, 376
Boase, Shannon, 111
Bodog.cpm, 161
The Body Shop, 524
Boeing Canada, 266
Boeing Co., 23, 48, 60, 141, 142, 190, 191, 291, 416, 515
Boldue, Sylvie, 333
Boliden Ltd., 84
Bombardier Inc., 141, 142, 144, 245t, 271, 514–515, 519, 633, 676
Bond, Chris, 236, 237
Boster, Adam, 198
Boston Pizza, 179
Bouchard, Gabriel, 247
Bowersox, Bob, 570
BP, 155, 524
Brascan Ltd., 197
Bre-X, 649
Brin, Sergey, 8, 420
Brison, Scott, 141
Bristol Aerospace, 186
British Airways, 190
Bronfman, Edgar, Jr., 208
Bronfman, Sam, 208
Brookfield Asset Management, 197
Brown, David, 179
Brown, Jamie, 236, 237
Brown, Michael, 273
Brown & Williamson, 551
Bryan, John H., 238
Bryson, Reid, 100
BSX Ltd., 632–633
Buchanan, Richard, 616
Buck or Two, 551
Budget, 556
Budweiser, 579
Buick, 548
Bullfrog Power, 600
Burbank Tournament of Roses Association, 374

Burbank Water and Power Department, 374
Burberry, 488
Bureau en gros, 519
Burger King, 40, 123, 252, 356, 523
Busch, August III, 580
Busch, August IV, 580
Business Development Bank of Canada (BDBC), 152, 607
Business Development Canada, 9

C

Cadbury, 85
Cadbury PLC, 538
CAE Inc., 251
Caira, Marc, 200
Caisse Centrale Desjardins, 605*t*
Caisse de dépôt et placement du Québec, 678
Caldarelli, David, 682
Calvin Klein, 55, 171
Campbell Soup Co., 414
Can-Eng Manufacturing, 154
Canada Customs and Revenue Agency, 442
Canada Deposit Insurance Corp., 78
Canada Life, 93
Canada Mortgage and Housing Corporation (CMHC), 14*t*, 266, 607
Canada Pension Plan (CPP), 258, 439, 440
Canada Post Corp., 14*t*, 245*t*, 263, 266, 528, 596, 678
Canada Revenue Agency, 109, 212
Canada Safeway, 574
Canada Trust, 61, 595, 596
Canadian Airline Pilots Union, 287
Canadian Airlines, 173
Canadian Alliance Against Software Theft (CAAST), 425
Canadian Anti-Counterfeitting Network (CACN), 87
Canadian Auto Workers (CAW), 277, 278, 286, 289, 291, 300, 376
Canadian Auto Workers Union (CAW), 282, 320
Canadian Bankers Association, 682
Canadian Broadcasting Corp. (CBC), 301, 346, 528*t*, 548
Canadian Business, 185, 504, 532
Canadian Cancer Society, 17
Canadian Coalition Against Insurance Fraud (CCAIF), 671
Canadian Competition Bureau, 14, 78, 85, 524, 562
Canadian Congress of Labour, 279–280
Canadian Federation of Business School Deans, 255
Canadian Federation of Independent Business, 245
Canadian Federation of Labour, 279
Canadian Forces, 221
Canadian Foundation for Innovation, 617
Canadian Geographic, 529
Canadian Human Rights Commission, 261
Canadian Human Rights Tribunal, 263
Canadian Imperial Bank of Commerce (CIBC), 56, 72, 180, 217, 255, 466, 594, 598*t*, 602, 682
Canadian Institute of Chartered Accountants (CICA), 78, 442, 444
Canadian Labour Congress (CLC), 279–280, 282, 405
Canadian Labour Relations Board, 284
Canadian Labour Union, 279
Canadian Living, 529
Canadian National Railway (CN), 6, 12, 61, 89, 126, 196, 197, 261, 273, 292, 298, 658
Canadian Natural Resources Ltd., 5, 6, 623*t*
Canadian Pacific Railways, 62, 127, 266
Canadian Payroll Association, 303
Canadian Petroleum, 638
Canadian Pharmacists Association (CPhA), 436
Canadian Public Accountability Board (CPAB), 466
Canadian Radio-Television and Telecomminications Commission (CRTC), 13, 508, 548
Canadian Real Estate Association (CREA), 562
Canadian Senate Banking Committee, 466
Canadian Standards Association, 84, 524
Canadian Tire Corp Ltd., 186, 245*t*, 518, 519, 551, 564, 566*t*, 596, 603
Canadian Transport Commission (CTC), 13
Canadian Union of Public Employees, 282, 287, 295
Canadian Union of Public Employees (CLC), 287*t*
Canadian Venture Exchange (CDNX), 626
Canadian Wheat Board, 6, 13, 14*t*, 212
Canfor Corp., 274, 384
Canon, 529
CanWest Global Communications Corp., 528*t*, 661
Career Magazine, 271
Careerbuilder, 271
Cargill Corn Milling North America (CCM), 393, 394
Carleton University, 100
Carlson Wagonlit Travel Canada, 259, A-1
Cartier, 86–87
Case Corp., 222
Cash, Johnny, 291
Cassano, Paul, 682
Cassis Monna & Filles, 106
Catalyst, 262
Caterpillar Tractor, 198
Catholic Children's Aid Society, 259
CBS, 301
C.D. Howe Institute, 405
CDNOW, 569
Céline Dion, 87
Central 1 Credit Union, 605*t*
Central Bank, 589
Centre for Education and Work, 317
Centre for Outsourcing Research and Education, 59
Centre for Philanthropy, 93
Certified Chartered Accountants, 81
Certified General Accountants Association of Canada, 442
Certified General Accountants of Canada, 259
CGI Group Inc., 415*t*
Chamitoff, Ken, 198
Chaparral Steel, 419
Chartered Financial Analyst (CFA), 625
Chartwell Technology, 16
Chateau Mouton Rothschild, 87
Chatelaine, 529
ChemLawn, 514
Chesebrough Ponds, 63
Chi-X Canada, 624
Chicago Stock Exchange, 626
Chicago Transit Authority, 50
Chinese Petroleum, 145
Chiquita, 160
Christian Network, 265
Chronicle-Herald, 337
Chrysler, 69, 144, 193, 203, 290, 294, 300, 320, 375, 376
Chubb Corp., 679
CI Financial Corp, 631*t*
CIBC Asset Management, 631*t*
CIBC Visa, 594
CIBC World Markets, 72, 130, 273
Circle K, 566
Circuit City, 518
Cisco Systems Inc., 181, 197, 203, 633
Citicorp, 599
Citigroup, 69, 625
City of Burbank, 374
Clarica Canadian Diversified, 646
Clark, Dick, 568
Clark, Larry, 201
Clark Equipment Corp., 223
Clarke, Consuelo, 136
Clarkson, Max, 91
Clean Environment Equity, 630
Clearwater Seafoods Income Fund, 127
Cleyn & Tinker, 171
Click Forensics Inc., 547
Co-operators Life Insurance Co., 672*t*
Coach Inc., 207
Coalition for Community Services (CCS), 505
Coast Capital Savings Credit Union, 241, 605*t*
Coca-Cola, 39, 69, 153, 182, 186, 480, 487, 518, 533, 539, 540, 548, 551, 552
Cogeco Inc., 528*t*
Coldplay, 530
College Grad Job Hunter, 271
Collins Barrow National Cooperative Inc., 443*t*
Comcast, 508
Comedy Central, 105, 546
Comfort Inn, 122
Commercial Alert, 88
Communications, Energy and Paperworkers Union of Canada (CLC), 287*t*
Community Marketing Inc., 488
Compaq Computer, 109, 190, 556
Complaints.com, 379, 497
Computer Associates, 28
Computing Technology Industry Association, 321
comScore, 547
Conexus Credit Union, 605*t*
Conference Board of Canada, 165
Conquest Vacations, 379
Consumer Affairs.com, 379–380
Consumer and Corporate Affairs Canada, 14
Consumer Reports, 496
Consumers Association of Canada (CAC), 34
Continental Airlines, 66
Cook, Scott, 666
Cooper, Roy, 557
Cooper, Simon, 328
Coppotelli, Blake, 446
Corber, Deborah, 333
Corus Entertainment Inc., 266, 301, 508, 528*t*
Costco Wholesale Canada Ltd., 156*t*, 566*t*
Cott Corp., 520
CP Ships, 62
Craib, Chris, 71
Craigslist, 530, 569
Crawford, Purdy, 678
Credit Suisse First Boston, 328
Credit Union Central of Saskatchewan, 605*t*
Crestine Coach Ltd., 52
Crichton, Michael, 521

Crothers, Melvin, 89–90
Crown Investments Corp of Saskatchewan, 14*t*
Cruise, Tom, 180, 336
Crull, Kevin, 508
CryptoLogic Inc., 16
Cuddy, Brian, 105–106
Cuddy, Bruce, 105–106
Cuddy, Mac, 105
Cuddy, Peter, 105–106
Cuddy International Corp., 105
Cummins Inc., 155
Cunningham Sheet Metal, 615
CUPE, 298
Curtis Mathes, 556
Cutler, Stephen, 647
Cypress Semiconductor, 230

D

Daewoo, 144, 221, 488
DaimlerChrysler, 50, 392
Dallas Texas, 155
Dallner, Crystal, 112
Dana Corp., 367
Dancescape, 584
Danone Group, 227–228
Danso, Kwasi, 482
Dantra, 138
Danyluk, Dan, 596
DC Comics, 490
de Boer, Garrit, 226
de Grandpré, Jean, 201
DeBeers, 385
DeBeers Canada, 385
Del Monte, 162
Delahaye Paine, Katie, 423
Delgratia Mining Corp., 649
Dell, Michael, 8, 506
Dell Corporation, 8, 396, 506–507, 562, 569, 594, 627
Deloitte & Touche LLP, 71, 443*t*, 444, 465
Delphi Automotive Systems, 369
Delta Chelsea Hotel, 316
Delta Whistler Village Suites, 229
Denomme, Robb, 9
Department of Foreign Affairs and Internatioanl Trade (DFAIT), 9, 16
Department of National Defence (DND), 172
Department of Regional Industrial Expansion (DRIE), 607
DesignShop, 395
Desjardins Group, 241, 589
Desjardins Financial Security Life Assurance, 672*t*
Detroit Red Wings, 552
Deutsche Bank, 625
Deutsche Lufthansa AG, 141
Deutsche Telekom AG, 291
Development Dimensions International (DDI), 188, 248
Devon Energy Corporation, 21
Diamond and Schmitt Architects, 229
Diamond State Insurance Company, 679
Diasqua Group, 560
Diavik Diamond Mines Inc., 385
Diochon, Monica, 104
Direct Energy Marketing Ltd., 156*t*
Dirt Devil, 562
Discover, 593
Disney, Walt, 201
Disney Channel, 236
Disney World, 367, 548
Dofasco, 271
Dole, 160, 162
Dollar, 556, 568
Dollarama, 551
Donna Karen, 207
Dorval, Yves-Thomas, 478
Dosanjh, Ujjal, 436
Dow Chemical, 83
Dow Jones Industrial Average (DJIA), 619, 620, 636, 641, 642
Dow-Jones World Sustainability Index, 195
Downe, Bill, 667
Doyle, William, 254
Drabinsky, Garth, 71, 465
Dragonfly Nightclub, 600
Draper, Tim, 584
Drbul, Bob, 207
DreamWorks Animation, 532
DriveSavers, 114
DRN Commerce, Inc., 107*t*
Dchesne, Rupert, 485
Dudley, Robert, 155
Duic, Daniel, 648
Dumas, Alexandre, 9
Dun & Bradstreet, 59
Dunkin Donuts, 112, 154
Dunn, Brian, 537
DuPont Co., 393
Durst, Fred, 679
Dyck, Cal, 468

E

E!, 538
Eagle Professional Resources Inc., 257
Eaglesham, Kyla, 111
Earthcycle, 111
Earthlink, 570
EarthLink Inc., 676
Eastman Kodak Co., 196
Eaton, Timothy, 201
Eaton Corporation, 138, 201, 315
eBay, 88–418, 434, 569, 594
Ebbers, Bernie, 71, 466
Eckerd Drugs, 61
Eckstein, Gordon, 71
The Economist, 609
Edwards Deming, W., 384
1867 Confederation Log Homes, 142
Eisner, Michael, 188, 326
Electra, 208
Electrolux, 81
Electronic Data Systems (EDS), 353
Electrovert Ltd., 153, 459
Ellis, Craig, 137
ELPRO International Inc., 656
Embraer, 142
Emerson Electric, 568
EMI Group PLC, 208
Emily Carr Institute, 468
En-lai, Zhou, 499
The Enamoured Heart, 136
EnCana Corp., 6, 68, 126*t*, 623*t*
Encyclopedia Britannica, 57
Enron, 56, 65, 72, 74, 91, 315, 326, 465, 619
Ensyn Corp., 84
Entrepreneurship Research Consortium (ERC), 107
Environics, 93
Environmental Careers Organization of Canada, 247
Envision Financial, 605*t*
EPIC Newsgroup Inc., 152
Equifax Canada, 424
Ernst & Young LLP, 443*t*, 483
Espirit, 115
Essa, Mohammad, 592
Estée Lauder, 523
Ethical Growth, 630, 646
European Commission, 639
Everex Systems Inc., 501
Exide Corp., 217
Expedia, 328, 568
Export Development Canada, 143
Export Development Corporation, 16, 607

F

Facebook, 8, 108, 511, 531, 584
Fairmont Hotels & Resorts, 260
Fantastic Sam's, 123
Farnborough International Airshow, 141
Farrell, Mike, 337
Fastow, Andrew, 91
FBI, 21, 87
Feathercraft, 500
Federal Express (FedEx), 24, 186, 220, 350, 360, 444
Federal Home Mortgage Corporation (Freddie Mac), 651, 652
Federal Industries, 197
Federal National Mortgage Association (Fannie Mae), 651, 652
Fédération de la santé et des services sociaux (CSN), 287*t*
Federation of Independent Business, 679
FedEx Kinko's, 360
Fendi, 168, 207
Ferique Equity, 646
Ferrero, 68
Fidelity Investments Canada ULC, 631*t*
Fields, Debbi, 215
Filter UK Ltd., 548
Financial Post Magazine, 254, 598*n*
Financial World, 662
Fischer, Jonathan, 158
Fisher-Price, 562
Flair, 173
Flavelle, Joseph, 26
Floors Plus, 138
Food Brokers Inc., 560
Ford, Henry, 26, 201
Ford Motor Co. of Canada Ltd., 156*t*, 241, 289, 300
Ford Motor Company, 5, 12, 50, 86, 144, 153, 213, 217, 300, 358, 366, 375, 376, 392, 419, 540, 554
Fording Coal, 62
Forest Stewardship Council, 195
Forge, Bharat, 359
Forrester Research, 581
Fort Saskatchewan, 83
Fortinos, 406
Four Seasons Hotels and Resorts, 155, 179, 194, 200, 202
Fox, 301, 546
Fox, Sally, 115
Frankfort, Lew, 207, 208
Franklin, John, 334
Franklin Templeton, 631*t*
Frantic Films, 212, 236, 237, 237*f*
Frantic Films Commercial Projects Inc., 236
Frantic Films Live Action Productions Inc., 236
Frantic Films Software Inc., 237
Frantic Films VFX Services Inc., 236
Fraser, John, 678
Free Range Graphics, 60
FreeMarkets Inc., 568
French, Neil, 263
French Canadian Network, 265
Friis, Janus, 434
Fuel Industries, 532
Fukui, Takeo, 195
Fuller Brush Company, 559, 567
Fur Council of Canada, 524
Furse, Clara, 328

G

Gagliardi, John, 108
Gaidano, Scott, 114
Galleon Energy Inc., 127

Gallup Organization, 303
Galt, Donald, 274, 275
Galt Contracting, 274
Gandalf Group, 524
Gap Inc., 535, 663
Gartner, 434
Gateway, 506
Gaunt, Bobbie, 241
GAX, 423
Geist, Michael, 535
Gemological Institute of Americas (GIA), 74
General Electric (GE), 182, 193, 194, 220, 228, 344, 380, 571
General Foods, 23, 252
General Mills, 23, 551
General Motors Acceptance Corporation (GMAC), 606
General Motors Canada, 6, 11–12, 39, 241, 300, 368, 405, 439, 485, 549
General Motors Corp., 39, 63, 69, 122, 144, 158, 221–241, 290, 294, 298, 300, 375, 376, 389, 392, 484, 551
Genuity Capital Markets, 72
Genuwine Cellars, 9
George, Barbara, 172
George Weston Ltd., 126*t*, 127, 245*t*
Georger, Rick, 179
Gerdau, Ameristell Corp., 156*t*
German Environment Ministry, 247
Giannulli, Massimo, 486
Gibralter Solutions Inc., 107*t*
Gibson, Daniel, 138
Gibson, Larry, 138
Gibson, Patricia, 138
Gibson, Tracy, 138
Gilbreth, Frank, 309
Gilbreth, Lillian, 309
Gildan Activewear Inc., 127, 171, 198, 290
Gill, Baljit, 112, 387
Gill, Gary, 71
Gillespie, John, 444
Girl Guides, 92
Gladstone Hotel, 111
Global Pulse, 68
Glenora Distilleries, 54
Global Crossings, 619
Global Research Consortium (GRC), 230
Global Training Systems, 399
Globe and Mail, 126, 304, 504
GlobeScan, 10
GM Canada, *see* General Motors Canada.
Godfrey, Paul, 179
Godiva, 556
Goldcorp Inc., 286, 623*t*
Golden Rule Resources Ltd., 648
Gompf, Tyler, 112
Goodyear, 560
Google Inc., 8, 68, 69, 195, 409, 418, 420, 511, 519, 521, 547, 569, 606
Gorman Brothers, 274
Gottlieb, Myron, 71, 465
Gourmet, 529
Government and Service Employees Union, 34
Graef, Ailin, 409
Graham, Billy, 568
Grameen Bank, 602
Grant Thorton Canada, 443*t*
Great Blue Heron Charity Casino, 291
Great Little Box Company Ltd., 257
Great-West Life Assurance Company, 93, 316, 672*t*
Green, Eryn, 120
Green Enterprise Toronto (GET), 111
Green Gardeners, 247
Green Realty Association, 229
Green Shift, 111
Green World Solutions (GWS), 482
Greener Footprints, 195
Greenlite Lighting Corp., 112
Greenpeace, 67
Greyhound Lines of Canada, 393
Griffith, Scott, 112
Grokster, 581
Group Aeroplan Inc., 485
Gucci Group, 87, 168, 207, 396, 488
Guinness, 538
Gulak, Ben, 346
Gupta, Nina, 112
Gurden, Derek, 580
GYNite, 423

H

Hagan, Jay, 114
Halde, Jean-René, 152
Hallmark Cards, 525
Hallmark/Westland, 389
Hamilton, Alexander, 604
Hampton Inn & Suites, 286, 399
Hanley, Wayne, 277
Hanshin Tigers, 183
Harbour Consulting, 404
Hargrove, Buzz, 300
Harlequin Enterprises, 499
Harley-Davidson, 451, 480, 520, 537
Harley Owners Group (H.O.G.), 480
Harper, Glen, 648
Harper, Stephen, 141
Harris Bank, 604
Harris Interactive Inc., 68
Hartco Income Fund, 415*t*
Harvard University, 205, 309, 596
Hawthorne Works, 309
HBO, 225, 301
Health Canada, 478
Healthtech Consultants, 107*t*
Hefner, Hugh, 538
Heinekey, Sabrina, 152
Heritage Foundation, 108
Herjavec, Robert, 584
Herold, Cameron, 201
Hershey, 85
Hertz, 556
Herzberg, Frederick, 311
Hewitt Associations, 260
Hewlett-Packard Canada, 64, 393
Hewlett-Packard (HP), 109, 181, 182, 190, 201, 506, 507, 556, 570
H.J. Heinz Co., 49, 217, 224, 388, 540
HKMB International Impact, 387
HLB/Schwartz Levitsky Feldman, 443*t*
HMV, 215
Hoefer, Tom, 385
Hollinger International, 72
Home Depot, 451, 548, 564
Home Depot Canada, 548, 566*t*
Home Hardware Stores Ltd., 566*t*
Home Shopping Network (HSN), 420
Honda Canada Inc., 156*t*
Honda Motor Co. Ltd., 50, 147, 195, 286, 300, 358, 376
Hong Kong Owners Association, 102
Hood Grou, 107*t*
Hoshino, Senichi, 183
Hostess Frito-Lay, 491
Hotmail, 584
Household Finance Corp., 659
Houston Astros Enron Field, 65
Howard Johnson, 122
HSBC Bank Canada, 266, 598*t*
Hubbert, H.K., 32, 33
Hudson's Bay Company (HBC), 197, 247, 492, 533
Hudson's Bay Oil and Gas, 656
Humane Society, 389
Humber College, 88
Humphries, Stephen, 680
Hunt, Chad, 247
Hunter Exploration Group, 63
Huntingdon Mills, 171
Husky Energy Inc., 156*t*
Husky Injection Molding Systems, 247, 260
Hyatt, John W., 482
Hydro One Inc., 678
Hydro-Quebec, 14*t*, 226
Hyundai Motor Company, 16, 145, 355, 488

I

I Love Rewards Inc., 250, 314
Ibis Sofitel, 154
IBM, 28, 153, 271, 422, 506, 518, 519, 527, 540–541, 556, 622, 626, 633
Ice.com, 569
ICICI OneSource, 381
Identity Theft Resource Center, 428
Idomo Furniture Co., 226
IGM Financial Inc., 631*t*
IKEA, 68, 567
Ikon Office Solutions Inc., 321
Illinois Central Railroad, 61
Imagine Canada's Caring Company, 93
ImClone, 619
Immersion, 412
Imperial Oil Ltd., 8, 9, 126, 126*t*, 156*t*, 249, 622, 623*t*
Imperial Tobacco, 551
Imperial Tobacco Canada Ltd., 478
Inc., 198
Inco Ltd., 155, 157
Independent Grocers Alliance (IGA), 564
India Post, 24
Industrial Alliance Insurance and Financial Services Inc., 672*t*
Industry Canada, 16, 107
iNetPrivacy, 481
The Influencers, 511
Infosys Technologies, 60, 307
ING Direct, 596
Install-a-Flor, 138
Institute of Chartered Accountants of Ontario (ICAO), 465
Insurance Brokers Association of Canada, 596
Intel, 627
Interac Association, 594, 601
Interbrand Best Global Brands, 518
Interface Inc., 345
Intergovernmental Panel on Climate Change, 82
International Accounting Standards Board (IASB), 460, 462
International Association of Independent Tanker Owners, 102
International Association of Machinists and Aerospace Workers (IAMAW), 291
International Association of Skateboard Companies, 521
International Brotherhood of Teamsters, 282
International Chamber of Commerce, 87
International Energy Agency (IEA), 32
International Financial Standards, 444–445
International Maritime Organization, 101
International Monetary Fund (IMF), 37, 590, 611
International Olympic Committee, 520
International Organization for Standardization, 393, 401
Intuit, 666
Intuit Canada, 64, 179
Invesco Trimark Ltd., 631*t*
Investors Canadian Enterprise, 646
Investors Group, 193

Investors Group Financial Services, 315
Ipsos Reid, 250, 511
Irving, Arthur, 105, 211
Irving, Jack, 105, 211
Irving, J.D., 105, 211
Irving, Jim, 105, 211
Irving, J.K., 105, 211
Irving, K.C., 105, 211
Irving, Kenneth, 105, 211
Irving Vorest Productions, 197
ISCM Investment Network, 119
Ishikawa, Kaoru, 384
ISL Engineering and Land Services, 107t
iTunes, 506, 508, 581

J

J. Sainsbury PLC, 520
Jackson, Samuel L., 511
Jaguar, 362
Japan Air Lines, 190
Jarislowsky, Stephen, 616
Jay-Z, 616
JCPenny, 568–569
J.D. Power and Associates, 376, 384
Jean Coutu Group Inc., 61, 68
Jennings, Christina, 112
Jentink, Reuben, 95
Jewish Network, 265
Jobs, Steve, 326, 328
John Deere, 564
Johnson, Mike, 247
Johnson & Johnson (J&J), 68, 69, 77, 411
Jonas, Julie, 111, 136
Joon-yang, Chung, 397
Jordan, Michael, 499
Jung, Andrea, 327
Juran, Joseph, 384

K

Kalyani, Baba, 359
Kantain Products Ltd., 670
Kastner, Peter, 506
Kazaa, 434
KDPaine & Partners, 423
Keds, 137
Keilhauer, Mike, 615
Kellogg Co., 23, 562, 571
Kelly, Bob, 328
Kelly Workforce Index, 303
Kempston-Darkes, Maureen, 241
Kentain Products, 679
Kerbel, Mark, 119
Kerviel, Jérôme, 680
Key Small Business Statistics, 107
KFC, 62
Kia, 488
Kijiji, 569
Kimberly-Clark Corp., 490, 518
Kingma, Lance, 9
Kitsch, Trent, 119
Kitwanga Lumber Company, 112
Kitwanga Mills Ltd., 387
Kivenko, Ken, 646
Kiwi, 492
KLM, 190
Kmart, 85, 197, 532, 533
Knights of Labour, 279
Ko, Lina, 584
Kolida, Bob, 247
Kolko, Jed, 507
KPMG Canada, 266
KPMG/Ipsos-Reid, 68
KPMG LLP, 71, 273, 443t, 483
Kraft Foods, 22, 69, 260, 518, 520, 551, 574
Krakoff, Reed, 207
Kroc, Ray, 500
Kroeker Farms, 127
Kroll Global Fraud Report, 446
Krugman, Paul, 142
Kulyk, Roman, 119

L

La Capitale Civil Service Mutual, 672t
Labatt Brewing Co. Ltd., 14, 260, 521, 522, 579
Labour Relations Board of British Columbia, 277
Lacroix, Vincent, 648
Lafferty and Co., 560
Lain Kennedy, Joyce, 271
Lakeport Brewing, 14
Landen, Barry, 90, 648
Land's End, 115, 569
Lang, Yolanda, 168
Langlitz Leathers, 525
Lantz, Jeff, 663
Lantz, Kelly, 663
Larsen & Shaw Ltd., 257
Lasser, Lawrence, 647
Laurentian Bank of Canada, 598t
Lawless Container Corp., 562
Lay, Kan, 72
Lazardis, Michael, 254
Leclerc, Jennifer, 603
Lee, David, 679–680
Lee Jeans, 511
Leeson, Nicholas, 680
Lefebvre, John, 161
Lego AS, 521
Lehman Brothers, 652
Leno, Jay, 301, 346
Leroux, Monique, 241
Les Petroles Therrien Inc., 86
Lever Brothers, 63
Levi Strauss & Co., 115, 216, 318, 514, 535, 655, 676
Levitt, Tammy, 136
Lewenza, Ken, 278
Lexus, 152, 207
Lietzke, Ron, 376
The Limited, 564
Limited Brands, 22
Limp Bizkit, 679
Lincoln, 554
Lingo Media Inc., 153, 155
Lion's Club, 95
Lippert, Glen, 679
Lipton, 63
Liquor Control Board of Ontario (LCBO), 34, 566t
LiveNation, 530
Livent Inc., 71, 465
LivePerson.com, 570
Livermore, Ann, 182
Livingston Healthcare Services Inc., 368
Liz Clairborne, 22
L.L. Bean, 115, 569
Lloyd's of London, 67
Loblaw Companies Limited, 79, 195, 260, 277, 406, 520, 551, 567, 596
Lockheed Martin, 416, 419
Loews Hotels, 185
Logan Aluminum Inc., 363
London Life, 93
London Stock Exchange, 328
Lorillard Tobacco, 551
Lotus Software, 319
Lou Lou, 173
Louis Vuitton, 86–87, 207, 358, 396, 488
Lowry, Chris, 111
Lucent, 519
Lululemon Athletica Ltd., 260, 524

M

Macauley, Fraser, 172
MacDonald, Dettwiler and Associates, 415t
MacDonald, John, 26
MacKean, J., 9
MacLean, Lauchie, 54
MacMillan, Gavin, 336
Madeleines Cherry Pie and Ice Cream, 111
Madoff, Bernie, 72, 640, 648
Magna International Inc., 200, 201, 245t, 300
Magnotta Winery Corporation, 34
Maiden Group PLC, 548
Malcolm, Grant, 71
Mandel, Steve, 434
Manitoba Hydro, 226
Manitoba Labour Board, 273, 284, 286, 293
Manitoba Liquor Control Commission (MLCC), 34
Manulife Financial Corp., 6, 126–127, 126t, 155, 672t
Maple Leaf Angels, 119
Maple Leaf Foods, 77, 85, 105, 200, 294
Maple Leaf Gardens Ltd., 197
Maple Leaf Sports & Entertainment, 314
Marriott, 314
Mars, 85
Mars Canada, 93
Marsden Corp., 505
Martha Stewart Living Omnimedia Inc., 227
Martin, Barry, 414
Martin, Darlene, 173
Marvel Entertainment, 490
Marx, Karl, 10
Mary Kay, 569
Maslow, Abraham, 310, 311
MasterCard, 127, 193, 593
Mathlouthi, Tawfik, 158
Mattel Inc., 85, 343, 498–499
Max Factor, 500
Maxi, 277
Maytag, 387
Mazda, 147
MBNA Canada Bank, 598t, 682
MCA Inc., 208
McArthur, Steven, 328
McCain, Harrison, 105
McCain, Michael, 200
McCain, Wallace, 105
McCain Foods Ltd., 105, 153, 158, 459
McCormick, Sean, 112
McDonald's, 39–40, 49, 55, 92, 122, 152, 154, 182, 196, 220, 251, 271, 286, 355–356, 363, 364, 369–370, 414, 499, 500, 518, 529–530, 532, 539, 551
McDonald's Restaurants of Canada Ltd., 245t
McGill University, 184
McGinty, Sarah, 205
McGregor, Douglas, 310
McKinnell, Henry, 328
McKinsey & Company, 328, 398
McLean's, 314
McManus, Geraldine, 112
McMillan, C. Steven, 238
Mecca-Cola, 158
Mediacorp, 266
Mega Brands Inc., 521
Mercedes-Benz, 198, 539
Mercury Marine, 361
Meridian Credit Union Ltd., 605t
Merkel, Angela, 327
Merrill Lynch & Co., 652
Merry Maids, 514
Mesley, Wendy, 583
Messerschmitt-Boelkow-Blohm, 388
Messier, Jean-Marie, 208
Messina, Carlo, 435
Messina, Gianpaolo, 435
Messina, Grant, 71
Metallon Corp., 157

Metro Inc., 245*t*
Meyers Norris Penhy LLP, 443*t*
MGM, 301
Michalowski, Sharon, 273, 284
Michelin, 144
Microsoft, 28, 49–50, 57, 155, 181, 220, 314, 319, 409, 508, 518, 519, 570, 581, 627
Microsoft Canada Co., 415*t*
Midwest Stock Exchange, 626
Miele Canada Limited, 107*t*
Millar Western Pulp Ltd., 83
Miller, Robin, 317
Miller Brewing Company, 580
Mintz, Jack, 405
Mintzberg, Henry, 184
MIT, 346
Mitchell, Camille, 105
Mitchell, Charles, 105
Mitchell, Fred, 105
Mitchell, LuAn, 105
Mitchell's Gourmet Foods Inc., 105
Mizrahi, Isaac, 486
Moffat, Edward, 333
Moge, Victor, 682
Mold-Masters Ltd., 158
Molson Canadian, 579
Molson Inc., 27, 61, 521, 537
Mompreneur Network Group, 112
Monkey Red Designs, 137
Monna, Anne, 106
Monna, Bernard, 106
Monna, Catherine, 106
Monster.ca, 247
Monster.com, 246, 271
Montblanc, 86
Montreal Canadiens, 201
Moody's, 627, 663
Moore, Paul, 646
Morgan Stanley, 625
Morin, Guy Paul, 481
Morpheus, 581
Motorola, 159, 220, 388, 392, 399
Mount Sinai Hospital, 368
Mountain Equipment Co-op (MEC), 78, 78*f*, 81, 93, 567
Mouvement des Caisses Desjardins, 605*t*
Movers and Shakers, 336
Mr. Big-and-Tall, 485
Mr. Coffee, 562
Mrs. Fields Cookies, 215
MTV, 105
Muolo, Paul, 651
Murty, Tad, 100
Music Store, 506
MusicNet, 581
MySpace, 423, 530

N

Napster, 581
Nardelli, Robert, 203
NASDAQ Composite, 619
NASDAQ Composite Index, 637
Nathan Phillips Square, 478
National Angels Organization, 119
National Association of Securities Dealers Automated Quotation (NASDAQ), 627, 637
National Association of Securities Dealers (NASD), 627, 640, 647
National Automobile, Aerospace, Transportation and General Workers Union of Canada (CAW Canada) (CLC), 287*t*
National Bank, 602
National Bank Financial, 379, 440
National Bank of Canada, 598*t*
National Football League, 294
National Hockey League (NHL), 292, 294, 301
National Public Relations, 584
National Railways Union, 287
National Research Council, 9, 236
National Semiconductor, 575
National Union of Public and General Employees (CLC), 287
Natural Resource Defense Council, 524
Natural Resources Canada, 16
Nature's Path Foods, 567
Nav Canada, 678
NBC, 301
NBC-Universal, 344
Nearing, Carnie, 136
NebuAd, 530
Neiman Marcus, 168
Nelvana, 520
Nestlé, 85, 144, 153, 522, 539–540
Neteller PLC, 161
Netflix, 514
Netscape, 49, 423
New York Metropolitan Opera, 196
New York Stock Exchange (NYSE), 626, 627, 641
New York Yankees, 192
Newfoundland Aquaculture Industry Association (NAIA), 617
Newman, David, 379
Nexfor Fraser Inc., 198
NFL, 528
NFO WorldGroup, 465
Niagara Fallsview Casino, 600
Nickelodeon, 105
Nickelodeon Enterprises, 520
Nielsen Media Research, 511, 546, 547
Nike, 79, 192, 489, 511, 520
Niko Resources, 157
Nippon Steel, 145
Nisker, Sari, 120
Nissan Motor Co. Ltd., 144, 147, 300, 358, 376
No Frills, 406, 567
No Kidding, 337
Nobis, 314
Nokia, 208, 548
NoKu, 434
Nooyi, Indra, 217
Norbourg Asset Management Inc., 648
Nortel Networks, 6, 89, 155, 203, 619, 622, 676
North American Palladium Ltd., 6
Northern Empire, 63
Northern Lights, 570
Northern Transportation Company Ltd., 572
Novelis Inc., 156*t*
Novotel, 154
NWT Chamber of Mines, 385
Nygard International Ltd., 273
Nylon, 658

O

O'Brien, Conan, 301
Office Depot, 563
Office Max, 563
Ogilvy & Mather, 263
Ohmes, Robert, 207
Old El Paso, 560
Olive Garden, 538
1-800-GOT-JUNK, 201
O'Neal, Shaquille, 499
Onex Corp., 60, 130*t*, 188, 245*t*, 254
Ontario Human Rights Commission, 78
Ontario Hydro, 202
Ontario Labour Relations Board (OLRB), 277, 285
Ontario Lottery and Gaming Corp., 14*t*
Ontario Ministry of Labour, 262
Ontario Power Generation Inc., 14*t*, 678
Ontario Securities Commission (OSC), 90, 467, 648
Ontario Teachers' Pension Plan, 439
Ontario Tobacco-Free Network, 478
Open Text Inc., 415*t*
Opera Company of Brooklyn, 383
Oppenheim, Matt, 434
Optionable Inc., 680
Oracle, 28, 627
Oracle Corp. Canada Inc., 415*t*
Orans, Lawrence, 434
Organic Trade Association (OTA), 60
Organization for Economic Co-operation and Development (OECD), 161, 241, 292, 381, 615
Organization of Petroleum Exporting Countries (OPEC), 33, 162
Orser, Barbara, 137
Ottawa Senators, 552
OutsideéIn Cosmetics Inc., 136
Outward Bound, 252

P

Pace Productivity, 184
Pacesetter Directional and Performance Drilling, 314
Packaging Association of Canada, 95
Pacific Stock Exchange, 626
Page, Larry, 8, 195, 420
Palliser Furniture Ltd., 258
Pan-Canadian Investors Committee, 678
PanCanadian Petroleum, 62
Panerai, 86
Para Paints, 127, 564
Paramount Digital Entertainment, 508
Paramount Pictures, 105, 301
Park, Andrew, 583
Park, Charles, 583
Parmalat Finanziaria S.p.A., 200, 465
Parrett, William, 465
Pasadena Tournament of Roses Parade, 374
Patterson, Tim, 100
Patti, Joe, 580
PDL Contact Centres Ltd., 107*t*
Pearson, Andrall (Andy), 324
Pearson Education Canada, 184
Pearson International Airport, 200
Peerless Clothing Inc., 171
Pellat, Henry, 26
Pembina Institute, 600
People, 484
People's Education Press, 155
People's Bank of China, 599
PepsiCo, 62, 217, 324
Petro-Canada, 5, 93, 294, 445
Petro-T., 86
Petrolifera Petroleum Ltd., 677
Pfizer Inc., 521
Philip Morris, 22, 435, 551
Philips, 532
PH&N Dividend Income, 646
Photo-Kicks, 198
Piccadilly Restaurants, 360
Pierre Bourgeois, 459
Pillsbury, 560
Pirate Bay, 581
Pixar Animation Studios, 214, 532
Pizza Hut, 62
Pizza Pizza Ltd., 122, 520
Playboy, 538
Plummer, Leanne, 88
Pohang Steel and Iron Corporation (POSCO), 384, 397
Polet, Robert, 488
Polo, 87
Polygram NV, 208
Ponoko, 409, 410

Pontiac, 511
Popular Photography, 529
Popular Science, 346
Porter, Michael, 57, 57*f*, 58, 198, 382
Post, Sandra, 583
Potash Corporation, 127, 199, 254, 292, 295, 623*t*
Powell, Michael, 434
Power Corp of Canada, 126*t*
PowerForward Inc., 119
PQ Media, 511, 548
Prada, 207
Prairie Centre for Business Intelligence, 9
Pratt & Whitney, 142
Prentice, Jim, 141
President's Choice Financial, 596
Pressplay, 581
PriceScan.com, 568
PricewaterhouseCoopers LLP, 443*t*, 581
Proctor & Gamble Canada, 236, 265
Proctor & Gamble (P&G), 27, 71, 85, 109, 144, 186, 197, 217, 225, 259, 411, 453, 480, 492, 493, 500, 511, 519, 527, 549, 551, 559, 565
Profit Magazine, 236, 314
Protega Inc., 107*t*
Provigio, 406
Prudential Financial, 625
Public Service Alliance Canada (CLC), 287*t*
Pure Trading, 624
Putnam Investments, 647
Pyo, Marina, 184

Q

Q-Ray, 583
Quaker Oats, 23, 568
Quebec Labour Relations Board, 277
Queen's Centre for Business Venturing, 107
Quinn, Kevin, 119
Quixstar, 569
QVC, 570

R

RadioShack, 518
Ralph Lauren, 171, 207
Randstad USA, 303
Rankin, Andrew, 90, 648
Rawlings, 417
RBC Asset Management, 631*t*
RBC Dominion Securities, 73, 90, 648
RBC Life Insurance Co., 672*t*
RCMP, 157, 172–180
Re/Max, 122, 181
Reader's Digest, 529
Real Canadian Superstores, 406, 567
Recording Industry Association of America (RIAA), 434, 581
Red Cross, 212
Red Lobster, 252
Redefining Progress, 42
Redstone, Brent, 105
Redstone, Shari, 105
Redstone, Sumner, 105
Reebok, 192
REGEN Energy Inc., 119
Renault, 144
Renfolds Grange, 87
Report on Business Magazine, 260
Reputation Institute, 68
Research in Motion (RIM), 8, 68, 254, 421, 521, 623*t*
Reuters, 181
Revlon, 499–500
Rexall, 122
Richard Ivey School of Business, 120
Ritz-Carlton Hotel Company, 328
Riverside, 274
R.J. Reynolds, 551
Robeez Footwear, 137–173
Roberts, Julia, 180
Rogers Cablesystems Ltd., 89, 528*t*
Rogers Cablevision, 262
Rogers Communications, 314, 488
Rogers Media Inc., 528*t*
Rolex, 87, 193, 532, 539
Rolling Stone, 484
Rollins, Kevin, 506
Rolls Royce, 388, 556
Romero, Chris, 423
Rona Inc., 195, 518, 566*t*
Ronald McDonald House, 92
Rosen, Al, 444
Rosenblum, Larry, 658
Rothmans Benson & Hedges, 478
Rowley, Rich, 590
Roy, Andrew, 247
Royal Bank of Canada (RBC), 53, 68, 89, 126*t*, 179, 196, 202, 245*t*, 255, 271, 519, 594–595, 596, 598*t*, 602, 604, 622, 623*t*, 648
Royal Bank Visa, 594
Royal Canadian Mint, 589, 591
Royal Caribbean, 102
Royal Dutch/Shell, 144, 153
Royal LePage, 229
Royal LePage Commercial, 399
Royal Mail Group, 24
Royal Winnipeg Ballet, 236
Royale Tissue, 197
RSM Richter LLP, 443*t*
RT Capital Management, 619, 649
Rubbermaid, 109
Rusnak, John, 680
Ryder System, 574

S

S&P/TSX, 636, 637, 642
Sabian Cymbals, 153, 459
Safeway, 485, 490
Salvation Army, 93
Samsonite, 87
Samsung, 145, 506
SAP Canada Inc., 415*t*
Sara Lee Corp., 238, 492
SAS, 513
SAS Institute, 513
Saturn Corp., 241, 574–575
Saucony, 137
Save-a-Lot, 350
Savvy.com, 136
Saxx & Co., 119
Schlimm, Dirk, 247
Schwartz, Gerald, 188, 254
Scotch Whisky Association, 54
Scott, Robert, 334, 335
Seagate Technology, 395
Seagram, 155, 208
Sears, 23, 88, 485, 520, 596
Sears Canada Inc., 566*t*, 568
Second Cup Ltd., 251
Second Life, 409
Secor Consulting, 155
Securities and Exchange Commission (SEC), 640, 647
Segal, Alvin, 171
Segal School of Business (Simon Fraser University), 191
Seldman, Neil, 482
Seneca College, 247
Sensory Logic Inc., 493
Service Employees International Union (CtW/CLC), 288*t*, 291
ServiceMaster, 514
Servus Credit Union Ltd., 605*t*
SES Canada Research Inc., 593
7-Eleven, 122, 566
Shackleton, Ernest, 334, 335
Shaftesbury Films, 112
Shamil Bank, 603
Shapiro, Gary, 555
Shaw Comminications Inc., 528*t*
Shell Oil Co., 197, 231, 524
Shep, Walter, 354
Shermag Inc., 615
Shift Selling Inc., 137
Shoppers Drug Mart, 6, 93, 518, 520
Shore Gold, 385
Show my Pony, 423
Siber, Brigit, 229
Sidetack Technologies Inc., 529
Siekaczek, Reinhard, 170
Siemens AG, 144, 170, 260
The Silver Dollar, 551
Simpson, O.J., 481
Singapore Airlines, 190
Sirius Diamond Inc., 385
Sirius Satellite, 548
Sirota Survey Intelligence, 247, 303
Skilsel, Denise, 545
Skymeter Corp., 553
Small Investor Protection Association, 646
Smith, Adam, 26
Smith, Richard, 418
Snoop Doggy Dogg, 679
Sobeys, 93, 406
Social Networks for Everything, 423
Société de alcools du Québec (SAQ), 34
Société Générale SA (SocGen), 680
Society of Management Accountants of Canada, 443
Soer, Casey, 120
Sofer, Oren, 385
Sola Optical, 268
Solutions 2 GO Inc., 107*t*
Sony BMG Music Entertainment, 208
Sony Corporation, 69, 186, 193, 201, 301, 506, 514, 548
Sony Ericsson, 88
Southwest Airlines, 379
Spamhaus Project, 429
Spar Aerospace, 201
Sperry, 137
Spitzer, Elliot, 646
Spoon Fed Soup, 136
Sprinkles Cupcake, 511
Spring, Charlie, 62
Springsteen, Bruce, 525
Sprott Canadian Equity, 646
SSQ, Socité d'assurance-vie Inc., 672*t*
St. Francis Xavier University, 104
Stallone, Sylvester, 525
Standard & Poor's Composite Index (S&P 500), 181, 636, 642, 641, 663
Standard Aero, 386–387
Standard Life Assurance Co. of Canada, 672*t*
Staples, 563
Star-Kist, 224
Starbucks Coffee Company, 179, 202, 260, 489, 519
Starlund, Mark, 387
Statistics Canada, 107, 111, 137, 156, 241, 376, 381, 404, 491, 504, 600
Steelcase, 186
Steeves, Tiffany, 152
Steinberg, Jerry, 337
Steinway & Sons, 398
Stevens, Bruce, 398
Stewart, Martha, 90
Stornoway, 63
StreamCast Networks, 581
Stride Rite Corporation, 137, 173
Stronach, Frank, 200, 201
Strong, Richard, 647

Strong Mutual Funds, 647
Student Workforce, 88
Sukufatu, Henry, 589
Suleman, Razor, 314
Sullivan, Scott, 466
Summa Investors, 630
Summerhurst, Bob, 337
Sun Life Financial Inc., 672, 672*t*
Sun Microsystems of Canada, 333
Suncor Energy Inc., 5, 126*t*, 179, 259, 439
Sunglass Hut International, 566
Sunkist, 560
Sunova Credit Union, 229
Super Lube, 122
Suzuki, 87–144
Sweetpea, 120
Swiss Chalet, 122
Swiss International Air Lines, 483
SXC Health Solutions Corp., 415*t*
Sylvan Learning Centre, 122
Syncrude, 5
Syncsort Inc., 540
Synovate, 605

T

T. Rowe Proce, 635
Taco Bell, 62, 356
Tang, Beverly, 584
Tang, Robert, 584
Target, 207, 486
Tata, Ratan, 359
Tata Consultancy Service, 60
Tata Group, 359
Tata Motors, 359, 405
Taylor, Frederick, 308–309
TD Asset Management, 631*t*
TD Canada Trust, 519, 594, 595–596, 598, 598*t*, 600, 602, 657, 658
TD Canada Trust Toronto Jazz Festival, 478
Teamsters Canada (CtW/CLC), 287*t*
Teck Cominco Ltd., 224
Teck Resources Ltd., 224
Telecommunications Workers Union (TWU), 294
Tell Us About Us (TUAU), 112
TELUS Corp., 93, 294
Terminix, 514
Terrapin Communications Inc., 60
Textile Canada Business Centre, 49
Thomson Reuters, 518
Thornhill, Stewart, 120
Thorpe, Greg, 137
3M Corp., 109, 216, 350
Thunder Oak Cheese, 354
Tiffany & Co., 88
Tim Hortons, 489, 519
Timbuktu Gold Corp., 649
TIME, 327
Tingling, Peter, 191
TMZ.com, 423
TNK, 155
TNT Post Group N.V., 12
Tobacco Institute, 17
Togo, 112
Tokyopop, 490
Tommy Hilfiger, 207
Tommy Hilfiger Footwear, 137
Top-Sider, 137
Toronto Association of Business Improvement Areas, 111
Toronto Blue Jays Baseball Club, 179
Toronto-Dominion Bank, 61, 196, 245*t*, 249, 260, 594, 595, 596, 604, 623*t*, 648
Toronto Hospital, 392
Toronto Maple Leafs, 197, 552
Toronto Police Service, 64
Toronto Raptors, 197
Toronto Star, 528
Toronto Stock Exchange (TSX), 619, 620, 624, 625, 626, 640, 648–649
Toshiba, 145, 389, 514
Tourism New Zealand, 147
Tournament of Roses Parade, 374
Toyota Motor Corp., 12, 16, 68, 145, 147, 152, 195, 200, 259, 286, 300, 350, 358, 361, 368, 376, 384, 386, 388, 392, 570
Trade and Labour Congress 279
Trades and Labour Congress(TLC), , 279–280
Transat A.T. Inc., 379
Transition Plus Sustainability Solutions (TPSS), 110, 111
Transparency International (TI), 162
TransTex Technologies, 49
Travel Industry Council of Ontario (TICO), 379
TrendLines, 32
Tricon Global Restaurants, 62
Trident Precision Manufacturing, 399
Trimark Investment Managemant Inc., 260
TriStar Oil & Gas Ltd., 127
Trudell, Cynthia, 241
TruGreen, 514
TSE, 637
Tupperware, 560, 567, 569–570
Turcotte, Denis, 185
TVI Pacific Inc., 157
Twain, Shania, 216

U

U-Exchange.com, 590
U.K. Advertising Standards Authority, 524
Ultramar Ltd., 156*t*, 86
Uniglobe Travel International, 562
Unilever, 62, 63, 144
Unilever Canada Ltd., 93, 551
Unite Here, 291
United Auto Workers (UAW), 281, 300
United Food and Commercial Workers (CtW/CLC), 277, 286, 287*t*
United Grain Growers, 61
United Nations, 82, 101, 143, 611
United Nations Environment Program, 247
United Nations Intergovernmental Panel on Climate Change (IPCC), 100
United Parcel Service (UPS), 24, 360, 444, 573, 575
United Way, 95, 180
United Steel, Paper and Forestry, Rubber, Manufacturing, Energy, Allied Industrial and Service Workers International Union (AFL-CIO/CLC), 287*t*
Universal, 208, 225, 553
University of British Columbia, 81
University of Guelph, 336
University of Manitoba Faculty Association, 287
University of Ottawa, 100, 137, 535
University of Saskatchewan, 212
University of Toronto, 91, 180, 212, 229, 583
Us, 484
U.S. Air Force, 424
U.S. Coast Guard, 102
U.S. Commerce Department, 159
U.S. Federal Aviation Administration (FAA), 199, 379
U.S. Federal Communications Commission (FCC), 434, 508
U.S. Federal Reserve, 37, 590, 616, 619, 651
U.S. Geological Services (USGS), 33
U.S. Justice Department, 170
U.S. National Cancer Institute, 478
U.S. Treasury, 589

V

Vacheron, 86
Vale Inco, 633, 634
van Herten, Ashley, 482
van Wiltenburg, Erin, 95
Vancouver City Savings Credit Union, 241, 605*t*
Vanier Institute, 136
Venture, 336
Verizon, 570
Versace, 396
Versace, Candice, 120
Versatile, 293
Viacom Inc., 105
Victoria's Secret, 88, 238, 569
Videotron Ltd., 528*t*
Virtual Worlds Management, 532
Visa, 127, 593, 594, 601
Visa Gold Exploration, 648
Vivendi SA, 155, 208
Vivendi Universal Music Group, 208
Viz Medin, 490
Vocalpoint, 511
Volkswagen, 144, 355, 488
Volkswagen Canada, 183, 511
Volvo, 198
VoxPop, 535
Vuze, 508

W

Wagman, Tamar, 120
Waite, Jonathan, 475
Wal-Mart, 6, 39, 57, 58, 153, 161, 195, 198, 202, 207, 227, 228–229, 271, 277, 278, 298, 351, 355, 367, 368, 398, 405, 406, 411, 420, 482, 485, 494, 514, 520, 551, 557, 558, 564, 566, 567, 596, 622
Wal-Mart Canada Corp., 156*t*, 245*t*, 566*t*
Walker, John, 110, 111
Wall, George, 469
Wall & Associates, 469
The Wall Street Journal, 504
Walsh, David, 649
Walt Disney Productions, 39, 155, 180, 188, 214, 326, 367
Walter Reed NAtional Military Medical Centre, 418
Ward, Max, 201
Wardair, 201
Warner Bros., 208, 514
Warner Music Group Corp., 208
Waterstone Human Capital, 179, 201
Watson, Michael, 646
Watson Wyatt Canada, 303
Watson Wyatt Worldwide, 439
Waugh, Rick, 678
Weener, Jann, 484
Welch, Jack, 220
Wellington West Holdings Inc., 62, 179
Wendy's, 39–40
Western Compensation & Benefits Consultants, 62
Western Electric Company, 309
Western Rice Mills Ltd., 21
WestJet Airlines, 57, 68, 74, 89–90, 181, 182, 194, 200, 278, 286, 316, 638
Weston, Galen, 79
Westport Innovations, 155
White Pages, 197
Wilkinson, Kendra, 538
Wilkinson, Pat, 548
Willard, Bob, 247
Williams, Theresa, 337

Wilson, Brett, 346
Wilson, Sandra, 137–173
Winfrey, Oprah, 511
Wipro, 60
Wisconsin Department of Financial Institution, 647
Wm. Wrigley Jr. Co., 61
Wolff, Jonathan, 482
Women's Leadership Council, 265
Wong, Sara, 247
Woo, Dolly, 120
Woods, Ken, 108
Word of Mouth Marketing Association, 530
Workopolis.com, 246, 271
Workplace Safety & Insurance Board, 14*t*
WorkSafe BC, 64
World Bank, 21, 611
World Economic Forum, 147
World Health Organization, 478
World Intellectual Property Organization (WIPO), 87
World Music, 216
World of Warcraft, 409
World Records, 208
World Trade Organization (WTO), 141, 142, 143, 159, 160, 162, 163, 171
World Wildlife Fund (WWF), 524
WorldBlu, 314
WorldCom Inc., 71, 466, 619
WPP Group PLC, 263
Wrangler, 228–229
Writers Guild of America (WGA), 301
WSI Inc., 521
Wyeth, 451

X

Xerox, 109, 230, 252, 389, 521, 539

Y

Yahoo! Inc., 181, 227, 519, 531, 569, 581, 622
Yellow Pages, 197, 532, 540
Yesmoke, 435
Yip, Christopher, 583
Yogen Früz, 122
YouTube, 423, 511, 531, 538
Yum! Brands Inc., 62, 324
Yunus, Muhammad, 602

Z

Zaccardelli, Giuliano, 172, 179
Zellers, 93, 197, 527, 551, 557, 566
Zemmström, Niklas, 434
Zia and Tia Luxury Organics, 111, 136
Zorniak, Ken, 236, 237
Zuckerberg, Mark, 8, 108

Subject Index

A

ABMs, 599–600
Aboriginal people, and employment initiatives, 266
absenteeism, 304
absolute advantage, 146
accommodative stance, 92
accountability, 219
 see also business accountability
accountants
 certified general accountant (CGA), 442
 certified management accountant (CMA), 443
 chartered accountant (CA), 442, 443*t*
 controller, 441
 forensic accountants, 443–446
 private accountants, 445
 professional accountants, 442–443
 role of, 441–446
accounting
 auditing, 443–445
 defined, 440
 described, 440–441
 double-entry accounting system, 447
 financial accounting, 441
 financial statements. *See* financial statements
 generally accepted accounting principles (GAAP), 444
 greening of business, 460
 international accounting, 459–460
 management consulting services, 445
 managerial accounting, 442
 offshore oversights, 444
 paperless system, 460
 pensions, 439–440
 services, 443–445
 tax services, 445
 users of accounting information, 441
accounting equation
 assets, 447
 defined, 447
 liabilities, 447
 owners' equity, 447
accounting information system (AIS), 441
accounts payable, 654
accounts receivable, 449, 654–655, 657, 658
acquisitions, 61–62
activity ratios, 458–459
adding value, 115
administered VMS, 564
administrative law, A-1
advertising
 advertising campaign, 533–534
 advertising media, 527–533
 advocacy advertising, 533
 brand advertising, 533
 changes in, 547–549
 cigarettes, 478–479
 co-operative advertising, 533
 comparative advertising, 527
 counterfeit brands, 86–88
 defined, 527
 ethics in, 86–88
 global advertising, 539
 guerilla advertising, 88
 industrial advertising, 533
 informative advertising, 527
 institutional advertising, 533
 measurement of effectiveness, 546–547
 morally objectionable advertising, 88
 persuasive advertising, 527
 product advertising, 533
 reminder advertising, 527
 retail advertising, 533
 small business, 540
 stealth advertising, 88
 strategies, 527
 trade advertising, 533
 truth in advertising, 86
 types of, 533
 undercover advertising, 88
advertising agencies, 534
advertising campaign, 533–534
advertising media
 defined, 527
 direct mail, 528–529
 internet marketing, 530–531
 magazines, 529
 newspapers, 528
 other advertising media, 532–533
 outdoor advertising, 529–530
 radio, 529
 television, 528
 top ten multimedia companies in Canada, 528*t*
 virtual advertising, 532
 word-of-mouth advertising, 530
advocacy advertising, 533
agency, 21.40
agency-principal relationship, 21.40
agency shop, 288
agents, 562, 565
aggregate output, 41
agreeableness, 305
agreement, A-2
Agreement on Internal Trade (AIT), 161
air pollution, 82–83
airplanes, 572
alternative plans, 199
alternative trading systems (ATSs), 624
alternatives, 190–191, 496
American Stock Exchange (AMEX), 626
Americas Free Trade Area (AFTA), 165
analysis of organization and environment, 194–196
analytic process, 348
Andean Pact, 165
angel investing, 119
anti-discrimination laws, 261–262
anti-unionization activities, 281
anti-virus software, 428
Antinori family, 106
application forms, 246–248
application server, 420
application software, 422
applied R&D, 49
approaching, 536
arbitration, 295
areas of management, 186–187
artificial intelligence (AI), 414
Asia-Pacific, 143, 144–145
Asia-Pacific Economic Cooperation, 165
assembly lines, 358
assembly processes, 348
assessment centre, 248
asset allocation, 633–634
assets
 accounts receivable, 449
 on balance sheet, 449–450
 current assets, 449
 defined, 447
 fixed assets, 449
 intangible assets, 449
 liquidity, 449
 merchandise inventory, 449
 prepaid expenses, 449
assignment of tasks, 219
Association of Southeast Asian Nations (ASEAN), 165, 165*f*
assurance, 400
attitudes, 307
audit, 443–445, 465–466
authority
 committee and team authority, 223–224
 defined, 219
 distribution of, 219–224
 forms of, 223–224
 line authority, 223, 224*f*
 staff authority, 223, 224*f*
autocratic style, 324
automated banking machines (ABMs), 599–600

B

bailment, A-3
bailor–bailee relationship, A-3
balance of payments, 148–149*f*
balance of trade, 43,147–148, 150
balance sheets
 assets, 449
 defined, 449
 liabilities, 450
 owners' equity, 450
Bank Act, 598
bank credit, 665
bank deposits, 601–602
bank loans. *See* loans
Bank of Canada
 bank rate, 597
 defined, 597
 described, 597
 inflation concerns, 37
 member bank borrowing from, 597
 monetary policies, 48
 monetary policy, 597, 597*f*
 operation of, 597
bank rate, 597
banker's acceptance, 599
bankrupt person or company, A-5
bankruptcy, A-5
banks
 alternate banks, 605
 Bank of Canada. *See* Bank of Canada
 Canadian *vs.* U.S. banks, 604
 chartered banks. *See* chartered banks
 international bank structure, 610–611
bargain retailers, 566
bargaining perspectives, 282
bargaining unit, 286
bargaining zone, 289*f*
barriers to trade
 business-practice laws, 161–162
 cartels, 162
 cultural differences, 156–158

dumping, 162
economic differences, 158–159
embargo, 159
legal differences, 159–162
local-content laws, 160
overcoming, 162–165
political differences, 159–162
protectionism, 160
quotas, 159
social differences, 156–158
subsidy, 159–160
tariff, 159
barter economy, 590, 591
basic R&D, 49
Batman movies, 475
bear markets, 636
bearer bonds, 628
behaviour-based interviewing, 249
behaviour modification theory, 313–314
behavioural approach, 324
behavioural aspects of decision making, 191–192
behavioural theory, 309–311
benchmarking, 392
benefits, and value, 477
benefits (employee)
cafeteria-style benefit plans, 259
collective bargaining issue, 290
defined, 258
mandated protection plans, 258
optional protection plans, 258–259
other types, 259–260
paid time off, 259
universal health care system, 258
best practices, 392
bill of materials, 369
biomass, 84
BlackBerry, 414–415, 421*f*
blank endorsement, A-4
blue-chip stock, 622
blue-sky laws, 640
BNA Act, 283
board of directors, 126–127
bona fide occupational requirement, 261
bond indenture, 660
bond quotations, 634–635, 635*f*
bond yield, 635
bonds
bearer bonds, 628
callable bonds, 629
convertible bonds, 629
corporate bonds, 628
coupon bonds, 628
debentures, 628
defined, 44, 627
government bonds, 629–630
interest payment, 628
as long-term funding, 659–660
ratings, 627
registered bonds, 628
retirement of bonds, 628–630
secondary securities market, 621, 630
secured bonds, 628
serial bonds, 629
sinking fund provisions, 629
unsecured bonds, 628
bonuses, 256
book value, 621
bookkeeping, 440
bootstrapping, 117
the bottom line, 450
boundaries. *See* organizational boundary
boundaryless organization, 228
boycotts, 294
branch offices, 154
brand advertising, 533
brand competition, 483
brand equity, 518–519
brand loyalty, 520–521
branding
brand equity, 518–519
brand loyalty, 520–521
copyrights, 521
defined, 518
ebusiness, 519
international branding, 519
licensed brands, 520
national brands, 519
patent, 521
private brands, 520
trademark, 521
types of brand names, 519–520
Brazil, and *jeitinho*, 73
breach of contract, A-2
break-even analysis, 554–556, 555*f*
break-even point, 554
bribes, 74, 161–162, 170–171
brokers, 560–565, 624
budget, 453, 453*f*
budget deficits
annual deficits, 44
defined, 44
budget surpluses, 44
bull markets, 636
business
charitable donations, 93
concept of, 6–7
defined, 6
ethics. *See* business ethics; ethics
family businesses, 105–106
goals of, 6–7
government, influences of, 13–17
government, influences on, 17–18, 17*f*
government, interactions with, 5–18
history of, in Canada, 24–28, 24*t*
internet, growth of, 28
management of. *See* management
nature of, 6–7
pro- and anti-business sentiment, 53
social responsibility. *See* corporate social responsibility (CSR)
standards of business conduct, 55–56
business accountability
Canadian *vs.* U.S. banks, 604
cigarettes, advertising of, 478
counterfeit brands, 87–88
financial advisers, 625
high prices, impact of, 21
managers, roles of, 184
mining business, 157
the Nano, 359
offshore oversights, 444
outsourcing, 59–60
perks, importance of, 260
product *vs.* geographical departmentalization, 217
professional accountability, 625
quality of diamonds, 385
Quicken, 666
social marketing, 423
business analysis, 515
business continuation agreements, 673
business cycle, 41–41*f*
Business Development Bank of Canada (BDC), 607
business distribution, 562–563
business environment
business process management, 61
core competencies, 58
described, 56
emerging challenges and opportunities, 58–61
industry environment, 57–58
outsourcing, 58–60
viral marketing, 60–61
business ethics
codes of ethics, adoption of, 77–78
and company practices, 77–79
defined, 72
ethics programs, 79
business law
see also law
breach of contract, A-2
contracts, A-2
defined, A-2
business-level strategy, 196, 198
business ownership
co-operative, 128–130
corporation, 126–128
forms of, 123–130, 131*t*
partnership, 125–126
sole proprietorship, 123–124
business plan, 116, 116*t*, 174–175, 338–339, 470–471, 585, 683
business-practice laws, 161–162
business process management, 61
business process outsourcing, 444
business process re-engineering, 394
buyers, 58
buying and selling securities
financial information services, 634–637
financing securities purchases, 637–639
stocks, 637
buzz marketing, 497

C

cafeteria-style benefit plans, 259
caisses populaires, 605
call option, 632
call price, 623, 629
callable bonds, 629
callable stock, 623
Canada
Agreement on Internal Trade (AIT), 161
balance of payments, 148–149*f*
banks, top ten, 598*t*
budget surpluses, 44
business, history of, 24–28, 24*t*
businesses, nature and goals of, 6
Canadian companies, top ten, 623*t*
Canadian *vs.* American management style, 328
chartered accountant firms, top ten, 443*f*
corporations, top ten, 126*t*
credit unions, top ten, 605*t*
Crown corporations, top ten, 14*t*
economy. *See* Canadian economy
employers, top ten, 245*t*
exports, 153
financial system. *See* Canadian financial system
foreign-controlled companies, top ten, 156*t*
foreign ownership of Canadian industry, 155
French and English cultures, 490
gross domestic product (GDP), 49
imports and exports, 148*f*, 149*t*
information technology companies, top ten, 415*t*
international economy, role in, 144
labour unions, 291
life insurance companies, top ten, 672*t*
multimedia companies, top ten, 528*t*
mutual funds, top ten, 631*t*

natural resources, 5–6
preferences and tastes, regional variations in, 55
price increases, rate of, 46*f*
retailers, top ten, 565*t*
securities regulations, 640
small- and medium-sized employers, top ten, 107*t*
softwood lumber dispute, 159–160
unions, top ten, 287*t*
universal health care system, 258
Canada Business Corporations Act, 127–128
Canada Labour Code, 283–284
Canada Pension Plan, 258
Canada Savings Bonds, 629
Canada Water Act, 16
Canadian economy
competition, 20–24
demand and supply, 18–20
high prices, impact of, 21
history of business in Canada, 24–28
management of, 48
new venture, role of, 111–112
private enterprise system, 20–24
small business, role of, 109–111
Canadian financial system
alternate banks, 605
chartered banks, 598–604
financial institutions, 595–597
investment dealers, 607
other sources of funds, 607–608
specialized lending and savings intermediaries, 606–607
Canadian Human Rights Act, 261
Canadian Human Rights Commission, 261
Canadian Mortgage and Housing Corporation (CMHC), 607
Canadian Radio-Television and Telecommunications Commission (CRTC), 13
Canadian stock exchanges, 624–626
Canadian Transport Commission (CTC), 13
Canadian Venture Exchange (CDNX), 626
Canadian Wheat Board, 13
capacity DSS, 413
capacity planning, 354–355
capital
defined, 8
as factor of production, 8
insufficient capital, 132
paid-in capital, 450
working capital, 655
capital expenditures, 655–656
capital items, 513
capital services, 513
capital structure, 662
capitalism, 12
carbon dioxide (CO2) levels, 82, 83*f*
Caribbean Common Market, 165
cartels, 162
cases
see also video cases
"Are We Running Out of Oil?", 32–33
"Bailout or Bust?", 375–376
"Bribery on the International Scene," 170–171
"Business of Bagging Customers," 207
"Business *vs.* Government in the Liquor Industry," 33–34
"Changing Distribution Channels in the Music Business," 581
"The Changing Face of Advertising," 547–549
"Commercial Paper Crisis," 677–678
"Continuing Concerns in the Accounting Profession," 466–467
"Cooking Up a New Structure," 238
"Coping with Currency Fluctuations," 615–616
"Corporate Reputations Are on The Line," 68–69
"Debate over Global Warming," 100–101
"Dell-ivering on Consumer Electronics," 506–507
"Do We Need to Audit the Auditors?", 465–466
"Galt Contracting," 274–275
"Getting In On the Ground Floor," 138
"How to Keep a Project Afloat," 374–375
"If At First You Don't Succeed," 208
"Impact of External Environment on Business Firms," 67–68
"International Challenges in the Clothing Industry," 171
"Internet Wars," 435–436
"It's the Latest Crisis in the Automobile Business," 299–300
"Labour Relations in Hollywood," 301
"Leadership and Management," 334–335
"Measuring the Effectiveness of Advertising," 546–547
"Mompreneurs," 136–137
"An Old Company with New Potential," 508
"Pollution on the High Seas," 101–102
"Poor Productivity: Canada's Biggest Problem?", 404–405
"Pursuing Effective Risk Management," 678–680
"Scandal in the Mutual Fund Industry," 646–647
"Sharing the Wealth," 434–435
"Stock Market Shenanigans," 648–649
"Structure Evolves at Frantic Films," 236–237
"The Struggle to Finance Fish Farming," 616–617
"Supply Chain Management at Loblaw," 406
"This Distribution Net's for You," 579–580
"What About Telecommuting?", 333–334
"Who Should Get Overtime Pay?", 273
cash, 449
cash discounts, 558
cash flow management, 653
cash-flow planning, 665–666
cash flows from financing, 452
cash flows from investing, 452
cash flows from operations, 452
casual gaming industry, 532
casualty, 670
catalogue marketing, 567
catalogue showrooms, 566
category killers, 566
cause-and-effect diagram, 386*f*
cellular layouts, 356–358
Central American Common Market, 165
centralized organizations, 220
certificates of deposit (CDs), 593
certification process, 286
certification vote, 286
certified general accountant (CGA), 442
certified management accountant (CMA), 443
Chain of Blame (Muolo), 651
chain of command, 213–214
change management, 202–203
channel captain, 564
channel conflict, 564
charismatic leadership, 326, 326*f*
charitable donations, 93
chartered accountant (CA), 442, 443*t*
chartered banks
bank loans, 602
Canadian *vs.* U.S. banks, 604
as creators of money, 602–604, 603*f*
defined, 598
deposits, 601–602
described, 598
electronic funds transfer (EFT), 599–601
financial advice, 599
international services, 599
online banking, 600
pension services, 598
reserve requirement, 603
services, 598–601, 602, 602*f*
top ten banks in Canada, 598*t*
trust services, 599
chemical processes, 348
chequable deposit, 601
cheque kiting, 90, 593
cherry-picking consumers, 551
chief executive officer (CEO), 127
China
counterfeit products, 87
gold farming, 409
choice, 85
cigarette advertising, 478
circuit breakers, 641
circular flow in market economy, 11*f*
classical theory of motivation, 308–309
classification of goods and services, 513
clerical processes, 348
client relationships, 319
client-server networks, 420
clients, 420
closed shop, 288
closing, 536
clothing industry, 171
co-operative, 128–130
co-operative advertising, 533
coaching perspective, 326–327
codes of ethics
adoption of, 77–78
defined, 77
personal codes of ethics, 72–73
collaboration, 416
collateral, 118, 657
collective bargaining
see also labour relations
bargaining zone, 289*f*
benefits, 290
compensation, 290
contract issues, 289–291
defined, 278
failure of, 292–294
impasse, 292
job security, 290
mandatory items, 289
other issues, 290–291
permissive items, 289
process, 288–289
reaching agreement, 288–289
union tactics, 292–294
collusion, 85
command economy, 10

commercial paper, 658, 677–678
commercialization, 516
commitment fee, 658
committee and team authority, 223–224
commodities
  decline in prices, 37
  demand, effect of, 21
  high prices, effect of, 21
  investments in, 632
  ups and downs of, 5–6
commodities market, 632
common carriers, 574
common law, A-1
common stock, 450, 621–622, 660
communication of information, 523
communism, 10
company productivity, 384
comparable worth, 262–263
comparative advantage, 146
comparative advertising, 527
compensating balance, 657
compensation
  basic compensation, determination of, 255–256
  collective bargaining issue, 290
  defined, 254
  executive compensation, 254–255
  incentive programs, 256–258
  job evaluation, 255
  overtime pay, 273
  pay structure, 256
  pay surveys, 255
  performance-based compensation, 256–258
competence, A-2
competition
  brand competition, 483
  competitive strategy, 57
  defined, 20
  degrees of competition, 21–24, 21*t*–22*t*
  and exchange rates, 150
  international competition, 147, 483
  in market economy, 20–24
  marketing environment, 482–483
  monopolistic competition, 22–23
  monopoly, 23–24
  oligopoly, 23
  perfect competition, 22
  and private enterprise, 20–21
  promotion of, 14
  and technology, 51
Competition Act 13, 14*t*
competitive advantage
  absolute advantage, 146
  comparative advantage, 146
  diversity as, 266
  forms of, 145–147
  national competitive advantage, 146–147, 147*f*
  sustaining, 115
competitive product analysis, 389
competitive strategy, 57, 196, 198
competitors
  government as, 13
  rivalry among, 57
  threat of potential entrants, 57
complaints, 85, 497
compressed workweek, 320
compulsory arbitration, 295
computer-aided design (CAD), 412
computer-aided manufacturing (CAM), 413
computer-assisted instruction, 251
computer graphics, 422
computer network, 420
computer operations control, 413
computer viruses, 426, 428
concentration strategy, 196
concept testing, 515
conceptual skills, 188
Confederation, 44
conflict of interest, 74
conglomerate diversification, 197
conglomerate merger, 61
conscientiousness, 305
conservative strategy, 662
consideration, A-2
Constitution Act, 283
consumer behaviour
  consumer buying process, 495–497, 495*f*
  cultural influences, 494–495
  defined, 494
  influences on, 494–495
  personal influences, 494–495
  psychological influences, 495
  social influences, 494–495
  understanding, 494–497
consumer buying process
  described, 495–497, 495*f*
  evaluation of alternatives, 496
  information seeking, 496
  post-purchase evaluations, 496–497
  problem/need recognition, 495–496
  and promotional mix, 525, 526*f*
  purchase decisions, 496
consumer co-operatives, 129
consumer finance company, 606
consumer goods, 477
Consumer Packaging and Labelling Act, 522
consumer price index (CPI), 45, 290
consumer products, 513, 559–561
consumer protection, 14
consumerism, 85
consumers
  see also customers
  cherry-picking consumers, 551
  money, and banking, 596
  purchase decision, 45
  rights of consumers, 85
contagion, 633
containerization, 572
contemporary motivation theory, 311–313
contingency approach, 324–325
contingency planning, 199
contingent workers, 267–268
continuous improvement, 399
contract carriers, 574
contracting out, 294
contracts, A-2
contractual VMS, 564
control charts, 390, 391*f*
control process, 183*f*
control systems, 131
controller, 441
controlling
  described, 182–183
  for quality, 388–389
convenience goods, 513
convenience services, 513
convenience stores, 566
convertible bonds, 629
copyrights, 521
core competencies, 58
core principles, 78*f*
corporate bonds, 628
corporate boundaries. *See* organizational boundary
corporate charitable donations, 93
corporate culture
  change management, 202–203
  communication of, 202
  defined, 200
  examples of, 179–180, 200–201
  forces shaping corporate culture, 201
  strong culture, 201
corporate environments. *See* external environment
corporate finance, 652
corporate-level strategy, 196, 197
corporate social responsibility (CSR)
  accommodative stance, 92
  approaches, 91–93, 92*f*
  areas of social responsibility, 82–91
  corporate charitable donations, 93
  customers, responsibility toward, 84–88
  defensive stance, 92
  defined, 79
  described, 55–56
  employees, responsibility toward, 88–90
  environmental responsibilities, 82–84
  ethical funds, 630
  vs. ethics, 79
  implementation of social responsibility programs, 91–94
  investors, responsibility toward, 90–91
  management of social responsibility programs, 93–94, 94*f*
  obstructionist stance, 92
  opponents of, 91
  organizational stakeholders, 79–80*f*
  proactive stance, 92
  and small business, 95
  social audits, 94
  social consciousness, 80–81
  supporters of, 91
  triple bottom line reporting, 94
corporate VMS, 564
corporation
  advantages of incorporation, 128
  board of directors, 126–127
  defined, 126
  disadvantages of incorporation, 128
  dividend, 128
  double taxation, 128
  employee-owned corporations, 62
  financial corporations, 606
  formation of, 127–128
  income trust, 127
  initial public offering (IPO), 127
  parent corporation, 63
  private corporation, 127
  public corporation, 127
  stockholders, 126
  subsidiary corporation, 63
  top ten corporations in Canada, 126*t*
  types of, 127
cost leadership, 198
cost of goods sold, 450–451
cost-of-living adjustment (COLA), 290
cost-oriented pricing, 553–554
costs
  exit costs, 116
  fixed costs, 554
  holding costs, 366–367
  personal selling, 534
  quality/cost studies, 391–392
  variable costs, 554
  warehousing, 571
counterfeit brands, 86–88
counterfeiting, 593
counterproductive behaviours, 304–305
coupon bonds, 628
coupons, 537
court system, A-1

courteous service, 85
craft unions, 286–287
creative selling, 535
credit card fraud, 594
credit cards, 593–595
credit default swaps, 651–652
credit policy, 655
credit unions, 605, 605*t*
creditors, 441
crisis management, 200
critical incident method, 253
cross-cultural leadership, 327–328
Crown corporations, 13*t*
Cuddy family, 105–106
cultural change, 179–180
cultural differences, 156–158
cultural receptiveness, 539
culture
- collectivism, 327
- cross-cultural leadership, 327–328
- described, 327
- and ethics, 73
- individualism, 327

culture surveys, 179
cumulative preferred stock, 623
currency, 592–593
currency exchange, 599
currency fluctuations, 615–616
current assets, 449
current liabilities, 450
current ratio, 456
customer departmentalization, 215–216
customer-service link, 352–353
customers
- *see also* consumers
- getting closer to, 392–393
- going international and customers' needs, 152
- government as, 13
- preferences and tastes, 55
- responsibility toward, 84–88
- satisfaction, 367
- services and, 363
- virtual presence, 353

customization, 352, 417
cybermalls, 569
cycle time, 51
cyclical unemployment, 46

D

damages, A-2
data, 410, 491
data collection, 491
data mining, 494
data warehousing, 493–494
day traders, 639
debentures, 628
debit card, 601
debt, 456, 681
debt financing, 118, 659–660, 661–663, 662*f*
debt-to-owners' equity ratios, 456
decentralized organizations, 220–221
decertification, 286
decision making
- behavioural aspects, 191–192
- defined, 189
- opportunity decision, 190
- problem decision, 190
- rational decision-making process, 189–191, 189*f*

decision-making hierarchy
- assignment of tasks, 219
- authority, distribution of, 219–224
- establishment of, 218–224
- performance of tasks, 219

decision-making skills, 189–192
decline stage, 517
dedication, 130
deductible, 668
deed, A-3
default, 44
defensive stance, 92
deflation
- defined, 46
- and economic stability, 46
- *vs.* inflation, 37–38
- predictions about, 37–38

degrees of competition, 21–24, 21*t*–22*t*
delegation, 219
demand
- conditions, 146
- defined, 18
- demand and supply schedule, 18
- demand curve, 19–20, 19*f*
- human resources and, 243–244
- international demand, 151
- law of demand, 18
- in market economy, 18–21
- prices and, 21
- and small business success, 130

demand and supply schedule, 18
demand curve, 19–20, 19*f*
demand deposits, 593
democratic style, 324
demographic variables, 487–488, 487*f*
denial of service (DOS) attacks, 424
department stores, 216, 565–566
departmentalization
- customer departmentalization, 215–216
- defined, 215
- described, 214
- functional departmentalization, 215
- geographic departmentalization, 216–217
- multiple bases of, 218*f*
- process departmentalization, 216–218
- product departmentalization, 216, 217
- profit centre, 215

deposits, 601–602
depreciation, 449
depression, 41
deregulation, 13, 595
developing countries, 143
diamonds, 385
differentiation strategy, 198
direct channel, 559
direct deposits and withdrawals, 600
direct mail, 528–529
direct-response retailing, 567
direct selling, 567
directing, 182
- *see also* leadership

discharge, A-2
discount brokers, 624
discount houses, 566
discounts, 558
discussion approach, 251
distribution
- business distribution, 562–563
- channels. *See* distribution channels
- consumer products, 559–561
- distribution mix, 559–564
- exclusive distribution, 563
- hubs, 574–575
- industrial distribution, 562–563
- intensive distribution, 563
- intermediaries, 559–563
- international distribution, 499–500
- in marketing mix, 485
- as marketing strategy, 574–575
- non-direct distributions, 561–562
- physical distribution, 570–575
- retailing, 565–570
- selective distribution, 563–564
- small business distribution, 501
- strategies, 563–564, 563*f*
- wholesaling, 564–565

distribution centres, 571
distribution channels
- channel captain, 564
- channel conflict, 564
- defined, 559
- types of, 559–563
- vertical marketing system (VMS), 564

distribution mix, 559–564
distribution-side hubs, 575
diversification, 197, 633
diversity in the workforce, 265–266
divestitures, 62
dividend, 128
divisional structure, 224–225, 225*f*, 225*t*
domestic productivity, 382
double-entry accounting system, 447
double taxation, 128
Dow Jones Industrial Average (DJIA), 636, 641
downsizing, 222, 282
drive, 130
drop shipper, 565
drug tests, 249
dumping, 162
dynamic pricing, 557

E

e-agents, 565, 568
e-intermediaries, 561, 568–570
early behavioural theory, 309–311
earnings per share, 457
Eastern Europe, 144
easy monetary policy, 48
ebrokers, 561
ebusiness. *See* ecommerce
ecash, 601
ecatalogues, 569
ecommerce
- *see also* internet
- agents, 562
- analysis of price of doing ebusiness, 30–31
- branding and, 519
- business-to-business (B2B) transactions, 10
- business-to-consumer (B2C) transactions, 10
- defined, 530
- fixed *vs.* dynamic pricing, 557
- order fulfillment, 573
- virtual presence of customer, 353

Economic Community of Central African States, 165
economic differences, 158–159
economic environment
- Canadian economy, management of, 48
- defined, 39
- economic growth, 40–44
- marketing environment, 481–482
- stability, 44–48

economic growth
- aggregate output, 41
- balance of trade, 43–44
- business cycle, 41–41*f*
- gross domestic product (GDP), 42–43
- gross national product (GNP), 42–43
- national debt, 44
- productivity, 43
- real growth rates, 42
- standard of living, 41

economic stability, 44–48
economic systems
- command economy, 10

defined, 7
factors of product, 7–9
goals of Canadian economic system, 40
market economies, 10–12, 11*f*
mixed market economy, 12–13
types of, 10–13
economic theory, 21
effectiveness, 181
efficiency, 181, 416
electronic conferencing, 419–420
Electronic Data Systems (EDS), 353
electronic funds transfer (EFT), 599–601
electronic purses, 601
electronic retailing, 568–570
electronic spreadsheets, 423–424
electronic storefronts, 569
email
spam, 427, 428–429
and time management, 189
email server, 420
embargo, 159
emissions trading, 639
emotional intelligence, 306, 324
emotional motives, 496
emotional quotient (EQ), 306
emotionality, 306
empathy, 324, 400
employee behaviour
counterproductive behaviours, 304–305
defined, 304
forms of, 304–305
organizational citizenship, 304
performance behaviours, 304
employee information systems, 244
employee-oriented, 324
employee-owned corporations, 62
employee stock ownership plans (ESOPs), 62
employees
accounting information, use of, 441
benefits, 258–259
compensation, 254–258
desires of, 302–304
discretion, control of, 362–363
empowerment, 316–316, 399
engagement and alignment, 314
idea sharing, encouragement of, 317
independence, 416
individual differences, 305–307
legal and social commitments, 89–90
managerial ethics, and behaviour toward employees, 73–74
market value of, 256
matching people and jobs, 307–308
monitoring of, 89
motivation. *See* motivation
new employee orientation, 250
performance appraisal, 252–253
person–job fit, 308
privacy, 89
psychological contracts, 307–308, 308*f*
responsibility toward, 88–90
safety and health, 264
training. *See* training and development
employers
see also management
anti-unionization activities, 281
small- and medium-sized employers, top ten, 107*t*
top ten in Canada, 245*t*
employers' associations, 294
Employment Equity Act, 262
employment insurance, 258
employment standards, 284
employment tests, 248
empowerment, 316–316, 399
encryption software, 428
encryption system, 428
endorsement, A-4
enterprise resource planning (ERP), 52–53*f*
entrepreneur
see also entrepreneurship; small business
after the start-up, 121–123
attributes of, 108–109
characteristics, 113*t*
defined, 8, 108
emergence of, 26
employee engagement, 314
entrepreneur-opportunity fit, 121
entrepreneur-resources fit, 121
and entrepreneurial process, 113
EPIC Newsgroup Inc., 152
as factor of production, 8
index of economic freedom, 108
Kitwanga Mills Ltd., 387
"Mompreneurs," 136–137, 173
women entrepreneurs in Canada, 111
entrepreneurial era, 26
entrepreneurial process
described, 112–113, 113*f*
the entrepreneur, 113
entrepreneur-opportunity fit, 121
entrepreneur-resources fit, 121
fit between elements, 120–121
opportunities, development of, 116–117
opportunities, identification of, 113–117
opportunity-resources fit, 121
resources, assessment of, 117–120
entrepreneurship
see also entrepreneur
branded entertainment, 532
defined, 108
men and cars, 555
"A Shrine to Wine," 9
social responsibility, 95
entry strategies, 116
the environment. *See* greening of business
environment, organizational. *See* external environment
environmental analysis, 195–196
Environmental Contaminants Act, 16
environmental management system (EMS), 393–394
environmental performance, 393
environmental protection, 16
environmental responsibilities, 82–84
equal employment opportunity regulations, 261–262
equilibrium price, 20
equity financing, 118, 660–661, 662*f*, 663
equity theory, 312–313
escalation of commitment, 192
essential services, 17
esteem needs, 311
etailing, 568–570
ethical behaviour
see also ethics
assessment of, 75–77, 76*f*
defined, 72
encouragement of, 77–79
ethical funds, 630
ethical leadership, 328
ethics
see also ethical behaviour
in advertising, 86–88
behaviour toward other economic agents, 74
business ethics, 72, 77–79
codes of ethics, 72–73, 77–78
and company practices, 77–79
conflict of interest, 74
vs. corporate social responsibility (CSR), 79
and culture, 73
defined, 72
ethical judgment making, 76*f*
ethics programs, 79
individual ethics, 72–73
Livent Inc., 71–72
managerial ethics, 73–74
and socio-cultural environment, 55–56
and technological developments, 77
in the workplace, 72–79
euro, 150
Europe, 143, 144
European settlers, 24
European Union (EU), 163–164*f*
exchange rate
and balance of trade, 150
and competition, 150
defined, 149–150
described, 149–150
fixed exchange rates, 150
floating exchange rates, 150
government influences, 609
and international trade, 608–609
law of one price, 608–609
exchange-traded fund (ETF), 631
exclusive distribution, 563
executive compensation, 254–255
executive support system (ESS), 414
existing products, pricing, 556–557
exit costs, 116
expansion into additional capabilities, 350
expectancy theory, 311–312, 313*f*
expense items, 513
experimentation, 493
expert system, 414
exporters, 153
exports, 142, 148*f*, 149*t*, 153
express warranty, A-3
external benchmarking, 392
external environment
business environment, 56–61
defined, 38, 480
dimensions of, 40*f*
economic environment, 39–48
marketing environment, 480–483
multiple organizational environments, 39
political-legal environment, 53–54
socio-cultural environment, 55–56
technological environment, 48–52
external failures, 392
external recruiting, 245–246
extranets, 419
extroversion, 306
extroverts, 306

F

fabrication processes, 348
factoring accounts receivable, 658
factoring company, 606
factors of production
capital, 8
defined, 7
described, 7–9, 8*f*
entrepreneurs, 8
factor conditions, 146
information resources, 9
labour, 7
natural resources, 9
factory outlets, 566
factory system, 24–25

failure of small business, 131*t*, 131–132
family businesses, 105–106, 122
features, 512–513
federal labour legislation, 283–284
feedback, performance, 252–253
finance
  Canadian financial system. *See* Canadian financial system
  debt financing, 118, 659–660, 661–663, 662*f*
  defined, 652
  equity financing, 118, 660–661, 662*f*, 663
  funds, need for, 654–656
  hybrid financing, 661
  international banking and finance, 608–611
  long-term expenditures, 655–656
  long-term funds, 659–664
  short-term expenditures, 654–655
  short-term funds, 656–658
  small businesses, 664–666
finance era, 27
financial accounting system, 441
financial advice, 599
financial advisers, 625
financial co-operatives, 129
financial control, 653–654
financial corporations, 606
financial crisis, 651–652, 667
financial forecasts, 115
financial information services
  bond quotations, 634–635, 635*f*
  market indexes, 636–637
  mutual funds quotations, 635–636*f*
  stock quotations, 634, 634*f*
financial institutions
  Bank of Canada, 597
  changes, 595–596
  chartered banks. *See* chartered banks
  consumer demands, changing, 596
  credit unions, 605
  deregulation, 595
  four financial pillars, 595
  international banking, changes in, 596
  investment dealers, 607
  specialized lending and savings intermediaries, 606–607
  trust company, 605
  types of, 595
financial managers
  cash flow management, 653
  defined, 187, 652
  financial control, 653–654
  financial plan, 654
  financial risk indexes, 662–663
  objectives, 652
  responsibilities, 653–654
  risk-return relationship, 664, 664*f*
  role of, 652
financial mismanagement, 90
financial misrepresentation, 91
financial plan, 654
financial ratios
  activity ratios, 456, 458–459
  classifications, 456
  current ratio, 456
  debt-to-owners' equity ratios, 456
  earnings per share, 457
  inventory turnover ratio, 458–459
  profitability ratios, 456, 457
  return on equity, 457
  return on sales, 457
  solvency ratios, 456
financial report, 445
financial resources, 118–119
financial risk indexes, 662–663
financial statements
  analysis, 455–459
  balance sheets, 449–450
  budget, 453, 453*f*
  defined, 448
  full disclosure, 455
  income statements, 450–452
  matching principle, 454–455, 455*t*
  reporting standards and practices, 453–455
  revenue recognition, 454, 455*t*
  statement of cash flows, 452
financial system. *See* Canadian financial system
financially viable ideas, 115
financing securities purchases, 637–639
finished goods inventory, 655
firewalls, 427–428
first-line managers, 186, 412
fiscal policies, 48
fish farming, 616–617
fishbone diagram, 386*f*
Fisheries Act, 16
five forces model, 57–58, 57*f*
fixed assets, 449
fixed costs, 554
fixed exchange rates, 150
fixed pricing, 557
flat organizational structure, 221
flexibility for customization, 417
flexible manufacturing system (EMS), 358
flextime, 319–320*f*
floating exchange rates, 150
focus groups, 492–493
focus strategy, 198
follow-up, 366, 536
Food and Drug Act, 14
forced distribution method, 253
forecast
  defined, 353–354
  demand and supply of labour, 243–244
  importance of, 442
foreign currency exchange rates, 459
foreign direct investment (FDI), 155–156
Foreign Investment Review Agency, 155
foreign ownership of Canadian industry, 155
foreign stock exchanges, 626–627
forensic accountants, 443–446
form utility, 347
formal organization, 231
forms of business ownership. *See* business ownership
formulation of strategy, 194–196, 194*f*
four-day workweek, 320, 322
franchise, 116, 122–123, 122*t*
franchising, 154
franchising agreement, 122
fraud, 443, 594
free-rein style, 324
free samples, 537
free trade agreements, 164–165
freedom of choice, 20
freight forwarder, 574
frictional unemployment, 46
friendly takeover, 62
full disclosure, 455
full-service brokers, 624
full-service merchant wholesaler, 565
functional departmentalization, 215
functional strategies, 196, 198
functional structure, 224, 224*t*
funds
  factoring accounts receivable, 658
  long-term expenditures, 655–656
  long-term funds, 659–664
  need for, 654–656
  short-term expenditures, 654–655
  short-term funds, 656–658
futures contracts, 632

G

G-3 group, 165
gain-sharing plans, 258
gaming industry, 532
Gantt chart, 364, 365*f*
gays, and employment initiatives, 266
GDP per capita, 42
gender, and leadership, 327
General Agreement on Tariffs and Trade (GATT), 162
general partners, 125
general partnership, 125
generally accepted accounting principles (GAAP), 444
Genuine Progress Indicator (GPI), 42
geographic departmentalization, 216–217
geographic expansion, 196–197
geographic variables, 487
Germany, and labour unions, 292
glass ceiling, 241
global economy
  see also international trade
  advertising, 539–540
  balance of payments, 148–149*f*
  balance of trade, 147–148
  banking services, 599
  branding, 519
  bribes, 74
  competitive advantage, forms of, 145–147
  corruption, 162
  described, 142–150
  exchange rates, 149–150
  geographic clusters, 144–145
  global exchange, improved, 416
  gold farming, 409
  growth of global operations, 345
  import-export balances, 147–148
  inflation, 45
  interconnectedness, 37
  international banking, 596
  international business management. *See* international business management
  international trade, 142–143
  major world marketplaces, 143–145
  per capita income, 143
  political stability, 53–54
  productivity, 381–382
  promotion strategies, 538–540
  sovereign governments, relations between, 54
global era, 27–28
global perspective, 538
global warming, 83, 100–101
globalization, 142–143
goal setting theory, 315
goals
  defined, 193
  green goals, 195
  intermediate goals, 194
  kinds of goals, 193–194
  long-term goals, 193
  management by objectives (MBO), 315, 316*f*
  purposes of goal setting, 193
  setting goals, 193–195
  short-term goals, 194
  SMART goals, 194, 315
  strategic goals, 192, 194
going international, 151–152, 151*f*
gold farming, 409
goods
  see also product

classification of, 513–514
consumer goods, 477
convenience goods, 513
industrial goods, 479
manufacturing operations. *See* manufacturing operations
marketing of, 477–480
shopping goods, 513
specialty goods, 513
goods-producing processes, 348
goods production, 344
see also manufacturing operations
goodwill, 449
government
administrative boards, 13
and business, interactions between, 5–18
commissions, 13
competition, promotion of, 14
as competitor, 13
consumer protection, 14
as customer, 13
environmental protection, 16
exchange rate, influences on, 609
fiscal policies, 48
influences of business, 17–18, 17*f*
influences on business, 13–17
market, 497
monetary policies, 48
as provider of essential services, 17
as provider of incentives, 16–17
as regulator, 15–16
regulatory agencies, 441
social goals, 16
stabilization policy, 48
as taxation agent, 16
top ten Crown corporations in Canada, 14*t*
tribunals, 13
government bonds, 629–630
grapevine, 232–233
graphic rating scale, 253, 254*f*
Great Depression, 80
greening of business
accounting, 460
emissions trading, 639
four-day workweek, 322
green goals, 195
green organizational structure, 229
green recruiting, 247
green trading, 639
Green World Solutions, 482
hydrogen fuel cell, 50
Mountain Equipment Co-op (MEC), 81
online banking, 600
promotion of green image, 524
retailing, 567
small businesses, 110–111
steel making, 397
telecommuting, 322
Wal-Mart, 368
grievance, 296, 296*f*
gross domestic product (GDP), 42–43, 49
gross margin, 451
gross national product (GNP), 42–43
gross profit, 451
group-based training, 252
group incentives, 257–258
group life insurance, 672
groupware, 423
growth
economic growth. *See* economic growth
of global operations, 345
and specialization, 215
growth stage, 517
growth strategies, 196
guerilla advertising, 88
Gulf Cooperation Council, 165

H

hackers, 424–425
handling objections, 536
harassment, 263–264, 305
hard work, 130
hardware, 421
Hawthorne effect, 309
Hazardous Products Act, 14
health and safety, 264
health insurance, 258
hedge funds, 631
hierarchy of human needs model, 310–311, 310*f*
high-contact processes, 349, 361
high-contact system, 349, 360
high-income countries, 143
high-tech bubble, 41
history of business in Canada
early years, 24
entrepreneurial era, 26
factory system, 24–25
finance era, 27
global era, 27–28
important dates, 24*t*
Industrial Revolution, 24–25
internet era, 28
marketing era, 27
production era, 26
sales era, 26–27
holding costs, 366–367
holidays, 284
horizontal integration, 197
horizontal merger, 61
hostile takeover, 62
hostile work environment, 263
hotspots, 421
housing co-operatives, 129
hubs, 574–575
human relations skills, 188, 309
human resource management (HRM)
anti-discrimination laws, 261–262
benefits, 258–259
challenges, 265–268
comparable worth, 262–263
compensation, 254–258
contingent workers, 267–268
defined, 242
development of human resources, 249–252
employee safety and health, 264
equal employment opportunity, 261–262
evaluation of employee performance, 252–253
human resource planning, 242–244
knowledge workers, 266–267
legal context, 261–264
orientation, 250
recruiting, 245–247
retirement, 264
selection, 246–249
sexual harassment, 263–264
staffing the organization, 245–249
strategic importance, 242
workforce diversity, 265–266
human resource managers, 186
human resource planning
described, 242, 243*f*
forecasting HR demand and supply, 243–244
job analysis, 243
matching supply and demand, 244
replacement charts, 244
skills inventories, 244
human resources, 7
human-resources model, 310
hybrid financing, 661
hydrogen fuel cell, 50
hygiene factors, 311

I

ideas
generation, 114
marketing of, 477–480
product ideas, 515
screening, 114–116
sharing ideas, encouragement of, 317
identifying products, 518–522
identity theft, 425–428
image differences, 540
impasse, 292
implied warranty, A-4
import-export balances, 147–148
importers, 153
imports, 142, 148*f*, 149*t*
incentive programs, 256–258
incentives, 16–17
income statement
cost of goods sold, 450–451
defined, 450
operating expenses, 451–452
revenues, 450
income trust, 127
incorporation, 127
independence, 416
independent agents, 154
independent local union, 287
index of economic freedom, 108
India, outsourcing to, 444
individual differences
attitudes, 307
defined, 305
personality, 305–306, 306*f*
individual ethics, 72–73
individual incentive plans, 256–257
industrial advertising, 533
Industrial Disputes Investigation Act, 283
industrial distribution, 562–563
industrial goods, 479
industrial market, 497
industrial products, 513–514
industrial relations, 284
Industrial Revolution, 24–25, 278
industrial selling, 535
industrial unions, 287
industry environment, 57–58
industry productivity, 383–384
inflation
consumer price index (CPI), 45
defined, 44–45
vs. deflation, 37–38
and economic stability, 44–46
global variations, 45
measurement of, 45–46
predictions about, 37–38
infocard, 428
informal groups, 231–233
informal organization
advantages and disadvantages, 231
defined, 231
grapevine, 232–233
informal groups, 231–233
information, 410
information management
defined, 410
information system (IS), 411–414
information technology (IT). *See* information technology (IT)
information managers, 186, 410
information resources
defined, 9
as factor of production, 9

information seeking, 496
information system (IS)
- artificial intelligence (AI), 414
- decision support system (DSS), 413
- defined, 411
- described, 410–411
- executive support system (ESS), 414
- key users, 411–412
- management information systems (MIS), 413
- system operations personnel, 412
- transaction processing systems (TPS), 412
- types of, 412–414

information technology (IT)
- anti-virus software, 428
- building blocks, 419–420
- collaboration, 416
- communication technologies, 419–420
- computer viruses, 426, 428
- defined, 414
- encryption system, 428
- firewalls, 427–428
- flexibility for customization, 417
- global exchange, improved, 416
- hackers, 424–425
- identity theft, 425–428
- impact of developments, 414–415
- independence, 416
- intellectual property theft, 426
- internet, 419
- leaner corporations, 416
- management processes, improved, 417
- networks, 420–423
- new business opportunities, 418
- and organizational processes, 415–420
- remote deliveries, 415
- risks and threats, 424–427
- security measures, 427–429
- social marketing, 423
- software piracy, 425
- spam, 427, 428–429
- spyware, 426–429
- top information technology companies in Canada, 415*t*
- Trojan horse, 426
- world improvements, 418
- World Wide Web, 419
- worms, 426

informative advertising, 527
initial public offering (IPO), 127
innovation, 398
input market, 11
inside directors, 127
insider trading, 90
insolvent person or company, A-5
institutional advertising, 533
institutional market, 497
instructional-based programs, 251
insufficient capital, 132
insurable risks, 670
insurance
- business continuation agreements, 673
- business insurance, special forms of, 672–673
- group life insurance, 672
- insurable *vs.* uninsurable risks, 670
- insurance product, 670–672
- key person insurance, 672
- liability insurance, 670–671
- life insurance, 672
- premiums, 669
- property insurance, 671–672
- as risk management, 669–673
- top ten life insurance companies in Canada, 672*t*

insurance co-operatives, 129
insurance company, 668
insurance policy, 668
intangibility, 352
intangible assets, 449
integration strategies, 197
intellectual property, 426, 521–522
intentional tort, A-4
interactive marketing, 570
interest rates, 659
intermediaries, 559–563, 562*f*
intermediate goals, 194
intermodal transportation, 572
internal benchmarking, 392
internal failures, 392
internal recruiting, 245
international accounting
- foreign currency exchange, 459
- international accounting standards, 460
- international transactions, 459

international banking and finance
- Canadian chartered banks and, 596
- described, 608
- exchange rates and international trade, 608–609
- international bank structure, 610–611
- international payments process, 609–610, 610*f*

international branding, 519
international business management
- adapting to customer needs, 152
- basic decisions, 151
- exporters, 153
- going international, 151–152, 151*f*
- importers, 153
- international demand, gauging, 151
- international firms, 153
- international organizational structures, 154–156
- involvement levels, 153–154
- multinational firms, 153–154

international competition, 483
international competitiveness, 147
international economy. *See* global economy
international firms, 153
international marketing mix
- described, 498–500
- distribution, 499–500
- price, 499
- products, 498–499
- promotion, 499

International Monetary Fund (IMF), 37, 611
international organizational structures
- branch offices, 154
- defined, 227
- emergence of different structures, 227–228
- foreign direct investment (FDI), 155–156
- independent agents, 154
- international division structure, 228*f*
- licensing arrangements, 154
- strategic alliances, 155

international payments process, 609–610, 610*f*
international pricing, 499, 559
international productivity comparisons, 381–382, 382*f*
international promotion strategies, 538–540
international trade
- *see also* global economy
- barriers, 156–165
- business-practice laws, 161–162
- cartels, 162
- cultural differences, 156–158
- dumping, 162
- economic differences, 158–159
- embargo, 159
- and exchange rates, 608–609
- history of, 142–143
- legal differences, 159–162
- local-content laws, 160
- overcoming barriers to trade, 162–165
- political differences, 159–162
- protectionism, 160
- quotas, 159
- social differences, 156–158
- subsidy, 159–160
- tariff, 159

international transactions, 459
international union, 287
internet
- *see also* ecommerce
- advertising, 530–531
- communication technologies, 419–420
- cybermalls, 569
- defined, 419
- e-agents, 565, 568
- e-intermediaries, 568–570
- ecatalogues, 569
- electronic retailing, 568–570
- electronic storefronts, 569
- employees, market value of, 256
- etailing, 568–570
- growth of, 28
- interactive marketing, 570
- internet-based stores, 569
- as market, 10
- multilevel marketing, 569
- online banking, 600
- online trading, 624
- remote deliveries, coordination of, 415
- shopping agents, 568
- start-ups in Europe, 144
- syndicated selling, 568
- video marketing, 570

internet-based stores, 569
internet era, 28
internet marketing, 530–531
internet service providers (ISPs), 429
internships, 246
interviews, 249
intraday trades, 639
intranets, 419
intrapreneuring, 109
introduction stage, 517
introverts, 306
intuition, 192
inventory
- as expenditure, 655
- finished goods inventory, 655
- raw materials inventory, 655
- types of, 655
- work-in-process inventory, 655

inventory control, 366, 571
inventory turnover ratio, 458–459
investment banker, 620–652
Investment Canada, 155
investment dealers, 607
investment reduction, 197
investments
- asset allocation, 633–634
- commodities, 632
- contagion, 633
- diversification, 633
- emissions trading, 639

innovation and technology, 398
risk-return relationship, 664, 664f
securities. See securities
investor relations, 621
investors
accounting information, use of, 441
angel investing, 119
responsibility toward, 90–91
Iran, 626
Irving family, 105, 211
ISO 9000, 393–394
ISO 14000, 393–402

J

Japan
cultural differences, 158
deflation, 37
job analysis, 243
job commitment, 307
job description, 243
job enrichment, 318–319
job evaluation, 255
job redesign, 319
job satisfaction, 307, 312f
see also motivation
job security, 290
job sharing, 321
job specialization, 214–215
job specification, 243
joint venture, 62–63
just-in-time (JIT) production systems, 367–369

K

key person insurance, 672
knowledge workers, 266–267, 412–414
Kyoto Summit, 82

L

label, 85, 522
labour
defined, 7–8
as factor of production, 7
forecasting demand and supply, 243–244
and knowledge workers, 266–267
shortage, during low unemployment, 46
specialization, 25
labour contract issues, 289–291
labour productivity, 381
labour relations
administration of labour agreement, 295–296
arbitration, 295
bargaining perspectives, 282
boycotts, 294
collective bargaining, 278, 288–291
contracting out, 294
defined, 278
employers' associations, 294
failure of collective bargaining, 292–294
federal legislation, 283–284
global perspective, 291–292
grievance, 296, 296f
important dates in Canadian history, 280t
labour unions. See labour unions
legal environment, 283–285
lockouts, 294
management tactics, 294
mediation, 295
picketing, 293–294
plant closures, 294
provincial legislation, 285
shop steward, 295
strikebreakers, 294
strikes, 292–293
trends in union-management relations, 282
union tactics, 292–294
work slowdown, 294
labour unions
see also labour relations
accounting information, use of, 441
anti-unionization activities, 281
bargaining unit, 286
boycotts, 294
certification process, 286
certification vote, 286
craft unions, 286–287
decertification, 286
defined, 278
development of Canadian labour unions, 279
future of, 282–283
global perspective, 291–292
grievance, 296, 296f
independent local union, 287
industrial unions, 287
international union, 287
legal environment, 283–285
local union, 287
national union, 287
non-agricultural workforce, 281f
organizing strategy, 286–288
picketing, 293–294
reasons for unionizing, 278
shop steward, 295
strikes, 292–293
tactics, when bargaining fails, 292–294
top ten unions in Canada, 287t
trends in union-management relations, 282
trends in union membership, 280–281
types of unions, 286–287
union security, 287–288
women and, 280
work slowdown, 294
workforce, composition of, 281
land pollution, 83–84
language differences, 539
law
administrative law, A-1
agency, A-3
bailment, A-3
bankruptcy, A-5
business law, A-1
common law, A-1
contracts, A-2
court system, A-1
defined, A-1
negotiable instruments, A-4
property, law of, A-3
role of, in Canadian society, A-1
sources of law, A-1
statutory law, A-1
torts, A-4
warranty, A-3
law of demand, 18
law of one price, 608–609
law of supply, 18
layout planning, 356–360
lead times, 367
leadership
approaches, 323–325
autocratic style, 324
behavioural approach, 324
charismatic leadership, 326, 326f
coaches, leaders as, 326–327
continuum, 325, 325f
cross-cultural leadership, 327–328
defined, 322
democratic style, 324
employee-oriented, 324
ethical leadership, 328
free-rein style, 324
and gender, 327
vs. management, 322, 323t
recent trends, 325–329
situational (contingency) approach, 324–325
strategic leadership, 328
task-oriented, 324
trait approach, 323–324
transactional leadership, 326
transformational leadership, 325–326
virtual leadership, 328–329
leading
see also leadership
described, 182
for quality, 388
lean manufacturing, 358
leaner corporations, 416
learning organization, 230–231
lease, A-3
lecture approach, 251
legal context of HRM, 261–265
legal differences, 159–162
legal organization, forms of. See business ownership
legal purpose, A-2
legislation
federal labour legislation, 283–284
human resource management, 261–265
provincial labour legislation, 285
securities regulation. See securities regulation
lesbians, and employment initiatives, 266
letters of credit, 599
levels of management, 184–186, 185f
leverage, 456–457
leveraged buyouts, 456–457
liabilities (accounting)
on balance sheet, 450
current liabilities, 450
defined, 447
long-term liabilities, 450
liability insurance, 670–671
liability (legal)
limited liability, 126, 128
product liability, A-4
unlimited liability, 124
licensed brands, 520
licensing arrangements, 154
lie detectors, 249
life insurance, 672
life insurance company, 635
limit buy order, 637
limit sell order, 637
limited-function merchant wholesalers, 565
limited liability, 126, 128
limited partners, 125
limited partnership, 125
line authority, 223, 224f
line departments, 223
line of credit, 657, 665
liquidation plan, A-5
liquidity, 449
liquor industry, 33–34
living standards. See standard of living
load funds, 630
loans
bank loans, 602
long-term loans, 659
secured loans, 656–657
unsecured loans, 657–658
Lobbying Act, 17
lobbyist, 17
local area networks (LANs), 420
local-content laws, 160
local union, 287

location planning, 355
lockouts, 294
long-run perspective, 399
long-term expenditures, 655–656
long-term funds
 debt financing, 659–660, 661–663, 662*f*
 equity financing, 660–661, 662*f*, 663
 hybrid financing, 661
 need for, 659
 sources of, 659–664
long-term goals, 193
long-term liabilities, 450
long-term loans, 659
long-term solvency, 456
losses, 667–668
low-contact processes, 349, 361
low-contact system, 349
low-income countries, 143
low middle-income countries, 143
luck, 131
Luxembourg, 42

M

M2, 593
M-1, 592–593
magazine advertising, 529
mail order, 567
management
 see also employers
 areas of management, 186–187
 basic management skills, 187–192
 Canadian *vs.* American management style, 328
 contingency planning, 199
 controlling, 183
 corporate culture, 179–180, 200–203
 crisis management, 200
 defined, 180
 glass ceiling, 241
 human resource management (HRM). *See* human resource management (HRM)
 improved processes, and information technology, 417
 vs. leadership, 322, 323*t*
 leading, 182
 levels of management, 184–186, 185*f*
 management process, 180–184
 organizing, 182
 participative management and empowerment, 316
 planning, 181–182
 strategic management, 192–198
 tactics, when bargaining fails, 294
 team management, 318
management accounting, 442
management by objectives (MBO), 315, 316*f*
management consulting services, 445
management development programs, 251
management information systems (MIS), 413
management skills
 combinations of, 187*f*
 conceptual skills, 188
 decision-making skills, 189–192
 human relations skills, 188
 technical skills, 187–188
 time management skills, 188–189
managerial accounting, 442
managerial capitalism, 79
managerial competence, 130
managerial ethics
 behaviour toward employees, 73–74
 behaviour toward organization, 74
 bribes, 74
 conflict of interest, 74
 defined, 73
managerial incompetence or inexperience, 131
managers
 accounting information, use of, 441
 described, 180
 financial managers. *See* financial managers
 first-line managers, 186, 412
 human resource managers, 186
 information managers, 186, 410
 marketing managers, 186–187, 483
 middle managers, 185, 412
 operations managers, 186
 production managers, 347
 roles of, 184
 sexual harassment and, 263–264
 top managers, 185, 412
 types of, 184–187
mandated protection plans, 258
manufacturing operations
 see also goods
 capacity planning, 354
 cellular layouts, 356–358
 flexible manufacturing system (EMS), 358
 layout planning, 356–358, 357*f*
 lean manufacturing, 358
 location planning, 355
 master production schedule, 363
 methods planning, 361
 process layout, 356
 product layout, 358
 productivity, 383
 scheduling, 363
 vs. service operations, 349–350
 soft manufacturing, 358
 U-shaped production lines, 358
manufacturing resource planning (MRP II), 369
margin, 604–632
margin credit, 639
margin trading, 638–639
market
 bear markets, 636
 bull markets, 636
 commodities market, 632
 defined, 10–11
 government market, 497
 industrial market, 497
 input market, 11
 institutional market, 497
 output market, 11
 over-the-counter (OTC) market, 627
 reseller market, 497
 securities markets, 620–621
 speed to market, 515
market capitalization, 622, 623*t*
market economy
 in Canada. *See* Canadian economy
 circular flow, 11*f*
 competition, 20–24
 demand and supply, 18–21
 described, 10–12
 private enterprise, 20–24
market indexes, 636–637
market order, 637
market penetration, 196
market price, 20
market research
 data mining, 494
 data warehousing, 493–494
 defined, 490
 described, 490, 491*f*
 experimentation, 493
 focus groups, 492–493
 observation, 492
 research methods, 492–493
 research process, 491
 surveys, 492
market segmentation
 caution, 489–490
 defined, 485
 demographic variables, 487–488, 487*f*
 described, 485–486, 486*t*
 geographic variables, 487
 identification of market segments, 487–489
 product-use variables, 488–489
 psychographic variables, 488
market share, 553
market value, 621
marketable ideas, 115
marketable securities, 449
 see also securities
marketing
 buzz marketing, 497
 consumer behaviour, 494–497
 defined, 476
 described, 476–485
 distribution, as marketing strategy, 574–575
 goods, 477–480
 ideas, 477–480
 interactive marketing, 570
 international marketing mix, 498–500
 market research, 490–494
 market segmentation, 485–490
 marketing environment, 480–483
 organizational marketing and buying behaviour, 497–498
 process, 490, 491*f*
 services, 477–480
 small business, 500–501
 target marketing, 485–490
 and value, 476–477
 video marketing, 570
 word-of-mouth marketing, 497
marketing co-operatives, 129
marketing concept, 476
marketing environment
 competitive environment, 482–483
 economic environment, 481–482
 external marketing environment, 480, 480*f*
 political-legal environment, 480
 socio-cultural environment, 480
 technological environment, 481
marketing era, 27
marketing managers, 186–187, 483
marketing mix
 choosing, 483*f*
 defined, 483
 distribution (place), 485
 international marketing mix, 498–500
 price, 484
 product, 483–484
 promotion, 485
 small business, 500–501
marketing plan, 483
markups, 561
Maslow's hierarchy of human needs model, 310–311, 310*f*
mass-customization, 417
mass production, 24–25
master production schedule, 363
matching organization and environment, 196
matching people and jobs, 307–308
matching principle, 454–455, 455*t*
materials handling, 571
materials management, 366–367
materials requirement planning (MRP), 369

matrix organization, 226–227
maturity stage, 517
McCain family, 105
media. *See* advertising media
media mix, 527
mediation, 295
meetings, 188
mentoring, 251
merchandise inventory, 449
merchant wholesalers, 565
mergers, 61–62
merit pay plans, 255
methods planning, 360–363
Mexico, 144
middle managers, 185, 412
mining business, 157
misrepresentation of finances, 91
mission statement, 193
missionary selling, 536
Mitchell family, 105
mixed market economy, 12–13
mobile messaging, 415
modified work schedules
  compressed workweek, 320
  flextime, 319–320*f*
  four-day workweek, 320, 322
  telecommuting, 320–321, 322
  worksharing, 321
monetary policies, 48
money
  banks as creators of money, 602–604, 603*f*
  characteristics of money, 590–591
  credit cards, 593–595
  currency, 592–593
  currency fluctuations, 615–616
  defined, 590
  divisibility, 591
  durability, 591
  functions of money, 591–592
  importance of, 589–590
  M2, 593
  M-1, 592–593
  medium of exchange, 592
  portability, 590
  stability, 591
  store of value, 592
  unit of account, 592
money economy, 592
money market mutual funds, 593
monitoring of employees, 89
monopolistic competition, 22–23
monopoly, 23–24
morale, 307
morally objectionable advertising, 88
motivating factors, 311
motivation
  behaviour modification theory, 313–314
  classical theory of motivation, 308–309
  contemporary motivation theory, 311–313
  defined, 308
  early behavioural theory, 309–311
  equity theory, 312–313
  expectancy theory, 311–312, 313*f*
  goal setting theory, 315
  Hawthorne effect, 309
  hierarchy of human needs model, 310–311, 310*f*
  human relations skills, 309
  human-resources model, 310
  job enrichment, 318–319
  job redesign, 319
  and leadership. *See* leadership
  management by objectives (MBO), 315, 316*f*
  modified work schedules, 319–321
  motivation-hygiene theory, 311
  participative management and empowerment, 316
  reinforcement, 313–314
  scientific management, 308–309
  strategies, 313–321
  team management, 318
  Theory X, 310
  Theory Y, 310
  trait approach, 324
  two-factor theory, 311, 312*f*
motivation-hygiene theory, 311
multilevel marketing, 569
multinational firms
  defined, 153
  described, 153–154
  in Eastern Europe, 144
multiple organizational environments, 39
mutual funds, 630–631, 631*t*, 646–647
mutual funds quotations, 635–636*f*

N

Nano, 359
NASDAQ Composite Index, 637
National Association of Securities Dealers Automated Quotation (NASDAQ), 627
national brands, 519
national competitive advantage, 146–147, 147*f*
national debt, 44
national union, 287
nationalization, 13
natural monopolies, 24
natural resources
  in Canada, 4–6
  defined, 9
  as factor of production, 9
natural work groups, 319
negative reinforcement, 313–314
neglect, 131
negligence, A-4
negotiable instruments, A-4
net asset value (NAV), 635
net earnings, 452
net income, 452
net profit, 452
networking, 251
networks
  client-server networks, 420
  computer network, 420
  hardware for, 421
  local area networks (LANs), 420
  software for, 422
  Wi-Fi, 421
  wide area networks (WANs), 420
  wireless local area network (wireless LAN or WLAN), 421
  wireless wide area networks (WWANS), 421
new employee orientation, 250
new firm. *See* new venture
new product development
  described, 514
  product mortality rates, 515
  risk of, 514
  seven-step development process, 515–516, 516*f*
  speed to market, 515
  time frame, 514–515
new product pricing, 557
new venture
  see also entrepreneur
  defined, 108
  entry strategies, 116
  role of, in Canadian economy, 111–112
  sharing ownership, 120
New York Stock Exchange (NYSE), 626, 641
newspaper advertising, 528
NINJA loans, 651
no-load funds, 630
nominal GDP, 42
non-direct distributions, 561–562
non-store retailing, 567–570
North America, 143, 144
North American Free Trade Agreement (NAFTA), 164–165
Nova Scotia, 54

O

objections, 536
observation, 492
obstructionist stance, 92
occupational health and safety, 284
Occupational Health and Safety Act (Ontario), 264
odd-even pricing, 558
odd lots, 637
off-the-job training, 251
office applications, 412–414
office-products industry, 563
oil, 32–33
oil sands development projects, 5
oligopoly, 23
omission, 313
on-the-job training, 250
online banking, 600
online trading, 624
Ontario Labour Relations Act, 285
Ontario Securities Act, 640
open-book credit, 656
open shop, 288
openness, 306
operating expenses, 451–452, 654–655
operating income, 452
operational plans, 182
operations capability, 350, 351*f*
operations control
  computer operations control, 413
  defined, 365–366
  follow-up, 366
  just-in-time (JIT) production systems, 367–369
  materials management, 366–367
  materials requirement planning (MRP), 369
  purchasing processes, 366–367
  quality control, 369
  tools, 367–369
  worker training, 367
operations management
  business strategy as driver of operations, 349–350
  defined, 347
  global operations, 345
  goods-producing processes, 348
  manufacturing operations *vs.* service operations, 349–350
  operations capability, 350, 351*f*
  operations control, 365–370
  operations planning, 353–363
  operations processes, 347–349
  operations scheduling, 363–364
  production. *See* production
  service-producing processes, 349
  service *vs.* manufacturing operations, 351–353
operations managers, 186
operations planning
  capacity planning, 354–355
  described, 353–354, 354*f*
  layout planning, 356–360
  location planning, 355
  methods planning, 360–363
  quality planning, 360
operations processes, 347–349
operations scheduling, 363–364
opportunities
  analysis of, 195

development of, 116–117
entrepreneur-opportunity fit, 121
identification of, 113–117
information technology (IT) and, 418
opportunity-resources fit, 121
opportunity decision, 190
optional protection plans, 258–259
order fulfillment, 573
order processing, 535
organization charts, 213*f*, 213–214
organizational analysis, 194–195
organizational boundary
acquisitions, 61–62
defined, 38
described, 38–39
divestitures, 62
employee-owned corporations, 62
joint venture, 62–63
mergers, 61–62
redrawing boundaries, 61–63
spinoff, 62
strategic alliances, 62–63
subsidiary and parent corporations, 63
organizational buying behaviour, 497–498
organizational citizenship, 304
organizational commitment, 307
organizational environments. *See* external environment
organizational markets, 497
organizational politics, 192
organizational stakeholders, 79–80*f*
organizational structure
authority, distribution of, 219–224
authority, forms of, 223–224
basic organizational structures, 224–231
boundaryless organization, 228
building blocks of organizational structure, 214–218
centralized organizations, 220
chain of command, 213–214
decentralized organizations, 220–221
decision-making hierarchy, 218–224
defined, 212
departmentalization, 214, 215–218
determinants of, 212–213
divisional structure, 224–225, 225*f*, 225*t*
downsizing, 222
flat organizational structure, 221
functional structure, 224, 224*t*
green organizational structure, 229
international organizational structures, 154–156, 227–228
learning organization, 230–231
matrix organization, 226–227
organization charts, 213*f*, 213–214
organizational design for twenty-first century, 228–231
project organization, 225–227
span of control, 221–222, 222*f*
specialization, 214, 215
tall organizational structure, 221
team organization, 230
virtual organization, 230, 230*f*
organizational values, 78*f*
organizing
described, 182
for quality, 388
orientation, 250
outcome, 352
outdoor advertising, 529–530
output market, 11
outside directors, 127
outsourcing, 58–60, 291, 444
over-the-counter (OTC) market, 627
overtime pay, 273
owners' equity, 447, 450
ownership utility, 347

P

packaging, 522
paid-in capital, 450
paid time off, 259
paperless system, 460
paperwork, and time management, 188
par value, 621
parent corporation, 63
participative management and empowerment, 316
partnerships, 125–126
patent, 521
pay-by-phone, 600
pay-for-knowledge, 256
pay-for-performance, 256
pay structure, 256
pay surveys, 255
peak oil, 32–33
penetration pricing, 557
pension funds, 607
pensions, 259, 439–440, 598
people with disabilities, and employment initiatives, 266
per capita income, 143
perfect competition, 22
performance, 351
performance appraisal
conducting, 252
defined, 252
methods, 253
performance feedback, 252–253
process, 252–253
ranking methods, 253
rating methods, 253
360-degree feedback, 252
performance-based compensation, 256–258
performance behaviours, 304
performance of tasks, 219
performance quality, 387–388
performance ratios. *See* profitability ratios
performance-reward link, 312
perks, importance of, 260
person-job fit, 308
personal property, A-3
personal selling
approaching, 536
closing, 536
costs of, 534
creative selling, 535
defined, 534
demonstrating, 536
follow-up, 536
handling objections, 536
industrial selling, 535
missionary selling, 536
order processing, 535
personal selling situations, 535
presenting, 536
process, 536
prospecting, 536
qualifying, 536
retail selling, 535
sales force management, 535–536
small business, 540
tasks, 535
personality, 305–306, 306*f*
persuasive advertising, 527
PERT charts, 364–365*f*
physical distribution
defined, 570
transportation operations, 571–574
warehousing, 570–571
physiological needs, 310
picketing, 293–294
piece-rate incentive plan, 256
pipeline, 572
place. *See* distribution
place utility, 346–347
planes, 572
planning
alternative plans, 199
defined, 181
hierarchy of plans, 182
human resource planning, 242–244
operations planning, 353–363
process, 181
for quality, 387–388
plans, 182
plant closures, 294
pledging accounts receivable, 657
point-of-purchase (POP) displays, 537
point-of-sale transfers, 600–601
poison pill, 62
political differences, 159–162
political-legal environment, 53–54, 480
political stability, 53–54
pollution
air pollution, 82–83
concerns, 84
control of, 82
defined, 82
land pollution, 83–84
shipping industry, 101–102
water pollution, 83
polygraph tests, 249
Ponzi scheme, 640
Porter's five forces model, 57–58, 57*f*
positive reinforcement, 313
possession utility, 347
post-purchase evaluations, 496–497
pre-staging hubs, 574
predictability, 670
prediction markets, 181
preferences, 55
preferred stock, 622–623, 661
premiums, 537, 668, 669
prepaid expenses, 449
prescription drugs, 85
presenting, 536
price
see also pricing
call price, 623, 629
collusion, 85
defined, 484
equilibrium price, 20
high prices, effect of, 21
increases in Canada, 46*f*
law of one price, 608–609
market price, 20
and productivity, 43
price fixing, 557
price gouging, 74, 86
price leadership, 557
price lining, 558
price points, 558
price-setting tools, 553–556
price skimming, 557
pricing
see also price
break-even analysis, 554–556, 555*f*
buyers *vs.* sellers, 551–555
cost-oriented pricing, 553–554
defined, 551–552
discounts, 558
ebusiness pricing, 557
existing products, 556–557
fixed *vs.* dynamic pricing, 557
international pricing, 499, 559
and marketing mix, 484–485
new products, 557
odd-even pricing, 558

penetration pricing, 557
price fixing, 557
price leadership, 557
price lining, 558
price-setting tools, 553–556
price skimming, 557
pricing objectives, 552–553
psychological pricing, 558
small business pricing, 501
strategies, 556–557
tactics, 558–559
unfair pricing, 85–86
pricing objectives, 552–553
primary data, 491
primary securities markets, 620
prime rate of interest, 602
The Principles of Scientific Management (Taylor), 308
print server, 420
privacy, 89
private accountants, 445
private brands, 520
private carriers, 574
private corporation, 127
private enterprise
defined, 20
degrees of competition, 21–24, 21*t*–22*t*
described, 20–24
elements of, 20
monopolistic competition, 22–23
monopoly, 23–24
oligopoly, 23
perfect competition, 22
private property rights, 20
private warehouses, 571
privatization, 12
Privy Council Order 1003, 283
proactive stance, 92
problem decision, 190
problem/need recognition, 495–496
process, 61, 352, 415–420
process departmentalization, 216–218
process layout, 356
process re-engineering, 394
process technologies, 51–52
process variation, 390, 391*f*
product
see also goods; services
branding, 518–521
business products, 562–563
consumer products, 513, 559–561
defined, 483–484
features, 512–513
identifying products, 518–522
industrial products, 513–514
international products, 498–499
labelling, 522
market demand, 130
marketing mix, 483–484
mortality rates, 515
new product development, 514–516
packaging, 522
promotion. *See* promotion
sales forecast, 115
small business products, 500–501
substitute products, 483
substitutes, 58
testing, 516
value package, 512–513
variations, 539
product adaptation, 518
product advertising, 533
product departmentalization, 216, 217
product development, 196
product differentiation, 484
product extension, 518
product ideas, 515
product layout, 358
product liability, A-4
product life cycle (PLC)
defined, 516
extending product life, 518
stages, 517–518, 517*f*
product line retailers, 565–566
product lines, 514
product mix
defined, 514
product lines, 514
product positioning, 489*f*, 523
product safety, 85
product technologies, 49–52
product-use variables, 488–489
production
see also operations management
goods production, 344
inputs and outputs, 348*f*
master production schedule, 363
meaning of, 344–346
operations processes, 347–349
transformation system, 347*f*, 348*f*
U-shaped production lines, 358
value creation, 346–353
production capability, 350, 351*f*
production era, 26
production management. *See* operations management
production managers, 347
productivity
among global competitors, 381–382
challenge, 380–384
company productivity, 384
as competitive tool, 398–400
defined, 43, 380
domestic productivity, 382
high productivity levels, 43
industry productivity, 383–384
international productivity comparisons, 381–382, 382*f*
labour productivity, 381
manufacturing *vs.* service productivity, 383
measurement of, 381
and price, 43
productivity-quality connection, 380–384
quality of work life, 399
professional accountability, 625
professional accountants, 442–443
profit
concept of, 6–7
defined, 6
gross profit, 451
net profit, 452
and private enterprise, 20
profit-and-loss statement. *See* income statement
profit centre, 215
profit-maximizing objectives, 552–553
profit-sharing, 257–258
profitability ratios, 456, 457
program trading, 641
progressive revenue taxes, 16
project organization, 225–227
projections, 442
promissory notes, 656
promotion
adding value, 523
advertising promotions, 527–534
communication of information, 523
control of sales volume, 524–525
defined, 522–523
green business image, 524
information and exchange values, 523
international promotion, 499
international promotion strategies, 538–540
in marketing mix, 485
objectives, 523–525
personal selling, 534–536
product positioning, 523
promotional mix, 525, 526*f*
public relations, 538
publicity, 538
pull strategy, 525
push strategy, 525
sales promotions, 536–538
small business promotion, 501, 540–541
strategies, 525
promotional mix, 525, 526*f*
property
defined, A-3
law of property, A-3
personal property A-3
real property, A-3
transfer of property, A-3
property insurance, 671–672
proposal, A-5
prospecting, 536
prospectus, 640
protection plans, 258
protectionism, 160
protectionist tariffs, 159
prototype development, 516
provincial labour legislation, 285
psychographic variables, 488
psychological contracts, 307–308, 308*f*
psychological pricing, 558
public corporation, 127
public relations, 538
public warehouses, 571
publicity, 538
pull strategy, 525
punishment, 313
purchase decisions, 45, 496
purchase of existing business, 122
purchasing power parity, 43, 366
purchasing processes, 366–367
pure R&D, 49
pure risks, 667
push strategy, 525
put option, 632

Q

qualified endorsement, A-4
qualifying, 536
quality
as competitive tool, 398–400
continuous improvement, 399
defined, 380
of diamonds, 385
performance quality, 387–388
productivity-quality connection, 380–384
and services, 379–380, 400
total quality management. *See* total quality management (TQM)
quality assurance. *See* total quality management (TQM)
quality circle, 316
quality control, 369–385
quality/cost studies, 391–392
quality improvement, 384
quality improvement (QI) teams, 392
quality of work life, 399
quality ownership, 388
quality planning, 360, 384
quality reliability, 388
quantity discounts, 559
quid pro quo harassment, 263
quotas, 159

R

racial harassment, 305

rack jobbers, 565
radio advertising, 529
railroads, 572
R&D intensity, 50
ranking methods, 253
rating methods, 253
rational decision-making process, 189–191, 189*f*
rational motives, 496
ratios. *See* financial ratios
raw materials inventory, 655
re-engineering, 394
re-engineering process, 394, 395*f*
real GDP, 42, 43
real growth rates, 42
real property, A-3
receiving order, A-5
recession, 41
recruiting
  defined, 245
  external recruiting, 245–246
  green recruiting, 247
  internal recruiting, 245
  internships, 246
recycling, 84
rediscount rate, 597
Redstone family, 105
regional stock exchanges (U.S.), 626
registered bonds, 628
regressive revenue taxes, 16
regulations
  see also government
  competition, promotion of, 14
  consumer protection, 14
  environmental protection, 16
  and government, 15–16
reinforcement, 313–314
reintroduction, 518
related diversification, 197
related industries, 146
relationship marketing, 479–480
reliability, 400
reminder advertising, 527
remote deliveries, 415
reorganization, A-5
repayment plan, A-5
repetitive strain injuries (RSIs), 264
replacement charts, 244
research and development (R&D), 48–49, 51*f*
research methods, 492–493
reseller market, 497
reserve requirement, 603
resources
  angel investing, 119
  assessment of, 117–120
  bootstrapping, 117
  entrepreneur-resources fit, 121
  financial resources, 118–119
  opportunity-resources fit, 121
responsibility, 219
responsiveness, 400
restrictive endorsement, A-4
restrictive taxes, 16
retail advertising, 533
retail selling, 535
retailers, 559, 560
retailing
  bargain retailers, 566
  direct-response retailing, 567
  e-intermediaries, 568–570
  electronic retailing, 568–570
  etailing, 568–570
  green retailing, 567
  non-store retailing, 567–570
  product line retailers, 565–566
  top ten retailers in Canada, 565*t*
  types of retail outlets, 565–567
retained earnings, 450, 661
retirement, 264
retirement of bonds, 628–630
retrenchment, 197
return on equity, 457
return on sales, 457
revenue recognition, 454, 455*t*
revenue tariff, 159
revenue taxes, 16
revenues, 450
revolving credit agreements, 657–658
rewards-personal goals link, 312
right monetary policy, 48
rights of consumers, 85
risk
  coping with risk, 667–669
  defined, 667
  identification of, 667
  insurable risks, 670
  pure risks, 667
  speculative risks, 667
  uninsurable risks, 670
risk avoidance, 667
risk control, 668
risk management
  defined, 667
  implementation of risk-management program, 669
  insurance, 669–673
  process, 667–669, 668*f*
risk propensity, 192
risk retention, 668
risk-return relationship, 664, 664*f*
risk-reward ratings, 663
risk transfer, 668
rivalries, 146
robotics, 414
round lot, 637
router, 428
rumours, 621

S

sabbaticals, 259
sabotage, 305
safety, 264
salary, 255
sales agents, 560
sales commission, 256
sales era, 26–27
sales finance company, 606
sales force management, 535–536
sales forecast, 115
sales offices, 562
sales promotions
  defined, 536–537
  small business, 541
  types of, 537–538
sales volume, 524–525
samples, free, 537
S&P/TSX Index, 636–637
satellite communications, 419, 420
savings certificates, 593
scheduling, 363–364
scheduling tools, 364
scientific management, 308–309
screening of ideas, 114–116, 515
seasonable unemployment, 46
seasonal discounts, 558
secondary data, 491
secondary securities market, 621, 630
secondary strikes, 293
secured bonds, 628
secured loans, 656–657
secured short-term loans, 656–657
securities
  see also investments
  bonds. *See* bonds
  buying and selling, 634–639
  defined, 620
  financing securities purchases, 637–639
  hedge funds, 631
  investment banker, 620–621
  margin trading, 638–639
  markets, 620–621
  mutual funds, 630–631, 631*t*
  prospectus, 640
  regulation. *See* securities regulation
  stock. *See* stock
  underwriting, 621
Securities and Exchange Commission (SEC), 640
securities markets, 620–621
securities regulation
  blue-sky laws, 640
  Canadian securities regulations, 640
  U.S. securities regulation, 640–641
security needs, 310
security policy, 428
selection process
  application forms, 246–248
  interviews, 249
  other techniques, 249
  steps in, 248*f*
  tests, 248
  validation, 246
selective distribution, 563–564
self-actualization needs, 311
self-awareness, 324
self-fulfilling prophecies, 38
self-regulation, 324
serial bonds, 629
servers, 420
service co-operatives, 129
service flow analysis, 361–362, 362*f*
service operations, 344
  see also services
service package, 515
service process design, 516
service-producing processes, 349
service technologies, 49–52
services
  capacity planning, 355
  capital services, 513
  characteristics, 352
  classification of, 513–514
  convenience services, 513
  customer contact, 363
  customer-service link, 352–353
  customization, 352
  defined, 479
  employee attitudes, 400
  employee discretion, control of, 362–363
  intangibility, 352
  layout planning, 360, 360*f*
  location planning, 355
  vs. manufacturing operations, 349–350
  market demand, 130
  marketing of, 477–480
  methods planning, 361–363
  productivity, 383
  promotion. *See* promotion
  quality considerations, 353, 400
  quality problems, 379–380
  sales forecast, 115
  scheduling, 363–364
  service flow analysis, 361–362, 362*f*
  shopping services, 513
  specialty services, 513
  unstorability, 352
setting goals, 193–195
sexual harassment, 263–264, 305
shareholder return ratios. *See* profitability ratios
shop steward, 295
shopping agents, 568
shopping goods, 513
shopping services, 513

short sale, 639
short-selling, 631
short-term expenditures, 654–655
short-term funds
  secured short-term loans, 656–657
  sources of, 656–658
  trade credit, 656
  unsecured short-term loans, 657–658
short-term goals, 194
short-term loans
  secured short-term loans, 656–657
  unsecured short-term loans, 657–658
short-term solvency ratios, 456
shortage, 20
sick leave, 259
Sig Sigma program, 399
simple ranking method, 253
sinking fund provisions, 629
situational approach, 324–325
skills. *See* management skills
skills inventories, 244
small business
  see also entrepreneur
  advertising, 540
  bank credit, 665
  cash-flow planning, 665–666
  defined, 107
  described, 106–107
  distribution, 501
  failure, 131*t*, 131–132
  family businesses, 105–106
  financial management, 664–666
  green business, 110–111
  marketing mix, 500–501
  personal selling, 540–541
  pricing, 501
  products, 500–501
  promotion, 501, 540–541
  role of, in Canadian economy, 109–111
  sales promotions, 541
  and social responsibility, 95
  start-up, 121–123
  success, 130–131
  top ten small- and medium-sized employers in Canada, 107*t*
  venture capital, 665
smart cards, 601
SMART goals, 194, 315
social audits, 94
social consciousness, 80–81
social differences, 156–158
social goals, 16
social marketing, 423
social needs, 311
social responsibility. *See* corporate social responsibility (CSR)
social skill, 324
socialism, 10
socio-cultural environment
  customer preferences and tastes, 55
  defined, 55
  ethics, 55–56
  influence of, 55
  marketing environment, 480
  social responsibility, 55–56
soft manufacturing, 358
software, 422
software piracy, 425
softwood lumber dispute, 159–160
sole proprietorship, 123–124
solvency ratios, 456
South American Free Trade Area (SAFTA), 165
spam, 427, 428–429
span of control, 221–222, 222*f*
special endorsement, A-4
specialization, 25, 214, 215
specialized lending and savings intermediaries, 606–607
specialty goods, 513
specialty services, 513
specialty stores, 566
specific performance, A-2
speculative risks, 667
speed to market, 515
spinoff, 62
spreadsheets, 423–424
spyware, 426–429
stability, 44–48
stabilization policy, 48
staff authority, 223, 224*f*
staffing
  described, 245
  recruiting, 245–247
  selection, 246–249
Standard & Poor's Composite Index (S&P 500), 636
standard of living
  defined, 41
  and productivity increases, 43
  purchasing power parity, 43
standard work hours, 284
standardization, 366
start-up
  after the start-up, 121–123
  franchises, 122–123
  purchase of existing business, 122
  small business, 121–123
  taking over family business, 122
statement of cash flows, 452
statements of financial position. *See* balance sheets
statistical process control (SPC), 390
statutory law, A-1
stealing, 21
stealth advertising, 88
steam power, 25
steel making, 397
stock
  blue-chip stock, 622
  buying and selling, 637
  common stock, 621–622, 660
  defined, 128
  market capitalization, 622, 623*t*
  preferred stock, 622–623, 661
  secondary securities market, 621
  stock exchanges, 623–627
stock exchange
  brokers, 624
  Canadian stock exchanges, 624–626
  defined, 623
  foreign stock exchanges, 626–627
  memberships, 624
  over-the-counter (OTC) market, 627
  trading floor, 624
stock markets
  frauds, 648–649
  program trading, 641
  volatility, 619–620
stock option, 632–633
stock quotations, 634, 634*f*
stockbroker recommendations, 621
stockholders, 126
stop order, 637
storage warehouses, 571
Store Wars: The Organic Rebellion (Organic Trade Association), 60
strategic alliances, 62–63, 155
strategic goals, 192, 194
strategic leadership, 328
strategic management
  defined, 192
  formulation of strategy, 194–196, 194*f*
  setting goals, 193–195
  strategies, levels of, 196–198
strategic plans, 182
strategy
  advertising, 527
  business-level strategy, 196, 198
  competitive strategy, 196, 198
  concentration strategy, 196
  conservative strategy, 662
  corporate-level strategy, 196, 197
  cost leadership, 198
  defined, 193
  differentiation strategy, 198
  distribution strategies, 563–564, 563*f*
  diversification strategies, 197
  as driver of operations, 349–350
  focus strategy, 198
  formulation of strategy, 194–196, 194*f*
  functional strategies, 196, 198
  growth strategies, 196
  hierarchy of strategy, 196*f*
  integration strategies, 197
  investment reduction, 197
  levels of, 196–198
  marketing mix, 483–485
  motivation, enhancement of, 313–321
  and national competitive advantage, 146
  and operations capability, 349–350
  pricing strategies, 556–557
  promotional strategies, 525
  pull strategy, 525
  push strategy, 525
  supply chain, 396
  unitization, 571
strategy formulation, 194–196, 194*f*
strikebreakers, 294
strikes, 292–293
structural unemployment, 46
structures, 146
subsidiary corporation, 63
subsidy, 159–160
substitute products, 483
substitutes, 58
success in small business, 130–131
supermarkets, 565–566
supplier selection, 367
suppliers, 58
supply
  defined, 18
  demand and supply schedule, 18
  human resources and, 243–244
  law of supply, 18
  in market economy, 18–21
  shortage, 20
  supply curve, 19–20, 19*f*
  surplus, 20
supply chain, 394–396, 396*f*, 397–398
supply chain management (SCM), 396–397, 406
supply chain strategy, 396
supply curve, 19–20, 19*f*
supply-side hubs, 574
support systems, 412
supporting industries, 146
surplus, 20
surveys, 492
SWOT analysis, 194
sympathy strikes, 293
syndicated selling, 568
synthetic process, 348
system architecture, 420–423
system operations personnel, 412
system software, 422

T

tactical plans, 182

takeover, 62
tall organizational structure, 221
tangibles, 400
target markets, 485–490
tariff, 159
task-oriented, 324
tasks
  assignment of, 219
  combining tasks, 319
  performance of, 219
  personal selling, 535
tastes, 55
tax authorities, 441
tax services, 445
taxes
  double taxation, 128
  government as taxation agent, 16
  progressive revenue taxes, 16
  regressive revenue taxes, 16
  restrictive taxes, 16
  revenue taxes, 16
team building, 252
team incentives, 257–258
team organization, 230
teams
  natural work groups, 319
  quality improvement (QI) teams, 392
  team building, 252
  team incentives, 257–258
  team management, 318
  team organization, 230
technical skills, 187–188
technological environment. *See* technology
technology
  and competition, 51
  defined, 48
  information technology (IT). *See* information technology (IT)
  investments, 398
  marketing environment, 481
  and new ethical problems, 77
  process technologies, 51–52
  product technologies, 49–52
  research and development (R&D), 48–49, 51*f*
  service technologies, 49–52
  technology transfer, 51
  transformation technology, 348
technology transfer, 51
telecommuting, 320–321, 322, 333–334
telemarketing, 567
telephone, and time management, 188
television advertising, 528
term deposit, 602
test marketing, 516
tests, employment, 248
Textile Labelling Act, 14
theft, 21, 305
Theory X, 310
Theory Y, 310
threat of potential entrants, 57
threats, analysis of, 195
360-degree feedback, 252
time deposits, 593
time management skills, 188–189
time utility, 346
title, A-3
Tobacco Act, 14
top managers, 185, 412
Toronto Stock Exchange (TSX), 624–626, 640
torts, A-4
total quality management (TQM)
  benchmarking, 392
  commitment to, 386–387
  competitive product analysis, 389
  control charts, 390, 391*f*
  controlling for quality, 388–389
  customer focus, 386
  customers, getting closer to, 392–393
  defined, 386
  ISO 9000, 393–394
  ISO 14000, 393–402
  leading for quality, 388
  organizing for quality, 388
  performance quality, 387–388
  planning for quality, 387–388
  process re-engineering, 394
  process variation, 390, 391*f*
  quality/cost studies, 391–392
  quality improvement (QI) teams, 392
  quality reliability, 388
  statistical process control (SPC), 390
  strategic approach, 386
  supply chain, 394–396, 396*f*, 397–398
  supply chain management (SCM), 396–397
  tools, 389–398
  value-added analysis, 389
toxic wastes, 84
toy recall, 343
trade acceptance, 656
trade advertising, 533
trade associations, 17
trade credit, 656
trade credit insurance, 656
trade deficit, 148
trade discounts, 558
trade draft, 656
trade shows, 537
trade surplus, 148
trade unions. *See* labour unions
trademark, 521
trading floor, 624
training and development
  assessment of needs, 250
  group-based training, 252
  instructional-based programs, 251
  off-the-job training, 251
  on-the-job training, 250
  and productivity improvement, 399
  team building, 252
  work-based programs, 250
  worker training, 367
trait approach, 323–324
transaction processing systems (TPS), 412
transactional leadership, 326
transfer of property, A-3
transformation system, 347*f*, 348*f*
transformation technology, 348
transformational leadership, 325–326
transport processes, 348
transportation, 366
transportation operations
  changes in, 572–573
  companies specializing in, 574
  containerization, 572
  intermodal transportation, 572
  major transportation modes, 571, 572
  order fulfillment, 573
trends in union membership, 280–281
triple bottom line reporting, 94
Trojan horse, 426
trucks, 572
trust company, 605
trust services, 599
truth in advertising, 86
turnover, 304–305
two-factor theory, 311, 312*f*

U

U-shaped production lines, 358
unconnectedness, 670
undercover advertising, 88
underwriting, 621
unemployment
  cyclical unemployment, 46
  defined, 46
  and economic stability, 46
  frictional unemployment, 46
  historical unemployment rate, 47*f*
  seasonable unemployment, 46
  structural unemployment, 46
unethical behaviour, 72
unfair pricing, 85–86
uninsurable risks, 670
union density, 280
union security, 287–288
union shop, 288
unions. *See* labour unions
United Nations, 82
United States
  American *vs.* Canadian management style, 328
  Canadian *vs.* U.S. banks, 604
  financial crisis, 651–652
  international economy, role in, 144
  labour unions, 291
  regional stock exchanges, 626
  securities regulation, 640–641
  softwood lumber dispute, 159–160
unitization, 571
universal health care system, 258
unlimited liability, 124
unsecured bonds, 628
unsecured loans, 657–658
unsecured short-term loans, 657–658
unstorability, 352
upper-middle-income countries, 143
utility
  defined, 346
  types of, 347
  and value, 477

V

vacation pay, 259
vacations, 284
validation, 246
value
  adding, through promotion, 523
  and benefits, 477
  book value, 621
  brand equity, 518–519
  defined, 477
  exchange, 523
  information, 523
  intermediaries, 561
  market value, 621
  in marketing, 476–477
  and utility, 477
value-added analysis, 389
value package, 512–513
variable costs, 554
variable pay, 256–257
vending machines, 567
venture capital, 665
venture capital firms, 606
verifiability, 670
vertical integration, 197
vertical marketing system (VMS), 564
vertical merger, 61
vestibule training, 251
video assessment, 248
video cases
  see also cases
  "African Accountants," 469
  "Card Tricks," 682
  "Clash of the Co-workers," 336–337
  "Debt Nation," 681
  "The 'Feel-Better' Bracelet," 583

"Flair Bartending," 336
"Mompreneurs," 173
"Shall We Dance?", 584
"Tree Planters," 468
"Whistle-blowers at the RCMP," 172
video marketing, 570
videoconferencing, 251, 419
violence in the workplace, 305
viral marketing, 60–61
virtual advertising, 532
virtual leadership, 328–329
virtual organization, 230, 230*f*
virtual presence, 353
virtual storefront, 569
viruses. *See* computer viruses
visible minorities, and employment initiatives, 266
VMS arrangements, 564
voluntary arbitration, 295
VSAT satellite communications, 419, 420

W

wage reopener clauses, 290
wages, 255, 284
warehouse club, 566
warehousing, 366, 570–571
warranty, A-3
water carriers, 572
water pollution, 83
weak control systems, 131
The Wealth of Nations (Smith), 26
Weights and Measures Act, 14
whistle-blowing, 89–90, 172
wholesale club, 566
wholesalers
agents, 565
brokers, 565
business retailers, 563
consumer products, 560
defined, 559
industrial products, 563
merchant wholesalers, 565
Wi-Fi, 421
wide area networks (WANs), 420
wikis, 316
wildcat strikes, 293
wireless fidelity, 421
wireless local area network (wireless LAN or WLAN), 421
wireless mooching, 425
wireless wide area networks (WWANS), 421
women
employment initiatives and, 266
entrepreneurs in Canada, 111
glass ceiling, 241
and leadership, 327
"Mompreneurs," 136–137, 173
and unions, 280
wooden pallets, 84
word-of-mouth advertising, 530
word-of-mouth marketing, 497, 511–512
work-based programs, 250
work-in-process inventory, 655
work life quality, 399
work slowdown, 294
workers' compensation, 258, 671
workforce diversity, 265–266
workforce management systems, 257
working capital, 655
workplace aggression, 305
worksharing, 321
World Bank, 143, 611
world marketplaces, 143–145
world product mandating, 154
World Trade Organization (WTO), 162–163
World Wide Web, 419
worms, 426

Z

Zimbabwe, 45